Gematria and the Tanakh

By Brian Pivik

ISBN 978-1-257-09404-2

Table of Contents:

Table of Contents: *i*

Introduction *1*

What is this Book? 1

So What is Gematria? 2

Chapter One: Types of Gematria *3*

- Mispar Ragil (Standard Gematria) 3
- Mispar soduwriy (Ordinal Value) 5
- Mispar katan (Small Number) 5
- Mispar hakadmi (Preceding Number) 5
- Mispar musaphi or kolel value (Standard + Letters) 5
- Mispar hameruva haklali (Squaring of the Total) 6
- Mispar hameruba haperati (Squaring of the Letters) 6
- Mispar shemi or miluy (Filling) 6
- Temurah 6
- Atbash 6
- Aiq Bekar 6
- Achas B'tay-ah 7
- Notarikon 7

Notes About the Text 7

Hebrew Language Conventions: 9

How to Reference this Book: 10

Chapter 2: Gematria and the Tanakh *13*

100 120

200 184

300 239

400 287

500 324

600 354

700 394

800 438

900 467

1000 489

2000 **558**

601,730 **572**

Biblical and Midrashic Bibliography ***573***

Hebrew Language Bibliography ***574***

Traditional Jewish Gematria Bibliography ***574***

Judaic Kabbalah Bibliography ***575***

Western Hermetic Gematria Bibliography ***576***

Guide to the Comprehensive Index ***579***

COMPREHENSIVE INDEX ***581***

Introduction

This book has been one of the most important parts of my life for the last ten years. Ever since I first read Kabbalah by Gershom Scholem, and my subsequent inquiries into this mysterious tradition, I felt that an incorporative, comprehensive listing of the Hebrew and Aramaic *gematria*[1] from the *Tanakh* was missing from the corpus of literature devoted to biblical exegesis. Disappointed every time I searched for a word that numerically matched a given term in a lexicon, I was frustrated by the lack of results as well as the time wasted trying to find words. Even worse, there were few books out there to answer my questions. What word meant what in the *Tanakh*? Is this word in the present or past tense; is it singular or plural?[2] Strong's Exhaustive Concordance of the Bible helped answer some of my questions, although the words listed were in alphabetical and not numerical terms and only contain the roots of most words. I decided that with the help of this book along with several other indispensable texts such as Godwin's Cabalistic Encyclopedia, The Spice of Torah-Gematria, and various lexicons and commentaries, I could create an exhaustive numerical concordance the *Tanakh*, as well as other traditions (including those used by the Golden Dawn and its subsequent organizations and personalities, as well as some important Talmudic references), thus completing my goal of one book to supplement others. In effect, I could help create the most comprehensive listing of Hebrew and Aramaic terms in order of *gematria* equivalency to date. Above all, I have endeavored to keep this book easy to use and geared toward anyone with any interest in *gematria* whatsoever. Over the course of this creating this text, I have taught myself Biblical Hebrew/Aramaic, graduated from the University of Wyoming with my Master's in Literary Criticism, and above all, learned valuable lessons about the nature of humanity. All of these and the people met along this path have contributed to the writing of this text. I could not begin to thank them all by name, and their mention in this context may embarrass them, but they know who they are, and I thank them all deeply.

What is this Book?

I have tried to incorporate an extensive reading of the adverbs, nouns, verbs, and adjectives that make up the entire Biblical Hebraic language. Also, a comprehensive listing of all persons and places in the Hebrew Bible is given. This book is not a word-by-word literal *gematria* of the Hebrew Bible (see Spice of Torah: Gematria for an example of this type of analysis). As this book cannot possibly give all permutations of every word without going beyond the scope of the limits of page length, etc., there is still a great deal of work to be done. Overall I find that one's investigation into the various *gematriot* of a word lead one to discover that the entirety of permutations is important to the overall interpretation, and that while there seems to be an amalgam of associations, all of these can be found to give meaning to the text or word in question.

While I have borrowed extensively from the texts noted above, most notably Godwin's and Locks's works, all the information contained within those texts are easily referenced in other places, thus most of their work (and my own for that matter) is public domain. One more note about the difference between this work and Locks: while Locks's excellent *gematria* book covers the entirety of Torah by taking each word as itself, I have relied upon the concordances and lexicons easily available to the interested reader. Thus, the words you will find in this text are the roots and basic terms that are used in the Tanakh, but not necessarily the words themselves. For instance, the word *mowrag* (מורג - 249), meaning "threshing instrument" or "thresher," is used in 2 Samuel 24:22, "And Arunah said to David, 'Let my lord the king take it and offer up whatever he sees fit. Here are oxen for a burnt offering, and the **threshing boards** and the gear of the oxen for wood.'" However, the term used here is actually והמורגים, *vehamuriygiym* (320 or 880), which literally means "and the threshing instruments," but the root of the word is *mowrag*. With a little ingenuity and basic knowledge of Hebrew/Aramaic, one may find new words from either the Bible or modern Hebrew to match almost any number in this text.

---

[1] *Gematria* (gemahtria – emphasis on the middle syllable) is the singular, *gematriot* is the plural.

[2] Given the fact that there are only two tenses in Biblical Hebrew, I have decided to call them either past or present and forgo any discussion of the meanings of perfect and imperfect tenses, which would require more space than necessary. Instead, I refer the reader to the bibliography.

So What is Gematria?

Gematria is a time-honored tradition in Judaism that dates back to the Talmudic interpretation of the Tanakh through the *Baraita of 32 Rules.*[3] It is not, however, a strictly Jewish practice. Rather, the Babylonians and the Gnostics of the early Christian era used the concept of *gematria*, and was widespread in the Magi literature and interpreters of dreams in Hellenistic Greece.[4] One example of non-Biblical use of *gematria* is Sargon II, the Assyrian King, who built a wall near Khorsabad 16,283 cubits long to match the numerical value of his name. Gershom Scholem, the seminal Kabbalistic scholar of the 20th century feels that the rise of Jewish *gematria* was a new introduction resulting from the use of Greek letters during the time of the Second Temple (Kabbalah, 337).

Whatever its origins, *gematria* is currently used by various groups and individuals to "prove" or "disprove" various points (usually theological). While non-Biblical in practice (as far as we can discern), the early development of Kabbalah led to the increasingly abstruse interpretation of Biblical passages. The growth of esotericism in Judaism led to a surprisingly large variety of interpretive methods, one of which was *gematria.* In Judaic hermeneutics (the study and interpretation of sacred texts), there are four methods of interpretation: *Peshat*, meaning "plain sense" or "literal" reading. *Peshat* draws upon context, grammar, philology, history, etc. to explain the passage(s) given. *Derash* is the method that translates "seek:(to)" and is almost exclusively the method employed by the writers of the Midrash. It employs a great deal of homily and parable to expand upon a given text. *Remez* literally means "hint" and this system seeks the allegorical meaning of a text, philosophizing upon the words and their meanings. Finally *sod*, meaning "secret," is the method that suggests words cannot express meaning or truth. Truth is beyond ordinary human conception and cognizance. Therefore, the *sod* interpreter reads the *Tanakh* as a sort of codebook, and various wordplays (such as *gematria*, *notarikon* and all the methods given below) help interpret a text.

In the medieval era, Hermetic scientists, magicians and mystics appropriated the language and methodology of the world of Kabbalah. The influence of the Kabbalah on the development of western mystery traditions is well documented and highly important to understand when dealing with the mindset of many references within this text. I refer the interested reader to the bibliography under the section "Western Hermetic *Gematria* Bibliography," which lists many works on the subject. On the other hand, there are also many Judaic references in the bibliography that give a more strict religious interpretation of the terms and numerical equivalencies in this book. In many cases, the relationships between Hermetic and Rabbinical interpretations do not overlap, as Christian mystery traditions influence the former far more than Judaism. These varied meanings often lead the reader to rethink oft-cited numerical proofs, and as such are valuable for comparison. However, I make no claims that either is more correct than the other is. Hebrew, as a sacred language, gives meanings through the relationships of words and phrases, no matter if they are modern Hebrew or medieval "appropriations" of the language. It has been said that Hermetic philosophers use the square peg of Christianity to fit into the round hole of Jewish Kabbalah, but as far as *gematria* is concerned, I leave conclusions up to the reader.

How are we to come up with those conclusions, then? By comparing two or more words or phrases in Hebrew or Aramaic with the same numerical total, we can draw conclusions about their relationship through further analysis. As an obvious example, the number 130 contains two phrases which relate on an esoteric level: sullam and Sinai. Obviously, the latter refers to Mount Sinai, where Moses received the Ten Commandments. The former word (sullam) is the word for "ladder," used in Jacob's famous vision. From the two, we infer that the way to heaven and inspiration is the "ladder" of the Law given by Moses. In many cases, the relationship is not so easily inferred, but must be carefully interpreted in relation to the words and a variety of methods. The following section explains these, and outlines the most important forms of gematria interpretation.

---

[3] Scholem, Gershom. Kabbalah. pp. 337. The Baraita of 32 Rules examines Genesis 14:14 among other passages, wherein Abram gathers 318 men, which is the numerical equivalent of his servant's name, Eliezer (אליעזר), meaning that the 318 men were really only one. Other Talmudic references to *gematria*: Shabbat 70a, 145b, 149b; Eruvin 65a; Yuma 54a; Succah 28a, 45b; Megillah 15b; Moed Katan 17a, 19b, 28a; Nedarim 32a (2x), 32b (2x); Makkot 23b-24a

[4] *Gematria* was referred to as "τὸ ἰσψηΦου"

Chapter One: Types of Gematria

There are many types of *gematria*, and this book (despite its length) could not possibly include all variations of every word in the Tanakh. I have included all the following types of *gematria* in the book with an analysis of YHVH, the Tetragrammaton, personally feeling it is the most important name of God in the Tanakh. The following list is by no means exhaustive, as there are many and various types of interpretation from the shape of the letters to the breath sounds.[5]

• *Mispar Ragil (Standard Gematria)*

This book is based on *Mispar Ragil* – within these pages are the root words used in the Tanakh. In this system of *gematria*, every letter in a Hebrew word or phrase equals a letter. The chart on the following page outlines the standard usage of the Hebrew letters and their equivalents, which can be found in nearly every work relating to Kabbalah or *gematria*.

---

[5] For a great introduction to this type of interpretation, see The Wisdom in the Hebrew Alphabet.

Letter	Name	English	Meaning	Number
א	aleph	’	ox	1
ב	beth	b, v	house	2
ג	gimel	g, gh	camel	3
ד	daleth	d, dh	door	4
ה	heh	h	window	5
ו	vav	w or v	nail	6
ז	zayin	z	sword	7
ח	cheth	ch	fence	8
ט	teth	t	serpent	9
י	yod	y	hand	10
כ, ך	kaph	k, kh	palm or fist	20, 500
ל	lamed	l	ox goad	30
מ, ם	mem	m	water	40, 600
נ, ן	nun	n	fish	50, 700
ס	samekh	s	prop	60
ע	ayin	‘	eye	70
פ, ף	peh	p, ph	mouth	80, 800
צ, ץ	tzaddi	ts or tz	fishhook	90, 900
ק	qoph	q	back of head	100
ר	resh	r	head	200
ש	shin	s, sh	tooth	300
ת	tau	t, th	tau cross, mark	400

As one can discern from the chart, some letters have a larger value (Kaf, Mem, Nun, Peh, Tzaddi). This is because when those letters are used at the end of words, they take the final (and thus larger) numerical value of that letter. However, the final letters were a late addition to Biblical Hebrew, an innovation of the later prophets, who introduced them for the purpose of easier reading.[6] When the numerical value of the final letters are taken into account, this is called *Mispar gadol* in Hebrew. In this text, I have given both *ragil* and *gadol* for each word.[7]

In *gematria* exegetical practice, two or more words or phrases or any combination thereof with the same numerical equivalency create an association with one another. This association is not concrete, but abstract in the sense of the perception, knowledge, wisdom and theological background of the reader. One may say that the interpretations given are of no use because of their abstract qualities, but it is the argument of the author that any information that adds to the meaning of a sacred text is by no means worthless. After all, if one stays true to the essential meaning of the words, then it is difficult to wander too far astray. One other important item to keep in mind is that many numerical equivalencies may have one or more exceedingly "holy" or "good" association and one or more that is "unholy." The typical explanation for this is that of the Delphic Maxim, or more familiarly the Emerald Tablet of Hermes, which states, "As above, so below," meaning that two apparantly opposing forces can exist within one paradigm because the heavenly or "holy" association has its opposing force below. One common Kabbalistic theme the reader will find alongside "holy" terms is that of the *Qlippoth* or "shells," who are associated with the broken vessels of Lurianic Kabbalah. There is not enough room here to go into full detail, and the many books in the Bibliography will help the reader to greater understand this theory.

Example of standard *Gematria* interpretation:

In Genesis 32:5, Jacob sends a message to his brother, Esau, saying: "I sojourned with Laban." The Hebrew for "I sojourned" is גרתי, "*garti*," gimel =3, resh=200, tav=400, and yod=10, totaling 613, which is the number of commandments specified in the Torah. By this it is inferred that Jacob was really stating: "Although I sojourned with Laban, I kept the 613 commandments."

---

[6] See Talmudic texts: *Shabbat* 104a, *Megillah* 2b, *Bereshit Rabbah* 1:15, *BaMidbar Rabbah* 18:17, *Tanchuma, Korach* 12, *Pirkey Rabbi Eliezer* 48.

[7] **An important note** on this in the text – I have rendered words that have final letters in both manners, e.g. "טרם," *terem* is listed as "טרמ" for numerical equivalent 249 and "טרם," for number 809. This has been done not only for ease of reference, but because the finals were such a late innovation to Biblical Hebrew.

In *mispar ragil*, the numerical equivalent of YHVH is 26. (yod=10 + heh=5 + vav=6 + heh=10)

• *Mispar soduwriy (Ordinal Value)*

Mispar soduwriy uses the ordinal values of the letters thus:

א = 1	מ = 13
ב = 2	נ = 14
ג = 3	ס = 15
ד = 4	ע = 16
ה = 5	פ = 17
ו = 6	צ = 18
ז = 7	ק = 19
ח = 8	ר = 20
ט = 9	ש = 21
י = 10	ת = 22
כ = 11	
ל = 12	יהוה = 26

• *Mispar katan (Small Number)*

Here, the numerical equivalents for each letter are rounded down from the tens and hundreds, giving each letter a limit from 1 to 9. This obviously limits the numerical amount that a word or phrase is given.

א = 1	מ = 4
ב = 2	נ = 5
ג = 3	ס = 6
ד = 4	ע = 7
ה = 5	פ = 8
ו = 6	צ = 9
ז = 7	ק = 1
ח = 8	ר = 2
ט = 9	ש = 3
י = 1	ת = 4
כ = 2	
ל = 3	יהוה = 23

• *Mispar hakadmi (Preceding Number)*

In this type of *gematria*, all the preceding letters' value are added to an individual letter's value. For example, the letter Heh (5) would be 1+2+3+4+5, resulting in a total of 15. This type of *gematria* results in a higher value for words and phrases in Hebrew. For example, יהוה = (1+2+3+4+5+6+7+8+9+10 [Yod]) + (1+2+3+4+5 [Heh]) + (1+2+3+4+5+6 [Vahv]) + (1+2+3+4+5 [Heh]) = 106

• *Mispar musaphi or kolel value (Standard + Letters)*

This *gematria* uses the number of letters in a word added to the standard value of the number.
יהוה = 26 + 4 letters = 30

• *Mispar hameruva haklali (Squaring of the Total)*

The total of a word's numerical equivalent is squared.
יהוה = 26
$26^2 = 676$

• *Mispar hameruba haperati (Squaring of the Letters)*

In squared number *gematria*, the value of a given letter is multiplied by itself.
יהוה $= 10^2 + 5^2 + 6^2 + 5^2 = 186$

• *Mispar shemi or miluy (Filling)*

Each letter has the numerical value of the sum of the Ragil values of all the letters that make up the names of the letter. In this method the Name YHVH ([yod + vav + dalet] + [heh + alef] + [vav + alef] + [vav + heh + alef]) equals 45, or ([yod + vav + dalet] + [heh + heh] + [vav + vav] + [heh + heh]) equals 52. This use of filling can be very complex, because there are various ways to spell each letter in Hebrew.

• *Temurah*

Temurah is a means whereby various letters in a word are substituted for other letters, creating an entirely new word. The system of *Temurah* is actually found in the Hebrew Bible at least twice, in the book of Jeremiah. Here, 25:26 and 51:41 speak of "Sheshach," ששך, which is actually a reference to Babylon – see *Atbash* below. I have given the most common types of *Temurah* along with the divine name YHVH and its permutations both here and in the text of the book itself.

• *Atbash*[8]

In this system of *gematria*, the first letter of the alphabet (Aleph, א) is substituted for the last letter (Tau, ת), the second letter (Bet, ב) is substituted for the penultimate (Shin, ש), and so on, according to the following chart:

אבגדהוזחטיכ
תשרקצפעסנמל

Example of *Atbash*:
ששך = בבל (Babylon = Sheshach)
יהוה = מצפצ or מצפץ

• *Aiq Bekar*

This relatively simple cipher uses the following chart, wherein any letter in the same box can be substituted for another:

ג ל ש	ב כ ר	א י ק
ו ס ם	ה נ ך	ד מ ת
ט צ ץ	ח פ ף	ז ע ן

Example of *Aiq Bekar*:
יהוה = אדמנ, קנסך, קדסך, etc.[9]

---

[8] Talmudic references to *Atbash*: *Shabbat* 104a

• *Achas B'tay-ah*

Very similar to *Aiq Bekar*, in that any of the other letters in a corresponding box can be substituted for each other:

ד כ צ	ג י פ	ב ט ע	א ח ס
ת	ז נ ש	ו מ ר	ה ל ק

Example of *Achas B'tay-ah*:
יהוה = גלרל, פקרק, פלמל, etc.

• *Notarikon*

This simplistic use of the Hebrew alphabet uses the first letters of a phrase in Hebrew to create a new word. According to the Jewish Encyclopedia, notarikon was used "in haggadic interpretation only, not in halakic matters" (340), meaning that interpretation was limited to nonlegal text, and legal text was out of bounds for this type of interpretation. The most common example of notarikon is the word *Tanakh*, a *notarikon* for ***Torah*** (Pentateuch), ***Neviim*** (Prophets), and ***Ketuvim*** (Writings) – i.e. the Hebrew Bible or Old Testament. Another example of this is the word *Amen*, אמן, which is a *notarikon* for *El Melek Ne'eman,* אל מלך נאמן, meaning "Lord, Faithful King." *Notarikon* can also be used for the last letters in a phrase that spell out a word. For example, YHVH can be spelled from the last letters of the phrase *Mi Iolah Lanuw Heshememah,* מי יעלה־לנו השמימה from Deut. 30:12, which translates to "Who shall go up for us to heaven?" The first letters of this phrase also spell the word *milah,* מילה, which means "circumcision." As the reader can infer, many meanings come about through the combination of biblical exegesis and *notarikon.*

Notes About the Text

Overall, I have tried to apply all standard transliterations of the text into English. This has often clashed with the transliterations given in other books and works about Kabbalah. When it interferes with standard transliterations, I have either changed the transliteration for ease of pronunciation or stayed with the most familiar term. Above all, I have endeavored to keep the transliterations easy to pronounce.

You will also notice that the Masoretic Points common to modern Hebrew are missing from this book. This is because points were added long after the words were written merely for ease of reading and also tend to complicate the format of this book – even today, Torah scrolls are unpointed. The transliterations of some words are multiple, simply because the (mental) vowels were added to the words themselves, and thus there are different meanings. This does not mean that two words with two separate transliterations and two meanings are directly interchangeable, but rather that the words take on a spiritual relationship with each other, leaving a mystically-inclined reader to see varied meaning in even one word. For example the Hebrew term *Chalaq* means "to divide," but when the vowel points are different, and it is pronounced *Cheleq*, it can mean "flattery," or even "portion." Again, we are dealing with a very ancient language here, and even when modern Hebrew or even Biblical scholarship illuminates meaning, there are various translations that can occur. This does not obscure meaning, but indeed helps create it.

Explanation of my Transliterations of the Masoretic Points and Letters:

ָ	*a*
ַ	*a*
ֻ	*u*
ֲ	*a*

---

[9] There is no reason for assuming that a final letter within a word is incorrect, for the *Tanakh* also contains instances of the same.

ֶ	*e*
ֳ	*o*
א	*'a*
ב	*v*
בּ	*b*
ג גּ	*g*
ד	*d*
ה	*h*
הָ	*ah*
וֹ	*ow*
וּ	*u*
ז	*z*
ח	*ach*
ט	*t*
ֵי	*ey*
ִי	*iy*
כּ	*k*
כ	*ch*
ל	*l*
מ ם	*m*
נ ן	*n*
ס	*s*
ע	*a'*
פּ	*p*
פ	*f*
צ	*tz*
ק	*q*
ר	*r*
שׂ	*s*
שׁ	*sh*
ת תּ	*t*

Gematria does leave itself open for different meanings, and of extreme interest to the beginner is knowledge of the Hebrew itself. I recommend three books written for college-level students who may not be able to take Biblical Hebrew. These are Biblical Hebrew (vols. 1 & 2) by Menahem Mansoor and Kittell's Yale Language Series (see the bibliography for further information). Together, these books provide a student with the willpower to learn Hebrew in several self-guided steps. For the purposes of this book, I find it necessary to explain some of my transliterations. For example, ויסרתי meaning "and I will chastise" is spelled *ve-Yisartiy* when transliterated here. This is merely for ease of understanding for the beginner, as the prefix ־ו means "and." In all cases when the word is to be properly transliterated, there is no space nor dash between the prefix "*ve*" and the rest of the word. This adaptation has been used merely for reading convenience, and the proper spelling of the word is "*veyisartiy*." The same motive is applied for the prefix *heh*, or "the." When using inseparable prepositions (see below), one can see that several meanings make themselves apparent in Biblical text.

Common Hebraic conventions that may be useful to the reader/*gematria*-minded person are given below. Remember that using the rules below change both the meaning and the *gematria* of a given word and/or phrase.

Hebrew Language Conventions:

Conjunction:

־ו	"and"

Definite Article

־ה	"the"

Direct Object

word used to indicate ־את

Personal Pronouns

הוא	he – m. sing.
היא	she – f. sing.
אתה	thou, you – f. sing.
אתה	you – m. sing.
הם	they – m. pl.
אתם	you – m. pl.
הן	they – f. pl.
אנחנו	we – pl.
אני	I

Prepositions

Inseparable

־ב	in, with
־כ	as, like
־ל	to, for
־מ	from

Separable

על	upon, over
אל	to
עם	with (beings)
עם	with (beings)
מן	from
תחת	under, instead of
בלי	without

How to Reference this Book:

I have tried to examine the elements of Hebrew language through *gematria* in an easy-to-read format. However, due to the length of this book, I had to abbreviate and shorten some elements of Hebrew and rely on the knowledge of the reader. Someone who is familiar with Jewish or Western Esoteric Kabbalah will find the terminology recognizable. Even then, the design of this book may confuse, and so I give these short examples for the easier interpretation of the reader:

1. For each number with a corresponding Hebrew letter, there is a short explanation of the numerical significance, in terms of the letter, etc. I have provided a short area for the reader to insert his or her own remarks in the "notes" section. There are also many excellent books listed in the bibliography, which explain various methods of interpreting letters. Indeed, the reader is encouraged to begin his or her own "book of letters," which can easily be done with various word processing or spreadsheet programs. These can be as lengthy as necessary. There is no end to the analytic methods of *gematria.*

2. I culled the various Western Esoteric References mostly from David Godwin's excellent Cabalistic Encyclopedia. I have not referenced the page numbers from his book, as the items there are easily found in the sections of his book. I must stress that my book does not replace his, as the divisions of his book called "Transliterated Hebrew" and "Hebrew" are still indispensable for their reference. My book is merely to serve as an addendum. Another excellent reference for those items the reader is unfamiliar with is Hulse's The Eastern Mysteries. The information for both books is found in the Bibliography.

Examples from this book along with explanations:

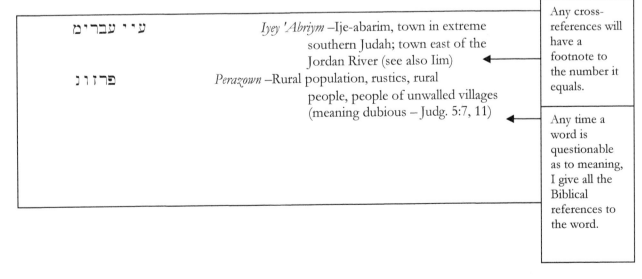

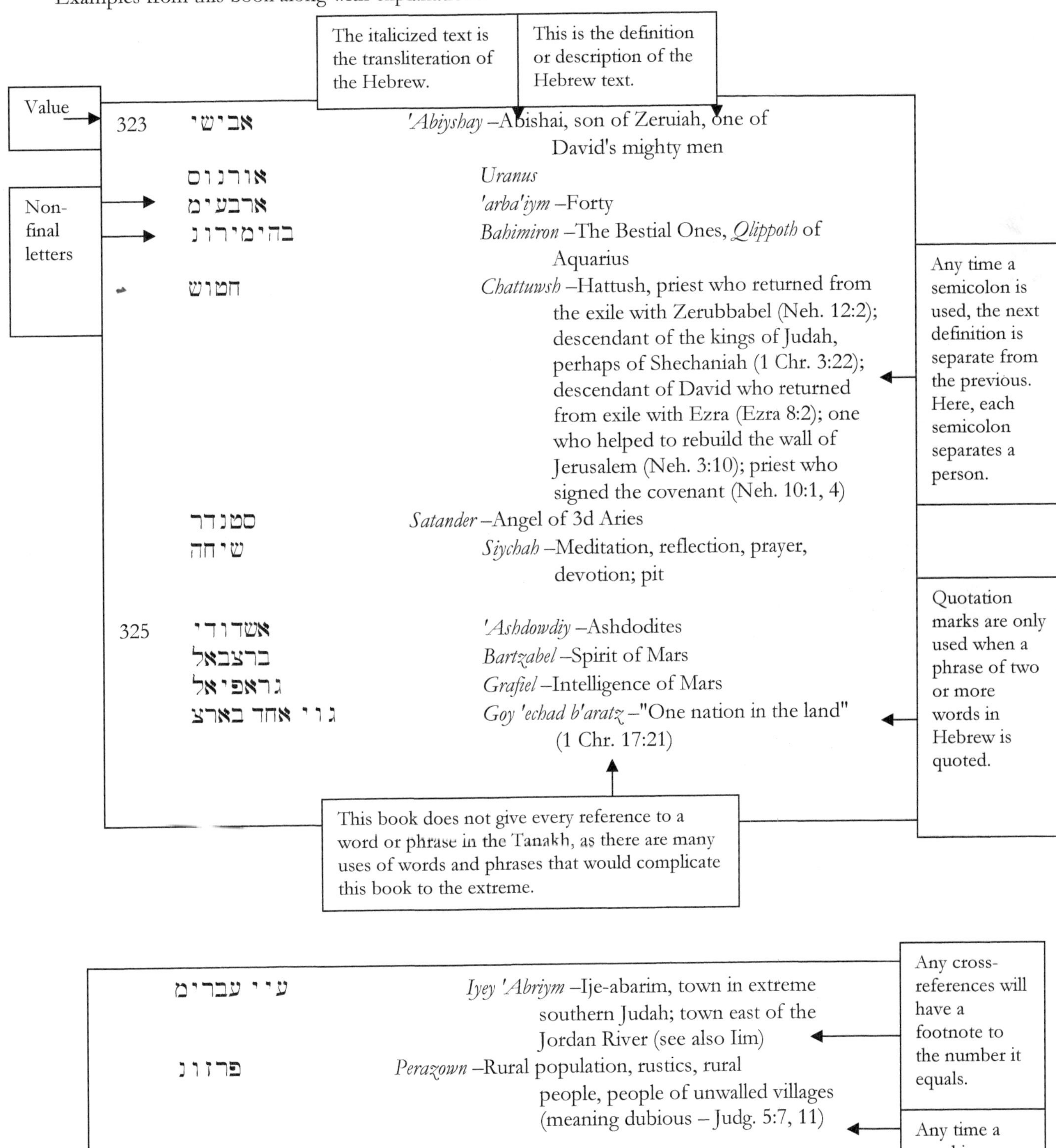

Chapter 2: Gematria and the Tanakh

#	Hebrew	Meaning and Translation

000 –The associated number of *Ain Sof Aur* (according to A.C.)[10]

00 –The associated number of *Ain Sof* (according to A.C.)

0 –The associated number of *Ain* (according to A.C.)
–Tarot Card: The Fool (The 11th Path; *Alef*; Air – G.D.) [11]

1 **א** *Alef*–First letter of Hebrew alphabet
–The 1st Path is the *Sefira Keter*, Crown
–Unity; the monad
–Mystic number of 1st path (*Keter*)
–Tarot Card: The Magician (The 12th Path; *Bet*; Mercury – G.D.)

The letter *alef* is the first letter and the first number of the Hebrew numerical system. It represents unity and the geometric symbol of the single point. *Alef* represents the unity of God and the singular nature of the Jewish deity. *Elohim*, the sacred name of God begins with an *alef*, and begins the name of the first human, Adam. Also, the introduction to the Ten Commandments begins with *alef*:

> אנכי יהוה אלקיך אשר הוצאתיך מארץ מצרים מבית עבדים, "I am God your God who has taken you out of the land of Egypt, out of the house of bondage" (Ex. 20:2).

Because the Torah begins with *bet*, not *alef*, it is intimated that there was a time not recorded in the Bible, and this is the basis for Isaac Luria's theory of the contraction or *tzimtzum* of God.[12]

In its shape, *alef* is similar to a human being with two arms upstretched and two legs down. The Zohar thus says that it represents the "image of God." In this way, the translation of *alef* as "ox" is apt, as it represents the human and physical nature of our everyday world. The shape of *alef* is also similar to two yods (one on top and one on the bottom) and one *vav*. Thus, the numerical value of one is also twenty-six, the number equivalent to the Tetragrammaton, YHVH. In this way, we see that God and man are both represented by this letter. When the Tetragrammaton is seen in the Torah scroll, the Name *Adonai* is pronounced instead, a Name that begins with *alef*. Indeed, the letter is a paradox and a deep mystery. It is no coincidence that *alef* (אלף) spelled backwards becomes *Pele'* (פלא) or "mystery."

NOTES:

---

[10] All references from 777 by Aleister Crowley – hereafter referred to as "A.C."

[11] All Tarot references from The Golden Dawn by Israel Regardie – hereafter referred to as G.D.

[12] Excellent examinations of Luria's theory can be found in nearly every introductory book on Kabbalah – see the bibliography.

2 ב *Bet* –Second letter of Hebrew alphabet; when used as a prefix, it often connotes "in" or "with"

–The 2nd Path is the *Sefira Chokmah*, Wisdom
–Duality; the duad
–Tarot Card: The High Priestess (The 13th Path; *Gimel*; Luna – G.D.)
–Prime number

The number two is represented by *bet*, the second letter of the Hebrew alphabet. The letter begins the *Tanakh*, and is thus very symbolic and important in gematria. It is also the only other letter besides *alef* that occupies only one number. In other words, there is no combination of letters that equal the number two. There are no words that have only two *alefs*, thus *bet* is the only letter equaling two. Duality is a concept associated with the relationship between God and Israel, the Oral and Written Torah, the two tablets of the Ten Commandments, the two genders of human beings, and heaven and earth.

Bet is composed of three *vavs*, which gives it the internal numerical value of thirty, a number also equaling יהוה plus the number of letters in the name.

Bet begins the word *Berakah*, or blessing. Thus, the Talmud relates that the *Tanakh* begins with *bet* because in that way, the entire world blesses God with the pronunciation of the letter. The letter also begins such notable words as *Beriy'ah*, or creation, *Ben*, or son, and *Beth*, or daughter. There are of course, a number of other important words. Arguably the most important is the word *Bereshit*, בראשית. This word can be translated in other ways than "In the beginning," including "At the beginning," or "With beginning," etc.[13] Because the *Tanakh* begins with the second letter, it is implied that there was a "pre-beginning" that existed before the creation of the world. What exists before the universe? God, the *alef*.

NOTES:

[13] For an excellent example of the various types of Kabbalistic interpretation of this first word of the Hebrew Bible, see chapter three "In the beginning" of David Sheinkin's book Path of the Kabbalah, which examines this in great detail.

3 אב *Ab* –Father (of an individual, of God as father of his people), head or founder of a household; ancestor; originator of a class, profession or art; of producer, generator; of benevolence & protection; term of respect & honor; ruler or chief; a title of *Chokmah*; the first two letters of the 42-letter name of God, corresponding to *Keter*; the initials of *Alef Bet* (the alphabet); 1st Gate of the 231 Gates[14]

Av –11th month of the Jewish Calendar – it is associated with Leo and the tribe Judah

Eb –Freshness, fresh green, green shoots, greenery; fruit, fresh, young, greening (Aramaic)

בא *Ba'* –Has come, came, went, go; set

Bo' –Come

ג *Gimel* –Third letter of Hebrew alphabet

–The 3rd Path is the *Sefira Binah*, Understanding
–The Triangle; the triad
–The number of persons in the Christian Trinity
–The number of elements mentioned in the *Sefer Yetzirah* (air, water, and fire)[15]
–The number of the three Patriarchs: Abraham, Isaac, and Jacob
–The number of divisions of Jews: *kohanim, leviim* and *Yisraelim*[16]
–The number of the parts of *Tanakh*: *Torah, Neviim* and *Kethuvim*
–The number of alchemical elements (sulfur, mercury, salt)
–The number of Mother Letters (*Alef, Mem, Shin*)[17]
–Mystic number of 2nd Path (*Chokmah*)
–Tarot Card: The Empress (The 14th Path; *Dalet*; Venus – G.D.)
–Prime number

Three is very important for Jewish mysticism, as can be seen in the above symbols that are all related to three. Triads allude to the conjunction of two opposing forces coming together in a third force. A *Midrashim* relates a triad through Solomon's words: "Have I not written for you threefold things of counsel and knowledge?" (Prov. 22:20). To this the *Midrash* states, "This verse refers to the Torah, which was written with an Alef-Bet that forms sets of three letters, alef-bet-gimel" (*Tanchuma Yisro*). Another clarification from *Anaf Yosef* is needed to explain this midrash: "The twenty-seven letters of the Hebrew *Aleph-Beis* (twenty-two regular plus five final letters) can be divided into sets of three. When they are set in triplets the *gematria* of the middle letter of each triplet is the average of the other two" (Munk, 76). In this way, a triad is again a representation of the completeness of two opposing forces, cf. Hegelian philosophy. To approach this same concept from a different perspective, consider that *gimel* can be translated "camel," and that an ancient *Midrash* written by Rabbi Eliezer relates that the third person in the Creation story (*nachash*) was a camel rather than a serpent. Thus, when he relates that the serpent is represented by a camel, he is intimating the importance of the number three to this story.

Gimel, the letter representing three, is related to *gamol*, a word that means "nourish until completely ripe," whether of a child growing or of a plant or animal. In this way, the letter represents the begininng of Torah study, study of *Kabbalah* or any such study that begins with small steps that must be practiced and nurtured to the point of second nature reaction. In other words, when one is learning to see and act upon everything through a Kabbalistic viewpoint, one is attuning themself to the *gimel*.

---

[14] The 231 Gates are essentially the maximum number of permutations of any two Hebrew letters without repetition. See Sefer Yetzirah for a full explanation.
[15] All Sefer Yetzirah references are from R. Aryeh Kaplan's edition.
[16] *Kohanim* = priestly caste; *Leviim* = levites; *Yisraelim* = Israelites
[17] Sefer Yetzirah, pp. 23-32.

The Jewish Encyclopedia mentions that three was very important to early peoples, especially in regard to its use in the three regions, "heaven, earth, and water, respectively represented in Babylonian mythology by the divinities Anu, Bel and Ea." The comparison to the creation story of Genesis comes easy with this information as well.

Some biblical passages where three is very important are:

1 Kings 17:21
1 Chr. 21:12
Dan. 6:10

NOTES:

4 אבא *'avo'* –I will come
אג *'ag* –To spell letters, to curse, swear; the initials of *Elohim Gibor*; 2nd Gate of the 231 Gates
גא *Ge'* –Proud
ד *Dalet* –Fourth letter of Hebrew alphabet
–The number of letters in the Tetragrammaton
–The 4th Path is the *Sefira Hesed*, Mercy
–The square; the tetrad
–The number of elements (fire, water, air, earth)
–The number of cardinal points (north, south, east, west)
–The number of seasons in the year
–The number of worlds of the Kabbalah (Assiah, Briah, Yetzirah, Aztilut)[18]
–The number of matriarchs: Sarah, Rachel, Rebecca, and Leah
–The number of Jacob's wives: Rachel, Bilhah, Zilpah, and Leah
–The number of cups of wine of the *Seder*
–The number of cardinal virtues (fortitude, justice, prudence, and temperance)
–The number of human limbs
–The number of levels of Biblical interpretation (literal, allusion, allegory, and secret)[19]
–Tarot Card: The Emperor (The 15th Path; *Heh*; Aries – G.D.)

Four is represented by the letter *dalet*, of which R. Yitzchak Ginsburg writes "the full meaning of the *dalet* is the door through which the humble enter into the realization of G-d's dwelling place below" (67). This means that in Jewish Kabbalistic thought, the *dalet* is related to *Malkut* as well as the means to get to *Malkut*. The shape of *dalet* is similar to a man bent over, bowing, and thus represents the selflessness that humans must have in order to begin the movement from physical to spiritual. This letter can be translated "door," as in the door to the higher levels of spirituality, "a poor man," representing the fact that one must be humble in order to attain these levels (as in the Hebrew word *dal* or דל, meaning pauper), "lifting up," intimating the soul's movement to a spiritual ideal, and "elevation," indicating the same as the latter. About the letter, the Sefer Bahir states, "What is this like? Ten kings were in a certain place. All of them were wealthy, but one was not quite as wealthy as the others. Even though he is still very wealthy, he is poor (*Dal*) in relation to the others" (11). R. Kaplan says about this passage, "(Dalet) is said to represent Malkhut-Kingship, the last of the Ten Sefirot. While each of the other nine give to the one below it, Malkhut-Kingship, being the lowest, cannot give.... Like the absolutely destitute, it only receives, but cannot give" (103). For a more indepth examination of the relationship between humility, poverty and giving, see the discussion of *dalet* in R. Michael Munk's book, The Wisdom in the Hebrew Alphabet, pp. 78-84, which provides a more thorough explanation of the associations given here.

NOTES:

[18] According to Isaac Luria, there are actually five worlds of the Kabbalah.

[19] See Introduction for a fuller explanation.

5	אגא	*'Age'* –Agee, one of David's mighty men
	אד	*Edh* –Mist, vapor; 3rd Gate of the 231 Gates
	בבא	*B'vo'* –As they were coming; gate
	בג	*Bagh* –Spoil, booty; back; food, delicacy, bread; 22nd Gate of the 231 Gates
	גב	*Gab* –Elevation, top; convex surface, back; back (Aramaic)
		Geb –Pit, water hole, beam, ditch; locust; den (Aramaic)
		Gob –Gob, site of several battles during Israel's wars with the Philistines – may be the same as Gezer or Gath
	דא	*Da'* –This one, another, this (Aramaic)
	ה	*Heh* –5th letter of Hebrew alphabet; when used as a prefix, it means "the"

–The 5th Path is the *Sefira Giburah*, Severity
–The pentagon; the pentad
–The number of senses
–The number of total elements (including Spirit)
–The number of fingers on one hand
–The number of toes on one foot
–The number of human limbs counting the head
–The number of lumbar vertebrae in the human spine
–The number of vanities in Ecclesiastes
–The number of times "Bless God, my soul" is stated in Psalms 103, 104
–The number of final letters in Hebrew
–The number of orders of architecture (Tuscan, Doric, Ionic, Corinthian, and Composite)
–Tarot Card: The Hierophant (The 16th Path; *Vav*; Taurus – G.D.)
–The number of books in the Torah
–Prime number

The Hebrew letter *heh* represents the number five, and is very important for gematria, especially concerning its use in the divine Tetragrammaton. It is the first letter of the Name that we encounter in the alphabet, and is also used by itself to represent *Ha-Shem* (the name), like so:

ה'

When used in this manner, observant Jews will pronounce the divine name *Adonai*, or whenever the Tetragrammaton is used.

Not only does *heh* represent an entire ½ of the Tetragrammaton, it is also symbolic of God's ability to forgive sinners, as the left leg of the letter is opened, symbolizing the path through which one can return to the one God.

Heh was given to various Biblical characters, from Abram to Sarai. The reader should take note of the numerical changes in their respective names.

NOTES:

6 אה *Ah* –Ah!; the initials of *Adam HaAretz*; 4th Gate of the 231 Gates

בד *Bad* –Alone, by itself, besides, apart, separation, being alone; linen, white linen; empty talk, idle talk, liar, lie; bar, limb, arm; a measure of weight (*Bad*); 23rd Gate of the 231 Gates

גבא *Gebe* –Cistern, pool

גג *Gagh* –Flat roof, roof, top, housetop; cover of an altar

דב *Dob* –A bear (see also דוב)[20]

הא *He'* –Behold!, lo!; even as, like as (Aramaic)

ו *Vav* –Sixth letter of Hebrew alphabet; when used as a prefix, it means "and"[21]

–The 6th Path is the *Sefira Tiferet*, Beauty
–The hexagon; the heptad
–Mystic number of the 3rd Path (*Binah*)
–Number of days the earth was created in Genesis
–Number of *alefs* in the first verse of Torah
–The number of orders of the *Misnah*
–The number of directions the world was sealed with (*Sefer Yezirah* 4:3)
–Tarot Card: The Lovers (The 17th Path; *Zayin*; Gemini – G.D.)
–Perfect number

Six is the number of days the earth was created in Genesis, and so represents physical completeness. Since *Tiferet* is also the sixth *sefirot*, we can see that the importance of this ordinal number, and of the letter *vav*.

Vav can be used for two different changes in the Hebrew language. Firstly, it is prefixed to a word to mean "and." This indicates its usage as a joiner, and thus links sentences into paragraphs and chapters, even joining books together. Its second use is termed "conversive" and changes the tense of a particular word from past to future or vice versa.[22] For example, the Hebrew ויאמר is translated "and he said," with the *vav* preceding the root אמר, meaning "say" or "command." The *yod* here is a prefix, indicating the masculine gender. Thus, the two uses of the *vav* are valuable for the meaning and interpretation of any given Biblical verse or name of an entity.

Interestingly, R. Ginsburgh gives another in-depth examination of the letter in its full spelling, stating that the Tabernacle's curtains were held together by "ווי העמודים, 'the *hooks* [*vavs*] of the pillars.'" He goes on to explain that this term is used a total of six times in the Hebrew Bible, and gives and excellent comprehensive meaning for the usage of this phrase. (Ginsburgh, 100).

NOTES:

---

[20] דוב (12).

[21] For a more in-depth examination of the various meanings of the prefix *vav*, see Munk's book The Wisdom in the Hebrew Alphabet, p. 99.

[22] For an excellent discussion of the *vav* conversive, consult the books listed in the bibliography under "Hebrew Language Bibliography."

7 אבד *Abad* –Destroy, perish
Avad –Perish, vanish, go astray, be destroyed; you perish, will perish; to perish, vanish (Aramaic)
Ovad –Void, lost
Oved –Destruction
אגג *Agag* –Agag, king of Amalek, spared by Saul but slain by Samuel
אדב *Adab* –To grieve, cause grief
אהא *Aha* –Name of God attributed to Venus. Initials of *Adonai HaAretz*
או *'O* –Desire; either, or, rather; whether, not the least; if, otherwise, and, then; 5th Gate of the 231 Gates
בדא *Bada'* –To devise, contrive, invent (in a bad sense)
בה *Bah* –To be broken into, confounded, confused, to burst forth, to be stirred up; in it, with her, with it, upon him; 24th Gate of the 231 Gates
גד *Gad* –Gad, seventh son of Jacob and an ancestor of a tribe of Israel (associated with Aries); Gad, David's seer who frequently advised him (1 Sam. 22:5; 1 Chr. 21:9-19); Gad, a Babylonian deity; fortune; 42nd Gate of the 231 Gates; coriander; who advised him (1 Sam. 22:5; 1 Chr. 21:9-19); Gad, the territory settled by the tribe of Gad
דאב *Da'ab* –To pine, mourn, be sorrowful; was weary (according to A.C.)
דבא *Dobe'* –To be sluggish; strength; riches, power (last two meanings according to A.C.)
דג *Dagh* –Fish
האא *Haa* –26th name of *Shem HaMeforash* (2 Sagittarius)
ז *Zayin* –7th letter of Hebrew alphabet

–The 7th Path is the *Sefira Netzach*, Victory
–The heptagon; the heptad
–The number of Hebrew words in Genesis 1:1
–The number of traditional planets (Moon, Sun, Mercury, Venus, Mars, Jupiter, Saturn)
–The number of days in the week
–The number of weeks of counting the Omer
–The number of lamps of the menorah
–The number of rabbinic *mitzvot*
–The number of vertebrae in the human neck
–The number of spinal chakras in Yoga
–The number of deadly sins, popularized by Heironymos Bosch's painting by the same name (envy, covetousness, lust, pride, anger, gluttony, and sloth)
–The number of liberal arts (grammar, rhetoric, logic, arithmetic, geometry, music, and astronomy), according to Nicomachus Capella
–Tarot Card: The Chariot (The 18th Path; *Chet*; Cancer – G.D.)
–Prime number

Seven is used almost exclusively in reference to the holiness of God. It is the last day of the Creation story, the climax (or some say anti-climax) to the story, rounding out the holiest day of the week, *Shabbat.* Nearly every reference in Biblical or post-biblical texts to the number seven relates to God and his dominion. Even Christian writers like John of the Apocalypse used this symbol to the point where its use is clichéd.

However, it is important that whenever one comes across this number, the student of *gematria* should be attentive.

The mathematical value of seven is interesting, especially as described by R. Michael Munk:

> Within the common decimal method – which is also the basis of the Torah's counting system – the following set of properties is common to one and seven: (a) neither of these numbers can be expressed as the product of any two whole numbers other than itself and one; (b) neither is a prime factor of any other number betwen one and ten. The combination of such properties can be found in no other number between one and ten. (105)

Using simple deduction and association, one can see the similarities between the significance of one and seven. Both represent God in one form or another, and both share properties that no other number between one and ten share.

NOTES:

8	אבה	*Abah* –To be willing, consent
		Abeh –Entreat, longing, desire
		Ebeh –Reed, papyrus
	אגד	*Agad* –To bind
	אהב	*Ahab* –Love, desired, beloved; to love, to like; loves, amours (only in plural)
		Ohab –Loved object; love
	אז	*Az* –Then, at that time, before, because of that; 6th Gate of the 231 Gates
	באה	*Be'ah* –Entrance, a coming in, entering, entry (of the temple)
	בו	*Bow* –To go in, enter, come, go, come in, within, split, insert, sexual union, in it, him
		Vo –In itself, in the ... is, that in it, on it, in it, with it, upon him; 25th Gate of the 231 Gates
	גה	*Geh* –This, such; 43rd Gate of the 231 Gates
	דאג	*Da'ag* –To be anxious, concerned, grieve; fear, sorrow
		Do'eg –Doeg, servant of Saul who executed the priests of Nob on Saul's orders (see also דואג)[23]
	דבב	*Dabab* –Move gently, glide, glide over
	דאג	*Da'g* –Fish (see also דג)[24]
	דד	*Dadh* –Love; beloved, breast, teat, nipple; pleasures of love
		Dod –Beloved, love, uncle (see also דוד)[25]
	הבא	*Haveh* –Bring
	ח	*Chet* –8th letter of Hebrew alphabet

–The 8th Path is the *Sefira Hod*, Splendor
–The octagon; the ogdoad
–The number of trigrams in the I Ching
–The number of days of *Chanukah*
–The number of *Sefirot* on the Sufi Tree of Life
–Tarot Card: Strength (The 19th Path; *Teth*; Leo – G.D.)

Eight is the number assigned to the letter *chet*, a symbol of transcendence. According to R. Michael Munk, "the number eight symbolizes man's ability to transcend the limitations of physical existence" (112). Thus, the number is heavily involved wherever humanity reaches beyond the mortal, such as the Temple services in Biblical times, the day of circumcision, the days of *Hannukah*, the list goes on and on. *Chet* means "fence," and is often referred to as a doorway to the spiritual. It should rather be thought of as the first gate into a new world of such life as well as holiness. Its form is said to consist of the previous two letters, *vav* and *zayin*, along with a bridge, called the *chatoteret*, or "hunchback." The combination of these two letters equals seventeen, which when reduced to its digit sum, equals eight.

Chet begins important terms such as *chavvah*, or "life;" *chen*, or "grace;" *cheta'*, or "sin;" *chuppah*, or "wedding canopy." The relationship of such terms to the meanings of the letter given above are an exercise for the reader.

NOTES:

---

[23] דואג (14).

[24] דג (7).

[25] דוד (14).

9 אדד — *'Adad* –Hadad, an Edomite

אוב — *Owb* –Water skin bottle; necromancer, one that has a familiar spirit

אזא — *Aza* –Make hot, heat

אח — *Ach* –Brother; ah!, alas!, woe!; Fire-pot, brazier; initials of *Adam Chavvah* (Adam and Eve); 7th Gate of the 231 Gates
Oach –Howling animal

בבה — *Babah* –The apple (pupil) of the eye

בגד — *Bagad* –To act treacherously, deceitfully, deal treacherously; fortune is come (only in relation to Gen. 30:11)
Beged –Treachery, deceit; garment, clothing (used indiscriminately)

בוא — *Vo'* –Come, come in, come out, come upon, go down

בז — *Baz* –Booty, spoil, robbery, spoiling; to prey, plunder, conquer, shutter, tread upon; give away, squander, treat lightly; cut into pieces; prey, spoil; 26th Gate of the 231 Gates

גאה — *Ga'ah* –To rise up, grow up, be exalted in triumph
Ge'ah –Pride
Ge'eh –Proud

גו — *Gav* –The back; the middle (Aramaic); 44th Gate of the 231 Gates
Gev –Among, back, body, middle

דה — *Dah* –61st Gate of the 231 Gates

הגא — *Hege'* –Hege, chamberlain of Ahasuerus (see also הגי)[26]

הד — *Hed* –A shout of joy, shout

ובא — *Vova'* –He shall come (Lev. 13:16)

זב — *Zav* –Issue

ט — *Teth* –9th letter of Hebrew alphabet

–The 9th Path is the *Sefira Yesod*, Foundation
–The number of squares in the magic square of Saturn[27]
–The number of months of pregnancy
–The number of blessings of *Musaf* on *Rosh HaShanah*
–Number of blasts of the *shofar*
–Tarot Card: The Hermit (The 20th Path; *Yod*; Virgo – G.D.)

Nine is the penultimate number before the completion of the *sefirot*. *Teth*, the 9th letter, begins the word *Tov*, or "good," the first word containing a *teth* in the Hebrew Bible. The shape of the letter is indicative of a womb in many Talmudic texts, which also relates to its association with the *sefira Yesod*. In this way, we see that good is one of the "curses" of the Genesis story.[28] Note that there are also nine months in a pregnancy.

Kabbalah teaches that nine represents the qualities of truth and eternity, identical with divine properties. Several Hebrew words' numerical equivalents can be reduced to nine: אמת (*emet*, truth – 441); ברית (*berith*, covenant – 612); אור (*aur*, light – 207); שבת (*Shabbat* – 702). All of these words, along with

---

26 הגי (18).

27 All references to magical squares or "kameas" are taken from Regardie's The Golden Dawn.

28 Again, I refer the reader to the many examinations of the Creation story told from a Kabbalistic bent. These will illuminate and impress with their ingenious and sometimes all too eye-opening perspectives.

others in their numerical categories, represent various aspects of the above.

NOTES:

10 אבוא *'avo'* –I will come
אהד *'Ohad* –Ohad, a son of Simeon
אט *'at* –Whisper; gentleness, softness; secret, charmers, enchanter, fortuneteller, soothsayer, diviner; 8th Gate of the 231 Gates
בדד *Badad* –To withdraw, be separate, be isolated; isolation, withdrawal, separation; alone
Bedad –Father of Hadad, a King of Edom
בזא *Baza'* –To divide, cleave, cut through
בח *Bach* –To look out, be cautious; 27th Gate of the 231 Gates
גבה *Gabahh* –To be high, be exalted; high, proud
Gaboahh –Haughty, height, high(-er), lofty, proud, exceed
Gobahh –Excellency, haughty, high, height, loftiness, pride
גז *Gaze* –Fleece, mowing, mown grass, shear; 45th Gate of the 231 Gates
דאה *Da'ah* –Fly swifly, dart through the air; a bird forbidden as food (probably a kite or vulture)
דו *Daw* –62nd Gate of the 231 Gates
הה *Hah* –Alas!
Heh –Window; 5th letter of Hebrew alphabet
ואבא *Va'avo'* –And I came, and I brought
זאב *Ze'eb* –Wolf; Zeeb, prince of Midian slain by Gideon (Judg. 7:25; 8:3 – see also Oreb)[29]
זג *Zag* –Name of some insignificant product of the vine, husks? or skins? (meaning uncertain – Num. 6:4)
חב *Chob* –Bosom
טא *Ta* –To sweep away
י *Yod*–10th letter of Hebrew alphabet

–The 10th Path is the *Sefirah Malkut*, Kingdom
–The decagon; the decad
–Mystic number of 4th Path (*Hesed*)
–The number of *Sefirot*
–The number of fingers
–The number of toes
–Pythagorean "divine tetrarkus"
–The number of utterances through which the world was created in Genesis
–The number of things created on the first day
–The number of generations from Adam to Noah and from Noah to Abraham
–The number of nations given to Abraham
–Number of Commandments
–Number of plagues of Egypt
–Tarot Card: The Wheel of Fortune (The 21st Path; *Kaf*; Jupiter – G.D.)

Finally we arrive at ten, the number associated with the *sefirot* and the number most related to completion. For example, we can see that there were ten utterances by God that created the world.

Yod begins many important words in Hebrew, all of which are important Kabbalistic terms. *Yetzirah*,

[29] Oreb (272).

Yom, *Yetzer*, *Yisrael*, *Yaakob*, *Yehudah* and the Name יהוה of course. There is also an important addition of the letter to the Ten Commandments. In the first reference to them (Ex. 20:12), the word *Ya'arikown*, which means "may be long" is spelled יארכון. In the second version (Deut. 5:16), it is spelled יאריכן. According to R. Munk, the inclusion of the *Yod* here "alludes to the fact that the promise of long life does not apply to life in This World. The omitted י, on the other hand, implies that the bliss of the World to Come is concealed from man on earth" (126).

NOTES:

11 אדו *'Iddow* –Iddo, official of Casiphia who provided Levites for Ezra

אהה *Ahah* –Alas!, oh!, ah!

אוד *Uwd* –Brand, firebrand

אחב *Achab* –Ahab, 7th King of Israel (spelling used only in Jer. 29:22 – see also אחאב)[30]

אי *Ai* –Where?, whence?; which?, how? (in prefix w/other adverb); island; not; alas!, woe!; howling beast, jackal; coast, island, shore, region; impossible; 9th Gate of the 231 Gates

בבאו *Bavouw* –When he came (goes)

בבגד *B'veged* –In a garment of

Baveged –In the garment

בבוא *Bavuwa'* –Coming of

בט *Bat* –To swell, burst forth, shine; to tread, to dash to pieces; 28th Gate of the 231 Gates

גדד *Gadad* –To penetrate, cut, attack, invade

Gedad –To cut down, hew down (Aramaic)

גוב *Gowb* –Grasshopper; locust; Gob, site of several battles during Israel's wars with the Philistines – may be the same as Gezer or Gath

Guwb –Husbandman; to dig; ditch, trench

גח *Goach* –Break forth, labor to bring forth, come forth, draw up, take out; 46th Gate of the 231 Gates

דבה *Dibbah* –Whispering, defamation, evil report

דהב *Dehab* –Gold, golden (Aramaic)

דז *Daz* –63rd Gate of the 231 Gates

הו *Hoo* –He, she, it; that

How –Alas!, ah!; he, she, it (Aramaic); 79th Gate of the 231 Gates

ואד *Veyd* –And a cloud, mist

ובבא *V'oa'* –And when he would come

זד *Zed* –Arrogant, proud, insolent, presumptuous

חבא *Chaba'* –To withdraw, hide

חג *Chag* –Festival, feast, festival-gathering, pilgrim-feast

טב *Tab* –Good (Aramaic)

–The 11th Path is between *Keter* and *Chokmah* and corresponds to *Alef*, Air, and the Tarot card The Fool – G.D.

–The number of magic (A.C.)

–Tarot Card: Justice (The 22nd Path; *Lamed*; Libra – G.D.)

–The sum of the first and tenth *sefira*

–Prime number

12 אבדה *Abedah* –A lost thing, something lost

Abaddoh –A lost thing, something lost, a perishing

אוה *Avah* –Desire, incline, covet, wait longingly, wish, sigh, want, to be greedy, prefer; to sign, mark, describe with a mark

Awah –Desire, lust, will (not necessarily evil)

---

[30] אחאב (12).

	אזאד	*Azad* –To be gone
	אחאב	*Achab* –Ahab, 7th King of Israel
	בטא	*Bata* –To speak rashly or angrily, speak thoughtlessly
	בי	*Biy* –If it please, pray excuse me, excuse me please; to dwell within, in me, at me, with me, by me; to pray, please; the Temple's innermost sanctuary; 29th Gate of the 231 Gates
	גדה	*Gadah* –River bank
	גוג	*Gog* –Gog, descendant of Joel; prince of Rosh, Meshech, and Tubal; Gog, a nation in the north
	גט	*Gat* –47th Gate of the 231 Gates
	דאבה	*De'abah* –Faintness, failure of mental energy, dismay, sorrow
	דגה	*Dagah* –Fish; to multiply, increase
	דוב	*Dowb* –A bear *Duwb* –Pine away, sorrow
	דח	*Dach* –64th Gate of the 231 Gates
	הבה	*Havah* –Come, give, prepare for this (Gen. 11:3)
	הוא	*Hava'* –To breathe; to be, to exist; to come to pass, become, be (Aramaic) *Hiva'* –He *Hu'*–He; a name of God and title of *Keter*
	הז	*Haz* –80th Gate of the 231 Gates
	וו	*Vav* –Nail, peg, hook, pin; 6th letter of Hebrew alphabet
	זה	*Zeh* –This, this one, here, which, this...that, the one...the other, another, such, this is; lamb, sheep (may be a typographical error for "seh" – 1 Sam. 17:34)[31] *Zoh* –This
	חבב	*Chabab* –To love fervently, cherish *Chobab* –Hobab, father-in-law or brother-in-law of Moses – see Num. 10:29 & Judg. 4:11 (in the latter Jethro is called the brother-in-law of Moses)
	חגא	*Chaga'* –Terror, a reeling (in terror – Is. 19:17); this
	חד	*Chad* –One (number), same, single, first, each, once; sharp
	טאב	*Te'eb* –To be glad, be good (Aramaic)

–The 12th Path is between *Keter* and *Binah* and corresponds to *Bet,* Mercury, and the Tarot card The Magician – G.D.
–The number of signs in the Zodiac
–The number of pairs of ribs in the human body
–The number of thoracic vertebrae in the human spine
–The number of Israelite tribes
–The number of Ishmaelite tribes
–The number of Jesus' disciples
–Tarot Card: The Hanged Man (The 23rd Path; *Mem*; Water – G.D.)

13	אבי	*'abowy* –Oh!, Woe! (exclamation of pain – indicates desire or uneasiness) *'Abiy* –Abi, daughter of Zechariah and the wife of Ahaz

[31] Seh, (305).

and mother of Hezekiah
'avi –Father, my father

אגדה *Aggadah* –Legend, tale; a type of presentation in the *Talmud*
Aguddah –Band, binding

אהבה *Ahabah* –Love, beloved; God's love to His people

אהוא *Ahava* –Ahava, site north of Babylon

אחד *Achad* –One; unity; to go one way or another, to be sharp
Echad –One (number); one of

איב *Ayab* –To be hostile to, to be an enemy to
Oyeb –Enemy (either personal or national)

באי *Ba'ey* –Those coming
Bo'i –I came

בהו *Bohu* –Waste, emptiness, void

בחג *Bochag* –On the feast (Deut. 16:16)

גבח *Gibbeach* –To be high in the forehead, bald

גהה *Gahah* –To cure; to remove (a bandage from a wound), healing, health
Gehah –Medicine; to cure

גוד *Guwd* –To invade, attack, overcome

גי *Gay* –Valley
Gi –The second two letters of the 42-letter name of God, corresponding to *Chokmah*; 48th Gate of the 231 Gates
Goy –Nation, people, namely gentile people or nation

דאגה *Dayagah* –Anxiety, anxious care, care
De'agah –Carefulness, fear, heaviness, sorrow, anxiety

דדה *Dadah* –To move slowly

דוג *Davvag* –A fisherman, fisher

דודוהו *Dowdavahuw* –Dodavah, father of Eliezer of Mareshah

דט *Dat* –65th Gate of the 231 Gates

הבאה *Haba'ah* –Which is coming

הבו *Havuw* –Give, ascribe

הגה *Hagah* –To moan, growl, utter, muse, mutter, meditate, devise, plot, speak; to remove, drive out
Hegeh –A rumbling, growling, moaning; to separate; to imagine

הדד *Hadad* –Hadad, a king of Edom who fought Midian (Gen. 36:35-36; 1 Chr. 1:46); the last of Edom's early kings (1 Chr. 1:50-51 – see also Hadar)[32]; member of the royal family of Edom who opposed Israel's rule of Edom (1 Kings 11:14-22, 25); an ancient Syrian god of storms

הח *Hach* –81st Gate of the 231 Gates

ובה *Vabah* –And through her

והב *Vaheb* –Vaheb, a place in Moab, site unknown

וז *Vuz* –96th Gate of the 231 Gates

זבד *Zabad* –To endow, bestow, endow with, bestow upon;

---

[32] Hadar, (209).

Zabad, descendant of Jerahmeel of Judah; man of Ephraim; son of Alai and one of David's mighty men; three who married foreign wives during the Ezile (see also Jozachar)[33]
Zeved –Endowment, gift, dowry, portion

זו — *Ziv* –Glory, splendor
Zow –This, such; which
Zuw –This, such; (of) which, (of) whom
Ziv –Glory, splendor; Ziv, the month of beginning the building of the Temple (1 Kings 6:1)

חגב — *Chagab* –Locust, grasshopper; Hagab, ancestor of captives returning with Zerubbabel (this name only used in Ezra 2:46 – see also Hagabah)[34]

יאב — *Ya'ab* –To long for, desire

יבא — *Ya'vo'* –Shall come

–The 13th Path is between *Keter* and *Tiferet* and corresponds to *Gimel,* Luna, and the Tarot card The High Priestess– G.D.
–The *Sefirot* of the Pillar of Mercy are 2 + 4 + 7 = 13
–Tarot Card: Death (The 24th Path; *Nun*; Scorpio – G.D.)
–Prime number

14 אביא — *'avia'* –Will I bring

אהבו — *'ahayvo'* –Loves him

אטד — *Atad* –Bramble, thorn, buckthorn

בבי — *Bebay* –Bebai, ancestor of captives returning from exile; ancestor of some returning from the exile with Ezra (may be the same as the latter)

בדח — *Badach* –To gladden, rejoice

בזה — *Bazah* –To despise, hold in contempt, disdain
Bazeh –With this, here, for this
Bazoh –Scorned, despised
Bizzah –Spoil, booty
Vazeh –Here

גוה — *Gevah* –Back; put out of mind, ignore, reject; arrogance, pride

גיא — *Gaye* –Valley, rising earth; one of the Seven Earths (associated with *Giburah* – A.C.)

דואג — *Dow'eg* –Doeg, servant of Saul who executed the priests of Nob on Saul's orders (see also דאג)[35]

דבח — *Debach* –To sacrifice (an animal), to offer sacrifice; sacrifice (all Aramaic)

דדו — *Dodow* –His uncle

דוד — *David* –David, King of Israel (see also דויד)[36]
Dowd –Beloved, love, uncle
Duwd –Basket, cauldron, kettle, (seething) pot

די — *Day* –Sufficiency, plenty, enough, abundance; 66th Gate of the 231 Gates

---

[33] Jozachar, (243).
[34] Hagabah (18).
[35] דאג (8).
[36] דויד (24).

האח *Heach* –Aha!
הבהב *Habhab* –Gift, offering, sacrificial offering
הבגד *HaBeged* –The garment
הבוא *Havoa'* –Shall come
הבז *HaBaz* –The booty
הדה *Hadah* –To direct out with the hand
הובא *Hava'* –Was brought
הזב *HaZav* –The issue (male) (Lev. 15:4)
הט *Hat* –82nd Gate of the 231 Gates
ואז *va-'az* –And then
ואהב *va-'ahev* –And loves
ובו *va-Vow* –And be in it, and to him
והבא *vu-Haba'* –And he that comes
וח *Vuch* –97th Gate of the 231 Gates
זבה *Zavah* –An issue of (female) (Lev. 15:19)
Zovah –Her issue
זהב *Zahav* –Gold, the metal of Sol
Z'hav –The gold of
חבד *Chabad* –An acronym for *Chokmah, Binah, Da'at* and the name of a branch of *Chassidut*
חגג *Chagag* –To hold a feast, hold a festival, make pilgrimage, keep a pilgrim-feast, celebrate, dance, stagger
יבב *Yabab* –To cry, cry shrilly
יד *Yod* –Hand
–The 14th Path is between *Chokmah* and *Binah* and corresponds to *Dalet,* Venus, and the Tarot card The Empress – G.D.
–The number of phalanges in the human hand
–The number of phalanges in the human foot
–The number of bones in the human face
–Tarot Card: Temperance (The 25th Path; *Samekh*; Sagittarius – G.D.)

15 אבוהא *Aboha* –Angel of 3rd decanate Sagittarius[37]
אביב *Aviv* –Spring, month of ear-forming, of greening of crop, of growing green, Abib (month of exodus & passover – March or April); fresh, young barley ears, barley
אוח *Och* –Olympic Planetary Spirit of Sol[38]
אחו *Achuw* –Reeds, marsh plants, rushes
איד *Eyd* –Distress, burden, calamity
באחד *Ba'achad* –In one of
Ba'echad –On the first
בבאי *B'vo'i* –When I came
בגדו *Bagdow* –His garment
בגוד *Bagowd* –Treacherous, deceitful
בגי *Vagai* –In the valley
בוז *Buwz* –To despise, hold in contempt, hold as

[37] All angels referenced as belonging to decanates and houses from Regardie's The Golden Dawn, p. 86. *Aboha* may Possibly relate to *'avia'* meaning "will I bring."
[38] All references to Olympic Planetary Spirits are taken from Regardie's The Golden Dawn.

insignificant; contempt; Buz, second born of Nahor; descendant of Gad; place in northern Arabia from which Elihu's father came

גאוה *Ga'avah* –Pride, excellency, haughtiness, majesty, a rising up

גבהה *Ge'vohah* –High

גבי *Gabbay* –Gabbai, chief of the tribe of Benjamin after the return from the exile

גזה *Gazah* –To cut off, portion out

Gazzah –Fleece

דוה *Davah* –To be ill, unwell

Daveh –Faint, unwell, menstrous

האזב *Ha'ayzov* –The hyssop

הדאה *HaDa'ah* –The kite

הדו *Hoduw* –Hodu, (India), land on the eastern limit of the Persian Empire, surrounding the Indus River (Est. 1:1; 8:9)

ההה *Hehah* –41st name of *Shem HaMeforash* (5 Aquarius)

הוד *Hod* –Splendor, majesty, vigor; Hod, one of the sons of Zophah, among the descendants of Asher; the eighth *Sefira*h (occurs 24 times in the *Tanakh*)

הי *Hiy* –Lamentation, wailing; 83rd Gate of the 231 Gates

ובאו *ve-Va'uw* –And they shall come

ve-Vo'uw –And you come

ובגד *ve-Vagad* –And rainment, and garment

וט *Vat* –98th Gate of the 231 Gates

זח *Zach* –112th Gate of the 231 Gates

זוב *Zowv* –A flow, issue, discharge, flux

Zuwb –To flow, gush, issue, discharge

חבה *Chabah* –To withdraw, hide, hide oneself

חוא *Chava'* –To show, interpret, explain, inform, tell, declare

יגב *Yagab* –To till, be a husbandman

Yegeb –Field, plowed field

ידא *Yada'* –To praise, give thanks (Aramaic)

יה *Yah* –Divine name associated with *Chokmah*

–The 15th Path is between *Chokmah* and *Tiferet* and corresponds to *Heh,* Aries (or Aquarius) , and the Tarot card The Emperor – G.D.

–Mystic number of the 5th Path *(Giburah)*

–Magic sum of the magic square of Saturn

–The number of rare earth elements (atomic numbers 57-71)

–The number of actinides (elements 89-103)

–Tarot Card: The Devil (The 26th Path; *Ayin*; Capricorn – G.D.)

16 אבחה *'ibchah* –Slaughter, flesh, meat, slaughtered meat

אהי *'ahiy* –Where

אודה *'odah* –I will thank; thank

אהוד *Ehud* –The 2nd judge of Israel

אזוב *'ezowb* –Hyssop, a plant used for medicinal and religious purposes

אחז *Achaz* –Ahaz, son of Micah and father of Jehoadah (1 Chr. 8:35-36; 9:41-42); the 11th judge of Israel

(1 Kings 15:38-16:20)
'achaz –Grasp, take hold, seize, take possession
'achuz –Percent

איה *'ayah* –Hawk, falcon, kite
'ayeh –Where? (of persons, things; rhetorical), where is?
'Ayah –Aiah, Ajah, father of Saul's concubine Rizpah

בדי *Badey', Vadey'* –Staves of

בגיא *ba-Gaya* –In the valley

בהט *Behat* –A costly stone (perhaps porphyry), red marble

בזהב *be-Zahav* –In gold

בזז *Bazaz* –Spoil, plunder, prey upon, seize

בטה *Batah* –To speak rashly or angrily, speak thoughtlessly

ביד *ba-yod* –By, into the hand, by hand
va-yad –By a hand, by the hand of

גבוה *Gabowahh* –Haughty, height, high(-er), lofty, proud, exceed

גוז *Guwz* –Pass over, away

דהוא *Dahava'* –Dehavites

הבט *Habet* –Look

הוה *Havah* –Desire (in bad sense); chasm (figuratively – destruction), be
Hovah –Ruin, disaster

היא *Hi* –She
Hia' –Which is

ואהד *va-'Ohad* –And Ohad

ואזב *va-'ayzov* –And hyssop

וי *Vaw* –99th Gate of the 231 Gates

זט *Zach* –113th Gate of the 231 Gates

חבו *Chebo* –68th name of *Shem HaMeforash* (2 Cancer)

חדד *Chadad* –To be sharp, be alert, be keen; Hadad, one of the twelve sons of Ishmael and grandson of Abraham (1 Chr. 1:30 – see also Hadar)[39]

חוב *Chowb* –A debt, debtor
Chuwb –To be guilty, make guilty

חזא *Chaza'* –To see, behold (Aramaic)

חח *Chach* –Hook, fetter, brooch, ring, nose ring

טוא *Tuw'* –To sweep, sweep away

יאה *Ya'ah* –To pertain to, befit, be befitting

–The 16th Path is between *Chokmah* and *Hesed* and corresponds to *Vav*, Taurus, and the Tarot card The Hierophant – G.D.
–The number of geomantic figures– G.D.
–The number of squares on the magic square of Jupiter
–The *Sefirot* on the Pillar of Severity are 3 + 5 + 8 = 16
–Tarot Card: The Tower (The 27th Path; *Peh*; Mars – G.D.)

17 אגגי *'Agagiy* –Agagite, descendant of Agag

אגוז *'egowz* –Nuts

אהו ה *'ahuw-ah* –God's secret name from Creation (*Zohar Chadash* 8a)

[39] Hadar (209).

אוי — *'owiy* –Woe!, Alas!, oh! (passionate cry of grief or despair)
'evi –Evi, one of the five kings of Midian (Num. 31:8)

באחו — *ba-'achuw* –In the reed grass

בבגדו — *be-Vigedow* –By his garment

גדוד — *Geduwd* –A band, troop, marauding band; something cut, furrow, cutting

גדי — *Gedi* –Kid, young male goat; Capricorn
Gadi –Gaddi, one of the persons sent to spy out Canaan; Gadi, father of King Menahem of Israel; Gadites

גיד — *Giyd* –Sinew, tendon

גזז — *Gazaz* –To cut off, shear, to destroy (an enemy); shave
Gazez –Gazez, son of Caleb; grandson of Caleb

דגי — *Dagay* –Fish of

דחה — *Dachah* –To chase, drive away, overthrow, outcast, thrust, totter

דיג — *Dayag* –Fisherman
Diyg –Fish for, catch

הגדה — *Haggadah* –Telling; text used for the story of the Exodus

הדגה — *HaDagah* –The fish

ההוא — *Hahia'* –That

הזה — *Hazah* –To dream, sleep, rave
Hazeh –This; sprinkle

והו — *Vehu* –1st name of *Shem HaMeforash* (1 Leo)
Vaho –49th name of *Shem HaMeforash* (1 Aries)

זבוב — *Zebuwb* –Fly

זבח — *Zabach, zavach* –To slaughter, kill, sacrifice, slaughter for sacrifice
Zebach –Sacrifice; Zebah, one of two Midianite kings slain by Gideon (see also Zalmunna)[40]

זדו — *Zaduw* –Wickedly

זוד — *Zuwd* –To boil, boil up, seethe, act proudly, act presumptuously, act rebelliously, be presumptuous, be arrogant, be rebelliously proud; to act proudly, be presumptuous (Aramaic)

זי — *Ziy* –114th Gate of the 231 Gates

חדה — *Chadah* –To rejoice

חגו — *Chagav* –Clefts, places of concealment, retreats

חוג — *Chuwg* –To encircle, encompass, describe a circle, draw round, make a circle; circle, circuit, compass; vault of the heavens (Job 22:14; Prov. 8:27; Isa. 40:22)

חט — *Chat* –127th Gate of the 231 Gates

טבו — *Tovuw* –Goodly

טוב — *Towb* –Tob, area east of the Jordan between Gilead and the eastern deserts
Tov –To be good, be pleasing, be joyful, be beneficial,

---

[40] Zalmunna (280).

be pleasant, be favorable, be happy, be right; good, pleasant, agreement; a good thing, benefit, welfare; welfare benefit, good things

Tuv –Good, good things, goodness

יגד *Yagud* –Shall troop

יהב *Yahab* –To give, provide, ascribe, come

Yehab –Burden, lot (that which is given)

–The 17th Path is between *Binah* and *Tiferet* and corresponds to *Zayin,* Gemini, and the Tarot card The Lovers – G.D.

–According to A.C., the masculine unity," the trinity of *Alef, Vav,* and *Yod* (1 + 6 + 10)

–Prime number

–The number of historical books in the Old Testament Protestant Bible

–The number of prophetical books in the Old Testament Protestant Bible

–Tarot Card: The Star (The 28th Path; *Tzaddi*; Aquarius – G.D.)

18 אביה *Abiyah* –Abijah, 2nd King of Judah

אהבי *'ahabiy* –Favority, beloved

אזי *Azay* –Then, in that case

איבה *Eyvah* –Enmity, hatred

בוי *Bavvay* –Bavai, one who helped rebuild the wall of Jerusalem

דוגה *Duwgah* –Fishhook

דוח *Duwach* –Rinse, cleanse away by rinsing, washing

האחד *HaEchad* –The first, this one, the one

הביא *Heviya'* –Brought

הגי *Hegay* –Hegai, chamberlain of Ahasuerus (see also הגא)[41]

החגב *HeChagav* –The grasshopper

ואחבא *va-Echbe'* –And I hid myself (Gen. 3:10; 1 Kings 18:13)

ובאזב *ve-Va'ezov* –And with the hyssop

והגד *ve-Hugad* –When it is told

והוא *ve-Hua* –And he, and it is, and he is

ve-Hiah –And she

חגבה *Chagabah* –Hagabah, ancestor of captives returning with Zerubbabel (this name only used in Ezra 2:45; Neh. 7:48 – see also Hagab)[42]

חוד *Chuwd* –To propose a riddle, propound a riddle

חטא *Chata'* –To sin, miss, miss the way, go wrong, incur guilt, forfeit, purify from uncleanness

Chatta' –Sinners; sinful; exposed to condemnation, reckoned as offenders

Cheta' –Sin

חי *Chai* –Living, alive; relatives; life; living thing, animal; community; alive, living, life (Aramaic); 128th Gate of the 231 Gates

יאבה *Yo'aveh* –Will be willing

ידד *Yadad* –To throw lots, cast lots; love, loving-one, friend

יגה *Yagah* –To afflict, grieve, suffer, cause grief; to repel,

---

[41] הגא (56).

[42] Hagab (13).

push away

יוב — *Iyyob* –Job, pious man of Uz after whom the book is named; third son of Issachar (see also Jashub)[43]

–The 18th Path is between *Binah* and *Giburah* and corresponds to *Chet,* Cancer, and the Tarot card The Chariot – G.D.

–Tarot Card: The Moon (The 29th Path; *Qof;* Pisces – G.D.)

–The number of the "Veils of Ain."

19 אבוי — *Abowy* –Oh!, woe!, (exclamation of pain – indicates desire or uneasiness)

אביו — *'aviyu* –His father

אהובה — *'ahuwvah* –Beloved

אהוז — *Ahoz* –Lord of Triplicity by Day for Sagittarius

אויב — *Owyeb* –Hating; an adversary; enemy, foe

אחוד — *'Echuwd* –Ehud, the 2nd judge of Israel

אחי — *'achai* –My brethren

'achiy –My brother, brother of

'Achi, 'Eychi –"Unity," Ehi, son of Benjamin

בגדי — *be-Giyd* –In the sinew (vein)

Vegaday –Garments of

בטוב — *ba-Tov* –Good, in the best, for good

בטח — *Batach* –To trust, be confident

Betach –Security, safety; securely; Betah, city of Amam-Zobah, identified with Tibhath

גדגדה — *Gudgodah* –Gudgodah, place where the Israelites camped in the wilderness

גוי — *Gowy* –Nation, people, namely gentile people or nation

דודה — *Dowdah* –Aunt, father's sister, uncle's wife

דיה — *Dayah* –Vulture, falcon

האטד — *HaAtad* –The Atad (of Goren HaAtad – a place stopped along the route to bury Jacob)

הגדגד — *Hagidgad* –Haggidgad, a place where Israel camped (Num. 33:32)

הגיא — *HaGaya'* –Of the valley, the valley

הדי — *Hidday* –Hiddai, one of David's mighty men (2 Sam. 23:30 – see also Hurai)[44]

הזהב — *HaZahav* –The gold[45]

היד — *HaYad* –Is the hand? (Ex. 14:31; Num. 11:23; Deut. 34:12; 2 Sam. 14:19; Is. 8:11; 14:26)

HaYod –The hand

ואבי — *va-'aviy* –And the father of

ואחד — *ve-'echad* –And one

ובאי — *va-Vi'iy* –And you go

ובהו — *va-Bohu* –And void (Gen. 1:2)

---

[43] Jashub (322).

[44] Hurai (224).

[45] *Sefer Bahir* says about the three letters of *Zahav, zayin, heh,* and *bet* "The first attribute is male...the *Zayin.* The second is the Soul...the *Heh.* The numerical value of *Heh* is five, alluding to the five names of the soul: *Nefesh, Ruach, Neshamah, Chayah, Yechidah.* The *Bet* is the sustenance. It is thus written, *Bereshit*" (19). About this, R. Kaplan says, "In the sense that it is represented here, the word *HaZahav* ('the gold,' HZHV) is actually a reversal of the Tetragrammaton YHVH, with the *Zayin* replacing the *Yud*" (123)

	ובחג	*va-Vachag* –And on the feast
	ויבא	*va-Yave'* –And he brought *va-Yavo'* –And he came
	זבוד	*Zabud* –Zabud, friend and officer of Solomon; Zabbud, one who returned from the exile with Ezra
	זבי	*Zabbay* –Zabbai, one who divorced his foreign wife after the exile; father of Baruch
	חבט	*Chabat* –To beat, beat out, beat off, thresh
	חהו	*Chaho* –24th name of *Shem HaMeforash* (6 Scorpio)
	חוה	*Chavah* –To tell, declare, show, make known; to breathe *Chavvah* –Eve, wife of Adam; village, town, tent village
	חטב	*Chatab* –To cut, gather
	חיא	*Chaya'* –To live
	טבח	*Tabach* –To slaughter, slay, butcher, kill ruthlessly *Tabbach* –Executioner, cook, bodyguard, guardsman; bodyguard, executioner, guardsmen (Aramaic) *Tebach* –Slaughter, slaughtering, animal; Tebah, son of Nahor, brother of Abraham
	טי	*Tiy* –141st Gate of the 231 Gates
	יבאו	*Yavo'* –Shall come
	ידה	*Yadah* –To throw, shoot, cast; her hand
	יהד	*Yahad* –To become a Jew (in fact or in fraud), become Judaised *Yehud* –Jehud, town of the tribe of Dan located between Baalath and Bene-berak – probably modern el-Yehudiyeh
	יואב	*Yow'ab* –Joab, son of Zeruiah, David's sister – he was captain of David's army; descendant of Judah (1 Chr. 2:54)[46]
	יובא	*Yuva'* –Will be brought

–The 19th Path is between *Hesed* and *Giburah* and corresponds to *Teth,* Leo, and the Tarot card Strength – G.D.
–Tarot Card: The Sun (The 30th Path; *Resh*; Sol – G.D.)
–Prime number

20	אזבי	*'Ezbay* –Ezbai, father of one of David's mighty men
	אחוה	*Achvah* –Declaration *Achavah* –Declaration, a declaring; fraternity, brotherhood
	באיבה	*Ve'eyvah* –In enmity
	בוזה	*Buwzah* –Contempt
	דודו	*Dowdow* –Dodo, grandfather of the judge Tola; commander of one of the divisions of David's army and father of Eleazar; father of Elkanan
	דוי	*Davvay* –Faint *Devay* –Languishing, sorrow
	דחה	*Dachah* –To chase, drive away, overthrow, outcast, thrust, totter (see also דחוה)[47]

[46] Some scholars believe a city is referred to here; one of the tribe of Judah; ancestor of the returned captives
[47] דחוה (23).

דיו *Deyow* –Ink

הובאו *Huv'uw* –They were brought

היה *Hayah* –To be, become, come to pass, exist, happen, fall out; destruction, calamity

הטאה *Hattaah* –Sin

ודי *Vediy* –And sufficiency

והבגד *Vehabeged* –And the garment

והובא *Vehuwva'* –He shall be brought

והזב *Vahazav* –And the issue

וזהב *ve-Zahav* –And gold

ויד *ve-Yad* –And hand, and a place

זהוב *Zahov* –Golden

זובה *Zovah* –Her issue

חזה *Chazah* –To see, perceive, look, behold, prophesy, provide
Chazeh –Breast (of animals), breast of an animal sacrifice
Chozeh –Seer

טוה *Tavah* –To spin

ידאה *Yide'eh* –Will swoop down

ידו *Yado* –His hand, his place
Yiddow –Iddo, captain of the tribe of Manasseh in Gilead (1 Chr. 27:21)

יהה *Yehah* –62nd name of *Shem HaMeforash* (2 Gemini)

יובב *Yobab* –Jobab, son of Joktan – may refer to an unknown Arabian tribe (Gen. 10:29; 1 Chr. 1:23; a King of Edom (Gen. 36:33-34; 1 Chr. 1:44-45); king of Canaan conquered by Joshua (Josh. 11:1); descendant of Benjamin (1 Chr. 8:9); another descendant of Benjamin (1 Chr. 8:18)

יוד *Yod* –Hand; 10th letter of Hebrew alphabet

יי *Yeya* –A name of God

כ *Kaf* –11th letter of Hebrew alphabet; when used as a prefix, it means "as" or "like"

–The 20th Path is between *Hesed* and *Tiferet* and corresponds to *Yod*, Virgo, and the Tarot card The Hermit – G.D.
–The number of years that Jacob worked for Laban
–The amount of silver that Joseph was sold for (Gen. 37:28)
–The maximum permissible height of a *sukah* (*Sukah* 1:1)
–Tarot Card: Judgment (The 31st Path; *Shin*; Fire – G.D.)

Kaf, the number equaling twenty, begins the word *Keter*, an important word in Kabbalah and the Tanakh. It is the name of a *sefirah* and is used as a reference to God and Israel several times. This implies that the word crown and by proxy *Kaf* is the means to approach God. Similarly, this letter begins the words *kippah*, the Hebrew word for *yarmulke*, an item worn in recognition of the commandment to cover one's head when in the presence of God. It also begins the word *kavannah*, a word implying "aiming" our hearts toward God. Thus, *Kaf* intimates a deep potential relationship with God.

Kaf as a verb means "subdue:(to)" or "coerce," which brings to mind the subduing of the Israelites under the Egyptians. In this way, the *kaf* hints that our release from bondage is only possible through interaction with God.

NOTES:

21 אהיה *Eheieh* –"I am" or "I will be" or "let there be;" name of God associated with *Keter*

אחזה *Achuzzah* –Possession, property

איי *Ayey* –Isles

אכ *Akh* –Indeed, surely (emphatic); howbeit, only, but, yet (restrictive); 10th Gate of the 231 Gates

בגוי *Beguwy* –With a nation

Bigvay –Bigvai, head of one of the families who returned with Zerubbabel; one who sealed the covenant with Nehemiah

בדיה *Bedeyah* –Bedeiah, one who divorced his pagan wife after the exile

בידה *Biyadah* –In her hand

גיח *Giyach* –Break forth, labor to bring forth, come forth, draw up, take out; strive; Giah, settlement between Gibeon and a ford across the Jordan River

האחז *HaAchez* –The percent

האיה *HaA'yah* –The falcon

הגיג *Hagiyg* –Whisper, musing, murmuring; meditation

הובה *Howvah* –Hobah

החבאה *Hachaba'h* –Hiding, concealment

הטבה *HaTavah* –The good

חגי *Chaggay* –Haggai, first of the prophets who prophesied after the exile

Chaggiy –Haggi, second son of Gad; Haggites

Chagiy –My feast

הוי *Howy* –Ah!, alas!, ha!, ho!, O!, woe!

היו *Hayuw* –Were, to be

חגי *Chaggai* –Haggai, first of the prophets who prophesied after the Exile

חזו *Chazuw* –Hazo, son of Nahor and nephew of Abraham

Chezev –Vision, appearance

ואבואה *Va'avo'ah* –That I may go in

זובו *Zovo* –His issue

יגח *Yigach* –Will gore

יזד *Yazad* –Comes presumptuously

יטב *Yatab* –To be good, be pleasing, be well, be glad

טוו *Tavuw* –Did spin

–The 21st Path is between *Hesed* and *Netzach* and corresponds to *Kaf*, Jupiter, and the Tarot card The Wheel of Fortune – G.D.

–Mystic number of 6th Path (*Tiferet*)

–Tarot Card: The Universe (The 32nd Path; *Tau*; Saturn – G.D.)

22 אכא *Aka* –7th name of *Shem HaMeforash* (1 Virgo)

אויה *Owyah* –Oh!, woe!, alas! (feminine of אוי)

בבאאהוה *Baba'ahaweh*–The intials of the first seven words of Genesis

בדיו *Badayuw* –Its staves

בזזו *Bazazuw* –They took for a prey

בידו *Biyado* –His hand

בכ *Bak* –To cause to weep, make cry, lament; the first and last letter of the *Sefer Yetzirah*; over you, in you, among you, by thee; 30th Gate of the 231 Gates

גדודה *Geduwdah* –Furrow, cutting

גדיה *Gediyah* –Kids, young female goats

Gidyah –A river bank, shore

דחי *Dechiy* –Stumbling

האאיה *Haayah* –Angel of 2q Sagittarius and night angel 8 Wands

הגדי *HaGadi* –The Gadites

HaGediy –The kid, the goat

הגיד *Higiyd* –Told

הזבח *HaZavach* –The sacrifice

הזי *Hezi* –9th name of *Shem HaMeforash* (3 Virgo)

הטח *Hitoch* –Was plastered

הטוב *Hatov* –What is good, proper

ואזוב *ve-'ezov* –And hyssop

ואחז *ve-'echoz* –And take it

ואיה *ve-'ayah* –And Ayah

ve-'ayeh –And where, and is

וביד *ve-Viyad* –And in his hand

ובזהב *Vavazahav* –And in gold

וביד *ve-Viyd* –And the hand

והיא *ve-Hiya'* –And she

ווי *Vavey* –Hooks

חביב *Chaviv* –Beloved, cherished

חדוד *Chadduwd* –Sharp, pointed, sharpened

חדי *Chadiy* –Breast, chest

חוח *Chavach* –Rock, crevice (a hiding place)

Chowach –Thorn, brier, bramble, thorn bush, thicket; hook, ring, fetter

חטה *Chittah* –Wheat

טובה *Towvah* –Favor, kindness, welfare, good

טחה *Tachah* –To hurl, shoot

Tuwchah –Inner regions, hidden recesses, inward parts

יהוא *Yehu'* –Jehu, prophet who brought tidings of disaster to Baasha of Israel; 10th King of Israel; descendant of Hezron; descendant of Simeon; one who joined David at Ziklag

יזה *Yazeh* –Sprinkled

Yazih –He shall sprinkle

יחד *Yachad* –To join, be joined, unite, be united; union, unitedness; together, altogether, all together

–The 22nd Path is between *Giburah* and *Tiferet* and corresponds to *Lamed,* Libra, and the Tarot card Justice – G.D.

–The number of letters in the Hebrew alphabet

–The number of Tarot trumps (including The Fool, 0)

–The number of scrolls of the original *Tanakh* (according to Sabas ?–532 C.E.)

23 אבכ *Abak* –To roll, turn
אחוח *'Achowach* –Ahoah, son of Bela, (see also Ahijah)[48]
איבי *'oyvay* –My enemies
באכ *Ba'ak* –Thou be come
בזובו *be-Zovo* –In his issue
בכא *Baka'* –Balsam tree; a shrub which drips sap when it is cut; Baca, valley of Palestine (Ps. 84:7)
גכ *Gak* –49th Gate of the 231 Gates
דחוה *Dachavah* –Musical instrument with strings (Aramaic)
הביאה *Haviya'ah* –Bring
הוזה *Huwzah* –Dreamer, visionary
החי *HaChai* –The living, the raw
הידד *Heydad* –A shout, cheer, shouting
ואיו *ve-'ayuw* –And where [is] he?
והדגה *ve-HaDagah* –And the fish
והזה *ve-Hizah* –And he shall sprinkle
וטוב *ve-Tov* –And good
וטח *ve-Tach* –And plaster
ויגד *va-Yaged* –And he told, was told
ויז *va-Yaz* –And he sprinkled
זבדי *Zabdiy* –Zabdi, father of Carmi (Josh. 7:1, 17-18 see also Zimri)[49]; descendant of Benjamin (1 Chr. 27:27); one of David's storekeepers (1 Chr. 27:27); ancestor of Mattaniah (Neh. 11:17 – see also Zichri and Zakkur)[50]
זבחו *Zivchu* –You sacrifice, his sacrifice
זוטא *Zuta* –Lesser (Aramaic)
זחח *Zachach* –To remove, displace
זיו *Ziyv* –Brightness, splendor
חדוה *Chedvah* –Joy, gladness; joy (Aramaic)
חוט *Chuwt* –To repair, join (Aramaic); a thread, cord, line, string
חטאה *Chata'ah* –Sin offering, offering (Aramaic); sinful, sin
חיה *Chayah* –To live, have life, remain alive, sustain life, live prosperously, live forever, be quickened, be alive, be restored to life or health
Chayeh –Vigorous, lively, having the vigor of life
Chayyah –Life, living, living things, animals
Chiah –Part of the soul referred to *Chokmah*
טיד *Tiyd* –Defender
יביא *Yabiya'* –He brings
יהוה YHVH by "small numbers" (1+5+6+5)[51]
טוח *Tuwach* –To spread over, overlay, plaster, cover over, coat, besmear; to be besmeared

[48] Ahijah (24).
[49] Zimri (257).
[50] Zichri (237), Zakkur (233).
[51] See introduction.

כאב *Ka'ab* –To be in pain, be sore, have pain, be sorrowful
Ke'ab –Pain (mental and physical), sorrow
כבא *Kaba'* –When entered
–The 23rd Path is between *Giburah* and *Hod* and corresponds to *Mem*, Water, and the Tarot card The Hanged Man – G.D.
–Number of "judgment," from Exodus and 1st Corinthians (23,000 men punished for fornication and idolatry)
–Prime number

24 אוזי *'Uwzay* –Uzai, father of Palal
אחיה *'acheyha* –Her brothers
'achiyha –Her brother
'Achiyah –Ahijah, son of Bela, (this spelling used only in 1 Chr. 8:7 – see also אחוח)[52]
בטחה *Bitkaw* –Trust, trusting, confidence
גויה *Geviyah* –A body, corpse, carcass, dead body
דודי *Duwday* –Mandrake (as an aphrodisiac)
דויד *David* –David, King of Israel (see also דוד)[53]
דכ *Dakh* –Oppressed, crushed; 67th Gate of the 231 Gates
Dek –This (Aramaic)
האהובה *Ha'Ahuwvah* –The beloved
הביאו *Haviyuw* –Carry, bring; they brought; he has brought
הגדגדה *HaGudgodah* –The Gudgod – a place in the wilderness (see also גדגדה)[54]
הגוי *HaGoy* –The nation
הטי *HaTiy* –Let down
הידה *Huyedah* –Songs of praise
ואביה *ve-'aviyha* –And her father
ואיבה *ve-'eyvah* –And enmity
והאחד *ve-Ha'Echad* –And the one
והביא *ve-Heviya'* –And he shall bring
וחטא *ve-Chite'* –And he shall cease
וחי *va-Chai* –And live, and life, and he live, and may live
ויאהב *va-Ye'ehav* –And he loved
ויבאה *va-Yeveha* –And he brought her
וייב *ve-Yov* –And Job
זיז *Ziyz* –Moving creatures, moving things; abundance, fullness
חוי *Chivviy* –Hivite, Hivites
חטאו *Chatuw* –They sinned; his sin
חטבה *Chatubah* –Colored fabric, dark-hued fabric
חיו *Chayuw* –They lived
טבחה *Tabbachah* –Female cook, cook
Tibchah –Slaughtered meat, a slaughter, flesh, meat, thing slaughtered
יבאהו *Yovehuw* –He shall bring it

---

52 אחוח (23).
53 דוד (14).
54 גדגדה (19).

ידי *Yadai* –My hands
Yadiy –My hand

יחו *Yecho* –33rd name of *Shem HaMeforash* (3 Capricorn)

יטה *Yuttah* –Juttah, city in the mountains of Judah, near Maon, Carmel, and Ziph (this spelling used only in Josh. 21:16 – see also יוטה)[55]

כד *Kad* –Jar, large jar (portable), bucket, pail, vessel

–The 24th Path is between *Tiferet* and *Netzach* and corresponds to *Nun*, Scorpio, and the Tarot card Death – G.D.
–The number of hours in a day
–The number of books in the Hebrew Bible (*Tanakh*)
–The number of letters in the Greek alphabet
–The number of ribs in the human body
–The number of vertebrae in the human spine

25 אביהוא *'aviyhu'* –Abihu, son of Aaron

אחיו *'achiyu* –His brother, his brethren; another
'Achyow –Ahio, descendant of Benjamin; descendant of Saul; son of Abinadab

אכד *Akkad* –Akkad, city built by Nimrod north of Babylonia, later the norther division of Babylonia

בבאך *B'vo'eka* –When you come in

בגדיו *Begada'yu* –His clothes

בוזי *Buwziy* –Buzite; Buzi, descendant of Aaron and father of Ezekiel

בחטאה *B'chata'ah* –When he sins

דודאי *Duwda'ey* –Mandrakes, violets, jasmine

דכא *Daka'* –To crush, be crushed, be contrite, be broken
Dakka' –Dust; contrite

הזדוג *Hazaduwg* –To be paired, mated

החזה *Hechazah* –Breast

היי *Hayay* –Be, to be
Hayeya –71st name of *Shem HaMeforash* (5 Cancer)

הך *Hak* –84th Gate of the 231 Gates

ואביו *ve-'aviyu* –But his father

ואחי *va-'achiy* –And brother of, and my brethren

ובטוב *vu-V'tuwv* –And with gladness

וגוי *ve-Goy* –And a nation of

והיד *ve-haYad* –And the hand

וטבח *vu-Tevoha* –And slaughter

ויבאו *va-Yavi'uw* –And they brought
va-Yavo'uw –And they came in, and they went in

ויבז *va-Yivez* –And he despised

ויט *Vayet* –Stretched out, turned away; bowed; and he pitched; turned in, extended

זיזא *Ziyza'* –Ziza, chief of Simeon; son of King Rehoboam

חביה *Chabayah* –Habaiah, ancestor to a priestly family (Ezra 2:61; Neh. 7:63)

---

[55] יוטה (30).

	חיוא	*Cheyva'* –Beast, animal (Aramaic) *Chioa* –The Beast; the union or offspring of Samael and Isheth Zenunim; acc. to A.C., archdemon of *Tiferet*
	טבוח	*Tavuwcha* –Will be slain
	יגבהה	*Yobehah* –Jogbehah, city east of the Jordan River, inhabited by the tribe of Gad – modern Jubeihat
	יהי	*Yehi* –Let there be, there was, let it be
	יואח	*Yow'ach* –Joah, son of Asaph, the recorder in the time of Hezekiah; descendant of Gers; porter in the tabernacle; Levite commissioned to repair the Lord's house
	יוחא	*Yowcha'* –Joha, descendant of Benjamin; one of David's valiant men
	יזוב	*Yazuv* –Will issue
	יזח	*Yizach* –And garments of
	יחבה	*Yechubbah* –Jehubbah, descendant of Asher
	כה	*Kah* –Here, so far, thus (Aramaic) *Koh* –Thus, here, in this manner

–The 25th Path is between *Tiferet* and *Yesod* and corresponds to *Samekh,* Sagittarius, and the Tarot card Temperance – G.D.

–The number of squares in the magic square of Mars

26	אחזי	*'Achzay* –Ahasai or Jahzerah, priest whose descendants dwelt in Jerusalem after the Babylonian exile
	בחטאו	*V'chetuw* –In his own sin
	בידי	*B'yadiy* –Into my hand
	הביט	*Hibiyt* –Has beheld
	הודוה	*Howdevah* –Hodevah, an ancestor of returning captives (Neh. 7:43 – see also Hodaviah)[56]
	הויה	*Huwyah* –It is
	החגי	*Hachagiy* –Haggites
	היטב	*Heytev* –Do good, well, diligently
	והדוה	*ve-Hadah* –And of her that is sick
	והיה	*ve-Hayah* –And became, will come to pass *va-Hayeh* –And will be *ve-H'yeh* –And be
	וחזה	*va-Chazeh* –And the breast of
	ויגז	*va-Yagaz* –And it caused to fly
	וידו	*ve-Yaduw* –And his hand
	וכ	*Vak* –100th Gate of the 231 Gates
	חגיה	*Chaggiyah* –Haggiah, descendant of Levi (1 Chr. 6:15)
	חדיד	*Chadiyd* –Hadid, Benjamite town east-northeast of Lydda
	חוזה	*Chuwzah* –Seer, prophet; pact
	חול	*Chowl* –Sand *Chuwl* –To twist, whirl, dance, writhe, fear, tremble, travail, be in anguish, be pained; Hul, grandson of Shem (Gen. 10:23; 1 Chr. 1:7)[57]

[56] Hodaviah (36).

	יהוה	YHVH –Tetragrammaton, Yahweh, Jehovah
	יטבה	*Yotbah* –Jotbah, home of Haruz, whose daughter was the mother of King Amon of Judah
	כאה	*Ka'ah* –To be sad, be disheartened, be cowed
	כבד	*Kabad* –To be heavy, be weighty, be grevious, be hard, be rich, be honorable, be glorious, be burdensom, be honored
		Kabed –Heavy, great; the liver (as heaviest organ); honor
		Kobed –Weight, heaviness, mass, great
	כדב	*Kedab* –False, lying (Aramaic)
	כו	*Kav* –Window

–The 26th Path is between *Tiferet* and *Hod* and corresponds to *Ayin,* Capricorn, and the Tarot card The Devil – G.D.
–The *Sefirot* of the Middle Pillar are 1 + 6 + 9 + 10 = 26
–The number of letters in the English alphabet
–The number of references to YHVH in the *Amidah*, the "standing prayer."

27	אבדכ	*'avadka* –You perish
	אכבד	*'ekavayd* –Will be glorified
	באחיו	*Bi'achiyuw* –Over his brother, over another
		B'achiy' –Against his brother
	בדודאי	*B'duwday* –Mandrakes, violets, jasmines
	בכה	*Bakah* –To weep, bewail, cry, shed tears; wept, mourned
		Bekeh –A weeping
	גדיי	*G'dayey* –Kids, goats
	גזזי	*Goz'zey* –Shearers
	דבאכ	*Dav'aka* –Your old age
	הגידה	*Hagiydah* –Tell
	הטובה	*Hatovah* –Is good?
		HaTuwvah –The goodness, the good
	ואהיה	*ve-'ehoieh* –And I will be
	ואכ	*va-'ak* –And I will smite
		ve-'ak –And surely
	והיו	*ye-Hayuw* –And let them be
	וחגי	*ye-Chagiy* –And Haggai
	ויזד	*ya-Yazed* –And he boiled, and he cooked
	זבחי	*Ziv'chiy* –My sacrifice; sacrifice of; sacrifice, offer
	זכ	*Zak* –Clean, pure; the pure one; 115th Gate of the 231 Gates
	חטי	*Chatiy* –Sin (Aramaic)
	חידה	*Chiydah* –Riddle, difficult question, parable, enigmatic saying or question, perplexing saying or question
	טובי	*Tuwviy* –My goodness
	טיח	*Tiyach* –A coating, plaster
	יגיד	*Yagiyd* –Utter
	ייז	*Yeyaz* –40th name of *Shem HaMeforash* (4 Aquarius)

57 Possibly an Aramean tribe is referred to; some have postulated the people of Hulia near Mount Masius.

כבה — *Kabah* –To quench, put out, be put out, be quenched, be extinguished

–The 27th Path is between *Netzach* and *Hod* and corresponds to *Peh,* Mars, and the Tarot card The Tower – G.D.

–The number of books in the Protestant New Testament Bible

28 אביהוד — *'Abihuwd* –Abihud, the name of two Israelites

אבכה — *'ibkah* –Slaughter, flesh, meat, slaughtered meat

אהבכ — *'aheveka* –He loves you

אחידה — *Achiydah* –Puzzle, riddle

באכה — *Bu'akah* –As you come, as you go toward

בוכ — *Buwk* –To perplex, confuse, be confused

ביהוה — *ba*-YHVH –By YHVH, in YHVH

va-YHVH –Against YHVH, by YHVH

גחזי — *Gechaziy* –Gehazi, dishonest servant of Elisha (see also גיחזי)[58]

די זהב — *Diy Zahab* –Dizahab, place in the Arabian desert near where Moses gave his farewell speech to Israel

האבידו — *Ha'aviydo* –He has destroyed

הגידו — *Hagiyduw* –Tell

החיה — *Hachaiah* –Living

הטוח — *Hituwch* –It is plastered

ובכ — *va-Vak* –And against you

vu-Veka –And you

והאבי — *ve-He'eviyd* –And he shall destroy

והגיד — *ve-Higiyd* –And tell

והטוב — *ve-HaTov* –And the good

ויחד — *va-Yichad* –And he rejoiced

זבדיה — *Zebadyah* –Zebadiah, descendant of Benjamin; son of Elpaal; one who joined David; son of Asahel; head of a family that returned from exile; priest who had taken a foreign wife; (see also Zebadiahu and Zebadiah)[59]

זבידה — *Zebiydah* –Zebudah, wife of Josiah, king of Judah

חטאי — *Chata'ay* –My sins

חטיא — *Chattaya'* –Sin offering (Aramaic)

חיי — *Chayay* –To live, have life, remain alive, sustain life, live prosperously, live forever, be quickened, be alive, be restored to life or health

חכ — *Chek* –Palate, mouth, taste, gums; 129th Gate of the 231 Gates

טיט — *Tiyt* –Mud, clay, mire, damp dirt

יביאה — *Y'viyaha* –Shall bring it

ידיד — *Yedid* –One beloved, beloved; lovely

יחדו — *Yachdaw* –Together, alike, as one

Yachdow –Jahdo, descendant of Gad (1 Chr. 5:14)

יחוד — *Yichudh* –Union with God

---

58 גיחזי (38).

59 Zebadiahu (34), Zebadiah (28).

	יחטא	*Yecheta'* –Shall sin, has sinned
	יחי	*Y'chiy* –Let live
	כח	*Koach* –Strength, power, might; a small reptile, probably a kind of lizard which is unclean

–The 28th Path is between *Netzach* and *Yesod* and corresponds to *Tzaddi*, Aquarius (or Aries) , and the Tarot card The Star – G.D.
–The height in cubits of the curtains in the Tabernacle in the Wilderness (Ex. 26:2)
–Number of letters in Genesis 1:1
–Mystic number of the 7th path (*Netzach*)
–Number of letters in the Arabic alphabet
–Perfect number

29	איביו	*'oyvayu* –His enemies
	גויי	*Goyey* –Nations
	דכה	*Dakah* –To crush, be crushed, be contrite, be broken
		Dakkah –A crushing
	הדך	*Hadak* –To cast down, tread down
	הודיה	*Havadiyah* –Thanks
	החוי	*HaChioiy* –The Hivite
	החיו	*Hachayuw* –You keep alive
	ואגידה	*ve-'agiydah* –And tell, that I may tell
	והביאה	*ve-Haviyah* –And bring it
		ve-Heviya'ah –And he shall bring it
	וזבחו	*ve-Zavchuw* –And they sacrifice
	וזיו	*Vezuw* –With splendor
	וחטאה	*ve-Chata'ah* –And sin
	וחיה	*ve-Chyeh* –And you shall live
		Vechiyah –Then she shall live
	ויאבדו	*va-Yovduw* –And they perished
	ויאהבה	*va-Ye'ehabeha* –And he loved her
	ויגידו	*va-Yagiyduw* –And they told
	וידגו	*ve-Yidguw* –And let them grow
	וכבא	*vo-K'voa'* –And is entered
	זיזה	*Zizah* – Zizah, Second son of Shimi (1 Chr. 23:11 – see also Zina)[60]
	טכ	*Tak* –142nd Gate of the 231 Gates
	יביאו	*Yaviya'uw* –They bring in, shall they bring
	ידיה	*Yadeyha* –Her hands
		Yedayah –Jedaiah, son of Shimri (1 Chr. 4:37); Judahite who helped repair the walls of Jerusalem (Neh. 3:10)
	יהדי	*Yehday* –Jehdai, one of the family of Caleb the spy
	יהיד	*Yehuwd* –Jewry, Judah, Judea
	יוזבד	*Yowzabad* –Jozabad, one who joined David at Ziklag; two descendants of Manasseh who joined David at Ziklag; overseer of the dedicated things of the Temple under Hezekiah; chief of the Levites in Josiah's time; one who helped weigh the sanctuary vessels; two who had married foreign

[60] Zina (68).

wives; one who interpreted the Law; chief Levite after the exile (not to be confused with Jehozabad)

כבוא *K'voa'* –When came, when goes

כדה *Kadah* –Her pitcher

כזב *Kazab* –To lie, tell a lie, be a liar, be found a liar, be in vain, fail; a lie, untruth, falsehood, deceptive thing

–The 29th Path is between *Netzach* and *Malkut* and corresponds to *Qof*, Pisces, and the Tarot card The Moon – G.D.

–According to A.C., the number of magic force

–The number of talents of gold used in the construction of the Tabernacle in the Wilderness (Ex. 38:24)

–Prime number

30 אבטיח *Abaittiyach* –Watermelon, Egyptian fruit (Num. 11:5)

אביטוב *'Abiytuwb* –Abitub, descendant of Benjamin

אכזב *Akzab* –Deceitful, treacherous, deception, lie, deceptive, disappointing

בחיי *Bichayay* –In my life

בכח *ba-Kocha* –In power

b'-Kocha –With power

דוך *Duwk* –To pound, beat (in mortar)

דכו *Dakuw* –Beat it

הודיה *Howdiyah* –Hodiah, brother-in-law of Naam (1 Chr. 4:19); Hodijah, Levite in the time of Nehemiah; one who sealed the covenant with God after the exile

הכה *Hakah* –And smite, smote; smite

Hukah –Was slain

ואחיה *ye-'achayeh* –And I make alive

והביאו *ye-Habiyaw* –And bring them, and bring, and put

והדיה *ye-Hadayah* –And the kite

וחטאו *ye-Chit'uw* –And he shall purify him

וחיו *ye-Chaiuw* –And they live

ye-Chiyuw –And live

וידי *vi-Y'diy* –And the hands of

חזיה *Chazayah* –Hazaiah, descendant of Judah (Neh. 11:5)

ידיו *Yadayuw* –His hands

יהודה *Yehudah* –Judah, son of Jacob and Leah and ancestor of a tribe of Israel (assoc. w/Leo); ancestor of one who helped to rebuild the Temple; one who married a foreign wife during the Exile; one who came up to Jerusalem with Zerubbabel; prince of Judah; priest and musician; Judah, the territory of one of the original twelve tribes

יהיה *Yiheyeh* –It shall be (Gen. 1:29)

יחזה *Yachazah* –Seeing

יוטה *Yuttah* –Juttah, city in the mountains of Judah, near Maon, Carmel, and Ziph (this spelling used only in Josh. 15:55 – see also יטה)[61]

ייי *Yeyaya* –22nd name of *Shem HaMeforash* (4 Scorpio)

יכ *Yak* –Hand, (way) side (1 Sam. 4:13); 154th Gate of the 231 Gates

כהה *Kahah* –To grow weak, grow dim, grow faint, falter, be weak, be dim, be darkened, be restrained, be faint, fail

Kehah –A quenching, dulling, lessening, healing, alleviation

Keheh –Dim, dull, colorless, be dark, faint

כזבא *Kozeba'* –Chozeba, village of Judah inhabited by the descendants of Shelah (see also Achzib and Chezib)[62]

כי *Kiy* –Branding, burning; that, for, because, when, as though, as, because that, but, then, certainly, except, surely, since

ל *Lamed* –12th letter of Hebrew alphabet; when used as a prefix, it means "to" or "for"

–The 30th Path is between *Hod* and *Yesod* and corresponds to *Resh,* Sol, and the Tarot card The Sun – G.D.

–The count of יהוה + the number of letters in the Name

–The number of days in a full month of the Hebrew calendar

–The height of the ark of Noah in cubits (Gen. 6:15)

Lamed is a *notarikon* for לב מבין דעת, "a heart that understands knowledge," and this phrase equals 608. If one multiplies heart (לב, 32) and Eve (חוה, 19), this intimates that *Lamed* is the same as the heart of Eve. Far from simply explaining the Adam and Eve story as a simple metaphor for the limitations of human behavior, the Kabbalah and Judaism delve deep into the mystical and theoretical interpretations of the story. The interested reader should refer to "The Path of Kabbalah" by David Sheinkin.

Note that *Lamed*, surrounded by *Mem* and *Kaf*, and from these letters we can form the word *melek* or "king." Furthermore, the *lamed* consists of a *kaf* with a *vav* on top. Adding these two numerical values together, we reach 26 – the same value as the Tetragrammaton.

NOTES:

[61] יטה (24).

[62] Achzib (40), Chezib (39).

31	אחזיה	*Achaziah* –Ahaziah, 8th King of Israel; alternate name for Jehoahaz, 6th King of Judah
	אחיחד	*'Achiychuwd* –Ahihud, prince of Asher who helped divide the land upon entering Canaan; member of the family of Ehud, descended from Benjamin
	איכ	*Eyk* –How? (interrog. adv.); how! (interj. – in lamentation); expression of satisfaction; no, not, nor, neither, nothing (as wish or preference); no, not (Aramaic)
	אל	*Al* –Do not, have not
		El –God, god-like one, mighty one; mighty things in nature; strength, power; these, those; Divine name assoc. w/*Hesed*; into, to, toward, unto (of motion); into; toward (of direction, not necessarily physical motion); against (motion or direction of a hostile character); in addition to; concerning, in regard to, in reference to, on account of; according to (rule or standard); at, by, against (of one's presence); in between, in within, to within, unto (idea of motion to); 11th Gate of the 231 Gates
	בידיה	*be-Yadiyha* –With her hands
	הוכ	*Huwk* –To go, come, walk, be brought
	הכבד	*Hakabod* –Wealth
		HaKavd –The liver
	הכו	*Hikuw* –They smote
	זהב טוב	*Zahav Tov* –Good gold (Gen. 2:12)
	חבויה	*Chabuyah* –Angel of 2q Cancer and night angel 2 Cups
	חוזי	*Chowzay* –Hozai, an unknown prophet who recorded some events of King Manasseh's life (2 Chr. 33:19); seers
	ואביהוא	*va-'avyhuwa'* –And Abihu
	ואחיו	*ve-'echayuw* –And his brethren, and his brother
	ואכד	*ve-'akad* –And Akkad
	ובגדיו	*ve-V'gadayu* –And his garments
	ובחיה	*vu-Bachayah* –And beast
	והכ	*ye-Hak* –And smite
	וטבחו	*yu-Tivachuw* –And kill it
	ויבזו	*va-Yabozuw* –And they spoiled
	ויגבהה	*ve-Yagebhah* –And Jogbehah
	ויהי	*va-Y'hiy* –And there was, there became
		vi-Y'hiy –And let it
	וכה	*va-Koh* –And that, and so, and here, and thus
	יביט	*Yabiyt* –Does he behold
	יהיו	*Yihiyuw* –Shall they be
	יזיד	*Yaziyd* –Shall presumptuously
	ייטב	*Y'ytav* –May be well
	כבדה	*Kavdah* –Severe, grievous
	כוה	*Kavah* –To burn, scorch, brand
	לא	*Lo, La* –Not, no, nothing

–The 31st Path is between *Hod* and *Malkut* and corresponds to *Shin,* Fire, and the Tarot card

Judgment – G.D.
–Prime number

32 אהיהוה *Ehyahweh* –Combination of the divine names *Eheieh* and YHVH
איטיב *'aytiyv* –I do good
אלא *Elah* –4th King of Israel (variant spelling)
בידיו *V'yadayv* –His hands
בכי *Bekiy* –A weeping, weeping
בל *Bal* –Not, hardly, else, no; mind, heart, center (Aramaic); care, anxiety; the first and last letters of the *Torah*; 31st Gate of the 231 Gates
Bel –Bel, chief god of the Babylonians[63]
הגידי *Hagiydi* –Tell
והויה *Vahaviah* –Angel of 1q Leo and day angel 5 Wands
ויהוה *va*-YHVH –And YHVH
וכבד *va-Kaved* –And sore
vu-K'vad –And heavy, slow, difficult
זכה *Zakah* –To be clean, be pure, be clear
חזיז *Chaziyz* –Thunderbolt, lightning flash, lightning, storm, cloud
טוביה *Towbiyah* –Tobiah, ancestor of returning captives who had lost their genealogy; Ammonite servant of Sanballat who opposed Nehemiah; leader who returned from the exile
יואחז *Yehoachaz* –Jehoahaz, 6th King of Judah; 16th King of Judah; 11th King of Israel
יזיה *Yezav'el* –Jeziah, one who took a foreign wife (Ezra 10:25)
יחיד *Yachiyd* –Only, only one, solitary
כבדו *Kavdu* –Were dim
K'vodo –His glory
כבוד *Kavod* –Glory, honor, glorious, abundance
כזה *Kazeh* –As this
כחד *Kachad* –To hide, conceal, cut off, cut down, make desolate, kick
לב *Leb* –Inner man, mind, will, heart, understanding; heart, mind (Aramaic)
–The 32nd Path is between *Yesod* and *Malkut* and corresponds to *Tau,* Saturn, and the Tarot card The Universe – G.D.
–The number of Paths of Wisdom
–The number of human teeth

33 אביכ *'abiyka* –Your father, your father's
אבל *Abal* –To mourn, lament; truly, verily, surely, but, however, howbeit, contrariwise, nay rather
Abel –To languish or mourn; mourning, desolate; meadow; Abel, second son of Adam and Eve, slain by his brother Cain

[63] Bel is associated with Enlil, Marduk who is associated with the earth and air.

Ebel –Mourning, lament
אחוחי *'Achowachiy* –Ahohite
איבכ *'obia'aka* –Your enemy
'oybeka –Your enemies
באל *Bael* –Goetic demon #1[64]
B'el –As God
בחגכ *B'chagela* –In your feast
בלא *Bela* –To wear away, wear out (Aramaic)
B'lia' –Not in, without; with no, not in
גל *Gal* –Ruins; well, fountain; billow, heap, spring, wave; 50th Gate of the 231 Gates
Gel –Dung
Gol –Oil vessel; bowl
ובאחיו *vu-Va'achiyu* –And against his brother
ובכה *vu-V'kah* –And upon you
והאחזו *va-He'achizuw* –And you get possessions
והחטה *ve-Hachitah* –And the wheat
ויזבח *va-Yizbach* –And he offered
ויחגו *ve-Yachoguw* –That they may hold a feast
זכו *Zakuw* –Purity, innocence, innocence (in God's sight)
חכה *Chakah* –To wait, wait for, await
Chakkah –Hook, angle, hook fastened in jaw, fishhook
יבאכ *Yabia'aka* –Shall bring you
יגידו *Yagiyduw* –They shall declare
ידידה *Yediydah* –Jedidah, mother of King Josiah
יזבחו *Yiz'bachuw* –And they shall sacrifice, they sacrificed
יחיה *Yechiyah* –Jehiah, Levite gatekeeper of the Ark (this name used in 1 Chr. 15:24 – see also Jeiel)[65]
Yicheh –Shall live
כאחד *K'achad* –As one
כבאי *K'voiy* –When I come
כחה *Kochah* –Her strength
לאב *La'av* –To the father, to a father
לבא *Lavoa'* –To come, to go in; at the entrance
לג *Log* –Basin (a liquid measure equal to about 1/2 liter)

34 אגל *Egel* –Drop, reserve supply, collections, stores
אחיהוד *'a'chiyhud* –Ahihud, prince of Asher who helped divide the land upon entering Canaan; member of the family of Ehud, descended from Benjamin
בבכי *Bivkiy* –In his crying
בבל *Babel* –Babel or Babylon, capital of the Babylonian empire
בלב *Belev* –The heart
גאל *Ga'al* –To redeem, act as kinsman-redeemer, avenge, revenge, ransom, do the part of a kinsman; to defile, pollute, desecrate

[64] All references to Goetic Demons come from Godwin's Cabalistic Encyclopedia.
[65] Jeiel (121).

		Go'el –Defilement, defiling
	דכי	*Dokiy* –Crushing, dashing, crashing, pounding of waves
	דל	*Dal* –Low, poor, weak, thin, one who is low; –68th Gate of the 231 Gates
	ואהבכ	*va-'ahevka* –And he will love you
	והגידו	*ve-Higiyduw* –And they shall declare
	ויחדו	*ve-Yachdaw* –And to be together
	ויחטא	*va-Y'chatee'* –And he purified
	ויחי	*va-Y'Chiy* –And lived
		va-Yechiy –And it live
	זבדיהו	*Zebadyahuw* –Zebadiahu, descendant of Levi through Kohath; Levite sent by Jehoshaphat to teach the Law; son of Ishmael
	חהויה	*Chahaviah* –Angel of 6q Scorpio and night angel 7 Cups
	חייו	*Chaya'uw* –His life
	ידכ	*Yadak, yadaka* –Your hand
	יהדיה	*Yehudiyah* –Jehudijah, wife of Ezra and descendant of Caleb
	יהוזבד	*Yehowzabad* –Jehozabad, servant who killed Jehoash; gatekeeper descended from Korah; chief captain of Jehoshaphat
	יזיז	*Yaziyz* –Jaziz, David's chief shepherd (1 Chr. 27:31)
	יחיו	*Y'chaiuw* –They will keep alive
	כדי	*Kediy* –To the extent of, in order that
	כיד	*Kiyd* –Ruin, destruction
	לבב	*Labab* –To ravish, become intelligent, get a mind; to make cakes, bake cakes, cook bread
		Levav –Inner man, mind, will, heart, soul, understanding; heart, mind (Aramaic); to heart
	לד	*Lodh* –Lod, city of Benjamin in the Plain of Sharon – modern Ludd

–Magic sum of the magic square of Jupiter

35	אגלא	*Agla* –A name of God; acronym for *Ateh Gibor le-Olam Adonai*, "Thou art mighty forever, O Lord."
	אלד	*Elad* –10th name of *Shem HaMeforash* (4 Virgo); I shall give birth
	בחייה	*B'chayeyha* –In her lifetime
	בלג	*Balag* –To gleam, smile
	גבל	*Gabal* –To bound, border
		Gebal –Gebal, Phoenician seaport north of Zidon (see also Byblos; northern portion of the mountains of Edom
		Gebul –Border, bound, coast, landmark, limit, quarter, space, great
	גלב	*Gallab* –A barber
	היכ	*Heyk* –How
	הכי	*Yakiy* –Is it?; because of
	הל	*Hal* –85th Gate of the 231 Gates
	ויביאו	*va-Yaviya'uw* –And they brought

	וכדה	*ve-Kadah* –With her pitcher
	יהודי	*Yehuwdiy* –Jehudite, Jew; Jehudi, man who brought Baruch to the princes and read the king Jeremiah's prophecies
	יכה	*Yakeh* –Smite, kills
	לה	*Lah* –To her, for it, unto; it

–Pythagorean number of "harmony," so called because 35 is the sum of the intervals in music. (12:9:8:6)

36	אהל	*'ahal* –To be clear, shine; to pitch a tent, to move a tent
		'ohel –Tent
		Ohel –Ohel, son of Zerubbabel
	אהיטוב	*'Achiytuwb* –Ahitub, son of Phinehas; father of Zadok the priest; father of Meraioth
	איכה	*'ayekah* –Where are you
		'ekah –How; Hebrew title of the book of Lamentations
	אלה	*'alah* –To lament, wail; to swear, curse; oath; oath of covenant; curse; execration; adjuration
		'allah –Oak, terebinth
		'elah –Terebinth, terebinth tree; Elah, valley where David killed Goliath; Goddess; a Duke of Edom assoc. w/*Giburah*; 4th King of Israel
		'eloah –God, god, false god (see also אלוה)[66]
		'elleh –These; these are; these (Aramaic)
	בדל	*Badal* –To divide, separate; a piece, severed piece, a piece (of an ear – Amos 3:12)
	בידכ	*Biyadeka* –In your hand
	בכחו	*be-Kocho* –With his power
	בלה	*Balah* –To wear out, become old
		Balahh –To trouble
		Baleh –Worn out, old
	הודויה	*Howdavyah* –Hodaviah, an ancestor of returning captives (Ezra 2:40 – see also Hodevah)[67]; chief of the tribe of Manasseh (1 Chr. 5:24); descendant of Benjamin (1 Chr. 9:7)
	היטיב	*Heytiyv* –He dealt well
	הייטב	*Hayiytav* –Would it have been pleasing, good; and his hands
	הלא	*Hala'* –To be removed far away, be removed far off
		Helo' –(is) Not?
		Halo' –Has not?, must I not?
	והכה	*ve-Hikah* –And smite
		ve-Hukah –And he be smitten
	וכי	*ve-Kiy* –And when, and if, and as, and that, and because
	ול	*Vak* –101st Gate of the 231 Gates
	יהודאי	*Yehuwda'iy* –Judaite, i.e. Jew
	כביד	*Kabiyd* –Weighty, influential
	לאה	*La'ah* –To be weary, be impatient, be grieved, be

[66] אלוה (42).

[67] Hodevah (26).

offended
Leah –Leah, Jacob's wife through the deception of her father, Laban (Gen. 29-31)

לבד *L'vad* –Aside from, besides; to themselves

לו *Lo* –Not, no; to him, for it, to it, regarding him

–Mystic number of 8th Path (*Hod*)
–The number of decanates in the Zodiac
–The number of squares in the magic square of Sol
–The "*Lamed Vav*" (LV), the 36 righteous men (and women?) in each generation around whom the world revolves, saints unknown even to themselves. (See *Sanhedrin* 97b) A similar Islamic tradition posits the existence of 4,000 such men.

37 אחזיהו *Achaziahu* –Ahaziah, 8th King of Israel; alternate name for Jehoahaz, 6th King of Judah (variant spelling)

אול *'uwl* –Powerful, mighty, strength; prominence (in belly – contemptuous)

אחאיה *Akaiah* –Angel of 1q Virgo and day angel 8 Pentacle

אלו *'aluw* –Behold!, lo! (Aramaic)
'illuw –If, though (contrary to fact)

בהל *Bahal* –To disturb, alarm, terrify, hurry, be disturbed, be anxious, be afraid, be hurried, be nervous
Behal –To frighten, alarm, dismay; to hurry, hasten; alarmed (Aramaic)

בלה *Balah* –Balah, Simeonite town in southern Judah (this spelling used only in Josh. 19:3 – see also Baalah and Bilhah)[68]

גדל *Gadal* –To grow, become great or important, promote, make powerful, praise, magnify, do great things; grown up
Gadel –Becoming great, growing up
Gedil –Twisted threads, tassels, festoons
Giddel –Giddel, head of a family of Solomon's servants; one whose descendants returned to Jerusalem with Zerubbabel
Godel –Greatness

גלד *Geled* –Skin (of man)

דגל *Dagal* –Look, behold; (set up) standards, banners
Degel –Standard, banner

דלג *Dalag* –To leap

הבל *Habal* –To act emptily, become vain, be vain
Hebel –Abel, son of Adam; vapor, breath, vanity

ואל *Valu* –Goetic demon #62
va-Al –And not
ve-El –And unto; and God

גדל *Gadil* –Let grow
Gadol –Great, greatness; to Gad

ואיב *ve-'eyk* –And how

והכבד *Y'hakved* –Then he hardened

ויהיו *va-Yihyuw* –And they became; and they shall be

---

[68] Baalah (107), Bilhah (42).

	ויחזו	*va-Yechezuw* –And they beheld
	וייטב	*va-Yiytav* –And was good
		va-Yiytev –And dealt well
	ולא	*ve-Lo'* –And not, neither
	זכי	*Zakkay* –Zaccai, one whose descendants returned from exile (see also the second Zabbai)[69]
	זל	*Zal* –116th Gate of the 231 Gates
	חטיטא	*Chatiyta'* –Hatita, Temple gatekeeper or porter whose descendants returned from the exile
	יהואחז	*Yehoachaz* –Jehoahaz, 6th King of Judah; 16th King of Judah; 11th King of Israel (variant spelling – see also Shallum)
	יחידה	*Yechidah* –Part of the soul referred to *Keter*
	כבודה	*Kebuwdah* –Abundance, riches, wealth; gloriousness, glorious
	כטוב	*ka-Tov* –As good
	לאו	*Lav* –11th name of *Shem HaMeforash* (5 Virgo)
		Lau –17th name of *Shem HaMeforash* (5 Libra)
	לבה	*Libbah* –Heart
		Labbah –Flame; tip of weapon, point, of spear
	להב	*Lahab* –Flame, blade
	לוא	*Luw'* –If, oh that!, if only!; for naught; not
	–Prime number	
38	אגדל	*'egdal* –I will be greater
	אדבאל	*'Adbe'el* –Adbeel, son of Ishmael
	אואל	*Uvall* –Goetic demon #47
		'Uwel –Uel, son of Bani
	אזל	*Azal* –To go, to go away, to go about; to go off; to depart
		Ezel –Memorial stone between Ramah & Nob – scene of final farewell between David and Jonathan
	באהל	*Ba'ohel* –In the tent
	באלה	*bi-'eleh* –By these
	בול	*Buwl* –Produce, outgrowth; Bul, eighth month in the ancient Hebrew calendar (1 Kings 6:38)
	בכבדי	*bi-Kavodiy* –In my glory
	בלו	*Below* –Tribute (Aramaic); worn out things, rags
	גיחזי	*Geychaziy* –Gehazi, dishonest servant of Elisha (also spelled גחזי)
	גלה	*Galah* –Uncover, remove
		Gelah –Uncover, remove (Aramaic)
		Giloh –Giloh, town in the hill country of Judah, north-northwest of Hebron (see also גילה)[70]
		Golah –Exile, captivity, removed
		Gullah –Bowl, pommel, spring
	האבל	*Ha'Abel* –The mourning

[69] Zabbai (19).

[70] גילה (48).

	הגל	*HaGal* –The heap
	ואכבדה	*ve-'ikavdah* –And I will be honored
	והביטו	*ve-Hibiytuw* –And they looked
	ויאחזו	*va-Ya'achazuw* –And they got them possessions
	ויבך	*va-Y'bak* –And he wept
	וכבוד	*vu-Kavod* –And the glory
	זכאי	*Zakkai* –Zaccai, one whose descendants returned from Exile
	חל	*Chel* –Bulwark, wall, rampart; 130th Gate of the 231 Gates
		Chol –Profaneness, commonness, unholy, profane, common, sand
	טוביהו	*Towbiyahuw* –Tobiahu or Tobiah, Levite sent by Jehoshaphat to teach the Law (2 Chr. 17:8)
	יבכו	*Yivkuw* –Bewail, they be weeping
	יכח	*Yakach* –To prove, decide, judge, rebuke
	לבו	*Libow* –To his heart
	להג	*Lahag* –Study, studying, devotion to study
	לח	*Lach* –Moist, fresh, green, new
		Leach –Moistness, freshness, vigor
	כחי	*Kohiy* –My power, might
39	אובל	*Uwbal* –Stream, river
	אחיך	*'acheyka* –Your brethren
		'achiyka –Your brother
	אחל	*'achel* –Will begin
	אלדד	*Eldad* –Eldad, one of two elders who received the prophetic powers of Moses (Num. 11:26-27)
	אלח	*Alach* –To be corrupt morally, tainted
	בגדל	*Bi-Gedol* –By the greatness
	בזיך	*Beziyk* –Censer
	גאלה	*Geullah* –Kindred, redemption, right of redemption, price of redemption
	גול	*Guwl* –To be glad; joy, be joyful, rejoice
	דלה	*Dalah* –To draw (of water), dangle
		Dallah –Hair, threads, thrum; poor; poorest, lowest
	הגאל	*Hago'el* –Who has redeemed
	הוכח	*Hokecha* –Rebuke
	הלבב	*HaLevav* –The heart
	והכח	*Vehakocha* –The land crocodile
	ויזבחו	*ve-Yizbechuw* –And they sacrificed, that they may sacrifice
	זבל	*Zabal* –To exalt, honor, (possibly) dwell exaltedly
		Zebul –Zebul, ruler of Shechem (Judg. 9:28-41)
	חלא	*Chala'* –To suffer, be sick, be diseased
	טל	*Tal* –Dew, night mist (of heaven – Gen. 27:28; 27:39); dew (Aramaic – Dan. 4:12, 20, 22, 30; 5:21); 143rd Gate of the 231 Gates
	ידכה	*Yadkah* –Your hand
	יהוה אחד	YHVH *Achad* –"יהוה is One"

יחויה *Yechaviah* –Angel of 3q Capricorn and day angel 3 Pent.

כוזו *Kuzu* –A name of God by Temurah

כזבי *Kazbiy* –Cozbi, Midianite woman slain by Phinehas at Shittim (Num. 25:6-18)

כזיב *Keziyb* –Chezib, a Canaanite city in the lowlands of Judah, captured by Joshua (this spelling used only in Gen. 38:5 – see also Achzib, Chozeba)[71]

לבז *Lavaz* –Prey

לבוא *lavua'* –To come, to enter

להד *Lahad* –Lahad, descendant of Judah

לט *Lat* –Secrecy, mystery, enchantment

Lot –Laudanum; myrrh

–The number of books in the Hebrew Bible

40 אכזיב *'Akziyb* –Achzib, Canaanite city in Judah; town in western Galilee near ancient Phoenicia

בחל *Bachal* –To loathe, abhor, feel loathing

בלבו *be-Lebuw* –In his heart

בלגה *Bilgah* –Bilgah, priest in the tabernacle service; priest who came up to Jerusalem with Zerubbabel

בלדד *Bildad* –Bildad, one of Job's friends (Job 2:11; 8:1; 18:1; 25:1; 42:9)

גאלו *Gi'aluw* –His kinsman

גבלה *Gebulah* –Border, bound, coast, landmark, place

גזל *Gazal* –Tear away, seize, rob

Gazel –Robbery, thing taken away by violence

Gezel –Violent perverting, violence

Gozal –Robbery, thing taken as plunder; young

הגבל *Hagbel* –Set bounds

Hagbul –Border

הלה *Hiloh* –Is not?

ובלב *vu-Velev* –And in the heart

וגאל *ve-Ga'al* –And shall redeem

ודל *ve-Dal* –And a poor man

ויביאהו *va-Yaviy'ahuw* –And he brought him

ולד *Valad* –Child, offspring

חבל *Chabal* –To bind; to take a pledge, lay to pledge; to destroy, spoil, deal corruptly, offend; to bring forth, travail; to hurt, destroy (Aramaic); hurt, damage, injury (Aramaic)

Chabol –Pledge

Chebel –A cord, rope, territory, band, company; pain, sorrow, travail, pang; union; destruction; one of two staffs named by Zechariah (Zech. 11:7)

Chibbel –Mast (meaning uncertain – Prov. 23:34)

Chobel –Sailor, seaman

חלב *Chalab* –Milk, sour milk, cheese

Chalav –Milk

Cheleb –Heleb (see also Heldai)[72]

---

[71] Achzib (40), Chozeba (30).

	Chelev –Fat; best of (the fattest part)
טלא	*Tala'* –To patch, spot, be spotted, be colored
	Tela' –Lamb (Isa. 40:11)
יחזיה	*Yachzeyah* –Jahaziah, son of Tikvah – one of four men who opposed Ezra's condemnation of marriage to foreign women (Ezra 10:15)
יל	*Yal* –155th Gate of the 231 Gates
כחזה	*ka-Chazeh* –As breast
לאט	*Lawat* –To cover
	La't –Secrecy, mystery
לבבו	*Levavuw* –To his heart
לבדד	*Levadad* –Alone
לגז	*Lagiz* –To shear
להה	*Lahah* –To languish, faint; to amaze, startle
לוד	*Luwd* –Lud, fourth son of Shem – possibly the Lydians are intended (Gen. 10:22)
לי	*Liy* –To me, I have, mine, for me
מ	*Mem* –13th letter of Hebrew alphabet; when used as a prefix, it means "from"

–The number of days Moses spent on Mount Sinai (Ex. 24:18)
–The number of days Noah and his family spent on the ark (Gen. 8:6)
–The amount (in *seah*) of water in a *kosher mikveh*
–The height of the entrance to the Sanctuary of the Temple (Ezek. 41:2)
–The number of years the Israelites ate manna (Ex. 16:35)

The Hebrew equivalent of thirty is *mem*, a letter that has two distinct versions. The first is open, and the *Midrash* states that the letter indicates kingship (מלכות). From the opened top of the letter, we learn that God is open to our search for spiritual enlightenment. The closed form of the letter, ם, intimates hidden or secret methods to explore this illumination. The latter form is only used at the end of a word, except in rare cases such as the word *lemarbeh* (לםרבה), used in Isaiah 9:06. The word means "to multiply," and is equinumerical with *Tath Zel* (תת זל), the Profuse Giver, which is a title of *Keter*. From this we learn that through *gematria* and its subdivisions, we can approach even the highest of the *sephirot*. As a warning, it is noted that the *gematria* is equal to *Paimon*, one of the Demon Kings of the Goetia. As above, so below.

NOTES:

[72] Heldai (52).

41	אהלה	*'ahaloh* –His tent
		'Oholah –Oholah, a name for Samaria (Ezek. 23:4-5, 36, 44)
	אחלב	*'Achlab* –Ahlab, town assigned to Asher, but never captured
	אלי	*'elay* –To me
		'eliy –My God (Ex. 15:2)
		Ulay –If not; if so be, may be, peradventure, unless; perhaps
	איל	*Ayyal* –Hart; a title of *Malkut*; ram; pillar, door post, jambs, pillaster; strong man, leader, chief; mighty tree, terebinth
		Eyal –Strength; help
		Ayal –Stag, deer, hart
	אמ	*Em* –Mother, source, womb, beginning, origin, crossroads; point of departure or division; if; 12th Gate of the 231 Gates
		'im –If, not, only, or, when
	באחיכ	*Be'achiyka* –Against your brother (Deut. 15:9)
	בטל	*Batel* –To cease
		Betel –To cease (Aramaic)
	בכזיב	*Vikziyv* –At Chezib (Gen. 38:5)
	גאואל	*Gehooale* –Geuel, the Gadite chosen to spy out the land, son of Machi
	גבול	*Gebuwl* –Border, bound, coast, landmark, limit, quarter, space, great
	גבלו	*Gebulo* –Its border
	גחל	*Gechel* –Coal, burning coal, ember
	גלח	*Galach* –Shave, shave off, be bald
	דבלה	*Debelah* –Lump of pressed figs, pressed fig-cake
		Diblah –Diblah, place or city in Palestine (see also Riblah)[73]
	האלה	*Ha'alah* –Cursing, the oath (Num. 5:21; Deut. 29:13)
		Haelah –These
		Ha'Ohal –The tent
	הלאה	*Haleah* –Out there, outwards, further
	וגבל	*ve-Gebul* –And (the) border (Deut. 3:16)
	ולה	*ve-Lah* –And to her, and she had
	טבל	*Tabal* –To dip, dip into, plunge
	יאל	*Ya'al* –To be foolish, become fools, act foolishly; to begin, make a beginning, show willingness
	ייטיב	*Yeytiyv* –Shall (do) good
	כויה	*Keviyah* –Burning, branding, branding scar, burn
	לבדה	*Levadah* –Only
	לבט	*Labat* –To throw down, thrust down, thrust out, thrust away
	לוה	*Lavah* –To join, be joined; to borrow, lend
	מא	*Ma'* –What, whatever (Aramaic)
	–Prime number	

[73] Riblah (237).

42	אהלו	*'ahalo* –His tent, its tent
	איאל	*Ayel* –Angel of 1st astrological house[74]
	אלוה	*Eloah* –God; false god
	אמא	*Ama* –Mother; a title of *Binah*
	בגזל	*Vegazel* –In robbery
	בהלה	*Behalah* –Dismay, sudden terror or ruin, alarm
	בחלב	*Bahalev* –In the milk of (Ex. 23:19)
	בלבבו	*Vilevavo* –In his heart
	בלהה	*Ballahah* –Terror, destruction, calamity, dreadful event
		Bilhah –Bilhah, Rachel's handmaiden, mother of Dan and Naphtali (Gen. 29:29); Bilhah, Simeonite city in southern Judah (this spelling used only in 1 Chr. 4:29 – see also Baalah and Balah)[75]
	בלי	*Beliy* –Wearing out; without; no, not (adv. of negation)
	במ	*Bam* –In them, them, upon them; 32nd Gate of the 231 Gates
		Bem –Entrance, gathering place, ascent
	גדלה	*Gadolah* –Great
	דחל	*Dechal* –To make afraid, dreadful, fear, terrible (Aramaic)
	דלח	*Dalach* –To stir up, make turbid
	הגדל	*HaGadhol* –The greater; the great, the elder
	הודיוהו	*Howdayevahuw* –Hodaiahu, son of Elioenai and descendant of Zerubbabel and David (1 Chr. 3:24)
	היטיבו	*Heytiyvuw* –They have (said) well
	הלוא	*Haloa'* –Wouldn't it?, is it not?
	הלז	*Halaz* –This, this one, yonder
	ואלה	*ve-'elah* –And these
	והכהו	*ve-Hikahuw* –And smite it, and smite him; and he shall beat him (Deut. 25:2)
	וול	*Vaval* –43rd name of *Shem HaMeforash* (1 Pisces)
	ויכבד	*ve-Yakbed* –And he hardened (Ex. 8:28)
	ויכי	*va-Yakuw* –And they smote (Gen. 14:7)
		ve-Yukuw –And were beaten (Ex. 5:14)
	ולאה	*ve-Le'ah* –And Leah
	ולו	*Valu* –Goetic demon #62 (Aurum Solis spelling)
		Velo –And unto him (Gen. 49:10); would that (Num. 20:3)
	חדל	*Chadal* –To stop, cease, desist, forego, cease to be, leave undone, forbear
		Chadel –Rejected, forbearing, transient, fleeting, lacking
		Chedel –Rest, cessation

[74] May mean "island of God."
[75] Baalah (107), Balah (37).

חלד *Cheled* –Age, duration of life, the world; one of the Seven Earths (corr., w/Tebhel, to *Yesod* and *Malkut*); our own Earth

Choled –Weasel, mole (meaning unknown – Lev. 11:29)

טבאל *Tabe'el* –Tabeal, father of a man the kings of Israel and Damascus planned to make king of Judah (Is. 7:6); Persian official who tried to hinder the rebuilding of the wall of Jerusalem

יבל *Yabal* –Jabal; to bring, lead, carry, bear along; a stream, watercourse

Yabbel –Running sore, runnings, ulcer (Lev. 22:22)

יוד ה וו ה *Yod H Vav H* –Tetragrammaton with the masculine consonants spelled out

יוד הה וו *Yod Heh Vav* –The three consonants of Tetragrammaton, spelled out

יוכבד *Yokeved* –Jochebed, descendant of Levi and mother of Moses

כבודי *Kevodiy* –My glory

לבדו *Lebado* –Alone, only

לבטא *Levatea'* –Uttering, pronouncing (Lev. 5:4)

לבי *Lawbee* or *Lebeya* –Lion; lioness

Libiy –My heart

Luwbiy –Lubims, Libyans (see also לובי)[76]

להבה *Lehabah* –Flame; tip of weapon, point, head of spear

לוו *Levo* –19th name of *Shem HaMeforash* (1 Scorpio)

לחבב *Lechovav* –To Hobab

–The number of children of Azmaveth who returned from exile (Ezra 2:24)

43 גדול *Gadhol* –Great

גיל *Giyl* –To be glad; joy; to be joyful, rejoice

גמ *Gam* –Together; also; become much or abundant, collection, company, addition; 51st Gate of the 231 Gates

דגול *Daguwl* –Flag, insignia

זול *Zuwl* –To pour out, lavish; to despise

חלה *Chalah* –To be or become sick, be or become weak, be or become diseased, be or become grieved, be or become sorry

Challah –Cake, perforated cake

ידידיה *Yedidah* –Jedidiah, the name God gave Solomon through Nathan (2 Sam. 12:25)[77]

יחדיהו *Yechdiyahuw* –Jehdeiah, descendant of Levi in David's time; overseer of David's donkeys

להח *Lehach* –34th name of *Shem HaMeforash* (4 Capricorn)

לוז *Luwz* –To depart, turn aside (from the right path); almond tree, almond wood; Luz, city north of

---

[76] לובי (48).

[77] This name literally means "one beloved by God."

		Jerusalem (see also Bethel)[78]; town of the Hittites
	מג –Prime number	*Mag* –Magus, magician; to shake, melt
44	אביאל	*Abiyel* –Abiel, ancestor of Saul; Arbathite who served as one of David's thirty mighty men (see also Abi Albon)[79]
	אגמ	*Agam* –Pool, troubled pool
		Agem –Stagnant pond
	אוזל	*'Uwzal* –Uzal, son of Joktan
	אי־כבוד	*'Iy-kabowd* –Ichabod, son of Phinehas
	אלזבד	*'Elzabad* –Elzabad, one who joined David at Ziklag; descendant of Levi
	אליאב	*Eliab* –Eliab, son of Helon, leader of Zebulun in the wilderness; a Reubenite chief, father of Dathan & Abiram; David's oldest brother; a Levite musician; a Gadite warrior for David; a Kohathite
	בדלח	*Bedolach* –Bdellium (i.e. gum resin)
	בבלי	*Babliy* –Babylonia
	גולה	*Gowlah* –Exile, captivity, removed
	גיאל	*Giel* –Angel of 3rd astrological house[80]
	גמא	*Gama'* –Swallow, drink
		Gome' –Rush, reed, papyrus
	דלי	*Deliy* –Bucket; Aquarius
	דמ	*Dam* –Blood (also of wine – fig.); 69th Gate of the 231 Gates
	חלאה	*Chel'ah* –Rust, scum; Helah, wife of Asher
	טלה	*Taleh* –Lamb (1 Sam. 7:9; Isa. 65:25); Aries
	יגאל	*Yig'al* –Igal, one of twelve spies sent to search out Canaan (Num. 13:7); one of David's heroes (2 Sam. 23:36); descendant of the royal house of Judah (1 Chr. 3:22)
	ילד	*Yalad* –To bear, bring forth, beget, engender
		Yeled –Child, son, boy, offspring[81]
	כידוד	*Kiydowd* –Spark
	להט	*Lahat* –To burn, blaze, scorch, kindle, blaze up, flame; flame (of angelic sword Gen. 3:24; Ex. 7:11)
	לוח	*Luwach* –Board, slab, tablet, plank
	מד	*Madh* –Measure, cloth, garment
45	אגיאל	*Agiel* –Intelligence of Saturn[82]
	אדמ	*Adam* –Adam; a title of *Tiferet*; to be red
		Adhom –Red, ruddy (of man, horse, heifer, garment, water, lentils)

[78] Bethel (443).

[79] Abi Albon (171, 821).

[80] May mean "valley of God."

[81] It should be noted that adding father, **אב**, 3 and mother, **אמ**, 41 equals 44.

[82] All references to Planetary Intelligences are taken from Regardie's The Golden Dawn.

Edom –Edom, the twin-brother of Jacob

Odem –Ruby, carnelian, sardius (precious stone in the High Priest's ephod – represents the tribe Reuben)

בלגי — *Bilgay* –Bilgai, one who sealed the new covenant with God after the exile (Neh. 10:9 – see also second Bilgah mentioned in Neh. 12:5, 18)[83]

גבלי — *Gibliy* –Giblites

גזלה — *Gezelah* –Robbery, thing taken away by violence

הם — *Ham* –Ham, name for Egypt used only in poetry (Ps. 78:51); place between Ashteroth Karnaim in Bashan – possibly modern Ham; 86th Gate of the 231 Gates

Hem –Abundance, clamor (meaning uncertain – Ezek. 7:11); they, these, the same, who

זאזל — *Zazel* –Spirit of Saturn[84]

זבול — *Zebuwl* –Exalted, residence, elevation, lofty abode, height, habitation, dwelling; the 4th Heaven (corr. to *Tiferet*)

זחל — *Zachal* –To shrink back, crawl away; to fear, be afraid

חלבה — *Chelbah* –Helbah, town of the tribe of Asher on the Phoenician plain northeast of Tyre

טול — *Tuwl* –To hurl, cast

יוד הא ואו הא — YHVH by a system of "filling"[85]

ילה — *Yelah* –44th name of *Shem HaMeforash* (2 Pisces)

ככה — *Kakah* –Like this, thus

לוט — *Lot* –Lot, Abraham's nephew who escaped from Sodom

Lowt –Covering, envelop

Luwt –To wrap closely or tightly, enwrap, envelop

ליה — *Loyah* –Wreath, garland (meaning dubious – 1 Kings 7:29, 30, 36)

לתאה — *Leta'ah* –A kind of lizard, exact meaning unknown (Lev. 11:30)

מאד — *Me'od* –Exceedingly, much; might, force, abundance; muchness, force, abundance, exceedingly

מה — *Mah* –What, which, why, how, of what kind; anything, something, aught, what may; what, whatever (Aramaic); secret name of the World of Yetzirah

–Mystic number of 9th Path (*Yesod*)

–The sum of all the numbers (1 through 9) on the magic square of Saturn

46 אביגל — *Abiygal* –Abigail, wife of Nabal the Carmelite – after his death, became the wife of David (this spelling used only in 1 Sam. 25:3 – see also אביגיל)[86]

אדליא — *'Adalya'* –Adalia, son of Haman

אילה — *Ayalah* –Doe, deer, hind

---

[83] Bilgah (40).

[84] Regardie, 65.

[85] See Introduction.

[86] אביגיל (56).

אליה *Alyah* –Tail, fat-tail (of sheep – an Eastern delicacy)
Eliyah–Elijah, the prophet; the younger man who rebuked Job and his three friends; an Ephraimite, Samuel's great-grandfather; a Manassite warrior chief for David; son of Shemaiah & Korhite gatekeeper; David's brother

אמה *Amah* –Maidservant, female slave, handmaid, concubine
Ammah –Cubit (a measure of distance – the forearm, roughly 18 in.)[87]; Cubit, a hill in the country of Benjamin where Joab and Abishai stopped
Ummah –People, tribe, nation

בדיל *Bediyl* –Alloy, dross, tin (the metal of Jupiter)

גבולה *Gebuwlah* –Border, bound, coast, landmark, place

גוזל *Gowzal* –Robbery, thing taken as plunder

דמב *Dameb* –65th name of *Shem HaMeforash* (5 Gemini)

האהלה *Ha'Ohela* –The tent

ההאל *Hahahel* –Angel of 5q Aquarius & day angel 7 Swords

ומ *Vam* –102nd Gate of the 231 Gates

חגלה *Choglah* –Hoglah, daughter of Zelophehad

חזאל *Chaza'el* –Hazael, murderer of Ben-hadad II who usurped the throne of Syria (see also חזהאל)[88]

חלח *Chalach* –Halah, portion of the Assyrian kingdom, encompassing the basin of the Habor and Saorkas Rivers

טואל *Toel* –Angel of 2nd astrological house

יהאל *Yahel* –Angel of 7th astrological house[89]

כבדכ *Kivodek* –Your glory, your honor

כדכב *Kadkob* –A precious stone (maybe ruby, agate – Is. 54:12; Ezek. 27.16)

לוי *Levi* –Levi, third son of Jacob who avenged Dinah's wrong and the founder of the priestly tribe of Israel; the tribe descended from Levi; Levites

לטבה *Litovah* –To do goodness, good

מאה *Ma'ah* –Hundred, one hundred (Aramaic)
Me'ah –Hundred; Meah, tower at Jerusalem not far from the Sheep Gate

–The number of books in the Roman Catholic Bible

47 אויל *Eviyl* –Silly; fool (-ish) man

אולי *Eviliy* –Silly, foolish; impious
Uwlay –If not; if so be, may be, peradventure, unless; suppose; Ulai, river surrounding Shushan in Persia

---

[87] There are several cubits used in the *Tanakh*, the cubit of a man or common cubit (Deut. 3:11), the legal cubit or cubit of the sanctuary (Ezek. 40:5) plus others – see a Bible dictionary for a complete treatment.

[88] חזהאל (51).

[89] *Yahel* may mean "Lord of God," as odd as that sounds, or there may be a letter omitted before or after "Yah" in this name.

במה *Bamah* –High place, ridge, height, technical name for cultic platform – Bamah, mentioned in Ezek. 20:29 – see also 1 Kings 3:4

בטול *Betuwl* –Selflessness, self-nullification

גמד *Gomed* –Cubit (measure from elbow to knuckles)

הלזה *Halazeh* –This, this one, yonder

ויאל *Veyel* –Angel of 6th astrological house

זככ *Zakak* –To be pure, be bright, be clean, be bright, clean

זם *Zam* –117th Gate of the 231 Gates

חלדה *Chuldah* –Huldah, prophetess in the days of King Josiah

חלט *Chalat* –To take up, catch, pick up (a word) (1 Kings 20:33)

טבול *Tabuwl* –Turban

יואל *Yoel* –Joel, firstborn son of Samuel the prophet (see also Vashni)[90]; descendant of Simeon; father of Shemaiah, a descendant of Reuben; chief of the tribe of Gad; ancestor of the prophet Samuel; descendant of Tola; one of David's mighty men; Levite in David's time; keeper of the treasures of the Lord's house; prince of Manasseh west of the Jordan; Levite who aided in cleansing the Temple; one who married a foreign wife during the exile; overseer of the descendants of Benjamin in Jerusalem; prophet in the days of Uzziah – a book written by him survives in the *Tanakh*

יזל *Yezel* –13th name of *Shem HaMeforash* (1 Libra)

כי טוב *Ki Tov* –That it was good

מבה *Mebah* –14th name of *Shem HaMeforash* (2 Libra)
Mabeh –55th name of *Shem HaMeforash* (1 Taurus)

מגד *Meged* –Excellence

–Prime number

48 במו *Bemow* –In, at, by

גדולה *Gedulah* –Greatness, magnificence; a title of *Hesed*

גדיאל *Gaddiy'el* –Gaddiel, one of the spies sent to Canaan (Num. 13:10)

גילה *Giylah* –Joy, rejoicing
Giyloh –Giloh, town in the hill country of Judah, north-northwest of Hebron (see also גלה)[91]

הלזו *Halezuw* –This, this one, yonder

והואל *Vehuel* –Angel of 1q Aries & day angel 2 Wands

ומב *Vameb* –61st name of *Shem HaMeforash* (1 Gemini)

זולה *Zuwlah* –A removal, a putting away; except, besides, with the exception of, with the removal of; except that

חיל *Chayil* –Strength, might, efficiency, wealth, army; strength, army, power (Aramaic)

---

[90] Vashni (366).
[91] גלה (38).

		Cheyl –Rampart, fortress, wall
		Chiyl –Pain, agony, sorrow, a writhing, anguish
	חלי	*Chaliy* –Jewelry, ornament; Hali, town of Judah, located near the border of Asher
		Choliy –Sickness
	חמ	*Cham* –Ham, son of Noah; father in law, husband's father; warm, hot; warmth, heat; Ham, name for Egypt used only in poetry (Ps. 78:51); place between Ashteroth Karnaim in Bashan and the Moabite country – possibly modern Ham; 131st Gate of the 231 Gates
		Chom –Heat, hot
	יבול	*Yebuwl* –Produce, fruit, produce (of the soil)
	יובל	*Yowbal* –Ram, ram's horn, trumpet, cornet
		Yubal –Jubal, son of Lamech – he was skilled with musical instruments (Gen. 4:21)
		Yuwbal –Stream
	יחל	*Yachal* –To wait, hope, expect
	כוכב	*Kowkab* –Stars (of Messiah, brothers, youth, numerous progeny, personification, God's own omniscience – fig. – Ezek. 32:7, Dan. 8:10; 12:13); Mercury
	לובי	*Luwbiy* –Lubims, Libyans (see also לבי)[92]
	לחי	*Lechiy* –Jaw, cheek; Lehi, location in Judah where Samson slew many Philistines (see also Ramath-lehi)[93]
	מבו	*Mabow'* –Entrance, a coming in, entering; sunset
	מדד	*Madad* –To measure, stretch
		Midad –To make extension, continue
	מח	*Meach* –Fatling, fat one, fat
		Moach –Marrow
	–The number of occurences of the Divine Name *El Shaddai*	
49	אהליאב	*'Oholiyab* –Aholiab, a worker on the Tabernacle
	אוביל	*'Owbiyl* –Obil, manager of David's camels
	אחלי	*'Achalay* –Oh that…!; oh would that!; ah that!
		'Achlay –Ahlai, daughter of Sheshan; father of one of David's mighty men
	אלידד	*Eliydad* –Elidad, a Benjamite chief who helped apportion his tribe's allotment to the Promised Land
	גולחב	*Golachab* –The Arsonists, *Qlippoth* of *Giburah*
	דהמ	*Daham* –Astonish, astound
	דליה	*Daliyah* –Branch, bough
		Delayah –Delaiah, one of David's priests; prince who urged Jehoiakim not to destroy the scroll containing Jeremiah's prophecies; ancestor of a postexilic family that had lost its genealogy; father of Shemaiah (see also Delaiahu)[94]

[92] לבי (42).

[93] Ramath-Lehi (688).

דמה *Damah* –To be like, resemble; to cease, cause to cease, cut off, destroy, perish

Demah –To be like (Aramaic)

Dummah –One silenced, one quieted by destruction, one destroyed

הגיאל *Hagiel* –Intelligence of Venus

הדמ *Hadam* –Member, limb, member of the body (Aramaic)

Hadom –Stool, footstool

הילד *HaYeled* –The baby

חיאל *Chiy'el* –Hiel, man who rebuilt Jericho (1 Kings 16:34) and sacrificed his sons, in fulfillment of Joshua's curse (Josh. 6:26)

חמא *Chema'* –Anger, rage (Aramaic)

ילדה *Yaldah* –Girl, damsel, marriageable girl

טמ *Tam* –144th Gate of the 231 Gates

לביבה *Labiybah* –Cakes, bread

מדה *Middah* –Measure, measurement, stature, size, garment; tribute

מואב *Moab* –Moab, son of Lot by his daughter and an ancestor of the Moabites; Moab, land that consisted of the plateau east of the Dead Sea between the wadis Arnon and Zered, though sometimes extending to the north of the Arnon

בובא *Mowba'* –Entrance, entering, in-coming

מוג *Muwg* –To melt, cause to melt

מחא *Macha'* –To strike, clap (the hands)

Mecha' –To strike, smite, kill (Aramaic)

–The number of squares in the magic square of Venus

50 אדמה *Adamah* –Earth, ground, land; Adamah, city in Naphtali; one of the Seven Earths (corr. to *Hesed*)

אטמ *Atam* –To shut, shut up, close

איזבל *Iyzebel* –Jezebel, queen of Israel, wife of Ahab, daughter of Ethbaal[95]

אלדיה *Aldiah* –Angel of 4q Virgo and night angel 9 Pent.

גזמ *Gazam* –Locusts

Gazzam –Gazzam, one whose descendants returned from Exile

דג גדול *Dagh Gadhol* –Great fish

המה *Hamah* –To murmur, growl, roar, cry aloud, mourn, rage, sound, make noise, tumult, be clamorous, be disquieted, be loud, be moved, be troubled, be in an uproar

Hemmah –They

טמא *Tame'* –To be unclean, become unclean, become impure; unclean, impure

ידאלה *Yidalah* –Idalah, city of the tribe of Zebulun – modern Khirbet el-Huvara

---

[94] Delaiahu (55).

[95] Jezebel's name literally means "Baal exalts" or "Baal is husband to" or "unchaste."

ייל	*Yeyal* –58th name of *Shem HaMeforash* (4 Taurus)
ילוד	*Yillowd* –Born
ילי	*Yeli* –2nd name of *Shem HaMeforash* (2 Leo)
ים	*Yam* –Sea; 156th Gate of the 231 Gates
	Yem –Mules (meaning uncertain – Gen. 36:24)
כל	*Kal* –Every; 166th Gate of the 231 Gates
	Kol –All, the whole, all, whole, the whole (Aramaic)
לודי	*Luwdiy* –Lydians (see also לודיי)[96]
מדו	*Medev* –Garment
מהה	*Mahah* –To linger, tarry, wait, delay
מוד	*Muwd* –To shake
מזג	*Mezeg* –Mixture, mixed wine
מטע	*Meta'* –To reach, to come upon, to attain (Aramaic)
מי	*Miy* –Who?, which?, whom?, would that, whoever, whosoever, every one
נ	*Nun* –14th letter of Hebrew alphabet

–The width of the ark of Noah in cubits
–The number of confrontory questions God makes to Job (Job 38, 39)

Nun is the letter equaling 50, a letter that reminds one of the profile of a human returning to standing after bowing or prostrating themself. From this we learn that *nun* represents the ability of humans to worship God, an action not possible for any other creature on the planet.

The letter itself means "fish," the object of desire of *tzaddi*, which means "fishhook." Contained within this teaching is wisdom.

There is a brief passage in the *Tanakh* where there are two inverted *nun*s. In Numbers 10:35, 36, separating the passage:

When the ark was to set out, Moses would say:
"Advance, O Adonai!
May Your enemies be scattered,
And may Your foes flee before You!
And when it halted, he would say:
Return, O Lord,
You who are Israel's myriad of thousands!"

According to the Zohar, the inverted *nun* symbolizes the *Shekinah* hovering over the Holy Ark. Thus, the *Shekinah* turned its face toward the children of Israel when this phrase was spoken.

NOTES:

[96] לודיי (60).

51 אדום *Edom* –The Kings and Dukes of Edom (Gen. 36:31, 43), of the line of Esau, who sold his birthright, "symbolize unlawful and chaotic forces" and are associated with the *Sefirot*; Edom, twin-brother of Jacob

אים *Ayom* –Frightful, terrible, dreadful

Aim –Goetic Demon #23

Aum –30th name of *Shem HaMeforash* (6 Sagittarius)

אכל *Akal*–To eat, devour, burn up, feed; to eat, devour

Okel –Food; food supply; meal, dinner

'Ukal –Ucal, man of the tribe of Benjamin (see also Ithiel)[97]; person to whom the proverbs of Agur were directed (Prov. 30:1)

אלכ *Illek* –These, those

אמי *'Amiy* –Ami, servant of Solomon

אנ *'an* –Where?, whither? (of place); when?, until when?, how long? (of time); pain, sorrow; Heliopolis, a city in lower Egypt; 13th Gate of the 231 Gates

גחם *Gacham* –Gaham, son of Nahor

הום *Huwm* –To distract, ring again, make a (great) noise, murmur, roar, discomfit, be moved

המו *Himmow* –They, them

חבולה *Chabuwlah* –Hurtful act, crime, harm, wicked deed, a wrong

חזהאל *Chazah'el* –Hazael, murderer of Ben-hadad II who usurped the throne of Syria (see also חזאל)[98]

יההאל *Yehohel* –Angel of 2q Gemini & night angel 8 Swords

ילוה *Yelaveh* –Attached

כלא *Kala'* –To restrict, restrain, withhold, shut up, keep back, refrain, forbid

Kele' –Imprisonment, confinement, restraint

לויה *Livyah* –Wreath

מבט *Mabbat* –Expectation, object of hope or confidence

מודא *Mowda'* –Kinsman, relative

מחבא *Machabe'* –Hiding place; bosom

נא *Na* –I (we) pray, now, please; raw, rare; a name of God

No –Thebes, the capital of Upper Egypt

52 אבא ואמא *'Aba ve-'Ama'* –"Father and mother"

אביטל *'Abiytal* –Abital, a wife of David

אימא *Aima* –The Supernal Mother; a title of *Binah*

אליהו *Eliyahuw* or *Elijah* –Elijah, the great prophet of the reign of Ahab; Benjamite son of Jeroham; a son of Elam with foreign wife during exile; a son of Harim, and priest, with foreign wife during exile

אליחבא *Elyachba* –Eliahbah, one of David's mighty warriors

אנא *'ana'* –I (Aramaic)[99]

---

[97] Ithiel (452).

[98] חזאל (46).

	'anna' –Ah now!, I/we beseech you, oh now!, pray now![100]
בהמה	*Behemah* –Beast, cattle, animal
בימ	*Bime'* –Goetic demon #26
בכל	*Bakol* –Among all
בנ	*Ben* –Son, grandson, child, member of a group, child (Aramaic); a title of *Tiferet*; the secret name of the world of Assiah; Ben, assistant in the temple musical service during David's reign (1 Chr. 15:18); 33rd Gate of the 231 Gates
גדליה	*Gedalyah* –Gedaliah, Levite musician; grandfather of the prophet Zephaniah; chief of Jerusalem that imprisoned Jeremiah; governor of Jerusalem after the exile; priest who had married a foreign wife during the exile
זהמ	*Zaham* –To loathe, be foul, be loathsome; Zaham, son of Rehoboam (2 Chr. 11:19)
זמה	*Zimmah* –Plan, device, wickedness, evil plan, mischievous purpose; Zimmah, Levite of the family of Gershon; Levite in the fourth or fifth degree of temple service; Levite who assisted in cleansing the temple
חדלי	*Chadlay* –Hadlai, father of Amasa, a chief man in the tribe of Ephraim (2 Chr. 28:12)
חלדי	*Chelday* –Heldai, captain of the temple service; an Israelite who returned from the exile and was given special honors (Zech. 6:10 – see also Helem)[101]
חמד	*Chamad* –To desire, covet, take pleasure in, delight in; desirableness, preciousness
	Chemed –Desire, delight, beauty, desirable, pleasant
יבמ	*Yabam* –To perform levirat marriage; brother-in-law, husband's brother
	Yebem –70th name of *Shem HaMeforash* (4 Cancer)
יהואל	*Yehoel* –Angel of *Keter* in the World of *Briah*[102]
יוד הה וו הה	*Yod Heh Vav Heh* –The consonants of Tetragrammaton spelled out; the expanded Name; YHVH by a system of "filling"[103]
כבל	*Kebel* –Bond(s), fetter(s)
כלב	*Kaleb* –Caleb, son of Hezron and grandson of Perez and great grandson of Judah and the father of Hur and grandfather of Caleb the spy; the godly son of Jephunneh and the faithful spy who reported the Promised Land faithfully and urged its capture; son of Hezron and grandson of Perez; son of Hur (1 Chr. 2:24) (some translations have this as a place – see also Caleb

---

[99] First person singular – usually used for emphasis.

[100] Participle of entreaty usually followed by the imperative verb.

[101] Helem (78, 638).

[102] *Yehoel* may mean "YHVH is Lord."

[103] See Introduction.

Ephrathah)[104]

Keleb –Dog

לאויה *Laviah* –Angel of 5q Virgo & day angel 10 Pentacles; Angel of 5q Libra & day angel 4 Swords

לכב *Lekab* –31st name of *Shem HaMeforash* (1 Capricorn)

מבטא *Mibta'* –Rash utterance, hasty vow

מגוג *Magog* –Magog, country of undetermined location, generally described as being in a northerly direction from Palestine[105]; Magog, second son of Japheth – possibly a people inhabiting the north land – the name may denote the Scythians or a term for northern barbarians

מזה *Mazeh* –Sucked out, empty, exhausted

Mizzah –Mizzah, a Chief of Edom (Gen. 36:13, 17; 1 Chr. 1:37)

נב *Nob* –Nob, city of the tribe of Benjamin northeast of Jerusalem

–The number of children of Nebo who returned from exile (Ezra 2:29)

53 אבים *Abiyam* –Abijam, 2nd King of Judah

אבן *Aben* –Stone (large or small)

Eben –Stone (Aramaic)

Oben –Wheel, disk

אהליבה *'Ohoiybah* –Oholibah, a symbolic name for Jerusalem (Ezek. 23:4-44)

אליהוא *Eliyhuw*–Elijah, the prophet; the younger man who rebuked Job and his three friends; an Ephraimite, Samuel's great-grandfather; a Manassite warrior chief for David; son of Shemaiah & Korhite gatekeeper; David's brother

בהילו *Behiyluw* –Haste, hastily (Aramaic)

בנא *Bena'* –To build (Aramaic)

גן *Gan* –Garden, enclosure; 52nd Gate of the 231 Gates

הזיאל *Haziel* –Angel of 3q Virgo & day angel 9 Pent.

חילה *Cheylah* –Bulwark, entrenchment, rampart, fortress

חליה *Chelyah* –Jewels, jewelry

חמה *Chammah* –Sun, heat of the sun, heat

Chemah –Heat, rage, hot displeasure, indignation, anger, wrath, poison, bottles

יגלי *Yogliy* –Jogli, prince of Dan (Num. 34:22)

כלאב *Kil'ab* –Chileab, son of David[106]

מבוה *Mebowah* –Entry, entrance, a coming in, entering

מגדו *Megiddown* –Megiddo, ancient city of Canaan assigned to Manasseh & located on the southern rim of the plain of Esdraelon 6 miles from Mt. Carmel & 11 miles from Nazareth (see also מגדון)[107]

---

[104] Caleb Ephrathah (738).

[105] Josephus identified Magog with the Scythians

[106] Chileab is called Daniel in 1 Chr. 3:1 (95).

[107] מגדון (103, 753).

מזו *Mezev* –Garner, granary

מחה *Machah* –To wipe, wipe out; to strike; full of marrow

נבא *Naba'* –To prophesy
Neba' –To prophesy (Aramaic)

–Prime number

54 אגן *Aggan* –Bowl, basin

דן *Dan* –Dan, fifth son of Jacob and progenitor of a tribe of Israel (assoc. w/Scorpio); Dan, town of the tribe of Dan in the northwest portion of Palestine
Den –This, on account of this; therefore; 70th Gate of the 231 Gates

דמי *Demiy* –Cessation, quiet, rest, silence, pause, peacefulness

זבדיאל *Zabdiy'el* –Zabdiel, father of Jashobeam, David's captain; overseer of the priests

חום *Chuwm* –Dark color, darkened, dark brown or black

חמאה *Chem'ah* –Curd, butter

טמה *Tamah* –To be stopped up, unclean

יזואל *Yezav'el* –Jeziel, man of valor who joined David at Ziklag (1 Chr. 12:3)

לכד *Lakad* –To capture, take, seize
Leked –A taking, capture

מדבח *Madbach* –Altar (Aramaic)

מדי *Maday* –What is enough, sufficiency, enough, sufficiently; Mede(s) ; Median; Madai, son of Japheth

מטה *Mattah* –Downwards, below
Matteh –Tribe; branch, staff
Mittah –Couch, bed, bier
Muttah –Spreading out, outspreading, spreading
Mutteh –A perversion, that which is perverted or warped, perverted

נבב *Nabab* –To hollow out

נד *Ned* –Heap, wall

55 אדמי *'Adamiy* –Adami, a place in Palestine
'Edomiy –Edomite, descendant from Edom

אדן *Eden* –Base, pedestal, socket (strong, firm)
'Addan –Addan, the man who could not prove his ancestry after the exile (Neh. 7:61; Ezra 2:59)

אחילוד *'Achiyluwd* –Ahilud, father of Jehoshaphat

גבים *Gebiym* –Gebim, settlement just north of Jerusalem near Michmash

גבן *Gibben* –Hump-backed, crooked-backed

גנב *Ganab* –To steal, steal away, carry away
Gannab –Thief

דגדגיאל *Dagdagiel* –Guardian of the 14th Tunnel of Set

דומה *Duwmah* –Silence; Dumah, descendant of Ishmael

דליהו *Delayahuw* –Delaiahu, one of David's priests; prince who urged Jehoiakim not to destroy the roll containing Jeremiah's prophecies; ancestor of a postexilic family that had lost its genealogy; father of Shemaiah (see also Delaiah)[108]

הנ *Hane* –They, these, the same, who; behold!, lo!; whether, if (Aramaic); 87th Gate of the 231 Gates

הלכ *Halak* –To go, walk, come; toll, custom duty, tribute (Aramaic)

Helek –Traveller

טמאה *Tum'ah* –Uncleanness (sexually and religiously)

יחואל *Yechav'el* –Jehiel, son of Heman the singer (2 Chr. 29:14)

כהל *Kehal* –To be able

כלה *Kalah* –To accomplish, cease, consume, determine, end, fail, finish, be complete, be accomplished, be ended, be at an end, be finished, be spent; completion, termination, full end, complete destruction, consumption, annihilation

Kaleh –Failing with desire, longing, longing for

Kallah –Bride, daughter-in-law; a title of *Malkut*

לכה *Lekah* –Lekah, a town in Judah; site unknown

מדוה *Madveh* –Sickness, disease

מוט *Mowt* –To totter, shake, slip; a shaking, wavering, pole, bar of yoke

מיה *Miah* –48th name of *Shem HaMeforash* (6 Pisces)

נאד *No'd* –Skin, bottle, skin-bottle

נגב *Negeb* –South-country; Nekeb, town on the boundary of the territory of Naphtali; south

נה *Noahh* –Eminency, distinction, splendor, eminence

–Mystic number of 10th Path (*Malkut*)

56 **אביגיל** *Abiygayil* –Abigail, wife of Nabal, then of David; sister of David (see also **אביגל**)[109]

אחזמ *'Achuzzam* –Ahuzam, son of Ashur

אימה *Eymah* –Terror, dread

Aim –Goetic demon #23 (Aurum Solis spelling)

אכלה *Oklah* –Food

אנה *'anah* –To mourn; to meet, encounter, approach, be opportune

בדנ *Bedan* –Bedan, leader of Israel mentioned as a deliverer of the nation (1 Sam. 12:11)[110]; descendant of Manasseh

גמזו *Gimzow* –Gimzo, town of northern Judah, southeast of Lydda

הוהמ *Howham* –Hoham, Amorite king slain by Joshua

הייאל *Hayayel* –Angel of 5q Cancer & day angel 4 Cups

ונ *Van* –103rd Gate of the 231 Gates

---

[108] Delaiah (49).

[109] **אביגל** (46).

[110] Many think that Bedan is a reference to Abdon (132, 782).

חזיאל *Chaziy'el* –Haziel, descendant of Levi in the time of David

יומ *Yom* –Day

Yowm –Day, time, year; 24-hour time period (1 day)

כול *Kuwl* –To seize, contain, measure

מדהבה *Madhebah* –Boisterous, raging, behavior, boisterous behavior; golden city, exactness of gold

נאה *Na'ah* –To be comely, be beautiful, be befitting; pasture, abode, abode of shepherd, habitation, meadow

נדב *Nadab* –To incite, impel, make willing; Nadab, firstborn of Aaron, struck dead for offering "strange fire" to God (Ex. 6:23; Lev. 10:1-3); descendant of Jerahmeel; brother of Gibeon; 2nd King of Israel

Nedab –To volunteer, offer freely (Aramaic)

נו *Nuw'* –To hinder, hold back, forbid, disallow, restrain, frustrate

Nu –Egyptian Goddess

–The number of men of Netophah who returned from exile (Ezra 2:22)

57 אבדנ *Abdan* –Destruction

און *Aven* –Trouble, vanity, wickedness (in regards to an idol)

Avnas –Goetic demon #58

On –Strength; wisdom; sorrow

Own –Ability, power, wealth, force, goods, might, substance; On, a Reubenite who rebelled against Moses and Aaron; On, city of Lower Egypt

אלוכ *Alloces* –Goetic demon #52

אנו *'anuw* –We (1st person plural – usually used for emphasis)

'Onow –Ono, city of Benjamin

אנח *'anach* –Sigh, groan (in pain or grief), gasp

בהנ *Bohan* –Bohan, descendant of Reuben for whom a boundary stone was named (Josh. 15:6); stone named for Bohan (Josh. 18:17)

Bohen –Thumb, great (big) toe (always used as both together – Ex. 29:20)

בנה *Banah* –To build (Aramaic); to build, rebuild, establish, cause to continue

דגימ *Dagim* –Fishes; Pisces

דגנ *Dagan* –Corn, grain

הבנ *Hoben* –Ebony

ווליה *Vavaliah* –Angel of 1q Pisces & day angel 8 Cups

זנ *Zan* –Species, kind, sort; 118th Gate of the 231 Gates

חטיל *Chattiyl* –Hattil, ancestor of some who returned from exile (Ezra 2:57; Neh. 7:59)

חטמ *Chatam* –To hold in, restrain

חמדה *Chemdah* –Desire, that which is desirable; pleasant, precious

חמט *Chomet* –A kind of lizard, an unclean animal (Lev. 11:30)

לוויה *Luviah* –Angel of 1q Scorpio & day angel 5 Cups
מאביד *Ma'aviyd* –Perished
מאוי *Ma'avay* –Desire
מדחה *Midcheh* –Occasion of stumbling, means of stumbling; ruin
מוטב *Motev* –Better
מזבח *Mizbeach* –Altar
מידבא *Meydeba'* –Medeba, Moabite town on the Jordan in the territory of Reuben east of the Arnon – modern Madaba
נגד *Nagad* –To be conspicuous, tell, make known
Negad –To stream, flow
Neged –What is conspicuous, what is in front of; in front of, straight forward, before, in sight of; in front of oneself, straightforward; before your face, in your view or purpose with; what is in front of, corresponding to; in front of, before; in the sight or presence of; parallel to; over, for; in front, opposite; at a distance; from the front of, away from; from before the eyes of, opposite to, at a distance from; from before, in front of; as far as the front of; in front of, facing (Aramaic)

58 אביהיל *Abiyhayil* –Abihail, wife of Abishur; wife of Rehoboam
אבנה *'Abanah* –Abana, river running through Damascus
אזן *Azan* –To hear, listen; weigh, test, prove, consider
Azen –Tools, implements, weapons
Ozen –Ear, as part of the body; ear as organ of hearing; (subjective) to uncover the ear to reveal; the receiver of divine revelation
גדליהו *Gedalyahuw* –Gedaliahu, Levite musician (see also Gedaliah)[111]; governor of Jerusalem after the exile
גנה *Gannah* –Garden, orchard
Ginnah –Garden
דדן *Dedan* –Dedan, descendant of Cush, possibly a people of Arabia in the neighborhood of Edom (Gen. 10:7); son of Jokshan and grandson of Abraham (Gen. 25:3 – see also דדנה)[112]
חן *Chen* –Favor, grace, charm; Hen, son of Zephaniah (Zech. 6:14 – see also Josiah in verse 10)[113]; 132nd Gate of the 231 Gates
טליהד *Taliahad* –Angel of Water[114]
יחיל *Yachiyl* –Waiting, hoping
יחם *Yacham* –To be hot (lust), conceive

[111] Gedaliah (52).
[112] דדנה (63).
[113] Josiah (326). The word *chen* is often considered a notarikon for חכמה נסתרה, "secret wisdom."
[114] Taliahad may derive from the name Elijah, the prophet. The relationship to his prophecy of the drought in Ahab's time may be indicative of this. In 1 Kings, Elijah was directed to show himself to Ahab as the herald of rain from YHVH.

	ייזאל	*Yeyazel* –Angel of 4q Aquarius & night angel 6 Swords
	כבול	*Kabul* –Cabul, town of the tribe of Asher noted for its dry climate; district of Galilee – the northern part of the territory of Naphtali
	כחל	*Kachal* –To paint (eyes), adorn with paint
	כלבו	*Kalibbow* –Calebite (this spelling used only in 2 Sam. 25:3 – see also כלבי)[115]
	כלוב	*Kelub* –Cage, basket, dog cage
		Kaluwb –Chelub, descendant of Judah; father of Ezri and one of David's officers
	כלח	*Kelach* –Full strength, firm or rugged strength, vigor; Calah, city built by Nimrod that later became the capital of the Assyrian Empire
	להחיה	*Lehachiah* –Angel of 4q Capricorn & night angel 3 Pentacles
	לחכ	*Lachak* –To lick, lick up
	מדוח	*Madduwach* –Seduction, enticement, a thing to draw aside
	מחי	*Mechi* –Stroke (of a battering-ram); 64th name of Shem *HaMeforash* (4 Gemini)
	מידד	*Meydad* –Medad, one of the elders of the Hebrews on whom the spirit fell (Num. 11:26-27)
	נבו	*Nebow* –Nebo, an ancestor of Jews who divorced their foreign wives after the Exile (Ezra 10:43)[116]
	נגה	*Nagahh* –To shine
		Nogahh –Brightness; daylight (Aramaic); Nogah, son of David
	נדד	*Nadad* –To retreat, flee, depart, move, wander abroad, stray, flutter
		Nadud –Tossing (of sleeplessness)
		Nedad –To flee (Aramaic)
	נהג	*Nahag* –To drive, lead, guide, conduct; to moan, lament
	נוב	*Nuwb* –To bear fruit
		Nowb –Fruit
	נח	*Noach* –Noah, son of Lamech
59	דנה	*Dannah* –Dannah, village in the hill country of Judah – modern Deir esh-Shemish or Simya
	המטה	*HaMateh* –The rod
	זבנ	*Zeban* –To buy, gain
	זנב	*Zanab* –To cut off; tail, end, stump
	חוילה	*Chaviylah* –Havilah, region of central Arabia populated by the descendant of Cush[117]
	חומה	*Chowmah* –Wall
	חלכא	*Cheleka'* –Hapless, poor, unfortunate person
	טנ	*Tan* –145th Gate of the 231 Gates

---

115 כלבי (62).

116 Some scholars believe this term may have referred to a city.

117 This term may have referred to the territory of the Arabian Desert for several hundred miles north of modern Al-Yamanah.

	יחיאל	*Yechiy'el* –Jehiel, singer in the Tabernacle in David's time; descendant of Gershon; companion of the sons of David; son of Jehoshaphat; Levite in charge of the dedicated things in the Temple; chief priest in Josiah's day; father of one who returned from exile; father of the one who first admitted taking a foreign wife during the exile; two who divorced their foreign wives after the exile
	מבטח	*Mibtach* –Trust, confidence, refuge
	מואבי	*Mow'abiy* –Moabite (see also מואבית, מואביה)[118]
	מטבח	*Matbeach* –Slaughtering place, slaughter
	נדה	*Nadah* –Exclude, drive away, thrust aside; cast out, put away
		Nedeh –Gift
		Niddah –Impurity, filthiness, menstrous, set apart
	–Prime number	
60	**אחיאמ**	*'Achiyam* –Ahiam, son of Sharar the Hararite and one of David's mighty men
	אמתי	*'Amittay* –Amittai, father of the prophet Jonah
	בחנ	*Bachan* –To examine, try, prove; watchtower
		Bochan –Testing, tested, tried
	גאונ	*Ga'own* –Exaltation, majesty, pride; genius, excellency
	גבנה	*Gebinah* –Cheese, curd
	גנבה	*Genebah* –Thing stolen, theft
	גנז	*Genaz* –Treasure (Aramaic)
		Genez –Treasury, chests
	דונ	*Duwn* –Judge, to judge
	הלכה	*Halakhah* –Practice; the parts of the Talmud dealing with matters of law
	המיה	*Hemyah* –Sound, music (of instruments)
	הנה	*Hennah* –They, these, the same, who; here, there, now, hither
		Hinneh –Behold!, lo!, see, if
	ודנ	*Vedan* –Vedan, a place, site uncertain, perhaps near Medina in Arabia, or may simple be read "and Dan" (Ezek. 27:19)
	זגנ	*Zagan* –Goetic demon #61 (Aurum Solis spelling)
	טנא	*Tene'* –Basket
	יכל	*Yakol* –To prevail, overcome, endure, to be able
	ילהיה	*Yelahiah* –Angel of 2q Pisces & night angel 8 Cups
	ילכ	*Yalak* –To go, walk, come
	ינ	*Yan* –157th Gate of the 231 Gates
	כלי	*Keliy* –Article, vessel, implement, utensil, instrument, tool; 18th name of *Shem HaMeforash* (6 Libra)
	כמ	*Kam* –167th Gate of the 231 Gates
	לודיי	*Luwdiyiy* –Lydians (see also לודי)[119]

---

[118] מואביה (64), מואבית (459).

מוטה	*Mowtah* –Pole; bar of yoke
מחזה	*Machazeh* –Vision (in the ecstatic state) (Gen. 15:1; Num 24:4, 16; Ezek. 13:7)
	Mechezah –Light, window, place of seeing
מטאטא	*Mat'ate'* –Broom, besom
מטוה	*Matveh* –That which is spun, yarn
נבח	*Nabach* –To bark
	Nobach –Nobah, descendant of Manasseh who conquered Kenath (Num. 32:42); Nobah, town of Gad east of the Jordan; city in Gilead
נוד	*Nuwd* –To shake, waver, wander, move to and fro, flutter, show grief, have compassion on; to flee (Aramaic)
	Nod –Nod, unidentified land east of Eden to which Cain fled after the murder of Abel (Gen. 4:16)
	Nowd –Wandering (of aimless fugitive)
נהה	*Nahah* –To wail, lament
ני	*Niy* –Wailing, lament
ס	*Samekh* –15th letter of Hebrew alphabet

Samekh is a letter with multiple and important meanings. It begins the word *sod*, (סוד), or "secret," the method of interpretation that includes kabbalah and *gematria*. In this way, the letter indicates the use of secret or esoteric information to apply new meanings to biblical passages. *Samekh* also means "support" and indicates that God supports all that humanity does or is capable of doing. In these two ways, the invisible support of God underlies the importance of Torah study as well as everyday life.

Samekh and *mem* are the only letters totally surrounded and these two letters are representative of two parts of Torah: "ם (=40) for the written torah, which was given to Moses during his forty days and nights in Heaven and ס (=60) for the Oral Law, which consists of sixty Talmudic tractates" (Munk, 160). Again we see that the *samekh* is representative of not only hidden meaning, but also that part of Jewish literature that explains the *Tanakh*. Thus, we can see that *Talmud* is a hidden interpretation of the Hebrew Bible, and clarifies the words given to us by God.

NOTES:

119 לודי (50).

61 אביחיל *Abiychayil* –Abihail, Levite who was the father of Zuriel; head of a family of Gad; father of Esther

אדומי *'Edowmiy* –Edomite, descendant from Edom

אדון *Adown* –Firm, strong, lord, master

'Addown –Addan, the man who could not prove his ancestry after the exile (Neh. 7:61; Ezra 2:59)

אחבן *'Achban* –Ahban, son of Abishur

אין *Ain* –Nothing; No-thing, not, nought; nothing, nought; not; to have (of possession); without; for lack of

Aiyn –Where?, whence?

Iyn –Is there not?, have you not?

אמך *Amak* –Thy mother; thy source

אני *Ani* –I (1st person singular – usually used for emphasis); 37th name of *Shem HaMeforash* (1 Aquarius)

'oniy –Fleet of ships

אס *'as* –Rim, edge; initials of *Ain Sof*; 14th Gate of the 231 Gates

בטן *Beten* –Belly, womb, body; bowels, the inmost part; Beten, village of the tribe of Ashur

Boten –Pistachio nuts – delicacy given to Joseph by Jacob through his sons

דמביה *Damabiah* –Angel of 5q Gemini & day angel 10 Swords

הון *Hown* –Wealth, riches, substance; enough, sufficiency

Huwn –To be easy, be ready

זאגן *Zagan* –Goetic demon #61

ייאל *Yeyayel* –Angel of 4q Scorpio & night angel 6 Cups

כליא *Keliy'* –Imprisonment

לאל *la-El* –To God

La'el –Lael, descendant of Gershon

מחוז *Machowz* –City, haven

מיטב *Meytab* –The best

נבט *Nabat* –To look, regard

Nebat –Nebat, father of Jeroboam I (1 Kings 11:26)

נגח *Nagach* –To push, thrust, gore

Naggach –Addicted to goring, apt to gore

נדבה *Nedavah* –Voluntariness, free-will offering

נוה *Navah* –To beautify; to dwell; rest

Naveh –Abode, habitation, abode of shepherds or flocks, pasture; dwelling, abiding

–Prime number

62 אבנט *Abnet* –Girdle, sash, waist band (of High Priest)

אסא *Asa* –3rd King of Judah; head of a Levite family

בהחמי *Behahemi* –Angel of 2d Aries

בין *Beyn* –Between, among, in the midst of, from between; between (Aramaic)

Biyn –To discern, understand, consider; prudent, regard

בלל *Balal* –To mix, mingle, confuse, confound

בני *Baniy* –Bani, descendant of Merari; one of David's mighty men; descendant of Judah; father of a family that returned from the exile (see

		Binnui)[120]; one whose descendants had taken foreign wives during exile; descendant of the latter; Levite who helped repair the wall of Jerusalem; Levite who assisted in the devotions of the people; one who sealed the new covenant with God after the exile; Levite whose son was an overseer of the Levites after the exile; three Levites who participated in the temple worship
		Bunniy –Bunni, ancestor of Shemaiah; Levite who helped Ezra teach the Law; one who sealed the covenant with God after the exile (see also Buni)[121]
	בס	*Bas* –To trample, step, pile up; to establish firmly, rest safely; 34th Gate of the 231 Gates
	דחנ	*Dochan* –Millet
	ווימ	*Vawvem* –Hooks
	זנה	*Zanah* –To commit fornication, be a harlot, play the harlot
	חמטה	*Chumtah* –Humtah, city in the mountains of Judah near Hebron
	טבליהו	*Tebalyahuw* –Tebaliah, Levite gatekeeper in the days of David
	טמא הוא	*Tamai Hua* –"He is unclean"
	כלבי	*Kalebiy* –Calebite (see also כלבו)[122]
	לבל	*Labal* –A demon king attendant upon Paimon[123]
	מבהיה	*Mebahiah* –Angel of 1q Taurus & day angel 5 Pentacles
	מחוגה	*Mechuwgah* –Circle-instrument, compass
	נאוה	*Na'veh* –Comely, beautiful, seemly
	נבי	*Nabiy'* –Spokesman, speaker, prophet
		Nebiy' –Prophet (Aramaic)
	נדח	*Nadach* –To impel, thrust, drive away, banish
	נזה	*Nazah* –To spurt, spatter, sprinkle; to spring, leap
63	אבדונ	*Abaddon* –Place of destruction, destruction, ruin, Abaddon; the angel of the bottomless pit; the Sixth Hell (corr. to *Hesed*)
	אבס	*Abas* –To feed, fatten
	אונו	*'Ownow* –Ono, city of Benjamin
	בונה	*Boneh* –Builder; beaver
		Buwnah –Bunah, son of Jerahmeel
	גלל	*Galal* –On account of, for the sake of; Galal, a returned exile; Levite who returned from the exile
		Gelal –Great (Aramaic)
		Gelel –Heap of dung
		Gillul –Idol
	גס	*Gas* –53rd Gate of the 231 Gates

[120] Binnui (68).

[121] Buni (68).

[122] כלבו (58).

[123] See Paimon (186, 836; 187, 837) and *Abalim* (83, 643).

	דאבונ	*De'abown* –Faintness, languishing, sorrow
	דגונ	*Dagon* –A god of the Philistines
	דדנה	*Dedaneh* –Dedan, district near Edom between Sela and the Dead Sea (Jer. 25:23; Ezek. 25:13 – see also דדן in Is. 21:13)[124]
	דונג	*Downag* –Wax
	ויאבדמ	*Va-Abdam* –And He destroyed them
	זונ	*Zuwn* –To feed
	חנה	*Chanah* –To decline, incline, encamp, bend down, lay siege against
		Channah –Hannah, prophetess, mother of Samuel
	יוד הי ואו הי	YHVH by a system of "filling"[125]
	יזליאה	*Yizliy'ah* –Jezliah, descendant of Benjamin
	יחדיאל	*Yachdiy'el* –Jahdiel, head of a family of Manasseh east of the Jordan (1 Chr. 5:24)
	ימחה	*ye-Macheh* –Be blotted out, wiped out
	מחידא	*Mechiyda* –Mehida, ancestor of returned captives
	מחיה	*Michyah* –Preservation of life, sustenance
	מכאב	*Mak'ob* –Pain, sorrow
	נביא	*Navia'* –Prophet
	נגהה	*Negohah* –Brightness
	נחה	*Nachah* –To lead, guide
	נטה	*Natah* –To stretch out, extend, spread out, pitch, turn, pervert, incline, bend, bow
	סבא	*Saba'* –To drink heavily or largely, imbibe
		Seba' –Seba, eldest son of Cush; Seba, African nation bordering the land of Cush[126]
		Sobe' –Drink, liquor, wine
	סג	*Seg* –The secret name of the World of *Briah*
64	אנחה	*'anachah* –Sighing, groaning (expression of grief or physical distress)
	גונה	*Gonah* –Serenity
	דינ	*Dayan* –Judge
		Diyn –Justice; judge, to judge; judgment (Aramaic); a title of *Giburah*
	דלל	*Dalal* –To hang, languish, hang down; below
	דני	*Dani* –50th name of *Shem HaMeforash* (2 Aries)
		Daniy –Danites, of Dan
	דס	*Das* –71st Gate of the 231 Gates
	זוזימ	*Zuwziym* –Zuzims, primitive tribe that lived in Ham, a place east of the Jordan River between Bashan and Moab, they were conquered by King Chedorlaomer (Gen. 14:15)
	חוימ	*Chivim* –Hivites
	מואביה	*Mow'abiy* –Moabite (see also מואבית, מואבי)[127]

[124] דדן (58, 708).

[125] See Introduction.

[126] There is some confusion between Sheba and Seba, but they are probably two distinct locations.

	מיזהב	*Mezahab* –Mezahab, mother of Matred, the grandfather of Mehetabel, wife of Hadar, a King of Edom (assoc. w/*Malkut*)
	נבואה	*Nebuw'ah* –Prophecy; prophesying (Aramaic)
	נוגה	*Nogah* –Venus
	נוח	*Nuwach* –To rest; resting place
	ניד	*Niyd* –Quivering (motion) of lips
	סבב	*Sabab* –To turn, turn about or around or aside or back or towards, go about or around, surround, encircle, change direction
	סד	*Sadh* –Stocks (for feet)

–The number of hexagrams in the I Ching
–The number of squares in the magic square of Mercury

65	אדין	*Edayin* –Then, afterwards, thereupon, from that time (Aramaic)
	אדני	*Adonai* –My lord; a name of God
	אחומי	*'Achuwmay* –Ahumai, son of Jahath
	בנ־הדד	*Ben-Hadad* –Ben-hadad I of Syria who invaded Israel (1 Kings 15:18, 20; 2 Chr. 10:2, 4); Ben-hadad II, laid siege to Samaria itself (1 Kings 20; 2 Kings 6:24; 8:7, 9); son and successor of Hazael who reigned over Syria as it disintegrated (2 Kings 13:3, 24-25); possibly a general title of the Syrian kings (Jer. 49:27)
	גמ יחד	*Gam Yechad* –"Together in unity" (Ps. 133:1)
	דומיה	*Duwmiyah* –Silence, quietness, still waiting, repose
	הדונ	*Haduwn* –Beautifully formed
	היכל	*Heykal* –Temple, palace, mansion, nave, sanctuary[128]
	הינ	*Hiyn* –Hin (unit of measurement, about 5 quarts)
	הליכ	*Haliyk* –Step
	הלל	*Halal* –To shine; to praise, boast, be boastful; Hillel, father of Abdon the judge
	הס	*Has* –Silence!; 88th Gate of the 231 Gates
	זנח	*Zanach* –To cast off, reject, spurn; to stink, emit stench, become odious
	ינה	*Yanah* –To oppress, suppress, treat violently, maltreat
	כליה	*Kilyah* –Kidneys; reins
	כמה	*Kamah* –To long for, faint, faint with longing
	ללה	*Lelah* –6th name of *Shem HaMeforash* (6 Leo)
	LVX	*LUX* –Light (Latin: L = 50, V = 5, X = 10)
	מזוזה	*Mezuwzah* –Doorpost, gatepost
	מזיח	*Maziyach* –Girdle
	מכה	*Makkah* –Blow, wound, slaughter
	נהי	*Nehiy* –Wailing, lamentation, mourning song
	נוט	*Nuwt* –To quake, shake, dangle

–The magic sum of the magic square of Mars

127 מואבית (459), מואבי (59).

128 From this, according to the Zohar, we learn that Adonai is the palace of YHVH

66 אטון *'etuwn* –Linen, yard, thread

אכילה *'akiylah* –Food, a meal, an eating, meat

אניה *'aniyah* –Mourning, lamentation

'oniyah –Ship

'Aniah –Araunah, a Jebusite (2 Sam. 26:16-24 – see also Ornan)[129]

בחון *Bachown* –Assayer (an inspector and valuer of metals)

גוזן *Gowzan* –Gozan, district and town of Mesopotamia, located on the Habor River

גלגל *Galgal* –Wheel (Aramaic)

Gilgal –Wheel; Gilgal, first campsite of the Israelites after they crossed the Jordan River into Canaan; village northeast of Bethel, from which Elijah and Elisha began their journey; town on the edge of the Plain of Sharon, north-northeast of Antipatris

דיבן *Diybon* –Dibon, city of the tribe of Gad located north of the Arnon River (see also Dimon – Num. 21:30; 32:3; Is. 15:9)[130]; village of southern Judah near the boundary of Edom (see also Dimonah – Neh. 11:25; Josh. 15:22; see also דיבון)[131]

דנהבה *Dinhabah* –Dinhabah, capital city of Bela, king of Edom (Gen. 36:32; 1 Chr. 1:43)

והנה *VeHinneh* –And behold!

וס *Vas* –104th Gate of the 231 Gates

חנדד *Chenadad* –Henadad, head of a Levite family that helped to rebuild the temple

יוכל *Yuwkal* –Jucal, messenger of King Zedekiah (this spelling used only in Jer. 38:1 – see also Jehucal)[132]

יון *Yavan* –Javan, fourth son of Japheth (Gen. 10:2, 4; 1 Chr. 1:5,7)[133]; Javan, trading post in southern Arabia (Ezek. 27:13)

Yaven –Mire, mirer (Ps. 40:3; 69:3)

יחזיאל *Yachaziy'el* –Jahaziel or Jaziel, Benjamite warrior who joined David at Ziklag; priest who helped bring the Ark of the Covenant in the Temple; Levite, son of Hebron; Levite who encouraged Jehoshaphat's army against the Moabites; tribal leader whose son returned from Babylon

כמו *Kemow* –Like, as, the like of which; when, according as, as it were

לול *Luwl* –Staircase, winding stair, shaft or enclosed space with steps or ladder

---

[129] Ornan (301, 951).

[130] Dimon (110, 760).

[131] Dimonah (115), דיבון (72, 722).

[132] Jehucal (71).

[133] The name corresponds etymologically with Ionia and may denote the Greeks (see Is. 66:19).

	ללאה	*Lula'ah* –Loop (used in attaching curtains to hooks – Ex. 26:4, 5, 10, 11; 36:11, 12, 17)
	מוכ	*Muwk* –To be low, grow poor, be depressed, be poor
	נבזבה	*Nebizbah* –Reward (Aramaic)
	נדיב	*Nadiyb* –Inclined, willing, noble, generous; noble one
	סאה	*Seah* –Seah, a measure of flour or grain (probably equal to 1/3 *efah*)
	–Mystic number of 11th Path (*Keter-Chokmah*; א; Air)	
	–The number of books in the Protestant Bible	
67	אבידנ	*Abidan* –Abidon, son of Gideoni and Prince of the tribe of Benjamin[134]
	אלול	*Eluwl* –Worthless, something worthless; ineffective; worthless gods, idols
		Elul – The 12th Jewish month, corresponding to Aug. or Sept. – it is associated with Virgo and the tribe Zebulun[135]
	בינה	*Binah* –Understanding, discernment; the third *Sefirah* (occurs 38 times in the *Tanakh*)
	בניה	*Benayah* –Benaiah, father of one of David's counselors; third leader of David's army; one of David's mighty men; one of David's priests and a Temple musician; grandfather of Jahaziel; head of a family of the tribe of Simeon; overseer of the temple during Hezekiah's reign; father of Pelatiah; four men who married foreign wives during the exile (see also בניהו)[136]
		Binyah –Structure, building
	גחונ	*Gachown* –Belly, womb
		Gichown –A river of Eden (assoc. w/Water); Gihon, intermittent spring outside the walls of Jerusalem, south of the Temple area
	וינא	*Vine'* –Goetic demon #45
	זדונ	*Zadown* –Pride, insolence, presumptuousness, arrogance
	זינ	*Zayin* –Sword; 6th letter of Hebrew alphabet
	זלל	*Zalal* –To be worthless, be vile, be insignificant, be light; to shake, tremble, quake
	זס	*Zas* –119th Gate of the 231 Gates
	חנט	*Chanat* –To embalm, spice, make spicy; to ripen; embalming
	טחנ	*Tachan* –To grind, crush
	יבמיה	*Yebamiah* –Angel of 4q Cancer & night angel 3 Cups
	יבנה	*Yabneh* –Jabneh, city marking the northern border of Judah – modern Yebnah (see also Jabneel)[137]
	לולא	*Luwle'* –Unless, if not, except
	נבחז	*Nibchaz* –Nibhaz, an idol worshipped by the Arites (2

134 Abidan represented his tribe when a census was taken during their trek in the wilderness.

135 *Elul* literally means "nothingness."

136 בניהו (73).

137 Jabneel (93).

		Kings 17:31)
	נביה	*Nebiy'ah* –Prophetess
	נגיד	*Nagiyd* –Leader, ruler, captain, prince
	סבה	*Sibbah* –Turn of events, turn of affairs
	סגד	*Sagad* –To prostrate oneself (in worship)
		Segid –To prostrate oneself, do homage, worship (Aramaic)
	סוא	*Sow'* –So, king of Egypt, either Osorkon IV or Tefnakht[138] (2 Kings 17:3-7)
	–Prime number	
68	אזני	*'Ozniy* –Ozni, alternate name for Ezbon, son of Gad (used in Num. 26:16); descendant of Benjamin
	בוס	*Buws* –To tread down, reject, trample down
	בנוי	*Binnuwy* –Binnui, Levite appointed by Ezra to weigh gold; two men who married foreign wives during the exile; one who repaired the wall of Jerusalem; Levite who came up with Zerubbabel (Neh. 12:8) (see also Bani)[139]
		Buwniy –Buni, ancestor of Shemaiah; Levite who helped Ezra teach the Law; one who sealed the covenant with God after the exile (see also Bunni)[140]
	הגינ	*Hagiyn* –Appropriate, suitable; directly ahead of
	הנחה	*Hanachah* –A day of rest, holiday, a giving of rest, holiday making
	זינא	*Ziyna'* –Zina, second son of Shimi (1 Chr. 23:10 – see also Zizah)[141]
	חיימ	*Chayim* –Life
	חינ	*Chiyn* –Beauty, grace
	חכמ	*Chakam* –To be wise; wise, wise man – it should be noted that Solomon said "The teaching of the wise is a fountain of life (Prov. 13:14)
	חלל	*Chalal* –To profane, defile, pollute, desecrate, begin; to wound (fatally), bore through, pierce, bore; to play the flute or pipe; slain, fatally wounded, pierced; profaned
	חנטא	*Chinta'* –Wheat (Aramaic)
	חס	*Chas* –133rd Gate of the 231 Gates
	יגדליהו	*Yigdalyahuw* –Igdaliah, ancestor of persons who had a "chamber" in the Temple (Jer. 35:4)
	יחמי	*Yachmay* –Jahmai, tribal leader of Issachar (1 Chr. 7:2)
	ינח	*Yanach* –To rest
	כלובי	*Keluwbay* –Chelubai, son of Hezron and the grandfather of Caleb
69	אבוס	*Aybuws* –Crib, manger, feeding trough

[138] Some believe this name is a reference to a city.
[139] Bani (62).
[140] Bunni (62).
[141] Zizah (29).

אביון *Ebyown* –In want, needy, chiefly poor, needy person; subject to oppression and abuse; needing help, deliverance from trouble, especially as delivered by God; general reference to lowest class

אחין *'Achyan* –Ahian, descendant of Manasseh

גויים *Goyim* –Nations; gentiles

גוני *Guwniy* –Guni, son of Naphtali found in three lists; father of Abdiel; Gunites

גלול *Gilluwl* –Idol

דינה *Diynah* –Dinah, daughter of Jacob by Leah, sister of Simeon & Levi

הדס *Hadas* –Myrtle tree

וכביאל *Vakabiel* –"Increase of the Concealment of God," Angel of Pisces

טין *Tiyn* –Clay

טלל *Talal* –To cover with a roof, cover over, roof
Telal –To seek shade, have shade (Aramaic)

טס *Tas* –146th Gate of the 231 Gates

יגון *Yagown* –Grief, sorrow, anguish

נוחה *Nowchah* –Nohah, son of Benjamin

נידה *Niydah* –Impure, filthiness, impurity

סוג *Suwg* –To move, go, turn back, move away, backslide; to fence about

מדכה *Medokah* –Mortar

סט *Set* –Transgression, error, sin

70 אדם וחוה *Adam ve-Chavvah* –Adam and Eve

אדניה *'Adoniyah* –Adonijah, son of David

בחין *Bachiyn* –Siege towers, watchtower

גאיון *Ga'ayown* –Proud, haughty

גוג ומגוג *Gog ve-Magog* –Gog and Magog

הליכה *Haliykah* –Going, doing, travelling company, way

הללה *Howlelah* –Madness

הסה *Hasah* –Hush, keep silence, be silent, hold peace, hold tongue; to hush

זבינא *Zebiyna'* –Zebina, one who divorced his foreign wife after the exile

ידון *Yadown* –Jadon, Judahite who helped repair the walls of Jerusalem after the exile

יין *Yayin* –Wine

ילל *Yalal* –To howl, wail
Yelal –A howling (of beasts)

יס *Yas* –158th Gate of the 231 Gates

כילי *Kiylay* –Scoundrel, knave

כל־חזה *Kol-Chozeh* –Col-hozeh, father of Baruch of the tribe of Judah; father of Shallum, who helped to rebuild the wall of Jerusalem (Neh. 3:15)[142]

כן *Ken* –So, therefore, thus; right, just, honest, true,

[142] These two may be the same person.

veritable; thus, so, as follows (adv. – Aramaic); base, stand, pedestal, office, foot, place, estate; gnat, gnats, gnat-storm[143]; 168th Gate of the 231 Gates

ליל *Layil* –Night

למ *Lam* –177th Gate of the 231 Gates

מיכ *Mik* –42nd name of *Shem HaMeforash* (6 Aquarius)

מכי *Makiy* –Machi, father of one of the spies sent into Canaan

נהיה *Nihyah* –Wailing, lament, lamentation, mourning, song of mourning

נחבי *Nachbiy* –Nahbi, spy of Naphtali whom Moses sent out to explore Canaan

סוד *Sowd* –Council, counsel, assembly; secret

Sod –Torah interpretation that focuses on the esoteric, mystical in the text

סחב *Sachab* –To drag

ע *Ayin* –Eye; source, well, spring, fountain, origin; 16th letter of Hebrew alphabet

–The age of Terah when his son Abram was born (Gen. 11:26)

–The number of words in Jacob's dream of heaven, where he wrestles with the angel (Gen. 28:12-15, beginning with the word *Ve-Hinneh*)

–The number of Jacob's direct descendents who accompanied him to Egypt (Gen. 46:27; Ex. 1:5)

–The number of days that the Egyptian nation mourned after the death of Jacob (Gen. 50:3 – some translators state that the Israelites mourned instead of the Egyptians)

–The number of Israelite leaders that accompanied Moses to the base of Mount Sinai (Ex. 24:1, 9)

–The number of Israelite leaders that accompanied Moses to the Tabernacle (Num. 11:16; 24-25)

–The number of Gideon's sons, later killed by Abimelech (Judg. 8:30)

–The number of silver coins given to Abimelech by the people of Shechem (Judg. 9:4)

–The number of donkeys that Abdon's sons and grandsons rode upon (Judg. 12:14)

–The number of people from Beth Shemesh struck down by the Lord for looking into the Ark (1 Sam. 6:19)

–The number of King Ahab's descendants in Samaria, slain in part by Jehu's planning (2 Kings 10:1-11)

–The number of years Tyre will be forgotten (Is. 23:15-17)

–The number of years that Israel will serve Babylon (Jer. 25:11)

–The number of elders that Ezekiel saw performing detestable things in his vision (Ezek. 8:11)

–The number of years that Israel fasted and lamented their sins (Zech. 7:4)

–The number of years given to us as human beings (Ps. 90:10)

–The number of weeks (viz. years) before Israel is holy after desecrating their gift of the chosen nation (Dan. 10:24)

–The number of cattle brought by the Israelites as burnt offerings to sacrifice to the Lord in 2 Chr. 29:32

–The number of years that Israel was desolate in 2 Chr. 36:21

–The number separating "male" [זכר = 227] and "female" [נקבה = 157], thus "secret," סוד separates the two

–The number separating "Torah" [תורה = 611] and "Israel" [ישראל = 541], again "secret," סוד separates the two

---

[143] It should be noted that this word, used as "and it was so" in Gen. 1:1 six times, implies that the phrase could mean "and it was 70," meaning that *Ken* or 70 separated Light & Darkness, Evening & Morning, the Upper Waters & the Lower Waters, etc.

As one can see by the above numerous references to seventy in the *Tanakh,* the meaning behind the letter *ayin* is one of great importance. *Ayin* literally means "eye" and points to the most important sense that humans possess. Above any other sense that humans have, sight is our most used and vital not only for our survival, but the ability to read Torah.

Kabbalah teaches that God possesses seventy names or "faces." According to R. Ginsburgh, the Name YHVH occurs 1820 times in the *Tanakh*; 1820 = 70 x 26. Since 26 is the number equivalent to YHVH itself, the seventy is the hidden number of God's face, each of which is turned away from humanity, for as it is written, "...for no man shall see Me and live ...and My Face shall not be seen." (Ginsburgh, 249).

NOTES:

71 **אדינו**

Adinow –Adino, name given Jashobeam when he killed 800 men at one time (this spelling used only in 2 23:8 – see also Josheb-Basshebeth, Joshebeth)[144]

אכן

Aken –Surely, truly, indeed

אליל

Eliyl –Of nought, good for nothing, worthless

Elil –Idol

אללי

Elelay –Woe!, alas!

אלם

Alam –To bind (to be bound)

Elem –In silence, silent

Illem –Mute, silent, dumb, to be unable to speak

Ulam –Vestibule, porch

אמדוך

Amdukias –Goetic demon #67

אמל

Amal –To be weak, to droop, to languish, to be exhausted

אנך

'anak –Plummet, plumb, lead-weight

Anakh –Plumbline (Amos 7:7-8)

אע

'a' –Wood, beam, timber; initials of *Aur Oguwl* (the circular light which descends through the ten *Sefiroth*; 15th Gate of the 231 Gates

הלול

Hilluwl –Rejoicing, praise

וניה

Vanyah –Vaniah, son of Bani who divorced his foreign wife after the exile

זנוח

Zanowach –Zanoah, one of the family of Caleb

חזון

Chazown –Vision, prophecy

יהוכל

Yehuwkal –Jehucal, messenger of King Zedekiah (this spelling used in Jer. 37:3 – see also Jucal)[145]

יונה

Yonah –Dove, pigeon; Jonah, prophet sent to preach to Nineveh in the days of Jeroboam II – he was the first Hebrew prophet sent to a heathen nation

כלוהי

Keluwhay –Chelluh, man who married a foreign wife during the exile

לאם

Leom –A people, nation

מיכא

Miyka' –Mica, son of Mephibosheth (this spelling used only in 2 Sam. 9:12 – see also מיכה); son of Zabdi (this spelling used only in Neh. 10:12 – see also מיכה); son of Zichri (this spelling used only in 1 Chr. 9:15 – see also מיכה)[146]; one who signed the covenant

מכוה

Mikvah –Burnt spot, burn scar

מלא

Male' –To fill, be full; full, fullness, that which fills

Mela' –To fill

Melo' –Fullness, that which fills

Millu' –Setting, installation

נדביה

Nedabyah –Nedabiah, descendant of King Jehoiakim of Judah (1 Chr. 3:18)

נדיבה

Nediybah –Nobility, nobleness, noble deeds

נזיד

Naziyd –Boiled food, soup, pottage, thing sodden or

---

[144] Josheb-Basshebeth (1016), Joshebeth (422, 982).

[145] Jucal (66).

[146] מיכה (75).

boiled

נכא — *Naka'* –To strike, scourge, smite
Nake' –Stricken

–Prime number

72 אליאל — *Eliy'el* –Eliel, an ancestor of Samuel; chief in David's army (might be two or three different men); a Levite with David in moving the Ark; a chief of Manasseh; two chiefs of Benjamin; a chief Bohathite; a Levite

בליל — *Beliyl* –Fodder

בלמ — *Balam* –To curb, hold in, restrain

בכימ — *Bokiym* –Bochim or Bokim, site near Gilgal where the Israelites repented of their sins (Judg. 2:1-5)

בסי — *Besay* –Besai, one who returned to Jerusalem with Zerubbabel (Ezra 2:49; Neh. 7:52)

בע — *Bo'* –To seek, request, petition, pray; 35th Gate of the 231 Gates

גלגול — *Gilgul* –Revolving; transmigration, reincarnation, turning over, rolling over

דביונ — *Dibyown* –Dove's dung (meaning dubious – see 2 Kings 6:25)

דיבונ — *Diybown* –Dibon, city of the tribe of Gad located north of the Arnon River (see also Dimon – Num. 21:30; 32:3; Is. 15:9)[147]; village of southern Judah near the boundary of Edom (see also Dimonah – Neh. 11:25; Josh. 15:22; see also דיבן)[148]

יבינ — *Yabiyn* –Jabin, king of Hazor defeated by Joshua; another king of Hazor who oppressed Israel and was defeated by Deborah

יוד הי ויו הי — YHVH by a system of "filling"[149]

יונדב — *Yownadab* –Jonadab, descendant of Rechab, who forbade his followers and descendants to drink wine and live in houses; sly son of David's brother, Shimeah (see also Jehonadab)[150]

חסד — *Chased* –To be good, be kind; to be reproached, be ashamed
Hesed –Goodness, kindness, faithfulness, mercy; a reproach, shame; the fourth *Sefira*h (this word occurs 248 times in the *Tanakh*); Hesed, father of an officer of Solomon (1 Kings 4:10)

טחנה — *Tachanah* –Mill

נבכ — *Nebek* –Spring, springs

עב — *Ab* –The secret name of the World of *Atzilut*; density; thicket, darkness, cloud; an architectural term (meaning dubious – 1 Kings 7:6; Ezek. 41:25,

---

[147] Dimon (110, 760).

[148] Dimonah (115), דיבן (66, 716).

[149] See Introduction.

[150] Jehonadab (77).

26)

–The number of quinances in the Zodiac
–The number of names of *Shem HaMeforash*
–The number of Goetic demons
–The number of joints in the human body (acccording to the Kabbalah)
–The number of letters on the stones of the ephod

73	אגדה הלכה	*Aggadah* + *Halakhah* –The two types of presentation in the *Talmud*
	אזניה	*'Azanyah* –Azaniah, father of Jeshua, signer of covenant
	בליאל	*Belial* –Goetic demon #68; *Qlippoth* of *Ain Sof*; Archdemon corresponding to *Hod*
	בניהו	*Benayahuw* –Benaiah, father of one of David's counselors; third leader of David's army; one of David's mighty men; one of David's priests and a Temple musician; grandfather of Jahaziel; head of a family of the tribe of Simeon; overseer of the temple during Hezekiah's reign; father of Pelatiah; four men who married foreign wives during the exile (see also בניה)[151]
	בעא	*Be'a'* –To ask, seek, request, desire, pray, make petition (Aramaic)
	גליל	*Galiyl* –Turning, folding (of leaves of doors)
	גללי	*Gilalay* –Gilalai, one of a party of priests who played on David's instruments at the consecration of the Jerusalem walls under Ezra
	גלמ	*Galam* –Wrap together
		Golem –Golem; substance yet being unperfect, unformed mass
	גליל	*Galiyl* –Galil, one of the largest districts of Palestine (see also Galilee)[152]
	גמל	*Gamal* –To deal fully with, recompense; to wean a child, to be weaned; to ripen, bear ripe (almonds); camel
		Gimel –Camel; third letter of Hebrew alphabet
	גע	*Go* –54th Gate of the 231 Gates
	חכילה	*Chakiylah* –Hachilah, hill in the wilderness southeast of Hebron, near Maon (1 Sam. 26:1-3)
	חכליה	*Chakalyah* –Hachaliah, father of Nehemiah, the governor of Israel
	חכמה	*Chokmah* –Wisdom; the second *Sefira*h (occurs 149 times in *Tanakh*)
	חסה	*Chosah* –Hosah, one of the first doorkeepers of the Ark of the Covenant (1 Chr. 16:38; 26:10-11, 16)
	טחונ	*Techown* –Mill, grinding mill, hand mill
	יומ טוב	*Yom Tov* –Good day
	כומז	*Kuwmaz* –Ornaments, golden ornament, (maybe armlets of gold); tablets
	כחמה	*Kockmah* –A title of *Chokmah*

[151] בניה (67).

[152] Galilee (78).

מבוכה *Mebuwkah* –Confusion, perplexity, confounding
מגל *Maggal* –Sickle
סבאי *Seba'iy* –Sabean
סחה *Sachah* –To scrape
סיג *Siyg* –A moving back or away; dross (usually of silver)
—Prime number

74 אביונה *Abiyownah* –Desire (Eccl. 12:5)
גיהונ *Gihon* –A river of Eden (assoc. w/Water)
דכנ *Dikken* –This, that (Aramaic)
דיני *Diynay* –Dinaite
דע *Dea'* –Knowledge, wisdom, opinion; 72nd Gate of the 231 Gates
הגיונ *Higayown* –Meditation, resounding music, musing
הדסה *Hadassah* –Hadassah, Hebrew name of Esther (see also Esther)[153]
וחכמ *Ve-Chakam* –And wise
זלזל *Zalzal* –(quivering) tendrils, twig, shoot, tendrils
חוס *Chuws* –To pity, have compassion, spare, look upon with compassion
ינוח *Yanowach* –Janoah, city of the tribe of Naphtali, north of Galilee – probably modern Yanuh
יסד *Yasad* –To found, fix, establish, lay foundation
Yesud –A beginning, foundation, that being founded
למד *Lamed* –Ox goad; 12th letter of Hebrew alphabet
נכד *Neked* –Progeny, posterity
סביב *Sabiyb* –Places round about, circuit, round about; in a circuit, a circuit, round about; in the circuit, from every side
סוח *Suwach* –Suah, son of Zophah, descendant of Asher
עד *'ad* –Perpetuity, forever, continuing future; as far as, even to, until, up to, while; until, while, to the point that, so that even; even to, until, up to, during; until, up to the time that, ere that; booty, prey
'ed –Witness, menstruation
–The number of Levites who returned from exile (Ezra 2:40)

75 אחינדב *'Achiynadab* –Ahinadab, son of Iddo
בזיונ *Bizzayown* –Contempt
בטחונ *Bittachown* –Trust, confidence, hope
גבע *Geba'* –Gaba, Geba, Gibeah, Benjamite city in the extreme northern portion of Judah, north-northeast of Jerusalem
הדד בנ בדד *Hadad ben Bedad* –Hadad, son of Bedad; a king of Edom (assoc. w/*Tiferet*)
הילל *Heylel* –Brightness; shining one, morning star; "light-bearer" – Lucifer
הללי *Halliy* –Praise

[153] Esther (661).

הלמ *Halam* –To smite, strike, hammer, strike down
Halom –Here, hither
Helem –Helem, descendant of Asher

הע *Ha'* –89th Gate of the 231 Gates

יללה *Yelalah* –A howling (of distress), wailing

כהנ *Kahan* –To act as a priest, minister in priest's office
Kahen –Priest (Aramaic)
Kohen –Priest, principal officer or chief ruler

כימה *Kiymah* –Pleiades, the astronomical constellation (Amos 5:8)

כנה *Kanah* –To title, surname, be surnamed, give an epithet or congnomen, give a flattering title (Job 32:21, 22; Isa. 44:5; 45:4)
Kannah –Root, support (of tree), shoot, stock
Kanneh –Canneh, town on the southern coast of Arabia

להמ *Laham* –To gulp, swallow greedily
La-hem –Unto them

לילה *Laylah* –Night

למד *Lamad* –To learn, teach, exercise in

מהודכ *Mehowdka* –From your glory

מהל *Mahal* –To circumcise, weaken, cut down

מיכה *Miykah* –Micah, owner of a small private sanctuary (Judg. 17:1-5); descendant of Reuben; son of Merib-Baal, Mephibosheth (see also מיכא); descendant of Kohath, son of Levi; father of Abdon (see also מיכיה)[154]; the prophet whose name bears a book (see also מיכהו)[155]; son of Zichri (see also מיכא); one who signed the covenant (see also מיכא) [156]

מלה *Melah* –23rd name of *Shem HaMeforash* (5 Scorpio)
Millah –Word, speech, utterance; thing (Aramaic)

נכה *Nakah* –To strike, smite, hit, beat, slay, kill
Nekeh, nakeh –Stricken, smitten

סחבה *Sechabah* –Rag, clout (stuff pulled or dragged about)

עגב *'agab* –To have inordinate affection or lust
'egeb –(sensuous) love

עדא *'ada'* –To pass on, pass away

76 אדניהו *'Adoniyahuw* –Adonijah, son of David

אלילה *Elilah* –Goddess

אלמה *Alummah* –Sheaf (as something bound); (fig. – of Israel returning from exile)

בעד *Be'ad* –Behind, through, round about, on behalf of, away from, about

גבעא *Gib'a'* –Gibeah, Benjamite city in the extreme northern portion of Judah, north-northeast of Jerusalem;

---

[154] מיכיה (86).
[155] מיכהו (81).
[156] מיכא (71).

Gibea, descendant of Caleb

גזוני *Gizowniy* –Gizonite

הוללה *Howlelah* –Madness

חביונ *Chebyown* –Concealment, covering, hiding, hiding place

וע *Va'* –105th Gate of the 231 Gates

יוני *Yevaniy* –Jevanite

כונ *Kavvan* –Cake, sacrificial cake

Kuwn –To be firm, be stable, be established; Chun, town in Syria

למו *Lamow* –At, for, to, in, of, by, in reference to (poetic form of inseparable preposition)

מול *Muwl* –To circumcise, let oneself be circumcised, be cut off; front; in front of

מלאה *Mele'ah* –Fullness, full produce

Millu'ah –Setting (of jewel)

נדבכ *Nidbak* –Row, layer, course (of stones)

נכו *Nekow* –Necho, Pharaoh of Egypt who fought Josiah at Megiddo

עבד *'abad* –To work, serve; to make, do (Aramaic); servant, slave (Aramaic); work

'ebed –Slave, servant; Ebed, father of Gaal who rebelled against Abimelech; companion of Ezra on his return to Jerusalem

77 אולמ *Uwlam* –Vestibule, porch; as for, but, howbeit, in very deed, surely, truly, wherefore; Ulam, descendant of Manasseh; descendant of Benjamin

במהל *Bimhal* –Bimhal, descendant of Asher

בעה *Ba'ah* –To seek out, swell, cause to swell, boil up, enquire

Be'ah –To ask, seek, request, desire, pray, make petition (Aramaic)

גדע *Gada'* –To cut, hew, chop, cut down, hew down, hew off, cut off, cut in two, shave off

גיחונ *Giychown* –A river of Eden (assoc. w/Water); Gihon, intermittent spring outside the walls of Jerusalem, south of the Temple area

זידונ *Zeydown* –Churning, raging, turbulent, proud, insolent

זע *Za'* –120th Gate of the 231 Gates

יבניה *Yibneyah* –Ibneiah, son of Jeroham, head of a Benjamite family that returned from exile

Yibniyah –Ibnijah, father of Reuel (1 Chr. 9:8)

יהונדב *Yehownadab* –Jehonadab, descendant of Rechab, who forbade his followers and descendants to drink wine and live in houses (Jer. 35:6-19; 2 Kings 10:15, 23); sly son of David's brother, Shimeah (2 Sam. 13:3, 5, 32, 35)

מגדל *Migdal* –Tower; Migdol, watchtower between Hebron and Bethlehem where Jacob once camped – identified with modern Siyar El-Ghanam (see also מגדול)[157]

מזל *Mazzel* –Destiny, fate, luck; constellation or planet

עבדא *'Abda* –Abda, father of Solomon's tribute officer, Adoniram; chief Levite after the Exile (see also Obadiah)[158]

עבה *'abeh* –To be thick, be fat, be gross

עוא *'Avva'* –Ava, Assyrian city that sent settlers to colonize Samaria (see also Ivah)[159]

עז *'az* –Strong, mighty, fierce

'ez –Female goat, she-goat, goat (also Aramaic)

'oz –Might, strength; violence; glory

78 אומאל *Avamel* –Angel of 6q Sagittarius & night angel 10 Wands

איואס *Aiwass*–The author of A.C.'s The Book of the Law

בעו *Ba'uw* –Petition, request; prayer (all Aramaic)

גלילה *Geliylah* –Border, coast, country, territory

Galiylah –Galilee, one of the largest districts of Palestine

געה *Ga'ah* –To low, bellow (of cattle)

Go'ah –Goath, site near Jerusalem, exact location unknown (Jer. 31:39)

היכל אהבה *Hekel Ahbah* –Palace of Love, Heavenly Mansion corr. to *Hesed*

זאמל *Zamael* –Angel ruling Mars and Tuesday

חכימ *Chakkiym* –Wise man, wise (Aramaic)

חליל *Chaliyl* –Pipe, flute

חלמ *Chalam* –To dream; to be healthy, be strong

Chelem –Dream (Aramaic); Helem, descendant of Asher; man of whom the prophet Zechariah speaks (see also Heldai)[160]

חמל *Chamal* –To spare, pity, have compassion on

חנכ *Chanak* –To train, dedicate, inaugurate

חע *Cha'* –134th Gate of the 231 Gates

יבוס *Yebuws* –Jebus, early name for Jerusalem (Judg. 19:10-11)

יזלאל *Yezalel* –Angel of 1q Libra & day angel 2 Swords

יסח *Yasak* –To anoint, be poured

כבונ *Kabbown* –Cabbon, town of lowland Judah

כדמדי *Kedamidi* –Angel of 1d Taurus

לחמ *Lacham* –To fight, do battle, make war; to eat, use as food

Lachem –War (meaning uncertain – Judg. 5:8)

Lechem –Bread, food, grain; feast (Aramaic)

מבהאל *Mebahel* –Angel of 2q Libra & day angel 2 Swords

מבול *Mabbuwl* –Flood, deluge, the Flood (Gen. 6:17; 7:6, 7,

---

157 מגדול (83).

158 Obadiah (91).

159 Ivah (81).

160 Heldai (52).

10, 17; 9:11, 15, 28; 10:1, 32; 11:10; Ps. 29:10)

מגלה *Megillah* –Roll, book, writing; scroll, roll, book (Aramaic)

מלח *Malach* –To tear away, dissipate; to salt, season; rag
Mallach –Mariner, sailor, seaman
Melach –Salt (Aramaic); to eat salt (Aramaic)

נכח *Nekach, nokach* –Be in front of; in front of, opposite to, in the sight of, before, to the front, right on; towards the front of, in front of, on behalf of, as far as in front of
Nakoach –Straight, right, straightness, be in front of

סחי *Sechiy* –Offscourings

עגה *'uggah* –Disc or cake (of bread)

עדד *'Oded* –Oded, prophet of Samaria who persuaded the northern army to free their Judean slaves

עוב *'uwb* –To becloud

עזא *Ezah* –Uzza, man who was struck dead by God when he touched the Ark of the Covenant; person in whose garden Manasseh, king of Judah, and Amon, also a king of Judah were buried; descendant of Ehud; ancestor of a Nethinim family that returned from Babylon

–The number of Tarot cards
–Mystic number of 12th Path (*Keter-Binah*; ב; Mercury)

79 בעז *Boaz* –Boaz, one of the pillars in the temple of Solomon; Bethlehemite of Judah who became the husband of Ruth

גולם *Golem* –Shapeless mass; artificial man

גוע *Gava'* –Die, be dead, give up the ghost, perish

גלומ *Gelowm* –Clothes

גמול *Gamuwl* –Gamul, chief priest who was the leader of the 22nd course in the service of the sanctuary (1 Chr. 24:17)

דלילה *Delilah* –Delilah, Philistine woman whom the Philistines paid to find Samson's source of strength (Judg. 16)

דעה *De'ah* –Knowledge (of God)

ומבאל *Vemibael* –Angel of 1q Gemini & day angel 8 Swords

חלאמ *Chel'am* –Helam, descendant of Asher; man of whom the prophet Zechariah speaks (Zech. 6:14) – may be another name for the second Heldai (see also חילם)[161]

טע *Ta'* –147th Gate of the 231 Gates

טלמ *Telem* –Telem, gatekeeper who divorced his foreign wife after the exile (Ezra 10:24)

יחלאל *Yachle'el* –Jahleel, son of Zebulun, ancestor of the Jehleelites

ינוחה *Yanowach* –Janohah, town on Ephraim's border –

---

[161] חילם (88, 648).

		probably modern Yanuh
	מלט	*Malat* –To slip away, escape, deliver, save, to be delivered
		Melet –Mortar, cement, clay (flooring)
	סוחה	*Suwchah* –Offal
	סיט	*Sit* –3rd name of *Shem HaMeforash* (3 Leo)
	עדה	*'adah* –To pass on, advance, go on, pass by, remove
		'Adah –Adah, one of the two wives of Lamech and the mother of Jabal and Jubal; one of the wives of Esau and the daughter of Elon the Hittite (the mother of Eliphaz, Esau's firstborn son)
		'edah –Congregation, gathering; testimony, witness
	עוג	*'Owg* –Og, giant king of Bashan, defeated at Edrei
		'uwg –To bake, bake a cake
	עזב	*'azab* –To leave, loose, forsake; to restore, repair
	עט	*'et* –Stylus
	–Prime number	
80	גבעה	*Gib-ah* –Hill
	גזע	*Geza'* –Stock, stem
	גנזכ	*Ginzak* –Treasury
	ההע	*Hehau* –12th name of *Shem HaMeforash* (6 Virgo)
	המלה	*Hamullah* –Rushing, roaring, rainstorm, roaring sound, rushing sound
	יה אדני	*Yah Adonai* –God, my Lord, Lord God
	יסוד	*Yesod* –Foundation, base, the ninth *Sefira* (occurs 47 times in the *Tanakh*)
	יע	*Ya'* –Shovel; 159th Gate of the 231 Gates
	כהנה	*Kehunnah* –Priesthood
	כלל	*Kalal* –To complete, perfect, make complete, make perfect
		Kelal –To finish, complete (Aramaic); Chelal, man who married a foreign wife during the exile
	כס	*Kes* –Seat (of honor), throne, seat, stool (Ex. 17:16); 169th Gate of the 231 Gates
	למוד	*Limmuwd* –Taught, learned, discipled
	לנ	*Lan* –178th Gate of the 231 Gates
	מגבלה	*Migbalah* –Twisted, cords
	מזלג	*Mazleg* –Three-pronged fork (a sacrificial implement)
	מכב	*Makak* –To be low, be humiliated
	סודי	*Sowdiy* –Sodi, father of one of the spies sent into Canaan
	סכ	*Sak* –Crowd, throng, multitude
		Sok –Thicket, lair, covert, booth
	עגבה	*'agabah* –Lustfulness
	עדו	*'Iddow* –Iddo, descendant of Gershon (see also Adaiah)[162]; captain of the tribe of Manasseh in Gilead
	עוד	*'owd* –A going round, continuance; still, yet, again, besides; still, while, yet (Aramaic)

[162] Adaiah (89).

	'uwd –To return, repeat, go about, do again; to bear witness
עטא	*'eta'* –Counsel (Aramaic)
עי	*'Ai* –Ai, city of the Ammonites
	'iy –Ruin, heap of ruins
פ	*Peh* –17th letter of Hebrew alphabet

–The age of Moses at the time of the Exodus

Peh is the letter corresponding to eighty, a number also equal to *Yah Adonai*, a phrase used only in Psalms 130:3, "If You keep account of sins, O **Lord, Lord**, who will survive?" *Yah* is the divine name attributed in Jewish Kabbalah to the *sephirah Hokmah*, referring to wisdom, and *Adonai* is attributed to *Malkut.* Thus, *peh* can be seen as a window to God's wisdom implanted on earth and in the physical realm. It is no coincidence that Moses was eighty when the Torah was received and the Exodus began. Since the word *limmuwd*, or "taught, learned, discipled" also equals eighty, we can infer that learning of wisdom takes place through the letter *peh* as well. Who then teaches this wisdom? *Kehunnah* or "priesthood," which is used in the passage of Ex. 29:9, "And so they shall have **priesthood** as their right for all time." Now, by referencing back to our original passage, we can see that the priesthood intercedes on our behalf for our sins, and thus we attain wisdom and become *kalal*, or "perfect" again in the eyes of God.

In another meaning, *peh* translates as "mouth," and again references to one of humanity's senses, that through which we openly praise God indeed the most important attribute that humans share with God and no other animal possesses. Speech is very important in the story of creation, and the interested reader should refer to Aryeh Kaplan's translation and explanation of *Sefer Yetzirah.*

NOTES:

81 אחסבי *'Achasbay* –Ahasbai, father of one of David's mighty men

אילם *Eylam* –Porch, vestibule, portico

'Eylim –Elim, resting place of the Israelites after the crossing of the Reed Sea

איע *Aya* –67th name of *Shem HaMeforash* (1 Cancer)

אלן *Illen* –These, those (see also אלין)[163]

אמם *'Amam* –Amam, village in southern Judah

אנכי *Anoki* –I (1st person singular)[164]

אף *'af* –Also, yea, though, so much the more (conj. – denoting addition, especially of something greater); furthermore, indeed; also, yea (Aramaic); nostril, nose, face; anger; the initials of *Aur Pesuwt*; 16th Gate of the 231 Gates

בעט *Ba'at* –To kick, kick at

חזיון *Chezyown* –Hezion, grandfather of Ben-Hadad I, king of Syria[165]

Chizzayown –Vision

חלחלה *Chalchalah* –Pain, trembling, terror, writhing, anguish

טבע *Taba'* –To sink, sink into, sink down, pierce, settle down, drown, be settled, be planted

יילאל *Yeyalel* –Angel of 4q Taurus & night angel 6 Pentacles

יכליהו *Yekolyahuw* –Jecholiah, mother of Uzziah, king of Judah (this spelling used in 2 Kings 15:2 – see also יכיליה)[166]

יליאל *Yelayel* –Angel of 2q Leo & night angel 5 Wands

ימלא *Yimla'* –Imla, father of Maachah (this spelling used only in 2 Chr. 18:7, 8 – see also ימלה)[167]

כאין *Camio* –Goetic demon #53

כסא *Kese'* –Full moon

Kise' –Seat (of honor), throne, seat, stool

ליליא *Leyleyaw* –Night (Aramaic)

מבדלה *Mibdalah* –Separate place

מולה *Muwlah* –Circumcision

מיכהו *Miykahuw* –Michaiah (Micah), the prophet whose name bears a Biblical book (this name used only in 2 Chr. 18:8 – see also מיכה)[168]

עבדה *'abodah* –Labor, service

'abbudah –Service, household servants

עבט *'abat* –To take a pledge, give a pledge (for a debt)

עדוא *'Iddow'* –Iddo, grandfather of the prophet Zechariah;

---

163 אלין (91, 741).

164 According to Shabbat 105a, the use of *anoki* in the beginning of the decalogue is a notarikon for אנא נפשי כתבית יהבית, "I myself have written [the Torah] and delivered it," or אמירה נעימה כתיבה יהיבה, "a pleasant saying, written and delivered."

165 Many scholars identify Hezion with Rezon (263, 913).

166 יכיליה (85).

167 ימלה (85).

168 מיכה (75).

		priest who returned to Jerusalem with Zerubbabel
	עוגב	*'uwgab* –A musical instrument (perhaps a flute, reed-pipe, or panpipes)
	עוה	*'avah* –To bend, twist, distort; to commit iniquity, do wrong, pervert
		'avvah –Distortion, ruin
		'Ivvah –Ivah, city located on the Euphrates River (see also Ava)[169]

–The number of magic squares in the magic sqare of Luna

82	אנאל	*Anael* –Angel ruling Venus and Friday[170]
	בעי	*Be'iy* –Ruin, heap of ruins
	בפ	*Baf* –Ball, stone, lump, hailstone, resin; 36th Gate of the 231 Gates
	זעה	*Ze'ah* –Sweat
	חלחול	*Chalachuwl* –Halhul, Judean village located north of Hebron – said to be the burial place of Jonah
	חסיד	*Chasiyd* –Faithful, kind, godly, holy one, saint, pious
	יזניה	*Yezanyah* –Jezaniah, captain of the forces who joined Gedaliah (this spelling used in Jer. 42:1 – see also יזניהו and Azariah)[171]
	כבס	*Kabas* –To wash (by treading), be washed, perform the work of a fuller
	לבנ	*Laban* –White; to be white; to make bricks; Laban, obscure place in the Sinai Peninsula (see also the first Libnah)[172]; Laban, brother of Rebekah and father of Rachel and Leah
	מזלה	*Mazzalah* –Constellations (2 Kings 23:5)
	נבל	*Nabal* –Foolishness, senseless, fool; Nabal, wealthy Carmelite who refused David and his men food
		Nabel –To be senseless, be foolish; to sink or drop down, languish, wither and fall, fade
		Nebel –A skin-bag, jar, pitcher; harp, lute, guitar, musical instrument
	ניחוח	*Nichowach* –Soothing, quieting, tranquilizing (also Aramaic)
	סבכ	*Sabak* –To interweave
		Sobek, *sebak* –Thicket
	עבי	*'abiy* –Thickness
	עובד	*'Owbed* –Obed, son of Boaz and Ruth, father of Jesse; descendant of Judah; one of David's warriors; Levite gatekeeper in David's time; father of Azariah, who helped make Joash king of Judah
	עזה	*'Azzah* –Gaza, southernmost of the five chief Philistine cities
		'Uzzah –Uzzah, descendant of Merari

---

[169] Ava (77).
[170] Anael may mean "Sorrow of God."
[171] יזניהו (88), Azariah (292).
[172] Libnah (87).

83	אביע	*'Abia'* –Notariqon for the four worlds of the Kabbalah (Atziluth, Briah, Yetzirah, Assiah)
	אבלים	*Abalim* –One of two demon kings attendant upon *Paimon*[173]
		Ebelim –Mournings, laments
	גלים	*Galliym* –Gallim, village near Gibeah of Saul, modern Kirbet Kakul
	גלמוד	*Galmuwd* –Desolate, solitary; sterile
	גמלי	*Gemalliy* –Gemalli, father of Ammiel
	גפ	*Gaf* –Back, top; body, person, self; height, elevation; wing (of bird – Aramaic); 55th Gate of the 231 Gates
	זוע	*Zuwa'* –To tremble, quiver, quake, be in terror
	חלילה	*Chaliylah* –Far be it from me, God forbid that, let it not be
	חמלה	*Chemlah* –Mercy, pity, compassion
	חנכא	*Chanukka'* –Dedication (Aramaic)
	טלטלה	*Taltelah* –A hurling, captivity
	יאזניה	*Ya'azanyah* –Jaazaniah, chief of the tribe of Rechabites, a son of a certain man named Jeremiah but not the prophet (Jer. 35:3); wicked prince of Judah seen in Ezekiel's vision (Ezek. 11:1)
	יגע	*Yaga'* –To toil, labor, grow weary, be weary; earnings, gain
		Yagea' –Weary, wearisome
	לבנא	*Lebana'* –Lebanah, chief of a family of returning exiles (see also לבנה)[174]
	לכבאל	*Lekabel* –Angel of 1q Capricorn & day angel 2 Pentacles
	מגדול	*Migdowl* –Migdol, watchtower between Hebron and Bethlehem where Jacob once camped – identified with modern Siyar El-Ghanam (see also מגדל)[175]
	מהזאל	*Mahazael* –Demon Prince of Earth
	מחלה	*Machaleh* –Disease, sickness; Mahalah, descendant of Manasseh
		Machlah –Mahlah, eldest daughter of Zelophehad allowed a share of the land because her father had no sons
		Mechillah –Hole, cavern
		Mechowlah –Dancing, dance
	מלחה	*Melechah* –Saltness, barrenness, saltiness
	נכחה	*Nekuchah* –Straight in front, be in front of, straight, right, straightness
	סבכא	*Sabbeka* –Trigon (a triangular musical instrument with four strings, similar to a lyre – Aramaic)

[173] See Paimon (186, 836; 187, 837) and *Labal* (62).

[174] לבנה (87).

[175] מגדל (77).

	עוז	*'uwz* –To take refuge, bring to refuge, seek refuge
	פג	*Pag* –Unripe fig, green fig
	–Prime number	
84	אבימאל	*'Abiyma'el* –Abimael, son of Joktan
	אגלים	*'Eglayim* –Eglaim, place in Moab
	אגף	*Aggaf* –Wing of an army, band, army, hordes
	אחלמה	*Achlamah* –Amethyst, or crystal; (precious stone in the High Priest's ephod – represents the tribe Gad – indentification unclear – Ex. 28:19; 39:12)
	גמולה	*Gamuwlah* –Dealing, recompense
	דמם	*Damam* –To be silent, be still, wait, be dumb, grow dumb
	דפ	*Dap* –73rd Gate of the 231 Gates
	חלום	*Chalowm* –Dream
	חמול	*Chamuwl* –Hamul, younger son of Perez
	חנוכ	*Chanokh* –Enoch, eldest son of Cain (Gen. 4:17-18); son of Jared (Gen. 5:18-19, 21; 1 Chr. 1:3)
	טעה	*Ta'ah* –To wander, stray, wander astray, err
	ידע	*Yada'* –To know; Jada, son of Onam and grandson of Jerahmeel
	יעד	*Ya'ad* –To fix, appoint, assemble, meet, set, betroth
	לחום	*Lachuwm* –Intestines, bowels (meaning uncertain – Job 20:23; Zeph. 1:17); food, something eaten
	מגדל־גד	*Migdal-Gad* –Migdalgad, lowland city of Judah
	מחול	*Machowl* –Dance, dancing; Mahol, father of renowned wise men (1 Kings 5:11)
	מלוח	*Malluwach* –Mallow (a type of plant)
	ממד	*Memad* –Measurement
	עדי	*'adiy* –Ornaments
	עודד	*'Owded* –Oded, father of Azariah the prophet
	עזגד	*'Azgad* Azgad, one whose descendants returned from the Exile with Zerubbabel; one who came back to Jerusalem with Ezra; one who sealed the new covenant with God after the Exile
	עזז	*'azaz* –Azaz, descendant of Reuben; to be strong; strength
	עטה	*'atah* –To cover, enwrap, wrap oneself, envelop oneself; to grasp
85	אלמודד	*Almodad* –Almodad, a descendant of Shem
	אפד	*'afad* –Bind, gird
		'Efod –Ephod, father of Hanniel
	גביע	*Gabiya* –Cup, bowl, a goblet (by analogy the calyz of a flower); house, cup, pot
	דנאל	*Dani'el* –Daniel, one of the sons of David; prophet at the time of Nebuchadnezzar and Cyrus; Levite of the line of Ithamar – this spelling used in Ezek. 14:14, 20; 28:3 (also spelled דניאל)
	הלנ	*Helon* –Father of Eliab, Prince of Zebulun

הממ *Hamam* –To move noisily, confuse, make a noise, discomfit, break, consume, crush, destroy, trouble, to vex

הפ *Hap* –90th Gate of the 231 Gates

חמואל *Chammuw'el* –Hamuel, descendant of Simeon

יהלמ *Yahalom* –Pearl, (precious stone in the High Priest's ephod – represents the tribe Judah – known for its hardness – perhaps jasper, onyx or diamond)

יכיליה *Yekiyleyah* –Jecholiah, mother of Uzziah, king of Judah (this spelling used in 2 Chr. 26:3 – see also יכליהו)[176]

ימלה *Yimlah* –Imlah, father of Maachah (this spelling used only in 1 Kings 22:8, 9; Job 8:21 – see also ימלא)[177]

יסודה *Yesuwdah* –Foundation

יעה *Ya'ah* –To sweep, sweep away, sweep together

כסה *Kasah* –To cover, conceal, hide

להנ *Lahen* –Therefore, on this account

Lawhen –Therefore; except, but (Aramaic)

מולדה *Mowladah* –Moladah, southern city of Judah

מיכיה *Miykayah* –Michaiah, a prophet whose name bears a Biblical book (see also מיכה)[178]

מילה *Milah* –Circumcision

נהל *Nahal* –To lead, give rest, lead with care, guide to a watering place or station, cause to rest, bring to a station or place of rest, guide, refresh

נלה *Nalah* –To complete, bring to an end (meaning doubtful – Isa. 33:1)

סוטי *Sowtay* –Sotai, head of a family of servants

סכה *Sukkah* –Thicket, covert, booth

עדיא *'Iddiy'* –Iddo, priest who returned to Jerusalem with Zerubbabel

עיה *'Aya'* –Aija, one of the strongest Canaanite cities (this spelling used only in Neh. 11:31 – see also עית)[179]

פה *Peh* –Mouth; 17th letter of Hebrew alphabet; a weight equal to one third of a shekel, occurs only in 1 Sam. 13:21

Poh –Here, from here, hither

86 אב לאבנ *Ab La'ben* –"Father of fathers"

אהלימ *Ahaliym* –Aloes, aloe tree

אלהימ *Elohim* –Rulers, judges, divine ones, angels, gods, god, goddess: godlike one; works or special possessions of God, the God; angelic choir

---

176 יכליהו (81).

177 ימלא (81).

178 מיכה (75).

179 עית (480).

assoc. w/*Netzach* & the sphere of Venus
אפה *'afah* –To bake
דבלים *Diblayim* –Diblaim, father-in-law of Hosea
הללויה *Haleluyah* –Hallelujah; praise the Lord
הנאל *Hanael* –"Presence of God," Archangel of Capricorn[180]
ופ *Vap* –106th Gate of the 231 Gates
כוס *Kows* –Cup; a kind of owl (an unclean bird)
כיונ *Kiyuwn* –Chiun or Kaiwan, a Saturnian deity during the time of Amos (Amos 5:26)[181]
לוים *Levim* –Levites; the priest tribe of Israel
לונ *Luwn* –To lodge, stop over, pass the night, abide; to grumble, complain, murmur
מבדיל *Mavedil* –To divide
מיהאל *Mihael* –Angel of 6q Pisces & night angel 10 Cups
מום *Mum* –Blemish; 72nd name of *Shem HaMeforash* (6 Cancer)
סוכ *Suwk* –To anoint, pour in anointing
עבדי *'Abdiy* –Abdi, grandfather of Ethan, whom David set over the song service; father of Kish, a Levite contemporary with Hezekiah; one who took a foreign wife during the Exile
עוי *'Avviy* –Avites
פאה *Pa'ah* –To cleave in pieces, break into pieces, shatter
Pe'ah –Corner, edge, side, quarter, extremity

87 אבידע *'Abiyda* –Abida, son of Abraham
אלונ *Allown* –Oak, great tree
'Allown –Allon, son of Jedidah and father of Shiphi
Elon–The tenth judge of Israel
Elown –Tree, great tree, terebinth; plain
אסוכ *'asuwk* –Flask, small oil jug
אפו *'efow* –Then, now, so
בהלמי *Bihelami* –Angel of 1d Pisces
בלאדנ *Bal'adan* –Baladan, father of Merodach-Baladan, king of Babylon in Hezekiah's time
בלהנ *Bilhan* –Bilhan, descendent of Seir; descendant of Benjamin
בלימה *Beliymah* –Nothingness
בסודיה *Besowdeyah* –Besodeiah, one of the repairers of the old gate of Jerusalem (Neh. 3:6)
גדפ *Gadaf* –To revile men, to blaspheme God
Gidduf –Revilings, reviling words
זיע *Ziya'* –Zia, descendant of Gad (1 Chr. 5:13)
זממ *Zamam* –To have a thought, devise, plan, consider, purpose; wicked device, evil plan; to appoint a time, be fixed, be appointed
Zemam –To agree together, appoint a time (Aramaic); a set time, appointed time, time; a set time, time,

---

[180] See also הניאל (96).

[181] The etymology of this word is related to the Babylonian deity Komananu, familiar to a G.D. ritual.

season (Aramaic)

זפ — *Zap* –121st Gate of the 231 Gates

חסידה — *Chasiydah* –Stork

יזע — *Yeza'* –Sweat, perspiration (Ezek. 44:18)

ימואל — *Yemuw'el* –Jemuel, son of Simeon (this name used only in Gen. 46:10 & Ex. 6:15 – see also Nemuel)[182]

יעז — *Ya'az* –To be strong, be fierce (meaning dubious – Isa. 33:19)

לבנה — *Libnah* –Tile, pavement, brick; Libnah, an encampment of the Israelites during their journey in the wilderness (see also Laban)[183]; Levitical city of Jerusalem

Libneh –Poplar, white poplar

Levanah –The Moon; frankincense, one of the ingredients of the holy incense

Lebenah –Tile, brick

Lebanah –Lebanah, chief of a family of returning exiles (see also לבנא)[184]

להבימ — *Lehabiym* –Lehabim, descendant of Mizraim (possibly a reference to a tribe of Egyptians)

מאומ — *M'uwm* –Blemish, spot, defect

נבלה — *Nebalah* –Senselessness, folly

Nebelah –Carcass, corpse

נזל — *Nazal* –To flow, distill, flow forth or down, trickle, drop

עבודה — *'abowdah* –Employment (mod. Hebrew)

עבומ — *'abowt* –Pledge, a thing given as security, article pledged as security for debt

עויא — *'ivya'* –Perversity, iniquity (Aramaic)

עזי — *'Uzziy* –Uzzi, descendant of Issachar; chief of a priestly family of Jedaiah; descendant of Benjamin; overseer of the Levites at Jerusalem; father of Elah, a descendant of Benjamin; son of Bukki (1 Chr. 6:5-6, 51; Ezra 7:4)[185]

פז — *Paz* –Refined or pure gold

88 זועה — *Zeva'ah* –A horror, an object of terror, a trembling, an object of trembling

זעוה — *Za'avah* –A horror, trembling, object of terror or trembling

חילמ — *Cheylam* –Helam, descendant of Asher; man of whom the prophet Zechariah speaks (Zech. 6:14) – may be another name for the second Heldai (see also חלאם)[186]

חלנ — *Chelon* –Helon, father of Eliab, the prince of Zebulun

Cholon –Holon, Moabite town, possibly modern

[182] Nemuel (127).

[183] Laban (82, 732).

[184] לבנא (83).

[185] Even though in the line of High Priests, he does not seem to have held this office.

[186] חלאם (79, 639).

		Horon; town in the hill country of Judah west of Hebron (see also Hilen, חלון)[187]
	חממ	*Chamam* –To be hot, become hot
	חניכ	*Chaniyk* –Trained, instructed, trained servant, tried, experienced
	חנכי	*Chanokiy* –Hanochites
	חנכאה	*Chanukah* –Dedication, consecration; Hanukkah, the 8-day festival of the same name (see also חנוכה)[188]
	חייכמ	*Chayaychem* –"...it is your very life;" (Deut. 32:47)
	חפ	*Chaf* –Pure, innocent, clean; 135th Gate of the 231 Gates
	יבוסי	*Yebuwsiy* –Jebusite(s)
	יגעה	*Yegi'ah* –A weaning, a tiring
	יזניהו	*Yezanyahuw* – Jezaniah, captain of the forces who joined Gedaliah (this spelling used in Jer. 40:8 – see also יזניה and Azariah)[189]
	כסח	*Kasach* –To cut down, cut away, cut off (of plants)
	לחמי	*Lachmiy* –Lahmi, brother of Goliath the giant
	מגדיאל	*Magdiel* –Magdiel, Duke of Edom (Gen. 36:43; 1 Chr. 1:54 – assoc. [with Mibzar] w/*Yesod*)
	מחלי	*Machliy* –Mahlites; Mahli, son of Merari; descendant of Levi
		Machluy –Sickness, suffering
	נחל	*Nachal* –To get as a possession, acquire, inherit, possess; torrent, valley, wadi, torrent-valley; palm-tree
	עזיא	*'Uzziya'* –Uzzia, one of David's valiant men
	פכ	*Pach* –Snare, danger, trap, bird trap; plate (of metal)
89	אדמדמ	*Adamdam* –Reddish, be reddish
	גולנ	*Gowlan* –Golan, city of Bashan east of the Jordan River, assigned to the Levites, probably modern Sam el-Haulan
	גופ	*Guwf* –Shut, close
	דממה	*Demamah* –Silence, whisper, calm
	הדפ	*Hadaf* –To thrust, push, drive, cast away, cast out, expel, thrust away
	חנוכה	*Chanukah* –Dedication, consecration; Hanukkah, the 8-day festival of the same name (see also חנכאה)[190]
	חפא	*Chafa'* –To cover, do secretly
	טפ	*Taf* –Children, little ones, little children; 148th Gate of the 231 Gates
	יאזניהו	*Ya'azanyahuw* –Jaazaniah, captain of the forces who joined Gedaliah (2 Kings 25:23) – he is the Jezaniah of Jer. 40:8; 42:1 and possibly the

[187] חלון (94, 744), Hilen (98, 748).

[188] חנוכה (89).

[189] יזניה (82), Azariah (292).

[190] חנכאה (88).

Azariah of Jeremiah 43:2[191]; leader of elder who were enticing the people to idolatry (Ezek. 8:11)

יחלאלי *Yachle'eliy* –Jahleelites

יעט *Ya'at* –To cover

Ye'at –To advise, counsel; counsellor (Aramaic)

מחיאל *Mochayel* –Angel of 4q Gemini & night angel 9 Swords

מטיל *Metiyl* –Hammered bar, wrought iron bar, wrought metal rod

מלוחה *Meluwkah* –Kingship, royalty, kingly office

נטל *Natal* –To lift, bear, bear up

Netal –To lift (Aramaic)

Netel –Burden, weight

עדיה *'Adayah* –Adaiah, son of Shimhi found in 1 Chr. 8:12-21; Levite ancestor of Asaph (see also Iddo)[192]; father of Jedidah, the mother of King Josiah; one whose descendants resided in Jerusalem and a member of the royal line of David; one who married a foreign wife; another who did the same; Levite descendant from Aaron who settled in Jerusalem after the Exile

עיט *'ayit* –Bird of prey, a swooper

'iyt –To scream, shriek; to dart greedily, swoop upon, rush upon

פדה *Padah* –To ransom, redeem, rescue, deliver

פוג *Puwg* –To grow numb, to be feeble, be benumbed

–Prime number

90 אפדה *'efuddah* –Ephod (priestly garment)

גואפ *Goap* –Demon King of the South and of Fire (Goetia)

דוממ *Duwmam* –Silence, dumb

טלאימ *Tela'iym* –Telaim, place where Saul gathered and numbered his forces before the attack on Amalek

ידוע *Yadduwa'* –Jaddua, Levite who sealed the covenant; the last High Priest mentioned in the Tanakh (Neh. 12:11, 22)

יועד *Yow'ed* –Joed, son of Pedaiah, a descendant of Benjamin

יכינ *Yakiyn* –Jachin, son of Simeon (Gen. 46:10; Ex. 6:15; Num. 26:12 – see also Jarib); priest in Jerusalem after the exile (1 Chr. 9:10; Neh. 11:10); head of a family of Aaron (1 Chr. 24:17 – see also Jarib)[193]; Jachin, the right hand pillar of Solomon's porch on the temple (1 Kings 7:21)[194]

יפ *Yaf* –160th Gate of the 231 Gates

כידונ *Kiydown* –Javelin, short sword, dart; gorget, a piece of armor for the throat (1 Sam. 17:6, 45); Chidon, place where Uzzah was struck dead for touching

---

[191] Azariah (292).

[192] Iddo (80).

[193] Jarib (222).

[194] Boaz (79).

	the Ark of the Covenant (1 Chr. 13:9) (see also Nachon)[195]
כיס	*Kiys* –Bag, purse
כליל	*Kaliyl* –Entire, all, perfect; entirety; whole, whole burnt offering, holocaust, entirety
כללי	*Kelali* –General, universal, collective
כלם	*Kalam* –To insult, shame, humiliate, blush, be ashamed, be put to shame, be reproached, be put to confusion, be humiliated
כע	*Ka'* –170th Gate of the 231 Gates
למכ	*Lamekh* –Lamech, father of Noah; father of Jabal and Jubal
לס	*Las* –179th Gate of the 231 Gates
מוליד	*Mowliyd* –Molid, descendant of Judah
מים	*Mem* or *Mayim* –Water, waters; 13th letter of Hebrew alphabet
מלכ	*Malak* –To be or become king or queen, reign; to counsel, advise
	Melak –Counsel, advise (Aramaic)
	Melek –King; a title of *Tiferet*; one of the Melekim; Melech, a Benjamite, the 2nd son of Micah and grandson of Mephibosheth
	Molek –Molech, the god of the Ammorites and Phoenicians to whom some Israelites sacrificed their infants in the valley of Hinnom (see also Milcom)[196]
	Moloch –Archdemon corr. (w/Satan) to *Keter*
מנ	*Man* –Manna; who?, what?, whoever, whosoever (Aramaic); 187th Gate of the 231 Gates
	Men –String (of harp); portion
	Min –From, out of, on account of, off, on the side of, since, above, than, so that not, more than; that; from; out of, by, by reason of, at, more than (Aramaic); when used as a prefix, it means "from"
סכי	*Sukkiy* –Sukkiims or Sukkites
סל	*Sal* –Basket
עזובה	*'azuwbah* –Azubah, wife of Caleb, the son of Hezron; mother of King Jehoshaphat; forsakenness, desolation
עזוז	*'ezuwz* –Strength, fierceness, might
	'izzuwz –Powerful, mighty
פוד	*Fudh* –Furcus, Goetic demon #50 (a misprint and false enumeration in *Sefer Sefirot*, A.C.)
צ	*Tzaddi* –18th letter of Hebrew alphabet

"The *tzaddik* (righteous) is an everlasting foundation" (Prov. 10:25). This phrase refers to the letter as well as the concept of the *tzaddik* in kabbalah. The ancient spelling of the letter *tzaddi* is צדי, but can also be spelled צדיק. In this way, the *tzaddik*'s role in Hasidism is represented by the letter. *Tzaddi* is formed from a

[195] Nachon (126, 776).
[196] Milcom (130, 690).

bent *nun* (standing for humility) and a *yod*, standing for the Tetragrammaton (*Magen David*). Thus the righteous person is a foundation for the extension of God's power on the earth. Also, *tzaddi* is numerically equivalent to the *ephuddah*, the priestly garment, thus pointing to the *tzaddik*'s role as priest since the destruction of the Temple. *Melek*, the word for "king" in Hebrew also equals *tzaddi*, and indicates that God as king must occupy the foundation for true righteousness.

NOTES:

91	אילנ	*Iylan* –Tree (Aramaic)
		'Eylown –Elon, father of a wife of Esau; son of Zebulun; tenth judge of Israel
	אלינ	*Illeyn* –These, those
	אמנ	*'aman* –To support, confirm, be faithful; to take the right hand, to turn right, choose to the right, go to the right, use the right hand; master-workman, artist, steady-handed one, artisan
		Amen –Verily, truly, amen, so be it; firm, faithful; a title of *Keter*; the first letters of *Elem Melek Ne'eman* (Lord, faithful king)
		Amon –14th King of Judah
		'omen –Faithfulness
	אונמ	*'Ownam* –Onam, grandson of Seir; son of Jerahmeel
	אלני	*'Eloniy* –Elonites
	אפוד	*'efowd* –Ephod (priestly garment)
	אצ	*Atz* –To hasten, urge, press, hurry; 17th Gate of the 231 Gates
	הוממ	*Howmam* –Homam or Hemam, Horite descendant of Esau
	יאהדונהי	*'Ahadonhai* –A god-name, combining YHVH and Adonai
	כאמל	*Kamael* –"He who sees God," archangel assoc. w/*Giburah* and w/Mars
	כלולה	*Keluwlah* –Betrothals, espousals
	כליאל	*Kaliel* –Angel of 6q Libra & night angel 4 Swords
	כניהו	*Konyahuw* –Coniah, alternate name for Jehoiachin, 18th King of Judah
	מאכל	*Ma'akal* –Food, fruit, meat
	מאנ	*Ma'n* –Vessel, utensil (Aramaic)
		Ma'en –To refuse; refusing, unwilling to obey
		Me'en –Refusing
	מלאכ	*Melek* –Angel; messenger, representative (Aramaic)
	מלכא	*Malka'* –Queen (Aramaic)
	מנא	*Mena'* –To number, reckon (Aramaic)
		Mene' –Mina, maneh (a weight of measurement; usually 50 shekels but maybe 60 shekels – Aramaic)
	נאמ	*Na'am* –To prophesy, utter a prophesy, speak as a prophet, say
		Ne'um –Utterance, declaration (of prophet)
	נבלט	*Neballat* –Neballat, town of Benjamin repopulated after the Exile
	סאל	*Sael* –45th name of *Shem HaMeforash* (3 Pisces)
	סוכה	*Sukah* –Hut; place resided in on the holiday of *Sukkot*
	סלא	*Sala'* –To weigh, compare
		Silla' –Silla, place near Millo where King Joash was murdered
	עבדיה	*Obadyah* –Obadiah, descendant of David; chief of the tribe of Issachar; descendant of King Saul; chief of the Gadites who joined David at Ziklag; one of the princes whom Jehoshaphat commissioned

to teach the Law; chief of a family that returned to Jerusalem; one who sealed the covenant with Nehemiah; gatekeeper for the sanctuary of the Temple; fourth of the "minor prophets" whose message was directed against Edom (see also the second Abda) [197]

עבידה *'abiydah* –Work, service, ritual, worship

פוה *Puvvah* –Puah, second son of Issachar (see also פואה)[198]

–Mystic number of 13th Path (*Keter-Tiferet*; ג; Moon)

92 אלהימו *Elohamow* –Their gods

אניאל *Aniel* –Angel of 1q Aquarius & day angel 5 Swords

אצא *Atza* –I will depart (Gen. 11:8)

בעיי *Bieyay* –Waste land in the wilderness (Num. 21:11)

בטמאם *Bitama'am* –Through their uncleanness (Lev. 15:31)

במלך *Bimelek* –Against the king (Num. 21:26)

במימ *Bimayem* –In [the] waters (Ex. 12:9, 15:10, 20:4)

בלס *Balas* –To gather figs, tend sycamore trees

בסל *Basal* –In the basket (Ex. 29:3; Lev. 8:31)

בצ *Botz* –Mud, mire, swamp, pond, puddle; bubbles; bubble forth, burst forth; 37th Gate of the 231 Gates

גדפה *Giddufah* –Revilings, reviling words

דחפ *Dachaf* –To drive on, hurry, hasten

החסידה *HaChasidah* –The stork (Lev. 11:19)

הלבנה *HaLevanah* –The Moon; the frankincense (Lev. 6:8)

העבוט *HaAvot* –The pledge

ואלהימ *ve-Elohim* –And God

והעבט *vi-Ha'avait* –And lend (Deut. 15:8)

וכסו *vi-Chesuw* –And they [the sons of Aaron shall] cover (Num. 4:5)

ועבדי *vi-Avdi* –But my servant (Num. 14:24)

חסדכ *Chasdek* –"Loving kindness" (Num. 14:19)

יכבס *Yi-Kabas* –In [the] water (Lev. 11:25)

לבני *Libniy* –Libnite; Libni, son of Merari (see also Laadan)[199]

לנדח *Lendoch* –Wield, forcing

מאומה *Meuwmah* –Anything

מבנ *Miben* –From [the] age [of twenty] (Ex. 30:14)

מזמה *Mezimmah* –Purpose, discretion, device, plot

מחמד *Machmad* –Desire, desirable thing, pleasant thing

Machmud –Desirable, precious thing

נולו *Nevaluw* –Refuse heap, dunghill, outhouse (Aramaic)

סבכי *Sibbekay* –Sibbechai, mighty man who killed a Philistine giant (2 Sam. 21:18; 1 Chr. 11:29; 20:4) (see also Mebunnai)

---

[197] Abda (77).

[198] פואה (92).

[199] Laadan (154, 804).

סבל *Sabal* –To bear, bear a load, drag oneself along
Sabbal –Burden-bearer
Sebal –To bear a load
Sebel, *sobel* –Load, burden

עזיה *Uzziah* –Uzziah, alternate name for Azariah, ninth King of Judah (variant spelling – this spelling used only in 2 Kings 15:1-8 – see also עזיהו)[200]; Levite descended from Kohath and ancestor of Samuel; priest who had married a foreign wife; descendant of Judah

פואה *Puw'ah* –Phuvah, second son of Issachar (this spelling used only in 1 Chr. 7:1 – see also פוה) [201]; father of Tola the judge

פחד *Pachad* –Fear; a title of *Giburah*; to fear, tremble, revere, dread, be in awe or dread, terror; thigh

צב *Tzab* –Litter; wagon; an unclean lizard (perhaps tortoise)
Tzav –Covered

93 אבצ *'Ebetz* –Abez, town in northern Palestine

אהליבמה *Aholibamah* –Aholibamah, wife of Esau; a Duke of Edom (assoc. w/*Hesed*)

גדופ *Gidduwf* –Revilings, reviling words

גצ *Gatz* –56th Gate of the 231 Gates

הפגה *Hafugah* –Ceasing, stopping, benumbing

חמוטל *Chamuwtal* –Hamutal, one of King Josiah's wives (this spelling used only in 2 Kings 23:31 – see also חמיטל)[202]

חפה *Chafah* –To cover, overlay; wainscotted, covered with boards or panelling
Chuppah –Chamber, room, canopy, closet; Huppah, priest in the time of David who had charge of one of the courses of service in the sanctuary

טוב אדניהו *Towb Adoniyahuw* –Tob-Adonijah, one of the Levites sent by Jehoshaphat through the cities of Judah to teach the law to the people

יבנאל *Yabne'el* –Jabneel, city marking the northern border of Judah – modern Yebnah (see also Jabneh)[203]; border town of the tribe of Naphtali – probably modern Khirbet Yeman

יגיע *Yagiya'* –Weary, tired
Yegiya' –Toil, work; product, produce

לבונה *Lebownah* –Frankincense, one of the ingredients of the Holy incense; Lebonah, a place north of Bethel

לחנה *Lechenah* –Concubine (Aramaic)

מגנ *Magan* –To deliver up, give, deliver
Magen –Shield, buckler

---

200 עזיהו (98).
201 פוה (91).
202 חמיטל (97).
203 Jabneh (67).

	נחלה	*Nachalah* –Possession, property, inheritance, heritage
	פחה	*Pechah* –Governor
	צבא	*Tzaba'* –To go forth, wage war, fight, serve *Tzava* –Host, army *Tzeba'* –To desire, be inclined, be willing, be pleased (Aramaic)
94	אופז	*'Uwfaz* –Uphaz, city reknowned for its gold
	גופה	*Guwfah* –A corpse, body
	דמנ	*Domen* –Dung
	דעכ	*Da'ak* –To go out, be extinguished, dry up
	דפי	*Dofiy* –A blemish, fault
	דצ	*Datz* –74th Gate of the 231 Gates
	זמזמ	*Zamzom* –Zamzummim, Ammonite name for the people called Rephaim (giants) by the Jews during the conquest of Canaan (Deut. 2:20)
	חופ	*Chowf* –Seashore, coast, shore
	חלונ	*Chalown* –Window *Cholown* –Holon, Moabite town, possibly modern Horon; town in the hill country of Judah west of Hebron (see also Hilen, חלן)[204]
	חמולי	*Chamuwliy* –Hamulites
	יעדי	*Ye'diy* –Iddo, a prophet who wrote about the kings of Israel (this spelling used only in 2 Chr. 9:29 – see also ועדו)[205]
	כלמד	*Kilmad* –Chilmad, nation on the Euphrates River that traded with Tyre
	כסדי	*Kasday* –Chaldean (this spelling used only in Ezra 5:12 – see also כשדים)[206]
	מדימ	*Madim* –Mars
	מדנ	*Medan* –Strife, contention; Medan, son of Abraham by Keturah
	מזל מוב	*Mazzel Tov* –Congratulations, good luck
	מחמאה	*Machama'ah* –Curd-like, smooth, unctuous, hypocritical (words of flattery – fig.)
	מלטיה	*Melatyah* –Malatiah, an assistant wall-builder
	מנד	*Menadh* –Prickly; 36th name of *Shem HaMeforash* (6 Capricorn)
	סלד	*Salad* –To leap, jump, spring, leap for joy *Seled* –Seled, descendant of Judah
	פוגה	*Puwgah* –Benumbing, cessation, rest, relief
	פוח	*Puwach* –To breathe, blow
	פזז	*Pazaz* –To refine, be refined; to bound, be agile, be supple
	פיד	*Piyd* –Ruin, disaster, destruction
	צד	*Tzadh* –Side; beside, against

---

[204] חלן (88, 738), Hilen (98, 748).

[205] ועדו (150).

[206] כשדים (374, 934).

95 אדמימ *'Adummiym* –Adummim, a place in Palestine

דניאל *Daniel* –Daniel, one of the sons of David; prophet at the time of Nebuchadnezzar and Cyrus; Levite of the line of Ithamar (also spelled דנאל); Angel of 2q Aries & night angel 2 Wands

ההעיה *Hihayah* –Angel of 6q Virgo & night angel 10 Pentacles

הימם *Heymam* –Hemam, son of Lotan and the grandson of Seir

המימ *HaMayim* –The water

המלכ *HaMelek* –The king

המנ *Haman* –Haman, prime minister of Ahasuerus who plotted against the Jews (Est. 3-9)

הנמ *Hinnom* –Hinnom, unknown person who had a son after whom a valley near Jerusalem was named – human sacrifices took place there in Jeremiah's day, and garbage was later incinerated in this defiled place (Josh. 15:8; 18:16; Neh. 11:30; Jer. 7:31-32)

הצ *Hatz* –91st Gate of the 231 Gates

זבולנ or זבלונ *Zebulun* –Zebulun, tenth son of Jacob and progenitor of a tribe of Israel (assoc. w/Capricorn) (from right to left – first spelling used only in Gen. 30:20; 35:23; 46:14; Josh. 19:27, 34; Judg. 4:6; 5:18; Judg. 6:35; 1 Chr. 2:1; 12:33; 12:41; 2 Chr. 30:10, 11, 18; Ps. 68:28; Is. 8:23 – second spelling only used in Gen. 49:13; Ex. 1:3; Num. 1:30, 31; 2:7; 7:24; 10:16; 13:10; 26:26; 34:25; Deut. 33:18; Josh. 19:10, 16; 21:7, 34; Judg. 1:30; 4:10; 1 Chr. 6:62, 77; Ezek. 48:26, 27, 33); Zebulun, territory given to the tribe of Zebulun

זחעי *Zachi* –Angel of 2d Leo

חלבנה *Chelbenah* –Galbanum, ingredient of the holy incense (Ex. 30:34)

חפז *Chafaz* –To hurry, flee, hasten, fear, be terrified

יכניה *Yekonyah* –Jeconiah, alternate name for Jehoiachin, 18th King of Judah

יסכה *Yiskah* –Iscah, daughter of Haran, sister of Milcah, and niece of Abraham

יפה *Yafah* –To be bright, be fair, be handsome; fair, beautiful, handsome

כלמה *Kelimmah* –Disgrace, reproach, shame, confusion, dishonor, insult, ignominy

לוטנ *Lowtan* –Lotan, Edomite chief (Gen. 36:20-29)

מהלכ *Mahlek* –Walk, journey, going, place to walk

מחויאל *Mechuwya'el* –Mehujael, descendant of Cain (see also מחייאל)[207]

מכלה *Miklah* –Completeness, perfection

מלכה *Malkah* –Queen; a title of *Malkut*

---

[207] מחייאל (99).

Milkah –Milcah, daughter of Haran, Abraham's brother, and wife of Nahor; daughter of Zelophehad

מנה *Manah* –To count, reckon, number, assign, tell, appoint, prepare; part, portion

Maneh –Maneh, mina, pound (60 shekels and 1/50 talent (of silver); 100 shekels and 1/100 talent (of gold)).

Moneh –Something weighed out, counted number, time

נהמ *Naham* –To growl, groan; growling, roaring

סלה *Salah* –To make light of, toss aside; to weigh, balance

Selah –To lift up, exalt; Selah (a technical musical term probably showing accentuation, pause, interruption)

עדיהו *'Adayahuw* –Adaiah, father of a captain who aided Jehoiada

עזיזא *'Aziyza'* –Aziza, son of Zattu (Ezra 10:27)[208]

פומ *Puwt* –Phut, son of Ham; a word for Libya or Libyans

פחז *Pachaz* –To be wanton, be reckless, be frothy; reclessness, wantonness, unbridled license, frothiness[209]

פיה *Peyah* –Edge (of a sword)

צדא *Tzeda* –Purpose; true

–The number of children of Gibbar who returned from exile (Ezra 2:20)

96 איפה *Eyfah* –Ephah (a unit of liquid measurement)

Eyfoh –Where?; what kind?

אמנה *'Amana* –Amana, mountains in Lebanon

'amanah –Faith, support, sure, certain

Emunah –Firmness, fidelity, steadfastness, steadiness (see also אמונה)[210]

'omnah –Bringing up, nourishment, rearing, training, providing for (as a parent); verily, truly, indeed

'omenah –Pillar, supporters of the door; confirm, support, uphold

הניאל *Hanael* –"Presence of God," Archangel of Capricorn[211]

וצ *Vatz* –107th Gate of the 231 Gates

חלבונ *Chelbown* –Helbon, village of Syria near Damascus, known for its wines – probably modern Khalbun

יוממ *Yowmam* –By day, in the daytime; daytime

ילונ *Yalown* –Jalon, descendant of Caleb the spy

יפו *Yafow* –Japha, Palestinian city on the Mediterranean coast northwest of Jerusalem (this name used only in Josh. 19:46 – see also Joppa)[212]

כסוי *Kasuwy* –Covering, outer covering

---

[208] Aziza divorced his pagan wife after the Exile.

[209] According to Midrash Aggadat Bereshit, the use of *Pachaz* in Gen. 49:4 is a notarikon for פחזת חטאת זנית, "you have been wanton; you have sinned; you have commited adultery."

[210] אמונה (102).

[211] See also הנאל (86).

[212] Joppa (97).

ללהאל *Lehahel* –Angel of 6q Leo & night angel 7 Wands

מהומה *Mehuwmah* –Tumult, confusion, disquietude, discomfiture, destruction, trouble, vexed, vexation

מכלאה *Mikla'ah* –Fold, enclosure

מלאכה *Mela'kah* –Occupation, work, business, employment

מלוכ *Malluwk* –Malluch, descendant of Levi; two who took foreign wives during the exile; priest who sealed the covenant; leader who sealed the new covenant with God after the exile; one of the priests who returned with Zerubbabel (see also מלוכי)[213]

מלכו *Malkuw* –Royalty, reign, kingdom

נומ *Nuwm* –To be drowsy, slumber, sleep

סלו *Salluw* –Sallu, priest who returned with Zerubbabel from the Exile (this spelling used only in Neh. 12:7 – see also סלי)[214]

עכו *'Akkow* –Accho, town of Palestine on the Mediterranean coast apportioned to the tribe of Asher

פוי *Poi* –56th name of *Shem HaMeforash* (2 Taurus)

פחח *Pachach* –To ensnare, trap

צאה *Tza'ah* –Filth, human excrement, feces

צו *Tzav* –Statute, command, oracle (meaning dubious – Hos. 5:11; Isa. 28:10, 13)

97 אוצ *Uwtz* –To press; to be close, hurry, withdraw, haste

אילונ *'Eylown* –Elon, father of a wife of Esau; son of Zebulun; tenth judge of Israel

'Ayalown –Aijalon, Ajalon, town northwest of Jerusalem; site where judge Elon was buried

אלוני *'Elowniy* –Elonites

אמונ *Amown* –Artificer, architect, master workman, skilled workman; throng, multitude

Emuwn –Faithfulness, trusting

Amon –Goetic demon #7; Amon, chief god of the Egyptians; 14th King of Judah; governor of Samaria in Ahab's time; a form of Ami

בצה *Bitstsah* –Swamp, marsh

האניאל *Haniel* –"Glory or grace of God" or "he who sees God," archangel assoc. w/*Netzach* and Venus

זיפ *Ziyph* –Ziph, grandson of Caleb; son of Jehaleleel; Ziph, city in southern Judah, located between Ithnan and Telem – probably modern ez-Teifah; town in Judah's hill country – probably present-day Tell Zif

זעכ *Za'ak* –To extinguish, be extinct, be extinguished

זצ *Zatz* –122nd Gate of the 231 Gates

חמיטל *Chamuwtal* –Hamutal, one of King Josiah's wives (this

213 מלוכי (106).

214 סלי (100).

spelling used only in 2 Kings 24:18; Jer. 52:1 – see also חמוטל)[215]

חטף — *Chataf* –To catch, seize

טפח — *Tafach* –To extend, spread, trip, take quick little steps

Tefach –Span, width of the hand, hand breadth; coping (an architectural term)

Tippuch –Tender care, dandling

יפוא — *Yafow'* –Joppa, Palestinian city on the Mediterranean coast northwest of Jerusalem (this name used only in Ezra 8:7 – see also Japha)[216]

מבנה — *Mibneh* –Structure, building

מהיטבאל — *Mehetabel* –Mehetabel, wife of Hadar, a King of Edom (Gen. 36:39; 1 Chr. 1:50); father of Delaiah who defied Nehemiah (Neh. 6:10)

נזמ — *Nezem* –Ring, nose ring, earring

סבלה — *Sebalah* –Burden, forced labor, compulsory service, burden bearing

סלוא — *Salluw'* –Sallai, chief man of the tribe of Benjamin; descendant of Benjamin dwelling in Jerusalem

עבדיהו — *'Obadyahuw* –Obadiah, governor or prime minister of Ahab who tried to protect the prophets against Jezebel; man of the tribe of Zebulun; Levite overseer in work done on the Temple

עובדיה — *'ovadyah* –Of Obadiah

פחדה — *Pachdah* –Dread, fear, awe, religious awe

צבה — *Tzabah* –To swell, swell up

Tzabeh –Swelling, swollen

Tzobah –Zoba, portion of Syria east of Coelesyria that was a separate empire during the days of Saul, David, and Solomon (see also צובה, צובא)[217]

צהב — *Tzahab* –To gleam, shine

Tzahov –Yellow; gleaming, yellow (of hair)

צוא — *Tzowa* –Filthy; filth

–Prime number

98 בוצ — *Buwts* –Byssus, a costly, fine white linen cloth made in Egypt

גדופה — *Geduwfah* –A taunt

Giddufah –Revilings, reviling words

חילנ — *Chiylen* –Hilen, city of the tribe of Judah, alloted to the Levites

חכליל — *Chakliyl* –Dull; dark-flashing, brilliant (Gen. 49:12)

חמנ — *Chamman* –Incense-altar, sun-pillar, idol, image

חנמ — *Chinnam* –Freely; for nothing, without cause

חסל — *Chasal* –To consume, finish off, bring to an end

חצ — *Chetz* –Arrow; lightning; punishment; wound; 136th Gate of the 231 Gates

---

[215] חמוטל (93).

[216] Japha (96).

[217] צובה (100), צובא (99).

Chotz –Out!, Avaunt!, Go away!

יחף *Yachef* –Barefoot

יפח *Yafach* –To breathe, breathe hard, puff

כובע *Kowba'* –Helmet

מאזן *Mo'zen* –Scales, balances; scale, balance (Aramaic)

מבון *Mabown* –Ones who taught, ones who gave understanding, teacher

מגנה *Meginnah* –Covering

מנהג *Minhag* –Driving, charioteering

נחם *Nacham* –To be sorry, console oneself, repent, regret, comfort, be comforted; Naham, descendant of Judah, a chieftain

Nocham –Repentance, sorrow

סגלה *Segullah* –Possession, property

סלח *Salach* –To forgive, pardon

Sallach –Ready to forgive, forgiving

עזיהו *Uzziahuw* –Uzziah, alternate name for Azariah, ninth King of Judah (this spelling used only in 2 Chr. 26 – see also עזיה)[218]; father of Jonathan

פטדה *Pitdah* –Topaz or chrysolite (precious stone in the High Priest's ephod – represents the tribe Simeon)

פיח *Piyach* –Soot, ashes

צבו *Tzebuw* –Thing, anything, matter (Aramaic)

צדד *Tzedad* –Zedad, northern boundary mark of Canaan

צח *Tzach* –Bright, dazzling, glowing, clear, bright

–The number of children of Ater who returned from exile (Ezra 2:16)

99 אפיח *'Afiyach* –Aphiah, a Benjamite

גליון *Gillayown* or *Gillyown* –Table, tablet

דמנה *Dimnah* –Dimnah, border town in Zebulun assigned to Levites of the Merari family

ובידו אנך *'owbiydow 'anak* –"And in his hand a lead plumbline" (Amos 7:7)

חניאל *Channiy'el* –Hanniel, prince of the tribe of Manasseh (Num. 34:23); hero of Asher (1 Chr. 7:39)

טיט היון *Tit HaYaven* –Miry Clay; the 4th Hell (corr. to *Tiferet*)

טמן *Taman* –To hide, conceal, bury

טצ *Tatz* –149th Gate of the 231 Gates

ידעיה *Yeda'yah* –Jedaiah, priest of Jerusalem (1 Chr. 9:10; 24:7; Ezra 2:36; Neh. 7:39); priest who returned with Zerubbabel (Neh. 11:10; 12:6, 19); another priest who came up with Zerubbabel (Neh. 12:7, 21); one who brought gifts to the temple (Zech. 6:10, 14)

מחיאל *Mechiyya'el* –Mehujael, descendant of Cain (see also מחויאל)[219]

נטיל *Netiyl* –Laden

---

218 עזיה (92).

219 מחויאל (95).

פדיה — *Pedayah* –Pedaiah, descendant of Jeconiah and the father of Zerubbabel; grandfather of King Josiah; son or grandson of Jeconiah; one who helped rebuild the wall of Jerusalem; one who stood with Ezra when he read the Law; descendant of Benjamin

צבבה — *Tzobebah* –Zobebah, descendant of Judah

צדה — *Tzadah* –To lie in wait; to lay waste

צובא — *Tzowba'* –Zoba, portion of Syria east of Coelesyria that was a separate empire during the days of Saul, David, and Solomon (this spelling used only in 2 Sam. 10:6, 8 – see also צובה, צבה)[220]

צחא — *Tziycha'* –Ziha, one whose children returned from Exile (this spelling used only in Neh. 7:46 – see also ציחא)[221]

–The number of occurences of ויהוה ("and YHVH") in *Tanakh*

100 אגמון — *Agmown* –Rush, bulrush, sad, drooping

בן־חיל — *Ben-Chayil* –Ben-Hail, prince of Judah under Jehoshaphat; son of Shimon of Judah

דוצ — *Duwts* –Spring, leap, dance

חצב — *Chatsab* –To dig, cleave, divide, hew, make, cut out, dig out, cut down, quarry, hewer, mason

יהועדה — *Yehow'addah* –Jehoadah, son of Ahaz of the family of Saul (this name only used in 1 Chr. 8:36 – see also Jarah)[222]

יוידע — *Yowyada'* –Joiada, ancestor of the priest Jeshua (see also Jehoiada)[223]

יכיני — *Yakiyniy* –Jachinites

ימימ — *Yamiym* –Right, right hand, right side

ימלכ — *Yamlek* –Jamlech, prince of Simeon (1 Chr. 4:34, 41)

ימנ — *Yaman* –To choose the right, go to the right, be right-handed

יפי — *Yafiy* –Beauty

יצ — *Yatz* –161st Gate of the 231 Gates

כלכל — *Kalkol* –Calcol, descendant of Judah

כפ — *Kaf* –Palm, hand, sole, palm of the hand, hollow or flat of the hand; 11th letter of Hebrew alphabet; 171st Gate of the 231 Gates

Kef –Rock, hollow of a rock

לדינו — *Ladino* –Language of the Sephardic Jews

לע — *Loa'* –Throat; 180th Gate of the 231 Gates

מדונ — *Madown* –Strife, contention; stature, size; Madon, city of northern Canaan

מיכל — *Miykal* –Brook, stream (meaning dubious – 2 Sam. 17:20); Michal, youngest daughter of Saul

---

220 צובה (100), צבה (97).

221 ציחא (109).

222 Jarah (285).

223 Jehoiada (105).

	whom David married
מין	*Min* –Species, kind
מלכי	*Malkay* –Kings
מנוד	*Manowd* –Shaking, wagging
מני	*Meniy* –Meni, a god that represented Destiny (Is. 65:11 – the god Gad is mentioned in this verse as well); Minni, portion of the land of Armenia
מס	*Mas* –A suffering, discouraged one; tax; gang or body of forced laborers, taskworkers, labor band or thing, forced service, taskwork, serfdom, tributary, tribute, levy, taskmasters, discomfited; despairing; 188th Gate of the 231 Gates
נהמה	*Nehamah* –Growling, groaning
נכל	*Nakal* –To be deceitful, be crafty, be knavish
	Nekel –Cunning, wiliness, craft, knavery
נלכ	*Nelakh* –21st name of *Shem HaMeforash* (3 Scorpio)
סכך	*Sakak* –To hedge, fence about, shut in; to block, overshadow, screen, stop the approach, shut off, cover; to cover, lay over; to weave together
סלי	*Salluw* –Sallu, priest who returned with Zerubbabel from the Exile (this spelling used only in Neh. 12:20 – see also סלו)[224]
סמ	*Sam* –Spice; drug; poison; as a spice, part of the holy incense
עבטיט	*'abtiyt* –Weight of pledges, heavy debts
עודכ	*'uwdka* –My testimony
על	*'al* –Height; above, upwards, on high; upon, on the ground of, according to, on account of, on behalf of, concerning, beside, in addition to, together with, beyond, above, over, by, onto, towards, to, against; because that, because, not withstanding, although; upon, over, on account of, above, to, against (Aramaic)
	'ol –Yoke
פדוי	*Paduwy* –Ransom
פכ	*Pakh* –Flask, bottle, vial
צובה	*Tzowba'* –Zoba, portion of Syria east of Coelesyria that was a separate empire during the days of Saul, David, and Solomon (see also צובא, צבה)[225]
צוד	*Tzuwd* –To hunt
צי	*Tzi* –Dryness; ship
ק	*Qof* –19th letter of Hebrew alphabet

Qof begins the word *kedushah*, קדושה, or "holiness." In ancient times, an object that was considered holy implied separateness from the ordinary world. Thus, the Ark of the Covenant, a holy implement, was separated from the Israelite camp and was placed in a special room inside the Temple. *Qof* alludes to holiness in its sum parts, a כ and a ו, two letters whose combined gematria equals 26, the number of YHVH. If we take the first part, כ, and make it a final ך, the sum of the two equals 86, the number of *Elohim*. Thus, we see

224 סלו (96).

225 צובא (99), צבה (97).

that the letter itself represents holiness and God. The letter also begins the word *qareban*, "temple offering" (קרבן) and again implies the separateness of an offering to God versus the ordinary meal that we might partake of. It is no coincidence that the letter *qof* equals *paduwy*, or "ransom" as well.

NOTES:

101 אימימ — *'Eymiym* –Emims, early Canaanite tribe

אכפ — *Akaf* –Press, urge, bend

Ekef –Pressure, urgency, burden

אמלל — *'amelal* –Weak, feeble

Umlal –Weak, feeble

אננ — *'anan* –Complain, murmur

אנפינ — *Anpin* –Face, countenance

אסמ — *'asam* –Storehouse, barn

אק — *Aq* –She-goat; initials of *Adam Qadmon*; 18th Gate of the 231 Gates

המונ — *Hamown* –Murmur, roar, crowd, abundance, tumult, sound

ויהי כנ — *Va-yehi khen* –"And it was so" (Gen. 1:7, 9, 11, 15, 24, 30; Judg. 6:38)

יכוניה or יכניהו — *Yekowneyah* or *Yekonyahuw* –Jeconiah, alternate name for Jehoiachin, 18th King of Judah

יצא — *Yatza'* –To go out, come out, exit

Yetza –To bring to an end, finish (Aramaic)

כלאימ — *Kil'ayim* –Two kinds, mixture

מאס — *Ma'as* –To reject, despise, refuse; to flow, run

מומיה — *Mevamiah* –Angel of 6q Cancer & night angel 4 Cups

מיכאל — *Michael* –"Who is as God," archangel assoc. w/*Hod*, w/Mercury, w/ South, & w/Fire (see Dan. 10:21; 12:1); Angel ruling Sol and Sunday; Angel of 6q Aquarius & night angel 7 Swords; Michael, one sent to spy out Canaan; descendant of Gad another descendant of Gad; ancestor of Asaph; chief of the tribe of Issachar; one residing in Jerusalem; warrior who joined David at Ziklag; father of Omri, a prince of Issachar; son of Jehoshaphat; ancestor of one who returned from the exile

מלאכי — *Meleaki* –Malachi, last of the prophets recorded in the Hebrew Bible

נומה — *Nuwmah* –Drowsiness, somnolence, indolence (fig.)

ננא — *Nena* –53rd name of *Shem HaMeforash* (5 Aries)

עלא — *'ella'* –Above (Aramaic)

'Ulla' –Ulla, descendant of Asher

צבט — *Tzabat* –To reach, hold out

צוה — *Tzavah* –To command, charge, give orders, lay charge, give charge to, order

קא — *Qe* –Vomit, what is vomited up

–Prime number

102 אמונה — *Emuwnah* –Firmness, fidelity, steadfastness, steadiness, faith

בלע — *Bala'* –To swallow down, swallow up, engulf, eat up

Bela'–A swallowing, devouring (fig. for ruin); a thing swallowed; Bela, son of Benjamin and one of the left-handed heroes (Gen. 46:21; 1 Chr. 7:6-7); a King of Edom (assoc. w/*Daath* - Gen.

		36:32-33; 1 Chr. 1:43-44); descendant of Reuben; Bela, one of the Cities of the Plain, probably Zoar (Gen. 14:2)
	בנימ	*Benayim* –Between, space between two armies
	בעל	*Ba'al* –To marry, rule over, possess, own; owner, husband, lord
		Baal –Lord, owner; archdemon corr. to *Netzach* (Mathers); Goetic demon #1 (Aurum Solis spelling); Baal, descendant of Reuben; fourth of ten sons of Jehiel
		Be'el –Owner, lord (Aramaic)
	בצי	*Betzay* –Bezai, ancestor of 323 captives returning from the exile; one who sealed the new covenant with God after the exile
	בק	*Baq* –Gnat, to enter into, search, investigate, examine, find out; initials of *Beth Quwl* (Daughter of the Voice); 38th Gate of the 231 Gates
		Boq –Daughter of the Voice, Muse, Echo; gnat, to enter into, search, investigate, examine, find out
	וילונ	*Vilon* –Veil; the First Heaven (corr. to *Yesod* and *Malkut*)
	זיפה	*Ziyphah* –Ziphah, son of Jehaleleel
	חמדנ	*Chemdan* –Hemdan, descendant of Seir (the KJV wrongly rendered his name Amram in 1 Chr. 1:41 – the reading there is Hamran)
	יצב	*Yatzab* –To place, set, stand still, set oneself
		Yetzeb –To make stand, make certain, gain certainty, know the truth (Aramaic)
	לעב	*La'ab* –To joke, jest
	מבני	*Mebunnay* –Mebunnai, a mighty man who killed a Philistine giant (2 Sam. 23:27 – see also Sibbechai)[226]
	מגדנה	*Migdanah* –Choice thing, excellent thing
	מסב	*Mesab* –Round thing, surrounding, round about, that which surrounds, that which is round
	צבי	*Tzebiy* –Beauty, glory, honor; roebuck, gazelle (meaning unknown)
	צואה	*Tzowah* –Filth, excrement
	קב	*Qab* –A dry measure –*cab/kab* (2 Kings 6:25)
103	אבימלכ	*Abimelech* –A King of the Philistines
	אבק	*Abaq* –To wrestle, grapple, bedust; dust
	גילני	*Giyloniy* –Gilonite
	גלע	*Gala'* –To be obstinate; meddle
	גננ	*Ganan* –To defend, cover, surround
	געל	*Ga'al* –To abhor, loathe, be vilely cast away, fall; Gaal, son of Ebed who tried to lead a rebellion against Abimelech
		Go'al –Loathing

[226] Sibbechai (92).

גק *Gaq* –57th Gate of the 231 Gates
חצה *Chatsah* –To divide, cut in two, cut short, live half (of one's life)
יצג *Yatzag* –To place, set, establish
לעג *La'ag* –To mock, deride, ridicule; mocking, derision, stammering
La'eg –Mocking
מגדון *Megiddown* –Megiddo, ancient city of Canaan assigned to Manasseh & located on the southern rim of the plain of Esdraelon 6 miles from Mt. Carmel & 11 miles from Nazareth (see also מגדו)[227]
מזון *Mazown* –Food, sustenance; food, feed (Aramaic)
מנחה *Minchah* –Gift, tribute, offering, present, oblation, sacrifice, meat offering; gift, offering (Aramaic)
נגן *Nagan* –To play or strike strings, play a stringed instrument
נחילה *Nechiylah* –(meaning uncertain – Ps. 5:1)
נחמה *Nechamah* –Comfort
עגל *'agol* –Round
'egel –Calf, bull-calf
עלג *'illeg* –Speaking inarticulately, stammering
פתיש *Pattiysh* –Forge hammer, hammer
צביא *Tzibya'* –Zibiah, descendant of Benjamin
ציבא *Tziyba'* –Ziba, steward of Saul
צחה *Tzicheh* –Parched
–Prime number

104 דק *Daq* –Crushed, fine, thin, small, gaunt
Doq –Veil, curtain; 75th Gate of the 231 Gates
חוצ *Chotz* –Out!, avaunt!, go away!
Chuwts –Outside, outward, street, the outside
חמון *Chammown* –Hammon, frontier village of the tribe of Asher, assigned to the Levites – may be the same as Hammath
מלך דוד *Melekh David* –King David
מדין *Midian* –Midian, son of Abraham by Keturah and founder of the Midianites; Midian, land of the descendants of Midian beyond the Jordan – included Edom, the Sinai Peninsula and Arabian Petra
Midyan –Strife, contention
Middiyn –Middin, village in the wilderness of Judah
מדני *Medaniy* –Midianite
מחוימ *Machaviym* –Mahavite
מנוח *Manowach* –Resting place, state or condition of rest, place; Manoah, father of Samson the judge
מסד *Masad* –Foundation
נדן *Nadan* –Gift (of a harlot's bribe); sheath

[227] מגדו (53).

	נחומ	*Nachum* –Nahum, one of the later prophets; Nehum, chief man that returned from Exile with Zerubbabel (this spelling used only in Neh. 7:7 – see also Rehum)
		Nichuwm –Comfort, compassion
	נמבזה	*Nemibzeh* –Vile, despised, disdained, held in contempt
	סדמ	*Sodom* –Sodom, one of the five cities of the plain, destroyed because of its wickedness
	צדי	*Tzaddi* –Fishhook; 18th letter of Hebrew alphabet
	צוח	*Tzavach* –To shout, cry aloud, cry out
	ציד	*Tzayid* –Hunting, game; provision, food
		Tzayad –Hunter
	קבב	*Qabab* –To curse, utter a curse against
105	אדמני	*Admoniy* –Red, ruddy(of Esau as infant)
	אלעד	*Elead* –Elead, a descendant of Ephraim
	גבננ	*Gabnon* –Peak, rounded summit, a mountain peak
	גבעל	*Gib'ol* –Bud
	גלבע	*Gilboa'* –Gilboa, mountain overlooking the Plain of Jezreel, site of Saul's death – modern Jebel Fuku'a
	הימנ	*Heyman* –Heman, wise man with whom Solomon was compared (1 Kings 5:11; 1 Chr. 2:6 – see also Ps. 88); musician and seer appointed by David as a leader in the Temple's vocal and instrumental music
	המס	*Hamas* –Brushwood
	הפכ	*Hafak* –To turn, overthrow, overturn, change, transform
		Hefek –Contrary, opposite, a difference, reversed, contrariness, perversity
		Hofek –Perverseness, perversity
	הק	*Haq* –92nd Gate of the 231 Gates
	זבולני	*Zebuwloniy* –Zebulonite, member of the tribe of Zebulun
	יהוידע	*Yehowyada'* –Jehoiada, father of Benaiah, one of David's officers; chief priest of the temple for many years of the monarchy; one who joined David at Ziklag; counselor of David; priest replaced by Zephaniah
	יהצ	*Yahatz* –Jahaz, battlefield on the wastelands of Moab (this spelling used only in Is. 15:4; Jer. 48:34 – see also יהצה)[228]
	ימימה	*Yemiymah* –Jemimah, first daughter of Job to be born after his restoration from affliction
	ימנה	*Yimnah* –Imna, a descendant of Asher (this spelling used in Gen. 46:17 – see also ימנע)[229]; Imnah, son of Asher (Num. 26:44; 1 Chr. 7:30); father of Kore in Hezekiah's reign (2 Chr. 31:14)

[228] יהצה (110).

[229] ימנע (170).

כלנה *Kalneh* –Calneh, city in Mesopotamia belonging to Nimrod; city located 6 miles from Arpad – probably modern Kullani (see also כלנו)[230]

כמהמ *Kimham* –Chimham, friend and political supporter of David

כפה *Kafah* –To sooth, subdue, pacify

Kippah –Branch, leaf, frond, palm frond, palm branch, skullcap, yarmulka

מהלל *Mahalal* –Praise, boast

מלכיה *Malkiyah* –Malchiah, leader of singing under David's reign; Aaronite whose descendants dwelled in Jerusalem after the Exile; head of a priestly family; three who married foreign wives during the Exile; three who helped to rebuild the wall of Jerusalem; prince or Levite who stood beside Ezra as he read the Law; priest who helped to purify the wall of Jerusalem; father of Pashur (see also מלכיהו)[231]

מסה *Massah* –Massah, name of a spot in the vicinity of Horeb where the Israelites tempted God (Ex. 17:7; Deut. 6:16 – see also the first Meribah)[232]

סככה *Sekakah* –Secacah, city of Judah near the Dead Sea

עזזיהו *'Azazyahuw* –Azaziah, father of a prince of Ephraim in David's time; Levite who took part in the musical service when the Ark was brought to the Temple; Levite who had the oversight of the dedicated things of the Temple under Hezekiah

עלה *'alah* –To go up, ascend, climb; burnt offering, holocaust (Aramaic)

'aleh –Leaf, leafage

'illah –Matter, affair, occasion (Aramaic)

'olah –Whole burnt offering; ascent, stairway, steps

פדיהו *Pedayahuw* –Pedaiah, father of Joel

פכה *Pakah* –To trickle, pour or flow forth

ציה *Tziyah* –To glow, burn, glitter; dryness, drought, desert; one of the Seven Earths (corr. to *Tiferet* or *Netzach*)

קוב *Qowba* –Helmet

–Mystic number of 14th Path (*Chokmah-Binah*; ד; Venus)

106 אלהיכמ *Elohikam* –Your God

בדק *Badaq* –To mend

Bedeq –Fissure, rent, breach, leak (in a building)

דבק *Dabaq* –Cling, cleave, keep close

Dabeq –Cleave, joining, stick closer

Debeq –Joint, solder

המונה *Hamownah* –Hamonah, symbolic name of the city where

---

230 כלנו (106).

231 מלכיהו (111).

232 Meribah (257).

Gog is to be defeated (Ezek. 39:16)

וק *Vaq* –108th Gate of the 231 Gates

יהללאל *Yehallel'el* –Jehaleleel, descendant of Judah through Caleb the spy; descendant of Merari in the time of Hezekiah

יויכין *Yehoiakin* –Jehoiachin, 18th King of Judah

כלנו *Kalnow* –Calneh, city in Mesopotamia belonging to Nimrod; city located 6 miles from Arpad – probably modern Kullani (this spelling used only in Is. 10:9 – see also כלנה)[233]

לוע *Luwa'* –To swallow, swallow down

מלהאל *Melahel* –Angel of 5q Scorpio & day angel 7 Cups

מלוכי *Malluwkiy* –Melicu, one of the priests who returned with Zerubbabel (this spelling used only in Neh. 12:14 – see also מלוך)[234]

נון *Nun* –Continue, to increase, propagate; fish; 14th letter of Hebrew alphabet; Nun or Non, descendant of Ephraim; father of Joshua

סאליה *Saliah* –Angel of 3q Pisces & day angel 9 Cups

עול *'aval* –To act wrongfully or unjustly, deviate from
'avval –unjust one, perverse one, unrighteous one
'evel –Injustice, unrighteousness, wrong
'uwl –To give suck, suckle, nurse; suckling, sucking child

פוכ *Fukh* –Furcas, Goetic demon #50 (A.C., 777)
Pukh –Antimony, stibium, black paint (eye cosmetic)

צחח *Tzachah* –To be dazzling, be aglow, glow

קו *Qav* –Line, cord, measuring-line

107 אונן *Onan* –Onan, second son of Judah who was slain by God for his disobedience (Gen. 38:4-10; Num. 26:19)

אנון *'innuwn* –These, those, they (Aramaic)

אקו *'aqqow* –Wild goat

בהק *Bohaq* –A harmless eruption of the skin, skin spot

ביצה *Beytsah* –Egg

בעלה *Ba'alah* –Mistress, female owner; sorceress, necromancer; Baalah, Simeonite town in southern Judah (see also Bilhah and Balah)[235]; hill in Judah between Ekron and Jabneel; (see also Kirjath-Jearim)[236]

גלעד *Gilead* –Gilead – area east of the Jordan River, from Moab to the Yarmuk River; mountain jutting onto the Plain of Jezreel; city in the region of Gilead; Gilead, son of Machir; father of Jephthah the judge; descendant of Gad

זיפי *Ziphiy* –Zimphim, Ziphite

---

[233] כלנה (105).
[234] מלוך (96, 576).
[235] Bilhah (42), Balah (37).
[236] Kirjath-Jearim (1040, 1600).

	זנימ	*Zonim* –To go astray
	זק	*Zaq* –Chain; flaming arrow; 123rd Gate of the 231 Gates
	למואל	*Lemuw'el* –Lemuel, unknown king often supposed to be Solomon or Hezekiah, whose words are recorded in Prov. 31:1-9
	לעז	*La'az* –To speak indistinctly, speak unintelligibly
	מאומ	*Ma'ows* –Refuse, trash
	מגנ דוד	*Magen David* –Star of David, hexagram
	עבדאל	*'Abe'el* –Abdeel, father of Shelemiah, who was commanded by Jehoiakim, king of Judah to arrest Baruch the scribe and Jeremiah the prophet
	עואל	*Oel* –Angel of 5th astrological house
	עכביה	*'akkabiyah* –Spider
	עלז	*'alaz* –To exult, rejoice, triumph
		'alez –Exultant, jubilant
	צביה	*Tzebiyah* –Gazelle, doe
		Tzibyah –Zibiah, mother of King Joash of Judah
	קבה	*Qebah, qobah* –Stomach, belly, maw
		Qubbah –Large vaulted tent, tent
	קוא	*Qowa* –To vomit up, spue out, disgorge
	–Prime number	
108	אבקה	*Abaqah* –Aromatic powders, powder
	בונימ	*Bonim* –Builders
	דדנימ	*Dedaniym* –Dodanim, son of Javan (Gen. 10:4) – 1 Chr. 1:7 has his name as Rodanim, and many scholars consider the latter to be his original name – it may also be a reference to the inhabitants of Rhodes and the neighboring islands
	חטיפא	*Chatiyfa* –Hatipha, ancestor of returning captives (Ezra 2:54; Neh. 7:56)
	חיצ	*Chayits* –Wall, party-wall, thin wall
	חמס	*Chamas* –To wrong, do violence to, treat violently, do wrongly; violence, wrong, cruelty, injustice
	חנ נ	*Chanan* –To be gracious, show favor, pity; to be loathsome; to show favor (Aramaic); Hanan, descendant of Benjamin (1 Chr. 8:23); one of David's heroes (1 Chr. 11:43); descendant of Benjamin through Saul (1 Chr. 8:38; 9:44); a returned captive (Ezra 2:46; Neh. 7:49); temple officer whose sons had a chamber in the Temple (Jer. 35:4) – this name should not be confused with Baal Hanan; Levite who assisted Ezra when reading the Law (Neh. 8:7); Levite who sealed the covenant with Nehemiah (Neh. 10:11; 13:13 – may be the same as the latter Levite); chief or family who also sealed the covenant (Neh. 10:27); chief or family who sealed the covenant with Nehemiah (Neh. 10:23)
	חסיל	*Chasiyl* –Locust

	חסמ	*Chasam* –To stop up, muzzle
	חצי	*Chetsiy* –Half, middle
		Chitstsiy –Arrow
	חק	*Choq* –Statute, ordinance, limit, something prescribed, due; share; task; boundary; 137th Gate of the 231 Gates
	יעזיהו	*Ya'aziyahuw* –Jaaziah, descendant of Merari living in Solomon's day
	יפיח	*Yafeach* –To breathe out, puffing out
	מוסב	*Musab* –Encompassing, surrounding, round about
	מגדל-אל	*Migdal-'El* –Migdalel, fortified city of Naphtali
	מחנה	*Machaneh* –Encampment, camp
	מנהיג	*Manhig* –Leader
	מסח	*Masach* –Guard; alternately, by turns (meaning uncertain – 2 Kings 11:6)
	עגלה	*'agalah* –Cart, wagon
		'eglah –Heifer; Eglah, one of David's wives and mother of Ithream
	עובל	*'Owbal* –Obal, son of Joktan, descendant of Shem (see also עיבל)[237]
	עזאל	*Azael* –Demon Prince of Water
		Ezal –A giant chained in Arqa
	קדד	*Qadad* –To bow down
109	אחימלכ	*'Achiymelek* –Ahimelech, friend of David; priest of Nob (see also Abimelech)[238]; son of Abiathar
	אחימנ	*'Achiyman* –Ahiman, son of Anak; Levite gatekeeper in the Temple
	בזק	*Bazaq* –Lightning flash, lightning
		Bezeq –Bezek, town near Jerusalem; place where Saul assembled his army
	בעל גד	*Ba'al Gad* –Baal Gad, town at the foot of Mount Hermon that marked the northern limite of Joshua's conquest
	טק	*Taq* –150th Gate of the 231 Gates
	יפדיה	*Yifdeyah* –Iphedeiah, descendant of Benjamin
	לעדה	*La'dah* –Laadah, descendant of Judah
	לעט	*La'at* –To swallow greedily, devour
	מאבוס	*Ma'abuws* –Storehouse, granary
	מדינה	*Mediynah* –Province, district
	מנוחה	*Menuwchah* –Resting place, rest
	נדנה	*Nidneh* –Sheath (meaning uncertain – Dan. 7:15)
	סחיאל	*Sachiel* –"Covering of God,"angel ruling Jupiter and Thursday
	צדיה	*Tzediyah* –Lying in wait, ambushing
	צוחה	*Tzevachah* –Outcry, shout
	צידה	*Tzeydah* –Provision, food

[237] עיבל (112).
[238] Abimelech (103, 583).

	צִיחָא	*Tziycha'* –Ziha, one whose children returned from Exile (this spelling used only in Ezra 2:43 – see also צחא)[239]; ruler of the Nethinim
	קדה	*Qiddah* –A spice – cassia (Ex. 30:24; Ezek. 27:19)
	קט	*Qat* –Small thing, little time (Meaning dubious – Ezek. 16:47)
	–Prime number	
110	אלדעה	*Elda'ah* –Eldaah, son of Midian
	אלעדה	*Eladah* –Eladah, a descendant of Ephraim
	אנחנא	*'anachna'* –We (1st person plural – Aramaic)
	דוק	*Duwq* –To be shattered, fall to pieces (Aramaic)
	דימון	*Diymown* –Dimon, city of the tribe of Gad located north of the Arnon River (this spelling used only in Is. 15:9 – see also Dibon, Dimonah)[240]
	דמיון	*Dimyon* –Resemblance, image, like
	הפכה	*Hafekah* –Overthrow (n. fem.)
	חבק	*Chabaq* –To embrace, clasp
		Chibbuq –Fold (hands), a folding (of the hands), clasping (of the hands)
	יהצה	*Yahatzah* –Jahazah, battlefield on the wastelands of Moab (see also יהץ)[241]
	ילע	*Yala'* –To speak rashly; devour, swallow
	ימין	*Yamiyn* –Right-hand or side; Jamin, son of Simeon; descendant of Ram; priest who explained the Law
	ימני	*Yamaniy* –Right, right-hand
	ינים	*Yaniym* –Janum, town in the mountains of Judah, west-southwest of Hebron
	יעל	*Ya'al* –To gain, profit, benefit, avail
		Ya'el –Mountain goat; Jael, wife of Heber, who killed Sisera
	יק	*Yaq* –162nd Gate of the 231 Gates
	כמנ	*Kamon* –Cumin
	כסל	*Kasal* –To be foolish, be stupid
		Kesel –Loins, flank; stupidity, folly, confidence, hope
	כצ	*Katz* –172nd Gate of the 231 Gates
	לפ	*Lap* –181st Gate of the 231 Gates
	מוסד	*Mowsad* –Foundation
		Muwsad –Foundation, laying of foundation, foundation laying
	מללי	*Milalay* –Milalai, priest who aided in the purification of the wall
	מע	*Ma'* –189th Gate of the 231 Gates
	ניננ	*Niyn* –Offspring, posterity
	נס	*Nes* –Something lifted up, signal, signal pole, ensign,

[239] צחא (99).
[240] Dibon (66, 716; 72, 722), Dimonah (115).
[241] יהץ (105, 915).

sail, banner, sign, standard; 196th Gate of the 231 Gates

סיטאל — *Sitael* –Angel of 3q Leo & day angel 6 Wands

סכל — *Sakal* –To be foolish, be a fool; fool
Sekel –Folly

עלי — *'eliy* –Pestle; Eli, High Priest at Shiloh and judge of Israel (1 Sam. 1-4)
'illay –Highest, the Most High (Aramaic)
'illiy –Upper

עמ — *'am* –Nation, people, populace; kinsman, kindred; people (Aramaic)
'im –With, against, toward, as long as, beside, except, in spite of; with (Aramaic)

פיכ — *Peyka* –Your word, your mouth

ציי — *Tziyiy* –A wild beast, desert-dweller, crier, yelper (an animal of some type)

קהה — *Qahah* –To be blunt, be dull
–The number of years that Joseph lived (Gen. 50:26)

111 אבנ חנ — *Eben Chen* –Precious stone

אחד הוא אלהימ — *Achad Hua Elohim* –"He is One God"

אלפ — *Alaf* –To learn; to make thousand-fold, bring forth thousands; producing thousands; chief, chiliarch; 1000 (Aramaic)
Alef –Ox; 1st letter of Hebrew alphabet
Alluf –Tame, docile; friend, intimate; chief (see also אלוף)[242]
Elef –Thousand; cattle, oxen; a thousand, company (as a company of men under one leader, troops); a city in the territory of Benjamin

אנס — *'anas* –To compel, to constrain; to oppress, compel, constrain (Aramaic)

אסנ — *'asan* –Sudden death

אפל — *'afel* –Gloomy, dark
'ofel –Darkness, gloom; spiritual unreceptivity, calamity (figurative)

דעואל — *De'uw'el* –Deuel, father of Eliasaph (Num. 1:14 – see also Reuel)[243]

יהויכינ — *Yehoiakin* –Jehoiachin, 18th King of Judah

יעלא — *Ya'ala'* –Jaala, servant of Solomon whose descendants returned from the Exile (this spelling used only in Neh. 7:58 – see also יעלה)[244]

יציא — *Yatziy'* –Coming forth (2 Chr. 33:21)

כנמא — *Kenema'* –Thus, so, accordingly, as follows (Aramaic)

מלכיהו — *Malkiyahuw* –Malchijah, father of Pashur (this spelling used only in Jer. 38:6 – see also מלכיה)[245]

---

[242] אלוף (117, 837).
[243] Reuel (307).
[244] יעלה (115).

	מסוה	*Masveh* –Veil
	נכיאל	*Nakhiel* –Intelligence of Sol
	סאנ	*Sa'an* –To tread, tramp
	עלוה	*'alvah* –Injustice, unrighteousness, iniquity
		Alvah –Alvah, a Duke of Edom (this spelling used only in Gen. 36:40 – see also Aliah)[246] (assoc. w/Daath)
	פלא	*Pala'* –To be marvelous, be wonderful, be surpassing, be extraordinary, separate by distinguishing action
		Pele –The Wonder; a title of *Keter*; wonder, marvel
	קוה	*Qavah* –To wait, look for, hope; to collect, bind together
		Qaveh –Line
	קטב	*Qeteb* –Destruction
	קיא	*Qi* –Vomit
	–Magic sum of the magic square of the Sun	
112	איעאל	*Ayoel* –Angel of 1q Cancer & day angel 2 Cups
	בטמאכמ	*Bitamakem* –Defile it
	בלעי	*Bal'iy* –Belaites
	בנינ	*Binyan* –Structure, building
	בנס	*Benas* –To be angry (Aramaic)
	בעלי	*Ba'aliy* –Baali, a symbolic name for YHVH (Hos. 2:18); my Baal (my Lord)
	בקי	*Buqqiy* –Bukki, prince of the tribe of Dan; son of Abishua who was an ancestor of Ezra and descendant of Aaron
	דחק	*Dachaq* –Thrust, crowd, oppress
	הקבה	*Haqabah* –A name of God; notariqon for *HaQadosh Barukh Hu*, "The Holy One, blessed be He."
	ולאדמ לא	*Uladam La* –"But for the man there was not" (Gen. 2:20)
	חדק	*Chedeq* –Brier, thorn, prick
	יבק	*Yabboq* –Jabbok, eastern tributary of the Jordan River, which served as the western border of Ammon
	יהוה אלהימ	YHVH *Elohim* –The Lord God, divine name assoc. w/*Binah*
	יציב	*Yatztzeeb* –The truth; surely, reliably, truly; reliable, true, certain, sure (Aramaic)
	יקב	*Yeqeb* –Wine vat, wine press
	נדחימ	*Nedachiym* –Driven away (Deut. 22:1)
	עיבל	*'Owbal* –Obal, son of Joktan, descendant of Shem (see also עובל)[247]
	עילב	*'Eybal* –Ebal, mountain north of Shechem and beside Mount Gerizim
	קדח	*Qadach* –To kindle, be kindled

[245] מלכיה (105).

[246] Aliah (115).

[247] עובל (108).

–The number of children of Jorah who returned from exile (Ezra 2:18)

113	אקדח	*'eqdach* –Fiery glow, sparkle; name of a gem – carbuncle
	בוקה	*Buwqah* –Emptiness
	המונ גוג	*Hamown Gowg* –Hamon Gog, valley where Gog and his armies will be defeated in their final struggle against Israel (Ezek. 39:11-15)
	זנונ	*Zanuwn* –Adultery, fornication, prostitution
	חקה	*Chaqah* –To cut, carve, cut in
		Chuqqah –Statute, ordinance, limit, enactment, something prescribed
	מבוסה	*Mebuwsah* –Downtreading, subjugation
	מוסבה	*Muwsabbah* –To be turned; surrounded, set (participle)
	מחסה	*Machaseh* –Refuge, shelter
	מכבנא	*Makbena'* –Machbenah, descendant of Caleb; a place named after him identical with Cabbon
	מעג	*Ma'owg* –Cake
	נחמיה	*Nechemiyah* –Nehemiah, governor of Jerusalem who helped to rebuild the fallen city; chief man who returned from the Exile; one who repaired the wall of Jerusalem
	נסג	*Nasag* –To move away, backslide, move, go, turn back
	סליחה	*Seliychah* –Forgiveness
	עגיל	*'agiyl* –Hoop, ring, earring
	עגמ	*'agam* –To be grieved
	פלג	*Palag* –To divide, split
		Pelag –To divide (Aramaic); half (Aramaic)
		Peleg –Channel, canal; Peleg, son of Eber and father of Reu
		Phaleg–Olympic Planetary Spirit of Mars
	סגנ	*Sagan* –Ruler, prefect, governor, a subordinate ruler
		Segan –Prefect, governor

–Prime number

114	גיהנומ	*Ge-Hinnom* –Gehenna, Hell; the First Hell (corr. to *Yesod* & *Malkut*)
	גמיאל	*Gamaliel* –The Obscene Ones, *Qlippoth* of *Yesod*; Prince of the Tribe of Manasseh
	דיק	*Dayeq* –Bulwark, siege wall, sidewall
	דלפ	*Dalaf* –To drop, drip(especially of tears)
		Delef –A dropping, dripping
	דמע	*Dama'* –To weep
		Dema' –Juice
	חנונ	*Chanuwn* –Gracious; Hanun, king of Ammon who involved the Amonites in a disastrous war with David; one who repaired the wall; one who repaired the valley gate of Jerusalem
	יקד	*Yaqad* –To burn, kindle, be kindled
	מדיני	*Medyaniy* –Medianite
	מדע	*Madda'* –Knowledge, thought

	מלמד	*Malmad* –Ox goad
	מעד	*Ma'ad* –To slip, slide, totter, shake
	נחנו	*Nachnuw* –We
	עדלי	*'Adlay* –Adlai, father of Shaphat, an overseer of David's herds
	עלטה	*'alatah* –Thick darkness
	עמד	*'amad* –To stand, remain, endure, take one's stand; to be at a stand *'immad* –With *'omed* –Standing place
115	אלידע	*Elyada'* –Eliada, a son of David; a Benjamite warrior chief; an Aramean, the father of an enemy of Solomon
	אנחנו	*'anachnuw* –We (1st person plural – usually used for emphasis)
	דימונה	*Diymownah* –Dimonah, city of the tribe of Gad located north of the Arnon River (this spelling used only in Josh. 15:22 – see also Dibon, Dimonah)[248]
	הנס	*Hanes* –Hanes, the name of an Egyptian city in Upper Egypt (Is. 30:4)
	חזק	*Chazaq* –To strengthen, prevail, harden, be strong, be firm, grow firm, be resolute, be sore; strong, stout, mighty *Chazeq* –Stronger, louder *Chezeq, Chozeq* –Strength
	העמ	*HaAwm* –The people
	יעלה	*Ya'alah* –Female mountain goat; Jaalah, servant of Solomon whose descendants returned from the Exile (this spelling used only in Ezra 2:56 – see also יעלא)[249] *Ya'aleh* –To rise up, to go up
	יקדה	*Yeqeda'* –A burning (Aramaic)
	יקה	*Yaqeh* –Jakeh, father of Agur, the wise man
	כסלה	*Kislah* –Confidence; folly, stupidity
	מוסדה	*Mowsadah* –Foundation *Muwsadah* –Foundation, appointment
	מכנה	*Mekonah* –Mekonah, city in southern Judah, between Ziklag and En Rimmon *Mekunah* –Resting place, base
	מלילה	*Meliylah* –Ear (of wheat), head (of wheat)
	מעה	*Me'ah* –External belly, abdomen (Aramaic); internal organs, inward parts, bowels, intestines, belly; grain (of sand)
	נהלל	*Nahalal* –Nahalal, city of Zebulun assigned to the Levites *Nahalol* –Pasture, watering place
	נסה	*Nasah* –To test, try, prove, tempt, assay, put to the proof

[248] Dibon (66, 716; 72, 722), Dimonah (115).
[249] יעלא (111).

		or test
	סלכה	*Salkah* –Salcah, city located at the extreme limits of Bashan – modern Salkhad
	סנה	*Senah* –Seneh, southerly of two rocks in the passage between Michmash and Geba (1 Sam. 14:4-5); a bush, thorny bush, the burning bush of Moses
	עדיאל	*'Adiy'el* –Adiel, father of David's treasurer, Asmaveth; descendant of Simeon in the time of Hezekiah; Levite priest whose son Maasai helped rebuild the Temple after the Captivity
	עזאזל	*'aza'zel* –Entire removal, scapegoat (meaning dubious – Lev. 16:8, 10, 26)
		Azazel –Demon Prince of Air
	עליה	*'aliyah* –Roof-room, roof-chamber
		'Alyah –Aliah, a Duke of Edom (this spelling used only in 1 Chr. 1:51 – see also Alvah)[250] (assoc. w/Daath)
	עמה	*'ummah* –Juxtaposition; Ummah, city of Asher on the Mediterranean coast – modern Alma
	פהל	*Pahel* –20th name of *Shem HaMeforash* (2 Scorpio)
	פלה	*Palah* –To be distinct, marked out, be separated, be distinguished
	קוט	*Quwt* –To loathe, be grieved, feel a loathing
	קיה	*Qayah* –To vomit up, disgorge
116	אדנכיאל	*Adnakhiel* –"Lord of the Mark of God," Archangel of Sagittarius
	אחזק	*'achazaq* –Hardness (only used in regards to the hardness Israel suffered at the hands of the Egyptians – Ex. 4:21)
	אלכימיה	*'alkiymiyah* –Alchemy (mod. Hebrew)
	אסנה	*'asnah* –Asnah, one whose descendants returned from exile
	אפלה	*'afelah* –Darkness, gloominess, calamity; wickedness
	בלעדי	*Biladey* –Apart from, except, without, besides
	גמיגין	*Gamigin* –Goetic demon #4
	האלפ	*Halphas* –Goetic demon #38
	המליאל	*Hamaliel* –"Abundance of God," Archangel of Virgo
	כליונ	*Killayown* –Completion, destruction, consumption, annihilation; failing, pining; Chilion, son of Naomi and husband Orpah
	כסלו	*Kislev* –"His confidence" – the 3rd month of Jewish calendar corresponding to Nov. – Dec. It is associated with Sagittarius and the tribe Asher
	מכונ	*Makhon* –Emplacement, fixed or established place, foundation; the 6th Heaven (corr. to *Hesed*)
	מודה אני	*Modeh Ani* –"I acknowledge;" prayer recited upon awakening in the morning

[250] Alvah (111).

מעבד — *Ma'bad* –Work; action (of God in history – Aramaic)
נוס — *Nuws* –To flee, escape
סון — *Seven* –Syene, town on the southern frontier of Egypt (see also סונה)[251]
סנאה — *Sena'ah* –Senaah, place where many of inhabitants returned after the Exile; Senuah, father of Hodaviah (1 Chr. 9:7); ancestor of those who rebuilt the Fish Gate at Jerusalem (Neh. 3:3)
עויל — *'aviyl* –Young male or man or boy, boy; perverse one, unjust one
פול — *Phul* –Olympic Planetary Spirit of Luna
Powl –Beans
Puwl –Pul, country of undetermined location, sometimes considered to be Libya (Is. 66:19); Pul, another name for Tiglath-Pileser, king of Assyria who invaded Naphtali during the time of Pekah of Israel (this name used only in 2 Kings 15:19 – see also Tiglath-Pileser)[252]
צחיח — *Tzechiyach* –Shining or glaring surface, glow (Ezek. 24:7, 8, 26:4, 14)

–The number of years of Israel's slavery in Egypt

117 אלופ — *Aluf* –Tame, docile; friend, intimate; chief
אסון — *'asown* –Evil, mischief, harm, hurt
בעליה — *Be'alyah* –Bealiah, man who joined David at Ziklag (1 Chr. 12:5)
בקיה — *Buqqiyah* –Bukkiah, son of Heman and musician in the temple
גדעם — *Gid'om* –Gidom, village of the tribe of Benjamin
גלעדי — *Gil'adiy* –Gileadite
זעם — *Za'am* –To denounce, express indignation, be indignant; anger
יעואל — *Ye'uw'el* –Jeuel, descendant of Judah (1 Chr. 9:6); Jeiel, ancestor of Saul (1 Chr. 9:35); one of David's mighty men (1 Chr. 11:44); scribe or recorder of Uzziah (2 Chr. 26:11); Levite in Hezekiah's time (2 Chr. 29:13);
מעבה — *Ma'abeh* –Thickness, compactness
נסבה — *Nesibbah* –Turn of affairs, a bringing about
סאון — *Se'own* –Sandal, boot (of soldier)
עבדיאל — *'Abdiy'el* –Abdiel, ancestral head of the tribe of Gad
עליז — *'alliyz* –Exultant, jubilant
פלוא — *Palluw'* –Phallu, son of Reuben

118 אדם בליאל — *Adam Belial* –Archdemon corr. to *Chokmah* (Waite)
בנינו — *Beniynuw* –Beninu, Levite who sealed the new covenant with God after the exile
זימימאי — *Zimimay* –Demon King of the North and of Earth

---

[251] סונה (121).
[252] Tiglath-Pileser (1204).

(Goetia)

חיק *Cheyq* –Bosom, hollow, bottom, midst

חלפ *Chalaf* –To pass on or away, pass through, pass by, go through, grow up, change, to go on from, pass over

Chelef –In exchange for; in return for; Heleph, town marking the boundary of the tribe of Naphtali, northeast of Mount Tabor

חנני *Chananiy* –Hanani, musician and head of one of the courses of the temple services; father of the prophet Jehu – cast into prison by Asa; priest who married a foreign wife; brother of Nehemiah and a governor of Jerusalem under him; priest and musician who helped to purify the walls of Jerusalem

חנס *Chanes* –Hanes, unidentified place in Egypt (Is. 30:4)

חסנ *Chasan* –To be treasured up, be hoarded, be laid up, be stored; to take possession of (Aramaic)

Chason –Strong

Chesen –Power, strength, power of the king, royal power

Chosen –Riches, treasure, wealth

חעמ *Cham* –38th name of *Shem HaMeforash* (2 Aquarius)

לחממ *Lachmam* –Lahmam, a city located in the lowlands of Judah (see also לחמס)[253]

מבוע *Mabbuwa'* –Spring of water

מחמל *Machmal* –Object of compassion or pity, thing pitied; object of deep love

נגינה *Negiynah* –Music, song, taunt, song (taunting)

נסח *Nasach* –To pull or tear away

Nesach –To pull or tear away (Aramaic)

עזיאל *'Aziy'el* –Aziel, Levite musician who participated in the return of the Ark of the Covenant to Jerusalem (see also Jaaziel)[254]

'Uzziy'el –Uzziel, ancestor of the Uzzielites, the son of Kohath; captain of the sons of Simeon; son of Bela and grandson to Benjamin; assistant wall-builder; Levite, son of Jeduthun, who helped to cleanse the Temple; musician set by David over the service of song in the temple (see also Azareel)[255]

פלגה *Pelaggah* –Stream, division, river

Peluggah –Division, section

פלח *Palach* –To cleave, slice

Pelach –To serve, worship, revere, minister for, pay reverence to (Aramaic); cleavage, mill-stone; to cut, slice; part cut off

קטט *Qatat* –To be cut off, snap, break (meaning dubious –

---

[253] לחמס (138).

[254] Jaaziel (128).

[255] Azareel (308).

		Job 8:14)
119	בעל זבוב	*Beelzebub* –Lord of the Flies; archdemon corr. to *Chokmah*
	בנ־אוני	*Ben-'Owniy* –Ben-oni, name given to Rachel's child as she died bearing him; Jacob changed his name to Benjamin (Gen. 35:18)
	דמעה	*Dim'ah* –Tears
	טעמ	*Ta'am* –To taste, perceive, eat; taste, judgment; taste, judgment, command (Aramaic)
		Te'am –To feed, cause to eat (Aramaic)
		Te'em –Decree, taste, judgment, command (Aramaic)
	טפל	*Tafal* –To smear, plaster over, stick, glue
	מטע	*Matta'* –Place or act of planting, planting, plantation
	מיסדה	*Meyusadah* –To be founded, be laid
	מעת	*Ma'at* –To be or become small, be few, be diminished
		Ma'ot –Wrapped, grasped (meaning uncertain – Ezek. 21:15)
		Me'at –Littleness, few, a little, fewness
	עמדה	*'emdah* –Standing ground
	פגול	*Pigguwl* –Foul thing, refuse
	פלדה	*Peladah* –Iron, steel
	פלחא	*Pilcha'* –Pilcha, one who sealed the new covenant
	פלט	*Palat* –To escape, save, deliver, slip away
		Pallet –Deliverance, escape
		Pelet –Pelet, son of Jahdai of the family of Caleb; one who joined David at Ziklag
	קיט	*Qayit* –Summer
120	אליהו הנביא	*'eliyhu HaNevia'* –"Elijah the prophet"
	דמיוני	*Dimyoni* –Imaginary, fanciful
	הנניה	*Hananiah* –Hananiah, original name of Shadrach[256]
	חזקה	*Chezqah* –Strength, strong, being strong, force
		Chozqah –Force, might, strength, violence
	הסנה	*HaSeneh* –The bush (Ex. 3:2)
	ימיני	*Yemiyniy* –Right, on the right, right hand; Yemenite; Jaminites
	יקהה	*Yiqqahah* –Obedience, cleansing, purging
	יקוד	*Yaqowd* –A burning
	כנימ	*Kinnim* –Vermin
	כננ	*Kanan* –Root, support (of tree), shoot, stock
	כמס	*Kamas* –To store up, save
	כסיל	*Kesiyl* –Fool, stupid fellow, dullard, simpleton, arrogant one; the constellation Orion (Job 9:9; 38:31; Amos 5:8); Chesil, village in the southernmost portion of Judah (see also Bethuel)[257]
	כסמ	*Kasam* –To cut, clip, trim, shear
	כק	*Kaq* –173rd Gate of the 231 Gates

[256] Shadrach (524, 1004).
[257] Bethuel (438).

לצ	*Letz* –Mocker; 182nd Gate of the 231 Gates
מגבעה	*Migba'ah* –Turban, head-gear
מדוע	*Madduwa'* –Why?, on what account?, wherefore?
מהלמה	*Mahalumah* –Strokes, blows
מועד	*Moedh* –Season
	Mow'ad –Appointed place (in army)
	Mow'ed –Appointed place, appointed time, meeting
מכלל	*Miklal* –Completeness, perfection
	Miklul –A thing made perfect, perfect thing, gorgeous garment or stuff; all sorts of things
מכס	*Mekes* –Computation, proportion to be paid, tribute, tax
מסך	*Masak* –To mix, mingle, produce by mixing; covering, screen (of the Tabernacle)
	Mesek –Mixture
מעי	*Ma'ai* –Maai, priest who helped to purify the people who returned from the Exile (Neh. 12:36)
	Me'iy –Ruin, heap
מפ	*Mof* –Memphis, Egypt; 190th Gate of the 231 Gates
ניס	*Niys* –Refuge, a fleeing one
נמל	*Namal* –To circumcise, become clipped, be circumcised, be cut off
נע	*Na'* –197th Gate of the 231 Gates
סין	*Siyn* –Sin, city on the eastern side of the Nile – possibly Pelusium, but also identified with Syene; wilderness area located between the Gulf of Suez and Sinai
סלל	*Salal* –To lift up, cast up, exalt
סמך	*Samekh* –To lean, lay, rest, support, uphold, lean upon; prop, support; 15th letter of Hebrew alphabet
סס	*Sas* –Moth
עוגיאל	*Ogiel* –The Hinderers, *Qlippoth* of *Chokmah*
עילי	*'Iylay* –Ilai, one of David's mighty men (see also Zalmon)[258]
עים	*'ayam* –Glow, heat (meaning dubious – Isa. 11:5)
עמוד	*'ammuwd* –Pillar, column
פדהאל	*Pedah'el* –Pedahel, Prince of Naphtali
פמ	*Pum* –Mouth (Aramaic)
פנצ	*Phenex* –Goetic demon #37 (Aurum Solis spelling)
צל	*Tzal* –Shadow; shelter
	Tzel –Shadow, shade

–Mystic number of 15th Path (*Chokmah-Tiferet*; ה; Aries)
–The number of days God's breath will "abide" with man (Gen. 6:3)
–The age when Moses could "no longer come and go" (Deut. 31:2); the age when Moses died (Deut. 34:7)
–The number of years it took to build Noah's ark
–The number of years that Christian Rosenkreutz would be hidden from his followers (see *Fama Fraternatis*)

[258] Zalmon (216, 866).

121 אלמלכ *Allammelek* –Alammelech, a town or site in Asher

אלמנ *Alman* –Widowed, forsaken, forsaken of a widow

Almon –Widowhood

אלצ *Alats* –To urge

אפיל *'afiyl* –Late, ripe

אצל *'atsal* –To lay aside, reserve, withdraw, withhold

'Atzel –Azal, a place near Jerusalem; Azel, son of Eleasah

'etsel –Beside, by, near, nearness, joining, proximity

'Ezel –Ezel, a hiding place of David

בנ־אבינדב *Ben-'Abiynadab* –Ben-Abinadab, one of Solomon's twelve officers, married to Solomon's daughter Taphath (1 Kings 4:11)

יעיאל *Ye'iy'el* –Jeiel, chief of the tribe of Reuben; singer and gatekeeper of the Tabernacle; descendant of Asaph; chief Levite in the days of Josiah; one who returned to Jerusalem with Ezra; one who married a foreign wife during the Exile

כסיאל *Cassiel* –Angel ruling Saturn and Saturday

כעאל *Kael* –Angel of 4th astrological house

לאמימ *Le'ummiym* –Leummim, son of Dedan

מטבע *Matbea* –Coin

מכונה *Mekownah* –Fixed resting place, base, pedestal

נינוה *Nineveh* –Nineveh, capital of Assyria

סונה *Seveneh* –Syene, town on the southern frontier of Egypt (this spelling used only in Ezek. 29:10; 30:6 – see also סון)[259]

עכאל *Akel* –Lord of Triplicity by Night for Cancer

פאנצ *Phenex* –Goetic demon #37

פלאי *Pallu'iy* –Palluites

Pil'iy –Wonderful, incomprehensible, extraordinary

צאל *Tze'el* –A kind of lotus

צחיחה *Tzechiychah* –Scorched land, parched, scorched

צלא *Tzela* –To pray (Aramaic) (Dan. 6:11, Ezek. 6:10)

122 אבל מחולה *'Abel Mechowlah* –Abel-Meholah, home of Elisha

אסמודאי *Asmodai* –Asmodeus; archdemon corr. to *Giburah* or *Netzach*; Goetic demon #32

בענ *Be'on* –Beon, ancient Amorite city located east of the Jordan river and north of Moab (this spelling used only in Num. 32:3 – see also Baal Meon and Beth Baal Meon)[260]

בצל *Betsiyl* –Onion

דיבוק *Dibbuk* –Evil possessing spirit

זיקה *Ziyqah* –Spark, missile, firebrand, flaming arrow; fetters (Isa. 50:11)

זלפה *Zilpah* –Zilpah, the Syrian given by Laban to Leah as a handmaid, a concubine of Jacob, mother of Gad

---

[259] סון (116, 766).

[260] Baal Meon (278, 837), Beth Baal Meon (680, 1330).

and Asher

	יועאלה	*Yow'e'lah* –Joelah, one who joined David at Ziklag
	מכבני	*Makbannay* –Machbanai, a warrior who joined David at Ziklag; Macbannite
	מלבנ	*Malben* –Brick mold, brick kiln, quadrangle
	נבע	*Naba'* –To flow, pour out, pour, gush forth, spring, bubble up, ferment
	סנואה	*Senuw'ah* –Senuah, descendant of Benjamin (Neh. 11:9)
	ענב	*'Anab* –Anab, town in the mountains of Judah *'enab* –Grape(s)

–The number of men of Michmas who returned from exile (Ezra 2:27)

123	אבל מימ	*'Abel Mayim* –Abel Mayim, place in Palestine
	בנעא	*Bin'a'* –Binea, descendant of Jonathan, son of Saul (see Bineah)[261]
	חנינה	*Chaniynah* –Favor, compassion
	חנניה	*Chananyah* –Hananiah, descendant of Benjamin; leader of the sixteenth division of David's musicians (see also חנניהו)[262]; grandfather of Irijah; false prophet who opposed Jeremiah; one of Daniel's friends at Babylon (see also Shadrach)[263]; son of Zerubbabel; priest present at the dedication of the walls of Jerusalem; Levite who married a foreign wife during the exile; druggist and priest who helped to rebuild the wall of Jerusalem; one who helped rebuild the gate of Jerusalem – perhaps the same as the latter; faithful Israelite placed in charge of Jerusalem; one who sealed the new covenant with God after the exile
	כהנ הגדול	*Kohen HaGodhol* –High Priest
	מחסיה	*Machseyah* –Mahseiah, grandfather of Baruch, Jeremiah's scribe (not to be confused with Maaseiah)
	מלחמה	*Milchamah* –War
	מעוז	*Ma'owz* –Place or means of safety, protection, refuge, stronghold
	נגע	*Naga'* –To touch, reach, strike *Nega'* –Stroke, plague, disease, mark, plague spot
	עגנ	*'agan* –To shut oneself in or off or up
	ענג	*'anag* –To be soft, be delicate, be dainty *'anog* –Dainty, delicate *'oneg* –Exquisite delight, daintiness, delight, pleasantness

–The number of children of Bethlehem who returned from exile (Ezra 2:21)

124	אלמגימ	*Almuggiym* –A tree from Lebanon, almug trees (sandalwood?), almug wood

[261] Bineah (127).

[262] חנניהו (129).

[263] Shadrach (524, 1004).

	אלעוזי	*Eluzai* –Eluzai, a Benjamite warrior who joined David
	בנ־חסד	*Ben-Chesed* –Ben-Hesed, one of Solomon's twelve supply officers
	חלופ	*Chalowf* –Destruction, passing away, vanishing, appointed to destruction
	ידלפ	*Yidlaf* –Jidlaph, son of Nahor and nephew of Abraham (Gen. 22:22)
	יוחננ	*Yowchanan* –Johanan, captain who allied with Gedaliah after the fall of Jerusalem; eldest son of Josiah, king of Judah; son of Elioenai; father of a priest in Solomon'stime; two valiant men who joined David at Ziklag; returned exile; priest in the days of Joiakim
	לפיד	*Lappiyd* –Torch
	מעדי	*Ma'aday* –Maadai, one who married a foreign wife
	מעתה	*Ma'ateh* –Wrap, mantle
	סדינ	*Sadiyn* –Linen wrapper (a type of garment)
	עדנ	*'adan* –To luxuriate, delight oneself
		'aden –Hitherto, still, yet
		Eden –Eden, descendant of Gershom; Levite in the time of Hezekiah; Eden, garden that God created as the first residence of man; region in Mesopotamia; luxury, dainty, delight, finery; delight
		'iddan –Time (Aramaic)
	ענד	*'anad* –To bind, tie up, bind around or upon
125	המניכ	*Hamniyk* –Necklace, chain (Aramaic)
	הנע	*Hena'* –Hena, city 20 miles from Babylon, probably modern Anah
	חזקי	*Chizqiy* –Hezeki or Hizki, son of Elpaal and descendant of Benjamin (1 Chr. 8:17)
	ידיעאל	*Yediy'a'el* –Jediael, son of Benjamin (1 Chr. 7:6, 10-11) – possibly the same as Ashbel (1 Chr. 8:1); one of David's mighty men (1 Chr. 11:45); one who joined David at Ziklag (1 Chr. 12:20); descendant of Korah, son of Meshelemiah (1 Chr. 26:2)
	מועדה	*Muw'adah* –Cities appointed (of refuge)
	מכסה	*Mekaseh* –Covering, that which covers
		Mikseh –A covering (of the Ark; of the skins of the Tabernacle); computation
	מנדאל	*Mendel* –Angel of 6q Capricorn & night angel 4 Pentacles
	מנלה	*Minleh* –Gain, wealth, acquisition (meaning dubious – Job 15:29)
	מסכה	*Masekah* –A pouring, libation, molten metal, cast image, drink offering; web, covering, veil, woven stuff
		Mesukkah –Covering
	נמלה	*Nemalah* –Ant
	נעה	*Ne'ah* –Neah, landmark boundary of Zebulun; Noah,

daughter of Zelophehad

סללה *Solelah* –Mound

עדנא *'Adna'* –Adna, priest listed in Nehemiah who returned with Zerubbabel from the Captivity; one who took a foreign wife

ענה *'anah* –To answer, respond, testify, speak, shout; to sing, utter tunefully; to dwell; to be occupied, be busied with; to afflict, oppress, humble, be afflicted, be bowed down; to answer, respond (Aramaic); to be humble, be low (Aramaic); poor, needy (Aramaic); Anah, Zibeon's daughter and one of Esau's wives (Gen. 36:2, 14, 18, 25);[264] son of Seir and a chief of Edom; son of Zibeon

פליה *Pelayah* –Pelaiah, son of Elioenai

צהל *Tzahal* –To neigh, cry shrilly; to make shining

צלה *Tzillah* –Zillah, wife of Lamech (Gen. 4:19, 22-23)

126 אלמנה *Almanah* –Widow; desolate house

הנניהו *Hananiahu* –Original name of Shadrach (variant spelling)[265]

כוק *Keveq* –35th name of *Shem HaMeforash* (5 Capricorn)

לוצ *Luwtz* –To scorn, make mouths at, talk arrogantly

מאפה *Ma'afeh* –Baked, thing baked

מכלול *Miklowl* –Perfection, gorgeous attire; perfectly, most gorgeously

מכנדבי *Maknadbay* –Machnadebai, one who had a foreign wife

מלונ *Malown* –Place of lodging, inn, khan

נוע *Nuwa'* –To quiver, totter, shake, reel, stagger, wander, move, sift, make move, wave, waver, tremble

נכונ *Nakown* –Nachon, either a combined name of two individuals, or two place names, or a combination of both (1 Sam. 6:6; 1 Chr. 13:9)[266]

סומכ *Sumk* –Supporting

סוס *Suws* –Swallow, swift; horse

סיונ *Siyvan* –Sivan, the 9th month of the Jewish calendar – it is associated with Gemini and the tribe Benjamin

סנוי *Senoy* –One of the three angels invoked against Lilith

עוימ *'Avviym* –Avim, city of the tribe of Benjamin, probably near Bethel (Deut. 2:23; Josh. 13:3)[267]

עונ *'avan* –To eye, look at

'avon –Perversity, depravity, iniquity, guilt or punishment of iniquity

ענו *'anav* –Poor, humble, afflicted, weak

Anu –63rd name of *Shem HaMeforash* (3 Gemini)

---

[264] If the father, he is the same as Beeri the Hittite (Gen. 26:34).

[265] Shadrach (524, 1004).

[266] Literally "destruction" or a "javelin."

[267] Some translate "Bethel and (the village of) the Avvim," thus indicating a group of people.

פלאיה *Pela'yah* –Pelaiah, Levite who explained the Law when Ezra read it; Levite who sealed the new covenant – may be the same as the previous Pelaiah

צחיחי *Tzechiychiy* –Shining or glaring surface, bare places

צלאה *Tzalah* –To roast

127 אהללה יהוה בחיי *'ahallah* YHVH *Bichayay* –"With my life I will praise YHVH"

בנעה *Bin'ah* –Bineah, descendant of Jonathan, son of Saul (see Binea)[268]

בענה *Ba'anah* –Baanah, one of David's mighty men (2 Sam. 23:29; 1 Chr. 11:30); captain in Ishbosheth's army; one of Solomon's royal merchants; another of Solomon's merchants, responsible for Asher; one who returned from the exile with Zerubbabel; father of Zadok, builder of the temple

מוטבע *Mevetbau* –Material, natural (Aramaic)

נמואל *Nemuw'el* –Nemuel, descendant of Reuben; son of Simeon (see also Jemuel)[269]

עבד אדום *'Obed 'Edowm* –Obed-edom, man who housed the Ark for three months (2 Sam. 6:10-12; 1 Chr. 13:13-14); one of the chief Levitical singers and doorkeepers (1 Chr. 15:18, 21, 24; 16:5, 38; 26:4, 8, 15); Temple treasurer or official, or perhaps the tribe that sprang from him (2 Chr. 25:24); Levite musician who ministered before the Ark when it was placed in the Tabernacle (1 Chr. 16:5, 38 – he may be the same as the second Obed-edom)

עזן *'Azzan* –Azzan, father of a chief of Issachar (Num. 34:26)

פויאל *Poyel*–Angel of 2q Taurus & night angel 5 Pentacles

סאסאה *Sa'se'ah* –To drive away

–The number of provinces of King Ahasuerus (Esth. 1:1)

–Prime number

128 אופיאל *Ophiel* –Olympic Planetary Spirit of Mercury

אליפז *Eliyfaz* –Eliphaz, Esau's son, father of Teman; the Temanite friend of Job

בינוני *Beinoniy* –Intermediate; a Jew who doesn't sin but still has evil urges

חלצ *Chalats* –To remove, draw out, draw off, take off, withdraw, equip (for war), arm for war, rescue, be rescued; to draw off or out, withdraw; loins

Cheletz –Helez, one of David's mighty men; descendant of Judah

חנמל *Chanamal* –Frost, flood, sleet (meaning uncertain – Ps.

[268] Binea (123).

[269] Jemuel (87).

78:47)

חסינ — *Chasiyn* –Strong, mighty

יבוסימ — *Yebusim* –Jebusites

יעזיאל — *Ya'aziy'el* –Jaaziel, temple musician in David's time (this name used only in 1 Chr. 15:18 – see also Aziel)[270]

לחצ — *Lachatz* –To squeeze, press, oppress; oppression, distress, pressure

מגפה — *Maggefah* –Blow, slaughter, plague, pestilence, strike, smite

מלחמה — *Milchamah* –Battle, war

מפח — *Mappach* –Breathing out, expiring, exhaling (of life)

סיחנ — *Sihown* –Sihon, King of the Ammorites defeated by Israel (see also סיחון)[271]

עזיאלי — *'Ozziy'eliy* –Uzzielites

ענוב — *'Anuwb* –Anub, descendant of Judah through Caleb

פחמ — *Pecham* –Coal, charcoal, ember

צלח — *Tzalach* –To rush; to advance, prosper, succeed
Tzelach –To prosper (Aramaic)

–The number of letters in The 10 Commandments
–The number of men of Anathoth who returned from exile (Ezra 2:23)
–The number of singers, children of Asaph, who returned from exile (Ezra 2:41)

129 היכל גונה — *Hekel Gonah* –Palace of Serenity; Heavenly Mansion corr. to *Hod*

חנמאל — *Chanam'el* –Hanameel, cousin of Jeremiah's who sold him a field (Jer. 32:6-9)

חנניהו — *Chananyahuw* –Hananiahu, a form of Hananiah, leader of the sixteenth division of David's musicians (this name used in 1 Chr. 25:23 – see also חנניה)[272]; officer of Uzziah; father of a prince under Jehoiakim

טענ — *Ta'an* –To load; to pierce

יהוחננ — *Yehowchanan* –Jehohanan, gatekeeper of the tabernacle in David's time; chief captain of Judah; father of Ishmael; one who divorced his wife after the exile; priest who returned to Jerusalem with Zerubbabel; singer at the purification of the wall of Jerusalem; son of Tobiah the Ammonite; son of Eliashib

יפלט — *Yaflet* –Japhlet, descendant of Asher

מעדיה — *Ma'adyah* –Maadiah, priest who returned from the Exile (see also Moadiah)[273]

נחליאל — *Nachaliy'el* –Nahaliel, an Israelite encampment north of the Arnon River and east of Moab

נטע — *Nata'* –To plant, fasten, fix, establish

---

270 Aziel (118).
271 סיחון (134, 784).
272 חנניה (123).
273 Moadiah (135).

Neta' –Plantation, plant, planting

עדנה *'Adnah* –Adnah, captain who joined David at Ziklag; chief captain of Jehoshaphat

עיטמ *'Eytam* –Etam, town of the tribe of Simeon; cleft of rock near Zorah; resort town near Jerusalem used by King Solomon

עמידה *Amidah* –Standard prayer recited while standing

פליט *Paliyt* –Refuge, fugitive, escaped one

פלטי *Paltiy* –Palti, man selected from Benjamin to spy out the land; man who married David's wife (this spelling used only in 1 Sam. 25:44 – see also פלטיאל)[274]; Paltite

Piltay –Piltai, priest in Jerusalem in the days of Joiakim

130 אלגומימ *Alguwmmiym* –A tree from Lebanon, almug trees

הצלה *Hatsalah* –Deliverance, escape (n. fem.)

חזקיה *Chezeqiah* –Hezekiah, 12th King of Judah (see also חזקיהו, יחזקיה, and יחזקיהו)[275]; one who returned from Babylon (this spelling used in Neh. 2:16; 10:18–see also יחזקיה)[276]; son of Neariah, descendant of the royal family of Judah (1 Chr. 3:23); great-grandfather of the prophet Zephaniah (Zeph. 1:1)

יענ *Ya'an* –Because, therefore, because that; because of, on account of

Ya'en –Ostrich (ceremonially unclean bird)

כנס *Kanas* –To gather, collect, wrap

כנני *Kenaniy* –Chenani, Levite in the time of Ezra

כפל *Kafal* –To double, fold double, double over

Kefel –Double, a doubling

לילינ *Lilin* –A class of demons

לק *Laq* –183rd Gate of the 231 Gates

מיסכ *Meysak* –Covered structure, covert

מלכמ *Malkam* –Malcham, descendant of Benjamin; Milcom, a god of the Ammonites (see also Molech)[277]

מעכ *Ma'ak* –To press, squeeze

מצ *Mots* –Chaff (always as driven by wind); 191st Gate of the 231 Gates

נכס *Nekas* –Riches, property (Aramaic)

Nekes –Riches, treasures

נממ *Nemem* –57th name of *Shem HaMeforash* (3 Taurus)

נסכ *Nasak* –To pour out, pour, offer; to set, install; to weave

Nesak –To pour out, offer sacrifice (Aramaic); something poured out, libation, drink offering, libation offering (Aramaic)

Nesek –Drink offering, libation, molten image,

---

274 פלטיאל (160).

275 חזקיהו (136), יחזקיה (140), יחזקיהו (146).

276 יחזקיה (140).

277 Molech (134, 784).

		something poured out
	נפ	*Nof* –Noph, another name for Memphis, Egypt; 198th Gate of the 231 Gates
	סיני	*Sinai* –Sinite; Sinai[278]
	סכנ	*Sakan* –To be of use or service or profit or benefit; to incur danger; to be poor
		Saken –To shut up, stop up
	סלמ	*Sullam* –Ladder (Gen. 28:12)
	סמל	*Semel* –Image, statue, idol
	סע	*Sa'* –204th Gate of the 231 Gates
	עיימ	*'Iyiym* –Iim, town in extreme southern Judah; town east of the Jordan River (see also Ije-Abarim)[279]
	עינ	*Ayin* –Ain, town of Judah near Rimmon, assigned to the Levites serving the tribe of Simeon; site on the boundary line of the Promised Land; eye; spring, fountain; 16th letter of Hebrew alphabet
	עלל	*'alal* –To act severely, deal with severely, make a fool of someone; to glean; to act or play the child; to insert, thrust, thrust in, thrust upon; to thrust in, go in, come in (Aramaic)
	עני	*'aniy* –Poor, afflicted, humble, wretched
		'oniy –Affliction, poverty, misery
		'Unniy –Unni, one of the Levites chosen as singers; Levite that returned to the land with Zerubbabel
	פהליה	*Pahaliah* –Angel of 2q Scorpio & night angel 5 Cups
	פלכ	*Pelek* –Whirl of spindle, stick, district
	פנ	*Pen* –Corner; lest, not, beware lest; lest
	צלי	*Tzaliy* –Roasted, roast; roasted
	קל	*Qal* –Swift, light, fleet; voice, sound (Aramaic)
131	אלימלכ	*Elimelech* –Elimelech, Naomi's husband and father-in-law of Ruth
	אלמני	*Almoniy* –Someone, a certain one
	אמנמ	*'omnam* –Verily, truly, surely
		'umnam –Verily, truly, indeed
	אמצ	*'amats* –To be strong, alert, courageous, brave, stout, bold, solid, hard
		Ammits –Strong, mighty (see also אמיץ)[280]
		'amots –Strong, bay, dappled, piebald (of color)
		'omets –Strength
	אנפ	*'anaf* –To be angry, to be displeased, to breathe hard (of God's anger); face, nose (Aramaic)
	אפימ	*'Appayim* –Appaim, son of Nadab and the father of Ishi
	אפנ	*'ofen* –Circumstance, condition, timely
	אציל	*'atsiyl* –Side, corner, chief; nobles (figurative)
		'atstsiyl –Joining, joint (such as elbow, etc.)

278 From the correspondence of "ladder" and "Sinai," we learn that the ladder to heaven – i.e., Jacob's ladder – is provided by the Law given on Sinai – see introduction.

279 Ije Abarim (343, 903).

280 אמיץ (141, 951).

אצמ 'Otzem –Ozem, brother of David; son of Jerahmeel

גבעונ Gib'own –Gibeon, chief city of the Hivites, assigned to the tribe of Benjamin

ויחזק Vayachazek –And he hardened

יאמאטע Yamatu –Guardian of the 20th Tunnel of Set

מלונה Meluwnah –Lodge, hut

מלכיאל Malkiy'el –Malchiel, descendant of Asher

מסוכה Mesukah –Hedge

מצא Matsa' –To find, attain to

נאפ Na'af –To commit adultery

Ni'uf –Adultery

נלכאל Nelakiel –Angel of 3q Scorpio & day angel 6 Cups

סוסה Suwsah –Mare

סמאל Samael –Angel of Death; Prince of Demons; Demon Prince of Fire; *Qlippoth* of *Hod*; archdemon corr. to *Chokmah* (A.C.)

עונה 'ownah –Cohabitation, conjugal rights

ענוה 'anvah, 'anavah –Humility, meekness

פלוטו *Pluto*

צולה Tzuwlah –Ocean-deep, deep, ocean depth

צמא Tzama –Thirst

Tzame' –To be thirsty

–Prime number

132 אלעלא *El'ale'* –Elealeh, a Reubenite village near Heshbon (in ruins)

בלק *Balaq* –To waste, lay waste, devastate

Balak –Balak, King of Moab who had Balaam curse Israel

לבעל *Li-Ba'al* –To Ba'al

מצב *Matstsab* –Station, garrison, standing-place

Mutstsab –Entrenchment, siege work, palisade, post

מעזיה *Ma'azyah* –Maaziah, priest who sealed the new covenant with God after the exile

ננאאל *Nanael* –Angel of 5q Aries & day angel 4 Wands

סאסיא *Sasia* –Lord of Triplicity by Night for Virgo

עבדונ *Abdown* –Abdon, 11th Judge of Israel; descendant of Benjamin who dwelt in Jerusalem; firstborn son of Jeiel and an ancestor of King Saul, mentioned in Chronicles; official sent by King Josiah to Huldah to inquire of the meaning of the Law (see also Achbor – possibly the same as the second Abdon)[281]

קבל *Qabal* –To take, receive, be before (occurs in 1 Chr. 12:18, 21:11; 2 Chr. 29:16, 29:22; Esth. 4:4, 9:23, 9:27; Ex. 26:5, 36:12; Ezra 8:30; Job 2:10 [2x]; Prov. 19:20)

Qebel –In front of, before, because of; because that, inasmuch as, although; accordingly, then

---

[281] Achbor (298).

Qobel–Battering-rams (Ezek. 26:9)
–In Arabic, the number for Muhammed's name and the word *Qalb*, Heart

133 גדעונ *Gideon* –5th Judge of Israel
גפנ *Gefen* –Vine, vine tree
זעונ *Za'avan* –Zaavan, descendant of Seir
חליפה *Chaliyfah* –A change, change (of garments), replacement
חעמיה *Chamiah* –Angel of 2q Aquarius & night angel 5 Swords
כמיגינ *Gamigin* –Goetic demon #4 (Aurum Solis spelling; probably a misprint)
נגפ *Nagaf*–To strike, smite
Negef–Blow, striking, plague
נפג *Nefeg* –Nepheg, brother of Korah; son of David
עמיזבד *'Ammiyzabad* –Ammizabad, one of David's captains
פנג *Pannag* –An edible food, perhaps pastry (meaning dubious – Ezek. 27:17)

134 דלק *Dalaqh* –To burn, hotly pursue
Delaqh –To burn (Aramaic)
חופמ *Chuwfam* –Hupham, head of a family descendant from Benjamin (Num. 26:39)[282]
חכמוני *Chakmowniy* –Hachmonite
מדמנ *Madmen* –Madmen, location in Moab – may be modern Khirbet Dimneh
מחלונ *Machlown* –Mahlon, first husband of Ruth who died in Moab
מפוח *Mappuach* –Bellows
מצד *Metsad* –Fort, stronghold, fastness
נדפ *Nadaf* –To drive, drive away, drive asunder
סיחונ *Sihon* –Sihon, King of the Ammorites defeated by Israel (see also סיחן)[283]
סעד *Sa'ad* –To support, sustain, stay, establish, strengthen, comfort
Se'ad –To support, sustain
עדינ *'adiyn* –Voluptuous; Adin, ancestor of returned captives; one whose descendant returned with Ezra; Jewish leader who sealed the covenant in Nehemiah's time
פדנ *Paddan* –Padan, plain region of Mesopotamia from the Lebanon Mountains to beyond the Euphrates, and from the Taurus Mountains on the north to beyond Damascus on the south (this spelling used only in Gen. 48:7 – see also פדן ארם)[284]
פלטיה *Pelatyah* –Pelatiah, one who sealed the new covenant with God after the Exile; descendant of David; captain of Simeon

---

282 In Gen. 46:21 and 1 Chr. 7:12, Hupham's name is listed as Huppim.
283 סיחן (128, 778).
284 פדן ארם (375, 1585).

	פליטה	*Peleytah* –Escape, deliverance
	צמד	*Tzamad* –To bind, join, fasten
		Tzemed –Couple, pair, team, yoke
135	אפדן	*'appeden* –Palace
	גבעני	*Gib'oniy* –Gibeonite
	גוסיון	*Gusion* –Goetic demon #11
	טלמון	*Talmown* –Talmon, Levite in Ezra's day – a temple porter
	יענה	*Ya'anah* –Ceremonially unclean bird – owl, ostrich, perhaps extinct
	כנניה	*Kenanyah* –Chenaniah, head Levite when David brought the Ark of the Covenant to the Temple (this spelling used only in 1 Chr. 15:27 – see also כנניהו)[285]
	מועדיה	*Mow'adyah* –Moadiah, priest who returned from the Babylonian exile (this spelling used only in Neh. 12:17 – see also Maadiah)[286]
	מלכידאל	*Malkidiel* –"King of the hand of God," Archangel of Aries
	ממלכה	*Mamlakah* –Kingdom, dominion, reign, sovereignty
	מסלה	*Mesillah* –Highway, raised way, public road
	מעכה	*Ma'akah* –Maachah, son of Nahor, Abraham's brother; one of David's wives and mother of Absalom; king of Maachah; father of Achish, king of Gath (see also Maoch)[287]; mother of Asa (see also Michaiah)[288]; concubine of Caleb; wife of Machir, son of Manasseh; wife of Jehiel; father of one of David's warriors; father of Shephatiah, ruler of Simeon
	מצה	*Matsah* –To drain, drain out
		Matstsah –Unleavened (bread, cake), without leaven; strife, contention
		Motzah –Mozah, city alloted to Benjamin (Josh. 18:26)
	נפה	*Nafah* –A lofty place, height; sieve, winnowing implement
	סמיכה	*Semichah* –Support
	סעה	*Sa'ah* –To rush (of storm winds)
	עבד נגו	*'Abed Negow* –Abed-nego, Chaldean name given to Azariah, one of the three friends of Daniel who were carried captive to Babylon (see also Azariah, עבד נגוא)[289]
	עדינא	*'Adiyna'* –Adina, son of Shiza the Reubenite, one of David's mighty men
	עזבון	*'izzabown* –Wares, goods

285 כנניהו (141).
286 Maadiah (129).
287 Maoch (136, 616).
288 Michaiah (81; 85).
289 עבד נגוא (136).

	עללה	*'olelah* –Gleaning
	עמיהוד	*Ammihud* –Ammihud, father of Elishama, prince of Ephraim; Simeonite whose son helped to divide the Promised Land; Naphthalite whose son helped divide the Promised Land; descendant of Judah through Perez and a son of Omri
	עניה	*'Anayah* –Anaiah, one who stood with Ezra at the reading of the Law (Neh. 8:4); one who sealed the covenant with God after the Exile (Neh. 10:22)
	פימה	*Piymah* –Super abundance (of fat), excessive fat
	פנה	*Panah* –To turn
		Pinnah –Corner
	צמה	*Tzammah* –Veil, woman's veil
	קהל	*Qahal* –To assemble, gather; assembly, congregation
	קלה	*Qalah* –To roast, parch; to disgrace, dishonor, be dishonored, be despised
		Qalahh –To assemble, be gathered together
136	אלעלה	*El'ale'* –Elealeh, a Reubenite village near Heshbon (in ruins)
	אמצה	*'amtsah* –Strength
	אנפה	*'anafah* –An unclean bird (perhaps a heron)
	אצליהו	*'Atzalyahuw* –Azaliah, father of Shaphan the scribe
	הסמאל	*Hismael* –Spirit of Jupiter
	חזקיהו	*Chezeqiahu* –Hezekiah, 12th King of Judah (variant spelling – see also חזקיה, יחזקיה, and יחזקיהו)[290]
	יהפיאל	*Iophiel* –Intelligence of Jupiter
	מהללאל	*Mahalaleel* –Mahalaleel, son of Cainan & father of Jared; one whose descendants lived at Jerusalem
	מוצ	*Muwtz* –Squeezer, executioner, oppressor
	מעוכ	*Ma'owk* –Maoch, father of Achish, king of Gath (this spelling used only in 1 Sam. 27:2 – see also Maachah)[291]
	נופ	*Nowf* –Elevation, height
		Nuwf –To move to and fro, wave, besprinkle
	סוסי	*Suwsiy* –Susi, father of one of the spies
	עבד נגוא	*Abedh Nego* –Abed-nego, Chaldean name given to Azariah, one of the three friends of Daniel who were carried captive to Babylon (see also Azariah)[292]
	עולל	*'owlel* –Child, boy
	עיונ	*'Iyown* –Ijon, city of northern Palestine belonging to the tribe of Naphtali
	פוטיאל	*Puwtiy'el* –Putiel, father-in-law of Eleazar, son of Aaron
	פונ	*Puwn* –To be perplexed, be distracted (meaning dubious

[290] חזקיה (130), יחזקיה (140), יחזקיהו (146).
[291] Maachah (135).
[292] Azariah (292).

		– Ps. 88:15)
	צומ	*Tzuwm* –To abstain from food, fast *Tzowm* –Fast, fasting
	צמאה	*Tzim'ah* –Parched condition, thirst, dehydration
	קול	*Qowl* –Voice, sound, noise; lightness, frivolity

–Mystic number of 16th Path (*Chokmah-Hesed*; ו; Taurus)
–The sum of all the numbers (1 through 16) on the magic square of Jupiter

137	אופנ	*Ofan* –Wheel, to revolve; one of the *Ofanim* (the wheel in Ezekiel's vision)
	אמוצ	*'Amowtz* –Amoz, father of the prophet Isaiah
	גדעני	*Gidonee* –Gideoni, descendant of Benjamin, father of Abidan
	זקנ	*Zaqan* –Beard, chin *Zaqen* –To be old, become old, old (of humans), elder *Zaqun* –Old age, extreme old age *Zoqen* –Old age
	מדחפה	*Medachfah* –Push, thrust
	מוצא	*Mowtsa'* –Act or place of going out or forth, issue, export, source, spring
	מצבה	*Matstsabah* –Guard, watch, army *Matstsebah* –Pillar, mastaba, stump
	נמואלי	*Nemuw'eliy* –Nemuelite
	קבלה	*Kabbalah* –Tradition

–The reciprocal of the fine structure constant
–The number of years that Ishmael (Gen. 25:17), Levi (Ex. 6:16), and Amram (Ex. 6:20) lived
–Prime number

138	בנ־אלהימ	*Ben-Elohim* –"Son of God"
	חלק	*Chalaq* –To divide, share, plunder, allot, apportion, assign; to be smooth, slippery, deceitful; portion, possession, lot (Aramaic); flattering, smooth; Halak, mountain in southern Palestine possibly modern Jebel Halaq *Challaq*, *Challuq* –Smooth *Cheleq* –Portion, share, part, territory; smoothness, seductiveness; flattery; Helek, descendant of Manasseh
	חמצ	*Chamets* –To be leavened, be sour; to be cruel, oppress, be ruthless; to be red *Chametz* –The thing leavened, leaven *Chomets* –Vinegar
	חנפ	*Chanef* –To be profaned, be defiled, be polluted, be corrupt; hypocritical, godless, profane, hypocrite, irreligious *Chonef* –Hypocrisy, godlessness, hypocrite, profaneness
	חפימ	*Chuppiym* –Huppim, head of a family descendent from Benjamin (this name used only in Gen. 46:21 and 1 Chr. 7:12 – see also Hupham)[293]

[293] Hupham (134, 694).

	חפנ	*Chofen* –Handfuls, hollow of the hand
	לבנונ	*Lebanown* –Lebanon, one of two ranges of mountains in northern Palestine
	לחמס	*Lachmas* –Lahmas, a city located in the lowlands of Judah (possibly an error for לחמם in Josh. 15:40)[294]
	לקח	*Laqach* –To take, get, fetch, lay hold of, seize, receive, acquire, buy, bring, marry, take a wife, snatch, take away *Leqach* –Learning, teaching, insight
	מחצ	*Machats* –To smite through, shatter, wound severely; severe wound, contusion
	מנחמ	*Menachem* –Menahem, 17th King of Israel
	מצח	*Metsach* –Brow, forehead
	מעזיהו	*Ma'azyahuw* –Maaziah, priest to whom certain sanctuary duties were charged (1 Chr. 24:18)
	נחלמי	*Nechelamiy* –Nehelamite
	נפח	*Napach* –To breathe, blow, sniff at, seethe, give up or lose (life) *Nofach* –Nophah, city in Moab (Num. 21:30 – this name is not referred to anywhere else and may not be a place – see also Nobah)[295]
	צמח	*Tzamach* –To sprout, spring up, grow up *Tzemach* –Sprout, branch, growth
	קלט	*Qalat* –To be stunted, be handicapped
139	אחיסמכ	*'Achysamak* –Ahisamach, craftsman who helped build the Tabernacle in the Wilderness
	אלחננ	*'Elkanan* –Elkanan, Jair's son who fought the Gittites; Dodo's son who was a chief of David
	דקלה	*Diqlah* –Diklah, son of Joktan
	חננאל	*Chanan'el* –Hananel, tower of Jerusalem, located near the Sheep's Gate (Jer. 31:38; Zech. 14:10)
	טנפ	*Tanaf* –To defile, soil
	יחצאל	*Yachtze'el* –Jahzeel, son of Naphtali listed three times (this name used in Gen. 46:24; 1 Chr. 7:13 – see also יחציאל)[296]
	יפלטי	*Yafletiy* –Japhletites
	לקט	*Laqat* –To pick up, gather, glean, gather up *Leqet* –Gleaning
	מדמנה	*Madmannah* –Madmannah, town near Gaza in southern Judah (see also Beth-Marcaboth – may be the same town)[297] *Madmenah* –Dung place, dung pit, dung hill; Madmenah, village north of Jerusalem in the territory belonging to Benjamin

[294] לחמם (118, 678).

[295] Nobah (60).

[296] יחציאל (149).

[297] Beth-Marcaboth (1080, 1085).

נטיע *Natia'* –Plant (fig. of vigorous sons)

נטפ *Nataf* –To drop, drip, distill, prophesy, preach, discourse; drop, gum, drops of stacte (an aromatic gum resin of a shrub used in the Holy incense)

עטינ *'atiyn* –Bucket, pail

קטל *Qatal* –To slay, kill

Qetel –Slaughter

–The children of the porters who returned from exile (Ezra 2:42)

–Prime number

140 יחזקיה *Yechizqiyah* –Hezekiah, 12th King of Judah (see also חזקיהו, חזקיה, and יחזקיהו)[298]; one who returned from Babylon (this spelling used in Ezra 2:16 –see also חזקיה)[299]

ילק *Yeleq* –Cankerworm, caterpillar

יעני *Ya'anay* –Jaanai, chief of a family descended from Gad

כילפ *Keylaf* –Large axes, axe

כנע *Kana'* –To be humble, be humbled, be subdued, be brought down, be low, be under, be brought into subjection

כסס *Kasas* –To estimate, reckon, compute

כענ *Ke'an* –Now, at this time, until now (Aramaic)

להקה *Lahaqah* –Company, group, band

מחצב *Machtseb* –Hewing, hewn (of stones)

מימנ *Miyamin* –Miamin, priest in the time of David; one who sealed the new covenant; one who divorced his foreign wife after the Exile; chief of the priests who returned with Zerubbabel from Babylon (this spelling used only in Neh. 12:5 – see also מנימין)[300]

מיצ *Miyts* –Squeezing, pressing, wringing

מלכימ *Melekim* –Kings; Angelic Choir assoc. w/ *Tiferet*

מעל *Ma'al* –To act unfaithfully, act treacherously, transgress, commit a trespass; unfaithful or treacherous act, trespass; higher part, upper part

Me'al –Going in (Aramaic)

Mo'al –Lifting

מצוד *Matsowd* –Siege works, bulwark; hunting implement, net; fastness, stronghold

Matsuwd –Net, prey, net prey; fastness, stronghold

מק *Maq* –Rottenness, decay; 192nd Gate of the 231 Gates

נסיכ *Nesiyk* –Poured out, libation, molten image, one anointed; prince, anointed one

נצ *Netz* –Blossom; an unclean bird of prey (perhaps hawk); 199th Gate of the 231 Gates

ספ *Saf* –A spreading out; basin, goblet, bowl; sill,

---

[298] חזקיהו (136), חזקיה (130), יחזקיהו (146).

[299] חזקיה (130).

[300] מנימין (200, 850).

threshold, entrance; Saph, descendant of Rapha the giant (see also Sippai)[301]; 205th Gate of the 231 Gates

עדינו *'adiynow* –Adina, son of Shiza the Reubenite and one of David's mighty warriors (1 Chr. 11:42)

עכן *'Akan* –Achan, one who stole part of the spoil of Jericho and brought "trouble" on his people and was killed for this (Josh. 7:1-24 – see also Achar, Achor)[302]

עליל *'aliyl* –Furnace, crucible

עלם *'alam* –To conceal, hide, be hidden, be concealed, be secret; perpetuity, antiquity, forever (Aramaic)

Alem –4th name of *Shem HaMeforash* (4 Leo)

'elem –Young man

עמל *'amal* –To labor, toil; Amal, son of Helem in the line of Ashur

'amel –Laborer, sufferer, wretched one; toiling

פדון *Padown* –Padon, one who returned with Zerubbabel

פדיום *Pidyowm* –Ransom, redemption

פיכל *Piykol* –Phichol, captain or captains of the army of Abimelech, king of the Philistines (Gen. 21:22; 26:26)[303]

פלטיהו *Pelatyahuw* –Pelatiah, wicked prince seen in Ezekiel's vision

פלל *Palal* –To intervene, interpose, pray; Palal, one who helped rebuild the wall

פני *Pene* –Face

פס *Pas* –Flat (of the hand or foot), palm, sole; palm of the hand

צן *Tzen* –Thorn, barb (meaning dubious – Job 5:5; Prov. 22:5); Zin, wilderness on the southern border of Canaan (not to be confused with Sin)

קהלה *Qehillah* –Assembly, congregation

קלי *Qallay* –Kallai, priest who returned with Zerubbabel

Qaliy –Parched grain, roasted grain

141 אמיץ *Ammiyts* –Strong, mighty

אמצי *'Amtziy* –Amzi, Levite of the family of Merari; ancestor of returned exiles

אסף *'asaf* –To gather, receive, remove, gather in; Asaph, one whose descendants were porters in David's time; one of David's three musicians; a Levite; father of Joah; keeper of the royal forests in Judah

'asuf –What is gathered, store, storing, storehouse

'osef –Gathering, collection, harvest

אפלל *'Eflal* –Ephlal, descendant of Perez

אפס *'afes* –To cease, break, come to an end

'efes –Ceasing, end, finality

[301] Sippai (150).

[302] Achar (290), Achor (296).

[303] Some scholars think this is not a proper name, but a Philistine military title.

כוקיה *Keveqiah* –Angel of 5q Capricorn & day angel 4 Pentacles

כנניהו *Kenanyahuw* –Chenaniah, head Levite when David brought the Ark of the Covenant to the Temple (this spelling used only in 1 Chr. 15:22 – see also כנניה)[304]; an officer of David

מהומנ *Mehuwman* –Mehuman, one of the chamberlains of Ahasuerus

מלכימ א *Melekim* –The Name of 1 Kings in Hebrew

מלאכימ *Malakim* –Angels; messengers

מלכיאלי *Malkiy'eliy* –Malchielite

מצוה *Mitzvah* –Commandment (of man, of God, of code of wisdom)

נאמנ *Ne'eman* –Faithful, loyal

נאצ *Na'ats* –To spurn, condemn, despise, abhor

נצא *Natsa'* –To fly

סיעא *Siy'a'* –Sia, an ancestor of returned captives (see also סיעהא)[305]

סמכיהו *Semakyahuw* –Semachiah, gatekeeper of the Tabernacle in David's day

פכיאל *Pakiel* –"Flask of God," Angel of Cancer

צנא *Tzona'* –Flock, sheep

142 אליקא *Eliyqa'* –Elika, one of David's mighty warriors

אסמודאל *Asmodel* –"Hawk of the Storehouse," Archangel of Taurus

בליעל *Belial* –Goetic demon #68; *Qlippoth* of *Ain Sof*; Archdemon corresponding to *Hod* (alternate spelling)

בלעמ *Balaam* –Balaam, prophet that the king of Moab induced to curse Israel (Num. 22-24; 31:8); Bileam, settlement on the western side of the Jordan assigned to Manasseh; Goetic demon #51 (Aurum Solis spelling)

בעלי יהודה *Ba'aley Yehuwdah* –Baale Yehuwdah (Judah), one of the cities of the Gibeonites located at the northwestern boundary of Judah (this spelling used only in 2 Sam. 6:2 – see also Baalah, Kirjath-Arim, Kirjath-Baal)[306]

בעלמ *Balam* –Goetic demon #51

בעמיכ *Biamek* –In your people

זולל וסבא *Zolel VeSove'* –"Glutton and drunkard" (Deut. 21:20)

חדקל *Chiddeqel* –Hiddikel, modern Tigris, a river of Eden (assoc. w/Air) (Gen. 2:14; Dan. 10:4)

מוצאה *Mowtsa'ah* –Origin, place of going out from

מלכימ ב *Melekim* –The Name of 2 Kings in Hebrew

---

304 כנניה (135).

305 סיעהא (146).

306 Baalah (107), Kirjath-Arim (1030, 1590), Kirjath-Baal (812).

	נצב	*Natsab* –To stand, take one's stand, stand upright, be set (over), establish
		Nitstsab –Haft, hilt (of sword)
	עזניה	*'ozniyah* –An unclean bird of prey (perhaps osprey, black eagle, buzzard)
	צבימ	*Tzebiyim* – Zeboim, one of the five cities of the Plain (this spelling used only in Gen. 10:19 – see also צביים, צבאים)[307]
143	אבצנ	*Ibtzan* –Ibzan, 9th Judge of Israel, a Betelemite judge (Judg. 12:8, 10)
	אצבנ	*'Etzbon* –Ezbon, son of Gad (see also Ozni, אצבון)[308]; descendant of Benjamin
	חליצה	*Chaliytsah* –What is stripped off (a person in war), armor, spoils, belt
	חלקה	*Chalaqqah* –Flattery, smoothness, fine promises
		Chaluqqah –Division, part, portion
		Chelqah –Portion, parcel; smooth part, smoothness, flattery
	חנפה	*Chanufah* –Profaneness, pollution, hypocrisy, godlessness
	מחצה	*Mechetsah* –Half (of spoils)
	מעגל	*Ma'gal* –Entrenchment, track
	מצחה	*Mitschah* –Greave(s), leg armor
	נזופ	*Nozuf* –Hated one
	פסג	*Pasag* –To pass between or within (meaning dubious – Ps. 48:14)
	צבאימ	*Tzebo'iym* –Zeboiim, one of the five cities of the Plain (see also צביים, צבים)[309]
144	חופמי	*Chuwfamiy* –Huphamites
	חמוצ	*Chamowts* –The oppressor, the ruthless (Isa. 1:17)
	ידעני	*Yidde'oniy* –One who has a familiar spirit, wizard, necromancer, soothsayer, diviner
	יחסיונ	*Ye-chesayun* –His [God's] refuge
	ועבדי כלב	*Ve-ovdi Kaleb* –"My servant Caleb"
	נטפה	*Netofah* –Netophah, city of Judah[310]
	ספד	*Safad* –To wail, lament, mourn
	עדלמ	*'Adullam* –Adullam, town of Judah near Succoth[311]
	צדימ	*Tziddiym* –Ziddim, fortress city of Naphtali
	צמיד	*Tzamiyd* –Bracelet, cover (of vessel)
	קדמ	*Qadam* –To meet, confront, go before
		Qedem –Before; the East; ancient things
		Qodam –Before, in front (Aramaic)

---

[307] צבאים (143, 703), צביים (152, 712).

[308] אצבון (149, 799), Ozni (68).

[309] צבים (142, 702), צביים (152, 712).

[310] A Netophathite is one from this city (549).

[311] David made the headquarters of his rebellion against Saul in a cave near this town (Josh. 12:7-15; 1 Sam. 22: 2 Sam. 23:13)

145

הצנ — *Hotzen* –Armor?, weapons?, chariots? (meaning uncertain – Ezek. 23:24)

הקמ — *Haqem* –16th name of *Shem HaMeforash* (4 Libra)

יהועדנ — *Yehow'addan* –Jehoaddan, mother of King Amaziah and wife of King Joash (this spelling used only in 2 Chr. 25:1 - see also יהועדין)[312]

יפנה — *Yefunneh* –Jephunneh, man of Judah and father of Caleb the spy; head of a family of the tribe of Asher

כנעה — *Kin'ah* –Bundle, bag, pack

מטמונ — *Matmon* –Treasure; hidden treasure, hidden or secret thing

מעלה — *Ma'alah* –What comes up, thoughts; step, stair
Ma'aleh –Ascent, incline; above

נממיה — *Nemamiah* –Angel of 3q Taurus & day angel 6 Pentacles

נועדיה — *Now'adyah* –Noadiah, son of Binnui to whom Ezra entrusted the sacred vessels of the Temple; prophetess opposed to Nehemiah

נצה — *Natsah* –To fly; to struggle; to strip off, make desolate, all in ruins
Nitstsah –Blossom

ספה — *Safah* –To sweep or snatch away, catch up, destroy, consume

עלילה — *'aliylah* –Wantonness, deed, doing

עלמה — *'almah* –Young woman

פסה — *Pissah* –Abundance, fullness, plenty (meaning dubious – Ps. 72:16)

צנה — *Tzinnah* –Something piercing, hook, barb; coolness, cold (of snow); shield, large shield, buckler

קליה — *Qelayah* –Kelaiah, one of the priests who divorced his foreign wife after the Exile (see also Kelita)[313]

קמה — *Qamah* –Standing grain

146

אמציה — *Amatziah* –Amaziah, 8th King of Judah; Levite descended from Merari; idolatrous priest of Bethel; father of Joshah

אספה — *'asefah* –A collecting, gathering
'asufah –Collection
'asfeh –Collection, rabble, connected multitude

בבא קמא — *Bava Kama* –The "first gate," one of the tractates of the Talmud

בכל לבבכמ — *Bakal Lababakam* –"With all your heart" (1 Sam. 12:24)

המצוה — *HaMitzvah* –The commandment

ויסע — *ve-Yisa'* –And he journeyed, led, set forward (Gen. 12:9; Ex. 15:22)

וסעדו — *ve-Sa'edo* –And comfort yourselves (Gen. 18:5)

יהוה נסי — YHVH *Nissi* –Adonai-nissi, an altar that Moses built at Rephidim in honor of Israel's victory over

---

312 יהועדין (155, 805).

313 Kelita (150).

Amalek (Ex. 17:15)

יחזקיהו *Yechizqiyahuw* –Hezekiah, 12th King of Judah (see also יחזקיה, חזקיהו, and חזקיה)[314]

מוק *Muwq* –To mock, deride, jeer

מנונ *Manown* –Grief, progeny, thankless one (meaning uncertain – Prov. 29:21)

נאצה *Ne'atsah* –Contempt, contumely; blasphemy

נוצ *Nuwts* –To fly, flee; to bloom, blossom

סופ *Suwf* –To cease, come to an end; to be fulfilled, be completed, come to an end (Aramaic); reed, rush, water, plant; Suph, unknown place or region opposite the campsite in the Transjordan where Moses explained the Law to the Israelites (Deut. 1:1)[315]

Sowf –End, conclusion (also Aramaic)

סיעהא *Siy'aha'* –Siaha, an ancestor of returned captives (see also סיעא)[316]

סלונ *Sillown* –Brier, thorn

עולמ *'owlam* (often *Olam*) –Long duration, antiquity, futurity, forever, ever, everlasting, evermore, perpetual, old, ancient, eternity, world; Elam, ancestor of some who married foreign wives during the Exile (Ezra 10:2)

עיניו *'eynayev* –His eyes (Gen. 13:10)

עלומ *'aluwm* –Youth, youthful, vigor

פוני *Puwniy* –Punites

פניו *Panayev* –His countenance, his face (Gen. 4:5; 31:21; 32:21)

Panav –Depressed (Gen. 4:5)

קולי *Qoliy* –My voice (Gen. 4:23)

קומ *Quwm* –To rise, arise, stand, rise up, stand up

147 אמנונ *'Amnown* –Amnon, son of David

כונניהו *Kownanyahuw* –Conaniah, chief of the Levites who assisted in the Passover celebration during King Josiah's reign

מצביה *Metzobayah* –Mesobaite

מקבה *Maqqabah* –Hammer

נצבה *Nitsbah* –Firmness (Aramaic)

עינ גדי *'Eyn Gediy* –En-Gedi, town on the western shore of the Dead Sea assigned to the tribe of Judah (see also Hazazon Tamar)[317]

עינ חדה *'Eyn Chaddah* –En Haddah, village of the tribe of Issachar

–The number of years that Jacob lived

---

314 חזקיהו (136), יחזקיה (140), חזקיה (130).

315 Some translations give this as the Red (Reed) Sea.

316 סיעא (141).

317 Hazazon Tamar (878, 1528; 884, 1534).

148	אהיה יה יהוה אלהימ	*Eheieh Yah* YHVH *Elohim* –A name of God
	אמאימונ	*Amaimon* –Demon King of Earth and the North; Demon King of the East and Air (Goetia)
	אנסואל	*Ansuel* –Angel of 11th astrological house
	בני אלהימ	*Beni Elohim* –Sons of the Gods; Angelic Choir assoc. w/*Hod*
	ויהי לה לבנ	*VaYehiy Lah Leven* –"And he became to her as a son" (Ex. 2:10)
	זולל וסובא	*Zolel VeSove'* –"Glutton and drunkard" (Deut. 21:20)[318]
	חלקי	*Chelqay* –Helkai, head of a priestly family
		Chelqiy –Helkite
	חמיצ	*Chamiyts* –Seasoned
	חמק	*Chameq* –To withdraw, turn around, turn away
	חספ	*Chasef* –Clay, potsherd
	חפני	*Chofniy* –Hophni, unholy son of Eli slain at the battle of Aphek (1 Sam. 1:3; 2:22-24, 34)
	חצנ	*Chetsen* –Bosom, bosom of a garment
		Chotsen –Bosom, lap
	לקחי	*Liqchiy* –Likhi, descendant of Benjamin
	מאזנימ	*Moznaim* –Scales; (i.e. Libra)
	מחנימ	*Machanayim* –Mahanaim, place on the boundary between Reuben and Gad
	מחק	*Machaq* –To utterly destroy, annihilate (Judg. 5:26)
	מקח	*Miqqach* –Taking, acceptance, receiving (of a bribe)
	נחצ	*Nachats* –To urge
	נצח	*Natsach* –To excel, be bright, be preeminent, be perpetual, be overseer, be enduring
		Netzach –To excel, distinguish oneself (Aramaic); juice (of grapes); eminence, perpetuity, strength, victory, enduring, everlastingness, eternity. Seventh *Sefira* (occurs 43 times in the *Tanakh*)
	סחפ	*Sachaf* –To prostrate, beat down
	ספח	*Safach* –To join, attach to, join together; to cause a scab upon, smite with scab
	פסגה	*Pisgah* –Pisgah, mountain ranges from which Moses viewed the Promised Land
	פסח	*Paseach* –Paseah, descendant of Judah through Caleb; one whose family returned from Exile; father of Jehoiada, who helped repair the wall; Passover
	צנח	*Tzanach* –To go down, descend
	קמח	*Qemach* –Flour, meal, meal flour
149	אצבונ	*'Etzbown* –Ezbon, son of Gad (see also Ozni, אצבן)[319]; descendant of Benjamin
	יחצאלי	*Yachtze'eliy* –Jahzeelites
	יחציאל	*Yachtziy'el* –Jahziel, son of Naphtali listed three times (this name used only in Num. 26:48 – see also

[318] A.C., 777 – Deut. 21:20 – actual spelling is זולל וסבא, giving a total gematria of 142.

[319] אצבן (143, 793), Ozni (68).

יחצאל)[320]

מקדה *Maqqedah* –Makkedah, city of the Canaanites located on the Plain of Judah – modern Mughar

קדמה *Qadmah* –Antiquity, former state; former time or situation (Aramaic)
Qedemah –Kedemah, son of Ishmael, head of a clan
Qidmah –Forward; east, eastward

קמט *Qamat* –To seize
–Prime number

150 אבעבעה *Aba'bu'ah* –Blisters, boils

אלפלט *Elifelet* –Eliphalet, Eliphelet, or Elpalet, David's youngest son; one of David's mighty warriors; a Benjamite descendant of Jonathan; a leader of the clan of Donikam; one of the line of Hashum

יעדו *Ya'dow* –Iddo, prophet who wrote about the kings of Israel (see also יעדי)[321]

יסף *Yasaf* –To add, increase, do again
Yesaf –To add (Aramaic)

יעכן *Ya'kan* –Jachan, descendant of Gad

יעלם *Ya'lam* –Jaalam, chief of Edom (Gen. 36:5, 14, 18; 1 Chr. 1:35)

כנף *Kanaf* –To be put or thrust in or into a corner, be hidden from view, be cornered, be thrust aside; wing, extremity, edge, winged, border, corner, shirt

כעס *Ka'as* –To be angry, be vexed, be indignant, be wroth, be grieved, provoke to anger and wrath; anger, vexation, provocation, grief

כפן *Kafan* –To hunger, be hungry, hungrily desire; to twist, bend; hunger, famine, painful hunger

מהפכה *Mahpekah* –Overthrow, destruction (always of Sodom & Gomorrah)[322]

מוקד *Mowqed* –A burning mass, burning, hearth

מכמן *Mikman* –Hidden stores, hidden treasure

מעיל *Me'iyl* –Robe

מנין *Minyan* –Number (Aramaic)

מפל *Mappal* –Refuse, hanging parts

נעל *Na'al* –To bar, lock, bolt; to furnish with sandals, to shoe; sandal, shoe

נפכ *Nofek* –Carbuncle or emerald (precious stone in the High Priest's ephod – represents the tribe Judah) (perhaps an emerald, turquoise, or ruby); jewels imported from Tyre

נק *Naq* –200th Gate of the 231 Gates

סמן *Saman* –To mark off

ספי *Sippay* –Sippai, descendant of Rapha the giant (see also

---

320 יחצאל (139).

321 יעדי (94).

322 Sodom (104, 664), Gomorrah (315), "Sodom and Gomorrah" (425, 985).

		Saph)[323]
	סצ	*Satz* –206th Gate of the 231 Gates
	עילמ	*'Eylam* –Elam, son of Shem; descendant of Benjamin; descendant of Korah; leader of the people who sealed the new covenant with God after the Exile; priest of Nehemiah's time who helped to cleanse Jerusalem; three whose descendants returned from the Exile
	עכס	*'akas* –To shake bangles, rattle, tinkle
		'ekes –Anklet, bangle
	עלמי	*'Almiy* –Elamite
	עממ	*'amam* –To darken, dim, grow dark
		Amem –52nd name of *Shem HaMeforash* (4 Aries)
	עפ	*'Ap* –211th Gate of the 231 Gates
	פליל	*Paliyl* –Judge, assessment, estimate
	צלל	*Tzalal* –To sink, be submerged; tingle, quiver; to be or become or grow dark
		Tzelel –Shadow, shade
	קדומ	*Qaduwm* –Ancient (meaning dubious – Judg. 5:21)
	קימ	*Qayam* –Secure, enduring (Aramaic)
		Qeyam –Decree, stature (Aramaic)
		Qiym –Adversary
	קליטא	*Qeliyta'* –Kelita, priest who explained the Law when it was read by Ezra; one of those who sealed the covenant – possibly the same as the first Kelita (see also Kelaiah)[324]
	קנ	*Qen* –Nest
151	אליעמ	*Eliyam* –Eliam, Bathsheba's father; a Gilonite warrior of David
	אליפל	*Elifal* –Eliphal, one of David's mighty warriors
	אנק	*'anaq* –To cry, groan
	אסיפ	*'asiyf* –In gathering, harvest
	אפע	*'efa* –Worthless, of nought
	ויקהל	*VaYakhel* –And he gathered together; a Torah portion
	חפזונ	*Chippazown* –Hurriedly, in haste, trepidation, hurried flight
	יסמכיהו	*Yismakyahuw* –Ismachiah, an overseer under King Hezekiah
	לא עמי	*Lo' 'Ammiy* –Lo-Ammi, symbolic name of Hosea's son (Hos. 1:9)[325]
	מאלפ	*Malphas* –Goetic demon #39
	מאפל	*Ma'afel* –Darkness
	מקוה	*Miqvah* –Reservoir; collection, collected mass
		Miqveh –Hope; collection, collected mass
	נאק	*Na'aq* –To groan
	נוצה	*Nowtsah* –Plumage, feathers

[323] Saph (140, 860).
[324] Kelaiah (145).
[325] Meaning "Not my people."

	נקא	*Neqe'* –Clean, pure
	סנבלט	*Sanballat* –Sanballat, leading opponent of the Jews at the time they were rebuilding the walls of Jerusalem (Neh. 2:10; 3:33, 7; 6:1-14)
	עועה	*'av'eh* –Distorting, perverting, warping
	עמיאל	*'Ammiy'el* –Ammiel, one of those sent by Moses to spy out the Promised Land; father of Machir, David's friend; father of Bathsheba; son of Obed-edom who served as a gatekeeper of the Tabernacle in the time of David
	עפא	*'ofe'* –Branch, foliage
	קוליה	*Qowlayah* –Kolaiah, descendant of Benjamin; father of the false prophet Ahab
	קומה	*Qowmah* –Height
	קנא	*Qana'* –To envy, be jealous
		Qanna' –Jealous (only of God)
		Qena' –To acquire, buy, purchase (Aramaic)
	–Prime number	
152	**אמציהו**	*Amatziah* –Amaziah, 8th King of Judah; Levite descended from Merari; idolatrous priest of Bethel; father of Joshah
	בנימנ	*Benjamin* –Benjamin, youngest son of Jacob and progenitor of a tribe of Judah (assoc. w/Sagittarius); descendant of Benjamin (1 Chr. 7:10); descendant of Harim; one who helped to repair the wall of Jerusalem; one who helped to dedicate the wall of Jerusalem
	יבלעמ	*Yible'am* –Ibleam, city of the tribe of Manasseh (see also Bileam)[326]
	נקב	*Naqab* –To pierce, perforate, bore, appoint; to curse, blaspheme
		Neqeb –Groove, socket, hole, cavity, settings; Nekeb, town on the boundary of the territory of Naphtali (see also Adami)[327]
	נציב	*Netsiyb* –Set over, something placed, pillar, prefect, garrison, post; Nezib, city in the lowlands of Judah
	צבייմ	*Tzebiyiym* –Zeboim, one of the five cities of the Plain (this spelling used only in Gen. 14:2, 9 – see also צבאים, צבים)[328]; Zebaim, home of one whose descendants returned from the Exile
153	**אביספ**	*'Ebyasaf* –Ebiasaph, a Levite
	בני האלהימ	*Beney HaElohim* –"Sons of God"
	בצלאל	*Betzalel* – Bezaleel, son of Uri and grandson of Hur; a skilled Judahite artisan in all works of metal, wood, and stone and one of the architects of the

[326] Bileam (142, 702).
[327] Adami (55).
[328] צבאים (143, 703), צבים (142, 702).

Tabernacle; an Israelite, one of the sons of Pahath-Moab, in the time of Ezra who had taken a strange wife

געפ — *Gaap* –Goetic demon #33

ה־פסש — *HaPesash* –The Passover

חדקיאל — *Chedeqiel* –"Thorn of God," Angel of Libra

חלקיה — *Chilqiyah* –Hilkiah, Levite who kept the children of the temple officials; father of Gemariah; cheif of priests who returned from captivity and his later descendants; one who stood with Ezra at the reading of the Law (see also חלקיהו – commonly translated Hilkiah, but another group of persons)[329]

מבוקה — *Mebuwqah* –Emptiness, void (Nah. 2:11)

מקחה — *Maqqachah* –Ware

עדעדה — *'Ad'adah* –Adadah, town in the southern district of Judah

פגע — *Paga'* –To encounter, meet, reach, entreat, make intercession

Pega' –Occurrence, happening, chance

צחנה — *Tzachanah* –Stench, foul odor

–Mystic number of 17th Path (*Binah-Tiferet*; ז; Gemini)

–The number of fishes caught by the disciples when Jesus appeared to them after the Resurrection (John 21:11)

154 אביאספ — *Abeawsaf* –Son of Korah

דלענ — *Dil'an* –Dilean, city in the lowlands of Judah, possible the same as Tell en-Najileh

חמוק — *Chammuwq* –Curve, curving

לעדנ — *La'dan* –Laadan, descendant of Ephraim; Levite from the family of Gershon (see also Libni)[330]

מחסומ — *Machsown* –Muzzle

מעמד — *Ma'amad* –Attendance, office, function, service

Mo'omad –Foothold, standing ground

נטיפה — *Netiyfah* –Drop (pendant, ornament – Judg. 8:26; Isa. 3:19)

נקד — *Naqod* –Speckled, marked with points (of sheep and goats)

Niqqud –Crumbled things, thing easily crumbled, crumbs

Noqed –Sheep-raiser, sheep-dealer, sheep-tender

עדלמי — *'Adullamiy* –Adullamite

עדפ — *'adaf* –To remain over, be in excess

פדע — *Pada'* –To deliver (meaning uncertain – Job 33:24)

צידנ — *Tziydon* –Zidon, ancient city of Canaan (this spelling used only in Gen. 10:15 – see also צידון)[331]

קדימ — *Qadiym* –East, east wind

קדמי — *Qodmay* –Former, first (Aramaic)

---

[329] חלקיהו (159).

[330] Libni (92).

[331] צידון (160, 810).

155 יהועדינ *Yehow'addiyn* –Jehoaddan, mother of King Amaziah and wife of King Joash (this spelling used only in 2 Kings 14:2 - see also יהועדן)[332]

ילקוט *Yalquwt* –Wallet, purse, pouch, bag

יסיסיה *Yasyasyah* –Angel of 2d Capricorn

לענה *La'anah* –Wormwood, hemlock

מוקדה *Mowqedah* –Hearth

מפלה *Mappalah* –A ruin

נהק *Nahaq* –To bray, cry, cry out

נקה *Naqah* –To be empty, be clear, be pure, be free, be innocent, be desolate, be cut off

סנהמ *Sanahem* –Lord of Triplicity by Day for Leo

עכסה *'Aksah* –Achsah, only daughter of Caleb, who married her cousin Othniel

עליליה *'aliyliyah* –Deed

עלמיה *Elemiah* –Angel of 4q Leo & night angel 6 Wands

פלילה *Peliylah* –Office of judge or umpire; judgment, decision

פלליה *Pelalyah* –Pelaliah, priest whose grandson dwelled in Jerusalem after the Exile

פעה *Pa'ah* –To groan, cry out, scream

קימה *Qiymah* –Rising up

קנה *Qanah* –To get, acquire, create, buy, possess; Kanah, stream that divided the territories of Ephraim and Manasseh; city in Asher not far from Zidon

Qaneh –Reed, stalk, bone, balances

156 אהל מועד *'ohel Muwa'yd* –"Tent of Meetings"

אנקה *'anaqah* –Crying, groaning, lamentation; an unclean animal, ferret, shrewmouse, gecko (perhaps extinct animal, exact meaning unknown – Lev. 11:30)

אפעה *'ef'eh* –A viper, snake

באבאלענ *Babalon* –An important figure in the mysticism of A.C.

וכל חכמ לב *vi-Kal Chakam Laiv* –"And all skillful" (Ex. 31:6)

ופסי *Vofsi* –Vophsi, descendant of Naphtali, father of Nahbi the spy

יוספ *Yosef* –Joseph, son of Jacob and Rachel; father of one of the spies sent into Canaan; son of Asaph; one who married a foreign wife during the exile; priest of the family of Shebaniah

יחזקאל *Yechzeqel* –Ezekiel, the prophet of a priestly family carried captive to Babylon and the author of the book bearing his name; Jehezekel, priest with sanctuary duty (1 Chr. 24:16)

יקומ *Yaquwm* –Living substance, that which stands or exists, existence

כמוצ *Kamotz* –Angel of 1d Scorpio

---

332 יהועדן (145, 795).

ממוכנ or מומכנ — *Memuwkan* –Memucan, a Persian prince (Esth. 1:14-15, 17-21 – the second spelling used only in Esth. 1:16)
מנוס — *Manows* –Flight, refuge, place of refuge
מפלאה — *Mifla'ah* –Wondrous work
נאקה — *Ne'aqah* –Groan, groaning
נוק — *Nuwq* –To suckle, nurse
עופ — *'owf* –Flying creatures, fowl, insects, birds; fowl (Aramaic)
'uwf –To fly about, fly away; to cover, be dark; gloom
עילומ — *'eylowm* –Forever, ever, everlasting, evermore, perpetual, old, ancient, world
עלונ — *'Alvan* –Alvan, oldest son of Shobal and descendant of Seir (this spelling used only in Gen. 36:23 – see also Aliah)[333]
פעו — *Pa'uw* –Pau, a city of Edom, that of King Hadar (this spelling used only in Gen. 36:39 – see also פעי)[334]
ציונ — *Tzion* –Zion, one of the hills on which Jerusalem stood[335]
Tziyown –Dryness, parched land or ground
Tziyuwn –Signpost, monument, market
צלול — *Tzeluwl* –Cake, round loaf, round, rolling
קונ — *Quwn* –To chant a dirge, wait, lament
קנאה — *Qin'ah* –Ardor, zeal, jealousy
קנו — *Qannow* –Jealous
–The number of children of Magbish who returned from exile (Ezra 2:30)

157 אמינונ — *'Amnown* –Amnon, son of David
ויאספ — *VaYe'asef* –And he was gathered (Gen. 25:8; 49:33)
זנק — *Zanaq* –To leap, spring
זעפ — *Za'af* –To fret, be sad, be wroth, be vexed, be enraged, be out of humor; rage, raging, storming, indignation
Za'ef –Angry, raging, out of humor, vexed
מופלא — *Mopla* –Wonderful, admirable; hidden, mystical
מזיק — *Mazziq* –Demon; injurer
מחנה־דנ — *Machaneh-Dan* –Mahaneh-Dan, campsite between Zorah and Eshtaol (Judg. 18:12)
נזק — *Nezaq* –To suffer injury
Nezeq –Injury, damage
נקבה — *Neqebah* –Female
ענואל — *Anevel* –Angel of 3q Gemini & day angel 9 Swords
קנז — *Qenaz* –Kenaz, a Duke of Edom (Gen. 36:42; 1 Chr. 1:53 – assoc. w/*Netzach*); fourth son of Eliphaz; father of Othniel the judge; grandson of Caleb

–Prime number

---

333 Aliah (115).

334 פעי (160).

335 Zion became applied to the Temple and the whole of Jerusalem and its people as a community whose destiny depends on God.

158 אזקימ *Aziqqiym* –Chains, manacles
חנק *Chanaq* –To strangle, strangle oneself
מחלפ *Machalaf* –Knife
מנגינה *Mangiynah* –Mocking or derisive song
מפלגה *Miflaggah* –Division (of priests for service)
נחמני *Nachamaniy* –Nahamani, one who returned with Zerubbabel
נצחי *Nitzchi* –Eternal, perpetual, enduring
ספיח *Safiyach* –Outpouring; growth from spilled kernels, after-growth, volunteer plants

159 אחיקמ *'Achiyqam* –Ahikam, officer in Josiah's court
חלקיהו *Chilqiyahuw* –Hilkiah, gatekeeper of the tabernacle (1 Chr. 26:11); master of the household of King Hezekiah (2 Kings 18:18, 26; Is. 22:20; 36:3); High Priest and the discoverer of the Book of the Law in the days of Josiah (2 Kings 22:4, 8, 14; 23:4); priest of Anathoth and father of Jeremiah (see also חלקיה – commonly translated Hilkiah, but another group of persons)[336]
מטעמ *Mat'am* –Tasty or savory food, delectable food, dainties
מפלט *Miflat* –Escape, place of escape
נקדה *Nequddah* –Point, drop (of silver)
נקט *Naqat* –To loathe, be grieved, feel a loathing
עגלונ *'Eglown* –Eglon, king of Moab who oppressed Israel in the days of the judges
עטפ *'ataf* –To turn aside; to envelop oneself; to be feeble, be faint, grow weak
קטנ *Qatan* –Young, small, insignificant, unimportant
Qaton –To be small, be insignificant
Qoten –Little finger

160 אליפלט *Eliyfelet* –Eliphalet, Eliphelet, or Elpalet, David's youngest son; one of David's mighty warriors; a Benjamite descendant of Jonathan; a leader of the clan of Donikam; one of the line of Hashum
בנ־בננ *Ben-Chanan* –Son of Hanan
הקמיה *Haqmiah* –Angel of 4q Libra & night angel 3 Swords
ינק *Yanaq* –To suckle, nurse, suck
יעפ *Ya'af* –To be or grow weary, be fatigued
Ya'ef –Faint, weary, fatigued
Ye'af –Weariness, fatigue, faintness
יפע *Yafa'* –To shine, shine forth or out
יקימ *Yaqiym* –Jakim, descendant of Benjamin; head of a priestly family descended from Aaron
כספ *Kasaf* –To long for, yearn for, long after
Kesaf –Silver (Aramaic)
Kesef –Silver (the metal of Luna), money

---

336 חלקיה (153).

מכמס	*Mikmas* –Michmas, town of Benjamin (this spelling used only in Ezra 2:27; Neh. 7:31 – see also מכמש)[337]
מלצ	*Malats* –To be smooth, be slippery
ממסכ	*Mamsak* –Mixed drink, mixed wine, drink-offering
מנע	*Mana'* –To withhold, hold back, keep back, refrain, deny, keep restrain, hinder
מסס	*Masas* –To dissolve, melt
מענ	*Ma'an* –Purpose, intent
נינטיאל	*Niantiel* –Guardian of the 24th Tunnel of Set
נעמ	*Na'am* –Naam, son of Caleb
	Na'em –To be pleasant, be beautiful, be sweet, be delightful, be lovely
	No'am –Kindness, pleasantness, delightfulness, beauty, favor; one of two staffs named by Zechariah (Zech. 11:7)
נפל	*Nafal* –To fall, lie, be cast down, fail
	Naphula –Goetic demon #60 (Aurum Solis spelling)
	Nefal –To fall (Aramaic)
	Nefel –Untimely birth, abortion, miscarriage
נקי	*Naqiy* –Clean, free from, exempt, clean, innocent
סלע	*Sela'* –Crag, cliff, rock; Sela, capital of Edom; rock formation which dominates the city of Petra (Judg. 1:36) – modern Ummel-Bizarah
סק	*Saq* –207th Gate of the 231 Gates
עיפ	*'ayef* –To be faint, be weary; faint, exhausted, weary
עלינ	*'Alyan* –Alian, oldest son of Shobal and descendant of Seir (this spelling used only in 1 Chr. 1:40 – see also Alvan)[338]
עלס	*'alas* –To rejoice
ענמ	*'Anem* –Anem, Levitical city of the tribe of Issachar (see also En-Gannim)[339]
עפי	*'ofiy* –Leafage, foliage (Aramaic)
עצ	*'etz* –Tree, wood, timber, stock, plant, stalk, stick, gallows; 212th Gate of the 231 Gates
פלטיאל	*Paltiy'el* –Paltiel, Prince of Issachar; man who married David's wife (see also פלטי)[340]
פלילי	*Peliyliy* –For a judge, calling for judgment, judicial, assessable, criminal
פסכ	*Pasak* –Pasach, descendant of Asher
פעי	*Pa'iy* –Pai, a city of Edom, that of King Hadar (this spelling used only in 1 Chr. 1:50 – see also פעו)[341]
צידונ	*Tziydown* –Zidon, eldest son of Canaan, son of Ham; Zidon, ancient city of Canaan (this spelling used

337 מכמש (400).
338 Alvan (156, 806).
339 En-Gannim (233, 1443).
340 פלטי (129).
341 פעו (156).

only in Josh. 11:8 – see also צידן)[342]

צליל — *Tzelil* –Ring; sound, tone

צלמ — *Tzelem* –Image, idol; the astral body in some Kabbalistic texts (Gen. 1:27; 9:6; Num. 14:9; 33:52; 1 Sam. 6:5, 11; 2 Kings 11:18; 2 Chr. 23:17; Ps. 39:7; 73:20; Ezek. 7:20; 16:17; 23:14; Dan. 2:31, 32, 34, 35; 3:1-3; 5, 7, 10, 12, 14, 15, 18, 19; Amos 5:26)[343]

קיימ — *Qayyam* –Existing, stable

קינ — *Qayin* –Spear

Qayin –Cain, eldest son of Adam who killed his brother Abel (see also Tubal-cain)[344]; town in the hill country of Judah

קלל — *Qalal* –To be slight, be swift; burnished, polished

161 אדמ עילאה — *Adam Illah* –The heavenly man

אנסנ — A permutation of יהוה by *Aiq Bekar*[345]

אפפ — *'afaf* –To surround, encompass

העלנו — *He'elanu* –Brought us up

יהוספ — *Yehowsef* –Joseph, son of Jacob and Rachel (this name is only used in Ps. 81:6 – see also יוסף)[346]

כי עבדי המ — *Ki 'avadai Haim* –"For they are My servants" (Lev. 25:42)

מנוסה — *Menowsah* –Flight, retreat

נעיאל — *Ne'iy'el* –Neiel, landmark boundary of Asher

נקודא — *Neqowda'* –Nekoda, head of a family of Nethinim (Ezra 2:48; Neh. 7:50); the head of a family without geneaology after the Exile (Ezra 2:60; Neh. 7:62)

פועה — *Puw'ah* –Puah, one of two midwives whom Pharaoh ordered to kill Hebrew males at their birth (Ex. 1:15)

162 אליפלהו — *Eliyfelehuw* –Eliphal, a Levite gate-keeper and musician for David

בנימינ — *Binyamiyn* –Benjamin, the youngest son of Jacob; descendant of Benjamin (1 Chr. 7:10); descendant of Harim; one who helped repair the wall at Jerusalem; one who helped dedicate the wall of Jerusalem

בצע — *Batsa'* –To cut off, break off, gain by unrighteous violence, get, finish, be covetous, be greedy

Betsa' –Profit, unjust gain, gain (profit) acquired by violence

גלאסלבול — *Glasya Labolas* –Goetic demon #25

---

[342] צידן (154, 804).

[343] See Gershom Scholem's "The Concept of the Astral Body," in On the Mystical Shape of the Godhead, pp. 251-273. Also refer to R. Aryeh Kaplan's Meditation and the Bible.

[344] Tubal-cain (598, 1248).

[345] See Introduction.

[346] יוסף (156, 876).

זקנה *Ziqnah* –Old age

סוסול *Sosul* –Angel of 8th astrological house

עצב *'atsab* –To hurt, pain, grieve, displease, vex, wrest; to shape, fashion, make, form, stretch into shape; to worship; to pain, grieve (Aramaic); idol, image

'atseb –Laborer, toiler, labor

'etseb –Pain, hurt, toil, sorrow, labor, hardship; vessel, creation, object; idol

'otseb –Pain, sorrow; idol

צבע *Tzeva* –Color

163 אצבע *'etsba* –Finger, toe; finger, toe (Aramaic)

מחלפה *Machlafah* –Braid, lock, plait

עולמ הזה *'olam Hazeh* –This world

–Prime number

164 הקטנ *Haqatan* –Hakkatan, father of Johanan, who returned with Ezra

חיצונ *Chiytsown* –Outer, external, outward

מעדנ *Ma'adan* –Dainty (of food), delight

מנדע *Manda'* –Knowledge, power of knowing

צידני *Tziydoniy* –Sidonian

צעד *Tzawad* –To step, march, stride, pace, step

165 הכספ *HaKasaf* –The money

הנפל *HaNofal* –The one who falls (Deut. 22:8)

הסלע *HaSela'* –The rock

העצ *Ha'Atz* –The gallows

חבצניה *Chabatstsanyah* –Habazaniah, grandfather of Jaazaniah, the founder of a Jewish sect (Jer. 35:3)

חזקימ *Chazokim* –Strength, energy

יפעה *Yif'ah* –Splendor, brightness, shining (Ezek. 28:7; 28:17)

יקמיה *Yeqamyah* –Jekamiah, descendant of Judah; son of King Jeconiah

מענה *Ma'aneh* –Answer, response; place for task; plowing ground, place for task

מצלה *Metsillah* –Bell

Metsullah –Ravine, basin, hollow

נעילה *Neilah* –Closing, locking; the final prayer recited on *Yom Kippur*

נעמה *Na'amah* –Naamah, daughter of Lamech and Zillah; wife of Solomon and mother of Rehoboam; town in the south-western lowlands of Judah; a queen of demons; archdemon corr. to *Malkut*

נקודה *Nekudah* –Point

עממיה *Amamiah* –Angel of 4q Aries & night angel 3 Wands

עיפה *'eyfah* –Darkness; Ephah, concubine of Caleb; descendant of Judah; grandson of Abraham

עצה *'atsah* –To shut

'atseh –Spine, backbone, sacrum

'etsah –Trees, wood; counsel, advice, purpose

פליליה *Peliyliyah* –The giving a decision, pronouncement of judgment, reasoning

צעה *Tza'ah* –To stoop, bend, incline

קינה *Qiynah* –Lamentation, dirge, elegy; Kinah, city on the extreme southern boundary of Judah

קללה *Qelalah* –Curse, vilification, execration

166 יונק *Yowneq* –Sucker, suckling, young plant

יוקימ *Yowqiym* –Jokim, descendant of Judah

כסלונ *Kesalown* –Chesalon, town near Mount Jearim of Judah

Kislown –Chislon, prince of the tribe of Benjamin and father of Elidad

מאפליה *Ma'feleyah* –Deep darkness, darkness

מסלול *Masluwl* –Highway

מעונ *Maon* –Dwelling, habitation, refuge, residence; Maon, son of Shammai or a city he founded (1 Chr. 2:45); Maon, a mountain city of Judah; wilderness east of the city, Maon, and west of the Dead Sea where David and his men hid from King Saul; Maon, the Fifth Heaven, corr. to *Giburah*

נפול *Naphula* –Goetic demon #60

עבד מלכ *'Ebed Melek* –Ebed-Melech, Ethiopian eunuch who served Zedekiah and rescued Jeremiah

עופי *'Owfay* –Ephai, one whose children were left in Judah during the Exile

עוצ *'uwts* –To counsel, plan; Uz, eldest son of Aram (Gen. 10:23); son of Shem[347]; son of Dishon, son of Seir; son of Nahor by Milcah; Uz, the country where Job lived; kingdom not far from Edom, perhaps the same as the latter

עליונ *'elyown* (often *Elyon*) –High, upper; Highest, Most High (of God); the Most High (of God – Aramaic); a name of God and title of *Keter*

עמונ *'Ammown* –Ammon, son of Lot (see also Ben-ammi)[348]; land settled by the Ammonites located north and east of Moab

167 המול לו כל *He-Mohl Lo Kal* –Every circumcised male

פנואל *Penuw'el* –Penuel, chief or father of Gedar; Penuel, encampment of the Hebrews east of Jordan (see also פניאל)[349]

קנזי *Qenizziy* –Kenezite

–Prime number

168 כסלחימ *Kasluchiym* –Casluhim, son of Mizraim, but possibly a

---

[347] The Septuagint makes this Uz identical with the first Uz, naming Aram as his father. It is also possible the Hebrew was abbreviated here.

[348] Ben-ammi (172, 822).

[349] פניאל (171).

people related to the Egyptians who were ancestors of the Philistines

חפפ *Chapaf*–To cover, protect
Chofaf–To cover, enclose, shelter, shield, surround
פלחנ *Polchan* –Service, worship (Aramaic)
צבוע *Tzabuwa'* –Colored, variegated, speckled
צבע *Tzeba'* –To dip, wet (something) (Aramaic)

169 טפפ *Tafaf*–To skip, trip, take quick little steps
יקטנ *Yoqtan* –Joktan, son of Eber of Shem's line (Gen. 10:25-26; 1 Chr. 1:19-20, 23)[350]
מעדנה *Ma'adannah* –Bonds, bands
צעדה *Tzehadah* –Marching; armlet, anklet, stepping chains

170 אצעדה *'ets'adah* –Armlet, bracelet, ankle chain
דלפונ *Dalfown* –Dalphon, son of Haman who was an advisor to King Ahasuerus
ימנע *Yimna'* –Imna, descendant of Asher (this spelling used only in 1 Chr. 7:35 – see also ימנה)[351]
יעצ *Ya'atz* –To advise, consult, give counsel
יפיע *Yafiya'* –Japhia, Amorite king of Lachish defeated by Joshua; son of David; Japhia, boundary town of Zebulun, southwest of Nazareth
יצע *Yatza'* –To spread out, make a bed
כסילימ *Kesilim* –Fools; the constellation Orion
כפיס *Kafiys* –Rafter, girder (meaning dubious – Hab. 2:11)
לפני *Lihpnay* –Before; to the face of
מועדימ *Moadim* –Seasons
מכנס *Miknas* –Underwear, drawers, trousers
מלק *Malaq* –To nip off (head of a bird)
מסכנ *Misken* –Poor, poor man
מסע *Masa'* –A pulling up (of stakes), breaking camp, setting out, journey; quarry, quarrying, breaking out (of stones); missile, dart
מענ *Ma'yan* –Spring
מעלל *Ma'alal* –Deed, practice
מפימ *Muppiym* –Muppim, son of Benjamin (see also Shuppim, Shupham, and Shephuphan)[352]
מצהלה *Matsalah* –Neighing
מקל *Maqqel* –Wands, rod, staff
ניסנ *Nisan* –The 7th month of the Jewish calendar – it is associated with Aries and the tribe Naphtali
נסס *Nasas* –To be sick; to be lifted up (meaning dubious – Zech. 9:16)
נעימ *Na'iym* –Pleasant, delightful, sweet, lovely, agreeable; singing, sweetly sounding, musical

---

350 The reference here may be to an Arabian tribe from whom many other Arabian groups sprang.
351 ימנה (105).
352 Shuppim (430, 990), Shupham (506, 1066), Shephuphan (516, 1166).

	נעמי	*Na'amiy* –Naamites
		No'omiy –Naomi, mother-in-law to Ruth
	נפיל	*Nefiyl* –Giants, one of the Nefilim (Gen. 6:4; Num. 13:33)
	נצל	*Natsal* –To snatch away, deliver, rescue, save, strip, plunder
		Netsal –To rescue, extricate, deliver
	סינים	*Siyniym* –Sinim, land from which the scattered Israelites were again to be gathered (Is. 49:12)[353]
	סלפ	*Salaf* –To twist, pervert, distort, overturn, ruin
		Selef –Crookedness, perverseness, crooked dealing
	ססמי	*Sismay* –Sisamai, descendant of Jerahmeel, son of Perez
	ספל	*Sefel* –Bowl, basin, cup
	עלע	*'ala'* –To suck up (meaning uncertain – Job 39:30); rib (Aramaic)
	עמס	*'amas* –To load, carry, carry a load
	ענימ	*'Aniym* –Anim, town in the hills of Judah
	ענן	*'anan* –To make appear, produce, bring; to practice soothsaying, conjure; cloud (Aramaic); cloud, cloudy, cloud-mass (of theophanic cloud); Anan, one who sealed the new covenant with God after the Exile
	עק	*'Aq* –213th Gate of the 231 Gates
	פלני	*Peloniy* –A certain one
	פלס	*Palas* –To weigh, make level, balance
	פסל	*Pasal* –To cut, hew, hew into shape
		Pesel –Idol, image
	פצ	*Patz* –217th Gate of the 231 Gates
	קיני	*Qeyniy* –Kenite
	קמל	*Qamal* –To be decayed, be withered
171	אבי עלבונ	*'Abiy 'albown* –"Father of strength;" Abi Albon, an Arbathite who served as one of David's thirty mighty men (this spelling used only in 2 Sam. 23:31 – see also Abiel)[354]
	אניעמ	*'Aniy'am* –Aniam, descendant of Manasseh
	יהוקימ	*Yehoiaqim* –Jehoiakim, 17th King of Judah
	יוספיה	*Yowsifyah* –Josiphiah, father of one who returned from exile
	כספיא	*Kasifya'* –Casiphia, unidentified place in Babylon to which Ezra sent for ministers of the house of God (Ezra 8:17)
	מאמצ	*Ma'amats* –Strength, force, power
	מעונה	*Me'ownah* –Dwelling, habitation, refuge
	מצולה	*Metsowlah* –Straitness, straits, distress, stress, anguish
	פלאינ	*Polayan* –Lord of Triplicity by Night for Aquarius

[353] Probably a reference to Syene on the southern Egyptian frontier wher there was a Jewish garrison. Earlier scholars believed that China was indicated, but that view has been discredited.

[354] Abiel (44).

	פניאל	*Peniy'el* –Penuel, descendant of Benjamin; Penuel, encampment of the Hebrews east of Jordan (this spelling used only in Gen. 32:30 – see also (פנואל)[355]
	–Mystic number of 18th Path (*Binah-Giburah*; ח; Cancer)	
172	בן־ימיני	*Ben-Yaminiy* –Benyemini, Benjamite (1 Sam. 9:21; Ps. 7:1)
	בן־עמי	*Ben-'Ammiy* –Ben-ammi, ancestor of the Ammorites, born to Lot and his daughter
	בעלים	*Ba'alis* –Baalis, king of the Ammonites after Jerusalem was taken (Jer. 40:14)
	בקע	*Baqa'* –To split, cleave, break open, divide, break through, rip up, break up, tear *Beqa'* –Half a shekel[356]
	יעבצ	*Ya'betz* –Jabez, head of a family of Judah; Jabez, dwelling place of scribes, probably in Judah
	מקבל	*Mekubbal* –Kabbalist
	עקב	*'aqab* –To supplant, circumvent, take by the heel, follow at the heel, assail insidiously, overreach *'aqeb* –Heel, rear, footprint, hinder part, hoof, rear of a troop, footstep; overreacher, supplanter *'aqob* –Deceitful, sly, insidious; steep, hilly *'eqeb* –Consequence, as a consequence, because, consequently, as a consequence of, that, because
	צלמ דהבא	*Tzelem Dahava* –"Golden image" (Dan. 3:5, 7, 10, 12, 14, 18)
	קבע	*Qaba'* –To rob (Meaning dubious – Mal. 3:8, 9; Prov. 22:13)
	–The number of words in the Ten Commandments	
173	אבינעמ	*'Abiyno'am* –Abinoam, father of Barak
	אנכי יהוה אלהיכ	*Anoki* YHVH *Eloheka* –"I am the Lord thy God"
	בקעא	*Biq'a'* –Plain (Aramaic – n. fem.)
	מחלצה	*Machalatsah* –Robe of state
	–Prime number	
174	אדני בזק	*Adonai Bezeq* – Adoni-bezek, king of Bezek
	לספד	*Lispod* –To mourn
	מסעד	*Mis'ad* –Support, pillar
	עקד	*'aqad* –To bind, tie *'aqod* –Streaked, striped
	צפד	*Tzafad* –To draw together, contract, draw up
175	יניקה	*Yaniqah* –Young plant, twig, young shoot
	מכפלה	*Makpelah* –Machpelah, place where the burial cave of Abraham is located
	מליצה	*Meliytsah* –Satire, mocking poem, mocking song,

[355] פנואל (167).

[356] There appear to be at least three different shekels, consult a Bible dictionary.

taunting, figure, enigma

	מסכנה	*Miskenah* –Supply, storage, storage house, magazine
	מקהל	*Maqhel* –Assembly, choir
	ענגה	*'ananah* –Cloud, cloudy
	עקה	*'aqah* –Oppression, pressure
	פצה	*Patzah* –To part, open, separate, set free
	צפה	*Tzafah* –To look out or about, to spy, keep watch, observe, watch; to lay out, lay over, overlay, cover; outflow, overflow, discharge
	קדמאל	*Qedemel* –Kedemel, spirit of Venus

–Magic sum of the magic square of Venus
–The number of years that Abraham lived (Gen. 25:7)

176	יויקים	*Yowyaqiym* –Joiakim, son of Jeshua who returned from exile – not to be confused with Jehoiakim
	יעוצ	*Ye'uwtz* –Jeuz, son of Shaharaim, a descendant of Benjamin
	יצוע	*Yatzuwa'* –Couch, bed
	לצונ	*Latzown* –Scorning, bragging
	לקומ	*Laqquwm* –Lakum, one of the landmarks on the boundary of Naphtali
	מעוני	*Me'uwniy* –Mehunites
	נסיונ	*Nisyon* –Trial, temptation
	עוק	*'uwq* –To totter, cause to totter, crush (meaning dubious – Amos 2:13)
	עמוני	*'Ammowniy* –Ammonite(s)
	עמוס	*Amos* –Amos, prophet during the reigns of Uzziah and Jeroboam whose book bears his name
	עמינדב	*Amminadab* –Amminadab, son of Kohath (see also Izhar)[357]; Aaron 's father-in-law; one of the Levites who helped to bring the Ark of the Covenant from the house of Obed-edom; Prince of Judah
	פוצ	*Puwtz* –To scatter, be dispersed, be scattered; to flow, overflow; to break
	פלוני	*Pelowniy* –Pelonite
	צופ	*Tzuwf* –To flow, overflow, flood, float; honeycomb (Prov. 16:24; Ps. 19:11); Zuph, land or district where Saul searched for his father's donkeys; Zuph, brother of Samuel (this spelling used only in 1 Chr. 6:20 – see also צופי)[358]
	צפו	*Tephow* –Zepho, son of Eliphaz (this spelling used only in Gen. 36:11, 15 – see also צפי)[359]
	קוע	*Qowa'* –Koa, prince or people dwelling between Egypt and Syria – named as an enemy of Jerusalem (Ezek. 23:23)

---

[357] Izhar (305).
[358] צופי (186).
[359] צפי (180).

177	אלקומ	*Alquwm* –No, not, nor, neither (neg. adv.); band of soldiers; no rebellion, no uprising (lit.)
	בנ־הימיני	*Ben-HaYaminiy* –Benhayemini, Benjamite (Judg. 3:15; 2 Sam. 16:11; 19:17; 1 Kings 2:8)
	בקעה	*Biq'ah'* –Valley; plain, level valley
	גנ עדנ	*Gan Eden* –"Garden of Eden"
	זעק	*Za'aq* –To cry, to cry out, call, call for help; cry, outcry *Ze'iq* –To cry, cry out, call (Aramaic)
	עזק	*'azaq* –To dig about
	עקבה	*'oqbah* –Subtlety, insidiousness, craftiness
	קמואל	*Qemuw'el* –Kemuel, son of Nahor and a nephew of Abraham; prince of Ephraim
178	חפצ	*Chafets* –To delight in, take pleasure in, desire, be pleased with; to move, bend down; desiring, delighting in, having pleasure in *Chefets* –Delight, pleasure
	חצפ	*Chatsaf* –To be urgent, harsh, show insolence
	מלקח	*Melqach* –Snuffers (for lamps in Temple or Tabernacle), tongs (for altar use)
	עזקא	*'izqa'* –Signet-ring
	עקוב	*'Aqquwb* –Akkub, ancestor of a family of a family of porters; ancestor of Nethinim who returned from the Exile; porter in the Temple after the Exile; priest who helped the people understand the Law; one descendant from David mentioned in 1 Chr. 3:24
	פצח	*Patzach* –To cause to break or burst forth, break forth with, break out
	קבוע	*Qavua* –Constant, fixed
179	אחינעמ	*'Achiyno'am* –Ahinoam, wife of Saul; mother of Amnon
	מקלט	*Miqlat* –Refuge, asylum
	נטעימ	*Neta'iym* –Netaim, place in Judah where some royal potters lived
	–Prime number	
180	דיונסימ	*Dionsim* –Last seven letters of the 22-letter name of God
	זהב וכספ	*Zahav Vikesef* –"Gold and silver" (Ex. 25:3; 35:5; 1 Kings 10:22; 1 Chr. 18:10; 29:3; 2 Chr. 9:14, 21; 24:24; Est. 1:6; Ezek. 16:13; 28:4; Hab. 2:19; Zech. 14:14)
	טופפה	*Towfafah* –Bands, phylacteries, frontlets, marks
	יסגנזנ	*Yasaganotz* –Angel of 3d Taurus (according to Regardie)
	יקע	*Yaqa'* –To be disclosed, be alienated
	כפפ	*Kafaf* –To bend, bend down, bow down, be bent, be bowed
	מסעי	*Masay* –Journies
	מפני	*Mipnay* –From the presence
	נסע	*Nasa'* –To pull out, pull up, set out, journey, remove, set

forward, depart

עינן *Enan* –Enan, father of a prince of Naphtali

עלפ *'alaf* –To cover

עניג *'inyan* –Occupation, task, job

ענני *'Ananiy* –Anani, descendant of David who lived after the Exile

עפל *'afal* –To lift up, swell, be lifted up; to presume, be heedless

'ofel –Hill, mount, fort, stronghold; tumor, hemorrhoid; Ophel, hill in southeastern Jerusalem

פנימ *Paniym* –Face

פסיל *Pesiyl* –Image, idol, graven image

פעל *Pa'al* –To do, make

Po'al –Work, deed, doing

פק *Paq* –218th Gate of the 231 Gates

צמימ *Tzamiym* –Snare, trap, noose (meaning dubious – Job 5:5, 18:9 – Robber)

צנמ *Tzanam* –To dry up, harden, wither

צפי *Tzephiy* –Zephi, son of Eliphaz (this spelling used only in 1 Chr. 1:36 – see also צפו)[360]

–The number of years that Isaac lived (Gen. 35:28)

181 אליספ *Eliasaf* –Eliasaph, a Gadite chief in the wilderness census; a head of the Gershonites

אליעיני *Eliyeynay* –Elienai, son of Shimi

אלקימ *'Elokim* –The alternate name of *Elohim* used in Rabbinical texts in deference to the use of the name of God

אפק *'afaq* –To hold, be strong, restrain, hold back

'Afeq –Aphek, Aphik, city north of Zidon; town assigned to Asher but never captured; town on the plain of Sharon; town between Shunem and Jezreel

קפא *Qafa'* –To thicken, condense; congelation

–Prime number

182 אל קנא *El Qanna* –A jealous god (Ex. 20:5)

בני ימיני *Beniy Yemiyniy* –Benjamite

בקיע *Beqiya'* –Fissure, breach, cleft

יעקב *Yaaqob* –Jacob – it should be noted that י = 10, corresponding to the ten commandments; the rest of the letters add to 172, the number of words in the ten commandments

לב קמי *Lev Qamay* –An *Atbash* for Chaldea (כשדימ *Chasdim*)

מלאכ האלהימ *Malakh HaElohim* –Angel of God

עזקה *'Azeqah* –Azekah, city in the lowlands of Socoh[361]

צאצא *Tze'etza'* –Offspring, produce, issue

183 מחלקה *Machleqah* –Class, division (of priests and Levites)

---

[360] צפו (176).

[361] The kings besieging Gibeon were driven here.

184	דנ יענ	*Dan Ya'an* –Dan Jaan, place or city in northern Palestine between Gilead and Zidon, possibly Dan
	דפק	*Dafaq* –To beat, knock
	מלקוח	*Malqowach* –Booty, prey, jaw
	מספד	*Misefed* –Wailing
	עמעד	*'Am'ad* –Amad, frontier town of the tribe of Asher
	פקד	*Paqadh* –To number; to attend to, muster, number, reckon, to visit, punish, appoint, look after, care for; to inspect; musterings, expenses
	צופח	*Tzowphach* –Zophah, descendant of Asher
	קפד	*Qafad* –To gather together, harvest
185	אני לדודי ודודי לי	*Ani Leduwdo VeDuwdiy Liy* –"I am my beloved's and my beloved is mine" (Song 6:3)
	להצילכ	*Lihatzelik* –To rescue you
	מנ המימ	*Min HaMayim* –"From the waters" (Ex. 2:10)
	סלסלה	*Salsillah* –Basket
	עזבוק	*'Azbuwq* –Azbuk, father of a man named Nehemiah
	עלפה	*'ulpeh* –Wilted, fainted
	עמסיה	*'Amasyah* –Amasiah, son of Zichri and chief captain of Jehoshaphat
	ענניה	*'Ananyah* –Ananiah, grandfather of Azariah; Ananiah, town inhabited by the tribe of Benjamin after the Exile
	פיפיה	*Piyfiyah* –Tooth, edge, mouth
	פנימה	*Peniymah* –Toward the inside, within, faceward
	פננה	*Peninnah* –Peninnah, second wife of Elkanah, father of Samuel
	פעלה	*Pa'ullah* –Work, recompense, reward
	צפיה	*Tzefiyah* –Lookout post, lookout, watchtower
	קדמיאל	*Qadmiy'el* –Kadmiel, one whose descendants returned from the Exile; one who helped rebuild the Temple; Levite who led the devotions of the people
186	אלקנה	*Elkanah* –Elkanah, Samuel's father; a ruler in Jerusalem in the time of king Ahaz; one of David's mighy warriors; son of Korah; several Levites
	אפקה	*'Afeqah* –Aphekah, city of Judah
	בעלידע	*Be'elyada* –Beeliada, son of David (1 Chr. 14:7) also known as Eliada (2 Sam. 5:16; 1 Chr. 3:8)
	יהוה	YHVH by "preceding numbers addition": {(1+2+3+4+5+6+7+8+9+10 [*Yod*]) + (1+2+3+4+5 [*Heh*]) + (1+2+3+4+5+6 [Vahv]) + (1+2+3+4+5 [*Heh*]) [362]
	מוספ	*Musaf* –Additional; prayer added during Shabbat, *Rosh Chodesh,* and *Yom Tov*
	מספו	*Mispow'* –Fodder, feed

[362] See Introduction.

	מקומ	*Maqowm* –Place, standing place
	נסיוני	*Nisyoni* –Experimental, tentative
	פונן	*Puwnon* –Punon, Israelite encampment during the last portion of the wilderness wandering
	פוק	*Puwq* –To reel, totter, stumble; to bring out, furnish, promote, go out, issue
	פימונ	*Paimon* –Goetic demon #9 (Aurum Solis spelling)
	צולס	*Tzolas* –Stolas, Goetic demon #36 (Aurum Solis spelling)
	צופי	*Tzowphay* –Zophai, brother of Samuel (see also צוף)[363]
	צוצ	*Tzuwtz* –To blossom, shine, sparkle; to gaze, peep, glance, make the eyes sparkle
	צפוי	*Tzippuwy* –Plating (of metal), metal plating
	קופ	*Qof* –Back of head; 19th letter of Hebrew alphabet; ape
	קלונ	*Qalown* –Shame, disgrace, dishonor
187	אופנימ	*Ofanim* –Wheels; Angelic Choir assoc. w/*Chokmah*
	זקפ	*Zaqaf* –To raise up
		Zeqaf –To raise, lift up (Aramaic)
	יעקבה	*Ya'aqobah* –Jaakobah, descendant of Simeon
	פאימונ	*Paimon* –Goetic demon #9; Demon King of Fire and the South
	צמאונ	*Tzimma'own* –Thirsty (parched) ground
	קפז	*Qippowz* –Arrow, snake, owl (meaning dubious – Is. 34:15)
188	בוצצ	*Bowtzetz* –Bozez, a rock near Michmash
	חצי הלילה	*Chatzi HaLaylah* –Midnight
	חצצ	*Chatsats* –To divide; to shoot arrows; gravel
	כבד בכספ	*Kabad Bavasaf* –"[Abram] was rich in silver" (Gen. 13:2)
	פקח	*Paqach* –To open (the eyes)
		Peqach –Pekah, 19th King of Israel
		Piqqeach –Seeing, clear-sighted
189	דפקה	*Dofqah* –Dophkah, place in the wilderness of Sinai between the Reed Sea and Rephidim
	עטלפ	*'atallef* –Bat
	פקדה	*Pequddah* –Oversight, care, custody, mustering, visitation, store
	קפדה	*Qefadah* –Shuddering, anguish
	קתפ	*Qataf* –To pluck off or out, cut off
190	כנענ	*Kenaan* –Canaan, son of Ham and grandson of Noah; Canaan, native name of Palestine, the land given to Abraham and his descendants
	מנעל	*Man'al* –Shoe
	מנק	*Menaq* –66th name of *Shem HaMeforash* (6 Gemini)

[363] צוף (176, 896).

נצן *Nitstsan* –Blossom
נקם *Naqam* –To avenge, take vengeance, revenge, avenge oneself, be avenged, be punished; vengeance
סלק *Seliq* –To ascend, come up (Aramaic)
ספן *Safan* –To cover, cover in; wainscotted, covered with boards or panelling
Sippun –Cover, cover in, panel, wainscotting
סקל *Saqal* –To stone (to death), put to death by stoning
עלצ *'alats* –To rejoice, exult
עצל *'atsal* –To be sluggish
'atsel –Sluggish, lazy
פינן *Pinon* –A Duke of Edom (assoc. w/*Tiferet*); darkness
פיק *Piyq* –Tottering, staggering, stagger, stumble
פנימי *Peniymiy* –Inner
פנין *Panin* –Pearl; a precious stone (perhaps corals, rubies, jewels); a title of *Malkut*
פעם *Pa'am* –To thrust, impel, push, beat persistently; stroke, beat, foot, step, anvil, occurrence
פקוד *Peqowd* –Pekod, minor Aramean tribe in eastern Babylonia (Jer. 50:21)[364]
Piqquwd –Precept, statute
ציצ *Tzyitz* –Flower, bloom; feather, wing (meaning dubious); Ziz, pass that runs from the western shore of the Dead Sea north of En-Gedi to the wilderness of Judah
צלע *Tzala* –To limp, be lame
Tzela –Rib (of the Adam), side, beam; limping, stumbling; Zelah, town of Benjamin containing Kish's tomb
צנן *Tzenan* –Zenan, village in the allotment of Judah (see also Zaanan)[365]
צק *Tzaq* –222nd Gate of the 231 Gates
קלס *Qalas* –To mock, scoff
Qeles –Derision, ridicule
קמטיאל *Qemetiel* –The Crowd of Gods; *Qlippoth* of Ain
קצ *Qetz* –End
קפוד *Qippowd* –Porcupine, hedgehog
–Mystic number of 19th Path (*Hesed-Giburah*; ט; Leo)

191 אליקימ *Eliakim* –Eliakim, the son of Hilkiah, master of Hezekiah's household; Josiah's son, enthroned by Pharaoh; a priest who assisted Nehemiah; (alternate name for Jehoiakim)
אלנעמ *Elnaam* –Elnaam, the father of two of David's mighty warriors
אפיק *'afiyq* –Channel; ravine; of hollow bones (figurative)
פוקה *Puwqah* –Tottering, staggering, stumbling (of qualm of conscience)

---

[364] Literally "visited by judgment."
[365] Zaanan (191, 841).

	צאנן –Prime number	*Tza'anan* –Zaanan, town in Judah (see also Zenan)[366]
192	אליהועיני	*Elyehoweynay* –Elioenai, a korahite temple doorkeeper, son of Meshelemiah; two men with foreign wives during the exile (one a priest); a son of Neariah; a Simeonite; a Benjamite, son of Becher
	בצק	*Batseq* –To swell, become blistered; dough (unleavened)
	זלעפה	*Zal'afah* –Burning heat, raging heat (n. fem.)
	יפה־פיה	*Yefeh-fiyah* –Very beautiful
	קבצ	*Qabatz* –To gather, assemble
	קול־יהוה בכח	*Qol*-YHVH *Bakocha* –"The voice of the Lord is power" (Ps. 29:4)
	קצב	*Qatzab* –To cut off, shear *Qetzeb* –Cut, shape, extremity, form, base
193	הפכפח	*Hafakpak* –Crooked, perverted
	מספחה	*Mispachah* –Long veil, veil (as spread out)
	מפגע –Prime number	*Mifga'* –Thing hit, mark, target, object of assault
194	פגעיאל	*Pag'iy'el* –Pagiel, chief of Asher
	פקיד	*Paqiyd* –Commissioner, deputy, overseer, officer
	צדק	*Tzadaq* –To be just, be righteous *Tzedek* –Jupiter; righteousness, justice, rightness
	קדמנ	*Qadmon* –East (Ezek. 47:8)
195	חפצי בה	*Chephtziy bahh* –Hephzibah, mother of King Manasseh
	חקופא	*Chaquwfa'* –Hakupha, ancestor of a family returning from captivity
	כנענה	*Kena'anah* –Chenaanah, son of Bilhan; father of the false prophet Zedekiah
	מקנה	*Miqnah* –Purchase *Miqneh* –Cattle, livestock
	נפטונ	*Neptun* –Neptune
	נקמה	*Neqamah* –Vengeance
	עצלה	*'atslah* –Sluggishness, laziness
	ציצה	*Tziytzah* –Blossom, flower
	קלסה	*Qallasah* –Mocking, derision
	קצה	*Qatzah* –To cut off *Qatzeh* –End, extremity
196	מועפ	*Muw'af* –Gloom, darkness
	מנעול	*Man'uwl* –Bolt
	מעופ	*Ma'uwf* –Gloom
	עלמונ	*'Almown* –Almon, priestly town near the territory of Benjamin (see also Alemeth)[367]

[366] Zenan (190, 840).
[367] Alemeth (540).

עולמימ — *Olamim* –Ages; worlds

צוק — *Tzoq* –Narrowness; oppression

Tzowq –Constraint, distress, strait; pressure, distress

Tzuwq –To constrain, press, bring into straits, straiten, oppress; to pour out, melt

קוצ — *Qotz* –Thorn, thorn bush

Qowtz –Koz, ancestor of a priestly family returning from captivity (see also Hakkoz)[368]; ancestor of one who helped to repair the walls of Jerusalem

Quwtz –To spend the summer; to be greived, loathe, abhor, feel a loathing; to awake, wake up

קמונ — *Qamown* –Camon, place where Jair the Gileadite was buried

קצו — *Qetzev* –End, border, boundary

197 אל עליונ — *El Elyon* –Most high God

במקנה — *Bamiqneh* –In cattle (Gen. 13:2)

בצקה — *Batzeqah* –Swell (Deut. 8:4)

בקמיהמ — *Beqameyhem* –Their enemies (Ex. 32:25)

בקצה — *Biqetzeh* –In end, edge, uppermost parts (Gen. 23:9; Num. 11:1)

הנחבימ — *Hanitzaviym* –That stood (Gen. 45:1)

ואקצ — *va-'Aqetz* –And I abhorred (Ex. 20:23)

ויצפהו — *va-Tzafeho* –And he overlaid it (Ex. 37:2)

ונאמנימ — *ve-Ne'emaniym* –And long continuance (Deut. 28:59)

זקנמ — *Zeqanam* –Their beard (Ex. 21:5)

ימצאונ — *Imatze'on* –Shall be found (Gen. 18:29)

הבחק — *HaBatzeq* –The dough (Ex. 12:39)

לזקני — *Lezaqney* –To the elders of (Ex. 19:7)

מזקנ — *Mizqen* –For age (Gen. 48:10)

מצאוני — *Metza'oniy* –And come upon us (Deut. 31:17)

עמנואל — *'Immanuw'el* –Immanuel, Isaiah's son (Isa. 7:14; 8:8)[369]

קבצה — *Qebutzah* –Gathering, assembly (Ezek. 22:20)

–Prime number

198 מחנק — *Machanaq* –Strangling, suffocation (as a mode of death)

צחק — *Tzachaq* –To laugh, mock, play

Tzechoq –Laughter, laughing stock

קבוצ — *Qibbutz* –Assembly, companies, gathering

קצח — *Qetzach* –Cumin

199 אמונה אמונ — *'Emunah 'Amown* –"Former of Faith" (*Sefer Yetzirah*)

הצדק — *HaTzedeq* –The righteousness, the right

יהוה מסיני בא — YHVH *Mesinai Ba'* –"YHVH came from Sinai" (Deut. 33:2)

צדקה — *Tzidqah* –Right doing, doing right, righteousness

Tzedaqah –Justice, righteousness

–Prime number

---

[368] Hakkoz (201, 1011).

[369] Literally "God with us" or "with us is God."

200 יצק *Yatẓoq* –To pour, flow, cast, pour out

יקצ *Yaqatẓ* –To awake, awaken, become active

כנעני *Kena'aniy* –Canaanite

מנימינ *Minyamiyn* –Miniamin, priest in the days of Joiakim; priest who helped dedicate the wall

מנעמ *Man'am* –Delicacies, dainties

מעצ *Ma'atẓ* –Maaz, oldest son of Ram

מצע *Matstsa'* –Couch, bed

סלעמ *Sol'am* –Locust

ענפ *'anaf* –Bough, branch
'anef –Full of branches, dense

עקל *'aqal* –To bend, twist

עצמ *'atsam* –To be vast, be numerous, be mighty; to shut (the eyes), close (the eyes)
'etẓem –Bone, substance, essence; Ezem, village south of Beersheba, near the border of Edom
'otẓem –Power, bones, might

פלצ *Palatẓ* –To shudder, tremble

פסס *Pasas*–To disappear, vanish, cease, fail

פצל *Patẓal* –To peel

צדוק *Tẓadowq* –Zadok, high priest in the time of David; father of Jerusha, wife of Uzziah and mother of Jotham, both kings of Judah; son of Ahitub and father of Shallum or Meshullam; young man of valor; two who repaired the wall of Jerusalem; one who sealed the covenant with Nehemiah; scribe under Nehemiah

צלפ *Tẓalaph* –Zalaph, father of one who repaired the wall of Jerusalem

צנינ *Tẓaniyn* –Thorn, prick

קיצ *Qayitẓ* –Summer, summer-fruit

קלע *Qala'* –To sling, hurl forth; to carve
Qalla' –Slinger
Qela' –Sling, slingstones; curtain, drape, hanging

קננ *Qanan* –To make a nest

קסמ *Qasam* –To practice divination, divine
Qesem –Divination, witchcraft

ר *Resh* –20th letter of Hebrew alphabet

The Talmud states that *resh* stands for רשע, *rasha'*, meaning "wickedness" or "a wicked person." The ability of humans to repent and truly turn their faces toward God is represented by the phrase "Who is a hero? He who masters his impulses" (Avot 4:1). Thus we see that just as a human can return to God, so can the letter *resh* also indicate possibility of reformation. "The use of the letter ר to symbolize both רשע, wicked person, and ראש, leader, is significant. It teaches that a penitant can attain the extraordinary accomplishment of transforming himself completely from the lowest status to the highest" (*Midrash Alpha Beita*)

NOTES:

201	אר	*Ar*–Light (of the sun); 19th Gate of the 231 Gates
	הקוצ	*Haqowtz*–Hakkoz, priest and chief of the seventh course of service in the sanctuary (this spelling used only in 1 Chr. 24:10 – see also Koz)[370]
	צחצחה	*Tzachtsachah*–Scorched region, parched land
	קוצה	*Qevutztzah*–Lock, locks of hair
202	ארא	*'ara'*–Ara, son of Jether
	בקק	*Baqaq*–To empty
	בר	*Bar*–Son (Aramaic); son, heir; pure, clear, sincere; clean, empty; purely; corn, grain; field; the first two letters of the Torah; exterior, outside, clear; 39th Gate of the 231 Gates
		Bor–Purity, innocence, cleanness; lye, potash, alkali used in smelting metal
	סאיציאל	*Saitziel*–"Going Forth of the Measure of God," Angel of Scorpio
	רב	*Rab*–Many; much; great, mighty; captain, chief; archer
		Rob–Multitude, abundance, greatness
203	אבר	*Abar*–Lead, the metal of Saturn; to fly (to move wings)
		Eber–Pinion, wing
	ארב	*'arab*–To lie in wait, ambush, lurk; Arab, town in the hills of Judah
		'ereb–A lying-in-wait; covert, lair, den
		'oreb–Ambuscade, hiding place; treachery, deceit (figurative)
	באר	*Ba'ar*–To make plain, distinct, to make clear, to declare, letters on a tablet
		Be'er–Beer, temporary encampment of the Israelites, (see also Beer Elim)[371]; place where Jotham sought refuge from his brother Abimelech, possibly the same as Beeroth
		Be'ayr–Well, pit, spring; a title of *Malkut*
		Bo'r–Cistern, pit, well
	בעל המונ	*Ba'al Hamown*–Baal Hamon, place where Solomon had a vineyard (Song 8:11)
	ברא	*Bara'*–To create, form, shape
	גר	*Gar*–Dwelling; 58th Gate of the 231 Gates
		Ger–Sojourner
		Gir–Chalk, lime
		Gur–Whelp, young one
	פקחיה	*Peqachiah*–Pekahiah, 18th King of Israel
	רבא	*Rabba*–Greater (Aramaic)
204	אגר	*Agar*–To gather
	ארג	*'arag*–To weave
		'ereg–Loom, shuttle
	בארא	*Be'era*–Beera, descendant of Asher

[370] Koz (196, 1006).
[371] Beer Elim (284, 844).

בקבק — *Baqbuk* –Flask, bottle

גרא — *Gera'* –Gera, son of Benjamin; son of Bela; father of Ehud; father of Shimi (all of these may be identical)

דקק — *Daqaq* –To crush, pulverize, thresh

Deqaq –To break into pieces, fall into pieces, be shattered (Aramaic)

דר — *Dar* –Pearl; mother of pearl; generation (Aramaic); 76th Gate of the 231 Gates

Dor –Period, generation, dwelling

יהוה מצליח — YHVH *Matzliyach* –"YHVH made it prosper" (Gen. 39:23)

מעטפה — *Ma'atafah* –Overtunic

מעצד — *Ma'atsad* –Axe

מצעד — *Mits'ad* –Step

פסח ליהוה — *Pesach Lah*-YHVH –(To offer the) "Pesach offering to YHVH"

צדיק — *Tzaddiyq* –Just, lawful, righteous

קדמני — *Qadmoniy* –Former, ancient, eastern; Kadmonites

רבב — *Rabab* –To be or become great, to be or become many, ten thousand; to shoot

205 אגאר — *Agares* –Goetic demon #2

אגרא — *Iggera* –Letter, missive (Aramaic loan-word used in last Hebrew Bible books: Ezra 4:8, 11, 5:6)

אדניקמ — *'Adoniyqam* –Adonikam, man who returned to Palestine after the exile (Ezra 2:13)

אדר — *Adar* –The 6th month of the Jewish calendar – it is associated with Pisces and the tribe Simeon; to be great, majestic, wide, noble (poetic)

Eder –Glory, magnificence; mantle, cloak

Iddar –Threshing floor (Aramaic)

ארד — *'Ard* –Ard, son of Benjamin; son of Bela

גבר — *Gabar* –To prevail, have strength, be strong, be powerful, be mighty, be great

Gebar –Man, man (of uprightness); a man, a certain (one – Aramaic)

Geber –Man, strong man, warrior; Geber, father of one of Solomon's officers; one of Solomon's commissaries

Gibbar –Mighty one, might; Gibbar, one who returned to Jerusalem with Zerubbabel

Gibbor –Champion, chief, giant, man, mighty (man, one), strong (one), valiant man (see also גבור)[372]

גרב — *Garab* –Itch, scab

Gareb –Gareb, one of David's mighty men (2 Sam. 23:38; 1 Chr. 11:40)

דאר — *Dowr* –Dor, Canaanite town on the Mediterranean coast

---

[372] גבור (211).

north of Caesarea – (see also דור)[373]

הפכפך *Hafakpak* –Crooked, perverted

הר *Har* –Hill, mountain, hill country, mount; 93rd Gate of the 231 Gates
Hor –Hor, mountain on the boundary of Edom; mountain between the Mediterranean Sea and the entrance of second Hamath – possibly in the Lebanon range

יצקה *Yetuqah* –A casting (of metal)

ספינה *Sefiynah* –Ship, vessel

עצמה *'atstsumah* –Defense, argument, strong
'otsmah –Power, strength, might

פצלה *Petsalah* –Stripe, peeled spot or stripe or strip

רגב *Regeb* –Clod (of earth)

206 אדרא *Idra* –Assembly (Aramaic)

ארגב *'Argob* –Argob, officer of Pekahiah slain by Pekah

ארה *'arah* –To pluck, gather

בדר *Bedar* –To scatter (Aramaic)

ברד *Baradh* –To hail
Barod –Spotted, marked
Bered –Bered, descendant of Ephraim (1 Chr. 7:20) – perhaps the same as Becher (Num. 26:35)

דבר *Dabar* –Speak, answer, appoint, bid, command, commune, declare, give, name, pronounce, say, talk, teach, tell, think, utter (all verbs); act, advice, affair, answer, decree (all adverbs)
Davar –Word, thing
Deber –Pestilence, plague, murrain
Debir –Hindmost chamber, innermost room of the Temple, Holy of Holies, most holy place (the place of the Ark and the cherubic images, the throne room of YHVH), Sanctuary of the Temple; Debir, king of Eglon defeated by Joshua; Debir, town in the hill country of Judah (see also Kirjath Sannah (Josh. 15:49) and Kirjath Sepher (Judg. 1:11-13), דביר)[374]
Dever –Murrain
Dober –Pasture

הרא *Hara'* –Hara, place in Assyria where the captive Israelites were taken

ור *Var* –109th Gate of the 231 Gates

עצום *'atsuwm* –Mighty, vast, numerous

ראה *Raah* –To see, observe, perceive, consider; 69th name of *Shem HaMeforash* (3 Cancer)
Ra'ah –To see, to look; bird of prey (hawk or kite)
Ra'eh –Seeing
Ro'eh –Seer, prophet, vision

---

373 דור (210).

374 דביר (216), Kirjath Sannah (825), Kirjath Sepher (1050).

רבד *Rabad* –To spread, be spread, deck
רו *Rev* –Appearance

207 אדונ אולמ *Adon Awlum* –Lord of the World
אור *Aur* –Light
Owr –Luminous, illumination, break of day, glorious, kindle, light, set on fire, shine
Ur –A city of Mesopotamia, birthplace of Abram
Uwr –Flame; the East (as the region of light), morning; sun
אינ־סופ *Ain Sof* –Infinity
ארו *'aruw* –Behold, lo
ברה *Barah* –To eat, consume
גדר *Gadar* –To wall up, wall off, close off, build a wall, enclose; boundary, limit
Gader, Geder –Fence, wall; Geder, town in the extreme southern portions of Judah, captured by Joshua – may be modern Beth Gador or Gedor; Gedor, descendant of Judah (1 Chr. 4:18); descendant of Judah (1 Chr. 4:4); ancestor of Saul (1 Chr. 8:31)
גרד *Garad* –To scrape, scratch
דגר *Dagar* –To gather together as a brood
הבר *Habar* –To divide; to be an astrologer
ה־רב *HaRab* –The Rabbi
זקנימ *Zeqanem* –Elders, wise ones
זקק *Zaqaq* –To purify, distill, strain, refine
זר *Zar* –Strange, foreign; 124th Gate of the 231 Gates
Zer –Border, moulding, circlet; crown, wreath, rim
מזיקימ *Mezziqim* –Demons; injurers
מעצבה *Ma'atsebah* –Place of pain, place of grief; terror
רבה *Rabbah* –Rabbah, chief city of the Ammonites; city in Judah near Kirjath-Jearim
Ravah –To multiply, increase, be or become many; to shoot
רהב *Rahab* –To behave proudly, act stormily; pride, blusterer; proud, defiant
Rohab –Arrogance, pride, object of pride
רז *Raz* –Secret (mod. Hebrew)

208 אברה *'ebrah* –Pinion, wing
אזר *'azar* –Gird, encompass, equip, clothe
ארבה *'arbeh* –Locust swarm, a kind of locust
'arubbah –Lattice, window, sluice; chimney
'orobah –Artifice, deceit, trick
ארז *'araz* –To be firm; made firm; firm, strong
'erez –Cedar
בארה *Be'erah* –Beerah, prince of the Reubenites who was taken into captivity by Tiglath-Pileser, king of Assyria
בור *Bowr* –Pit, well, cistern

Buwr –To make clear, clear up, explain, prove

גהר *Gahar* –To prostrate oneself; to put one's head between one's knees (like Elijah)

גרה *Garah* –To cause strife, stir up, contend, meddle, strive, be stirred up

Gerah –Cud; *gerah* (a weight, a 20th part of a shekel, equal to the weight of 16 barley grains or four to five carob beans)

Gorah –Whelp

הגר *Hagar* –Sarah's Egyptian maid; mother of Ishmael

הרג *Harag* –To kill, slay, murder, destroy, murderer, slayer, out of hand

Hereg –A killing, slaughter

וארא *Vara'* –I [God] revealed myself

Ve'Ere' –And I saw (Gen. 31:10)

זרא *Zara'* –Nausea, loathsome thing, loathing

חספס *Chaspas* –To peel, flake off (only in the participle)

חקק *Chaqaq* –To cut out, decree, inscribe, set, engrave, portray, govern

Cheqeq –Decree, resolve, statute, action prescribed

Chuqqoq –Hukkok, place on the border of Naphtali, probably modern Yakuk (see also חיקק)[375]

חר *Chor* –A noble, freeborn one; 138th Gate of the 231 Gates

יצחק *Itzchaq* –Isaac – it should be noted that י = 10, corresponding to the ten commandments, צ = 90, the age of Isaac's mother when she gave birth, ח = 8, the day when Isaac was circumcised, ק = 100, the age of Abraham at the birth of Isaac

לחם עני *Lechem 'Oniy* –"Bread of anguish" (Deut. 16:3)

פינחס *Piynechas* –Phinehas, grandson of Aaron and High Priest; younger son of Eli and a priest who abused his office; father of Eleazar

פענח *Panach* –The last name given to Joseph by Pharaoh (Gen. 41:45)

קדקד *Qodqod* –Head, crown of head, top of head, hairy crown, scalp

רבו *Rebuw* –Greatness (Aramaic); ten thousand, myriad

רדד *Radad* –To beat down, beat out, subside

209 אחר *Achar* –To delay, hesitate, tarry, defer, remain behind; after the following part, behind (of place), hinder, afterwards (of time); after

Acher –Another, other, following; Aher, descendant of Benjamin (see also Ahiram and Aharah)[376]

ארח *'arach* –To wander, journey, go, keep company with; Arah, son of Ulla; ancestor of a family returned

---

[375] חיקק (218).

[376] Ahiram (259, 819), Aharah (217).

from exile

'orach –Way, path, course of life

בואר *Buer* –Goetic demon #10

בזר *Bazar* –To scatter, disperse

גדבר *Gedebar* –Treasurer (Aramaic)

גור *Gowr* –Whelp

Gur –Whelp, young one; Gur, hill near Ibleam where Jehu killed Ahaziah

דהר *Dahar* –Rush, dash (of horse)

הדר *Hadar* –To honor, adorn, glorify, be high; to glorify God (Aramaic); honor, majesty (Aramaic); ornament, splendor, glory; Hadar, a King of Edom (Gen. 25:15 – see also Hadad)[377] (assoc. w/*Malkut*)

Heder –Ornament, splendor, adornment, glory

זרב *Zarab* –To dry up, be warmed, be burned, be scorched

חרא *Chere'* –Dung, excrement

טר *Tar* –151st Gate of the 231 Gates

צדקיה *Tzedeqiah* –Zedekiah, 19th and last King of Judah (see also צדקיהו)[378]; false prophet who encouraged Ahab to attack the Syrians at Ramoth-Gilead (see also צדקיהו)[379]; Zidkijah, chief prince of the Jews (Neh. 10:2)

רבבה *Rababah* –Multitude, myriad, ten thousand

רדה *Radah* –To rule, have dominion, dominate; to scrape out

210 אגור *'Aguwr* –Agur, son of Jakeh, author of Proverbs 30

אטר *Atar* –Shut

Itter –Bound, impeded (on the right, i.e., left-handed), shut, shut up

'Ater –Ater, one who sealed the covenant after the exile; ancestor of a family of gatekeepers; ancestor of a family that returned from exile

בחר *Bachar* –To choose, elect, decide for

בעל חנן *Baal-Hanan* –Baal-hanan, a King of Edom (assoc. w/*Yesod*); archdemon corr. to *Netzach* (Waite); Baal-hanan, tender of olive and sycamore trees in David's time (1 Chr. 27:28)

בקבוק *Baqbuwq* –Bakbuk, one whose descendant returned from exile (Ezra 2:51; Neh. 7:53)

ברח *Barach* –To go through, flee, run away, chase, drive away, put to flight, reach, shoot (extend), hurry away

גזר *Gazar* –To cut, divide

Gezar –Cut out, determine – thus soothsayer (Aramaic)

Gezer –Portion, piece; Gezer, Canaanite town beside the Mediterranean Sea near Lachish and Lower Beth Horon

---

[377] Hadad (209).

[378] צדקיהו (215).

[379] צדקיהו (215).

גרז	*Garaz*–To cut, cut off
דור	*Dowr*–Period, generation, dwelling; Dor, Canaanite town on the Mediterranean coast north of Caesarea – (see also דאר)[380]
	Duwr–To dwell; to heap up, pile; to dwell (Aramaic); circle, ball
הרה	*Harah*–To conceive, become pregnant, bear, be with child, be conceived; progenitor
	Hareh–Pregnant
חבר	*Chabar*–To unite, join, bind together, be joined, be coupled, be in league, heap up, have fellowship with, be compact, be a charmer; associate, companion, friend, comrade, fellow (Aramaic)
	Chabbar–Associate, partner (in trade)
	Chaber–United; associate, fellow, worshippers; companion
	Cheber–Association, company, band; shared, association, society; a magician, charmer, spell; Heber or Eber, descendant of Asher (Gen. 46:17; 1 Chr. 7:31-32); husband of Jael, who killed Sisera (Judg. 4:11, 17, 21; 5:24); head of a clan of Judah (1 Chr. 4:18); descendant of Benjamin (1 Chr. 8:17); head of a family of Gad (1 Chr. 8:17); descendant of Benjamin (1 Chr. 8:22)
חרב	*Charab*–To be waste, lay waste, make desolate, be desolate, be in ruins; to be dry, be dried up; to attack, smite down, slay, fight; to dry up, be wasted (Aramaic)
	Chareb–Waste, desolate, dry
	Chereb–Sword, knife
	Choreb–Dryness, desolation, drought, heat; Horeb, mountain in the Sinai Peninsula where Moses heard God speak to him through the burning bush
יוצדק	*Yowtzadaq*–Jozadak, priest and father of Jeshua the High Priest (see also Jehozadek)[381]
יר	*Yar*–163rd Gate of the 231 Gates
לצצ	*Latzatz*–To scorn, make mouths at, talk arrogantly
מסנינ	*Misnin*–Angel of 1d Capricorn
מפצ	*Mappats*–Shattering (of type of weapon)
	Mappets–War club, club, battle axe, hammer
נסק	*Nasaq*–To ascend
	Nesaq–To ascend, come up (Aramaic)
נעמנ	*Na'aman*–Pleasantness; Naaman, Syrian general who was healed of leprosy by bathing in the Jordan; grandson of Benjamin; son of Benjamin and founder of a tribal family
נפלימ	*Nefilim*–"Giants" (Gen. 6:4; Num. 13:33)
סעפ	*Sa'af*–To cut off, lop off boughs

380 דאר (205).

381 Jehozadek (215).

		Sa'if–Ambivalence, division, divided opinion
		Se'ef–Ambivalent, divided, half-hearted
	עמק	*'amaq* –To be deep, be profound, make deep
		'ameq –Deep, unfathomable
		'amoq –Deep, mysterious, depths
		'emeq –Valley, vale, lowland, open country
		'omeq –Depth
	ענמימ	*'Anamim* –Anamim, descendants of Mizraim (Gen. 10:13; 1 Chr. 1:11)[382]
	ענמלכ	*'Anammelek* –Anammelech, one of the gods worshipped by the people of Sepharvaim[383]
	עפני	*'Ophniy* –Ophni, city of Benjamin
	עצנ	*'etsen* –Sharp, strong, spear (meaning uncertain – 2 Sam. 23:8)
	פלמני	*Palmowniy* –A certain one
	פצמ	*Patzam* –To split or break open
	צנע	*Tzana'* –To be humble, be modest, be lowly; modest
	צענ	*Tza'an* –To wander, travel; Zoan, ancient Egyptian city on the eastern bank of the Nile Delta on the Tanitic branch of the river (Ezek. 30:14)
	קיננ	*Kenan* –Cainan, son of Enosh
	קמע	*Kamea* –Amulet, magic square
	קנינ	*Qinyon* –Thing acquired, acquisition, possession
	רגז	*Ragaz*–Tremble, quake, rage, quiver
		Raggaz–Trembling, quivering, quaking
		Regaz–To rage, enrage (Aramaic)
		Rogaz–Agitation, excitement, raging, trouble
	רדו	*Redu* –To go down (Gen. 42:12)
	רהה	*Rahah* –To fear (Isa. 44:8)
	רוד	*Ruwd* –To wander restlessly, roam
	רחב	*Rachab* –To be or grow wide, be or grow large; breadth or wide expanse; broad or open place or plaza; Rahab, harlot of Jericho who helped the Hebrew spies (Josh. 2:1-21; 6:17-25)
		Rechob –Rehob, father of Hadadezer, king of Zobah; Rehob, two towns of Asher (see also Beth-Rehob)[384]
	רי	*Ri* –Rushing water; moisture

–Mystic number of 20th Path (*Hesed-Tiferet*; י; Virgo)
–The number of years of Egyptian bondage

211	איר	*Iyar* –8th month of Jewish calendar – it is associated with Taurus and the tribes Ephraim and Manasseh
	אלפעל	*Elpaal* –Elpaal, a Benjamite
	ארגז	*'argaz* –Box, chest, coffer
	ארוד	*'Arowd* –Arod, son of Gad

[382] Possibly an unknown Egyptian tribe.
[383] It is possible that Anammelech represented the moon, with Adrammelech representing the sun.
[384] One of these two towns was given to the Levites and one remained in the hands of the Canaanites. Beth-Rehob (628).

		'Arvad –Arvad, Phoenician city, modern Ruwad
	ארי	*'ariy* –Lion
	גבור	*Gibbowr* –Champion, chief, giant, man, mighty (man, one), strong (one), valiant man
	גחר	*Gachar* –Gahar, one whose family returned from the exile
	דברה	*Dabbarah* –Word
		Deborah –Deborah, the name of Rebekah's nurse; the name of the 4th Judge of Israel (see also דבורה)[385]
		Dibrah –Cause, reason, manner; intent, sake (Aramaic)
		Doberah –Floats, rafts
	הדבר	*Haddabar* –Counsellor, ministry (Aramaic)
	הראה	*HaRo'eh* –Haroeh, descendant of Judah (see also Reaiah)[386]
	דורא	*Duwra'* –Dura, Babylonian plain where King Nebuchadnezzar set up a golden idol
	ואדר	*Veadar* –The Jewish intercalary month
	זרד	*Zered* –Zared or Zered, brook and valley that marks the greatest limit of the Hebrews' wandering in the wilderness
	חגר	*Chagar* –To gird, gird on, gird oneself, put on a belt
	חרג	*Charag* –To shake from fear, tremble, quake
	יאר	*Ye'or* –River, stream, canal, the Nile
	ירא	*Yare'* –To fear, revere, be afraid; fearing, reverent, afraid
	מועצה	*Mow'etsah* –Counsel, plan, principal, device
	מקניהו	*Miqneyahuw* –Mikneiah, Levite musician (1 Chr. 15:18, 21)
	סופניה	*Siyfoneya* –A musical instrument, wind instrument, bagpipe, double pipe, panpipes (Aramaic)
	עלוקה	*'aluwqah* –Leech
	צאען	*Tzo'n* –Small cattle, sheep, flock, flocks
	ראי	*Re'iy* –Mirror
		Ro'iy –Looking, appearance, seeing, sight
	רוה	*Ravah* –To be satiated, have or drink one's fill
		Raveh –Watered, saturated
	רטב	*Ratab* –To be moist
		Ratob –Moist, juicy, fresh
	–Prime number	
212	אורה	*'averah* –A stall (for animals)
		'owrah –Luminousness; prosperity (fig.)
	ארוה	*'urvah* –Manger, crib, stall (for animals)
	ברי	*Beriy* –Fat; fatter, fed, firm, plenteous, rank; Berites; Beri, descendant of Asher
	גדרה	*Gederah* –Wall, hedge; sheepfold; Gederah, town in the lowlands of Judah, northwest of Zorah, present-day Jedireh

385 דבורה (217).

386 Reaiah (216).

גזבר *Gizbar* –Treasurer

דרח *Darak* –To tread, bend, lead, march

האור *Haures* –Goetic demon #64

זהר *Zahar* –To admonish, warn, teach, shine, send out light, be light, be shining

Zehar –Brightness, shining

Zohar –Splendor, brightness, shining; the *Sefer Ha Zohar*

זרה *Zarah* –To scatter, fan, cast away, winnow, disperse, compass, spread, be scattered, be dispersed

חדר *Chadar* –To encompass, surround, enclose; Hadar, one of the twelve sons of Ishmael and grandson of Abraham (Gen. 25:15) – he is called Hadad in 1 Chr. 1:30; the last of Edom's early kings (Gen. 36:39) – he is called Hadad in 1 Chr. 1:50-51

Cheder –Chamber, room, parlor, innermost or inward part, within

חרד *Charad* –To tremble, quake, move about, be afraid, be startled, be terrified

Chared –Trembling, fearful, afraid

ירב *Yareb* –Jareb, king of Assyria (Hos. 5:13; 10:6 – this must be a nickname)

צבעימ *Tzebo'iym* –Zeboim, valley between Michmash and the wilderness to the east; Benjamite town, probably north of Lydda

צלפחד *Tzelophechad* –Zelophehad, grandson of Gilead

קוקו *Qav-qav* –Might

ראוה *Ra'avah* –To behold

רבי *Rebbe* –Teacher

רזה *Razah* –To move or become or grow lean

Razeh –Lean

ריב *Riyb* –To strive, contend; strive, controversy, dispute

213 אביר *Abir* –The Almighty, strong, mighty – used only to describe God; "The Strong" – old name for God (poetic)

Abbiyr –Mighty, valiant

ארבי *'Arbiy* –Arbite, a native of Arab

ארזה *'arzah* –Cedar panels, cedar work

בארי *Be'eriy* –Beeri, father of Judith, wife of Esau; father of the prophet Hosea

בהור *Bohuwr* –Clarity

בירא *Biyra* –Castle, citadel, palace (Aramaic); palace, castle; temple

בריא *Bariy'* –Fat; fatter, fed, firm, plenteous, rank

גדור *Gedowr* –Gedor, town in the extreme southern portions of Judah, captured by Joshua – may be modern Beth Gador or Gedor; Gedor, descendant of Judah (1 Chr. 4:18); descendant of Judah (1 Chr. 4:4); ancestor of Saul (1 Chr. 8:31)

	גיר	*Giyr* –Plaster
	הרגה	*Haregah* –A killing, slaughter (n. fem.)
	הרח	*Harach* –59th name of *Shem HaMeforash* (5 Taurus)
	וזר	*Vazar* –Guilty, burdened with guilt, strange; criminal, guilty
	זור	*Zuwr* –To be strange, be a stranger; to press, squeeze, crush, press down and out
	חרה	*Charah* –To be angry; anger
	טרד	*Tarad* –To pursue, chase, be continuous
		Terad –To drive away, drive from, chase away (Aramaic)
	יגר	*Yagor* –To fear, dread, be afraid
	כוזו במוכסז כוזו	*Kuzu Bemuksuk Kuzu* –A name of God derived from the phrase "*Adonai Elohainu Adonai*" through *Aiq Bekar*
	צלחה	*Tzelachah* –Cooking pot, pot
	רחה	*Recheh* –Handmills (for grinding)
214	אזור	*Ezowr* –Waist cloth, the innermost piece of clothing; waist band
	ארחה	*'aruchah* –Meal, allowance, ration
		'orechah –Caravan, travelling company
	דההר	*Dahahar* –Dashing, rushing, galloping (of riders)
	הדרה	*Hadarah* –Adornment, glory
	זזר	*Zazer* –Angel of 1d Aries
	חור	*Chavar* –To be white, grow white, grow pale
		Chivvar –White (Aramaic)
		Chowr –Hole, cave
		Chuwr –Hole; white cloth, white stuff; Hur, son of Caleb; one of the men who held up Moses' arms during the battle with Amalek; Midianite king slain by Israel; officer of Solomon on Mount Ephraim; father of Rephaiah, who helped rebuild the wall of Jerusalem in Nehemiah's time; son of Judah
	טהר	*Tahar* –To be clean, be pure
	ירד	*Yarad* –To go down, descend, decline
		Yared –Jared, descendant of Seth
	רביב	*Rabiyb* –Copious showers, heavy showers
	רדי	*Radday* –Raddai, brother of David
	רהט	*Rahat* –Trough, hollow; lock of hair
	רוח	*Revach* –Space
		Ruach –Breath, wind, spirit; middle part of the tripartite soul; the element Air
	–The number of bones in the human body	
215	אגורה	*Agowrah* –Payment, piece, coin
	אדיר	*Addiyr* –Great, majestic; great one, majestic one
	אחור	*Achowr* –The back side, the rear
	ארדי	*'Ardiy* –Ardites
	גביר	*Gebiyr* –Lord

גזרה *Gezerah* –Separation, cut off; decree (Aramaic)
Gizrah –Cutting, separation

הרי *Hari* –Aspect, characteristic; 15th name of Shem HaMephorash (3 Libra)

זרח *Zerach* –Zerah, son of Reuel;Father of Jobab, a King of Edom; son of Judah; descendant of Gershon; a Levite; king of Ethiopia who warred with Asa – also called a Cushite or Ethiopian
Zarach –To rise, come forth, break out, arise, rise up, shine
Zerach –Dawning, shining

חברה *Chabburah* or *Chaburah* –Bruise, stripe, wound, blow
Chabrah –Associate, fellow, companion (Aramaic)
Chebrah –Company, association

חרבה *Charabah* –Dry land, dry ground
Charabhah –Parched Land; one of the Seven Earths (corr. to *Giburah*)
Chorbah –A place laid waste, ruin, waste, desolation

טור *Tuwr* –Row; mountain (Aramaic)

יהוצדק *Yehowtzadaq* –Jehozadek, priest and father of Jeshua the High Priest (see also Jozadak)[387]

ירה *Yarah* –To throw, cast, pour

מעמסה *Ma'amasah* –Load, burden

מעקה *Ma'aqeh* –Parapet

מצפה *Mitzpeh* –Watchtower, lookout point; Mizpeh or Mizpah, a mound of stones on Mount Gilead; Hivite settlement in northern Palestine at the foot of Mount Hermon; city in the lowlands of Judah; town in Gilead east of the Jordan; town of Benjamin just north of Jerusalem; place in Moab

סעפה *Se'appah* –Bough, branch

צדקיהו *Tzedeqiahu* –Zedekiah, 19th and last King of Judah (variant spelling – see also Mattaniah)[388]; Zedekiah, false prophet who encouraged Ahab to attack the Syrians at Ramoth-Gilead (see also צדקיה)[389]; false prophet; prince of Judah in the days of Jehoiakim

צלמנה *Tzalmonah* –Zalmonah, Israelite encampment in the desert (Num. 33:41-42)

קעילה *Qe'iylah* –Keilah, descendant of Caleb; Keilah, town in the lowlands of Judah

רגזה *Rogzah* –Trembling, quivering, quaking

216 אוראוב *Orobas* –Goetic demon #55

אזרח *Ezrach* –A native (one rising from the soil)

אריה *'aryeh* –Lion (Aramaic); Arieh, man killed by Pekah

---

[387] Jozadak (210).
[388] Mattaniah (505).
[389] צדקיה (209).

בחור *Bachuwr* –Youth, young man

דברי *Dibriy* –Dibri, descendant of Dan whose daughter married an Egyptian, her son was stoned for blasphemy

גבורה *Giburah* –Severity, force, mastery, might, mighty (act, power), power, strength; might (Aramaic); the 5th *Sefira*h (occurs 61 times in the *Tanakh*)

דביר *Debiyr* –Hindmost chamber, innermost room of the Temple, Holy of Holies, most holy place (the place of the Ark and the cherubic images, the throne room of YHVH), Sanctuary of the Temple; Debir, king of Eglon defeated by Joshua; Debir, town in the hill country of Judah (see also Kirjath Sannah (Josh. 15:49) and Kirjath Sepher (Judg. 1:11-13), דבר)[390]

היאר *HaYar* –The river (Gen. 41:1)

חבור *Chabowr* –Habor, tributary of the Euphrates River, probably modern Khabur River

ורדו *Orduw* –And dominate (Gen. 1:28)

חבקוק *Chabaqquwq* –Habakkuk, prophet during the reign of Jehoiakim and Josiah

יראה *Yir'ah* –Fear, terror, fearing

נקיון *Niqqayown* –Innocency

על־פי יהוה *Al-pey* YHVH –"On God's order" (occurs 25 times in *Tanakh*)

עמוק *'Amowq* –Amok, priest who returned to Jerusalem with Zerubbabel

צלמון *Tzalmown* –Zalmon, wooded area in Shechem; father of Boaz (see also Salma)[391]

ראומה *Re'uwmah* –Reumah, Nahor's concubine

ראיה *Re'ayah* –Reaiah, descendant of Reuben; one whose descendants returned from the Exile; descendant of Judah (see also Haroch)[392]

רביד *Rabiyd* –Chain (for necklace)

רחוב *Rechowb* –Rehob, Levite who sealed the covenant (Neh. 10:12)

217 אדרזדא *Adrazda* –Correct, exactly, diligently, earnestly (Aramaic)

אויר *Avir* –Ether; the 8th Heaven according to the *Zohar*

אורי *Uwriy* –Uri, son of Hur; father of Geber; porter of Levi

אחרח *'Achrach* –Aharah, son of Benjamin (see also Ehi (Gen. 46:21) and Ahiram (Num. 26:38))[393]

בהיר *Bahir* –Bright, brilliant (of light), shining

בריה *Biryah* –Food

גדרי *Gederiy* –Gederite

---

390 דבר (206), Kirjath Sannah (825), Kirjath Sepher (1050).

391 Salma (371).

392 Haroeh (211).

393 Ehi (19), Ahiram (259, 819).

	דבורה	*Debowrah* –Deborah, the name of Rebekah's nurse; the name of the 4th Judge of Israel
	חגור	*Chagowr* –Clothed, girded, girt; girdle, belt; loin-covering, belt, loincloth, armor
	חטת	*Choter* –Branch, twig, rod
	חרדה	*Charadah* –Fear, anxiety, quaking, trembling, extreme anxiety, anxious care; Haradah, place where the Israelites camped during their wilderness wanderings
	חרט	*Cheret* –An engraving tool, stylus, chisel, graving tool
	טבור	*Tabbuwr* –Center, midst, navel, highest part
	טחר	*Techor* –Tumors, hemorrhoids
	טרח	*Tarach* –To burden, toil, be burdened (Job 37:11)
		Torach –Burden
	מזיקינ	*Mazziqin* –A class of demons
	נאפופ	*Na'afuwf* –Adultery
	סהקנב	*Sahaqnab* –Lord of Triplicity by Night for Scorpio
	רזי	*Razi* –Leanness; secret
218	בראיה	*Bera'yah* –Beraiah, chief of the tribe of Benjamin
	בריאה	*Briah* –A creation, created thing, new thing, marvel, Creation; the Archangelic or Creative World
	הגרי	*Hagriy* –Hagarite (see also הגריא)[394]
	זורה	*Zuwrah* –A thing that is crushed
	חיקק	*Chuqqoq* –Hukkok, place on the border of Naphtali, probably modern Yakuk (see also חקק)[395]
	חרי	*Choriy* –Heat (of anger), burning (of anger);white bread, cake; a Horite; Hori, descendant of Esau
	יחר	*Yachar* –To delay, tarry, defer
	ירח	*Yerach* –Month (lunar cycle), moon; Jerah, son of Joktan (Gen. 10:26; 1 Chr. 1:20 – the name may refer to an Arabian tribe)
		Yereach –Moon
	עצבונ	*'itstsabown* –Pain, labor, hardship, sorrow, toil
	צבעונ	*Tzib'own* –Zibeon, Hivite man; son of Seir
	צלצח	*Tzeltzach* –Zelzah, town near Rachel's tomb
	רדיד	*Radiyd* –Something spread; large veil
	רטט	*Retet* –Trembling, panic
	ריח	*Reyach* –Scent, fragrance, aroma, odor
219	אחימעצ	*'Achiyma'atz* –Ahimaaz, father of Ahinoam; one of Solomon's officers; son of Zadok
	אחרי	*Ochoriy* –Other, another, after
	בקבקיה	*Baqbukyah* –Bakbukiah, Levite who returned with Zerubbabel; Levite and guard of the Temple storehouse; Levite who lived in Jerusalem – perhaps identical with Bakbakkar

394 הגריא (219).

395 חקק (208).

הגריא *Hagri'* –Hagarite (see also הגרי)[396]
טרי *Tariy* –Fresh, new
יגור *Yagowr* –Fearful, fearing
Yaguwr –Jagur, town in extreme southern Judah – probably modern Tell Ghurr
ירט *Yarat* –To precipitate, be precipitate, push headlong
רוהגה *Rowhagah* –Rohgah, chief of Asher (1 Chr. 7:34)
רוחה *Revachah* –Respite, relief

220 בחיר *Bachiyr* –Chosen, chosen one, choice one, elect (of God)
בריח *Bariyach* –Fleeing; fugitive; Bariah, son of Shemaiah of the tribe of Judah
Beriyach –Bar of tribulation, a fortress of the earth as a prison (fig.); Beriah, descendant of Asher; descendant of Ephraim; descendant of Benjamin; descendant of Levi
גבירה *Gebiyrah* –Queen
גזרי *Gizriy* –Gezrite, Gezrites
הכרה *Hakkarah* –The look, appearance, expression
חברי *Chebriy* –Heberites
טהור *Tahowr* –Table
יבחר *Yibchar* –Ibhar, one of David's sons born at Jerusalem
כר *Kar* –174th Gate of the 231 Gates
מפיצ *Mefits* –Scatterer, disperser, scattering, club
נקע *Naqa'* –To be estranged, be alienated
סעיפ *Sa'iyf* –Cleft, branch
ספפ *Safaf* –To stand at or guard the threshold
טהור *Tahur* –Clean, purified
כר *Kar* –Howdah, palanquin, basket saddle; pasture, meadow; ram, lamb, he-lamb; battering-ram
Kor –Kor, a measure (usually dry)
מפעל *Mif'al* –Work, thing made
מצצ *Matsats* –To drain out, suck
נפצ *Nafats* –To shatter, break, dash, beat in pieces; to scatter, disperse, overspread, be scattered
Nefets –Driving storm
סנסנ *Sansin* –Bough, fruit-stalk (of date trees)
ספלימ *Sefalim* –Cups
עמיק *'amiyq* –Deep (subst.); deep things, deep mysteries
ענק *'anaq* –To serve as a necklace, adorn with a neck ornament; necklace, neck-pendant; neck
Anaq –Anak, ancestor of the giant Anakim (Num. 13:22, 28, 33; Josh. 15:14)
עסיס *'asas* –To press, crush, press by treading, tread down or out, press (grapes)
'asiys –Sweet wine, wine, pressed out juice
עקנ *'Aqan* –Akan, son of Ezer and grandson of Seir
צלק *Tzeleq* –Zelek, Ammonite who was a valiant man of

[396] הגרי (218).

David

צנפ *Tzanaf* –To wrap, wrap or wind up together, wind around

צפימ *Tzophiym* –Zophim, place on top of Pisgah where Balaam viewed the Israelite camp

צפנ *Tzafan* –To hide, treasure, treasure or store up

קסס *Qasas* –To strip off, cut off

ריי *Riyi* –29th name of *Shem HaMeforash* (5 Sagittarius)

רכ *Rak* –Tender, soft, delicate, weak; soft (Prov. 15:1)[397]

Rok –Tenderness, delicacy (of woman)

Rokh –Softness

221 אכר *Ikkar* –Plowman, husbandman, farmer

ארודי *'Arowdiy, 'Arvadiy* –Arvadite

ארכ *'arak* –To be long, prolong; to be long, reach, meet; fitting, proper

'arek –Long (pinions); patient, slow to anger

'arok –Long (of time; of God's wisdom [figurative])

Erech –Uruk, a city of ancient Mesopotamia

'orek –Length; forbearance, self-restraint (of patience)

חבורה *Chabbuwrah* –Bruise, stripe, wound, blow

חרוז *Charuwz* –A beaded necklace, string of beads

יאיר *Yair* –Jair, descendant of Judah through his father and of Manasseh through his mother; 7th Judge of Israel; father of Mordecai, Esther's cousin; father of Elkanan, slayer of Goliath the Gittite (2 Sam. 21:19 – here called Jaare-Oregim) – may be a copyist's error for Jair in 1 Chr. 20:5

יארי *Ya'iriy* –Jairite

יורה *Yowrah* –Jorah, head of a family who sealed the new covenant with God after the exile (this spelling used only in Ezra 2:18 – see also the second Hariph)[398]

Yowreh –Early rain, autumn shower

מועקה *Muw'aqah* –Compression, distress, pressure

מנקאל *Menqel* –Angel of 6q Gemini & night angel 10 Swords

רויה *Revayah* –Saturation

222 אוריה *'Uwriyah* –Urijah, Hittite soldier in David's army; priest under Ahaz; prophet who offended Jehoiakim; priest father of Meremoth; man who stood by Ezra; priest whom Isaiah took as a witness

ארכא *'arka'* –Prolongation, lengthening, prolonging (Aramaic)

בכר *Bakar* –To be born first

Beker –Young male camel, dromedary; Becher, son of Ephraim; son of Benjamin

ברכ *Barakh* –To kneel, bless; to praise, salute, curse

Berak –To bless, kneel (Aramaic)

Berekh –Knee, lap; weak from fear (fig.); knee

---

[397] Rakh is one of the ten words in the Tanakh with a Dagesh in the letter Resh.

[398] Hariph (298, 1018).

		(Aramaic)
	ויידבר	*va-Yidabar* –And spoke
	חרדי	*Charodiy* –Harodite
	יריב	*Yariyb* –Contender, opponent, adversary; Jarib, tribal leader in the time of Ezra; priest who divorced his foreign wife after the exile[399]
	כבר	*Kabar* –To be much, be many, be in abundance, intertwine, multiply
		Kebar –Already, long ago, a great while
		Khebar –Chebar, a river in Mesopotamia
	מקבלימ	*Mekubbaliym* –Kabbalists
	רבכ	*Rabak* –To mix, stir
		Ravakh –To be mixed, mingled
	ריבי	*Riybay* –Ribai, father of Ittai, one of David's valiant men (2 Sam. 23:29; 1 Chr. 11:31)
	רכב	*Rakab* –To mount and ride, ride
		Rakav –To ride, drive; horseman, driver
		Rekab –Rechab, descendant of Benjamin who murdered Ishbosheth; founder of a tribe called Rechabites; descendant of Hamath Rabah; one who helped to build the wall of Jerusalem
		Rekev –Vehicle; a team, chariotry; mill-stone
223	אברכ	*Abrek* –A shout made to announce Joseph's chariot (meaning dubious – Gen. 41:43)
	חירה	*Chiyrah* –Hirah, friend of Judah (Gen. 38:1, 12)
	כיאני יהוה אלהיכמ	*Ki ahni* YHVH *elohaychem* –"For I am YHVH, your God" (Lev. 11:44; 20:7; 24:22; 25:17; 26:1)
	צקלג	*Tziqlag* –Ziklag, city in the south of Judah (see also ציקלג)[400]
	קבצאל	*Qabtze'el* –Kabzeel, city in Judah (see also Jekabzeel)[401]

–The number of children of Hashum who returned from exile (Ezra 2:19)
–The number of men of Betel and Ai who returned from exile (Ezra 2:28)
–Prime number

224	דכר	*Dakar* –Ram (Aramaic)
	דרכ	*Darak* –To tread, bend, lead, march
		Derek –Way, road, distance, journey, manner
	חורי	*Chowriy* –Hori, father of one of the men sent to spy out the Promised Land
		Chuwray –Hurai, one of David's mighty men ((1 Chr. 11:32) – see also Hiddai (2 Sam. 23:30))[402]
		Chuwriy –Huri, descendant of Gad
	טירה	*Tiyrah* –Encampment, battlement
	יקדעמ	*Yoqde'am* –Jokdeam, city in the mountains of Judah south of Hebron
	ירוח	*Yarowach* –Jaroah, descendant of Gad (1 Chr. 5:14)

---

[399] See also the first Jachin (90, 740).
[400] ציקלג (233).
[401] Jekabzeel (233).
[402] Hiddai (19).

	ירחו	*Yerechow* –Jericho, fortified city of Canaan located northwest of the Jordan River (see also יריחו and יריחה)[403]
	מפקד	*Mifqad* –Muster, appointment, appointed place; number
	סנדלעי	*Sandali* –Lord of Triplicity by Day for Capricorn
225	ארידי	*'Ariyday* –Aridai, son of Haman slain by the Jews
	הכר	*Hakar* –To deal wrongly with
	זרחי	*Zarchiy* –Zarchite
	חזיר	*Chaziyr* –Hog, swine, boar
		Cheziyr –Hezir, Levite in the time of David (1 Chr. 24:15); chief of the people that sealed the new covenant with God after the exile (Neh. 10:21)
	יהיר	*Yahiyr* –Proud, arrogant, haughty
	יזרח	*Yizrach* –Izrahite or descendant of Zerah
	יטור	*Yetuwr* –Jetur, son of Ishmael
	יריה	*Yeriyah* –Jeriah, descendant of Hebron in the days of David (this spelling used only in 1 Chr. 26:31 – see also יריהו)[404]
	כרה	*Karah* –To dig, excavate, dig through; to give a banquet or feast; to get by trade, trade, buy, bargain over; cottage
		Kerah –Feast
	סנסנה	*Sansannah* –Sansannah, village in extreme southern Judah
	פספה	*Pispah* –Pispah, descendant of Asher
	צנפה	*Tzenefah* –Winding, thing wrapped, ball
	רחביה	*Rechabyah* –Rehabiah, eldest son of Eliezer, son of Moses (1 Chr. 23:17; 24:21 – see also רחביהו)[405]
	רכה	*Rekah* –Rechah, village in Judah (1 Chr. 4:12)
226	אזרחי	*'Ezrachiy* –Ezrahite
	אכלה	*'oklah* –Food
	והמצפה	*ve-HaMitzpah* –And the Watchtower (Gen. 31:49; Josh. 15:38, 18:26; 1 Sam. 7:16; Neh. 3:7)
	ויברח	*ve-Yivrach* –And he fled (Gen. 31:21; Ex. 2:15; Judg. 9:21; 11:3; 1 Sam. 19:12, 20:1, 21:10, 11; 22:20; 2 Sam. 13:34; 1 Kings 11:17, 40; Job 14:2; Jer. 26:21; Hos. 12:14)
	יורי	*Yowray* –Jorai, chief of the tribe of Gad
	יסוד עולם	*Yesod Olam* –Eternal Foundation of the World, a title of *Yesod*
	כור	*Kuwr* –Furnace, forge, smelting furnace or pot; to bore, pierce, dig, hew
	צפון	*Tzafon* –North (of direction), northward; Zaphon, place

[403] Jericho is the oldest continually inhabited city in the world. יריחו (234), יריחה (233)

[404] יריהו (231).

[405] רחביהו (231).

allotted to the tribe of Gad in the Jordan Valley east of the river
Tzephown –Zephon, son of Gad (see also Ziphion)[406]

227 בכרה
Bakkurah –First ripe fig, early fig
Bekowrah –Birthright, primogeniture, right of the first born (see also בכורה)[407]
Berakah –Berachah, valley in Judah near Tekoa, named by Jehoshaphat (2 Chr. 20:26)
Bikrah –A young female camel, young camel, dromedary

ברכה
Berakah –Blessing
Berekah –Pool, pond

זכר
Zakar –To remember, recall, call to mind; male (n. mas.); male (of humans and animals – adj.)
Zeker –Memorial, remembrance; Zacher, son of Jeiel (see also Zechariah (1 Chr. 8:31))[408]

חר הגדגד
Chor Hagidgad –Hor Hagidgad, place where the wandering Israelites camped – probably located on modern Gadi Ghadaghed (see also Gudgodah)[409]

חריט
Chariyt –Bag, purse

כברה
Kibrah –Distance (undetermined length)
Kebarah –Sieve, sifter

כרז
Keraz –To herald, proclaim, make proclamation

רכבה
Rikbah –Riding, act of riding

–Prime number

228 אלהי יעקב
Elohi Yaaqob –The God of Jacob

אזכר
Ezkor –I will remember

אוריהו
'Uwriyahuw –Urijah, Hittite soldier in David's army; priest under Ahaz; prophet who offended Jehoiakim; priest father of Meremoth; man who stood by Ezra; priest whom Isaiah took as a witness

ארכבה
'arkubah –Knee (Aramaic)

בכור
Bekowr –Firstborn, firstling
Bikkuwr –Firstfruits

בכרו
Bokeruw –Bocheru, son of Azel, also a descendant of King Saul; firstborn

ברוך
Barukh –Blessed
Baruwk –Baruch, Jeremiah's friend and scribe; descendant of Perez who returned from the exile; one who helped to rebuild the wall of Jerusalem (Neh. 3:20; 10:7); man who sealed the covenant with Nehemiah (Neh. 10:7) – may be the same as the third

---

[406] Ziphion (236, 886).
[407] בכורה (233).
[408] Zechariah (242).
[409] Gudgodah (19).

	ובךכ	*Uwvarek* –And He will bless
	חרהיה	*Charhayah* –Harhaiah, father of Uzziel, a builder of the wall of Jerusalem
	כרוב	*Kerub* –Cherub, one of the cherubim (pl.); Cherub, place in Babylonia where some Jewish citizens lived during the Exile from which some persons of doubtful extraction returned with Zerubbabel (Ezra 2:59; Neh. 7:61); Ruler of Earth; one of the Kerubim
	רכוב	*Rekuwb* –Chariot
229	הדרך	*HaDarak* –The way
	המפקד	*Hamifqad* –Hammiphkad, gate in or near the northern end of the east wall of Jerusalem (Neh. 3:31)[410]
	וגרך	*ve-Gayrika* –"And your convert [stranger]" (Ex. 20:10; Deut. 29:10)
230	הכרה	*Hakkarah* –The look, appearance, expression
	זרחיה	*Zerachyah* –Zerahiah, priest of the line of Eleazar; head of a family who returned from the exile
	יגלפזק	*Yaglepzeq* –31st-36th letters of the 42-letter name of God (assoc. w/*Hod* or Friday)
	יחזרה	*Yachzerah* –Jahzerah, priest of the family of Immer whose descendants dwelt in Jerusalem after the exile (see also Ahasai – may be another name)[411]
	יעקן	*Ya'aqan* –Jaakan, son of Ezer, son of Seir (this name used only in Deut. 10:6; 1 Chr. 1:42 – he is also called Akan in Gen. 36:27)[412]
	ירך	*Yarek* –Thigh, side, loin, base
	כיר	*Kiyr* –Stove, range, cooking furnace
	כרי	*Kariy* –A group of foreign mercenary soldiers serving as bodyguard for King David; also executioners (2 Sam. 20:23; 2 Kings 11:4, 19)
	לקק	*Laqaq* –To lap, lick, lap up
	לר	*Lar* –184th Gate of the 231 Gates
	מקצ	*Maqatz* –Makaz, place mentioned in 1 Kings 4:9
	נפק	*Nefaq* –To go or come out, bring or come forth
	נצצ	*Natsats* –To shine, sparkle, gleam
	נקפ	*Naqaf* –To strike, strike off; to go around, compass, round
		Noqef –Striking off
	ענקי	*'Anaqiy* –Anakim or Anakite
	פנק	*Panaq* –To indulge, pamper, bring up, treat delicately
	צניפ	*Tzaniyf* –Turban, headdress
	צפינ	*Tzafiyn* –Treasure, a hidden thing
	קמצ	*Qamatz* –To grasp, take a handful
		Qometz –Closed hand, fist, handful

[410] Literally "the Muster" (see מפקד - 224).

[411] Ahasai (26).

[412] Some scholars feel that the reference in Deut. 10:6 may refer to a city, perhaps Beeroth (609). Akan (220, 870).

	ראידיה	*Rayadyah* –Angel of 2d Virgo
231	ארכי	*'Arkiy* –Archite
	ירי הו	*Yeriyahuw* –Jeriah, descendant of Hebron in the days of David (this spelling used only in 1 Chr. 23:19; 24:23 – see also יריה)[413]
	ירכא	*Yarka'* –Thigh, loin, flank, side (Aramaic)
	כארי	*Ka'ari* –Like a lion
	נפקא	*Nifqa'* –Outlay, expense (Aramaic)
	רחביהו	*Rechabyahuw* –Rehabiah, eldest son of Eliezer, son of Moses (this spelling used only in 1 Chr. 24:21; 26:25 – see also רחביה)[414]

–Mystic number of 21st Path (*Hesed-Netzach*; כ; Jupiter)

–The number of Gates of Wisdom, according to the *Sefer Yetzirah*; that is, the number of possible combinations of two Hebrew letters, disregarding order

232	אמניציאל	*Amnitziel* –"Coming forth of the Faithful of God," Archangel of Pisces
	אראל	*'er'el* –Hero, valiant one (form and meaning dubious – Isa. 33:7)
		Aral –Angel of Fire
	ארוכה	*'aruwkah* –Healing, restoration
	בכרי	*Bakriy* –Bachrites
		Bikriy –Bichri, ancestor of Sheba who rebelled against David
	חדרך	*Chadrak* –Hadrach, Syrian country associated with Hamath and Damascus, along the Orontes River south of Hamath
	טהור הוא	*Tahuwr Hua* –He is clean
	יברך	*Yivarak* –Bless
	יהי אור	*Yehi Aur* –"Let there be light" (Gen. 1:3)
	יריבי	*Yeriybay* –Jeribai, one of David's mighty men (1 Chr. 11:46)
	כביר	*Kebiyr* –(Something) netted, a quilt, fly net, pillow; mighty, great, powerful, many, much
233	אזכרה	*Azkarah* –Memorial offering – portion of food that's burned
	בכורה	*Bekowrah* –Birthright, primogeniture, right of the first born
		Bikkuwrah –First-ripe fig, early fig; firstfruits
	גרל	*Garol* –Harsh, rough; lot, portion
		Goral –A lot cast for certain decisions, small rock used for same (see Urim and Thummim)[415]
	והרבך	*ve-Hirebeka* –And multiply you (Deut. 7:13)
	וזקניכם	*Vizeknaychem* –And your elders
	זכור	*Zakowr* –Remember

[413] יריה (225).

[414] רחביה (225).

[415] Urim (257, 817), Thummim (490, 1050).

		Zakkuwr–Zakkur or Zacchur, descendant of Simeon; father of Shammua, one of the spies; descendant of Merari; Levite who sealed the covenant; father of Hanan; one who rebuilt part of the wall of Jerusalem (see also Zabbud and Zabdi)[416]
		Zakuwr–Male
	יקבצאל	*Yeqabtze'el*–Jekabzeel, city in Judah, probably modern Khirbet Hora (this name used only in Neh. 11:25 – see also Kabzeel)[417]
	יריחה	*Yeriychoh*–Jericho, fortified city of Canaan located northwest of the Jordan River (see also יריחו and ירחו)[418]
	כרוז	*Karowz*–A herald (Aramaic)
	עין גנים	*'Eyn Ganniym*–En-Gannim, town of lowland Judah; border town of the tribe of Issachar (see also Anem)[419]
	עץ החיים	*Etz HaChayim*–Tree of Life
	ציקלג	*Tziyqlag*–Ziklag, city in the south of Judah (this spelling used only in 1 Chr. 12:1, 20 – see also צקלג)[420]
	רגל	*Ragal*–To go on foot, spy out, foot it, go about
		Regal–Foot (Aramaic)
	–Prime number	
234	דכאוראב	*Decarabia*–Goetic demon #69
	יריחו	*Yeriychow*–Jericho, fortified city of Canaan located northwest of the Jordan River (see also ירחו and יריחה)[421]
	פס דמים	*Pas Dammiym*–Pas-Dammim, Philistine settlement near Socoh, apportioned to the tribe of Judah (this spelling used only in 1 Chr. 11:13 – see also Ephes Dammim)[422]
235	אפס דמים	*'Efes Dammiym*–Ephes Dammim, Philistine settlement near Socoh
	ירכה	*Yerekah*–Flank, side, extreme parts
	נקפה	*Niqpah*–Tether, rope, encircling rope
	צדקיאל	*Tzadqiel*–Archangel assoc. w/*Hesed*, and Jupiter
	צפניה	*Tzephanyah*–Zephaniah, prophet in the days of Josiah; Levite or priest, ancestor of Samuel (see also Uriel)[423]; son of Josiah the priest; priest who opposed Babylonian rule (this spelling used only in Jer. 21:1 – see also צפניהו)[424]

---

[416] Zabbud (19), Zabdi (23).

[417] Kabzeel (223).

[418] Jericho is the oldest continually inhabited city in the world. יריחו (234), ירחו (224)

[419] Anem (160, 720).

[420] צקלג (224).

[421] Jericho is the oldest continually inhabited city in the world. ירחו (224), יריחה (233)

[422] Ephes Dammim (235, 795).

[423] Uriel (248).

–235 lunar months = 19 solar years = 1 "year of Meton"

236 הראל *Har'el* –Altar, altar hearth
ודפקומ *Uwdfaquwm* –And if they overdrive them (Gen. 33:13)
ויכר *Awyakar* –And he acknowledged, knew
ומקלכמ *Uwmaqelkem* –And your staff
יורידו *Yowriyduw* –And they shall take down
יראייה *Yir'iyayh* –Irijah, captain of the gate who arrested Jeremiah
כאזרח *Ki'ezrach* –As a native, homeborn, like the native born
כאריה *Ki'aryah* –Like a lion, as a lion
כיור *Kiyowr* –Pot, basin, laver, pan
לדבר *Lidabayr* –To speak, communicate
Lidbir or *Lodebar* –Lo-Debar, place east of the Jordan River (see also לא דבר, לו דבר)[425]
מוצק *Muwtsah* –Constraint, distress; a casting
מצוק *Matsowq* –Straitness, straits, distress, stress, anguish
Matsuwq –Molten support, pillar, column
סנסנוי *Sansenoy* –One of three angels invoked against Lilith
ספעטאוי *Sapatavi* –Lord of Triplicity by Night for Aries
צמוק *Tzammuwq* –Bunch of raisins; raisin-bunch
צפוני *Tzafoni* –Zephonites; the Northern One; northern; northern one, northerner; Lilith
צפיונ *Tziphyown* –Ziphion, son of Gad (this spelling used only in Gen. 46:16 – see also צפון)[426]

237 אריוכ *'Aryowk* –Arioch, king of Ellasar; captain of Nebuchadnezzar's guard
ארכוי *'Arkevay* –Archevite
בכירה *Bekiyrah* –Firstborn, firstborn (of women)
ברכיה *Berekyah* –Berachiah, father of Asaph, the chief singer; one of the tabernacle doorkeepers; descendant of Ephraim in the time of Pekah; father of the prophet Zechariah; descendant of Jehoiakim; father of one who repaired the wall of Jerusalem; Levite who lived near Jerusalem (see also Berekyahu)[427]
זכרי *Zikriy* –Zichri, son of Izhar; descendant of Benjamin; descendant of Benjamin of Shishak; descendant of Benjamin of Jeroham; descendant of Eliezer in the days of Moses; father of Eliezer, descendant of Reuben; father of Amaziah; father of Elishaphat; man of valor who slew the son of King Ahaz; father of Joel; priest of the sons of Abijah (see Zabdi)[428]

[424] צפניהו (241).
[425] לא דבר (237), לו דבר (242).
[426] צפון (226, 876).
[427] Berekyahu (243).
[428] Zabdi (23).

לא דבר — *Lo' Debar* –Lo-Debar, place east of the Jordan River (this spelling used only in 2 Sam. 17:27; Amos 6:13 – see also לו דבר, לדבר)[429]

סויעסאל — *Soyasel* –Angel of 9th astrological house

ענואנינ — *A'ano'nin* –Guardian of the 26th Tunnel of Set

עצמ הכבוד — *Etzem HaKabodh* –Essence of glory

ראהאל — *Rahael* –Angel of 3q Cancer & day angel 3 Cups

רבלה — *Riblah* –Fertility; Riblah, city on the Orontes where the sons of Zedekiah were slain; border city of the Promised Land

238 אכזרי — *Akzariy* –Cruel

דכארביא — *Decarabia* –Goetic demon #69 (Aurum Solis spelling)

ויברכ — *ve-Yibarak* –And He blessed

יויריב — *Yowyariyb* –Joiarib, one whom Ezra sent to persuade ministers to return to the land of Israel; ancestor of a family living in Jerusalem; priest who returned from the exile (this spelling used in Neh. 11:10; 12:6, 19 – see also Jehoiarib)[430]

סזיעסאל — *Sizajasel* –Angel of 9th astrological house (variant or misprint; see 237, Soyasel)

רחל — *Rachel* –Rachel, younger daughter of Laban, wife of Jacob and mother of Joseph and Benjamin; ewe

239 ברזל — *Barzel* –Iron (the metal of Mars); tool of iron; harshness, strength, oppression (fig.)

גורל — *Gowral* –A lot cast for certain decisions, small rock used for same (see Urim and Thummim)[431]

ויבנ נח מזבח ליהוה — *Vahyeven Noach Mezbayach la* YHVH –"And he, Noah, built an altar to YHVH" (Gen. 8:20)

יכסגנוצ — *Yakasaganotz* –Angel of 3d Taurus

חקבטנע — *Chaqbatna* –25th-30th letters of the 42-letter name of God, assoc. w/Thursday (Kaplan, *Sefer Yetzirah*)

לגור — *Lagowr* –To be a stranger; to be fearful

–Prime number

240 העסקה — *Ha'asaqah* –Employment; dealing; activity

יזרחיה — *Yizrachyah* –Izrahiah, descendant of Issachar (1 Chr. 7:3); Jezrahiah, an overseer of the singers at the purification of the people (Neh. 12:42)

כידור — *Kiydowr* –Attack, onslaught, onset

ככר — *Kikkar* –Round

Kikker –Talent (a unit of money – Aramaic)

כנענימ — *Kanannim* –Canaanites

מקסמ — *Miqsam* –Divination

מקק — *Maqaq* –To decay, pine away, rot, fester

---

[429] לו דבר (242), לדבר (236).

[430] Jehoiarib (243).

[431] Urim (257- 817), Thummin (490, 1050).

	מר	*Mar* –Bitter, bitterness; bitterly; a drop, a flowing down; sad; fierce, violent, wild; sadness; 193rd Gate of the 231 Gates
		More –Myrrh
	ססםם	*Saspam* –Angel of 1d Aquarius
	ספק	*Safaq* –To clap, slap
		Sefeq –Handclapping, mocking, mockery, scorn (meaning dubious – Job 20:22; 36:18)
	עמלק	*'Ameleq* –Amelek, grandson of Esau and son of Eliphaz and progenitor of the Amalekites (Gen. 36:12, 16; 1 Chr. 1:36 – see also Ex. 17:8-9)
	פנינים	*Peninim* –Rubies, gems
	פעמנ	*Pa'amon* –Bell (on High Priest's robe)
	פצע	*Patza'* –To bruise, wound, wound by bruising
		Petza' –Bruise, wound
	פקדונ	*Piqqadown* –Deposit, store, supply
	צלצל	*Tzelatzal* –Whirring, buzzing; spear; whirring locust
	צמק	*Tzamaq* –To dry up, shrivel (of women's breasts)
	צפע	*Tzefa'* –Poisonous serpent
	קנצ	*Qenetz* –Snare, net (meaning dubious – Job 18:2)
	רכב	*Rakak* –To be tender, be soft, be weak
	רמ	*Ram* –Ram, ancestor of David (Ruth 4:19); son of Jerahmeel of Judah (1 Chr. 2:27); head of the family of Elihu (Job 32:2)
241	אמר	*'amar* –To say, speak, utter; to say, to speak, to command, to tell, to relate
		'emer, 'omer –Word, command, utterance, speech, word, saying, promise, command
		'immar –Lamb (Aramaic)
		'Immer –Immer, a place or person unknown (Ezra 2:59; Neh. 7:61)
	אריל	*'ariy'el* –Meaning uncertain, perhaps lion-like (1 Chr. 11:22; 2 Sam. 23:20)
		Ari'el –"lion of God" or "lioness of God" (a name applied to Jerusalem; the name of a chief of the returning exiles)
	ארמ	*'Aram* –Aram, son of Shem; son of Abraham's nephew, descendent from Asher; Ram, the father of Amminadab; Aram, location occupied by the Aramaenans
	זכר ואז	*Zakar Vi-az* –May come
	זרבבל	*Zerubbabel* –Zerubbabel, leader of a group who returned from exile – he began the rebuilding of the Temple
	חקדטנע	*Chaqdatna* –25th-30th letters of the 42-letter name of God (Trachtenberg, 1939)
	חרגל	*Chargol* –A kind of locust, locust, a leaping creature (Lev.11:22)
	מאר	*Ma'ar* –To pain, prick, irritate, be in pain
	מוצקה	*Muwtsaqah* –Pipe; a casting

מצוקה *Metsuwqah* –Straitness, distress, straits, stress

מרא *Mara'* –To beat (the air), flap (the wings) (meaning dubious – Job 39:18); filthy (Zeph. 3:1); Mara, name assumed by Naomi after the death of her husband (Ruth 1:20)[432]

Mare' –Lord (of king, of God – Dan. 2:47; 4:16, 21; 5:23 – Aramaic)

סמקיאל *Sameqiel* –"Vomiting Forth of the Poison of God," Angel of Capricorn

צפניהו *Tzephanyahuw* –Zephaniah, a priest who opposed Babylonian rule (this spelling used only in 2 Kings 25:18; Jer. 37:3 – see also צפניה)[433]

ראמ *Re'am* –To rise

Re'em –Great aurochs or wild bulls now extinct

242 אראיל *Ari'eyl* –Hearth, altar hearth, altar

אראלי *'Ar'eliy* –Areli, son of Gad; Arelites

אריאל *Ariel* –Ruler of Air; one sent by Ezra to secure the temple ministers (Ezra 8:16); name of Jerusalem (Isa. 29:1-2)

ברמ *Beram* –Only, nevertheless, but (Aramaic)

זכריה *Zekaryah* –Zechariah, chief of the tribe of Reuben–; Levite gatekeeper in the days of David; Levite set over the service of song in the days of David; priest in the days of David; descendant of Levi through Kohath; descendant of Levi through Merari; father of Iddo; prince of Jehoshaphat sent to teach the people; Levite who encouraged Jehoshaphat against Moab; son of Jehoshaphat; son of Jehoiada who was stoned; prophet in the days of Uzziah; Levite who helped to cleanse the temple; descendant of Levi; prince of Judah in the days of Josiah; a minor prophet whose book is named after him; chief man of Israel; one who returned from the exile; one who took a foreign wife during the exile; prince with Ezra; descendant of Perez; one whose descendants dwelled in Jerusalem; a priest; Levite trumpeter; priest who took part in the dedication ceremony; one whom Isaiah took as a witness (see also Zaker)[434]; Zachariah, 15th King of Israel; father of Abi or Abijah (written Zechariah in 2 Chr. 29:1)

יהוה יראה YHVH *Jireh* –Adonai-Jireh, place where Abraham attempted to offer Isaac as a sacrifice (Gen. 22:14)

כרכב *Karkob* –Edge, rim

לו דבר *Lo' Debar* –Lo-Debar, place east of the Jordan River

---

[432] Mara derives from *marah* or "bitter."

[433] צפניה (235).

[434] Zacher (227).

(this spelling used only in 2 Sam. 9:4, 5 – see also לא דבר, לדבר)[435]

מרב *Merab* –Merab, daughter of Saul promised to David but given to Adriel

קבצים *Qibtzayim* –Kibzaim, city of Ephraim given to the Levites (see also Jokmeam)[436]

243 אברם *Abram* –Abram

אגרטל *Agartal* –Vessel, basket, leather bag, basin

ברכיהו *Berekyahuw* – Berekyahu, father of Asaph, the chief singer; one of the tabernacle doorkeepers; descendant of Ephraim in the time of Pekah; father of the prophet Zechariah; descendant of Jehoiakim; father of one who repaired the wall of Jerusalem; Levite who lived near Jerusalem (see also Berachiah)[437]

גמר *Gamar* –To end, come to an end, complete, cease; to fail, perfect, perform

Gemar –To complete (Aramaic)

Gomer –Gomer, eldest son of Japheth; immoral wife of Hosea

גרם *Garam* –To cut off, reserve, lay aside, leave, save; to break bones, gnaw bones, break

Gerem –Bone, strength, bare, self; bone (Aramaic)

יהויריב *Yehowyariyb* –Jehoiarib, head of a family of Aaron (1 Chr. 24:7)

יוזכר *Yozakar* –Jozachar, son of Shimeath, who collaborated in the slaying of King Joash of Judah (see also Zabad)[438]

מארב *Ma'arab* –Ambush, (hunter's) blind

Marbas –Goetic demon #5

מגר *Magar* –To throw, cast, toss

Megar –To overthrow (Aramaic)

רגלי *Ragliy* –On foot; footman

רגם *Ragam* –To stone, slay or kill by stoning

Regem –Regem, descendant of Caleb (see also Regem-melech)[439]

244 גמרא *Gemara* –Commentary on the Mishnah

הרחאל *Herachiel* –Angel of 5q Taurus & day angel 7 Pentacles

חרול *Charuwl* –Nettles, weeds, kind of weed

מרד *Marad* –To rebel, revolt, be rebellious; rebellious (Aramaic)

Merad –Rebellion (Aramaic)

Mered –Rebellion, revolt (always against YHVH); Mered, son of Ezra, descendant of Judah

---

435 לא דבר (237), לדבר (236).

436 Jokmeam (260, 820).

437 Berachiah (237).

438 Zabad (13).

439 Regem-Melech (333, 1373).

	רדמ	*Radam* –To be asleep, unconscious
245	אדמ קדמו ן	*Adam Qadmon* –The archetypal man
	אדרמ	*'Adoram* –Adoram, alternate name for Adoniram
	הרמ	*Harum* –Harum, descendant of Judah *Horam* –Horam, king of Gezer defeated by Joshua
	מהר	*Mahar* –To hasten; to obtain or acquire by paying purchase price, give a dowry *Maher* –Hurrying, speedy, swift, hastening; quickly, speedily *Mohar* –Purchase price for wife, wedding money
	מרה	*Marah* –To be contentious, be rebellious, be refractory, be disobedient towards, be rebellious against *Morah, morrah* –Bitterness, grief; Marah, fountain of bitter water in the wilderness of Shur where the Israelites first halted after crossing the Reed Sea
	צפעה	*Tzefiah* –Offshoot, leaf, shoot (meaning dubious – Isa. 22:24)
	רב־מג	*Rab-Mag* –Rabmag, official position of some sort (Jer. 39:3, 13)[440]
	רמה	*Ramah* –To cast, shoot, hurl; to beguile, deceive, mislead; height, high place; Ramah, town in Benjamin; frontier town of Asher; fortified city of Naphtali *Remah* –To cast, throw (Aramaic) *Rimmah* –Maggot, worm *Rowmah* –Proudly, haughtily
	–The number of mules brought out of exile (Ezra 2:66)	
246	אדמה ללי ו ן	*'adamah le'livan* –I will be like the One on High
	אמרה	*'imrah* –Utterance, speech, word (word of God, the Torah)
	ג ברי אל	*Gabriel* –Archangel assoc. w/*Yesod*, Luna (both archangel and angel), the West, and Water (Biblical references – Dan. 8:16; 9:21)
	הרי אל	*Hariel* –Angel of 3q Libra & day angel 3 Swords
	מארה	*Me'erah* –Curse
	מדבר	*Midbar* –Wilderness; mouth
	מ ור	*Muwr* –To change, exchange
	מראה	*Mar'ah* –Vision (as mode of revelation); mirror *Mar'eh* –Sight, appearance, vision *Mur'ah* –Crop or craw (of a bird), alimentary canal (of a bird)
	מרבד	*Marbad* –Spread, coverlet
	נ יצוצ	*Niytsowts* –Spark
	צלמ אלהימ	*Tzelem 'Elohim* –"Image of God"
	צפ וע	*Tzefuwa'* –Dung (of cattle), manure, cattle dung
	ראידאל	*Raydel* –Lord of Triplicity by Day for Taurus
	ראמה	*Rawmah* –Corals

[440] It is unclear whether it is a high religious or governmental position – Nergal-Sharezer of Babylonia bore this title.

	רומ	*Ruwm* –To rise, rise up, be high, be lofty, be rotten, be wormy; haughtiness, height, elevation
247	אחרחל	*'Acharchel* –Aharhel, descendant of Judah
	אלויר	*Aloyar* –Lord of Triplicity by Night for Capricorn
	זמר	*Zamar* –To sing, sing praise, make music; to trim, prune
		Zammar –Singer (Aramaic)
		Zemar –Instrumental music, music (Aramaic)
		Zemer –Mountain sheep, mountain goat, moufflon, gazelle, chamois (meaning uncertain – Deut.14:5)
	זרמ	*Zaram* –To pour out, pour forth in floods, flood away
		Zerem –Rain-shower, thunderstorm, flood of rain, downpour, rainstorm
	ירואל	*Yeruw'el* –Jeruel, wilderness area in Judah near the cliff of Ziz and En-Gedi (2 Chr. 20:16)
	מאור	*Ma'owr* –Light, luminary
	מורא	*Mowra'* –Fear, reverence, terror
	מרבה	*Marbeh* –Abundance, increase
		Mirbah –Much
	ראומ	*Raum* –Goetic demon #40
	רמז	*Remez* –Torah interpretation that focuses on hints and allusions in the text
	רזמ	*Razam* –To wink; flash (of eyes)
248	אברהמ	*Abraham* –Abraham
	אוריאל	*Auriel* –Archangel assoc. w/North and Earth; Uriel, chief of the sons of Kohath (see also Zephaniah)[441]; father of Michaiah, one of Rehoboam's sons
	במרבר	*Bamidbar* –"In the Wilderness," Hebrew title of the Book of Numbers
	ברומ	*Berowm* –Variegated cloth, damask
	וברכב	*vo-Verakika* –And bless you (Deut. 7:13)
	זכריהו	*Zekaryahu* –Zachariah, 15th King of Israel (variant spelling)
	חמר	*Chamar* –To boil, foam, foam up, ferment; to be reddened; to daub, seal up, cover or smear with asphalt; wine (Aramaic)
		Chemar –Slime, pitch, asphalt, bitumen
		Chemer –Wine
		Chomer –Cement, mortar, clay; heap; Homer – a unit of dry measure about 65 imperial gallons
	חרמ	*Charam* –To ban, devote, destroy utterly, completely destroy, dedicate for destruction, exterminate; to split, slit, mutilate (a part of the body)
		Charim –Harim, priest in charge of the third division of temple duties; ancestor of some returning from captivity – his descendants took foreign wives during the exile; one who sealed the new covenant with God after the exile; family that

[441] Zephaniah (235).

sealed the new covenant with God after the exile
Chorem –Horem, fortress of the tribe of Naphtali – modern Hurah

מגרה *Megarah* –Saw (for stone cutting)
מחר *Machar* –Tomorrow, in time to come, in the future
מרח *Marach* –To rub
רגמה *Rigmah* –Heap (of stones)
רזיאל *Raziel* –Archangel assoc. w/ *Chokmah*
רחמ *Racham* –To love, love deeply, have mercy; womb (n. mas.); compassion; carrion vulture (extinct bird); Raham, descendant of Caleb
רמח *Romach* –Spear, lance
–The number of positive Commandments in Torah
–The number of columns of text in the Torah (when written on a scroll)
–The number of parts of the human skeleton

249 ארזיאל *Araziel* –"Firmness of God," Angel of Taurus
ברזלי *Barzillay* –Barzillai, husband of Merab, Saul's eldest daughter, and father of Adriel; one who befriended David when he fled from Absalom; priest whose genealogy was lost during the exile
גמור *Gamori* –Goetic demon #56
הדרמ *Hadoram* –Hadoram, superintendent of forced labor under David, Solomon, and Rehoboam (2 Chr. 10:18) (see also Adoniram (1 Kings 4:6); and Adoram (2 Sam. 20:24; 1 Kings 12:18))[442]
הצדיקמ *HaTzedekim* –The righteous
טרמ *Terem* –Before, not yet, before that
מגור *Magowr* –Fear, terror
Maguwr –Sojourning place, dwelling place, sojourning
מורג *Mowrag* –Thresher, threshing-sledge
מטר *Matar* –To rain; rain
מרט *Marat* –To bare, polish, make smooth or bald or bare
Meret –To pluck, pull off (Aramaic)
קומו צאו *Quwmu Tzuuw* –Go!, get out!, leave!

250 דרומ *Darom* –South
ימר *Yamar* –To exchange
ירמ *Yoram* –Joram, 5th King of Judah; 9th King of Israel
למענכמ *Lima'ankem* –Through your fault, for your sake
מבחר *Mibchar* –Choicest, best; Mibhar, one of David's mighty men (1 Chr. 11:38)
מברח *Mibrach* –Fugitive, flight
מדור *Medowr* –Dwelling place
מהרה *Meherah* –Haste, speed
מורד *Mowrad* –Descent, slope, steep place, hanging work, bevelled work
מטרא *Mattara'* –Guard, ward, prison, mark, target
מעמק *Ma'amaq* –Depths

---

[442] Adoniram (305, 865), Adoram (245, 805).

מרוד *Maruwd* –Restlessness, straying, wanderer, refugee
מרחב *Merchab* –Broad or roomy place, wide, expanses
מרי *Meriy* –Rebellion
נפיסימ *Nefiysiym* –Nephusim, ancestor of returned captives (this name used only in Ezra 2:50 – see also נפושסים, Naphish)[443]
נר *Ner* –Lamp; prosperity; instruction; Ner, father of Abner, Saul's commander-in-chief; grandfather of Saul (see also Abiel)[444]; 201st Gate of the 231 Gates
עמלקי *'Amaleqiy* –Amalekite(s)
עצמנ *'Atzmon* –Azmon, place on the western boundary of Canaan (this spelling used only in Num. 34:4; – see also עצמון)[445]
פקע *Peqa'* –Knob-shaped or ball-shaped or gourd-shaped carved wood or metal ornament
צינק *Tiynoq* –Pillory, stocks
צעיפ *Tza'iyf* –Wrapper, shawl, veil
צפפ *Tzafaf* –To chirp, peep
קיצנ *Qiytzown* –At the end, outermost, outer
קסמימ *Qesemim* –Practicing a form of divination
קצינ *Qatziyn* –Chief, ruler, commander
רכל *Rakal* –Merchant(s); Rachal, town in Judah (1 Sam. 30:29 – see also Carmel)[446]
רמי *Rammiy* –Syrian
רנ *Ron* –Shout, rejoicing, ringing cry, shout, cry (of joy)
–The number of Isralites who rebelled against Moses and Aaron with Korah and other insurrectors (Num. 16)

251 אמיר *Amiyr* –Top, summit (of tree or mountain)
אמרי *'Emoriy* –Amorite
'Imriy –Imri, descendant of Judah; father of Zakkur, one of Nehemiah's assistants
ארמי *'Arammiy* –Aramitess
ארנ *Aran* –Aran, son of Dishon
Aron –Ark (of the covenant)
'Oran –Fir tree, cedar; Oren, son of Jerahmeel of Judah
יאמר *Yomar* –Said, will say, shall say
יריאל *Yeriy'el* –Jeriel, descendant of Issachar
מורה *Mowrah* –Razor
Mowreh –Rain; teacher; Moreh, first stopping place of Abraham after he entered Canaan; hill lying at the foot of the valley of Jezreel
מריא *Meriy'* –Well-fed, fatling
נאר *Na'ar* –To abhor, spurn

---

[443] נפושסים (546, 1106), Naphish (440).
[444] The relationships here are unclear – Abner may have been Saul's uncle. If so, both Ner's are the same. It is possible that the second Ner had sons named Ner and Kish, the father of Saul. Abiel (44).
[445] עצמון (256, 906).
[446] Carmel (290).

סומפניה | *Suwmponeyah* –A musical instrument, wind instrument, bagpipe, double pipe, panpipes (Aramaic)
רומה | *Ruwmah* –Rumah, town whose locality is uncertain
רייאל | *Reyayel* –Angel of 5q Sagittarius & day angel 10 Wands
–Prime number

252 ארומה | *'Aruwmah* –Arumah, town near Shechem
המאור | *HaMa'or* –The light
זמרה | *Zimrah* –Music, melody, song; choice fruits, choice products
זרמה | *Zirmah* –Flow, issue (of semen)
חזק ואמצ | *Chazaq ve-Ematz* –To be strong and brave
כרבל | *Karbel* –To put a mantle on, be-mantle, bind around
מאורה | *Meuwrah* –Light hole, den
מדרגה | *Madregah* –Steep place, steep
מזרה | *Mazzarah* –(Mazzaroth – the 12 signs of the Zodiac and their 36 constellations. See Job 38:32)
Mizreh –Pitchfork
Mezarch –Scatterer
נבר | *Naberius* –Goetic demon #24

253 אבירמ | *'Abiyram* –Abiram, a Reubenite who conspired against Moses and was destroyed; firstborn son of Hiel who died when his father began to rebuild Jericho
אבנר | *'Abner* –Abner, captain of the army under Saul
ברכאל | *Barak'el* –Barachel, father of Elihu, a figure in Job
גרמי | *Garmiy* –Garmite
גרנ | *Goren* –Threshing floor; barn, barn-floor, corn floor, void place
חמרה | *Chamorah* –Heap
חרמה | *Chormah* –Hormah, Canaanite city located near Ziklag, called Zephath in 1 Sam. 30:30 – perhaps modern Tell el-Milk
יברכיהו | *Yeberekyahuw* –Jeberechiah, father of the Zechariah whom Isaiah took as a witness (Is. 8:2)
כרבלא | *Karbela'* –Mantle, robe, cap, turban, helmet
מזור | *Mazowr* –Net, trap (meaning dubious – Ob. 1:7); wound
מטרד | *Matred* –Matred, mother of Mehetabel, and wife of Hadar, a King of Edom (Gen. 36:39; 1 Chr. 1:50)
מרוז | *Merowz* –Meroz, place near Kishon (Judg. 5:23)
נגר | *Nagar* –To pour, run, flow, pour down
רגנ | *Ragan* –To murmur, whisper
רחמה | *Rachamah* –Womb
–Mystic number of 22nd Path (*Giburah-Tiferet*; ל; Libra)

254 אלהי יצחק | *Elohi Itzchaq* –The God of Isaac
גרודיאל | *Gerodiel* –Angel of 3d Aquarius
ואברהמ | *ve-Avraham* –And Abraham

	ורחמ	*ve-Racham* –And of the womb
	זוריאל	*Zuriel* –"Binding of God," Archangel of Libra
	חורמ	*Churam* –Huram, descendant of Bela and a grandson of Benjamin (1 Chr. 8:5); king of Tyre who formed an alliance with David and Solomon; skilled craftsman from Tyre employed by Solomon (2 Chr. 4:16) (see also Hiram (2 Kings 7:13))[447]
	חמור	*Chamowr* –He-ass; Hamor, prince of Shechem whose son Shechem brought destruction on himself and his family (Gen. 33:19; 34:2-26)
	מגורה	*Megowrah* –Fear, terror
		Meguwrah –Fear, terror; storehouse, granary
	מחראה	*Machara'ah* –Sewer, cesspool, cloaca; draught house
	מרוח	*Merowach* –Bruised, crushed, rub (meaning dubious – Lev. 21:20)
	נדר	*Nadar* –To vow, make a vow
		Neder –Vow, votive offering
	נרד	*Nerd* –Spikenard, nard
	צדיכימ	*Tzadikim* –Righteous ones
	רחומ	*Rachum* –Merciful, compassion (of God)
		Rechuwm –Rehum, chief man that returned from Exile with Zerubbabel (see also Nehum)[448]; chancellor of Artaxerxes; Levite who helped to repair the wall of Jerusalem; one who sealed the covenant (Neh. 10:26)
255	אנדר	*Andras* –Goetic demon #63
	הדורמ	*Hadowram* –Hadoram, son of Joktan (Gen. 10:27; 1 Chr. 1:21); son of Tou, king of Hamath (1 Chr. 18:10) – called Joram in 2 Sam. 8:9-10; (see also Jehoram)[449]
	הרנ	*Haran* –Haran (ancient Mesopotamian city); Haran, brother of Abraham who died before his father; descendant of Levi; son of Caleb
	טרומ	*Terowm* –Before, not yet, before that, ere (of time)
	ימרה	*Yimrah* –Imrah, descendant of Asher
	מגזרה	*Magzerah* –Axe, cutting instrument
	מדורה	*Meduwrah* –Pile (of fuel), pyre, pile (of wood)
	מהיר	*Mahiyr* –Quick, prompt, skilled, ready
	מהרי	*Maharay* –Maharai, one of David's warriors (2 Sam. 23:28; 1 Chr. 11:30; 27:13)
	מורט	*Mowrat* –Scoured, polished, smooth
	מזרח	*Mizrach* –East, place of sunrise
	מחברה	*Mechabberah* –Binder, clamp, joint
	מריה	*Mowriyah* –Moriah, elevation in Jerusalem on which Solomon built the Temple; hill on which Abraham was prepared to sacrifice Isaac (see also

[447] Hiram (258, 818).
[448] Nehum (104, 664).
[449] Joram (256, 816), Jehoram (261, 821).

(מוריה)[450]
Merayah –Meraiah, priest of Jerusalem in the days of Joiakim

מרזח *Mirzach* –Cry of joy, revelry

נהר *Nahar* –To shine, beam, light, burn; to flow, stream; stream, river
Nehar –River (Aramaic)

פקעה *Paqqu'ah* –Gourds

רכלה *Rekullah* –Merchandise, traffic, trade

רמיה *Ramyah* –Ramiah, one who married a foreign wife during the Exile
Remiyah –Laxness, slackness, slackening

רנה *Ranah* –To rattle (Job 39:23)
Rinnah –Ringing cry; Rinnah, descendant of Judah

256 אהרן *Aaron* –Brother of Moses

אמריה *'Amaryah* –Amariah, son of the priest Meraioth; son of Azariah; name of a Levite; chief priest during the time of Jehoshaphat; ancestor of Zephaniah; Levite who distributed tithes; one who sealed the covenant with God after the exile; one who took a foreign wife during the exile; one whose descendents dwelled in Jerusalem after the exile

דברים *Devarim* –Words; Hebrew title of the book of Deuteronomy

יורם *Yoram* –Joram, descendant of Moses (1 Chr. 26:25) 5th King of Judah; 9th King of Israel (see also Hadoram – also Jehoram)[451]

מבחור *Mibchowr* –Choice

נור *Nur* –Fire, fiery (Aramaic)

עצמון *'Atzmown* –Azmon, place on the western boundary of Canaan (this spelling used only in Num. 34:5; Josh. 15:4 – see also עצמן)[452]

257 אבניצדק *Avinitzedek* –Just scales, accurate scales

אורים *Urim* –Lights; Urim, a material object used (along with the Thummim) for divination by the High Priest[453]

ארומי *'Arowmiy* –Edomites, clerical error for אדומי in 2 Kings 16:6[454]

ארון *'arown* –Chest, ark, Ark of the Covenant; coffin

בן־גבר *Ben-Geber* –Ben-geber, one of Solomon's officers who provided food for the king and his household (1 Kings 4:13)

זמיר *Zamiyr* –Song, psalm; trimming, pruning

---

[450] מוריה (261).
[451] Hadoram (255, 815), Jehoram (261, 821).
[452] עצמן (250, 900).
[453] Thummim (490, 1050).
[454] אדומי (61).

זמרי — *Zimri* –Zimri, disobedient Israelite slain by Phinehas; captain who slew Elah, becoming fifth King of Israel; son of Zerah of Judah; descendant of Benjamin; unknown place or tribe of peoples

חרטמ — *Chartom* –Diviner, magician, astrologer (Gen. 41:8, 24; Ex. 7:11, 22; 8:7, 18, 19; 9:11; Dan. 1:20; 2:2); magician, magician-astrologer (Aramaic – Dan. 2:10, 27; 4:4, 6; 5:11)

מריבה — *Meriybah* –Strife, contention; Meribah, desert location where Moses smote the rock; another name for Kadesh Barnea in the wilderness of Zin, where the Israelites rebelled against Moses

נורא — *Nuwra* –Fiery

נזר — *Nazar* –To dedicate, consecrate, separate; to be a Nazarite, live as a Nazarite

Nezer –Consecration, crown, separation, Nazariteship

סומפוניה — *Suwpowneyah* –A musical instrument, wind instrument, bagpipe, double pipe, panpipes (Aramaic)

רזנ — *Razan* –To be weighty, be judicious

Razown –Leanness, scantness, wasting; potentate, ruler

–Prime number

258 גמריה — *Gemaryah* –Gemariah, one who sought to stop Jehoiakim from burning Jeremiah's prophecies; one of Zedekiah's ambassadors to Babylon (see also Gemaryahu)[455]

זמורה — *Zemowrah* –Branch, twig, shoot

חירמ — *Chiram* –Hiram, King of Tyre; architect of the Temple of Solomon

חרנ — *Charan* –Haran, brother of Abraham who died before his father; descendant of Levi; son of Caleb; Haran, Mesopotamian city northwest of Ninevah

ירחמ — *Yerocham* –Jeroham, Levite, the grandfather of Samuel; descendant of Benjamin; head of a family of Benjamin; priest whose son lived in Jerusalem after the exile; father of two who joined David at Ziklag; father of Azareel, prince of Dan; father of one who helped Jehoiada to set Joah on the throne of Judah; father of Adaiah the priest (this latter may be the same as the fourth Jeroham)

מזהור — *Mazohir* –Illuminating, radiant

מחיר — *Mechiyr* –Price, hire; Mehir, descendant of Caleb of Hur

נחר — *Nachar* –Snorting

259 אדני־צדק — *'Adoniy-Tzedeq* –Adoni-zedek, king of Jerusalem

אחרימ — *Achrowm* –Another

'Achiyram –Ahiram, descendant of Benjamin (see also Ehi, may be Aher as well)[456]

אחרנ — *Achron* –Short for *Acharown*, meaning behind,

---

[455] Gemaryahu (264).

[456] Ehi (19), Aher (209).

following, subsequent, western
Ochoran –Other, another

גרונ *Garown* –Neck, throat

מטרי *Matriy* –Matri, ancestor of a tribe of Benjamin to which Saul belonged

נטר *Natar* –To keep, keep guard, reserve, maintain
Netar –To keep (Aramaic)

ראובנ *Re'uwben* –Reuben, eldest son of Jacob and Leah; descendants of Reuben who made up the tribe of Israel with the same name (assoc. w/Aquarius)

260 ארגונ *'argevan* –Purple, red-purple

בחרימ *Bachuriym* –Bahurim, village near the Mount of Olives
Bechuriym –Youth

ברחמי *Barchumiy* –Barhumite

ברטחיאל *Baratchial* –Guardian of the 12th Tunnel of Set

גרזימ *Gerizim* –Gerizim, the mountain whereupon six of the tribes of Israel stood to bless (Deut. 11:29)

גרזנ *Garzen* –Axe

דרונ *Darown* –South

המריה *HaMoriah* –The land of Jerusalem

טיריאל *Tiriel* –Intelligence of Mercury

יקמעמ *Yeqam'am* –Jekameam, descendant of Levi (1 Chr. 23:19; 24:23)
Yoqme'am –Jokmeam, city of the tribe of Ephraim, given to the Levites (probably the same as Kibzaim)

ירמי *Yeremay* –Jeremai, one who divorced his foreign wife after the exile

כמר *Kamar* –To yearn, be kindled, be black (hot), grow warm and tender, be or grow hot, become hot, become emotionally agitated (with love or anger); priest, idolatrous priest

כרמ *Kerem* –Vineyard
Korem –To tend vines or vineyards, to dress vines or vineyards

לריכ *Leraikha* –Goetic demon #14 (Aurum Solis spelling)

מכר *Makar* –To sell
Makkar –Acquaintance, friend
Meker –Merchandise, value, price

מצפנ *Mitspun* –Hidden treasure, treasure

מרכ *Morek* –Weakness

נהרה *Neharah* –Light, daylight

ניר *Niyr* –To break up, freshly plow or till; tillable or untilled or fallow ground; lamp

נקיק *Naqiyq* –Cleft (of a rock)

סר *Sar* –Stubborn, implacable, rebellious, resentful, sullen, ill-humored; 208th Gate of the 231 Gates

צענימ *Tza'ananniym* –Zaannanim, place on the southern border of Naphtali (this spelling used only in Judg.

4:11 – see also צענ נ ימ)[457]

צעק *Tza'aq* –To cry, cry out, call, cry for help

קלקל *Qeloqel* –Contemptible, worthless

קנ נ י נ *Qinnamon* –Cinnamon

קנסנ A permutation of יהוה by *Aiq Bekar*[458]

קצע *Qatza'* –To scrape, scrape off; to be cornered, be set in corners

רכיל *Rakiyl* –Slander, slanderer, tale-bearer

רמכ *Rammak* –Steeds, mules (meaning dubious – Esth. 8:10)

–The number of chapters in the New Testament Protestant Bible (keep in mind that chapters were not added to the Bible till long after the destruction of the Temple)

261 אדורימ *'Adowrayim* –Adoraim, city in Judah

אליצפנ *Eliytsafan* –Elizaphan or Elzaphan, a Kohathite chief in the wilderness; a Zebulunite chief; Uzziel's son, Mishael's brother in time of Moses

אסר *'asar* –To tie, bind, imprison

'esar –Bond, binding obligation, obligation; interdict, decree, decree of restriction (Aramaic); connecting, shackling

ארדונ *'Ardown* –Ardon, son of Caleb

דראונ *Dera'own* –Aversion, abhorrence

הרונ *Herown* –Physical conception, pregnancy, conception

יהורמ *Yehoram* –Jehoram, son of Tou, king of Hamath; alternate name for Joram, 5th King of Judah, and for Joram, 9th King of Israel; priest commissioned to teach the people

לראיכ *Leraikha* –Goetic demon #14

מוריה *Mowriyah* –Moriah, elevation in Jerusalem on which Solomon built the Temple; hill on which Abraham was prepared to sacrifice Isaac (see also מריה)[459]

מחזור *Machzor* –Festival prayer book

262 אהרונ *'Aharown* –Aaron

אורנה *'Owrnah* –Araunah, a Jebusite (2 Sam. 26:16-24), called Ornan in 1 Chr. 21:15-25[460] – see Arnaunah below

אל מלכ נאמנ *El Melek Ne'eman* –The Lord and faithful king – it is important to notice the first letters of this phrase (see introduction)

אמריהו *'Amaryahuw* –Amariah, son of the priest Meriaoth; son of Azariah; name of a Levite; chief priest during the time of Jehoshaphat; ancestor of Zephaniah; Levite who distributed tithes; one who sealed the covenant with God after the exile; one who took

---

457 צענ נ ימ (310, 870).

458 See Introduction.

459 מריה (255).

460 Ornan (301, 951).

a foreign wife during the exile; one whose descendents dwelled in Jerusalem after the exile

ארונה *'Aravnah* –Araunah, a Jebusite (2 Sam. 26:16-24), called Ornan in 1 Chr. 21:15-25[461] – see Araunah above

בסר *Beser* –Unripe or sour grapes

Boser –Unripe grape, sour grapes

זמירה *Zemiyrah* –Zemira, son of Becher, a descendant of Benjamin

מברכ *Mabrak* –Consecrated

מכבר *Makbar* –Netted cloth, coverlet

Makber –Grating, latticework

מרכב *Merkab* –Chariot, place to ride, riding seat (Lev. 15:9; 1 Kings 4:26; Song 3:10)

סבר *Sebar* –To think, intend

סרב *Sarab* –Brier, rebel (meaning dubious – Ezek. 2:6)

עינ בעינ *'Ayin Be'ayin* –"Eye to eye" (Is. 52:8)

263 אבינר *'Abiyner* –Abner, captain of the army under Saul

אבדרונ *Abdaron* –Angel of 2d Aquarius

אורונ *Avron* –Angel of 2d Pisces

ברכיאל *Barkiel* –"Son of God's Prospering," Archangel of Scorpio

גמטריא *Gematria* –Hebrew numerology

גרס *Garas* –To be crushed, broken

סגר *Sagar* –To shut, close

Segar –To shut; shirt (both Aramaic)

רזונ *Rezown* –Rezon, Syrian rebel who set up his own government in Damascus (1 Kings 11:23)[462]

–Prime number

264 גמריה *Gemaryahuw* – Gemaryahu, one who sought to stop Jehoiakim from burning Jeremiah's prophecies; one of Zedekiah's ambassadors to Babylon (see also Gemariah)[463]

חורנ *Chavran* –Hauran, district bordering the region of Gilead south of Damascus, noted for the fertility of its soil

חרונ *Charown* –Anger, heat, burning of anger (always used of God's anger)

יחמור *Yachmuwr* –A kind of deer, red in color – perhaps extinct

ירדנ *Yordan* –Jordan, major river of Palestine (Gen. 13:10; Josh. 2:7)

מדרכ *Midrak* –Treading or stepping place, place to tread on

מרדכ *Merodak* –Merodach, the name of a Babylonian deity, possibly representing Mars or may be a

---

461 Ornan (301, 951).

462 Some scholars think Rezon simply is a title denoting a prince and identify him with Hezion (81, 731).

463 Gemariah (258).

		Hebraized form of "Marduk" (Jer. 50:2)
	נחור	*Nachowr* –Nahor, Abraham's grandfather; Abraham's brother
	סדר	*Seder* –Arrangement, order
	סרד	*Sered* –Sered, eldest son of Zebulun (Gen. 46:14; Num. 26:26)
265	אור החמה	*'Auwr HaChamah* –"Light of the sun" (Is. 30:26)
	אחרונ	*Acharown* –Behind, following, subsequent, western
	הפצצ	*HaPitztzetz* –Happizzez, priest on whom fell the lot for the 18th of the 24 courses which David appointed for the temple service (1 Chr. 24:15)
	הרס	*Haras* –To tear down, break down, overthrow, beat down, break, break through, destroy, pluck down, pull down, throw down; ruined, destroyer, utterly
		Heres –Overthrow, destruction; city in Egypt, probably On-Heliopolis
	ימ הקדמוני	*Yawm HaQadmoni* –"The eastern sea" (Joel 2:20)
	ירמיה	*Yirmeyah* –Jeremiah, head of a family of the tribe of Manasseh (1 Chr. 5:24); one who joined David at Ziklag (1 Chr. 12:4); man of Gad who joined David at Ziklag (1 Chr. 12:10); priest who sealed the new covenant with God after the exile (Neh. 10:3; 12:1, 12) – (see also ירמיהו)[464]
	מחבא רוח	*Machava' Rocha* –"Refuge from gales" (Is. 32:2)
	מכרה	*Mekerah* –Swords, weapons, devices (meaning dubious – Gen. 49:5)
		Mikreh –Pit, salt pit (meaning uncertain – Zeph. 2:9)
	נהיר	*Nehiyr* –Light (Aramaic)
	נריה	*Neriah* –Neriah, father of Baruch (see also נריהו)[465]
	סהר	*Sahar* –Roundness
		Sohar –House of roundness, roundhouse, prison
	סרה	*Sarah* –Apostasy, defection, turning aside, withdrawal
		Sirah –Sirah, well near Hebron where Abner was recalled by Joab (2 Sam. 3:26)
	צעקה	*Tza'aqah* –Cry, outcry
	רסה	*Risah* –Rissah, encampment in the wilderness
266	והנהר	*Vaserah* –I will turn aside
	בחורימ	*Bachuwriym* –Bahurim, village near the Mount of Olives
	בחרומי	*Bacharuwmiy* –Baharumite
	בנ־חור	*Ben-Chuwr* –Ben-Hur, one of Solomon's twelve supply officers, in charge of supplying food to Solomon's household
	הראני	*Hare'niy* –Show me
	חברונ	*Chebrown* –Hebron, city in the hills of Judah, south of Jerusalem; town of the tribe of Asher, more

[464] ירמיהו (271).

[465] נריהו (271).

		frequently called Abdon
	חרבונ	*Charabown* –Drought
	כמראה	*Kemar'eh* –An appearance
	סור	*Suwr* –To turn aside, depart; degenerate; Sur, a gate in Jerusalem, possibly leading from the king's palace to the Temple (2 Kings 11:6) (compare with 2 Chr. 23:5, where it is called the Gate of the Foundation)
	צמצומ	*Tzimtzum* –Contraction
	קוליל פי	*Qulielfi* –Guardian of the 29th Tunnel of Set
267	אסור	*'esuwr* –Band, bond; house of bonds, prison (figurative); band, bond, imprisonment
	ורכיאל	*Verkiel* –"Gentle one of God," Archangel of Leo
	חרבונא	*Charbowna'* –Harbona, chamberlain under Ahasuerus (see also Harbonah)[466]
	יראונ	*Yirown* –Iron, city of the tribe of Naphtali – probably modern Yarun
	מרכבה	*Merkabah* –Chariot (Gen. 41:43; 46:29; Ex. 14:25; 15:4; Josh. 11:6, 9; Judg. 4:15; 5:28; 1 Sam. 8:11; 2 Sam. 15:1, 1 Kings 7:33; 10:29; 12:18; 20:33; 22:35; 2 Kings 5:21, 26; 9:27; 10:15; 23:11; 1 Chr. 28:18; 2 Chr. 1:17; 9:25; 10:18; 14:8; 18:34; 35:24; Song 6:12; Isa. 2:7; 22:18; 66:15; Jer 4:13; Joel 2:5; Mic. 1:13; 5:10; Nah. 3:2; Hab. 3:8; Hag. 2:22; Zech 6:1, 2, 3)
	נזיר	*Nazir* –Consecrated or devoted one, Nazarite
268	חסר	*Chaser* –To lack, be without, decrease, be lacking, have a need; in need of, lacking, needy, in want of
		Cheser –Poverty, want
		Choser –Want, lack, want of, lack of
	חרני	*Choroniy* –Horonite
	חרס	*Cheres* –Itch, an eruptive disease; sun; Heres, mountain near Ailalon and Shaalbin on the border between Judah and Dan
	נחיר	*Nechiyr* –Nostril
	נחרי	*Nacharay* –Naharai, Joab's armor-bearer
	סחר	*Sachar* –To go around, go about, travel about in, go about in trade; traffic, gain, profit, gain from merchandise
	סרח	*Sarach* –To go free, be unrestrained, be overrun, exceed, overhang, grow luxuriously
		Serach –Excess, overhanging
	רונוו	*Ronove* –Goetic demon #27 (Aurum Solis Spelling)
269	אחירמי	*'Achiyramiy* –Ahiramites
	אחרינ	*Ochoreyn* –End, outcome
	דרבונ	*Dorbown* –Goad

[466] Harbonah (271).

	סגור	*Segowr* –Enclosure, encasement, fine gold
	סוגר	*Suwgar* –Cage, prison, cage with hook
	סמנגלופ	*Semangelof* –One of three angels invoked against Lilith
	ראובני	*Re'uwbeniy* –Reubenites
	–Prime number	
270	חברני	*Chebroniy* –Hebronites (see also חברוני)[467]
	יסר	*Yasar* –To chasten, discipline, instruct, admonish
	יקנעמ	*Yoqne'am* –Jokneam, city in Zebulun allotted to the Levites
	כרמי	*Karmiy* –Carmi, son of Reuben who went to Egypt with him; descendant of Judah; another son of Judah – may be the same as the second Carmi; Carmites
	כרנ	*Keran* –Cheran, son of Dishon (Gen. 36:26; 1 Chr. 1:41)
	מכיר	*Makiyr* –Machir, son of Manasseh; descendant of Manasseh living near Mahanaim
	מכרי	*Mikriy* –Michri, ancestor of a clan of Benjamin in Jerusalem
	נכר	*Nakar* –To recognize, acknowledge, know, respect, discern, regard; to act or treat as foreign or strange, disguise, misconstrue
		Nekar –Foreign, alien, foreignness, that which is foreign
		Neker –Calamity, disaster, misfortune
	סיר	*Siyr* –Pot; thorn, hook, brier
	ער	*'ar* –Enemy, adversary, foe (also Aramaic); 214th Gate of the 231 Gates
		Er –Er, eldest son of Judah, slain by God; son of Shelah
	צקלנ	*Tziqlon* –Sack, bag (meaning dubious – 2 Kings 4:42)
	קיקינ	*Qiyqayown* –A plant (perhaps a gourd)
	קפצ	*Qafatz* –To draw together, close, shut, shut up, stop up
	קצפ	*Qatzaf* –To be displeased, angry
		Qetzaf –Wrath (of God) , anger
	רע	*Ra'* –Bad, evil; evil, misery (Jer. 39:12, Prov. 11:21; 20:22)[468]
		Rea –Friend, companion; shouting, roar (dubious – Ex. 32:17; Job 36:33; Mic. 4:9); purpose, aim, thought
		Roa' –Badness, evil
271	אסיר	*'asiyr* –Prisoner, captive, bondman
		'assiyr –Prisoners (collective); prisoner, captive; Assir, son of Korah; son of Ebiasaph, son of king Jehoiachin
	ארע	*'ara'* –Earth, world, ground
	והרינ	*Vehrin* –Angel of 2d Sagittarius
	חרבונה	*Charbownah* –Harbonah, chamberlain under Ahasuerus

---

[467] חברוני (276).

[468] Ra is one of the ten words in the Tanakh with a Dagesh in the letter Resh.

(see also Harbona)[469]

ירמיהו *Yirmeyahuw* –Jeremiah, father of Hamutal (Jer. 52:1); woman of Libnah whose daughter married King Josiah (2 Kings 23:31; Jer. 52:1); man who joined David at Ziklag (1 Chr. 12:13); descendant of Jonadab (Jer. 35:3); prophet whose activity covered the reigns of the last five kings of Judah – also wrote the Biblical book (see also ירמיה)[470]

לאמר *le-Mor* –Spoke to

מכורה *Mekuwrah* –Origin (Ezek. 16:3; 21:30; 29:14)

נריהו *Neriahuw* –Neriah, father of Baruch (this spelling used only in Jer. 36:14, 32; 43:6 – see also נריה)[471]

–Prime number

272 בער *Ba'ar* –To burn, consume, kindle, be kindled; to be stupid, brutish, barbarous; brutishness, stupidity, brutish (person)

ברע *Bera'* –Bera, king of Sodom in the time of Abram (Gen. 14:2)

וירנו *VeYarnuw* –They shouted, and they praised (Lev. 9:24)

מכביר *Makbiyr* –To be in abundance

עבר *'abar* –To pass over or by or through, alienate, bring, carry, do away, take, take away, transgress; region beyond or across (Aramaic)

'eber –Region beyond or across, side; Eber, great-grandson of Shem; descendants of Eber or those who lived "across" the Euphrates; family of the tribe of Gad; descendant of Benjamin; head of a priestly family

ערב *'arab* –To pledge, exchange, mortgage, engage, occupy, undertake for, give pledges, be or become surety, take on pledge, give in pledge; to become evening, grow dark; to mix, join together (Aramaic); poplar, willow; Arabia

'areb –To be pleasant, be sweet, be pleasing; sweet, pleasant

'erev –Evening, night, sunset; woof (as knitted material); mixture, mixed people, mixed company

'arob – Swarm

'oreb –Raven; Oreb, one of two Midianite chieftains defeated by Gideon and beheaded by the Ephraimites (see also Zeeb)[472]; Oreb, the rock east of Jordan near Bethbareh where the Midianite chieftain Oreb died

רבע *Raba'* –To lie stretched out, lie down; to square, be squared; fourth part, four sides

---

[469] Harbona (276).

[470] ירמיה (265).

[471] נריה (265).

[472] Zeeb (10).

		Reba' –Reba, one of the Midianite chieftans slain by the Israelites under Moses
	רינוו	*Ronove* –Goetic demon #27
	רעב	*Ra'ab* –Famine, hunger
		Ra'eb –To be hungry, be voracious
273	אבנ מאסו הבונימ	*Eben Maasu HaBonim* –"The stone that the builders rejected" (Ps. 118:22)
	ארבע	*'arba* –Four; Arba, ancestor of the Anak and founder of Kirjath Arba
	בערא	*Ba'ara'* –Baara, Moabite wife of Shaharaim
	גער	*Ga'ar* –To rebuke, reprove, corrupt
	גרע	*Gara'* –To diminish, restrain, withdraw, abate, keep back, do away, take from, clip
	חורמ ביו	*Churam Abiv* –Huram Abiv, "Huram his father" = Hiram Abiff[473]
	חלקלקה	*Chalaqlaqqah* –Flattery, slipperiness, fine promises, smoothness
	חסרה	*Chasrah* –Hasrah, grandfather of Shallum (see also Harhas)[474]
	ערג	*'arag* –To long for, pant after
	רגע	*Raga'* –To act in an instant, stir up, disturb; to rest or repose; to harden
		Ragea' –Restful, quiet
		Rega' –A moment; for a moment
	מעצ החיימ	*Maetz HaChayim* –From the Tree of Life
274	דרע	*Dara'* –Dara, son of Zerah of the tribe of Judah, possibly the same as Darda
		Dera' –Arm (Aramaic)
	מרדכי	*Mordekay* –Mordecai, Jewish exile who became a vizier of Persia; leader who returned from the captivity
	סרדי	*Sardiy* –Sardites
	עדר	*'adar* –To help; to hoe; to be lacking, fail
		'eder –Flock, herd; Ader, grandson of Merari, son of Levi; Eder, tower or possibly a town between Bethlehem and Hebron; town of southern Judah
	ערד	*'arad* –Wild ass; Arad, one of the chief men of Aijalon; Arad, Canaanite city in the wilderness of Judea
	רוחני	*Ruwchaniy* –Spiritual (mod. Hebrew)
	רוחינ	*Ruachin* –A class of demons
	רעד	*Ra'ad* –To tremble, quake
275	אדרכנ	*Adarkan* –Drachma, dram, daric – unit of weight and value (of gold, money) equal to 128 grains or 4.32 grams
	אדרע	*Edra'* –Strong, force, arm, power
	ערה	*'arah* –To be bare, be nude, uncover, leave destitute,

[473] Hiram Abiff is the mythological founder of the Freemason movement.
[474] Harhas (276).

discover, empty, raze, pour out; bare place

קציעה *Qetziyah* –Cassia (a spice); Kezia, second daughter of Job to be born after his restoration from affliction

קצפה *Qetzafah* –Snapping or splintering, something fragmented or splintered

רהע *Reha* –39th name of *Shem HaMeforash* (3 Aquarius)

רעה *Raah* –Evil

Ra'ah –To pasture, tend, graze; to associate with, to be a special friend

Re'eh –Friend of the king

Ro'ah –Broken

276 אחודראון *Achodraon* –Lord of Triplicity by Night for Libra

אריטון *Ariton* –Demon King of Water and the West

דרדע *Darda'* –Darda, wise man with whom Solomon was compared ((1 Kings 5:11) – see also Dara)[475]

חברוני *Chebrowniy* –Hebronites (see also חברני)[476]

חרחס *Charchas* –Harhas, grandfather of Shallum, husband of the prophetess Huldah (see also Hasrah)[477]

יהוה צדקנו YHVH *Tzidqenuw* –"The Lord is our Vindicator" (Jer. 23:6; 33:16)

יסור *Yasuwr* –Those departing, revolting

Yissowr –Fault-finder, reprover, one who reproves

כנור *Kinnowr* –Lyre, harp

כרוכל *Crocell* –Goetic demon #49

עור *'avar* –To blind, make blind, put out the eyes of

'ivver –Blind

'owr –Skin, hide

'uwr –To rouse oneself, awake, awaken, incite; to be exposed, be bared, be laid bare; chaff (Aramaic)

רעו *Reu* –Reu, son of Peleg and father of Serug

–Mystic number of 23rd Path (*Giburah-Hod*; מ; Water)

277 בערה *Be'erah* –Burning, fire

זרע *Zara'* –To sow, scatter seed (of semen)

Zera' –Seed, sowing, offspring (also Aramaic)

Zeroa' –Vegetables (as sown)

כימאור *Kimaris* –Goetic demon #66

סהיבר *Sahiber* –Angel of 3d Leo

סגריד *Sagriyd* –Steady or persistent rain

עברה *'abarah* –Ford

'ebrah –Outpouring, overflow, excess, fury, wrath, arrogance

עזר *'azar* –To help, succor, support

'Azzur –Azzur, father of a prince that Ezekiel saw in a vision

---

[475] Dara (274).

[476] חברני (270).

[477] Hasrah (273).

		'ezer –Ezer, son of Seir (see also Abiezer, Romamtiezer)[478]; son of Ephraim slain by the inhabitants of Gath; descendant of Judah through Caleb (see the second Ezra)[479]; valiant man who joined David at Ziklag; Levite who assisted in repairing the wall of Jerusalem; priest in Nehemiah's time; help, succor
	ערבה	*'arabah* –Desert plain, steppe, desert, wildness
		'arubbah –Pledge, token, bond, surety, thing exchanged
	רזע	*Raziy* –Leanness, wasting
	–Prime number	
278	ארבעה	*Arbaah* –Four
	בעור	*Beor* –Beor, father of Bela, a King of Edom; father of the prophet Balaam
	בעל מעונ	*Ba'al Me'own* –Baal Meon, Amorite city on the northern border of Moab (this spelling used only in Jer. 48:23 – see also Beon, Beth Baal Meon)[480]
	גערה	*Ga'arah* –A rebuke, reproof
	ויראו מאד	*Vahyiruw Mi'od* –"Greatly frightened" (Ex. 14:10)
	ועבר	*Vi'avar* –Pass through
	חסיר	*Chassiyr* –Lacking, wanted, deficient (Aramaic)
	חרכ	*Charak* –To set in motion, start; to roast; to singe (Aramaic)
		Cherek –Lattice, other opening through which one may look
	כרובימ	*Kerubim* –Cherubs, Angelic Choir assoc. w/*Yesod*
	כרדמדי	*Keradamidi* –Regardie's spelling for *Kedamidi*, angel of 1d Taurus
	מרגלה	*Margelah* –Place at the feet, feet
	סחרה	*Sechorah* –Merchandise
		Socherah –Buckler, shield
	עולמ המומבע	*Olam HaMevethau* –Natural World, third face of Adam Qadmon
	עבור	*'abuwr* –For the sake of, on account of, because of, in order to; in order that; produce, yield
	עזרא	*Ezra* –Ezra, head of one of the courses of priests that returned from the Exile (see also Azariah)[481]; descendant of Judah through Caleb; prominent scribe and priest descended from Hilkiah the High Priest
	ערוב	*Arov* –Wild beasts
279	עגור	*'aguwr* –Name of a bird (perhaps a thrust, swallow, crane – Isa. 38:14; Jer. 8:7)
	עמר	*'atar* –To surround; to crown, give a crown

[478] Abiezer (290), Romamtiezer (973).
[479] Ezra (278).
[480] Beon (122, 772), Beth Baal Meon (680, 1330).
[481] Azariah (292).

280	דגדגירונ	*Dagdagiron* –The Snakey Ones, *Qlippoth* of Capricorn
	דכרונ	*Dikrown* –Record, memorandum (Aramaic)
	הריסה	*Hariysah* –Ruin (n. fem.)
	יער	*Ya'ar* –Forest, thicket, wood, wooded height
	ירע	*Yara'* –To tremble, quiver
	כרכמ	*Karkom* –Saffron (Song 4:14)
	מכירי	*Makiyriy* –Makirite
	ממר	*Memer* –Bitterness
	מנענע	*Mena'ana'* –A kind of rattle (as a musical instrument)
	מצפונ זהב	*Metzafon Zahab* –"Refined gold" (1 Kings 10:18)
	נכרי	*Nokriy* –Foreign, alien
	סנדלפונ	*Sandalfon* –Archangel assoc. w/*Malkut*
	סרכ	*Sarek* –Chief, overseer (Aramaic)
	עיר	*'ayir* –He-ass, male ass
		'iyr –Excitement, anguish; city, town; waking, watchful, wakeful one, watcher, angel; Ir, descendant of Benjamin (see also Iri)[482]
	ערוד	*'arowd* –Wild ass
	ערי	*Eri* –Eri, son of Gad (Gen. 46:16; Num. 26:16); 46th name of *Shem HaMeforash* (4 Pisces)
	פר	*Par* –Bull, young bull, steer, bullock; victim; offering; 219th Gate of the 231 Gates
	צלמנע	*Tzalmunna'* –Zalmunna, one of two Midianite kings slain by Gideon (see Zebah)[483]
	קצצ	*Qatzatz* –To cut off
	רכס	*Rakas* –To bind
		Rekes –Rough places
		Rokes –Snares, plot, band
	רממ	*Ramam* –To be exalted, be lifted up
	רעי	*Re'iy* –Pasture; Rei, friend of David (1 Kings 1:8)
		Ro'iy –Shepherd
281	אפר	*'afer* –Covering, bandage
		'efer –Ashes; worthlessness (figurative)
	אריסי	*'Ariysay* –Arisai, son of Haman
	כרסא	*Korse'* –Throne, royal chair
	מאמר	*Ma'amar* –Word, command
		Me'mar –Word, command (Aramaic)
	ממרא	*Mamre'* –Mamre, an Amorite chief who allied with Abraham
	עירא	*'Iyra'* –Ira, priest to David; one of David's mighty men and captain of the Temple guard; another of David's mighty men
	ערוה	*'arvah* –Dishonor, nakedness (Aramaic)
		'ervah –Nakedness, nudity, shame, pudenda
	פאר	*Pa'ar* –To glorify, beautify, adorn; to go over the boughs
		Pehayr –Headdress, ornament, turban

[482] Iri (290).
[483] Zebah (17).

פרא *Para'* –To bear fruit, be fruitful
Pere' –Wild ass
רפא *Rafa'* –To heal, make healthful; ghosts of the dead, spirits; giants; Rapha, fifth son of Benjamin (see also Rephaiah)[484]; Refaim

282 ארא לימ *Aralim* –Angelic Choir assoc. w/*Binah*
בעיר *Beir*–Beasts, cattle
עברי *'Ibri* –A designation of the patriarchs and the Israelites – Hebrew or Hebrewess; Ibri, descendant of Merari in the time of David
עזרה *'azarah* –Enclosure
'ezrah –Ezrah, descendant of Judah through Caleb (see also the third Ezer)[485]; help, succor, assistance
ערבי *'Arabiy* –Arabian

283 גפר *Gofer*–Cypress? (wood of which the ark was made); gopher, gopher wood
גרפ *Garaf*–To sweep away, sweep
זכרונ *Zikrown* –Memorial, reminder, remembrance
זרוע *Zerowa'* –Arm, forearm, shoulder, strength
Zeruwa' –That which is sown, sowing, thing sown
נרגל *Nergal*–Nergal, a Babylonian deity identified with Mars (2 Kings 17:30)
עזור *'Azzuwr*–Azzur, father of the false prophet Hananiah; leader who signed the covenant renewal with God
עינ עגלימ *'Eyn 'Eglayim* –En Eglaim, place on the northwest coast of the Dead Sea
פגר *Pagar*–To be exhausted, be faint
Peger–Corpse, carcass, monument, stela
רגלימ *Rogeliym* –Rogelim, dwelling place of Barzillai

284 אגרפ *Egrof*–Fist
אזרוע *Ezrowa* –Arm
אמבריאל *Ambriel*–"Mother of the Plenty of God," Archangel of Gemini
באר אלימ *Be'er 'Eliym* –Beer Elim, village in southern Moab
לא רחמה *Lo' Ruchamah* –Lo-Ruhamah, figurative name of Hosea's daughter, indicating God's rejection of Israel[486] (Hos. 1:6)
עירד *Irad*–Irad, father of Mehujael and descendant of Enoch
עטרה *'atarah* (often *Atarah*) –Atarah, wife of Jerahmeel and mother of Onam; crown, wreath diadem; a title of *Malkut*
ערוגה *'aruwgah* –Garden terrace or bed
פדר *Peder*–Fat, suet

---

[484] Rephaiah (295).
[485] Ezer (277).
[486] Lo-ruhamah literally means "not pitied."

	פרד	*Parad* –To separate, divide
		Pered –Mule
	רדפ	*Radaf* –To follow, to pursue
	רפד	*Rafad* –To spread
285	אדרעי	*Edre'iy* –Edrei, a chief city of Bashan, north of Jabbok river
	ארפד	*'Arpad* –Arpad, a Syrian city north of Aleppo (Is. 36:19; Jer. 42:23)
	יערה	*Ya'arah* –Forest; honeycomb; Jarah, son of Ahaz of the family of Saul (see also Jehoadah (1 Chr. 8:36))[487]
	מרמה	*Mirmah* –Deceit, treachery; Mirma, descendant of Benjamin
	עריה	*'eryah* –Nudity, nakedness
	פרה	*Parah* –To bear fruit, be fruitful, branch off; cow, heifer; Parah, town of Benjamin
		Perah –Mole
		Purah –Phurah, servant of Gideon
	רעיה	*Ra'yah* –Attendant maidens, companion
	רפה	*Rafah* –To sink, relax, sink down; slack; Rapha, descendant of King Saul

–The number of times the term "YHVH of Hosts" occurs in the *Tanakh*

286	ויקצפ	*ve-Yektzof* –Anger (of Moses)
	ופר	*Vepar* –Goetic demon #42 (Aurum Solis spelling)
	יעור	*Ya'owr* –Wood, forest, thicket, wooded height
		Ya'uwr –Jair, father of Elkanan, who slew the brother of Goliath the Gittite
	מורמ	*Murmus* –Goetic demon #54 (note the last *Mem* is not a *Samekh*)
	מרומ	*Marowm* –Height
		Merowm –Merom, lake north of the Sea of Galilee
	עירו	*'Iyruw* –Iru, son of Caleb
	פארה	*Pehorah* –Bough, branch, shoot
	פור	*Puwr* –To break, crush
	רוממ	*Romam* –Praise, exaltation, extolling
	רופ	*Ruf* –To shake, rock
	רפאה	*Refu'ah* –Remedy, medicine
287	אופר	*'Owphiyr* –Ophir, the son of Joktan; the name of a city
	ופאר	*Vepar* –Goetic demon #42
	זעיר	*Ze'eyr* –A little (of quantity or of time); a little, small (Aramaic)
	זפר	*Zepar* –Goetic demon #16 (Aurum Solis spelling)
	יארכונ	*Ya'arikown* –May be long
	יובב בנ זרח	*Yobab ben Zerach* –Jobab, son of Zerah; a King of Edom (assoc. w/*Hesed*)
	יעזר	*Ya'zer* –Jaazer, fortified Amorite city east of the Jordan

[487] Jehoadah (100).

		River (see also יעזיר)[488]
	מוריאל	*Muriel*–"Water of God," Archangel of Cancer
	ממזר	*Mamzer*–Bastard, child of incest, illegitimate child
	עזרי	*'Ezriy*–Ezri, one of David's superintendents of farm workers
	פזר	*Pazar*–To scatter, disperse
	פרז	*Paraz*–Chieftan, leader, warrior (meaning dubious – Hab. 3:14)
	רפוא	*Raphuw'*–Raphu, father of a spy sent into Canaan
288	איעזר	*'Iy'ezer*–Jeezer, descendant of Manasseh
	זפאר	*Zepar*–Goetic demon #16
	חפר	*Chafar*–To dig, search for
		Chafer–To be ashamed, be confounded, be abashed, feel abashed
		Chefer–Hepher, youngest son of Gilead and founder of the Hepherites; man of Judah; one of David's heroes; Hepher, town west of the Jordan River – probably modern Tell Ibshar
		Chofer–Mole (as digger)
	חרפ	*Charaf*–To reproach, taunt, blaspheme, defy, jeopardise, rail, upbraid; to winter, spend harvest time, remain in harvest time; to acquire, be betrothed
		Charef–Hareph, son of Caleb (do not confuse with Hariph)
		Choref–Harvest time, autumn; winter
	ירחע	*Yarcha'*–Jarha, Egyptian servant who married his master's daughter (1 Chr. 2:34-35)
	ממגרה	*Mammegurah*–Granary, storehouse
	מרגמה	*Margemah*–Sling; heap of stones
	פחר	*Pechar*–Potter (Aramaic)
	פרח	*Parach*–To bud, sprout, shoot, bloom; to break out (of leprosy); to fly
		Perach–Bud, sprout
	רחפ	*Rachaf*–To grow soft, relax; to hover
	רפח	*Rephach*–Rephah, descendant of Ephraim
289	אחירע	*Achira*–Ahira, chief of the tribe of Naphtali
	אפרח	*'efroach*–Young, young one (of birds); young birds
	טפר	*Tefar*–Fingernail, nail, claw (Aramaic)
	טרפ	*Taraf*–To tear, rend, pluck; freshly picked, freshly plucked, fresh-plucked
		Teref–Prey, food, leaf
	ירחמאל	*Yerachme'el*–Jerahmeel, son of Hezron, grandson of Judah; son of Kish; officer of Jehoiakim
	פטר	*Patar*–To separate, set free, remove, open, escape, burst through
		Peter–Firstborn, firstling, that which separates or first

[488] יעזיר (297).

opens

פרדה *Perudah* –Seed; grain of seed
Pirdah –She-mule, mule

פרט *Parat* –To improvise carelessly, chant, stammer (meaning dubious – Amos 6:5)
Peret –The broken off, something scattered

290 אביעזר *'Abiyezer* –Abiezer, descendant of Manasseh; one of David's mighty warriors

הדדעזר *Hadad'ezer* –Hadadezer, king of Zobah in Syria that warred against David and Joab (see also Hadarezer)[489]

כרמל *Karmel* –Plantation, garden-land, orchard, fruit orchard; fruit, garden-growth; Carmel, string of mountains that run through central Palestine and jut into the Mediterranean Sea; town in the mountains of Judah – modern Kermel

כרע *Kara'* –To bend, kneel, bow, bow down, sink down to one's knees, kneel down to rest (of animals), kneel in reverence; leg

מהמרה *Mahamorah* –A flood, a pit of water, watery pit

מרים *Miryam* –Miriam, sister of Moses and Aaron[490]; descendant of Judah

נמר *Nemar, namer* –Leopard

עכר *'akar* –To trouble, stir up, disturb, make (someone) taboo

עירי *'Iyriy* –Iri, descendant of Benjamin (see also Ir)[491]

עכר *'Akar* –Achar, one who stole part of the spoil of Jericho and brought "trouble" on his people, and he was killed for this (see also Achan, Achor)[492]

ערך *'arak* –To arrange, set or put or lay in order, set in array, prepare, order, ordain, handle, furnish, esteem, equal, direct, compare; to value, tax
'erek –Order, row, estimate, things that are set in order, layer, pile

פרי *Peri* –Fruit, offspring, produce

צר *Tzar* –Persecutor, enemy; narrow, tight; straits, distress, adversary, foe, enemy, oppressor, danger; hard pebble, flint, stone; 223rd Gate of the 231 Gates
Tzer –Zer, fortress city of Naphtali (see also Madon)[493]
Tzor –Tyre, city of Phoenicia (see also צור)[494]; flint, pebble

קיקלן *Qiyqalown* –Disgrace, shame

קציץ *Qetziytz* –Keziz, valley and town of Benjamin

רמן *Rimmon* –Pomegranate

רץ *Ratz* –Piece, bar (meaning dubious – Ps. 68:31)

---

[489] Hadarezer (486).
[490] Miriam rebelled against Moses with Aaron at Hazeroth.
[491] Ir (280).
[492] Achan (140, 790), Achor (296).
[493] Madon (100, 750).
[494] צור (296).

291	אלסר	*Ellasar* –Ellasar, a town in Babylonia, c. 28 miles (50 km.) East of Ur
	אמרים	*Emorim* –Ammorites
	אפיר	*'Owphiyr* –Ophir, the son of Joktan; the name of a city
	אצר	*'atsar* –To store up, save, lay up
		'Etzer –Ezer, son of Seir; son of Ephraim; descendant of Judah; valiant man who joined David at Ziklag; Levite who helped repair the wall at Jerusalem; priest in Nehemiah's time
	ארצ	*Aretz* –Earth; one of the four elements; one of the Seven Earths (corr. to Supernals)
		'erets –Land, earth
	פורה	*Puwrah* –Winepress
	פרודא	*Peruwda'* –Peruda, one whose descendants returned from the Exile (this spelling used only in Ezra 2:55 – see also פרידא)[495]
	צכמקיאל	*Tzakmiqiel* –"Brightness and Foulness of God," Angel of Aquarius
	רוממה	*Romamah* –Uplifting, arising
	רמליהו	*Remalyahuw* –Remaliah, father of Pekah (2 Kings 15:25-37)[496]
	רצא	*Ratza'* –To run
292	ארצא	*'artsa'* –Arza, housekeeper of Elah, king of Israel
	בני יעקן	*Beney Ya'aqan* –Bene Jaakan, place on the border of Edom where the wandering Israelites camped (see also Beeroth)[497]
	בצר	*Batsar* –To gather, restrain, fence, fortify, make inaccessible, enclose
		Betsar –Precious ore, gold
		Betser –Gold, precious ore, ring-gold; Bezer, fortified city within the territory of Reuben
	בריעי	*Beriy'iy* –Beerites
	זמרדיאל	*Zamradiel* –Guardian of the 17th Tunnel of Set
	מזמרה	*Mazmerah* –Pruning knife
		Mezzamerah –Snuffers (temple utensil)
	סרבל	*Sarbal* –Mantle, coat (meaning dubious; perhaps also "a babouche" (oriental slipper) – Dan. 3:21, 27)
	עזריה	*Azaryah* –Azariah, 9th King of Judah; alternate name for Jehoahaz, 6th King of Judah; original name of Abed-nego; error for Ahaziah, 8th King of Israel in 2 Chr. 22:6; son of Ahimaaz; ancestor of Samuel the prophet; descendant of Jerahmeel; ancestor of Zadok and Ezra; High Priest and grandson of the latter; son of Hilkiah the High Priest under Josiah; captive carried to Babylon

[495] פרידא (295).

[496] This is perhaps not a proper name, but a sarcastic slur on Pekah's impoverished background. The name literally means "whom YHVH has adorned."

[497] Beeroth (609).

		with Daniel (see also Abed-nego)[498]; one who charged Jeremiah with false prophecy; one who came up to Jerusalem with Zerubbabel – this may be another name of Seraiah[499]; one who repaired the wall of Jerusalem; priest who explained the Law; prince of Judah; descendant of Judah
	עכבר	*'akbar* –Mouse
	פרזה	*Perazah* –Open region, hamlet, unwalled village, open country
	צבר	*Tzabar* –To heap up, pile up
		Tzibbur –Heap, pile
	צרב	*Tzarab* –To burn, scorch
	רבצ	*Rabatz* –To stretch oneself out, lie down
		Rebetz –Resting or dwelling place, place of lying down
	רביעי	*Rebiy'iy* –Fourth
293	חרפה	*Cherpah* –Reproach, scorn
	יועזר	*Yow'ezer* –Joezer, warrior who joined David at Ziklag
	מזמור	*Mizmowr* –Melody, Psalm
294	אלהי אברהמ	*Elohi Abraham* –The God of Abraham
	ארגמנ	*'argaman* –Purple, red-purple
	המאור הגדל	*HaMaor HaGadhol* –The greater light
	טרפה	*Terefah* –That which is torn, animal torn (by beasts)
	מלכי־צדק	*Malkiy-Tzedeq* –Melchizedek, King and High Priest of Salem (Gen. 14:18-20; Ps. 110:4)
	נמרד	*Nimrowd* –Nimrod, son of Cush and leader of a kingdom stretching from Babel, Erech, Accad, Calneh, and Assyria (see also נמרוד)[500]
	פרוח	*Paruwach* –Paruah, father of Jehoshaphat
	רצד	*Ratzad* –To watch stealthily, watch with enmity (or envy)
295	אדרמלכ	*Adramelek* –Archdemon corr. to *Hod*
	יריעה	*Yeriy'ah* –Curtain, drape
	מנרה	*Menorah* –Candlestick
	נמרה	*Nimrah* –Nimrah, fortified city built by the tribe of Gad east of the Jordan (only called Nimrah in Num. 32:3 – see also Beth Nimrah)[501]
	פטור	*Patuwr* –Opened
	פרידא	*Peruwda'* –Peruda, one whose descendants returned from the Exile (this spelling used only in Neh. 7:57 – see also פרודא)[502]
	צהר	*Tzahar* –To press oil, press out oil, glisten

[498] Abed-nego (135; 137).
[499] Seraiah (521).
[500] נמרוד (300).
[501] Beth-Nimrah (707).
[502] פרודא (291).

		Tzohar –Noon, midday; roof (meaning dubious)
	צרה	*Tzarah* –Straits, distress, trouble; vexer, rival; wife
	ריפה	*Riyfah* –A grain or fruit (meaning dubious)
	רפיה	*Rephayah* –Rephaiah, head of a family of the house of David; captain of Simeon; son of Tola; one who helped to rebuild the wall of Jerusalem (see also Rapha)[503]
	רצה	*Ratzah* –To be pleased with, be favorable to, accept favorably
296	אחיעזר	*Achiezer* –Ahiezer, Prince of the tribe of Dan; one who joined David at Ziklag
	מנור	*Manowr* –Beam
	עכור	*'Akowr* –Achor, valley south of Jericho, in which Achan was stoned and which formed the northern boundary of Judah
	פרחח	*Pirchach* –Brood
	צור	*Tzor* –Tyre, city of Phoenicia (see also צר)[504]
		Tzuwr –To bind, besiege, confine, cramp; to show hostility to, be an adversary, treat as foe; to form, fashion, delineate; rock, cliff; Zur, prince of Midian slain by Phinehas; son of Jehiel
	רוצ	*Rutz* –To run
	רמונ	*Rimmown* –Rimmon, town in southern Judah; rock near Gibeah; border town of Zebulun (see also Dimnah)[505]; Rimmon, Syrian god whose temple was at Damascus (2 Kings 5:18)[506]; father of Ishbosheth's murderers (2 Sam. 4:2-9)
297	אופיר	*'Owphiyr* –Ophir, the son of Joktan; the name of a city
	אוצר	*Otsar* –A depository, armory, cellar, garner, store (–house), treasure (–house)
	אלה הרורימ	*Eleh Hadevarim* –"These be the words"; Hebrew title of the book of Deuteronomy
	אלהימ גבור	*Elohim Gibor* –Almighty God; divine name assoc. w/*Giburah*
	ארמונ	*'armown* –Citadel, palace, fortress
	בצרה	*Botsrah* –Enclosure, fold, sheepfold
		Bozrah –Bozrah, capital and city of Edom (that of King Jobab); city of Moab, probably Bezer (Jer. 48:24)
	וארצ	*VeEretz* –And land
	זמרנ	*Zimran* –Zimran, son of Abraham by Keturah
	זרעכ	*Zaracha* –Your seed
	כורסיא	*Korsia* –Throne; a title of *Binah*
	יעזיר	*Ya'azeyr* –Jaazer, fortified Amorite city east of the

[503] Rapha (285).
[504] צר (290).
[505] Dimnah (99).
[506] He has been identified with Rammanu, the Assyrian god of wind, rain and storm.

Jordan River (this spelling used only in 1 Chr. 6:66; 26:31 – see also יעזר)[507]

מנזר *Minezar* –Princes, anointed ones, consecrated ones (meaning dubious – Nah. 3:17)

עזרכ *'Ezireka* –Your help

פרזי *Perizziy* –Perizzite

צואר *Tzawa'r* –Neck (Aramaic)

Tzavvar –Neck, back of neck

298 איעזרי *'Iy'ezriy* –Jezerite, a descendant of Jeezer

ביפרו *Bifrons* –Goetic demon #46

בצור *Batsowr* –Vintage; inaccessible; in rock

חמרנ *Chamran* –Hamran, son of Dishon (1 Chr. 1:41)

חפרי *Chefriy* –Hepherites

חצר *Chatsar* –To sound a trumpet

Chatser –Court, enclosure; settled abode, settlement, village, town

חריפ *Chariyf* –Hariph, ancestor of returning captives; head of a family who sealed the new covenant with God after the exile (see also Jorah)[508]

חרצ *Charats* –To cut, sharpen, decide, decree, determine, maim, move, be decisive, be mutilated; loin, hip, hip joint (Aramaic)

יפרח *Yefrach* –Shall bud

עזריהו *'Azaryahuw* –Azariah, descendant of David's High Priest; ruler of Solomon's officers; prophet who went to Asa; son of King Jehoshaphat; captain who helped to place Joash on the throne; another man who helped Joash; High Priest who opposed Uzziah; chief of Ephraim; descendant of Kohath and father of Joel; one who helped cleanse the Temple; chief of the family of Zadok, priest in Hezekiah's time

עכביר *Achbowr* –Achbor, father of Baal-Hanan, a King of Edom; father of Elnathan, who was sent by Jehoiakim to bring Urijah from Egypt (see also Abdon)[509]

צחר *Tzachar* –Reddish-gray, tawny, white (Ezek. 27:18)

Tzachor –Tawny (Judg. 5:10)

Tzochar –Zohar, father of Ephron, from whom Abraham bought a field; son of Simeon of Judah (see also Zerah)[510]; son of Helah, of the tribe of Judah

צרח *Tzarach* –To cry, roar, make a shrill or clear sound

רחמימ *Rachamim* –Compassion, a title of *Tiferet*

רחצ *Rachatz* –To wash, wash off, wash away; to trust; washing

רצח *Ratzach* –To murder, slay, kill

---

[507] יעזר (287).

[508] Jorah (221).

[509] Abdon (134, 784).

[510] Zerah (215).

Retzach –Shattering

299 הפטרה *Haftorah* –Dessert; the reading of the prophets accompanying the Torah-portion

ירחמאלי *Yerachme'eliy* –Jerahmeelites

מגרון *Migrown* –Migron, Benjamite village north of Michmash

פטיר *Patiyr* –Unoccupied, free to work

צרדה *Tzeredah* –Zereda, village in Manasseh (see also צרדתה, צרתן)[511]

רהדצ *Rahadetz* –Angel of 2d Cancer

רפידה *Refiydah* –Support

300 אור בפאהה *Or be-Pe'ahah* –Light in Extension

אלף למד הה יוד מם *Alef Lamed Heh Yod Mem* –The full spelling of *Elohim*

יצר *Yatzar* –To bind, be distressed, be in straits; to form, fashion

Yatzur –Forms, members (of the body)

Yetzer –Form, forming, purpose, framework; Jezer, third son of Naphtali

כרמלי *Karmeliy* –Carmelite

כפר *Kafar* –To cover, purge, make an atonement, make reconciliation, cover over with pitch; village

Kippur –Atonement

Kofer –Price of a life, ransom, bribe; asphalt pitch; the henna plant; village

כרכס *Karkas* –Carcas, chamberlain of Ahasuerus

כרמיל *Karmiyl* –Crimson, red, carmine

מכמר *Makmar* –Net, snare

ממכר *Mimkar* –Sale, ware, thing sold

מנהרה *Minharah* –Crevices, ravines, mountain clefts, den, dugout holes (meaning dubious – Judg. 6:2)

מסר *Masar* –To set apart, deliver up, offer

Mosar –Discipline, correction

מצפצ *Matz-Patz* –A name of God by Temurah

מרס *Meres* –Meres, one of the seven princes of Persia

נמרוד *Nimrowd* –Nimrod, son of Cush and leader of a kingdom stretching from Babel, Erech, Accad, Calneh, and Assyria (this spelling used only in 1 Chr. 1:10 – see also נמרד)[512]

סכסכסלים *Saksaksalim* –Guardian of the 25th Tunnel of Set

סמר *Samar* –To bristle up, shiver, stand up; bristling, rough

עפעפ *'af'af* –Eyelid

ערל *'arel* –To remain uncircumcised, count uncircumcised, count as foreskin; uncircumcised, having foreskin

פרכ *Perek* –Harshness, severity, cruelty

---

511 צרדתה (700), צרתן (740, 1390).

512 נמרד (294).

צ י ר — *Tzayar* –To supply oneself w/provisions; to act as an envoy

Tziyr –Envoy, messenger; pivot of door, hinge; pang, distress; image, idol

צ ר י — *Tzeriy* –A kind of balsam, balm, salve; Zeri, musician in the days of David (see also Izri)[513]

Tzoriy –Zorite

קר — *Qar* –Cool, calm, self-possessed; 226th Gate of the 231 Gates

Qor –Cold

רוח אלהים — *Ruach Elohim* –The Spirit of God

רק — *Raq* –Thin, lean; only, altogether, surely

Roq –Saliva, spittle

רמס — *Ramas* –To trample; to creep, move lightly, move about

רנן — *Ranan* –To overcome; to cry out, shout for joy

Rannen –Cry, shout

Renen –Plumage (Job 39:13)

רעל — *Ra'al* –To quiver, shake, reel; reeling

ש — *Shin* –21st letter of Hebrew alphabet

–Mystic number of 24th Path (*Tiferet-Netzach*; נ ; Scorpio)

–The number of foxes Samson let loose and used to burn down the Philistinian fields (Judg. 15:1-6)

–The length of the ark of Noah in cubits

Shin is the letter associated with the number 300. Glancing through the various numerical correspondences above, it is obvious that *shin* is equivalent to a number of words and phrases associated with God and reconciliation. From *tzaddi* to *qof* to *resh* to *shin*, we can see three distinct phases: there is the holy *tzaddik*, the human who is righteous, the utter Godly holiness of *qedushah*, the sinfulness of *rasha'* the wicked human, and the uplifting nature of *kafar*, which means atonement. *Shin* also stands for *shalom*, meaning peace and perfection.

The three heads of the *shin* are indicative several important concepts in Judaism as well as Kabbalah:

1. The three worlds in which humanity lives: this world, the Messianic era, and the world to come.
2. The *nefesh* through which God breathes life, the *neshamah* or soul which humans only have, and the *guf* or body.
3. The Holy One, the holiness of the Sabbath, and the holiness of Israel. (*Otiot deR'Akiva*)

The three heads also point to the three Temples, the last of which will be built in the time of the Messiah.

NOTES:

[513] Izri (310).

301 ארמני *'Armoniy* –Armoni, son of Saul

ארנן *'Arnan* –Arnan, descendant of David and founder of a family
'Arnon –Arnon, river that pours into the Dead Sea
'Ornan –Ornan, a Jebusite from whom David bought land and upon which the Temple was built (called Araunah in 2 Sam. 24:16)[514]

ארק *'araq* –Earth, the earth (Aramaic)

אש *'esh* –Fire, fever, heat; 20th Gate of the 231 Gates
'ish –There is, there are
'osh –Foundation

הצור *HaTzor* –The rock

הצללפוני *Hatzelelpowniy* –Hazelelponi, daughter of Etam in the genealogy of Judah

הרמון *Harmown* –"High fortress" – a place, site unknown (see Amos 4:3)

מנורה *Menowrah* –Lamp stand

צורה *Tzuwrah* –Form, fashion, design

קרא *Qara'* –To call, call out, recite, read, proclaim; to encounter, befall
Qora' –Partridge
Qore' –Kore, Levite in charge of the freewill offerings in Hezekiah's time; son of Asaph whose descendants were gatekeepers at the tabernacle (this spelling used only in 1 Chr. 26:1 – see also קורא)[515]

רציא *Rezia* –Rezia, descendant of Asher

שא *Sho* –Destruction

302 ארקא *Arqa* –Earth; one of the Seven Earths (corr. to *Hod*)

בקר *Baqar* –To seek, enquire, consider; cattle, herd, oxen, ox
Beqar –To seek, enquire (Aramaic)
Boqer –Morning
Bowker –Herdsman

בציר *Batsiyr* –Vintage

ברק *Baraq* –To flash lightning, cast forth (lightning), lightning; Barak, general of the judge Deborah

בש *Bash* –Troubled mind; to be ashamed; to act shamefully; initials of *Beth Shamash* (House of the Sun); 40th Gate of the 231 Gates

סראיאל *Sarayel* –"Sullen of God," Angel of Gemini

צופליפו *Tzuflifu* –Guardian of the 28th Tunnel of Set

קבר *Qabar* –To bury
Qeber –Grave, sepulchre, tomb

קדד *Qedad* –To bow down

קרב *Qarab* –To come near, approach, enter into
Qerab –Battle, war
Qereb –Midst, among, inner part, middle

---

[514] Araunah (66; 262).
[515] קורא (307).

	רמונו	*Rimmownow* –Rimmono, Levitical city of Zebulun (1 Chr. 6:77)
	רקב	*Raqab* –To rot; rotteness, decay
303	באש	*Ba'ash* –To have a bad smell, stink, smell bad; to abhor *Ba'osh* –Stench, foul odor *Be'esh* –To be evil, be bad, be displeasing (Aramaic)
	גש	*Gash* –59th Gate of the 231 Gates
	וירא אלהים	*Va-ya-re Elohim* –And God saw
	מסגר	*Masger* –A shutting up, locksmith, smith, dungeon, enclosure, builder of bulwarks
	נרגן	*Nirgan* –To murmur, whisper
	רחצה	*Rachtzah* –Washing
	שאב	*Sha'ab* –To draw water
	שבא	*Sheba* –Sheba, grandson of Abraham; descendant of Shem; descendant of Ham[516]; Sheba, country in south-west Arabia whose capital was Ma'rib
304	דקר	*Daqar* –To pierce, thrust through, pierce through *Deqer* –Dekar, father of one of Solomon's commissaries (1Kings 4:9)
	דש	*Dash* –77th Gate of the 231 Gates
	זרזיפ	*Zarziyf* –Drip, drop, dripping, a soaking, a saturation
	חצור	*Chatzowr* –Hazor, captial of the Canaanite kingdom, later included in the territory of Naphtali in northern Palestine; place in extreme southern Judah – possibly modern el-Jebariyeh; another city in southern Judah (Josh. 15:25 – see also Hazor Hadattah)[517]; village of the tribe of Benjamin, to which the Jewish exiles returned; region of the Arabian Desert east of Palestine
	חצרו	*Chetzrow* –Hezro or Hezrai, one of David's warriors (see also Hezro in 1 Chr. 11:37)
	חרופי	*Charuwfiy* –Haruphite
	חרוצ	*Charuwts* –Sharp-pointed, sharp, diligent; strict decision, decision; trench, moat, ditch; gold (poetically); Haruz, man of Jotbah in Judah
	חרמון	*Chermown* –Hermon, highest mountain of the Anti-Lebanon range, marking the northeast boundary of Palestine
	כאמבריאל	*Kambriel* –"Assimilation of God," Archangel of Aquarius
	סמדר	*Semadar* –Grape blossom, grape bud
	קדר	*Qadar* –To be dark, to grow dark *Qedar* –Kedar, second son of Ishmael; tribe which sprang from Kedar, as well as the territory which they inhabited in the northern Arabian desert
	רדנימ	*Rodaniym* –Rodanim (see also Dodanim)[518], son of

[516] Some scholars believe that the latter two Shebas are either the same person, or refers to a tribe and stress that close genealogical ties account for the occurence of the name in both Ham's and Shem's genealogy.
[517] Hazor Hadattah (721).

		Javan (1 Chr. 1:7) – many scholars consider Rodanim to be his original name – it may also be a reference to the inhabitants of Rhodes and the neighboring islands
	רקד	*Raqad* –To skip about
	שאג	*Showag* –To roar
	שבב	*Showbab* –Backsliding, backturning, apostate
	שגא	*Sagaw* –To increase, grow, magnify
		Shage' –Shage, father of one of David's mighty men (see also Shammah, Agee)[519]
	שד	*Shad* –Teat
		Shed –Demon; idol
		Shod –Violence, ruin, destruction, devastation
305	אבי העזרי	*'Abiy HaEzriy* –Father of the Ezrite; a descendant of Abiezer
	אדנירמ	*Adoniram* –Solomon's tribute officer
	אדש	*Adash* –To tread, tread on, thresh, trample on
	אשד	*'eshed* –Bottom, slope, foundation, lower part
	דשא	*Dasha'* –To sprout, shoot, grow green
		Deshe' –Grass, new grass, green herb, vegetation, young
	הסה	*Hasah* –Keep silence!, Quiet!, Hush!
	הש	*Hash* –94th Gate of the 231 Gates
	הקממנע	*Haqamamna* –The 25th-30th letters of the 42-letter name of God, assoc. w/*Netzach* (A.C.)
	חרצבה	*Chartsubbah* –Bond, fetter, pang, hands
	יצהר	*Yitzhar* –Fresh oil, shining (pure) oil; Izhar, Levite father of Korah
	כפרה	*Keforah* –Atonement
	מקצעה	*Maqtsu'ah* –Scraping tool (used in fashioning idol – Is. 44:13)
		Mequts'ah – Place of corner structure, corner buttress, inner corner butress
	ערלה	*'orrlah* –Foreskin, uncircumcised
	קרה	*Qarah* –Cold; to encounter, meet, befall; to build with beams
		Qareh –Chance, accident
	רננה	*Renanah* –Ringing shout, shout (for joy)
	רעלה	*Ra'alah* –Veil
	רקה	*Raqqah* –Temple, the temple (of the head)
	שגב	*Shagab* –To be high, inaccessibly high
	שה	*She* –Sheep, goat
		She –One of a flock, lamb, sheep, goat, young sheep
306	אשה	*'eshshah* –Fire
		'ishshah –Burnt-offering, offering made by fire, fire offering; woman, wife, female
	בדקר	*Bidqar* –Bidkar, captain in the service of Jehu who

[518] Dodanim (108, 668).
[519] Shammah (345), Agee (5).

executed the sentence on Ahab's son (2 Kings 9:25)

דבש *Debash* –Honey, honeycomb

ויפרדו *Vayeparedow* –They parted from each other (Gen. 13:11)

וש *Vash* –110th Gate of the 231 Gates

יהוה רעי YHVH *Ra'ah* –"The Lord my shepherd" (Ps. 23:1)

ופחד יצחק *ve-Pachad Yitzachq* –"The fear of Isaac" (Gen. 31:24)

כפור *Kefowr* –Bowl, basic; hoarfrost, frost

מוסר *Mowser* –Band, bond
Muwsar –Discipline, chastening, correction

מקצוע *Maqtsowa'* –Place of corner structure, corner buttress, inner corner butress

נעצוצ *Na'atsuwts* –Thorn bush

פורכ *Furcas* –Goetic demon #50

קור *Quwr* –To dig, cast out; destroy, break down; thread, film, web

קראה *Qir'ah* –To encounter, befall, meet

רהעאל *Rehael* –Angel of 3q Aquarius & day angel 6 Swords

רוק *Ruwq* –To make empty, empty out

שאה *Shaah* –To lay waste, devastate; 28th name of Shem HaMephorash (4 Sagittarius)
Shah –Calamity, devastation, ruin

שגג *Shagag* –To go astray, err, commit sin or error

307 ארנונ *'Arnown* –Arnon, river that pours into the Dead Sea

בקרה *Baqqarah* –A seeking, a care, concern

וריאצ *Oriax* –Goetic demon #59

זרק *Zaraq* –To scatter, sprinkle, toss, throw, scatter abundantly, strew

זש *Zash* –125th Gate of the 231 Gates

טברמונ *Tabrimmown* –Tabrimmon, father of Ben-Hadad I, king of Syria

מאלכונעפאט *Malkunofat* –Guardian of the 23rd Tunnel of Set

קורא *Qowre'* –Kore, Levite in charge of the freewill offerings in Hezekiah's time; son of Asaph whose descendants were gatekeepers at the tabernacle (see also קרא)[520]

קרבה *Qerabah* –An approach, drawing near

רבקה *Rivqah* –Rebekah, wife of Isaac and mother of Jacob and Esau

רעואל *R'uw'el* –Reuel, son of Esau by Basmath; descendant of Benjamim (see also Jethro, Deuel)[521]

שבה *Shabah* –To take captive; return

שוא *Shavi* –Falsehood

–Prime number

---

[520] קרא (301).

[521] Jethro (616), Deuel (111).

308 אלעזר *Eleazar* –Eleazar, the High Priest son of Aaron; Abinadab's son who cared for the Ark; the priest who rebuilt and dedicated the restored walls of Jerusalem in the time of Ezra; one of David's mighty warriors; a Levite; one of the line of Parosh

באשה *Bo'shah* –Stinking things, stinking or noxious weeds, stinkweed

בוקר *Bowker* –Herdsman

בוש *Buwsh* –To put to shame, be ashamed, be disconcerted, be disappointed

ואשא *Vaesa'* –Very lifted up

חסה *Chasah* –To seek refuge, flee for protection

חציר *Chatsiyr* –A dwelling, an abode, settled abode, haunt; grass, leek, green grass, herbage

חקר *Chaqar* –To search, search for, search out, examine, investigate, seek

Cheqer –A search, investigation, searching, enquiry, thing to be searched out

חריץ *Chariyts* –A cut, thing cut, sharp instrument, sharp cutting instrument, harrow, hoe

חרנים *Choronayim* –Horonaim, sanctuary town of Moab, near Zoar

חרק *Charaq* –To gnash, grind the teeth

Korach –Korah, son of Esau; son of Hebron; son of Eliphaz; grandson of Kohath; one of the persons who rebelled against Moses and Aaron

חש *Chash* –139th Gate of the 231 Gates

מסחר *Mischar* –Merchandise (meaning dubious – 1 Kings 10:15)

עזראל *'Azar'el* –Azarael, Korahite who joined David at Ziklag; one who ministered in the song service of the Temple; prince of Dan; one who took a foreign wife; priest of the family of Immer; one who played the trumpet at the dedication of the new Temple

צריח *Tzeriyach* –Excavation, underground chamber, cellar, underground room (meaning dubious – 1 Sam. 13:6; Judg. 9:46, 49)

קרוב *Qarowb* –Near

קרח *Qarach* –To be bald, make bald

Qareach –Kareah, father of Johanan and Jonathan

Qerach –Frost, ice, ice crystal

Qereach –Bald

Qorach –Korah, son of Esau by Aholibamah; son of Eliphaz; son of Hebron; grandson of Kohath and ancestor of some sacred musicians[522]

רחמני *Rachmaniy* –Compassionate, compassionate woman

רחק *Rachowq* –Remote, far, distant; distance

---

522 This last Korah was one of the leaders of the rebellion against Moses and Aaron – the earth swallowed them up (Num. 16:1-35).

רקצ *Raqach* –To mix, compound
Raqqach –Ointment-maker, perfumer
Raqquach –Perfumery, perfume, unguent
Reqach –Spice, spicery
Roqach –Spice mixture, perfume, ointment
שבו *Shebuw* –Agate (precious stone in the High Priest's ephod – represents the tribe Naphtali)
שבעה *Shib'ah* –Shebah, well at Beer-sheba where Isaac made a covenant with Abimelech (Gen. 26:33)
שגה *Saga7h* –To grow, increase
Shagah –To go astray, stray, err
שדד *Sadad* –To harrow
Shadad –To despoil, devastate, ruin, destroy
שוב *Shuwb* –To return, turn back; repentance
שח *Shach* –Depressed, low, lowly
Seach –Thought

309 גוש *Guwsh* –A clod of earth, lump of earth
טש *Tash* –152nd Gate of the 231 Gates
קטר *Qatar* –To sacrifice, burn incense, burn sacrifices; incense; incense-altar; to shut in, close (meaning dubious – Ezek. 46:22)
Qetar –Knot, joint, problem
שאגה *Sha'agah* –Roaring
שדה *Sadeh* –Field, land
Shiddah –Concubine, wife, harem
שהד *Sahed* –Witness
שוג *Suwg* –To move, go, turn back, turn away
שזב *Shezab* –To deliver (Aramaic)
שט *Set* –Transgression; swerver, revolter, rebel
Showt –Scourge, whip

310 אשדה *'ashedah* –Foundation, slope
דוש *Duwsh* and *Dowsh* –Tread, thresh; to trample, tread down (Aramaic)
חבש *Chabash* –To tie, bind, bind on, bind up, saddle, restrain, bandage, govern
חצר גדה *Chatzar Gaddah* –Hazar Gaddah, village on the southern border of Judah southwest of Ras Zuiveira – possibly modern Khirbet Ghazza
חשב *Chashab* –To think, plan, esteem, calculate, invent, make a judgment, imagine, count; to think, account (Aramaic)
Chesheb –Girdle, band, "ingenious work" (name of the girdle or band of the ephod – Ex. 28:8, 27, 28; 29:5; 39:5, 20, 21; Lev. 8:7)
יצרי *Yitzriy* –Izri, Levite and head musician for the sanctuary (see also Zeri)[523]; Jezerites
יקר *Yaqar* –To esteem, be prized, be valuable

[523] Zeri (300).

		Yeqar –Price, value, preciousness, honor; honor, esteem (Aramaic)
	ירק	*Yaraq* –To spit; herbs, herbage, vegetables
		Yereq –Green, greenness, green plants
	יש	*Yesh* –Existence, being, substance; there is/are; 164th Gate of the 231 Gates
	כפיר	*Kefiyr* –Young lion; village
	מער	*Ma'ar* –Bare, naked place, nakedness
	מרע	*Mera'* –Mischief; confidential friend
		Merea' –Companion, friend, confidential friend, confidant
	סרנ	*Seren* –Lord, ruler, tyrant; axle
	עמר	*'amar* –To bind sheaves; to manipulate, deal tyrannically with; wool (Aramaic)
		'omer –Omer (a dry measure of 1/10 ephah (about 2 liters)); sheaf
	ערמ	*'aram* –To be subtle, be shrewd, be crafty, beware, take crafty counsel, be prudent; to heap up, pile, be heaped up
		'arem –Heap, pile (Jer. 50:26)
		'orem –Subtlety, shrewdness, craftiness
	צעננימ	*Tza'ananniym* –Zaannanim, place on the southern border of Naphtali (this spelling used only in Josh. 19:33 – see also **צענים**)[524]
	צרכ	*Tzorek* –Need
	קיר	*Qiyr* –Wall (of house); side (of altar); Kir, eastern country whose location has not been determined (2 Kings 16:9; Amos 9:7 – see also Kir-Haraseth)[525]
	קרי	*Qeriy* –Opposition, contrariness, encounter
	ריק	*Riyq* –Emptiness, vanity, empty, idle
		Reyq –Empty, vain
	רסנ	*Resen* –Something that restrains, halter; Resen, city between Nineveh and Calah in Assyria
	רעמ	*Ra'am* –To thunder; thunder
		Raum –Goetic demon #40 (Aurum Solis spelling)
	שאט	*Shehat* –Despise, contempt
		Shawt –To treat with contempt or despise
	שבח	*Shabach* –To soothe; to laud, praise
		Shebach –To laud, praise
	שובב	*Showbab* –Shobab, son of David; son of Caleb
	שוד	*Shuwd* –To ruin, destroy, spoil, devastate
	שי	*Shai* –Gift, tribute
311	אויל מרדכ	*'Eviyl Merodak* –Evil-Merodach, king of Babylon
	איש	*Ish* –Man; a title of *Tiferet*
		Iysh –Man; whosoever; each; to be a man, show masculinity; champion, great man

---

[524] **צענים** (260, 820).

[525] Kir-Haraseth (1218).

	גור־בעל	*Guwr-Ba'al* –Gur Baal, desert district south of Beersheba between Canaan and the Arabian peninsula
	זהב אופיר	*Zahav 'avpiyr* –Arabic gold, gold of Ophir (1 Chr. 29:4)
	יאש	*Ya'ash* –To despair; It is hopeless!
		Joash –7th King of Judah (also known as Jehoash), 13th King of Israel (also known as Jehoash)
	כמראה אדם	*Kemar'eh 'Adam* –"Semblance of a man" (Ezek. 1:26)
	מוסרה	*Mowserah* –Mosera, location of an Israelite wilderness encampment near Mount Hor on the border of Edom (see also מסרות)[526]
	מסורה	*Masorah* –Tradition
	עריאל	*Ariel* –Angel of 4q Pisces & night angel 9 Cups
	צפקיאל	*Tzafqiel* –Archangel assoc. w/*Binah* & Saturn
	צרויה	*Tzeruwyah* –Zeruiah, daughter of Jesse and David's sister
	קורה	*Qowrah* –Rafter, beam
	קריא	*Qariy'* –Called, summoned, called one
		Qirya' –City (Aramaic)
	רפאל	*Rafael* –Rephael, firstborn son of Obed-edom and tabernacle gatekeeper; Archangel assoc. w/*Tiferet*, w/Sol, w/the East, & w/Air; Angel ruling Mercury and Wednesday – means "Healing of God"
	שגח	*Shagach* –To gaze, stare
	שבט	*Shevet* –The 5th month of the Jewish calendar – it is associated with Aquarius and the tribe Reuben
		Shebet –Rod, staff, branch
	שגגה	*Shagagah* –Sin, inadvertent sin
	שגוב	*Seguwb* –Segub, younger son of Hiel who rebuilt Jericho in the days of Ahab; grandson of Judah
	שוה	*Shavah* –To agree with, to be like; to set, place
		Shaveh –Shaveh, place near Salem mentioned as the King's Valley
	שיא	*Sheya'* –Sheva, son of Caleb; scribe of David (see also Seraiah, Shavsha and Shisha)[527]
		Siy –Loftiness (of pride)
	–Prime number	
312	ושו	*Voso* –Goetic demon #57
	חדש	*Chadash* –To be new, renew, repair; new, new thing, fresh
		Chodesh –Month, monthly, new moon; Hodesh, a wife of Shaharaim
	יבש	*Yabesh* –To make dry, wither, be dry, become dry; dry, dried; Jabesh, father of Shallum, who killed Zechariah and reigned in his place
	ירבעל	*Yerubba'al* –Jerubbaal, name given to Gideon by his

---

[526] מסרות (706).

[527] Seraiah (515), Shavsha (676), Shisha (611).

		father (Judg. 6:32; 7:1; 8:29)
	ישב	*Yashab* –To dwell, remain, sit, abide
	מעבר	*Ma'abar* –Ford, pass, passing
	מערב	*Ma'arab* –Merchandise, articles of exchange; setting place, west, westward
	סברימ	*Sibrayim* –Sibraim, northern boundary marker of Canaan
	שאוה	*Shahavah* –Devastating storm
	שבי	*Shebiy* –Captivity, captives; captive (n. fem.)
		Shobay –Shobai, tabernacle gatekeeper whose descendants returned from the Exile
		Shobiy –Shobi, man who helped David when he fled from Absalom (2 Sam. 17:27)
	שחד	*Shachad* –To give a present, bribe or ransom
	שיב	*Siyb* –To be hoary, be grey
313	אבשי	*'Abshay* –Abishai, son of Zeruiah, one of David's mighty men
	אננאורה	*Ananaurah* –Angel of 1d Virgo
	באיש	*Bi'uwsh* –Evil, bad, be evil (Aramaic)
	בושה	*Buwshah* –Shame
	גש	*Giysh* –A clod of earth, lump of earth
	החש	*Hachash* –51st name of *Shem HaMeforash* (3 Aries)
	חשה	*Chashah* –To be silent, quiet, still, inactive
	קבורה	*Qebuwrah* –Grave, burial, burial site
	קרחה	*Qorchah* –Baldness, bald
	רקחה	*Raqqachah* –Ointment-maker, perfumer
	שבאי	*Sheba'iy* –Sabean
	שובה	*Shuwbah* –Retirement, withdrawal
	שחה	*Shachah* –To swim; to bow down
	שיג	*Siyg* –A moving away
	–Prime number	
314	בראדכ בלאדנ	*Bero'dak Bal'adan* –Berodach-Baladan, form of Merodach-Baladan, son of Baladan king of Babylon (2 Kings 20:12)
	דיש	*Day'yish* –Threshing (the process)
		Diysh –Tread, thresh
	ויאספ אל־עמיו	*VaYe'asef El-'Amayuw* –"He was gathered to his people" (Gen. 49:33)
	חוש	*Chuwsh* –To haste, make haste, hurry
	מחסור	*Machsowr* –Need, poverty, thing needed
	מטטרונ	*Metatron* –Archangel assoc. w/*Keter*
	מעדר	*Ma'der* –Hoe
	שביב	*Sebiyb* –Flame (Aramaic)
		Shabiyb –Flame (Job 18:5) –meaning dubious
	שגיא	*Saggiy* –Great (of God – Job 36:26, 37:23)
	שדי	*Shaddai* –Almighty
	שוח	*Suwach* –To meditate, muse, commune, speak
		Shuwach –To sink down, be bowed down; Shuah, son of Abraham by Keturah

	שחו	*Shachuw* –Swimming (Ezek. 47:5)
	שטה	*Shittah* –Acacia wood
	שיד	*Siyd* –To whitewash; lime
315	אשדוד	*'Ashdowd* –Ashdod, one of the five chief Canaanite cities
	גביש	*Gabish* –Pearl, crystal; piece of ice, hail
	טוש	*Tuws* –To dart, flutter, rush
	חשבה	*Chashubah* –Hashubah, son of Zerubbabel
	יצהרי	*Yitzhariy* –Izeharites
	יצירה	*Yetzirah* –Formation; the Angelic or Formative World
	ישבאב	*Yesheb'ab* –Jeshebeab, head of the fourteenth course of priests (1 Chr. 24:13)
	כורגסיטז	*Kurgasiax* –Guardian of the 21st Tunnel of Set
	כפירה	*Kefiyrah* –Chephirah, city of Gibeon given to the tribe of Benjamin – modern Kefireh
	מנחראי	*Minacharai* –Angel of 2d Taurus
	מערה	*Me'arah* –Mearah, place (possibly a cavern) in Zidon in northern Canaan (Josh. 13:4)
	עמרה	*Amorah* –Gomorrah, one of the five cities of the plain destroyed along with Sodom[528]
	מערה	*Ma'arah* –Army, battle-line; nakedness
		Ma'areh –Bare space, open plain; nakedness
		Me'arah –Cave, den, hole
	מרעה	*Mir'eh* –Pasture, pasturage
	עדריאל	*'Adriy'el* –Adriel, son of Barzillai the Meholathite, of the tribe of Issachar[529]
	ערמה	*'ormah* –Shrewdness, craftiness, prudence
	קוטר	*Qiytowr* –Thick smoke, smoke
	קריה	*Qiryah* –City, town
	רעליה	*Re'elayah* –Reeliah, chief who returned to the land (this spelling used only in Ezra 2:2 – see also Raamiah)[530]
	רעמה	*Ra'mah* –Vibration, quivering; Raamah, place near Ma'in in southwest Arabia
	שוט	*Suwt* –To swerve, fall away
		Shuwt –To go, rove about; to row
	שיה	*Shayah* –To forget, deprive
316	אבישג	*'Abiyshag* –Abishag, a concubine of David
	ולפר	*Valefor* –Goetic demon #6 (Aurum Solis spelling)
	ושאגו	*Vassago* –Goetic demon #3
	חשוב	*Chashuwb* –Hashub or Hasshub, father of Shemaiah (1 Chr. 9:14; Neh. 11:15); Israelite who helped rebuild the wall of Jerusalem (Neh. 3:11, 23); head of a family who sealed the covenant after the Captivity (Neh. 10:24)
	חשח	*Chashach* –To need, have need; the thing needed (all

[528] Many scholars believe it was submerged by the southeastern tip of the Dead Sea.
[529] This is the man whom Merab married although she had been promised to David. (1 Sam. 18:19; 2 Sam. 21:8)
[530] Raamiah (325).

		Aramaic)
	ידבש	*Yidbash* –Idbash, one of the sons of the father of Etam (1 Chr. 4:3)
	ירוק	*Yarowq* –Greens, green plants, green thing
	מעור	*Ma'owr* –Nakedness, pudendum (Hab. 2:15)
	סנור	*Sanver* –Sudden blindness
	ערומ	*'arowm* –Naked, bare
		'aruwm –Subtle, shrewd, crafty, sly, sensible
	קריאה	*Qeriy'ah* –Proclamation, preaching
	שאיה	*She-iyah* –Ruin
	שחח	*Shachach* –To bow, crouch down
317	גדיש	*Gadiysh* –Heap, stack, pile; tomb
	גורובעל	*Guwr-Baal* –"Dwelling of Baal"
	ואלפר	*Valefor* –Goetic demon #6
	ויקרא	*Vayiqra* –"And He called;" Hebrew title of Leviticus
	חדשה	*Chadashah* –Hadashah, village in the lowlands of Judah
	יבשה	*Yabbashah* –Dry land, dry ground; one of the Seven Earths (corr. to *Netzach*)
	יואש	*Joash* –Joash, father of Gideon (Judg. 6:11); man commanded by King Ahab to imprison the prophet Maachah; 7th King of Judah (also known as Jehoash); 13th King of Israel (also known as Jehoash); descendant of Shelah, the family of Judah; commander of the warriors who left Saul and joined David's army at Ziklag
	מזער	*Miz'ar* –A little, a trifle, a few
	מזרע	*Mizra'* –Seed-land, place of sowing
	פרזל	*Parzel* –Iron (Aramaic)
	שביה	*Shibyah* –Captivity, captives
		Shobyah –Shachia, descendant of Benjamin
	שחט	*Sachat* –To squeeze, press out
		Shachat –To kill, slaughter, beat; to beat, hammer
	שטח	*Shatach* –To spread, spread abroad, stretch out
	שיבה	*Shiybah* –Restoration; sojourn
		Seybah –Age, grey hair, old age
	–Prime number	
318	אליעזר	*Eliezer* –Eliezer, Abraham's Damascene servant; a son of Moses; a Benjamite; a priest who helped move the Ark; a Reubenite; a prophet who spoke to Jehoshaphat; a Levite chief; son of Harim; priest with foreign wife
	אמרי בינה	*'Imeray Binah* –"Words of understanding"
	חיש	*Chiysh* –To haste, make haste, hurry; quickly
	יזרעאל	*Yizre'el* –Jezreel, descendant of Etam; symbolic name of a son of Hosea (Hos. 1:4); Jezreel, city on the Plain of Jezreel between Mount Gilboa and Mount Carmel; town in Judah's hill country – probably modern Khirbet Terama on the Plain of Dibleh; name of the entire valley that separates

Samaria from Galilee

יחש *Yachash* –To reckon genealogically, genealogy

ישבו *Yoshuwv* –Dwell

ישוב *Yashuwb* –Jashub, one who divorced his foreign wife (Ezra 10:29) (see also Jashubi-Lehem, the second Job)[531]

ישח *Yeshach* –A sinking feeling, emptiness

מגרעה *Migra'ah* –Recess, edge, rebatement

מרגעה *Marge'ah* –Rest, repose, place of rest

מרובע *Meruba* –Square; the "square" Hebrew alphabet

עזריאל *'Azriy'el* –Azriel, father of Jeremoth, a ruler of Naphtali in David's time; chief of the tribe of Manasseh; father of Seraiah, an officer sent to capture Baruch

קרחי *Qorchiy* –Korahite

רחיק *Rachiyq* –Far, far off, distant

Rechiyt –Rafters, boards

שטט *Shotet* –Scourge

שיזא *Shiyza'* –Shiza, father of one of David's valiant men

שיח *Siyach* –To put forth, mediate, speak; meditation, complaint, musing; bush, plant, shrub

–The number of men in Genesis 42:12 who accompanied Abram to follow Kedorlaomer's army (it is intimated that Eleazar was in fact the only person with him because of the gematriot here – see the introduction to gematria)

319 חושה *Chuwshah* –Hushah, descendant of Judah (1 Chr. 4:4)

ישט *Yashat* –To hold out, extend

ישימה *Yeshiymah* –Desolation

מרגוע *Margowa'* –Rest

סרגון *Sargown* –Sargon, important king of Assyria and Babylonia who finished the siege of Samaria and carried away Israel (this spelling used only in Is. 20:1)

סרתן *Sarton* –Crab; Cancer

קיטר *Qiytowr* –Thick smoke, smoke

שגיאה *Shegiyah* –Error

שוחה *Shuwchah* –Pit; Shuah, brother of Chelub

שיט *Shayit* –Rowing

320 דרכמון *Darkemown* –Daric, drachma, dram

הרעמה *HaRimah* –Would taunt her (1 Sam. 1:6)[532]

יקיר *Yaqqiyr* –Rare, very precious, honor, dear, noble, famous (Aramaic)

ישבח *Yishbach* –Ishbah, descendant of Judah

ישי *Yishay* –Jesse, father of David (Ruth 4:17, 22; 1 Sam. 17:17)

כטורה *Keturah* –Beautiful

כרסם *Kirsem* –To tear apart, ravage, tear off

---

[531] Jashubi-Lehem (400, 960), Job (18).

[532] HaRimah is one of the ten words in the Tanakh with a Dagesh in the letter Resh.

	כש	*Kash* –175th Gate of the 231 Gates
	נבוזראדנ	*Nebuwzaradan* –Nebuzaradan, Babylonian captain of the guard at the siege of Jerusalem (2 Kings 25:8, 11, 20)
	נער	*Na'ar* –To growl; to shake, shake out or off; a boy, lad, servant, youth, retainer; a shaking, scattering
		No'ar –Youth, boyhood, early life
	סריטיאל	*Saritiel* –"Extending of the Rebellion of God," Angel of Sagittarius
	סרינ	*Siyron* –Armor
	עירמ	*'eyrom* –Naked; nakedness
		Eram –A Duke of Edom (Gen. 36:43 – assoc. w/*Malkut*)
	עמיר	*'amiyr* –Swath, a row of fallen grain
	עמרי	*'Omriy* –Omri, 6th King of Israel and founder of the third dynasty;[533] descendant of Benjamin, the son of Becher; descendant of Perez living at Jerusalem; Prince of Issachar in the days of David
	ענר	*'Aner* –Aner, Amorite chief; Aner, city of the tribe of Manasseh located west of the Jordan assigned to the Levites
	ערנ	*'Eran* –Eran, Ephraim's grandson
	פרמ	*Param* –To tear, rend garment, rip
	צעצע	*Tza'tzua'* –Things formed, images, sculpted figures
	קטורה	*Qetowrah* –Smoke of sacrifice, incense
		Qetuwrah –Keturah, wife of Abraham
	רחבעמ	*Rechabam* –Rehoboam, son of Solomon and first King of Judah
	רסס	*Rasas* –To moisten
	שכ	*Sekh* –Thorn; enclosure
		Sok –Booth, pavilion
		Suwk –To hedge or fence up or about
	–The number of children of Harim who returned from exile (Ezra 2:32)	
321	אדימירונ	*Adimiron* –The Bloody Ones, *Qlippoth* of Taurus
	אלינכיר	*Alinkir* –Angel of 3d Cancer
	אשכ	*'eshek* –Testicle, stone
	בלפגור	*Belphegor* –Archdemon corr. to *Tiferet*
	יושה	*Yowshah* –Joshah, descendant of Simeon
	ירפאל	*Yirpe'el* –Irpeel, city of the tribe of Benjamin (Josh. 18:27) – perhaps modern Rafat
	ישוה	*Yishvah* –Ishvah, second son of Asher
	לסלרא	*Laslara* –Lord of Triplicity by Day for Virgo
	מרפא	*Marpe'* –Health, healing, cure
	פראמ	*Pir'am* –Piram, Amorite king slain by Joshua
	שאהיה	*Sahiah* –Angel of 4q Sagittarius and night angel 9 Wands
322	אשויה	*'ashuwyah* –Buttress, support

[533] Omri founded Samaria and made it Israel's capital.

	דברי הימימ א	*Debere HaYamim* –"Events of the days"; Hebrew title of 1 Chronicles
	יהואש	*Yehoash* –Jehoash, alternate name for Joash, 7th King of Judah; alternate name for Joash, 13th King of Israel
	ירבעמ	*Yeroboam* –Jeroboam, Son of Solomon and first King of Israel; 14th King of Israel (Jeroboam II)
	ישבי	*Yashubiy* –Jashubites
	ישיב	*Yashiyb* –Jashub, son of Issachar and founder of a tribal family, the Jashubites (Num. 26:24 – see also Job)[534]
	כבש	*Kabash* –To subject, subdue, force, keep under, bring into bondange
		Kebes –Lamb, sheep, young ram
		Kebesh –Footstool
	כשב	*Keseb* –Lamb, young ram, sheep
	לברמימ	*Lebarmim* –Lord of Triplicity by Night for Sagittarius
	עברימ	*'Abarim* –Abarim, large mountain range in Moab near Heshbon[535]
		'Ibrim –Hebrews
	עברנ	*'Ebron* –Ebron, town of the tribe of Asher (see also Abdon, Hebron – Josh. 19:28)[536]
	רעבנ	*Reabown* –Hunger, lack of food, famine
	שבכ	*Sabak* –Network, latticework, net, netting; network of boughs
	שכב	*Shakab* –To lie down with sexually
323	אבישי	*'Abiyshay* –Abishai, son of Zeruiah, one of David's mighty men
	אורנומ	*Uranus* – Uranus
	ארבעימ	*'arba'iym* –Forty
	בהימירונ	*Bahimiron* –The Bestial Ones, *Qlippoth* of Aquarius
	דברי הימימ ב	*Debere HaYamim* –"Events of the days"; Hebrew title of 2 Chronicles
	חטוש	*Chattuwsh* –Hattush, priest who returned from the exile with Zerubbabel (Neh. 12:2); descendant of the kings of Judah, perhaps of Shechaniah (1 Chr. 3:22); descendant of David who returned from exile with Ezra (Ezra 8:2); one who helped to rebuild the wall of Jerusalem (Neh. 3:10); priest who signed the covenant (Neh. 10:5)[537]
	סטנדר	*Satander* –Angel of 3d Aries
	שיחה	*Siychah* –Meditation, reflection, prayer, devotion; pit
324	חושי	*Chuwshay* –Hushai, friend and counselor of David, probably the father of Baana (1 Kings 4:16)
	חסרונ	*Chesrown* –The thing lacking, defect, deficiency

534 Job (18).
535 Abarim includes Mount Nebo from which Moses surveyed the Promised Land before he died.
536 Abdon (134, 784), Hebron (266, 916).
537 Entries 1, 2, 3, and 5 may refer to the same person.

	כשד	*Kesed* –Chesed, son of Nahor and Milcah and nephew of Abraham (Gen. 22:22)
	מרדפ	*Murdaf* –Persecution
	שוחי	*Shuchiy* –Shuhite
325	אשדודי	*'Ashdowdiy* –Ashdodites
	ברצבאל	*Bartzabel* –Spirit of Mars
	גראפיאל	*Grafiel* –Intelligence of Mars
	גוי אחד בארצ	*Goy 'echad b'aratz* –"One nation in the land" (1 Chr. 17:21)
	חשביה	*Chashabyah* –Hashabiah, descendant of Levi; son of Kemuel who was a prince of the Levites; chief of a Levite clan; descendant of Levi; attendant of the Temple; priest in the days of Jeshua; one who repaired the wall of Jerusalem; one who sealed the covenant with Nehemiah; Levite in charge of certain temple functions; Levite who returned with Ezra from Babylon; chief of the family of Kohath; chief Levite[538]
	ישיה	*Yishshiyah* –Isshiah, Levite who was head of the house of Rehabiah; Levite of the house of Uzziel; second son of Uzziel; son of Harum who divorced his foreign wife (see also ישיהו)[539]
	כשה	*Kasah* –To become sated, be gorged with food
	ניגדוהר	*Nundohar* –Angel of 2d Scorpio
	נערה	*Na'arah* –Girl, damsel, female servant; Naarah, wife of Ashur
	רעמיה	*Ra'amyah* –Raamiah, chief who returned to the land (see also Reelaiah)
	שכה	*Shakah* –Lustful *Sukkah* –Barb, spear *Sokoh* –Shocho, place in one of Solomon's administrative districts (1 Kings 4:10)

–Sum of all the numbers (1-25) on the magic square of Mars
–Mystic number of 25th Path (*Tiferet-Yesod*; ס; Sagittarius)

326	אישהוד	*'Iyshowd* –Ishod, a man of Manasseh
	יאשיה	*Yosiah* –Josiah, 15th King of Judah (see also יאשיהו)[540]; son of Zephaniah living in Jerusalem (see also Hen)[541]
	יהוה ראפכ	YHVH *Rafak* –"God thy Healer" – God-name used in Ex. 15:26
	יהושה	*Yehovashah* –Variation on Yehoshuah (see below)
	יהשוה	*Yehoshuah* –Jesus according to Hermetic tradition; spirit (ש) descended into matter (YHVH)
	ישוי	*Yishviy* –Jesuites; Ishvi, third son of Asher; son of King

[538] Entries 7, 9, 14 may refer to the same person.
[539] ישיהו (331).
[540] יאשיהו (332).
[541] Hen (58, 708).

Saul by Ahinoam[542]

כוש *Kush* –Cush, a land that bordered the Gihon River, which was one of the four rivers of the Garden of Eden; an area South of Egypt which incluedes part of the countries Sudan and Ehiopia – also called Nubia; Cush, eldest son of Ham; descendant of Benjamin and enemy of David

נעור *Na'uwr* –Youth, early life

שכו *Sekuw* –Sechu, location with a well on the route from Gibeah to Ramah

327 בוטיש *Botis* –Goetic demon #17

כבשה *Kibsah* or *Kabsah* –Ewe-lamb, lamb

כשבה *Kisbah* –Ewe-lamb, lamb, sheep

לכסף מוחא *Lekasaf Muwcha'* –"A mine for silver" (Job 28:1)

עברנה *'Ebronah* –Ebronah, one of Israel's halting-places in the desert

שבכה *Sabakah* –Network, latticework, net, netting

שכבה *Shekabah* –The act of lying with another person (sexually)

328 איש־טוב *'Iysh Tov* –Ish-Tob, an area east of the Jordan River

בעל צפון *Ba'al Tzephown* –Baal Zephon, site that the Israelites faced when they encamped between Migdol and the Red Sea during the Exodus (Ex. 14:2; Num. 33:7)

החשיה *Hechashiah* –Angel of 3q Aries & day angel 3 Wands

חשך *Chasak* –To withhold, restrain, hold back, keep in check, refrain; to be or become dark, grow dim, be darkened, be black, be hidden

Chashok –Obscure, insignificant, low

Choshek –Darkness, obscurity

טו בשבט *Tu b'Shevat* –The fifteen day of *Shevat*

יזרעאלי *Yizre'e'liy* –Jezreelite

כחש *Kachash* –To deceive, lie, fail, grow lean, be disappointing, be untrue, be insufficient, be found liars, belie, deny, dissemble, deal falsely; lying, deception; leanness, failure

Kechash –Deceitful, false, deceptive, lying

מגרפה *Migrafah* –Shovel

ערבון *'arabown* –Pledge, security

שובך *Showbak* –Shobach, captain of the army of Hadarezer of Zobah (see also Shophach)[543]

שכח *Shakach* –To forget, ignore, wither

Shekach –To find

Shakeach –Forgetting, forgetful, forget

329 אליחרף *Eliychoref* –"God of winter (harvest-time)" –Elihoreph, a

[542] Some believe that Ishvi is identical with Ishbosheth (1013).

[543] Shophach (406, 886).

scribe in Solomon's court

אסר־חדונ *'Esar-Chaddown* –Esar-Haddon, son of Sennacherib and king of Assyria

טרסני *Tarasni* –Angel of 1d Libra

טרפלי *Tarpelay* –Tarpelites, members of an Assyrian tribe transported to Samaria by Shalmaneser of Assyria (Ezra 4:9 – Aramaic)

330 יערימ *Ye'ariym* –Jearim, mountains marking the boundary of Judah northeast of Beth Shemesh

לש *Lash* –185th Gate of the 231 Gates

מערכ *Ma'arak* –Arrangement, plan, preparation

מצר *Metzar* –Distress, straits; isthmus

Metzer –Boundary; 60th name of *Shem HaMeforash* (6 Taurus)

מרצ *Marats* –To be or make sick

נסרכ *Nisrok* –Nisroch, Assyrian god with a temple in Ninevah

נערי *Na'aray* –Naarai, one of David's mighty men (this spelling used only in 1 Chr. 11:37 – see also Paarai)[544]

סנחריב *Sancheriyb* –Sennacherib, Assyrian king who killed his brother to usurp the throne[545]

סער *Sa'ar* –To storm, rage; tempest, storm, whirlwind

סרים *Sariys* –Official, eunuch

עקלקל *'aqalqal* –Winding, devious, crooked

ערני *'Eraniy* –Eranite(s)

פרימ *Puriym* –Purim, Jewish holiday observed a month before Passover in commemoration of Jewish deliverance from massacre led by Esther and Mordecai (see also פורים)[546]

פספסימ *Paspasim* –10th – 15th letters of the 22-letter name of God

צמר *Tzemer* –Wool

רסים *Rasiys* –Drop (of dew); fragment

רעינ *Ra'yown* –Longing, striving; thought

של *Shal* –Transgression, fault, crime, error

Shel –Who, which

331 אכיש *'Akiysh* –Achish, king of Gath during the time of David; king of Gath during the time of Solomon; the two may be identical

אפרימ *'Efrayim* –Ephraim, second son of Joseph and ancestory of the tribes of Israel (assoc. w/Taurus)

אשל *'eshel* –Tamarisk tree

חשביהו *Chashabyahuw* –Hashabiah or Hashabiahu, son of Jeduthun; descendant of Kohath

ישיהו *Yishshiyahuw* –Isshiah, Levite who was head of the

---

544 Paarai (360).

545 Sennacherib unsuccessfully invaded Judah – see 2 Kings 19 for a full account of the destruction of his army.

546 פורים (336, 896).

		house of Rehabiah; Levite of the house of Uzziel; second son of Uzziel; son of Harum who divorced his foreign wife (see also ישיה)[547]
	סיסרא	*Siysera'* –Sisera, captain of the army of Jabin who was murdered by Jael; one whose descendants returned
	פארן	*Pa'ran* –Paran, wilderness seven days' march from Mount Sinai – it is located east of the wilderness of Beer-Sheba (see also El-Paran)[548]
	שאל	*Shaowl* –Sheol, underworld, grave, pit, (mistranslated as) hell
		Shawal –To ask, enquire, borrow, beg
		She'al –Sheal, Israelite who divorced his foreign wife after the Exile
		Sheh'el –To ask (Aramaic)
	שוכה	*Sowkoh* –Shocho, town in lowland Judah or the hilly country (this spelling used only in Josh. 15:35 and 1 Sam. 17:1 – see also שוכו)[549]
332	אנדרומאל	*Andromalius* –Goetic demon #72
	אפראים	*Ephraim* –Ephraim, second son of Joseph by Asenath and progenitor of a tribe of Israel (assoc. w/Taurus); Ephraim, territory allotted to the tribe of Ephraim; city near Baal-hazor, probably the same as "Ephraim near the Wilderness" (2 Sam. 13:23); gate on the north wall of old Jerusalem (2 Kings 14:13; 2 Chr. 25:23); rough area (not forest) where Absalom was slain (2 Sam. 18:6); mountains west of the Jordan River (1 Sam. 1:1; 2 Chr. 13:4), allotted to the tribe of Ephraim
	בשל	*Bashal* –To cook, boil, bake, roast, ripen, grow ripe
		Bashel –Cooked, boiled
	יאשיהו	*Yosiahu* –Josiah, 15th King of Judah (alternate spelling – see also יאשיה)[550]
	לבש	*Labash* –To dress, wear, clothe, put on clothing, be clothed
		Lebash –To be clothed (Aramaic)
	מאראצ	*Marax* –Goetic demon #21
	מבצר	*Mibtsah* –Fortification, fortress, fortified city, stronghold
		Mibzar –Mibzar, Duke of Edom (Gen. 36:42; 1 Chr. 1:53 – assoc. [w/Magdiel] w/*Yesod*)
	מרבצ	*Marbets* –Place of lying down, resting or dwelling place
	עורונ	*'iwarown* –Blindness
	ערבס	*Orobas* –Goetic demon #55 (Aurum Solis spelling)
	שאלא	*She'elaw* –Affair, request

---

[547] ישיה (325).

[548] El-Paran (372, 1022).

[549] שוכו (332).

[550] יאשיה (326).

	שבל	*Shebel* –Flowing skirt, train
		Shibbol –Flowing stream, ear of grain
	שוכו	*Sowkow* –Shocho, town in lowland Judah or the hilly country (this spelling used only in 2 Chr. 11:7 – see also שוכה)[551]
	שלב	*Shalab* –To be bound, be joined, be joined together; joining (of bases)
333	איק בכר	*Aiq Bekar* –The cabala of the nine chambers
	אשבל	*'Ashbel* –Ashbel, son of Benjamin
	גלש	*Galash* –To lie down, to sit up
	חשכה	*Chashekah* –Darkness
		Cheshkah –Darkness, obscure, low
	רגמ מלכ	*Regem Melek* –Regem-Melech, messenger sent out by some Jews (Zech. 7:2)[552]
	שגל	*Shagal* –To be sexually excited; to lie with; to violate, ravish
		Shegal –Royal paramour, consort, queen; king's wife or concubine, consort (Aramaic)
	שלג	*Shaleg* –To snow
		Sheleg –Snow
334	חרי־יונימ	*Charey-yowniym* –Dung, dove's dung
	חשוכ	*Chashowk* –Darkness (Aramaic)
	כשדי	*Kasdiy* –Chaldeans (this spelling used only in Dan. 2:5, 10; 4:4; 5:7, 30 – see also כשדימה)[553]
		Kasday –Chaldean (by association, an astrologer)
	לשד	*Leshad* –Juice, juicy bit, dainty bit
	עינ־דר	*'Eyn-Dor* –En-Dor, town of the tribe of Manasseh where Saul consulted a witch about his future (this spelling used only in Josh. 17:11 – see also עין־דאר, and עין־דור)[554]
	עמיחור	*'Ammiychuwr* –Ammihur, father of Talmai, king of Geshur
335	אבנ העזר	*'Eben Ha'Ezer* –Ebenezer, a place in Palestine
	הר סיני	*Har Sinai* –Mount Sinai
	מערכה	*Ma'arakah* –Row, rank, battle-line
	מרצה	*Merutsah* –Crushing, oppression
	נעריה	*Ne'aryah* –Neariah, descendant of David; descendant of Simeon who smote the Amalekites in Mount Seir
	עינ־דאר	*'Eyn-Do'r* –En-Dor, town of the tribe of Manasseh where Saul consulted a witch about his future (this spelling used only in 1 Sam. 83:11 – see also עין־דר, and עין־דור)[555]

---

551 שוכה (331).

552 Some scholars believe this is not a proper name but the passage should read "...Sherezer, the friend of the king."

553 כשדימה (379).

554 עין־דאר (335, 985), עין־דור (340, 990).

שכיה — *Sekiyah* –Image, ship, craft (Isa. 2:16)

שלה — *Shalah* –To be at rest, prosper, be quiet; to be negligent; to mislead; to draw out, extract; neglect
Shelah –At ease; Shelah, youngest son of Judah
Shiloh –Shiloh, town in Ephraim (see also שילה, שילו, and שלו)[556]

336 כושי — *Kuwshiy* –Cushites; Cushi, great-grandfather of Jehudi; father of Zephaniah

לוש — *Luwsh* –To knead (dough); Laish, northern limit of the tribe of Dan; place named in Is. 10:30 with Gallim and Anathoth

מצור — *Matsowr* –Siege enclosure, siege, entrenchment, siege works; "Matsor" – a name for Egypt

מרוצ — *Merowts* –Running, race, course

פורימ — *Puwriym* –Purim, Jewish holiday observed a month before Passover in commemoration of Jewish deliverance from massacre led by Esther and Mordecai (this spelling used only in Est. 9:26, 28 – see also פרים)[557]

פרוימ — *Parvayim* –Parvaim, place where gold was obtained for the decoration of Solomon's Temple

שאלה — *Sha'elah* –Request, thing asked for, demand

שול — *Shuwl* –Skirt of High Priest's robe

שלו — *Selav* –Quail
Shelev –Ease, prosperity
Shaluw –Neglect, remissness (Aramaic)
Shalev –Quiet, at ease, prosperous
Shilow –Shiloh, town in Ephraim (see also שילה, שילו, and שילו)[558]

שכוי — *Sekviy* –A celestial appearance (Job 38:36)

337 אלוש — *'Aluwsh* –Alush, site where the Israelites camped on their journey from Egypt to Mount Sinai

אליצור — *Elitzur* –Elizur a chief of Reuben in the wilderness

זהב שחוט — *Zahav Shechuwt* –"Beaten gold" (2 Chr. 9:15)

זפרנ — *Zifron* –Ziphron, place specified by Moses as the northern boundary of the Promised Land (Num. 34:9) – probably modern Za'feranh

יושויה — *Yowshavyah* –Joshaviah, one of David's valiant men (1 Chr. 11:46)

מוראצ — *Marax* –Goetic demon #21 (Aurum Solis spelling)

פורלאכ — *Phorlakh* –Angel of Earth

פרזימ — *Perizzim* –Perizzites

צוריאל — *Tzuwriy'el* –Zuriel, chief of the Levites, descendant from

---

555 עין־דור (340, 990), עין־דר (334, 984).

556 שילה (345), שילו (346), שלו (336).

557 פרים (330, 890).

558 שילה (345), שילו (346), שלה (335).

Merari

שאול *Saul* –Shaul, sixth King of Edom (Gen. 36:37-38; 1 Chr. 1:48-49 – assoc. w/*Hod*); descendant of Levi; son of Simeon found in several lists; the first king of the United Kingdom of Israel

–Prime number

338 אבי גבערנ *Abiy Gibown* –Abi Gibon, father of Gibeon

חלש *Chalash* –To be weak, be prostrate; to weaken, disable, prostrate

Challash –Weak

חפרימ *Chafarayim* –Haphraim, frontier town assigned to the tribe of Issachar – may be modern Khirbet el-Farriyah or et Faryibeh

חשל *Chashal* –To shatter; to subdue, crush, shatter (Aramaic)

לבוש *Lebuwsh* –Clothing, garment, apparel, rainment

לחש *Lachash* –To whisper, charm, conjure; whispering, charming

שובל *Showbal* –Shobal, son of Seir; son of Caleb, son of Hur; son of Judah

שחל *Shachal* –Lion

שלח *Shelah* –Selah

Shalach –To send, send away, let go

Shelach –Weapon, missile, sprout; Shelah, youngest son of Judah; Shiloah, waterway of Jerusalem

339 ישוחיה *Yeshowchayah* –Jeshoaiah, descendant of Simeon (1 Chr. 4:36)

לתש *Latash* –To sharpen, hammer, whet

שבואל *Shebuw'el* –Shebuel, son of Gershom

שובאל *Shuwbael* –Shubael, son of Haman

שלט *Shalat* –To domineer, dominate, have mastery, be master, lord it over

Shelet –Shield

340 יסגדיברודיאל *Yasgedibarodiel* –Angel of 3d Capricorn

כימער *Kimaris* –Goetic demon #66 (Aurum Solis spelling)

ליש *Layish* –Lion; Laish, northern limit of the tribe of Dan; place named in Is. 10:30 with Gallim and Anathoth

מלכירמ *Malkiyram* –Malchiram, descendant of King Jehoiakim

מסה *Masah* –To melt, dissolve, be liquified

Massah –Despair, test

Missah –Sufficient, sufficiency

מסמר *Masmer* –Nail

מצרי *Mitzriy* –Mitsrite (inhabitant of Egypt)

מרמס *Mirmas* –Trampling place, trampling

מרק *Maraq* –To scour, polish; broth, juice cooked from meat

מש *Mash* –Mash, son or grandson of Shem (Gen. 10:23 –

see also Meshech)[559]; 194th Gate of the 231 Gates

נמרימ *Nimriym* –Nimrim, brook in Moab

נצר *Natsar* –To guard, watch, watch over, keep

Netser –Sprout, shoot, branch (always figurative)

ספר *Safar* –To count, recount, relate; enumerator, muster-officer, secretary, scribe

Safer –Scribe, secretary

Sefar –Book (Aramaic); census, enumeration; Sephar, area in the southeastern portion of Arabia (Gen. 10:30)

Sefer –Book, missive, document, writing

סרפ *Saraf* –To burn

עינ־דור *'Eyn-Do'r* –En-Dor, town of the tribe of Manasseh where Saul consulted a witch about his future (this spelling used only in 1 Sam. 28:7 – see also עין־דר, and עין־דאר)[560]

עכרנ *'Okran* –Ocran, descendant of Asher

פרס *Paras* –To break in two, to divide; Persia

Peras –To break in two, divide; half-mina, half-shekel

Peres –Bird of prey (perhaps vulture, perhaps extinct)

צמרי *Tzemariy* –Zemarite

קעקע *Qa'aqa'* –Incision, tattoo, mark (Lev. 19:28)

קרמ *Qaram* –To spread something over, cover

רעע *Ra'a'* –To be bad, be evil; to break, shatter

Re'a' –To crush, break, shatter

רפינ *Rifyown* –Sinking

רפס *Rafas* –To humble thyself, submit thyself

Refas –To tread, trample down (Aramaic)

רקמ *Raqam* –Embroidered with needlework

Reqem –Rekem, Midianite king slain by the Israelites; son of Hebron; Rekem, city of Benjamin

שככ *Shakak* –To subside, abate, decrease

שלי *Sheliy* –Quiet, private, quietness

שמ *Sham* –There, then, thither

Shem –Name; Shem, eldest son of Noah & progenitor of the tribes

341 אמש *'emesh* –Yesterday, last night; recently (figurative)

אשמ *'asham* –To offend, be guilty, trespass; to be desolate, acknowledge offense; guilt, offense, sin, guiltiness

'ashem –Guilty, faulty (and obliged to offer a guilt-offering)

מצורה *Metsuwrah* –Siege works, stronghold, rampart

מקרא *Miqra'* –Convocation, convoking, reading, a calling together, assembly

מרוצה *Meruwtsah* –Running, course (of life)

---

[559] Meshech (360, 840).

[560] עין־דר (334, 984), עין־דאר (985, 335).

	משא	*Mashsha'* –Lending on interest, usury (Neh. 5:7, 10)
		Massa' –Load, bearing, tribute, burden, lifting; utterance, oracle, burden; Massa, son of Ishmael
		Masso' –A lifting up
		Mesha' –Mesha, boundary marker of the descendants of Joktan
	ספרא	*Sifra* –Book (Aramaic)
	צלמ אלקימ	*Tzelem Aleqiym* –"Image of God"
	שלוה	*Shalvah, shelevah* –Quietness, ease, prosperity
	שמא	*Shamma'* –Shamma, descendant of Asher
	–Sum of the three mother letters (א, מ, and ש)	
342	ביפרנ	*Bifrons* –Goetic demon #46 (Aurum Solis spelling)
	בשמ	*Basam* –Spice, balsam; sweet, sweet smell, sweet odor
		Besem –Spice, balsam; sweet, sweet smell, sweet odor; balsam tree, perfume
	כורסונ	*Korson* –Demon King of the West and Water (Goetia)
	מבש	*Mabush* –Private parts, his privates, male genitals (literally "that excites shame" – Deut. 25:11)
	מרבק	*Marbeq* –Stall (of animals)
	פוכלור	*Focalor* –Goetic demon #41
	שביל	*Shevil* –Path
		Shabiyl –Way, path
	שבמ	*Sebam* –Shebam, city east of the Jordan given to the tribes of Reuben and Gad (see also Sibmah)[561]
343	אבל כרמימ	*'Abel Keramiym* –Abel-Keramim, a city in Palestine
	אבשלי	*'Ashbeliy* –Ashbelites
	גשמ	*Gasham* –To rain
		Geshem –Rain, shower; body (Aramaic); Geshem, Arabian opponent of Nehemiah – also known as Gashmu
		Goshem –To be rained upon; to rain
	ויאמר אלהימ	*Vay-yomer Elohim* –And God said
	משאב	*Mash'ab* –Drawing place of water, place to draw water
	עיי עברימ	*Iyey 'Abriym* –Ije-Abarim, town in extreme southern Judah; town east of the Jordan River (see also Iim)[562]
	פרזונ	*Perazown* –Rural population, rustics, rural people, people of unwalled villages (meaning dubious – Judg. 5:7, 11)
	שלחה	*Shilluchah* –Shoot, branch
	$–7^3$	
344	ארמ צובה	*'Aram Tzobah* –Aramzobah (Ps. 60:2)
	ספרד	*Sefarad* –Sepharad, place where the Jerusalem exiles lived (Ob. 20)
	סרפד	*Sarpad* –An unidentified desert plant (meaning

561 Sibmah (347).
562 Iim (130, 690).

doubtful; perhaps brier, nettle – Isa. 55:13)

פרדס *Pardes* –Park, preserve, enclosed garden, forest, orchard; notarikon for the four levels of Torah study (*peshat, remez, derush, sod*)

קרדמ *Qardom* –Axe

רפידימ *Rephiydiym* –Rephidim, Israelite encampment between the Wilderness of Sin and Mount Sinai

שלוח *Shulluwach* –Sending away, parting gift

שמד *Shamad* –To destroy

345 אל שדי *El Shaddai* –God Almighty

ה י כ ה ש ה *Heh, Yod, Kaf, Heh, Shin, Heh* –The first letters of each verse of Deut. 32:1-6 [563]

המצרי *HaMitzeriy* –The Egyptian (Ex. 2:12)

השמ *Hashem* –Hashem, father of several of David's guards (1 Chr. 11:34)

HaShem –The Name; Tetragrammaton

Husham –A King of Edom (assoc. w/ *Giburah*)

מחש *Mahash* –5th name of *Shem HaMeforash* (5 Leo)

מקרה *Meqareh* –Beam work

Meqerah –Coolness, cooling

Miqreh –Unforeseen meeting or event, accident, happening, chance, fortune

מרעלה *Mar'alah* –Maralah, boundary village of Zebulun

משה *Mashah* –To draw

Mashsheh –Loan

Mosheh –"Drawn" – Moses

משגב *Misgab* –High place, refuge (of God), secure height, retreat; a place in Moab

ספרה *Seforah* –Number (Ps. 71:15)

עריסה *'ariysah* –Dough, meal, coarse meal, kneading trough (meaning dubious – Num. 15:20, 21; Neh. 10:38; Ezek. 44:30)

פרסה *Parsah* –Hoof (of horses)

צפצפה *Tzaftzafah* –A kind of willow, willow tree

רקמה *Riqmah* –Broidered work, needlework

שהמ *Shoham* –Shoham, descendant of Merari; Malachite (precious stone in the High Priest's ephod – represents Joseph)

שילה *Shiyloh* –Shiloh, town in Ephraim (see also שלה, שילו, and שלו)[564]

שליה *Shilyah* –Afterbirth

שמה *Shammah* –Waste, horror, apallment; Shammah, grandson of Esau; son of Jesse (see also Shimeah or Shimea)[565]; one of David's mighty men or the father of one of David's mighty men (2 Sam. 23:11); another of David's mighty men

---

[563] The final Heh is enlarged in the original.

[564] שלה (335), שילו (346), שלו (336).

[565] Shimeah (415), Shimea (411).

(2 Sam. 23:33 – see also Shammoth)[566]; another of David's mighty men (2 Sam. 23:25)

–The number of children of Jericho who returned from exile (Ezra 2:34)

346 אלגביש *Elgabiysh* –Hail (literally, "pearls of God")

אלישה *Elishah* –Elisha, descendant of Noah, son of Javan (perhaps ancestor of the Aeolians)

אשמה *'ashmah* –Guiltiness, guilt, offense, sin, wrongdoing

מוש *Muwsh* –To feel; to depart, remove

מקור *Maqowr* –Spring, fountain

מרוק *Maruwq* –Scraping, rubbing (Esth. 2:12)

משאה *Mashsha'ah* –Loan

Massa'ah –The uplifted, uplifting

צנור *Tzinnuwr* –Pipe, spout, water conduit

רצון *Ratzon* –Pleasure, delight, favor

שילו *Shiylow* –Shiloh, town in Ephraim (see also שלה, שילה, and שלו)[567]

שמאה *Shim'ah* –Shimah, one of the family of King Saul whose descendants dwelled in Jerusalem (this spelling used only in 1 Chr. 8:32 – see also שמאם)[568]

347 אפריון *'appiryown* –Sedan, litter, palanquin; chariot

מזרק *Mizraq* –Bowl, basin

נער בכה *Na'ar Bokeh* –"Crying boy" (Ex. 2:4)

שבמה *Sibmah* –Sibmah, town of Reuben and Gad (see also Shebam)[569]

348 בצרון *Bitstsarown* –Stronghold

הגשם *HaGashem* –The rain showers

חמש *Chamash* –To arrange in multiples of five, take one fifth

Chamesh –Five

Chamush –In battle array, arrayed for battle by fives, armed

Chomesh –Fifth part; belly, abdomen, fifth, ribs

חצרים *Chatzeriym* –Villages

חשם *Chashum* –Hashum, one whose descendants returned from exile; one who sealed the covenant; priest who helped Ezra at the reading of the Law

Chusham –Husham, descendant of Esau who became king of Edom – this spelling used in Gen. 36:34-35 (see also חושם)[570]

Chushim –Hushim, descendant of Benjamin (1 Chr. 7:12)

חרצן *Chartsan* –Kernels, seeds, insignificant vine product (Num. 6:4)

---

566 Shammoth (746).

567 שלה (335), שילה (345), שלו (336).

568 שמאם (381, 941).

569 Shebam (342, 902).

570 חושם (354, 914).

	מושב	*Mowshab* –Seat, assembly, dwelling-place, dwelling, dwellers
	מחקר	*Mechqar* –Range, space, field
	מרחק	*Merchaq* –Distant place, distance, far country
	מרקח	*Merqach* –Spice, perfume, aromatic spices
	מושב	*Mowshav* –Dwelling place
	משגה	*Mishgeh* –Mistake
	משח	*Mashach* –To smear, anoint, spread a liquid
		Meshach –Oil (Aramaic)
	שלחי	*Shilchiy* –Shilhi, grandfather of King Jehoshaphat
	שמח	*Sameach* –Joyful, merry, glad
		Samach –To rejoice, be glad
349	גשמו	*Gashmuw* –Gashmu, Arabian opponent of Nehemiah – also known as Geshem
	הלוחש	*Hallohesh* –Hallohesh, father of one who repaired the wall; man or family that sealed the new covenant with God after the Exile – may be the same as the first Hallohesh
	חלושה	*Chaluwshah* –Weakness, defeat, prostration
	טפסר	*Tifsar* –Scribe, official, marshal
	מדקרה	*Madqarah* –Thrust, stab, piercing
	מדשה	*Medushshah* –That which is threshed, thing threshed
	מקטר	*Miqtar* –Place of sacrificial smoke, altar, hearth, incense
	רפסדה	*Rafsodah* –Raft
	שדמה	*Shedemah* –Field
	שליט	*Shalliyt* –Having mastery, domineering, master
	שמט	*Shamat* –To release, let go
350	אלינוש	*Eligos* –Goetic demon #15
	וירא אלהים כי טוב	*Va-ya-re Elohim ki tov* –"And God saw that it was good."(Gen. 1:10, 12, 18, 21, 25)
	זהב פרוים	*Zahav Peruwym* –"Red-orange gold from Parvaim" (2 Chr. 3:6)
	ימש	*Yamash* –To touch, feel
	ישם	*Yasham* –To put, place, set, appoint, make; to ruin, be desolate
	כפרים	*Kiporim* –Many atonements
	כשל	*Kashal* –To stumble, stagger, totter
	מערם	*Ma'arom* –Naked thing, nakedness
		Murmas –Goetic demon #54 (Aurum Solis spelling)
	משובב	*Meshowbab* –Meshobab, prince of Simeon (1 Chr. 4:34)
	משי	*Meshiy* –A costly material for garments (perhaps silk)
		Mushshiy –Mushi, son of Merari, son of Levi (see also מושי)[571]
	נציר	*Natsiyr* –Preserved
	נקר	*Naqar* –To bore, pick, dig, pick out
	נש	*Nash* –202nd Gate of the 231 Gates

571 מושי (356).

ספיר *Sappiyr*–Sapphire (precious stone in the High Priest's ephod – represents the tribe Issachar), lapis lazuli

עמרמ *'Amram*–Amram, son of Kohath and descendant of Levi and father or ancestor of Aaron, Moses, and Miriam; one who had taken a foreign wife (see also Hemdan)[572]

עפר *'afar*–To dust, powder

'afer–Dry earth, dust, powder, ashes, earth, ground, mortar, rubbish

'Epher–Epher, grandson of Abraham and son of Midian; one of the descendants of Judah; chief of the tribe of Manasseh

'ofer–Deer, fawn, stag, young hart

ערפ *'araf*–To drop, drip; to break the neck (of an animal)

'oref–Neck, back of the neck, back

פער *Pa'ar*–To open wide, gape

פרנכ *Parnak*–Parnach, descendant of Zebulun

פרסי *Parsiy*–Persian

פרע *Para'*–To lead, act as leader; to let go, let loose, ignore, let alone

Pera'–Hair, long hair (of head), locks; leader

קרנ *Qaran*–To shine

Qeren–Horn (n. fem.); a place conquered by Israel

רעפ *Ra'af*–To trickle, drip

ריקמ *Reyqam*–Vainly, emptily

רצינ *Retziyn*–Rezin, last king of Syria who, along with Pekah, fought Judah; one whose descendants returned from the Exile

שכל *Sakal*–To be prudent, prosper; to lay cross-wise, cross (hands)

Sekal–To consider, contemplate

Sekel–Prudence, insight, understanding

Sekhel–Understanding, "intelligence," consciousness, wisdom

Shakol–To be bereaved, make childless

שלכ *Shalak*–To throw, cast, hurl, fling; bird of prey (probably the cormorant)

שליטא *Shlita*–Notarikon for לאורך ימים טובים אמן שיהיה, ("May he live for long and good days, Amen") a phrase used when mentioning a living rabbi or sage

שמי *Shammay*–Shammai, descendant of Judah; descendant of Caleb, son of Hezron; son or grandson of Ezra

שנ *Shen*–Tooth; Shen, place near which Samuel erected a stone memorial to the victory over the Philistines

351 אמרפל *'Amrafel*–Amraphel, king of Shinar (Gen. 14:1, 9)

---

[572] Hemdan (102, 752).

	אנש	*'anash* –To be weak, sick, frail
		'enash –Man, human being (Aramaic); mankind (Aramaic)
	אשימ	*Eshim* –Flames; Angelic Choir assoc. w/*Malkut*
	אשכל	*'Eshkol* –Eshcol, brother of Mamre who helped Abraham; valley north of Hebron famous for its grapes
	ישמא	*Yishma'* –Ishma, brother of Jezreel and Idbash, all descendants of Caleb
	לוסנהר	*Losanahar* –Angel of 1d Leo
	מישא	*Meysha'* –Mesha, descendant of Benjamin; Mesha, boundary marker of the descendants of Joktan
	מרסנא	*Marsena'* –Marsena, prince of Persia
	נשא	*Nasa'* –To lift, bear up, carry, take
		Nasha' –To beguile, deceive; to lend on interest or usury, be a creditor
		Nesa' –To lift, bear, take, carry (Aramaic)
	שאנ	*Shawan* –To be at ease, rest, be quiet
	שנא	*Sane'* –To hate, be hateful
		Shana –To change, alter
		Shena' –Sleep (this spelling used only in Ps. 127:2)

–Mystic number of the 26th Path (*Tiferet-Hod*; ע; Capricorn)

352	אשימא	*'Ashiyma'* –Ashima, a god of Hamath (2Kings 17:30)
	ברקנ	*Barqan* –Briers, briars
	בשנ	*Bashan* –Bashan, area stretching from the Upper Jordan Valley to the Arabian Desert
	ופרינו	*Uwfarinuw* –And we shall be fruitful
	ושמו	*Visamuw* –They shall bestow
	יבשמ	*Yibsam* –Jibsam, descendant of Tola (1 Chr. 7:2)
	מראדכ בלאדנ	*Mero'dak Bal'adan* –Merodach-Baladan, king of Babylon in the days of Hezekiah (this spelling used only in Jer. 50:2 – see also Berodach-baladan)[573]
	משואה	*Masshuw'ah, meshow'ah* –Desolation, ruin
	נשב	*Nashab* –To blow
	קרבנ	*Qorban* –Offering, oblation
	רקבנ	*Riqqabown* –Rottenness, decay, decayed
353	אלישיב	*Eliashib* –Eliashib, a priest in David's reign; a descendant of David; a High Priest in Nehemiah's time; a temple singer with foreign wife; one of the line of Zattu; one of the line of Bani
	אשבנ	*'Eshban* –Eshban, son of Dishon
	אשנב	*'eshnab* –Window lattice
	באשימ	*Be'ushiym* –Stinking or worthless things, wildgrapes, stinkberries
	גשנ	*Goshen* –Goshen, cattle-raising district of the Nile

[573] Berodach-Baladan (314, 1444).

assigned to the Israelites before they were placed in bondage; town in the hill country of Judah; region of Judah

חמשה *Chamishah* –Five

מרקחה *Merqachah* –A seasoning, compounding, spice-seasoning; ointment pot

משובה *Meshubah* –Turning away, turning back, apostasy, backsliding

משחה *Mishchah* –Consecrated portion, anointing oil, portion, ointment, anointing portion

נגש *Nagas* –To press, drive, oppress, exact, exert demanding pressure

Nagash –To draw near, approach

נשג *Nasag* –To reach, overtake, take hold upon

פנ ינחמ העמ *Pen Yenacham HaAm* –"The people might change their minds" (Ex. 13:17)

שבנא *Shebna'* –Shebna, scribe or secretary of Hezekiah replaced by Eliakim (see also שבנה)[574]

שמ אחד *Shem Achad* –The name of unity

שמחה *Simchah* –Joy, mirth, gladness

שנאב *Shin'ab* –Shinab, king of Admah attacked by Chedorlaomer and his allies

–Prime number

354 דשנ *Dashen* –To be fat, grow fat, become fat, become prosperous, anoint, fat; vigorous, stalwart ones

Deshen –Fat ashes, fatness

Dishon –Dishon, son of Seir; grandson of Seir (see also דישון, דישן, and דשון)[575]

חושמ *Chuwsham* –Husham, descendant of Esau who became king of Edom – this spelling used in 1 Chr. 1:45-46 (see also חשם)[576]

חצרונ *Chetzrown* –Hezron, son of Reuben; son of Perez

חרמונימ *Chermowniym* –Hermonites

מגדל-עדר *Migdal-'Eder* –Migdal Eder, watchtower betweeen Hebron and Bethlehem where Jacob once camped

מריב בעל *Meriyb Ba'al* –Merib-Baal, grandson of Saul – he was loyal to David, even though Ziba told David he was a traitor (this spelling used only in 1 Chr. 8:34; 9:40 –see also Mephibosheth)[577]

משוגה *Meshuwgah* –Error

ספרדי *Sefardi* –Spanish Jew

שדימ *Shedim* –Demons

Siddiym –Siddim, valley near the Dead Sea, full of bitumen pits (Gen. 14:3, 8, 10)

---

[574] שבנה (357).

[575] דישון (370, 1020), דישן (257, 817), דשון (360, 1010).

[576] חשם (348, 908).

[577] Mephibosheth (822; 832).

שוחמ *Shuwcham* –Shuham, son of Dan (this spelling used only in Num. 26:42 – see also Hushim)[578]

שמטה *Shemittah* –Release (from debt)

355 לשכה *Lishkah* –Room, chamber, hall, cell

מגביש *Magbiysh* –Magbish, unidentified town in Benjamin (Ezra 2:30)

מחשבה *Machashabah* –Thought, device

משוט *Mashowt* –Oar

נקרה *Neqarah* –Hole, crevice

נשה *Nashah* –To forget, deprive; to lend, be a creditor
Nasheh –Vein, nerve, tendon (in the thigh)

ספירה *Sefirah* –Sphere; number; emanation

עפרה *'Ophrah* –Ophrah, descendant of Judah; Ophrah, city of Benjamin; city in Manasseh

ערפה *'Orpah* –Mane, neck; Orpah, daughter-in-law of Naomi

פרסי *Parsiy* –Persian

פרעה *Par'ah* –Leader, commander
Par'oh –Pharaoh

שנה *Senah* –Sleep
Shanah –Year; to repeat, do again, change, alter
Shenah –Sleep; year (Aramaic)
Shaneh –Year

356 אשנה *'Ashnah* –Ashnah, the name of two villages in the lowlands of Judah

בנ־דקר *Ben-Deqer* –Ben-dekar, one of Solomon's twelve officers who provided food for the royal household (1 Kings 4:9)

ירקומ *Yeraqown* –Mildew, paleness, lividness

מושי *Muwshiy* –Mushite; Mushi, son of Merari, son of Levi (see also משי)[579]

מירמוני *Mormowniy* –Mormon, a member of the Church of Jesus Christ of Latter-Day Saints (mod. Hebrew)

נוצרי *Notzeriy* –Christian (mod. Hebrew)

נוש *Nuwsh* –To be sick

ספרוי *Sefarviy* –Sepharvite

פעור *Pe'owr* –Peor, mountain peak near Pisgah in Moab

רקונ *Raqqown* –Rakkon, place near Joppa in the territory of Dan

שכול *Shakkuwl* –Childless, bereaved, robbed of offspring

שנאה *Sin'ah* –Hating, hatred, hate

357 אנוש *'enowsh* –Man, mortal man, person, mankind
Enosh –Enos, son of Seth & father of Cainan

אשכול *'eshkowl* –Cluster (of grapes or flowers)

בשנה *Boshnah* –Shame

---

578 Hushim (358, 918).

579 משי (350).

כגדיכש — *Kegadikesh* –The 13th-18th letters of the 42-letter name of God, assoc. w/*Giburah* (A.C., 777)

קול יהוה על־המימ — *Qol* YHVH *'Al-HaMayim* –"The voice of YHVH is over the waters" (Ps. 29:3)

שבנה — *Shebnah* –Shebnah, scribe or secretary of Hezekiah replaced by Eliakim (see also שבנא)[580]

358 אליהוא בנ ברכאל — *'elihua ben Barakel* –"Elihu, son of Barakel" (Job 32:2, 6)

חשימ — *Chushiym* –Hushim, son of Dan (Gen. 46:23) – in Num. 26:42, his name is Shuham; one of the two wives of Shaharaim (1 Chr. 8:11 – in verse 8 of this her name is spelled חושים)

חשנ — *Chassan* –Angel of Air

Choshen –Breastplate, breastpiece; breastplate of the High Priest (also sacred pouch of the High Priest designed to hold the Urim and Thummim; Ex. 25:7; 28:4, 15, 22-24, 26, 28, 29, 30; 29:5; 35:9, 27; 39:8, 9, 15-17, 19, 21; Lev. 8:8)[581]

מחודש — *Mechudash* –Renewed, restored

שחנ — *Shachan* –To be hot

משיח — *Meshiyach* –Anointed, anointed one, Messiah

נחש — *Nachash* –To practice divination, divine, observe signs, learn by experience, diligently observe, practice fortunetelling, take as an omen; divination, enchantment; snake, serpent; the name of a staff created by Moses; Nahash, father of Abigail and Zeruiah; Ammonite king that was defeated by Ammon (not to be confused with Ir-Nahash)

Nechash –Copper, bronze (Aramaic)

359 זרע לבנ — *Zera' Lavan* –"White seed," i.e. sperm

נטש — *Natash* –To leave, permit, forsake, cast off or away, reject, suffer, join, spread out or abroad, be loosed, cease, abandon, quit, hang loose, cast down, make a raid, lie fallow, let fall, forgo, draw

סטריפ — *Satrip* –Angel of 3d Pisces

שטימ — *Shittiym* –Shittim, final Israelite encampment before crossing the Jordan[582] (Num. 25:1; Josh. 2:1); dry and unfruitful valley (Joel 4:18)

שטנ — *Satan* –Adversary, accuser; archdemon corr. (with Moloch) to *Keter*

–Prime number

360 דרקונ — *Darqown* –Darkon, servant of Solomon whose descendants returned to Palestine after the exile

דשונ — *Diyshon* –Dishon, son of Seir (also known as Dishon);

---

580 שבנא (353).

581 Urim (257, 817), Thummim (490, 1050).

582 At Shittim, Moses bade farewell and the Law was completed.

	grandson of Seir (see also דישון, דישן, and דשן)[583]
ישן	*Yashan* –Old, store, storage
	Yashen –To sleep, be asleep; sleeping; Jashen, father of some, or one, of David's mighty men – Jashen may be one of David's men himself
כרפס	*Karpas* –Cotton or fine linen
כשיל	*Kashshiyl* –Axe
לכיש	*Lachiysh* –Lachish, southern city of Judah midway between Jerusalem and Gaza
מהשיה	*Mahashiah* –Angel of 5q Leo & day angel 7 Wands
מלצר	*Meltsar* –Guardian, an officer of the court (meaning dubious – Dan. 1:11, 16)
מסדרון	*Misderown* –Porch, colonnade (meaning dubious – Judg. 3:23)
משך	*Mashak* –To draw, drag, sieze
	Meshek –A drawing, drawing up, drawing up a trail; Meshech, son of Japheth; possibly a people inhabiting the land in the mountains north of Assyria; tribe mentioned in association with Kedar; son or grandson of Shem (this spelling used only in 1 Chr. 1:18 – see also Mash)[584]
נשי	*Nasiy'* –One lifted up, chief, prince, captain, leader; rising mist, vapor
	Neshiy –Debt
סש	*Sash* –209th Gate of the 231 Gates
עמרמי	*'Amramiy* –Amramite
עפיר	*'ofir* –Earth, dust, ground, ashes, mortar, powder, rubbish
עצר	*'atsar* –To restrain, retain, close up, shut, withhold, refrain, stay, detain
	'etser –Restraint, oppression
	'otser –Restraint, coercion
עריפ	*'ariyf* –Cloud, mist
פערי	*Pa'aray* –Paarai, one of David's mighty men (see also Naarai)[585]
צער	*Tza'ar* –To be or grow insignificant, grow small
	Tzo'ar –Zoar, one of the five cities of the Plain of the Jordan (Gen. 14:2; 19:22)
צרע	*Tara'* –To be diseased of skin, be leprous; to be a leper
קדרון	*Qidrown* –Kidron, valley in Jerusalem between the Mount of Ophel and the Mount of Olives
קרס	*Qaras* –To bend down, stoop down, crouch
	Qeres –Hook
	Qeros –Keros, ancestor of a clan who returned from Exile to the land of Israel (this spelling used only in Ezra 2:44 – see also קירס)[586]

---

583 דישון (370, 1020), דישן (257, 817), דשן (354, 1004).
584 Mash (340).
585 Naarai (330).

	רעצ	*Ra'atz* –To shatter
	רצע	*Ratza'* –To pierce the ear
	שינ	*Shin* –Tooth; 21st letter of Hebrew alphabet
		Shayin –Urine
	שכלי	*Shikkuliym* –Childlessness, bereavement
	שכמ	*Shakam* –To rise or start early
		Shekem –Shoulder, back; Shechem, son of Hamor who defiled Dinah (Gen. 33:19; 34); two descendants of Manasseh; Shechem, ancient city in central Palestine
	שלל	*Shalal* –To spoil, plunder, take spoil
		Showlal –Barefoot
	שני	*Shani* –Crimson
		Sheni –Second
361	אדני הארצ	*Adonai HaAretz* –Lord of the Earth; divine name assoc. w/*Malkut*, Earth, and the North
	מצראל	*Mitzrael* –Angel of 6q Taurus& night angel 7 Pentacles
	נשיא	*Nisia'* –Prince
	סמגר נבו	*Samgar Nebow* –Samgar-Nebo, Babylonian officer who sat with other officials in the middle gate of Jerusalem (Jer. 39:3)[587]
	שאס	*Shawas* –To plunder, spoil
	שניא	*Saniy* –Hated, held in aversion
362	אריכ־אפימ	*Arik Apim* –Long of Face; a title of *Keter*
	אשמודאי	*Asmodai* –Goetic demon #32 (Aurum Solis spelling)
	בטול היש	*Bitul HaYeish* –"Nullification of somethingness"
	בשס	*Bashas* –To tread down, trample
	יומ כפור	*Yom Kippur* –Day of Atonement; holiest day of the Jewish year
	משכב	*Mishkab* –Couch, bed; a lying down, couch, bier; act of lying (for sexual contact)
	נשואה	*Nesuw'ah* –What is borne or carried about, load
363	גישנ	*Geyshan* –Geshan, descendant of Caleb
	מגור מסביב	*Magowr Misabiyb* –Magor-Missabib, symbolic name given to Pashur by Jeremiah (Jer. 20:1-3) – means literally "terror on every side"
	משטוח	*Mishtowach* –Spreading place
	עינ רגל	*'Eyn Rogel* –En Rogel, spring outside the city of Jerusalem near the Hinnom Valley
	עיר המלח	*'Iyr HaMelech* –Ir Hammelech, city in the wilderness of Judah near Engedi (Josh. 15:62)[588]
	שדי אל חי	*Shaddai El Chai* –Almighty Living God; divine name assoc. w/*Yesod*, Air, & the East

586 קירס (370).

587 Some scholars take this as a proper name (perhaps meaning "be gracious, Nebo"), and others view it as a title of Nergal-Sharezer.

588 Some translate "City of Salt."

364	אור מופלא	*Aur Mopla* –The Hidden Light; a title of *Keter*
	בני־ברק	*Beney Baraq* –Bene Berak, town of the tribe of Dan east of modern Jaffa
	דישנ	*Diyshon* –A clean animal (perhaps antelope, gazelle, or mountain goat)
		Diyshon –Dishon, son of Seir (also known as Dishon); grandson of Seir (see also דישון, דשון, and דשן)[589]
	חושימ	*Chuwshiym* –Hushim, one of the two wives of Shaharaim (1 Chr. 8:8 – in verse 11 of this her name is spelled חשים)[590]
	חצרוני	*Chetzrowniy* –Hezronites
	חשונ	*Cheshvan* –The 2nd month of the Jewish calendar – it is associated with Scorpio and the tribe Dan
	נחוש	*Nachuwsh* –Bronze
	שוחמי	*Shuwchamiy* –Shuhamites
	שמיטה	*Shmitah* –Release; the sabbatical year
	שטנה	*Sitnah* –Accusation, enmity; Sitnah, second well dug by Isaac (Gen. 26:21)
365	העמרמי	*Ha'ameramiy* –The Amramites (Num. 3:27)
	השכמ	*Hashekem* –Rise up early (Ex. 8:16)
	השליכ	*Hishliyka* –Hurled, thrown (Num. 35:20)
	השלל	*HaShalal* –The spoil (Num. 31:11)
	השמידו	*Hishemiyduw* –Has destroyed them (Deut. 4:3); he has destroyed (Deut. 28:48)
	השני	*HaShaniy* –The scarlet (Gen. 38:30)
		HaSheniy –The second (Gen. 2:13)
	ואשלחכ	*Ve-'ashalechaka* –That I might have sent you away (Gen. 31:27)
		Ve-'eshelachaka –And I will send you (Gen. 37:13)
	וישלחהו	*Ve-Yeshalechhuw* –And he sent him forth (Gen. 3:23)
	וישטמ	*Ve-Yisetim* –And he hated (Gen. 27:41)
	ונגשו	*Venigeshuw* –And they shall come near (Deut. 21:5)
	חשבנה	*Chashabnah* –Hashabnah, one who sealed the new covenant with God after the exile
	ישנה	*Yeshanah* –Jeshanah, city in the hill country of Ephraim; the Old Gate in the northwest corner of Jerusalem at the time of Nehemiah (Neh. 3:6; 12:39)
	כמשה	*Kemosheh* –Like Moses (Deut. 34:10)
	לשלה	*Leshelah* –To Shelah (Gen. 38:26)
	משכה	*Mashkah* –Has drawn (Deut. 21:3)
	נשיה	*Neshiah* –Forgetfulness, oblivion; one of the Seven Earths (corr. to *Tiferet*)
	עצרה	*'atsarah* –Assembly, solemn assembly

[589] דישון (370, 1020), דשון (360, 1010), דשן (354, 1004).

[590] חשים (358, 918).

	צערה	*Tzo'arah* –To Zoar (Gen. 19:23)
	צרעה	*Tzirah* –Hornets
		Tzor'ah –Zorah, city in the lowlands of Judah allotted to the tribe of Dan
	קטרון	*Qitrown* –Kitron, one of the towns of Zebulun (see also Kattath)[591]
	שכמה	*Shekemah* –To Shechem (Gen. 37:14)
		Shikmah –Shoulder, shoulder blade, back; her shoulder (Gen. 21:14)
	שללה	*Shelalah* –Its spoil (Deut. 13:17)

–The number of years Enoch lived (Gen. 5:23)
–The number of negative commandments in the Tanakh
–The number of main nerves and blood vessels in the human body
–The number of days in one year

366	אנדראלפ	*Andrealphus* –Goetic demon #65
	ושני	*Vashniy* –Vashni, firstborn of Samuel (1 Chr. 6:13 – also see 1 Sam. 8:2)
	חשבון	*Cheshbown* –Account, reasoning, reckoning; Heshbon, Amorite capital on the boundary between Reuben and Dan, standing between the Arnon and Jabbok Rivers
		Chishshabown –Device, invention
	כמוש	*Kemowsh* –Chemosh, a god of Moabites (see also כמיש)[592]
	מושכ	*Moshek* –Attractive (mod. Hebrew)
	ספר יהוה	*Sefer* YHVH–"Book of YHVH" (Is. 34:16)
	ערוצ	*'aruwts* –Dreadful; chasm, ravine, steep slope
	ערמון	*'armown* –Plane-tree (as stripped of bark – Gen. 30:37; Ezek. 31:8)
	צוער	*Tzuw'ar* –Zuar, father of Nethaneel and a chief of Issachar
	שוני	*Shuwniy* –Shuni, son of Gad; Shunites
367	שבניה	*Shebanyah* –Shebaniah, Levite who guarded the devotions of the people; two priests who sealed the new covenant
	שיאון	*Shi'yown* –Shihon, town near Mount Tabor
368	ברקוס	*Barqows* –Barkos, a family of temple servants who returned from the exile with Zerubbabel
	חמישי	*Chamiyshiy* –Fifth
	מחשכ	*Machshak* –Dark place, darkness, secrecy
	שבלול	*Shabluwl* –Snail
	שחין	*Shechin* –Boils, inflamed spot, inflammation
369	חשבדנה	*Chashbaddanah* –Hasbadana, assistant to Ezra at the reading of the Law

591 Kattath (509).

592 כמיש (370).

חשמודאי *Chasmodai* –Spirit of Luna

נחושה *Nechuwshah* –Copper, bronze

עולמ הבריאה *Olam HaBriah* –The World of Creation

שהדני *Shehadani* –Angel of 2d Gemini

–Magic sum of the magic square of Luna

370 דישונ *Diyshown* –Dishon, son of Seir (also known as Dishon); grandson of Seir (see also דישן, דשון, and דשן)[593]

כמיש *Kemiysh* –Chemosh, a god of Moabites (this spelling used only in 2 Chr. 35:20; Is. 10:9; Jer. 48:7 – see also כמוש)[594]

כנש *Kanash* –To gather (Aramaic)

לשמ *Leshem* –Ligure, jacinth, or opal; probably jacinth or ligure (precious stone in the High Priest's ephod – represents the tribe Dan); Leshem, northern limit of the tribe of Dan; place named in Is. 10:30 with Gallim and Anathoth

מישכ *Meshakh* –Meshach, the name given to Mishael after he went into Babylonian captivity

משל *Mashal* –To rule, have dominion, reign; to represent, liken, be like; to speak in a proverb, use a proverb, speak in parables, speak in sentences of poetry; proverb, parable; Mashal, city in Asher given to the Levites (see also Mishal)[595]

Meshowl –Byword

Moshel –Dominion

נערנ *Na'aran* –Naaran, border town of Ephraim east of Bethel

נשכ *Nashak* –To bite; to pay, give interest, lend for interest or usury

Neshek –Interest, usury

עקר *'aqar* –To pluck up, root up; to cut, hamstring; to pluck, be rooted up (Aramaic); barren, sterile

'eqer –Member, offspring, offshoot; Eker, son of Ram and descendant of Judah

'iqqar –Root, stock (Aramaic)

עריצ *'ariyts* –Awe-inspiring, terror-striking, awesome, terrifying, ruthless, might

עש *'ash* –Moth; herbage, grass; 215th Gate of the 231 Gates

Ayish –Arcturus, the Great Bear of Astronomy (this spelling used only in Job 9:9 – see also עיש)[596]

פצר *Patzar* –To press, push

פרצ *Paratz* –To break through or down or over, burst, breach

Peretz –Breach, gap, bursting forth; Perez, eldest son of Judah

ציער *Tziy'or* –Zior, city in Judah near Hebron (see also

---

593 דישן (257, 817), דשון (360, 1010), דשן (354, 1004).

594 כמוש (366).

595 Mishal (371).

596 עיש (380).

Zair below)

צעיר — *Tza'iyr* –Little, insignificant, young; Zair, place in or near Edom where Joram defeated the Edomites (see also Zior above)

צפר — *Tzafar* –To go early, depart early (meaning dubious – Judg. 7:3)
Tzefar –Bird (Aramaic)

צרעי — *Tzor'iy* –Zorites (see also צרעתי)[597]

צרפ — *Tzaraf* –To smelt, refine, test

קירס — *Qeyros* –Keros, ancestor of a clan who returned from Exile to the land of Israel (this spelling used only in Neh. 7:47 – see also קרס)[598]

קרע — *Qara'* –To tear, tear in pieces
Qera' –Torn pieces of garment or fabric

רענן — *Ra'anan* –Flourishing; to grow green; luxuriant, fresh

רצפ — *Ratzaf* –To fit together, fit out, pattern
Retzef –Hot stove, glowing stone, flame; Rezeph, city of Syria taken by Sennacherib

שכמי — *Shikmiy* –Shechemites

שכנ — *Shakan* –To settle down, abide, dwell
Sheken –Dwelling
Shaken –Inhabitant, neighbor

שלמ — *Shalam* –To be in a covenant of peace, be at peace, be complete, be sound
Shelem –Peace offering
Shalem –Perfect, whole; Salem, city of Melchizedek (Gen. 14:18; Ps. 76:3)
Shallum –16th King of Judah, aka Jehoahaz; 16th King of Israel (variant spelling); Shallum, youngest son of Naphtali (this spelling used only in Gen. 46:24; Num. 26:49 – see also שלומ)[599]; descendant of Simeon; husband of Huldah the prophetess; father of Hezekiah; one who married a foreign wife during the Exile; uncle of Jeremiah; father of one who was a temple officer in the days of Jehoiakim
Shillem –Recompense, requittal

שמימ — *Shamayim* –Heaven, sky

371 אפרסכי — *'Afarsekay* –Apharsachites

יהוה שמה — YHVH *Shammah* –Adonai is there – symbolic name for Jerusalem (Ezek. 48:35)

מושכה — *Mowshekah* –Cord

משוכה — *Mesuwkah* –Hedge

משאל — *Mish'al* –Mishal, territorial town of Asher

צרועה — *Tzeruw'ah* –Zeruah, mother of Jeroboam I

---

597 צרעתי (770).

598 קרס (360).

599 שלומ (376, 936).

שלמא — *Salma'* –Salma, son of Caleb, son of Hur (1 Chr. 2:51, 54); Salma, father of Boaz (this spelling used only in Ruth 4:20 – see also שלמון)[600]

שמאל — *Sama'l* –To take the left, go to the left
Semol –Left-hand or left side

372 איל פארן — *'Eyl Paran* –El-Paran, place in the Wilderness of Paran

בשלם — *Bishlam* –Bishlam, foreign colonist who wrote a letter of complaint against the Jews (Ezra 4:7)

יהוה שמו — YHVH *Shemo* –"יהוה is His Name"

ישבו בנב — *Yishbow be'Nob* –Ishbi-Benob, one of the sons of Rapha the Philistine[601]

כבשן — *Kibshan* –Kiln (pottery or lime), smelting forge, furnace

עבש — *'abash* –To shrivel, waste away

עקרב — *'aqrab* –Scorpion; Scorpio

עשב — *'eseb* –Herb, herbage, grass, green plants

שבים — *Shabise* –Front band for a woman's head

–The number of children of Shephatiah who returned from exile (Ezra 2:4)

373 אלהי העברים — *Elohi HaIbrim* –God of the Hebrews

אשבע — *'Ashbea* –Ashbea, place where linen workers lived (1 Chr. 4:21)

בעשא — *Baasha* –3rd King of Israel

געש — *Ga'ash* –To shake, quake; Gaash, hill in the territory of Ephraim, south of Timnath Serah, burial place of Joshua

הא־לכם זרע — *HaLakem zera'* –"Take for yourselves seed" (Gen. 47:23)

קול־יהוה בהדר — *Qol*-YHVH *Behadar* –"The voice of the Lord is majesty" (Ps. 29:4)

שבניהו — *Shebanyahuw* –Shebaniah, priest who aided in bringing the Ark of the Covenant to the Temple (1 Chr. 15:24)

שגע — *Shagah* –To be mad (insane)

–Prime number

374 בכבשים — *Bakevasiym* –Among sheep

בכשבים — *Bakesaviym* –Among sheep

בשבע — *Bisheva'* –In seven

ובירקון — *VeVayiraquwn* –And with mildew, a dryness

וישבנו — *VeYashavnuw* –And we will dwell

כשדים — *Kasdiym* –Chaldees

לשלחו — *Leshalcho* –Let him go

מרפידם — *Merefiydim* –From Rephidim

נטישה — *Netiyshah* –Twig, tendril, tendrils of a vine (as spread out)

עדש — *'adash* –Lentil

---

600 שלמון (426, 1076).

601 Ishbi-Benob attacked David but was killed by Abishai (2 Sam. 21:15-22)

375 חשבניה *Chashabneyah* –Hashabniah, father of Hattush who helped to rebuild the wall of Jerusalem; Levite who officiated at the fast under Ezra and Nehemiah when the covenant was sealed

נשכה *Nishkah* –Chamber, room, cell

עשה *'asah* –To yield; to do, fashion, accomplish, make; to press, squeeze

'oseh –Yielding (Gen. 1:11, 12)

פדן ארם *Paddan 'Aram* –Padan-Aram, plain region of Mesopotamia from the Lebanon Mountains to beyond the Euphrates, and from the Taurus Mountains on the north to beyond Damascus on the south (see also פדן)[602]

צעירה *Tze'iyrah* –Youth

צפרה *Tzipporah* –Zipporah, wife of Moses and daugher of Reuel

קערה *Qe'arah* –Dish, platter

רצפה *Ritzpah* –Pavement; live coal; Rizpah, concubine of Saul

שלמה *Salmah* –Garment, outer garment

Shelomoh –Solomon, son of David by Bathsheba and king of a united, strong Israel for forty years

Shillumah –Reward, requittal, retribution

שמיכה *Semiykah* –Rug, coverlet, thick coverlet (Judg. 4:18 – the death of Sisera)

שמלה *Samlah* –Samlah, a King of Edom (Gen. 36:36; 1 Chr. 1:47-48 – assoc. w/*Netzach*)

Simlah –Garment, clothes, a cloth

שעה *Shaah* –Hour

Sha'ah –To look at, regard, gaze at; brief time, moment (Aramaic)

376 כושן *Kuwshan* –Cushan, the name of a place or people (see also Cushan-Rishathaim, Midian)[603]

משאלה *Mish'alah* –Request, petition, desire

עוש *'uwsh* –To lend aid, come to help, hasten

עשו *Esau* –Esau, eldest son of Isaac and twin brother of Jacob – he was the progenitor of the tribe of Edom and also sold his birthright to Jacob

צופר *Tzowphar* –Zophar, Naamathite and friend of Job

צפור *Tzippowr* –Bird, fowl; Zippor, father of Balak, king of Moab

שוע *Shavah* –To cry out, shout (for help)

Showa' –Shoa, location mentioned along with Babylon, Chaldea, and Assyria

Shuwa' –Shua, Canaanite whose daughter Judah married

שלום *Shalom* –Peace

Shallum –16th King of Judah, aka Jehoahaz; 16th King

---

[602] פדן (134, 784).

[603] Cushan-Rishathaim (1396, 2606), Midian (104, 754).

of Israel; Shallum, youngest son of Naphtali (see also שלם)[604]; descendant of Judah; descendant of Aaron and an ancestor of Ezra (this spelling used only in 1 Chr. 5:38-39; Ezra 7:2 – see also Meshullam)[605]; gatekeeper of the tabernacle; one who married foreign wives during the Exile; one who helped to repair the wall of Jerusalem

Shilluwm –Requital, reward

377 מבשלה *Mebashshelah* –Cooking places

שבעה *Shivah* –Seven

שועא *Shuw'a'* –Shua, daugher of Heber

שמאול *Semo'wl* –The left, the left-hand side

שמואל *Shemuel* –Samuel, prophet and last judge of Israel; Shemuel, one appointed to divide the land of Canaan; head of a family of Issachar

378 אשכנז *'Ashkenaz* –Ashkenaz, son of Gomer; possibly a race or tribe who dwelt in eastern Armenia

חשמל *Chashmal* –A shining substance, amber or electrum or bronze (meaning uncertain – Ezek. 1:4, 27; 8:2); shining metal

מלבוש *Malbuwsh* –Clothing, apparel, vestments, raiment, attire

שבוע *Shavua* –Week

Shabuwah –Seven, period of seven (days or years), heptad, week

שבנוכ *Sabnock* –Goetic demon #43

שמואל א *Shemuel* –The Hebrew name of 1 Samuel

שחים *Shachiys* –Grain

–Mystic number of 27th Path (*Netzach-Hod*; פ; Mars)

379 אבשלומ *'Abshalowm* –Absalom, son of David

כשדימה *Kasdiymah* –Chaldeans (see also כשדי)[606]

שמואל ב *Shemuel* –The Hebrew name of 2 Samuel

380 ישע *Yasha'* –To save, be saved, be delivered

Yesha' –Deliverance, salvation, rescue

לשנ *Lashan* –To use the tongue, slander

מספר *Mispar* –Number, tale; Angel of 3d Virgo (Regardie's spelling); Mispar, one who returned from captivity (this spelling used only in Ezra 2:2 – see also מספרת)[607]

מצרימ *Mitzraim* –Egypt; Mizraim (Egyptians); Mizraim, the second son of Ham

משלי *Mishle* –Proverbs, the Hebrew name of the book

נשל *Nashal* –To slip off, drop off, clear away, draw off

---

[604] שלם (370, 930).

[605] Meshullam (410, 970).

[606] כשדי (334).

[607] מספרת (780).

עיש *Ayish* –Arcturus, the Great Bear of Astronomy (this spelling used only in Job 38:32 – see also עש)[608]

ערפל *'arafel* –Cloud, heavy or dark cloud, darkness, gross darkness, thick darkness

ערקי *'Arqiy* –Arkite(s)

פלער *Flauros* –Goetic demon #64 (Aurum Solis spelling; more commonly known as Haures)

פריצ *Periytz* –Violent one, robber, breaker

פרצי *Partziy* –Pharzite

פרק *Paraq* –To tear apart or away, tear off, break away; fragment, broken crumb, broth

Peraq –To tear away, break off (sins)

Pereq –Parting of ways, breaking in upon, plunder, crossroad

פש *Pash* –Folly, weakness, stupidity; 220th Gate of the 231 Gates

צמרימ *Tzemarayim* –Zemaraim, city north of Jericho; mountain in Ephraim's hill country

צפיר *Tzafiyr* –He-goat

Tzefiyr –He-goat (Aramaic)

צרפי *Tzorephiy* –Goldsmiths

רפק *Rafaq* –To support

רצצ *Ratzatz* –To crush, oppress

רקיע *Raqia* –Firmament (of water above); the Second Heaven (corr. to *Hod* or *Yesod*)

רקעי *Raqay* –To beat, stamp, spread out

Riqquay –Expansion, hammered, broad (Num. 17:3)

שכינ *Sakkiyn* –Knife

שלמי *Salmay* –Shalmai, ancestor of returned exiles

Shelomiy –Shelomi, father of a prince of Asher

Shillemiy –Shillemites

שממ *Shamem* –To be desolate, to be apalled; devastated, deserted, desolate

שמלי *Shamlay* –Shalmai, Temple servant whose descendants returned to Jerusalem after the Exile

381 **אשפ** *'ashshaf* –Astrologer, enchanter, magician, necromancer, exorcist, conjurer

הושע *Hoshea* –20th and last King of Israel; Hosea, one of the 12 minor prophets; chief of the tribe of Ephraim in the days of David; one who sealed the covenant with Nehemiah; original name of Joshua

מישאל *Mishael* –Mishael, one who carried away the dead Nadab and Abihu; one who stood with Ezra at the reading of the Law; one of the companions of Daniel in Babylon (see also Meshach)[609]

שאפ *Sha'af* –To gasp, pant, breathe heavily; to crush, trample

---

608 עש (370).

609 Meshach (370, 850).

שועה *Shavaw* –Cry for help
שמאלי *Sema'lee* –Left, left side, on the left
שמאמ *Shim'am* –Shimeam, one of the family of King Saul whose descendants dwelled in Jerusalem (this spelling used only in 1 Chr. 9:38 – see also שמאה)[610]

382 בלשנ *Bilshan* –Bilshan, prince who returned from the exile (Ezra 2:2: Neh. 7:7)
מבשמ *Mibsam* –Mibsam, son of Ishmael; son of Simeon
שבניכ *Sabnock* –Goetic demon #43 (A.C., 777; probably a misprint for שבנוך)[611]

383 פגש *Pagash* –To meet, join, encounter
שבועה *Shebuwah* –Oath, curse

384 גשפא *Gishpa'* –Gishpa, overseer of the Temple servants
משלוח *Mishlowach* –Outstretching, sending, sending forth; undertaking (that to which one stretches out the hand), place of letting or turning loose, pasture (place where animals are let free)
פקדר *Peqiduth* –Oversight, overseer, guard
שדפ *Shadaf* –To scorch, blight
שעטה *Sha'atah* –Stamping (of hoofs), crushing noise

385 לטושמ *Letuwshim* –Letushim, son of Dedan
משמה *Meshammah* –Devastation, horror
עשיה *Assiah* –Action; the Material World
פצירה *Petziyrah* –Price, charge (meaning dubious – 1 Sam. 13:21)
צפירה *Tzefiyrah* –Plait, chaplet, wreath, crown (Ezek. 7:7, 10; Isa. 28:5)
עשיה *'Asayah* –Asaiah, descendant of Merari who helped bring up the Ark of the Covenant; prince of Simeon who helped defeat the people of Gedor; resident of Jerusalem after the Exile; Asahiah, one sent to inquire of the Lord concerning the Book of the Law
פוטיפר *Powtiyphar* –Potiphar, Egyptian captain of the guard who became the master of Joseph
פשה *Pashah* –To spread
שכינה *Shekanyah* –Shechaniah, head of a family of the house of David; two whose descendants returned from the Exile; one who took a foreign wife during the exile; father of one who repaired the wall of Jerusalem; father-in-law to one who opposed Nehemiah; priest who returned from the Exile
Shekinah –Divine Presence; a title of *Malkut*; a Hebrew

---

610 שמאה (346).

611 שבנוך (378, 858).

goddess

שלמיה *Shelemyah* –Shelemiah, one who married a foreign wife during the Exile; father of Hananiah; priest over the treasury; father of one sent to Jeremiah to ask for prayers; father of the guard who apprehended Jeremiah

שממה *Shemamah* –Devastation, waste, desolation

שפה *Safah* –Lip, language, speech; shore, edge, border

Shafah –To sweep bare, scrape; cream, cheese (dubious)

386 אשפה *'ashpah* –Quiver (for arrows)

יעוש *Ye'uwsh* –Jeush, son of Esau (Gen. 36:18 and 1 Chr. 1:35); son of Eshek and a descendant of King Saul; descendant of Gershon and the head of a clan; son of Rehoboam

יעשו *Ya'asuw* –Jaasau, one who married a foreign wife after the exile

ישוע *Yeshuwa'* –Jeshua, town in southern Judah that was repopulated by Jews returning from the exile – probably modern Tell es-Sa'roeh; Jeshua, priest of the sanctuary; Levite in charge of various offering to the temple; priest who returned to Jerusalem with Zerubbabel; father of Jozabad the Levite; one whose descendants returned from the exile; father of one who repaired the wall of Jerusalem; Levite who explained the Law to the people; one who sealed the new covenant with God after the exile (some think this latter is the same as the sixth Jeshua) (see also Joshua)[612]

לשון *Lashown* –Tongue

פוש *Puwsh* –To spring about; to be scattered, be spread

שופ *Shuwf* –To bruise, crush, to fall upon

שפו *Shefow* –Shepho, descendant of Seir the Horite (this spelling used only in Gen. 36:23 – see also שפי)[613]

שלון *Shalluwn* –Shallun, one who helped to repair the gate of Jerusalem

387 בעשיה *Ba'aseyah* –Baaseiah, ancestor of Asaph and descendant of Gershon

יסנדיברודיאל *Yasnadibarodiel* –Angel of 3d Capricorn (according to 777; probably a misprint)

נגדיכש *Negadikesh* –The 13th-18th letters of the 42-letter name of God (assoc. w/Tuesday)

שזפ *Shazaf* –To catch sight of, look on

388 אשכנזי *Ashkenazi* –German Jew

---

[612] Joshua (391).

[613] שפי (390).

חלמיש *Challamiysh* –Flint, rock

חפש *Chafas* –To search, search for, to search out, disguise oneself

Chafash –To be free, be freed

Chefes –Trick, plot, shrewd device

Chofesh –Precious

חשפ *Chashaf* –To strip, strip off, lay bare, make bare, draw out

Chasif –Small flocks, little flocks

ממשח *Mimshach* –Anointed, expansion (meaning uncertain – Ezek.28:14)

פשח *Pashach* –To tear, rip, tear in pieces

שחפ *Shachaf* –Cuckow, gull, sea-gull (ceremonially unclean bird)

שלחימ *Shilchiym* –Shilhim, city in southern Judah near Lebaoth (see also Shaaraim)[614]

שלחנ *Shulchan* –Table

389 אבישוע *'Abiyshuwa'* –Abishua, son of Phinehas; descendant of Benjamin

אבישלומ *'Abiyshalowm* –Abishalom, son of David

חשפא *Chasuwfa* –Hashupha, ancestor of a family of Temple servants who returned from the Captivity with Zerubbabel (Ezra 2:43 – see also חשופא)[615]

טפש *Tafash* –To be gross, be insensitive, be fat

מוגשמ *Mughsham* –Realized, materialized, corporeal

פשט *Pashat* –To strip, invade, strip off, make a dash, raid, spread out

Peshat –Torah interpretation that focuses on literal meaning of the text

שדפה *Shedefah* –Blighted, blasting, blighted thing

שלטנ *Shiltown* –Mastery; governor, ruler, official (Aramaic)

Sholtan –Dominion, sovereignty (Aramaic)

שטפ *Shataf* –To wash, rinse, engulf

Shetef –Flood, downpour

שפט *Shafat* –Judge; Shaphat, one sent to spy out the land of Canaan; father of Elisha the prophet; one of the family of David; chief of Gad; overseer of David's herds in the valley

Shefet –Judgment

–Prime number

390 יושב חסד *Yuwshab Chesed* –Jushab-Hesed, son of Zerubbabel (1 Chr. 3:20)

ישעי *Yish'iy* –Ishi, member of the family of Jerahmeel; descendant of Judah; descendant of Simeon; chief of the tribe of Manasseh

מכשל *Michshol* –Stumbling-block

614 Shaaraim (620, 1180).

615 חשופא (395).

	משיזבאל	*Mesheyzab'el* –Meshezabeel, priest who helped rebuild the wall at Jerusalem; one who signed the new covenant with God; descendant of Judah
	נשמ	*Nasham* –To pant
	צש	*Tzash* –224th Gate of the 231 Gates
	קצר	*Qatzar* –To be short, be impatient, be vexed, be grieved; to reap, harvest
		Qatzer –Short, impatient
		Qotzer –Shortness, impatience, anguish
	קרסל	*Qarsol* –Ankle
	קרצ	*Qaratz* –To narrow, pinch, squeeze
		Qeretz –Nipping, nipper, stinger (of insect)
	שלני	*Shelaniy* –Shelanites
		Shiloniy –Shiloni, father of Zechariah
	שמימ	*Shamayim* –Heaven, sky
	שמנ	*Shaman* –To be or become fat, grow fat
		Shemen –Fat, oil
		Shamen –Fat, rich, robust
	שפי	*Shefiy* –Bareness, high place; Shephi, descendant of Seir the Horite (this spelling used only in 1 Chr. 1:40 – see also שפו)[616]
	שצ	*Shax* –Goetic demon #44
391	אסנפר	*'Osnappar* –Asnapper or Osnapper, Ashurbanipal, king of Assyria
	אשמנ	*'ashman* –The stout, among the stout; the desolate, like dead
	יהושע	*Yehoshua* –Joshua, successor of Moses (see also יהושוע)[617]
	ישועה	*Yeshuw'ah* –Salvation, deliverance
	ישימאל	*Yesiyma'el* –Jesimael, descendant of Simeon
	נשמא	*Nishma'* –Breath, spirit (Aramaic)
	רומ־מעלה	*Rom Maalah* –The Inscrutable Height, a title of *Keter*
	שכניהו	*Shekanyahuw* –Shechaniah, priest in the time of David (1 Chr. 24:11); priest in Hezekiah's day (2 Chr. 31:15)
	שלמיהו	*Shelemyahuw* –Shelemiah, descendant of Levi (this spelling used only in 1 Chr. 26:14 – see also Meshelemiah)[618]; one who married a foreign wife during the exile; ancestor of one who was sent by the princes to get Baruch; one ordered to capture Baruch and Jeremiah; father of one sent to Jeremiah to ask for prayers
392	אספרנא	*'osparna'* –Thoroughly; eagerly, diligently (Aramaic)
	שבילימ	*Shevilim* –Paths
	שביעי	*Shebiy'iy* –Seventh

[616] שפו (386).

[617] יהושוע (397).

[618] Meshelemiah (425 or 431).

שבצ *Shabbats* –To weave
Shabats –Cramp, agony, anguish (2 Sam. 1:9)
–The number of Nethinims and children of Solomon's servants who returned from exile (Ezra 2:43-58)

393 גרגופיאצ *Gargophias* –Guardian of the 13th Tunnel of Set
חפשה *Chufshah* –Freedom
חצצרה *Chatsotserah* –Trumpet, clarion
יהושבע *Yehowsheba'* –Jehosheba, daughter of Jeohoram, king of Judah, who helped conceal Joash (this name only used in 2 Kings 1:2 – see also Jehoshabeath)[619]
שפחה *Shifchah* –Maid, maidservant, slavegirl

394 משטמה *Mastemah* –Animosity, enmity
ספרדימ *Sefardim* –Spanish Jews
עטישה *'atiyshah* –Sneezing

395 אביר יעקב *'Abiyr Yaqob* –"Mighty One of Jacob" (Gen. 49:24)
השמימ *HaShamaim* –The heaven
השמנ *HaShamen* –The oil
חשופא *Chasuwfa* –Hashupha, ancestor of a family of Temple servants who returned from the Captivity with Zerubbabel (see also חשפא)[620]
ישעיה *Yeshayah* –Isaiah, the great prophet who wrote the book bearing his name; Jesaiah, grandson of Zerubbabel; one who returned from the exile; descendant of Merari who returned from exile; one whose descendants dwelled in Jerusalem (see also ישעיהו)[621]
ישפה *Yashefeh* –Jasper (precious stone in the High Priest's ephod – represents the tribe Benjamin)
Yishpah –Ispah, descendant of Benjamin
מנשה *Manasseh* –Manasseh, first son of Joseph who was the founder of a tribe of Israel (assoc. w/Gemini); idolatrous 13th King of Judah; one whose descendants set up graven images at Laish (Judg. 18:30)[622]; two who had taken foreign wives (Ezra 10:30, 33)
מכשלה *Makshelah* –Overthrown mass, stumbling-block, something overthrown, decay, ruin
משנה *Mishnah* –Codified Jewish law
Mishneh – Double, copy, second, repetition
נשמה *Neshamah* –Breath, spirit; highest part of the soul
עריהנס *Uriens* –Guardian of the 16th Tunnel of Set

---

619 Jehoshabeath (793).
620 חשפא (389).
621 ישעיהו (401).
622 Some scholars feel we should read Moses here – some ancient manuscripts (Septuagint, Old Latin, and the Vulgate) read Moses

פשוט *Pashuwt* –Undressed
שמנה *Shemonah* –Eight, eighth

396 הושעיה *Howsha'yah* –Hoshaiah, father of Jezaniah or Azariah; man who led half of the princes of Judah in procession at the dedication of the walls
יפוש *Ipos* –Goetic demon #22
מושכל *Mevshekal* –Intellectual (Aramaic)
Muskal –Idea, concept (Mod. Hebrew)
מכשול *Mikshowl* –A stumbling, means or occasion of stumbling, stumbling-block
ספרוים *Sefarvayim* –Sepharvaim, city formerly identified with Sippar on the east bank of the Euphrates, now believed to be the Syrian city Shabara (Is. 37:13)
שונם *Shuwnem* –Shunem, town near Jezreel that was allotted to the tribe of Issachar

397 אבל השטים *'Abel HaShittim* –Abel-Shittim, a location in Palestine
אור פנימי *Aur Penimi* –The Internal Light; a title of *Keter*
יהושוע *Yehowshuwa'* –Joshua (more properly Jehoshua), successor of Moses (this spelling only used in Deut. 3:21; Judg. 2:7 – see also יהושע)[623]
משאון *Mashsha'own* –Guile, dissimulation, deceit
–Prime number

398 חמשים *Chamishshiym* –Fifty
חפשי *Chofshiy* –Free
חשמן *Chashman* –Ambassadors, bronze (meaning uncertain – Ps. 68:32)
סתרעתן *Sateraton* –Lord of Triplicity by Day for Aries
עכשוב *'akshuwb* –Asp, viper
שחצ *Shachatz* –Dignity, pride

399 פטיש *Pattiysh* –Forgehammer, hammer; a garment, coat, tunic (Aramaic – meaning dubious – Dan. 3:21)

400 ישבי לחמ *Yashubiy Lechem* –Jashubi-Lehem, descendant of Judah
כפש *Kafash* –To make bent, press or bend together; to bend down
כשפ *Kashaf* –To practice witchcraft or sorcery, use witchcraft
Kashshaf –Sorcerer, witch
Keshef –Sorcery, witchcraft
לשע *Lesha'* –Lasha, Canaanite boundary somewhere in the southeast of Palestine
מכמש *Mikmash* –Michmash, town of Benjamin (see also מכמס)[624]

---

623 יהושע (391).
624 מכמס (160).

מנשי	*Menashshiy* –Manassites
מעצר	*Ma'tsar* –Restraint, control
מצער	*Mits'ar* –A small thing; Mizar, hill east of the Jordan, probably within sight of Mount Hermon (Ps. 42:7)
מרצע	*Martsea'* –Awl, boring-instrument
משכיל	*Maskiyl* –Poem, song of contemplation
נמשי	*Nimshiy* –Nimshi, ancestor of Jehu
נשימ	*Nashim* –Women, wives
סנפיר	*Senappiyr* –Fin
עשל	*Ashel* –47th name of *Shem HaMeforash* (5 Pisces)
קציר	*Qatziyr* –Harvest, harvesting; boughs, branches
קש	*Qash* –Straw, chaff, stubble; 227th Gate of the 231 Gates
רקק	*Raqaq* –To spit
שכלימ	*Sekhelim* –Intelligences
שמינ	*Shamayin* –Heaven, sky (Aramaic)
שנימ	*Shanim* –Years
	Shenaim –Two
שננ	*Shanan* –To sharpen, whet
שעל	*Sho'al* –Hollow hand, hollow of hand, handful
שפכ	*Shafak* –To pour, pour out, spill
	Shefek –Place of pouring
שק	*Saq* –Sack; mesh, sackcloth, sacking
	Shaq –Leg (lower)
ת	*Tau* –22nd letter of Hebrew alphabet

Tau represents truth through the word *emet* (אמת). Unlike meanings previously given, the letter here occurs at the end of the word it represents. This points to the final nature of the letter itself as well as the accumulation of truth through the study of the letters. It also indicates that the study of Torah means truth. תורת אמת, "proper rulings," or "Torah of truth" (Mal. 2:6). *Emet* is an acrostic of אלהים מלך תמיד, "God is the eternal King," and indicates that God is truth and perfection, as *tau* is also the first letter of תמימות, "divine perfection."

NOTES:

401 אכשפ *Akshaf* –"I shall be bewitched" – city in North Canaan at the foot of Mount Carmel

אמפרודים *Amprodias* –Guardian of the 11th Tunnel of Set

אנשימ *'anashim* –Men of distinction

ארר *'arar* –To curse

את *'ath* –Sign, miraculous signs, wonder (Aramaic); essence, the thing itself; the first and last letters of the Hebrew alphabet; letter, sign, mark; plowshare, spade; 21st Gate of the 231 Gates

Ate –Thou (f.)

'eth –Word used to indicate a direct object; in G.D. usage, essence or Spirit; with, near, together with; plowshare

ואשמידמ *vi-Ashmidaym* –That I may destroy them (Deut. 9:14)

ישעיהו *Yeshayahuw* –Jesaiah, one appointed to the song service; grandson of Moses (see also ישעיה)[625]

נשיאמ *Nisiem* –Princes

Nosiem –Burdened, laden

קשא *Qishshu'* –Cucumber

שאננ *Shahanan* –At ease, quiet, secure

שנאנ *Shin'an* –Repetitions (Ps. 68:18– Thousands of thousands)

תא *Ta* –Room, guardroom, chamber

–Prime number

402 בקש *Baqash* –To seek, require, desire, exact, request

ברר *Barar* –To purify, select, polish, choose, purge, cleanse or make bright, test or prove

בת *Bath* –Daughter (n. fem.); young women, women, girl, daughter; unit of liquid measure, equal to dry measure ephah (about 40 litres – 22 litres in some places); initials of *Bayith Thabel* (House of the World); 41st Gate of the 231 Gates

יהוה שלומ YHVH *Shalowm* –Adonai Shalom, an altar built by Gideon in Ophrah (Judg. 6:24)

נבשנ *Nibshan* –Nibshan, wilderness town of Judah

קשב *Qashab* –To hear, be attentive, heed

Qashshab –Attentive

Qesheb –Attentiveness, attention

שבק *Shebeq* –To leave, let alone (Aramaic)

403 אבת *Oboth* –Waterskins; undetermined site of an Israelite camp in the wilderness (perhaps at east boundary of Moab)

אשבעל *'Ashba'al* –Ashbaal, alternate name for Ishbosheth, son and successor of Saul (this name used in 1 Chr. 8:33; 9:39)

גרר *Garar* –To drag, drag away

Gerar –Gerar, Philistine city on the southern edge of

[625] ישעיה (395).

Palestine, near Gaza

גת *Gath* –Wine press, wine vat; 60th Gate of the 231 Gates; Gath, one of the five chief Philistine cities, home of the giant Goliath

חשמנה *Chashmonah* –Hashmonah, place where the Israelites camped in the wilderness – possibly modern Wadi el-Hashim

תאב *Tawab* –To long for; to loath, abhor

404 בקבקר *Baqbaqqar* –Bakbakkar, Levite who returned from the exile – may be the same as Bakbukiah

ברבר *Barbur* –Fowl, birds; birds fattened for table of Solomon

דת *Dath* –Royal command, law, decree, edict, regulation, usage; decree, law (Aramaic); 78th Gate of the 231 Gates

חשמונ *Cheshmown* –Heshmon, place in the far southern region of Judah – possibly same as Azmon

רברב *Rabrab* –Great; captain, chief (n) (Aramaic)

קדש *Qadash* –To consecrate, sanctify, be hallowed, be set apart, be sanctified

Qadesh –Male temple prostitute; Kadesh, wilderness on Palestine's southern frontier – it was on the border between the wilderness of Paran on the south and the wilderness of Zin on the north (see also Kadesh Barnea)[626]

Qodesh –Apartness, holiness, sacredness

שקד *Saqad* –To bind, bind on, be kept on

Shaqad –Cups shaped like almond blossoms

Shaqed –Almond tree, almonds

שפטיה *Shefatyah* –Shephatiah, son of David by Abital; father of Meshullam who dwelled in Jerusalem; ancestor of returned captives; one of Solomon's servants whose descendants returned from the Exile; ancestor of returned captives; descendant of Perez whose descendants dwelled in Jerusalem; prince of Judah in Zedekiah's time

405 דתא *Dethe'* –Grass

הרר *Harar* –Mountain, hill, hill country, mount

הת *Hath* –95th Gate of the 231 Gates

יושפט *Yowshafat* –Joshaphat, one of David's valiant men (1 Chr. 11:43); priest who preceded the Ark when it was moved to Jerusalem (1 Chr. 15:24)

מערצה *Ma'aratsah* –Awful shock, crash, terror

משסה *Mechissah* –Booty, spoil, plunder

סהרנצ *Saharnatz* –Angel of 2d Libra

קשה *Qasah* –A kind of jug, jar

Qashah –To be hard, be severe, be fierce

Qasheh –Hard, cruel, severe

שפכה *Shofkah* –Penis, urethra, male organ

---

[626] Kadesh Barnea (726).

שקה *Shaqah* –To give to drink, irrigate, drink, water

406 אלעשה *Elasah* –Elasah, a descendant of Judah, son of Helez; a priest of Pashur's line with a foreign wife during Ezra's time; Shaphan's son, Zedekiah's servant; a descendant of Benjamin, son of Rapha, father of Azel

אתה *'athah* –To come, arrive; used in the New Testament in the phrase "marantha" (Lord come)

'attah –You (second person singular masculine)

בגתא *Bigtha'* –Bigtha, chamberlain of Ahasuerus

בעל חצור *Ba'al Chatzowr* –Baal Hazor, place near Ephraim where Absalom's servants killed Ammon (2 Sam. 13:23)

בעל חרמונ *Ba'al Chermown* –Baal Hermon, mountain east of Lebanon (Judg. 3:3); city near Mount Hermon where Canaanite worship took place (1 Chr. 5:23)

בקדש *Ba-Qodesh* –In Holiness

גרגר *Gargar* –Berry, olive berry

האת *HaOth* –The sign

הנשאימ *HaNisi'im* –The rulers

ולמשל *Vilimshol* –And to rule

וקציר *Viqatzir* –And harvest

ושנימ *Vishanim* –And years

ות *Vath* –110th Gate of the 231 Gates

כשלונ *Kishshalown* –A stumbling, a fall, a calamity

מעצור *Ma'tsowr* –Restraint, hindrance

עפרונ *'Ephrown* –Ephron, Hittite from whom Abraham bought a field with a cave, which became Sarah's burial place

עשהאל *'Asah'el* –Asahel, son of David's sister, Zeruiah – he was slain by Abner; Levite sent to teach the Law, Levite employed as an officer of the offerings and tithes; father of Jonathan, appointed to take a census of foreign wives

קוש *Qowsh* –To lay bait or snare, lure

רור *Ruwr* –To flow

רפליפו *Raflifu* –Guardian of the 30th Tunnel of Set

שועל *Shuwal* –Fox, a burrower; Shual, third son of Zophah; Shual, district north of Michmash

שופכ *Showphak* –Shophach, captain of the army of Hadarezer of Zobah (see also Shobach)[627]

שוק *Shuwq* –To be abundant; street

Showq –Leg, thigh

שילוני *Shiylowniy* –Shilonite

שימונ *Shiymown* –Shimon, descendant of Caleb

שקו *Shequ* –37th-39th letters of the 42-letter name of God

Shiqquv –Drink, refreshment

---

627 Shobach (328, 808).

תאה *Ta'ah* –To mark out, point out; cross; 22nd letter of Hebrew alphabet
–Mystic number of 28th Path (*Netzach-Yesod*; צ; Aries or Aquarius)

407 אבגתא *Abagtha* –Abagtha, a eunuch of Xerxes
אות *Oth* –Sign, token; token, ensign, standard, miracle, proof
Uwth –To consent, agree
ארור *Arur* –Cursed
בקשה *Baqqashah* –Request, entreaty, position
בתה *Bathah* –End, destruction
Battah –Cliff, precipice, steep
זרר *Zarar* –To sneeze
זת *Zath* –126th Gate of the 231 Gates שנהבים
שנהבים *Shenhabbiym* –Ivory
תבה *Tebah* –Ark (Noah's); the basket in which the baby Moses was placed

408 בות *Buwth* –To pass the night, lodge (Aramaic)
דרדר *Dardar* –Thistles, thorns
זאת *Zo'oth* –This, this one, here, which, this...that, the one...the other, such
חרר *Charar* –To burn, be hot, be scorched, be charred
Charer –Dry regions, parched place
חשק *Chashaq* –To love, be attached to, long for; fillet
Chashuq –Fillets, binders (rings clasping a pillar of the Tabernacle or silver rods between the pillars – Ex. 27:10, 11; 36:38; 38:10-12, 17, 19)
Chesheq –Desire, thing desired
Chishshuq –Spoke, spoke of a wheel
חת *Chath* –Fear, terror; shattered, dismayed; broken; terrified; 140th Gate of the 231 Gates
Cheth –Heth, son of Canaan (Gen. 10:15; 1 Chr. 1:13) – possibly a reference to the Hittite people
קשח *Qashach* –To treat hardly, treat severely
שובק *Showbeq* –Shobek, one who sealed the covenant with Nehemiah
שחק *Sachaq* –To laugh, play, mock
Sechowq –Laughter, laughing stock, mocking
Shachaq –To rub away, pulverize; dust, cloud
תאבה *Ta'abah* –Longing

409 אחת *Achath* –One (feminine)[628]
בזתא *Biztha'* –Biztha, one of Ahasuerus' eunuchs
ויגוע ויאסף אל־עמיו *VaYiga' VaYe'asef El-'Amayuw* –"And, breathing his last, he was gathered to his people" (Gen. 49:33)
טת *Tath* –153rd Gate of the 231 Gates
קדשה *Qedushah* –Prayer extolling God's holiness
Qedeshah –Female temple prostitute, harlot

[628] It should be noted that 4+0+9=13, the same amount as "one" in the masculine. Adding these two together equals 26, the number of YHVH.

	קשט	*Qoshet* –Bow; truth, balanced verity
	שקט	*Shaqat* –To be quiet, be tranquil, be at peace
		Sheqet –Quiet, tranquility, quietness
	תדה	*Towdah* –Confession, praise, thanksgiving
	–Prime number	
410	אררט	*'Ararat* –Ararat, a mountainous, hilly land in western Asia later known as Armenia – Noah's ark rested on mountains in this region
	גאות	*Ge'uwth* –Majesty
	דרור	*Derowr* –A flowing, free run, liberty; a swallow, bird
	הרהר	*Harhor* –Mental conception, fantasy, image, mental picture, fancy, imagining (Aramaic)
	חבת	*Chabeth* –Flatcakes, bread wafers (1 Chr. 9:31)
	יהושפט	*Yehowshafat* –Jehoshaphat, recorder of David (2 Sam. 8:16; 20:24; 1 Kings 4:3); officer of Solomon (1 Kings 4:17); father of Jehu, who conspired against Joram (2 Kings 9:2, 14); priest who helped to bring the Ark of the Covenant from Obed-edom (1 Kings 15:24); 4th King of Judah (1 Kings 22:41)
	יקש	*Yaqosh* –To lure, entice, snare, lay a snare or lure
	ית	*Yath* –Marks the direct object or the accusative case. Is not translated (Aramaic); 165th Gate of the 231 Gates
	ממשל	*Mimshal* –Dominion, ruler
	מפרצ	*Mifrats* –Landing place
	מצרפ	*Mitsaref* –Crucible
	משכנ	*Mishkan* –Abode (of God - Aramaic); dwelling place, Tabernacle
	משלמ	*Meshullam* –Meshullam, grandfather of Shaphan; descendant of King Jehoiakim; head of a family of Gad; descendant of Benjamin; one whose son lived in Jerusalem; one who lived in Jerusalem; descendant of Aaron and an ancestor of Ezra (see also Shallum)[629]; priest (1 Chr. 9:12); overseer of the Temple work; chief man who returned with Ezra to Jerusalem; one who assisted in taking account of those who had foreign wives after the Exile; one who took a foreign wife during the Exile; two who rebuilt part of the wall of Jerusalem; prince or priest who stood with Ezra while he read the Law; priest who sealed the new covenant with God after the Exile; one whose descendants lived in Jerusalem; priest who assisted in the dedication of the wall of Jerusalem; descendant of Ginnethon; Levite and gatekeeper after the Exile
	נשינ	*Nashiyn* –Wives (Aramaic)
	פלש	*Palash* –To roll

[629] Shallum (376, 936).

קדוש *Qadosh* –Holy
Qadesh –Holiness, sacred, holy, Holy One, saint, set apart
Qiddush –Sanctification; prayer recited on Shabbat and during festivals

קיש *Qiysh* –Kish, son of Gibeon; Levite in David's time; descendant of Levi who assisted in the cleansing of the Temple under Hezekiah; great-grandfather of Mordecai; father of King Saul

קשי *Qeshiy* –Stubborness, obstinancy

ריר *Riyr* –Slime juice or liquid, spittle

רקיק *Raqiyq* –Thin cake, wafer

שלפ *Shalaf* –To draw out or off, take off
Shelaf –The second son of Joktan & a descendant of Shem

שמיני *Shemiyniy* –Eighth

שמע *Shama'* –To hear, listen, obey; sound
Shema' –Report, a hearing; Shema, son of Hebron; descendant of Reuben; chief of the tribe of Benjamin; one who stood with Ezra when he read the law; Shema, city of Judah in the Negeb
Shoma' –Report , rumor, news, fame

שנס *Shanas* –To gird up

שפטיהו *Shefatyahuw* –Shephatiah, valiant man who joined David at Ziklag; prince of Simeon; son of Jehoshaphat

שפל *Shafel* –To be or become low, sink, be humbled
Shefel –Low, lowliest (of station – Aramaic)

שקי *Sheqi* –37th-39th letters of the 42-letter name of God, assoc. w/*Yesod* (A.C., 777)

411 אלישע *Elisha* –Elisha, the great prophet who succeeded Elijah

אתי *'Ittay* –Ittai, Philistine friend and general of David; one of David's mighty men (see also איתי)[630]

היכל רצונ *Hekel Ratzon* –Palace of Delight, Heavenly Mansion corr. to *Tiferet*

ויצמח יהוה אלהימ מנ האדמה *Vahyatzmach* YHVH *Elohim men HaAdamah* –"And from the ground the Lord God caused to grow" (Gen. 2:9)

טבת *Tabbath* –Tabbath, place where the Midianites stayed after Gideon's attack (Judg. 7:22)
Tebeth –Tebeth, the ancient Hebrew tenth month (Est. 2:16)

יומ הכפרימ *Yom HaKipurim* –"The Day of Many Atonements," Yom HaKippurim, a variation of Yom Kippur

משוסה *Meshuwsah* –Booty, spoil, plunder

טבת *Tevet* –The 4th month of the Jewish calendar – it is associated with Capricorn and the tribe Gad

עשיאל *'Asiy'el* –Asiel, descendant of Simeon and grandfather of

---

[630] איתי (421).

Jehu

עמשא *'Amasa'* –Amasa, nephew of David who became the commander of Absalom's army; leader of the Ephraimites and son of Hadlai who opposed making slaves of captured Israelites

שלמיאל *Shelumiy'el* –Shelumiel, chief of Simeon appointed to assist Moses

שמעא *Shim'a'* –Shimea, descendant of Merari; father of Berachiah; one of the family of King Saul whose descendants dwelled in Jerusalem (see also Shimeam)[631]; son of Jesse (this spelling used only in 2 Sam. 21:21; 1 Chr. 20:7 – see also Shammah and Shimeah)[632]; one of David's sons (this spelling used only in 1 Chr. 3:5 – see also Shammua)[633]

תהו *Tohu* –Desolation, "without form"

412 בית *Bayith* –House; place; receptacle; home (house with family); household, family; household affairs; inwards (metaphor); temple; on the inside; within; house of God (Aramaic); Bajith, Moabite city or temple (Is. 15:2)

Bet –House; 2nd letter of Hebrew alphabet

התבה *HaTayvah* –The ark (of Noah)

חדת *Chadath* –New (Aramaic)

יומ הכפארימ *Yom HaKipariym* –"Day of the atonements," Yom HaKippurim, a variation of Yom Kippur

ישבק *Yishbaq* –Ishbak, son of Abraham and father of a northern Arabian tribe

יתב *Yethiyb* –To sit, dwell

תאוה *Ta'avah* –Desire, lust, passion; boundary, limit

413 אבל מצרימ *'Abel Mitzrayim* –"Meadow of Egypt," Abel Mizraim, a place in Palestine

אלישבע *Elisheba* –Elisheba, Aaron's wife

גבחת *Gabbachath* –Bald in the forehead

גתי *Gittiy* –Gittite

חתה *Chathah* –To take hold of, seize, take away, pile up, snatch up (coals)

Chittah –Terror, fear

414 אזות *'Azoth* –The first matter of the Alchemists placed into Hebrew letters (one possible spelling)[634]

אינ־סופ אור *Ain-Sof Aur* –The Limitless Light

אני יהוה אלהי אברהמ אביכ *'Ani* YHVH *'Elohey 'Avraham 'Aviyka* –"I am the Lord, the God of your father Abraham" (Gen. 28:13)

הגות *Haguwth* –Meditation, utterance, musing

זתוא *Zattuw'* –Zattu, one whose descendants returned from

---

631 Shimeam (381, 941).

632 Shammah (345), Shimeah (415).

633 Shammua (416).

634 Azoth (478).

		the exile; cosealer of the new covenant
	יתד	*Yathed* –Pin, stake, peg, nail
	מקור חיים	*Maquwr Chaim* –"The fountain of life" (Ps. 36:10)
	משוטטים	*Mashuwtim* –A going forth, emanation
	נחשונ	*Nachshown* –Naashon, descendant of Judah (perhaps Aaron's brother-in-law – Ex. 6:23; Num. 1:7)
	עינ יהוה אל־יראיו	*'Ayin* YHVH *'El-Yere'ayo* –"The eye of the Lord is on those who fear Him" (Ps. 33:18)
	פלדש	*Pildash* –Pildash, son of Nahor, Abraham's brother
	קדיש	*Qaddiysh* –Holy, separate; angels, saints
	שחוק	*Sekhoq* –Laughter, laughing, mirth
	תבואה	*Tebuwah* –Produce, product, revenue
		Tuwgah –Grief, heaviness, sorrow
	תוח	*Towach* –Toah, ancestor of Samuel the prophet (see also Tohu below and Nahath)[635]
	תחו	*Tochuw* –Tohu, ancestor of Samuel the propet (this spelling used only in 1 Sam. 1:1 – see also Toah above and Nahath)[636]
415	אדרגזר	*Adargazer* –Judge (diviner), counselor
	אחות	*Achowth* –Sister
	בגדות	*Bogedowth* –Treacherous, treacherousness of treacherous behavior
	הקדוש	*HaQadosh* –The holy
	הררי	*Harariy* –Hararite (see also הארריּ)[637]
	השפל	*Hashpala* –Humiliation, degradation, demeaning
	זאויר אנפינ	*Zauir Anpin* –The Lesser Countenance, a title of *Tiferet*
	זוחת	*Zowcheth* –Zoheth, descendant of Judah (1 Chr. 4:20)
	טות	*Tevath* –Fasting, fastingly, hungrily
	ממשלה	*Memshalah* –Rule, dominion, realm
	מצעירה	*Mitstse'iyrah* –Little, insignificant, a small thing
	סרעפה	*Sar'appah* –Bough
	עשליה	*Asaliah* –Angel of 5q Pisces & day angel 10 Cups
	קדישא	*Qadisha* –Holy (Aramaic)
	קשוט	*Qeshowt* –Truth
	שמעה	*Shim'ah* –Shimeah, son of Jesse (this spelling used only in 1 Chr. 20:7 – see also Shammah, Shimea)[638]; Shemaah, father of two valiant men who joined David
	שנינה	*Sheniynah* –Sharp word, cutting word, taunt
	שפלה	*Shiflaw* –Lowliness, humiliation, a low place
		Shefelah –Lowland, valley
416	אחזת	*'Achuzzath* –Ahuzzath, friend of Abimelech, king of Philistia

[635] Nahath (458).
[636] Nahath (458).
[637] הארריּ (416).
[638] Shammah (345), Shimea (411).

	גבהות	*Gabhuwth* –Haughtiness, loftiness, lofty
	המאור הקטנ	*HaMaor HaQaton* –The lesser light
	חרחר	*Charchur* –Extreme heat, inflammation, violent heat, fever
	הארריּ	*Ha'rariy* –Hararite – this spelling only used in 2 Sam. 23:34 (see also הררי)[639]
	יקוש	*Yaqowsh* –Fowler, bait-layer, trapper
	ישימונ	*Yeshiymown* –Waste, wilderness, desert, desolate place
	קפצפוני	*Qaftzafoni* –Prince and King of Heaven, husband of Mehetabel, and father of Lilith the Younger
	שמוע	*Shammuwa'* –Shammua, one sent to spy out the land of Canaan; one of David's sons (see also Shimea)[640]; Levite who led the Temple worship after the Exile (see also Shemaiah)[641]; head of a priestly family in Nehemiah's day
	שקוי	*Shiqquwy* –Drink, refreshment
417	אדמ דוד משיח	*Adam David Mashiach* –The lineage of the Messiah – "Adam, David, Messiah"
	אודות	*Owdowth* –Cause
	אלישוע	*Elishua* –Elishah, a son of David
	בתיה	*Bithyah* –Daughter of Yah; Bithiah, daughter of Pharaoh and wife of Mered (1 Chr. 4:18)
	זית	*Zayith* –Olive, olive tree; mountain facing Jerusalem on the east side (Mount of Olives)
	חברברה	*Chabarburah* –Spots, stripe, mark
	נבושזבנ	*Nebuwshazban* –Nebushazban, a Babylonian prince (Jer. 39:13)
	נבכדנאצר	*Nebukadne'tztzar* –Nebuchadnezzar, king of the Babylonian Empire; he captured Jerusalem three times and carried Judah into captivity (this spelling used only in 2 Kings 24:1, 10; 25:1, 8; 1 Chr. 6:15; Jer. 28:11, 14 – see also נבוכדנאצר, נבוכדנצר, נבוכדראצר, and נבוכדראצור)[642]
	עיי העברימ	*'Iyey HaAbariym* –Ije-Abarim, place where the Israelites camped in the territory of Moab
	שכאנומ	*Shakanom* –A title of *Tiferet*
418	אבראהאדאברא	*Abrahadabra* –A.C.'s spelling of Abracadabra; i.e., the "Word of the Aeon"
	בולשכינ	*Boleskine* –A.C.'s retreat in Scotland
	חית	*Chayyath* –Beast
		Chet –Fence, enclosure; 8th letter of Hebrew alphabet
	חטאת	*Chattath* –Sin; atonement
	חתי	*Chittiy* –Hittite, Hittites

639 הררי (415).

640 Shimea (411).

641 Shemaiah (47).

642 נבוכדנאצר (423), נבוכדנצר (422), נבוכדראצר (573), נבוכדראצור (579).

	יחת	*Yachath* –Jahath, descendant of Judah, son of Reaiah; three descendants of Levi: a son of Libni, a son of Shimi, a son of Shelomoth; Levite who helped oversee temple repair
	ישחק	*Yischaq* –Isaac, son of Abraham and Sarah, born to them in their old age (this spelling used only in Jer. 33:26; Amos 7:9, 16 – see also יצחק)[643]
	רא הור	*Ra-Hoor* –Ra-Horus, an Egyptian god
419	אחדות	*Achdoth* –Unity, oneness
	טבחת	*Tibchath* –Tibhath, city of Amam-Zobah (see also Betah)[644]
	טית	*Teth* –Serpent; 9th letter of Hebrew alphabet
	–Prime number	
420	גזית	*Gaziyth* –Hewed, hewn stone, wrought
	ויקדש	*ve-Yiqadosh* –And He sanctified
	ירקעם	*Yorqe'am* –Jorkeam or Jorkoam, son of Raham, or a city he founded (1 Chr. 2:44)
	כסף נבחר	*Kesaf Nevachar* –"Choice silver" (Prov. 10:20)
	כרר	*Karar* –To whirl, dance
	כת	*Kath* –176th Gate of the 231 Gates
	מישע	*Meysha'* –Mesha, king of Moab who rebelled against Ahaziah; eldest son of Caleb
	מעשי	*Ma'say* –Maasai, Aaronite priest whose family lived in Jerusalem after the exile
	משעי	*Mish'iy* –Cleansing (Ezek. 16:4)
	עמשי	*'Amasay* –Amasai, son of Elkanah in the genealogy of Kohath; captain who joined David at Ziklag; priest who assisted in bringing up the Ark of the Covenant to Jerusalem
	ענש	*'anash* –To fine, amerce, punish, condemn, mulct; to fine (Aramaic); confiscation, fining, amercing (Aramaic)
		'onesh –Fine, penalty, indemnity
	עשן	*'ashan* –To smoke, be angry, be wroth; smoke; Ashan, lowland town assigned to the tribe of Judah, then to Simeon
		'ashen –Smoking
	פרצימ	*Peratziym* –Perazim, a mountain in Palestine; "breaches"
	צפרנ	*Tzipporen* –Fingernail, stylus point
	קישי	*Qiyshiy* –Kishi, father of Ethan, also known as Kushaiah
	שלמנ	*Shalman* –Shalman, king who sacked Beth-Arbel[645]
		Shalmon –Reward, bribe
	שמעי	*Shim'iy* –Shimi, son of Gershon and a grandson of Gershon; descendant of Benjamin who cursed David when he was fleeing from Absalom; loyal

[643] יצחק (208).

[644] Betah (19).

[645] Scholars argue that Shalman is actually Shalmaneser V of Assyria or Shalman king of Moab.

officer of David; officer of Solomon; grandson of King Jeconiah; man who had sixteen sons and six daughters (1 Chr. 4:26-27); descendant of Reuben; son of Libni; father of a chief of Judah; Levite; Levite in the Temple song service in the days of David; one in charge of many vineyards; one who helped to cleanse the Temple; Levite in charge of the temple offerings under Hezekiah; three men who took foreign wives during the Exile; grandfather of Mordecai; Shimeites

שסס *Shasas* –To plunder, spoil

שען *Sha'an* –To lean on, trust in, support

שפמ *Safam* –Moustache

Shafam –Shapham, chief of Gad

Shefam –Shepham, location on the northeastern boundary of the Promised Land near Riblah

תכ *Tokh* –Oppression

421 איתי *Iythay* –There is, there are; particle denoting existence; to be

'Ittay –Ittai, Philistine friend and general of David; one of David's mighty men

אשען *'Esh'an* –Eshean, mountain village near Dumah

הגית *Hagith* –Olympic Planetary Spirit of Venus

הושמע *Howshama'* –Hoshama, son or descendant of Jeconiah

הרורי *Harowriy* –Harorite

התבודד *Hitboded* –To meditate

חגית *Chaggiyith* –Haggith, wife of David and mother of Adonijah

חזות *Chazowth* –Visions; view, sight, visibility (Aramaic)

Chazuwth –Vision, conspicuousness

יעשיאל *Ya'asiy'el* –Jaasiel, one of David's mighty men (1 Chr. 11:47); leader of the tribe of Benjamin during David's reign (1 Chr. 27:21)

מושעה *Mowsha'ah* –Saving act, deliverance

מי הירקונ *Mey he-Yarqown* –Me-Jarkon, city in the territory of Dan near Joppa

פשיאל *Pasiel* –Angel of 12th astrological house

שמועה *Shemuw'ah* –Report, news, rumor

–Prime number

422 אריכ־אנפינ *Arik Anpin* –The Vast Countenance, a title of *Keter*

חרחור *Charchuwr* –Harhur, ancestor of returned captives

ישבעמ *Yashob'am* –Jashobeam, one who joined David at Ziklag (1 Chr. 12:6) (see also Adino)[646]

כתב *Kathab* –To write, record, enroll; a writing, document, edict

Kethab –To write (Aramaic); a writing

נבוכדנצר *Nebuwkadne'tztzar* –Nebuchadnezzar, king of the

[646] Adino (71).

Babylonian Empire; he captured Jerusalem three times and carried Judah into captivity (this spelling used only in Ezra 1:7; 5:12, 14; 6:5; Neh. 7:6; Esth. 2:6; Dan. 2:28, 46; 3:1-3, 5, 7, 9, 13, 16, 19, 24, 26, 28; 4:1, 4, 18, 28, 31, 33, 34, 37; 5:2 – see also נבכדנאצר, נבוכדנצר, נבוכדנאצר, נבוכדראצר, and נבוכדראצור)[647]

שבעים *Shivim* –Seventy

423 בהיות *Biheyot* –There was

זוית *Zaviyth* –Corner

נבוכדנאצר *Nebuwkadne'tztzar* –Nebuchadnezzar, king of the Babylonian Empire; he captured Jerusalem three times and carried Judah into captivity (this spelling used only in 2 Kings 24:11, 25:22; 36:6, 7, 10, 13; Jer. 27:6, 8, 20; 28:3; 29:1, 3; Dan. 1:1 – see also נבכדנאצר, נבוכדנצר, נבוכדראצר, and נבוכדראצור)[648]

פילגש *Piylegesh* –Concubine, paramour

שגענ *Shiggawown* –Madness

424 ויזתא *Vahyezatha'* –Vajezatha, one of the 10 sons of Haman who were hanged with their father (Est. 9:9)

זרזיר *Zarziyr* –Girded, girt, alert, perhaps an extinct animal (meaning unkown – Prov. 30:31)

חיות *Chayoth* –Living Creatures

Chayuwth –Living; animals

טוטת *Totath* –Lord of Triplicity by Night for Taurus

ידדות *Yediduwth* –One dearly beloved, object of love

קשיטה *Qesiytah* –A unit of unknown value (Gen. 33:19; Job 42:11; Josh. 24:32)

שמידע *Shemiyda'* –Shemida, grandson of Manasseh

425 אידית *Yiddith* –Yiddish, the language of the Ashkenazic Jews

בטחות *Battuchowth* –Security, safety

גור אריה *Gur Arieh* –Lion's whelp

התכ *Hathak* –Hatach, chamberlain of Ahasuerus (Est. 4:5-10)

כהת *Kahath* –8th name of *Shem HaMeforash* (2 Virgo)

מעשיה *Ma'aseyah* –Maaseiah, four men who took foreign wives during the Exile (Ezra 10:18, 21-22, 30); father of Azariah, who repaired part of the wall of Jerusalem (Neh. 3:23); priest who stood with Ezra while he read the Law (Neh. 8:4); priest who explained the Law (perhaps the same as the latter – see Neh. 8:7); one who sealed the new covenant with God after the Exile (Neh. 10:26); descendant of Perez living in Jerusalem (Neh.

---

[647] נבכדנאצר (417), נבוכדנצר (422), נבוכדנאצר (423), נבוכדראצר (573), נבוכדראצור (579).

[648] נבכדנאצר (417), נבוכדנצר (422), נבוכדראצר (573), נבוכדראצור (579).

11:5); one whose descendants lived in Jerusalem (Neh. 11:7); two priests who took part in the purification of the wall of Jerusalem (Neh. 12:41-42); priest whose son was sent by King Zedekiah to inquire of the Lord (Jer. 21:1; 29:25); father of a false prophet (Jer. 29:21)

משלמיה *Meshelemyah* –Meshelemiah, descendant of Levi (this spelling used only in 1 Chr. 9:21 – see also משלמיהו and Shelemiah)[649]

סדם ועמרה *Sodom ve-Amorah* –"Sodom and Gomorrah" (Gen. 14:10, 11; 18:20; 19:28; Deut. 29:22; Jer. 49:18)

שמעיה *Shema'yah* –Shemaiah, prophet who warned Rehoboam; descendant of David; head of a family of Simeon; son of Joel; descendant of Merari; one who helped to bring the Ark of the Covenant to the Temple; Levite who recorded the allotment in David's day; gatekeeper for the Tabernacle; one who helped to cleanse the Temple; Levite in Hezekiah's day; one who returned with Ezra; person sent to Iddo to enlist ministers; two who married foreign wives during the Exile; one who helped to repair the wall of Jerusalem; one who tried to intimidate Nehemiah; one who sealed the new covenant with God after the exile; one who helped to purify the wall of Jerusalem; one at the dedication of the wall of Jerusalem; prince of Judah who took part in the dedication of the wall; Levite of the line of Asaph; chief of the priests who returned with Zerubbabel

תכה *Takah* –To lay down, recline

426 הרגו בחרב *Harguw Becharev* –They killed with the sword

יטבתה *Yotbathah* –Jotbathah, encampment of the Israelites in the wilderness

כבדת *Kebeduth* –Heaviness, difficulty

כות *Kuwth* –Cuth, Babylonian city – probably modern Tell Ibrahim (see also Cuthah)[650]

נושע *Nowsha* –To be redeemed

עין רמון *'Eyn Rimmown* –En Rimmon, city of Judah, south of Jerusalem, where the tribe of Judah settled on their return from the Exile (Neh. 11:29)

עקרון *'Eqrown* –Ekron, northernmost of the five chief cities of Palestine, apportioned to the tribe of Judah

שלמון *Salmown* –Salmon, father of Boaz (this spelling used only in Ruth 4:21 – see also שלמא)[651]

תוח *Tavech* –Amidst us

427 עזריקם *'Azriyqam* –Azrikam, son of Azel of the family of Saul;

---

649 משלמיהו (431), Shelemiah (385 or 391).

650 Cuthah (431).

651 שלמא (371).

governor of Ahaz's house; descendant of Merari; one of the family of David

קושיהו — *Quwshayahuw* –"bow of יהוה;" father of Ethan the Merarite

428 אור חוזר — *'or Chozer* –Returning light

אשכנזימ — *Ashkenazim* –German Jews

געשכלה — *Gasheklah* –The Smiters, the Disturbers of All Things, the Breakers in Pieces, *Qlippoth* of *Hesed*

המשכנ אחד — *HaMishkon echad* –One dwelling (of God's dwelling place)

חשמלימ — *Chashmalim* –Angelic Choir assoc. w/*Hesed*

חתכ — *Chathak* –To divide, determine

מחשפ — *Machsof* –A stripping, a laying bare (of bark)

משפח — *Mispach* –Bloodshed, outpouring (of blood)

–The difference between life (*chai*) and death (*maveth*) – (446-18)

429 חצר סוסה — *Chatzar Suwsah* –Hazar Susah, small village in the extreme south of the territory of Simeon – may be modern Susiyeh

משפט — *Mishpat* –Judgment, justice, ordinance

430 אלישפט — *Elishafat* –Elishaphat, a captain for the High Priest Jehoiada

כתי — *Kittiy* –Chittim or Kittim (see also כתיי)[652]

לקש — *Laqash* –To glean, gather, take the aftermath, take everything

Leqesh –After-growth, aftermath, spring-crop, late crop after-growth

לת — *Lath* –186th Gate of the 231 Gates

משמנ — *Mashman* –Fatness, fat piece, fertile place, richly prepared food; fatness

נפש — *Nafash* –To take breath, refresh oneself

Nefesh –Soul, self, life, creature, person, appetite, mind, living being, desire, emotion, passion, lowest part of the tripartite soul

נשפ — *Nashaf* –To blow

Neshef –Twilight

עקרני — *'Eqroniy* –Ekronite (see also עקרוני)[653]

פרעה נכה — *Par'oh Nekoh* –Pharaoh-Nechoh, an Egyptian king, the son and successor of Psammetichus and the contemporary of Josiah, king of Judah (see also פרעה נכו)[654]

צדיק־יסוד־עולמ — *Tzadiq-Yesod-Olam* –"The Righteous Is the Foundation of the World," a title of *Yesod*

רעמסס — *Ra'meses* –Rameses, royal city of the Egyptian King Ramses II which the ancestors of Israel were

---

652 כתיי (440).

653 עקרוני (436).

654 פרעה נכו (431).

forced to help build (Ex. 1:11); "land of Ramses" is used to describe the fertile district of Egypt where the Israelites settled (Gen. 47:11; Ex. 12:37)

שממנ *Shimamon* –Horror, dismay, apallment

שמצ *Shemets* –Whisper, little

שסע *Shasa'* –To divide, cleave, part, split
Shesa' –Cleft, clovenfooted

שפימ *Shuppiym* –Shuppim, gatekeeper in the days of David; son of Benjamin (this spelling used only in 1 Chr. 7:12, 15; 26:16 – see also Shupham, Shephuphan, Muppim)[655]

שפמי *Shifmiy* –Shiphmite

שפנ *Safan* –To cover, cover in, panel, hide
Shafan –Rock badger, coney, the hyrax; Shaphan, scribe of Josiah who read him the Law; father of a chief officer under Josiah; father of Elasah; father of Jaazaniah whom Ezekiel saw in a vision; father of Gemariah[656]

שפעי *Shif'iy* –Shiphi, father of a chief of Simeon

שקל *Shaqal* –To weigh, weigh out, pay out
Seqel –Shekel

תכי *Tukkiy* –Peacock; baboon, ape

תל *Tel* –Mound

431 איש ימיני *'Iysh Yemiyniy* –Man of Yemini, Yemenite (Judg. 19:16; 1 Sam. 9:1; 2 Sam. 20:1; Est. 2:5)

התוכ *Hittuwk* –A melting

כותה *Kuwthah* –Cuthah, Babylonian city – probably modern Tell Ibrahim (see also Cuth)[657]

מעשיהו *Ma'aseyahuw* –Maaseiah, Levite of the praise service (1 Chr. 15:18, 20); captain who helped to make Joash king (2 Chr. 23:1); officer of King Uzziah (2 Chr. 26:11); son of Ahaz, king of Judah (2 Chr. 28:7); governor of Jerusalem under Josiah's reign (2 Chr. 34:8); officer of the Temple (Jer. 35:4)

משלמיהו *Meshelemyah* –Meshelemiah, descendant of Levi (this spelling used only in 1 Chr. 26:1-2, 9 – see also משלמיה and Shelemiah)[658]

נוטריקונ *Notariqon* –The kabbalistic theory of acronyms

עציונ גבר *'Etzyown Geber* –Ezion Geber, village west of the port of Elath on the Gulf of Aqaba

פרעה נכו *Par'oh Nekow* –Pharaoh-Necho, an Egyptian king, the son and successor of Psammetichus and the contemporary of Josiah, king of Judah (see also פרעה נכה)[659]

---

[655] Shupham (506, 1066), Shephuphan (516, 1166), Muppim (170, 730).
[656] Many scholars consider all of the above to be the same person.
[657] Cuth (426).
[658] משלמיה (425), Shelemiah (385 or 391).

	שמעיהו	*Shema'yahuw* –Shemaiah, Levite whom Jehoshaphat sent to teach the people; Levite in Hezekiah's day; chief Levite in Josiah's day; father of the prophet Urijah; one who wanted the priests to reprimand Jeremiah; father of a prince of the Jews
	שלאנן	*Shel'anan* –At ease, quiet, secure
	תיטיב	*Taytev* –You do good
	–Prime number	
432	בכית	*Bekiyth* –Weeping
	בלע בן בעור	*Bela ben Beor* –Bela, son of Beor; a King of Edom (assoc. w/Daath)
	בן עיש	*Ben Ayish* –Son of Ayish; Ursa Minor
	וישמעו	*Yayishmio* –"They [Adam and Eve] heard" (Gen. 3:8)
	תבל	*Tebhel* –World; one of the Seven Earths (corr. [w/Cheled] to *Yesod* and *Malkut*)
		Tubal –Tubal, son of Japheth; trader with Tyre (this spelling used only in Ezek. 27:13 – see also תובל)[660]
433	בלאת	*Beleth* –Goetic demon #13
	זכות	*Zakoth* –Merit, privilege, right
	משפחה	*Mishpachah* –Clan, family
	תכחה	*Towkechah* –Rebuke, correction, reproof, punishment; argument
	תלג	*Telag* –Snow (Aramaic)
	–Prime number	
434	גאלת	*Giulath* –Redemption
	דלת	*Dalet* –Door, gate; 4th letter of Hebrew alphabet
	עין חצור	*'Eyn Chatzowr* –En Hazor, fortified city of the tribe of Naphtali
	עמישדי	*'Ammiyshadday* –Ammishadai, Father of Ahiezer, Prince of Dan during the wilderness journey
	שמידעי	*Shemiyda'iy* –Shemidaites
435	גבלת	*Gabluth* –A twisting (by analogy – chain, rope)
	הנפש	*HaNefesh* –The soul
	התל	*Hathal* –To mock, deceive; deceive
		Hathol –Mockery, mocker
	יהודית	*Yehuwdiyth* –Judith, wife of Esau; Jew's language
	ישמעיה	*Yishma'yah* –Ishmaiah, chief of Gibeon who joined David at Ziklag (1 Chr. 12:4)
	משמנה	*Mishmannah* –Mishmannah, one who joined David at Ziklag
	שמצה	*Shimtsah* –Whisper, derision, whispering

[659] פרעה נכה (430).

[660] תובל (438).

תלה *Talah* –To hang
–The number of camels brought out of exile (Ezra 2:67)
–Mystic number of 29th Path (*Netzach-Malkut*; ק; Pisces)

436 לות *Levath* –To, at, beside, near, with (Aramaic)
עקרוני *'Eqrowniy* –Ekronite (see also עקרני)[661]
שופמי *Shuwphamiy* –Shuphamite
תאלה *Ta'alah* –Curse
תלאה *Tela'ah* –Toil, hardship, distress

437 אולת *'iweleth* –Foolishness, folly, silliness
משבצה *Mishbetsah* –Plaited or filigree or chequered work (of settings for gems)
שבענה *Shib'anah* –Seven

438 אשפנז *'Ashpenaz* –Ashpenaz, prince of Nebuchadnezzar's eunuchs who was in command of the captives from Judah
בתול *Bethuwl* –Bethuel, town apportioned to the tribe of Simeon (Josh. 19:4; 1 Chr. 4:30) (see also Bethel (1 Sam. 30:27))[662]
בית הגלגל *Beyth HaGilgal* –Beth-Gilgal, place in Palestine (Jer. 12:29)
חתל *Chathal* –To entwine, enwrap, be swaddled
תובל *Tuwbal* –Tubal, a trader with Tyre (this spelling used only in Is. 66:19 – see also תבל)[663]
תלח *Telach* –Telah, descendant of Ephraim

439 בתואל *Bethuw'el* –Bethuel, son of Nahor, Abraham's brother
גלות *Galuwth* –Exile, exiles, captives; captivity (Aramaic)
לבאות *Leba'owth* –Lebaoth, one of the towns of southern Judah in Simeon (see also Beth-Birei)[664]
עוגרמענ *Ogarman* –Lord of Triplicity by Night for Gemini
שפטים *Shofetim* –Judges
שפטן *Shiftan* –Shiphtan, father of Kemuel, chief of Ephraim
תלדה *Towledah* –Descendents, results, proceedings, genealogies
–Prime number

440 בזיותיה *Bizyowtheyah* –"Contempt of יהוה" – a town in southern Judah near Beersheba
ישפן *Yishpan* –Ishpan, descendant of Benjamin and son of Shashak
כתיי *Kittiyiy* –Chittim or Kittim (see also כתי)[665]

---

661 עקרני (430).
662 Bethel (443).
663 תבל (432).
664 Beth-Birei (625).
665 כתי (430).

	מרר	*Marar* –To be bitter; to be strong, strengthen
		Meror –Bitter thing, bitter herb, bitterness
	משק	*Mashshaq* –Running, rushing
		Mesheq –Acquisition, possession, son of possession, heir
	מת	*Mat* –Male, man; 195th Gate of the 231 Gates
		Met –Dead
	נפיש	*Nafiysh* – Naphish, ancestor of returned captives (see also נפושסים, Nephusim)[666]
	ערצ	*'arats* –To tremble, dread, fear, oppress, prevail, break, be terrified, cause to tremble
	פסש	*Pasash* –To pass over, spring over; to limp
		Pesash –Passover
		Peseash –Lame
	שכל כללי	*Sekhel Kelali* –Collecting or Collective Intelligence (30th Path)
	שמנימ	*Shemonim* –Eighty, forescore
	שספ	*Shasaf* –To hew in pieces (meaning dubious – 1 Sam. 15:33)
	שעע	*Sha'a'* –To stroke, be smeared over, be blinded; to sport, take delight in
	שקמ	*Shaqam* –Sycamore tree
	תהלה	*Tehillah* –Psalm, praise, song or hymn of praise
	תולד	*Towlad* –Tolad, town southeast of Beersheba in southern Judah
	תלי	*Theli* –Dragon; Satan
		Teliy –Quiver of arrows
	תמ	*Tam* –Whole, complete; simple, pious, innocent, sincere, mild, perfect; to be complete, be finished
		Tom –Wholeness; simplicity, piety, innocence, sincerity, mildness, perfection
441	אילת	*Ayeleth* –Doe, deer, hind; ("Aijeleth Shahar" is part of the title of Ps. 22 and probably describes to the musicians the melody to which the psalm was to be played)
		'Eylowth –Elath, port city of the Gulf of Elath on the Reed Sea
	אלקשי	*Elkoshiy* –Elkoshite
	אמת	*'emeth* –Firmness, faithfulness, truth;in truth, truly[667]
	אתמ	*Atem* –You (m. pl.)
		'Etham –Etham, place where the Israelites camped before they entered the wilderness of Sinai
	גחלת	*Gacheleth* –Coal, burning coal, ember
	ישמעיהו	*Yishma'yahuw* –Ishmaiah, chief of Zebulun in David's time (1 Chr. 27:19)
	רמרא	*Ramara* –Lord of Triplicity by Day for Pisces
	תאמ	*Ta'am* –To match

---

[666] נפושסים (546, 1106), Nephusim (250, 810).

[667] *Émeth* is a notarikon of the the final letters of the words ברא אלהים את (Gen. 1:1).

		To'am –Harmony
	תמא	*Tema'* –Tema, place where Tema's descendants dwelt (Job 6:19)
	–21²	
442	בלתי	*Biltiy* –Not, except, not, except; except; so as not, in order not; an account of not, because...not; until not
	בעל שמ	*Baal Shem* –"Master of the Name," a Jewish kabbalist
	היכל בשלמה	*Heykal Solmon* –"Temple of Solomon"
	עינ הקורא	*'Eyn haq-Qowre'* –En Hakkore, spring at Lehi, which God brought forth as an answer to Samson's prayer (Judg. 15:18-19)
443	בית־אל	*Betel* –House of God; Bethel, name of an important city north of Jerusalem, formerly called Luz[668]
	בתולה	*Betulah* –Virgin; Virgo; a title of *Malkut*
	גילת	*Giylath* –Joy, rejoicing
	גלית	*Golyath* –Goliath, Philistine giant slain by David (1 Sam. 17:4-54); another giant, possibly the son of the first Goliath (2 Sam. 21:19)
	זלות	*Zulluwth* –Vileness, worthlessness
	חתלה	*Chathullah* –Swaddling-band, navel-band (Job 38:9)
	לזות	*Lezuwth* –Deviation, perversity, crookedness
	מתג	*Metheg* –Bridle
	תחלה	*Techillah* –Beginning, first
	–Prime number	
444	דמשק	*Dammeseq* –Damascus, important Syrian trade center, also the captial of Syria (see also דומשק, דרמשק)[669] – this spelling used in Gen. 14:15; 15:2; 2 Sam. 8:5, 6; 1 Kings 11:24; 15:18; 19:15; 20:34; 2 Kings 5:12; 8:7, 9; 14:28; 16:9, 10 (here also spelled דומשק), 11, 12; Song 7:5; Is. 7:8; 8:4; 10:9; 17:1, 3; Jer. 49:23, 24, 27; Ezek. 27:18; 47:16, 17, 18; 48:1; Amos 1:3, 5; 5:27; Zech. 9:1
		Demesheq –Damask?, silk? (meaning uncertain – Amos 3:12)
	השפטימ	*HaShofetim* –The Judges
	יאר יהוה פניו אליכ	*Ya'ar* YHVH *Panavi 'aliyk* –"May YHVH bestow His favor upon you..." (Num. 6:26)
	חתול	*Chittuwl* –Bandage
	לחות	*Luchoth* –The tablets the Ten Commandments were written upon
		Luchowth –Luhith, town in Moab, between Aeropolis and Zoar (this spelling used only in Jer. 48:5 – see also לוחית)[670]

668 Luz (43).
669 דומשק (450), דרמשק (644).

מקדש *Miqdash* –Sacred place, sanctuary, holy place; the Holy Sanctuary
Mikodesh –From the Holy Place
צפרדע *Tzefardea* –Frogs
שחצומ *Shachatzowm* –Shahazimah, city of Issachar
תלאובה *Tal'uwbah* –Drought

445 זחלת *Zocheleth* –Zoheleth, stone beside Enrogel near the Well of the Virgin – here Adonijah sacrificed animals (1 Kings 1:9)
יתלה *Yithlah* –Jethlah, town of Dan (Josh. 19:42)
כרכרה *Karkarah* –Dromedary, dromedary camel, beasts
מכשפה *Mekshepah* –Sorcerer
מקשה *Miqshah* –Hammered work, finely decorated cultic objects of gold or silver; place or field of cucumbers
Miqsheh –Turned work, well-dressed hair, well-set hair, turner's work (meaning uncertain – possibly referring to artistry of the hairdo – Is. 3:24)
מררה *Mererah* –Gall
Merorah –Bitter thing, gall, poison
משקה *Mashqeh* –Irrigation, drink; butter, cup-bearer
מתה *Metah* –To die, be dead
שופטימ *Shofetim* –The Hebrew name of the book of Judges
תחבלה *Tachbulah* –Direction, counsel, guidance
תחלוא *Tachaluw* –Diseases
תל אביב *Tel 'Abiyb* –Tel-Aviv, town of Babylonia near the river Chebar where Jewish exiles were placed (Ezek. 3:15)
תמה *Tummah* –Integrity
Tamahh –To be astounded, amazed, dumb-founded

446 אתמדא *'Admatha'* –Admatha, a prince of Persia
ינשופ *Yanshuwf* –Great owl, eared owl
מוקש *Mowqesh* –Bait, lure, snare
מות *Maveth* –Death, dying, Death (personified), realm of the dead
Mowth –Death (Aramaic)
Muwth –To die, kill, have one executed; an unknown translation used in Ps. 48:15 – here translated as "evermore"
משעול *Mish'owl* –Hollow way, narrow way
פישונ *Pison* –A river of Eden (Gen. 2:11 – assoc. w/Fire)
קמוש *Qimmowsh* –Thistles or nettles, a thorny or useless plant

447 אותמ *'Awotam* –Them, themselves (Gen. 41:8)
אילות *'Eylowth* –Elath, port city of the Gulf of Elath on the Reed Sea
Eyaluwth –Strength, my help

---

670 לוחית (454).

	אליאתה	*Eliylathah* –Eliathah, a Hemanite musician in David's court
	אמות	*'Amot* –I die (Gen. 26.9); cubits (Ex. 26:16) *'Emot* –A people (Num. 25:15)
	אמתו	*'Amatow* –His bondswoman (Ex. 21:20)
	בהמת	*Behemot* –Cattle (Num. 3:41); beasts (Num. 32:24)
	בהררמ	*Behareram* –In their mount (Gen. 14:6)
	גדלתי	*Giddaltiy* –Giddalti, son of Heman in charge of one of the courses at the temple
	השביעני	*Hisheviy'ani* –Made me swear (Gen. 50:5)
	ואמת	*Ve'amet* –And truly, and truth (Gen. 24:49)
	ואתמ	*Ve'atem* –And you (Gen. 9:7) *Ve-'otam* –And those (Lev. 14:11)
	ובשפטימ	*Ve-Vishefatiym* –And with judgements (Ex. 6:6)
	והבדלת	*Ve-Hivedaleta* –And you shall separate (Num. 8:14)
	ומאת	*Vome'ath* –And a hundred *Vo-me'et*-And of (Lev. 16:5)
	זתמ	*Zetham* –Zetham, son or grandson of Laadan
	יהוה אחד נשמה אחד	YHVH *Echad Neschamah Echad* –One God, one soul
	לחטת	*Lechatat* –For a sin offering (Num. 15:24)
	מאות	*Me'avot* –Hundreds (Gen. 5:5)
	מאתו	*Mei'tow* –From him (Gen. 8:8)
448	במות	*Bamowth* –Bamoth, an Israelite encampment north of the Arnon River (Num. 21:19) – may be the same as Bamoth Baal of Num. 22:41
	חמת	*Chamath* –Hamath, Hittite city on the Orontes River north of Damascus – a supply base for Solomon's armies; ideal northern boundary of Israel *Chammath* –Hammath, city on Naphtali alloted to the Levites (see also Hammon and Hammoth dor)[671] *Chemeth* –Bottle, waterskin
	חתמ	*Chatham* –To seal, seal up, affix a seal; seal (Aramaic)
	מחת	*Machath* –Mahath, descendant of Kohath who helped to purify the sanctuary (1 Chr. 6:20; 2 Chr. 29:12); a Levite overseer of dedicated things during Hezekiah's reign
	מספר חיימ	*MiSefer Chayiym* –"Book of Life" (Ps. 69:29)
	משחק	*Mishchaq* –Object of derision
	מתח	*Mathach* –To spread out
	פרצ עזא	*Peretz 'Uzza'* –Perez-Uzzah, name David gave to the place Uzzah was struck by God (2 Sam. 6:8)
	תמח	*Temach* –Thamah, one whose descendants returned from the Exile
449	–Prime number	
450	אחמתא	*'Achmetha'* –Achmetha or Ecbatana, capital of the

[671] Hammon (104, 754), Hammoth dor (653).

	Median empire, later Persian and Parthian capitals, conquered by Alexander the Great
דומשק	*Duwmeseq* –Damascus, important Syrian trade center, also the captial of Syria (see also דמשק, דרמשק)[672] – this spelling used in 2 Kings 16:10 (here also spelled דמשק)[673]
דמות	*Demuwth* –Likeness, similitude; in the likeness of, like as
הזחלת	*HaZoheleth* –The serpent
המדתא	*Hammedatha* –Hammedatha, father of Haman the Agagite
ילדות	*Yalduwth* –Childhood, youth
כשפים	*Keshafim* –Witchcrafts, sorceries
כתל	*Kethel* –A wall (Aramaic)
	Kothel –Wall (of house)
לתכ	*Lethek* –Barley-measure (uncertain measurement but thought to be 1/2 an homer - 5 ephahs)
מדות	*Midowth* –Virtues
מחבת	*Machabath* –Flat plate, pan, griddle
מפלש	*Miflas* –Swaying, poising, balancing
מררי	*Merariy* –Merari, third son of Levi and founder of a priestly clan; Merarite
משמע	*Mishma'* –Thing heard, rumor; Mishma, son of Ishmael; descendant of Simeon
משעמ	*Mish'am* –Misham, descendant of Benjamin
מתי	*Mathay* –When?
נקש	*Naqash* –To knock, strike, bring down; to ensnare
	Neqash –To knock (of knees – Aramaic)
נשק	*Nasaq* –To kindle, burn
	Nashaq –To put together, kiss; to handle, be equipped with
	Nesheq –Equipment, weapons, armory
נת	*Nath* –203rd Gate of the 231 Gates
ערק	*'araq* –To gnaw, chew
פארפאחיטאס	*Parfaxitas* –Guardian of the 27th Tunnel of Set
פרי עצ	*Peri Etz* –"Fruit of a tree" (Gen. 1:29)
פשע	*Pasa'* –To step, march, step forward
	Pasha' –To rebel, transgress, revolt
	Pesa' –Step
	Pesha' –Transgression, rebellion
קנה חכמה קנה בינה	*Qeneh Chakmah Qeneh Biynah* –"Acquire wisdom, acquire discernment" (Prov. 4:5)
רצונ באינ גבול	*Ratzon Be'iyn Gebul* –"Good will with no limit"
שוכנ עד	*Shoken 'Ad* –"Dwelling in eternity"
שעלימ	*Sha'aliym* –Shalim, unidentified region, perhaps in the region of Ephraim or Benjamin, where Saul searched for his father's donkeys (1 Sam. 9:4)

[672] דמשק (444), דרמשק (644).

[673] דמשק (444).

שעפ *Sha'aph* –Shaaph, descendant of Judah; son of Caleb

שפע *Shefa'* –Abundance

תלכ *Talak* –Go

תנ *Tan* –Jackal; the great dragon

451 אלישמע *Elishama* –Elishama, an Ephraimite chief in the wilderness; a son of David; Jehoiakim's secretary; a priest who taught the law; a man of Judah

יארמלקע *Yarmulka* –Skullcap (Yiddish)

ישמעאל *Yishma'el* –Ishmael, son of Abraham and Hagar whose descendants are the Arabian nomads; descendant of Benjamin; father of Zebadiah; captain in the time of Jehoiada and Joash; cunning son of Nethaniah and traitor of Israel; Levite who married a foreign wife during the exile

שנאנימ *Shinanim* –Angelic Choir sometimes assoc. w/*Tiferet*

תהומ *Tehom* –Abyss, "deep"

תימא *Teyma'* –Tema, son of Ishmael

תנא *Tana* –Teacher

452 איתיאל *'Iythiy'el* –Ithiel, man of the tribe of Benjamin; person to whom the proverbs of Agur were directed (Prov. 30:1)

שעלבימ *Sha'albiym* –Shaalabim, city of the tribe of Dan (this spelling used only in Judg. 1:35 – see also שעלבין)[674]

453 בהמות *Behemowth* –The great land-monster of Hebrew mythology (exact meaning unkown – Job 40:15 –24)[675]

גתימ *Gittayim* –Gittaim, Benjamite town of refuge near Beeroth

זכוכת *Zekuwkith* –Glass, crystal, fine glass

מחתה *Machtah* –Fire-holder, censer, firepan, snuff dish, tray

Mechittah –Destruction, ruin, terror, a breaking

נפש חיה *Nefesh Chayyah* –Life, living creature

תמוז *Tammuz* –The 10th month of the Jewish calendar – it is associated with Cancer and the tribe Issachar; Tammuz, a near-Eastern god associated with the sun

454 איכה ירדפ אחד אלפ *'eykah yirdof 'echad 'alef* –"How does one pursue a thousand?" (Deut. 33:30)

דתנ *Dathan* –Dathan, chief of the tribe of Reuben who tried to overthrow Moses and Aaron

Dothan –Dothan, city of the tribe of Manasseh west of the Jordan River, near Mount Gilboa, here

---

674 שעלבין (462, 1112).

675 Some scholars speculate that it is perhaps an extinct dinosaur – Diplodocus or Brachiosaurus,

Joseph was sold into slavery (see also דתין)[676]

זהראריאל *Zahărariel* –A title of *Tiferet*

חותמ *Chowtham* –Seal, signet, signet-ring; Hotham, descendant of Asher (1 Chr. 7:32); father of two of David's best men (1 Chr. 11:44)

חמות *Chamowth* –Mother-in-law, husband's mother

לוחית *Luwchiyth* –Luhith, town in Moab, between Aeropolis and Zoar (this spelling used only in Is. 15:5 – see also לחות)[677]

רברבנ *Rabreban* –Lord, noble (Aramaic)

תמיד *Tamidh* –Continually

–The number of children of Adin who returned from exile (Ezra 2:15)

455 בגתנ *Bigthan* –Bigthan, chamberlain who conspired against Ahasuerus

גנבת *Genubath* –Genubath, son of Hadad the Edomite

נתה *Nethah* –25th name of *Shem HaMeforash* (1 Sagittarius)

יתמה *Yithmah* –Ithmah, a Moabite, one of David's guards (1 Chr. 11:46)

פוטי פרע *Powtiy Phera'* –Potipherah, priest of On and father-in-law of Joseph (Gen. 41:45, 50)

שפעה *Shif'ah* –Abundance, quantity, multitude

תכלה *Tiklah* –Perfection, completeness, completion

456 אנתה *'antah* –You, thou (2nd person singular – Aramaic)

אתנה *'atenah* –You (f. pl.)

'ethnah –Hire, price (of a harlot); reward

בגתנא *Bigthana'* –Bigthana, chamberlain who conspired against Ahasuerus

יותמ *Yotham* –Jotham, son of Gideon who managed to escape from Abimelech; son of Jahdai; 10th King of Judah

יתומ *Yathowm* –An orphan, fatherless

כהתאל *Kehethel* –Angel of 2q Virgo & night angel 8 Pentacles

פרצופ *Partzuf* –Face, person

תאנה *Ta'anah* –Occasion, opportunity

457 אתונ *'athown* –She-ass, she-donkey

'attuwn –Furnace

זנת *Zonowth* –Armor (used in warfare not sanctioned by YHVH)

–Prime number

458 בית האלי *Beyth HaEliy* –Bethelite, inhabitant of Bethel

בית חגלה *Beyth Choglah* –Beth Hogla, Benjamite village southeast of Jericho

---

676 דתין (464, 1114).

677 לחות (444).

בעל פעור *Baal Peor* –"Lord of the opening," Baal-peor a Moabite fertility god
ויהי יהוה את *Vahe* YHVH *Eth* –"YHVH was with" (Gen. 39:2, 21; Josh. 6:27; Judg. 1:19)
חמתי *Chamathiy* –Hamathite
חתאתמ *Chata'tem* –You have sinned (Ex. 32:30, 32, 34; Lev. 10:19; 16:16, 21, 34; Num. 5:7; 16:26; 18:9; 32:23; Deut. 9:16, 18; Ps. 85:3; Is. 58:1; Jer. 14:10; 40:3; 44:23)
חתימ *Chittim* –Hittites
חתנ *Chathan* –To become a son-in-law, make oneself a daughter's husband; son-in-law, daughter's husband, bridegroom, husband
כל נשיא בהמ *Kal Nasiy' VaHem* –"All were leaders" (Num. 13:2)
נבות *Nabowth* –Naboth, the owner whom Jezebel had killed in order to obtain his vineyard (1 Kings 21:1-18)
נחת *Nachath* –To go down, descend; Nahath, descendant of Esau; overseer of the offerings at the Temple (see also Toah)[678]
Nacheth –Descending
Nechath –To descend
נתח *Nathach* –To cut, cut up, cut in pieces, divide
Nethach –Piece, a piece of flesh or metal
שחקימ *Shechaqim* –Clouds; the 3rd Heaven (corr. to *Netzach*)
תחנ *Tachan* –Tahan, the name of two descendants of Ephraim

459 בעל שמ טוב *Baal Shem Tov* –Master of the Good Name, given to R. Yisrael ben Eliezar
גנתו *Ginnethow* –Ginnetho, priest or prince who sealed the new covenant with God after the exile (see also Ginnethon)[679]
מואבית *Mow'abiy* –Moabite (see also מואביה, מואבי)[680]
פסנטרינ *Pisanteriyn* –A stringed instrument (perhaps a lyre or a harp)

460 יהוה איש מלחמה YHVH *Ish Milchamah* – "The Lord is a man of war"
יקשנ *Yoqshan* –Jokshan, son of Abraham by Keturah
כתמ *Katham* –To be stained, be defiled, be deeply stained
Kethem –Gold, pure gold
מרירי *Meriyriy* –Bitter
משענ *Mish'en* –Support, staff
נית *Nith* –54th name of *Shem HaMeforash* (6 Aries)
סרר *Sarar* –To rebel, be stubborn, be rebellious, be refractory
סת *Sath* –210th Gate of the 231 Gates
צללדמירונ *Tzelilimiron* (or *Tzeleldimiron*?) – The Changers,

[678] Toah (414).
[679] Ginnethon (509, 1159).
[680] מואביה (64), מואבי (59).

		Qlippoth of Gemini (spelling given in 777; probably a misprint)
	קדש ליהוה	*Qadesh la*-YHVH –"Holy to the Lord"
	תהלכה	*Tahalukah* –Procession
	תלל	*Talal* –To exalt; exalted, lofty
	תמכ	*Tamak* –To grasp, hold, support, attain
461	איתנ	*Eythan* –Perpetual, constant, perennial, ever-flowing, permanent; Ethan, wise man in the time of Solomon; descendant of Judah; descendant of Levi
	אתני	*'Ethniy* –Ethni, one whom David set over the song service of the Temple (1 Chr. 6:26)
	גבתונ	*Gibbethown* –Gibbethon, village of the tribe of Dan where Nadab was assassinated
	הלכות	*Halachot* –Practice; the parts of the Talmud dealing with matters of law (pl.)
	ישמעאלי	*Yishma'e'liy* –Ishmaelite
	קרנ הפוכ	*Qeren Happuwk* –Keren-Happuch, third daughter of Job to be born after his restoration to health
	–Prime number	
462	באר לחי ראי	*Be'er LaChay Ro'iy* –Beer Lahai Roi, the well of Hagar
	ביתנ	*Biythan* –House, palace
	מכתב	*Miktab* –Writing, thing written
	נבית	*Nebayowth* –Nebaioth, oldest son of Ishmael; an Israelite tribe descended from Nebaioth (possibly identifiable with the later Naoteans – Is. 60:7 – see also נביות)[681]
	נתיב	*Nathiyb* –Trodden with the feet, path, pathway; path, pathway, traveller
	שעלבינ	*Sha'albiym* –Shaalabim, city of the tribe of Dan (this spelling used only in Josh. 19:42 – see also שעלבים)[682]
	שעלבני	*Sha'alboniy* –Shaalbonite
	תבלל	*Teballul* –Obscurity, confusion
	תבני	*Tibni* –Tibni, one who rivaled Omri for the throne of Israel (1 Kings 16:21-22)
	תנואה	*Tenuw'ah* –Opposition, enmity
		Tenuwbah –Fruit, produce
463	באתינ	*Bathin* –Goetic demon #18
	גינת	*Giynath* –Ginath, father of Tibni
	ולבחתה	*ve-Livchotah* –And to lament, to wail, to weep
	זנות	*Zenuwth* –Fornication, harlotry
		Zonowth –Fornications (armor worn that is not sanctioned by God – 1 Kings 22:38)

---

[681] נביות (468).

[682] שעלבים (452, 1012).

חתנה *Chathunnah* –Wedding, marriage
סבתא *Sabta'* –Sabta, third son of Cush (possibly a people of southern Arabia is intended – this spelling used only in 1 Chr. 1:9 – see also סבתה)[683]
תחנה *Tachanah* –Encamping, encampment
Techinnah –Favor, supplication, prayers; Tehinnah, descendant of Judah
–Prime number

464 דתין *Dothayin* –Dothan, city of the tribe of Manasseh west of the Jordan River, near Mount Gilboa, here Joseph was sold into slavery (see also דתן)[684]
חנות *Chanuwth* –Cell, vaulted room
Channowth –Intent; to pity, be gracious; gracious
תמידי *Temidi* –Constant, perpetual
תנחו *Tanchum* –Consolation (s)

465 אחימות *'Achiymowth* –Ahimoth, son of Elkanah
כשניעיה *Kashenyayah* –Angel of 10th astrological house
מכתה *Mekittah* –Crushed or pulverised fragments
משענה *Mish'enah* –Support (of every kind), staff
נשיקה *Neshiyqah* –Kiss
–Mystic number of 30th Path *Hod-Yesod*; ר; Sol)

466 גלגלת *Gelgoleth* –Golgotha; skull, head, every man
יונת *Yownath* –Meaning uncertain – title of Psalm 56
נוית *Naviyth* –Naioth, place in Ramah where a community of prophets gathered around Samuel (1 Sam. 19:18-23; 20:1 – see also the second Ramah)[685]
Nuit –Egyptian sky goddess (cf. The Book of the Law)
סות *Suwth* –To incite, allure, instigate, entice; garment, vesture
סתו *Sethav* –Fall, autumn, rainy season
עולם היצירה *Olam HaYetzirah* –World of Formation
קול־יהוה יחיל מדבר *Qol-YHVH Yachiyl Midbar* –"The voice of YHVH convulses the wilderness" (Ps. 29:8)
קישון *Qiyshown* –Kishon, river in central Palestine which rises in Mount Tabor and drains the valley of Esdraelon
קשיון *Qishyown* –Kishion, city on the boundary of the tribe of Issachar
שמעון *Simeon* –Simeon, second son of Jacob by Leah, a progenitor of a tribe of Israel (assoc. w/Pisces)
תאניה *Ta'aniyah* –Mourning, grieving
תמכו *Tamakuw* –Supported

467 בן־זוחת *Ben-Zowcheth* –Ben-zoheth, son of Ishi and descendant

---

683 סבתה (467).
684 דתן (454, 1104).
685 Ramah (245).

of Judah
זיתנ *Zeythan* –Zethan, descendant of Benjamin (1 Chr. 7:10)
יאתונ *Ye'ithown* –Entrance (Ezek. 40:15)
נתיבה *Netivah* –Path
סבתה *Sabta'* –Sabta, third son of Cush (possibly a people of southern Arabia is intended – this spelling used only in Gen. 10:7 – see also סבתא)[686]

–Prime number

468 ביתונ *Beton* –Angel of 3d Gemini
בעל פעור *Ba'al Pe'owr* –Baal-peor, Moabite god of fertility (Deut. 4:3; Hos 9:10)
חנית *Chaniyth* –Spear
נביות *Nebayowth* –Nebaioth, oldest son of Ishmael; an Israelite tribe descended from Nebaioth (possibly identifiable with the later Naoteans – Is. 60:7 – see also נבית)[687]
עזרמ ומגנמ הוא *Ezram ve-magenawm hu* –He (God) is their help and shield (Psalms 115:10-13)
תחני *Tachaniy* –Tahanites

469 בית אונ *Beyth 'Aven* –Beth Aven, town of the tribe of Benjamin

470 ידתונ *Yeduwthuwn* –Jeduthun, one of the three chief musicians of the service of song (this name only used in 1 Chr. 25:1-6 – see also ידותון, ידיתון – he was also named Ethan in 1 Chr. 6:29; 15:17, 19)[688]
כמריר *Kimriyr* –Blackness, gloominess, darkness
כנת *Kenath* –Associate, colleague, companion; companion, associate (Aramaic)
משקל *Mishqal* –Heaviness, weight
נכת *Nekoth* –Treasure
נתהיה *Nithahiah* –Angel of 1q Sagittarius & day angel 8 Wands
נתכ *Nathak* –To pour out or forth, drop (of rain), be poured, be poured out, be melted, be molten
עקש *'aqash* –To be perverse, twist, pervert, make crooked, prove perverse, declare perverse
'iqqesh –Twisted, distorted, crooked, perverse, perverted; Ikkesh, father of Ira, one of David's mighty men
ערר *'arar* –To strip, make bare, strip oneself
עשק *'asaq* –To strive, contend, quarrel
'ashaq –To press upon, oppress, violate, defraud, do violence, get deceitfully, wrong, extort
'Esheq –Eshek, well dug by Isaac in the Valley of Gerar

---

686 סבתא (463).

687 נבית (462).

688 ידותון (476, 1126), ידיתון (480, 1130), Ethan (461, 1111).

		– claimed by the Philistines
		'osheq –Oppression, extortion, injury
	עת	*'eth* –Time; 216th Gate of the 231 Gates
	קרקע	*Qarqa'* –Floor, bottom; Karkaa, unknown site on the southern boundary of the tribe of Judah
	שכל דמיוני	*Sekhel Dimyoni* –Imaginative Intelligence (24th Path)
	שצפ	*Shetsef* –Flood, downpour, overflowing
	שקע	*Shaqa'* –To sink, sink down, subside
	תכנ	*Takan* –To measure
		Token –Measurement, measured amount; Tochen, town of Simeon (see also Ether)[689]
	תלמ	*Telem* –Furrow, ridge
	תמל	*Temowl* –Before, yesterday, already
	תנכ	*Tanakh* –Jewish Bible
471	אלתולד	*Eltowlad* –Eltolad, a city in southern Judah
	הללות	*Howleluwth* –Madness
	מלאת	*Mille'th* –Fullness, setting, border, rim
	נכאת	*Neko'th* –A spice (perhaps tragacanth gum)
472	בעת	*Ba'ath* –To terrify, startle, fall upon, dismay, be overtaken by sudden terror
	ויעש אלהימ	*Va-ya-as Elohim* –"And God made"
	מהציאות	*Machaziy'owth* –Mahazioth, one set over the song service of the Temple (1 Chr. 25:4, 30)
	עבת	*'abath* –To wind, weave, weave together
		'aboth –Having interwoven foliage, leafy, dense with foliage; cord, rope, cordage, foliage, interwoven foliage
	תעב	*Tawab* –To abhor, be abominable
473	מחלת	*Machalath* –Mahalath (meaning dubious, probably a catchword in a song giving name to tune – Ps. 53:1; 88:1)
474	אל ביתאל	*El Betel* –"The God of the House of God" – the place where God revealed Himself to Jacob (Gen. 35:7)
	דעת	*Daath* –Knowledge; the pseudo-*Sefira*h (occurs 93 times in the *Tanakh*)
	חכמות	*Chokmowth* –Wisdom (n. fem.)
	חסות	*Chasuwth* –Refuge, shelter
	חצר סוסימ	*Chatzar Suwsiym* –Hazar Susim, small village in the extreme south of the territory of Simeon – may be modern Susiyeh
	עתד	*'athad* –To be ready, make ready, prepare
	רעדר	*Raadar* –Lord of Triplicity by Day for Cancer
475	בית־דגונ	*Beyth-Dagown* –Beth Dagon, town located on the border

[689] Ether (670).

between Asher and Zebulun (Josh. 19:27); town in the Judean lowlands (Josh. 15:33, 41)

גבעת *Gib'ath* –Gibeath, city in the hill country of Judah southwest of Bethlehem

כהנת *Koheneth* –Priestess

עשקה *'oshqah* –Oppression, abuse, distress

עתה *'attah* –Now

תעה *Tawah* –To err, wander astray

476 ביתחון *Betchon* –Lord of Triplicity by Day for Scorpio

ידותון *Yeduwthuwn* –Jeduthun, one of the three chief musicians of the service of song (this name only used in 1 Chr. 9:16 – see also ידיתון ,ידתון – he was also named Ethan in 1 Chr. 6:29; 15:17, 19)[690]

מלכישוא *Malkiyshuwa'* –Malchishua, third son of King Saul

מלקוש *Malqowsh* –Latter rain, spring rain

משקול *Mishqowl* –Heaviness, weight

מתלאה *Mattela'ah* –What a weariness, toil, hardship, weariness

עות *'avath* –To be bent, be crooked, bend, make crooked, pervert

'uwth –To hasten to, help, succor (meaning dubious – Isa. 50:4)

עשוק *'ashowq* –Oppressor, extortioner

'ashuwq –Oppression, extortion

צלילימירון *Tzelilimiron* –The Clangers, *Qlippoth* of Gemini

שכל נעבד *Sekhel Ne'evad* –Administrative or Assisting Intelligence (32nd Path)

תנוך *Tenuwk* –Tip, lobe (of ear)

477 אתמול *'ethmowl* –Yesterday, recently, formerly; before, before that time, before the time, heretofore, of late, of old, these days, time(s) past

בעתה *Be'athah* –Terror, dismay

הוללות *Howleluwth* –Madness

הנה אלקינו זה קוינו לו *Haneh 'elqeynuw Zeh Qeviynuw Luw* –"Behold, this is our God that we have been waiting for" (Is. 25:9)

שכל מוטבע *Sekhel Motba* –Active Intelligence (28th Path)

תעבה *Tow'ebah* –A disgusting thing, abomination

478 אזעת *'Azo'th* –The first matter of the Alchemists placed into Hebrew letters (one possible spelling)[691]

חצר עינן *Chatzar 'Eynan* –Hazar Enan, small village on the northern border of Palestine (this name used only in Num. 34:9, 10; Ezek. 48:1 – see also חצר עינון)[692]

---

690 ידתון (470, 1120), ידיתון (480, 1130), Ethan (461, 1111).

691 Azoth (414).

692 חצר עינון (484, 1134).

כתובימ *Ketuvim* –Hagiographia,[693]
מחלת *Machalath* –Mahalath, daughter of Ishmael and wife of Esau; wife of Rehoboam; this name was later used for a major demon

479 גלילות *Geliylowth* –Geliloth, landmark on the southern boundary of Benjamin
תגמול *Tagmuwl* –Benefit, act of grace
–Prime number

480 ידיתונ *Yediythuwn* –Jeduthun, one of the three chief musicians of the service of song (this name only used in Neh. 11:17 – see also ידתון, ידותון – he was also named Ethan in 1 Chr. 6:29; 15:17, 19)[694]; father of Obededom (1 Chr. 16:38) – he may be the same as the first Jeduthun[695]
כסת *Keset* –Band, fillet, covered amulets, false phylacteries (Ezek. 13:18, 20)
לילית *Lilith* –Name of a female goddess known as a night demon who haunts the desolate places of Edom, Queen of the Night, Queen of Demons, wife of Samael, wife of Asmodai, first wife of Adam, archdemon corr. to *Yesod*, *Qlippoth* of *Malkut*
מהתלה *Mahathalah* –Deceptions, illusions
מולדת *Mowledeth* –Kindred, birth, offspring, relatives
ממרר *Mamror* –Bitter thing, bitterness
ממשק *Mimshaq* –Possession, place possessed
מתמ *Methom* –Soundness, entirely, entire
סכת *Sakath* –To be silent
Sukkoth –Succoth, first camping ground of the Israelites after leaving Israel
עדות *'eduwth* –Testimony
עית *Ayeth* –The last three letters of the 42-letter name of God, assoc. w/*Malkut* (A.C.)
'Ayath –Aiath, one of the strongest Canaanite cities (this spelling used only in Is. 10:28 – see also עיה)[696]
עמשסי *'Amashsay* –Amashai, priest of the family of Immer
עתוד *'athuwd* –Ready, prepared
'attuwd –Ram, he-goat, chief one
עתי *'Attay* –Attai, one who joined David at Ziklag; son of king Rehoboam; grandson of Sheshan the Jerahmeelite, son of Ahlai and Jarha
'ittiy –Timely, ready
פרר *Parar* –To break, frustrate; to split, divide

---

[693] Term given for the third division of the Hebrew Bible, including Psalms, Proverbs, Job, Song of Solomon, Ruth, Lamentations, Ecclesiastes, Esther, Daniel, Ezra, Nehemiah, and 1 and 2 Chronicles
[694] ידותון (476, 1126), ידתון (470, 1120), Ethan (461, 1111).
[695] Jeduthun (470, 1120; 476, 1120; 480, 1130).
[696] עיה (86).

פשק *Pasaq* –To part, open wide

פת *Path* –Bit, morsel (of bread), fragment, piece; 221st Gate of the 231 Gates

Poth –Opening, pudenda, sockets, hinges, secret parts (meaning dubious – 1 Kings 7:50; Isa. 3:17)

קלשנ *Qilleshown* –Forks, three-pronged pitchfork, goad (meaning dubious – 1 Sam. 13:21)

שקפ *Shaqaf* –To overlook, look down or out, overhand

Shaquf –Frame, window casing, beams laid over

Sheqef –Framework, casing, door, lintel

תלמוד *Talmud* –Teaching

תלמי *Talmay* –Talmai, man or clan defeated by Caleb; King of Geshur and father-in-law of David

תעו *To'uw* –Tou, king of Hamath who sent his son to congratulate David on his victory over Hadadezer

תפ *Tof* –Hand-drum; bezel; timbrel, tambourine

–The number of years from the Exodus to the building of the Temple (1 Kings 6:1)

481 אדירירונ *Adiryaron* –"The Mighty One Sings"(?); a title of *Tiferet*

הלמות *Halmuwth* –Hammer, mallet

כפר העמוני *Kefar Ha'Ammowniy* –Chephar Haammonai, town assigned to the tribe of Benjamin – probably modern Khirbet Kafr'Ana

טבעת *Taba'ath* –Ring, signet, signet-ring

עותה *'avvathah* –Subversion, bending

תכונה *Tekuwnah* –Arrangement, preparation, fixed place

482 עבדות *'abduwth* –Servitude, bondage

483 בית מלא *Beyth Millo'* –Beth Millo, ancient fortification in or near Shechem

בנ־איש ימיני *Ben-'Iysh Yemiyniy* –Benish Yemini, Benjamite (1 Sam. 9:1; 2 Sam. 20:1; Est. 2:5)

לא תחמד *Lo tha-chemodh* –"Thou shalt not covet" (Ex. 20:14)

מגמת *Megammath* –Meaning uncertain, perhaps hordes, accumulation, assembling, eagerness (of Babylonians – Hab. 1:9)

מזלות *Mazloth* –Constellations; the Sphere of the Zodiac corresponding to *Chokmah*

מלתחה *Meltachah* –Wardrobe, wearing apparel, vestment

סבתכא *Sabteka* –Sabtecha, fifth son of Cush (possibly a people of southern Arabia is intended)

פרבר *Parbar* –Parbar, area on the west side of the Temple containing officials' chambers and cattle stalls

שוא *Shavi* –Falsehood (here, the *alef* has been extended out using the complete numerical equivalency of each letter)

תועבה *Toyava* –Abomination

484 בנ־אשה אלמנה *Ben-Ishah Almanah* –"Widow's son" (1 Kings 7:14)

חלמות *Challamuwth* –Purslane, a tasteless plant with thick slimy juice (Job 6:6)

חצר עינונ *Chatzar 'Eynown* –Hazar Enan, small village on the northern border of Palestine (this name used only in Ezek. 47:17 – see also חצר עינן)[697]

עתיד *'athiyd* –Ready, prepared (also Aramaic)

תלמיד *Talmiyd* –Scholar

485 גבעתי *Gib'athiy* –Gibeathite

דנתאל *Dantalion* –Goetic demon #71

עתיה *'Athayah* –Athaiah, son of Uzziah and descendant of Judah dwelling in Jerusalem

פתבג *Pathbag* –Portion of food for king, delicacies

פתה *Pathah* –To be spacious, be open, be wide; to be simple, entice, deceive, persuade

תהלימ *Tehillim* –Psalms

תעודה *Tehuwdah* –Testimony, confirmation

486 הדרעזר *Hadar'ezer* –Hadarezer, king of Zobah in Syria that warred against David and Joab (2 Sam. 10:16; 1 Chr. 18:3-10 – see also Hadadezer)[698]

כסות *Kesuwth* –Covering, clothing

לא תגנב *Lo thi-genov* –"Thou shalt not steal" (Ex. 20:13)

מלותי *Mallowthiy* –Mallothi, one who was set over the song service of the Temple

ממות *Mamowth* –Death

סכות *Sikkuwth* –Tabernacle

Sukkowth –Succoth, town where Jacob built himself a house

עוית *Avith* –Avith, a city of Edom ruled by King Hadad (this spelling used only in Gen. 36:35 – see also עיות below)

עיות *Avith* –Avith, same as previous (this spelling used only in 1 Chr. 1:46 – see also עוית above)

עותי *'Uwthay* –Uthai, son of Bigvai who returned to the land of Israel with Ezra; descendant of Judah

פרור *Paruwr* –Pan

487 אשקלונ *'Ashqelown* –Ashkelon or Askalon, one of five chief Canaanite cities located north of modern Gaza

זפת *Zepeth* –Pitch, tar, asphalt

טבעות *Tabba'owth* –Tabbaoth, one whose descendants returned with Zerubbabel (Ezra 2:43; Neh. 7:46)

עזתי *'Azzathiy* –Gazathite or Gazite

פארור *Pa'ruwr* –Glow, heat (meaning dubious – Joel 2:6; Nah. 2:11)

---

[697] חצר עינן (478, 1128).

[698] Hadadezer (290).

–Prime number

488 במותמ *Bamuwtham* –High places, altars
בתולימ *Betuwliym* –Virginity
התועבה *HaTowayvah* –The abominations
חסידות *Chassidut* –Lovingkindness; the movement within Judaism
חתלנ *Chethlon* –Hethlon, mountain pass at the northern border of Palestine, connecting the Mediterranean coast with the Plain of Hamath (Ezek. 47:15; 48:1)
חתפ *Chathaf* –To seize, take away, snatch away
Chethef –Prey; robber
לבעל פעור *Li-Ba'al Pe'or* –To Baal-Peor
מחלתי *Mecholathiy* –Mecholathite
נבלות *Nabluwth* –Immodesty, shamelessness, lewdness, pudenda (of female) (Hos. 2:12)
פחת *Pachath* –Pit, hole
פתח *Pathach* –To open; to carve, engrave
Pethach –To open; opening, doorway, entrance, unfolding
תאומיאל *Thaumiel* –Twins of God, *Qlippoth* of *Keter*

489 בית מלוא *Beyth Millow'* –Beth Millo, ancient fortification in or near Shechem
טפת *Tafath* –Taphath, daughter of Solomon
רוח רעה *Ruach Raah* –Evil spirit

490 בית־לחמ *Beth-Lechem* –Bethlehem, town south of Jerusalem, originally called Ephrath; city of the tribe of Zebulun northwest of Nazareth; Bethlehem, son of Salma, a descendant of Caleb
יוכבד בת לוי *Yokeved Beth Layvi* –"Perfect without blemish"
יפת *Yafeth* –Japheth, son of Noah[699]
מכלת *Makkoleth* –Food, food stuff
מלכת *Meleketh* –Queen
מנת *Menath* –Portion
מתנ *Mattan* –Gifts, offerings, presents; Mattan, priest of Baal slain by the Hebrews (2 Kings 11:18; 2 Chr. 23:17); father of a prince of Judah (Jer. 38:1)
Mothen –Loins, hips
סלת *Soleth* –Fine flour
ערירי *'ariyriy* –Stripped, childless, bare of children
עתכ *'Athak* –Athach, town in southern Judah to which David sent some of the spoil of Ziklag
פדות *Paduwth* –Ransom; redemption
פתי *Pethiy* –Simplicity, naïveté (n.fem.); simple, foolish, open-minded
Pethay –Width; breadth
צרר *Tzarar* –To bind, be narrow, be in distress, make narrow,

[699] Japheth is considered the father of the Indo-European races (cf. Gen. 5:32; 6:10; 7:13; 9:18, 23, 27; 1 Chr. 1:4-5)

cause distress, besiege, be straitened, be bound; to show hostility toward, vex

צת *Tzath* –225th Gate of the 231 Gates

שקצ *Shaqats* –To detest, make abominable

Sheqets –Detestable thing or idol, an unclean thing, an abomination

תמימ *Thummim* –Thummim, a material object used (along with the Urim) for divination by the High Priest[700]

תצ *Tatz* –The third two letters of the 42-letter name of God (assoc. w/*Binah*)

–The number of times one should forgive his brother's sins (Matt. 18:22)

491 בית גמול *Beyth Gamuwl* –Beth Gamul, city of Moab

מאכלת *Ma'akeleth* –Knife

Ma'akoleth –Fuel

מתנא *Mattena'* –Gift (Aramaic)

ניתאל *Nithael* –Angel of 6q Aries & night angel 4 Wands

שכל נאמנ *Sekhel Ne'eman* –Faithful Intelligence (22nd Path)

תלונה *Teluwnah* –Murmuring

–Prime number

492 סבלת *Sibboleth* –An ear of grain or wheat; mispronunciation of "Shibboleth"

מתבנ *Mathben* –Straw heap

סוכות *Sukkot* –Huts; the 8-day holiday celebrating the gathering of the harvest and the clouds of glory during the trek of the desert

צבת *Tzebet* –Bundles (of grain)

תבצ *Tebetz* –Thebez, place in the district of Neapolis

תולונ *Tuwlon* –Tilon, descendant of Judah

493 פתחה *Pethikhah* –Drawn sword, sword

494 דיפת *Diyphath* –Riphath, son of Gomer (this spelling used only in 1 Chr. 1:6 – see also ריפת)[701]

חכללות *Chakliluwth* –Redness, dullness

מלכדת *Malkodeth* –A catching instrument, snare, trap

מתג האמה *Metheg ha-'Ammah* –Metheg-Ammah, stronghold of the Philistines captured by David (2 Sam. 8:1)[702]

פתוח *Pittuwach* –Engraving, carving

תפוח *Tappuwach* –Apple, apple tree; Tappuah, descendant of Judah

495 המלכת *Hammoleketh* –Hammoleketh, ancestor of Gideon (1 Chr. 7:18)

---

[700] Thummim may literally be "perfection" as an intensive plural.

[701] Possibly a reference to the Paphlagonians on the Black Sea. Some scholars think this spelling is a copyist's mistake. ריפת (690).

[702] Many scholars believe that the name refers to Gath

מבליגית *Mabliygiyth* –Smiling, cheerfulness, source of cheerfulness or brightening
מפשעה *Mifsa'ah* –Hip, buttock, stepping region of body
מתנה *Mattanah* –Gift; Mattanah, encampment during the latter part of Israel's wandering (Num. 21:18-19)
צררה *Tzererah* –Zererath, town in the Jordan River Valley through which the Midianite army fled when defeated by Gideon's army
תמנה *Timnah* –Timnah, town on the northern border of Judah; town in the hill country of Judah

496 כלמות *Kelimmuwth* –Shame, disgrace, ignominy
לויתנ *Leviathan* –The great sea-monster of Hebrew mythology, dragon (Isa. 27:1; Job 3:8, 40:25; Ps. 74:14, 104:26)
מלכות *Malkut* –Kingdom, royalty, royal power, reign, sovereign power; the 10th *Sefira*h (it is interesting to note that the word *Keter* appears 91 times in the *Tanakh* [9+1=10])
פותי *Puwthiy* –Puhites
צות *Tzuwth* –To kindle, burn, set on fire
צרור *Tzorowr* –Bundle, parcel, pouch, bag (as packed); pebble
קמשונ *Qimmashown* –Thistles or nettles, thorny or useless plant
שקוצ *Shiqquwts* –Detestable thing or idol, abominable thing, abomination, idol
תצאה *Towtsa'ah* –Outgoing, border, a going out, end, escape
–Mystic number of 31st Path (*Hod-Malkut*; ש; Fire)
–Perfect number

497 אשקלוני *'Eshqelowniy* –Eshkalonites
זאת חנוכה *Zot Chanukah* –This is the Dedication; last day of *Chanukkah*
תאומימ *Teomim* –Twins; Gemini

498 בית אלהימ *Beth Elohim* –House of God
היכל זכות *Hekel Zakoth* –Palace of Merit, Heavenly Mansion corr. to *Giburah*
יפתח *Yefthach* –Jephthah, the 8th Judge of Israel
מנחת *Manachath* –Manahath, descendant of Seir; Manahath, city of Benjamin

499 –Prime number

500 יצת *Yatzath* –To kindle, burn, set on fire
ך *Kaf* (final) –11th letter of Hebrew alphabet
כפת *Kefath* –To bind
כתפ *Kathef* –Shoulder, shoulder-blade, side, slope
מנית *Minniyth* –Minnith, location east of the Jordan where Jephthah slaughtered the Ammonites

מכתמ *Miktam* –Michtam (a technical term found in Psalm titles, meaning uncertain – Ps. 16:1; 56:1; 57:1; 58:1; 59:1; 60:1)

מתני *Mattenay* –Mattenai, two who married foreign wives during the Exile (Ezra 10:33, 37); priest who returned after the Exile (Neh. 12:19)

Mithniy –Mithnite

נתנ *Nathan* –To give, put, set; Nathan, prophet and royal advisor to David; son of David; father of Igal; descendant of Jerahmeel; companion of Ezra; one of those who had married a foreign wife; brother of Joel, one of David's valiant men; father of Solomon's chief officer; chief man of Israel (see also Nathan-Melech)[703]

Nethan –To give (Aramaic)

סתמ *Satham* –To stop up, shut up, keep close

פרו ורבו *Peru u-revu* –"Be fruitful and multiply" (Gen. 1:22)

צית *Tzit* –Last three letters of the 42-letter name of God

קת *Qath* –228th Gate of the 231 Gates

שלקע or שעליכע *Shalicu* –Guardian of the 31st Tunnel of Set

שקק *Shaqaq* –To run about, rush to and fro

רש *Rash* –229th Gate of the 231 Gates

שר *Sar* –Master, prince, head, chief, ruler, leader

Shor –Navel, umbilical cord

תימנ *Teman* –Teman, grandson of Esau; Duke of Edom (Gen. 36:42; 1 Chr. 1:53 – assoc. w/*Hod*)

Teyman –South, southward

תלע *Tala'* –To be clad in scarlet

תמני *Timna'* –Timnite

תמס *Temes* –Dissolving, melting

תנימ *Tannim* –Whale (Ezra 32:2); jackals, wild beasts; denizens of 31st Tunnel of Set

501 אך *Akh* –Indeed, surely (emphatic); howbeit, only, but, yet (restrictive); 10th Gate of the 231 Gates

אמתני *'emtaniy* –Terrible (Aramaic)

ארש *'aras* –To betroth, engage

אשר *'ashar* –To go straight, walk, go on, advance, make progress

Asher –Asher, eighth son of Jacob and progenitor of a tribe of Israel (assoc. w/Libra); Asher, town on the southern border of Manasseh; which, whose,wherein, that

'ashur –Step, going; one from the tribe of Asher; Assyria

'esher –Happiness, blessedness

'osher –Happiness

אתננ *'ethnan* –Hire of prostitue, price; Ethnan, grandson of Ashur through Caleb, son of Hur

דצכ עדש באחב *Detzakh Adhash Beachav* –The 10 Plagues of Egypt

---

[703] Nathan-Melech (590, 1720).

		(taking the first letter of each)
	יתניאל	*Yathniy'el* –Jathniel, gatekeeper of the tabernacle (1 Chr. 26:2)
	כי קדוש אני	*Ki Qodesh Ani* –"Holy am I" (Lev. 11:44, 45)
	מלאכית	*Mal'akuwth* –Message
	פחזות	*Pachazuwth* –Recklessness, extravagance, frivolity
	קאת	*Qa'ath* –Ceremonially unclean bird (perhaps the pelican or cormorant)
	ראש	*Re'sh* –Chief, head
		Ro'sh –Head, top, summit, chief, total, sum; gall, venom, poison; Rosh, descendant of Benjamin; northern people mentioned with Meshech and Tubal (Ezek. 38:2-3; 39:1); top, roof (Hab. 3:13)[704]
	שאר	*Seere* –Goetic demon #70
		Sehor –Leaven
		Shawar –To remain, be left over
		Shehar –Rest, residue, remnant, remainder
		She'er –Flesh, food, body, near kin
	שרא	*Shere'* –To loosen, abide, begin
	תמונה	*Temuwnah* –Form, likeness, semblance
	תנאים	*Tannaim* –Teachers in the Mishnah
	תנומה	*Tenuwmah* –Slumber, sleep
502	ארור המנ	*'Arrur Haman* –"Cursed be Haman"
	בך	*Bak* –To cause to weep, make cry, lament; the first and last letter of the *Sefer Yetzirah*; over you, in you, among you, by thee; 30th Gate of the 231 Gates
	בעלת	*Ba'alath* –Baalath, town of the tribe of Dan, near Gezer
	ברוב מרדכי	*Barukh Mordekai* –"Blessed be Mordecai"
	בשר	*Basar* –To bear news, bear tidings, publish, preach, show forth; flesh
		Besar –Flesh (Aramaic)
	בתק	*Bathaq* –To cut, cut up, cut off, cut down
	שבר	*Sheber* –Sheber, descendant of Jephunneh
	שרב	*Sharab* –Burning or scorching heat, parched ground
503	אבך	*Abak* –To roll, turn
	אתבעל	*'Ethbaal* –Ethbaal, king of Zidon and father of Ahab's wife Jezebel
	באך	*Ba'ak* –Thou be come
	גך	*Gak* –49th Gate of the 231 Gates
	גרש	*Garash* –To drive out, expel, cast out, drive away, divorce, put away, thrust away, trouble, cast up
		Geres –A crushing, grain, grits, groats
		Geresh –A thing put forth, yield, produce, thing thrust forth
	יחוה־דעת	*Yechaueh-Daath* –"Speaks out" (Ps. 19:3)
	חצר אדר	*Chatzar Addar* –Hazar Addar, fortress town located on

[704] Rosh is one of the ten words in the Tanakh with a Dagesh in the letter Resh.

the southwestern border of Judah between Kadesh Barnea and Karka (this name is only used in Num. 34:4 – see also Adar)[705]

מגפיעש *Magpiy'ash* –Magpiash, one who sealed the new covenant with God after the exile

פתחיה *Pethachyah* –Pethahiah, chief Levite in the time of David; Levite having a foreign wife; descendant of Judah; Levite who regulated the devotions of the people after Ezra had finished reading the Law

רגש *Ragash* –To rage; to be in a tumult; to conspire, plot
Regash –To be in tumult
Regesh –Throng, in company; throng

שגר *Sheger* –Offspring, young or offspring of wild beasts

שרג *Sarag* –To be intertwined

504 במותימו *Bamuwtaymuw* –"...their high places" [in some translations – "their backs"] (Deut. 33:29)

דרש *Darash* –To resort to, seek, seek with care, enquire, require

דך *Dakh* –Oppressed, crushed; 67th Gate of the 231 Gates
Dek –This (Aramaic)

ויהי ביום השמיני *Vahi Bayom HaShimini* –"On the eighth day..." (Lev. 9:1)

חצות *Chatzoth* –Middle, mid-, half, division; midnight (modern Hebrew)

מחתו *Minchatuw* –His [Abel's] offering (Gen. 4:4)

שדר *Shedar* –To struggle, strive (Aramaic)

שרד *Sarad* –To escape, survive
Serad –Plaited or braided work
Sered –Stylus, a line, marker

תדעל *Tid'al* –Tidal, King of Goyim (nations) who, with his allies, invaded the Cities of the Plain (Gen. 14:1, 9)

505 בבאך *B'vo'eka* –When you come in

בית הלחמי *Beyth HaLachmiy* –Bethlehemite

הך *Hak* –84th Gate of the 231 Gates

ויצב שמ מזבח *Vayatzev Sham Mizbach* –"He [Jacob] erected there an altar" (Gen. 33:20)

מתניה *Mattaniah* –Mattaniah, brother of Jehoiakim, made puppet king of Judah by Nebuchadnezzar and renamed Zedekiah (2 Kings 24:17); descendant of Asaph whose family dwelt at Jerusalem (1 Chr. 9:15; 2 Chr. 20:14; Neh. 11:17, 22; 13:13); four who married foreign wives during the Exile (Ezra 10:26-27, 30, 37); one of the gatekeepers (Neh. 12:25)

קהת *Qehath* –Kohath, second son of Levi and beginning of a priestly clan

---

[705] Adar (274).

שרה — *Sarai* –Sarah, given name of the wife of Abraham and mother of Isaac (Gen. 17:15)[706]
Sarah –Contend, have power, contend with, persist; princess
Sharah –To let loose, free; wall, vine row
Sherah –Bracelet
Sowrah –Row (meaning uncertain – Isa. 28:25)

תעלה — *Tehalah* –Healing (of new flesh)

506 אבגיתצ — *Abgitatz* –First six letters of the 42-letter name of God (assoc. w/Sunday)

אשרה — *'asherah* –The name (and groves of worship of) a Babylonian (Astarte) – Canaanite goddess (of fortune and happiness), the consort of Baal; her images (1 Kings 14:15, 23; 15:13; 16:33; 18:19; 2 Chr. 14:2; 15:16; 17:6; 19:3; 24:18; 31:1; 33:3, 19; 34:3, 4, 7; 2 Kings 13:6; 17:10, 16; 18:4; 21:3, 7; 23:4, 6, 7, 14, 15; Deut. 7:5; 12:3; 16:21; Ex. 34:13; Isa. 17:8; 27:9; Jer. 17:2; Judg. 3:7; 6:25, 26, 28, 30; Mic. 5:14)

וך — *Vak* –100th Gate of the 231 Gates

ושר — *Vesher* –32nd name of *Shem HaMeforash* (2 Capricorn)

נתונ — *Nathiyn* –Nethinims (Temple-servants – this spelling used only in Ezra 8:17 – see also נתינ)[707]

פרצופימ — *Partzufim* –Persons, faces

ראשה — *Ri'shah* –Beginnings
Ro'shah –Top, topmost

רוש — *Ruwsh* –To be poor, be in want, lack

שארה — *Shaharah* –Kinswoman
Sheherah –Sherah, female descendant of Ephraim who built or fortified three villages

שור — *Shor* –Ox, bull; Taurus
Shur –Shur, desert in the northwest part of the Sinai Peninsula

שפופמ — *Shefuwfam* –Shupham, son of Benjamin (this spelling used only in Num. 26:39 – see also Shuppim, Shephuphan)[708]

תולע — *Towla'* –Tola, son of Issachar; the 6th Judge of Israel

507 אבדך — *'avadka* –You perish

אנתונ — *'antuwn* –You, thou (2nd person plural – Aramaic)

אשור — *Ashur* –Assyria

אתוק — *'attuwq* –Gallery, porch

בעלי השמימ — *Baali HaShamaim* –Masters of the heavens, astrologers

בשרה — *Besorah* –News, good news, tidings, reward for good news

---

706 Sarah literally means "princess."

707 נתינ (510, 1160).

708 Shuppim (430, 990), Shephuphan (516, 1166).

	גוגול הנפש	*Gilgul Hanefesh* –The rolling or the transmigration of the soul (reincarnation)
	דבאך	*Dav'aka* –Your old age
	ואך	*va-'ak* –And I will smite
		ve-'ak –And surely
	זך	*Zak* –Clean, pure; the pure one; 115th Gate of the 231 Gates
	זרש	*Zeresh* –Zeresh, wife of Haman
	שזר	*Shazar* –To twist, be twisted
	שכל מופלא	*Sekhel Mopla* –Admirable or Mystical Intelligence (1st Path)
508	בוך	*Buwk* –To perplex, confuse, be confused
	בנות האדמ	*Beniyth HaAdam* –"Daughters of Man (Adam)"
	בעלות	*Be'alowth* –Bealoth, village in southern Judah (Josh. 15:24 – may be the same as Baalath Beer – Josh 19:8)
	ברוש	*Berowsh* –Cypress, fir, juniper, pine
	בשור	*Besowr* –Besor, brook south of Ziklag
	גרשה	*Gerushah* –Expulsion, violence, dispossession, act of expulsion
	ובך	*va-Vak* –And against you
		vu-Veka –And you
	והוצאת	*Vihotzayt* –Then bring forth
	חדוהי ודרעוהי די כספ	*Cheduwhiy VeDara'vehiy Diy Kasaf* –"Its breasts and its arms were of silver" (Dan. 2:32)
	חנתנ	*Channathon* –Hannathon, town of the tribe of Zebulun located on a road between Megiddo and Accho
	חך	*Chek* –Palate, mouth, taste, gums; 129th Gate of the 231 Gates
	חקת	*Chuqath* –Statutes, laws
	חרש	*Charash* –To cut in, plow, engrave, devise; to be silent, be dumb, be speechless, be deaf; craftsman; artisan, engraver, graver, artificer
		Cheres –Earthenware, clay pottery, shard, potsherd, earthen vessel
		Cheresh –Silently, secretly; magic art, magician; deaf; Heresh, head of a Levite family
		Choresh –Wood, wooded height, forest, wooded area; metal craftsman
	חשר	*Chishshur* –Hub, hub of a wheel, nave
	רחש	*Rachash* –To keep moving, stir
	שחר	*Shachar* –Dawn; to be black; to seek
		Shachor –Black
		Shechowr –Blackness, pit
		Shichor –Shihor, east branch of the Nile River (see also שיחור, שחור)[709]
	שכל נצחי	*Sekhel Nitzchi* –Triumphant or Eternal Intelligence (16th Path)

[709] שחור (514), שיחור (524).

	שרח	*Serach* –Serah, daughter of Asher (compare Num. 26:46)
	תחמס	*Tachmas* –Ostrich, a ceremonially unclean bird
	תל מלח	*Tel Melach* –Tel-Melah, Babylonian town mentioned in Ezra 2:59; Neh. 7:61, location unknown
	תקח	*Tekahach* –Take
509	גנתון	*Ginnethown* –Ginnethon, priest or prince who sealed the new covenant with God after the exile (see also Ginnetho)[710]
	הדך	*Hadak* –To cast down, tread down
	חרשא	*Charsha'* –Harsha, ancestor of returning captives
	טך	*Tak* –142nd Gate of the 231 Gates
	קטת	*Qattath* –Kattath, town in Zebulun (see also Kitron)[711]
	רטש	*Ratash* –To dash to pieces
	שדרה	*Sederah* –Row, rank (of soldiers)
	שטר	*Shoter* –Official, officer
	שרוג	*Serug*–Serug, father of Nahor and son of Reu and great-grandfather of Abraham
	שרט	*Sarat* –To incise, scratch, tattoo, cut
		Seret –Incision, cut
	–Prime number	
510	דוך	*Duwk* –To pound, beat (in mortar)
	דרוש	*Derush* –Torah interpretation that focuses on additional meanings derived by verbal analogy
	יך	*Yak* –Hand, (way) side (1 Sam. 4:13)
	ירש	*Yarash* –To seize, dispossess, take possession of, inherit, disinherit
	ישר	*Yashar* –To be right, go straight, be level, be upright, be just; straight, upright
		Yesher –Jesher, son of Caleb
		Yosher –Straightness, uprightness
	יתנן	*Yithnan* –Ithnan, town in extreme southern Judah
	לפת	*Lafath* –To twist, grasp, turn, grasp with a twisting motion
	מעקש	*Ma'aqesh* –Crooked place, twisted, crooked things
	משקע	*Mishqa'* –What is settled or clarified, clear
	מתניהו	*Mattaniahu* –Mattaniah, brother of Jehoiakim, made puppet king of Judah by Nebuchadnezzar and renamed Zedekiah (alternate spelling)
	נתין	*Nathiyn* –Nethinims (Temple-servants – this spelling used only in 1 Chr. 9:2; Ezra 2:43, 58, 70; 7:7, 24; 8:20; Neh. 3:26, 31; 7:46, 60, 73; 10:28; 11:3, 21 – see also נתון)[712]
	נתס	*Nathas* –To tear down, break down
	עלית	*'alliyth* –Roof-room, roof-chamber

[710] Ginnetho (459).
[711] Kitron (365, 1015).
[712] נתון (506, 1156).

	עתלי	*'Athlay* –Athlai, son of Bebai who divorced his pagan wife
	עתם	*'atham* –To be burned up, be scorched (meaning dubious – Isa. 9:19)
	פלת	*Peleth* –Peleth, father of On; son of Jonathan and a descendant of Perez
	פתל	*Pathal* –To twist
	ריש	*Resh* –Head; 20th letter of Hebrew alphabet
		Reysh –Poverty
	שיר	*Shir* –Song; to sing
	שכל קיים	*Sekhel Qayyam* –Stable Intelligence (23rd Path)
	שרי	*Sarai* –Sarai, the original name of the wife of Abraham and mother of Isaac; Sharai, one who took a foreign wife
	תהפכה	*Tahpukah* –Perversity, perverse thing
	תימני	*Teymeniy* –Temeni, son of Ashur; Temanite
	תיצי	*Tiytziy* –Tizite
	תנין	*Tannin* –Whale (Gen. 1:21; Job 7:12), dragon, serpent, sea-monster
		Tinyan –Second (Aramaic)
	תפל	*Tafel* –Foolish, insipid; tastlessness, unseasoned (n. masc.)
		Tofel –Tophel, area north of Bozra, toward the southeast corner of the Dead Sea
511	איך	*Eyk* –How? (interrog. adv.); how! (interj. – in lamentation); expression of satisfaction; no, not, nor, neither, nothing (as wish or preference); no, not (Aramaic)
	אסנת	*'Asenath* –Asenath, wife of Joseph
	אשרי	*'Asheriy* –Asherites
		'Ashrei –Happy; the name of a prayer consisting of Psalm 145
	הוך	*Huwk* –To go, come, walk, be brought
	והך	*ye-Hak* –And smite
	מתניהו	*Mattanyahuw* –Mattaniah, son of Heman the singer (1 Chr. 25:4, 16); one who helped to cleanse the Temple (2 Chr. 29:13)
	עתיאל	*Athiel* –"Uncertainty"; *Qlippoth* of *Ain Sof Aur*
	רישא	*Risha* –Head; a title of *Keter*
	תקוה	*Tiqvah* –Hope, expectation; Tikvah, father-in-law of Huldah the prophetess; father of Jahaziah
512	קדחת	*Qaddachath* –Fever
	שחדר	*Shachdar* –Angel of 3d Libra
513	אביך	*'abiyka* –Your father, your father's
	איבך	*'obia'aka* –Your enemy
		'oybeka –Your enemies
	בחגך	*B'chagela* –In your feast
	בשורה	*Besowrah* –News, good news, tidings, reward for good

		news
	געתמ	*Ga'tam* –Gatam, Edomite chief, grandson of Esau
	הרגשה	*Hargashah* –Feeling, sensation
	חשרה	*Chashrah* –Collection, mass, an accumulation of water
	יבאך	*Yabia'aka* –Shall bring you
	שריג	*Sariyg* –Tendril, twig, branch
514	ואהבך	*va-'ahevka* –And he will love you
	ידך	*Yadak, yadaka* –Your hand
	שחור	*Shachor* –Black
		Shichowr –Shihor, east branch of the Nile River (see also שיחור, שחר)[713]
	שכל מעמיד	*Sekhel Maamid* –Constituting Intelligence (15th Path)
	שריד	*Sariyd* –Survivor, remnant; Sarid, landmark in the territory of Zebulun
515	אלונ בכות	*'Allown Bakuwth* –Allon Bachuth, burial place of Deborah, nurse of Rebekah
	אשחור	*'Ashchuwr* –Ashur, son of Hezron and Abiah, father of Tekoa
	היך	*Heyk* –How
	ואהבכ וברככ והרבכ	*Ve-'Aheveka ve-Verakeka ve-Hirebeka* –"He will favor you and bless you and multiply you" (Deut. 7:13)
	ירשה	*Yereshah* –Possession, property, inheritance
	ישרה	*Yishrah* –Uprightness
	נתניה	*Nethanyah* –Nethaniah, musician in David's worship services (1 Chr. 25:2); father of Jehudi (Jer. 36:14); father of Ishmael, the murderer of Gedaliah (Jer. 40:14-15; 41:11) (see also נתניהו)[714]
	עתליה	*Athalyah* –Athaliah, daughter of Jezebel and 12th King of Israel; son of Jeroham; father of a returned exile
	קהתי	*Qohathiy* –Kohathites
	יד ראש	*Yod Rosh* –"Arm head" (literally the two places where the *tefillim* are placed on the human body)
	שריה	*Serayah* –Seraiah, scribe of David (see also Sheva, Shavsha, Shisha)[715]; chief priest of Jerusalem; one whom Gedaliah advised to submit to Chaldea; brother of Othniel; descendant of Simeon; priest that returned to Jerusalem with Zerubbabel (see also Seraiah)[716]; prince of Judah who went to Babylon; son of Hilkiah dwelling in Jerusalem after the Exile; chief of the priests who returned from Babylon

[713] שיחור (524), שחר (508).

[714] נתניהו (521).

[715] Sheva (311), Shavsha (676), Shisha (611).

[716] Seraiah (521).

	תפלה	*Tiflah* –That which is empty, folly, silly, foolish *Tefillah* –Prayer
	–The total gematria of Isaac and Rivkah, Jacob's parents (208+307)	
516	בידך	*Biyadeka* –In your hand
	גרגשי	*Girgashiy* –Girgashite
	יונתנ	*Yownathan* –Jonathan, grandson of Onam (1 Chr. 27:32); father of one who returned with Ezra (Ezra 8:6); one involved with the foreign wife controversy (Ezra 10:15); descendant of Jeshua the High Priest (Neh. 12:11); priest (Neh. 12:14); one who joined Gedaliah after the fall of Jerusalem (Jer. 40:8)
	כסלות	*Kesullowth* –Chesulloth, town southeast of Nazareth in the territory of Issachar
	סכלות	*Sikluwth* –Folly, foolishness
	שפופנ	*Shefuwfan* –Shephuphan, son of Benjamin (this spelling used only in 1 Chr. 8:5 – see also Shuppim, Shupham)[717]
	תולעי	*Towla'iy* –Tolaites
	תמוע	*Timnah* –A Duke of Edom (assoc. w/Daath)
517	אשורי	*'Ashuwriy, 'Ashshuwriy* –Ashurites
	ירושא	*Yeruwsha'* –Jerusha, wife of King Uzziah (this spelling used only in 2 Kings 15:33 – see also ירושה)[718]
	פתואל	*Pethuw'el* –Pethuel, father of Joel the prophet
	שרביה	*Sherebyah* –Sherebiah, priest who returned from the Exile; Levite who sealed the new covenant with God after the Exile
518	בנתינו	*Beniteynuw* –Our daughters (Gen. 34:9)
	ובישר	*ve-Veyisher* –And in uprightness (Deut. 9:5)
	ובשרי	*ve-Vesariy* –And my flesh (Gen. 29:14)
	והוצאתי	*ve-Hotze'tiy* –And I will bring out (Ex. 6:6)
	ויבך	*va-Y'bak* –And he wept
	ויחזק לב פרעה	*Vayachazek Lev Para'oh*–And he Pharaoh hardened his heart
	וישבר	*ve-Yeshaber* –And he broke (Ex. 32:19) *ve-Yishbir* –And he sold (Gen. 41:56)
	ויתיצב	*ve-Yityatzev* –And he stood (Ex. 34:5)
	ולבנתיכ	*ve-Livnoteyka* –And to your daughters (Num. 18:11)
	ושורו	*ve-Shoro* –And his ox (Ex. 20:14)
	חלפת	*Chalifir* –Changes (Gen. 45:22)
	חקתי	*Cheqitay* –My statutes (Lev. 18:4)
	חריש	*Chariysh* –Plowing, plowing time (Gen. 45:6)
	ישברו	*Yoshberuw* –They shall break (Num. 9:12)

717 Shuppim (430, 990), Shupham (506, 1066).

718 ירושה (521).

	כחצת	*Kachtzith* –About midnight (Ex. 11:4)
	כמנחת	*Keminechat* –Like the meal offering (Ex. 29:41)
	לפתח	*Lapetach* –At the door (Gen. 4:7); to the door (Ex. 26:36)
	מלחמת	*Milechamit* –Wars of (Num. 21:14)
	מנחתכ	*Minchateka* –Your meal offering (Lev. 2:13)
	תקטט	*Teqowtet* –A rising against (Ps. 139:21)
519	אבישור	*'Abishuwr* –Abishur, son of Shammai
	אחיך	*'acheyka* –Your brethren *'achiyka* –Your brother
	אחישר	*'Achiyshar* –Ahishar, officer of Solomon
	בזיך	*Beziyk* –Censer
	ברבטוש	*Barbatos* –Goetic demon #8
	שטרי	*Shitray* –Shitrai, man in charge of David's herds in Sharon
	שעטנז	*Sha'atnez* –Mixed fabric
520	דוכיפת	*Duwkiyfath* –An unclean bird, perhaps houpee or the grouse
	דריוש	*Dar'yavesh* or *Dareyavesh* –Darius, sub-king of Cyrus who received the kingdom of Belshazzar, also known as Darius the Mede; fourth king of Persia; Darius II who ruled Persia and Babylon
	ילפע	*Yallefeth* –Scab, sore, scales, scurf
	כסמת	*Kussemeth* –Spelt –a wheat-like crop planted and harvested in the fall or spring
	כרש	*Keres* –Belly *Koresh* –Cyrus, ruler of the Persian Empire who returned the Jews to their land (this spelling used only in Gen. 18:25; Ezra 1:1, 2; 3:7; Esth. 1:14; Job 27:7; Jer. 51:34; Ezek. 31:11 – see also כרוש)[719]
	כשר	*Kasher* –To succeed, please, be suitable, be proper, be advantageous, be right and proper to *Kosher* –Ritually clean, wholesome
	מודעת	*Mowda'ath* –Kindred, kinship
	מועדת	*Muw'edeth* –Sliding
	מלל	*Malal* –To speak, utter, say *Melal* –To speak, say (Aramaic)
	מסכת	*Masseketh* –Web
	נתע	*Natha'* –To break, break down, break out
	עמית	*'amiyth* –Neighbor, relation, associate, fellow
	ענת	*Anath* –Anath, father of the judge Shamgar
	פלתי	*Pelethiy* –Pelethites
	פתיל	*Pathiyl* –Cord, thread (twisted)
	פתמ	*Pithom* –Pithom, Egyptian store-city built by the Israelites (Ex. 1:11)

---

719 כרוש (526).

	רכש	*Rakash* –Got, gather *Rekesh* –Steeds, horses
	שכר	*Sakar* –To hire; Sacar, father of one of David's mighty men (see also Sharar)[720]; Levite tabernacle gatekeeper in the days of David *Shakar* –To be drunk, to become drunk *Seker* –Hire, wages *Shekar* –Strong drink, intoxicating drink *Shikkowr* –Drunken, drunkard
	שפיפנ	*Shefiyfon* –Horned snake, adder (Gen. 49:17)
	שרכ	*Sarak* –To twist *Serowk* –Sandal thong *Sharekh* –Traverse (Ezek. 16:4)[721]
521	אשכר	*'eshkar* –Gift
	ויבנשמ מזבח לי יהוה	*Vayivensham Mizbayach La* YHVH –"Noah built an altar to YHVH" (Gen. 12:8)
	ושריה	*Veshriah* –Angel of 2q Capricorn & night angel 2 Pentacles
	יהונתנ	*Yehownathan* –Jonathan, priest of an idol shrine in the territory of Ephraim; son of Abiathar the High Priest; son of Shimea, David's brother; one of David's mighty men; uncle of David; scribe in whose house Jeremiah was kept prisoner; son of Saul and close friend of David
	ירושה	*Yeruwsha'* –Jerusha, wife of King Uzziah (this spelling used only in 2 Chr. 27:1 – see also ירושא)[722]
	נתניהו	*Nethanyahuw* –Nethaniah, musician in David's worship services (1 Chr. 25:12); Levite whom Jehoshaphat sent to teach in Judah's cities (2 Chr. 17:8); father of Ishmael, the murderer of Gedaliah (Jer. 40:8; 41:9) (see also נתניה)[723]
	עתליהו	*Athaliahuw* –Athaliah, daughter of Jezebel and 12th King of Israel
	שדיאור	*Shedey'uwr* –Shedeur, one who helped number the people
	שרבימ	*Sharbiyt* –Sceptre; dart, spear
	שריהו –Prime number	*Serayahuw* –Seraiah, leader sent to capture Jeremiah
522	בעל פרצימ	*Ba'al Peratziym* –Baal Perazim, place near the valley of Rephaim, where David won a battle with the Philistines (2 Sam. 5:20); called Perazim in Is. 28:21
	ועבדתמ	*va-Avadtem* –You shall serve
523	אלפ בית	*Alef Bet* –The Hebrew alphabet

[720] Sharar (700).
[721] Sharekh is one of the ten words in the Tanakh with a Dagesh in the letter Resh.
[722] ירושא (517).
[723] נתניה (515).

	כהנת הגדול	*Koheneth HaGadhol* –High Priestess
	עזמות	*'Azmaveth* –Azmaveth, one of David's mighty men; descendant of Saul; father of two men who joined David at Ziklag; treasury officer during David's reign
	פתגמ	*Pithgam* –Edict, decree, command, work, affair
	שחריה	*Shecharyah* –Sheheriah, descendant of Benjamin
	–Prime number	
524	ויהי נעמ אדני אלהינו עלינו	*Vihi No'am Adonai Elohenu Alaynuw* –"May the favor of the Lord, our God, be upon us" (Psalms 90:17)
	כארי ידיי ורגליי	*Ka'ari yedi ve-ragoli* –"Like a lion, they are at my hands and my feet" (Psalm 22:17)
	כל עדת	*Kal 'adath* –All witnesses, entire congregation
	שדרכ	*Shadrakh* –Shadrach, name given to Hananiah at Babylon (Dan. 1:7; 3)[724]
	שיחור	*Shiychowr* –Shihor, east branch of the Nile River (this spelling used only in Josh. 13:3; 19:25; 1 Chr. 13:5 – see also שחור, שחר)[725]
525	יהוה צבאות	YHVH *Tzabaoth* –Lord of Hosts; divine name assoc. w/*Netzach*, w/Fire, & w/the South
	תלפיה	*Talpiyah* –Weapons, armory, armaments
526	אבראכאלא	*Abrakala* –Original name of Abracadabara
	ואברכה מברכיכ	*va-Avarkah Mivrakika* –"I will bless those who bless you" (Gen. 12:3)
	ואלה המשפטימ	*vi-Aleh HaMishpatem* –"And these are the laws" (Ex. 21:1)
	כבדך	*Kivodek* –Your glory, your honor
	כורש	*Kowresh* –Cyrus, ruler of the Persian Empire who returned the Jews to their land (this spelling used only in 2 Chr. 36:22, 23; Ezra 1:1, 7, 8; 3:7; 4:3, 5; 5:13, 14, 17; 6:3, 14; Is. 44:28; 45:1; Dan. 1:21; 6:29; 10:1 – see also כרש) [726]
	כסילות	*Kesiyluwth* –Foolishness, stupidity
	כרוש	*Koresh* –Cyrus, ruler of the Persian Empire who returned the Jews to their land (see also כרש)[727]
	מופת	*Mowfeth* –Wonder, sign, miracle, portent
	משקופ	*Mashqowf* –Lintel (of door)
	ענות	*'enuwth* –Affliction
	רכוש	*Rekuwsh* –Property, goods, possessions
527	אחישחר	*'Achiyshachar* –Ahishahar, son of Bilhah
	אלמנות	*Almanuwth* –Widowhood

---

[724] Hananiah (120; 123; 126).

[725] שחור (514), שחר (508).

[726] כרש (520).

[727] כרש (520).

	בינה נבחר מכספ	*Binah Nevacher Mekasaf*–"Understanding to be chosen above silver" (Prov. 16:16)
	זכך	*Zakak* –To be pure, be bright, be clean, be bright, clean
	מטבעות	*Matbeoth* –Coins
	פתאומ	*Pith'owm* –Suddenly, surprisingly; suddenness
528	בעותימ	*Bi'uwthiym* –Terrors, alarms (occasioned by God)
	בצלות	*Batzluwth* –Bazluth, one whose descendants returned from the exile – the same as Bazlith
	העגות	*Haagenti* –Goetic demon #48
	חרישי	*Chariyshiy* –Harsh, lot, sultry, silent (meaning uncertain – Jon. 4:8)
	מפתח	*Mafteach* –Key, opening instrument
		Miftach –Opening, utterance
	צלחת	*Tzallachath* –Dish, bowl
	שכל קבוע	*Sekhel Qavua* –Measuring, Cohesive, "Receptacular," Arresting, Receiving, Settled, or Constant Intelligence (4th Path)
	תחכמני	*Tachkemoniy* –Tachmonite
	–Mystic number of 32nd Path (*Yesod-Malkut*; ת; Saturn)	
529	אחיתפל	*'Achiythofel* –Ahithophel, real leader of rebellion against David
	יפתח־אל	*Yiftach-'el* –Jiphthah-el, valley that served as the boundary between the territories of Zebulun and Asher
	שיטרי	*Sitri* –Goetic demon #12
	תענוג	*Tahanuwg* –Daintiness, luxury, delight
530	והארצ אזכר	*Viha'aretz Ezkor* –"And I will remember the land" (Lev. 26:42)
	חבצלת	*Chabatstseleth* –Meadow-saffron, crocus, rose
	כנסת	*Keneset* –Synagogue
	לפידות	*Lappiydowth* –Lappidoth, husband of the prophetess Deborah
	מעכת	*Ma'akath* –Maachathite
	נסתכ	*Nasitek* –He might prove you
	נפת	*Nefeth* –Height
		Nofeth –Flowing honey, honey from the comb, a dropping down, honey, honeycomb
	עתני	*'Othniy* –Othni, Levite, son of Shemaiah and tabernacle gatekeeper in David's time
	פתנ	*Pethen* –A snake, venemous serpent (perhaps cobra, adder or viper)
	צלתי	*Tzillethay* –Zilthai, descendant of Benjamin; captain who joined David at Ziklag
	שכיר	*Sakiyr* –Hired laborer or mercenary
	תקל	*Teqal* –To weigh; tekel, shekel (Aramaic)
531	אלך	*Illek* –These, those

אלנתנ *Elnathan* –Elnathan, king Jehoiachin's maternal grandfather; three chief men in Ezra's time; son of Achbor, a military commander under Jehoiakim

אפתנ *'appethom* –Treasury, treasuries; revenue (Aramaic)

בית פלט *Beyth Pelet* –Beth-Palet, town in the southernmost part of Judah, probably modern el-Meshash

כושרה *Kowsharah* –Prosperity; singing

נתנאל *Nethan'el* –Nethaneel, chief of Issachar whom Moses sent to spy out the land of Canaan; fourth son of Jesse; one of the trumpet blowers when the Ark of the Covenant was brought up; Levite; son of Obed-edom and gatekeeper of the Tabernacle; prince commissioned by Jehoshaphat to teach the people; Levite in the days of Josiah; priest who married a foreign wife; priest in the days of Joiakim; Levite musician at the purification ceremony

532 אלתקא *Eltekay* –Eltekeh, Levitical city in the tribe of Dan, between Ekron and Timma

אשראל *'Asar'el* –Asareel, descendant of Judah through Caleb

בצלית *Batzliyth* –Bazlith, one whose descendants returned from the exile – the same as Bazluth

מצבת *Matstsebeth* –Pillar, mastaba, stump

רב־סרים *Rab-Sariys* –Rabsaris, an official position in the Babylonian and Assyrian governments whose precise nature is unknown; one of three officials sent from Lachish by Sennacherib, king of Assyria (2 Kings 18:17); official under Nebuchadnezzar, King of Babylon, who possibly ordered the release of Jeremiah (Jer. 39:3, 13)

533 טבל וילונ שמימ *Tebel Vilon Shamaim* –Veil of the Firmament; the First Heaven (corr. to *Yesod* and *Malkut*)

פתיגיל *Pethiygiyl* –Rich or expensive robe

534 בינותינו *Beynoteynuw* –Between us

בסבלתמ *Besivlotam* –With their burdens (Ex. 1:11)

דלקת *Dalaqta* –Hotly pursued (Gen. 31:36)

Dalleqeth –Inflammation

ומנחלת *VeMinachalat* –And from the inheritance (Num. 36:4)

ומפתח *VeMifetach* –And from (the) door

ותלחצ *VaTilachetz* –And she thrust herself (Num. 22:25)

VaTilechatz –And crushed (Num. 22:25)

ידעתנ *Yeda'ten* –You know

לדרש *Liderosh* –To inquire

לטוטפת *Letotafot* –As frontlets (Deut. 11:18)

עדיתימ *'Adiythayim* –Adithaim, town in the lowlands of Judah

תחלצו *Techaltuw* –You will arm yourself (Num. 32:20)

535	הלך	*Halak* –To go, walk, come; toll, custom duty, tribute (Aramaic) *Helek* –Traveller
	זקן ושבע	*Zaqan ve-Shavay* –"Old, wise and satisfied" (Gen. 25:8)
	קהלת	*Qoheleth* –Preacher, public speaker; the book of Ecclesiastes
	שכירה	*Sekiyrah* –Hired laborer or mercenary
536	אלתקה	*Eltekay* –Eltekeh, Levitical city in the tribe of Dan, between Ekron and Timma (see also אלתקא)[728]
	בית עדנ	*Beyth 'Eden* –Beth Eden, city-state in Mesopotamia
	ולמולדתח	*Vulimuwladtech* –And to your birthplace (Gen. 31:3)
	חכמת המדידה	*Chokmah HaMedidah* –"The measure of Wisdom"
	כישור	*Kiyshowr* –Spindle-wheel, distaff
	ממלכות	*Mamlakuwth* –Kingdom, dominion, reign, sovereignty
	מסלות	*Maslowth* –Illumination
	מצות	*Matstsuwth* –Strife, contention *Mitzvot* *Matzot* –Bread without leaven
	מקומ־סקיר	*Mequwm-Safiyr* –"Its rocks are a source of sapphires" (Job 28:6)
	עולמ העשיה	*Olam HaAssiah* –The World of Action; the Material World
	שיר יהוה	*Shiyr* YHVH –"The song of YHVH" (Ps. 137:4)
	שכל נסיוני	*Sekhel Nisyoni* –Intelligence of Probation or Tentative Intelligence or Intelligence of Temptation and Trial (25th Path)
	תעלול	*Tahaluwl* –Wantonness, caprice
537	אלוך	*Alloces* –Goetic demon #52
	אצילות	*Atzilut* –Nobility; the Divine or Archetypal World
	אשראלה	*'Asar'elah* –Asarelah or Asharelah, son of Asaph, musician in the Temple by David (1 Chr. 25:2, 14)
	מטפחת	*Mitpachath* –Cloak
	פחת מואב	*Pachath Mow'ab* –Pahath-Moab, Jewish family named after an ancestor of the above name or title (Ezra 2:6; Neh. 3:11 – see also Neh. 10:15, which refers to a person with the same family name)
538	בית האצל	*Beyth Ha'Etzel* –Beth-Ezel, town of Judah (Micah 1:11)
	בת קול	*Bath Qol* –Daughter of the Voice (the voice of God)
	חלקת	*Chelqath* –Helkath, town marking the boundary of the tribe of Asher – probably modern Tell el-Harboj
	חרנפר	*Charnefer* –Harnepher, descendant of Asher
	לחך	*Lachak* –To lick, lick up
	צלחית	*Tzelochiyth* –Jar, bowl

---

[728] אלתקא (532).

	קלחת	*Qallachath* –Cauldron, pot, kettle
539		
540	ולא תטמאו בהמ	*Viloh Tetamu Bahem* –"And you shall not defile yourselves through them" (Lev. 18:30)
	ילך	*Yalak* –To go, walk, come
	כענת	*Ke'eneth* –Now, and now
	מעכתי	*Ma'akathiy* –Maachathite
	מתק	*Mathaq* –To be or become sweet or pleasing; to feed sweetly *Metheq*, *motheq* –Sweetness
	נתצ	*Nathats* –To pull down, break down, cast down, throw down, beat down, destroy, overthrow, break out (of teeth)
	עלמת	*'Alemeth* –Alameth, son of Becher and grandson of Benjamin; descendant of Jonathan, son of Saul
	ערער	*'ar'ar* –Stripped, destitute *'Aro'er* –Aroer, town on the northern bank of the Arnon River (this spelling used only in Josh. 12:2 – see also ערוער)[729]; village of Judah
	קהלתה	*Qehelathah* –Kehelathah, desert encampment of the Israelites
	רמש	*Remes* –Creeping thing *Remesh* –Creeping things, moving things
	רשמ	*Rasham* –To inscribe, note *Resham* –To inscribe, sign
	שמר	*Shamar* –To keep, guard, observe, give heed *Shemer* –Lees, dregs; Shemer, owner of the hill which Omri bought and on which he built Samaria; son of Heber, of the tribe of Asher (see also Shomer)[730]; descendant of Asher (this spelling used only in 1 Chr. 7:32) *Shimmur* –Night watch, watching, vigil *Shomer* –Shomer, woman of Moab, mother of Jehozabad who killed Joash (this spelling used only in 2 Kings 12:21 – see also Shimrith)[731]
	תענכ	*Ta'anak* –Taanach, ancient city in Canaan whose king was conquered by Joshua
	תעע	*Tawah* –To deceive, misuse
541	אימצת	*'Ametzeth* –Strength
	אמך	*Amak* –Thy mother; thy source
	יקתאל	*Yoqthe'el* –Joktheel, city located in the lowlands of Judah; the name given to Sela, capital of the Edomites
	ישראל	*Yisra'el* –Israel, the name given to Jacob after he

[729] ערוער (546).
[730] Shomer (546).
[731] שחור (514), שחר (508).

wrestled with the being at Peniel (see also Jacob)[732]; the northern kingdom of the Hebrews in Palestine, inhabited by the ten tribes that followed Ishbosheth and Jeroboam – the cities of Jericho and Gezer marked its southern boundary

על איש ימינכ *'al Ish Yamiynk* –"Your right hand" (Ps. 80:17)

תנופה *Tenuwfah* –Swinging, waving

–The total of YHVH plus *tefillah* (26+515)

–Prime number

542 אספתא *'Aspatha'* –Aspatha, son of Haman (Est. 9:7)

אשראלי *'Asri'eliy* –Asrielites

אשריאל *'Asriy'el* –Ashriel or Asriel, son of Manasseh listed in second census in the Wilderness

עולמ מושכל *Olam Mevshekal* –Intellectual World, first face of Adam Qadmon

מקבת *Maqqebeth* –Hole, excavation, perforation; hammer, perforator

משבר *Mishbar* –Breaker, breaking (of sea)

Mishber –Place of breaking forth, place of breach, opening (of womb)

543 אהיה אשר אהיה *Eheieh Asher Eheieh* –Existence of Existences; "I AM WHAT I AM" (Ex. 13:14) ; a title of *Keter*

גרשמ *Gershom* –Gershom, firstborn son of Moses and Zipporah; father of Jonathan; descendant of Phinehas

וישכב במקומ ההוא *ve-Yishkav Bamaqom HaHowa'* –"And lay down in that place" (Gen. 28:11)

מגרש *Migrash* –Common, common land, open land, suburb

שמאבר *Shem'eber* –Shemeber, king of Zeboim in the days of Abraham

שמגר *Shamgar* –Shamgar, the 3rd Judge of Israel

544 ואינ ברוחו רמיה *ve-Ayin Baruchuw Remiyah* –"And in whose spirit there is no deceit" (Ps. 32:2)

ולקחת *Vilaqacht* –You will take

ומנחתמ *Vumenchatam* –With their meal offerings (Lev. 23:18)

חלמתינו *Chalomotaynu* –Interpreted our dreams (Gen. 41:12)

יערי ארגימ *Ya'arey 'Oregiym* –Jaare-Oregim, father of Elkanan, slayer of Goliath the Gittite[733]

מדרש *Midrash* –Study, exposition, Midrash, record, story

פתחונ *Pithchown* –Opening

תפוחימ *Tappuwachim* –Apple, apple tree

545 הליך *Haliyk* –Step

מהפכת *Mahpeketh* –Stocks (as in instrument of torture)

מלתעה *Malta'ah* –Tooth, great tooth

---

[732] Jacob (182).

[733] Some scholars feel that this is a copyist's error for Jair (cf. 1 Chr. 20:5).

	מרשה	*Mareshah* –Mareshah, father of Hebron; son of Laadah; Mareshah, city in the lowlands of Judah (this spelling used only in 2 Chr. 11:8 – see also מראשה)[734]
	משרה	*Mishrah* –Juice
		Misrah –Rule, dominion, government
	מתלעה	*Methalle'ah* –Teeth, fangs, incisors
	מתקה	*Mithqah* –Mithcah or Mithkah, an unidentified encampment of the Israelites in the Wilderness (Num. 33:28)
	נפתוח	*Neftowach* –Neptoah, spring that marks the boundary between Judah and Benjamin
	שמרה	*Shomrah* –Guard, watch
		Shemurah –Eyelid
	שרמה	*Sheremah* –Field
	תעלמה	*Tahalummah* –Hidden thing, secret (Job 11:6, 28:11, Ps. 44:22)
	תקומה	*Tequwmah* –Standing, ability or power to stand
546	ארמ נהרימ	*'Aram Naharayim* –Aham-Naharaim, location between the Tigris and Euphrates Rivers (Ps. 60:1)
	אשמרה	*'ashmurah* –Watch (a period of time), night-watch
	ישראלה	*Yesr'elah* –Jesharelah, son of Asaph, appointed by King David to be musician in the Temple (this spelling used only in 1 Chr. 25:14 – see also Asharelah)[735]
	מוך	*Muwk* –To be low, grow poor, be depressed, be poor
	מורש	*Mowrash* –Possession
	מראשה	*Mar'ashah* –Place at the head, dominion, head place; a head place
		Mar'eshah –Mareshah, city in the lowlands of Judah (this spelling used only in Josh. 15:44 – see also מרשה)[736]
	משור	*Massowr* –Saw
	מתוק	*Mathowq* –Sweet; sweetness, pleasant (thing)
	נפושסימ	*Nefuwshesiym* –Nephisesim, ancestor of returned captives (see also Naphish)[737]
	עלמות	*'Alamowth* –Alamoth, city given to the priests of the tribe of Benjamin (see also Almon)[738]
	ערוער	*'arow'er* –Naked, stripped, destitute; tree or bush (probably juniper or cypress)
		'Arow'er –Aroer, town on the northern bank of the Arnon River (this spelling used only in Josh. 12:2 – see also ערער)[739]; city of Gilead east of

[734] מראשה (546).
[735] Asharelah (537).
[736] מרשה (545).
[737] Nephusim (250, 810), Naphish (440).
[738] Almon (196, 846).
[739] ערער (540).

Rabbath-Ammon

ערעור — *'Ar'owr* –Aroer, town on the northern bank of the Arnon River (this spelling used only in Judg. 11:26)

פיתון — *Piythown* –Pithon, son of Micah and great-grandson of Saul

רישא דלא — *Risha Dela* –"The Head Which Is Not;" a title of *Keter*

שומר — *Showmer* –Shomer, descendant of Asher (this spelling used only in 1 Chr. 7:32 – see also Shamer)[740]

שמור — *Shamuwr* –Shamir, son of Micah, a Levite

שרהיאל — *Sharhiel* –"Ruling of God," Angel of Aries

547 בית מעכה — *Beyth Ma'akah* –Beth Maachah, city in Manasseh (2 Sam. 20:14, 15)

כתמ פז — *Katam Pez* –"Pure gold of the head" (Song 5:11)

–Prime number

548 בעירירון — *Beiriron* –The Herd, *Qlippoth* of Aries

חרמש — *Chermesh* –Sickle

יהוה אלוה ודעת — YHVH *Eloah va-Daath* –Lord God of Knowledge; divine name assoc. w/*Tiferet*

מחצית — *Machatsiyth* –Half, middle

משחר — *Mishchar* –Dawn

ספחת — *Sappachath* –Eruption, scab, lesion

עבירירון — *Abiriron* –The Clayish Ones, *Qlippoth* of Libra

תפסח — *Tifsach* –Tipsah, crossing located on the Euphrates River; place mentioned in connection wtih Tirzah (see also Tappuah)[741]

549 גרשומ — *Gershowm* –Gershom, important priest, eldest son of Levi ((Gen. 46:11; Ex. 6:16; 1 Chr. 6:1) – see also Gershon (גרשון)) [742]

מורגש — *Morgash* –Moral; felt, sensed

משטר — *Mishtar* –Rule, authority

נטפתי — *Netofathiy* –Netophathite

550 במות בעל — *Bamowth Ba'al* –Bamoth Baal, an Israelite encampment north of the Arnon River ((Num. 22:41) – see also as Bamoth of Num. 21:19)[743]

לשרכ — *LeSharekha* –For your navel (Prov. 3:8)[744]

מיך — *Mik* –42nd name of *Shem HaMeforash* (6 Aquarius)

מישר — *Meyshar* –Evenness, uprightness, straightness, equity

מפלת — *Mappeleth* –Carcass, ruin, overthrow

נשר — *Neshar, nesher* –Eagle, vulture, griffon-vulture; bird of prey

נתק — *Nathaq* –To pull or tear or draw off or away or apart,

---

740 Shamer (540).

741 Tappuah (494).

742 גרשון (559, 1209).

743 Bamoth (448).

744 LeSharekha is one of the ten words in the Tanakh with a Dagesh in the letter Resh.

		draw out, pluck up, break, lift, root out
		Netheq –Scab, skin eruption, scall (of leprosy)
	ערערי	*'Aro'eriy* –Aroerite(s)
	פללתי	*Pelawlitee* –I thought
	פתע	*Petha'* –Suddenness, in an instant
	קדמות	*Qedemowth* –Kedemoth, Levitical city east of the Dead Sea
	קנת	*Qenath* –Kenath, town on the extreme northeastern border of Israelite territory, the easternmost of the ten cities of the Decapolis
	שמיר	*Shameer* –Thorns; flint
		Shamiyr –Shamir, city in the mountainous district of Judah; town in Mount Ephraim
	שמרי	*Shimriy* –Shimri, head of a family of Simeon; father of one of David's mighty men; gatekeepr of the tabernacle in David's day; one who helped to cleanse the Temple
	שרטיאל	*Sharatiel* –"Cutting of God," Angel of Leo
	תקן	*Taqan* –To equalize, make straight
551	אמדוך	*Amdukias* –Goetic demon #67
	אנך	*'anak* –Plummet, plumb, lead-weight
		Anakh –Plumbline (Amos 7:7-8)
	דנתאליון	*Dantalion* –Goetic demon #71 (Aurum Solis spelling)
	חמת צובה	*Chamath Tzowbah* –Hamath Zobah, city captured by Solomon
	ישראלי	*Yisre'eliy* –Israelite
	מורשה	*Mowrashah* –A possession
	משורה	*Mesuwrah* –Measure
	ראשן	*Ri'shown* –First, primary; first, before, formerly
552	אשמראי	*Asmodai* –Goetic Demon #32 (a variant spelling)
	אשרנא	*'ushsharna'* –Wall, panelling, beams, structure (meaning unknown – Ezra 5:3, 9)
	ושמרו	*VeShamruw* –And they guard
	מצוסיו	*Mitzvotayv* –His commandments
	נבך	*Nebek* –Spring, springs
	פי־בסת	*Piy-Beseth* –Pibeseth, Egyptian town located on the west bank of the Pelusiac branch of the Nile (Ezek. 30:17)
	שברים	*Shebariym* –Shebarim, place to which the Israelites ran on their flight from Ai (Josh. 7:5)
553	מחרשה	*Machareshah* –Plowshare
	נברשא	*Nebresha'* –Lamp stand, candlestick (Aramaic)
554	זרע זרע	*Zorea Zara* –Bearing seed
	מרחוש	*Marchosias* –Goetic demon #35
555	הנשר	*HaNesher* –The eagle

מהודך *Mehowdka* –From your glory
שהרנ *Saharon* –Moon, crescent moon (as ornament)
שמריה *Shemaryah* –Shemariah, son of King Rehoboam; two who married foreign wives during the Exile
תעפה *Tow'afah* –Eminence, lofty horns, summit

556 אנדראש *Andras* –Goetic demon #63 (Aurum Solis spelling)
גרגשימ *Girgasim* –Girgashites
מישור *Miyshowr* –Level place, uprightness
נדבך *Nidbak* –Row, layer, course (of stones)
רשימו *Reshimu* –Impression
שרונ *Sharown* –Sharon, region that lies between the Mediterranean Sea from Joppa to Carmel and the central portion of Palestine; district east of the Jordan occupied by the tribe of Gad
תקונ *Tiqqun* –Restoration

557 יקותיאל *Yequwthiy'el* –Jekuthiel, descendant of the spy Caleb (1 Chr. 4:18)
ספר הזהר *Sefer HaZohar* –Book of Splendor
ראשונ *Rishon* –First, former, primary

558 חנך *Chanak* –To train, dedicate, inaugurate
שחרימ *Shacharayim* –Shaharaim, descendant of Benjamin who went to Moab (1 Chr. 8:8)

559 גרשונ *Gereshown* –Gershon, important priest, eldest son of Levi (Gen. 46:11; Ex. 6:16; 1 Chr. 6:1) – also called Gershom (גרשום)
נקדה פשות *Neqedah Peshutah* –The Simple Point; a title of *Keter*

560 בעל-חננ בנ עכבור *Baal-Chanan ben Akbor* –Baal-Hanan, son of Achbor, a King of Edom (assoc. w/*Yesod*)
בלק בנ צפור *Balak ben Tzepior* –"Balak, son of Zippor" (Num. 22:2)
בעלי במות *Ba'aley Bamowth* –"Lords of the High Places" (Num 21:28)
גנזך *Ginzak* –Treasury
ישמרי *Yishmeray* –Ishmerai, descendant of Benjamin
ישרימ *Yishawrim* –The righteous
מכך *Makak* –To be low, be humiliated
מכשר *Mekeshar* –Sorceress
מצלת *Metseleth* –Cymbals
סך *Sak* –Crowd, throng, multitude
Sok –Thicket, lair, covert, booth
פרפר *Parpar* –Pharpar, one of the two rivers of Damascus
קסת *Qeseth* –Pot (for ink), inkhorn, inkwell
רשינ *Rishyown* –Permission
סובב כל עלמינ *Sovev Kol Almin* –"Encompassing all worlds"
שניר *Sheniyr* –Senir, Ammorite name for Harim (see also

		Harim)[745]
	שרינ	*Shiryown* –Body armor; a weapon; Sirion, name given to Mount Hermon by the Sidonians (see also שריון)[746]
	תמנע	*Timna'* –Timna, concubine of a son of Esau; chief of Edom (Gen. 36:40; 1 Chr. 1:51); son of Eliphaz
	תפפ	*Tafaf* –To play the timbrel, to drum
561	עתניאל	*Ahniel* –Othniel, Caleb's younger brother who liberated Israel from foreign rule and the 1st Judge of Israel
	ראשני	*Ri'showniy* –First
	שמריהו	*Shemaryahuw* –Shamariah, one who joined David at Ziklag (1 Chr. 12:5)
	–The sum of the numbers 1 through 33	
562	לא תנאפ	*Lo thi-ne'af* –"Thou shalt not commit adultery" (Ex. 20:13)
	סבך	*Sabak* –To interweave
		Sobek, sebak –Thicket
	ספר ה־בהיר	*Sefer HaBahir* –A 12th century cabalistic text
	עצבת	*'atstsebeth* –Pain, hurt, injury, sorrow, wound
563	גרשני	*Gereshunniy* –Gershonite
	סגרש	*Sagarash* –Angel of 1d Gemini
	–Prime number	
564	אזנ שארה	*'Uzzen She'erah* –Uzzen-Sherah, town founded by Sherah, daughter of Ephraim
	חלמ יסודות	*Cholam Yesodoth* –The Breaker of Foundations; the Sphere of the Elements; the part of the material world corr. to *Malkut*
	חנוך	*Chanokh* –Enoch, eldest son of Cain (Gen. 4:17-18); son of Jared (Gen. 5:18-19, 21; 1 Chr. 1:3)
	חרוצ נבחר	*Cheruwtz Nevachar* –"Choice gold" (Prov. 8:10)
	כדרלעמר	*Kedorla'omer* –Chedorlaomer, king of Elam who came up against Sodom and Gomorrah (Gen. 14:1-24)
	שרוחנ	*Sharuwchen* –Sharuhen, city in Simeon near Beth-lebaoth
565		
566	יונקת	*Yowneqeth* –Young plant, twig, young shoot
	ישרונ	*Yesherown* –The righteous people (a fig. phrase for Israel – Deut. 32:15; Is. 44:2)
	מסתולל	*Mistuwlayl* –You exalt yourself
	נפתול	*Naftuwl* –Wrestlings (Gen. 30:8)
	סוך	*Suwk* –To anoint, pour in anointing

[745] Harim (248, 808).

[746] שריון (566, 1216).

	צלמות	*Tzal-Maveth* –Shadow of Death; the 2nd Hell (corr. to *Hod*), death-shadow, deep shadow, deep darkness, shadow of death
	שרוני	*Sharowniy* –Sharonite
	שריונ	*Shiryown* –Sirion, name given to Mount Hermon by the Sidonians (see also שרין)[747]
567	אסוך	*'asuwk* –Flask, small oil jug
	מעלה עקרבימ	*Ma'aleh 'Aqrabbiym* –Maaleh-Acrabbim, high place which marks part of the boundary of Judah between Kedish and the Dead Sea
	שכל בהיר	*Sekhel Bahir* –Intelligence of Transparency or of Light (12th Path)
568	חניך	*Chaniyk* –Trained, instructed, trained servant, tried, experienced
569	–Prime number	
570	יצר רע	*Yetzer Ra* –Evil inclination
	ישמרכ	*Yishmark* –Guard you
	כי יהוה אלהיכמ הוא אלהי האלהימ ואדני האדנימ האל הגדל	*Ki* YHVH *Elohaycham Hu Elohay HaElohim va-Adonai HaAdonim HaAl HaGadol* –"For the Lord your God is the God of gods and the Lord of lords, the Almighty, the great..." (Deut. 10:17)
	כנשר	*Kinesher* –Eagle
	כספית	*Kaspith* –Mercury, the metal of the planet Mercury
	למך	*Lamekh* –Lamech, father of Noah; father of Jabal and Jubal
	מודה אני לפניכ מלכ חי וקימ	*Modeh Ani Lifanek Melek Chai Ve-qayam* –"I am thankful before You, Living and Eternal King"
	מלך	*Malak* –To be or become king or queen, reign; to counsel, advise
		Melak –Counsel, advise (Aramaic)
		Melek –King; a title of *Tiferet*; one of the Melekim; Melech, a Benjamite, the 2nd son of Micah and grandson of Mephibosheth
		Molek –Molech, the god of the Ammorites and Phoenicians to whom some Israelites sacrificed their infants in the valley of Hinnom (see also Milcom)[748]
		Moloch –Archdemon corr. (w/Satan) to *Keter*
	מסכנת	*Miskenuth* –Poverty, scarcity
	מפתנ	*Miftan* –Threshold
	נעמתי	*Na'amathiy* –Naamathite
	נפתלי	*Naphtali* –Naphtali, sixth son of Jacob whose descendants became one of the tribes; the tribe

[747] שרין (560, 1210).

[748] Milcom (130, 690).

		of Israel (assoc. w/ Virgo); territory assigned to the tribe of Naphtali, located in mountainous northern Palestine
	ערש	*'eres* –Couch, divan, bed
	עשר	*'asar* –Ten (Aramaic); to tithe, take the tenth part of, give a tithe, take a tithe; –teen (in combination with other numbers)
		'ashar –To be or become rich or wealthy, enrich, pretend to be rich
		'eser –Ten
		'osher –Wealth, riches
	עתק	*'athaq* –To move, proceed, advance, move on, become old, be removed; forward, bold, arrogant
		'atheq –Handed forward, advanced, enduring, durable, valuable, eminent, surpassing
	צפת	*Tzephath* –Zephath, city of Canaan in the mountains of Kadesh near the Edomite border (see also Hormah)[749]
		Tzepeth –Plated capital (of pillar)
	רעש	*Ra'ash* –To quake, shake (A.C. has Earthquake here in 777)
	רשע	*Rasha'* –To be wicked, act wickedly; wicked, criminal
		Resha' –Wrong, wickedness, guilt
	שכל טהור	*Sekhel Tahur* –Purified or Pure Intelligence (9th Path)
	שכרנ	*Shikkarown* –Drunkenness
	שער	*Sa'ar* –To storm, shiver, dread, be afraid; to storm away, sweep away, whirl away
		Se'ar –Hair (Aramaic)
		Shar –Gate; a title of *Malkut*
		Sha'ar –To reason out, calculate; gate, door; unit of measure (Gen 26:12)
		Sho'ar –Horrid, disgusting, vile, offensive
		Showar –Gatekeeper, porter
	שרע	*Sara'* –To extend, stretch out
	תפלינ	*Tefillin* –Phylacteries (see Exod. 13:1-10, 11-16; Deut. 6:4-9, 11:13-21)
	תקע	*Taqowah* –A wind instrument, trumpet (Ezek. 7:14)
		Taqah –To blow, clap, strike
		Teqah –Sound, blast, trumpet blast
571	כרשנא	*Karshena'* –Carshena, one of the seven princes of Persia and Media during Ahasuerus's reign (Esth. 1:14)
	מלאך	*Melek* –Angel; messenger, representative (Aramaic)
	מתקלא	*Metheqela* –Balance
	–Prime number	
572	במלך	*Bimelek* –Against the king (Num. 21:26)
	ברשע	*Birsha'* –Birsha, king of Gomorrah in the days of Abraham (Gen. 14:2)
	חסדך	*Chasdek* –"Loving kindness" (Num. 14:19)

[749] Hormah (253).

	פורפור	*Furfur* –Goetic demon #34
	קבעת	*Qubba'ath* –Cup
573	נבוכדראצר	*Nebuwkadnetztzar* –Nebuchadnezzar, king of the Babylonian Empire; he captured Jerusalem three times and carried Judah into captivity (this spelling used only in Jer. 21:2, 7; 22:25; 24:1; 25:1, 9; 29:21; 32:1; 32:28; 34:1; 35:11; 37:1; 39:1; 39:5; 39:11; 43:10; 44:30; 46:2, 13, 26; 49:30; 50:17; 51:34; 52:4, 12, 28-30; 26:7; 29:18, 19; 30:10 – see also נבוכדנאצר, נבוכדנצר, נבכדנאצר, נבוכדנצר, and נבוכדראצור)[750]
574	דעך	*Da'ak* –To go out, be extinguished, dry up
575	באר שבע	*Be'er Sheba'* –Beersheba, city in southern Judah
	המלך	*HaMelek* –The king
	עשרה	*Asarah* –Ten
	מהלך	*Mahlek* –Walk, journey, going, place to walk
	מקהלת	*Maqheloth* –Makheloth, desert encampment of the Israelites – probably modern Kuntilet Krayeh or Ajurd
	צפתה	*Tzephathah* –Zephathah, valley in Judah's territory near Mareshah in which Asa and Zerah battled
	רשעה	*Rish'ah* –Wickedness, guilt
	שערה	*Sa'aroh* –A single hair
		Se'arah –Storm
		Se'orah –Barley
	תפצה	*Tefowtsah* –Dispersion
576	כשרון	*Kishrown* –Success, skill, profit
	מלוך	*Malluwk* –Malluch, descendant of Levi; two who took foreign wives during the exile; priest who sealed the covenant; leader who sealed the new covenant with God after the exile; one of the priests who returned with Zerubbabel (see also מלוכי)[751]
	מעונתי	*Me'ownothay* –Meonothai, descendant of Judah
	מקלות	*Maqqeloth* –Wands
		Miqlowth –Mikloth, descendant of Benjamin living in Jerusalem; chief military officer under David
	עמונית	*'Ammowniyth* –Ammonitess
	עשור	*'asowr* –Ten, decade, tenth
	שכרון	*Shikkerown* –Shicron, town on the northern boundary of Judah
	תקוע	*Teqowa'* –Tekoa, town of Judah on the hills near Hebron;

---

750 נבכדנאצר (417), נבוכדנצר (422), נבוכדנאצר (423), נבוכדראצור (579).

751 מלוכי (106).

577	אלה המצות	*Ayleh HaMitzuwth* –"These are the commands" (Lev. 27:34)
	זעך	*Za'ak* –To extinguish, be extinct, be extinguished
	כראשון	*Karishown* –As the first
	–Prime number	
578	בית מעון	*Beyth Me'own* –Baal's dwelling place; Beth Meon, Amorite city on the north border of Moab (this name only used in Josh. 13:17)
	חצ לילית	*Chotz Lilith* –Out Lilith!
	מחלקת	*Machaloqeth* –Division, course, class, share, allotment (often of priests and Levites)
	צפחת	*Tzappachath* –Jar, jug (for liquids)
579	ובידו אנך	*'owbiydow 'anak* –"And in his hand a lead plumbline" (Amos 7:7)
	חצות לילה	*Chatzoth Laylah* –Midnight
	נבוכדראצור	*Nebuwkadnetztzar* –Nebuchadnezzar, king of the Babylonian Empire; he captured Jerusalem three times and carried Judah into captivity (this spelling used only in Jer. 49:28 – see also נבוכדנאצר, נבוכדנצר, נבכדנאצר, נבוכדנצר, and נבוכדנאחר)[752]
	ערב זרק	*Oreb Zaraq* –Raven of Dispersion, *Qlippoth* of *Netzach*
580	אבל בית־מעכה	*'Abel Beyth-Ma'akah* –Abel of Beth-Maachah, a town near Dan
	גיא־צלמות	*Gey-Tzalmaveth* –Valley of the Shadow of Death
	ימלך	*Yamlek* –Jamlech, prince of Simeon (1 Chr. 4:34, 41)
	ממתק	*Mamtaq* –Sweetness, sweet thing
	משמר	*Mishmar* –Place of confinement, prison, guard, jail, guard post, watch, observance
	נלך	*Nelakh* –21st name of *Shem HaMeforash* (3 Scorpio)
	סכך	*Sakak* –To hedge, fence about, shut in; to block, overshadow, screen, stop the approach, shut off, cover; to cover, lay over; to weave together
	עודך	*'uwdka* –My testimony
	עשיר	*'ashiyr* –Rich, wealthy; the rich, the wealthy, rich man
	עתיק	*'athiyq* –Eminent, surpassing, choice, splendid; durable *'attiyq* –Removed, weaned, old, ancient, taken away; ancient, advanced, aged, old, taken away (Aramaic)
	פך	*Pakh* – Flask, bottle, vial
	פסתם	*Pastam* –6th - 9th letters of the 22-letter name of God
	פרש	*Parash* –To spread, spread out, stretch, break in pieces; to make distinct, declare, distinguish, separate; to pierce, sting; scatter; horse, steed, warhorse, horseman

---

752 נבכדנאצר (417), נבוכדנצר (422), נבוכדנאצר (423), נבוכדנאצר (423).

Perash –To specify, distinguish, make distinct
Peresh –Fecal matter, dung, offal; Peresh, son of Machir, son of Manasseh

פשר *Peshar* –To interpret; interpretation(of dream)
Pesher –Interpretation, solution

צפית *Tzafiyth* –Rug, carpet; watchtower

רפש *Rafash* –To stamp, tread, foul by stamping or treading
Refesh –Mire, mud

רשפ *Reshef* –Flame, coals, firebolt; Resheph, descendant of Ephraim; Canaanite deity worshipped as lord of the underworld

שיער *Sitri* –Goetic demon #12 (Aurum Solis spelling; probably a misprint for שיצר, 600)

שעיר *Sair* –Hairy one; he-goat; demon; hairy
Se'iyr –Seir, grandfather of Hori, ancestor of the Horites

שפר *Shafar* –To be pleasing, be beautiful
Shefer –Beauty, goodness, goodliness; Shepher, mountain encampment during the Hebrews' wanderings in the wilderness
Shofar –Horn, ram's horn

שרפ *Sar'af* –Disquieting thoughts, thoughts
Saraf –To burn; serpent, fiery serpent; *Seraf*, one of the *Serafim*; Saraph, descendant of Judah (1 Chr. 4:22)
Seraf –Ruler of Fire; one of the *Serafim*

שעיר *Sa'iyr* –Hairy; he-goat, buck; raindrops, rainshowers

תפילינ *Tefilin* –Leather boxes containing parchment, worn on the head and left arm by men during weekday morning prayer

תקפ *Taqaf* –To prevail, overcome, overpower
Teqef –To grow strong, be hardened (Aramaic)
Teqof –Strength, might (Aramaic)
Toqef –Authority, power, strength, energy

581 אור כשדימ *Ur Kasdim* –Ur of the Chaldees
אלתקנ *Elteqon* –Eltekon, a city in the territory of Judah north of Hebron
אשפר *'eshpar* –Piece of meat, measured portion, date-cake
עתיקא *Atiqa* –The Ancient One; a title of *Keter*
פראש *Foras* –Goetic demon #31 (Aurum Solis spelling)

582

583 אבימלך *Abimelech* –A King of the Philistines
אחד־עשר *Achad-Asar* –Eleven
טמירא־דטמירינ *Temira de-Temirin* –The Concealed of the Concealed, a title of *Keter*

584 חוצ לילית *Chotz Lilith* –Out Lilith!

585 אלהימ־צבאות *Elohim Tzabaoth* –God of Hosts; divine name assoc.

w/*Hod*, w/Water, & w/the West

הפך — *Hafak* –To turn, overthrow, overturn, change, transform
Hefek –Contrary, opposite, a difference, reversed, contrariness, perversity
Hofek –Perverseness, perversity

משמרה — *Masmerah* –Nail

פרשה — *Parashah* –Exact statement, declaration

שעירה — *Se'iyrah* –She-goat; Seirath, place in Mount Ephraim to which Ehud fled after he murdered Eglon

שעריה — *She'aryah* –Sheariah, descendant of Saul

שפרה — *Shifrah* –Fairness, clearness; Shiphrah, one of the Hebrew midwives at the time of the birth of Moses (Ex. 1:15)

שרפה — *Serefah* –Burning

586 בית עקד — *Beyth 'Eqed* –Beth Eked, a town on the road from Jezreel to Samaria where Jehu killed 42 relatives of King Ahaziah

ירושלמ — *Yeruwshalaim* –Jerusalem, capital of the southern kingdom of Judah until its destruction by Nebuchadnezzar in 586 B.C. (see also ירושלים)[753]

פוך — *Fukh* –Furcas, Goetic demon #50 (A.C., 777)
Pukh –Antimony, stibium, black paint (eye cosmetic)

פרוש — *Parush* –Hermit

שופר — *Shofar* –Ceremonial ram's horn, trumpet

תקועי — *Teqow'iy* –Tekoite

587 פוראש — *Foras* –Goetic demon #31

פרשז — *Parshez* –Spreading (verbal)

–Prime number

588 מספחת — *Mispachath* –Eruption, scab

נפתחימ — *Naftuchiym* –Naphtuhim, son of Mizraim (Gen. 10:13; 1 Chr. 1:11 – many people think this refers to a district in Egypt)

צפיחת — *Tzappiychith* –Flat cake, wafer

589 אחימלך — *'Achiymelek* –Ahimelech, friend of David; priest of Nob (see also Abimelech)[754]; son of Abiathar

כבוד־ראשונ — *Kabodh Rishon* –First Splendor, a title of *Keter*

רטפש — *Ruwtafash* –To grow fresh, become, be grown fresh

590 כרכמיש — *Kakemiysh* –Carchemish, city west of the Euphrates River

נתנ־מלכ — *Nethan-Melek* –Nathan-Melech, officer under Josiah (2 Kings 23:11)

---

[753] ירושלים (596, 1156).

[754] Abimelech (103, 583).

עשירי *'asiyriy* –A tenth (ordinal number)
פיך *Peyka* –Your word, your mouth
פקדות *Peqiduth* –Oversight, overseer, guard
ציצת *Tziytzith* –Fringe, tassel, lock
פעלתי *Peull'thay* –Peulthai, son of Obed-edom and gatekeeper in the time of David
קצת *Qetzath* –End, part
שפיר *Shappiyr* –Fair, beautiful (of foliage); Saphir, town in Judah
שרצ *Sharatz* –To bring forth abundantly
Sheretz –Creeping thing, moving creature
תקיפ *Taqqiyf* –Mighty

591 אני יהוה מקדשכמ *Ani* YHVH *Miqadishkem* –"I am YHVH who makes you holy" (Lev. 21:8)
אנקתמ *Anaqtam* –First five letters of the 22-letter name of God
הקפות *Hakafot* –Encircling; the procession of the Torah around the *bimah* on certain days
כל ישראל *Kol Israel* –All of Israel
תקופה *Tequwfah* –Coming round, a turning, circuit

592 בצקת *Botzqath* –Bozkath or Boscath, town near Lachish in southern Judah
שכל מצוחצח *Sekhel Metzochtzoch* –Scintillating or Fiery Intelligence (11th Path)

593 –Prime number

594 פקדתי *Pachadti* –I remember
פשחור *Pashchuwr* –Pashur, head of a priestly family; priest who sealed the covenant with God after the Exile; son of Immer the priest who put Jeremiah in stocks because Jeremiah's prophecies were so unpopular; priest, the "chief governor in the house of the Lord," who persecuted Jeremiah; son of Malchiah, whose family returned to Jerusalem

595 הפנימית *HaPeniymiyth* –The Penimith (Heb. uncertain – Ezek. 8:3)
יערשיה *Ya'areshyah* –Jareshiah, descendant of Benjamin son of Jehoram

596 בטול במציאות *Bitul Bimtziuwt* –Nullification of Existence
ירושלימ *Yeruwshalayim* –Jerusalem, capital of the southern kingdom of Judah until its destruction by Nebuchadnezzar in 586 B.C. (see also ירושלם)[755]
מופעת *Mowfa'ath* –Mephaath, city allotted to Reuben and

[755] ירושלם (586, 1146).

assigned to the Levites

עצלות *'atsluwth* –Sluggishness, laziness

שמרון *Shomrown* –Shimron, ancient city belonging to Zebulun; Shimron, fourth son of Issachar; Samaria, capital of the northern kingdom of Israel; another name for the kingdom of Israel

597

598 צבקות *Tzevakot* –Hosts; name of God used in place of *Tzeva'ot*

תובל קין *Tubal-Qayin* –Tubal-Cain, one of the sons of Lamech and an expert metal-smith (Gen. 4:22)

תחפנס *Tachpanches* –Tahapanes, Egyptian queen, wife of the Pharaoh, who received the fleeing Hadad, an enemy of Solomon (see also תחפנחס, תחפניס)[756]

599 אלופו של עולמ *'elifuw Shel 'olam* –Master of the Universe – a name of God

–Prime number

600 טהר *Taher* –To be clean, pure

Tohar –Purity, purification, purifying

ם *Mem* (final) –13th letter of Hebrew alphabet

מנקית *Menaqqiyth* –Sacrificial bowl or cup

מסך *Masak* –To mix, mingle, produce by mixing; covering, screen (of the Tabernacle)

Mesek –Mixture

מצרפ לכספ *Metzeraf Lekasaf* –"Fining pot is for silver" (Prov. 17:3)

סמך *Samekh* –To lean, lay, rest, support, uphold, lean upon; prop, support; 15th letter of Hebrew alphabet

קרקר *Qarqor* –Karkor, city in Gad, east of the Jordan[757]

קרש *Qeresh* –Board, boards, plank

קשר *Qashar* –To bind, tie, bind together, conspire

Qesher –Conspiracy, treason, (unlawful) alliance

Qishshur –Bands, sashes, headbands

רת *Rath* –230th Gate of the 231 Gates

שיצר *Sitri* –Goetic demon #12 (corrected Aurum Solis spelling)

שמרינ *Shomrayin* –Samaria, capital of the northern kingdom of Israel (this spelling used only in Ezra 4:10, 17 – see also שמרון)[758]

שמרני *Shimroniy* –Shimronites; Samaritans, natives or inhabitants of Samaria

שקר *Saqar* –To ogle, be wanton

Shaqar –To do or deal falsely, be false, trick

Sheqer –Lie, deception, disappointment; falsehood

---

756 תחפנחס (606), תחפניס (608).

757 Karkor is the site of Gideon's victory over Zebah and Zalmunna (Judg. 8:10).

758 שמרון (596, 1246).

שרק *Sharaq* –To hiss, whistle, pipe
Saruq –Sorrel, reddish, tawny, bay
Soreq –Choice grapes
שש *Shasah* –To spoil, plunder, take spoil
Shesh –White marble; something bleached white, linen; alabaster, marble; six
תפינ *Tufiyn* –Broken piece, baked piece, pieces cooked
–Noah's age at the time of the Flood (Gen. 7:6)

601 אלמלך *Allammelek* –Alammelech, a town or site in Asher
אם *Em* –Mother, source, womb, beginning, origin, crossroads; point of departure or division; if; 12th Gate of the 231 Gates
'im –If, not, only, or, when
אתר *'athar* –Track, place
ולא שמעו בקולי *Ve-lo Shamo Biqowli* –"...and [they] have disobeyed me" (Num. 14:22)
שכל מאיר *Sekhel Meir* –Illuminating Intelligence (14th Path)
תאר *Ta'ar* –To be drawn, incline, delineate
Ta'or –Curse
To'ar –Shape, form, outline, figure, appearance
–Prime number

602 אור־פשוט *Aur Pashot* –The Simple Light, a title of *Keter*
בם *Bam* –In them, them, upon them; 32nd Gate of the 231 Gates
Bem –Entrance, gathering place, ascent
בתר *Bathar* –To cut in two
Bether –Part, piece (of the parts of an animal cut in half for a sacrifice); Bether, range of hills located between Bethlehem and Jerusalem
ויסרם מעל פניו *Va-Yesirem Ma'al Panayv* –"and [He] banished them from His presence" (2 Kings 17:18)[759]
קוממיות *Qowmemiyuwth* –Uprightness
שבש *Shabash* –To confuse, to be perplexed (Aramaic)

603 בני ישראל *Beniy Yisrael* –Children of Israel
גם *Gam* –Together; also; become much or abundant, collection, company, addition; 51st Gate of the 231 Gates
גשש *Gashash* –To feel with the hand, grope, stroke, feel
גתר *Gether* –Gether, descendant of Shem or possibly an unknown family of Arameans; third of Aram's sons
שלהבירונ *Shalhebiron* –The Flaming Ones, *Qlippoth* of Leo
תרג *Tirgam* –To interpret, translate

604 אגם *Agam* –Pool, troubled pool
Agem –Stagnant pond

[759] This is the reference to the so-called lost tribes of Israel.

	אגרת	*Agrath* –A Queen of Demons *Iggereth* –Letter, missive
	דם	*Dam* –Blood (also of wine – fig.); 69th Gate of the 231 Gates
605	אדם	*Adam* –Adam; a title of *Tiferet*; to be red *Adhom* –Red, ruddy (of man, horse, heifer, garment, water, lentils) *Edom* –Edom, the twin-brother of Jacob *Odem* –Ruby, carnelian, sardius (precious stone in the High Priest's ephod – represents the tribe Reuben)
	אדרת	*Addereth* –Glory, cloak
	ארפכשד	*Arfaxad* –Arphaxad, son of Shem and father of Shelah; lived 438 years
	גברת	*Gebereth* –Lady, queen; mistress (of servants)
	המ	*Ham* –Ham, name for Egypt used only in poetry (Ps. 78:51); place between Ashteroth Karnaim in Bashan – possibly modern Ham; 86th Gate of the 231 Gates *Hem* –Abundance, clamor (meaning uncertain – Ezek. 7:11); they, these, the same, who
	המניך	*Hamniyk* –Necklace, chain (Aramaic)
	טהרה	*Tohorah* –Purifying, cleansing, purification, purity, cleanness
	רהט	*Rahat* –Trough, hollow; lock of hair
	שרקה	*Shereqah* –Hissing, whistling
	ששה	*Shishshah* –Six
606	דברת	*Daberath* –Daberath, city of the tribe of Issachar, assigned to the Levites (Josh. 19:12; 1 Chr. 6:57)
	דתבר	*Dethabar* –Lawyer, interpreter of decrees, judge (Aramaic)
	ום	*Vam* –102nd Gate of the 231 Gates
	טהור	*Tahowr* –Pure, clean *Tehowr* –Pureness, cleanness, clean, pure
	מוסך	*Musk* –Attractive (mod. Hebrew)
	סומך	*Sumk* –Supporting
	עליצות	*'aliytsuwth* –Exultation
	פלצות	*Pallatzuwth* –Shuddering, trembling
	רות	*Ruwth* –Friend, mate; Ruth, Moabite wife of Mahlon and Boaz
	שורק	*Sowreq* –Sorek, valley in Gaza where Delilah lived
	שרוק	*Saruwq* –Vine-tendrils or clusters
	ששו	*Shashah* –To give the sixth part, give the sixth part of *Shawshaw* –To lead, lead on
	תחפנחס	*Tachpanches* –Tahapanes, Egyptian queen, wife of the Pharaoh, who received the fleeing Hadad, an enemy of Solomon (see also תחפנס,

תחפניס)[760]

607 אום — *Aum* –30th name of *Shem HaMeforash* (6 Sagittarius)

בהרת — *Bohereth* –White patch of skin, brightness, bright spot (on skin); bright spot, scar, blister, boil

גדרת — *Gaderowth* –A town in the low country of Judah

זם — *Zam* –117th Gate of the 231 Gates

זרת — *Zereth* –Span (a unit of measure, approximately 1/2 cubit, or the distance between the thumb and little finger on an outstretched hand)

זתר — *Zethar* –Zethar, eunuch of Ahasuerus

רבשקה — *Rabshaqeh* –Rabshakeh, title of an office in the Assyrian government (2 Kings 18:17-28; 19:4, 8)[761]

שושא — *Shavsha'* –Shavsha, scribe of David (see also Seraiah, Sheva, and Shisha)[762]

–Prime number

608 ברות — *Baruwth* –Food

Berowth –Cypress, fir, juniper, pine

חית כפ ממ הה — *Cheth Kaf Mem Heh* –The letters *chet, kaf, mem, heh*, which spell *Chokmah*, wisdom

חם — *Cham* –Ham, son of Noah; father in law, husband's father; warm, hot; warmth, heat; Ham, name for Egypt used only in poetry (Ps. 78:51); place between Ashteroth Karnaim in Bashan and the Moabite country – possibly modern Ham; 131st Gate of the 231 Gates

Chom –Heat, hot

חרת — *Charath* –To engrave, graven

Chereth –Hereth, forest in the hill country of Judah – David hid from Saul in a cave near this place

חשש — *Chashash* –Chaff, dry grass

חתר — *Chathar* –To dig, row

לב מבין דעת — *Lev Meviyn Da'at* –"A heart that understands knowledge" (notarikon for *Lamed*)

רחת — *Rachath* –Shovel

רתח — *Rathach* –To boil

Rethach –Boiling

שכל מזהור — *Sekhel Mazohir* –Illuminating or Radiant Intelligence (2nd Path)

תבור — *Tabowr* –Tabor, mountain located in the northern part of the Valley of Jezreel (Judg. 4:6, 12, 14; Ps. 89:13) – modern Jebel el-Tur; town of Zebulun given to the Levites (1 Chr. 6:62); an oak in Benjamin (1 Sam. 10:3)

תחפניס — *Tachpanches* –Tahapanes, Egyptian queen, wife of the Pharaoh, who received the fleeing Hadad, an

---

[760] תחפנס (598), תחפניס (608).

[761] The precise function of this title is unknown, but suggestions include that of a field marshal or governor of the Assyrian provinces east of Haran.

[762] Seraiah (515), Sheva (311), Shisha (611).

		enemy of Solomon (see also תחפנס, תחפנחס)[763]
	תרח	*Terach* –Terah, father of Abraham
609	אברתו	*'evrato* –Her pinions (Deut. 32:11)
	אחרת	*'acheret* –Another (Gen. 26:21)
	ארבות	*'Arubbowth* –Aruboth, district belonging to Solomon
	ארחת	*'orchat* –Caravan (Gen. 37:25)
	בארות	*Be'erowth* –Beeroth, place on the border of Edom; city of Gibeon assigned to the tribe of Benjamin
	בבהרת	*Babaheret* –In the bright spot (Lev. 13:25)
	גרות	*Geruwth* –Lodging place, habitation
	דהם	*Daham* –Astonish, astound
	הדם	*Hadam* –Member, limb, member of the body (Aramaic)
		Hadom –Stool, footstool
	וארבת	*ve-'arubot* –And the windows (Gen. 7:11)
	טם	*Tam* –144th Gate of the 231 Gates
	רדתה	*Ridtah* –Fall, be subdued (Deut. 20:20)
	תאחר	*Te'acher* –You shall delay (Ex. 22:28)
	תגור	*Taguwr* –You shall be afraid (Deut. 18:22)
	תדהר	*Tedahr* –Favor
		Tidhar –Species of hardwood tree
	תהדר	*Tehidar* –You shall favor (Ex. 23:3)
	תחרא	*Tachra'* –Coat of mail (Ex. 28:32)
	תטר	*Titor* –Shall bear grudge (Lev. 19:18)
	תרדה	*Tirdeh* –You shall rule (Lev. 25:43)
610	אטם	*Atam* –To shut, shut up, close
	ברחת	*Borachat* –Flee (Gen. 16:8)
	בתרח	*Betarach* –In Terah (Num. 33:27)
	גברתה	*Gevirtah* –Her mistress (Gen. 16:4)
	גזם	*Gazam* –Locusts
		Gazzam –Gazzam, one whose descendants returned
	הרתה	*Haratah* –She had conceived (Gen. 16:4)
	הששה	*HaSishah* –The six (Ex. 28:10)
	ותרד	*ve-Tered* –And went down, let down (Gen. 24:16)
	חברת	*Chabereth* –Companion, wife, consort
		Chovereth –Junction, a thing joined (Ex. 26:3); curtain pieces of the Tabernacle
	טאמפיעת	*Temphioth* –Guardian of the 19th Tunnel of Set
	ים	*Yam* –Sea; 156th Gate of the 231 Gates
		Yem –Mules (meaning uncertain – Gen. 36:24)
	ירקרק	*Yeraqraq* –Greenish, pale green, greenish-yellow (Lev. 13:49)
	ירת	*Yereth* –27th name of *Shem HaMeforash* (3 Sagittarius)
	ישש	*Yashesh* –Aged, decrepit, feeble

[763] תחפנס (598), תחפנחס (606).

	יתר	*Yatar* –Leave, remain, rest, remainder, remnant
		Yeter –Rest, remnant, residue, abundance (Gen. 49:3); Jether, firstborn son of Gideon; son of Jerahmeel; descendant of Caleb the spy; descendant of Asher; a possible textual error in Ex. 4:18 for Jethro[764]
	לפרש	*Lifrosh* –To declare (Lev. 24:12)
	מיסך	*Meysak* –Covered structure, covert
	מעך	*Ma'ak* –To press, squeeze
	מעשר	*Ma'aser* –Tithe (Lev. 27:30), tenth part (Gen. 14:20)
	משער	*Misha'ar* –From the gate (Ex. 32:27)
	נסך	*Nasak* –To pour out, pour, offer; to set, install; to weave
		Nesak –To pour out, offer sacrifice (Aramaic); something poured out, libation, drink offering, libation offering (Aramaic)
		Nesek –Drink offering, libation, molten image, something poured out
	עצמתי	*'atzmotay* –My bones (Gen. 50:25)
	פלך	*Pelek* –Whirl of spindle, stick, district
	קרשי	*Qareshey* –Boards of (Num. 26:17)
	רבבות	*Rivavot* –Myriads (Num. 10:36)
		Rivivot –Ten thousands (Deut. 33:17)
	רחבת	*Rachavat* –Spread, width (Gen. 34:21)
		Rechovot –Rehoboth, suburb of Ninevah (Gen. 10:11)
	שיש	*Shayish* –Alabaster
	ששי	*Sheshai* –Shashai, one who married a foreign wife during the Exile (Num. 13:22)
		Shishshi –Sixth (Gen. 30:19)
	תדרו	*Tidruw* –You vow (Deut. 12:11)
611	אדום	*Edom* –The Kings and Dukes of Edom (Gen. 36:31, 43), of the line of Esau, who sold his birthright, "symbolize unlawful and chaotic forces" and are associated with the *Sefirot*; Edom, twin-brother of Jacob
	אים	*Ayom* –Frightful, terrible, dreadful
		Aim –Goetic Demon #23
		Aum –30th name of *Shem HaMeforash* (6 Sagittarius)
	אלימלך	*Elimelech* –Elimelech, Naomi's husband and father-in-law of Ruth
	אנסך	A permutation of יהוה by *Aiq Bekar*[765]
	אשיש	*'ashiysh* –With sense of pressing down, foundation
	אךסנ	A permutation of יהוה by *Aiq Bekar*[766]
	באברתו	*Be'evratow* –With his wings
	בני ישראל	*Beniy Yisrael* –Children of Israel (using *mispar musaphi* or *kolel* – see introduction)
	הום	*Huwm* –To distract, ring again, make a (great) noise,

[764] See Jethro (616).
[765] See Introduction.
[766] See Introduction.

murmur, roar, discomfit, be moved

וארפכשד *ve-'arfakshad* –And Arphaxad (Gen. 10:22)

וששה *ve-Shishah* –And six (Ex. 25:32)

ותהר *va-Tahar*–And she conceived, became pregnant (Gen. 4:1; 21:2)

חגרת *Chagorot* –Aprons (Gen. 3:7)

יראת *Yir'at* –Fear of (Gen. 20:11)

יתרא *Yithra'* –Ithra, an Israelite who fathered Amassa by David's sister or half-sister, Abigail (2 Sam. 17:25)

כמתאננימ *Kemit'oneniym* –As murmurers (Num. 11:1)

מסה אסרה *Moshe asurah* –"Moses turned aside" (Exod. 3:3, 4)

קשורה *Qishuwrah* –Is bound up (Gen. 44:30)

ראית *Ra'iyat* –You saw (Gen. 20:10)

Rehiyth –To look

שישא *Shiysha'* –Shisha, father of two of Solomon's scribes

שרוקה *Sheruwqah* –Piping, whistling, hissing

תורה *Torah* –Law, Torah, Pentateuch

תירא *Tiyra'* –You fear (Deut. 7:18); you shall fear (Gen. 15:1)

–603 + 8 letters (*Beniy Yisrael* + the number of letters)

612 אכנ יש יהוה במקומ הזה *'Aken Yesh* YHVH *Bamaquwm Hazeh* –"Surely the Lord exists in this place" (Gen. 28:16)

בחברת *Bachovaret* –In the set, joining (Ex. 26:4)

בים *Bime'* –Goetic demon #26

ברדתו *Beridto* –When he came down (Ex. 34:29)

ברית *Beriyt* –Covenant, alliance, pledge; Goetic demon #28; Berith, Shechemite deity (Judg. 9:46)

Boriyt –Lye, potash, soap, alkali (used in washing)

ברתי *Berothay* –Berothai, town in northern Palestine between Hamath and Damascus

Berothiy –Berothite

הבהרת *HaBaheret* –The bright spot (Lev. 13:23)

הראות *Haro'ot* –Have seen (Deut. 4:3)

Hera'ot –Where there appears (Lev. 13:14)

הראתו *Hera'oto* –He has shown himself (Lev. 13:7)

השלחנ הטהר *HaShulchan HaTahor* –"The pure table" (Lev. 24:5)

ואנכי לא ידעתי *ve-'Anokiy Lo' Yada'etiy* –"And I did not know it" (Gen. 28:16)

וברדת *ve-Veredet* –And when fell (Num. 11:9)

ודברת *ve-Dibarat* –And you shall speak (Num. 4:15)

והנשארימ *ve-Hanish'ariym* –And the remaining (Gen. 14:10)

וידעת כי־יהוה אלהיכ *ve-Yada'at Kiy*-YHVH *'Eloheyka* –"Know, therefore, that only the Lord your God is God" (Deut. 7:9)

וישרצו *va-Yishritzuw* –And they increased abundantly (Ex. 1:7)

ותדבר *va-Tidaber* –And she spoke (Gen. 39:17)

ve-Tedaber –And said (Ex. 32:13)

ותראה *ve-Tera'eh* –And let appear (Gen. 1:9)

זהם *Zaham* –To loathe, be foul, be loathsome; Zaham, son of Rehoboam (2 Chr. 11:19)

	יבם	*Yabam* –To perform levirat marriage; brother-in-law, husband's brother
		Yebem –70th name of *Shem HaMeforash* (4 Cancer)
	כי אמ ישראל	*Ki Em Israel* –For the people of Israel
	פסח ליהוה המול לו כל זכר ואז	*Pesach Lah*-YHVH *He-Mohl Lo Kal Zakar Vi-az* –(If a stranger...would offer the) passover to YHVH, all his males must be circumcised (Ex. 12:48)
	קצותיו	*Qetzotayev* –Its ends, corners (Ex. 25:19)
	רבית	*Rabbiyth* –Rabbith, boundary town of Issachar
	ריבת	*Riyvot* –Controversy (Deut. 17:8)
	תרזה	*Tirzah* –A type of tree, perhaps the cypress

–The total number of years that Abraham, Isaac, Jacob, and Joseph lived
–The total gematria of Eber and Shem, the sons of Noah

613	אביתר	*'Ebyathar* –Abiathar, High Priest
	את האור	*Eth HaOhr* –Is the light
	בארתי	*Be'erothiy* –Beerothite
	בראתי	*Barati* –I have created (Gen. 6:7; Is. 45:12; 54:16; Dan. 8:2, 15)
	ברותה	*Berowthah* –Berothah, town in northern Palestine between Hamath and Damascus (this name used only in Ezek. 47:16)
	ברעה שאלה	*Bira'ah Shiulah* –Gone to the grave in evil
	גדרות	*Gederowth* –Gederoth, town in the lowlands of Judah, modern Katrah
	גרתי	*Gartiy* –I have sojourned (Gen. 32:5)
	האור ובינ החשכ	*HaOhr Vuvayn HaChushek* –"the light and divided the darkness" (Gen. 1:4)
	הברות	*HaBorot* –The pits (Gen. 37:20)
	הרבות	*HaRebot* –The many (Deut. 17:16)
	וגדרת	*ve-Gidrot* –And folds, and corrals (Num. 32:24, 36)
	וזרת	*ve-Zeret* –And a span (Ex. 39:9)
	והאלהימ נסהאת	*ve-HaElohim Nisahath* –"And God tested" (Gen. 22:1)
	ותראו	*va-Tiraw* –And you have seen (Deut. 29:16)
	יגרת	*Yagorta* –You were afraid of (Deut. 28:60)
	למענ תחיה	*Li-Ma'an Tiachyeh* –"So that you might thrive" (Deut. 16:20)
	משה רבינו	*Mosheh Rabeyuw* –"Moses our teacher"
	תחרה	*Tacharah* –To burn, be kindled with anger

–The number of bones in the human body
–The number of "lights"
–Prime number
–The number of *mitzvoth*

614	בברית	*Bivriyt* –In the covenant (Deut. 29:11)
	האחרת	*Ha'acheret* –The next (Gen. 17:21)
	והרגת	*ve-Haragat* –And you shall kill (Lev. 20:16)
	והתגר	*ve-Hitgar* –And contend (Deut. 2:24)
	ויהי יהוה את יוספ	*Vahe* YHVH *Eth Yosief*–"YHVH was with Joseph"

		(Gen. 39:2, 21)
	חום	*Chuwm* –Dark color, darkened, dark brown or black
	חרות	*Charuwt* –Graven (Ex. 32:16)
	כל דברימ בכל דברימ	*Kol-Dabarim Be-Kol-Dabarim* –All Things in All Things
	תהרגו	*Taharoguw* –You shall slay (Lev. 20:15)
	תטהר	*Tithar* –She shall be clear (Lev. 15:28)
	תריד	*Tariyd* –You shall break loose (Gen. 27:40)
615	אבים	*Abiyam* –Abijam, 2nd King of Judah
	אחרות	*'acherot* –Other (Gen. 29:27)
	ברזות	*Birzowth* –Birzavith, descendant of Asher (1 Chr. 7:31)
	גבים	*Gebiym* –Gebim, settlement just north of Jerusalem near Michmash
	גברתי	*Gevirtiy* –My mistress (Gen. 16:8)
	החברת	*Hachoveret* –Joining (Ex. 36:17)
		HaChoveret –The set (Ex. 26:10
	המעשר	*HaMa'aser* –The tithe (Num. 18:26)
	הששי	*HaShishiy* –The sixth (Gen. 1:31)
	התיר	*Howthiyr* –Hothir, 13th son of Hemam & a Kohathite Levite
	והדרת	*ve-Hadarat* –And honor (Lev. 19:32)
	יתרה	*Yithrah* –Abundance, riches, wealth
	לשרפה	*Lisrefah* –Burn thoroughly (Gen. 11:3)
	מבאר שבע	*Mib'ed Shava'a* –"From Beer-Sheba" (Gen. 28:10)
	מלאכי אלהימ עלימ וירדימ בו	*Mal'akey 'Elohiym 'Oliym ve-Yirediym Bo* –"Angels of God were going up and down on it." (Gen. 28:12 – in reference to Jacob's ladder)
	ממקהלת	*Mimaqhelot* –From Makheloth (Num. 33:26)
	מעשה	*Ma'aseh* –Deed, work
	נכספתה	*Niksaftah* –You longed; desire (Gen. 31:30)
	שריקה	*Seriyqah* –Carded, combed, fine (of flax)
	תאחרו	*Ta'charuw* –Delay, hinder (Gen. 24:56)
	תגורו	*Taguwruw* –You shall fear (Deut. 1:17)
616	אחזם	*'Achuzzam* –Ahuzam, son of Ashur
	ארידתא	*'Ariydatha'* –Aridatha, son of Haman, hanged with his father
	אשישה	*'ashiyshah* –Raisin-cake, used in sacrificial feasts
	בחרות	*Bechurowth* –Youth
	בצדקתכ	*Betzidqatak* –In your righteousness (Deut. 9:5)
	דברתי	*Dibartiy* –I will speak, I have spoken (Gen. 24:33)
	הוהם	*Howham* –Hoham, Amorite king slain by Joshua
	הראית	*Har'eyat* –You have been shown (Ex. 26:30)
	התורה	*HaTorah* –The Torah, the law (Lev. 7:37)
	ובחרת	*Vevacharat* –Therefore
		ve-Vacharat –And choose
	וחברת	*ve-Chibarat* –And you shall couple (Ex. 26:6)
	ויתר	*ve-Yeter* –And the rest (Deut. 3:13); and the excellence (Gen. 49:3)

	ונצלתם	*ve-Nitzaltem* –And you shall spoil, empty (Ex. 3:22)
	ותברח	*ve-Tivrach* –And she fled (Gen. 16:6)
	ותורד	*ve-Tored* –And she let down (Gen. 24:46)
	חרבות	*Charavoth* –Swords
	יום	*Yom* –Day
		Yowm –Day, time, year; 24-hour time period (1 day)
	יותר	*Yowter* –Superiority, advantage, excess; excess, better; besides, moreover, more; let, leave (Ex. 16:19)
		Yivater –Shall remain (Ex. 29:34)
	יתור	*Yatuwr* –To remain over, leave; search
	יתרו	*Yitero* –Jethro, father-in-law of Moses (see also Reuel and Jether)[767]
	להתאפק	*Lehit'afeq* –To refrain himself (Gen. 45:1)
	מיניקות	*Meyniyqot* –Nursing (Gen. 32:16)
	מנקיתיו	*Menaqiyotayev* –Its bowls (Ex. 37:16)
	מעוך	*Ma'owk* –Maoch, father of Achish, king of Gath (this spelling used only in 1 Sam. 27:2 – see also Maachah)[768]
	עתיכ־יומינ	*Atik Yomin* –The Ancient of Days; a title of *Keter*
	קרשיו	*Qerashayev* –Its boards (Ex. 35:11)
	רחבות	*Rechovot* –Rehoboth, a well dug by Isaac in the Valley of Gerar (Gen. 26:22); city somewhere in northern Edom (Gen. 36:37; 1 Chr. 1:48)
	שערום	*Sa'ruwm* –Dreaded, feared (Deut. 32:17)
	תרגזו	*Tirgezuw* –Quarrel (Gen. 45:24)
617	אילונ בית חננ	*'Eylown Beyth Chanan* –Elon Beth Hanan, one of the three towns of the tribe of Dan
	גדרתי	*Gederathiy* –Gederathite
	דגים	*Dagim* –Fishes; Pisces
	הברית	*HaBirith* –The Covenant (namely between God and Israel)
	והותר	*ve-Hoter* –And too much (Ex. 36:7)
	וחגרת	*ve-Chagarat* –And you shall gird (Ex. 29:9)
	ויראת	*ve-Yare'at* –And you shall fear (Lev. 19:14)
	וראית	*ve-Ra'iyat* –And you shall see (Ex. 33:23)
	ותורה	*ve-Torah* –And Torah
	חתם	*Chatam* –To hold in, restrain
	חצי המנחות	*Chatziy Hamenuchowth* –"Half of the Menuhoth" (1 Chr. 2:52)
	יראתו	*Yir'ato* –His fear (Ex. 20:17)
	ראותי	*Re'otiy* –I have seen (Gen. 46:30)
	רחבית	*Rehoboth* –Rehoboth, city of King Saul of Edom
	תיראו	*Tiyra'uw* –You shall fear (Gen. 43:23; Deut. 13:5); you fear (Num. 14:9)
	–Prime number	

767 Reuel (307), Jether (610).

768 Maachah (135).

618 אל אלהי ישראל — *El elohey Yisra'el* –"The mighty God of Israel" – name given to an altar, a location, by Jacob (Gen. 33:20)

ביתור — *Bethor* –Olympic Planetary Spirit of Jupiter

בריתו — *Beriyto* –His covenant (Ex. 2:24)

הבריאת — *HaBeriy'ot* –The fat (Gen. 41:20)

הרגתי — *Haragtiy* –Have I slain (Gen. 4:23)

וביתר — *ve-Veyeter* –And in the remnant (Deut. 28:54)

ויבתר — *ve-Yevater* –And he divided (Ex. 15:10)

ורבית — *ve-Raviyat* –And multiply (Deut. 30:16)

ותראהו — *ve-Tir'ehuw* –And she saw him (Ex. 2:6)

יחם — *Yacham* –To be hot (lust), conceive

619 אחיסמך — *'Achysamak* –Ahisamach, craftsman who helped build the Tabernacle in the Wilderness

אחרית — *Achariyth* –After part, end, latter

בית ברה — *Beyth Barah* –Beth Barah, place in the vicinity of the Jordan Valley, possibly a ford or crossing

בית־גדר — *Beyth-Gader* –Beth-Gader, town of Judah founded by Hareph

בריאות — *Beriy'ot* –Rank, plump, healthy (Gen. 41:5)

המן בן־המדתא האגגי — *Haman Ben Hamedata' HaAgagiy* –"Haman son of Hammedatha the Agagite" (Esth. 3:1)

הרוחת — *HaRuwchot* –The spirits (Num. 16:22)

ובריאת — *ve-Veriy'ot* –And fat (Gen. 41:2)

–Prime number

620 אחיאם — *'Achiyam* –Ahiam, son of Sharar the Hararite and one of David's mighty men

וטהרת — *ve-Tiharat* –And cleanse (Num. 8:6)

חכמה בינה ודעת — *Chokmah Binah ve-Da'ath* –"Wisdom, Understanding and Knowledge," the second, third and pseudo-*sephiroth* of the Tree of Life

טהרות — *Tehorot* –Clean (pl. – Lev. 14:4)

טהרתו — *Taharato* –His cleaning (Lev. 13:35)

ישיש — *Yashiysh* –Aged, old man, aged one

Yasiys –Will rejoice (Deut. 28:63)

יתיר — *Yattiyr* –Extraordinary; exceedingly, extremely; Jattir, town in the mountains of Judah, assigned to the Levites – probably modern Khirbet 'Atti

יתרי — *Yithriy* –Ithrite

כם — *Kam* –167th Gate of the 231 Gates

כנשרים — *Kanishareem* –Like eagles

כרת — *Karat* –To cut, cut off, cut down, cut off a body part, cut out, eliminate, kill, cut a covenant; he cut (Gen. 15:18); to cut (Ezek. 16:4)[769]

כשש — *Keshesh* –About six (Ex. 12:37)

כתר — *Kathar* –To surround; to bear, wait

[769] Karat is one of the ten words in the Tanakh with a Dagesh in the letter Resh.

		Keter –Crown; the 1st *Sefira* (occurs 63 times in the *Tanakh* – Esth. 1:11; 2:17; 6:8)
	לציצת	*Letziytzit* –For a fringe (Num. 15:39)
	לצקת	*Latzeqet* –For casting (Ex. 38:27)
	לשמרנ	*Leshimron* –Of Shimron (Num. 26:24)
	מפרש	*Mifras* –Spreading out, thing spread out
	מרפש	*Mirpas* –Befouled, thing befouled
	משעיר	*Miseiyr* –From Seir (Deut. 33:2)
	משפר	*Mishpar* –Angel of 3d Virgo
	משרעי	*Mishra'iy* –Mishraites
	נסיך	*Nesiyk* –Poured out, libation, molten image, one anointed; prince, anointed one
	עשרימ	*'esriym* –Twenty, twentieth
	פרשמ	*Pirsham* –Their dung (Lev. 16:27)
	צורישדי	*Tzuwriyshadai* –Zurishaddai, father of Shelumiel
	צפנת	*Tzafnath* –Zaphenath, the first name of Joseph given by Pharaoh (Gen. 41:45)
	רוחות	*Ruachoth* –Spirits, ghosts
	רשעימ	*Rash'iym* –Wicked ones
	שנער	*Shin'ar* –Shinar, plains later known as Babylonia or Chaldea, through which the Tigris and Euphrates Rivers flow (Gen. 10:10)
	שערימ	*Se'oriym* –Barley (Lev. 27:16); Seorim, priest in the days of David
		Sha'riym –(A hundred)-fold (Gen. 26:12)
		Sha'arayim –Shaaraim, town in lowland Judah; town of Simeon
	ששכ	*Sheshak* –Sheshack, name used for Babylon in Jer. 25:26; 51:41 – it is an *Atbash*
	תטהרו	*Titharuw* –You shall be clean (Lev. 16:30)

–The number of letters in the Ten Commandments
–The number of Jewish laws (613) plus the seven major Rabbinical laws

621	באחרית	*Biacharit* –In the end, in the last (Gen. 49:1)
	הותיר	*Howthiyr* –Had left (Ex. 10:15); Hothir, son of Heman in charge of the twenty-first course of the tabernacle service
	חצי המנחתי	*Chatziy Hamenachtiy* –"Half of the Manahethites" (1 Chr. 2:54)
	יאתרי	*Ye'atheray* – Jeaterai, son of Zerah, descendant of Gershon
	יראתי	*Yare'tiy* –I was afraid (Gen. 31:31)
	כראשנימ	*Kari'shoniym* –Like unto the first (Ex. 34:1)
	כראת	*Kiyr'iy* –Fear (Gen. 21:17)
	ראיתי	*Ra'iytiy* –Have I seen (Gen. 7:1)
	ראתכ	*Ro'tak* –You see (Ex. 10:28)
	תיריא	*Tiyreya'* –Tiria, descendant of Judah

–The number of children of Ramah and Gaba who returned from exile (Ezra 2:26)

622	בדרתיו	*Bedorotayev* –In his generation (Gen. 6:9)

בחורות *Bechuwrowth* –Youth
בטהרתו *Betahorato* –For his cleansing (Lev. 14:32)
בעמיך *Biamek* –In your people
בעשרימ *Be'sriym* –For twenty (Gen. 37:30)
בריתי *Beriytiy, Veriytiy* –My covenant (Gen. 6:18; 17:2)
ברכת *Berakat* –You have blessed (Num. 23:11)
Birkat –Blessing (Gen. 28:4)
Birkot –Blessing (Gen. 49:25)
ודברתי *ve-Dibartiy* –And I will speak (Ex. 25:22)
והתורה *ve-HaTorah* –And the law (Ex. 24:12)
ווים *Vawvem* –Hooks
ויותר *ve-Yivater* –And he was left (Gen. 32:25)
ויתרו *ve-Yaruruw* –That they may spy out (Num. 13:2)
ומנקיתיו *ve-Menaqyotayev* –And its bowls (Ex. 25:29)
וראיתה *ve-Ra'iytah* –And when you have seen (Num. 27:13)
כברת *Kivrat* –Much, some (Gen. 35:6)
רכבת *Rakavat* –You have ridden (Num. 22:30)
תברכ *Tevarek* –You bless (Num. 22:6)

623 ביד משה ואהרנ *Be-yad Moshe Ve-Aharon* –"The leadership of Moses and Aaron" (Num. 33:1)
בלשאצר or בלאשצר or בלשאצר (From right to left) *Belsha'tztzar*, *Bel'shatztzar*, and *Belsha'tztzar* –Belshazzar, co-regent in Babylon from 550-539, he was in power when he saw the handwriting on the wall before he was overthrown by Persia (Dan. 5:1-2, 9, 22, 29-30; 7:1; 8:1)
בריתא *Baraita* –External (material), Tanaic traditions and teachings not included in the Misnah
החירת *Hachiyrot* –Hahiroth (Ex. 14:2)
ויאבדם *Va-Abdam* –And He destroyed them
ותחגרו *ve-Tachgeruw* –And you girded (Deut. 1:41)
יגרתי *Yagortiy* –I was in dread of (Deut. 9:19)
משפט צדק *Mishpat Tzedek* –Righteous justice
רוח הקדש *Ruach HaQodesh* –Holy spirit
ספר זכרונ *Sefer Zikarown* –"Book of Remembrance" (Mal. 3:16)
תריבהו *Teriyvehuw* –You did try him (Deut. 33:8)
–The number of children of Bebai who returned from exile (Ezra 2:11)

624 הבריאות *HaBiriy'ot* –The fat (Gen. 41:7)
והבריאת *ve-HaBeriy'ot* –And the fat (ones) (Gen. 41:4)
והרגתי *ve-Haragtiy* –And I will kill (Ex. 22:23)
זוזים *Zuwziym* –Zuzims, primitive tribe that lived in Ham, a place east of the Jordan River between Bashan and Moab, they were conquered by King Chedorlaomer (Gen. 14:15)
חוים *Chivim* –Hivites
נחשירונ *Nachashiron* –The Snakey Ones, *Qlippoth* of Sagittarius
עינ תפוח *'Eyn Tappuwach* –En Tappuah, town on the border of Ephraim

	תדרך	*Tidrok* –You shall tread (Deut. 11:24; 33:29)
	תפקדמ	*Tifeqdem* –You shall number them (Num. 3:15)
625	בית בראי	*Beyth Bir'iy* –Beth-Birei, town of southern Judah of the tribe of Simeon
	גברתכ	*Gevirtek* –Your mistress (Gen. 15:9)
	גם יחד	*Gam Yechad* –"Together in unity" (Ps. 133:1)
	הכרת	*Hikaret* –Cut off (Num. 15:31)
	העשרימ	*Ha'Esriym* –The twenty (Gen. 18:31)
	הריתי	*Hariytiy* –Conceived (Num. 11:12)
	הרשעימ	*HaResha'iym* –The wicked (Ex. 9:27)
	השעירמ	*HaSe'iyrim* –The he-goats (Lev. 16:7)
	כאדרת	*Ka'deret* –Like a mantle (Gen. 25:25)
	כרתה	*Karuthah* –Beams, hewn beams
	משרפה	*Misrafah* –A burning
626	הראתכ	*Har'otak* –Show you (Ex. 9:16)
	וכרת	*ve-Karat* –And cut down (Deut. 20:20)
	ועשרימ	*ve-'esriym* –And twenty (Gen. 6:3)
	ועשרנ	*ve-'isaron* –And a tenth part (Ex. 29:40)
	יותיר	*Yotiyr* –He shall leave (Deut. 28:54)
	כרתו	*Kartuw* –They cut down (Num. 13:24)
	עשרונ	*'issarown* –Tenth part, tithe
	קליפות	*Qlippoth* –Shells, demons
	רכות	*Rakot* –Weak (Gen. 29:17)
	תכרו	*Tikruw* –You shall buy (Deut. 2:6)
	תצפנו	*Tetzafenuw* –You shall overlay it (Ex. 25:11)
627	אעשרנו	*'a'srenuw* –I will give a tenth (Gen. 28:22)
	בית העמק	*Beyth Ha'Emeq* –Beth Emek, town near the border of Asher, modern Amkah
	וראיתי	*ve-Ra'iytiy* –And when I see (Ex. 12:13)
	ראיתיו	*Reiytiyev* –Seen him (Gen. 44:28)
	רשלייזדגנאיב	*Resheliyiyzadigna'yav* –One version of the 12-letter name of God[770]
	תזכר	*Tizakar* –You shall (sanctify the) male (Ex. 34:19)
		Tizkor –You shall remember (Deut. 7:18)
628	בית רחוב	*Beyth Rechowb* –Beth-Rehob, town of the Upper Jordan Valley
	בכרות	*Bekowrath* –Bechorath, ancestor of Saul (1 Sam. 9:1)
	בכרתו	*Bekorato* –His birthright (Gen. 25:33)
	ובכרת	*ve-Vekorot* –And the firstlings (Deut. 12:6)
	וברכת	*ve-Berakat* –And bless (Deut. 8:10)
	והזהרתה	*ve-Hizhartah* –And you shall admonish (Ex. 18:20); enlighten, caution (Rashi)
	חיים	*Chayim* –Life

[770] This name is derived from the first letters of the names of the tribes of Israel (*Benjamin, Joseph, Asher, Gad, Naftali, Dan, Zebulon, Issachar, Judah, Levi, Shimeon, Reuven*).

	חכם	*Chakam* –To be wise; wise, wise man
	ממחציתמ	*Mimachatziytam* –Of their half (Num. 31:29)
	תברכו	*Tevarakuw* –You shall bless (Num. 6:23)
629	**אחריתי**	*'achariytiy* –My end (Num. 23:10)
	גויים	*Goyim* –Nations; gentiles
630	**אדם וחוה**	*Adam ve-Chavvah* –Adam and Eve
	וירדתי	*ve-Yaradtiy* –And I will come down (Num. 11:17)
	ופקדתמ	*ve-Feqadtem* –You shall appoint (Num. 4:27)
	יכרת	*Yikaret* –Will be cut off, consumed (Gen. 9:11)
	יריתי	*Yariytiy* –I have cast (Gen. 31:51)
	ישישי	*Yeshiyshay* –Jeshishai, descendant of Gad
	כרית	*Keriyth* –Cherith, wadi of Gilead, east of the Jordan River, where birds fed the prophet Elijah
	לם	*Lam* –177th Gate of the 231 Gates
	כרתי	*Karatiy* –I have cut (covenant) (Ex. 34:27) *Kerethiy* –Cherethites
	לקרש	*Laqeresh* –To a board (Ex. 26:17)
	לשקר	*Lashaqer* –Falsely (Lev. 19:12) *Lasheqer* –To lie (Lev. 5:24)
	לשש	*Leshesh* –For six (Ex. 38:26)
	נפך	*Nofek* –Carbuncle or emerald (precious stone in the High Priest's ephod – represents the tribe Judah) (perhaps an emerald, turquoise, or ruby); jewels imported from Tyre
	סערש	*Sarash* –Lord of Triplicity by Day for Gemini
	עשרין	*'esriyn* –Twenty (Aramaic)
	פרשימ	*Parashiym* –Horsemen (Gen. 50:9)
	שלש	*Shalash* –To do a third time, do three times, divide in three parts (Gen. 5:22; 11:13) *Shalosh* –Three, triad *Shelash* –Three (Ex. 21:11) *Shelesh* –Shelesh, descendant of Asher *Shillesh* –Pertaining to the third, 3rd generation
	שעירמ	*Seirim* –Hairy ones; he-goats; demons
	שרסכימ	*Sarsekiym* –Sarsechim, prince of Babylon who sat at the gate (Jer. 39:3)
	שרפימ	*Serafim* –Angelic Choir assoc. w/*Giburah*
	תדרכו	*Tidrekuw* –You shall tread (Deut. 11:25)
	תכיר	*Takiyr* –Recognize (Deut. 16:19)
	תעניק	*Ta'aniyq* –You shall furnish (Deut. 15:14)
	–The sum of the numbers 1 through 35	
631	**אלם**	*Alam* –To bind (to be bound) *Elem* –In silence, silent *Illem* –Mute, silent, dumb, to be unable to speak *Ulam* –Vestibule, porch
	ואחריתו	*ve-'achriyto* –But his end (Num. 24:20)
	והרחבתי	*ve-Hirchavtiy* –And I will enlarge (Ex. 34:24)

	לאם	*Leom* –A people, nation
	לראת	*Lir'ot* –To see (Gen. 11:5)
	סנוי סנסנוי סמנגלופ	*Senoy, Sansenoy, Semangelof* –Three angels invoked against Lilith
	ספרא דצניעותא	*Sifra Dtzenioutha* –Book of Concealed Mystery
	פרנאש	*Forneus* –Goetic demon #30 (Aurum Solis spelling)
	תאריכ	*Ta'ariyk* –You may prolong (Deut. 4:40)
	–Prime number	
632	בלטשאצר	*Beltesha'tztzar* –Belteshazzar, Daniel's Babylonian name – Hebrew form of the Babylonian name, Balat-usu-usur (protect his life) (also Aramaic)
	בלם	*Balam* –To curb, hold in, restrain
	בכים	*Bokiym* –Bochim or Bokim, site near Gilgal where the Israelites repented of their sins (Judg. 2:1-5)
	בכרתי	*Bekoratiy* –My birthright (Gen. 27:36)
	בית כר	*Beyth Kar* –Beth Car, Philistine stronghold in Judah (1 Sam. 7:11)
	ברכתי	*Beraktiy* –I have blessed (Gen. 17:20)
		Birkatiy –My blessing, my gift (Gen. 27:36)
	והארכת	*ve-Ha'arakat* –That you may prolong (Duet. 22:7)
	וכרות	*ve-Karuwt* –And cut (Lev. 22:24)
		ve-Keruwt –And maimed (Deut. 23:2)
	ועשרונ	*ve-'isaron* –And a tenth part (Lev. 14:21)
	וראיתיה	*ve-Re'iytiyah* –And I will look upon it (Gen. 9:16)
	חטוטרת	*Chatoteret* –Hunchback
	כראותה	*Kir'otah* –When she saw (Gen. 39:13)
	עולמ יסודות	*Olam Yesodoth* –The World of Foundations; the Sphere of the Elements; the part of the material world corr. to *Malkut*
633	אזכרתה	*'azkaratah* –Memorial part of it (Lev. 2:2)
	גלם	*Galam* –Wrap together
		Golem –Golem; substance yet being unperfect, unformed mass
	הברכות	*HaBerakot* –The blessings (Deut. 28:2)
	וזכרת	*ve-Zakarat* –And you shall remember (Deut. 5:15)
	והרביתי	*ve-Hirbeytiy* –And I will multiply (Gen. 17:20)
	והתברכ	*ve-Hitbarek* –And he will bless himself (Deut. 29:18)
	יום טוב	*Yom Tov* –Good day
	כראותו	*Kira'oto* –When he sees (Gen. 44:31)
	פרשגנ	*Parshegen* –Copy
	תזכרו	*Tizkeruw* –You may remember (Num. 15:40)
	תרגל	*Tirgal* –To go on foot, spy out
634	וחכם	*ve-Chakam* –And wise
	לדרת	*Ledorot* –Unto generations (Gen. 9:12)
	לרדת	*Laredet* –To go down (Gen. 44:26)
635	הילל בנ שחר	*Helel ben Shachar* –"Son of the Dawn;" Lucifer (Is.

14:12)[771]

הלם *Halam* –To smite, strike, hammer, strike down
Halom –Here, hither
Helem –Helem, descendant of Asher
הפרשימ *HaParashiym* –The horsemen (Ex. 14:28)
השלש *HaShalesh* –The three (Deut. 19:9)
השרפימ *HaSerafiym* –The fiery (Num. 21:6)
HaSerufiym –The burned (Num. 17:4)
להם *Laham* –To gulp, swallow greedily
La-hem –Unto them
עינ התנימ *'Eyn HaTanniym* –En Hatannim, a pool near Jerusalem (Neh. 2:13)[772]
שלשה *Shalishah* –Shalisha, area near Mount Ephraim through which Saul passed when searching for his father's livestock
Shelshah –Three (Gen. 6:10)
Shilshah –Shilshah, son of Zophah

636 וסקלתמ *ve-Seqaltem* –And you shall stone them (Deut. 22:24)
ve-Seqaltam –And you shall stone them (Deut. 17:5)
ושלש *ve-Shalesh* –And three (Gen. 46:15)
ve-Shelesh –And three (Gen. 5:23)
לראתה *Lir'otah* –To see it (Deut. 28:68)
לשוש *Lasuws* –To rejoice (Deut. 30:9)
לתור *Latuwr* –To seek out, to spy out (Num. 10:33)
פרשונ *Purson* –Goetic demon #20 (Aurum Solis spelling)
צפרירונ *Tzafiriron* –The Scratchers, *Qlippoth* of Virgo
שלוש *Sallos* –Goetic demon #19 (Aurum Solis spelling)
Shaluwsh –Three (Num. 22:32)
תכירו *Takiyruw* –You shall respect (Deut. 1:17)
תראלה *Tar'alah* –Taralah, city allotted to the tribe of Benjamin

637 אולם *Uwlam* –Vestibule, porch; as for, but, howbeit, in very deed, surely, truly, wherefore; Ulam, descendant of Manasseh; descendant of Benjamin
והוריתי *ve-Horeytiy* –And I will teach (Ex. 4:15)
והותרכ *ve-Hotirak* –And (he) will make you over abundant (Deut. 28:11)
ויראתכ *ve-Yir'atak* –And the fear of you (Deut. 2:25)
ונאספתמ *ve-Ne'esaftem* –And you shall be gathered (Lev. 26:25)
ותצפנהו *ve-Titzfenehuw* –Then she hid him (Ex. 2:2)
לראות *Lera'ot* –To appear (Ex. 34:24)
Lir'ot –To see, gaze (Gen. 2:19)
פרשדנ *Parshedon* –Excrement, feces (meaning dubious – Judg.

---

[771] It should be noted that Lucifer, or "light bearer" is wrongly applied to the Christian devil, due to a misreading of Isaiah 14:12: "How are you fallen from heaven,/O Shining One, son of Dawn!" It is imperative that the reader understand that in context, this is part of a song of scorn to be recited over the king of Babylon (Nebuchadnezzar), and is not a reference to the devil of Christianity. The JPS Hebrew-English Tankah states that Lucifer may also refer to a character in some lost myth. Also see A Dictionary of Angels, p. 176 for more information.

[772] Some translate "Jackyl's Spring" or "Dragon well."

		3:22)
	שאלוש	*Sallos* –Goetic demon #19
	פורנאש	*Forneus* –Goetic demon #30
	תאריכו	*Ta'ariykuw* –You may prolong (Deut. 11:9)
638	הרגתיכ	*Haragtiyk* –I would kill you (Num. 22:29)
	ובריתכ	*ve-Beriytak* –And your covenant (Deut. 33:9)
	וברכתי	*ve-Veraktiy* –And I will bless (Gen. 17:16)
	ויותירו	*ve-Yotiyruw* –(but some) left (of it) (Ex. 16:20)
	חכים	*Chakkiym* –Wise man, wise (Aramaic)
	חלם	*Chalam* –To dream; to be healthy, be strong
		Chelem –Dream (Aramaic); Helem, descendant of Asher; man of whom the prophet Zechariah speaks (see also Heldai)[773]
	לחם	*Lacham* –To fight, do battle, make war; to eat, use as food
		Lachem –War (meaning uncertain – Judg. 5:8)
		Lechem –Bread, food, grain; feast (Aramaic)
	עיר נחש	*'Iyr Nachash* –Ir-Nahash, person or a town of the tribe of Judah (1 Chr. 4:12)
	–The total gematria of Abraham, Isaac, and Jacob	
639	גולם	*Golem* –Shapeless mass; artificial man
	גלום	*Gelowm* –Clothes
	גרלות	*Gorlot* –Lots (lottery) (Lev. 16:8)
	הושענא רבה	*Hoshanah Rabbah* –Great hosanna; the seventh day of *Sukkot*
	והתברכו	*ve-Hitbarkuw* –And shall be blessed, consecrated (Gen. 22:18)
	חלאם	*Chel'am* –Helam, descendant of Asher; man of whom the prophet Zechariah speaks (Zech. 6:14) – may be another name for the second Heldai (see also חילם)[774]
	טלם	*Telem* –Telem, gatekeeper who divorced his foreign wife after the exile (Ezra 10:24)
	כל הנגע בהמ יקדש	*Kal HaNogayah bahem yiqdash* –"Whatever touches them shall be consecrated" (see Ex. 30:29)
	משנה גמרא	*Mishnah* + *Gemara* –The Talmud consists of the *Mishnah* plus *gemara* (commentary)
	עצ הדעת	*Etz HaDaath* –Tree of Knowledge
	עשרימ ואחד	*Esrim ve-Achad* –Twenty-one
	–The total gematria of YHVH and the 613 commandments (26+613)	
640	השלשה	*HaShelshah* –The three (Num. 3:46)
	ויבאו שני המלאכימ סדמה	*VaYavo'uw Sh'ney HaMal'akiym Sodomah* –"The two angels arrived in Sodom" (Gen. 19:1)
	חאראכית	*Characith* –Guardian of the 18th Tunnel of Set
	יכרית	*Yakriyt* –Shall cut off (Deut. 12:29)

[773] Heldai (52).

[774] חילם (88, 648).

	ירשיענ	*Yarshiy'en* –Will condemn (Ex. 22:8)
	בריתי	*Kariytiy* –I have dug (Gen. 50:5)
	כשעירמ	*Kis'iyrim* –As the small rain (Deut. 32:2)
	לקרשי	*Leqarshey* –For (the) boards of (Ex. 26:26)
	ממסך	*Mamsak* –Mixed drink, mixed wine, drink-offering
	מפלצת	*Mifletseth* –Horrid thing, horrible thing
	מקלעת	*Miqla'ath* –Carving
	מרת	*Moret* –Bitterness (Gen. 26:35); bitterness (Prov. 14:10)[775]
	משמרכמ	*Mishmarkem* –Your prison (Gen. 42:19)
	משש	*Mashash* –To feel, grope
	פסך	*Pasak* –Pasach, descendant of Asher
	רמת	*Remeth* –Remeth, city of the tribe of Issachar
	רתמ	*Ratham* –To bind, attach
		Rethem –Juniper, juniper tree
	שליש	*Shaliysh* –Musical instrument; shield carrier, officer, captain
	שמש	*Shemash* –To minister, serve
		Shemesh, Shamesh –Sun (Sol)
	תמר	*Tamar* –Palm tree; Tamar, wife of Er, mother of Perez; daughter of David violated by Amnon; Tamar, place somewhere to the southwest of the Dead Sea; Tadmor, city known to the Greeks and Romans as Palmyra (this spelling used only in 1 Kings 9:18 – see also תדמר)[776]
		Tamer –Rebellious (Ex. 23:21)
		Timmor –Palm tree figure (Ezek. 40:16, 22, 26, 31, 34, 37; 41:18, 19, 20, 25, 26)
		Tomer –Post, column
641	אילמ	*Eylam* –Porch, vestibule, portico
		'Eylim –Elim, resting place of the Israelites after the crossing of the Reed Sea
	אממ	*'Amam* –Amam, village in southern Judah
	אמרת	*'amarat* –You said (Gen. 12:19)
	באחריתכ	*Be'achariyteka* –In your later end (Deut. 8:16)
	והכרתי	*ve-Hikratiy* –He will cut off, cut down (Lev. 17:10)
	ולשרקה	*ve-Lasreqah* –And unto the choice vine (Gen. 49:11)
	ונשרפה	*ve-Nisrefah* –And burn (Gen. 11:3)
	ושלשה	*ve-Shelshah* –And three (Ex. 25:32)
	חוות יאיר	*Chavvowth Ya'iyr* –Havoth Jair, area in the northwest part of Bashan, containing several unwalled cities
	ירתאל	*Yerathel* –Angel of 3q Sagittarius & day angel 9 Wands
	להורת	*Lehorot* –To show, teach (Gen. 46:28)
	מארת	*Me'orot* –Lights, luminaries (Gen. 1:14)
	מי יעלה ונל השמילה	*Mi Iolah Vinneh Heshemelah* –"Who will go up for us to

[775] Marat is one of the ten words in the Tanakh with a Dagesh in the letter Resh.

[776] תדמר (644).

heaven?" (Deut. 30:12) – It is important to notice the first letters of this phrase as well as the last letters (see introduction)

מראת *Mer'oth* –From seeing (Gen. 27:1)

ראמת *Ra'moth* –Ramoth, Levitical city of Gilead in Gad (see also Ramoth-Gilead)[777]

שנאצר *Shenatztzar* –Shenazar, son or grandson of Jeconiah

תאמר *To'mar* –Has said (Gen. 21:12); you should say (Gen. 14:23)

–Prime number

642 בכרתכ *Bekoratak* –Your birthright (Gen. 25:31)

ברכתכ *Birkateka* –Your blessing (Gen. 27:35)

בשעריכמ *Besha'areykem* –Within your gates (Deut. 12:12)

האחדות זוהר *HaAchdoth Zohar* –The Splendor of Unity, a title of *Chokmah* as the Second Path

ויכרתו *ve-Yikretuw* –And they cut (Gen. 21:27)

וירכתו *ve-Yarkato* –And his flank (Gen. 49:13)

כברכת *Kevirkat* –According to the blessing (Deut. 12:15)

לברית *Livriyt* –For a covenant (Gen. 17:7)

להראות *Lehar'ot* –To show (Deut. 3:24)

עפר בצר *'ofer Betzer* –"Gold dust" (Job 22:24)

פורשונ *Purson* –Goetic demon #20

תברככ *Tevarekak* –May bless you (Gen. 27:4)

–The number of children of Bani who returned from exile (Ezra 2:10)

643 אבלימ *Abalim* –One of two demon kings attendant upon Paimon[778]

Ebelim –Mournings, laments

אחשדרפנ *Achashdarpan* –Satrap, a governor of a Persian province

במראת *Bimar'ot* –In the visions (Gen. 46:2); in the mirrors (Ex. 38:8)

בראתמ *Bir'otam* –When they see (Ex. 13:17)

גלימ *Galliym* –Gallim, village near Gibeah of Saul, present-day Kirbet Kakul

וברכתיה *ve-Verketiyah* –And I will bless her (Gen. 17:16)

והרביתכ *ve-Hirbiytik* –And multiply you (Gen. 48:4)

וזכרתי *ve-Zakartiy* –And I will remember (Gen. 9:15)

ולבהרת *ve-Labeharet* –And to a bright spot (Lev. 14:56)

מבארת *Mib'erot* –From Beeroth (Deut. 10:6)

תזכירו *Tazkiyruw* –You shall mention (Ex. 23:13)

–Prime number

644 אגלימ *'Eglayim* –Eglaim, place in Moab

אדרא זוטא קדישא *Idra Zuta Qadisha* –Lesser Holy Assembly

אכזריות *Akzeriyuwth* –Cruelty, fierceness, cruel

דממ *Damam* –To be silent, be still, wait, be dumb, grow

[777] Ramoth-Gilead (747; 753).

[778] See Paimon (186, 836; 187, 837) and *Labal* (62).

dumb

דרמשק *Darmeseq* –Damascus, important Syrian trade center, also the captial of Syria (this spelling used in 1 Chr. 18:5, 6; 2 Chr. 16:2; 24:23; 28:5, 23 – see also דומשק, דמשק))[779]

חלומ *Chalowm* –Dream

חירמ מלכ־צור *Chiram Malakh-Tzor* –"Hiram, King of Tyre" (2 Sam. 5:11; 1 Kings 5:15; 9:11; 1 Chr. 14:1)

לחומ *Lachuwm* –Intestines, bowels (meaning uncertain – Job 20:23; Zeph. 1:17); food, something eaten

מרבבת *Merivevot* –From the myriads (Deut. 33:2)

תדמר *Tadmor* –Tadmor, city known to the Greeks and Romans as Palmyra (see also תמר)[780]

645 המם *Hamam* –To move noisily, confuse, make a noise, discomfit, break, consume, crush, destroy, trouble, to vex

השלשי *HaShelishiy* –The third (Ex. 19:11)

השמש *HaShamesh* –The sun (Num. 21:11)

HaShemesh –The sun (Gen. 15:12)

יהלמ *Yahalom* –Pearl, (precious stone in the High Priest's ephod – represents the tribe Judah – known for its hardness – perhaps jasper, onyx or diamond)

מהרת *Miharat* –You hastened (Gen. 27:20)

משרקה *Masreqah* –Masrekah, the city of King Samlah of Edom (Gen. 36:36; 1 Chr. 1:47)

מרתה *Maratah* –To Marah (Ex. 15:23)

רתמה *Rithmah* –Rithmah, fourteenth encampment of Israel in the wilderness

תרמה *Tormah* –Treachery, fraud, deceit

646 אהלימ *Ahaliym* –Aloes, aloe tree

אלהימ *Elohim* –Rulers, judges, divine ones, angels, gods, god, goddess; godlike one; works or special possessions of God, the God, God; Angelic Choir assoc. w/*Netzach* (this is not the usual enumeration, which is 86, with the final מ counted as 40)

בית ארבאל *Beyth 'Arbe'l* –Beth-Arbel, town destroyed by Shalman, modern Irbid

דבלימ *Diblayim* –Diblaim, father-in-law of Hosea

דברתמ *Dibartem* –You have spoken (Num. 14:28); you have said (Ex. 12:32)

האמרת *He'emarat* –You have avouched, set apart (Deut. 26:17)

המארת *HaMe'orot* –The lights (Gen. 1:16)

הראיתיכ *Her'iytiyak* –I have caused you to see it (Deut. 34:4)

והכריתה *ve-Hikriytah* –And destroy (Lev. 26:22)

---

[779] דמשק (444), דומשק (450).

[780] תמר (640).

	ותרמ	*ve-Taram* –And it was lifted up (Gen. 7:17)
	כור עשנ	*Kowr 'Ashan* –Chor-ashan or Chorashan, town in Judah given to Simeon (see also Ashan)[781]
	לוים	*Levim* –Levites; the priest tribe of Israel
	מום	*Mum* –Blemish; 72nd name of *Shem HaMeforash* (6 Cancer)
	מותר	*Mowthar* –Pre-eminence, abundance, profit, superiority
	מצלעתיו	*Mitzal'otayev* –Of his ribs (Gen. 2:21)
	מרות	*Marowth* –Maroth, town in the lowlands of Judah (see also Maarath – may be the same place)[782]
	משוש	*Masows* –Exultation, joy, rejoicing
	מתור	*Mituwr* –From spying (Num. 13:25)
	עבד מלך	*'Ebed Melek* –Ebed-Melech, Ethiopian eunuch who served Zedekiah and rescued Jeremiah
	רמות	*Ramuwth* –Heighty, lofty stature; a heap (of dead bodies), remains, corpses
	שלשיו	*Shalishayev* –His captains (Ex. 15:4)
647	ברתמה	*Beritmah* –In Rithmah (Num. 33:18)
	התנינמ הגדלימ	*HaTanninim HaGedholim* –"The great sea monsters" (Gen. 1:21)
	ואמרת	*ve-'amarat* –Then you shall say (Gen. 32:19)
	והותירכ	*ve-Hotiyrak* –And will make you over abundant (Deut. 30:9)
	ולהורת	*ve-Lehorot* –And that he may teach (Ex. 35:34)
	ותאמר	*ve-To'mer* –And she said (Gen. 3:2)
	זמם	*Zamam* –To have a thought, devise, plan, consider, purpose; wicked device, evil plan; to appoint a time, be fixed, be appointed *Zemam* –To agree together, appoint a time (Aramaic); a set time, appointed time, time; a set time, time, season (Aramaic)
	זמרת	*Zimrath* –Song of praise, song, music, melody
	להבים	*Lehabiym* –Lehabim, descendant of Mizraim (possibly a reference to a tribe of Egyptians)
	מאום	*M'uwm* –Blemish, spot, defect
	מראתו	*Mer'ato* –Its crop (Lev. 25:3)
	ראמות	*Ra'mowth* –Ramoth, city of Levi in Issachar (see also Jarmuth and Remeth)[783]
	תאמרו	*To'meruw* –You shall say (Gen. 34:11; 50:17)
	תזמר	*Tizmor* –You shall prune (Lev. 25:3)
	–Prime number	
648	אלהימ יראהלו השה	*Elohim Yerehlo Hasheh* –"God will see to the sheep..." (Gen. 22:7, 8)
	חייכם	*Chayaychem* –it is your very life (Deut. 32:47)
	חילם	*Cheylam* –Helam, descendant of Asher; man of whom

781 Ashan (420, 1070).
782 Maarath (710).
783 Jarmuth (656), Remeth (640).

the prophet Zechariah speaks (Zech. 6:14) – may be another name for the second Heldai (see also חלאם)[784]

חמם *Chamam* –To be hot, become hot
כבכרתו *Kivkorato* –His birthright (Gen. 43:33)
כברכתו *Kivirchatuw* –According to his blessing (Gen. 49:28)
מחרת *Mochorath* –The morrow, the day after
מתרח *Mitarach* –From Terah (Num. 33:28)
תגרמה *Togarmah* –Togarmah, son of Gomer (this spelling used only in 1 Chr. 1:6 – see also תוגרמה)[785]; country that supplied horses and mules to the Tyrians and soldiers to the army of Gog

649 אדמדם *Adamdam* –Reddish, be reddish
ולהרבות *ve-Leharbuwt* –And to multiply (Deut. 28:63)
ומגרת *ve-Migarat* –And of her that sojourned (Ex. 3:22)
ותפקחנה *ve-Tifaqachnah* –And were opened (Gen. 3:7)
תרגום *Targum* –Translation; Aramaic Bible
תרדמה *Tardemah* –Deep sleep, trance (Gen. 2:21)

650 דומם *Duwmam* –Silence, dumb
טלאים *Tela'iym* –Telaim, place where Saul gathered and numbered his forces before the attack on Amalek
ימשש *Yemashesh* –Gropes (Deut. 28:29)
כלם *Kalam* –To insult, shame, humiliate, blush, be ashamed, be put to shame, be reproached, be put to confusion, be humiliated
לדרתיו *Ledorotayev* –Throughout his generations (Lev. 25:30)
לחברתי *Lechaburatiy* –For bruising me (Gen. 4:23)
לטהרתו *Letaharato* –For his cleansing (Lev. 13:7)
לכרת *Likrot* –To make (Deut. 28:69); to cut down (Deut. 19:5)
למקמתמ *Limqomotam* –After their places (Gen. 36:40)
לשעירמ *Las'iyrim* –Demons (Lev. 17:7)
מים *Mem* or *Mayim* –Water, waters; 13th letter of Hebrew alphabet
מיתר *Meythar* –Cord, string
Miyeter –From the remnant (Deut. 3:11)
מחברת *Machbereth* –Thing joined, joint, seam, place of joining
מרדות *Marduwth* –Rebellion, rebelliousness
נרת *Nerot* –Lamps (Ex. 39:37)
נתר *Nathar* –To start up, tremble, shake, spring up; to loose, let loose, undo, be free, be loose
Nether –To strip off (Aramaic); natron, nitre, soda, carbonate of soda
פרעש *Par'osh* –Flea; Parosh, one whose descendants returned from the Exile; another whose family returned

---

[784] חלאם (79, 639).

[785] תוגרמה (654).

		from the Exile; one whose descendants had taken foreign wives during the Exile; one who sealed the covenant; father of one who helped repair the wall of Jerusalem[786]
	קרשימ	*Qerashiym* –Boards (Ex. 26:22)
	רמתי	*Ramathiy* –Ramathite
	שלישי	*Shelishiy* –Third, one third, third part, third time
	שמשי	*Shimshay* –Shimshai, scribe who, with Rehum, wrote to the king of Persia opposing the rebuilding of the wall of Jerusalem
	ששימ	*Shishshim* –Sixty, threescore
	ששנ	*Sasown* –Gladness, joy, exultation, rejoicing
		Sheshan –Sheshan, descendant of Judah through Jerahmeel
	תמרדו	*Timroduw* –Rebel (Num. 14:9)
	תרימ	*Toroym* –Turtle-doves (Lev. 5:7)
	תרנ	*Toren* –Beacon, mast, flagpole (Ezek. 27:5, Isa. 30:17, 33:23)
651	איתמר	*'iytamar* –Ithamar, a son of Aaron (Ex. 6:23; 28:1; 1Chr. 24:6)
	אמרתי	*'amartiy* –I said (Gen. 31:31)
		'imratiy –My speech (Gen. 4:23)
	אונם	*'Ownam* –Onam, grandson of Seir; son of Jerahmeel
	ארמית	*'Aramiyth* –Syrian language (2 Kings 18:26; Ezra 4:7; Isa. 36:11; Dan. 2:4)
	אתרימ	*'Athariym* –Spies (Num. 21:1)
	הומם	*Howmam* –Homam or Hemam, Horite descendant of Esau
	והרמת	*ve-Haremot* –And levy, you shall lift (Num. 31:28)
	ותמהר	*ve-Temaher* –And she hastened (Gen. 24:18)
	יראתמ	*Yere'tem* –You were afraid (Num. 12:8)
	מחגרת	*Machagoreth* –Wrapping, girding, sash, cincture
	נאם	*Na'am* –To prophesy, utter a prophesy, speak as a prophet, say
		Ne'um –Utterance, declaration (of prophet)
	ראיתמ	*Re'iytem* –You have seen (Gen. 45:13)
	שטוליש	*Stolas* –Goetic demon #36
	תיראמ	*Tiyra'em* –Fear them (Num. 14:9)
	תמורה	*Temurah* –That which is exchanged, exchange, substitute; permutation; Hebrew cryptology
	תרומה	*Teruwmah* –Contribution, offering, gift offering
652	בטמאם	*Bitama'am* –Through their uncleanness (Lev. 15:31)
	במחברת	*Bamachbaret* –In the joining (Ex. 36:11)
		Bamachberet –In the set, joining (Ex. 26:4)
	במים	*Bimayem* –"In [the] waters" (Ex. 12:9, 15:10, 20:4)
	ואלהים	*ve-Elohim* –And God

[786] All of these persons may be the same.

	ודברתמ	*ve-Dibartem* –And you speak (Num. 20:8)
	ותמרו	*ve-Tamruw* –And you rebelled (Deut. 1:26)
	מרבית	*Marbiyth* –Increase, great number, multitude, greatness
	מריבת	*Meriyvat* –Meribah, desert location where Moses smote the rock; another name for Kadesh Barnea in the wilderness of Zin, where the Israelites rebelled against Moses (Num. 27:14)
	–The number of children of Pelaiah, Tobiah, and Nekuda who returned from exile (Ezra 2:60)	
653	אנכי יהוה אלהיך	*Anoki YHVH Eloheka* – "I am the Lord thy God"
	ארנבת	*'arnebet* –Hare (exact meaning unknown – Deut. 14:7; Lev. 11:6)
	המחרת	*HaMacharat* –The next (Lev. 11:32)
	חמת דאר	*Chammoth Do'r* –Hammoth dor, city on Naphtali allocated to the Levites – see also Hammon and Hammath[787]
	וזמרת	*ve-Zomerat* –And song; and might (Ex. 15:2)
	ותאמרו	*ve-To'meruw* –And you said (Deut. 1:14)
	תגרנ	*Tageran* –Haggler
	–Prime number	
654	בוא השמש	*Bo hash-Shamesh* –"Going down of the sun"; sunset (Josh. 10:27)
	במריבת	*Bimeriyvat* –In the strife of (Num. 27:14)
	בת רבימ	*Bath Rabbiym* –Bath Rabbim, a gate of Heshbon (Song 7:5)
	ותגרמה	*ve-Togarmah* –And Togarmah (Gen. 10:3)
	זלברהית	*Zalbarhith* –Lord of Triplicity by Night for Leo
	זמזם	*Zamzom* –Zamzummim, Ammonite name for the people called Rephaim (giants) by the Jews during the conquest of Canaan (Deut. 2:20)
	מדים	*Madim* –Mars
	נדרת	*Nadarat* –You vow (Gen. 31:13)
	תוגרמה	*Towgarmah* –Togarmah, son of Gomer (this spelling used only in Gen. 10:3 – see also תגרמה)[788]
655	אדמים	*'Adummiym* –Adummim, a place in Palestine
	אשר אינ בה מומ	*Asher Ain Bah Muwm* –"In which there is no defect" (Num. 19:2)
	היכל עצמ שמימ	*Hekel Etzem Shamaim* –Palace of the Body of Heaven, Heavenly Mansion corr. to *Netzach* (see Ex. 24:10)
	הימם	*Heymam* –Hemam, son of Lotan and the grandson of Seir
	המים	*HaMayim* –The water
	הנם	*Hinnom* –Hinnom, unknown person who had a son after whom a valley near Jerusalem was named – human sacrifices took place there in Jeremiah's

[787] Hammon (104, 754), Hammath (448).

[788] תגרמה (648).

day, and garbage was later incinerated in this defiled place (Josh. 15:8; 18:16; Neh. 11:30; Jer. 7:31-32)

הנרת *HaNerot* –The lamps (Ex. 30:7)

הקדוש ברוכ הוא *HaQadosh Barukh Hu* –"The Holy One, blessed be He"

הקרשים *HaQerashiym* –The boards (Ex. 26:15)

הרמתי *HaRimotiy* –I have lifted up (Gen. 14:22)

השלישי *HaSheliyshiy* –The third (Gen. 2:14)

התרים *HaTariym* –The spies (Num. 14:6)
HaToriym –The turtle-doves (Lev. 1:14)

ותרדמה *ve-Tardemah* –And a deep sleep (Gen. 15:12)

חמת רבה *Chamath Rabbah* –Hamath Rabah, Hamath the great (Amos 6:2)

נהם *Naham* –To growl, groan; growling, roaring

תימרה *Tiymarah* –Pillar, column

656 האתרים *Ha'atariym* –The Atharim (meaning uncertain – see Num. 21:1)

הראיתם *HaR'item* –I have seen (1 Sam. 10:24, 17:25; 2 Kings 6:32; 20:15)[789]

התרומה *HaTeruwmah* –The offering, the gift offering (Ex. 25:3)

וימשש *ve-Yemashesh* –And he felt (Gen. 31:34)

ויתרם *ve-Yitram* –And what they leave (Ex. 23:11)

ומיתר *ve-Miyeter* –And from the remainder (Lev. 14:17)

יומם *Yowmam* –By day, in the daytime; daytime

ירמות *Yeremowth* –Jeremoth, son of Becher, of the tribe of Benjamin (1 Chr. 7:8); son of Beriah (1 Chr. 8:14); three who married foreign wives (Ezra 10:26-27, 29); son of Mushi, descendant of Levi (1 Chr. 23:23) – his name is spelled differently in 1 Chr. 24:30; one appointed by David to the song service of the temple (1 Chr. 25:22) – his name is spelled differently in 1 Chr. 25:4; Jarmuth, city in the lowlands of Judah – modern Khirbet Yarmuk; city of the tribe of Issachar assigned to the Levites[790]

וששים *ve-Shishiym* –And sixty (Gen. 5:15)

מחברתו *Machbarto* –Its coupling (Ex. 28:27)

ממעשרו *Mima'asro* –Of his tithe (Lev. 27:31)

מרחבות *Merechovot* –Of Rehoboth (Gen. 36:37)

מריות *Merayowth* –Meraioth, descendant of Aaron and ancestor of Azariah; another priest of the same line; a priest at the end of the Exile – may be the same as Meremoth

משרוקי *Mashrowqiy* –Pipe

נום *Nuwm* –To be drowsy, slumber, sleep

נותר *Noter* –Remained (Ex. 10:15)

עקלתון *'aqallathown* –Crooked

---

789 HaR'item is one of the ten words in the Tanakh with a Dagesh in the letter Resh.

790 The latter is probably the same as the third Ramoth

	שושנ	*Shuwshan* –Lily; Shushan, capital of Elam inhabited by the Babylonians – later a royal residence and capital of the Persian Empire
	תנור	*Tannuwr* –Furnace, oven (Gen. 15:17; Lev. 11:35); furnace of God's wrath
	תרימו	*Tariymuw* –You shall set apart (Num. 15:19)
657	בית הרמ	*Beyth HaRam* –Beth Aram, town of the tribe of Gad, noted for its hot springs
	גדרתימ	*Gederothayim* –Gederothaim, town of Judah, perhaps the same as Gederoth
	ואיתמר	*ve-'iytamar* –And Ithamar (Ex. 28:1)
	ואמרתי	*ve-'amartiy* –And I shall say (Gen. 24:43)
	והוריתיכ	*ve-Horeytiyak* –And I will teach you (Ex. 4:12)
	וכגבורתכ	*ve-Kigvuwrotek* –And according to your might (Deut. 3:24)
	וראיתמ	*ve-Re'iytem* –And you shall look, see (Ex. 16:7)
	ותרודיאל	*Uthrodiel* –Angel of 3d Scorpio
	ותרומה	*ve-Teruwmah* –And a gift offering (Ex. 29:28)
	נזמ	*Nezem* –Ring, nose ring, earring
	תיראומ	*Tiyra'uwm* –You shall fear (Deut. 3:22)
	תראנו	*Tir'enuw* –You may see them (Num. 23:13)
658	בתנור	*Batanuwr* –In oven (Lev. 7:9) *Betanuwr* –In oven (Lev. 26:26)
	בתרונ	*Bithrown* –Bithron, gorge in the Aravah east of the Jordan River
	הארנבת	*Ha'Arnevet* –The hare (Lev. 11:6)
	וברכתיכ	*ve-Varaktik* –And I [YHVH] will bless you (Gen. 26:24)
	והזרתמ	*ve-Hizartem* –Thus you shall separate (Lev. 15:31)
	ורביתמ	*ve-Reviytem* –And multiply (Deut. 8:1)
	חנמ	*Chinnam* –Freely, for nothing, without cause
	נחמ	*Nacham* –To be sorry, console oneself, repent, regret, comfort, be comforted; Naham, descendant of Judah, a chieftain *Nocham* –Repentance, sorrow
	על־פי יהוה יחנו ועל־פי יהוה יסעו	*al-Pi* YHVH *Yachanuw Vial-Pi* YHVH *Yisauw* –"On a sign from the Lord they made camp and on a sign from the Lord they broke camp" (Num. 9:23)
	תחרימ	*Tachariym* –You shall destroy (Deut. 7:2)
	תרבונ	*Tirbuwn* –May increase (Deut. 6:3)
659	אחריתמ	*'achriytam* –Their end (Deut. 32:20)
	אנחרת	*'Anacharath* –Anaharath, town of the tribe of Issachar
	ותחמרה	*ve-Tachmerah* –And daubed it (Ex. 2:3)
	טירתמ	*Tiyrotam* –Their encampments (Num. 31:10)
	–Prime number	
660	הנהרת	*HaNeharot* –The rivers (Ex. 8:1)

	ובמרבית	*ve-Vemarbiyt* –And for increase (Lev. 25:37)
	וטהרתמ	*ve-Tehartem* –And you shall be clean (Num. 31:24)
	ימים	*Yamiym* –Right, right hand, right side
	יתרנ	*Yithran* –Ithran, descendant of Seir; son of Zophah of Asher
	לשלש	*Lishelesh* –For three (Lev. 25:21)
	מצנפת	*Mitsnefeth* –Turban (of the High Priest – see Ex. 28:4)
	סם	*Sam* –Spice; drug; poison; as a spice, part of the holy incense
	סתר	*Sathar* –To hide, conceal
		Sethar –To hide, remove from sight; destroy (all Aramaic)
		Sether –Covering, shelter, hiding place, secrecy; shelter, protection
	צעקת	*Tza'aqat* –Cry (Ex. 3:9)
	רמנ פרצ	*Rimmon Peretz* –Rimmon-Parez, fifteenth encampment of the Israelites (Num. 33:19)
	תמכר	*Timaker* –Shall be sold (Lev. 25:23)
	תצעק	*Titz'aq* –You cry (Ex. 14:15)
	תרינ	*Tereyn* –Two (Aramaic)
661	אימים	*'Eymiym* –Emims, early Canaanite tribe
	אמרתכ	*'imrateka* –Your word (Deut. 33:11)
	אסם	*'asam* –Storehouse, barn
	אסתר	*Esater* –Shall I be hid (Gen. 4:14)
		Esther –Esther (see also Hadassah)[791]
	הנותר	*HaNotar* –The remainder (Ex. 29:34)
	הנרות	*HaNerot* –The lamps (Lev. 24:4)
	והורדתמ	*ve-Horadtem* –And you will bring down (Gen. 42:38)
	והנתר	*ve-Hanitar* –And that which remains (Ex. 12:10)
	והקשרימ	*ve-Haqshuriym* –And the stronger (Gen. 30:42)
	ועצמתיהמ	*ve-'atzmoteyhem* –And their bones (Num. 24:8)
	ישטולוש	*Stolas* –Goetic demon #36 (A.C., 777, probably a misprint)
	כלאים	*Kil'ayim* –Two kinds, mixture
	תרגבונ	*Thergebon* –Lord of Triplicity by Day for Libra
	תרומיה	*Teruwmiyah* –Portion, contribution
662	בנים	*Benayim* –Between, space between two armies
	בסתר	*Basater* –In secret (Deut. 27:15)
		Baseter –In secrecy (Deut. 13:7)
	הנוראת	*HaNora'ot* –The tremendous, terrible (Deut. 10:21)
	ונראתה	*ve-Nir'atah* –And shall be seen (Gen. 9:14)
	מברכת	*Mevoreket* –Blessed (Deut. 33:13)
	מרבכת	*Murbeket* –Scalded (Lev. 6:14)
	מרכבת	*Mirkevot* –Chariots (Ex. 15:4)
	תדברונ	*Tedabruwn* –Shall you speak (Gen. 32:20)

[791] Hadassah (74).

663	תסגר	*Tisager* –Let her be shut up (Num. 12:14)
664	במרכבת	*Bemirkevet* –In the chariot (Gen. 41:43)
	ורחמתי	*ve-Richamtiy* –And I will show mercy (Ex. 33:19)
	מחוים	*Machaviym* –Mahavite
	נחום	*Nachum* –Nahum, one of the later prophets; Nehum, chief man that returned from Exile with Zerubbabel (this spelling used only in Neh. 7:7 – see also Rehum) *Nichuwm* –Comfort, compassion
	סדם	*Sodom* –Sodom, one of the five cities of the plain, destroyed because its wickedness
	תהרגנו	*Tahargenuw* –You shall kill (Deut. 13:10)
	תרחנה	*Tirchanah* –Tirhanah, descendant of Hezron
665	המצנפת	*HaMitznafet* –The mitre (Ex. 28:37) *HaMitznefet* –The mitre (Ex. 28:37)
	הסתר	*Haster* –Hide (Deut. 31:18)
	הרימתי	*Hariymitiy* –I lifted up (Gen. 39:15)
	ותרגנו	*ve-Teragnuw* –And you murmured (Deut. 1:27)
	כי יהוה אלהיכ הואהלכ עמכ לאירפכ	*Ki* YHVH *Eloheka Huaholayk Aymak Layarpik* –"Your God [YHVH] Himself marches with you: He will not fail you or forsake you" (Deut. 31:6)
	כמהם	*Kimham* –Chimham, friend and political supporter of David
	להכרית	*Lehakriyt* –To destroy (Ex. 8:5)
	להצילך	*Lihatzelik* –To rescue you
	לשלשה	*Lishleshah* –Of three (Num. 29:14)
	נרתיה	*Neroteyha* –Its lamps (Ex. 25:37)
	סתרה	*Sitrah* –Protection (Deut. 32:38)
	תהרס	*Taharos* –You overthrow (Ex. 15:7)
666	אלהיכם	*Elohikam* –Your God
	ארנ הקדוש	*Aron HaQodesh*–Holy Ark (of the covenant)
	הנזופ לפתח	*HaNozuf Lapetach* –"The hated one at the door"
	התרומיה	*HaTeruwmiyah* –The portion, the contribution
	וישבר החנפה	*ve-Yeshaber HaChanufah* –"And he broke the profaneness"
	ויתרנ	*ve-Yitran* –And Ithran (Gen. 36:26; 1 Chr. 1:41; 7:37)
	ותסר	*ve-Tasar* –And she put off (Gen. 38:14, 19; Hos. 2:4)
	יוחננ פול וסשני	*Yown Puwl Vesshani* –John Paul II, pope currently at the writing of this book[792]
	ירימות	*Yeriymowth* –Jeremoth, son of Bela (1 Chr. 7:7); one who joined David at Ziklag (1 Chr. 12:5); ruler of the tribe of Naphtali (1 Chr. 27:19); son of David (2 Chr. 11:18); Levite overseer in the temple during the reign of King Hezekiah of

[792] Numerous popes' names were used throughout history to "prove" the evil nature of the Catholic Church

Judah (2 Chr. 31:13); son of Mushi, descendant of Levi (1 Chr. 24:30) – his name is spelled differently in 1 Chr. 23:23; one appointed by David to the song service of the Temple (1 Chr. 25:4) – his name is spelled differently in 1 Chr. 25:22

יתרונ *Yithrown* –Advantage, profit, excellency

מיתריו *Meytarayev* –Its cords (Ex. 39:40; Num. 3:26)

נשימירון *Nashimiron* –Malignant Women, *Qlippoth* of Pisces

סתרו *Sithro* –His secret place (Ps. 18:12), his covering

סורת *Sorath* –Spirit of the Sun

סתור *Sethuwr* –Sethur, one sent to spy out the land (Num. 13:13)

צדכוסינו *Tzedkosaynuw* –Our righteousness

צעקתו *Tza'aqato* –Their cry (Ex. 22:22; 1 Sam. 9:16)

קסר נרונ *Kesar Neron* –Nero Caeser

שמ יהשוה *Shem Yehoshuah* –The name Yehoshuah (i.e., Jesus)

תאכלו הצדיק *Ti'keluw HaTzadiyq* –"You shall eat the righteous"

תמכרו *Timkeruw* –You shall sell (Lev. 25:14; Neh. 5:8)

תסור *Tasuwr* –You shall turn aside (Deut. 17:11; 28:14; Josh. 1:7; 1 Sam. 6:3; 2 Sam. 12:10; Prov. 27:22)

תסרו *Tasuruw* –You shall turn aside (Deut. 5:29)

DICLVX *Diclux* –"Double-dealer" – Same as *Teitan* (Latin) (see below)

teitan *Teitan* –Teitan, Roman Emperor (Greek)[793]

–The number of the Beast of the Revelation (Rev. 13:18)
–The number of talents of gold that Solomon received in one year (I Kings 10:14; 2 Chr. 9:13)
–The number of children of Adonikam who returned from exile (Ezra 2:13)
–The sum of all the numbers (1 to 36) on the magic square of Sol

667 בית הרנ *Beyth HaRan* –Beth Haran, another name for Beth Aram, town of the tribe of Gad, noted for its hot springs

ובטירתמ *ve-Vetiyrotam* –And by their encampments (Gen. 25:16)

והנותר *ve-HaNotar* –And the remainder (Lev. 7:16)

וראיתנ *ve-R'iyten* –And you shall see (Ex. 1:16)

ותיראנ *ve-Tiyre'an* –But they feared (Ex. 1:17)

ותראני *ve-Tira'niy* –And saw me (Num. 22:33)

זנים *Zonim* –To go astray

מזכרת *Mazkeret* –Memory of (Num. 5:15)

תיראונ *Tiyr'uwn* –You will fear (Ex. 9:30); be afraid (Deut. 1:29)

668 בונים *Bonim* –Builders

גי הנם *Ge-Hinnom* –Gehenna; hell; specifically, the 1st Hell, corr. to *Yesod* and *Malkut*

דדנים *Dedaniym* –Dodanim, son of Javan (Gen. 10:4) – 1 Chr.

---

793 T=300; E=5; I=10; T=300: A=l; N=50 (This interpretation of the Beast of Revelation was favored by Victorinus, probably of Greek extraction, was first a rhetorician by profession, and became bishop of Petavium, or Petabio, in ancient Panonia (Petau, in the present Austrian Styria). He died a martyr in the Diocletian persecution (303).

1:7 has his name as Rodanim, and many scholars consider the latter to be his original name – it may also be a reference to the inhabitants of Rhodes and the neighboring islands

ובמצנפת *ve-Vemitznefet* –And with the mitre (Lev. 16:4)

וברכתמ *ve-Veraktem* –And you will bless (Ex. 12:32)

חסם *Chasam* –To stop up, muzzle

חסרת *Chasarat* –You have lacked (Deut. 2:7)

מבכרות *Mibkorot* –Of the firstlings (Gen. 4:4)

מרכבתו *Merkavto* –His chariot (Gen. 46:29)

סחרת *Sochereth* –A stone used in paving (w/marble)

תחסר *Techsar* –You shall lack (Deut. 8:9)

תסרח *Tisrach* –Shall hang (Ex. 26:12)

תריבונ *Teriyvuwn* –Do you quarrel (Ex. 17:2)

669 אחרנית *Achoraniyt* –Backwards, back part, the rear

והחרמתי *ve-Hacharamtiy* –And I will devote (Num. 21:2)

ותסגר *ve-Tisager* –And was shut up (Num. 12:15)

670 ינים *Yaniym* –Janum, town in the mountains of Judah, west-southwest of Hebron

כנרת *Kinnerowth* –Chinnereth, early name for the Sea of Galilee (see also כנרות)[794]; fortified city of Naphtali on the north shore of the Sea of Galilee; region of Naphtali surrounding the city of Chinnereth (see also כנרות)

לתמר *Letamar* –To Tamar (Gen. 38:11)

מכרתי *Mekerathiy* –Mecherathite

משלש *Meshulash* –Three years old (Gen. 15:9)

סתרי *Sithry* –Sithri, descendant of Levi through Kohath (Ex. 6:22)

עם *'am* –Nation, people, populace; kinsman, kindred; people (Aramaic)

'im –With, against, toward, as long as, beside, except, in spite of; with (Aramaic)

ערת *'orot* –Skins (Gen. 27:16)

עשרנימ *'esroniym* –Tenth parts (Lev. 14:10)

עשש *'ashesh* –To waste away, fail

עתר *'athar* –To pray, entreat, supplicate; to be abundant; supplicant, worshipper; odor, incense

'Ether –Ether, village of the tribe of Judah; village of the tribe of Simeon (see also Tochen)[795]

רעת *Ra'at* –Wickedness (Gen. 6:5)

שלשמ *Shilshown* –Day before yesterday, three days ago; idiom for "in times past"

תירס *Tiyras* –Tiras, youngest son of Japheth

תער *Ta'ar* –Razor, sheath

[794] כנרות (676).

[795] Tochen (470, 1120).

	תקפצ	*Tiqfotz* –You shall shut (Deut. 15:7)
	תקצפ	*Tiqtzof* –Will you be angry (Num. 16:22)
	תרע	*Tera'* –Gate, door (Aramaic); shall be evil (Deut. 28:54)
		Tara' –Porter, doorkeeper
	–The number of mysteries mentioned in the *Sefer HaZohar*	
671	אסתיר	*'astiyr* –I will hide (Deut. 31:18)
	ותהרינ	*ve-Tahareyn* –Became pregnant (Gen. 19:36)
	לפקערציאצ	*Lafcursiax* –Guardian of the 22nd Tunnel of Set
	לראתמ	*Lir'otam* –To see them (Ex. 14:13)
	תארע	*Ta'area'* –Tarea, son of Micah, descendant of Saul (see also Tahrea)[796]
	תרעא	*Throa* –Gate; a title of *Malkut*
672	אינ אינ סיפ אינ סופ אור	*Ain Ain Sof Ain Sof Aur* –Nought without limit light without limit
	ארונ הקדוש	*Arown HaQodesh* –The Ark of the Covenant, holy ark
	בית פצצ	*Beyth Patztzetz* –Beth Pazzez, town of the tribe Issachar, modern Kerm el-Had-datheh
	בטמאכמ	*Bitamakem* –Defile it
	בירנית	*Biyraniyth* –Fortress, fortified place
	בצרת	*Batstsoreth* –Dearth, drought, destitution
	והארכתמ	*ve-Ha'araktem* –And you may prolong (Deut. 5:30)
	ולאדם לא	*Uladam La* –"But for the man there was not" (Gen. 2:20)
	יהוה אלהים	YHVH *Elohim* –The Lord God; divine name assoc. w/*Binah*
	נדחימ	*Nedachiym* –Driven away (Deut. 22:1)
	ערבת	*'arvot* –Plains of (Num. 31:12)
	קופ בית למד	*Quwp Biyth Lamed* –"To receive illumination," written in full (notariqon of קבל)
	תבער	*Tiva'er* –You shall put away (Deut. 21:9)
	תוסרו	*Tivasruw* –You will be corrected (Lev. 26:23)
	תעבר	*Ta'avor* –You shall pass, go over (Gen. 18:3); there comes (Num. 5:30)
673	ארבעת	*'arba'at* –Four (Num. 7:7)
	וזכרתמ	*ve-Zekartem* –And remember (Num. 15:39)
	עגמ	*'agam* –To be grieved
	תגרע	*Tigra'* –You shall diminish (Deut. 13:1)
	תסגיר	*Tasgiyr* –You shall deliver (Deut. 23:16)
	–Prime number	
674	בערבת	*Be'arvot* –In the plains of (Num. 25:3)
	גיהנומ	*Ge-Hinnom* –Gehenna, Hell; the First Hell (corr. to *Yesod* & *Malkut*)
	דרתיכמ	*Doroteykem* –Your generations (Lev. 23:43)
	חרסות	*Charsuwth* –Potsherd
	לדרתמ	*Ledorotam* –Throughout their generations (Gen. 17:7)

[796] Tahrea (678).

	תסחרו	*Tischaruw* –You shall trade (Gen. 42:34)
675	בין האור ובין החשכ	*Bayn HaOhr Vuvayn HaChushek* –"divided the light and divided the darkness" (Gen. 1:4)
	הסירת	*HaSiyrot* –The pots (Ex. 38:3)
	העם	*HaAwm* –The people
	הקצפת	*Hiqtzafat* –Did make angry, provoke (Deut. 9:7)
	הרעת	*Hare'oat* –Afflicted, dealt ill (Num. 11:11)
	נכרתה	*Nikretah* –Let us cut (make) (Gen. 31:44)
676	אסתירה	*'astiyrah* –I will hide (Deut. 32:20)
	ויסתר	*ve-Yaster* –And he hid (Ex. 3:6)
	ולירכתי	*ve-Leyarketey* –And for the hinder part (Ex. 26:22)
	ולשמש	*ve-Lashemesh* –And to the sun (Deut. 17:3)
	ונכרת	*ve-Nikrat* –Shall be cut off (Ex. 30:33)
	וסתרי	*ve-Sitriy* –And Sithri (Ex. 6:22)
	וערת	*ve-'orot* –And skins (Ex. 25:5)
	ושלשמ	*ve-Shalishim* –And captains of the hosts (Ex. 14:7)
	ותער	*ve-Te'ar* –And she emptied (Gen. 24:20)
	ותירס	*ve-Tiyras* –And Tiras (Gen. 10:2)
	כנרות	*Kinnerowth* –Chinnereth, early name for the Sea of Galilee (see also כנרת); region of Naphtali surrounding the city of Chinnereth (see also כנרת)[797]
	מדברתיכ	*Midabroteyak* –Your words (Deut. 33:3)
	מתנוצצ	*Mit-Notzetz* –Resplendent
	עורת	*'averet* –Blindness (Lev. 22:22) *'avorot* –Skins (Ex. 39:34)
	ערות	*'ervat* –Nakedness (Gen. 9:22)
	עתור	*Athor* –Lord of Triplicity by Day for Aquarius
	רעות	*Ra'ot* –Evils, ills *Re'uwth* –Female companion, mate; longing, striving *Reuwth* –Good pleasure, will (Aramaic)
	רעתו	*Ra'ato* –His harm (Num. 34:23)
	שושע	*Shavsha* –Royal scribe or secretary for King David
	שלשומ	*Shilshom* –Before yesterday (Gen. 31:2)
	תרעו	*Tare'uw* –Be wicked (Gen. 19:7)
677	בית הכרמ	*Beyth HaKerem* –Beth Haccerem, town of Judah that maintained a beacon station, probably present-day Ain Karim
	גדעמ	*Gid'om* –Gidom, village of the tribe of Benjamin
	והאלהימ נסהאת אברהמ	*ve-HaElohim Nisahath Abraham* –"And God tested Abraham" (Gen. 22:1)
	זעם	*Za'am* –To denounce, express indignation, be indignant; anger
	זרעת	*Zero'ot* –Mighty, arms (Deut. 33:27)
	למאורת	*Lim'orot* –For lights (Gen. 1:15)

[797] כנרת (670).

תערבה *Taharubah* –Pledge, surety, hostage

תבערה *Tav'erah* –Taberah, place three days north of Mount Sinai where Israel was punished for murmuring against God

תזרע *Tizara'* –That is sown (Deut. 29:22)

Tizra' –You have sown (Deut. 22:9); you shall sow (Gen. 23:10; Lev. 19:19)

–Prime number

678 אדם בליאל *Adam Belial* –Archdemon corr. to *Chokmah* (Waite)

ברעתו *Bir'oto* –As he fed (Gen. 36:24)

ובערת *ve-Bi'arat* –And you shall put away (Deut. 13:6); and you shall exterminate (Deut. 17:12)

ותבער *ve-Tiv'ar* –And burned (Num. 11:1)

ותעבר *ve-Ta'avor* –And passed over (Gen. 32:22)

ותרעב *ve-Tir'av* –And was famished (Gen. 41:55)

חעם *Cham* –38th name of *Shem HaMeforash* (2 Aquarius)

לחמם *Lachmam* –Lahmam, a city located in the lowlands of Judah (see also לחמס)[798]

מרכבתיו *Markvotayv* –Of their chariots (Ex. 14:25)

ערבות *Arabhoth* –Plains; the 7th Heaven, corr. to the 3 Supernals

תבערו *Teva'aruw* –You shall kindle (Ex. 35:3)

תברכנו *Tevarakenuw* –Bless them (Num. 23:25)

תחרע *Tachrea'* –Tahrea, son of Micah, descendant of Saul

תעברו *Ta'avoruw* –You shall pass on, shall go (Gen. 18:5)

Ta'avruw –You shall pass over (Deut. 3:18)

679 טעם *Ta'am* –To taste, perceive, eat; taste, judgment; taste, judgment, command (Aramaic)

Te'am –To feed, cause to eat (Aramaic)

Te'em –Decree, taste, judgment, command (Aramaic)

עטרת *'atarot* –Ataroth, town east of the Jordan River rebuilt by the tribe of Gad (this spelling used only in Num. 32:34 – see also עטרות)[799]

תגרעו *Tigr'uw* –Shall diminish (Ex. 5:8)

680 בית בעל מעון *Beyth Ba'al Me'own* –Baal's dwelling place; Beth Baal Meon, Amorite city on the north border of Moab (this name only used in Josh. 13:17)

בערבות *Be'arvot* –In (the) plains (Num. 22:1)

הרעתה *Hare'otah* –You have dealt ill (Ex. 5:22)

כנים *Kinnim* –Vermin

כסם *Kasam* –To cut, clip, trim, shear

לנתר *Lenater* –To leap (Lev. 11:21)

לשׁשׁן *Lishshan* –Tongue, language (Aramaic)

ממשש *Mimashesh* –Grope (Deut. 28:29)

---

[798] לחמס (138).

[799] עטרות (685).

	עים	*'ayam* –Glow, heat (meaning dubious – Isa. 11:5)
	פם	*Pum* –Mouth (Aramaic)
	פרת	*Parot* –Cows (Gen. 41:26)
		Perath –Prath or Euphrates, a river of Eden (assoc. w/Earth)
		Porat –Fruitful (Gen. 49:22)
	פתר	*Patar* –He had interpreted (Gen. 40:16; 41:13)
	צנצנת	*Tzintzenet* –Jar, pot, receptacle
	רממת	*Romemut* –Uplifting, arising, lifting up of self
	רפת	*Refeth* –Stable, stall
	שלשימ	*Shelshim* –Thirty, thirtieth
	שעשגז	*Sha'ashgaz* –Shaashgaz, chamberlain of Ahasuerus
	תפר	*Tafar* –To sew together (Ezek. 13:18)
681	אמרתמ	*'amartem* –You spoke (Gen. 43:27)
	אני אעביר כל־טובי על־פניכ	*'Ani 'A'aviyr Kal-Toviy 'Al-Paneyka* –"I will make all My goodness pass before you" (Ex. 22:19)
	אעתיר	*'a'tiyr* –Shall I entreat (Ex. 8:5)
	אפרת	*'efrat* –Ephrath, another name for Bethlehem; second wife of Caleb
	ארעית	*'ar'iyth* –Bottom (Aramaic)
	הריסות	*Hariysuwth* –Destruction, ruin, overthrow
	הרעות	*HaRa'ot* –The evils (Deut. 31:17)
	והסרתי	*ve-Hasirotiy* –And I will remove (Ex. 23:25)
	והרעת	*ve-HaRa'ot* –And the bad (Gen. 41:27)
	ונכרתה	*ve-Nikretah* –Shall be cut off (Gen. 17:14)
	לאמים	*Le'ummiym* –Leummim, son of Dedan
	להורתמ	*Lehorotam* –That you may teach them (Ex. 24:12)
	ממארת	*Mam'eret* –Malignant (Lev. 13:51)
	ערותה	*'ervatah* –Her nakedness (Lev. 18:7)
	רעותה	*Ra'uwtah* –Another, her neighbor (Ex. 11:2)
	עלמנ דבלתימה	*'Almon Diblathayemah* –Almon Diblathaim, site between Dibon Gad and the mountains of Abarim where the Israelites camped during their wandering in the wilderness
	שלמנאסר	*Shalman'eser* –Shalmaneser, king of Assyria to whom Hoshea became subject was Shalmaneser V (2 Kings 17:3)[800]
	תאריכנ	*Ta'ariykun* –You shall prolong (Deut. 4:26)
	תפאר	*Tefa'er* –To remove (the fruits of the highest branch – Deut. 24:20)
	תרועה	*Teruw'ah* –Alarm, signal, shout; one of the three types of *shofar* blasts
682	בירכתימ	*Bayarkatayim* –In the hinder part (Ex. 26:23)
	בית חורונ	*Beyth Chowrown* –Beth Horon, twin town located between Ephraim and Benjamin, modern Beit 'Ur et Tahta and Beit 'Ur el Foka

[800] Either Shalmaneser or Sargon, his successor, was the king to whom Samaria fell after a long siege (2 Kings 17:6; 18:9).

	בערתי	*Bi'artiy* –I have consumed (Deut. 26:13) *Vi'artiy* –I have consumed (Deut. 26:14)
	ברכתני	*Beraktaniy* –You bless me (Gen. 32:27)
	ברעתי	*Bera'atiy* –In my wretchedness (Num. 11:15)
	ונכרתו	*ve-Nikretuw* –And they will be cut off (Lev. 18:29)
	וערות	*ve-'ervat* –And the nakedness (Gen. 9:23)
	ורעות	*ve-Ra'ot* –And bad (Gen. 41:19)
	ירק עשב	*Yereq Esev* –Green herb
	עברתי	*'avartiy* –I passed over (Gen. 32:11); I transgressed (Deut. 26:13)
	ערבתי	*'Arbathiy* –Arbathite(s)
	ערותו	*'ervato* –His nakedness (Lev. 20:17)
	רביעת	*Reviy'it* –The fourth part (Ex. 29:40)
	תברכני	*Tevarakaniy* –Shall bless me (Gen. 27:19)
	תרביע	*Tarvato* –Crossbred (Lev. 19:19)
683	אבל מים	*'Abel Mayim* –Abel Mayim, place in Palestine
	והלכת אל המקומ	*Vihalachath El HaMaqowm* –And go to the place [that God has chosen to dwell] (Deut. 26:2)
	והעברת	*Viha'avarat* –You shall set apart, bring (Ex. 13:12); you shall proclaim (Lev. 25:9)
	ותרכבנה	*ve-Tirkavnah* –And they rode (Gen. 24:61)
	עולמ אצילות	*Olam Atzilut* –The World of Nobility, the Divine or Archetypal World
	תזרעו	*Tizra'uw* –You shall sow (Lev. 25:11)
	תרגיע	*Targiya'* –You shall have rest, ease (Deut. 28:65)
	–Prime number	
684	אלמגים	*Almuggiym* –A tree from Lebanon, almug trees (sandalwood?), almug wood
	ברביעית	*Birvi'iyt* –With the fourth part (Num. 15:4)
	שלחנ ערוב	*Shulchan Aruch* –The Jewish Law, written by R. Josef Karo
	תרדפ	*Tirdof* –You shall follow, pursue (Deut. 16:20)
685	הפכפך	*Hafakpak* –Crooked, perverted
	הרעתי	*Hare'otiy* –I have hurt (Num. 16:15)
	ובתבערה	*ve-Vetav'erah* –And at Taberah (Deut. 9:22)
	לולב ואתרוג	*Lulav ve-Etrog* –"Palm stalk and citron;" two of the four plants waved during *Sukkot*
	ממשרקה	*Mimasreqah* –From Masrekah (Gen. 36:36)
	מרתמה	*Meritmah* –From Rithmah (Num. 33:19)
	עטרות	*'atarot* –Ataroth, town east of the Jordan River rebuilt by the tribe of Gad (this spelling used only in Num. 32:3 – see also עטרת)[801]; town on the edge of the Jordan Valley at the border of Ephraim; house of Joab mentioned in the genealogy of Judah (see also

801 עטרת (679).

Ataroth Addar)[802]

תפרה *Tifreh* –You be increased (Ex. 23:30)

686 אפרת *'efrathah* –Ephrath, another name for Bethlehem; second wife of Caleb (Gen. 35:16)

התפאר *Hitfa'er* –Have you this glory (Ex. 8:5)

התרועה *HaTeruw'ah* –The alarm (Num. 31:6)

ויסרתי *ve-Yisartiy* –And I will chastise (Lev. 26:28)

ויעתר *ve-Ye'atar* –And he entreated (Gen. 25:21)
ve-Ye'ater –And let be entreated (Gen. 25:21)

ויתנכר *ve-Yitinaker* –But he made himself strange (Gen. 42:7)

ופתר *ve-Foter* –And one to interpret (Gen. 40:8)

ושלשימ *ve-Shelishiym* –And thirty (Gen. 5:5); and third (Gen. 5:16)

מרמות *Meremowth* –Meremoth, priest who weighed the gold and silver vessels of the Temple; one who divorced his foreign wife after the Exile; one who sealed the new covenant with God after the Exile

נכריות *Nakriyot* –Strangers (Gen. 31:15)

סירתיו *Siyrotayev* –Its pots (Ex. 27:3)

עוים *'Avviym* –Avim, city of the tribe of Benjamin, probably near Bethel (Deut. 2:23; Josh. 13:3)[803]

פותר *Poter* –One who could interpret (Gen. 41:8)

פרות *Parot* –Cows (Gen. 32:16)

פתור *Pethowr* –Pethor, residence of Balaam, near the Euphrates River and the mountains of Aram

שושנכי *Shuwshankiy* –Susanchites

תפארה *Tifarah* –Beauty, splendor, glory

תריעו *Tariy'uw* –You shall sound an alarm (Num. 10:7)

687 העברית *Ha'Ivriyot* –The Hebrew women (Ex. 1:15)

הרביעת *HaReviy'it* –The fourth (Lev. 19:24)

ואמרתמ *ve-'amartem* –And you shall say (Gen. 32:21)

והרעות *ve-HaRa'it* –And the bad (Gen. 41:20)

ולאיתמר *ve-Le'iytamar* –And unto Ithamar (Lev. 10:6)

זכרתני *Zekartaniy* –Remember me (Gen. 40:14)

מזמרת *Mizmerat* –Of the choicest fruits (Gen. 43:11)

עבד אדום *'Obed 'Edowm* –Obed-edom, man who housed the Ark for three months (2 Sam. 6:10-12; 1 Chr. 13:13-14); one of the chief Levitical singers and doorkeepers (1 Chr. 15:18, 21, 24; 16:5, 38; 26:4, 8, 15); Temple treasurer or official, or perhaps the tribe that sprang from him (2 Chr. 25:24); Levite musician who ministered before the Ark when it was placed in the Tabernacle (1 Chr. 16:5, 38 – he may be the same as the second Obed-edom)

---

[802] Ataroth Addar (890).

[803] Some translate "Bethel and (the village of) the Avvim," thus indicating a group of people.

	פורתא	*Powratha'* –Poratha, son of Haman slain by the Jews
	רפאות	*Rif'uwth* –Healing
	תזריע	*Tazriya'* –Have conceived seed (Lev. 12:2)
688	ויתעבר	*ve-Yit'aber* –He was filled with wrath (Deut. 3:26)
	ועברתי	*ve-'avartiy* –For I will go (Ex. 12:12)
	ורביעת	*ve-Reviy'it* –And the fourth (Num. 28:14)
	יבוסים	*Yebusim* –Jebusites
	ממחרת	*Mimacharat* –On the morrow (Gen. 19:34; Lev. 23:15)
	נעשה אדמ בצלמנו	*Naaseh adham be-tzelmenu* –"Let us make the earth creature (אדמ) in our image" (Gen. 1:26)
	פחם	*Pecham* –Coal, charcoal, ember
	פרחת	*Porachat* –Breaking out (Lev. 13:42)
	רמת לחי	*Ramath Lechiy* –Ramath-Lehi, location in Judah where Samson slew many Philistines (this spelling used only in Judg. 15:17 – see also Lehi)[804]
	תעבירו	*Ta'aviyruw* –You shall make go through (Lev. 25:9)
	תפרח	*Tifrach* –Shall break out abroad (Lev. 13:12)
689	לאחריתמ	*La'chariytam* –Their latter end (Deut. 32:29)
	פטרת	*Pitrat* –That opens (Num. 8:16)
690	אלגומים	*Alguwmmiym* –A tree from Lebanon, almug trees
	הכצעקתה	*Hakitz'aqatah* –Whether according to the cry of it (Gen. 18:21)
	יריעת	*Yeriy'ot* –Curtains (Ex. 26:1)
	כמשלש	*Kemishlesh* –About three (Gen. 38:24)
	מלכם	*Malkam* –Malcham, descendant of Benjamin; Milcom, a god of the Ammonites (see also Molech)[805]
	מנרת	*Menorat* –Candlestick (Ex. 25:31)
	מריתמ	*Meriytem* –You rebelled (Num. 20:24)
	מרכלת	*Markoleth* –Market place, place of trade
	מרתימ	*Merathayim* –Merathaim, symbolic name for the country of the Chaldeans, also known as Babylon (Jer. 50:21)
	נמם	*Nemem* –57th name of *Shem HaMeforash* (3 Taurus)
	סלם	*Sullam* –Ladder (Gen. 28:12)
	עיטם	*'Eytam* –Etam, town of the tribe of Simeon; cleft of rock near Zorah; resort town near Jerusalem used by King Solomon
	עיים	*'Iyiym* –Iim, town in extreme southern Judah; town east of the Jordan River (see also Ije-Abarim)[806]
	ענמלך	*'Anammelek* –Anammelech, one of the gods worshipped by the people of Sepharvaim[807]
	צרת	*Tzarat* –Distress (Gen. 42:21)

[804] Lehi (48).
[805] Molech (134, 784).
[806] Ije Abarim (343, 903).
[807] It is possible that Anammelech represented the moon, with Adrammelech representing the sun.

		Tzereth –Zereth, descendant of Judah
	ריפת	*Riyphath* –Riphath, son of Gomer (Gen. 10:3 – see also דיפת)[808]
	תמרימ	*Temariym* –Palm trees (Ex. 15:27)
	תצר	*Tatzar* –Be at enmity, harass (Deut. 2:9)
691	אמנם	*'omnam* –Verily, truly, surely
		'umnam –Verily, truly, indeed
	אפים	*'Appayim* –Appaim, son of Nadab and the father of Ishi
	אפרתי	*'Efrathiy* –Ephraimite, Ephrathite
	אצם	*'Otzem* –Ozem, brother of David; son of Jerahmeel
	העתירו	*Ha'tiyruw* –Entreat (Ex. 8:4)
	הפרות	*HaFarot* –The cows (Gen. 41:3)
	והרמתמ	*ve-Haremotem* –And you shall set apart (Num. 18:26)
	ומהרתמ	*ve-Mihartem* –And you shall hasten (Gen. 45:13)
	לראתכמ	*Lar'otkem* –To show you (Deut. 1:33)
	פתורה	*Petorah* –Pethor, residence of Balaam, near the Euphrates River and the mountains of Aram
	תרופה	*Teruwfah* –Healing
	–Prime number	
692	ביריעת	*Biyriy'ot* –Of the curtains (Ex. 26:12)
	בצרת	*Betzurot* –Fortified (Deut. 3:5)
	צרבת	*Tzarebet* –Scab, scar of a sore (n. fem.) (Lev. 13:23); burning, scorching
	רביעית	*Rebiy'iyt* –Quarter (Num. 15:5)
	רבצת	*Rovetzet* –That coucheth (Gen. 49:25)
	תבצר	*Tivtzor* –You shall gather (Lev. 25:5)
693	בארצת	*Ba'rtzot* –In lands (Lev. 26:36)
	בית רפא	*Beyth Rapha'* –Beth Rapha, descendant of Judah and son of Eshton
	גפרות	*Gafrit* –Sulfur
		Gofriyt –Brimstone (of judgment – fig.; of YHVH's breath – fig., Gen. 19:24)
	העבריות	*Ha'Ivriyot* –The Hebrew women (Ex. 1:16)
	קול יהוה יחולל אילות	*Qol* YHVH *Yecholel 'Ayalot* –"The voice of YHVH causes hinds to calve" (Ps. 29:9)
694	בית הערבה	*Beyth Ha'Arabah* –Beth Arabah, village in the Judean wilderness on the boundary between Judah and Benjamin
	ובתנוריכ	*ve-Vetanuwreyak* –And in your ovens (Ex. 7:28)
	וממחרת	*ve-Mamacharat* –And on the morrow (Lev. 7:16)
	חופם	*Chuwfam* –Hupham, head of a family descendant from Benjamin (Num. 26:39)[809]

[808] Possibly a reference to the Paphlagonians on the Black Sea. דיפת (494).

[809] In Gen. 46:21 and 1 Chr. 7:12, Hupham's name is listed as Huppim.

695 הירינת *HaYeriy'ot* –The curtains (Ex. 26:2)
התמרימ *HaTemariym* –The palm trees (Deut. 34:3)
מהרתנ *Miharten* –So soon (Ex. 2:18)
נהרתמ *Naharotam* –Their rivers (Ex. 7:19)
עולמ מורגש *Olam Morgash* –Moral World, second face of Adam Qadmon
תרצה *Tirtzah* –Tirzah, youngest daughter of Zelophehad; Tirzah, Canaanite city located north of Jerusalem, which also was an early capital of Israel (Num. 36:11)
Tirzeh –Will appease, accept (Lev. 26:34; Deut. 33:11)

696 גתה־חפר or גת־החפר *Gittah-Chefer* or *Gath-HaChefer* –Gittah Hepher or Gittah-hepher, city of the tribe of Zebulun, northeast of Nazareth, home of the prophet Jonah
הארחת *Ha'Aratzot* –The lands (Gen. 26:3)
וייפתר *va-Yiftar* –And he solved, interpreted (Gen. 41:12)
וערכת *ve-'arakat* –And you shall arrange (Ex. 40:40)
וצרת *ve-Tzarat* –Bind up, you shall besiege (Deut. 16:25; 20:12)
וריפת *ve-Riyfat* –And Riphath (Gen. 10:3)
ותרצ *ve-Taratz* –And ran (Gen. 24:20)
ve-Tiretz –And shall be paid, enjoy, forgiven (Lev. 26:43)
יריעות *Yeriy'owth* –Jerioth, wife or concubine of Caleb (1 Chr. 2:18)
לא יהיה־לכ אלהימ אחרימ על־פני *Lo yiheyeh-leka Elohim acherim al-pana* –"Thou shalt have no other gods before me" (Ex. 20:3)
ערותכ *'ervatak* –Your nakedness (Ex. 20:23)
צומ *Tzuwm* –To abstain from food, fast
Tzowm –Fast, fasting
שמשונ *Shimshown* –Samson, the 12th Judge of Israel
תצור *Tatzuwr* –You shall besiege (Deut. 20:19)

697 והעתירו *ve-Ha'tiyruw* –And entreat (Ex. 10:17)
ותאמרנ *ve-To'maran* –And they said (Ex. 1:19)
תאמרונ *To'meruwn* –You shall say (Gen. 32:5)

698 בצרות *Betzurot* –Fortified, strength (Num. 13:28)
ובצרת *ve-Vetzurot* –And fortified (Deut. 9:1)
והזכרתני *ve-Hizkartaniy* –And mention me (Gen. 40:14)
ותרבצ *ve-Tirbatz* –And she lay down (Num. 22:27)
חפימ *Chuppiym* –Huppim, head of a family descendent from Benjamin (this name used only in Gen. 46:21 and 1 Chr. 7:12 – see also Hupham)[810]
חפרתי *Chafartiy* –I dug (Gen. 21:30)

[810] Hupham (134, 694).

	חרפתי	*Charfatiy* –My reproach (Gen. 30:23)
	מנחם	*Menachem* –Menahem, 17th King of Israel
	תבצרו	*Tivtzruw* –You shall gather them (Lev. 25:11)
	תחרימם	*Tachariymem* –You shall destroy (Deut. 20:17)
	תרצח	*Tirtzach* –Shall kill, murder (Ex. 20:13)
699	גת־רמון	*Gath-Rimmown* –Gath Rimmon, city of the tribe of Dan; town of the tribe of Manasseh
	וחפרתה	*ve-Chafartah* –And you shall dig (Deut. 23:14)
700	בחצרת	*Bachatzerot* –In 'Hazeroth (Num. 33:17)
	כפרת	*Kaporet* –Mercy Seat, place of atonement (the golden plate of propitiation on which the High Priest sprinkled the seat seven times on the Day of Atonement symbolically reconciling YHVH and His chosen people; slab of gold on top of the Ark of the Covenant which measured 2.5 by 1.5 cubits – on it and part of it were the two cherubim facing each other, whose out-stretched wings came together above and constituted the throne of God – see Ex. 37:6), literally "cover"
	כפתר	*Kaftor* –Bulb, knob, capital, capital of a pillar (Ex. 25:33); Caphtor, island or seacoast region from which the Philistines originally came (this spelling used only in Deut. 2:23 – see also כפתור)[811]
	כרמלית	*Karmeliyth* –Carmelites
	לרעת	*Lera'ot* –To do evil (Ex. 23:2)
	מכמרת	*Mikmereth* –Net, fishing net
	מכרתמ	*Mekartem* –You sold (Gen. 45:4)
	מלכים	*Melekim* –Kings; Angelic Choir assoc. w/*Tiferet*; a book of the Bible
	ממכרת	*Mimkeret* –Sale, be sold (Lev. 25:42)
	מסרת	*Masoreth* –Bond (of the covenant)
	מסתר	*Master* –Hiding, act of hiding, one who causes people to hide *Mistar* –Secret place, hiding place
	מרנתי	*Meronothiy* –Meronothite
	ן	*Nun* (final) –14th letter of Hebrew alphabet
	סרתמ	*Sartem* –You had turned aside (Deut. 9:16)
	עלם	*'alam* –To conceal, hide, be hidden, be concealed, be secret; perpetuity, antiquity, forever (Aramaic) *Alem* –4th name of *Shem HaMeforash* (4 Leo) *'elem* –Young man
	ערכתי	*'araktiy* –I have prepared (Num. 23:4)
	ערלת	*'arlat* –Foreskin (Ex. 4:25)
	פדיום	*Pidyowm* –Ransom, redemption
	פרכת	*Paroket* –Curtain, veil, partition (Ex. 26:31; 35:12)

[811] כפתור (706).

	צעקתמ	*Tza'aqatam* –Cry of them (Gen. 19:13)
	צרדתה	*Tzeredathah* –Zereda, village in Manasseh (see also צרדתה, צרתנ)[812]
	צרתי	*Tzaratiy* –My distress (Gen. 35:3)
	קרת	*Qereth* –City, town
	קשש	*Qashash* –To gather, assemble, collect
	רך	*Rak* –Tender, soft, delicate, weak; soft (Prov. 15:1)[813] *Rok* –Tenderness, delicacy (of woman) *Rokh* –Softness
	רקת	*Raqqath* –Rakkath, fortress city in Naphtali on the western shore of the Sea of Galilee
	רתק	*Rattowq* –Chain *Rathaq* –To bind
	שטה	*Satah* –To turn aside, go aside, turn, decline *Shittah* –Acacia tree, acacia wood
	שרר	*Sarar* –To be or act as prince, rule, contend, have power *Sharar* –To be an enemy; Sharar, father of one of David's mighty men (this spelling used only in 2 Sam. 23:33 – see also Sacar)[814] *Shorer* –Navel, umbilical cord
	ששק	*Shashaq* –Shashak, descendant of Benjamin
	שת	*Set* –Seth, son of Adam and Eve *Shat* –Pillar; prince, appointed, put (Gen. 4:25); 231st Gate of the 231 Gates *Shet* –Buttocks (Num. 24:17); noise
	תכפר	*Tekafer* –You shall make atonement (Ex. 29:37)
701	אלו מיכאל גבריאל ורפאל	*'elu Michael Gabriel ve-Rafael* –"These are Michael, Gabriel, and Rafael." – This tells who the three men representing God are when they confront Abraham (see below)
	אנסנ	A permutation of יהוה by *Aiq Bekar*[815]
	אן	*'an* Where?, whither? (of place); when?, until when?, how long? (of time); pain, sorrow; Heliopolis, a city in lower Egypt; 13th Gate of the 231 Gates
	ארך	*'arak* –To be long, prolong; to be long, reach, meet; fitting, proper *'arek* –Long (pinions); patient, slow to anger *'arok* –Long (of time; of God's wisdom [figurative]) *Erech* –Uruk, a city of ancient Mesopotamia *'orek* –Length; forbearance, self-restraint (of patience)
	אשת	*'eshet* –Wife of, woman of (Gen. 11:29)
	הנותרמ	*HaNotarim* –The remaining (Lev. 10:16)
	והנה שלשה	*ve-hinneh shelshah* –"And behold, three…"; the first words of Gen. 18:2, when three men confront Abraham

---

812 צרתן (740, 1390), צרדתה (700).

813 Rakh is one of the ten words in the Tanakh with a Dagesh in the letter Resh.

814 Sacar (520).

815 See Introduction.

והפרתי *ve-Hifretiy* –And I will make fruitful (Gen. 17:6)
והרצת *ve-Hirtzat* –And repay (Lev. 26:34)
ותרצה *ve-Tirtzah* –And Tirzah (Num. 26:33)
מלכים א *Melekim* –The Name of 1 Kings in Hebrew
מלאכים *Malakim* –Angels; messengers
רמות־נגב *Ramowth-Negeb* –"Ramoth of the south," sometimes called Ramoth-Negeb, city of Simeon
שאת *Shayth* –Ruin, devastation
Seheth –Elevation, exaltation, dignity, swelling
Se'et –Lifted up, dignity, rising (Gen. 4:7)
שכל הרצון *Sekhel HaRatzon* –Intelligence of Will (20th Path)
תקרא *Tiqra'* –You shall read (Deut. 31:11); shall call (Gen. 17:15)
תשא *Tisa'* –Shall bear, lift up (Gen. 18:24; Lev. 7:18)

702 בלעם *Balaam* –Balaam, prophet that the king of Moab induced to curse Israel (Num. 22-24; 31:8); Bileam, settlement on the western side of the Jordan assigned to Manasseh; Goetic demon #51 (Aurum Solis spelling)
בן *Ben* –Son, grandson, child, member of a group, child (Aramaic); a title of *Tiferet*; the secret name of the world of Assiah; Ben, assistant in the temple musical service during David's reign (1 Chr. 15:18); 33rd Gate of the 231 Gates
בעלם *Balam* –Goetic demon #51
בקרת *Biqqoret* –Punishment (after judicial enquiry), compensation, disciplinary punishment (Lev. 19:20)
ברך *Barakh* –To kneel, bless; to praise, salute, curse
Berak –To bless, kneel (Aramaic)
Berekh –Knee, lap; weak from fear (fig.); knee (Aramaic)
ברקת *Bareqath* –A gem, precious stone, emerald, carbuncle; (precious stone in the High Priest's ephod – represents the tribe Levi)
בשת *Bosheth* –Shame
הארצות *Ha'Aratzot* –The lands (Gen. 41:54)
ויתפרו *ve-Yitferuw* –And they sewed (Gen. 3:7)
וצרות *ve-Tzarot* –And troubles (Deut. 31:17)
ותאמרנה *ve-To'marnah* –And they said (Gen. 31:14)
מלכים ב *Melekim* –The Name of 2 Kings in Hebrew
צבים *Tzebiyim* – Zeboim, one of the five cities of the Plain (this spelling used only in Gen. 10:19 – see also צביים, צבאים)[816]
קברת *Qevurat* –Grave of (Gen. 35:20)
קרבת *Qaravat* –You did come near (Deut. 2:37)
רבך *Rabak* –To mix, stir
Ravakh –To be mixed, mingled

[816] צבאים (143, 703), צביים (152, 712).

	שבת	*Shabat* –Sabbath, day of rest *Shavat* –He rested, ceased (Gen. 2:3) *Shevet* –You have dwelt (Deut. 1:6)
	תקבר	*Tiqaver* –You shall be buried (Gen. 15:15)
	תקרב	*Taqriv* –You shall bring near (Lev. 2:4) *Tiqrav* –You draw near (Deut. 20:10); you shall approach (Lev. 18:14); draw nigh (Ex. 3:5)
	תשב	*Tashev* –Bring back *Towshab* –Soujourner, stranger *Teshev* –You shall dwell; abide, tarry, sit, stay
703	אבן	*'aben* –Stone (large or small) *'eben* –Stone (Aramaic) *Oben* –Wheel, disk
	אברך	*Abrek* –A shout made to announce Joseph's chariot (meaning dubious – Gen. 41:43)
	אסתאריאל	*Satariel* –The Concealors, *Qlippoth* of *Binah*
	בשאת	*Bas'et* –In the rising (Lev. 13:10) *Bis'et* –In bearing (Ex. 27:7)
	גן	*Gan* –Garden, enclosure; 52nd Gate of the 231 Gates
	מסגרת	*Misgereth* –Border, fastness, rim
	פי החרת	*Pi HaChiyroth* –Pi-hahiroth, location of the final Israelite encampment prior to crossing the Reed Sea
	צבאים	*Tzebo'iym* –Zeboiim, one of the five cities of the Plain (see also צביים, צבים)[817]
	רזי יסודות	*Razi Yesodoth* –Secret foundations
	תגש	*Tigos* –You shall exact, take (Deut. 15:3)
	–The sum of the numbers 1 through 37	
704	אגן	*Aggan* –Bowl, basin
	בטרצתג	*Batratztag* –19th-24th letters of the 42-letter name of God (assoc. w/Wednesday)
	בקברת	*Beqivrot* –In Kibroth (Num. 33:16)
	דן	*Dan* –Dan, fifth son of Jacob and progenitor of a tribe of Israel (assoc. w/Scorpio); Dan, town of the tribe of Dan in the northwest portion of Palestine *Den* –This, on account of this; therefore; –70th Gate of the 231 Gates
	דרך	*Darak* –To tread, bend, lead, march *Derek* –Way, road, distance, journey, manner
	ובצורת	*ve-Vetzuwrot* –And fortified (Deut. 1:28)
	וחצרת	*ve-Chatzerot* –And Hazeroth
	ורחצת	*ve-Rachatzat* –And you shall wash (Ex. 29:4)
	חצרות	*Chatzerot* –Hazeroth, place where the Israelites camped in the wilderness, possibly modern Ain Hudra
	חצר שועל	*Chatzar Shuw'al* –Hazar Shual, town in southern Judah apportioned to the tribe of Simeon – possibly modern el-Watan

817 צבים (142, 702), צביים (152, 712).

	לדרתיכמ	*Ledoroteykem* –Throughout your generations (Gen. 17:12)
	עדלם	*'Adullam* –Adullam, town of Judah near Succoth[818]
	צדים	*Tziddiym* –Ziddim, fortress city of Naphtali
	קדם	*Qedem* –Before; the East; ancient things
705	אדן	*Eden* –Base, pedestal, socket (strong, firm)
		'Addon –Addan, the man who could not prove his ancestry after the exile (Neh. 7:61; Ezra 2:59)
	אשדת	*'ashdot* –Slopes (Deut. 3:17)
		'eshdath –Fiery law, fire of a law, fire was a law (meaning uncertain – Deut. 33:2)
	בגשת	*Begeshet* –Through coming near (Num. 8:19)
	בעלת באר	*Ba'alath Be'er* –Baalath Beer, border town of the tribe of Simeon, sometimes called "Ramah of the South" (1 Sam. 30:27; Josh 19:8), identical with the city Baal, see also Bealoth[819]
	גבן	*Gibben* –Hump-backed, crooked-backed
	הכפרת	*HaKaforet* –The ark cover (Ex. 25:18)
	המקצעת	*HaMiqtzo'ot* –The corners (Ex. 26:24)
	הן	*Hane* –They, these, the same, who; behold!, lo!; whether, if (Aramaic); 87th Gate of the 231 Gates
	הפרכת	*HaFaroket* –The veil (Ex. 26:33)
	הקם	*Haqem* –16th name of *Shem HaMeforash* (4 Libra)
	מיתריהמ	*Meytreyhem* –Their cords (Ex. 35:18)
	קרתה	*Qartah* –Kartah, city in Zebulun given to the Merarite Levites
	רתקה	*Rethuqah* –Chain
	שתה	*Shathah* –To drink; foundation, support
		Shethah –To drink (Aramaic); buttocks
	תדשא	*Tadshe'* –Put forth grass (Gen. 1:11)
	תרעלה	*Tarelah* –Reeling, staggering
	תשה	*Tasheh* –You do lend (Deut. 24:10)
706	בדן	*Bedan* –Bedan, leader of Israel mentioned as a deliverer of the nation (1 Sam. 12:11)[820]; descendant of Manasseh
	בחצרות	*Bachatzerot* –In Hazeroth
	בכל לבבכם	*Bakal Lababakam* –"With all your heart" (1 Sam. 12:24)
	דבשת	*Dabbesheth* –Hump (of camel); Dabbesheth, border town of the tribe of Zebulun
	וכפרת	*ve-Kafarta* –And pitch it (Gen. 6:14)
	וכפתר	*ve-Kaftor* –And a knob (Ex. 25:35)
	ון	*Van* –103rd Gate of the 231 Gates
	וסרתמ	*ve-Sartem* –And you turn aside (Deut. 11:16)

---

818 David made the headquarters of his rebellion against Saul in a cave near this town (Josh. 12:7-15; 1 Sam. 22: 2 Sam. 23:13)

819 Bealoth (508).

820 Many think that Bedan is a reference to Abdon (132, 782).

	וצרתי	*ve-Tzartiy* –And I will be an adversary (Ex. 23:22)
	כפתור	*Kaftowr* –Caphtor, island or seacoast region from which the Philistines originally came (this spelling used only in Jer. 47:4; Amos 9:7 – see also כפתר)[821]
	לרעות	*Lir'ot* –To feed (Gen. 37:12)
	מסרות	*Moserowth* –Moseroth, location of an Israelite wilderness encampment near Mount Hor on the border of Edom (see also מוסרה)[822]
	מסתור	*Mistowr* –Place of shelter
	עולם	*'owlam* (often *Olam*) –Long duration, antiquity, futurity, forever, ever, everlasting, evermore, perpetual, old, ancient, eternity, world
	עלום	*'aluwm* –Youth, youthful, vigor
	ערלתו	*'arlato* –His foreskin (Gen. 17:14); closed, forbidden (Lev. 19:23)
	קום	*Quwm* –To rise, arise, stand, rise up, stand up
	שושק	*Shuwshaq* –Shishak, another name for Shishak I (this spelling used only in 1 Kings 14:25 – see also שישק)[823]
	שתו	*Shatuw* –Put on, returned his (Ex. 33:4)
	תשאה	*Tashuah* –Noise, clamor
707	אבדן	*Abdan* –Destruction
	און	*Aven* –Trouble, vanity, wickedness (in regards to an idol)
		Avnas –Goetic demon #58
		On –Strength; wisdom; sorrow
		Own –Ability, power, wealth, force, goods, might, substance; On, a Reubenite who rebelled against Moses and Aaron; On, city of Lower Egypt
	אם טבקשנה ככספ	*'as Tevuqshenah Kekasap* –If you seek her as silver (Prov. 2:4)
	אשתו	*'ishto* –His wife (Gen. 3:20)
	בהן	*Bohan* –Bohan, descendant of Reuben for whom a boundary stone was named (Josh. 15:6); stone named for Bohan (Josh. 18:17)
		Bohen –Thumb, great (big) toe (always used as both together – Ex. 29:20)
	בית נמרה	*Beyth Nimrah* –Beth-Nimrah, fortified city built by the tribe of Gad east of the Jordan River (Num. 32:36) (see also Nimrah (Num. 32:3))[824]
	דגן	*Dagan* –Corn, grain
	הבן	*Hoben* –Ebony
	השבת	*HaShabat* –The Sabbath, the seventh (Ex. 16:29; Lev. 23:16)

[821] כפתר (700).

[822] מוסרה (311).

[823] Shishak was king of Egypt who sheltered Jeroboam against Solomon and in later years invaded Judah. שישק (710).

[824] Nimrah (295).

ואשת *ve-'eshet* –And (the) wife (Gen. 7:13)
ve-'esht –And I drank (Gen. 24:46)

וקראת *ve-Qara't* –And shall call, befall (Gen. 16:11; Deut. 31:29)
ve-Qara'ta –And you shall call (Gen. 17:19)

ותקרא *ve-Tiqra'* –And she called (Gen. 4:25)

ותשא *ve-Tisa'* –And she lifted, and cast (Gen. 21:16; 39:7)

זן *Zan* –Species, kind, sort; 118th Gate of the 231 Gates

קברתה *Qevuratah* –Her grave (Gen. 35:20)

שאתו *Se'to* –To carry it (Deut. 14:24)

שבתה *Shavtah* –Rest (Lev. 26:35)

תזרק *Tizroq* –You shall dash (Num. 18:17)

תקראו *Tiqr'uw* –You shall proclaim (Lev. 23:2)

תשאו *Tis'uw* –You shall bear (Num. 14:34; 18:32)

708 אהיה יה יהוה אלהים *Eheieh Yah* YHVH *Elohim* –A name of God

אזן *Azan* –To hear, listen; weigh, test, prove, consider
Azen –Tools, implements, weapons
Ozen –Ear, as part of the body; ear as organ of hearing; (subjective) to uncover the ear to reveal; the receiver of divine revelation

בית צור *Beyth Tzuwr* –Beth Zur, city in the hill country of Judah; Bethzur, son of Maon

במסרות *Bemoserot* –In Moseroth (Num. 3:30)

בני אלהים *Beni Elohim* –Sons of the Gods; Angelic Choir assoc. w/*Hod*

ברוך *Barukh* –Blessed
Baruwk –Baruch, Jeremiah's friend and scribe; descendant of Perez who returned from the exile; one who helped to rebuild the wall of Jerusalem (Neh. 3:20; 10:7); man who sealed the covenant with Nehemiah (Neh. 10:7) – may be the same as the third

דדן *Dedan* –Dedan, descendant of Cush, possibly a people of Arabia in the neighborhood of Edom (Gen. 10:7); son of Jokshan and grandson of Abraham (Gen. 25:3) – (see also דדנה)[825]

המסגרת *HaMisgeret* –The border (Ex. 25:27)

השאבת *HaSho'avot* –The women (who draw water - Gen. 24:11)

וברך *Uwvarek* –And He will bless

וברקת *ve-Vareqet* –A tenant (Lev. 22:10)

וקרבת *ve-Qaravat* –And when you come near (Deut. 2:19)

ושבת *ve-Shavat* –And you will return (Deut. 4:30)

ותקבר *ve-Tiqaver* –And she was buried (Gen. 35:8)

ותשב *ve-Tashav* –And returned (Gen. 8:9)
ve-Teshev –And she sat, dwelt, remained (Gen. 21:16)

חן *Chen* –Favor, grace, charm; Hen, son of Zephaniah (Zech. 6:14 – see also Josiah in verse 10)[826];

---

[825] דדנה (63).

		132nd Gate of the 231 Gates
	חרך	*Charak* –To set in motion, start; to roast; to singe (Aramaic)
		Cherek –Lattice, other opening through which one may look
	כפרחת	*Keforachat* –Appearing to bud (Gen. 40:10)
	מאזנים	*Moznaim* –Scales; Libra
	מחנים	*Machanayim* –Mahanaim, place on the boundary between Reuben and Gad
	קברות	*Qivrot* –Kibroth
	קברתו	*Qevurato* –His grave (Deut. 34:6)
	קרחת	*Qarachath* –Baldness of head, back baldness, bald spot
	שבות	*Shauwth* –Captivity, captives
	שבתו	*Shivto* –Loss of his time (Ex. 21:19)
	שחת	*Shachath* –To destroy, corrupt, decay; pit, destruction, grave
	שכל מחודש	*Sekhel Mechudash* –Renovating or Renewing Intelligence (26th Path)
	שחת	*Shachet* –Destroyed (Gen. 13:10)
		Shichet –Have dealt corruptly
	תבוסה	*Tebusah* –A treading down, ruin, downfall, destruction
	תושב	*Toshav* –A tenant (Lev. 22:10); sojourner, settler (Ex. 12:45)
	תחש	*Tachash* –A kind of leather, skin, or animal hide (made out of ceremonially unclean animal); seal-skin (Num. 4:6, 10); Thahash, son of Nahor, Abraham's brother
	תקרבו	*Tiqrevuw* –Shall approach (Lev. 18:6)
	תרחק	*Tirchaq* –You shall keep you far (Ex. 23:7)
	תשבו	*Tashuvuw* –You shall return (Lev. 25:10)
		Teshevuw –You shall dwell (Gen. 34:10)
		Teshvuw –You shall abide (Lev. 8:35)
	תשוב	*Tashuv* –Will return; you shall go back, return (Deut. 24:19)
709	באוחרתי	*Be'otzrotay* –In my treasures (Deut. 32:34)
	באשתו	*Ba'sheto* –To his wife (Gen. 2:24)
	גשור	*Geshuwr* –Geshur, Aramean kingdom east of Maacah, between Mount Hermon and the district of Bashan, where Absalom sought refuge; Geshurite
	גשתו	*Gishto* –His approach (Gen. 33:3)
	הדרך	*HaDarak* –The way
	השדת	*HaSadot* –The fields (Ex. 8:9)
	ובאשת	*ve-Ve'shet* –And in, against the wife (Deut. 28:54)
	וגרך	*ve-Gayrika* –"And your convert [stranger]" (Ex. 20:10; Deut. 29:10)
	והבצרות	*ve-HaButzrot* –And the fortified (Deut. 28:52)

---

[826] Josiah (326). The word *chen* is often considered a notarikon for חכמה נסתרה, "secret wisdom."

	ותבאש	*ve-Tiv'ash* –And stank (Ex. 8:10)
	ותגש	*ve-Tigash* –And came near (Gen. 33:7)
	ותשאב	*ve-Tish'av* –And she drew (Gen. 24:20, 45)
	זבן	*Zeban* –To buy, gain
	טן	*Tan* –145th Gate of the 231 Gates
	קטרת	*Qetoreth* –Incense, smoke, odor of sacrifice
	תגשו	*Tigshuw* –You shall come (Ex. 19:15)
	תקטר	*Taqtar* –Shall be made to smoke, burnt (Lev. 6:15)
	תשגו	*Tishguw* –You shall err (Num. 15:22)
	–Prime number	
710	בחן	*Bachan* –To examine, try, prove; watchtower *Bochan* –Testing, tested, tried
	בקרחת	*Vaqarachat* –In the bald head (Lev. 13:42)
	בשבתו	*Beshebto* –Of every Sabbath (Num. 28:10)
	בשחת	*Beshachet* –When destroyed (Gen. 19:29)
	גאון	*Ga'own* –Exaltation, majesty, pride; genius, excellency
	דון	*Duwn* –Judge, to judge
	ובקברת	*ve-Beqivrot* –And in Kibroth (Deut. 9:22)
	ודן	*Vedan* –Vedan, a place, site uncertain, perhaps near Medina in Arabia, or may simple be read "and Dan" (Ezek. 27:19)
	ושדת	*ve-Sadet* –And plaster (Deut. 27:2)
	זגן	*Zagan* –Goetic demon #61 (Aurum Solis spelling)
	ין	*Yan* –157th Gate of the 231 Gates
	יעלם	*Ya'lam* –Jaalam, chief of Edom (Gen. 36:5, 14, 18; 1 Chr. 1:35)
	ירך	*Yarek* –Thigh, side, loin, base
	כפתרי	*Kaftoriy* –Caphtorite
	לירכתימ	*Layarkatayim* –For the hinder part (Ex. 26:27)
	לפתר	*Liftor* –To interpret (Gen. 41:15)
	מכנרת	*Mikineret* –From Kinnereth (Deut. 3:17)
	מערת	*Me'arath* –Maarath, town located in the mountains of Judah – modern Umman; cave (Gen. 23:9)
	משלשמ	*Mishilshom* –From the day before (Ex. 4:10)
	נסתר	*Nisater* –We are absent (Gen. 31:49) *Nisetar* –Hidden, secret
	עילם	*'Eylam* –Elam, son of Shem; descendant of Benjamin; descendant of Korah; leader of the people who sealed the new covenant with God after the Exile; priest of Nehemiah's time who helped to cleanse Jerusalem; three whose descendants returned from the Exile
	עממ	*'amam* –To darken, dim, grow dark *Amem* –52nd name of *Shem HaMeforash* (4 Aries)
	ערתמ	*'orotam* –Their skins (Lev. 16:27)
	קדומ	*Qaduwm* –Ancient (meaning dubious – Judg. 5:21)
	קדרות	*Qadruwth* –Darkness, gloom
	קימ	*Qayam* –Secure, enduring (Aramaic) *Qeyam* –Decree, stature (Aramaic)

Qiym –Adversary

קנסך — A permutation of יהוה by *Aiq Bekar*[827]

קדסנ — A permutation of יהוה by *Aiq Bekar*

קרתי — *Qoratiy* –My roof (Gen. 19:8)

רמיתני — *Rimiytaniy* –Beguiled me (Gen. 29:25)

שישק — *Shiyshaq* –Shishak, another name for Shishak I (see also שושק)[828]

שית — *Shiyth* –To put, set; garment
Shayith –Thorn bushes

שריר — *Shariyr* –Sinew, muscle

שתי — *Shetey* –Two
Shethiy –A drinking, drinking bout (Eccl. 10:17); warp, woven material
Shitiy –Show, my setting (Ex. 10:1)

תחשב — *Techashev* –Accounted (Deut. 2:20)

תיש — *Tayish* –He-goat

תרהקה — *Tirhaqah* –Tirhakah, king of Ethiopia and Egypt who aided Hezekiah in his fight against Sennacherib

תשי — *Teshiy* –You are unmindful (Deut. 32:18)

711 אדון — *Adown* –Firm, strong, lord, master
'Addown –Addan, the man who could not prove his ancestry after the exile (Neh. 7:61; Ezra 2:59)

אחבן — *'Achban* –Ahban, son of Abishur

אין — *Ain* –Nothing; No-thing, not, nought; nothing, nought; not; to have (of possession); without; for lack of
Aiyn –Where?, whence?
Iyn –Is there not?, have you not?

אליעם — *Eliyam* –Eliam, Bathsheba's father; a Gilonite warrior of David

אש מצרפ — *Esh Metzaref* –Purifying Fire, title of a 17th-century cabalistic alchemical text; "Smelter's fire" (Mal. 3:2)

אשית — *'ashiyt* –I will put (Gen. 3:15)

אשתי — *'ishtiy* –My wife (Gen. 20:11)

בטן — *Beten* –Belly, womb, body; bowels, the inmost part; Beten, village of the tribe of Asher
Boten –Pistachio nuts – delicacy given to Joseph by Jacob through his sons

הון — *Hown* –Wealth, riches, substance; enough, sufficiency
Huwn –To be easy, be ready

הנותרימ — *HaNotariym* –The remaining (Ex. 28:10)

הרקות — *HaRaqot* –The lean (Gen. 41:20)
Hareqot –Empty (Gen. 41:27)

השגגת — *Hashogeget* –That errs (Num. 15:28)

והפריתי — *ve-Hifreytiy* –And I will make fruitful (Gen. 17:20)

ומיתריהמ — *ve-Meytereyhem* –And their cords (Num. 3:37)

ושתה — *ve-Shatah* –That may drink (Ex. 17:6)

[827] See Introduction.

[828] Shishak was king of Egypt who sheltered Jeroboam against Solomon and in later years invaded Judah. שושק (706).

זאגן *Zagan* –Goetic demon #61

פרש הסוס *Peresh HaSuws* –"Dung of the Horse," an alchemical term

קראתי *Qara'tiy* –I have called (Ex. 31:2)

712 בין *Beyn* –Between, among, in the midst of, from between; between (Aramaic)

Biyn –To discern, understand, consider; prudent, regard

במערת *Bim'arat* –In the cave (Gen. 50:13)

בקירת *Beqiyrot* –In the walls (Lev. 13:49)

בשתי *Bashtiy, Bishtiy* –In the warp (Lev. 13:48, 49)

Bishtey –For two (Gen. 31:41)

דחן *Dochan* –Millet

ואשתה *ve-'eshteh* –That I may drink (Gen. 24:14)

וקששו *ve-Qeshesho* –And gather (Ex. 5:7)

ורקות *ve-Raqot* –And lean (Gen. 41:19)

ושתו *ve-Shato* –And to drink (Ex. 32:6)

חדרך *Chadrak* –Hadrach, Syrian country associated with Hamath and Damascus, along the Orontes River south of Hamath

יבלעם *Yible'am* –Ibleam, city of the tribe of Manasseh – see also Bileam[829]

יברך *Yivarak* –Bless

יבשת *Yabbesheth* –Dry land; the earth (as a planet), dry land (Aramaic)

Yevoshet –Dried (Gen. 8:7)

ישבת *Yeshebet* –Sits

מערבת *Ma'arvot* –From the plains (Deut. 34:1)

עברתמ *'avartem* –You are come, you passed (Gen. 18:5)

צביים *Tzebiyiym* –Zeboim, one of the five cities of the Plain (this spelling used only in Gen. 14:2, 9 – see also צבאים, צבים)[830]; Zebaim, home of one whose descendants returned from the Exile

קברתי *Qavartiy* –I buried (Gen. 49:31)

שבתי *Shabbethay* –Shabbethai, assistant to Ezra; one who explained the Law to the people; chief Levite in Jerusalem[831]

שגגתו *Shiggato* –His error (Lev. 5:18)

שיבת *Seyvat* –Grey hairs (Gen. 44:31)

תקריב *Taqriyv* –Will offer, bring, sacrifice (Lev. 2:1); you shall bring, offer (Ex. 29:4)

תשבי *Tishbiy* –Tishbite

תשיב *Tashiyv* –Bring back (Gen. 24:6)

713 אבדון *Abaddon* –Place of destruction, destruction, ruin, Abaddon; the angel of the bottomless pit; the Sixth Hell (corr. to *Hesed*)

---

[829] Bileam (142, 702).

[830] צבאים (143, 703), צבים (142, 702).

[831] All three Shabbethais may be the same.

	בני האלהים	*Beney HaElohim* –"Sons of God"
	דאבון	*De'abown* –Faintness, languishing, sorrow
	דגון	*Dagon* –A god of the Philistines
	הרחקת	*Harchoqot* –Which are far (Deut. 20:15)
	השחת	*HaShechet* –The corrupt
	התחש	*HaTachash* –The sealskin (Num. 4:25)
	ואשתו	*ve-'ishto* –And his wife, mate (Gen. 2:25)
	והקרבת	*ve-Hiqravat* –And you shall bring (Ex. 29:3)
	והרבך	*ve-Hirebeka* –And multiply you (Deut. 7:13)
	והשבת	*ve-Hashevota* –And consider it (Deut. 4:39)
	וזרקת	*ve-Zaraqat* –And you shall dash (it) (Ex. 29:16)
	ושבתה	*ve-Shavtah* –And shall keep (Lev. 25:2)
	זון	*Zuwn* –To feed
	מגערת	*Mig'ereth* –Rebuke, reproof
	פרעה חפרע	*Par'oh Chophra'* –Pharaoh-Hophra, an Egyptian king in the time of Zedekiah, king of Judah (Jer. 37:5; 44:30; Ezek. 29:6-7)
	שבתאי	*Shabbathai* –Saturn; the material world corr. to *Binah*
	תשובה	*Teshuvah* –Recurrence, an answer, return
	תשיג	*Tasiyg* –Suffice, reach (Lev. 5:11; 14:30)
714	אתון נורא	*Attun Nura* –"Fiery furnace" (Dan. 3:6, 11, 15, 17, 21, 23, 26)
	ביבשת	*Bayabashet* –Upon the dry land (Gen. 4:9)
	בעל ברית	*Ba'al Beriyth* –Baal-berith, literally "Baal of the covenant," a god of the Shechemites (Judg. 8:33; 9:4)
	בשבית	*Bashviyt* –Into captivity (Num. 21:29)
	דין	*Dayan* –Judge
		Diyn –Justice; judge, to judge; judgment (Aramaic); a title of *Giburah*
	הקטרת	*HaQetoret* –The incense (Ex. 30:27; Num. 16:35)
	וחקרת	*ve-Chaqarat* –And make search (Deut. 13:15)
	ושחת	*ve-Shichet* –And spilled it (Gen. 38:9)
	ותושב	*ve-Toshav* –And a sojourner (Gen. 23:4)
	ותשבו	*ve-Tashuvuw* –And you returned (Deut. 1:45)
		ve-Teshvuw –And you abode (Deut. 1:46)
	מחסום	*Machsown* –Muzzle
	קדים	*Qadiym* –East, east wind
	שחות	*Shechuwth* –Pit
	תשטה	*Tishteh* –Shall go aside (Num. 5:12, 29)
715	אדין	*Edayin* –Then, afterwards, thereupon, from that time (Aramaic)
	בן־הדד	*Ben-Hadad* –Ben-hadad, Ben-hadad I of Syria who invaded Israel (1 Kings 15:18, 20; 2 Chr. 10:2, 4); Ben-hadad II, laid siege to Samaria itself (1 Kings 20; 2 Kings 6:24; 8:7, 9); son and successor of Hazael who reigned over Syria as it disintegrated (2 Kings 13:3, 24-25); possibly a

general title of the Syrian kings (Jer. 49:27)

הדון *Haduwn* –Beautifully formed

הין *Hiyn* –Hin (unit of measurement, about 5 quarts)

הקצפתמ *Hiqtzaftem* –You made angry (Deut. 9:8)

הרעתמ *Hare'otem* –You deal so ill (Gen. 43:6)

השתי *HaShetiy* –The warp (Lev. 13:52)

ובאשתו *ve-Vi'sheto* –Or his wife (Gen. 26:11)

וקטרת *ve-Qetoret* –And the incense (Num. 4:16)

ישתה *Yashateh* –May be drunk (Lev. 11:34)
Yishteh –Drinks, shall drink (Gen. 44:5)

כפתריה *Kaftoreyah* –Its knobs (Ex. 25:31)

מכרתיהמ *Mekeroteyhem* –Their sword (Gen. 49:5)

מעשקה *Ma'ashaqqah* –Extortionate deed, extortion (Prov. 28:16; Isa. 33:15)

סנהם *Sanahem* –Lord of Triplicity by Day for Leo

רתיקה *Rattiyqah* –Chain

שתיה *Shethiyah* –Drinking (mode or manner or amount of)

תמכרנה *Timkerenah* –You shall sell her (Deut. 21:14)

716 אטון *Etuwn* –Linen, yard, thread

בחון *Bachown* –Assayer (an inspector and valuer of metals)

בקרחתו *Beqarachto* –On his baldness (Lev. 13:42)

גוזן *Gowzan* –Gozan, district and town of Mesopotamia, located on the Habor River

דיבן *Diybon* –Dibon, city of the tribe of Gad located north of the Arnon River (see also Dimon – Num. 21:30; 32:3; Is. 15:9)[832]; village of southern Judah near the boundary of Edom (also known as Dimonah – Neh. 11:25; Josh. 15:22) (see also דיבון)[833]

וחבשת *ve-Chavashat* –And you shall bind (Ex. 29:9)

וישת *va-Yesht* –And he drank (Gen. 9:21)
ve-Yashet –And he put (Gen. 30:40)

וכל חכם לב *vi-Kal Chakam Laiv* –"And all skillful" (Ex. 31:6)

ושתי *Vashti* –Vashti, queen of Persia who was divorced by King Ahasuerus
ve-Shetey –And two (Gen. 19:30)
ve-Shatiy –And I will set (Ex. 23:31)

יון *Yavan* –Javan, fourth son of Japheth (Gen. 10:2, 4; 1 Chr. 1:5,7) – the name corresponds etymologically with Ionia and may denote the Greeks (see Is. 66:19); Javan, trading post in southern Arabia (Ezek. 27:13)
Yaven –Mire, mirer (Ps. 40:3; 69:3)

יושת *Yuwshat* –Be placed upon (Ex. 21:30)

יקום *Yaquwm* –Living substance, that which stands or exists, existence

---

832 Dimon (110, 760).

833 דיבון (72, 722), Dimonah (115).

	ישתו	*Yishtuw* –They drank (Deut. 32:38)
	עילום	*'eylowm* –Forever, ever, everlasting, evermore, perpetual, old, ancient, world
	קריות	*Qeriyowth* –Kerioth, town in extreme southern Judah; city of Moab
	ראשיהמ כסכ	*Rashiyham Kasak* –"Capitals were silver" (Ex. 38:16)
	שבת בזה	*Shabbat Bazah* –"She insulted the Sabbath" (in reference to Vashti)
	שהדותא	*Sahaduwta'* –Sahadutha , heap of stones on Mount Gilead (see also Jegar-Sahadutha)[834]
717	אבידן	*Abidan* –Abidon, son of Gideoni and Prince of the tribe of Benjamin[835]
	אור ישר	*'or Yashar* –Straight light
	אריוך	*'Aryowk* –Arioch, king of Ellasar; captain of Nebuchadnezzar's guard
	גחון	*Gachown* –Belly, womb
		Gichown –A river of Eden (assoc. w/Water); Gihon, intermittent spring outside the walls of Jerusalem, south of the Temple area
	וקראתי	*ve-Qara'tiy* –And I will call (Ex. 2:7)
	זדון	*Zadown* –Pride, insolence, presumptuousness, arrogance
	זין	*Zayin* –Sword; 6th letter of Hebrew alphabet
	טחן	*Tachan* –To grind, crush
	ישבקשה	*Yoshbeqashah* –Joshbekashah, son of Heman, David's song leader (1 Chr. 25:4, 24)
	תשחט	*Tishachet* –Slaughtered (Lev. 6:17)
		Tishchat –You shall sacrifice (Ex. 34:25)
718	אזקים	*Aziqqiym* –Chains, manacles
	אשביתה	*'ashbiytah* –I would make cease (Deut. 32:26)
	הגין	*Hagiyn* –Appropriate, suitable; directly ahead of
	המגערת	*Hamig'eret* –And the rebuke (Deut. 28:20)
	ויברך	*ve-Yibarak* –And He blessed
	וישבת	*va-Yishbot* –And he rested (Gen. 2:2)
		ve-Yashavat –And dwelt (Deut. 8:12); and you tarry, dwell (Gen. 27:44)
	ועברתמ	*ve-'avartem* –And when you go over (Deut. 12:10)
		ve-'evratam –And their wrath (Gen. 49:7)
	ושבית	*ve-Shaviyat* –And you have taken captive (Deut. 21:10)
	ושבתי	*ve-Shavtiy* –So that I return (Gen. 28:21)
	חין	*Chiyn* –Beauty, grace
	חשתי	*Chushathiy* –Hushathite
	ישבתו	*Yishbotuw* –Cease (Gen. 8:22)
	שחיטה	*Shechiytah* –Slaughtering, killing, act of slaying
	שחית	*Shechiyth* –Pit
	תקריבו	*Taqriyvuw* –You shall offer (Lev. 22:20); you shall

[834] Jegar-Sahadutha (929)
[835] Abidan represented his tribe when a census was taken during their trek in the wilderness.

		bring, sacrifice (Lev. 1:2)
	תשיבו	*Tashiyvuw* –Carry back (Gen. 43:12)
719	אביון	*Ebyown* –In want, needy, chiefly poor, needy person; subject to oppression and abuse; needing help, deliverance from trouble, especially as delivered by God; general reference to lowest class
	אחין	*'Achyan* –Ahian, descendant of Manasseh
	אחיקם	*'Achiyqam* –Ahikam, officer in Josiah's court
	אשחית	*'ashchiyt* –I will destroy (Gen. 18:28)
	גשורי	*Geshuwriy* –Geshurites
	והשבתו	*ve-Hashevoto* –And you shall restore it (Deut. 22:2)
	ויספו ענוים ביהוה שמחה	*ve-Yisapho 'anuwyam Be-*YHVH *Shamachah* –"The humble shall increase joy in God" (Is. 29:19)
	טין	*Tiyn* –Clay
	יגון	*Yagown* –Grief, sorrow, anguish
	מטעם	*Mat'am* –Tasty or savory food, delectable food, dainties
	ושחתה	*ve-Shichatah* –And he will destroy it (Ex. 21:26)
	תקטיר	*Taqtiyr* –You shall burn (Num. 18:17)
	–Prime number	
720	בחין	*Bachiyn* –Siege towers, watchtower
	גאיון	*Ga'ayown* –Proud, haughty
	והקטרת	*ve-Hiqetarat* –And you shall make smoke (Ex. 29:13)
		ve-HaQetoret –And the incense (Ex. 30:37)
	ידון	*Yadown* –Jadon, Judahite who helped repair the walls of Jerusalem after the exile
	יין	*Yayin* –Wine
	יקים	*Yaqiym* –Jakim, descendant of Benjamin; head of a priestly family descended from Aaron
	ישית	*Yashiyt* –Shall put (Gen. 46:4)
	יתחשב	*Yitchashav* –Shall be reckoned (Num. 23:9)
	יתרעם	*Yithre'am* –Ithream, son of David probably by Eglah
	כן	*Ken* –So, therefore, thus; right, just, honest, true, veritable; thus, so, as follows (adv. – Aramaic); base, stand, pedestal, office, foot, place, estate; gnat, gnats, gnat-storm[836]; 168th Gate of the 231 Gates
	כתש	*Kathash* –To pound, mix by pounding, pound fine, bray
	מרעית	*Mir'iyth* –Pasturing, pasturage, shepherding
	נעם	*Na'am* –Naam, son of Caleb
		Na'em –To be pleasant, be beautiful, be sweet, be delightful, be lovely
		No'am –Kindness, pleasantness, delightfulness, beauty, favor; one of two staffs named by Zechariah (Zech. 11:7)
	נערת	*Ne'oreth* –A strand of flax, tow (as shaken from flax

[836] It should be noted that this word, used as "and it was so" in Gen. 1:1 six times, implies that the phrase could mean "and it was 70," meaning that *Ken* or 70 separated Light & Darkness, Evening & Morning, the Upper Waters & the Lower Waters, etc.

		when beaten)
	ענם	*'Anem* –Anem, Levitical city of the tribe of Issachar (see also En-Gannim)[837]
	עת קצין	*'Eth Qatziyn* –Eth Kazin, town on the eastern border of Zebulun
	פרתמ	*Partham* –Noble, nobleman
	צלם	*Tzelem* –Image, idol; the astral body in some Kabbalistic texts (Gen. 1:27; 9:6; Num. 14:9; 33:52; 1 Sam. 6:5, 11; 2 Kings 11:18; 2 Chr. 23:17; Ps. 39:7; 73:20; Ezek. 7:20; 16:17; 23:14; Dan. 2:31, 32, 34, 35; 3:1-3; 5, 7, 10, 12, 14, 15, 18, 19; Amos 5:26)[838]
	קיים	*Qayyam* –Existing, stable
	רכך	*Rakak* –To be tender, be soft, be weak
	שכל שלמ	*Sekhel Shalem* –Perfect or Absolute Intelligence (8th Path)
721	אדם עילאה	*Adam Illah* –Heavenly Man
	אכן	*Aken* –Surely, truly, indeed
	אשתכ	*'ishteka* –Your wife (Gen. 3:17)
	והרעתמ	*ve-Har'otem* –And you shall sound (Num. 10:9)
	והתעמר	*ve-Hit'amer* –And treats as a slave (Deut. 24:7)
	ונסתרה	*ve-Nisterah* –And secretly (Num. 5:13)
	חזון	*Chazown* –Vision, prophecy
	חצור חדתה	*Chatzowr Chadattah* –Hazor Hadattah, city in southern Judah (Josh. 15:25 – see also Hazor)[839]
	כי עבדי הם	*Ki 'avadai Haim* –"For they are My servants" (Lev. 25:42)
	נקדה ראשונה	*Neqedah Rishonah* –The Primordial Point, a title of *Keter*
722	דביון	*Dibyown* –Dove's dung (meaning dubious – see 2 Kings 6:25)
	דיבון	*Diybown* –Dibon, city of the tribe of Gad located north of the Arnon River (see also Dimon – Num. 21:30; 32:3; Is. 15:9)[840]; village of southern Judah near the boundary of Edom (also known as Dimonah – Neh. 11:25; Josh. 15:22) (see also דיבן)[841]
	וישתו	*ve-Yishtuw* –And drinks, drank (Gen. 24:54)
	חשחות	*Chashchuwth* –Things needed, requirements, that which is required
	יבין	*Yabiyn* –Jabin, king of Hazor defeated by Joshua; another king of Hazor who oppressed Israel and was defeated by Deborah

837 En-Gannim (233, 1443).
838 See Gershom Scholem's "The Concept of the Astral Body," in On the Mystical Shape of the Godhead, pp. 251-273. Also refer to R. Aryeh Kaplan's Meditation and the Bible.
839 Hazor (304).
840 Dimon (110, 760).
841 דיבן (66, 716), Dimonah (115).

	כבשת	*Kevast* –Ewe-lambs (Gen. 21:28, 29)
	שכבת	*Shekobet* –Copulation
		Shikvat –A layer, flow (Ex. 16:13: Lev. 15:16)
	שיבתי	*Seyvatiy* –My grey hairs (Gen. 42:38)
	תשבך	*Tishbek* –Shall carry you away captive (Num. 24:22)
	תשכב	*Tishkav* –She will lie, sleep (Lev. 15:20; 18:22)
723	ארבעתים	*'arba'tayim* –Fourfold
	השחית	*Hishchiyt* –Had corrupted (Gen. 6:12)
	ונזכרתם	*ve-Gizkartem* –And you shall be remembered (Num. 10:9)
	והעברתם	*ve-Ha'avartem* –And you shall cause to pass (Num. 26:8)
	והשבתי	*ve-Hashivotiy* –And I will bring back (Num. 22:8)
		ve-Hishbatiy –And I will cause to cease (Lev. 26:6)
	וזרעתם	*ve-Zera'tem* –And you shall sow (Gen. 47:23)
	וישבתה	*ve-Yishavtah* –And shall dwell (Deut. 17:14)
	ושחטת	*ve-Shachatat* –And you shall slaughter (Ex. 29:11)
	טחון	*Techown* –Mill, grinding mill, hand mill
	עולם הזה	*'olam Hazeh* –This world
	תשחטו	*Tishchatuw* –You shall slaughter (Lev. 22:28)
724	בשבתך	*Beshivtak* –When you sit (Deut. 6:7)
	גיחון	*Gihon* –A river of Eden (assoc. w/Water)
	דכן	*Dikken* –This, that (Aramaic)
	הגיון	*Higayown* –Meditation, resounding music, musing
	החרש ואאלפך חכמה	*Hecharosh ve-'alpek chekomah* –"Be still and I will teach you wisdom" (Job 33:33)
	וישבתו	*ve-Yishbetuw* –And they rested (Ex. 16:30)
	תרחיקו	*Tarchiyquw* –You shall go far (Ex. 8:24)
725	אשדודית	*'Ashdowdiyth* –The speech of Ashdod
	בזיון	*Bizzayown* –Contempt
	בטחון	*Bittachown* –Trust, confidence, hope
	הדד בן בדד	*Hadad ben Bedad* –Hadad, son of Bedad; a King of Edom (assoc. w/*Tiferet*)
	חזקים	*Chazokim* –Strength, energy
	כהן	*Kahan* –To act as a priest, minister in priest's office
		Kahen –Priest (Aramaic)
		Kohen –Priest, principal officer or chief ruler
	שער קימה	*Shi'ur Komah* –Measure of height, measure of body (used by some early Merkavah mystics and Kabbalists to imply the "measure" of God)
	תקטירו	*Taqtiyruw* –And you shall burn (Lev. 2:11)
	–The number of children of Lod, Hadid, and Ono who returned from exile (Ezra 2:33)	
726	ואשתחוה	*ve-'eshtachaveh* –And prostrated myself (Gen. 24:48)
	ויתריעל	VITRIOL –Acronym (rendered into Hebrew letters) for the alchemical formula "*Visita interiora terrae*

		rectificando invenies occultum lapidem" ("Visit the interior of the earth; by rectification, you shall find the hidden stone.")
	חביון	*Chebyown* –Concealment, covering, hiding, hiding place
	יוקים	*Yowqiym* –Jokim, descendant of Judah
	כון	*Kavvan* –Cake, sacrificial cake
		Kuwn –To be firm, be stable, be established; Chun, town in Syria
	מפתור	*Miftor* –From Pethor (Deut. 23:5)
	ערותנ	*'ervatan* –Their nakedness (Lev. 18:9)
	קדש ברנע	*Qadesh Barnea'* –Kadesh Barnea, wilderness on Palestine's southern frontier – it was on the border between the wilderness of Paran on the south and the wilderness of Zin on the north (see also Kadesh)[842]
	קירתיו	*Qiyrotayv* –It sides (Ex. 30:3)
	תפרמו	*Tifromuw* –Rend (Lev. 10:6)
727	גיחון	*Giychown* –A river of Eden (assoc. w/Water); Gihon, intermittent spring outside the walls of Jerusalem, south of the Temple area
	ואשתכ	*ve-'ishtak* –And your wife (Gen. 6:18)
	זידון	*Zeydown* –Churning, raging, turbulent, proud, insolent
	–Prime number	
728	וברכך	*vo-Verakika* –And bless you (Deut. 7:13)
	ותשכב	*ve-Tishkav* –And lay (Gen. 19:33)
	חשכת	*Chasakat* –Withheld (Gen. 22:12)
	יזרעאלית	*Yizre'e'liyth* –Jezreelitess
	כבון	*Kabbown* –Cabbon, town of lowland Judah
	כסלחים	*Kasluchiym* –Casluhim, son of Mizraim, but possibly a people related to the Egyptians who were ancestors of the Philistines
	כשבתו	*Keshivto* –When he sits (Deut. 17:8)
	כתושב	*Ketoshav* –As a settler (Lev. 25:40)
	מרחפת	*Merachefet* –Hovered (Gen. 1:2)
	שבותכ	*Shevuwtak* –Your captivity (Deut. 30:3)
	שכבתו	*Shekavto* –He lie, he lay (Lev. 20:15)
	תעברנו	*Ti'avirenuw* –Bring us over (Num. 32:5)
	תשכח	*Tishakach* –It shall be forgotten (Deut. 31:21); you shall forget (Deut. 25:19); you forget (Deut. 4:9)
729	לא תרצח	*Lo thi-retzach* –"Thou shalt not murder" (Ex. 20:13
	קרעשטנ	*Qerashaten* –7th-12th letters of the 42-letter name of God (assoc. w/Monday)
730	ברכת המזונ	*Birkat HaMazon* –"The blessing over food" (prayer recited after eating a meal containing bread)
	וישתחו	*ve-Yishtachavu* –And they bowed down (Gen. 27:29)

[842] Kadesh (404).

		ve-Yishtachuw –And he worshipped (Ex. 34:8); and he bowed down (Gen. 18:2)
	ורדפתמ	*ve-Redaftem* –And you shall chase (Lev. 26:7)
	ישתחוו	*Yishtachavuw* –Shall bow down (Gen. 49:8)
	כסילים	*Kesilim* –Fools; the constellation Orion
	כשית	*Kasiyat* –You are covered with fat (Deut. 32:15)
		Kushiyt –Cushite
	למקצעת	*Limqutz'ot* –For the corners (Ex. 26:23)
	לן	*Lan* –178th Gate of the 231 Gates
	לפרכת	*Lafaroket* –To (the) veil (Ex. 26:33)
	לקשש	*Leqoshesh* –To gather (Ex. 5:12)
	מועדים	*Moadim* –Seasons
	מערכת	*Ma'areketh* –Row, line
	מפים	*Muppiym* –Muppim, son of Benjamin (see also Shuppim, Shupham, and Shephuphan)[843]
	נעים	*Na'iym* –Pleasant, delightful, sweet, lovely, agreeable; singing, sweetly sounding, musical
	סינים	*Siyniym* –Sinim, land from which the scattered Israelites were again to be gathered (Is. 49:12)[844]
	עברתמ	*'akartem* –You have troubled (Gen. 34:30)
	ענים	*'Aniym* –Anim, town in the hills of Judah
	צמרת	*Tzammereth* –Treetop, top, highest branch (Ezek. 17:3, 22; 31:3, 10, 14)
	שתל	*Shathal* –To plant, transplant
		Shethiyl –Plant, cutting, slip
	תצרמ	*Tetzurem* –Harass them (Deut. 2:19)
	תרפימ	*Terafiym* –Teraphim, idolatry, idols, images
	תשיכ	*Tashiyk* –You are covered with fat (Deut. 32:15)

–The number of shekels of gold used in the construction of the Tabernacle in the Wilderness

731	אלן	*Illen* –These, those (see also אלין)[845]
	אניעם	*'Aniy'am* –Aniam, descendant of Manasseh
	בית השטה	*Beyth HaShittah* –Beth-Shittah, town of the Jordan Valley between Jezreel and Zerarah
	והריקתי	*ve-Hariyqotiy* –And I will draw out (Lev. 26:33)
	והשתחוו	*ve-Hishtachavuw* –And bow down, worshipped (Gen. 11:8)
	חזיון	*Chezyown* –Hezion, grandfather of Ben-Hadad I, king of Syria[846]
		Chizzayown –Vision
	יהוקים	*Yehoiaqim* –Jehoiakim, 17th King of Judah
	כאין	*Camio* –Goetic demon #53
	לקראת	*Liqra'at* –Over against, to meet (Gen. 15:10)
	לשאת	*Lase'at* –Bear, carry

[843] Shuppim (430, 990), Shupham (506, 1066), Shephuphan (516, 1166).

[844] Probably a reference to Syene on the southern Egyptian frontier wher there was a Jewish garrison. Earlier scholars believed that China was indicated, but that view has been discredited.

[845] אלין (91, 741).

[846] Many scholars identify Hezion with Rezon (263, 913).

	קראתיכ	*Qera'tiyak* –I called you (Num. 24:10)
	שאלת	*Sha'alat* –You did desire (Deut. 18:16)
	תשאל	*Tish'al* –Do you ask (Gen. 32:30)
732	אשתאל	*'Eshta'ol* –Eshtaol, settlement in the hills of Judah, also the burying place of Samson
	הנרות הללו	*HaNeirot Halalu* –These lamps; liturgy recited at *Chanukkah*
	לבן	*Laban* –White; to be white; to make bricks; Laban, obscure place in the Sinai Peninsula (see also the first Libnah)[847]; Laban, brother of Rebekah and father of Rachel and Leah
	לשבת	*Lashevet* –Toward the seat, dwelling (Num. 21:15); that they may dwell (Gen. 13:6) *Lashvet* –To dwell in (Num. 35:2)
	צלם דהבא	*Tzelem Dahava* –"Golden image" (Dan. 3:5, 7, 10, 12, 14, 18)
	שבלת	*Shibboleth* –Ear of corn; Gileadite password (Judg. 12:6)
	שכבתי	*Shakavtiy* –I lay (Gen. 19:34)
	תבשל	*Tevashel* –You shall cook, boil (Ex. 23:19; Deut. 14:21) *Tevushal* –Boiled (Lev. 6:21)
	תלבש	*Tilbash* –You shall wear (Deut. 22:11)
733	אבינעם	*'Abiyno'am* –Abinoam, father of Barak
	בארצתמ	*Be'artzotam* –In their lands (Gen. 10:5)
	רישא־הורה –Prime number	*Risha Havurah* –The White Head, a title of *Keter*
734	ושכחת	*ve-Shakachat* –And you forget (Deut. 8:14)
	ותחשכ	*ve-Techshak* –And was darkened (Ex. 10:15)
	ותכחש	*ve-Tekachesh* –Then denied (Gen. 18:15)
	ותשכח	*ve-Tishkach* –And did forget (Deut. 32:18)
	תכחשו	*Tekachashuw* –You shall deal falsely (Lev. 19:11)
	תשכחו	*Tishkechuw* –You forget (Deut. 4:23)
735	במרצתג	*Bamratztag* –19th-24th letters of the 42-letter name of God, assoc. w/*Tiferet* (A.C., 777)
	הכשית	*HaKushiyt* –The Cushite (Num. 12:1)
	המערכת	*HaMa'araket* –The row (Lev. 24:6, 7)
	הלן	*Helon* –Father of Eliab, Prince of Zebulun
	התרפימ	*HaTerafiym* –The Teraphim (Gen. 31:19)
	להן	*Lahen* –Therefore, on this account *Lawhen* –Therefore; except, but (Aramaic)
736	ארונ העדת	*Aron HaEdeth* –Ark of the Testimony
	וישתחוו	*ve-Yishtachavo* –And they prostrated themselves (Gen. 43:26); and bowed down (Gen. 27:29)

[847] Libnah (87).

	ולשת	*ve-Leshet* –And to Seth (Gen. 4:26)
	ושכתי	*ve-Sakotiy* –And I will cover (Ex. 33:22)
	ותרפימ	*ve-Terafim* –And Teraphim, idols, idolatry, images
	יויקים	*Yowyaqiym* –Joiakim, son of Jeshua who returned from exile – not to be confused with Jehoiakim
	כושית	*Kuwshiyth* –Female Cushite
	כיון	*Kiyuwn* –Chiun or Kaiwan, a Saturnian deity during the time of Amos (Amos 5:26)[848]
	לון	*Luwn* –To lodge, stop over, pass the night, abide; to grumble, complain, murmur
	לקום	*Laqquwm* –Lakum, one of the landmarks on the boundary of Naphtali
	לקראתה	*Liqra'tah* –To meet her (Gen. 24:17)
	מערכות	*Ma'arakot* –Rows (Lev. 24:6)
	פתרונ	*Pithrown* –Interpretion
	פתרנו	*Pitrono* –Its interpretation (Gen. 40:12)
	–The number of horses brought out of exile (Ezra 2:66)	
737	אלונ	*Allown* –Oak, great tree
		'Allown –Allon, son of Jedidah and father of Shiphi
		Elon–The tenth judge of Israel
		Elown –Tree, great tree, terebinth; plain
	אלקום	*Alquwm* –No, not, nor, neither (neg. adv.); band of soldiers; no rebellion, no uprising (lit.)
	בלאדן	*Bal'adan* –Baladan, father of Merodach-Baladan, king of Babylon in Hezekiah's time
	בלהן	*Bilhan* –Bilhan, descendent of Seir; descendant of Benjamin
	בעל שלשה	*Ba'al Shalishah* –Baal Shalisha, village of Ephraim that presented food to the prophet Elisha
	וישיתהו	*ve-Yeshiytehuw* –And set him (Gen. 41:33)
	ולשאת	*ve-Las'et* –And for a rising (Lev. 14:56)
	ושאלת	*ve-Sha'alat* –And ask (Deut. 13:15)
	לאשתו	*Le'ishto* –Of his wife (Gen. 26:7)
	לקראתו	*Liqra'to* –To meet him (Gen. 14:17)
	שלהבת	*Shalhebet* –Flame
738	אשתאול	*'Eshta'owl* –Eshtaol, settlement in the hills of Judah, also the burying place of Samson
	גחרפת	*Gecherefet* –Designated (Lev. 19:20)
	ובשלת	*ve-Vishalat* –And you shall roast (Ex. 29:31)
	ושכבתי	*ve-Shakavtiy* –And when I sleep (Gen. 47:30)
	ותלבש	*ve-Tilbash* –And she put on (Gen. 27:15; 38:19)
	חלן	*Chelon* –Helon, father of Eliab, the prince of Zebulun
		Cholon –Holon, Moabite town, possibly modern Horon; town in the hill country of Judah west of Hebron (see also Hilen, חלון)[849]

[848] The etymology of this word is related to the Babylonian deity Komananu, familiar to a G.D. ritual.

[849] חלון (94, 744), Hilen (98, 748).

	כלב אפרתה	*Kabel 'Ephrathah* –Caleb Ephrathah, place where Hezron died (1 Chr. 2:24) (see also Caleb)[850]
	כשביות	*Kishvuyot* –As though captives (Gen. 21:27)
	לשחת	*Leshachet* –To destroy (Gen. 6:17)
	מחצרת	*Mechatzerot* –From Hazeroth
	שחלת	*Shecheleth* –Onycha (ingredient used in the holy incense)
	שכחתי	*Shakachtiy* –I have forgotten (Deut. 26:13)
	שלחת	*Shalachat* –You did send (Num. 24:12)
	תבשלו	*Tevashlo* –You will cook (Num. 16:23)
	תשלח	*Tishalach* –You send forth, shall let go (Ex. 15:7)
		Tishlach –You will send (Ex. 4:13); send, will send (Gen. 22:12)
739	אחינעם	*'Achiyno'am* –Ahinoam, wife of Saul; mother of Amnon
	גולן	*Gowlan* –Golan, city of Bashan east of the Jordan River, assigned to the Levites, probably modern Sam el-Haulan
	למסגרתו	*Lemisgarto* –To its border (Ex. 25:25)
	לקטרת	*Liqtoret* –For incense (Ex. 40:5)
	נטעים	*Neta'iym* –Netaim, place in Judah where some royal potters lived
	שכל מוגשם	*Sekhel Mughsham* –Corporeal Intelligence (29th Path)
	שלטת	*Shalleteth* –Imperious, domineering
	–Prime number	
740	דיונסים	*Dionsim* –Last seven letters of the 22-letter name of God
	יכין	*Yakiyn* –Jachin, son of Simeon (Gen. 46:10; Ex. 6:15; Num. 26:12 – see also Jarib); priest in Jerusalem after the exile (1 Chr. 9:10; Neh. 11:10); head of a family of Aaron (1 Chr. 24:17 – see also Jarib)[851]; Jachin, the right hand pillar of Solomon's porch on the temple (1 Kings 7:21)[852]
	כידון	*Kiydown* –Javelin, short sword, dart; gorget, a piece of armor for the throat (1 Sam. 17:6, 45); Chidon, place where Uzzah was struck dead for touching the Ark of the Covenant (1 Chr. 13:9) (see also Nachon)[853]
	לריך	*Leraikha* –Goetic demon #14 (Aurum Solis spelling)
	לשתי	*Lishtey* –For two (Ex. 26:19)
	מכפתר	*Mikaftor* –From Caphtor (Deut. 2:23)
	מן	*Man* –Manna; who?, what?, whoever, whosoever (Aramaic); 187th Gate of the 231 Gates
		Men –String (of harp); portion
		Min –From, out of, on account of, off, on the side of, since, above, than, so that not, more than; that;

[850] Caleb (52).
[851] Jarib (222).
[852] See Boaz (79).
[853] Nachon (126, 776).

from; out of, by, by reason of, at, more than (Aramaic); when used as a prefix, it means "from"

מפרכת *Mifreketh* –Neck

מצרית *Mitzriyt* –Egyptian (Gen. 16:1)

מקשש *Meqoshesh* –Gathering (Num. 15:32)

מרך *Morek* –Weakness

ספרת *Sofereth* –Sophereth, servant of Solomon whose ancestors returned from exile

ערלתמ *'arlatam* –Their foreskin (Gen. 17:23)

פנים *Paniym* –Face

פרסת *Perasot* –Footed, hoofed (Lev. 11:3)

צמים *Tzamiym* –Snare, trap, noose (meaning dubious – Job 5:5, 18:9 – Robber)

צנם *Tzanam* –To dry up, harden, wither

צרתנ *Tzarethan* –Zarthan, village near Beth-Shean in the territory of Manasseh (see also Zereda)[854]

רמך *Rammak* –Steeds, mules (meaning dubious – Esth. 8:10)

שמת *Shemot* –Names

שעשע *Sha'shua'* –Delight, enjoyment

שתמ *Shatham* –To open (dubious meaning)
Shetem –Is opened (Num. 24:3)

תספר *Tesafer* –You may tell (Ex. 10:2)
Tisfar –You shall number (Deut. 16:9)

תשמ *Tesham* –Be desolate (Gen. 47:19)

741 אילן *Iylan* –Tree (Aramaic)
'Eylown –Elon, father of a wife of Esau; son of Zebulun; tenth judge of Israel

אלקים *'Elokim* –The alternate name of *Elohim* used in Rabbinical texts in deference to the use of the name of God

אמן *'aman* –To support, confirm, be faithful; to take the right hand, to turn right, choose to the right, go to the right, use the right hand; master-workman, artist, steady-handed one, artisan
Amen –Verily, truly, amen, so be it; firm, faithful; a title of *Keter*; the first letters of *Elem Melek Ne'eman* (Lord, faithful king)
Amon –14th King of Judah
'omen –Faithfulness

והשבתי *ve-Hashikotiy* –And I will make cease (Num. 17:20)

ונערתיה *ve-Na'aroteyha* –And her maidens (Gen. 24:64)

ותרעינה *ve-Tir'eynah* –And they fed (Gen. 41:2)

לקראתי *Liqera'tiy* –Against me

לראיך *Leraikha* –Goetic demon #14

מאן *M a'n* –Vessel, utensil (Aramaic)
Ma'en –To refuse; refusing, unwilling to obey
Me'en –Refusing

[854] Zereda (299; 700).

משאת *Mas'eth* –Uprising, utterance, burden, portion, uplifting
–The sum of the numbers 10 through 38

742 אל מלך נאמן *El Melek Ne'eman* –The Lord and faithful king – it is important to notice the first letters of this phrase (see introduction)
אשתאלי *'Eshta'uliy* –Eshtaulites
בעל תמר *Ba'al Tamar* –Baal Tamar, place in Benjamin near Gibeah and Bethel where the Israelites prepared for battle with the army of Gibeah (Judg. 20:33)
בשמת *Basemat* –Basmath, wife of Esau and daughter of Elon the Hittite (see also Adah)[855]; another of Esau's wives – daughter of Ishmael (Gen. 28:9) and may be the same person as the first; daughter of Solomon and wife of Ahimaaz
Beshemot –In names (Num. 32:38)
מבן *Miben* –"From [the] age [of twenty]" (Ex. 30:14)
מברך *Mabrak* –Consecrated
מקברת *Miqivrot* –From Kibroth (Num. 33:17)
משבת *Mishbath* –Cessation, annihilation
Mishevet –To dwell (Gen. 36:7)
שכבתכ *Shekavtak* –Your (carnal) lying (Lev. 18:20)
שבתמ *Shavtem* –You are turned back, away (Num. 14:43)

743 השחיתכ *Hashchiyteka* –Destroy you (Deut. 10:10)
והלבשת *ve-Hilbashat* –And you shall dress, clothe (Ex. 28:41)
והשבתיכ *ve-Hashivotiyka* –And will bring you back (Gen. 28:15)
ולאשתו *ve-Le'ishto* –And for his wife (Gen. 3:21)
לשחתה *Leshachatah* –To destroy it (Gen. 19:13)
מגן *Magan* –To deliver up, give, deliver
Magen –Shield, buckler
מגשת *Migeshet* –To come near (Ex. 34:30)
משגת *Maseget* –Suffice, reach, afford (Lev. 14:21)
–The number of children of Kirjatharim, Chephirah, and Beeroth who returned from exile (Ezra 2:25)
–Prime number

744 בקברתמ *Biqvuratam* –In their burying-place (Gen. 47:30)
בקרבתמ *Beqarvatam* –When they drew near (Lev. 16:1)
דמן *Domen* –Dung
ולתושב *ve-Latoshav* –And for the settler (Num. 35:15)
ושחלת *ve-Shechelet* –And Onycha (Ex. 30:34)
ותשלח *ve-Tishlach* –And she sent (Gen. 27:42)
חלון *Chalown* –Window
Cholown –Holon, Moabite town, possibly modern Horon; town in the hill country of Judah west of Hebron (see also Hilen, חלן)[856]
חצרמות *Chatzarmavet* –Hazarmaveth, small district of Arabia in

---

855 Adah (79).
856 חלן (88, 738), Hilen (98, 748).

the southern portion of the Arabian Peninsula (Gen. 10:26)

מדן *Medan* –Strife, contention; Medan, son of Abraham by Keturah

מדרך *Midrak* –Treading or stepping place, place to tread on

מחצרות *Mechatzerot* –From Hazeroth

מרדך *Merodak* –Merodach, the name of a Babylonian deity, possibly representing Mars or may be a Hebraized form of "Marduk" (Jer. 50:2)

שותלח *Shotalach* –Shuthelah, son of Ephraim

תשלחו *Teshalechuw* –You shall put out (Num. 5:3)
Tishlachuw –You shall send (Gen. 37:22; Num. 13:2)

745 בגשתמ *Vegishtam* –When they approach (Ex. 28:43)

בחמר ובזפת *VaChemar VeVazefer* –"With tar and pitch" (Ex. 2:3)

המן *Haman* –Haman, prime minister of Ahasuerus who plotted against the Jews (Est. 3-9)

המצרית *HaMitzriyot* –The Egyptian

ולקטרת *ve-Liqtoret* –And for the incense (Ex. 25:6)

זבלן or זבולן *Zebulun* –Zebulun, tenth son of Jacob and progenitor of a tribe of Israel (assoc. w/Capricorn) (from right to left – first spelling used only in Gen. 30:20; 35:23; 46:14; Josh. 19:27, 34; Judg. 4:6; 5:18; Judg. 6:35; 1 Chr. 2:1; 12:33; 12:41; 2 Chr. 30:10, 11, 18; Ps. 68:29; Is. 8:23 – second spelling only used in Gen. 49:13; Ex. 1:3; Num. 1:30, 31; 2:7; 7:24; 10:16; 13:10; 26:26; 34:25; Deut. 33:18; Josh. 19:10, 16; 21:7, 34; Judg. 1:30; 4:10; 1 Chr. 6:48, 77; Ezek. 48:26, 27, 33); Zebulun, territory given to the tribe of Zebulun

לוטן *Lowtan* –Lotan, Edomite chief (Gen. 36:20-29)

משתה *Mishteh* –Feast, drink, banquet

צנתרה *Tzantarah* –Pipe

746 אשתמה *'Eshtemoh* –Eshtemoa, village in the hill country of Judah, famed for its prophetic oracle

וספרת *ve-Safarat* –And you shall number (Lev. 25:8)

וערלתמ *ve-'arletem* –And you shall close (Lev. 19:23)

ושמת *ve-Samet* –And you shall put (Ex. 4:15)

ותשמ *ve-Tasem* –And she put, laid (Ex. 2:3)

חלבון *Chelbown* –Helbon, village of Syria near Damascus, known for its wines – probably modern Khalbun

ילון *Yalown* –Jalon, descendant of Caleb the spy

ממסרות *Mimoserot* –From Moseroth (Num. 33:31)

מקום *Maqowm* –Place, standing place

משתאה *Mishta'eh* –Astonished (Gen. 24:21)

פרסות *Perasot* –Hoofs

פתרוס *Pathrows* –Pathros, country of Upper Egypt inhabited by the Pathrusim, one of the seven peoples coming out of Egypt

שגגתמ *Shiggatam* –Their error (Num. 15:25)

	שמות	*Shammowth* –Shammoth, one of David's mighty men (this spelling used only in 1 Chr. 11:27 – see also Shammah)[857]
		Shemoth –Names; the Hebrew title of Exodus
	תמרוק	*Tamruwq* –A scraping, rubbing
	תספרו	*Tesafarat* –You shall number (Lev. 23:16)
747	אופנים	*Ofanim* –Wheels; Angelic Choir assoc. w/*Chokmah*
	אילון	*'Eylown* –Elon, father of a wife of Esau; son of Zebulun; tenth judge of Israel
		'Ayalown –Aijalon, Ajalon, town northwest of Jerusalem; site where judge Elon was buried
	אמון	*Amown* –Artificer, architect, master workman, skilled workman; throng, multitude
		Emuwn –Faithfulness, trusting
		Amon –Goetic demon #7; Amon, chief god of the Egyptians; 14th King of Judah; governor of Samaria in Ahab's time; a form of Ami
	אשמתו	*'ashmato* –His being guilty (Lev. 5:24)
	ברכת כהנים	*Birkat Kohaniym* –"The Priest's blessing" (recited as part of morning liturgy in the Temple and later in daily prayers – consists of Num. 6:24-26)
	וקראתם	*ve-Qera'tem* –And you shall proclaim (Lev. 23:21)
	רמת גלעד	*Ramoth Gil'ad* –Ramoth-Gilead, chief city of Gad, city of refuge ascribed to the Levites (see also רומת גלעד)[858]
748	בשמות	*Beshemot* –By names (Num. 1:17)
	הבאשתם	*Hiv'ashtem* –You made abhorred (Ex. 5:21)
	ובשמת	*ve-Vasemat* –And Basmath (Gen. 36:4)
		ve-Veshemot –And by name (Num. 4:32)
	ושבתם	*ve-Shavtem* –And you shall return (Ex. 25:10)
	חילן	*Chiylen* –Hilen, city of the tribe of Judah, alloted to the Levites
	חמן	*Chamman* –Incense-altar, sun-pillar, idol, image
	חמשת	*Chameshet* –Five
	ישחיתכ	*Yashchiyteka* –Will destroy you (Deut. 4:31)
	מאזן	*Mo'zen* –Scales, balances; scale, balance (Aramaic)
	מבון	*Mabown* –Ones who taught, ones who gave understanding, teacher
	מקברות	*Miqverot* –From Kibroth (Num. 4:31)
	מרקחת	*Mirqachath* –A seasoning, compounding, spice-seasoning; ointment pot
	משחת	*Mashachat* –You anoint (Gen. 31:13)
		Mashcheth –Ruin, destruction
		Mishchath –Disfigurement (of face), corruption
	שלחתי	*Shalachtiy* –I sent, I had put forth (Gen. 38:23)
	שתלחי	*Shuthalchiy* –Shuthalhites

[857] Shammah (345).
[858] רומת גלעד (753).

	תמשח	*Timshach* –You shall anoint (Ex. 30:30)
749	גליון	*Gillayown* or *Gillyown* –Table, tablet
	ושלחתה	*ve-Shilachtah* –And you shall let her go (Deut. 21:14)
	טיט היון	*Tit HaYaven* –Clay; the 4th Hell (corr. to *Tiferet*)
	טמן	*Taman* –To hide, conceal, bury
	מקטרת	*Miqtereth* –Censer
	סלע המחלקות	*Sela' Hammachleqowth* –Sela-Hammahlekoth, cliff in the wilderness near Moan where David escaped from Saul
	תשמט	*Tashmet* –Shall release (Deut. 15:3)
750	אגמון	*Agmown* –Rush, bulrush; sad, drooping
	בן־חיל	*Ben-Chayil* –Ben-Hail, prince of Judah under Jehoshaphat; son of Shimon of Judah
	ובקרבתמ	*ve-Veqarvatam* –And when they came near (Ex. 40:32)
	חשבתמ	*Chashavtem* –You meant (Gen. 50:20)
	ימן	*Yaman* –To choose the right, go to the right, be right-handed
	כפתרימ	*Kaftoriym* –Caphtorim, the people of Caphtor (Gen. 10:14; 1 Chr. 1:12)
	מדון	*Madown* –Strife, contention; stature, size; Madon, city of northern Canaan
	מחשבת	*Machshavet* –Workmanship (Ex. 35:33)
		Machshavot –Works, thoughts (Gen. 6:5; Ex. 31:4)
	מקרית	*Miqryat* –From (the) city (Num. 21:28)
	מין	*Min* –Species, kind
	נקם	*Naqam* –To avenge, take vengeance, revenge, avenge oneself, be avenged, be punished; vengeance
	נשת	*Nashath* –To be dry, be parched
	נתש	*Nathash* –To pull up, expel, root out, pluck up
	פעם	*Pa'am* –To thrust, impel, push, beat persistently; stroke, beat, foot, step, anvil, occurence
	פתרסי	*Pathrusiy* –Pathrusite
	קרנת	*Qarnot* –Horns (Ex. 29:12)
	קרתנ	*Qartan* –Kartan, city of Naphtali given to the Gershonite Levites
	שלכת	*Shalleketh* –Felling (of tree); Shalleketh, west gate of the Temple of Solomon in Jerusalem (1 Chr. 26:16)
	שמתי	*Samtiy* –I have set, put, done (Gen. 28:22)
		Shumathiy –Shumathites
	שנת	*Shenath* –Sleep; year (Gen. 41:50; Deut. 26:12)
	שתימ	*Shethiym* –Two
	שתנ	*Shathan* –To urinate
	תנקר	*Tenaqer* –You will put out (Num. 16:14)
	תשימ	*Tasiym* –You bring (Deut. 22:8); shall set (Gen. 6:16)
	תשכל	*Teshakel* –Shall bereave (Deut. 32:25)
751	אליקים	*Eliakim* –Eliakim, the son of Hilkiah, master of Hezekiah's household; Josiah's son, enthroned

by Pharaoh; a priest who assisted Nehemiah; (alternate name for Jehoiakim)[859]

אלנעם *Elnaam* –Elnaam, the father of two of David's mighty warriors

אנן *'anan* –Complain, murmur

אשכלת *'askelot* –Clusters (Deut. 32:32)

המון *Hamown* –Murmur, roar, crowd, abundance, tumult, sound

ויהי כן *Va-yehi khen* –"And it was so" (Gen. 1:7, 9, 11, 15, 24, 30; Judg. 6:38)

לקראתכ *Liqra'tak* –To meet you (Gen. 32:7)
Liqra'teak –To meet you (Ex. 4:14)

נשאת *Nisse'th* –Gift, portion (as something taken up)
Noso'ot –Laden (Gen. 45:23)

נתדורינאל *Nathdorinel* –Lord of Triplicity by Night for Pisces

שמהות *Shamhuwth* –Shamhuth, captain of David's army

תשאלכ *Tish'alak* –Shall ask of you (Deut. 14:26)

תשנא *Tisna'* –Shall hate (Lev. 19:17)

–Prime number

752 בנקרת *Beniqrat* –In a cleft (Ex. 33:22)

בשנת *Bishnat* –In the year of (Gen. 7:11)

המזרקת *HaMizraqot* –The basins (Ex. 38:3)

וילון *Vilon* –Veil; the 1st Heaven (corr. to *Yesod* & *Malkut*)

חמדן *Chemdan* –Hemdan, descendant of Seir (the KJV wrongly rendered his name Amram in 1 Chr. 1:41 – the reading there is Hamran)

ישבתמ *Yeshavtem* –You dwelt, abode (Lev. 18:3)

לשבתכ *Leshivtak* –You to dwell in (Ex. 15:17)

תשיבמ *Teshiyvem* –You shall bring them back (Deut. 22:1)

753 בשנאת *Besin'at* –In hate (Deut. 1:27)

גנן *Ganan* –To defend, cover, surround

השתלחי *HaShetalchiy* –The Shuthelahites (Num. 26:35)

ובשליתה *ve-Veshilyatah* –And in her afterbirth (Deut. 28:57)

והקרבתמ *ve-Hiqravtem* –And you shall bring present (Lev. 23:8)

והשבתמ *ve-Hishbatem* –And will you make rest (Ex. 5:5)

מגדון *Megiddown* –Megiddo, ancient city of Canaan assigned to Manasseh & located on the southern rim of the plain of Esdraelon 6 miles from Mt. Carmel & 11 miles from Nazareth (see also מגדו)[860]

מזון *Mazown* –Food, sustenance; food, feed (Aramaic)

נגן *Nagan* –To play or strike strings, play a stringed instrument

רמות גלעד *Ramowth Gil'ad* –Ramoth-Gilead, chief city of Gad, city of refuge ascribed to the Levites (this spelling used only in 2 Chr. 18:2, 19; 22:5 – see also

---

[859] Jehoiakim (171, 731).

[860] מגדו (53).

(רמת גלעד)[861]

754 והשגתמ — *ve-Hishagtam* –And when you overtake them (Gen. 44:4)

וחמשת — *ve-Chameshet* –And five (Num. 31:32)

ומשחת — *ve-Mashachat* –And you shall anoint (Ex. 28:41)
ve-Mishchat –And of the anointing (Lev. 7:35)

ושחתמ — *ve-Shichatem* –And so you will destroy (Num. 32:15)

ושלחתי — *ve-Shilachtiy* –And I will send (Gen. 27:45; Lev. 26:25)

ושמחת — *ve-Samachat* –And you shall rejoice (Deut. 12:18)

חמון — *Chammown* –Hammon, frontier village of the tribe of Asher, assigned to the Levites – may be the same as Hammath

חמשתו — *Chamishito* –Fifth thereof, its fifth (Lev. 27:27)

מדין — *Midian* –Midian, son of Abraham by Keturah and founder of the Midianites; Midian, land of the descendants of Midian beyond the Jordan – included Edom, the Sinai Peninsula and Arabian Petra
Midyan –Strife, contention
Middiyn –Middin, village in the wilderness of Judah

משחות — *Mashchith* –The Destroyer (Ex. 12:23

נדן — *Nadan* –Gift (of a harlot's bribe); sheath

755 גבנן — *Gabnon* –Peak, rounded summit, a mountain peak

הימן — *Heyman* –Heman, wise man with whom Solomon was compared (1 Kings 5:11; 1 Chr. 2:6 – see also Ps. 88); musician and seer appointed by David as a leader in the Temple's vocal and instrumental music

העפרת — *Ha'Ofaret* –The lead

כפתריהמ — *Kaftoreyhem* –Their knobs (Ex. 25:36)

נשתה — *Nishteh* –Shall we drink (Ex. 15:24)

שד השדימ הלבנה — *Shed HaShedim HaLebanah* –Intelligence of the Intelligences of the Moon (a literal Hebrew translation)

שנתה — *Shenatah* –First year (Lev. 14:10)

756 יויכין — *Yehoiakin* –Jehoiachin, 18th King of Judah

ויתשמ — *ve-Yitshem* –And he rooted/exiled them out (Deut. 29:27)

ושמתי — *ve-Samtiy* –And I will appoint (Ex. 21:13); and I will make (Gen. 13:16)

ושתימ — *ve-Shetayim* –And two (Num. 45:6)
ve-Sheteym –And two (Ex. 24:4)

ותרצני — *ve-Tirtzeniy* –And you were pleased with me (Gen. 33:10)

ותשלכ — *ve-Tashlek* –And she cast (Gen. 21:15)

כפתרונ — *Kefitron* –According to the interpretation (Gen. 40:5)

---

[861] רמת גלעד (747).

	נון	*Nun* –Continue, to increase, propagate; fish; 14th letter of Hebrew alphabet; Nun or Non, descendant of Ephraim; father of Joshua
	נשאתה	*Nasa'tah* –You have forgiven (Num. 14:19)
	ספירות	*Sefirot* –Spheres; numbers; emanations[862]
	עולמים	*Olamim* –Ages; worlds
	עופרת	*'owfereth* –Lead
	פרעות	*Par'aot* –Breaches (Deut. 32:42)
	קרנות	*Qarnot* –Horns (Lev. 4:7)
	שמתיו	*Shamtiyv* –I made him (Gen. 27:37)
	שנות	*Shenot* –Years of (Deut. 32:7) *Shinuwth* –Year *Shinuvoth* –Graduation
	שנתו	*Shenato* –First year, year old (Lev. 12:6)
	תקראנה	*Tiqre'nah* –Befallen us (Ex. 1:10)
	תשימו	*Tasiymuw* –You shall put (Gen. 32:17; Deut. 14:1)
757	אונן	*Onan* –Onan, second son of Judah who was slain by God for his disobedience (Gen. 38:4-10; Num. 26:19)
	אנון	*'innuwn* –These, those, they (Aramaic)
	אשתונ	*'Eshtown* –Eshton, descendant of Judah
	בקמיהם	*Beqameyhem* –Their enemies (Ex. 32:25)
	הנחבים	*Hanitzaviym* –That stood (Gen. 45:1)
	ונאמנים	*ve-Ne'emaniym* –And long continuance (Deut. 28:59)
	ותנשא	*ve-Tinase'* –And they shall be exalted (Num. 24:7)
	ותקראנ	*ve-Tiqre'at* –And they called (Num. 25:2)
	זקנם	*Zeqanam* –Their beard (Ex. 21:5)
	מגן דוד	*Magen David* –Star of David, hexagram
	–Prime number	
758	וישבתמ	*ve-Yeshavtem* –And you shall dwell (Lev. 25:18)
	חמשית	*Chamishiyt* –Fifth
	חנן	*Chanan* –To be gracious, show favor, pity; to be loathsome; to show favor (Aramaic); Hanan, descendant of Benjamin (1 Chr. 8:23); one of David's heroes (1 Chr. 11:43); descendant of Benjamin through Saul (1 Chr. 8:38; 9:44); a returned captive (Ezra 2:46; Neh. 7:49); temple officer whose sons had a chamber in the Temple (Jer. 35:4) – this name should not be confused with Baal Hanan; Levite who assisted Ezra when reading the Law (Neh. 8:7); Levite who sealed the covenant with Nehemiah (Neh. 10:11; 13:13 – may be the same as the latter Levite); chief or family who also sealed the covenant (Neh. 10:27); chief or family who sealed the covenant with Nehemiah (Neh. 10:23)
	מורמוניות	*Mormonism* –The Church of Jesus Christ of Latter-Day

[862] The *Sefirot* are explained by the *Sefer Bahir*, "Why are they called *Sephirot?* Because it is written (Psalm 19:2), 'The heavens declare (*me-SaPRim*) the glory of God" (47).

		Saints (Modern Hebrew)
	משחית	*Mashchiyth* –Ruin, destruction; will destroy (Gen. 19:14)
	נושבת	*Noshavet* –Inhabited (Ex. 16:35)
	נחשת	*Nechosheth* –Lust, harlotry; copper, brass; the metal of Venus
	שבתון	*Shabaton* –Solemn rest (Ex. 16:23)
	תחשים	*Techashiym* –Seals (animal) (Ex. 25:5)
	תקברנו	*Tiqberenuw* –You shall bury him (Deut. 21:23)
	תקרבון	*Taqrivuwn* –You shall bring (Deut. 1:17)
	תשובן	*Teshuwvun* –You will turn away (Deut. 32:15)
759	אחימן	*'Achiyman* –Ahiman, son of Anak; Levite gatekeeper in the Temple
	והשחתם	*ve-Hishchatem* –And shall deal corruptly (Deut. 4:25)
	והשלחתי	*ve-Hishlachtiy* –And I will send (Lev. 26:22)
	ותגשן	*ve-Tigashan* –And they came near (Gen. 33:6)
	נחשתא	*Nechushta'* –Nehushta, wife of Jehoiakim, mother of Jehoiachin
760	את שטן	*Eth Shatan* –"The essence of Satan"
	בשבתנו	*Beshivtenuw* –When we sat (Ex. 16:3)
	דימון	*Diymown* –Dimon, city of the tribe of Gad located north of the Arnon River (this spelling used only in Is. 15:9 – see also Dibon, Dimonah)[863]
	דמיון	*Dimyon* –Resemblance, image, like
	ימין	*Yamiyn* –Right-hand or side; Jamin, son of Simeon; descendant of Ram; priest who explained the Law
	כמן	*Kamon* –Cumin
	כשמת	*Kashemot* –After their name (Gen. 26:18)
	כתליש	*Kithliysh* –Kithlish, city located in the lowlands of Judah, perhaps the same as Dilean – modern Khirbet el-Mak-haz
	כתר חכמה־בינה	*Keter Chokmah Binah* –The Three Supernals combined; a name of God
	מכתש	*Maktesh* –Mortar; Maktesh, section of Jerusalem where merchants gathered
	מנעם	*Man'am* –Delicacies, dainties
	נין	*Niyn* –Offspring, posterity
	סלעם	*Sol'am* –Locust
	סרך	*Sarek* –Chief, overseer (Aramaic)
	עצם	*'atsam* –To be vast, be numerous, be mighty; to shut (the eyes), close (the eyes)
		'etzem –Bone, substance, essence; Ezem, village south of Beersheba, near the border of Edom
		'otzem –Power, bones, might
	עצרת	*'atzeret* –Assembly (Lev. 23:36)

863 Dibon (66, 716; 72, 722), Dimonah (115).

ערלתכמ *'arlatkem* –Your foreskin (Gen. 17:11)
צרעת *Tzarahath* –Leprosy
קריתימ *Qiryathayim* –Kiriathaim, Moabite city on the east of the Jordan (Gen. 14:5 –see also Kartan)[864]
קרעשמנ *Qerashamen* –7th-12th letters of the 42-letter name of God, assoc. w/*Hesed* (A.C.)
קסמ *Qasam* –To practice divination, divine
Qesem –Divination, witchcraft
שכלתי *Shakaltiy* –I am bereaved (Gen. 43:14)
שנית *Sheniyt* –A second time (Gen. 22:15)
שנתי *Shenatiy* –My sleep (Gen. 31:40)
שתינ *Shittiyn* –Sixty, threescore (Aramaic)
תערצ *Ta'arotz* –You shall be afraid (Deut. 7:21)
תרעצ *Tir'atz* –Dashes in pieces (Ex. 15:6)
תשמידו *Tashmiyduw* –Demolish (Num. 33:52)
–The number of children of Zaccai who returned from exile (Ezra 2:9)

761 אסן *'asan* –Sudden death
השנות *Hishanot* –Repeated (Gen. 41:32)
והקריתמ *ve-Hiqriytem* –And you shall appoint (Num. 35:11)
והשמתי *ve-Hashimotiy* –And I will bring desolation (Lev. 26:32)
ונשתה *ve-Nishteh* –That we may drink (Ex. 17:2)
יהויכין *Yehoiakin* –Jehoiachin, 18th King of Judah
יתנשא *Yitnasha'* –He lifts himself up (Num. 23:24)
משיתהו *Meshiytihuw* –I drew him (Ex. 2:10)
נשאתי *Nasa'tiy* –I have lifted up (Gen. 19:21)
סאן *Sa'an* –To tread, tramp
–Prime number

762 ביתשנ *Beyth Shan* –Beth-Shan, southern border town of the region of Galilee, largest of the ten cities of the Decapolis (Josh. 17:11; 1 Chr. 7:29) (see also בית שאן)[865]
בנין *Binyan* –Structure, building
וערפתו *ve-'arfto* –Then you shall break its neck (Ex. 13:13)
ותקראנה *ve-Tiqre'nah* –And have befallen (Lev. 10:19)
שבתכמ *Shabatkem* –Your Sabbath (Lev. 23:32)
תקברני *Tiqebreniy* –Bury me (Gen. 47:29; 50:5)

763 ביתשאנ *Beyth She'an* –Beth-Shean, southern border town of the region of Galilee, largest of the ten cities of the Decapolis (Josh. 17:11; 1 Chr. 7:29)
החמישת *HaChamiyshit* –The fifth (Lev. 19:25)
המון גוג *Hamown Gowg* –Hamon Gog, valley where Gog and his armies will be defeated in their final struggle against Israel (Ezek. 39:11-15)
המשחית *HaMashchiyt* –The destroyer (Ex. 12:23)

---

[864] Kartan (750, 1400).
[865] בית שאן (763, 1413).

	הנחשת	*Hanchoshet* –Brass, brazen (Ex. 35:16)
	התושבים	*HaToshaviym* –The strangers (Lev. 25:45)
	התחשים	*HaTechashiym* –The seals (Ex. 39:34)
	ותקרבנה	*Vatiqravnah* –Then drew near (Num. 27:1)
	זנון	*Zanuwn* –Adultery, fornication, prostitution
	נשחתה	*Nishchatah* –It was corrupt (Gen. 6:12)
	סגן	*Sagan* –Ruler, prefect, governor, a subordinate ruler *Segan* –Prefect, governor
764	בשבתכם	*Beshivtekem* –When you dwell (Lev. 26:35)
	הראני נא את־כבדך	*Hare'niy Na' 'Eth-Kevodeka* –"Oh, let me behold Your presence!" (Ex. 33:18)
	ולתושבך	*ve-Letoshavak* –And to your settler (Lev. 25:6)
	ונחשת	*ve-Nechoshet* –And brass (Ex. 25:3)
	ותושבים	*ve-Toshaviym* –And settlers (Lev. 25:23)
	ותקרבון	*ve-Tiqrevuwn* –And you came near (Deut. 1:22)
	חמישתו	*Chamiyshito* –Its fifth (Lev. 5:16)
	חמשיתו	*Chamishiyto* –Its fifth (Lev. 22:14)
	חנון	*Chanuwn* –Gracious; Hanun, king of Ammon who involved the Amonites in a disastrous war with David; one who repaired the wall; one who repaired the valley gate of Jerusalem
	קדרנית	*Qedoranniyth* –Mournfully
	תנחשו	*Tenachashuw* –Divination (Lev. 19:26)
765	אדניקם	*'Adoniyqam* –Adonikam, man who returned to Palestine after the exile (Ezra 2:13)
	בית המרחק	*Beyth HaMerchaq* –Beth Merhak, possibly a town on the bank of Kidron (2 Sam. 15:17)
	הצרעת	*HaTzara'at* –The leprosy (Lev. 13:12)
	השנית	*HaSheniyt* –The second (Gen. 4:19)
	התישים	*HaTiyashiym* –The he-goats (Gen. 30:35)
	והשמדתי	*ve-Hishmadtiy* –And I will destroy (Lev. 26:30)
	ויברך אתם אלהים	*Va-ye-varekh otham Elohim* –"And God blessed them" (Gen. 1:22, 28)
	שכל הקדוש	*Sekhel HaQodesh* –Sanctifying Intelligence (3rd Path)
766	אשכלתיה	*'ashkeloteyah* –Its clusters (Gen. 40:10)
	גמיגין	*Gamigin* –Goetic demon #4
	ובנחשת	*ve-Vanchoshet* –And in brass (Ex. 31:4)
	ותישים	*ve-Teyashiym* –And he-goats (Gen. 32:15)
	ותעצר	*ve-Ta'atzar* –And was stayed (Num. 17:13)
	כליון	*Killayown* –Completion, destruction, consumption, annihilation; failing, pining; Chilion, son of Naomi and husband Orpah
	מכון	*Makhon* –Emplacement, fixed or established place, foundation; the 6th Heaven (corr. to *Hesed*)
	סון	*Seven* –Syene, town on the southern frontier of Egypt

		(see also סונה)[866]
	עצום	*'atsuwm* –Mighty, vast, numerous
	קרנתיו	*Qarnotayv* –Its horns (Ex. 27:2)
	שנותי	*Shanotiy* –I whet (Deut. 32:41)
	תערצו	*Ta'artzuw* –You be terrified (Deut. 20:3)
	תפריעו	*Tafriy'uw* –Disturb, interfere (Ex. 5:4)
	תשכילו	*Taskiylo* –You may prosper (Deut. 29:8)
767	אסון	*'asown* –Evil, mischief, harm, hurt
	את־שמ יהוה	*'Eth-Shem* YHVH –"The Name of the Lord" (Ps. 135:1)
	והשמותי	*ve-Hashimotiy* –And bring to desolation (Lev. 26:31)
	ונשאתי	*ve-Nasa'tiy* –Then I will forgive (Gen. 18:26)
	זקנים	*Zeqanem* –Elders, wise ones
	מזיקים	*Mezziqim* –Demons; injurers
	מאון	*Se'own* –Sandal, boot (of soldier)
	תבל וישבי בה	*Tebel ve-Yoshvey Vah* –"World and all its inhabitants" (Ps. 24:1)
768	בית פעור	*Beyth Pe'owr* –Beth Peor, town of Moab near Pisgah where the Israelites placed their camp while warring against Og
	וקברתני	*ve-Qevartaniy* –And bury me (Gen. 47:30)
	ושכבתמ	*ve-Shekavtem* –And you shall lie down (Lev. 26:6)
	חמישית	*Chamiyshiyt* –A fifth (Gen. 47:24)
	חסן	*Chasan* –To be treasured up, be hoarded, be laid up, be stored; to take possession of (Aramaic) *Chason* –Strong *Chesen* –Power, strength, power of the king, royal power *Chosen* –Riches, treasure, wealth
	לחם עני	*Lechem 'Oniy* –"Bread of anguish" (Deut. 16:3)
	נחשתי	*Necheshethi* –Coppery, brassy *Nichashtiy* –I have observed the signs (Gen. 30:27)
	שלחתיכ	*Shelachtiyak* –Have sent you (Ex. 3:12)
	תשיבנו	*Teshiyvenuw* –You shall restore it (Ex. 22:25)
769	בן־אוני	*Ben-'Owniy* –Ben-oni, name given to Rachel's child as she died bearing him; Jacob changed his name to Benjamin (Gen. 35:18)
	ומזרקתיו	*ve-Mizreqotayv* –And its basins (Ex. 27:3)
	מעשה שדימ	*Ma'asheh Shedim* –"Demoniacal works"
	–Prime number	
770	וחמישתו	*ve-Chamiyshito* –And a fifth part of it (Lev. 5:24; Num. 5:7)
	ונטשתה	*ve-Netashtah* –And let it lie fallow (Ex. 23:11)
	כי באתי אל הארצ	*Ki vati el HaAretz* –"That I have entered the land" (Deut. 26:3)

[866] סונה (121).

	כנן	*Kanan* –Root, support (of tree), shoot, stock
	משכית	*Maskiyth* –Show-piece, figure, imagination, image, idol, picture; covering
	נפלים	*Nefilim* –"Giants" (Gen. 6:4; Num. 13:33)
	סין	*Siyn* –Sin, city on the eastern side of the Nile – possibly Pelusium, but also identified with Syene; wilderness area located between the Gulf of Suez and Sinai
	עין שמש	*'Eyn Shemesh* –En Shemesh, well and town east of Bethany on the road between Jerusalem and Jericho
	ענמים	*'Anamim* –Anamim, descendants of Mizraim (Gen. 10:13; 1 Chr. 1:11)[867]
	ערך	*'arak* –To arrange, set or put or lay in order, set in array, prepare, order, ordain, handle, furnish, esteem, equal, direct, compare; to value, tax
		'erek –Order, row, estimate, things that are set in order, layer, pile
	עשת	*'ashath* –To be smooth, be shiny, gleam; to think
		'ashith –To think, plan (Aramaic)
		'esheth –Plate, slab, something fabricated (Song 5:14)
	פצם	*Patzam* –To split or break open
	פרצת	*Paratzat* –You have made a breach (Gen. 38:29)
	צרעתי	*Tzor'iy* –Zorites (see also צרעי)[868]
	צרפת	*Tzarephath* –Zarephath, town located near Zidon that was the residence of Elijah
	קיתרס	*Qiytharos* –Musical instrument (probably zither or lyre – Aramaic)
	קערת	*Qa'arat* –Dish (Num. 7:13)
	שלמת	*Salmat* –Garment (Ex. 22:25)
	שמלת	*Semalot* –Raiment (Gen. 45:22)
		Shemilath –Garments
	תמשל	*Timshal* –May rule (Gen. 4:7)
		Timshol –Shall rule (Gen. 37:29)
	תעש	*Ta'as* –You make (Gen. 22:12)
	תשע	*Teshah* –Nine, nonad
771	אפרסתכי	*'Afarsathkay* –Apharsachites
	ארבעימ יומ וארבעימ לילה	*Arbawuwm Yom Viarbaim Layilaw* –"Forty days and forty nights" (Gen. 7:12)
	אלמן	*Alman* –Widowed, forsaken, forsaken of a widow
		Almon –Widowhood
	בן־אבינדב	*Ben-'Abiynadab* –Ben-Abinadab, one of Solomon's twelve officers, married to Solomon's daughter Taphath (1 Kings 4:11)
	והנסתרימ	*ve-Hanistariym* –And those that are hidden (Deut. 7:20)
	לאשמת	*La'shmat* –To bring guiltiness (Lev. 4:3)
	לקראתמ	*Liqra'tam* –To meet them (Gen. 18:2)

[867] Possibly an unknown Egyptian tribe.

[868] צרעי (370).

	שלתיאל	*Shelathiel* –Shealthiel, father of Zerubbabel (this spelling used only in Hag. 1:12, 14; 2:2); "Boon of God," Angel of Virgo
	שעיר אנפין	*Seir Anpin* –The Bearded Countenance; a title of *Tiferet*
	תשליכהו	*Tashliykuhuw* –You shall cast him (Ex. 1:22)
772	בען	*Be'on* –Beon, ancient Amorite city located east of the Jordan river and north of Moab (this spelling used only in Num. 32:3 – see also Baal Meon and Beth Baal Meon)[869]
	מלבן	*Malben* –Brick mold, brick kiln, quadrangle
	משלבת	*Meshulavot* –Joined (Ex. 26:17)
	צבעים	*Tzebo'iym* –Zeboim, valley between Michmash and the wilderness to the east; Benjamite town, probably north of Lydda
	שאלתיאל	*She'altiy'el* –Shealthiel, son of Jeconiah; father of Zerubbabel
	שבעת	*Shavu'at* –Oath (Ex. 22:10)
		Shavu'ot –Weeks, Shavuoth (Ex. 34:22)
		Siv'at –Seven (Gen. 8:10)
	תשבע	*Tishava'* –Swears (Lev. 5:4)
		Tishave'a –You shall swear (Deut. 6:13)
773	כהן הגדול	*Kohen HaGodhol* –High Priest
	עגן –Prime number	*'agan* –To shut oneself in or off or up
774	בן־חסד	*Ben-Chesed* –Ben-Hesed, one of Solomon's twelve supply officers
	בשבעת	*Bishvu'at* –With oath (Num. 5:21)
	בת־שבע	*Bath-Sheba'* –Bathsheba, beautiful wife of Urijah the Hittite and later wife of David (2 Sam. 11:3; 12:24; 1 Kings 1:11-2:19) – called Bathshua in 1 Chr. 3:5
	יוחנן	*Yowchanan* –Johanan, captain who allied with Gedaliah after the fall of Jerusalem; eldest son of Josiah, king of Judah; son of Elioenai; father of a priest in Solomon'stime; two valiant men who joined David at Ziklag; returned exile; priest in the days of Joiakim
	לשותלח	*Leshuwtelach* –Of Shuthelah (Num. 26:35)
	סדין	*Sadiyn* –Linen wrapper (a type of garment)
	עדן	*'adan* –To luxuriate, delight oneself
		'aden –Hitherto, still, yet
		Eden –Eden, descendant of Gershom; Levite in the time of Hezekiah; Eden, garden that God created as the first residence of man; region in Mesopotamia; luxury, dainty, delight, finery; delight
		'iddan –Time (Aramaic)

[869] Baal Meon (278, 837), Beth Baal Meon (680, 1330).

775 אדרמלך — *Adramelek* –Archdemon corr. to *Hod*
העשת — *Ha'osot* –That do (Lev. 18:29)
הקערת — *HaQa'rot* –The dishes (Num. 4:7)
ונשתחוה — *ve-Nishtachaveh* –And we will worship (Gen. 22:5)
עשתה — *'asatah* –She had prepared (Gen. 27:17)
'astah –She has done (Deut. 22:21)
תעשה — *Ta'aseh* –You shall do (Gen. 6:14; 26:29; Ex. 23:24)
Te'aseh –Shall be made (Lev. 2:11); shall be done (Ex. 35:2)
תשעה — *Tishah* –Nine
–The number of children of Arah who returned from exile (Ezra 2:5)

776 ומשלת — *ve-Mashalat* –And you shall rule (Deut. 15:6)
ועשת — *ve-'asat* –And it shall bring forth (Lev. 25:21)
ופרצת — *ve-Faratzat* –And you shall spread abroad (Gen. 28:14)
ושמלת — *ve-Semalot* –And raiment (Ex. 3:22)
ושמתיך — *ve-Samtiyak* –And I will put you (Ex. 33:22)
ותעש — *ve-Ta'as* –And made (Gen. 27:14)
ותשע — *ve-Tesha'* –And nine (Gen. 5:8)
כעופרת — *Ka'oferet* –As lead (Ex. 15:10)
לשמות — *Lishmot* –According to the names (Num. 26:55)
מלון — *Malown* –Place of lodging, inn, khan
נכון — *Nakown* –Nachon, either a combined name of two individuals, or two place names, or a combination of both (1 Sam. 6:6; 1 Chr. 13:9)[870]
סיון — *Siyvan* –Sivan, the 9th month of the Jewish calendar – it is associated with Gemini and the tribe Benjamin
עון — *'avan* –To eye, look at
'avon –Perversity, depravity, iniquity, guilt or punishment of iniquity
עשות — *'ashowth* –Smooth, shiny
'Ashvath –Ashvath, son of Japhlet and descendant of Asher
'asot –Made, will do (Gen. 2:4)
שלמות — *Shelomowt* –Unhewn, whole (Deut. 27:6); Shelomoth, descendant of Izhar; descendant of Gershon; one over the treasures in the days of David (this spelling used only in 1 Chr. 26:26)
שמלתו — *Simlato* –His garment (Ex. 22:26)
תעשו — *Ta'asuw* –You shall do, make (Gen. 19:8; Lev. 16:29)

777 אחת רוח אלהים חיים — *Achath Ruach Elohim Chayyim* –One is the Spirit of the Living God
בעשתה — *Ba'astah* –By its doing (Lev. 4:27)
בתשעה — *Betash'ah* –In the ninth day (Lev. 23:32; 2 Kings 25:3; Jer. 39:2; 52:6)
זרעך — *Zaracha* –Your seed

---

[870] Literally "destruction" or a "javelin."

מתושאל *Methusael* –Methusael, father of Lamech (Gen. 4:18)
עולמ חקליפות *Olam HaQlippoth* –The world of Shells or Demons
עזרך *'Ezireka* –Your help
עזן *'Azzan* –Azzan, father of a chief of Issachar (Num. 34:26)

–The number of years that Lamech lived (Gen. 5:31)
–The name of A.C.'s cabalistic treatise that included *Sefer Sefiroth.*

778 בשלמתו *Besalmato* –In his garment (Deut. 24:13)
בת־שוע *Bath-Shuwa'* –Bathshua, wife of Judah; another name of Bathsheba, beautiful wife of Urijah the Hittite and later wife of David (1Chr. 3:5)[871]
ושבעת *ve-Sava'at* –And be satisified (Deut. 6:11)
ve-Siv'at –And seven (Num. 31:36)
חסין *Chasiyn* –Strong, mighty
משלחת *Mishlachath* –Discharge, sending, sending away, deputation
סיחן *Sihown* –Sihon, King of the Ammorites defeated by Israel (see also סיחון)[872]
שבעות *Shavu'ot* –Weeks
שלחתמ *Shelachtem* –You sent (Gen. 45:8)
תשבעו *Tisba'uw* –You will be satisfied (Lev. 26:26); You shall be filled (Ex. 16:12)
Tishv'uw –You shall swear (Lev. 19:12)

779 טען *Ta'an* –To load; to pierce

780 ובשבעת *ve-Vashvi'it* –And in the eleventh (Ex. 21:2)
יהוחנן *Yehowchanan* –Jehohanan, gatekeeper of the tabernacle in David's time; chief captain of Judah; father of Ishmael; one who divorced his wife after the exile; priest who returned to Jerusalem with Zerubbabel; singer at the purification of the wall of Jerusalem; son of Tobiah the Ammonite; son of Eliashib
יען *Ya'an* –Because, therefore, because that; because of, on account of
Ya'en –Ostrich (ceremonially unclean bird)
לילין *Lilin* –A class of demons
מספרת *Mispereth* –Mispereth, one who returned from captivity (this spelling used only in Neh. 7:7 – see also מספר)[873]
מפרסת *Mafreset* –Parted, cloven (Lev. 11:3)
סכן *Sakan, sakan* –To be of use or service or profit or benefit; to incur danger; to be poor
saken –To shut up, stop up

---

[871] See Bathsheba (774).
[872] סיחון (134, 784).
[873] מספר (380).

ספלים *Sehalim* –Cups

עין *Ayin* –Ain, town of Judah near Rimmon, assigned to the Levites serving the tribe of Simeon; site on the boundary line of the Promised Land; eye; spring, fountain; 16th letter of Hebrew alphabet

עשית *'asiyat* –You have done (Gen. 3:13; 4:10)

עשתי *'ashtey* –One, eleven, eleventh

פן *Pen* –Corner; lest, not, beware lest; lest

פרך *Perek* –Harshness, severity, cruelty

פתרנימ *Pitroniym* –Interpretations (Gen. 40:8)

צפים *Tzophiym* –Zophim, place on top of Pisgah where Balaam viewed the Israelite camp

שלמית *Shelomiyt* –Shelomith, mother of one stoned for blasphemy in the wilderness; daughter of Zerubbabel; descendant of Levi and Kohath; child of Rehoboam

שמתמ *Shemotam* –Their names (Gen. 25:16)

שפת *Safat* –Speech, edge; lip (Gen. 11:7)
Shafath –To set, place, put, ordain

תעשי *Ta'asiy* –You shall do (Gen. 20:13)

תפש *Tafash* –To catch, sieze
Tofes –Handle (Gen. 4:21)

תשלימ *Tashliym* –Will make peace (Deut. 20:12)

–The sum of the numbers 1 through 39

781 אפן *'ofen* –Circumstance, condition, timely

אשפת *'ashpoth* –Ash-heap, refuse heap, dunghill

גבעון *Gib'own* –Gibeon, chief city of the Hivites, assigned to the tribe of Benjamin

ועשתה *ve-'astah* –And do (Lev. 5:17)

ממשאת *Mimas'ot* –Than the portions (Gen. 43:34)

שערורה *Sha'arurah* –Horrid thing

תשועה *Teshuwah* –Salvation, deliverance

782 אלהי אברהמ אלהי יצחק ואלהי יעקב *Elohi Abraham Elohi Itzchaq ve-Elohi Yaaqob* –"The God of Abraham, the God of Isaac, and the God of Jacob" (Ex. 3:6)

בעשתי *Ba'shetey* –Eleventh

בשמתמ *Bishmotam* –By their names (Gen. 25:13)

בשפת *Bisfat* –In the edge (Ex. 26:4)

מקבלים *Mekubbaliym* –Kabbalists

עבדון *Abdown* –Abdon, 11th Judge of Israel; descendant of Benjamin who dwelt in Jerusalem; firstborn son of Jeiel and an ancestor of King Saul, mentioned in Chronicles; official sent by King Josiah to Huldah to inquire of the meaning of the Law (see also Achbor – possibly the same as the second Abdon)[874]

[874] Achbor (298).

783 גדעון *Gideon* –The 5th Judge of Israel
כמיגין *Gamigin* –Goetic demon #4 (Aurum Solis spelling; probably a misprint)
גפן *Gefen* –Vine, vine tree
השבעות *HaShavu'ot* –The weeks (Deut. 16:16)
והלבשתמ *ve-Hilbashtam* –And you shall put upon them, and you shall clothe them (Ex. 29:8)
ומתושאל *ve-Metuwsha'el* –And Methusael
זעון *Za'avan* –Zaavan, descendant of Seir
כי אני יהוה אלהיכם *Ki ahni* YHVH *elohaychem* –"For I am YHVH, your God" (Lev. 11:44; 20:7; 24:22; 25:17; 26:1)

784 יקדעם *Yoqde'am* –Jokdeam, city in the mountains of Judah south of Hebron
מדמן *Madmen* –Madmen, location in Moab – may be modern Khirbet Dimneh
מחלון *Machlown* –Mahlon, first husband of Ruth who died in Moab
מתושלח *Methushelach* –Methuselah, longest living human recorded in the Hebrew Bible, grandfather of Noah (Gen. 5:21-27)
סיחון *Sihon* –Sihon, King of the Ammorites defeated by Israel (see also סיחן)[875]
עדין *'adiyn* –Voluptuous; Adin, ancestor of returned captives; one whose descendant returned with Ezra; Jewish leader who sealed the covenant in Nehemiah's time
פדן *Paddan* –Padan, plain region of Mesopotamia from the Lebanon Mountains to beyond the Euphrates, and from the Taurus Mountains on the north to beyond Damascus on the south (this spelling used only in Gen. 48:7 – see also פדן ארם)[876]
שבועות *Shavuot* –Weeks; the holiday celebrating the harvest and giving of the Torah
שיחרירונ *Shichiriron* –The Black Ones; *Qlippoth* of Cancer
תשלחומ *Teshalchuwm* –You shall put them (Num. 5:3)

785 אפדן *'appeden* –Palace
גוסיון *Gusion* –Goetic demon #11
טלמון *Talmown* –Talmon, Levite in Ezra's day – a temple porter
עזבון *'izzabown* –Wares, goods
פשתה *Pasatah* –Be spread (Lev. 13:23)
Pastah –Be spread (Lev. 13:8; 13:28)
Pishteh –Flax, linen
Pishtah –Flax
תיעשה *Tey'aseh* –Shall be made (Ex. 25:31)

---

875 סיחן (128, 778).
876 פדן ארם (375, 1585).

	תפשה	*Tifseh* –Shall spread abroad (Lev. 13:7)
786	אש מנ השמימ	*Esh Min HaShamaim* –"Fire from Heaven" (2 Kings 1:10)
	השמאלית	*HaSema'liyt* –The left (direction) (Lev. 14:15)
	וספרתמ	*ve-Sefartem* –And you shall count (Lev. 23:15)
	ועשית	*ve-'asiyat* –And do, and you shall make (Gen. 40:14)
	ופרקת	*ve-Faraqat* –And you will take off (Gen. 27:40)
	ושכנתי	*ve-Shachantiy* –That I may dwell (Ex. 25:8)
	ושמתמ	*ve-Samtam* –Then make them (Gen. 47:6)
		ve-Samtem –And you shall put (Ex. 3:22)
	ותשממ	*ve-Tesimem* –And put them (Gen. 31:34)
	יסוד עולם	*Yesod Olam* –Eternal Foundation of the World, a title of *Yesod*
	ישעות	*Yeshuw'at* –Salvation (Ex. 14:13)
	ישעתו	*Yeshuato* –His salvation (Deut. 32:15)
	כצערתו	*Kitz'irato* –According to his youth (Gen. 43:33)
	עיון	*'Iyown* –Ijon, city of northern Palestine belonging to the tribe of Naphtali
	פון	*Puwn* –To be perplexed, be distracted (meaning dubious – Ps. 88:16)
	פורך	*Furcas* –Goetic demon #50
	קערתיו	*Qa'rotayu* –Its dishes (Ex. 25:29; 37:16)
	שולמית	*Shuwlammiyth* –Shulamite, young woman mentioned in Song of Songs 7:1[877]
	שלומית	*Shelowmiyth* –Shelomith, ancestor of a family that returned from the Exile (not to be confused with Shelomoth)
	שמותמ	*Shemotam* –Their names (Ex. 28:12)
	שמלתיו	*Simlotayu* –His garments (Gen. 37:34)
	שפרור	*Shafruwr* –Canopy, royal pavilion
	שפתו	*Sefato* –Its edge (Ex. 28:27)
787	אופן	*Ofan* –Wheel, to revolve; one of the *Ofanim* (the wheel in Ezekiel's vision)
	השביעת	*Hashviy'it* –Weeks (Lev. 23:16)
		HaShviy'it –The seventh (Lev. 25:4)
	ואתפש	*ve-'etfos* –And I took hold (Deut. 9:17)
	זקן	*Zaqan* –Beard, chin
		Zaqen –To be old, become old, old (of humans), elder
		Zaqun –Old age, extreme old age
		Zoqen –Old age
	חשנ משפט	*Chashen Mishpat* –"Breastplate of decision" (Ex. 28:15)
	לקראתנו	*Liqra'tenuw* –To meet us (Gen. 24:65)
	–Prime number	
788	חכמה נסתרה	*Chokmah Nisetarah* –Secret Wisdom
	חפן	*Chofen* –Handfuls, hollow of the hand

[877] Many scholars interpret Shulamite as Shunammite – a woman from the city of Shunem (1 Sam. 28:4).

	לבנון	*Lebanown* –Lebanon, one of two ranges of mountains in northern Palestine
	למשחית	*Limaschit* –To destroy (Ex. 12:13)
	משחתמ	*Mashchatam* –Their anointing, their corruption (Lev. 22:25; 40:15)
	שפחת	*Shifchat* –Handmaid of (Gen. 16:8)
789	אלחנן	*'Elkanan* –Elkanan, Jair's son who fought the Gittites; Dodo's son who was a chief of David
	חצר התיכונ	*Chatzar Hatikown* –Hazar Hatticon, village on the border of Havran
	עטין	*'atiyn* –Bucket, pail
	תשפט	*Tishfot* –You shall judge (Lev. 19:15)
790	בחצצרת	*Bachtzotzrot* –With (the) trumpets (Num. 10:9)
	במושבתמ	*Bemoshvotam* –In their dwellings (Ex. 10:23)
	בשחפת	*Bashachefet* –With consumption (Deut. 28:22)
	ומשדמת	*ve-Mishadmot* –And of the fields of (Deut. 32:32)
	כען	*Ke'an* –Now, at this time, until now (Aramaic)
	מימן	*Miyamin* –Miamin, priest in the time of David; one who sealed the new covenant; one who divorced his foreign wife after the Exile; chief of the priests who returned with Zerubbabel from Babylon (this spelling used only in Neh. 12:5 – see also מנימין)[878]
	משנת	*Mishnat* –From the year (Lev. 25:50)
	נשמת	*Nishmat* –Breath of (Gen. 2:7)
	עכן	*'Akan* –Achan, one who stole part of the spoil of Jericho and brought "trouble" on his people and was killed for this (Josh. 7:1-24 – see also Achar, Achor)[879]
	ערסתכמ	*'arisotekem* –Of your dough (Num. 15:20)
	עשיתי	*'asiytiy* –I have made, done (Gen. 7:4)
	פדון	*Padown* –Padon, one who returned with Zerubbabel
	פתרסימ	*Patrusiym* –Pathrusim, descendant of Mizraim; possibly the inhabitants of Pathros (Gen. 10:14)
	צן	*Tzen* –Thorn, barb (meaning dubious – Job 5:5; Prov. 22:5); Zin, wilderness on the southern border of Canaan (not to be confused with Sin)
	צרך	*Tzorek* –Need
	שדפות	*Shedufot* –Blasted (Gen. 41:23)
	שכלתמ	*Shikaltem* –You have bereaved (Gen. 42:36)
	שמלתכ	*Shimelatak* –Your raiment (Deut. 8:4)
	שממית	*Semamiyth* –A kind of lizard (Prov. 30:28 – here translated as spider)
	שמנת	*Shamanat* –You did grow fat (Deut. 32:15)
		Shemonat –Eight (Gen. 17:12)

---

[878] מנימין (200, 850).

[879] Achar (290), Achor (296).

	תפשי	*Tofsey* –Them who took... in hand (Num. 31:27)
	תקצר	*Tiqtzar* –Too short (Num. 11:23) *Tiqtzor* –You reap (Deut. 24:19)
	תשיעי	*Teshiy'iy* –Ninth
791	אויל מרדך	*'Eviyl Merodak* –Evil-Merodach, king of Babylon
	התפרקו	*Hitfaraquw* –Let them take (it) off (Ex. 32:24)
	ותפשה	*ve-Tefasah* –And lay hold on her (Deut. 22:28)
	לקראתכמ	*Liqra'tkem* –Against you (Deut. 1:44)
	מהומן	*Mehuwman* –Mehuman, one of the chamberlains of Ahasuerus
	מתנשא	*Mitnasse'* –Exalted
	נאמן	*Ne'eman* –Faithful, loyal
	שנאתמ	*Sene'tem* –You have hated (Gen. 26:27)
	שראצר	*Shar'etzer* –Sharezer, son of the Assyrian king Sennacherib who, with his brother, killed their father (2 Kings 19:37; Is. 37:38); one sent to consult the priests and prophets (Zech. 7:2)[880]
792	ותפשו	*ve-Tafshovu* –Then they shall lay hold (Deut. 21:19)
	תשבצ	*Tashbetz* –Chequer work (Ex. 28:4)
793	אבצן	*Ibtzan* –Ibzan, 9th Judge of Israel, a Bethelemite judge (Judg. 12:8, 10)
	אצבן	*'Etzbon* –Ezbon, son of Gad (see also Ozni, אצבון)[881]; descendant of Benjamin
	השחפת	*Hashachafat* –Consumption (Lev. 26:16)
	והשביעת	*ve-Hashviy'it* –And in the seventh (Ex. 23:11)
	וזקניכם	*ve-Zeknaychem* –And your elders
	יהושבעת	*Yehowshab'ath* – Jehoshabeath, daughter of Jeohoram, king of Judah, who helped conceal Joash (this name only used in 2 Chr. 22:11 – see also Jehosheba)[882]
	פגשתי	*Pagashtiy* –I met (Gen. 33:8)
	שפחתה	*Shifchatah* –Her handmaid (Gen. 16:3)
794	ושמחתמ	*ve-Semachtem* –And you will rejoice (Lev. 23:40)
	ושפחת	*ve-Shefachot* –And maidservants (Gen. 12:16)
	יחסיון	*Ye-chesayun* –"His [God's] refuge"
	חפשות	*Chofshuwth* –Separateness, freedom
	חצוצרת	*Chatzotzrot* –Trumpets (Num. 10:2)
	פס דמים	*Pas Dammiym* –Pas-Dammim, Philistine settlement near Socoh, apportioned to the tribe of Judah (this spelling used only in 1 Chr. 11:13 – see also Ephes Dammim)[883]
	שלחתנו	*Shelachtanuw* –You sent us (Num. 13:27)

[880] Sharezer literally means "He has protected the king," which may be an ironic reference in the first case.

[881] אצבון (149, 799), Ozni (68).

[882] Jehosheba (393).

[883] Ephes Dammim (235, 795).

	שפחתו	*Shifchato* –His handmaid (Gen. 29:24)
	תשלחנו	*Teshalchenuw* –Let him go, send (Deut. 15:13); you shall let him go, send (Deut. 15:12)
795	אפס דמים	*'Efes Dammiym* –Ephes Dammim, Philistine settlement near Socoh
	הצן	*Hotzen* –Armor?, weapons?, chariots? (meaning uncertain – Ezek. 23:24)
	התשיעי	*HaTeshiy'iy* –The ninth (Num. 7:60)
	יהועדן	*Yehow'addan* –Jehoaddan, mother of King Amaziah and wife of King Joash (this spelling used only in 2 Chr. 25:1 - see also יהועדין)[884]
	לא תנחשו	*La Tenachashuw* –"You shall not guess," or "You shall not practice divination" (Lev. 19:26)
	מטמון	*Matmon* –Treasure; hidden treasure, hidden or secret thing
	שפתיה	*Sefateyah* –Her lips (Num. 30:9)
796	בחצצרות	*Bachatzotzruwt* –Trumpets (Num. 10:8)
	ודפקום	*ve-Defaquwm* –And if they overdrive them (Gen. 33:13)
	והפשתה	*ve-HaFishtah* –And the flax (Ex. 9:31)
	ולצרעת	*ve-Letzara'at* –And for the leprosy (Lev. 14:55)
	ומקלכם	*ve-Maqelkem* –And your staff (Ex. 12:11)
	ושדופת	*ve-Sheduwfot* –And blasted (Gen. 41:6)
	ושמנת	*ve-Shemonat* –And eight (Num. 2:24)
	ותקצר	*va-Tiqtzar* –And became impatient (Num. 21:4)
	מנון	*Manown* –Grief, progeny, thankless one (meaning uncertain – Prov. 29:21)
	משנתו	*Mishnato* –Out of his sleep (Gen. 28:16)
	סלון	*Sillown* –Brier, thorn
	תקצור	*Tiqtzor* –You shall reap (Lev. 25:5)
	תקצרו	*Tiqtzeruw* –Shall reap it (Lev. 25:11)
797	אמנון	*'Amnown –'Amnown* –Amnon, son of David
	ונשאתמ	*ve-Nesha'tem* –And bring (Gen. 45:19)
	עין גדי	*'Eyn Gediy* –En-Gedi, town on the western shore of the Dead Sea assigned to the tribe of Judah (see also Hazazon Tamar)[885]
	עין חדה	*'Eyn Chaddah* –En Haddah, village of the tribe of Issachar
	עצם הכבוד	*Etzem HaKabodh* –Essence of glory
	–Prime number	
798	אמאימון	*Amaimon* –Demon King of Earth and the North; Demon King of the East and Air (Goetia)
	ושבצת	*ve-Shibatzat* –And you shall weave (Ex. 38:39)

---

[884] יהועדין (155, 805).

[885] Hazazon Tamar (878, 1528; 884, 1534).

חצן *Chetsen* –Bosom, bosom of a garment
Chotsen –Bosom, lap
ויהי לה לבן *VaYehiy Lah Leven* –"And he became to her as a son" (Ex. 2:10)
משחתים *Mashchitiym* –Will destroy (Gen. 19:13)
משחיתם *Mashchiytam* –I will destroy them (Gen. 6:13)
שלחתני *Shilachtaniy* –Sent me away (Gen. 31:42)

799 אצבון *'Etzbown* –Ezbon, son of Gad (see also Ozni, אצבן)[886]; descendant of Benjamin
השפחות *HaShefachot* –The handmaids (Gen. 33:1)
פרקי אבות *Pirkei Avot* –Mishnah tractate

800 וחצצרות *ve-Chatzotzrot* –And the trumpets (Num. 31:6)
ושפחות *ve-Shefachot* –And maid servants (Gen. 30:43)
יעכן *Ya'kan* –Jachan, descendant of Gad
כנענים *Kanaanim* –Canaanites
כפן *Kafan* –To hunger, be hungry, hungrily desire; to twist, bend; hunger, famine, painful hunger
לעשת *La'ast* –That you should do, to work, to keep (Ex. 35:1)
מכמן *Mikman* –Hidden stores, hidden treasure
מנין *Minyan* –Number (Aramaic)
מצרעת *Metzora'at* –Leprous (Ex. 12:10); was leprous (Ex. 4:6)
מקסם *Miqsam* –Divination
סמן *Saman* –To mark off
ספסם *Saspam* –Angel of 1d Aquarius
ערסתיכם *'arisoteykem* –Your dough (Num. 15:21)
ף (final) *Peh* –17th letter of Hebrew alphabet
פנינים *Peninim* –Rubies, gems
קנסנ A permutation of יהוה by *Aiq Bekar*[887]
קן *Qen* –Nest
קשת *Qashat* –Bow; bowman, archer; Sagittarius
Qeshet –Bow (for hunting or war)
רם *Ram* –Ram, ancestor of David (Ruth 4:19); son of Jerahmeel of Judah (1 Chr. 2:27); head of the family of Elihu (Job 32:2)
רשש *Rashash* –To beat down, shatter
שך *Sekh* –Thorn; enclosure
Sok –Booth, pavilion
Suwk –To hedge or fence up or about
שנתים *Shenatayim* –Two years (Gen. 11:10)
שקת *Shoqeth* –Watering trough
שרש *Sharash* –To uproot, take root
Sheresh –Root; Sheresh, descendant of Judah through Jerahmeel
ששר *Shashar* –Red color, vermilion
שתק *Shataq* –To be quiet, be silent

886 אצבן (143, 793), Ozni (68).
887 See Introduction.

	תשמדון	*Tishameduwn* –Shall be destroyed (Deut. 4:26)
	תשפכ	*Tishfok* –You shall pour out (Ex. 29:12)
	תת	*Tet* –Yield, give (Gen. 4:12)
801	אף	*'af* –Also, yea, though, so much the more (conj. – denoting addition, especially of something greater); furthermore, indeed; also, yea (Aramaic); nostril, nose, face; anger; the initials of *Aur Pesuwt*; 16th Gate of the 231 Gates
	ארם	*'Aram* –Aram, son of Shem; son of Abraham's nephew, descendent from Asher; Ram, the father of Amminadab; Aram, location occupied by the Aramaenans
	אשך	*'eshek* –Testicle, stone
	אתת	*Othoth* –Signs, tokens
	חפזון	*Chippazown* –Hurriedly, in haste, trepidation, hurried flight
	ראם	*Re'am* –To rise
		Re'em –Great aurochs or wild bulls now extinct
802	בנימן	*Benjamin* –Benjamin, youngest son of Jacob and progenitor of a tribe of Judah (assoc. w/Sagittarius); descendant of Benjamin (1 Chr. 7:10); descendant of Harim; one who helped to repair the wall of Jerusalem; one who helped to dedicate the wall of Jerusalem
	בף	*Baf* –Ball, stone, lump, hailstone, resin; 36th Gate of the 231 Gates
	ברם	*Beram* –Only, nevertheless, but (Aramaic)
	בתת	*Betet* –When will give (Ex. 16:8)
	ויתפרקו	*ve-Yitfarquw* –And they took off (Ex. 32:3)
	ויתרצצו	*ve-Yitrotztzu* –And they struggled (Gen. 25:22)
	לשבעת	*Leshiv'at* –To seven (Gen. 7:10)
	קבצים	*Qibtzayim* –Kibzaim, city of Ephraim given to the Levites (see also Jokmeam)[888]
	שבך	*Sabak* –Network, latticework, net, netting; network of boughs
	תבקש	*Tevaqesh* –Do you seek (Gen. 37:15)
	תבת	*Tevet* –Ark of (Gen. 6:14)
803	אברם	*Abram* –Abraham
	באתת	*Bo'tot* –By signs (Deut. 4:34); with ensigns (Num. 2:2)
	גף	*Gaf* –Back, top; body, person, self; height, elevation; wing (of bird – Aramaic); 55th Gate of the 231 Gates
	ומשנאתו	*Vomisin'ato* –Because he hated (Deut. 9:28)
	רגם	*Ragam* –To stone, slay or kill by stoning
		Regem –Regem, descendant of Caleb (see also Regem-melech)[889]

[888] Jokmeam (260, 820).

	תגת	*Tiger* –To haggle
804	אגף	*Aggaf* –Wing of an army, band, army, hordes
	דלען	*Dil'an* –Dilean, city in the lowlands of Judah, possible the same as Tell en-Najileh
	דף	*Dap* –73rd Gate of the 231 Gates
	לעדן	*La'dan* –Laadan, descendant of Ephraim; Levite from the family of Gershon (see also Libni)[890]
	משתחוים	*Mishtachaviym* –Were bowing down (Gen. 37:9)
	צידן	*Tziydon* –Zidon, ancient city of Canaan (this spelling used only in Gen. 10:15 – see also צידון)[891]
	רדם	*Radam* –To be asleep, unconscious
	שפחתיו	*Shifchotayv* –His handmaids (Gen. 32:23)
	תקדש	*Tiqdash* –Be forfeited (Deut. 22:9)
	תשמטנה	*Tishmetenah* –You shall let it rest (Ex. 23:11)
805	אדרם	*'Adoram* –Adoram, alternate name for Adoniram
	הף	*Hap* –90th Gate of the 231 Gates
	הקשת	*HaQeshet* –The bow (Gen. 9:14)
	הרם	*Harum* –Harum, descendant of Judah
		Horam –Horam, king of Gezer defeated by Joshua
	השמינת	*HaShemiynit* –The eighth (Lev. 25:22)
	השקת	*HaShoqet* –The trough (Gen. 24:20)
	התת	*Hathath* –To shout at, be frantic at, assail, break in, overwhelm, imagine mischief
	ושפטתי	*ve-Shafatetiy* –And I will judge (Ex. 18:16)
	יהועדין	*Yehow'addiyn* –Jehoaddan, mother of King Amaziah and wife of King Joash (this spelling used only in 2 Kings 14:2 - see also יהועדן)[892]
	לעשתה	*La'astah* –To do it (Deut. 11:22)
	קשתה	*Qashatah* –Cruel (Gen. 49:7)
	שרשה	*Sharshah* –Chain
806	האתת	*Ha'Otot* –The signs (Ex. 4:17)
	וף	*Vap* –106th Gate of the 231 Gates
	ושפכת	*ve-Shafakat* –And pour upon (Ex. 4:9)
	ותקש	*ve-Teqash* –And she had hard labor (Gen. 35:16)
	ותשק	*ve-Tasheq* –And she (gave to) drink (Gen. 21:19)
	לעשות	*La'asot* –To do, observe (Gen. 2:3)
	לעשתו	*La'asto* –To do it (Gen. 41:32)
	לשמלתו	*Lesimlato* –To his garment (Deut. 22:3)
	מומכן or ממוכן	*Memuwkan* –Memucan, a Persian prince (Esth. 1:14-15, 17-21 – the second spelling used only in Esth. 1:16)
	נושנת	*Noshenet* –Old (Lev. 13:11)

---

[889] Regem-Melech (333, 1373).

[890] Libni (92).

[891] צידון (160, 810).

[892] יהועדן (145, 795).

נשתון *Nishtevan* –Letter (also Aramaic)
עלון *'Alvan* –Alvan, oldest son of Shobal and descendant of Seir (this spelling used only in Gen. 36:23 – see also Aliah)[893]
פרעתון *Pir'athown* –Pirathon, town where Abdon the judge was buried
ציון *Tzion* –Zion, one of the hills on which Jerusalem stood[894]
Tziyown –Dryness, parched land or ground
Tziyuwn –Signpost, monument, market
קון *Quwn* –To chant a dirge, wait, lament
קשות *Qashot* –Roughly (Gen. 42:7)
Qesot –Jars (Num. 4:7)
קשתו *Qashto* –His bow (Gen. 49:24)
רום *Ruwm* –To rise, rise up, be high, be lofty; be rotten, be wormy; haughtiness, height, elevation
שונמית *Shuwnammiyth* –Shunamite
שותק *Shotheq* –Silent
שכלתנו *Soklethanuw* –Insight
שרשו *Sheroshuw* –Uprooting, banishment
תוקש *Tivaqesh* –You be snared (Deut. 7:25)
תקשו *Taqshuw* –You should stiffen (Deut. 10:16)
תשימון *Tesiymuwn* –You shall lay (put) (Ex. 22:24)
תשלכון *Tashlikuwn* –You will cast (throw) (Ex. 22:30)
תשפכו *Tishfekuw* –You shed, spill (Gen. 37:32)
תתו *Tito* –Deliver him (Deut. 2:30)

807 אותת *'uwtot* –Signs (Deut. 6:22)
אמינון *'Amiynown* –*'Amnown* –Amnon, son of David
גדף *Gadaf* –To revile men, to blaspheme God
Gidduf –Revilings, reviling words
יהוה ראפך YHVH *Rafak* –"God thy Healer" – God-name used in Ex. 15:26
זף *Zap* –121st Gate of the 231 Gates
זרם *Zaram* –To pour out, pour forth in floods, flood away
Zerem –Rain-shower, thunderstorm, flood of rain, downpour, rainstorm
מחנה־דן *Machaneh-Dan* –Mahaneh-Dan, campsite between Zorah and Eshtaol (Judg. 18:12)
ראום *Raum* –Goetic demon #40
רזם *Razam* –To wink; flash (of eyes)
תאות *Ta'avat* –The utmost bound (Gen. 49:26)
תתאו *Teta'uw* –You shall mark out (Num. 34:7)

808 אברהם *Abraham* –Abraham
ברום *Berowm* –Variegated cloth, damask
בתתו *Betito* –When he gives (Lev. 20:4)

[893] Aliah (115).
[894] Zion became applied to the Temple and the whole of Jerusalem and its people as a community whose destiny depends on God.

חף — *Chaf*–Pure, innocent, clean; 135th Gate of the 231 Gates

חרם — *Charam* –To ban, devote, destroy utterly, completely destroy, dedicate for destruction, exterminate; to split, slit, mutilate (a part of the body)

Charim –Harim, priest in charge of the third division of temple duties; ancestor of some returning from captivity – his descendants took foreign wives during the exile; one who sealed the new covenant with God after the exile; family that sealed the new covenant with God after the exile

Chorem –Horem, fortress of the tribe of Naphtali – modern Hurah

חשך — *Chasak* –To withhold, restrain, hold back, keep in check, refrain; to be or become dark, grow dim, be darkened, be black, be hidden

Chashok –Obscure, insignificant, low

Choshek –Darkness, obscurity

חתת — *Chathath* –To be shattered, be dismayed, be broken, be abolished, be afraid; terror; Hathath, son of Othniel

Chitat –Terror of (Gen. 35:5)

נחשתנ — *Nehushtan* –Nehushtan, name given to the fiery serpent made by Moses[895]

רחם — *Racham* –To love, love deeply, have mercy; womb (n. mas.); compassion; carrion vulture (extinct bird); Raham, descendant of Caleb

שובך — *Showbak* –Shobach, captain of the army of Hadarezer of Zobah (see also Shophach)[896]

שמחתכמ — *Simchatkem* –Your gladness (Num. 10:10)

שפחתכ — *Shifchatek* –Your maid (Gen. 15:6)

תבקשו — *Tevaqshuw* –You shall seek out (Lev. 19:31)

תחת — *Tachath* –Under, beneath, the under part, instead of; Tahath, descendant of Kohath; descendant of Ephraim; grandson of the latter

Techat –Be dismayed (Deut. 1:21, 31:8)

תתח — *Towthach* –A weapon, perhaps a club or mace

809 אחשרש — *'Achashrosh* –Ahasuerus, father of Darius the Mede; king of Persia (Xerxes); Cambyses, king of Persia (see also אחשורוש)[897]

גוף — *Guwf*–Shut, close

הדרם — *Hadoram* –Hadoram, superintendent of forced labor under David, Solomon, and Rehoboam (2 Chr. 10:18) (see also Adoniram (1 Kings 4:6), and Adoram (2 Sam. 20:24; 1 Kings 12:18))[898]

הדף — *Hadaf*–To thrust, push, drive, cast away, cast out,

---

[895] This pole was set on a pole so that persons bitten by snakes could look at it and live – it was destroyed during the later reforms of Hezekiah because it had become an object of worship.

[896] Shophach (406, 886).

[897] אחשורוש (821).

[898] Adoniram (305, 865), Adoram (245, 805).

expel, thrust away

הצדיקם *HaTzedekim* –The righteous

טף *Taf* –Children, little ones, little children; 148th Gate of the 231 Gates

טרם *Terem* –Before, not yet, before that

עגלון *'Eglown* –Eglon, king of Moab who oppressed Israel in the days of the judges

קטן *Qatan* –Young, small, insignificant, unimportant
Qaton –To be small, be insignificant
Qoten –Little finger

תבואת *Tevuw'at* –Fruits, increases (Lev. 23:39; Deut. 14:22)
Tevuw'ot –Crops, fruits (Lev. 25:15, 16; Deut. 33:14)

–Prime number

810 בתחת *Betachat* –In Tahath (Num. 33:26)

גואף *Goap* –Demon King of the South and of Fire (Goetia)

דרום *Darom* –South

השקתה *Hishqatah* –She made drink (Gen. 24:46)

ונשמדתי *ve-Nishmadtiy* –And I shall be destroyed (Gen. 34:30)

וקדשת *ve-Qidashat* –And you shall sanctify (Ex. 28:41)

ותשלחוני *ve-Teshalchuwniy* –And you have sent me away (Gen. 26:27)

יף *Yaf* –160th Gate of the 231 Gates

ירם *Yoram* –Joram, 5th King of Judah; 9th King of Israel

יתת *Yetheth* –Jetheth, one of the Dukes of Edom who came of Esau (assoc. w/Daath – Gen. 36:40; 1 Chr. 1:51)

למענכם *Lima'ankem* –Through your fault, for your sake

לעשתי *La'shtey* –To eleven (Ex. 26:8)

מען *Ma'an* –Purpose, intent

מערך *Ma'arak* –Arrangement, plan, preparation

מעשת *Me'ast* –From doing (Gen. 18:25)

מרצפת *Martsefeth* –Pavement

משכיתם *Maskiytam* –Their figured (stones) (Num. 33:52)

משלמת *Meshullemeth* –Meshullemeth, wife of King Manasseh and mother of Amon (2 Kings 21:19)

נסרך *Nisrok* –Nisroch, Assyrian god with a temple in Ninevah

נפיסים *Nefiysiym* –Nephusim, ancestor of returned captives (this name used only in Ezra 2:50 – see also נפושסים, Naphish)[899]

עלין *'Alyan* –Alian, oldest son of Shobal and descendant of Seir (this spelling used only in 1 Chr. 1:40 – see also Alvan)[900]

פלשת *Pelesheth* –Pelesheth, the Hebrew name for Palestine, an ill-defined region consisting of the west coast of Canaan between the Jordan and the Dead Sea on the east and the Mediterranean on the west

---

[899] נפושסים (546, 1106), Naphish (440).

[900] Alvan (156, 806).

	צידון	*Tziydown* –Zidon, eldest son of Canaan, son of Ham; Zidon, ancient city of Canaan (this spelling used only in Josh. 11:8 – see also צידן)[901]
	קין	*Qayin* –Spear
		Qayin –Cain, eldest son of Adam who killed his brother Abel (see also Tubal-cain)[902]; town in the hill country of Judah
	קסמים	*Qesemim* –Practicing a form of divination
	קשתי	*Qashtiy* –My bow (Gen. 9:13)
	שלמתמ	*Shilamtem* –Have you rewarded (Gen. 44:4)
	שמינית	*Shemiyniyth* –Sheminith – perhaps a musical instrument or musical notation
	שמלתמ	*Simlotam* –Their clothes, garments (Gen. 44:13)
	שמעת	*Shama'at* –You have hearkened, heard (Gen. 3:17)
		Shimeath –Shimeath, mother of one who aided in killing King Joash
		Shoma'at –Heard (Gen. 18:10)
	שפתיכ	*Sefateyak* –Your lips (Deut. 23:24)
	תודת	*Todat* –Thanksgiving (Lev. 7:13)
	תשמע	*Tishma'* –You will hearken (Deut. 13:9); will hearken (Gen. 41:15)
	תתי	*Titiy* –I give (Gen. 29:19)
811	אשתמע	*'Eshtemoa'* –Eshtemoa, village in the hill country of Judah, famed for its prophetic oracle
	אתתי	*'ototay* –My signs (Ex. 7:3)
	בתבואת	*Batvuw'ot* –As the ingatherings (Gen. 47:24)
	הקשות	*HaQesaot* –The covers (Ex. 37:16)
	והשכמתמ	*ve-Hishkamtem* –And you may rise up early (Gen. 19:2)
	שראשי	*Sheroshi* –For my head (Song 5:2)[903]
	תשוקה	*Teshuwqah* –Desire, longing, craving
	–Prime number	
812	בהקשתה	*Behaqshotah* –When she was having difficulty (Gen. 35:17)
	בנימין	*Binyamiyn* –Benjamin, the youngest son of Jacob; descendant of Benjamin (1 Chr. 7:10); descendant of Harim; one who helped repair the wall at Jerusalem; one who helped dedicate the wall of Jerusalem
	בשמלתמ	*Besimlotam* –In their clothes (Ex. 12:34)
	גרגרות	*Gargerowth* –Neck (always fig.)
	דחף	*Dachaf* –To drive on, hurry, hasten
	האתות	*Ha'Otot* –The signs (Gen. 4:9)
	והאתת	*ve-Ha'Otot* –And the signs (Deut. 7:19)
	ולעשות	*ve-La'asot* –And to do (Deut. 24:8)
	למשבתמ	*Lemoshvotam* –According to their habitations (Gen.

901 צידן (154, 804).

902 Tubal-cain (598, 1248).

903 SheRoshi is one of the ten words in the Tanakh with a Dagesh in the letter Resh.

		36:43)
	משבתיכמ	*Meshvoteykem* –Your habitations (Ex. 35:3)
	קרית בעל	*Qiryath Ba'al* –Kirjath-Baal, originally one of the cities of the Gibeonites located at the northwestern boundary of Judah (this spelling used only in 2 Sam. 6:2 –see also Baalah, Kirjath-Arim, and Baale-judah)[904]
	תתאוה	*Tit'aeh* –You shall desire (Deut. 5:18)
813	אבירם	*'Abiyram* –Abiram, a Reubenite who conspired against Moses and was destroyed; firstborn son of Hiel who died when his father began to rebuild Jericho
	אראריתא	*Ararita* –A name of God; acronym for *Achad Rosh Achdotho Rosh Ichudo Temurahzo Achad*, "One is His Beginning, one is His individuality, His permutation is one"
	גדוף	*Gidduwf* –Revilings, reviling words
	גתית	*Gittiyth* –Gittith, a type of harp
	התחת	*Hatachat* –Instead of, in the place of (Gen. 30:2)
	ראש חדש	*Rosh Chodesh* –Head of the month; first day of the Jewish month
814	הקטן	*Haqatan* –Hakkatan, father of Johanan, who returned with Ezra
	ואברהם	*ve-Avraham* –And Abraham
	וחשקת	*ve-Chashaqat* –And you have a desire (Deut. 21:11)
	ורחם	*ve-Racham* –And of the womb
	ושחקת	*ve-Shachaqat* –And you shall beat (Dex. 30:36)
	ותחת	*ve-Tachat* –And under (Ex. 24:10)
	חוף	*Chowf* –Seashore, coast, shore
	חורם	*Churam* –Huram, descendant of Bela and a grandson of Benjamin (1 Chr. 8.5); king of Tyre who formed an alliance with David and Solomon; skilled craftsman from Tyre employed by Solomon (2 Chr. 4:16) (see also Hiram (2 Kings 7:13))[905]
	חיצון	*Chiytsown* –Outer, external, outward
	חשוך	*Chashowk* –Darkness (Aramaic)
	יתדת	*Yitdot* –Pins of (Ex. 27:19)
	מעדן	*Ma'adan* –Dainty (of food), delight
	צדיכים	*Tzadikim* –Righteous ones
	רחום	*Rachum* –Merciful, compassion (of God)
		Rechuwm –Rehum, chief man that returned from Exile with Zerubbabel (see also Nehum)[906]; chancellor of Artaxerxes; Levite who helped to repair the wall of Jerusalem; one who sealed the covenant (Neh. 10:26)

---

[904] Baalah (107), Kirjath-Arim (1030, 1590), Baale-judah (142).
[905] Hiram (258, 818).
[906] Nehum (104, 664).

	שכל תמידי	*Sekhel Temidi* –Perpetual Intelligence (31st Path)
	תבואתה	*Tavo'atah* –Let come (Deut. 33:16)
		Tavuw'atah –Increase thereof, produce (Ex. 23:10, Lev. 25:3)
	תקדיש	*Taqdiysh* –You shall sanctify (Deut. 15:19)
815	בעל תשובה	*Ba'al Teshuvah* –Returnee; one who returns to Judaism
	הדורם	*Hadowram* –Hadoram, son of Joktan (Gen. 10:27; 1 Chr. 1:21); son of Tou, king of Hamath (1 Chr. 18:10) – called Joram in 2 Sam. 8:9-10; (see also Jehoram)[907]
	התקדשו	*Hitqadshuw* –Sanctify yourself (Num. 11:18)
	ובאתות	*ve-V'otot* –And with signs (Deut. 26:8)
	ותבואת	*ve-Tevuw'at* –And the increase, produce (Deut. 22:9)
	טרום	*Terowm* –Before, not yet, before that, ere (of time)
	לתפשה	*Letafsah* –To take it (Deut. 20:19)
	משכנתה	*Mishkentah* –Of her neighbor (Ex. 3:22)
	שתיקה	*Shethiqah* –Silence
	תבואתו	*Tevuw'ato* –Its produce (Lev. 19:25)
	תעשמה	*Tahatsumah* –Mighty, power
816	דברים	*Devarim* –Words; Hebrew title of Deuteronomy
	וקדשתו	*ve-Qidashto* –And sanctify it/him (Ex. 19:23)
	ושמעת	*ve-Shama'at* –And you heard it (Deut. 17:4)
		ve-Shama'ta –And hear (Deut. 4:30)
	ותשמע	*ve-Tishma'* –And let hear (Deut. 32:1)
	חתחת	*Chathchath* –Terror
	יחזקאל ירמיה ישעיה	*Ezekiel, Jeremiah, Isaiah* –The three Major Prophets
	יורם	*Yoram* –Joram, descendant of Moses (1 Chr. 26:25) 5th King of Judah; 9th King of Israel (see also Hadoram – also Jehoram)[908]
	כסלון	*Kesalown* –Chesalon, town near Mount Jearim of Judah
		Kislown –Chislon, prince of the tribe of Benjamin and father of Elidad
	מעון	*Maon* –Dwelling, habitation, refuge, residence; Maon, son of Shammai or a city he founded (1 Chr. 2:45); Maon, a mountain city of Judah; wilderness east of the city, Maon, and west of the Dead Sea where David and his men hid from King Saul; Maon, the Fifth Heaven, corr. to *Giburah*
	מעשות	*Me'asot* –From doing (Gen. 44:7)
	משלמות	*Meshillemowth* –Meshillemoth, descendant of Ephraim; priest whose descendants lived in Jerusalem (this spelling used only in Neh. 11:13 – see also Meshillemith)[909]
	עליון	*'elyown* (often *Elyon*) –High, upper; Highest, Most High

[907] Joram (256, 816), Jehoram (261, 821).
[908] Hadoram (255, 815), Jehoram (261, 821).
[909] Meshillemith (820).

(of God); the Most High (of God – Aramaic); a name of God and title of *Keter*

עמון *'Ammown* –Ammon, son of Lot (see also Ben-ammi)[910]; land settled by the Ammonites located north and east of Moab

פרעתוני *Pir'athowniy* –Pirathonite

שועתמ *Shav'atam* –Their cry (for help) (Ex. 2:23)

שפלות *Shifluwth* –Sinking, idleness, inactivity

תערצונ *Ta'artzuwn* –Be terrified (Deut. 1:29)

תשמעו *Tishma'uw* –You shall hearken (Deut. 13:5); will hearken (Gen. 34:17; Ex. 19:5)

817 אורים *Urim* –Lights; Urim, a material object used (along with the Thummim) for divination by the High Priest[911]

אשתמוע *'Eshtemowa'* –Eshtemoa, village in the hill country of Judah, famed for its prophetic oracle

אתתיו *'ototayu* –His signs (Deut. 11:3)

ונשאתני *ve-Nesa'taniy* –And you shall carry me (Gen. 47:30)

ותשקהו *ve-Tashqehuw* –And gave him drink (Gen. 24:18)

זיף *Ziyph* –Ziph, grandson of Caleb; son of Jehaleleel; Ziph, city in southern Judah, located between Ithnan and Telem – probably modern ez-Teifah; town in Judah's hill country – probably present-day Tell Zif

חטף *Chataf* –To catch, seize

חרטם *Chartom* –Diviner, magician, astrologer (Gen. 41:8, 24; Ex. 7:11, 22; 8:7, 18, 19; 9:11; Dan. 1:20; 2:2); magician, magician-astrologer (Aramaic – Dan. 2:10, 27; 4:4, 6; 5:11)

פורלאך *Phorlakh* –Angel of the element of Earth

תתגדדי *Titgodduw* –You shall cut yourselves (Deut. 14:1)

818 ובקשתי *ve-Veqashtiy* –And with my bow (Gen. 48:22)

חורם *Chiram* –Hiram, King of Tyre; architect of the Temple of Solomon

חתית *Chittiyth* –Terror

יחף *Yachef* –Barefoot

ירחם *Yerocham* –Jeroham, Levite, the grandfather of Samuel; descendant of Benjamin; head of a family of Benjamin; priest whose son lived in Jerusalem after the exile; father of two who joined David at Ziklag; father of Azareel, prince of Dan; father of one who helped Jehoiada to set Joah on the throne of Judah; father of Adaiah the priest (this latter may be the same as the fourth Jeroham)

מושבתיכמ *Moshvoteykem* –Your habitations (Ex. 12:20)

פלחן *Polchan* –Service, worship (Aramaic)

---

910 Ben-ammi (172, 822).

911 Thummim (490, 1050).

	קיר חרש	*Qiyr Cheres* –Kir-Haresh, fortified city (see also Kir, Kir-Haraseth)[912]
	תחתי	*Tachtiy* –Low, lower, lowest
819	אחרים	*Achrowm* –Another
		'Achiyram –Ahiram, descendant of Benjamin (see also Ehi, may be Aher as well)[913]
	היתדת	*HaYetedot* –The pins (Ex. 38:20)
	הקדשתי	*Hiqdashtiy* –I hallowed (Num. 3:13)
	יקטן	*Yoqtan* –Joktan, son of Eber of Shem's line (Gen. 10:25-26; 1 Chr. 1:19-20, 23)[914]
	נטשתני	*Netashtaniy* –Suffer me, allow me (Gen. 31:28)
	שאר ישוב	*She'ar Yashuwb* –Shear-Jashub, symbolic name given a son of Isaiah in the days of King Ahaz of Judah (Is. 7:3)[915]
820	בחרים	*Bachuriym* –Bahurim, village near the Mount of Olives
		Bechuriym –Youth
	גרזים	*Gerizim* –Gerizim, the mountain whereupon six of the tribes of Israel stood to bless (Deut. 11:29)
	דלפון	*Dalfown* –Dalphon, son of Haman who was an advisor to King Ahasuerus
	וקדשתי	*ve-Qedashtiy* –And I will sanctify (Ex. 29:44)
	יקמעם	*Yeqam'am* –Jekameam, descendant of Levi (1 Chr. 23:19; 24:23)
		Yoqme'am –Jokmeam, city of the tribe of Ephraim, given to the Levites (probably the same as Kibzaim)
	יתקדשו	*Yitqadashuw* –Sanctify themselves (Ex. 19:22)
	כף	*Kaf* –Palm, hand, sole, palm of the hand, hollow or flat of the hand; 11th letter of Hebrew alphabet; 171st Gate of the 231 Gates
		Kef –Rock, hollow of a rock
	כרם	*Kerem* –Vineyard
		Korem –To tend vines or vineyards, to dress vines or vineyards
	כתת	*Kathath* –To beat, crush by beating, crush to pieces, crush fine
	מסכן	*Misken* –Poor, poor man
	מען	*Ma'yan* –Spring
	משלמית	*Meshillemiyth* –Meshillemith, priest whose descendants lived in Jerusalem (this spelling used only in 1 Chr. 9:12 – see also Meshillemoth)[916]
	משמתם	*Meshmotam* –From their names (Ex. 28:10)
	משפת	*Mishpath* –Fire-places, ash-heaps (meaning uncertain – Gen. 49:14); sheepfolds, saddle-bags (meaning uncertain – Judg. 5:16)

[912] Kir (310), Kir-Haraseth (1218).
[913] Ehi (19), Aher (209).
[914] The reference here may be to an Arabian tribe from whom many other Arabian groups sprang
[915] Shear-jashub literally means "a remnant returns."
[916] Meshillemoth (816).

ניסן *Nisan* –7th month of the Jewish calendar – it is associated with Aries and the tribe Naphtali

ענן *'anan* –To make appear, produce, bring; to practice soothsaying, conjure; cloud (Aramaic); cloud, cloudy, cloud-mass (of theophanic cloud); Anan, one who sealed the new covenant with God after the Exile

עשיתמ *'asiytem* –So doing (Gen. 44:5)
'asiytim –I have made them (Gen. 6:7)

פלשתי *Pelishtiy* –Philistine

צענים *Tza'ananniym* –Zaannanim, place on the southern border of Naphtali (this spelling used only in Judg. 4:11 – see also צעננים)[917]

שכך *Shakak* –To subside, abate, decrease

שמעתי *Shama'tiy* –I have heard, I heard, I have hearkened (Gen. 3:10; Num. 10:14)
Shim'athiy –Shimeathites

שפתמ *Sefatam* –Their language (Gen. 11:7)

תשעימ *Tishiym* –Ninety

–The sum of the numbers 1 through 40

821 אבי עלבון *'Abiy 'albown* –"Father of strength;" Abi Albon, an Arbathite who served as one of David's thirty mighty men (this spelling used only in 2 Sam. 23:31 – see also Abiel)[918]

אדורים *'Adowrayim* –Adoraim, city in Judah

אחשורוש *'Achashverowsh* –Ahasuerus, father of Darius the Mede; king of Persia (Xerxes); Cambyses, king of Persia

אכף *Akaf* –Press, urge, bend
Ekef –Pressure, urgency, burden

השמעות *Hashma'uwth* –A causing to hear, a report, a communication

והשקית *VeHishqiyat* –You shall give her to drink (Num. 20:8)

יהורם *Yehoram* –Jehoram, son of Tou, king of Hamath; alternate name for Joram, 5th King of Judah, and for Joram, 9th King of Israel; priest commissioned to teach the people

פלאין *Polayan* –Lord of Triplicity by Night for Aquarius

–Prime number

822 בן־ימיני *Ben-Yaminiy* –Benyemini, Benjamite (1 Sam. 9:21; Ps. 7:1)

בן־עמי *Ben-'Ammiy* –Ben-ammi, ancestor of the Ammorites, born to Lot and his daughter

כתבת *Katavat* –You have written (Ex. 32:32)
Kethobeth –Impression, inscription, mark

מפבשת *Mefibosheth* –Mephibosheth, son of Saul by his

---

917 צעננים (310, 870).

918 Abiel (44).

		concubine Rizpah (2 Sam. 21:8)
	משבעתי	*Mishve'atiy* –From my oath (Gen. 24:8)
	נשבעת	*Nishba'at* –You did swear (Ex. 32:13)
	שבעתימ	*Shivawthayim* –Sevenfold, seven times
	תכתב	*Tiktav* –You shall write (Num. 17:17)
823	תחתיה –Prime number	*Tachteyah* –In its place (Lev. 13:23)
824	אדרא רבא קדישא	*Idra Rabba Qadisha* –Greater Holy Assembly
	תחתיו	*Tachtayu* –In his stead, place (Gen. 36:33); under him (Ex. 17:12)
	תתחטאו	*Titchata'auw* –Purify yourselves (Num. 31:19) *Titchata'uw* –You shall purify yourselves (Num. 31:20)
825	בעל תשובה	*Ba'alei Teshuvah* –Returnees; people who return to Judaism
	ים הקדמוני	*Yawm HaQadmoni* –"The eastern sea" (Joel 2:20)
	נעשתה	*Ne'estah* –Being done (Num. 15:24)
	עשתנה	*'eshtunah* –Thought
	קרית סנה	*Qiryath Sannah* –Kirjath Sannah, town in the hill country of Judah assigned to the Levites (this spelling used only in Josh. 15:49 – see also the first Debir and Kirjath Sepher)[919]
826	בחורים	*Bachuwriym* –Bahurim, village near the Mount of Olives
	ועשיתמ	*ve-'asiytem* –And do them (Ex. 4:21; Lev. 19:37)
	וקשתכ	*ve-Qashteka* –And your bow (Gen. 27:3)
	ושמעתי	*ve-Shama'tiy* –And I will hear (Ex. 22:26)
	ותשעימ	*ve-Tish'iym* –And ninety (Gen. 5:17)
	לצון	*Latzown* –Scorning, bragging
	נסיון	*Nisyon* –Trial, temptation
	צמצום	*Tzimtzum* –Contraction
	שפמות	*Sifmowth* –Siphmoth, place in southern Judah frequented by David (1 Sam. 30:28)
	תעשונ	*Ta'asuwn* –You will do (Num. 32:23); shall do (Ex. 4:15)
	תעשנו	*Ta'asenuw* –You shall make it (Ex. 28:15)
827	בן־הימיני	*Ben-HaYaminiy* –Benhayemini, Benjamite (Judg. 3:15; 2 Sam. 16:11; 19:17; 1 Kings 2:8)
	התבודדות	*Hitbodedut* –Meditation
	לא־תכצור –Prime number	*La-Tiktzor* –Do not harvest (Lev. 25:5)
828	וכתבת	*ve-Katavat* –And you shall write (Deut. 27:3) *ve-Ketovet* –And imprints (Lev. 19:28)
	וקשותיו	*ve-Qesotayu* –And its jars (Ex. 25:29)

[919] Debir (206; 216), Kirjath Sepher (1050).

	משפחת	*Mishfachat* –Of the family (Lev. 25:47) *Mishfechot* –Families (Gen. 10:32)
	צפנת פענח	*Tzophnath Pa'neach* –Zaphnath-Paaneah, name given to Joseph by Pharaoh (Genesis 41:45)[920]
	תכתבו	*Tekatayvu* –May you be written (into the Book of Life)
829	כתבואת	*Ketevuw'at* –As the increase of (Num. 18:30)
	תבואתכ	*Tevuw'atak* –Of your produce, increase (Deut. 14:28)
	–Prime number	
830	ולשפחות	*ve-Lishfachot* –And for bondwomen (Deut. 28:68)
	יסגנזן	*Yasaganotz* –Angel of 3d Taurus (according to Regardie)
	יקנעם	*Yoqne'am* –Jokneam, city in Zebulun allotted to the Levites
	יששכר	*Issachar* –Issachar, ninth son of Jacob and ancestor of one of the twelve tribes of Israel (assoc. w/Cancer); a tabernacle porter (1 Chr. 26:5)
	יתדתיו	*Yetedotayu* –You did blow (Ex. 15:10)
	כתית	*Katiyt* –Beaten out, pure, pounded fine (in a mortar), costly
	לף	*Lap* –181st Gate of the 231 Gates
	לתת	*Latet* –To give, to fasten (Gen. 15:7; 29:26)
	נפשת	*Nefshot* –Body, person (Lev. 21:11); souls (Ex. 12:4)
	עינן	*Enan* –Enan, father of a prince of Naphtali
	ענין	*'inyan* –Occupation, task, job
	עשיתנ	*'asiyten* –Have you done (Ex. 1:18)
	פרנך	*Parnak* –Parnach, descendant of Zebulun
	פשתימ	*Pishtiym* –Linen (Lev. 13:47)
	רחבעם	*Rechabam* –Rehoboam, son of Solomon and first King of Judah
	שבע בנות	*Sheva' Banot* –"Seven daughters" (Ex. 2:16)
	שלך	*Shalak* –To throw, cast, hurl, fling; bird of prey (probably the cormorant)
	שסעת	*Shosa'at* –Clovenfooted (Lev. 11:26)
	שפתימ	*Sefatayim* –Lips (Ex. 6:12)
831	אלף	*Alaf* –To learn; to make thousand-fold, bring forth thousands; producing thousands; chief, chiliarch; 1000 (Aramaic) *Alef* –Ox; 1st letter of Hebrew alphabet *Alluf* –Tame, docile; friend, intimate; chief (see also אלוף)[921] *Elef* –Thousand; cattle, oxen; a thousand, company (as a company of men under one leader, troops); a city in the territory of Benjamin
	לאתת	*Le'otot* –For signs (Gen. 1:14)

[920] Often translated as "creator of life" or "God speaks; he lives" in Egyptian – some have "savior of the world," "revealer of secrets."

[921] אלוף (117, 837).

832	ארץ ישראל	*'eretz Yisrael* –Land of Israel
	בפשתימ	*Vafishtiym* –Of linen (Lev. 13:52)
	בשפתימ	*Visfatayim* –With lips (Lev. 5:4)
	וכתות	*ve-Katuwt* –And crushed (Lev. 22:24)
	ושמעתיו	*ve-Shema'tiyu* –And I will hear it (Deut. 1:17)
	יהוה איש מלחמה יהוה שמו	YHVH *Ish Milchamah* YHVH *Shemo* –The Lord is a man of war; YHVH is His Name (Ex. 15:3)
	כתבתי	*Katavtiy* –I have written (Ex. 23:12)
	מפיבשת	*Mefiybosheth* –Mephibosheth, grandson of Saul (see also Merib-Baal)[922]
	משבצת	*Mishbetzot* –Settings, fittings (Ex. 28:13)
	נשבעתי	*Nishba'atiy* –Have I sworn (Gen. 22:16)
833	חורם אביו	*Churam Abiv* –Huram Abiv, "Huram his father" = Hiram Abiff[923]
	חיות הקדש	*Chayoth HaQodesh* –Holy Living Creatures; Angelic Choir assoc. w/*Keter*
834	דלף	*Dalaf* –To drop, drip
		Delef –A dropping, dripping
	ומשפחת	*ve-Mishfachat* –And the family of (Num. 3:21)
	משפחות	*Mishfechot* –Families (Gen. 10:18)
	משפחתו	*Mishfachto* –His family (Lev. 25:10)
	תלדת	*Toldot* –Generations (Gen. 25:12)
835	הפשתימ	*HaPishtiym* –The linen, the flax (Lev. 13:59)
	ויתדתיה	*ve-Yitedoteyah* –And its pins (Ex. 39:40)
	וכתבואת	*ve-Kitvuw'at* –And as the produce (Num. 18:30)
	ושפטתמ	*ve-Sefattem* –And you will judge (Deut. 1:16)
	לתתה	*Letitah* –To give her (Ex. 22:16)
	נתפשה	*Nitfasah* –Coerced (Num. 5:13)
	תהלת	*Tehilot* –Praises (Ex. 15:11)
	תעשינה	*Ta'aseynah* –Do (Deut. 1:44); will be done (Lev. 4:2)
836	האלף	*Halfas* –Goetic demon #38
	וישׂשכר	*ve-Yishashkar* –And Issachar (Gen. 35:23)
	ולתת	*ve-Latet* –And to give (Gen. 45:25)
	ופשתימ	*ve-Pishtiym* –And linen (Deut. 22:11)
	וקצרתמ	*ve-Qetzretem* –And you harvest (Lev. 23:10)
	לישועתכ	*Lishuatich* –For your salvation
	נפשות	*Nafeshuwth* –Souls (Gen. 36:6)
	פונן	*Puwnon* –Punon, Israelite encampment during the last portion of the wilderness wandering
	פימון	*Paimon* –Goetic demon #9 (Aurum Solis spelling)
	צפנת פענח	*Tzafnat panach* –Zaphenath-Paneah, the name given to Joseph by Pharaoh (Genesis 41:45 – translated

[922] He was loyal to David, even though Ziba told David he was a traitor (2 Sam. 4:4; 9:6-13). Merib-baal (354).

[923] Hiram Abiff is the mythological founder of the Freemason movement.

		as "creator of life" or "God speaks; he lives" in Egyptian – Gematria Kotel)
	קלון	*Qalown* –Shame, disgrace, dishonor
837	אלוף	*Aluf* –Tame, docile; friend, intimate; chief
	המשבצת	*HaMishbetzot* –The settings (Ex. 28:14)
	לםרבה	*Lemarbah* –To multiply – this version of this word (final *Mem* in the middle of the word) only occurs in Isaiah 9:6
	פאימון	*Paimon* –Demon King of Fire; Goetic demon #9
	צמאון	*Tzimma'own* –Thirsty (parched) ground
	תת זל	*Tath Zel* –The Profuse Giver; a title of *Keter*
838	בתולת	*Betuwlat* –A virgin of (Deut. 22:19)
	וכתבתי	*ve-Katavtiy* –And I will write (Ex. 34:1)
	חלף	*Chalaf* –To pass on or away, pass through, pass by, go through, grow up, change, to go on from, pass over
		Chelef –In exchange for; in return for; Heleph, town marking the boundary of the tribe of Naphtali, northeast of Mount Tabor
	כרובים	*Kerubim* –Angelic Choir assoc. w/*Yesod*
	משבצות	*Mishbetzuwt* –Settings (Ex. 28:11)
	משפחתי	*Mishfachtiy* –My kindred (Gen. 24:38)
	עולם המוטבע	*Olam HaMevetbau* –Natural World, third face of Adam Qadmon
	תחלת	*Towcheleth* –Hope
	תחתיכ	*Tachteyak* –Under you (Deut. 28:23)
839	–Prime number	
840	דבר (משה) אל־בני ישראל	*Diber (Mosheh) 'El-Beney Yisra'el* –"(Moses) spoke to the children of Israel" (Deut. 4:45 – the name Moses is left out of the *gematria*)
	כנען	*Kenaan* –Canaan, son of Ham and grandson of Noah; Canaan, native name of Palestine, the land given to Abraham and his descendants
	כרכם	*Karkom* –Saffron (Song 4:14)
	לעשתמ	*La'astam* –To do them (Deut. 5:1)
	לממשלת	*Lememshelet* –To rule, dominate (Gen. 1:16)
	לתתי	*Letitiy* –To give me leave (Num. 22:13)
	מף	*Mof* –Memphis in Egypt; 190th Gate of the 231 Gates
	מררת	*Merorot* –Bitter (Deut. 32:32)
	משכנתיכ	*Mishkenoteyak* –Your dwellings (Num. 24:5)
	משך	*Mashak* –To draw, drag, sieze
		Meshek –A drawing, drawing up, drawing up a trail; Meshech, son of Japheth; possibly a people inhabiting the land in the mountains north of Assyria; tribe mentioned in association with Kedar; son or grandson of Shem (this spelling

used only in 1 Chr. 1:18 – see also Mash)[924]

מתת *Mattath* –Gift, reward
Mitet –He will give (Deut. 28:55)
נצן *Nitstsan* –Blossom
ספן *Safan* –To cover, cover in; wainscotted, covered with boards or panelling
Sippun –Cover, cover in, panel, wainscotting
פינן *Pinon* –A Duke of Edom (assoc. w/*Tiferet*); darkness
פנין *Panin* –Pearl; a precious stone (perhaps corals, rubies, jewels); a title of *Malkut*
צנן *Tzenan* –Zenan, village in the allotment of Judah (see also Zaanan)[925]
רמם *Ramam* –To be exalted, be lifted up
שלמתיכמ *Salmoteykem* –Your clothes (Deut. 29:4)
שמעתיכ *Shem'otiyak* –I have heard you (Gen. 17:20)
תולדת *Toldot* –Generations (Gen. 5:1)
תלדות *Toldot* –Generations (Gen. 36:1)
תמת *Tamot* –Let die (Num. 23:10)

841 אנפין *Anpin* –Face, countenance
הודעני נא את־דרכב *Howdi'eniy Na' 'Eth-Derakeka* "Pray let me know Your ways" (Ex. 33:13)
הנפשות *HaNefashot* –The souls, the persons (Lev. 18:19)
להשקות *Lehashqot* –To water (Gen. 2:10)
להשקתו *Lehashqoto* –To give him drink (Gen. 24:19)
צאנן *Tza'anan* –Zaanan, town in Judah (see also Zenan)[926]
תהלתו *Tehilatuw* –Praise (Is. 42:10, 12; Ps. 66:2; 149:1)

842 אראלים *Aralim* –Angelic Choir assoc. w/*Binah*
ובמשפחתו *ve-Vemishfachto* –And against his family (Lev. 20:5)
תבלות *Tabliyth* –Destruction
תשופנו *Teshuwfanuw* –Shall bruise (Gen. 3:15)

843 הבתולת *HaBetuwlot* –The virgins (Ex. 22:16)
המשבצות *HaMishbetzuwt* –The settings (Ex. 28:25)
רגלים *Rogeliym* –Rogelim, dwelling place of Barzillai

844 באר אלים *Be'er 'Eliym* –Beer Elim, village in southern Moab
בשבעתיכמ *Beshavu'oteykam* –In your weeks (Num. 28:26)
הכחות השכלים *HaKachoth HaSekhelim* –Intellectual virtues
חלוף *Chalowf* –Destruction, passing away, vanishing, appointed to destruction
ידלף *Yidlaf* –Jidlaph, son of Nahor and nephew of Abraham (Gen. 22:22)
קדמן *Qadmon* –East (Ezek. 47:8)
קדשתמ *Qidashtem* –You sanctified (Deut. 32:51)

[924] Mash (340).
[925] Zaanan (191, 841).
[926] Zenan (190, 840).

845	השליך	*Hishliyka* –Hurled, thrown (Num. 35:20)
	ואשלחך	*Ve-'ashalechaka* –That I might have sent you away (Gen. 31:27)
		Ve-'eshelachaka –And I will send you (Gen. 37:13)
	מתתה	*Mattattah* –Mattathah, one who divorced his foreign wife after the Exile (Ezra 10:33)
	נתטון	*Neptun* –Neptune
	תהמת	*Tehomot* –Deeps, depths (Ex. 15:5, 8)
846	ותלית	*ve-Taliyat* –And you shall hand (Deut. 21:22)
	ושננתם	*ve-Shinanetam* –And you shall teach (Deut. 6:7)
	ותמת	*ve-Tamat* –And died (Gen. 23:2)
	ותתם	*ve-Titom* –And was ended (Gen. 47:18)
	לעשותם	*La'asotam* –And do them (Deut. 7:11)
	מורם	*Murmus* –Goetic demon #54
	מושך	*Moshek* –Attractive (mod. Hebrew)
	מרום	*Marowm* –Height
		Merowm –Merom, lake north of the Sea of Galilee
	עלמון	*'Almown* –Almon, priestly town near the territory of Benjamin (see also Alemeth)[927]
	קמון	*Qamown* –Camon, place where Jair the Gileadite was buried
	רומם	*Romam* –Praise, exaltation, extolling
	תולדות	*Toldot* –Generations (Gen. 2:4)
	תמרור	*Tamruwr* –Bitterness
	תמות	*Tamuwt* –You shall die (Gen. 2:17)
	תמתו	*Tamutuw* –You shall die (Lev. 10:6)
847	אל עליון	*El Elyon* –Most High God
	ימצאון	*Imatze'on* –Shall be found (Gen. 18:29)
	מזקן	*Mizqen* –For age (Gen. 48:10)
848	ארבעה עשר	*Arbaah-Asar* –Fourteen
	ובקשתם	*ve-Viqashtem* –And you will seek (Num. 16:10)
	חתמת	*Chothemeth* –Signet-ring, signet seal
	מחשך	*Machshak* –Dark place, darkness, secrecy
	מחתת	*Machtot* –Firepans (Num. 16:17)
	מתחת	*Mitachat* –Beneath, from under, below; from Tahath (Ex. 20:4; Num. 33:27)
	שיחיה לאורכ ימימ טובימ אמנ	*Shichih Lavrak Yamiym Toviym Amen* –"May he live for long and good days, Amen," a phrase used when mentioning a living rabbi or sage
	תחתם	*Tachtam* –In their stead (Deut. 2:12)
849	אמונה אמון	*'Emunah 'Amown* –"Former of Faith" (*Sefer Yetzirah*)
	אמתחת	*'amtachath* –Sacks, flexible container (for grain); spread out

[927] Alemeth (540).

	מלאך המשחית	*Malakh HaMaschith* –Angel of Destruction
850	וקדשתמ	*ve-Qidashtem* –And you shall hallow (Deut. 25:10)
	ללשנתמ	*Lileshonotam* –According to their tongues (Gen. 10:20)
	מישך	*Meshakh* –Meshach, the name given to Mishael after he went into Babylonian captivity
	מנימין	*Minyamiyn* –Miniamin, priest in the days of Joiakim; priest who helped dedicate the wall
	מרים	*Miryam* –Miriam, sister of Moses and Aaron[928]; descendant of Judah
	משמעת	*Mishma'ath* –Subjects, body of subjects; bodyguard, listeners, obedient ones
	מתתי	*Mititiy* –Then I should give (Gen. 29:19)
	נף	*Nof* –Noph, another name for Memphis, Egypt; 198th Gate of the 231 Gates
	נשך	*Nashak* –To bite; to pay, give interest, lend for interest or usury *Neshek* –Interest, usury
	צנין	*Tzaniyn* –Thorn, prick
	קנן	*Qanan* –To make a nest
	שמעתמ	*Shema'tem* –You would hear, hearken (Gen. 42:22)
	שמשרי	*Shamsheray* –Shamsherai, descendant of Benjamin
	תכלת	*Tekhelet* –Blue
	תמית	*Tamiyt* –You shall slay (Gen. 42:37)
	תנקש	*Tinaqesh* –You shall be ensnared (Deut. 12:30)
	תתנ	*Titen* –You will put, give
851	אמרים	*Emorim* –Amorites
	אנף	*'anaf* –To be angry, to be displeased, to breathe hard (of God's anger); face, nose (Aramaic)
	אתנת	*'atonot* –She-asses (Gen. 32:16)
	באמתחת	*Be'amtachat* –In the sack of (Gen. 44:12)
	בית לבאות	*Beyth Le'Afrah* –Beth le-Aphrah, another name for Beth Aphrah
	ותהמת	*ve-Tehomot* –And depths (Deut. 8:7)
	נאף	*Na'af* –To commit adultery *Ni'uf* –Adultery
	שמש ומגנ יהוה אלהימ	*Shamash ve-Magen* YHVH *Elohim* –"A sun and shield are YHVH *Elohim*" (Ps. 84:12)
	תמותה	*Temuwthah* –Death (Ps. 79:11 & 102:21)
852	בתכלת	*Batkelet* –In blue (Ex. 35:35)
	ונושנתמ	*ve-Noshantem* –And you shall have been long (Deut. 4:25)
	פכרת צביימ	*Pokereth Tzebayiym* –Pochereth-Zebaim, one whose children returned
	תמנתו	*Tamuwtuw* –You shall die (Gen. 42:20)

[928] Miriam rebelled against Moses with Aaron at Hazeroth

853	בעל המון	*Ba'al Hamown* –Baal Hamon, place where Solomon had a vineyard (Song 8:11)
	החתמת	*HaChotemet* –The signets, the seals (Gen. 38:25)
	המחתת	*HaMachtot* –The firepans (Ex. 38:3)
	נגף	*Nagaf* –To strike, smite
		Negef –Blow, striking, plague
	–Prime number	
854	אלהי אברהם	*Elohi Abraham* –The God of Abraham
	ומתחת	*ve-Mitachat* –And underneath (Deut. 33:27)
	מחתות	*Machtot* –Censers, firepans (Num. 16:6)
	מחתתו	*Machtato* –His censer (Lev. 10:1)
	נדף	*Nadaf* –To drive, drive away, drive asunder
855	אמתחתו	*'amtachto* –His sack (Gen. 42:27)
	התכלת	*HaTekelet* –The blue (Ex. 28:5)
	מתתיה	*Mattithyah* –Mattithiah, Levite in charge of "things made in pans" (1 Chr. 9:31); Levite singer and gatekeeper (this spelling used only in 1 Chr. 16:5 – see also מתתיהו)[929]; son of Jeduthun (1 Chr. 25:3, 21); one who took a foreign wife during the Exile (Ezra 10:43); one who stood with Ezra when he read the Law (Neh. 8:4)
	נתתה	*Natatah* –You gave (Gen. 3:12)
	תהלתכ	*Tehilatka* –Your glory, your praise (Deut. 10:21)
856	ולתתכ	*ve-Letiteka* –And to make you, give you (Deut. 26:19)
	ונתת	*ve-Natata* –And you shall give, put (Gen. 40:13)
	ותכלת	*ve-Tekelet* –And blue (Ex. 25:4)
	ותתנ	*ve-Titen* –And she gave (Gen. 3:6; 30:4)
	מרירות	*Meriyruwth* –Bitterness
	נוף	*Nowf* –Elevation, height
		Nuwf –To move to and fro, wave, besprinkle
	תשפכנו	*Tishfekenuw* –You shall pour it out (Deut. 12:16)
	תתנו	*Titnuw* –You shall give, make (Gen. 34:9; Ex. 5:18; 22:29; Lev. 19:28)
857	אלה הדורים	*Eleh HaDevarim* –"These be the words" – Hebrew title of the book of Deuteronomy
	אלהים גבור	*Elohim Gibor* –Almighty God; divine name assoc. w/ *Giburah*
	ואתנת	*ve-'atonot* –And she-asses (Gen. 12:16)
	תבקשנה	*Tevaqshanah* –Did you require it (Gen. 31:39)
858	אראתרונ	*Arathron* –Olympic Planetary Spirit of Saturn
	אתה גבור לעולמ אדני	*Ateh Gibor le-Olam Adonai* –Thou art mighty forever, O Lord; usually abbreviated **אגלא** (*Agla*) and used as a name of God

[929] מתתיהו (861).

בצלמ אלהימ ברא אתו — *Be-tzelem Elohim bara othu* –In the image of God created he them (Gen. 1:27)

חנף — *Chanef* –To be profaned, be defiled, be polluted, be corrupt; hypocritical, godless, profane, hypocrite, irreligious

Chonef –Hypocrisy, godlessness, hypocrite, profaneness

למשפחת — *le-Mishfachat* –To the family, of families (Num. 3:30; 36:6)

ממושבתיכמ — *Mimoshvoteykem* –Out of your dwellings (Lev. 23:17)

רחמים — *Rachamim* –Compassion, a title of *Tiferet*

שבנוך — *Sabnock* –Goetic demon #43

תבקשנו — *Tevaqshenuw* –You shall require it (Gen. 43:9)

תחתימ — *Tachtiyim* –Lower (Gen. 6:16)

תנובת — *Tenuwvot* –Produce, fruitage (Deut. 32:13)

תנתח — *Tenatecha* –You shall cut (Ex. 29:17)

859 טנף — *Tanaf* –To defile, soil

נטף — *Nataf* –To drop, drip, distill, prophesy, preach, discourse; drop, gum, drops of stacte (an aromatic gum resin of a shrub used in the Holy incense)

–Prime number

860 בעל חנן — *Baal-Hanan* –Baal-hanan, a King of Edom (assoc. w/*Yesod*); archdemon corr. to *Netzach* (Waite); Baal-hanan, tender of olive and sycamore trees in David's time (1 Chr. 27:28)

ויתדתמ — *ve-Yetedotam* –And their pins (Num. 3:37)

ונתנה הארצ יבולה — *vi-Natnah ha-aretz Yibuwlah* –"And the earth shall give of its produce" (Lev. 26:4)

כי־טוב ויבדל אלהימ בינ האור ובינ החשכ — *Ki-towv ve-Yavdel Elohim Beyn ha-Owr vo-Beyn Ha-Chosheka* –"...was good, and God separated the light from the darkenss" (Gen. 1:4)

כילף — *Keylaf* –Large axes, axe

ליששכר — *le-Yisaskar* –Of Issachar (Num. 1:8)

לעשתכמ — *La'astkem* –That you might do (Deut. 4:17)

לפשתימ — *Lafishtiym* –Of linen (Lev. 13:48)

מסנין — *Misnin* –Angel of 1d Capricorn

נעמן — *Na'aman* –Pleasantness; Naaman, Syrian general who was healed of leprosy by bathing in the Jordan; grandson of Benjamin; son of Benjamin and founder of a tribal family

נתתי — *Natatiy* –I have given, I will give (Gen. 1:29)

סכסכסלים — *Saksaksalim* –Guardian of the 25th Tunnel of Set

סף — *Saf* –A spreading out; basin, goblet, bowl; sill, threshold, entrance; Saph, descendant of Rapha the giant (see also Sippai)[930]; 205th Gate of the

[930] Sippai (150).

		231 Gates
	עצן	*'etsen* –Sharp, strong, spear (meaning uncertain – 2 Sam. 23:8)
	פלשתים	*Pelishtiym* –Philistines (Gen. 10:14)
	צען	*Tza'an* –To wander, travel; Zoan, ancient Egyptian city on the eastern bank of the Nile Delta on the Tanitic branch of the river (Ezek. 30:14)
	קינן	*Kenan* –Cainan, son of Enosh
	קנין	*Qinyon* –Thing acquired, acquisition, possession
	רוח אלהים	*Ruach Elohim* –The Spirit of God
	שפרפר	*Shefarfar* –Dawn, early morning (Aramaic)
	תכלית	*Takliyth* –End, perfection, completion
	תלתל	*Taltal* –Wavy, branch
	תתני	*Tattenay* –Tatnai, Persian governor of Samaria in the days of Zerubbabel
861	אסף	*'asaf* –To gather, receive, remove, gather in; Asaph, one whose descendants were porters in David's time; one of David's three musicians; a Levite; father of Joah; keeper of the royal forests in Judah *'asuf* –What is gathered, store, storing, storehouse *'osef* –Gathering, collection, harvest
	באמתחתי	*Ve'amtachtiy* –In my sack (Gen. 42:28)
	ונתתה	*ve-Natatah* –And you shall give (Ex. 21:23)
	מתתיהו	*Mattithyahuw* –Mattithiah, Levite singer and gatekeeper (this spelling used only in 1 Chr. 15:18, 21 – see also מתתיה)[931]; son of Jeduthun (1 Chr. 25:3, 21)
	צאען	*Tzo'n* –Small cattle, sheep, flock, flocks
862	שבניך	*Sabnock* –Goetic demon #43 (A.C., 777, probably a misprint for שבנוך)[932]
	תבנית	*Tabniyth* –Pattern, plan, form, figure, pattern, likeness (Ex. 25:9)
863	וירא אלהים	*Va-ya-re Elohim* –And God saw
	מחתתיה	*Machtoteyha* –Its snuff dishes (Num. 4:9)
	נזוף	*Nozuf* –Hated one
	שכל ההרגש	*Sekhel HaHergesh* –Disposing Intelligence (17th Path)
	תזנות	*Taznuwth* –Fornication, harlotry
	תחתיהמ	*Tachteyhem* –Was under them (Num. 16:31)
	תחתנה	*Tachtenah* –Instead (Gen. 2:21)
	–Prime number	
864	אשדות הפסגה	*'Ashdowth HaPisgah* –Ashdothpisgah, literally "the ravines of Mt. Pisgah" (Deut. 3:17; Josh. 12:3; 13:20)

---

931 מתתיה (855).

932 שבנוך (378, 858).

אשת זנונימ *Isheth Zenunim* –Woman of Whoredom; Demon of Prostitution; archdemon corr. to *Chokmah* (A.C.)

חתנתו *Chotanto* –His mother-in-law (Deut. 27:23)

מתחתיו *Mitachtayu* –From his place (Ex. 10:23)

קדוש קדשימ *Qadosh Qadeshim* –Holy of Holies

רדנים *Rodaniym* –Rodanim (see also Dodanim)[933], son of Javan (1 Chr. 1:7) – many scholars consider Rodanim to be his original name – it may also be a reference to the inhabitants of Rhodes and the neighboring islands

865 אדנירם *Adoniram* –Solomon's tribute officer

נתתיה *Netatiyha* –I give it (Gen. 23:11)

תבואתנו *Tevuw'atenuw* –Our increase (Lev. 25:20)

866 ונתתי *ve-Natatiy* –And I will give (Gen. 17:8)

ותשקינ *ve-Tashqeyna* –And they made to drink (Gen. 19:33)

סוף *Suwf* –To cease, come to an end; to be fulfilled, be completed, come to an end (Aramaic); reed, rush, water, plant; Suph, unknown place or region opposite the campsite in the Transjordan where Moses explained the Law to the Israelites (Deut. 1:1)[934]

Sowf –End, conclusion (also Aramaic)

משענתו *Misha'anto* –His staff (Ex. 21:19)

נקיון *Niqqayown* –Innocency

נתתיו *Netatiyu* –Have given it (Lev. 17:11)

צלמון *Tzalmown* –Zalmon, wooded area in Shechem; father of Boaz (see also Salma)[935]

תשמעונ *Tishemuwn* –You shall hear (Deut. 1:17); you hearken (Deut. 7:12, 8:20)

867 ארוממכ יהוה כי דליתני *'aruwmamek* YHVH *Kiy Deliyteniy* –"I will exalt You, God, for You have lifted me up" (Ps. 30:2)

בית השפע *Beth HaShefa* –House of Influence

מזיקין *Mazziqin* –A class of demons

תנואתי *Tenuwatiy* –My displeasure (Num. 14:34)

868 והתאויתמ *ve-Hita'iytem* –And shall mark out (Num. 34:10)

וכתבתמ *ve-Ketavtam* –And you shall write (Deut. 6:9)

חסף *Chasef* –Clay, potsherd

חרנים *Choronayim* –Horonaim, sanctuary town of Moab, near Zoar

ממשפחת *Mimishpachat* –Of the families

משפחתמ *Mishpechotam* –Their families

נתיבות *Netivoth* –Paths

---

933 Dodanim (108, 668).

934 Some translations give this as the Red (Reed) Sea.

935 Salma (371).

	סחף	*Sachaf*–To prostrate, beat down
	עצבון	*'itstsabown* –Pain, labor, hardship, sorrow, toil
	פסח	*Pesach* –Passover
	צבעון	*Tzib'own* –Zibeon, Hivite man; son of Seir
869	ומחתתיה	*ve-Machtoteyha* –And its snuff dishes (Ex. 25:38)
	תגרירון	*Tageriron* –The Hagglers, *Qlippoth* of *Tiferet*
870	התהלכתי	*Hithalaktiy* –I had walked, had followed (Gen. 24:40)
	ומחתתיו	*ve-Machtotayuw* –And its firepans (Ex. 27:3)
	ונקדשתי	*ve-Niqdashtiy* –And I will be hallowed
	יסף	*Yasaf*–To add, increase, do again
		Yesaf–To add (Aramaic)
	כנף	*Kanaf*–To be put or thrust in or into a corner, be hidden from view, be cornered, be thrust aside; wing, extremity, edge, winged, border, corner, shirt
	כתנת	*Kethoneth* –Tunics, undergarments
	משקלת	*Mishqeleth* –Level, leveling tool or instrument, plummet
	סנסן	*Sansin* –Bough, fruit-stalk (of date trees)
	עף	*'Ap* –211th Gate of the 231 Gates
	עקן	*'Aqan* –Akan, son of Ezer and grandson of Seir
	ערם	*'aram* –To be subtle, be shrewd, be crafty, beware, take crafty counsel, be prudent; to heap up, pile, be heaped up
		'arem –Heap, pile (Jer. 50:26)
		'orem –Subtlety, shrewdness, craftiness
	צעננים	*Tza'ananniym* –Zaannanim, place on the southern border of Naphtali (this spelling used only in Josh. 19:33 – see also צענים)[936]
	צפן	*Tzafan* –To hide, treasure, treasure or store
	קדש קדשימ הוא	*Qodesh Qadashim Hua* –"It is Holy, most Holy" (Ex. 30:10; Lev. 6:10, 18, 22; 7:1, 6; 10:12, 17; 14:13; 24:9)
	רעם	*Ra'am* –To thunder; thunder
		Raum –Goetic demon #40 (Aurum Solis spelling)
	תעשק	*Ta'ashoq* –You shall oppress
871	אסיף	*'asiyf*–In gathering, harvest
	כמראה אדם	*Kemar'eh 'Adam* –"Semblance of a man" (Ezek. 1:26)
	מאלף	*Malphas* –Goetic demon#39
872	בנפשתמ	*Benafostam* –At the cost of ther own lives (Num. 17:3)
	ונושעתמ	*ve-Nosha'tam* –And you shall be saved (Num. 10:9)
	ונתתיו	*ve-Netatiyuw* –And I will make him (Gen. 17:20)
	סברים	*Sibrayim* –Sibraim, northern boundary marker of Canaan
	עבתת	*'avotot* –Chains (Ex. 28:24)

[936] צענים (260, 820).

תתעב — *Teta'ev* –You shall abhor (Deut. 23:8)

873 אביסף — *'Ebyasaf* –Ebiasaph, a Levite
געף — *Gaap* –Goetic demon #33

874 אביאסף — *Abeawsaf* –Son of Korah
למשפחתיו — *Lemishfechotayu* –According to its family (Num. 2:34)
ממשפחתו — *Mimishfachto* –Of his family (Lev. 25:49)
עדף — *'adaf* –To remain over, be in excess
עתדת — *'atidot* –Things that are to come (Deut. 32:35)

875 והתחתנו — *ve-Hitchatnuw* –And make you marriages (Gen. 34:9)
הכתנת — *HaKatnot* –The tunics (Ex. 39:27)
המשפתימ — *HaMishpetayim* –The sheepfolds (Gen. 49:14)

876 והתהלכתי — *ve-Hithalaktiy* –And I will walk (Lev. 26:12)
וכתנת — *ve-Ketonat* –And a tunic (Ex. 28:4)
ותשקע — *va-Tishqa'* –And abated
יוסף — *Yosef* –Joseph, son of Jacob and Rachel; father of one of the spies sent into Canaan; son of Asaph; one who married a foreign wife during the exile; priest of the family of Shebaniah
ותתע — *ve-Teta'* –And strayed (Gen. 21:14)
כתנות — *Katnot* –Garments (Gen. 3:21)
כתנתו — *Kutanto* –His coat (Gen. 37:23)
עוף — *'owf* –Flying creatures, fowl, insects, birds; fowl (Aramaic)
'uwf –To fly about, fly away; to cover, be dark; gloom
עקשות — *'iqqeshuwth* –Distortion, crookedness
ערום — *'arowm* –Naked, bare
'aruwm –Subtle, shrewd, crafty, sly, sensible
צפון — *Tzafon* –North (of direction), northward; Zaphon, place allotted to the tribe of Gad in the Jordan Valley east of the river
Tzephown –Zephon, son of Gad (see also Ziphion)[937]
שר שלומ — *Sar Shalom* –"Prince of Peace" (Is. 9:5)

877 העבתת — *Ha'avotot* –Wreathen (Ex. 28:25)
ויאסף — *VaYe'asef* –And he was gathered (Gen. 25:8; 49:33)
זעף — *Za'af* –To fret, be sad, be wroth, be vexed, be enraged, be out of humor; rage, raging, storming, indignation
Za'ef –Angry, raging, out of humor, vexed

–Prime number

878 ותחי רוח יעקב אביהמ — *Vatchi Ruach Yaaqob 'avhem* –"the spirit of their father Jacob revived" (Gen. 45:27)
חצצנ תמר — *Chatzetzon Tamar* –Hazazon Tamar, said to be another name for En-Gedi (Gen. 14:7; 2 Chr. 20:2) – this

[937] Ziphion (236, 886).

		name may in fact refer to modern Tamar (see also חצצון תמר)[938]
	מחלף	*Machalaf*–Knife
	ממשפחתי	*Mimishfachtiy* –Of my kindred (Gen. 24:40)
	תועבת	*Thoavath* –Abomination (Gen. 46:34; Ex. 8:22)
879	עטף	*'ataf*–To turn aside; to envelop oneself; to be feeble, be faint, grow weak
880	בתועבת	*Beto'ebot* –With abominations (Deut. 32:16)
	יעף	*Ya'af*–To be or grow weary, be fatigued *Ya'ef*–Faint, weary, fatigued *Ye'af*–Weariness, fatigue, faintness
	יעקן	*Ya'aqan* –Jaakan, son of Ezer, son of Seir (this name used only in Deut. 10:6; 1 Chr. 1:42 – he is also called Akan in Gen. 36:27)[939]
	כסף	*Kasaf*–To long for, yearn for, long after *Kesaf*–Silver (Aramaic) *Kesef*–Silver (the metal of Luna), money
	כרסם	*Kirsem* –To tear apart, ravage, tear off
	נתתיכ	*Netatiyka* –Have I made you, permitted you (Gen. 17:5)
	עיף	*'ayef*–To be faint, be weary; faint, exhausted, weary
	עירם	*'eyrom* –Naked; nakedness *Eram* –A Duke of Edom (Gen. 36:43 – assoc. w/*Malkut*)
	פרם	*Param* –To tear, rend garment, rip
	פתת	*Pathath* –To break up, crumble
	צפין	*Tzafiyn* –Treasure, a hidden thing
	שפך	*Shafak* –To pour, pour out, spill *Shefek* –Place of pouring
	תולדתמ	*Toldotam* –Their generations (Num. 1:20)
	תפת	*Tofeth* –Act of spitting, spit; Topheth, once a part of a king's garden in Hinnom – it became a place where the people of Jerusalem sacrificed their children (Jer. 19:6, 11-14; 2 Kings 23:10 – see also תפתה)[940]
881	אפף	*'afaf*–To surround, encompass
	דברי הימים א	*Debere HaYamim* –"Events of the days," Hebrew title of 1 Chronicles
	התעשקו	*Hit'asquw* –They contended (Gen. 26:20)
	יהוסף	*Yehowsef*–Joseph, son of Jacob and Rachel (this name is only used in Ps. 81:6 – see also יוסף)[941]
	פראם	*Pir'am* –Piram, Amorite king slain by Joshua
	שקערורה –Prime number	*Sheqa'ruwrah* –Depression, hollow

938 חצצון תמר (884, 1534).

939 Some scholars feel that the reference in Deut. 10:6 may refer to a city, perhaps Beeroth (609). Akan (220, 870).

940 תפתה (885).

941 יוסף (156, 876).

882 דברי הימימ ב — *Debere HaYamim* –"Events of the days"; Hebrew title of 2 Chronicles

ירבעם — *Yeroboam* –Jeroboam, son of Solomon and first King of Israel; 14th King of Israel (Jeroboam II)

לברמים — *Lebarmim* –Lord of Triplicity by Night for Sagittarius

עברים — *'Abarim* –Abarim, large mountain range in Moab near Heshbon[942]

'Ibrim –Hebrews

שכל מנהיג האחדות — *Sekhel Manhig HaAchdoth* –Uniting Intelligence or Inductive Intelligence of Unity (13th Path)

883 ארבעים — *'arba'iym* –Forty

התועבת — *HaTo'evot* –The abominations (Lev. 18:26)

חלקת הצרימ — *Chelqath Hatztzurim* –Helkath-Hazzurim, area of smooth ground near the pool of Gibeon (2 Sam. 2:16)

–Prime number

884 חצצון תמר — *Chatzetzown Tamar* –Hazazon Tamar, said to be another name for En-Gedi (Gen. 14:7; 2 Chr. 20:2) – this name may in fact refer to modern Tamar (see also חצצן תמר)[943]

885 הכסף — *HaKasaf* –The money

תפתה — *Tofteh* –Act of spitting, spit; Tophet, once a part of a king's garden in Hinnom – it became a place where the people of Jerusalem sacrificed their children (this spelling used only in 1 Kings 22:22; 2 Chr. 18:21; Is. 30:33 – see also תפת)[944]

886 ונתתיכ — *ve-Netatiyka* –And I will make of you (Gen. 17:6)

ותתכס — *va-Titekas* –And she covered herself (Gen. 24:65)

ותתצב — *ve-Tetatzav* –And she stood (Ex. 2:4)

פתות — *Fatot* –You shall break (Lev. 2:6)

צפיון — *Tziphyown* –Ziphion, son of Gad (this spelling used only in Gen. 46:16 – see also צפון)[945]

שופך — *Showphak* –Shophach, captain of the army of Hadarezer of Zobah (see also Shobach)[946]

שכל שפע נבדל — *Sekhel Shefa Nivdal* –Intelligence of the Mediating Influence (6th Path)

תלנות — *Telunot* –Murmurings (Ex. 16:12; Num. 14:27)

887 ענואנין — *A'ano'nin* –Guardian of the 26th Tunnel of Set

---

[942] Abarim includes Mount Nebo from which Moses surveyed the Promised Land before he died.

[943] חצצן תמר (878, 1528).

[944] תפת (880).

[945] צפון (226, 876).

[946] Shobach (328, 808).

888	אני יהוה לא שניתי	*'aniy* YHVH *Lah Sheniytiy* –"I am God, I have not changed" (Mal. 3:6)
	יהוה צבאות ה־משיח	YHVH *Tzabaoth HaMessiach* –God of hosts, the messiah
	חפף	*Chapaf* –To cover, protect
		Chofaf –To cover, enclose, shelter, shield, surround
	פחתת	*Pecheteth* –A boring or eating out, hole, hollow; a fret, a low place (meaning uncertain – see Lev. 13:55)
	קצ שמ לחשכ	*Qetz Shem Lechashak* –"He has set an end to darkness" (Job 28:3)
	תפתח	*Tefetech* –You shall engrave (Ex. 28:11)
		Tiftach –You shall open (Deut. 15:8)
	IHSOUS	*Iesous* –Jesus (Greek)
889	ויבן נח מזבח ליהוה	*Vahyeven Noach Mezbayach la* YHVH –"And he, Noah, built an altar to YHVH" (Gen. 8:20)
	טפף	*Tafaf* –To skip, trip, take quick little steps
890	יערים	*Ye'ariym* –Jearim, mountains marking the boundary of Judah northeast of Beth Shemesh
	מתנת	*Matanot* –Gifts (Gen. 25:6; Ex. 28:38)
	סלף	*Salaf* –To twist, pervert, distort, overturn, ruin
		Selef –Crookedness, perverseness, crooked dealing
	עטרות אדר	*'Atrowth 'Addar* –Ataroth Addar, village on the southern frontier of Ephraim (see also Ataroth)[947]
	פספסים	*Paspasim* –10th – 15th letters of the 22-letter name of God
	פעמן	*Pa'amon* –Bell (on High Priest's robe)
	פקדון	*Piqqadown* –Deposit, store, supply
	פרים	*Puriym* –Purim, Jewish holiday observed a month before Passover in commemoration of Jewish deliverance from massacre led by Esther and Mordecai (see also פורים)[948]
	צררת	*Tzerurot* –Being bound up (Ex. 12:34)
	תמימת	*Temiymot* –Complete (Lev. 23:15)
	תפתי	*Tiftay* –Magistrate (Aramaic)
891	אפרים	*'Efrayim* –Ephraim, second son of Joseph and ancestory of the tribes of Israel (assoc. w/Taurus)
892	אפראימ	*Ephraim* –Ephraim, second son of Joseph by Asenath and progenitor of a tribe of Israel (assoc. w/Taurus); Ephraim, territory allotted to the tribe of Ephraim; city near Baal-hazor, probably the same as "Ephraim near the Wilderness" (2 Sam. 13:23); gate on the north wall of old Jerusalem (2 Kings 14:13; 2 Chr. 25:23); rough area (not forest) where Absalom was slain (2

---

947 Ataroth (679; 685).

948 פורים (336, 896).

Sam. 18:6); mountains west of the Jordan River (1 Sam. 1:1; 2 Chr. 13:4), allotted to the tribe of Ephraim

בספר מלחמות יהוה *be-Sefer Milchamuwt* YHVH –"The Book of the Wars of the Lord" (Num. 21:14)

ששבחר *Sheshbatztzar* –Sheshbazzar, prince of Judah into whose hands Cyrus placed the Temple vessels (Ezra 1:8, 11; 5:14-16)[949]

893 שמרון מראון *Shimrown Mero'wn* –Shimon-Meron, royal city of the Canaanites, whose king was slain by Joshua (see also Shimron)[950]

894 ופתחת *ve-Fitachta* –And you shall engrave (Ex. 28:9)

ותפתח *ve-Tiftach* –And she opened (Ex. 2:6)

חרי-יונים *Charey-yowniym* –Dung, dove's dung

תתנחלו *Titenachaluw* –You receive inheritance (Num. 34:13)

Titenechaluw –You shall inherit (Num. 33:54)

895 בארת בני־יעקן *Be'eroth Beney-Ya'aqan* –Beeroth Bene Jaakan, a form of Beeroth, meaning a place on the border of Edom; city of Gibeon assigned to the tribe of Benjamin

יונת אלם רחקים *Yownath 'elem rechoqiym* –Title of Ps. 56:1 (meaning uncertain)

פרק שירה *Perek Shirah* –Chapter of song; Midrash tractate

תמנתה *Timnatah* –To Timnah

תנחמת *Tanchumeth* –Tanhumeth, father of one of Gedaliah's captains

–The number of years that Mahaleel lived (Gen. 5:17)

896 אדמה לליון *'adamah le'livan* –I will be like the One on High

ונתתם *ve-Netatem* –That you shall give (Gen. 47:24)

ve-Nitatem –And you shall be delivered, handed over (Lev. 26:25)

ותמנת *ve-Temunat* –And the similitude (Num. 12:8)

נפשתינו *Nafshoteynuw* –Our souls (Deut. 4:16)

פורים *Puriym* –Purim, Jewish holiday observed a month before Passover in commemoration of Jewish deliverance from massacre led by Esther and Mordecai (this spelling used only in Est. 9:26, 28 – see also פרים)[951]

פרוים *Parvayim* –Parvaim, place where gold was obtained for the decoration of Solomon's Temple

פתיות *Pethayuwth* –Simplicity, naïveté

צוף *Tzuwf* –To flow, overflow, flood, float; honeycomb (Prov. 16:24; Ps. 19:11); Zuph, land or district

---

[949] Many believe Sheshbazzar is the same as Zerubbabel, but others deny this. They claim Sheshbazzar was governor under Cyrus and Zerubbabel under Darius.

[950] Shimron (596, 1246).

[951] פרים (330, 890).

where Saul searched for his father's donkeys; Zuph, brother of Samuel (this spelling used only in 1 Chr. 6:20 – see also צופי)[952]

צררות *Tzerorot* –Bundles, tied (Gen. 42:35)

תמונת *Temuwnat* –Form (Deut. 4:16)

תמתון *Temuton* –You die (Gen. 3:3, 4; Is. 22:14)

תשקצו *Teshaqtzuw* –You shall (make) detest(able) (Lev. 11:43; 20:25)

Teshaqetzuw –You shall detest (Lev. 11:12)

תתצו *Titotzuw* –You shall break down (Deut. 7:5)

897 תוחאת *Totza'ot* –The ends (Num. 34:8)

פרזים *Perizzim* –Perizzites

898 בית דבלתימ *Beyth Diblathayim* –Beth Diblathaim, town in Moab, possibly the same as Almon Diblathaim

חפרים *Chafarayim* –Haphraim, frontier town assigned to the tribe of Issachar – may be modern Khirbet el-Farriyah or et Faryibeh

חצף *Chatsaf* –To be urgent, harsh, show insolence

כתועבת *Keto'avot* –As the abominations (Deut. 8:9)

למשפחתמ *Lemishfehcotam* –By their families (Gen. 10:5)

899 שכל מורגש *Sekhel Morgash*–Exciting or Natural Intelligence (27th Path)

900 זהב וכסף *Zahav Vikesef* –"Gold and silver" (Ex. 25:3; 35:5; 1 Kings 10:22; 1 Chr. 18:10; 29:3; 2 Chr. 9:14, 21; 24:24; Est. 1:6; Ezek. 16:13; 28:4; Hab. 2:19; Zech. 14:14)

כפף *Kafaf* –To bend, bend down, bow down, be bent, be bowed

כתולדתמ *Ketoldotam* According to their birth (Ex. 28:10)

כתפת *Kitefot* –Shoulder-pieces (Ex. 28:7, 12; 39:20)

מכמתת *Mikmethath* –Michmethath, landmark boundary of Manasseh on the western side of the Jordan, east of Sehechm

מלכירם *Malkiyram* –Malchiram, descendant of King Jehoiakim

נמרים *Nimriym* –Nimrim, brook in Moab

נפשתיכמ *Nafshoteykem* –Of your persons (souls) (Ex. 16:16)

נתתימ *Netatiym* –I have given them (Num. 18:8)

עלף *'alaf* –To cover

עצמן *'Atzmon* –Azmon, place on the western boundary of Canaan (this spelling used only in Num. 34:4; – see also עצמון)[953]

ץ *Tzaddi* (final) –18th letter of Hebrew alphabet

קיצן *Qiytzown* –At the end, outermost, outer

---

952 צופי (186).

953 עצמון (256, 906).

	קציין	*Qatziyn* –Chief, ruler, commander
	קרם	*Qaram* –To spread something over, cover
	רן	*Ron* –Shout, rejoicing, ringing cry, shout, cry (of joy)
	רקם	*Raqam* –Embroidered with needlework
		Reqem –Rekem, Midianite king slain by the Israelites; son of Hebron; Rekem, city of Benjamin
	רשת	*Resheth* –Net, network (Ex. 27:4)
	שם	*Sham* –There, then, thither
		Shem –Name; Shem, eldest son of Noah & progenitor of the tribes
	שרת	*Sharath* –To minister, serve, minister to
		Shareth –Ministry, religious ministry, service in the Tabernacle
	שתר	*Sathar* –To burst out, break out
		Shethar –Shethar, one of the seven princes of Persia and Media (Esth. 1:14)
	תך	*Tokh* –Oppression
	תרש	*Teresh* –Strictness; Teresh, chamberlain of the Persian court that plotted against the crown
901	אליסף	*Eliasaf* –Eliasaph, a Gadite chief in the wilderness census; a head of the Gershonites
	אץ	*Atz* –To hasten, urge, press, hurry; 17th Gate of the 231 Gates
	ארן	*'aron* –Ark (of the covenant) (see also ארון)[954]
		'oren –Fir tree, cedar
	ארשת	*'aresheth* –Desire, request
	אשם	*'asham* –To offend, be guilty, trespass; to be desolate, acknowledge offense; guilt, offense, sin, guiltiness
		'ashem –Guilty, faulty (and obliged to offer a guilt-offering)
	ראשת	*Rahashoth* –Head place, place at the head
	תארש	*Te'ares* –You shall betroth (Deut. 28:30)
	תשאר	*Tisha'er* –Shall be left behind (Ex. 10:26)
902	במשענתם	*Bimishanotam* –With their staves (Num. 21:18)
	בץ	*Botz* – Mud, mire, swamp, pond, puddle; bubbles; bubble forth, burst forth; 37th Gate of the 231 Gates
	בשם	*Basam* –Spice, balsam; sweet, sweet smell, sweet odor
		Besem –Spice, balsam; sweet, sweet smell, sweet odor; balsam tree, perfume
	היכל לבנת הספיר	*Hekel Lebanath HaSafir* –Palace of the Pavement of Sapphire Stone, Heavenly Mansion corr. to *Yesod* & *Malkut* (see Ex. 24:10)
	שבם	*Sebam* –Shebam, city east of the Jordan given to the tribes of Reuben and Gad (see also Sibmah)[955]

[954] ארון (257, 907).
[955] Sibmah (347).

	שברת	*Shibareta* –You did break (Ex. 34:1)
	תשבר	*Teshabur* –You shall break in pieces (Ex. 23:24)
903	אבל כרמים	*'Abel Keramiym* –Abel-Keramim, a city in Palestine
	אבץ	*'Ebetz* –Abez, town in northern Palestine
	גץ	*Gatz* –56th Gate of the 231 Gates
	גרן	*Goren* –Threshing floor; barn, barn-floor, corn floor, void place
	גרשת	*Girashta* –Driven out (Gen. 4:14)
	גשם	*Gasham* –To rain
		Geshem –Rain, shower; body (Aramaic); Geshem, Arabian opponent of Nehemiah – also known as Gashmu
		Goshem –To be rained upon; to rain
	ויאמר אלהים	*Vay-yomer Elohim* –And God said
	עיי עברימ	*Iyey 'Abriym* –Ije-Abarim, town in extreme southern Judah; town east of the Jordan River (see also Iim)[956]
	רגן	*Ragan* –To murmur, whisper
904	ארם צובה	*'Aram Tzobah* –Aramzobah (Ps. 60:2)
	בתבניתמ	*Betavniytam* –After their pattern (Ex. 25:40)
	דץ	*Datz* –74th Gate of the 231 Gates
	למשפחותמ	*Lemishpechotam* –By their families (Num. 4:38)
	לתלדתמ	*Letoldotam* –According to their generations (Ex. 6:16)
	קרדם	*Qardom* –Axe
	רפידים	*Rephiydiym* –Rephidim, Israelite encampment between the Wilderness of Sin and Mount Sinai
	תדרש	*Tidrosh* –You shall seek (Deut. 23:7); you inquire (Deut. 12:30)
905	הץ	*Hatz* –91st Gate of the 231 Gates
	השם	*Hashem* –Hashem, father of several of David's guards (1 Chr. 11:34)
		HaShem –The Name; Tetragrammaton
		Husham –A King of Edom (assoc. w/ *Giburah*)
	הרן	*Haran* –Haran (ancient Mesopotamian city); Haran, brother of Abraham who died before his father; descendant of Levi; son of Caleb
	הרשת	*HaReshet* –The network (Ex. 27:4)
	השרת	*HaSharet* –The ministry (Num. 4:12)
	התך	*Hathak* –Hatach, chamberlain of Ahasuerus (Est. 4:5-10)
	התלעת	*HaTola'at* –The worm (Deut. 28:39)
	שהם	*Shoham* –Shoham, descendant of Merari; Malachite (precious stone in the High Priest's ephod – represents Joseph)
	תהפכת	*Tahpukot* –Perverse
	תתנה	*Titnenah* –You shall give it (Deut. 14:21)
	–The number of years that Enos lived (Gen. 5:11)	

[956] Iim (130, 690).

906 אהרן — *Aaron* –Brother of Moses
בית תפוח — *Beyth Tappuwach* –Beth Tappuah, settlement in the hills of Judah west of Hebron
וץ — *Vatz* –107th Gate of the 231 Gates
ושרת — *ve-Sheret* –And will minister
ותלעת — *ve-Tola'at* –And scarlet (Ex. 26:1)
כתפות — *Kitpot* –Shoulder-pieces (Ex. 28:25)
מוסף — *Musaf* –Additional; prayer added during Shabbat, *Rosh Chodesh,* and *Yom Tov*
נתנות — *Netunot* –Shall be given
עצמון — *'Atzmown* –Azmon, place on the western boundary of Canaan (this spelling used only in Num. 34:5; Josh. 15:4 – see also עצמן)[957]
קוף — *Qof* –Back of head; 19th letter of Hebrew alphabet; ape
שקוצית — *Shequitzit* –Last six letters of the 42-letter name of God (assoc. w/Saturday)
שרות — *Sheruwth* –Remnant
תולעת — *Tola'at* –Scarlet
תורש — *Tiuarsh* –You come to poverty (Gen. 45:11)

907 אוץ — *Uwtz* –To press; to be close, hurry, withdraw, haste
ארון — *'arown* –Chest, ark, Ark of the Covenant; coffin
בן־גבר — *Ben-Geber* –Ben-geber, one of Solomon's officers who provided food for the king and his household (1 Kings 4:13)
זץ — *Zatz* –122nd Gate of the 231 Gates
זקף — *Zaqaf* –To raise up
Zeqaf –To raise, lift up (Aramaic)
רזן — *Razan* –To be weighty, be judicious
Razown –Leanness, scantness, wasting; potentate, ruler
תאשור — *Teashshuwr* –A species of tree, perhaps cypress or cedar
–Prime number

908 בוץ — *Buwts* –Byssus, a costly, fine white linen cloth made in Egypt
בתולעת — *be-Tola'at* –In yarn
הגשם — *HaGashem* –The rain showers
חץ — *Chetz* –Arrow; lightning; punishment; wound; 136th Gate of the 231 Gates
Chotz –Out!, Avaunt!, Go away!
חצרים — *Chatzeriym* –Villages
חרן — *Charan* –Haran, brother of Abraham who died before his father; descendant of Levi; son of Caleb; Haran, Mesopotamian city northwest of Nineveh
חרשת — *Charosheth* –Carving, skillful working; Harosheth, small village on the northern bank of the Kishon River
חשם — *Chashum* –Hashum, one whose descendants returned

---

[957] עצמן (250, 900).

		from exile; one who sealed the covenant; priest who helped Ezra at the reading of the Law
		Chusham –Husham, descendant of Esau who became king of Edom – this spelling used in Gen. 36:34-35 (see also חושם)[958]
		Chushim –Hushim, descendant of Benjamin (1 Chr. 7:12) (see also חושם)[959]
	חתך	*Chathak* –To divide, determine
	כבד בכסף	*Kabad Bavasaf* –"[Abram] was rich in silver" (Gen. 13:2)
	תחרש	*Tacharosh* –You shall plow
	תשברו	*Teshaberuw* –You shall break
		Tishberuw –You shall buy
909	אחרן	*Achron* –Short for *Acharown*, – behind, following, subsequent, western
		Ochoran –Other, another
	גרון	*Garown* –Neck, throat
	טץ	*Tatz* –149th Gate of the 231 Gates
	עטלף	*'atallef* –Bat
	קטף	*Qataf* –To pluck off or out, cut off
	ראובן	*Re'uwben* –Reuben, eldest son of Jacob and Leah; descendants of Reuben who made up the tribe of Israel with the same name (assoc. w/Aquarius)
	שרטת	*Saratet* –Cuttings (Lev. 21:5)
910	ארגון	*'argevan* –Purple, red-purple
	גרזן	*Garzen* –Axe
	דוץ	*Duwts* –Spring, leap, dance
	דרון	*Darown* –South
	ודרשת	*ve-Darashta* –And you shall inquire
	וירא אלהים כי טוב	*Va-ya-re Elohim ki tov* –"And God saw that it was good."(Gen. 1:10, 12, 18, 21, 25)
	זהב פרוים	*Zahav Peruwym* –"Red-orange gold from Parvaim" (2 Chr. 3:6)
	יץ	*Yatz* –161st Gate of the 231 Gates
	ירשת	*Yoreshet* –Who possesses
	ישם	*Yasham* –To put, place, set, appoint, make; to ruin, be desolate
	כמתנת	*Kematnat* –As gifts
	כפרים	*Kiporim* –Many atonements
	לתולדתמ	*Letoldotam* –According to their generations (Gen. 10:32)
	מערם	*Ma'arom* –Naked thing, nakedness
		Murmas –Goetic demon #54 (Aurum Solis spelling)
	מצפן	*Mitspun* –Hidden treasure, treasure
	מתכנת	*Mathkoneth* –Measurement, proportion, tale; count, amount

---

958 חושם (354, 914).

959 חושם (354, 914).

	עמרם	*'Amram* –Amram, son of Kohath and descendant of Levi and father or ancestor of Aaron, Moses, and Miriam; one who had taken a foreign wife (see also Hemdan)[960]
	קנמון	*Qinnamon* –Cinnamon
	ריקם	*Reyqam* –Vainly, emptily
	שרית	*Sariyta* –You have striven
	תדרשו	*Tidreshuw* –You shall seek
	תירש	*Tiyrowsh* –Wine, fresher new wine
	תשרי	*Tishri* –The 1st month of the Jewish calendar – it is associated with Libra and the tribe Levi
	–The number of years that Cainan lived (Gen. 5:14)	
911	אליצפן	*Eliytsafan* –Elizaphan or Elzaphan, a Kohathite chief in the wilderness; a Zebulunite chief; Uzziel's son, Mishael's brother in time of Moses
	ארדון	*'Ardown* –Ardon, son of Caleb
	אשים	*Eshim* –Flames; Angelic Choir assoc. w/*Malkut*
	אשתדור	*'eshtadduwr* –Revolt, sedition (Aramaic)
	באר שחת	*Bar Shachath*–Pit of Destruction; the 5th Hell (corr. to *Giburah*)
	דראון	*Dera'own* –Aversion, abhorrence
	הרון	*Herown* –Physical conception, pregnancy, conception
	התוך	*Hittuwk* –A melting
	התולעת	*HaTola'at* –The scarlet
	ראשית	*Rashith* –Beginning, first, best, chief
	שארית	*Sha'eriyth* –Rest, residue, remainder, remnant
	תוקהת	*Towqahath* –Tikvath, father-in-law of Huldah the prophetess; father of Jahaziah
	תשורה	*Teshuwrah* –Gift, present
	–Prime number	
912	אהרון	*'Aharown* –Aaron
	בכתנתמ	*be-Kutanotam* –In their tunics
	בת שיר	*Bath Shir* –Song-maiden; muse
	דרבון	*Dorbown* –Goad
	ושרתו	*Veshertuw* –That they may serve
	ותולעת	*ve-Tola'at* –And yarn
	יבשם	*Yibsam* –Jibsam, descendant of Tola (1 Chr. 7:2)
	ירבשת	*Yerubbesheth* –Jerubbesheth, name given to Jerubbaal (Gideon) by those who wanted to avoid pronouncing Baal (2 Sam. 11:21)[961]
	–The number of years Seth lived (Gen. 5:8)	
913	אבדרון	*Abdaron* –Angel of 2d Aquarius
	אורון	*Avron* –Angel of 2d Pisces
	באשים	*Be'ushiym* –Stinking or worthless things,

[960] Hemdan (102, 752).

[961] See Jerubbaal and Gideon.

		wildgrapes, stinkberries
	בית אשר	*Beyth 'asher* –House of happiness
	בראשית (ב = 2)	*Bereshit* –"In the beginning;" Hebrew title of Genesis[962]
	ויהושע בן נון מלא רוח חכמה	*Yeheshua ben Nun Malay Ruach Chamah* –"Yeheshua son of Nun was filled with the spirit of wisdom" (Deut. 34:9)
	למשפחתיהם	*Lemishpechoteyhem* –After their families (Gen. 8:19)
	ראש בית	*Ra'sh Beyth* –Head of the house
	רזון	*Rezown* –Rezon, Syrian rebel who set up his own government in Damascus (1 Kings 11:23)[963]
	שם אחד	*Shem Achad* –The name of unity
	תוצאתיו	*Totza'otayu* –Its ends, its going out (Num. 34:4, 5)
	תלה ארץ על בלימה	*Taleh 'aretz 'el Beliymah* –"He suspends the earth on nothingness" (Job 26:7)
	–300 more than the *mitzvot* of Torah (613)	
914	ובתולעת	*ve-Vetola'at* –And in yarn
	וממשפחתמ	*ve-Mimishpachtam* –And of the families
	חוץ	*Chotz* –Out!, avaunt!, go away!
		Chuwts –Outside, outward, street, the outside
	חורן	*Chavran* –Hauran, district bordering the region of Gilead south of Damascus, noted for the fertility of its soil
	חושם	*Chuwsham* –Husham, descendant of Esau who became king of Edom – this spelling used in 1 Chr. 1:45-46 (see also חשם)[964]
	חרון	*Charown* –Anger, heat, burning of anger (always used of God's anger)
	חרמונים	*Chermowniym* –Hermonites
	ירדן	*Yordan* –Jordan, major river of Palestine (Gen. 13:10; Josh. 2:7)
	שדים	*Shedim* –Demons
		Siddiym –Siddim, valley near the Dead Sea, full of bitumen pits (Gen. 14:3, 8, 10)
	שוחם	*Shuwcham* –Shuham, son of Dan (this spelling used only in Num. 26:42 – see also Hushim)[965]
	שחרות	*Shacharuwth* –Blackness of hair (indicating youth)
915	אחרון	*Acharown* –Behind, following, subsequent, western
	אמתחתינו	*'amtechoteynuw* –Our sacks (Gen. 43:21)
	יהץ	*Yahatz* –Jahaz, battlefield on the wastelands of Moab (this spelling used only in Is. 15:4; Jer. 48:34 – see also יהצה)[966]

[962] *Bereshit* is sometimes considered a notarikon for ברא רקיע ארץ שמים ים תהום, "He created the firmament, the earth, the heavens, the sea, and the abyss."

[963] Some scholars think Rezon simply is a title denoting a prince and identify him with Hezion (81, 731).

[964] חשם (348, 908).

[965] Hushim (358, 918).

[966] יהצה (110).

916	בן־חור	*Ben-Chuwr* –Ben-Hur, one of Solomon's twelve supply officers, in charge of supplying food to Solomon's household
	ובחרשת	*ve-Vacharoshet* –And in cutting, carving (Ex. 31:5)
	וירשת	*ve-Yarashta* –And possess, and inherit (Deut. 6:18, 16:20)
	וישרת	*va-Yesharet* –And he ministered (Gen. 39:4)
	ותירש	*ve-Tiyrosh* –And wine (Gen. 27:28)
	חברון	*Chebrown* –Hebron, city in the hills of Judah, south of Jerusalem; town of the tribe of Asher, more frequently called Abdon
	חרבון	*Charabown* –Drought
	ירקום	*Yeraqown* –Mildew, paleness, lividness
	ירשתו	*Yerushato* –His possession
	ישרתו	*Yershartuw* –They minister
	מועף	*Muw'af* –Gloom, darkness
	מעוף	*Ma'uwf* –Gloom
	רמתים צופים	*Ramathayim Tzowphiym* –Ramathaim-Zophim, town where Samuel was born (this spelling used only in 1 Sam. 1:11 – see also Ramah)[967]
	תנינות	*Tinyanuwth* –The second time, again (Aramaic)
	תירוש	*Tiyrosh* –Of the wine
	תירשו	*Tiyreshuw* –You will inherit (Lev. 20:24)
917	באמתחתינו	*be-'amotchoteynuw* –In our sacks (Gen. 43:18)
	במתכנתה	*Bematkuntah* –According to its composition
	וראשית	*ve-Re'ashiyt* –And first (fruits)
	יראון	*Yirown* –Iron, city of the tribe of Naphtali – probably modern Yarun
	קול יהוה על־המים	*Qol* YHVH *'Al-HaMayim* –"The voice of YHVH is over the waters" (Ps. 29:3)
918	ביתון	*Beton* –Angel of 3d Gemini
	ושברתי	*vo-Shavartiy* –And I will break (Lev. 26:19)
	חיץ	*Chayits* –Wall, party-wall, thin wall
	חשים	*Chushiym* –Hushim, son of Dan (Gen. 46:23) – in Num. 26:42, his name is Shuham; one of the two wives of Shaharaim (1 Chr. 8:11 – in verse 8 of this her name is spelled חושים)[968]
	תועבתמ	*To'avotam* –Their abominations (Deut. 20:18)
919	אחרין	*Ochoreyn* –End, outcome
	אחשתרי	*Achashtariy* –Ahashtariy, a descendant of Ashur of Judah (1 Chr. 4:6)[969]
	אמתחתיכמ	*'amtechoteykem* –Your sacks (Gen. 43:12)
	וגרשתי	*ve-Gerashtiy* –And I will drive out (Ex. 33:2)

[967] Ramah (245).

[968] חושים (364, 924).

[969] In 1 Chr. 4:6, this name is given with the "heh" preceding it, making his name Haahashtariy.

	שטים	*Shittiym* –Shittim, final Israelite encampment before crossing the Jordan[970] (Num. 25:1; Josh. 2:1); dry and unfruitful valley (Joel 4:18)
	–Prime number	
920	כץ	*Katz* –172nd Gate of the 231 Gates
	כרן	*Keran* –Cheran, son of Dishon (Gen. 36:26; 1 Chr. 1:41)
	עיר שמש	*'Iyr Shemesh* –Ir Shemesh, city of the tribe of Dan (see also Beth Shemesh)[971]
	ענף	*'anaf* –Bough, branch
		'anef –Full of branches, dense
	צלף	*Tzalaph* –Zalaph, father of one who repaired the wall of Jerusalem
	קיקין	*Qiyqayown* –A plant (perhaps a gourd)
	שכם	*Shakam* –To rise or start early
		Shekem –Shoulder, back; Shechem, son of Hamor who defiled Dinah (Gen. 33:19; 34); two descendants of Manasseh; Shechem, ancient city in central Palestine
921	באמתחתיכמ	*Be'amtechoteykem* –In your sacks (Gen. 43:23)
	והרין	*Vehrin* –Angel of 2d Sagittarius
	וירשתה	*viy-Rishtah* –And you shall possess it
	ישרתהו	*Yeshartuhu* –They shall minister
922	ותירוש	*ve-Tiyrosh* –And wine
	יום כפור	*Yom Kippur* –Day of Atonement; holiest day of the Jewish year
	מהר שלל חש בז	*Maher-shalal-hash-baz* –Maher-Shalal-Hash-Baz, symbolic name of Isaiah's son (Is. 8:1-4)[972]
	קול־יהוה שבר ארזימ	*Qol*-YHVH *Shover 'Araziym* –"The voice of the Lord breaks cedars" (Ps. 29:5)
	תורישו	*Toriysuw* –You will drive out
923	חמשה עשר	*Chamishah-Asar* –Fifteen
924	ובמתכנתו	*ve-Vematkunto* –And according to its composition (Ex. 30:32)
	ויברא אלהימ את האדמ בצלמו	*Vay-yi-vera Elohim eth HaAdham be-tzalmu* –"So God created man in his own image" (Gen. 1:27)
	חושים	*Chuwshiym* –Hushim, one of the two wives of Shaharaim (1 Chr. 8:8 – in verse 11 of this her name is spelled חשים)
	יאר יהוה פניו אליך	*Ya'ar* YHVH *Panavi 'aliyk* –"May YHVH bestow His favor upon you..." (Num. 6:26)
	רוחין	*Ruachin* –A class of demons

[970] At Shittim, Moses bade farewell and the Law was completed.
[971] Beth Shemesh (1052).
[972] The name means "Pillage hastens, looting speeds"

925 אדרכן *Adarkan* –Drachma, dram, daric – unit of weight and value (of gold, money) equal to 128 grains or 4.32 grams

השכם *Hashekem* –Rise up early (Ex. 8:16)

וגרשתיו *ve-Gerashtiyuw* –And I shall drive them out

וישטם *Ve-Yisetim* –And he hated (Gen. 27:41)

926 אחודראון *Achodraon* –Lord of Triplicity by Night for Libra

אריטון *Ariton* –Demon King of Water and the West

ענתות *'Anathowth* –Anathoth, son of Becher; one who sealed the new covenant with God after the Exile; Anathoth, town of the tribe of Benjamin (birthplace of the prophet Jeremiah)

תלונתמ *Taluwnotam* –Their murmurings

927

928 בעל מעון *Ba'al Me'own* –Baal Meon, Amorite city on the northern border of Moab (this spelling used only in Jer. 48:23 – see also Beon, Beth Baal Meon)[973]

כבד את־אביכ ואת־אמכ *Kabedh eth-abika ve-eth-immeka* –"Honor thy father and thy mother" (Ex. 20:12)

למשפחתיכמ *Lemishpachoteykem* –According to your families (Ex. 12:21)

מפתחת *Mefutachot* –Engraved

תתעבנו *Tita'evenuw* –You shall abhor it (Deut. 7:26)

929 היכל קדוש קדשימ *Hekel Qadesh Qadeshim* –Palace of the Holy of Holies; Heavenly Mansion corr. to Supernals

יגר שהדותא *Yegar Sahaduwtha'* –Jegar-Sahadutha, pile of stones erected by Laban to memorialize his pact with Jacob (Gen. 31:47) (Aramaic)

עולם הבריאה *Olam HaBriah* –World of Creation

930 דגדגירון *Dagdagiron* –The Fishy Ones, *Qlippoth* of Capricorn

דכרון *Dikrown* –Record, memorandum (Aramaic)

מצפון זהב *Metzafon Zahab* –"Refined gold" (1 Kings 10:18)

לנפשתיכמ *le-Napeshoteykem* –Of your lives, to yourselves

לץ *Letz* –Mocker; 182nd Gate of the 231 Gates

לרשת *Lareshet* –To possess

לשם *Leshem* –Ligure, jacinth, or opal; probably jacinth or ligure (precious stone in the High Priest's ephod – represents the tribe Dan); Leshem, northern limit of the tribe of Dan; place named in Is. 10:30 with Gallim and Anathoth

לשרת *Lesharet* –To minister

לתך *Lethek* Barley-measure (uncertain measurement but thought to be 1/2 an homer - 5 ephahs)

סנדלפון *Sandalfon* –Archangel assoc. w/*Malkut*

[973] Beon (122, 772), Beth Baal Meon (680, 1330).

	סעף	*Sa'af* –To cut off, lop off boughs *Sa'if* –Ambivalence, division, divided opinion *Se'ef* –Ambivalent, divided, half-hearted
	ענתתי	*'Anthothiy* –Antothite
	שלם	*Shalam* –To be in a covenant of peace, be at peace, be complete, be sound *Shelem* –Peace offering *Shalem* –Perfect, whole *Shallum* –16th King of Judah, aka Jehoahaz; 16th King of Israel (variant spelling) *Shillem* –Recompense, requittal
	תירשכ	*Tiyroshka* –Your wine
	תלך	*Talak* –Go
	תעינת	*Thaniyth* –Ascetic practice of fasting (Ezra 9:5 – heaviness)
	–The number of years that Adam lived (Gen. 5:5)	
931	אליץ	*Alats* –To urge
	רוח הרוחות הלבנה	*Ruach HaRuachoth HaLebanah* –Spirit of the Spirits of the Moon (a literal Hebrew translation; cf. 3321)
	תלאשר	*Tela'ssar* –Telassar, city near Harran and Orfa in western Mesopotamia
932	בית ענת	*Beyth 'Anoth* –Beth Anath, fortress town of the tribe of Naphtali; town in the mountains of Judah (see also בית ענות)[974]
	בשלם	*Bishlam* –Bishlam, foreign colonist who wrote a letter of complaint against the Jews (Ezra 4:7)
	עצ הדעת טוב ורע	*Etz HaDaath Tov va-Ra* –Tree of the Knowledge of Good and Evil
933	אלהי העברים	*Elohi HaIbrim* –God of the Hebrews
	הא־לכם זרע	*HaLakem zera'* –"Take for yourselves seed" (Gen. 47:23)
	זכרון	*Zikrown* –Memorial, reminder, remembrance
934	בכבשים	*Bakevasiym* –Among sheep
	בכשבים	*Bakesaviym* –Among sheep
	כשדים	*Kasdiym* –Chaldees
	מרפידם	*Merefiydim* –From Rephidim
935	בית עזמות	*Beyth 'Azmaveth* –Beth Azmaveth, town near Jerusalem, halfway between Geba and Anathoth
	התעללת	*Hita'alalet* –You have mocked, shamed
	לרשתה	*le-Rishtah* –To inherit it, to possess it (Gen. 15:7)
	ענתתיה	*'Anthothiyah* –Antothijah, son of Shashak
936	ותירשכ	*ve-Tiyroshka* –And your wine
	לוץ	*Luwtz* –To scorn, make mouths at, talk arrogantly

[974] בית ענות (938).

	לשרתו	*le-Sharto* –To minister to him
	שלום	*Shalom* –Peace
		Shallum –16th King of Judah, aka Jehoahaz; 16th King of Israel; Shallum, youngest son of Naphtali (see also שלם)[975]; descendant of Judah; descendant of Aaron and an ancestor of Ezra (this spelling used only in 1 Chr. 5:38-39; Ezra 7:2 – see also Meshullam)[976]; gatekeeper of the tabernacle; one who married foreign wives during the Exile; one who helped to repair the wall of Jerusalem
		Shilluwm –Requital, reward
	תנופת	*Tenuwpot* –Wave offering; offering
937	יארכון	*Ya'arikown* –May be long
	יובב בן זרח	*Yobab ben Zerah* –Jobab, son of Zerah; a King of Edom (assoc. w/*Hesed*)
	נאפוף	*Na'afuwf* –Adultery
	–Prime number	
938	בית ענות	*Beyth 'Anowth* –Beth Anoth, fortress town of the tribe of Naphtali; town in the mountains of Judah
	חלץ	*Chalats* –To remove, draw out, draw off, take off, withdraw, equip (for war), arm for war, rescue, be rescued; to draw off or out, withdraw; loins
		Cheletz –Helez, one of David's mighty men; descendant of Judah
	לחץ	*Lachatz* –To squeeze, press, oppress; oppression, distress, pressure
939	אבשלום	*'Abshalowm* –Absalom, son of David
	והתנחלתמ	*ve-Hichnachaltem* –And you shall inherit them (Lev. 25:46)
	חברה זרח בקר אור	*Chevrah Zerach Boqer Aur* –"Society of the Shining Light of Dawn"; official Hebrew name of the Hermetic Order of the Golden Dawn
	תל חרשא	*Tel Charsha'* –Tel-Harsa, Babylonian village used as a grouping point for Jews returning to Palestine
940	אבנ העופרת אל פיה	*'eben HaOfereth Al Peyah* –"Lead stone on its mouth" (Zech. 5:8)
	מץ	*Mots* –Chaff (always as driven by wind); 191st Gate of the 231 Gates
	מצרים	*Mitzraim* –Egypt; Mizraim (Egyptians); Mizraim, the second son of Ham
	משרת	*Mesharet* –Minister
		Masreth –Pan, dish
		Mishrat –Dipping, liquor, soaking
	סעיף	*Sa'iyf* –Cleft, branch
	ספף	*Safaf* –To stand at or guard the threshold

975 שלם (370, 930).

976 Meshullam (410, 970).

פתלתל *Pethaltol* –Twisted, crooked, tortuous
צמיתת *Tzemiythuth* –Completion, finality, in perpetuity
צמרים *Tzemarayim* –Zemaraim, city north of Jericho; mountain in Ephraim's hill country
צנף *Tzanaf* –To wrap, wrap or wind up together, wind around
קיקלן *Qiyqalown* –Disgrace, shame
רמן *Rimmown* –Pomegranate
שמם *Shamem* –To be desolate, to be apalled; devastated, deserted, desolate
תמך *Tamak* –To grasp, hold, support, attain
שמרת *Shimrath* –Shimrath, descendant of Benjamin
תעתע *Tahtuah* –Errors, delusion; mockery
תרמש *Tisrmosho* –That will crawl
תשמר *Tishmor* –You shall observe; you shall keep

941 אמץ *'amats* –To be strong, alert, courageous, brave, stout, bold, solid, hard
Ammits –Strong, mighty (see also אמיץ)[977]
'amots –Strong, bay, dappled, piebald (of color)
'omets –Strength
משארת *Mish'ereth* –Kneading trough or bowl
משראת *Mishrath* –Angel of 1d Sagittarius
שמאם *Shim'am* –Shimeam, one of the family of King Saul whose descendants dwelled in Jerusalem (this spelling used only in 1 Chr. 9:38 – see also שמאה)[978]
–Prime number

942 בני יעקן *Beney Ya'aqan* –Bene Jaakan, place on the border of Edom where the wandering Israelites camped (see also Beeroth)[979]
וישרתוכ *vi-Yeshartuwka* –And minister unto you (Num. 18:2)
מבשם *Mibsam* –Mibsam, son of Ishmael; son of Simeon

943 באשמרת *be-'ashmoret* –In the watch

944 ארגמן *'argaman* –Purple, red-purple
סכות בנות *Sukkowth benowth* –Succoth-benoth, Babylonian goddess, the mistress of Marduk (2 Kings 17:30)[980]

945 הרמשת *Haromasat* –That moves, creeps (Gen. 1:21)
התעללתי *Hetalalti* –I made a mockery (Ex. 10:2)
התשמר *Hetishmor* –Whether you would keep (Deut. 8:2)
ויחזק יהוה את לב פרעה *va-Yichzaq* YHVH *Eth Lav Para'oh* –"And the Lord

---

977 אמיץ (141, 951).
978 שמאה (346).
979 Beeroth (609).
980 Literally "the daughter's booth."

stiffened the heart of Pharaoh" (Ex. 9:12, 10:20, 27; 11:10; 14:8)

לטושם — *Letuwshim* –Letushim, son of Dedan
–The number of children of Zattu who returned from exile (Ezra 2:8)

946 ופתלתל — *ve-Petaltol* –And crooked
ושמרת — *ve-Shamarta* –And you shall keep
ליושתו — *li-Yerushato* –To his possession
מוץ — *Muwtz* –Squeezer, executioner, oppressor
משרתו — *Mersharto* –His minister
רמון — *Rimmown* –Rimmon, town in southern Judah; rock near Gibeah; border town of Zebulun (see also Dimnah)[981]; Rimmon, Syrian god whose temple was at Damascus (2 Kings 5:18)[982]; father of Ishbosheth's murderers (2 Sam. 4:2-9)
תשמרו — *Tishmeruw* –You shall observe; you shall keep; be mindful of; observe
תשקצנו — *Teshaqtzenuw* –You shall detest it
תתצון — *Titotzuwn* –You shall break down

947 אמוץ — *'Amowtz* –Amoz, father of the prophet Isaiah
ארמון — *'armown* –Citadel, palace, fortress
זמרן — *Zimran* –Zimran, son of Abraham by Keturah
מתראוש — *Mathravash* –Angel of 1d Cancer
שבעה־עשר — *Shivah-Asar* –Seventeen

948 ושברתמ — *ve-Shibartem* –And dash in pieces
חמץ — *Chamets* –To be leavened, be sour; to be cruel, oppress, be ruthless; to be red
Chametz –The thing leavened, leaven
Chomets –Vinegar
חמרן — *Chamran* –Hamran, son of Dishon (1 Chr. 1:41)
מחרשת — *Macharesheth* –Plowshare
מרחשת — *Marchesheth* –Saucepan, stew pan
שלחים — *Shilchiym* –Shilhim, city in southern Judah near Lebaoth (see also Shaaraim)[983]

949 אבישלום — *'Abiyshalowm* –Abishalom, son of David
מוגשם — *Mughsham* –Realized, materialized, corporeal
מגרון — *Migrown* –Migron, Benjamite village north of Michmash

950 במרחשת — *ba-Marchashat* –In the stewing pan
המתהפכת — *HaMithapeket* –Which turned every way (Gen. 3:24)
לרשתכ — *le-Rishteka* –That you may inherit
מיץ — *Miyts* –Squeezing, pressing, wringing
מרשית — *Mereshiyt* –From the beginning (Deut. 11:12)

---

[981] Dimnah (99).
[982] He has been identified with Rammanu, the Assyrian god of wind, rain and storm.
[983] Shaaraim (620, 1180).

	נץ	*Netz* –Blossom; an unclean bird of prey (perhaps hawk); 199th Gate of the 231 Gates
	נקף	*Naqaf* –To strike, strike off; to go around, compass, round *Noqef* –Striking off
	נשם	*Nasham* –To pant
	נתך	*Nathak* –To pour out or forth, drop (of rain), be poured, be poured out, be melted, be molten
	צניף	*Tzaniyf* –Turban, headdress
	רנן	*Ranan* –To overcome; to cry out, shout for joy *Rannen* –Cry, shout *Renen* –Plumage (Job 39:13)
	שכרתיכ	*Sekartiyka* –I hired you
	שמים	*Shamayim* –Heaven, sky
	שמרית	*Shimriyth* –Shimrith, woman of Moab, mother of Jehozabad who killed Joash (see also Shomer)[984]
	תלנתיכמ	*Telunoteykam* –Your murmurings
	תנך	*Tanakh* –Jewish Bible
951	אמיץ	*Ammiyts* –Strong, mighty
	ארנן	*'Arnan* –Arnan, descendant of David and founder of a family *'Arnon* –Arnon, river that pours into the Dead Sea *'Ornan* –Ornan, a Jebusite from whom David bought land and upon which the Temple was built (called Araunah in 2 Sam. 24:16)[985]
	הרמון	*Harmown* –High fortress – a place, site unknown (see Amos 4:3)
	והתעלמת	*ve-Hita'alamta* –And hide yourself
	ישראלית	*Yisra'eliyth* –Female Israelite
	מראשית	*Mere'ashiyth* –Of the first
	נאץ	*Na'ats* –To spurn, condemn, despise, abhor
	ראשיתמ	*Re'ashiytam* –The first part of them
	רום מעלה	*Rom Maalah* –The Inscrutable Height, a title of *Keter*
	שמע ישראל	*Shema Israel* –"Hear, O Israel"
952	ומשרתו	*ve-Mesharto* –And his minister
	שבילים	*Shevilim* –Paths
953	נרגן –Prime number	*Nirgan* –To murmur, whisper
954	והנגלת לנו ולבנינו עד עולמ	*Ve-Haneglot la-nu vuwlvanavinu ad olam* –"...with overt acts, it is for us and our children ever..." (Deut. 29:28)
	חרמון	*Chermown* –Hermon, highest mountain of the Anti-Lebanon range, marking the northeast boundary of Palestine

[984] Shomer (546).
[985] Araunah (66; 262).

תעמשו בכלו *Vo-shamatav Vi-koloh* –"and heed His command with all your heart and soul..." (Deut. 30:2)
חמוץ *Chamowts* –The oppressor, the ruthless (Isa. 1:17)
ספרדים *Sefardim* –Spanish Jews
רהב המ שבת *Rahab Hem Shebeth* –Rahab Hem Shebeth, "Rahab sits idle," a name given by the prophet Isaiah to Egypt, comparing Egypt to Rahab the dragon, a mythological sea monster of chaos (Is. 30:7)

955 השמים *HaShamaim* –The heaven
וגרשתמו *ve-Gerashtamo* –And you shall drive them out
על־ספר הישר *'al-Sefer HaYashar* –"The book of Jashar" (Josh. 10:13; 2 Sam. 1:18)

956 הנשארת *Hanisha'eret* –Which remains
הישראלית *HaYisra'eliyt* –The Israelite
וירשתמ *vi-Yerishtam* –And you do succeed them, and you have driven them out
ve-Yerishtem –And possess
מורשתי *Morashtiy* –Morashthite
נוץ *Nuwts* –To fly, flee; to bloom, blossom
ספר התורה *Sefer HaTorah* –Book of the Law
ספרוים *Sefarvayim* –Sepharvaim, city formerly identified with Sippar on the east bank of the Euphrates, now believed to be the Syrian city Shabara (Is. 37:13)
שונם *Shuwnem* –Shunem, town near Jezreel that was allotted to the tribe of Issachar
תנוך *Tenuwk* –Tip, lobe (of ear)
תשארנה *Tisha'arnah* –They shall remain

957 אבל השטים *'Abel HaShittim* –Abel-Shittim, a location in Palestine
ארנון *'Arnown* –Arnon, river that pours into the Dead Sea
והורשתמ *ve-Horashitem* –And you shall drive them out
טברמון *Tabrimmown* –Tabrimmon, father of Ben-Hadad I, king of Syria
מראשתיו *Mira'ashuwtav* –Above his head, around his head, under his head

958 חמיץ *Chamiyts* –Seasoned
חמשים *Chamishshiym* –Fifty
נחץ *Nachats* –To urge
תשברונ *Teshaberuwn* –You shall dash into pieces

959 אחשתרנ *Achastaran* –Royal steeds

960 ישבי לחם *Yashubiy Lechem* –Jashubi-Lehem, descendant of Judah
לצמתת *Litzmitut* –In perpetuity, irredeemably
משכרת *Maskoreth* –Wages
מתנתיכמ *Matnoteykam* –That is given by you (Num. 18:29)
נשים *Nashim* –Women, wives

סרן *Seren* –Lord, ruler, tyrant; axle
סץ *Satz* –206th Gate of the 231 Gates
רסן *Resen* –Something that restrains, halter; Resen, city between Nineveh and Calah in Assyria
שכלים *Sekhelim* –Intelligences
שנים *Shanim* –Years
Shenaim –Two
תדרשנו *Tidreshenuw* –You seek him

961 אנשים *'anashim* –Men of distinction
ואשמידם *vi-Ashmidaym* –That I may destroy them (Deut. 9:14)
נשיאם *Nisiem* –Princes
Nosiem –Burdened, laden

962 הראשנות *HaRi'ashonot* –The first
תורישמו *Toriyshemo* –Shall dispossess them
תשברני *Tashbirniy* –You shall sell to me (Deut. 2:28)
–The number of years that Jared lived (Gen. 5:20)

963

964 יהוה שלום YHVH *Shalowm* –Adonai Shalom, an altar built by Gideon in Ophrah (Judg. 6:24)
מטטרון *Metatron* –Archangel assoc. w/*Keter*
תחרשון *Tacharshuwn* –Shall hold your peace

965 שמ המפרש *Shem HaMeforash* –Name of Extension; the 72-fold name of God
שמנה־עשר *Shemonah-Asar* –Eighteen

966 הנשאים *HaNisi'im* –The rulers
והתחזקתמ *ve-Hitchazaqtam* –And be of good courage (Num. 13:20)
ושנים *vi-Shanim* –And years
כמוץ *Kamotz* –Angel of 1d Scorpio
תירשון *Tiyrashuwn* –You shall possess
מתנותיכמ *Matnoteykam* –Your gifts

967 ומשארתכ *ve-Misha'artaka* –And your kneading bowl (Deut. 28:5)
שנהבים *Shenhabbiym* –Ivory
–Prime number

968 בנות שיר *Banoth Shir* –Song maidens, muses

969 סרגון *Sargown* –Sargon, important king of Assyria and Babylonia who finished the siege of Samaria and carried away Israel (this spelling used only in Is. 20:1)
סרטן *Sarton* –Crab; Cancer
–The number of years that Methuselah lived (Gen. 5:27)

970 דרכמון *Darkemown* –Daric, drachma, dram
לצמיתת *la-Tzemiytut* –In perpetuity (Lev. 25:30)
לשרתמ *le-Shartam* –To minister unto them (Num. 16:9)
מלץ *Malats* –To be smooth, be slippery
משכרתי *Maskertiy* –My wages (Gen. 31:7)
משלם *Meshullam* –Meshullam, grandfather of Shaphan; descendant of King Jehoiakim; head of a family of Gad; descendant of Benjamin; one whose son lived in Jerusalem; one who lived in Jerusalem; descendant of Aaron and an ancestor of Ezra (see also Shallum)[986]; priest (1 Chr. 9:12); overseer of the Temple work; chief man who returned with Ezra to Jerusalem; one who assisted in taking account of those who had foreign wives after the Exile; one who took a foreign wife during the Exile; two who rebuilt part of the wall of Jerusalem; prince or priest who stood with Ezra while he read the Law; priest who sealed the new covenant with God after the Exile; one whose descendants lived in Jerusalem; priest who assisted in the dedication of the wall of Jerusalem; descendant of Ginnethon; Levite and gatekeeper after the Exile
נבוזראדן *Nebuwzaradan* –Nebuzaradan, Babylonian captain of the guard at the siege of Jerusalem (2 Kings 25:8, 11, 20)
נפתלתי *Niftaltiy* –Have I wrestled (Gen. 30:8)
סרין *Siyron* –Armor
עץ *'etz* –Tree, wood, timber, stock, plant, stalk, stick, gallows; 212th Gate of the 231 Gates
ערן *'Eran* –Eran, Ephraim's grandson
עשרת *'esarot* –Tens
'eseret –Ten
עתך *'Athak* –Athach, town in southern Judah to which David sent some of the spoil of Ziklag
צעיף *Tza'iyf* –Wrapper, shawl, veil
צפף *Tzafaf* –To chirp, peep
צקלן *Tziqlon* –Sack, bag (meaning dubious – 2 Kings 4:42)
שנים־עשר *Shenaim-Asar* –Twelve
שערת *Si'irot* –Hairy (Gen. 27:23)
תעשר *Ta'aser* –You shall tithe
תרשים *Tharsis* –Ruler of Water

971 אדימירון –Prime number *Adimiron* –The Bloody Ones, *Qlippoth* of Taurus

972 ברשעת *be-Risha'at* –In wickedness (Deut. 9:5)
ונדבתיך *Vinedvotecha* –And you [shall] give your free will offering

[986] Shallum (376, 936).

ספרא דצניעותא *Safra Detziuta* –Book of modesty, a section of the *Zohar*
עברן *'Ebron* –Ebron, town of the tribe of Asher (see also Abdon, Hebron – Josh. 19:28)[987]
רעבן *Reabown* –Hunger, lack of food, famine

973 אבל מצרים *'Abel Mitzrayim* –"Meadow of Egypt," Abel Mizraim, a place in Palestine
בהימירון *Bahimiron* –The Bestial Ones, *Qlippoth* of Aquarius
רוממתי עזר *Rowmamtiy 'Ezer* –Romamtiezer, son of Heman appointed over the service of song (1 Chr. 25:4, 31)
–The number of children of Jedaiah who returned from exile (Ezra 2:36)

974 חסרון *Chesrown* –The thing lacking, defect, deficiency
מקור חיים *Maquwr Chaim* –The fountain of life
משוטטים *Mashuwtim* –A going forth, emanation

975 העץ *Ha'Atz* –The gallows
התנפלתי *Hitnapaltiy* –I fell down
עיר התמרימ *'Iyr HaTemariym* –Ir Hatemariym, another name for Jericho (Deut. 34:3; Jdg. 1:16; 3:13; 2 Chr. 28:15)[988]
עשתרה *'ashterah* –Ewe, flock, increase, young
שתר בוזני *Shethar Bowzenay* –Shethar-Boznai, official of the king of Persia (Ezra 5:3, 6; 6:6, 13)

976 בטול במציאות ממש *Bitul Bimtziuwt Mamash* –Absolute nullification of existence
ושמרתיכ *ve-Shemartiyka* –And I will keep you
כל עשב זרע זרע *Kal esev zorea zara* –"Every herb bearing seed" (Gen. 1:29)
כתועפת *Ketoa'apot* –Like the strength
עוץ *'uwts* –To counsel, plan; Uz, eldest son of Aram (Gen. 10:23); son of Shem[989]; son of Dishon, son of Seir; son of Nahor by Milcah; Uz, the country where Job lived; kingdom not far from Edom, perhaps the same as the latter
רשעתו *Rishato* –His wickedness
שמונה עשרה *Shemoneh Esreh* –Eighteen; portion of the liturgy consisting of 19 blessings
תתקעו *Titqa'uw* –You shall blow

977 אדם דוד משיח *Adam David Mashiach* –The lineage of the Messiah – "Adam, David, Messiah"
בעשתרה *Be'eshterah* –Beeshterah, city east of the Jordan River which was given to the Levites of the family of

---

[987] Abdon (134, 784), Hebron (266, 916).
[988] This name is literally translated as "city of palm trees."
[989] The Septuagint makes this Uz identical with the first Uz, naming Aram as his father. It is also possible the Hebrew was abbreviated here.

Gershon – may be identical with Ashtaroth (literally "of Ashtaroth")

עיי העברים — *'Iyey HaAbariym* –Ije-Abarim, place where the Israelites camped in the territory of Moab

שכאנום — *Shakanom* –A title of *Tiferet*

–Prime number

978 בעל צפון — *Ba'al Tzephown* –Baal Zephon, site that the Israelites faced when they encamped between Migdol and the Red Sea during the Exodus (Ex. 14:2; Num. 33:7)

וברשעת — *ve-Barsha'ath* –And for the wickedness

מתלקחת — *Mitlaqachat* –Flashing up (Ex. 9:24)

ערבון — *'arabown* –Pledge, security

979 אסר־חדון — *'Esar-Chaddown* –Esar-Haddon, son of Sennacherib and king of Assyria

980 יעץ — *Ya'atz* –To advise, consult, give counsel

ירקעם — *Yorqe'am* –Jorkeam or Jorkoam, son of Raham, or a city he founded (1 Chr. 2:44)

משכרתכ — *Maskureteka* –Your wages

משמרת — *Mishmereth* –Guard, charge, function, obligation, service, watch

עשרית — *Asiriyt* –Tenth

פץ — *Patz* –217th Gate of the 231 Gates

פרצים — *Peratziym* –Perazim, a mountain in Palestine; "breaches"

רעין — *Ra'yown* –Longing, striving; thought

שערת — *Se'iyrat* –Kid, goat

שפם — *Safam* –Moustache

Shafam –Shapham, chief of Gad

Shefam –Shepham, location on the northeastern boundary of the Promised Land near Riblah

שרפת — *Sarefat* –Burning

תשרפ — *Tisaref* –She shall be burnt; shall be burned

Tisrof –You shall burn

981 דצך עדש באחב — *Detzakh Adhash Beachav* –The The 10 Plagues of Egypt (taking the first letter of each)

מאמץ — *Ma'amats* –Strength, force, power

פארן — *Pa'ran* –Paran, wilderness seven days' march from Mount Sinai – it is located east of the wilderness of Beer-Sheba (see also El-Paran)[990]

982 במשמרת — *Bemishmeret* –In charge (Num. 4:27)

ברוך מרדכי — *Barukh Mordekai* –"Blessed be Mordecai"

יעבץ — –Jabez, head of a family of Judah; Jabez, dwelling place of scribes, probably in Judah

ישבעם — *Yashob'am* –Jashobeam, one who joined David at Ziklag

---

[990] El-Paran (372, 1022).

		(1 Chr. 12:6) (see also Adino)[991]
	עורון	*'iwarown* –Blindness
	שבעים	*Shivim* –Seventy
983	קרית ארבע	*Qiryath 'Arba'* –Kirjath-Arba, early name for the city of Hebron (see also קרית הארבע, Hebron)[992]
	–Prime number	
984	עינ־דר	*'Eyn-Dor* –En-Dor, town of the tribe of Manasseh where Saul consulted a witch about his future (this spelling used only in Josh. 17:11 – see also עין־דאר, and עין־דור)[993]
985	אבן העזר	*'Eben Ha'Ezer* –Ebenezer, a place in Palestine
	העשרתי	*He'eshretiy* –Enriched
	ובמשארותיכ	*ve-Bemisha'aruwteyaka* –Your kneading bowls (Ex. 7:28)
	סדם ועמרה	*Sodom ve-Amorah* –"Sodom and Gomorrah" (Gen. 14:10, 11; 18:20; 19:28; Deut. 29:22; Jer. 49:18)
	עינ־דאר	*'Eyn-Dor* –En-Dor, town of the tribe of Manasseh where Saul consulted a witch about his future (this spelling used only in Josh. 17:11 – see also עין־דר, and עין־דור)[994]
986	ומשמרת	*ve-Mishmeret* –And the charge (Num. 3:25)
	ונתצתמ	*ve-Nitatztem* –And you shall break down (Deut. 12:3)
	ושמרתמ	*ve-Shemartem* –And you shall observe (Ex. 12:17)
	ושרפת	*ve-Sarafta* –And you shall burn (Ex. 29:34)
	ותשרפ	*ve-Tisaref* –And let her be burnt (Gen. 38:24)
	ותתעלפ	*ve-Tita'laf* –And wrapped herself (Gen. 38:14)
	יעוץ	*Ye'uwtz* –Jeuz, son of Shaharaim, a descendant of Benjamin
	משמרתו	*Mishmarto* –His duty (Num. 3:7)
	פוץ	*Puwtz* –To scatter, be dispersed, be scattered; to flow, overflow; to break
	שכל החפצ המבוקש	*Sekhel HaChafutz HaMevuqash* –Intelligence of Conciliation, Rewarding Intelligence of Those Who Seek, or Desired and Sought Consciousness (21st Path)
	תקופת	*Tequwfat* –At the turn of (Ex. 34:22)
	תשרפו	*Tisorofuw* –You shall burn (Ex. 12:10)
987	זפרן	*Zifron* –Ziphron, place specified by Moses as the northern boundary of the Promised Land (Num. 34:9) – probably modern Za'feranh
	עזריקם	*'Azriyqam* –Azrikam, son of Azel of the family of Saul;

991 Adino (71).
992 קרית הארבע (988), Hebron (266, 916).
993 עין־דאר (335, 985), עין־דור (340, 990).
994 עין־דר (334, 984), עין־דור (340, 990).

governor of Ahaz's house; descendant of Merari; one of the family of David

988 אבי גבערן — *Abiy Gibown* –Abi Gibon, father of Gibeon

אשכנזים — *Ashkenazim* –German Jews

חפץ — *Chafets* –To delight in, take pleasure in, desire, be pleased with; to move, bend down; desiring, delighting in, having pleasure in

Chefets –Delight, pleasure

חשמלים — *Chashmalim* –Angelic Choir assoc. w/*Hesed*

קרית הארבע — *Qiryath Ha'Arba'* –Kirjath-Haarba, early name for the city of Hebron (this spelling used only in Neh. 11:25 – see also קרית ארבע, Hebron)[995]

989 סמנגלוף — *Semangelof* –One of the three angels invoked against Lilith

990 משמרתי — *Mishmartiy* –My charge (Gen. 26:5)

עין־דור — *'Eyn-Dor* –En-Dor, town of the tribe of Manasseh where Saul consulted a witch about his future (this spelling used only in Josh. 17:11 – see also עין־דאר, and עין־דר)[996]

עכרן — *'Okran* –Ocran, descendant of Asher

צדיק־יסוד־עולם — *Tzadiq-Yesod-Olam* –The Righteous Is the Foundation of the World, a title of *Yesod*

קצף — *Qatzaf* –To be displeased, angry

Qetzaf –Wrath (of God), anger

רפין — *Rifyown* –Sinking

שפים — *Shuppiym* –Shuppim, gatekeeper in the days of David; son of Benjamin (this spelling used only in 1 Chr. 7:12, 15; 26:16 – see also Shupham, Shephuphan, Muppim)[997]

–The sum of the numbers 1 through 44

991 –Prime number

992 ביפרן — *Bifrons* –Goetic demon #46 (Aurum Solis spelling)

כורסון — *Korson* –Demon King of the West and Water (Goetia)

993 פרזון — *Perazown* –Rural population, rustics, rural people, people of unwalled villages (meaning dubious – Judg. 5:7, 11)

994

995 השרצת — *HaSoretzet* –That swarms (Lev. 11:46)

---

[995] קרית ארבע (983), Hebron (266, 916).

[996] עין־דאר (985, 335), עין־דר (334, 984).

[997] Shupham (506, 1066), Shephuphan (516, 1166), Muppim (170, 730).

996	ונשמרת	*ve-Nishmarta* –And you shall keep you (Deut. 23:10)
	ועשירית	*va-'asiyriyt* –And the tenth
	עתיקא קדישא	*Atiqa Qadisha* –The Most Holy Ancient One, a title of *Keter*
	צוצ	*Tzuwtz* –To blossom, shine, sparkle; to gaze, peep, glance, make the eyes sparkle
	רצון	*Ratzon* –Pleasure, delight, favor
	שמירמות	*Shemiyramowth* –Shemiramoth, Levite in the choral service (1 Chr. 15:18, 20; 16:5)
	שמרימות	*Shemariymowth* –Shemiramoth, one sent by Jehoshaphat to teach the Law (2 Chr. 17:8)
	תשמרונ	*Tishmeruwn* –You shall observe, you shall keep (Deut. 6:17)
997	אפריון	*'appiryown* –Sedan, litter, palanquin; chariot
	ונשארתמ	*Venisha'artem* –You shall be left (Deut. 4:27)
	–Prime number	
998	בוצץ	*Bowtzetz* –Bozez, a rock near Michmash
	בצרון	*Bitstsarown* –Stronghold
	ולבנתיך	*ve-Livnoteyka* –And to your daughters (Num. 18:11)
	חצץ	*Chatsats* –To divide; to shoot arrows; gravel
	חרצן	*Chartsan* –Kernels, seeds, insignificant vine product (Num. 6:4)
	מנחתך	*Minchateka* –Your meal offering (Lev. 2:13)
999	כספ צרופ בעליל לארצ	*Kesaf Tzeruwf Baliyl La'ratz* –"Silver refined in an earthen furnace" (Ps. 12:7)
	שפטים	*Shofetim* –Judges
1000	א (writ large)	*Alef* –1st letter of Hebrew alphabet, used to designate the number 1000
	כמתעתע	*Kimeta'atea* –As a mocker (Gen. 27:12)
	משמרתכ	*Mishmarteka* –Your duty
	עלץ	*'alats* –To rejoice, exult
	ציץ	*Tziytz* –Flower, bloom; feather, wing (meaning dubious); Ziz, pass that runs from the western shore of the Dead Sea north of En-Gedi to the wilderness of Judah
	קץ	*Qetz* –End
	קרן	*Qaran* –To shine
		Qeren –Horn (n. fem.); a place conquered by Israel
	רצין	*Retziyn* –Rezin, last king of Syria who, along with Pekah, fought Judah; one whose descendants returned from the Exile
	רתת	*Retheth* –Trembling
	שמנים	*Shemonim* –Eighty, forescore
	שן	*Shen* –Tooth; Shen, place near which Samuel erected a stone memorial to the victory over the Philistines

	שקם	*Shaqam* –Sycamore tree
	שרך	*Sarak* –To twist
		Serowk –Sandal thong
		Sharekh –Traverse (Ezek. 16:4)[998]
	ששת	*Sheshet* –Six
	תם	*Tam* –Whole, complete; simple, pious, innocent, sincere, mild, perfect; to be complete, be finished
		Tom –Wholeness; simplicity, piety, innocence, sincerity, mildness, perfection
	תפלצת	*Tifletseth* –Shuddering, horror
	תשקר	*Tishqor* –Deal falsely
1001	אתם	*Atem* –You (m. pl.)
		'Etham –Etham, place where the Israelites camped before they entered the wilderness of Sinai
	שאן	*Shawan* –To be at ease, rest, be quiet
	תאם	*Ta'am* –To match
		To'am –Harmony
1002	בעל שם	*Baal Shem* –"Master of the Name," a Jewish magician
	ברקן	*Barqan* –Briers, briars
	בשן	*Bashan* –Bashan, area stretching from the Upper Jordan Valley to the Arabian Desert
	קבץ	*Qabatz* –To gather, assemble
	קרבן	*Qorban* –Offering, oblation
	רקבן	*Riqqabown* –Rottenness, decay, decayed
1003	אשבן	*'Eshban* –Eshban, son of Dishon
	גרף	*Garaf* –To sweep away, sweep
	גשן	*Goshen* –Goshen, cattle-raising district of the Nile assigned to the Israelites before they were placed in bondage; town in the hill country of Judah; region of Judah
	תתגר	*Titgar* –Contend
1004	אגרף	*Egrof* –Fist
	דשן	*Dashen* –To be fat, grow fat, become fat, become prosperous, anoint, fat; vigorous, stalwart ones
		Deshen –Fat ashes, fatness
		Dishon –Dishon, son of Seir (also known as Dishon); grandson of Seir (see also דישון, דישן, and דשון)[999]
	השפטים	*HaShofetim* –The Judges
	חצרון	*Chetzrown* –Hezron, son of Reuben; son of Perez
	פרי עצ זרע זרע	*Peri etz zorea zara* –The fruit of a tree yielding seed
	רדף	*Radaf* –To follow, to pursue
	שדרך	*Shadrakh* –Shadrach, name given to Hananiah at Babylon (Dan. 1:7; 3)[1000]

[998] Sharekh is one of the ten words in the Tanakh with a Dagesh in the letter Resh.

[999] דישון (370, 1020), דישן (257, 817), דשון (360, 1010).

	שחצום	*Shachatzowm* –Shahazimah, city of Issachar
1005	שופטים	*Shofetim* –The Hebrew name of the book of Judges
	שרשרה	*Sharaherah* –Chain
1006	ואברכה מברכיך	*va-Avarkah Mivrakika* –"I will bless those who bless you" (Gen. 12:3)
	בן־דקר	*Ben-Deqer* –Ben-dekar, one of Solomon's twelve officers who provided food for the royal household (1 Kings 4:9)
	ויקצף	*ve-Yektzof* –Anger (of Moses)
	וששת	*ve-Sheshet* –And six
	ותקשר	*ve-Tiqshor* –And bound
	משנה תורה	*Mishneh Torah* –Rambam's codification of the Oral Torah
	קול־יהוה חצב להבות אש	*Qol*-YHVH *Chotzev Lahavoth 'Esh* –"The voice of YHVH kindles flames of fire" (Ps. 29:7)
	קוץ	*Qotz* –Thorn, thorn bush *Qowtz* –Koz, ancestor of a priestly family returning from captivity (see also Hakkoz)[1001]; ancestor of one who helped to repair the walls of Jerusalem *Quwtz* –To spend the summer; to be greived, loathe, abhor, feel a loathing; to awake, wake up
	רוף	*Ruf* –To shake, rock
	רקון	*Raqqown* –Rakkon, place near Joppa in the territory of Dan
	שיחור לבנת	*Shiychowr Libnath* –Shihor-Libnath, boundary stream of Asher
	תורת	*Torat* –Law (Ex. 13:9)
	תותר	*Totar* –Excellency (Gen. 49:4)
	תשקרו	*Teshaqruw* –You shall lie (Lev. 19:11)
1007	אותם	*'Awotam* –Them, themselves (Gen. 41:8)
	בהררם	*Behareram* –In their mount (Gen. 14:6)
	ואקץ	*va-'Aqetz* –And I abhorred (Ex. 20:23)
	ואתם	*Ve'atem* –And you (Gen. 9:7) *Ve-'otam* –And those (Lev. 14:11)
	ובשפטים	*Ve-Vishefatiym* –And with judgements (Ex. 6:6)
	זתם	*Zetham* –Zetham, son or grandson of Laadan
	תתראו	*Titra'uw* –Do you look upon one another (Gen. 42:1)
1008	אליהוא בן ברכאל	*'elihua ben Barakel* –"Elihu, son of Barakel" (Job 32:2, 6)
	חרף	*Charaf* –To reproach, taunt, blaspheme, defy, jeopardise, rail, upbraid; to winter, spend harvest time, remain in harvest time; to acquire, be betrothed *Charef* –Hareph, son of Caleb (do not confuse with

[1000] Hananiah (120; 123; 126).
[1001] Hakkoz (201, 1011).

Hariph)
Choref –Harvest time, autumn; winter

חשן *Chassan* –Angel of Air

Choshen –Breastplate, breastpiece; breastplate of the High Priest (also sacred pouch of the High Priest designed to hold the Urim and Thummim; Ex.25:7; 28:4, 15, 22-24, 26, 28, 29, 30; 29:5; 35:9, 27; 39:8, 9, 15-17, 19, 21; Lev. 8:8)[1002]

חתם *Chatham* –To seal, seal up, affix a seal; seal (Aramaic)

מספר חיים *MiSefer Chayiym* –"Book of Life" (Ps. 69:29)

קבוץ *Qibbutz* –Assembly, companies, gathering

רחף *Rachaf* –To grow soft, relax; to hover

שחן *Shachan* –To be hot

תרבות *Tarbut* –Increase, brood, progeny

1009 זרע לבן *Zera' Lavan* –"White seed"; sperm

טרף *Taraf* –To tear, rend, pluck; freshly picked, freshly plucked, fresh-plucked

Teref –Prey, food, leaf

שטן *Shatan* –Adversary, accuser; archdemon corr. to *Keter*

תתגרו *Titgaruw* –You contend (Deut. 2:5)

–Prime number

1010 דרקון *Darqown* –Darkon, servant of Solomon whose descendants returned to Palestine after the exile

דשון *Diyshon* –Dishon, son of Seir (also known as Dishon); grandson of Seir (see also דישון, דישן, and דשן)[1003]

יקץ *Yaqatz* –To awake, awaken, become active

ירקרקת *Yeraqraqot* –Greenish

ישן *Yashan* –Old, store, storage

Yashen –To sleep, be asleep; sleeping; Jashen, father of some, or one, of David's mighty men – Jashen may be one of David's men himself

יתרת *Yoteret* –Appendage, overhand, the caudate lobe of the liver of a sacrificial animal

כשפים *Keshafim* –Witchcrafts, sorceries

למשמרת *Lemishmaret* –To be kept

Lemishmeret –To be put away, kept

מסדרון *Misderown* –Porch, colonnade (meaning dubious – Judg. 3:23)

מעץ *Ma'atz* –Maaz, oldest son of Ram

מרשעת *Mirsha'ath* –Wickedness

משעם *Mish'am* –Misham, descendant of Benjamin

נסתך *Nasitek* –He might prove you

פלץ *Palatz* –To shudder, tremble

קדרון *Qidrown* –Kidron, valley in Jerusalem between the Mount of Ophel and the Mount of Olives

---

[1002] Urim (257, 817), Thummim (490, 1050).

[1003] דישון (370, 1020), דישן (257, 817), דשן (354, 1004).

קיץ *Qayitz* –Summer, summer-fruit

קיתרס *Qiyatharos* –Musical instrument, probably the zither or lyre (Aramaic)

שין *Shin* –Tooth; 21st letter of Hebrew alphabet

Shayin –Urine

שעלים *Sha'aliym* –Shalim, unidentified region, perhaps in the region of Ephraim or Benjamin, where Saul searched for his father's donkeys (1 Sam. 9:4)

1011 הקוץ *Haqowtz* –Hakkoz, priest and chief of the seventh course of service in the sanctuary (this spelling used only in 1 Chr. 24:10 – see also Koz)[1004]

התורת *HaTorot* –The laws (Ex. 18:20)

שנאנים *Shinanim* –Angelic Choir sometimes assoc. w/*Tiferet*

תהום *Tehom* –Abyss; "deep"

1012 שעלבים *Sha'albiym* –Shaalabim, city of the tribe of Dan (this spelling used only in Judg. 1:35 – see also שעלבין)[1005]

תרבית *Tarbiyth* –Increment, usury, interest, bonus (Ezek. 18:8, 13, 17, 22:12)

תתורו *Tatuwruw* –You go about (Num. 15:39)

1013 איש־בשת *'Iysh-Bosheth* –Ishbosheth, son of Saul and short king of Israel before his defeat by David

גישן *Geyshan* –Geshan, descendant of Caleb

גתים *Gittayim* –Gittaim, Benjamite town of refuge near Beeroth

עין רגל *'Eyn Rogel* –En Rogel, spring outside the city of Jerusalem near the Hinnom Valley

–Prime number

1014 דישן *Diyshon* –A clean animal (perhaps antelope, gazelle, or mountain goat)

Diyshon –Dishon, son of Seir (also known as Dishon); grandson of Seir (see also דישון, דשון, and דשן)[1006]

חותם *Chowtham* –Seal, signet, signet-ring; Hotham, descendant of Asher (1 Chr. 7:32); father of two of David's best men (1 Chr. 11:44)

חשון *Cheshvan* –The 2nd month of the Jewish calendar – it is associated with Scorpio and the tribe Dan

1015 היתרת *HaYotarat* –The lobe (Ex. 29:13)

הששית *HaShishiyt* –The sixth (Ex. 26:9)

קטרון *Qitrown* –Kitron, one of the towns of Zebulun (see also Kattath)[1007]

[1004] Koz (196, 1006).

[1005] שעלבין (462, 1112).

[1006] דישון (370, 1020), דשון (360, 1010), דשן (354, 1004).

1016 ויתרת — *ve-Yotarat* –And the lobe (Lev. 9:19)
ותקעתמ — *ve-Teqa'atam* –And you shall blow (Num. 10:5)
חשבון — *Cheshbown* –Account, reasoning, reckoning; Heshbon, Amorite capital on the boundary between Reuben and Dan, standing between the Arnon and Jabbok Rivers
Chishshabown –Device, invention
יותם — *Yotham* –Jotham, son of Gideon who managed to escape from Abimelech; son of Jahdai; 10th King of Judah
ישב בשבת — *Yosheb bash-Shebeth* –Josheb Basshebeth, one of David's mighty men (this spelling used only in 2 Sam. 23:8 – see also Jashobeam and Adino)[1008]
יתום — *Yathowm* –An orphan, fatherless
ערמון — *'armown* –Plane-tree (as stripped of bark – Gen. 30:37; Ezek. 31:8)

1017 והתורת — *ve-HaTorot* –And the laws
שיאון — *Shi'yown* –Shihon, town near Mount Tabor
–The number of children of Harim who returned from exile (Ezra 2:39)

1018 בתורתי — *be-Toratiy* –In my law
ותרבית — *ve-Terbiyt* –And increase
חריף — *Chariyf* –Hariph, ancestor of returning captives; head of a family who sealed the new covenant with God after the exile (see also Jorah)[1009]
חתאתם — *Chata'tem* –You have sinned (Ex. 32:30, 32, 34; Lev. 10:19; 16:16, 21, 34; Num. 5:7; 16:26; 18:9; 32:23; Deut. 9:16, 18; Ps. 85:3; Is. 58:1; Jer. 14:10; 40:3; 44:23)
חתים — *Chittim* –Hittites
יתבששו — *Yitbeshashuw* –Ashamed (Gen. 2:25)
כל נשיא בהם — *Kal Nasiy' VaHem* –"All were leaders" (Num. 13:2)
שחין — *Shechin* –Boils, inflamed spot, inflammation
שחקים — *Shechaqim* –Clouds; the 3rd Heaven (corr. to *Netzach*)

1019 באת בש שדי — *Beth Besh Shaddai* –"By signs troubles the mind the Almighty"
בעל שם טוב — *Baal Shem Tov* –Master of the Good Name, given to R. Yisrael ben Eliezar
–Prime number

1020 דישון — *Diyshown* –Dishon, son of Seir (also known as Dishon); grandson of Seir (see also דישן, דשון, and דשן)[1010]

[1007] Kattath (509).
[1008] Jashobeam (422, 982), Adino (71).
[1009] Jorah (221).
[1010] דישן (257, 817), דשון (360, 1010), דשן (354, 1004).

	כתם	*Katham* –To be stained, be defiled, be deeply stained *Kethem* –Gold, pure gold
	כתרת	*Kothereth* –Capital crown, capital of a pillar
	לצץ	*Latzatz* –To scorn, make mouths at, talk arrogantly
	מפץ	*Mappats* –Shattering (of type of weapon) *Mappets* –War club, club, battle axe, hammer
	נערן	*Na'aran* –Naaran, border town of Ephraim east of Bethel
	עפעף	*'af'af* –Eyelid
	רענן	*Ra'anan* –Flourishing; to grow green; luxuriant, fresh
	שכן	*Shakan* –To settle down, abide, dwell *Sheken* –Dwelling *Shaken* –Inhabitant, neighbor
	תכרת	*Tikrot* –Will be cut off (Num. 15:31); you shall cut off (Ex. 23:32, 34:12); perish (Gen. 41:36)
	תענך	*Ta'anak* –Taanach, ancient city in Canaan whose king was conquered by Joshua
1021	ויאמר הראני נא את־כבדכ	*VaYi'amar Hare'niy Na' 'Eth-Kevodeka* –"He said, 'Oh, let me behold Your presence!'" (Ex. 33:18)
	על איש ימינך	*'al Ish Yamiynk* –"Your right hand" (Ps. 80:17)
	פרמשתא	*Parmashta'* –Parmasta, son of Haman
	–Prime number	
1022	איל פארן	*'Eyl Paran* –El-Paran, place in the Wilderness of Paran
	במשמרתמ	*Bemishmerotam* –Regarding their duties (Num. 8:26)
	ותורתי	*ve-Torotay* –And my laws (Gen. 26:5)
	כבשן	*Kibshan* –Kiln (pottery or lime), smelting forge, furnace
	תורתיו	*Toratayu* –His laws (Ex. 18:16)
	תותירו	*Totiyruw* –Shall remain, will remain (Ex. 12:10) *Tuwtiyruw* –You let remain (Num. 33:55)
1023		
1024	ובירקון	*VeVayiraquwn* –And with mildew, a dryness
	זרזיף	*Zarziyf* –Drip, drop, dripping, a soaking, a saturation
	נחשתירונ	*Necheshthiron* –The Brazen Ones, *Qlippoth* of Scorpio
1025		
1026	ומשמרתמ	*ve-Mishmartam* –And their charge (Num. 3:31)
	ותכרת	*va-Tikrot* –And she cut off
	כושן	*Kuwshan* –Cushan, the name of a place or people (see also Cushan-Rishathaim, Midian)[1011]
	לא תעשה־לכ פסל	*Lo tha'aseh-leka pesel* –"Thou shalt not make unto thee any graven image" (Ex. 20:4)
	עולם היצירה	*Olam HaYetzirah* –World of Formation
	עשרימ ושנימ	*Esrim u-Shenaim* –Twenty-two
	שכל מתנוצצ	*Sekhel Mitnotzetz* –Resplendent Intelligence (10th Path)

[1011] Cushan-Rishathaim (1396, 2606), Midian (104, 754).

	שערי-מות	*Shaare-Maveth* –Gates of Death; the 3rd Hell (corr. to *Netzach*)
1027		
1028	ברייתית	*Baraitot* –External (materials), Tanaic traditions and teachings not included in the Misnah
1029	אחימעץ	*'Achiyma'atz* –Ahimaaz, father of Ahinoam; one of Solomon's officers; son of Zadok
1030	כריתת	*Keriytut* –Divorce (Deut. 24:1)
	לשן	*Lashan* –To use the tongue, slander
	לשרך	*LeSharekha* –For your navel (Prov. 3:8)[1012]
	לששת	*Lesheshet* –For six
	מפיץ	*Mefits* –Scatterer, disperser, scattering, club
	מצץ	*Matsats* –To drain out, suck
	נפץ	*Nafats* –To shatter, break, dash, beat in pieces; to scatter, disperse, overspread, be scattered *Nefets* –Driving storm
	פנץ	*Phenex* –Goetic demon #37 (Aurum Solis spelling)
	קרית ערים	*Qiryath 'Ariym* –Kirjath-Arim, originally one of the Gibeonites located at the northwestern boundary of Judah (see also Baalah, Kirjath-Jearim, Kirjath-Baal, and Baale-judah)[1013]
	שכין	*Sakkiyn* –Knife
	שלשת	*Shelishet* –Three
	שפן	*Safan* –To cover, cover in, panel, hide *Shafan* –Rock badger, coney, the hyrax; Shaphan, scribe of Josiah who read him the Law; father of a chief officer under Josiah; father of Elasah; father of Jaazaniah whom Ezekiel saw in a vision; father of Gemariah[1014]
	תלם	*Telem* –Furrow, ridge
1031	אלחי אלחי למא שבקתני	*Eloi, Eloi, lama sabachthani* –"My God, my God, why hast thou forsaken me?" (The last words of Jesus, according to Mark 15:34; a direct reference to Ps. 22:2)
	ויאמר אלהים נעשה אדם בצלמנו	*Vay-yomer Elohim naaseh adham be-tzelmenu* –"And God said let us make man in our image" (Gen. 1:26)
	פאנץ	*Phenex* –Goetic demon #37
	–Prime number	
1032	בלשן	*Bilshan* –Bilshan, prince who returned from the exile (Ezra 2:2: Neh. 7:7)
	ויעש אלהים	*va-Ya'as Elohim* –"And God made"

[1012] LeSharekha is one of the ten words in the Tanakh with a Dagesh in the letter Resh.
[1013] Baalah (107), Kirjath-Jearim (1040, 1600), Kirjath-Baal (812), Baale-judah (142).
[1014] Many scholars consider all of the above to be the same person.

	ותורתכ	*ve-Toratka* –And your instructions, and your laws (Deut. 33:10)
	צדק ושלומ נשקו	*Tzedeq ve-Shalowm Nifgashuw* –"Justice and well-being kiss" (Ps. 85:11)
	ראשית הגלגלימ	*Rashith HaGilgam* –The Beginning of Revolvings, the Primum Mobile; the Material World assoc. w/*Keter*
	תורת יהוה	*Torath* YHVH –"The Law of the Lord" (Ps. 19:7)
1033	–Prime number	
1034	זכר ונקבה ברא אתמ	*Zakhar u-neqevah bara otham* –Male and female created He them
	ויאסף אל־עמיו	*VaYe'asef El-'Amayuw* –"He was gathered to his people" (Gen. 49:33)
	חצר סוסים	*Chatzar Suwsiym* –Hazar Susim, small village in the extreme south of the territory of Simeon – may be modern Susiyeh
1035	אלחי אלחי למה שבקתני	*Eloi, Eloi, lama sabachthani* –"My God, my God, why hast thou forsaken me?" (The last words of Jesus, according to Mark 15:34; a direct reference to Ps. 22:1)
	פרשנדתא	*Parshandatha* –Parshandatha, son of Haman slain by the Jews
1036	ונשמרתמ	*ve-Nishmartem* –And take heed of yourselves (Deut. 2:4)
	ושלשת	*ve-Shloshet* –And three (Gen. 7:13)
		ve-Shilasheta –And divide into three parts (Deut. 19:3)
	לשון	*Lashown* –Tongue
	שדרכ מישכ ועבד נגוא	*Shadrakh Meshakh ve-Abedh Nego* –Shadrach, Meshach, and Abed-nego (Dan. 2:49)
	שלון	*Shalluwn* –Shallun, one who helped to repair the gate of Jerusalem
	תכריתו	*Takriytuw* –You cut off (Num. 4:18)
	תשרפונ	*Tisrefa'uwno* –You shall burn it (Lev. 13:55)
		Tisrefuwn –You shall burn (Deut. 7:5)
1037		
1038	כתובים	*Ketuvim* –Hagiographia,[1015]
	שלחן	*Shulchan* –Table
1039	שלטן	*Shiltown* –Mastery; governor, ruler, official (Aramaic)
		Sholtan –Dominion, sovereignty (Aramaic)
	–Prime number	
1040	מקץ	*Maqatz* –Makaz, place mentioned in 1 Kings 4:9
	משׁשת	*Mishashta* –You have felt

[1015] Term given for the third division of the Hebrew Bible, including Psalms, Proverbs, Job, Song of Solomon, Ruth, Lamentations, Ecclesiastes, Esther, Daniel, Ezra, Nehemiah, and 1 and 2 Chronicles

	מתם	*Methom* –Soundness, entirely, entire
	נצץ	*Natsats* –To shine, sparkle, gleam
	קמץ	*Qamatz* –To grasp, take a handful
		Qometz –Closed hand, fist, handful
	קרית יערימ	*Qiryath Ye'ariym* –Kirjath-Jearim, originally one of the Gibeonites located at the northwestern boundary of Judah (see also Baalah, Kirjath-Arim, Kirjath-baal, and Baale-judah)[1016]
	שלשית	*Shelishiyt* –Third part
	שמן	*Shaman* –To be or become fat, grow fat
		Shemen –Fat, oil
		Shamen –Fat, rich, robust
	תאנטיפצת	*Thantifaxath* –Guardian of the 32nd Tunnel of Set
	תרתמ	*Taretem* –You have spied out (Num. 14:34)
1041	אשמן	*'ashman* –The stout, among the stout; the desolate, like dead
1042		
1043		
1044	מרדף	*Murdaf* –Persecution
	מתרדת	*Mithredath* –Mithredath, treasurer of Cyrus through whom he restored the Temple vessels (Ezra 1:8); one who wrote to the king of Persia protesting the restoration of Jerusalem (Ezra 4:7)
1045	השלישת	*HaSheliyshit* –The third (Deut. 26:12)
	השמן	*HaShamen* –The oil
	תהלים	*Tehillim* –Psalms
1046	וקשרתמ	*ve-Qesharetam* –And you shall bind them (Deut. 6:8)
		ve-Qesharetem –And you shall bind (Deut. 11:18)
	ושלישת	*ve-Sheliyshit* –And the third
	ותרמת	*ve-Terumat* –And offerings of
	תרומת	*Teruwmot* –Offerings, gifts
1047	לכסף מוחא	*Lekasaf Muwcha'* –"A mine for silver" (Job 28:1)
	משאון	*Mashsha'own* –Guile, dissimulation, deceit
1048	במותם	*Bamuwtham* –High places, altars
	בתולים	*Betuwliym* –Virginity
	בתרומת	*Biteruwmat* –Of the sacred gifts (Lev. 22:12)
	חשמן	*Chashman* –Ambassadors, bronze (meaning uncertain – Ps. 68:32)
	מחתרת	*Machtereth* –A breaking in, burglary
	סתרעטן	*Sateraton* –Lord of Triplicity by Day for Aries

[1016] Baalah (107), Kirjath-Arim (1030, 1590), Kirjath-Baal (812), Baale-judah (142).

1049 אליחרף — *Eliychoref* –"God of winter (harvest-time)" –Elihoreph, a scribe in Solomon's court
יכסגנוץ — *Yakasaganotz* –Angel of 3d Taurus
–Prime number

1050 בית־לחמ — *Beth-Lechem* –Bethlehem, town south of Jerusalem, originally called Ephrath; city of the tribe of Zebulun northwest of Nazareth; Bethlehem, son of Salma, a descendant of Caleb
במחתרת — *Bamachteret* –In breaking in
ישמרך — *Yishmark* –Guard you
כשלשת — *Kishloshet* –About three
קנץ — *Qenetz* –Snare, net (meaning dubious – Job 18:2)
קרית ספר — *Qiryath Sepher* –Kirjath Sepher, town in the hill country of Judah assigned to the Levites (this spelling used only in Judg. 1:11-13 – see also the first Debir and Kirjath Sannah)[1017]
שמין — *Shamayin* –Heaven, sky (Aramaic)
שנן — *Shanan* –To sharpen, whet
תמים — *Thummim* –Thummim, a material object used (along with the Urim) for divination by the High Priest[1018]
תרתנ — *Tartan* –Tartan, title of a high Assyrian officer (2 Kings 18:17; Is. 20:1)[1019]

1051 המקשרות — *HaMequsharot* –The stronger
שאנן — *Shahanan* –At ease, quiet, secure
שנאן — *Shin'an* –Repititions (Ps. 68:18– Thousands of thousands)
–Prime number

1052 בית שמש — *Beyth Shemesh* –Beth Shemesh, town on the road from Ashkelon and Ashdod to Jerusalem; Canaanite city in the territory of Naphtali; city of the tribe of Issachar; another name for the Egyptian city of Heliopolis
ותרומת — *ve-Teruwmat* –And the offering
נבשן — *Nibshan* –Nibshan, wilderness town of Judah
–The number of children of Immer who returned from exile (Ezra 2:37)

1053

1054 המתטרת — *Hemethterith* –Guardian of the 15th Tunnel of Set
חשמון — *Cheshmown* –Heshmon, place in the far southern region of Judah – possibly same as Azmon
פתח משכנ אהל מועד — *Pethach Mishkon 'ahul Muwad* –"Open the door to the Tabernacle of the Tent of Meeting" (Ex. 40:6)

1017 Debir (206; 216), Kirjath Sannah (825).
1018 Thummim may literally be "perfection" as an intensive plural.
1019 There is evidence that the office was second only to the king.

1055

1056 בעל חרמון — *Ba'al Chermown* –Baal Hermon, mountain east of Lebanon (Judg. 3:3); city near Mount Hermon where Canaanite worship took place (1 Chr. 5:23)

כשלון — *Kishshalown* –A stumbling, a fall, a calamity

ניצוץ — *Niytsowts* –Spark

עפרון — *'Ephrown* –Ephron, Hittite from whom Abraham bought a field with a cave, which became Sarah's burial place

שימון — *Shiymown* –Shimon, descendant of Caleb

תרומתי — *Teruwmitiy* –My offering (Ex. 25:2)

Teruwmotay –My gifts (Num. 18:8)

1057 תאומים — *Teomim* –Twins; Gemini

1058 ותמורתו — *vu-Temuwrato* –And its exchange (Lev. 27:10)

1059

1060 לשלשת — *Lishleshet* –To the third

מכתם — *Miktam* –Michtam (a technical term found in psalm titles, meaning uncertain – Ps. 16:1; 56:1; 57:1; 58:1; 59:1; 60:1)

משכן — *Mishkan* –Abode (of God - Aramaic); dwelling place, Tabernacle

נשין — *Nashiyn* –Wives (Aramaic)

סתם — *Satham* –To stop up, shut up, keep close

סרף — *Saraf* –To burn

שכל נסתר — *Sekhel Nisetar* –Hidden or Occult Intelligence (7th Path)

תנים — *Tannim* –Whale (Ezra 32:2); jackals, wild beasts; denizens of 31st Tunnel of Set

1061 אדסך — A permutation of יהוה by *Aiq Bekar*[1020]

היכל רצון — *Hekel Ratzon* –Palace of Delight, Heavenly Mansion corr. to *Tiferet*

הנותרת — *HaNotarot* –The rest of

HaNoteret –The remainder

חזק ואמץ — *Chazaq ve-Ematz* –To be strong and brave

תנאים — *Tannaim* –Teachers in the Mishnah

–Prime number

1062

1063 –Prime number

1064 ויהי ביום השמיני — *Vahi Bayom HaShimini* –"On the eighth day..." (Lev.

[1020] See Introduction.

		9:1)
	נחשון	*Nachshown* –Naashon, descendant of Judah (perhaps Aaron's brother-in-law – Ex. 6:23; Num. 1:7)
	עין יהוה אל־יראיו	*'Ayin* YHVH *'El-Yere'ayo* –"The eye of the Lord is on those who fear Him" (Ps. 33:18)
1065	זאויר אנפין	*Zauir Anpin* –The Lesser Countenance, a title of *Tiferet*
	ויצב שם מזבח	*Vayatzev Sham Mizbach* –"He [Jacob] erected there an altar" (Gen. 33:20)
1066	אזנות תבור	*'Aznowth Tabowr* –Aznoth-tabor, an incline near Mount Tabor, west of Kadesh Barnea
	המאור הקטן	*HaMaor HaQaton* –The lesser light
	ישימון	*Yeshiymown* –Waste, wilderness, desert, desolate place
	כתרומת	*Kitruwmat* –As that which is set aside (Num. 15:20)
	פרצופים	*Partzufim* –Faces, persons
	שפופם	*Shefuwfam* –Shupham, son of Benjamin (this spelling used only in Num. 26:39 – see also Shuppim, Shephuphan)[1021]
1067	בית השמשי	*Beyth HaShimshiy* –Bethshemite
	בעלי השמים	*Baali HaShamaim* –Masters of the heavens, astrologers
	הנותרות	*HaNotarot* –That remain; and the remnant
	נבושזבן	*Nebuwshazban* –Nebushazban, a Babylonian prince (Jer. 39:13)
1068	בולשכין	*Boleskine* –A.C.'s retreat in Scotland
	בנות האדם	*Beniyth HaAdam* –"Daughters of Man (Adam)"
1069	–Prime number	
1070	משלשת	*Meshuleshet* –Three years old
	ערף	*'araf* –To drop, drip; to break the neck (of an animal)
		'oref –Neck, back of the neck, back
	עשן	*'ashan* –To smoke, be angry, be wroth; smoke; Ashan, lowland town assigned to the tribe of Judah, then to Simeon
		'ashen –Smoking
	עתם	*'atham* –To be burned up, be scorched (meaning dubious – Isa. 9:19)
	עתרת	*'athereth* –Abundance, excess, copiousness
	צפרן	*Tzipporen* –Fingernail, stylus point
	צרף	*Tzaraf* –To smelt, refine, test
	רעף	*Ra'af* –To trickle, drip
	שכל קיים	*Sekhel Qayyam* –Stable Intelligence (23rd Path)
	שלמן	*Shalman* –Shalman, king who sacked Beth-Arbel[1022]
		Shalmon –Reward, bribe
	שלשתמ	*Shelashtam* –They three

[1021] Shuppim (430, 990), Shephuphan (516, 1166).
[1022] Scholars argue that Shalman is actually Shalmaneser V of Assyria or Shalman king of Moab.

	שען	*Sha'an* –To lean on, trust in, support
1071	אשען	*'Esh'an* –Eshean, mountain village near Dumah
	מי הירקון	*Mey he-Yarqown* –Me-Jarkon, city in the territory of Dan near Joppa
	שוה קריתימ	*Shaveh Qiryathayim* –Shaveh-Kiriathaim, plain near Kirjathaim, the dwelling place of the Emim
1072		
1073	געתם	*Ga'tam* –Gatam, Edomite chief, grandson of Esau
	שגען	*Shiggawown* –Madness
1074	נרגל שראצר	*Nergal Shar'etzer* –Nergal-Sharezer, Babylonian officer who released Jeremiah
1075	הפצץ	*HaPitztzetz* –Happizzez, priest on whom fell the lot for the 18th of the 24 courses which David appointed for the temple service (1 Chr. 24:15)
	שיר השירימ	*Shir HaShirim* –The Song of Songs
1076	בעט ברזל ועפרת	*Ba'at Barzel Ve-Ofereth* –"With an iron and lead pen" (Job 19:24)
	לתרומת	*Literuwmat* –For the offering
	עקרון	*'Eqrown* –Ekron, northernmost of the five chief cities of Palestine, apportioned to the tribe of Judah
	שלמון	*Salmown* –Salmon, father of Boaz (this spelling used only in Ruth 4:21 – see also שלמא)[1023]
	תכרתונ	*Tikerotuwn* –You shall cut down
1077		
1078	המשכן אחד	*HaMishkon echad* –One dwelling (of God's dwelling place)
1079	סטריף	*Satrip* –Angel of 3d Pisces
1080	בית מרכבות	*Beyth Markabowth* –Beth-Marcaboth, city of the Simeonites in the Negeb near Ziklag
	מעשרתיכמ	*Ma'asroteykam* –Your tithes
	משמן	*Mashman* –Fatness, fat piece, fertile place, richly prepared food; fatness
	עריף	*'ariyf* –Cloud, mist
	פתם	*Pithom* –Pithom, Egyptian store-city built by the Israelites (Ex. 1:11)
	קפץ	*Qafatz* –To draw together, close, shut, shut up, stop up
	שממן	*Shimamon* –Horror, dismay, apallment
	תרעתי	*Tir'athiy* –Tirathite

[1023] שלמא (371).

1081 והסתרתי — *ve-Histaretiy* –And I will hide (Deut. 31:17)
נוטריקון — *Notariqon* –The kabbalistic theory of acronyms
עציון גבר — *'Etzyown Geber* –Ezion Geber, village west of the port of Elath on the Gulf of Aqaba
שלאנן — *Shel'anan* –At ease, quiet, secure
תפארת — *Tiferet* –Beauty; the 6th *Sefira*h (occurs 51 times in the *Tanakh*)
–The sum of the numbers 1 through 46

1082 בלע בן בעור — *Bela ben Beor* –Bela, son of Beor; a King of Edom (assoc. w/Daath)
בן עיש — *Ben Ayish* –Son of Ayish; Ursa Minor
בעל פרצים — *Ba'al Peratziym* –Baal Perazim, place near the valley of Rephaim, where David won a battle with the Philistines (2 Sam. 5:20); called Perazim in Is. 28:21
ועבדתם — *va-Avadtem* –You shall serve
ותרועת — *Vutruwa'at* –Trumpet blast
לראשי ישראל — *Lerashai Yisrael* –"For Israel began," "At beginning, Israel"

1083 פתגם — *Pithgam* –Edict, decree, command, work, affair

1084 ויהי נעם אדני אלהינו עלינו — *Vihi No'am Adonai Elohenu Alaynuw* –"May the favor of the Lord, our God, be upon us" (Psalms 90:17)
עין חצור — *'Eyn Chatzowr* –En Hazor, fortified city of the tribe of Naphtali

1085 בית המרכבות — *Beyth HaMarkabowth* –Beth Marcaboth, city of the Simeonites in the Negeb near Ziklag

1086 אנדראלף — *Andrealfus* –Goetic demon #65
ואלה המשפטים — *vi-Aleh HaMishpatem* –"And these are the laws" (Ex. 21:1)
תרומתמ — *Teruwmatam* –Their sacrifices of well-being (Ex. 29:28)
–The total gematria of Sarah, Rebecca, Rachel and Leah

1087 פתאום — *Pith'owm* –Suddenly, surprisingly; suddenness
–Prime number

1088 בעותים — *Bi'uwthiym* –Terrors, alarms (occasioned by God)

1089 עוגרמען — *Ogarman* –Lord of Triplicity by Night for Gemini
שפטן — *Shiftan* –Shiphtan, father of Kemuel, chief of Ephraim

1090 הרמש הרמש — *HaRemes HaRomes* –The creeping thing that creepeth
ישפן — *Yishpan* –Ishpan, descendant of Benjamin and son of Shashak
קצץ — *Qatzatz* –To cut off
רצף — *Ratzaf* –To fit together, fit out, pattern
Retzef –Hot stove, glowing stone, flame; Rezeph, city of

		Syria taken by Sennacherib
	שלשתכמ	*Shelashtekam* –You three
1091	והעתרתי	*ye-Ha'ataretiy* –And I will entreat (Ex. 8:25)
	ויבנשמ מזבח לי יהוה	*Vayivensham Mizbayach La* YHVH –"Noah built an altar to YHVH" (Gen. 12:8)
	–Prime number	
1092	דמות כמראה אדמ עליו מלמעלה	*Demuwth Kemar'eh 'Adam 'Alayuw Milema'elah* – "There was the semblance of a human form" (Ezek. 1:26)
	וידעת כי־יהוה אלהיך	*ve-Yada'at Kiy*-YHVH *'Eloheyka* –"Know, therefore, that only the Lord your God is God" (Deut. 7:9)
	עין הקורא	*'Eyn haq-Qowre'* –En Hakkore, spring at Lehi, which God brought forth as an answer to Samson's prayer (Judg. 15:18-19)
1093	–Prime number	
1094	בסבלתם	*Besivlotam* –With their burdens (Ex. 1:11)
	מכת בכורות	*Makath be-Khoroth* –The Slaying of the Firstborn
	עדיתים	*'Adiythayim* –Adithaim, town in the lowlands of Judah
1095		
1096	בצדקתך	*Betzidqatak* –In your righteousness (Deut. 9:5)
	ספר ספירות	*Sefer Sefirot* –Book of the Numbers
	עולם העשיה	*Olam HaAssiah* –The World of Action; the Material World
	מקום־ספיר	*Mequwm-Safiyr* –"Its rocks are a source of sapphires" (Job 28:6)
	פישון	*Pison* –A river of Eden (Gen. 2:11 – assoc. w/Fire)
1097	–Prime number	
1098	שני המארת הגדלימ	*Shene HaMeoroth HaGedholim* –"Two great lights"(Gen. 1:16)
1099	אהיה יה יהוה אדני אל אלוה אלהימ שדי צבאות	*Eheieh Yah* YHVH *Adonai El Eloah Elohim Shaddai Tzabaoth* –The name of God of 33 letters, composed of Names used in the Tanakh
	ברכי נפשי את יהוה	*Berakiy Nefashiy Eth* YHVH –"My soul, bless God" (Ps. 103:1, 2, 22; 104:1, 35)
	חיה נשמה ריח נפש	*Chiah, Neshamah, Ruach, Nefesh* –The five souls of Kabbalistic thought
1100	ולא תטמאו בהם	*Viloh Tetamu Bahem* –"And you shall not defile yourselves through them" (Lev. 18:30)
	קציץ	*Qetziytz* –Keziz, valley and town of Benjamin
	רץ	*Ratz* –Piece, bar (meaning dubious – Ps. 68:31)

	רשם	*Rasham* –To inscribe, note
		Resham –To inscribe, sign
	שוכן עד	*Shoken 'Ad* –"Dwelling in eternity"
	ששך	*Sheshak* –Sheshack, name used for Babylon in Jer. 25:26; 51:41 – it is an *Atbash*
	שתת	*Shathath* –To set, appoint
	תן	*Tan* –Jackal
	תרתק	*Tartaq* –Tartak, god of the Avites[1024]
	תשת	*Tashat* –Lay
		Tashet –Put
		Teshet –You shall drink
1101	ארץ	*Aretz* –Earth; one of the four elements; one of the Seven Earths (corr. to Supernals)
		'erets –Land, earth
	אשף	*'ashshaf* –Astrologer, enchanter, magician, necromancer, exorcist, conjurer
	ראתך	*Ro'tak* –You see (Ex. 10:28)
	שאף	*Sha'af* –To gasp, pant, breathe heavily; to crush, trample
1102	עולם מושכל	*Olam Mevshekal* –Intellectual World, first face of Adam Qadmon
	רבץ	*Rabatz* –To stretch oneself out, lie down
		Rebetz –Resting or dwelling place, place of lying down
	שבתת	*Shabatot* –Sabbaths
	תברך	*Tevarek* –You bless (Num. 22:6)
	תשבת	*Tishbat* –Shall rest
		Tishbot –It shall have rest; you shall rest
1103	גרשם	*Gershom* –Gershom, firstborn son of Moses and Zipporah; father of Jonathan; descendant of Phinehas
	וישכב במקום ההוא	*ve-Yishkav Bamaqom HaHowa'* –"And lay down in that place" (Gen. 28:11)
	–Prime number	
1104	דתן	*Dathan* –Dathan, chief of the tribe of Reuben who tried to overthrow Moses and Aaron
		Dothan –Dothan, city of the tribe of Manasseh west of the Jordan River, near Mount Gilboa, here Joseph was sold into slavery (see also דתין)[1025]
	ומנחתמ	*Vumenchatam* –With their meal offerings (Lev. 23:18)
	ותוצא הארצ דשא	*Va-totze HaAretz deshe* –And the earth brought forth grass
	יערי ארגים	*Ya'arey 'Oregiym* –Jaare-Oregim, father of Elkanan, slayer of Goliath the Gittite[1026]

[1024] The name Tartak may be a corruption of the Aramean goddess, Atargatis.

[1025] דתין (464, 1114).

[1026] Some scholars feel that this is a copyist's error for Jair (cf. 1 Chr. 20:5)

	רברבן	*Rabreban* –Lord, noble (Aramaic)
	שדף	*Shadaf* –To scorch, blight
	תדרך	*Tidrok* –You shall tread (Deut. 11:24; 33:29)
	תפוחים	*Tappuwachim* –Apple, apple tree
1105	בגתן	*Bigthan* –Bigthan, chamberlain who conspired against Ahasuerus
	גברתך	*Gevirtek* –Your mistress (Gen. 15:9)
	השתרר	*Histarar* –Ruling, prince
	תשתה	*Tishetah* –You shall drink; drinks
1106	הראתך	*Har'otak* –Show you (Ex. 9:16)
	ועשרן	*ve-'isaron* –And a tenth part (Ex. 29:40)
	ותשת	*Vatesht* –And drank
	נפושסים	*Nefuwshesiym* –Nephisesim, ancestor of returned captives (see also Nephusim, Naphish)[1027]
	רוץ	*Rutz* –To run
	שוף	*Shuwf* –To bruise, crush, to fall upon
	תרומתכמ	*Teruwmatekem* –Your gift; contribution, Terumah
1107	אתון	*'athown* –She-ass, she-donkey
		'attuwn –Furnace
	וארץ	*VeEretz* –And land
	כתם פז	*Katam Pez* –"Pure gold of the head" (Song 5:11)
	שזף	*Shazaf* –To catch sight of, look on

–The total gematria of Israel and Yesherown

1108	בשררות	*Bishriruwt* –In the stubbornness
	חרץ	*Charats* –To cut, sharpen, decide, decree, determine, maim, move, be decisive, be mutilated; loin, hip, hip joint (Aramaic)
	חשף	*Chashaf* –To strip, strip off, lay bare, make bare, draw out
		Chasif –Small flocks, little flocks
	חתן	*Chathan* –To become a son-in-law, make oneself a daughter's husband; son-in-law, daughter's husband, bridegroom, husband
	רחץ	*Rachatz* –To wash, wash off, wash away; to trust; washing
	שבתות	*Shabatot* –Weeks
	שחף	*Shachaf* –Cuckow, gull, sea-gull (ceremonially unclean bird)
	תחן	*Tachan* –Tahan, the name of two descendants of Ephraim
	תשבתו	*Tishbetuw* –You shall celebrate
	תשחת	*Tashchet* –Destory
		Tishachet –Was ruined

[1027] Nephusim (250, 810), Naphish (440).

1109 גרשום — *Gershowm* –Gershom, important priest, eldest son of Levi ((Gen. 46:11; Ex. 6:16; 1 Chr. 6:1) – see also Gershon (גרשון)) [1028]

פסנטרין — *Pisanteriyn* –A stringed instrument (perhaps a lyre or a harp)

רהדץ — *Rahadetz* –Angel of 2d Cancer

שטף — *Shataf* –To wash, rinse, engulf

Shetef –Flood, downpour

–Prime number

1110 יקשן — *Yoqshan* –Jokshan, son of Abraham by Keturah

מצפץ — *Matz-Patz* –A name of God by Temurah

משען — *Mish'en* –Support, staff

צללדמירון — *Tzelilimiron* (or *Tzeleldimiron*?) –The Clangers; *Qlippoth* of Gemini (A.C., 777, probably a misprint)

תתעמר — *Tite'amer* –You shall treat as a slave (Deut. 21:14)

1111 איתן — *Eythan* –Perpetual, constant, perennial, ever-flowing, permanent; Ethan, wise man in the time of Solomon; descendant of Judah; descendant of Levi

גבתון — *Gibbethown* –Gibbethon, village of the tribe of Dan where Nadab was assassinated

והתמכרתמ — *ve-Hitmakaretam* –And you shall be sold

תאריך — *Ta'ariyk* –You may prolong (Deut. 4:40)

1112 ביתן — *Biythan* –House, palace

כסלת תבר — *Kisloth Tabor* –Chisloth Tabor, city of Zebulun at the foot of Mount Tabor

שברים — *Shebariym* –Shebarim, place to which the Israelites ran on their flight from Ai (Josh. 7:5)

שבתתי — *Shabetitai* –My Sabbaths

שעלבין — *Sha'albiym* –Shaalabim, city of the tribe of Dan (this spelling used only in Josh. 19:42 – see also שעלבים)[1029]

תשבית — *Tashbiyt* –Shall you suffer to be lacking (Lev. 2:13)

1113 באתין — *Bathin* –Goetic demon #18

והתברך — *ve-Hitbarek* –And he will bless himself (Deut. 29:18)

1114 דתין — *Dothayin* –Dothan, city of the tribe of Manasseh west of the Jordan River, near Mount Gilboa, here Joseph was sold into slavery (see also דתן)[1030]

ותשחת — *va-Tishachet* –And was corrupted

חרוץ — *Charuwts* –Sharp-pointed, sharp, diligent; strict decision,

---

[1028] גרשון (559, 1209).

[1029] שעלבים (452, 1012).

[1030] דתן (454, 1104).

		decision; trench, moat, ditch; gold (poetically); Haruz, man of Jotbah in Judah
1115	הנסתרת	*HaNistarot* –The secret things (Deut. 29:28)
1116	גרגשים	*Girgasim* –Girgashites
	הבל הבלימ אמר קהלת הבל הבלימ הכל הבל	*Habal Habalim 'amer Qoholet Habal Habalim Hakal Habal* –"Vanity of vanities, says Ecclesiastes, vanity of vanities, all is vanity" (Ecc. 1:1)
	משרפות מימ	*Misrefowth Mayim* –Misrephoth-Maim, location in northern Palestine (Josh. 11:8; 13:6)
	נעצוץ	*Na'atsuwts* –Thorn bush
	עטרות בית יואב	*'Atrowth beyth Yow'ab* –"Ataroth the house of Joab"
	קישון	*Qiyshown* –Kishon, river in central Palestine which rises in Mount Tabor and drains the valley of Esdraelon
	קשיון	*Qishyown* –Kishion, city on the boundary of the tribe of Issachar
	שחרחרת	*Shecharchoreth* –Blackish
	שמעון	*Simeon* –Simeon, second son of Jacob by Leah, a progenitor of a tribe of Israel (assoc. w/Pisces)
1117	בן־זוחת	*Ben-Zowcheth* –Ben-zoheth, son of Ishi and descendant of Judah
	והותרך	*ve-Hotirak* –And (he) will make you over abundant (Deut. 28:11)
	ויראתך	*ve-Yir'atak* –And the fear of you (Deut. 2:25)
	ולתפארת	*ve-Letipa'aret* –And for beauty, honor, glory
	וריאץ	*Oriax* –Goetic demon #59
	זיתן	*Zeythan* –Zethan, descendant of Benjamin (1 Chr. 7:10)
	יאתון	*Ye'ithown* –Entrance (Ezek. 40:15)
	שבתתיה	*Shabetiteyha* –Its Sabbaths (Lev. 26:34)
	–Prime number	
1118	הרגתיך	*Haragtiyk* –I would kill you (Num. 22:29)
	ובריתך	*ve-Beriytak* –And your covenant (Deut. 33:9)
	חזוקותיכ אמצתיכ	*Chezowqowtik 'Ametzeth* –"Powerful strength"
	חריץ	*Chariyts* –A cut, thing cut, sharp instrument, sharp cutting instrument, harrow, hoe
	מנא מנא תקל ופרסינ	*Mena Mena Tekel Ufarsin* –"Numbered, numbered, weighed, and divisions"; the handwriting on the wall (alternate spelling)
	שמע ישראל יהוה אלהינו יהוה אחד	*Shema Israel* YHVH *Elohenu* YHVH *Echadh*–"Hear, O Israel: the LORD our God is one LORD" (Deut. 6:4)
	שחרים	*Shacharayim* –Shaharaim, descendant of Benjamin who went to Moab (1 Chr. 8:8)
	תשביתו	*Tashbiytuw* –You shall put away
	תשחית	*Tashchiyt* –You shall mar, destroy

1119	בית און	*Beyth 'Aven* –Beth Aven, town of the tribe of Benjamin
	ויבנשמ אברהמ את המזבח	*Vayiven Avraham Et HaMizbayach* –"And Abraham built an altar there" (Gen. 22:9)
	תשתחוה	*Tayshtachveh* –Shall bow down
1120	ידתון	*Yeduwthuwn* –Jeduthun, one of the three chief musicians of the service of song (this name only used in 1 Chr. 25:1-6 – see also ידותון, ידיתון – he was also named Ethan in 1 Chr. 6:29; 15:17, 19)[1031]
	ישרים	*Yishawrom* –The righteous
	כשף	*Kashaf* –To practice witchcraft or sorcery, use witchcraft
		Kashshaf –Sorcerer, witch
		Keshef –Sorcery, witchcraft
	שתיתי	*Shatiytiy* –Drank
	תכן	*Takan* –To measure
		Token –Measurement, measured amount; Tochen, town of Simeon (see also Ether)[1032]
1121	אכשף	*Akshaf* –"I shall be bewitched" – city in North Canaan at the foot of Mount Carmel
	באחריתך	*Be'achariyteka* –In your later end (Deut. 8:16)
	נחש הנחשת	*Nachash HaNechsheth* –"Brazen serpent" (2 Kings 18:4)
	עטרות שופנ	*'Atrowth Showfan* –Atroth-Shophan or Atroth, Shophan, one of the cities taken by the Israelites from kings Og and Sihon in the Bashan and rebuilt by the tribe of Gad (Num. 32:35)
1122	בכרתך	*Bekoratak* –Your birthright (Gen. 25:31)
	ברכתך	*Birkateka* –Your blessing (Gen. 27:35)
	תברכך	*Tevarekak* –May bless you (Gen. 27:4)
1123	והרביתך	*ve-Hirbiytik* –And multiply you (Gen. 48:4)
	התשחית	*Hatashchiyth* –Will you destroy? (Gen. 18:28)
	–Prime number	
1124	חלם יסודות	*Cholam Yesodoth* –The Breaker of Foundations; the Sphere of the Elements; the part of the material world corr. to *Malkut*
1125	בית־דגון	*Beyth-Dagown* –Beth Dagon, town located on the border between Asher and Zebulun (Josh. 19:27); town in the Judean lowlands (Josh. 15:33, 41)
	קברות התאוה	*Qibrowth HaTa'avah* –Kibroth-Hattaavah, campsite on the Sinai Peninsula where the Israelites grew tired of manna

---

1031 ידותון (476, 1126), ידיתון (480, 1130), Ethan (461, 1111).

1032 Ether (670).

1126 ביתחון — *Betchon* –Lord of Triplicty by Day for Scorpio

הראיתיך — *Her'iytiyak* –I have caused you to see it (Deut. 34:4)

ושתיתי — *ve-Shatiytiy* –And I may drink

ידותון — *Yeduwthuwn* –Jeduthun, one of the three chief musicians of the service of song (this name only used in 1 Chr. 9:16 – see also ידיתון, ידתון – he was also named Ethan in 1 Chr. 6:29; 15:17, 19)[1033]

מנה מנה תקל ופרסין — *Mene Mene Tekel Ufarsin* –"Numbered, numbered, weighed, and divisions"; the handwriting on the wall

צלילימירון — *Tzelilimiron* –The Clangers, *Qlippoth* of Gemini

1127 והותירך — *ve-Hotiyrak* –And will make you over abundant (Deut. 30:9)

מעלה עקרבים — *Ma'aleh 'Aqrabbiym* –Maaleh-Acrabbim, high place which marks part of the boundary of Judah between Kedish and the Dead Sea

1128 חצר עינן — *Chatzar 'Eynan* –Hazar Enan, small village on the northern border of Palestine (this name used only in Num. 34:9, 10; Ezek. 48:1 – see also חצר עינון)[1034]

1129 ויגוע ויאסף אל־עמיו — *VaYiga' VaYe'asef El-'Amayuw* –"And, breathing his last, he was gathered to his people" (Gen. 49:33)

–Prime number

1130 ידיתון — *Yediythuwn* –Jeduthun, one of the three chief musicians of the service of song (this name only used in Neh. 11:17 – see also ידותון, ידתון – he was also named Ethan in 1 Chr. 6:29; 15:17, 19)[1035]; father of Obededom (1 Chr. 16:38) – he may be the same as the first Jeduthun

לשתת — *Lishtoth* –To drink

מצרף — *Mitsref* –Crucible

פתן — *Pethen* –A snake, venemous serpent (perhaps cobra, adder or viper)

קלשן — *Qilleshown* –Forks, three-pronged pitchfork, goad (meaning dubious – 1 Sam. 13:21)

שלף — *Shalaf* –To draw out or off, take off

Shelaf –The second son of Joktan & a descendant of Shem

1131 אדירירון — *Adidyaron* –"The Mighty One Sings" (?); a title of *Tiferet*

אלתשחת — *Al-taschith* –"Do not destroy" – a command to the

[1033] ידתון (470, 1120), ידיתון (480, 1130), Ethan (461, 1111).

[1034] חצר עינון (484, 1134).

[1035] ידותון (476, 1126), ידתון (470, 1120), Ethan (461, 1111).

chief musician, or perhaps the title of a melody used for several Psalms

1132 תלבשת — *Talbosheth* –Garment, clothing

1133 בן־איש ימיני — *Ben-'Iysh Yemiyniy* –Benish Yemini, Benjamite (1 Sam. 9:1; 2 Sam. 20:1; Est. 2:5)

1134 בן־אשה אלמנה — *Ben-Ishah Almanah* –"Widow's son" (1 Kings 7:14)
חצר עינון — *Chatzar 'Eynown* –Hazar Enan, small village on the northern border of Palestine (this name used only in Ezek. 47:17 – see also חצר עינן)[1036]

1135 גוי אחד בארץ — *Goy 'echad b'aratz* –"One nation in the land" (1 Chr. 17:21)
הקדוש ברוך הוא — *HaQadosh Barukh Hu* –"The Holy One, blessed be He"
והשתחוית — *vi-Heshtachavet* –And you will bow down/worship (Deut. 4:19)

1136 לשתות — *li-Shetuwt* –To drink
שושן עדות — *Shuwshan 'Eduwth* –"Lily of the testimony," title of Psalm 60 (see also שושנים עדות)[1037]

1137 אשקלון — *'Ashqelown* –Ashkelon or Askalon, one of five chief Canaanite cities located north of modern Gaza
והוריתיך — *ve-Horeytiyak* –And I will teach you (Ex. 4:12)
וכגבורתך — *ve-Kigvuwrotek* –And according to your might (Deut. 3:24)

1138 וברכתיך — *ve-Varaktik* –And I [YHVH] will bless you (Gen. 26:24)
חתלן — *Chethlon* –Hethlon, mountain pass at the northern border of Palestine, connecting the Mediterranean coast with the Plain of Hamath (Ezek. 47:15; 48:1)

1139 אל תשחת — *'Al tashcheth* –Thou must not destroy

1140 כסף נבחר — *Kesaf Nevachar* –"Choice silver" (Prov. 10:20)
מרץ — *Marats* –To be or make sick
מתן — *Mattan* –Gifts, offerings, presents; Mattan, priest of Baal slain by the Hebrews (2 Kings 11:18; 2 Chr. 23:17); father of a prince of Judah (Jer. 38:1)
Mothen –Loins, hips
פסתם — *Pastam* 6th – 9th letters of the 22-letter name of God

1141 אור כשדים — *Ur Kasdim* –Ur of the Chaldees
אמרתך — *'imrateka* –Your word (Deut. 33:11)
שכל נאמן — *Sekhel Ne'eman* –Faithful Intelligence (22nd Path)

[1036] חצר עינן (478, 1128).
[1037] שושנים עדות (1186, 1746).

1142	מאראץ	*Marax* –Goetic demon #21
	מרבץ	*Marbets* –Place of lying down, resting or dwelling place
	מתבן	*Mathben* –Straw heap
	תולון	*Tuwlon* –Tilon, descendant of Judah
1143		
1144		
1145	אלהים צבאות	*Elohim Tzabaoth* –God of Hosts; divine name assoc. w/*Hod*, w/Water, & w/the West
1146	ירושלם	*Yeruwshalaim* –Jerusalem, capital of the southern kingdom of Judah until its destruction by Nebuchadnezzar in 586 B.C. (see also ירושלים)[1038]
	לויתן	*Leviathan* –The great sea-monster of Hebrew mythology, dragon (Isa. 27:1; Job 3:8, 40:25; Ps. 74:14, 104:26)
	מרוץ	*Merowts* –Running, race, course
	קמשון	*Qimmashown* –Thistles or nettles, thorny or useless plant
	תשומת	*Tesuwmeth* –Pledge, security, deposit
1147	מוראץ	*Marax* –Goetic demon #21 (Aurum Solis spelling)
1148	בתשומת	*Bitsomet* –Pledge, in the placing
	מחשף	*Machsof* –A stripping, a laying bare (of bark)
	נפתחים	*Naftuchiym* –Naphtuhim, son of Mizraim (Gen. 10:13; 1 Chr. 1:11 – many people think this refers to a district in Egypt)
1149	להשתחות	*Lehishtachawt* –To bow down (Gen. 37:10)
1150	נשף	*Nashaf* –To blow
		Neshef –Twilight
	נתן	*Nathan* –To give, put, set; Nathan, prophet and royal advisor to David; son of David; father of Igal; descendant of Jerahmeel; companion of Ezra; one of those who had married a foreign wife; brother of Joel, one of David's valiant men; father of Solomon's chief officer; chief man of Israel (see also Nathan-Melech)[1039]
		Nethan –To give (Aramaic)
	שתיתמ	*Shetiytem* –You have drunk
	תימן	*Teman* –Teman, grandson of Esau; Duke of Edom (Gen. 36:42; 1 Chr. 1:53 – assoc. w/*Hod*)
		Teyman –South, southward

[1038] ירושלים (596, 1156).

[1039] Nathan-Melech (590, 1720).

1151 אני יהוה מקדשכמ — *Ani* YHVH *Miqadishkem* –"I am YHVH who makes you holy" (Lev. 21:8)

אנקתם — *Anaqtam* –First five letters of the 22-letter name of God

אנסך — A permutation of יהוה by *Aiq Bekar*[1040]

אדסנ — A permutation of יהוה by *Aiq Bekar*

אתנן — *'ethnan* –Hire of prostitue, price; Ethnan, grandson of Ashur through Caleb, son of Hur

–Prime number

1152 ארור המן — *'Arrur Haman* –"Cursed be Haman"

1153 –Prime number

1154

1155

1156 ושתיתמ — *ve-Shetiytem* –And you may drink

ירושלים — *Yeruwshalayim* –Jerusalem, capital of the southern kingdom of Judah until its destruction by Nebuchadnezzar in 586 B.C. (see also ירושלם)[1041]

מדברתיך — *Midabroteyak* –Your words (Deut. 33:3)

נתון — *Nathiyn* –Nethinims (Temple-servants – this spelling used only in Ezra 8:17 – see also נתין)[1042]

1157 אנתון — *'antuwn* –You, thou (2nd person plural – Aramaic)

תתנשאו — *Titnasa'uw* –You do raise yourself up

1158 חנתן — *Channathon* –Hannathon, town of the tribe of Zebulun located on a road between Megiddo and Accho

תמנת חרס — *Timnath Sheres* –Timnath-Heres, village in Ephraim (identical with Timnath-Serah)

תמנת סרח — *Timnath-Serach* –Timnath-Serah, home and burial place of Joshua (identical with Timnath-Heres)

1159 אלופו של עולם — *'elifuw Shel 'olam* –Master of the Universe – a name of God

גנתון — *Ginnethown* –Ginnethon, priest or prince who sealed the new covenant with God after the exile (see also Ginnetho)[1043]

1160 יתנן — *Yithnan* –Ithnan, town in extreme southern Judah

נתין — *Nathiyn* –Nethinims (Temple-servants – this spelling used only in 1 Chr. 9:2; Ezra 2:43, 58, 70; 7:7,

---

[1040] See Introduction.

[1041] ירושלם (586, 1146).

[1042] נתין (510, 1160).

[1043] Ginnetho (459).

		24; 8:20; Neh. 3:26, 31; 7:46, 60, 73; 10:29; 11:3, 21 – see also נתון)[1044]
	קדסך	A permutation of יהוה by *Aiq Bekar*[1045]
	שסף	*Shasaf* –To hew in pieces (meaning dubious – 1 Sam. 15:33)
	תנין	*Tannin* –Whale (Gen. 1:21; Job 7:12), dragon, serpent, sea-monster
		Tinyan –Second (Aramaic)
1161	אני אעביר כל־טובי על־פניך	*'Ani 'A'aviyr Kal-Toviy 'Al-Paneyka* –"I will make all My goodness pass before you" (Ex. 22:19)
1162	ויסרם מעל פניו	*Va-Yesirem Ma'al Panayv* –"and [He] banished them from His presence" (2 Kings 17:18)[1046]
1163	–Prime number	
1164	תשחתון	*Tashchitun* –You deal corruptly
1165	אלון בכות	*'Allown Bakuwth* –Allon Bachuth, burial place of Deborah, nurse of Rebekah
	ארץ תחתונה	*Aretz HaTachtonah* –Nethermost Earth
1166	יונתן	*Yownathan* –Jonathan, grandson of Onam (1 Chr. 27:32); father of one who returned with Ezra (Ezra 8:6); one involved with the foreign wife controversy (Ezra 10:15); descendant of Jeshua the High Priest (Neh. 12:11); priest (Neh. 12:14); one who joined Gedaliah after the fall of Jerusalem (Jer. 40:8)
	ינשוף	*Yanshuwf* –Great owl, eared owl
	יסוד התפארת	*Yesod HaTiferet* –Foundation of Beauty
	שפופן	*Shefuwfan* –Shephuphan, son of Benjamin (this spelling used only in 1 Chr. 8:5 – see also Shuppim, Shupham)[1047]
1167 – 1169		
1170	רעץ	*Ra'atz* –To shatter
	שמיני עצרת	*Shmini Atzeret* –Eight [day] gathering; Festival occuring on the day immediately following the last day of *Sukkot*
	שעף	*Sha'aph* –Shaaph, descendant of Judah; son of Caleb
	שפיפן	*Shefiyfon* –Horned snake, adder (Gen. 49:17)
1171	אדני הארץ	*Adonai HaAretz* –Lord of the Earth; divine name assoc. w/*Malkut*, Earth, and the North

[1044] נתון (506, 1156).

[1045] See Introduction.

[1046] This is the reference to the so-called lost tribes of Israel.

[1047] Shuppim (430, 990), Shupham (506, 1066).

יהונתן *Yehownathan* –Jonathan, priest of an idol shrine in the territory of Ephraim; son of Abiathar the High Priest; son of Shimea, David's brother; one of David's mighty men; uncle of David; scribe in whose house Jeremiah was kept prisoner; son of Saul and close friend of David

כמתאננים *Kemit'oneniym* –As murmurers (Num. 11:1)

–Prime number

1172 והנשארים *ve-Hanish'ariym* –And the remaining (Gen. 14:10)

כי אם ישראל *Ki Em Israel* –For the people of Israel

1173 והאלהים נסהאת *ve-HaElohim Nisahath* –"And God tested" (Gen. 22:1)

1174 בשבתתיכמ *ve-Shabatitykem* –In your Sabbaths (Lev. 26:35)

ובתנוריך *ve-Vetanuwreyak* –And in your ovens (Ex. 7:28)

תשחיתונ *Tishchiytun* –You will become corrupt (Deut. 31:29)

1175 והשתחויתמ *ve-Hishtachaviytem* –And you worshipped them (Ex. 24:1)

ששה־עשר *Shishshah-Asar* –Sixteen

1176 ונצלתם *ve-Nitzaltem* –And you shall spoil, empty (Ex. 3:22)

ערוץ *'aruwts* –Dreadful; chasm, ravine, steep slope

ערותך *'ervatak* –Your nakedness (Ex. 20:23)

עשתות *'ashtuwth* –Thought, idea

פרצוף *Partzuf* –Person, face

שערום *Sa'ruwm* –Dreaded, feared (Deut. 32:17)

1177–1179

1180 ותשתחוינ *va-Tishtachaveyna* –And they bowed down

כנשרים *Kanishareem* –Like eagles

עריץ *'ariyts* –Awe-inspiring, terror-striking, awesome, terrifying, ruthless, might

עשרים *'esriym* –Twenty, twentieth

פרשם *Pirsham* –Their dung (Lev. 16:27)

פרץ *Paratz* –To break through or down or over, burst, breach

Peretz –Breach, gap, bursting forth; Perez, eldest son of Judah

רשעים *Rash'iym* –Wicked ones

שערים *Se'oriym* –Barley (Lev. 27:16); Seorim, priest in the days of David

Sha'riym –(A hundred)-fold (Gen. 26:12)

Sha'arayim –Shaaraim, town in lowland Judah; town of Simeon

תחתימ חדשי *Tachtiym Chodshiy* –Tahtim-Hodshi, location between Gilead and Dan-jaan visited by Joab during the census of Israel

1181 אלנתן *Elnathan* –Elnathan, king Jehoiachin's maternal

grandfather; three chief men in Ezra's time; son of Achbor, a military commander under Jehoiakim

אפתן — *'appethom* –Treasury, treasuries; revenue (Aramaic)

כראשנים — *Kari'shoniym* –Like unto the first (Ex. 34:1)

–Prime number

1182 בעשרים — *Be'sriym* –For twenty (Gen. 37:30)

1183 בית הישימות — *Beyth HaYeshiymowth* –Beth-Jeshimoth, town in Moab near the Dead Sea

1184 ידעתן — *Yeda'ten* –You know

תפקדם — *Tifeqdem* –You shall number them (Num. 3:15)

1185 העשרים — *Ha'Esriym* –The twenty (Gen. 18:31)

הרשעים — *HaResha'iym* –The wicked (Ex. 9:27)

השעירם — *HaSe'iyrim* –The he-goats (Lev. 16:7)

התשיעת — *HaTeshiy'ot* –The ninth

זקן ושבע — *Zaqan ve-Shavay* –"Old, wise and satisfied" (Gen. 25:8)

1186 בית עדן — *Beyth 'Eden* –Beth Eden, city-state in Mesopotamia

ועשרים — *ve-'esriym* –And twenty (Gen. 6:3)

שושנים עדות — *Shuwshanniym 'Eduwth* –"Lilies of the testimony," title of Psalm 80 (see also שושן עדות)[1048]

תאנת שלה — *Ta'anath Shiloh* –Taanath-Shiloh, border town between Manasseh and Ephraim – modern Khirbet Ta'na

1187 –Prime number

1188 ממחציתם — *Mimachatziytam* –Of their half (Num. 31:29)

1189

1190 ופקדתם — *ve-Feqadtem* –You shall appoint (Num. 4:27)

פרשים — *Parashiym* –Horsemen (Gen. 50:9)

רצץ — *Ratzatz* –To crush, oppress

שעירים — *Seirim* –Hairy Ones; he-goats; demons

שצף — *Shetsef* –Flood, downpour, overflowing

שרסכים — *Sarsekiym* –Sarsechim, prince of Babylon who sat at the gate (Jer. 39:3)

שרפים — *Serafim* –Angelic Choir assoc. w/*Giburah*

תנשמת — *Tanshemeth* –An unclean animal of some kind (usu. transl. as swan or mole. See Deut. 14:16 & Lev. 11:18, 30)

1191

1192 עולם יסודות — *Olam Yesodoth* –The World of Foundations; the Sphere

---

[1048] שושן עדות (1137, 1786).

		of the Elements; the part of the material world corr. to *Malkut*
1193	–Prime number	
1194	ואין ברוחו רמיה	*ve-Ayin Baruchuw Remiyah* –"And in whose spirit there is no deceit" (Ps. 32:2)
	פתחון	*Pithchown* –Opening
1195	הפרשים	*HaParashiym* –The horsemen (Ex. 14:28)
	השרפים	*HaSerafiym* –The fiery (Num. 21:6)
		HaSerufiym –The burned (Num. 17:4)
	התנשמת	*HaTinshemet* –The horned owl
1196	וסקלתם	*ve-Seqaltem* –And you shall stone them (Deut. 22:24)
		ve-Seqaltam –And you shall stone them (Deut. 17:5)
	פיתון	*Piythown Piythown* –Pithon, son of Micah and great-grandson of Saul
1197	ונאספתם	*ve-Ne'esaftem* –And you shall be gathered (Lev. 26:25)
	ותתפשהו	*ve-Titpeshu* –And she caught him (Gen. 39:12)
1198	בעירירון	*Beiriron* –The Herd, *Qlippoth* of Aries
	עבירירון	*Abiriron* –The Clayish Ones, *Qlippoth* of Libra
1199	כל הנגע בהמ יקדש	*Kal HaNogayah bahem yiqdash* –"Everything touching them shall be consecrated" (see Ex. 30:29)
	עשרים ואחד	*Esrim ve-Achad* –Twenty-One
1200	ויבאו שני המלאכים סדמה	*VaYavo'uw Sh'ney HaMal'akiym Sodomah* –"The two angels arrived in Sodom" (Gen. 19:1)
	לתשעת	*le-Tishat* –To nine (Num. 34:13)
	משמרכם	*Mishmarkem* –Your prison (Gen. 42:19)
	קרץ	*Qaratz* –To narrow, pinch, squeeze
		Qeretz –Nipping, nipper, stinger (of insect)
	קשקשת	*Qasqeset* –Scale (of fish, water animals)
	רתם	*Ratham* –To bind, attach
		Rethem –Juniper, juniper tree
	שכל נשרש	*Sekhel Nesharash* –Radical or Rooted Intelligence (5th Path)
	שץ	*Shax* –Goetic demon #44
	שקף	*Shaqaf* –To overlook, look down or out, overhand
		Shaquf –Frame, window casing, beams laid over
		Sheqef –Framework, casing, door, lintel
	שרשת	*Sharshat* –Chains
	תף	*Tof* –Hand-drum; bezel; timbrel, tambourine
	תקן	*Taqan* –To equalize, make straight
1201	אשתך	*'ishteka* –Your wife (Gen. 3:17)
	דנתאליון	*Dantalion* –Goetic demon #71 (Aurum Solis spelling)
	והתנשמת	*ve-HaTinshamet* –And the chameleon; and the horned

		owl (Deut. 14:16)
	ראשן –Prime number	*Ri'shown* –First, primary; first, before, formerly
1202	בשעריכם	*Besha'areykem* –Within your gates (Deut. 12:12)
	שבץ	*Shabbats* –To weave *Shabats* –Cramp, agony, anguish (2 Sam. 1:9)
	תשבך	*Tishbek* –Shall carry you away captive (Num. 24:22)
1203	בראתם	*Bir'otam* –When they see (Ex. 13:17)
	גרגופיאץ	*Gargofias* –Guardian of the 13th Tunnel of Set
	צרת השחר	*Tzereth HaShachar* –Zareth-Shahar, town allotted to the tribe of Reuben
1204	בשבתך	*Beshivtak* –When you sit (Deut. 6:7)
	החרש ואאלפך חכמה	*Hecharosh ve-'alpek chekomah* –"Be still and I will teach you wisdom" (Job 33:33)
	תגלת פלאסר	*Tiglath Pil'eser* –Tiglath-Pileser, king of Assyria who invaded Naphtali during the time of Pekah of Israel (2 Kings 15:29; 16:7, 10; 1 Chr. 5:6, 26)
1205	שהרן	*Saharon* –Moon, crescent moon (as ornament)
	שלשה־עשר	*Shelshah-Asar* –Thirteen
1206	דברתם	*Dibartem* –You have spoken (Num. 14:28); you have said (Ex. 12:32)
	וקשקשת	*ve-Qasqeset* –And scales (as on fish)
	ותרם	*ve-Taram* –And it was lifted up (Gen. 7:17)
	שרון	*Sharown* –Sharon, region that lies between the Mediterranean Sea from Joppa to Carmel and the central portion of Palestine; district east of the Jordan occupied by the tribe of Gad
	תקון	*Tiqqun* –Restoration
1207	ואשתך	*ve-'ishtak* –And your wife (Gen. 6:18)
	ראשון	*Rishon* –First, former, primary
1208	אלהים יראהלו השה	*Elohim Yerehlo Hasheh* –"God will see to the sheep..." (Gen. 22:7, 8)
	בשקתות	*Beshiqatut* –In the troughs
	חתף	*Chathaf* –To seize, take away, snatch away *Chethef* –Prey; robber
	שבותך	*Shevuwtak* –Your captivity (Deut. 30:3)
	שחץ	*Shachatz* –Dignity, pride
1209	גרשון	*Gereshown* –Gershon, important priest, eldest son of Levi (Gen. 46:11; Ex. 6:16; 1 Chr. 6:1) – also called Gershom (גרשום)
	תרגום	*Targum* –Translation; Aramaic Bible
1210	בלק בן צפור	*Balak ben Tzepior* –"Balak, son of Zippor" (Num. 22:2)

	למקמתם	*Limqomotam* –After their places (Gen. 36:40)
	לשעירם	*Las'iyrim* –Demons (Lev. 17:7)
	סובב כל עלמין	*Sovev Kol Almin* –"Encompassing all worlds"
	קרשים	*Qerashiym* –Boards (Ex. 26:22)
	רשין	*Rishyown* –Permission
	שרין	*Shiryown* –Body armor; a weapon; Sirion, name given to Mount Hermon by the Sidonians (see also שריון)[1049]
	ששים	*Shishshim* –Sixty, threescore
	תרים	*Toroym* –Turtle-doves (Lev. 5:7)
	תרשיש	*Tarshish* –Tarshish, son of Javan and grandson of Noah; one of the seven princes of Persia; descendant of Benjamin; Tarshish, ciy in southern Spain with which the Phoenicians traded; chrysolite (precious stone in the High Priest's ephod – represents the tribe Asher)
	תשיך	*Tashiyk* –You are covered with fat (Deut. 32:15)
1211	אתרים	*'Athariym* –Spies (Num. 21:1)
	יראתם	*Yere'tem* –You were afraid (Num. 12:8)
	קראתיך	*Qera'tiyak* –I called you (Num. 24:10)
	ראיתם	*Re'iytem* –You have seen (Gen. 45:13)
	תיראם	*Tiyra'em* –Fear them (Num. 14:9)
1212	ודברתם	*ve-Dibartem* –And you speak (Num. 20:8)
	תשוקתו	*Teshuqato* –His desire
1213	–Prime number	
1214	אזן שארה	*'Uzzen She'erah* –Uzzen-Sherah, town founded by Sherah, daughter of Ephraim
	בת רבים	*Bath Rabbiym* –Bath Rabbim, a gate of Heshbon (Song 7:5)
	ותחשך	*ve-Techshak* –And was darkened (Ex. 10:15)
	קרית חצות	*Qiryath Chutzowth* –Kirjath-Huzoth, town of Moab (see also Kerioth)[1050]
	שרוחן	*Sharuwchen* –Sharuhen, city in Simeon near Beth-lebaoth
1215	הקרשים	*HaQerashiym* –The boards (Ex. 26:15)
	התרים	*HaTariym* –The spies (Num. 14:6)
		HaToriym –The turtle-doves (Lev. 1:14)
	סהרנץ	*Saharnatz* –Angel of 2d Libra
1216	האתרים	*Ha'atariym* –The Atharim (meaning uncertain – see Num. 21:1)
	הראיתם	*HaR'item* –I have seen (1 Sam. 10:24, 17:25; 2 Kings 6:32; 20:15)[1051]

[1049] שריון (566, 1216).
[1050] Kerioth (716).

	ויתרם	*ve-Yitram* –And what they leave (Ex. 23:11)
	וששים	*ve-Shishiym* –And sixty (Gen. 5:15)
	ותרשיש	*ve-Tarshysh* –And Tarshish
	ישרון	*Yesherown* –The righteous people (a fig. phrase for Israel – Deut. 32:15; Is. 44:2)
	שריון	*Shiryown* –Sirion, name given to Mount Hermon by the Sidonians (see also שרין)[1052]
1217	בית הרם	*Beyth HaRam* –Beth Aram, town of the tribe of Gad, noted for its hot springs
	גדרתים	*Gederothayim* –Gederothaim, town of Judah, perhaps the same as Gederoth
	וראיתם	*ve-Re'iytem* –And you shall look, see (Ex. 16:7)
	שכל בית הקדנש	*Sekhel Beth HaShefa* –Intelligence of the House of Influence (18th Path)
	תיראום	*Tiyra'uwm* –You shall fear (Deut. 3:22)
	–Prime number	
1218	והזרתם	*ve-Hizartem* –Thus you shall separate (Lev. 15:31)
	ורביתם	*ve-Reviytem* –And multiply (Deut. 8:1)
	קיר חרשת	*Qiyr Chereseth* –Kir-Haraseth, fortified city (see also Kir, Kir-Haresh)[1053]
	תחרים	*Tachariym* –You shall destroy (Deut. 7:2)
	תחתית	*Tachtiyt* –Depth (Deut. 32:22)
1219	אחריתם	*'achriytam* –Their end (Deut. 32:20)
	טירתם	*Tiyrotam* –Their encampments (Num. 31:10)
1220	בתחתית	*Bethechtiyt* –At the foot of
	וטהרתם	*ve-Tehartem* –And you shall be clean (Num. 31:24)
	כתף	*Kathef* –Shoulder, shoulder-blade, side, slope
	מפרץ	*Mifrats* –Landing place
	מפתן	*Miftan* –Threshold
	שכרן	*Shikkarown* –Drunkenness
	תפלין	*Tefillin* –Phylacteries (see Exod. 13:1-10, 11-16; Deut. 6:4-9, 11:13-21)
1221	והורדתם	*ve-Horadtem* –And you will bring down (Gen. 42:38)
	והקשרים	*ve-Haqshuriym* –And the stronger (Gen. 30:42)
	ועצמתיהם	*ve-'atzmoteyhem* –And their bones (Num. 24:8)
1222	מלאך האלהים	*Malakh HaElohim* –Angel of God
	שכבתך	*Shekavtak* –Your (carnal) lying (Lev. 18:20)
	–The number of children of Azgad who returned from exile (Ezra 2:12)	
1223	והשבתיך	*ve-Hashivotiyka* –And will bring you back (Gen. 28:15)

[1051] HaR'item is one of the ten words in the Tanakh with a Dagesh in the letter Resh.

[1052] שרין (560, 1210).

[1053] Kir-Haresh (818), Kir (310).

השחיתך — *Hashchiyteka* –Destroy you (Deut. 10:10)
–Prime number

1224 וצדקתו עמדת לעד — *ve-Tzidqato 'Omedet La'ad* –"His beneficence is everlasting" (Ps. 111:3)

1225 זה־שמי לעלמ וזה זכרי לדר דר — *Zeh-Shemiy Leo'lam VeZeh Zikriy Ledor dor* –"This shall be My name forever, This My appellation for all eternity" (Ex. 3:15)
עתיקא דעתיקינ — *Atiqa de-Atiqin* –The Ancient of the Ancient Ones, a title of *Keter*
–Sum of all the numbers (1 to 49) on the magic square of Venus

1226 אלפ שנימ בעיניכ כיומ אתמול — *'alef Sheniym Be'yaniyk Kiyvom 'atemuwl* –"A thousand years in Your eyes are as a day of yesterday" (Ps. 90:4)
כשרונ — *Kishrown* –Success, skill, profit
שכרונ — *Shikkerown* –Shicron, town on the northern boundary of Judah
שם יהשוה — *Shem Yehoshuah* –The name Yehoshuah (i.e., Jesus)
תשוקתכ — *Teshuwqatek* –Your desire

1227 ובטירתם — *ve-Vetiyrotam* –And by their encampments (Gen. 25:16)
כראשונ — *Karishown* –As the first

1228 בית מעונ — *Beyth Me'own* –Baal's dwelling place; Beth Meon, Amorite city on the north border of Moab (this name only used in Jer. 48:23)
וברכתם — *ve-Veraktem* –And you will bless (Ex. 12:32)
חדוהי ודרעוהי די כסף — *Cheduwhiy VeDara'vehiy Diy Kasaf* –"Its breasts and its arms were of silver" (Dan. 2:32)
ישחיתך — *Yashchiyteka* –Will destroy you (Deut. 4:31)

1229 –Prime number

1230 עשרנים — *'esroniym* –Tenth parts (Lev. 14:10)
שלשם — *Shilshown* –Day before yesterday, three days ago; idiom for "in times past"
תפילינ — *Tefilin* –Leather boxes containing parchment, worn on the head and left arm by men during weekday morning prayer

1231 אלתקן — *Elteqon* –Eltekon, a city in the territory of Judah north of Hebron
לקראתך — *Liqra'tak* –To meet you (Gen. 32:7)
Liqra'teak –To meet you (Ex. 4:14)
לראתם — *Lir'otam* –To see them (Ex. 14:13)
עשרת הדברימ — *Asereth HaDavarim* –The 10 Commandments
תשאלך — *Tish'alak* –Shall ask of you (Deut. 14:26)
–Prime number

1232 והארכתם | *ve-Ha'araktem* –And you may prolong (Deut. 5:30)
לשבתך | *Leshivtak* –You to dwell in (Ex. 15:17)

1233 וזכרתם | *ve-Zekartem* –And remember (Num. 15:39)
טמירא דטמירין | *Temira de-Temirin* –The Concealed of the Concealed, a title of *Keter*

1234 דרתיכם | *Doroteykem* –Your generations (Lev. 23:43)
לדרתם | *Ledorotam* –Throughout their generations (Gen. 17:7)

1235

1236 ושלשם | *ve-Shalishim* –And captains of the hosts (Ex. 14:7)
ותשלך | *ve-Tashlek* –And she cast (Gen. 21:15)
שלשום | *Shilshom* –Before yesterday (Gen. 31:2)

1237 בית הכרם | *Beyth HaKerem* –Beth Haccerem, town of Judah that maintained a beacon station, probably present-day Ain Karim

–Prime number

1238

1239 כבור ראשון | *Kabodh Rishon* –First Splendor, a title of *Keter*

1240 שלשים | *Shelshim* –Thirty; thirtieth
שמץ | *Shemets* –Whisper, little

1241 אמרתם | *'amartem* –You spoke (Gen. 43:27)
להורתם | *Lehorotam* –That you may teach them (Ex. 24:12)

1242 בירכתים | *Bayarkatayim* –In the hinder part (Ex. 26:23)

1243 אלף בית | *Alef Bet* –The Hebrew alphabet
והלכת אל המקום | *Vihalachath El HaMaqowm* –And go to the place [that God has chosen to dwell] (Deut. 26:2)
עולם אצילות | *Olam Atzilut* –The World of Nobility , the Divine or Archetypal World

1244 הראני נא את־כבדך | *Hare'niy Na' 'Eth-Kevodeka* –"Oh, let me behold Your presence!" (Ex. 33:18)
ולתושבך | *ve-Letoshavak* –And to your settler (Lev. 25:6)

1245

1246 ושלשים | *ve-Shelishiym* –And thirty (Gen. 5:5); and third (Gen. 5:16)
משקוף | *Mashqowf* –Lintel (of door)
שמרון | *Shomrown* –Shimron, ancient city belonging to Zebulun; Shimron, fourth son of Issachar; Samaria, capital

of the northern kingdom of Israel; another name for the kingdom of Israel

1247 בינה נבחר מכסף — *Binah Nevacher Mekasaf* –"Understanding to be chosen above silver" (Prov. 16:16)
ואמרתם — *ve-'amartem* –And you shall say (Gen. 32:21)
–The number of children of Pashur who returned from exile (Ezra 2:38)

1248 נעשה אדם בצלמנו — *Naaseh adham be-tzelmenu* –Let us make man in our imagev
שלחתיך — *Shelachtiyak* –Have sent you (Ex. 3:12)
תובל קין — *Tubal-Qayin* –Tubal-Cain, one of the sons of Lamech and an expert metal-smith (Gen. 4:22)

1249 לאחריתם — *La'chariytam* –Their latter end (Deut. 32:29)
–Prime number

1250 מריתם — *Meriytem* –You rebelled (Num. 20:24)
מרתים — *Merathayim* –Merathaim, symbolic name for the country of the Chaldeans, also known as Babylon (Jer. 50:21)
ערץ — *'arats* –To tremble, dread, fear, oppress, prevail, break, be terrified, cause to tremble
קנסך — A permutation of יהוה by *Aiq Bekar*[1054]
קדסנ — A permutation of יהוה by *Aiq Bekar*
שמרין — *Shomrayin* –Samaria, capital of the northern kingdom of Israel (this spelling used only in Ezra 4:10, 17 – see also שמרון)[1055]
תמרים — *Temariym* –Palm trees (Ex. 15:27)
תפין — *Tufiyn* –Broken piece, baked piece, pieces cooked

1251 ואני דניאל נהייתי ונחלתי ימימ — *ve-'aniy Daniel Nehiytiy ve-Necheltiy Yamiym* –"And I, Daniel, was broken and became sick for many days" (Dan. 8:27)
והרמתם — *ve-Haremotem* –And you shall set apart (Num. 18:26)
ומהרתם — *ve-Mihartem* –And you shall hasten (Gen. 45:13)
לראתכם — *Lar'otkem* –To show you (Deut. 1:33)

1252

1253 שלהבירון — *Shalhebiron* –The Flaming Ones, *Qlippoth* of Leo

1254 –The number of children of Elam who returned from exile (Ezra 2:7)
–The number of children of "the other Elam" who returned from exile (Ezra 2:31)

1255 התמרים — *HaTemariym* –The palm trees (Deut. 34:3)
והתקדשתמ — *ve-Hitqadishtem* –And sanctify yourselves (Lev. 11:44)
נהרתם — *Naharotam* –Their rivers (Ex. 7:19)

[1054] See Introduction.
[1055] שמרון (596, 1246).

	עולם מורגש	*Olam Morgash* –Moral World, second face of Adam Qadmon
1256	ושמתיך	*ve-Samtiyak* –And I will put you (Ex. 33:22)
1257		
1258	לב מבין דעת	*Lev Meviyn Da'at* –"A heart that understands knowledge" (notarikon for *Lamed*)
	פרץ עזא	*Peretz 'Uzza'* –Perez-Uzzah, name David gave to the place Uzzah was struck by God (2 Sam. 6:8)
	תחרימם	*Tachariymem* –You shall destroy (Deut. 20:17)
	תתחתן	*Titachatan* –Shall marry (Deut. 7:3; 1 Sam. 18:21)
1259	–Prime number	
1260	מכרתם	*Mekartem* –You sold (Gen. 45:4)
	סרתם	*Sartem* –You had turned aside (Deut. 9:16)
	פרי עץ	*Peri Etz* –Fruit of a tree
	צעקתם	*Tza'aqatam* –Cry of them (Gen. 19:13)
	תרשישים	*Tarshishim* –Chrysolites; Angelic Choir sometimes assoc. w/*Netzach*
1261	הנותרם	*HaNotarim* –The remaining (Lev. 10:16)
1262		
1263	למען תחיה	*Li-Ma'an Tiachyeh* –"So that you might thrive" (Deut. 16:20)
1264	לדרתיכם	*Ledoroteykem* –Throughout your generations (Gen. 17:12)
1265	מיתריהם	*Meytreyhem* –Their cords (Ex. 35:18)
1266	וסרתם	*ve-Sartem* –And you turn aside (Duet. 11:16)
1267-1269		
1270	לירכתים	*Layarkatayim* –For the hinder part (Ex. 26:27)
	לשמרן	*Leshimron* –Of Shimron (Num. 26:24)
	משלשם	*Mishilshom* –From the day before (Ex. 4:10)
	ערתם	*'orotam* –Their skins (Lev. 16:27)
	שמלתך	*Shimelatak* –Your rainment (Deut. 8:4)
1271	הנותרים	*HaNotariym* –The remaining (Ex. 28:10)
	ומיתריהם	*ve-Meytereyhem* –And their cords (Num. 3:37)
1272	עברתם	*'avartem* –You are come, you passed (Gen. 18:5)
1273	ביד משה ואהרן	*Be-yad Moshe Ve-Aharon* –"The leadership of Moses

and Aaron" (Num. 33:1)
ספר זכרון *Sefer Zikarown* –"Book of Remembrance" (Mal. 3:16)

1274 נחשירון *Nachashiron* –The Snakey Ones, *Qlippoth* of Sagittarius
עין תפוח *'Eyn Tappuwach* –En Tappuah, town on the border of Ephraim

1275 הקצפתם *Hiqtzaftem* –You made angry (Deut. 9:8)
הרעתם *Hare'otem* –You deal so ill (Gen. 43:6)
וקראתי בשמ יהוה לפניכ *ve-Qara'tiy Vashem* YHVH *Lepaneyka* –"And I will proclaim before you the name YHVH" (Ex. 33:19)
מכרתיהם *Mekeroteyhem* –Their sword (Gen. 49:5)
–The sum of the numbers 1 through 50

1276 ועשרן *ve-'isaron* –And a tenth part (Ex. 29:40)
עשרון *'issarown* –Tenth part, tithe
שקערורת *Sheqa'aruroth* –Penetrating streaks (meaning uncertain – Lev. 14:37)

1277 –Prime number

1278 ועברתם *ve-'avartem* –And when you go over (Deut. 12:10)
ve-'evratam –And their wrath (Gen. 49:7)

1279 ויספו ענוים ביהוה שמחה *ve-Yisapho 'anuwyam Be-*YHVH *Shamachah* –"The humble shall increase joy in God" (Is. 29:19)
סנוי סנסנוי סמנגלופ אדמ והוה חצ לילות *Senoy, Sansenoy, Semangelof! Adam ve-Chavvah! Chotz Lilith!* –"Senoy, Sansenoy, Semangelof! Adam and Eve! Out, Lilith!" The formula used against Lilith
–Prime number

1280 יתרעם *Yithre'am* –Ithream, son of David probably by Eglah
עשרין *'esriyn* –Twenty (Aramaic)
פבו ורבו ומלאו את הארצ *Peru u-revu u-mileu eth HaAreth* –"Be fruitful and multiply and replenish the earth" (Gen. 1:28, 9:1)
פרתם *Partham* –Noble, nobleman
שכל שלם *Sekhel Shalem* –Perfect or Absolute Intelligence (8th Path)
תפף *Tafaf* –To play the timbrel, to drum
תשפך *Tishfok* –You shall pour out (Ex. 29:12)

1281 והרעתם *ve-Har'otem* –And you shall sound (Num. 10:9)

1282 לא תנאף *Lo thi-ne'af* –"Thou shalt not commit adultery" (Ex. 20:13)

1283 ארבעתים *'arba'tayim* –Fourfold
ונזכרתם *ve-Gizkartem* –And you shall be remembered (Num.

10:9)

והעברתם ve-Ha'avartem –And you shall cause to pass (Num. 26:8)

וזרעתם *ve-Zera'tem* –And you shall sow (Gen. 47:23)

פרשגן *Parshegen* –Copy

–Prime number

1284

1285 הילל בן שחר *Helel ben Shachar* –"Son of the Dawn;" Lucifer (Is. 14:12)[1056]

סנוי סנסנוי סמנגלופ אדמ חוצ לילות *Senoy, Sansenoy, Semangelof! Adam ve-Chavvah! Chotz Lilith!* –"Senoy, Sansenoy, Semangelof! Adam and Eve! Out, Lilith!" The formula used against Lilith (variant spelling)

1286 פרשון *Purson* –Goetic demon #20 (Aurum Solis spelling)

צפרירון *Tzafiriron* –The Scratchers, Qlippoth of Virgo

1287 פרשדן *Parshedon* –Excrement, feces (meaning dubious – Judg. 3:22)

1288 שפחתך *Shifchatek* –Your maid (Gen. 15:6)

1289 צללו כעופרת במימ אדירימ *Tzelelu Kofereth Bemayim Adirim* –"They sank like lead in mighty waters" (Exod. 15:10)

–Prime number

1290 ורדפתם *ve-Redaftem* –And you shall chase (Lev. 26:7)

ירשיען *Yarshiy'en* –Will condemn (Ex. 22:8)

עכרתם *'akartem* –You have troubled (Gen. 34:30)

שפתיך *Sefateyak* –Your lips (Deut. 23:24)

תצרם *Tetzurem* –Harass them (Deut. 2:19)

תרפים *Terafiym* –Teraphim, idolatry, idols, images

–The number of days from the time when the regular offering is banished and the appalling abomination is set up in Daniel 12:11

1291 –Prime number

1292 פורשון *Purson* –Goetic demon #20

1293 בארצתם *Be'artzotam* –In their lands (Gen. 10:5)

1294 אחשדרפן *Achashdarpan* –Satrap, a governor of a Persian province

---

[1056] It should be noted that Lucifer, or "light bearer" is wrongly applied to the Christian devil, due to a misreading of Isaiah 14:12: "How are you fallen from heaven,/O Shining One, son of Dawn!" It is imperative that the reader understand that in context, this is part of a song of scorn to be recited over the king of Babylon (Nebuchadnezzar), and is not a reference to the devil of Christianity. The JPS Hebrew-English TANAKH states that Lucifer may also refer to a character in some lost myth. Also see A Dictionary of Angels, p. 176 for more information.

1295 התרפים — *HaTerafiym* –The Teraphim (Gen. 31:19)

1296 ותרפים — *ve-Terafim* –And Teraphim, idols, idolatry, images
כור עשן — *Kowr 'Ashan* –Chor-ashan or Chorashan, town in Judah given to Simeon (see also Ashan)[1057]

1297 –Prime number

1298

1299 שכל מוגשם — *Sekhel Mughsham* –Corporeal Intelligence (29th Path)

1300 ערלתם — *'arlatam* –Their foreskin (Gen. 17:23)
רשף — *Reshef* –Flame, coals, firebolt; Resheph, descendant of Ephraim; Canaanite deity worshipped as lord of the underworld
שקץ — *Shaqats* –To detest, make abominable
Sheqets –Detestable thing or idol, an unclean thing, an abomination
שרף — *Sar'af* –Disquieting thoughts, thoughts
Saraf –To burn; serpent, fiery serpent; *Seraf*, one of the *Serafim*; Saraph, descendant of Judah (1 Chr. 4:22)
Seraf –Ruler of Fire; one of the *Serafim*
ששן — *Sasown* –Gladness, joy, exultation, rejoicing
Sheshan –Sheshan, descendant of Judah through Jerahmeel
שתם — *Shatham* –To open (dubious meaning)
תץ — *Tatz* –Third two letters of the 42-letter name of God (assoc. w/*Binah*)
תקיף — *Taqqiyf* –Mighty
תקף — *Taqaf* –To prevail, overcome, overpower
Teqef –To grow strong, be hardened (Aramaic)
Teqof –Strength, might (Aramaic)
Toqef –Authority, power, strength, energy
תרן — *Toren* –Beacon, mast, flagpole (Ezek. 27:5, Isa. 30:17, 33:23)
תשם — *Tesham* –Be desolate (Gen. 47:19)

1301 תרשתא — *Tirshatha'* –Tirshatha, title of the governor of Judea under Persian rule (Ezra 2:63; Neh. 7:65, 70; 8:9; 10:2)
–Prime number

1302 שבתם — *Shavtem* –You are turned back, away (Num. 14:43)
תבץ — *Tebetz* –Thebez, place in the district of Neapolis

1303 תגרן — *Tageran* –Haggler
–Prime number

[1057] Ashan (420, 1070).

1304	בקברתם	*Biqvuratam* –In their burying-place (Gen. 47:30)
	בקרבתם	*Beqarvatam* –When they drew near (Lev. 16:1)
1305	בגשתם	*Vegishtam* –When they approach (Ex. 28:43)
1306	וערלתם	*ve-'arletem* –And you shall close (Lev. 19:23)
	וקשתך	*ve-Qashteka* –And your bow (Gen. 27:3)
	ותשם	*ve-Tasem* –And she put, laid (Ex. 2:3)
	עקלתון	*'aqallathown* –Crooked
	שגגתם	*Shiggatam* –Their error (Num. 15:25)
	שושן	*Shuwshan* –Lily; Shushan, capital of Elam inhabited by the Babylonians – later a royal residence and capital of the Persian Empire
	שקוץ	*Shiqquwts* –Detestable thing or idol, abominable thing, abomination, idol
1307	אשתרות	*Ashtaroth* –Archdemon corr. to *Hesed* (Mathers and Waite) or to *Giburah* (A.C.); Goetic demon #29
	ברכת כהנים	*Birkat Kohaniym* –"The Priest's blessing" (recited as part of morning liturgy in the Temple and later in daily prayers – consists of Num. 6:24-26)
	וקראתם	*ve-Qera'tem* –And you shall proclaim (Lev. 23:21)
	–Prime number	
1308	בתרון	*Bithrown* –Bithron, gorge in the Aravah east of the Jordan River
	הבאשתם	*Hiv'ashtem* –You made abhorred (Ex. 5:21)
	ושבתם	*ve-Shavtem* –And you shall return (Ex. 25:10)
	תרבון	*Tirbuwn* –May increase (Deut. 6:3)
1309	תבואתך	*Tevuw'atak* –Of your produce, increase (Deut. 14:28)
1310	ובקרבתם	*ve-Veqarvatam* –And when they came near (Ex. 40:32)
	חשבתם	*Chashavtem* –You meant (Gen. 50:20)
	יתרן	*Yithran* –Ithran, descendant of Seir; son of Zophah of Asher
	כפתרים	*Kaftoriym* –Caphtorim, the people of Caphtor (Gen. 10:14; 1 Chr. 1:12)
	שתים	*Shethiym* –Two
	תרין	*Tereyn* –Two (Aramaic)
	תשים	*Tasiym* –You bring (Deut. 22:8); shall set (Gen. 6:16)
1311	תרגבון	*Thergebon* –Lord of Triplicity by Day for Libra
1312	ישבתם	*Yeshavtem* –You dwelt, abode (Lev. 18:3)
	תדברון	*Tedabruwn* –Shall you speak (Gen. 32:20)
	תשיבם	*Teshiyvem* –You shall bring them back (Deut. 22:1)
1313	והקרבתם	*ve-Hiqravtem* –And you shall bring present (Lev. 23:8)

והשבתם *ve-Hishbatem* –And will you make rest (Ex. 5:5)

1314 והשגתם *ve-Hishagtam* –And when you overtake them (Gen. 44:4)
ושחתם *ve-Shichatem* –And so you will destroy (Num. 32:15)

1315 כפתריהם *Kaftoreyhem* –Their knobs (Ex. 25:36)
שד השדים הלבנה *Shed HaShedim HaLebanah* –Intelligence of the Intelligences of the Moon (a literal Hebrew translation)

1316 אבגיתץ *Abgitatz* –First six letters of the 42-letter name of God (assoc. w/Sunday)
ארן הקדוש *Aron HaQodesh*–Holy Ark (of the covenant)
ויתרן *ve-Yitran* –And Ithran (Gen. 36:26; 1 Chr. 1:41; 7:37)
ויתשם *ve-Yitshem* –And he rooted/exiled them out (Deut. 29:27)
ושתים *ve-Shetayim* –And two (Num. 45:6)
ve-Sheteym –And two (Ex. 24:4)
יוחנן פול וסשני *Yown Puwl Vesshani* –John Paul II, pope currently at the writing of this book
יתרון *Yithrown* –Advantage, profit, excellency
לישועתכ *Lishuawtich* –For your salvation
קסר נרון *Kesar Neron* –Nero Caeser
נשימירון *Nashimiron* –Malignant Women, *Qlippoth* of Pisces

1317 בית הרנ *Beyth HaRan* –Beth Haran, another name for Beth Aram, town of the tribe of Gad, noted for its hot springs
וראיתן *ve-R'iyten* –And you shall see (Ex. 1:16)
ותיראן *ve-Tiyre'an* –But they feared (Ex. 1:17)
תיראון *Tiyr'uwn* –You will fear (Ex. 9:30); be afraid (Deut. 1:29)

1318 וישבתם *ve-Yeshavtem* –And you shall dwell (Lev. 25:18)
תחשים *Techashiym* –Seals (animal) (Ex. 25:5)
תחתיך *Tachteyak* –Under you (Deut. 28:23)
תריבון *Teriyvuwn* –Do you quarrel (Ex. 17:2)

1319 והשחתם –Prime number *ve-Hishchatem* –And shall deal corruptly (Deut. 4:25)

1320 משכנתיך *Mishkenoteyak* –Your dwellings (Num. 24:5)
ערלתכם *'arlatkem* –Your foreskin (Gen. 17:11)
קריתים *Qiryathayim* –Kiriathaim, Moabite city on the east of the Jordan (Gen. 14:5 –see also Kartan)[1058]
שמעתיך *Shem'otiyak* –I have heard you (Gen. 17:20)

1321 הודעני נא את־דרכך *Howdi'eniy Na' 'Eth-Derakeka* "Pray let me know Your

[1058] Kartan (750, 1400).

ways" (Ex. 33:13)

ותהרין *ve-Tahareyn* –Became pregnant (Gen. 19:36)
–Prime number

1322 ארון הקדוש *Arown HaQodesh* –The Ark of the Covenant, holy ark
שבתכם *Shabatkem* –Your Sabbath (Lev. 23:32)

1323 התושבים *HaToshaviym* –The strangers (Lev. 25:45)
התחשים *HaTechashiym* –The seals (Ex. 39:34)

1324 בשבתכם *Beshivtekem* –When you dwell (Lev. 26:35)
ותושבים *ve-Toshaviym* –And settlers (Lev. 25:23)

1325 התישים *HaTiyashiym* –The he-goats (Gen. 30:35)

1326 ותישים *ve-Teyashiym* –And he-goats (Gen. 32:15)

1327 את־שם יהוה *'Eth-Shem* YHVH –"The Name of the Lord" (Ps. 135:1)
–Prime number

1328 ושכבתם *ve-Shekavtem* –And you shall lie down (Lev. 26:6)

1329 מלאך המשחית *Malakh HaMashith* –"Angel of Destruction"
מעשה שדים *Ma'asheh Shedim* –"Demoniacal works"

1330 בית בעל מעון *Beyth Ba'al Me'own* –Baal's dwelling place; Beth Baal Meon, Amorite city on the north border of Moab (this name only used in Josh. 13:17)
לששן *Lishshan* –Tongue, language (Aramaic)

1331 והנסתרים *ve-Hanistariym* –And those that are hidden (Deut. 7:20)
לקראתם *Liqra'tam* –To meet them (Gen. 18:2)
עלמן דבלתימה *'Almon Diblathayemah* –Almon Diblathaim, site between Dibon Gad and the mountains of Abarim where the Israelites camped during their wandering in the wilderness
תאריכן *Ta'ariykun* –You shall prolong (Deut. 4:26)

1332 בית חורונ *Beyth Chowrown* –Beth Horon, twin town located between Ephraim and Benjamin, modern Beit 'Ur et Tahta and Beit 'Ur el Foka

1333

1334 ויהי יהוה את יוסף *Vahe* YHVH *Eth Yosief*–"YHVH was with Joseph" (Gen. 39:2, 21)

1335 תהלתך *Tehilatka* –Your glory, your praise (Deut. 10:21)
–The number of days of a happy man (Dan. 12:11)

1336 ולתתך *ve-Letiteka* –And to make you, give you (Deut. 26:19)

1337 אחת רוח אלהים חיים — *Achath Ruach Elohim Chayyim* –"One of the Spirit of the Living God"
עולם הקליפות — *Olam HaQlippoth* –The World of Shells or Demons

1338 שלחתם — *Shelachtem* –You sent (Gen. 45:8)

1339

1340 והארץ אזכר — *Viha'aretz Ezkor* –"And I will remember the land" (Lev. 26:42)
פתרנים — *Pitroniym* –Interpretations (Gen. 40:8)
שמתם — *Shemotam* –Their names (Gen. 25:16)
תשלים — *Tashliym* –Will make peace (Deut. 20:12)

1341

1342 אלהי אברהם אלהי יצחק ואלהי יעקב — *Elohi Abraham Elohi Itzchaq ve-Elohi Yaaqob* –"The God of Abraham, the God of Isaac, and the God of Jacob" (Ex. 3:6)
בשמתם — *Bishmotam* –By their names (Gen. 25:13)

1343 והלבשתם — *ve-Hilbashtam* –And you shall put upon them, and you shall clothe them (Ex. 29:8)

1344 ותלחץ — *VaTilachetz* –And she thrust herself (Num. 22:25)
VaTilechatz –And crushed (Num. 22:25)
תשלחום — *Teshalchuwm* –You shall put them (Num. 5:3)

1345 מהרתן — *Miharten* –So soon (Ex. 2:18)
תשעה־עשר — *Tishah-Asar* –Nineteen

1346 וספרתם — *ve-Sefartem* –And you shall count (Lev. 23:15)
ושמתם — *ve-Samtam* –Then make them (Gen. 47:6)
ve-Samtem –And you shall put (Ex. 3:22)
ותשמם — *ve-Tesimem* –And put them (Gen. 31:34)
שמותם — *Shemotam* –Their names (Ex. 28:12)
שמשון — *Shimshown* –Samson, the 12th Judge of Israel

1347 ארוממך יהוה כי דליתני — *'aruwmamek* YHVH *Kiy Deliyteniy* –"I will exalt You, God, for You have lifted me up" (Ps. 30:2)
ותאמרן — *ve-To'maran* –And they said (Ex. 1:19)
תאמרון — *To'meruwn* –You shall say (Gen. 32:5)

1348 אדון אולם — *Adon Awlum* –Lord of the World
בן־אלהים — *Ben-Elohim* –"Son of God"
משחתם — *Mashchatam* –Their anointing, their corruption (Lev. 22:25; 40:15)

1349 גת־רמון — *Gath-Rimmown* –Gath Rimmon, city of the tribe of Dan; town of the tribe of Manasseh

מורשת גת — *Mowresheth Gath* –Moresheth-Gath, hometown of Micah

1350 במושבתם — *Bemoshvotam* –In their dwellings (Ex. 10:23)
נתץ — *Nathats* –To pull down, break down, cast down, throw down, beat down, destroy, overthrow, break out (of teeth)
ערסתכם — *'arisotekem* –Of your dough (Num. 15:20)
פתרסים — *Patrusiym* –Pathrusim, descendant of Mizraim; possibly the inhabitants of Pathros (Gen. 10:14)
שכלתם — *Shikaltem* –You have bereaved (Gen. 42:36)

1351 לקראתכם — *Liqra'tkem* –Against you (Deut. 1:44)
סנוי סנסנוי סמנגלוף — *Senoy, Sansenoy, Semangelof* –Three angels invoked against Lilith
שכל הרצון — *Sekhel HaRatzon* –Intelligence of Will (20th Path)
שנאתם — *Sene'tem* –You have hated (Gen. 26:27)

1352 רחצתי את־רגלי — *Rachatztiy Eth-Ragelay* –"I had bathed my feet" (Song 5:3)

1353

1354 ושמחתם — *ve-Semachtem* –And you will rejoice (Lev. 23:40)

1355

1356

1357 ונשאתם — *ve-Nesha'tem* –And bring (Gen. 45:19)

1358 משחתים — *Mashchitiym* –Will destroy (Gen. 19:13)
משחיתם — *Mashchiytam* –I will destroy them (Gen. 6:13)

1359 אבנ מאסו הבונימ היתה לראש פנה — *Eben Maasu HaBonim HaYetah Lero'as Pinah* –"The stone that the builders rejected has become the chief cornerstone" (Ps. 118:22)
שמחת תורה — *Simchat Torah* –"Rejoicing of the Torah"; holiday celebrating the giving of the Torah after the Golden Calf incident

1360 נתתיך — *Netatiyka* –Have I made you, permitted you (Gen. 17:5)
ערסתיכם — *'arisoteykem* –Your dough (Num. 15:21)
שנתים — *Shenatayim* –Two years (Gen. 11:10)

1361 תקימ את משכנ — *Takim Eth Mishkon* –"Set up the Tabernacle of the Tent of Meeting" (Ex. 40:2)

–Prime number

1362

1363		
1364	אתון נורא	*Attun Nura* –"Fiery furnace" (Dan. 3:6, 11, 15, 17, 21, 23, 26)
	וכל־העמ ראימ את־הקולת	*VeKal-Ha'am Ro'iym 'Eth-HaQoliyth* –"All the people witnessed the thunder (or voices)" (Ex. 20:15)
	משתחוים	*Mishtachaviym* –Were bowing down (Gen. 37:9)
1365		
1366	ונתתיך	*ve-Netatiyka* –And I will make of you (Gen. 17:6)
	צלם אלהים	*Tzelem 'Elohim* –"Image of God"
1367	–Prime number	
1368	שמחתכם	*Simchatkem* –Your gladness (Num. 10:10)
1369		
1370	ארתחשסתא	*'Artachshast'* –Artaxerxes, king of Persia, Artaxerxes I Longimanus (spelling used in Ezra 7:1, 7, 11, 12, 21; 8:1; Neh. 2:1; 5:14; 13:6)
	משכיתם	*Maskiytam* –Their figured (stones) (Num. 33:52)
	עשתרת	*Ashtoreth* –Ashtoreth, a Phoenician goddess
	עת קצין	*'Eth Qatziyn* –Eth Kazin, town on the eastern border of Zebulun
	שלמתם	*Shilamtem* –Have you rewarded (Gen. 44:4)
	שמלתם	*Simlotam* –Their clothes, garments (Gen. 44:13)
1371	והשכמתם	*ve-Hishkamtem* –And you may rise up early (Gen. 19:2)
1372	בעשתרת	*Bashterot* –In Ashteroth
	בשמלתם	*Besimlotam* –In their clothes (Ex. 12:34)
	למשבתם	*Lemoshvotam* –According to their habitations (Gen. 36:43)
	משבתיכם	*Meshvoteykem* –Your habitations (Ex. 35:3)
1373	מלאכתו אשר עשה	*Melakhtu asher asah* –"His work which He had made" (Gen. 2:2)
	רגם מלך	*Regem Melek* –Regem-Melech, messenger sent out by some Jews (Zech. 7:2)[1059]
	–Prime number	
1374	חרוץ נבחר	*Cheruwtz Nevachar* –"Choice gold" (Prov. 8:10)
1375		
1376	ועשתרת	*ve-'oshterot* –And the flocks
	ערותן	*'ervatan* –Their nakedness (Lev. 18:9)

1059 Some scholars believe this is not a proper name but read "...Sherezer, the friend of the king."

עשתרות *'Ashtarowth* –Astaroth, the plural version of Ashtoreth (q.v.); city in the northern Transjordan region of Israel that served as one of the Cities of Refuge
שועתם *Shav'atam* –Their cry (for help) (Ex. 2:23)

1377

1378 מושבתיכם *Moshvoteykem* –Your habitations (Ex. 12:20)
–The sum of the numbers 1 through 52

1379 קרעשטן *Qerashaten* –7th-12th letters of the 42-letter name of God (assoc. w/Monday)

1380 ברכת המזון *Birkat HaMazon* –"The blessing over food" (prayer recited after eating a meal containing bread)
משמתם *Meshmotam* –From their names (Ex. 28:10)
עשיתם *'asiytem* –So doing (Gen. 44:5)
'asiytim –I have made them (Gen. 6:7)
עשתרתי *'Ashterathiy* –Asterathite(s)
שפתם *Sefatam* –Their language (Gen. 11:7)
תשעים *Tishim* –Ninety

1381 –Prime number

1382 ועשתרות *ve-'oshterut* –And the flocks
שבעתים *Shibawthayim* –Sevenfold, seven times

1383 – 1385

1386 ארון העדת *Aron HaEdeth* –Ark of the Testimony
הנזוף לפתח *HaNozuf Lapetach* –"The hated one at the door"
ועשיתם *ve-'asiytem* –And do them (Ex. 4:21; Lev. 19:37)
ותשעים *ve-Tish'iym* –And ninety (Gen. 5:17)
פתרון *Pithrown* –Interpretation

1387

1388 לישועתכ קויתי יהוה *Liyshuw'ateka Qiviytiy* YHVH –"For Your salvation do I hope, God" (Gen. 49:18)
חץ לילית *Chotz Lilith* –Out Lilith!

1389

1390 פשתים *Pishtiym* –Linen (Lev. 13:47)
צרתן *Tzarethan* –Zarthan, village near Beth-Shean in the territory of Manasseh (see also Zereda)[1060]
שפתים *Sefatayim* –Lips (Ex. 6:12)
תקצף *Tiqtzof* –Will you be angry (Num. 16:22)

[1060] Zereda (299; 700).

1391

1392 בפשתים — *Vafishtiym* –Of linen (Lev. 13:52)
בשפתים — *Visfatayim* –With lips (Lev. 5:4)

1393

1394 חוץ לילית — *Chotz Lilith* –Out Lilith!

1395 הפשתים — *HaPishtiym* –The linen, the flax (Lev. 13:59)
ושפטתם — *ve-Sefattem* –And you will judge (Deut. 1:16)
מן המים — *Min HaMayim* –"From the waters" (Ex. 2:10)

1396 ופשתים — *ve-Pishtiym* –And linen (Deut. 22:11)
וקצרתם — *ve-Qetzretem* –And you harvest (Lev. 23:10)
כושן רשעתים — *Kuwshan Rish'athayim* –Cushan-Rishathaim, king of Mesopotamia that God chose to punish Israel (Judg. 3:8, 10)

1397

1398

1399 –Prime number

1400 לעשתם — *La'astam* –To do them (Deut. 5:1)
קרתן — *Qartan* –Kartan, city of Naphtali given to the Gershonite Levites
שלמתיכם — *Salmoteykem* –Your clothes (Deut. 29:4)
שרץ — *Sharatz* –To bring forth abundantly
Sheretz –Creeping thing, moving creature
שרשרת — *Sharoshhrot* –Chains
שתן — *Shathan* –To urinate

1401

1402 אריך אפים — *Arik Apim* –Long of Face; a title of *Keter*

1403

1404 בשבעתיכם — *Beshavu'oteykam* –In your weeks (Num. 28:26)
הכחות השכלים — *HaKachoth HaSekhelim* –Intellectual virtues
קדשתם — *Qidashtem* –You sanctified (Deut. 32:51)
תרדף — *Tirdof* –You shall follow, pursue (Deut. 16:20)

1405

1406 ושננתם — *ve-Shinanetam* –And you shall teach (Deut. 6:7)
ותתם — *ve-Titom* –And was ended (Gen. 47:18)
כפתרון — *Kefitron* –According to the interpretation (Gen. 40:5)
לעשותם — *La'asotam* –And do them (Deut. 7:11)

1407	אשתון	*'Eshtown* –Eshton, descendant of Judah
	ותקראן	*ve-Tiqre'at* –And they called (Num. 25:2)
1408	ובקשתם	*ve-Viqashtem* –And you will seek (Num. 16:10)
	שבתון	*Shabaton* –Solemn rest (Ex. 16:23)
	תחתם	*Tachtam* –In their stead (Deut. 2:12)
	תקרבון	*Taqrivuwn* –You shall bring (Deut. 1:17)
	תשובן	*Teshuwvun* –You will turn away (Deut. 32:15)
1409	ותגשן –Prime number	*ve-Tigashan* –And they came near (Gen. 33:6)
1410	את שטן	*Eth Shatan* –"The essence of Satan"
	וקדשתם	*ve-Qidashtem* –And you shall hallow (Deut. 25:10
	ללשנתם	*Lileshonotam* –According to their tongues (Gen. 10:20)
	קרעשמן	*Qerashamen* –7th-12th letters of the 42-letter name of God, assoc. w/*Hesed* (A.C.)
	שמעתם	*Shema'tem* –You would hear, hearken (Gen. 42:22)
	שתין	*Shittiyn* –Sixty, threescore (Aramaic)
	תירשך	*Tiyroshka* –Your wine
1411	אבן חן	*Eben Chen* –Precious stone
1412	בית שן	*Beyth Shan* –Beth-Shan, southern border town of the region of Galilee, largest of the ten cities of the Decapolis (Josh. 17:11; 1 Chr. 7:29) (see also בית שאן)[1061]
	ונושנתם	*ve-Noshantem* –And you shall have been long (Deut. 4:25)
	פכרת צביים	*Pokereth Tzebayiym* –Pochereth-Zebaim, one whose children returned
1413	בית שאן	*Beyth She'an* –Beth-Shean, southern border town of the region of Galilee, largest of the ten cities of the Decapolis (Josh. 17:11; 1 Chr. 7:29)
1414	ותקרבון	*ve-Tiqrevuwn* –And you came near (Deut. 1:22)
1415		
1416	ותירשך	*ve-Tiyroshka* –And your wine
1417		
1418	אתה גבור לעולם אדני	*Ateh Gibor le-Olam Adonai* –"Thou art mighty forever, O Lord"; usually abbreviated **אגלא** (Agla) and used as a name of God
	ממושבתיכם	*Mimoshvoteykem* –Out of your dwellings (Lev. 23:17)

[1061] בית שאן (763, 1413).

תחתים *Tachtiyim* –Lower (Gen. 6:16)

1419

1420 ויתדתם *ve-Yetedotam* –And their pins (Num. 3:37)
לעשתכם *La'astkem* –That you might do (Deut. 4:17)
עין שמש *'Eyn Shemesh* –En Shemesh, well and town east of Bethany on the road between Jerusalem and Jericho
פלשתים *Pelishtiym* –Philistines (Gen. 10:14)

1421 שעיר אנפין *Seir Anpin* –The Bearded Countenance; a title of *Tiferet*

1422 וישרתוך *vi-Yeshartuwka* –And minister unto you (Num. 18:2)

1423 אות ברית קדש *'oth Beriyth Qadosh* –"Holy sign of the covenant"
תחתיהם *Tachteyhem* –Was under them (Num. 16:31)
–Prime number

1424 אשת זנונים *Isheth Zenunim* –Woman of Whoredom; Demon of Prostitution; archdemon corr. to *Chokmah* (A.C.)
קדוש קדשים *Qadosh Qadeshim* –Holy of Holies

1425

1426 והחיות רצוא ושוב כמראה הבזק *VeHachayot Ratzoa' Va-Shov Kemar'ah Habazaq* –"Dashing to and fro [among] the creatures was something that looked like flares" (Meaning of Heb. uncertain - Ezek. 1:14)

1427 אם טבקשנה ככסף *'as Tevuqshenah Kekasap* –"If you seek her as silver" (Prov. 2:4)
עופרת נתנו עזבוניכ *Owfereth Nathanu 'azabunik* –"Lead they gave for your wares" (Ezek. 27:12)
–Prime number

1428 והתאויתם *ve-Hita'iytem* –And shall mark out (Num. 34:10)
וכתבתם *ve-Ketavtam* –And you shall write (Deut. 6:9)
משפחתם *Mishpechotam* –Their families

1429 –Prime number

1430 לרשתך *le-Rishteka* –That you may inherit
קדש קדשים הוא *Qodesh Qadashim Hua* –"It is Holy, most Holy" (Ex. 30:10; Lev. 6:10, 18, 22; 7:1, 6; 10:12, 17; 14:13; 24:9)
שכרתיך *Sekartiyka* –I hired you

1431 אש מצרף *Esh Metzaref* –Purifying Fire, title of a 17th-century cabalistic alchemical text; "Smelter's fire" (Mal.

		3:2)
	תכונת הקדמות	*Tekunath HaQadmuth* –Treasure, or dwelling place of the primordial; the preparation of principles; a phrase used to describe the Eighth Path
1432	בנפשתם	*Benafostam* –At the cost of ther own lives (Num. 17:3)
	ונושעתם	*ve-Nosha'tam* –And you shall be saved (Num. 10:9)
1433	–Prime number	
1434	מצפון תפתח הרעה	*Mitzfon tefetach HaRa'ah* –"Evil begins from the north" (Jer. 1:14)
	שיחרירון	*Shichiriron* –The Black Ones; *Qlippoth* of Cancer
1435	המשפתים	*HaMishpetayim* –The sheepfolds (Gen. 49:14)
1436	שר שלום	*Sar Shalom* –"Prince of Peace" (Is. 9:5)
1437	חשן משפט	*Chashen Mishpat* –"Breastplate of decision" (Ex. 28:15)
1438	ותחי רוח יעקב אביהם	*Vatchi Ruach Yaaqob 'avhem* –"the spirit of their father Jacob revived" (Gen. 45:27)
1439	חצר התיכון	*Chatzar Hatikown* –Hazar Hatticon, village on the border of Havran
	–Prime number	
1440	תולדתם	*Toldotam* –Their generations (Num. 1:20)
1441	אליתרפ	*Eliychoref* –"God of winter (harvest-time)" – a scribe in Solomon's court
1442		
1443	חלקת הצרים	*Chelqath Hatztzurim* –Helkath-Hazzurim, area of smooth ground near the pool of Gibeon (2 Sam. 2:16)
	עין גנים	*'Eyn Ganniym* –En Gannim, town of lowland Judah; border town of the tribe of Issachar (see also Anem)[1062]
1444	בראדך בלאדן	*Bero'dak Bal'adan* –Berodach-Baladan, form of Merodach-Baladan, son of Baladan, king of Babylon (2 Kings 20:12)
1445		
1446		

[1062] Anem (160, 720).

1447 –Prime number

1448

1449 עץ הדעת *Etz HaDaath* –Tree of Knowledge

1450 תשמדון *Tishameduwn* –Shall be destroyed (Deut. 4:26)

1451 –Prime number

1452

1453 –Prime number

1454 אני יהוה אלהי אברהם אביך *'Ani* YHVH *'Elohey 'Avraham 'Aviyka* –"I am the Lord, the God of your father Abraham" (Gen. 28:13)

1455 אדם קדמון *Adam Qadmon* –The archetypal man

1456 ונתתם *ve-Netatem* –That you shall give (Gen. 47:24)
ve-Nitatem –And you shall be delivered, handed over (Lev. 26:25)
ושמרתיך *ve-Shemartiyka* –And I will keep you
נשתון *Nishtevan* –Letter (also Aramaic)
פרעתון *Pir'athown* –Pirathon, town where Abdon the judge was buried

1457

1458 בית דבלתים *Beyth Diblathayim* –Beth Diblathaim, town in Moab, possibly the same as Almon Diblathaim
למשפחתם *Lemishfehchotam* –By their families (Gen. 10:5)
נחשתן *Nehushtan* –Nehushtan, name given to the fiery serpent made by Moses[1063]

1459 –Prime number

1460 בן־בנן *Ben-Chanan* –Son of Hanan
כתולדתם *Ketoldotam* –According to their birth (Ex. 28:10)
משכרתך *Maskureteka* –Your wages
נפשתיכם *Nafshoteykem* –Of your persons (souls) (Ex. 16:16)
נתתים *Netatiym* –I have given them (Num. 18:8)

1461 צלם אלקים *Tzelem Aleqiym* –"Image of God"

1462 במשענתם *Bimishanotam* –With their staves (Num. 21:18)

1463

[1063] This pole was set on a pole so that persons bitten by snakes could look at it and live – it was destroyed during the later reforms of Hezekiah because it had become an object of worship.

1464	בתבניתם	*Betavniytam* –After their pattern (Ex. 25:40)
	למשפחותם	*Lemishpechotam* –By their families (Num. 4:38)
	לתלדתם	*Letoldotam* –According to their generations (Ex. 6:16)
1465	ובמשארותיך	*ve-Bemisha'aruwteyaka* –Your kneading bowls (Ex. 7:28)
	תשימון	*Tesiymuwn* –You shall lay (put) (Ex. 22:24)
	תשלכון	*Tashlikuwn* –You will cast (throw) (Ex. 22:30)
1466	תערצון	*Ta'artzuwn* –Be terrified (Deut. 1:29)
1467–1469		
1470	לתולדתם	*Letoldotam* –According to their generations (Gen. 10:32)
1471	–Prime number	
1472	בכתנתם	*be-Kutanotam* –In their tunics
1473	למשפחתיהם	*Lemishpechoteyhem* –After their families (Gen. 8:19)
1474	וממשפחתם	*ve-Mimishpachtam* –And of the families
1475		
1476	תעשון	*Ta'asuwn* –You will do (Num. 32:23); shall do (Ex. 4:15)
1477	גן עדן	*Gan Eden* –"Garden of Eden"
1478	תועבתם	*To'avotam* –Their abominations (Deut. 20:18)
1479	אמתחתיכם	*'amtechoteykem* –Your sacks (Gen. 43:12)
1480	משמרתך	*Mishmarteka* –Your duty
	עשיתן	*'asiyten* –Have you done (Ex. 1:18)
	תקפץ	*Tiqfotz* –You shall shut (Deut. 15:7)
1481	באמתחתיכם	*Be'amtechoteykem* –In your sacks (Gen. 43:23)
	לפקערציאץ	*Lafcursiax* –Guardian of the 22nd Tunnel of Set
	–Prime number	
1482	בית פצץ	*Beyth Patztzetz* –Beth Pazzez, town of the tribe Issachar, modern Kerm el-Had-datheh
	מראדך בלאדן	*Mero'dak Bal'adan* –Merodach-Baladan, king of Babylon in the days of Hezekiah (this spelling used only in Jer. 50:2 – see also Berodach-baladan)[1064]
	קול־יהוה שבר ארזים	*Qol*-YHVH *Shover 'Araziym* –"The voice of the Lord

[1064] Berodach-Baladan (314, 1444).

breaks cedars" (Ps. 29:5)

1483 אבן מאסו הבונים *Eben Maasu HaBonim* –"The stone that the builders rejected" (Ps. 118:22)

–Prime number

1484 אגרת בת מחלת *Agrath bath Mahalath* –Agrath, a queen of demons; one of the three wives of Samael

דן יען *Dan Ya'an* –Dan Jaan, place or city in northern Palestine between Gilead and Zidon, possibly Dan

1485

1486 מתנוצץ *Mit-Notzetz* –Resplendent

תלונתם *Taluwnotam* –Their murmurings

1487 –Prime number

1488 למשפחתיכם *Lemishpachoteykem* –According to your families (Ex. 12:21)

1489 היכל קדוש קדשים *Hekel Qadesh Qadeshim* –Palace of the Holy of Holies; Heavenly Mansion corr. to Supernals

–Prime number

1490 לנפשתיכם *le-Napeshoteykem* –Of your lives, to yourselves

1491

1492

1493 עין עגלים *'Eyn 'Eglayim* –En Eglaim, place on the northwest coast of the Dead Sea

–Prime number

1494

1495 –The sum of all the letters of the Hebrew alphabet

1496 – 1498

1499 והתנחלתם *ve-Hichnachaltem* –And you shall inherit them (Lev. 25:46)

–Prime number

1500 תשתרר *Tistarar* –You shall rule

תתן *Titen* –You will put, give

–The number of keys mentioned in the *Sefer HaZohar*

1501 ויאמר הראני נא את־כבדך *VaYi'amar Hare'niy Na' 'Eth-Kevodeka* –"He said, 'Oh, let me behold Your presence!'" (Ex. 33:18)

1502–1505

1506	ותרץ	*ve-Taratz* –And ran (Gen. 24:20) *ve-Tiretz* –And shall be paid, enjoy, forgiven (Lev. 26:43)
	ותתן	*ve-Titen* –And she gave (Gen. 3:6; 30:4)
	לא תעשה־לך פסל	*Lo tha'aseh-leka pesel* –"Thou shalt not make unto thee any graven image" (Ex. 20:4)
1507		
1508	אראתרון	*Arathron* –Olympic Planetary Spirit of Saturn
	ושברתם	*ve-Shibartem* –And dash in pieces
	ותרבץ	*ve-Tirbatz* –And she lay down (Num. 22:27)
1509		
1510	תלנתיכם	*Telunoteykam* –Your murmurings
	ראשיתמ –Prime number	*Re'ashiytam* –The first part of them
1512	ותורתך	*ve-Toratka* –And your instructions, and your laws (Deut. 33:10)
1513		
1514	והנגלת לנו ולבנינו עד עולם	*Ve-Haneglot la-nu vuwlvanavinu ad olam* –"...with overt acts, it is for us and our children ever..." (Deut. 29:28)
	רהב הם שבת	*Rahab Hem Shebeth* –Rahab Hem Shebeth, "Rahab sits idle," a name given by the prophet Isaiah to Egypt, comparing Egypt to Rahab the dragon, a mythological sea monster of chaos (Is. 30:7)
1515		
1516	וירשתם	*vi-Yerishtam* –And you do succeed them, and you have driven them out *ve-Yerishtem* –And possess
	ותשקין	*ve-Tashqeyna* –And they made to drink (Gen. 19:33)
	תשמעון	*Tishemuwn* –You shall hear (Deut. 1:17); you hearken (Deut. 7:12, 8:20)
1517	והורשתם	*ve-Horashitem* –And you shall drive them out
1518		
1519	תגרירון	*Tageriron* –The Hagglers, *Qlippoth* of *Tiferet*
	אברהמ יצחק יעקב שבטי ישרונ	*Abraham Yitzak Ya'aqov Shavoti Yeshrown* –"Abraham, Isaac, Jacob, the tribes of the righteous people" – a name of God of 22 letters

1520 מתנתיכמ *Matnoteykam* –That is given by you (Num. 18:29)

1521

1522 לא־תענה ברעב עד שקר *Lo-tha'aneh be-re'aka edh shaqer* –"Thou shalt not bear false witness against thy neighbor" (Ex. 20:13)

1523 –Prime number

1524

1525 שם המפרש *Shem HaMeforash* –Name of Extension; the 72-fold name of God

1526 מתנותיכם *Matnoteykam* –Your gifts

1527

1528 חצצן תמר *Chatzetzon Tamar* –Hazezon Tamar, said to be another name for En-Gedi (Gen. 14:7; 2 Chr. 20:2) – this name may in fact refer to modern Tamar (see also חצצון תמר)[1065]

1529

1530 לשרתם *le-Shartam* –To minister unto them (Num. 16:9)
שנים־עשר *Shenaim-Asar* –Twelve

1531 יום הכפרים *Yom HaKipurim* –"The Day of Many Atonements," Yom HaKippurim, a variation of Yom Kippur
מאשתמ עפרת *Mashatham Ofereth* –"The lead comes whole from the fire" (Jer. 6:29)
–Prime number

1532 יום הכפארים *Yom HaKipariym* –"Day of the atonements," Yom HaKippurim, a variation of Yom Kippur

1533

1534 חצצונ תמר *Chatzetzown Tamar* –Hazezon Tamar, said to be another name for En-Gedi (Gen. 14:7; 2 Chr. 20:2) – this name may in fact refer to modern Tamar (see also חצצן תמר)[1066]

1535 עיר התמרים *'Iyr HaTemariym* –Ir Hatemariym, another name for Jericho (Deut. 34:3; Jdg. 1:16; 3:13; 2 Chr. 28:15)[1067]

[1065] חצצון תמר (884, 1534).
[1066] חצצן תמר (878, 1528).

1536–1542

1543 –Prime number

1544

1545 בארת בני־יעקן *Be'eroth Beney-Ya'aqan* –Beeroth Bene Jaakan, a form of Beeroth, meaning a place on the border of Edom; city of Gibeon assigned to the tribe of Benjamin

1546 ונתצתם *ve-Nitatztem* –And you shall break down (Deut. 12:3)
ושמרתם *ve-Shemartem* –And you shall observe (Ex. 12:17)
על־ספר דברי שלמה *'al-Sefer divrey Solomoh* –"The book of the Annals of Solomon" (1 Kings 11:41)
תמתון *Temuton* –You die (Gen. 3:3, 4; Is. 22:14)

1547

1548

1549 –Prime number

1550

1551

1552 אריך אנפין *Arik Anpin* –The Vast Countenance, a title of *Keter*

1553 –Prime number

1554–1556

1557 ונשארתם *Venisha'artem* –You shall be left (Deut. 4:27)

1558

1559 –Prime number

1560

1561

1562 עין בעין *'Ayin Be'ayin* –"Eye to eye" (Is. 52:8)

1563–1566

1567 –Prime number

1568

[1067] This name is literally translated as "city of palm trees."

1569

1570 תערץ — *Ta'arotz* –You shall be afraid (Deut. 7:21)
תרעץ — *Tir'atz* –Dashes in pieces (Ex. 15:6)

1571 –Prime number

1572–1577

1576 והתחזקתם — *ve-Hitchazaqtam* –And be of good courage (Num. 13:20)
ותקעתם — *ve-Teqa'atam* –And you shall blow (Num. 10:5)

1577 אין־סוף — *Ain-Sof* –Infinity

1578

1579 –Prime number

1580 כי באתי אל הארץ — *Ki vati el HaAretz* –"That I have entered the land" (Deut. 26:3)

1581

1582 במשמרתם — *Bemishmerotam* –Regarding their duties (Num. 8:26)

1583 –Prime number

1584

1585 פדן ארם — *Paddan 'Aram* –Padan-Aram, plain region of Mesopotamia from the Lebanon Mountains to beyond the Euphrates, and from the Taurus Mountains on the north to beyond Damascus on the south (see also פדן)[1068]

1586 ומשמרתם — *ve-Mishmartam* –And their charge (Num. 3:31)

1587

1588 עזרם ומגנם הוא — *Ezram ve-magenawm hu* –"He (God) is their help and shield" (Psalms 115:10-13)

1589

1590 אבן העופרת אל פיה — *'eben HaOfereth Al Peyah* –"Lead stone on its mouth" (Zech. 5:8)
קרית ערים — *Qiryath 'Ariym* –Kirjath-Arim, originally one of the Gibeonites located at the northwestern boundary

---

1068 פדן (134, 784).

of Judah (see also Baalah, Kirjath-Jearim, Kirjath-Baal, and Baale-judah)[1069]

1591 קרן הפוך — *Qeren Happuwk* –Keren-Happuch, third daughter of Job to be born after his restoration to health

1592 צדק ושלום נשקו — *Tzedeq ve-Shalowm Nifgashuw* –"Justice and well-being kiss" (Ps. 85:11)

ראשית הגלגלים — *Rashith HaGilgam* –The Beginning of Revolvings, the Primum Mobile; the Material World assoc. w/*Keter*

1593

1594 זכר ונקבה ברא אתם — *Zakhar u-neqevah bara otham* –"Male and female created He them"

1595

1596 ונשמרתם — *ve-Nishmartem* –And take heed of yourselves (Deut. 2:4)

תתצון — *Titotzuwn* –You shall break down

1597 –Prime number

1598

1599

1600 קרית יערים — *Qiryath Ye'ariym* –Kirjath-Jearim, originally one of the Gibeonites located at the northwestern boundary of Judah (see also Baalah, Kirjath-Arim, Kirjath-baal, and Baale-judah)[1070]

תרתמ — *Taretem* –You have spied out (Num. 14:34)

1601 אדסך — A permutation of יהוה by *Aiq Bekar*[1071]

–Prime number

1602 תשבץ — *Tashbetz* –Chequer work (Ex. 28:4)

1603 עץ החיים — *Etz HaChayim* –Tree of Life

1604

1605

1606 וקשרתם — *ve-Qesharetam* –And you shall bind them (Deut. 6:8)

ve-Qesharetem –And you shall bind (Deut. 11:18)

1607 –Prime number

[1069] Baalah (107), Kirjath-Jearim (1040, 1600), Kirjath-Baal (812), Baale-judah (142).

[1070] Baalah (107), Kirjath-Arim (1030, 1590), Kirjath-Baal (812), Baale-judah (142).

[1071] See Introduction.

1608 תשברון *Teshaberuwn* –You shall dash into pieces

1609 אחשתרן *Achastaran* –Royal steeds

1610 ארתחששתא *'Artachshashta'* or *'Artachshasht'* –Artaxerxes, king of Persia, Artaxerxes I Longimanus; in Ezra 4:7 possibly the pseudo-Smerdis king of Persia, but most likely Artaxerxes I (spelling only used in Ezra 4:7, 8, 11, 23; 6:14)

1611

1612

1613 –Prime number

1614 תחרשון *Tacharshuwn* –Shall hold your peace

1615

1616 תירשון *Tiyrashuwn* –You shall possess

1617–1618

1619 –Prime number

1620

1621 ויצמח יהוה אלהים מן האדמה *Vahyatzmach* YHVH *Elohim men HaAdamah* –"And from the ground the Lord God caused to grow" (Gen. 2:9)

–Prime number

1622–1626

1627 –Prime number

1628–1630

1631 שוה קריתים *Shaveh Qiryathayim* –Shaveh-Kiriathaim, plain near Kirjathaim, the dwelling place of the Emim

–The number of letters in Genesis

1632

1633

1634

1635 שיר השירים *Shir HaShirim* –The Song of Songs

1636

1637 –Prime number

1638–1639

1640 מעשרתיכם *Ma'asroteykam* –Your tithes

1641

1642 ארץ ישראל *'eretz Yisrael* –Land of Israel

1643 מעץ החיים *Maetz HaChayim* –"From the Tree of Life"

1644

1645

1646 תשמרון *Tishmeruwn* –You shall observe, you shall keep (Deut. 6:17)

1647–1649

1650 שלשתכם *Shelashtekam* –You three

1651

1652 דמות כמראה אדם עליו מלמעלה *Demuwth Kemar'eh 'Adam 'Alayuw Milema'elah* – "There was the semblance of a human form" (Ezek. 1:26)

1653–1655

1656 –The year (of Creation) of the Flood

1657 –Prime number

1658 שני המארת הגדלים *Shene HaMeoroth HaGedholim* –"Two great lights"(Gen. 1:16)

1659 אהיה יה יהוה אדני אל אלוה אלהים שדי צבאות *Eheieh Yah* YHVH *Adonai El Eloah Elohim Shaddai Tzabaoth* –The name of God of 33 letters, composed of Names used in the Tanakh

1660

1661 שתי הצוצרת כסף *Shetiy Hatzuwtzerat Kesaf* –"Two trumpets of silver" (Num. 10:2)

1662

1663 –Prime number

1664

1665

1666 ארם נהרים — *'Aram Naharayim* –Aham-Naharaim, location between the Tigris and Euphrates Rivers (Ps. 60:1)

תרומתכם — *Teruwmatekem* –Your gift; contribution, Terumah

1667 –Prime number

1668

1669 –Prime number

1670–1673

1674 נחשתירון — *Necheshthiron* –The Brazen Ones, *Qlippoth* of Scorpio

1675

1676 משרפות מים — *Misrefowth Mayim* –Misrephoth-Maim, location in northern Palestine (Josh. 11:8; 13:6)

1677–1680

1681 אנקתמ פסתמ פספסימ דיונסימ — *Anaqtam Pastam Paspasim Dionsim* –The 22-letter name of God

1682

1683

1684 חירם מלך־צור — *Chiram Malakh-Tzor* –"Hiram, King of Tyre" (2 Sam. 5:11; 1 Kings 5:15; 9:11; 1 Chr. 14:1)

1685

1686 תשרפון — *Tisrefuwn* –You shall burn (Deut. 7:5)

1687–1690

1691 מה־טבו אהליכ יעקב משכנתיכ ישראל — *Mah-tovo 'ahaleyka ya'aqov mishkenoteyka yisrael* –"How fair are your tents, O Jacob, Your dwellings, O Israel!" (Num. 24:5)

1692

1693 –Prime number

1694

1695

1696

1697 –Prime number

1698

1699 –Prime number

1700 קדסך — A permutation of יהוה by *Aiq Bekar*[1072]
תרתן — *Tartan* –Tartan, title of a high Assyrian officer (2 Kings 18:17; Is. 20:1)[1073]
תשרף — *Tisaref*–She shall be burnt; shall be burned
Tisrof–You shall burn

1701

1702 שכל סוד הפעולות הרוחניות — *Sekhel Sod HaPauloth HaRuachnioth* – Intelligence of All the Activities of the Spiritual Beings or of the Secrets or Mysteries of All Spiritual Activities (19th path)

1703

1704 פתח משכן אהל מועד — *Pethach Mishkon 'ahul Muwad* –"Open the door to the Tabernacle of the Tent of Meeting" (Ex. 40:6)

1705

1706 ותשרף — *ve-Tisaref*–And let her be burnt (Gen. 38:24)
ותתעלף — *ve-Tita'laf*–And wrapped herself (Gen. 38:14)
תשוקתך — *Teshuwqatek* –Your desire

1707–1709

1710 שתיתם — *Shetiytem* –You have drunk

1711–1715

1716 ושתיתם — *ve-Shetiytem* –And you may drink

1717

1718

1719

1720 ועופרת בתוכ כור סיגימ כסף היו — *Ve-Ofereth Betuwk Kuwr Siygim HaYa* –"And lead in the middle of the furnace, they are the dross of silver" (Ezek. 22:18)

1072 See Introduction.

1073 There is evidence that the office was second only to the king.

נתן־מלך *Nethan-Melek* –Nathan-Melech, officer under Josiah (2 Kings 23:11)

1721 –Prime number

1722

1723 תלה ארץ על בלימה *Taleh 'aretz 'el Beliymah* –"He suspends the earth on nothingness" (Job 26:7)

–Prime number

1724

1725

1726 עין רמון *'Eyn Rimmown* –En Rimmon, city of Judah, south of Jerusalem, where the tribe of Judah settled on their return from the Exile (Neh. 11:29)

תכרתון *Tikerotuwn* –You shall cut down

1727–1732

1733 –Prime number

1734 בשבתתיכם *ve-Shabatitykem* –In your Sabbaths (Lev. 26:35)

כל דברים בכל דברים *Kol-Dabarim Be-Kol-Dabarim* –All Things in All Things

1735 והשתחויתם *ve-Hishtachaviytem* –And you worshipped them (Ex. 24:1)

1736–1740

1741 גדול אדונינוורב כח לתבונתו אינ מספר *Geduwl Adonainunuwve-rav Koah Lethvanthuw Ain Mesafer* –"Great is our Lord and abundant in strength; His understanding is infinite" (Ps. 147:5)

ככר עפרת נשאת *Kikkar Opereth Na-Shayth* –"A lead cover was lifted up" (Zech. 5:7)

–Prime number

1742 עץ הדעת טוב ורע *Etz HaDaath Tov va-Ra* –"Tree of the Knowledge of Good and Evil"

1743 האור ובינ החשב *HaOhr Vuvayn HaChushek* –"the light and divided the darkness" (Gen. 1:4)

טבל וילון שמים *Tebel Vilon Shamaim* –Veil of the Firmament; the First Heaven (corr. to *Yesod* and *Malkut*)

1744

1745

1746 עתיך יומין
שושנים עדות

Atik Yomin –"The Ancient of Days," a title of *Keter*
Shuwshanniym 'Eduwth –"Lilies of the testimony," title of Psalm 80 (see also שושן עדות)[1074]

1747 –Prime number

1748 התשעה בנות שיר

HaTishah Banoth Shir –The Nine Song-Maidens (The Nine Muses)

1749

1750 רצון באין גבול

Ratzon Be'iyn Gebul –"Good will with no limit"

1751–1752

1753 –Prime number

1754–1758

1759 –Prime number

1760–1766

1767 התנינם הגדלים

HaTanninim HaGedholim –"The great sea monsters" (Gen. 1:21)

1768 מנא מנא תקל ופרסין

Mena Mena Tekel Ufarsin –"Numbered, numbered, weighed, and divisions"; the handwriting on the wall (alternate spelling)

1769

1770 עשתרת קרנים

'Ashteroth Qarnayim –Ashtoreth Karnaim, town of Bashan, the seat of the worship of the goddess Ashtaroth – possibly the same as the city of Astaroth

1771 עטרות שופן

'Atrowth Showfan –Atroth-Shophan or Atroth, Shophan, one of the cities taken by the Israelites from kings Og and Sihon in the Bashan and rebuilt by the tribe of Gad (Num. 32:35)

1773–1774

1775 היכל עצם שמים

Hekel Etzem Shamaim –Palace of the Body of Heaven, Heavenly Mansion corr. to *Netzach* (see Ex. 24:10)

–The number of letters in the account of the seven days of Creation (Gen. 1 and 2:1-3)

[1074] שושן עדות (1137, 1786).

–The number of shekels of silver used in the construction of the Tabernacle in the Wilderness

1776 מנה מנה תקל ופרסין *Mena Mena Tekel Ufarsin* –"Numbered, numbered, weighed, and divisions"; the handwriting on the wall (Dan. 5:25)

1777 –Prime number

1778–1782

1783 –Prime number

1784 אין־סוף אור *Ain-Sof Aur* –The Limitless Light

1785 זה־שמי לעלם וזה זכרי לדר דר *Zeh-Shemiy Leo'lam VeZeh Zikriy Ledor dor* –"This shall be My name forever, This My appellation for all eternity" (Ex. 3:15)

1786 שושן עדות *Shuwshan 'Eduwth* –"Lily of the testimony," title of Psalm 60 (see also שושנים עדות)[1075]

1787 –Prime number

1788 בית עשתרות *Beyth 'Ashtarowth* –Beth Astaroth, House of Astaroth, a place in Palestine

1789 –Prime number

1790

1791 עשרת הדברים *Asereth HaDavarim* –Ten Commandments

1792–1795

1796 השתחוו ליהוה בהדרת קדש *HaShetachuw le*-YHVH *Behadarot Qadosh* –"Bow down to God in sacred splendor" (Ps. 96:9) – (this phrase is a notarikon for *Kabbalah* when spelled backwards)

שכל החפץ המבוקש *Sekhel HaChafutz HaMevuqash* –Intelligence of Conciliation, Rewarding Intelligence of Those Who Seek, or Desired and Sought Consciousness (21st Path)

1797–1779

1780 אתמ שמעימ ותמונה אינכמ ראימ *Atem Shome'iym VeTemonah 'Eynekem Ro'iym* –"You heard the sound of words but perceived no shape" (Deut. 4:12)

1781–1800

[1075] שושנים עדות (1186, 1746).

1801 –Prime number

1802–1810

1811 ואני דניאל נהייתי ונחלתי ימימ — *ve-'aniy Daniel Nehiytiy ve-Necheltiy Yamiym* –"And I, Daniel, was broken and became sick for many days" (Dan. 8:27)

–Prime number

1812

1813

1814 פרי עץ זרע זרע — *Peri etz zorea zara* –"The fruit of a tree yielding seed"

שלחן ערוך — *Shulchan Aruch* –The Jewish Law, written by R. Josef Karo

תשחתון — *Tashchitun* –You deal corruptly

1815 והתקדשתם — *ve-Hitqadishtem* –And sanctify yourselves (Lev. 11:44)

1816–1819

1820 תרשישים — *Tarshishim* –Chrysolites; Angelic Choir sometimes assoc. w/*Netzach*

– The number of occurrences of YHVH in the *Tanakh* (according to R. Yitzchak Ginsburgh in The Alef-Beit, p. 249)

1821

1822 אכן יש יהוה במקום הזה — *'Aken Yesh* YHVH *Bamaquwm Hazeh* –"Surely the Lord exists in this place" (Gen. 28:16)

1823 –Prime number

1824 תשחיתון — *Tishchiytun* –You will become corrupt (Deut. 31:29)

1825–1829

1830 ותשתחוין — *va-Tishtachaveyna* –And they bowed down

1831 –Prime number

1832–1835

1836 שכל מתנוצץ — *Sekhel Mitnotzetz* –Resplendent Intelligence (10th Path)

1837 זכור את־יומ השבת לקדשו — *Zakhor eth-yom HaShabath le-qadesho* –"Remember the sabbath day, to keep it holy" (Ex. 20:8)

1838–1844

1845 עין התנים — *'Eyn HaTanniym* –En Hatannim, a pool near Jerusalem (Neh. 2:13)[1076]

1846

1847 –Prime number

1848–1859

1860 בעל חנן בן עכבור — *Baal-Chanan ben Akbor* –Baal-Hanan, son of Achbor, a King of Edom (assoc. w/ *Yesod*)

1861 –Prime number

1862–

1865 אשר אין בה מום — *Asher Ain Bah Muwm* –"In which there is no defect" (Num. 19:2)

1866

1867 –Prime number

1868 לישועתכ קויתי יהוה — *Liyshuw'ateka Qiviytiy* YHVH –"For Your salvation do I hope, God" (Gen. 49:18)

1869

1870

1871 –Prime number

1872

1873 –Prime number

1874

1875 עתיקא דעתיקין — *Atiqa de-Atiqin* –"The Ancient of the Ancient Ones," a title of *Keter*

1876

1877 –Prime number

1878

1879 –Prime number

1880

1076 Some translate "Jackyl's Spring" or "Dragon well."

1881 כי סבבוני כלבים עדת מרעים הקיפוני כארי ידיי ורגליי — *Kiy Sababuwniy Kalubim Adath Mera'aim he-qifoni ka'ari yedi-i ve-ragoli-i* –"Dogs surround me; a pack of evil ones closes in on me, like lions [they maul] my hands and feet" (Psalm 22:17)

1882–1887

1888 חית כף מם הה — *Cheth Kaf Mem Heh* –The letters *chet, kaf, mem, heh,* which spell *Chokmah*, wisdom

כבד את־אביך ואת־אמך — *Kabedh eth-abika ve-eth-immeka* –"Honor thy father and thy mother" (Ex. 20:12)

1889 –Prime number

1890–1893

1894 איכה ירדף אחד אלף — *'eykah yirdof 'echad 'alef* –"How does one pursue a thousand?" (Deut. 33:30)

1895–1900

1901 –Prime number

1902 לא תשא את־שם־יהוה אלהיך לשוא — *Lo thisa eth-shem*-YHVH *Eloheka lashave* –"Thou shalt not swear falsely by the name of the Lord thy God" (Ex. 20:7)

1903–1906

1907 עופרת נתנו עזבוניך — *Owfereth Nathanu 'azabunik* –"Lead they gave for your wares" (Ezek. 27:12)

–Prime number

1908 תתחתן — *Titachatan* –Shall marry (Deut. 7:3; 1 Sam. 18:21)

1909–1912

1913 –Prime number

1914 ותותא הארץ דשא — *Va-totze HaAretz deshe* –"And the earth brought forth grass"

1915–1916

1917 אילון בית חנן — *'Eylown Beyth Chanan* –Elon Beth Hanan, one of the three towns of the tribe of Dan

1918

1919 המן בן־המדתא האגגי — *Haman Ben Hamedata' HaAgagiy* –"Haman son of Hammedatha the Agagite" (Esth. 3:1)

1920–1930

1931 –Prime number

1932

1933 –Prime number

1934–1948

1949 –Prime number

1950

1951 מכנפ הארצ זמירות שמענו צבי לצדיק — *Meknof Ha'Aretz Zemiyroth Shemonuw Tzeviy Letzadik* –"From the end of the earth we have heard songs, the desire of the *tzaddik*" (Is. 24:16)

–Prime number

1952–1953

1954

1954

1955 ואהבך וברכך והרבך — *Ve-'Aheveka ve-Verakeka ve-Hirebeka* –"He will favor you and bless you and multiply you" (Deut. 7:13)

1956–1972

1973 –Prime number

1974

1975 ארץ תחתונה — *Aretz HaTachtonah* –Nethermost Earth

1976

1977

1978 בצלם אלהים ברא אתו — *Be-tzelem Elohim bara othu* –"In the image of God created he them"

1979 –Prime number

1980–

1981 והאלהים נסהאת אברהם — *ve-HaElohim Nisahath Abraham* –"And God tested Abraham" (Gen. 22:1)

1986

1987 –Prime number

1988–1992

1993 –Prime number

1994

1995

1996 אש מן השמים — *Esh Min HaShamaim* –"Fire from heaven" (2 Kings 1:10)

ראשיהם כסף — *Rashiyham Kasak* –Capitals were silver (Ex. 38:16)

שדרך מישך ועבד נגוא — *Shadrakh Meshakh ve-Abedh Nego* –Shadrach, Meshach, and Abed-nego (Dan. 2:49)

1997 –Prime number

1998

1999 –Prime number

2000

2001

2002 לא־תענה ברעך עד שקר — *Lo-tha'aneh be-re'aka edh shaqer* –"Thou shalt not bear false witness against thy neighbor" (Ex. 20:13)

2003 –Prime number

2004–2010

2011 –Prime number

2012–2014

2015 יונת אלם רחקים — *Yownath 'elem rechoqiym* –Title of Ps. 56:1 (meaning uncertain)

2016

2017 –Prime number

2018–2026

2027 –Prime number

2028

2029 –Prime number

2030–2035

2036 רמתים צופים *Ramathayim Tzowphiym* –Ramathaim-Zophim, town where Samuel was born (this spelling used only in 1 Sam. 1:11 – see also Ramah)[1077]

2037

2038

2039 –Prime number

2040 מצרף לכסף *Metzeraf Lekasaf* –"Fining pot is for silver" (Prov. 17:3)

2041–2043

2044 ויברא אלהים את האדם בצלמו *Vay-yi-vera Elohim eth ha-adham be-tzalmu* –"So God created man in his own image"

2045–2052

2053 –Prime number

2054

2055

2056 –The number of children of Bigvai who returned from exile (Ezra 2:14)

2057–2060

2061 שמש ומגן יהוה אלהים *Shamash ve-Magen* YHVH *Elohim* –"A sun and shield are YHVH *Elohim*" (Ps. 84:12)

2062

2063 –Prime number

2064–2068

2069 –Prime number

2070–2077

2078 חזוקותיך אמצתיך *Chezowqowtik 'Ametzeth* –"Powerful strength"

2079

2080 פשטתי את־כתנתי *Pashatetiy Eth-Raglay* –"I had taken off my robe" (Song

---

[1077] Ramah (245).

5:3)

תפתרתרת Tafthartharath –The Spirit of Mercury

-The sum of all the numbers (1 to 64) on the magic square of Mercury

2081 –Prime number

2082

2083 –Prime number

2084 מצפון תפתח הרעה *Mitzfon tefetach HaRa'ah* –"Evil begins from the north" (Jer. 1:14)

2085

2086

2087 –Prime number

2088

2089 –Prime number

2090 מודה אני לפניך מלך חי וקים *Modeh Ani Lifanek Melek Chai Ve-qayam* –"I am thankful before You, Living and Eternal King"

פרו ורבו ומלאו את הארץ *Peru u-revu u-mileu eth HaAretz* –"Be fruitful and multiply and replenish the earth" (Gen. 1:28; 9:1)

2091 מאשתם עפרת *Mashatham Ofereth* –"The lead comes whole from the fire" (Jer. 6:29)

2092–2119

2120 ועשו לי מקדש ושכנתי בתוכמ *ve-aso liy miqdash ve-Shakantiy be-Tokam* –"And let them make Me a sanctuary that I may dwell among them" (Ex. 25:8)

רמן פרץ *Rimmon Peretz* –Rimmon-Parez, fifteenth encampment of the Israelites (Num. 33:19)

2121

2122

2123 פן ינחם העם *Pen Yenacham HaAm* –"The people might change their minds" (Ex. 13:17)

2124–2145

2146 עשרים ושנים *Esrim u-Shenaim* –Twenty-two

2147–2150

2151 אחד ראש אחדותו ראש יחודו תמורהזו אחד — *Achad Rosh Achdotho Rosh Ichudo Temurahzo Achad*–"One is His Beginning; one is His Individuality; His Permutation is One"; usually abbreviated אראריתא (*Ararita*) and used as a name of God

ויאמר אלהים נעשה אדם בצלמנו — *Vay-yomer Elohim naaseh adham be-tzelmenu* –"And God said let us make man in our image" (Gen. 1:26)

2152–2171

2172 –The number of children of Parosh who returned from exile (Ezra 2:3)

2173–2192

2193 שמרון מראון — *Shimrown Mero'wn* –Shimon-Meron, royal city of the Canaanites, whose king was slain by Joshua (see also Shimron)[1078]

2194–2212

2213 ויהושע בן נון מלא רוח חכמה — *Yeheshua ben Nun Malay Ruach Chamah* –"Yeheshua son of Nun was filled with the spirit of wisdom" (Deut. 34:9)

2224

2225 ואת העפרת כל דבר אשר בא באש — *Ve-eth HaOfereth Kol Debar Asher Be' Ba'ash* –"And the lead, everything that goes through the fire" (Num. 31:22, 23)

2226–2235

2236 הבל הבלים אמר קהלת הבל הבלים הכל הבל — *Habal Habalim 'amer Qoholet Habal Habalim Hakal Habal* –"Vanity of vanities, says Ecclesiastes, vanity of vanities, all is vanity" (Ecc. 1:1)

2237

2238

2239 ויבנשמ אברהמ את המזבח — *Vayiven Avraham Et HaMizbayach* –"And Abraham built an altar there" (Gen. 22:9)

2240–2248

2249 –The number of occurrences in the *Tanakh* of the Divine Name *Elohim* (according to James Eshelman in The Magical Pantheons, p. 206)

[1078] Shimron (596, 1246).

2250	כי יהוה אלהיכמ הוא אלהי האלהימ ואדני האדנימ האל הגדל	*Ki* YHVH *Elohaycham Hu Elohay HaElohim va-Adonai HaAdonim HaAl HaGadol* –"For the Lord your God is the God of gods and the Lord of lords, the Almighty, the great..." (Deut. 10:17)
2251–2294		
2295	מלאכי אלהים עלים וירדים בו	*Mal'akey 'Elohiym 'Oliym ve-Yirediym Bo* –"Angels of God were going up and down on it." (Gen. 28:12)
2296	לא יהיה־לך אלהים אחרים על־פני	*Lo yiheyah-leka Elohim acherim al-pana* –"Thou shalt have no other gods before me" (Ex. 20:3)
2297–2308		
2309	קדוש קדוש קדוש יהוה צבקות מלא כל הארצ כבודו	*Qadosh Qadosh Qadosh* YHVH *Tzebaquwth Mela' Kel HaAretz Kebuwdo* –"Holy, holy, holy is God of Hosts, the whole world is full of His glory" (Is. 6:3)
2310		
2311	באה הצפירה אליכ יושב הארצ בא העת קרוב היומ מהומה ולא־הד הרימ	*Ba'ah Hatzefiyrah 'Aleyka Yoshev Ha'Aretz Ba' Ha'et Qariov HaYom Mehomah Velo'-Hed Hariym* –"The cycle has come around for you, O inhabitants of the land; the time has come; the day is near. There is panic on the mountains, not joy." (Meaning uncertain – Ezek. 7:7)
2312–2314		
2315	וקראתי בשם יהוה לפניך	*ve-Qara'tiy Vashem* YHVH *Lepaneyka* –"And I will proclaim before you the name YHVH" (Ex. 33:19)
2316–2329		
2330	עשתרת קרנים	*'Ashteroth Qarnayim* –Ashtoreth Karnaim, town of Bashan, the seat of the worship of the goddess Ashtaroth – possibly the same as the city of Astaroth
2331–2364		
2365	ויברך אתם אלהים	*Va-ye-varekh otham Elohim* –"And God blessed them" (Gen. 1:22, 28)
2366–2380		

2381 שתי הצוצרת כסף — *Shetiy Hatzuwtzerat Kesaf* –"Two trumpets of silver" (Num. 10:2)

2382–2387

2391 גדול אדונינו ורב כח לתבונתו אין מספר — *Geduwl Adonainunuwve-rav Koah Lethvanthuw Ain Mesafer* –"Great is our Lord and abundant in strength; His understanding is infinite" (Ps. 147:5)

2392–2396

2397 זכור את־יום השבת לקדשו — *Zakhor eth-yom HaShabath le-qadesho* –"Remember the sabbath day, to keep it holy" (Ex. 20:8)

2398–2408

2409 צללו כעופרת במים אדירים — *Tzelelu Kofereth Bemayim Adirim* –"They sank like lead in mighty waters" (Ex. 15:10)

2410–2450

2451 ארבעים יום וארבעים לילה — *Arbawuwm Yom Viarbaim Layilaw* –"Forty days and forty nights" (Gen. 7:12)

2452–2454

2455 בין האור ובין החשך — *Bayn HaOhr Vuvayn HaChushek* –"divided the light and divided the darkness" (Gen. 1:4)

2456–2483

2484 וכל־העם ראים את־הקולת — *VeKal-IIa'um Ro'iym 'Eth-HaQoliyth* –"All the people witnessed the thunder (or voices)" (Ex. 20:15)

2485–

2569 אבנ מאסו הבונים היתה לראש פנה — *Eben Maasu HaBonim HaYetah Lero'as Pinah* –"The stone that the builders rejected has become the chief cornerstone" (Ps. 118:22)

2570

2571 תקים את משכן — *Takim Eth Mishkon* –"Set up the Tabernacle of the Tent of Meeting" (Ex. 40:2)

2570–2584

2585 כי יהוה אלהיך הואהלך — *Ki* YHVH *Eloheka Huaholayk*

	עמך לאירפך	*Aymak Layarpik* –"Your God [YHVH] Himself marches with you: He will not fail you or forsake you" (Deut. 31:6)
2586–2605		
2606	כושן רשעתים	*Kuwshan Rish'athayim* –Cushan-Rishathaim, king of Mesopotamia that God chose to punish Israel (Judg. 3:8, 10)
2607–2632		
2633	יש ששימ רבוא אותיות לתורה	*Yesh Sheshiym Ravuwa' 'avtiyvat Letuwrah* –"There are six hundred thousand letters in the Torah" (*Megaleh Amukot, VeEtchanan* 186)
2634–2650		
2651	מה־טבו אהליך יעקב משכנתיך ישראל	*Mah-tovo 'ahaleyka ya'aqov mishkenoteyka yisrael* –"How fair are your tents, O Jacob, Your dwellings, O Israel!" (Num. 24:5)
2652–2679		
2680	ועשו לי מקדש ושכנתי בתוכם	*ve-aso liy miqdash ve-Shakantiy be-Tokam* –"And let them make Me a sanctuary that I may dwell among them" (Ex. 25:8)
2681–2717		
2718	יברכב יהוה וישמרכ יאר יהוה פניו אליכ ויחנכ ישא יהוה פניו אליכ וישמ לכ שלומ	*Yebarakak* YHVH *ve-Yishmarak Ya'ar* YHVH *Peniyv 'aliyk ve-Yichnak Yisha'* YHVH *Peniyv 'aliyk ve-Yisham Lak Shelom* –"May God bless you and guard you. May God shine His Countenance upon you and give you grace. May God turn His Countenance toward you and grant you peace." (Num. 6:24 – 26)
2719–2728		
2729	אברהם יצחק יעקב שבטי ישרון	*Abraham Yitzak Ya'aqov Shavoti Yeshrown* –"Abraham, Isaac, Jacob, the tribes of the righteous people" – a name of God of 22 letters
2738	קץ שם לחשך	*Qetz Shem Lechashak* –"He has set an end to darkness" (Job 28:3)
2739–2808		
2809–2810		
2811		

2812 –The number of children of Pahathmoab who returned from exile (Ezra 2:6)

2813–2894

2895 ועופרת אל תוכ כור לפחת
עליו אש להנתיכ

Ve-Ofereth Al Tuwk Le-pachath Esh Lahentik –"And the lead into the middle of the furnace to blow the fire on it to melt it" (Ezek. 22:20)

2896–2910

2911 בראשית (ב = 2000)

Bereshith –"In the beginning;" Hebrew title of Genesis

2912–2941

2942 לא תשא את־שם־יהוה אלהיך
לשוא

Lo thisa eth-shem-YHVH *Eloheka lashave* –"Thou shalt not swear falsely by the name of the Lord thy God" (Ex. 20:7)

2243–3000

3001 כי סבבוני כלבים עדת מרעים
הקיפוני כארי ידיי ורגליי

Kiy Sababuwniy Kalubim Adath Mera'aim he-qifoni ka'ari yedi-i ve-ragoli-i –"Dogs surround me; a pack of evil ones closes in on me, like lions [they maul] my hands and feet" (Psalm 22:17)

3002–3027

3028 ויתאנפ יהוה מאד בישראל
ויסרמ מעל פניו לא נשאר
רק שבע יהודה לבדו

Va-Yite'anaf YHVH *Mea'd BeYisra'el*
Va-Yesirem Ma'al Panayv Loa' Nish'ar
Raq Shevet Yehuwdah Levado –"The Lord was incensed at Israel and He banished them from His presence; none was left but the tribe of Judah alone" (2 Kings 17:18)

3029–3097

3098 שיחיה לאורך ימים טובים אמן

Shichih Lavrak Yamiym Toviym Amen –"May he live for long and good days, Amen," a phrase used when mentioning a living rabbi or sage

3099–3118

3119 קדוש קדוש קדוש יהוה צבקות
מלא כל הארץ כבודו

Qadosh Qadosh Qadosh YHVH *Tzebaquwth*
Mela' Kel HaAretz Kebuwdo –"Holy, holy, holy is God of Hosts, the whole world is full of His glory" (Is. 6:3)

3120–3165

3166 –The total gematria of Reuben, Simeon, Levi, Judah, Issachar, Zebulon, Benjamin, Dan, Joseph,

3167–3192

3193 יש ששים רבוא אותיות לתורה

Yesh Sheshiym Ravuwa' 'avtiyvat Letuwrah –"There are six hundred thousand letters in the Torah" (*Megaleh Amukot, VeEtchanan* 186)

3194–3199

3200 כי־טוב ויבדל אלהים בין
האור ובין החשך

Ki-towv ve-Yavdel Elohim Beyn ha-Owr vo-Beyn Ha-Chosheka –"...was good, and God separated the light from the darkenss" (Gen. 1:4)

3201–3248

3249 כסף צרוף בעליל לארץ

Kesaf Tzeruwf Baliyl La'ratz –"Silver refined in an earthen furnace" (Ps. 12:7)

3250–3253

3254 חזון עובדיה כה אמר אדוני
יהוה לאדום שועה שמענו
מאת יהוה וציר בגוים שולח
קומו ונקומה עליה למלחמה

Chazon 'ovadyah. Koh 'amer Adonai YHVH *le-'adom, shevuw'ah shama'nuw me'et* YHVH *ve-tziyr bagoyim: shuvlach, qomo ve-naquwmah 'aleyah, lamilchamah.* –"The prophecy of Obadiah. We have received tidings from the Lord, And an envoy has been sent out among the nations: 'Up! Let us rise up against her for battle.'" (Obadiah 1:1)

3255–3320

3321 מלכא בתרשישים ועד ברוה
שהקים

Malka be-Tarshishim ve-Ad be-Ruah Shehaqim –The Intelligence of the Intelligences of Luna (ם in בתרשישים = 600; ם in שהקים = 700)

מלכא בתרשיסים ועד רוחות
שחלים

Malka be-Tarshisim ve-Ad Ruachoth Shechalim – Regardie's version of the Intelligence of the Intelligences of Luna

מלכא בתרשישים ועד ברוה

Malka be-Tarshishim ve-Ad be-Ruach Sheharim – A.C.'s version of the Intelligence of the Intelligences of Luna

מלכא בתרשישים עד ברוח
שחרים

Malka be-Tarshishim ve-Ad be-Ruach Shacharim – Queen of the Tarshishim forever, in the Spirit of the Dawning Ones; Paul Foster Case's version of the preceding

שד ברשמעת השרתתן

Shed Barshemath HaSharthathan –The Spirit of the Spirits of Luna

שד ברשהמעת שרתתן

Shed Barshehmath Sharthathan –A different version of the preceding

3322–3340

3341 רצית יהוה ארצכ שבת שבות יעקב — *Ratziyta* YHVH *'aretzeka shaveta shaviyt ya'aqiv* –"O Lord, You will favor Your Land, restore Jacob's fortune" (Ps. 85:2)[1079]

3342–3368

3369 סנוי סנסנוי סמנגלוף אדם והוה חץ לילות — *Senoy, Sansenoy, Semangelof! Adam ve-Chavvah! Chotz Lilith!* –"Senoy, Sansenoy, Semangelof! Adam and Eve! Out, Lilith!" The formula used against Lilith

3370–3374

3375 סנוי סנסנוי סמנגלוף אדם וחוה חוץ לילות — *Senoy, Sansenoy, Semangelof! Adam ve-Chavvah! Chotz Lilith!* –"Senoy, Sansenoy, Semangelof! Adam and Eve! Out, Lilith!" The formula used against Lilith (variant spelling)

3376–3479

3480 ועופרת בתוך כור סיגים כסף היו — *Ve-Ofereth Betuwk Kuwr Siygim HaYa* –"And lead in the middle of the furnace, they are the dross of silver" (Ezek. 22:18)

3481 מכנפ הארצ זמירות שמענו צבי לצדיק — *Meknof Ha'Aretz Zemiyroth Shemonuw Tzeviy Letzadik* –"From the end of the earth we have heard songs, the desire of the *tzaddik*" (Is. 24:16)

3482–3510

3511 אשר עשה האלקימ את האדמ ישר והמה בקשו חשבונות רבימ — *Asher 'oseh Ha'Elqiym 'eth HaAdam Yosher ve-Hamah Beqso Chashvonot Raviym* –"That God has made man upright, but they have sought out many schemes" (Ecc. 7:29)

3512–3545

3546 אלפ שנימ בעיניכ כיומ אתמול — *'alef Sheniym Be'yaniyk Kiyvom 'atemuwl* –"A thousand years in Your eyes are as a day of yesterday" (Ps. 90:4)

3547–3629

3630 –The number of children of Senaah who returned from exile (Ezra 2:35)

3631–3702

3703 אבגיתצ־קרעשטנ־נגדיכש — *Abgitatz-qerashaten-negadikesh-batratztag-*

[1079] This verse was traditionally used in the expulsion of demons.

בטרצתג־חקדטנע־יגלפזק־שקוצית *chaqdatna-yaglepzeq-shequtzit* –The name of God of 42 letters

3702–3782

3783 אבגיתצקרעשמנכגדיכשבמרצתג הקממנעיגלפזקשקיעית *Ab-gi-tatz-qerashamen-kegadikesh-bamratztag-haqamamna-yaglepzeq-sheqi-ayeth* –The name of God of 42 letters (A.C.)

3784–3820

3821 רצית יהוה ארצך שבת שבות יעקב *Ratziyta* YHVH *'aretzeka shaveta shaviyt ya'aqiv* –"O Lord, You will favor Your Land, restore Jacob's fortune" (Ps. 85:2)[1080]

3822–3854

3855 ועופרת אל תוך כור לפחת עליו אש להנתיך *Ve-Ofereth Al Tuwk Le-pachath Esh Lahentik* –"And the lead into the middle of the furnace to blow the fire on it to melt it" (Ezek. 22:20)

3856–3920

3921 אנקתם־פסתם־פספסים־דיונסים *Anaqtam Pastam Paspasim Dionsim* –The 22-letter name of God

3922–4019

4020 אתם שמעים ותמונה אינכם ראים *Atem Shome'iym VeTemonah 'Eynekem Ro'iym* –"You heard the sound of words but perceived no shape" (Deut. 4:12)

4021–4071

4072 אין אין סיף אין סוף אור *Ain Ain Sof Ain Sof Aur* –Nought without limit light without limit

4073–4307

4308 ויתאנפ יהוה מאד בישראל
ויסרמ מעל פניו לא נשאר
רק שבע יהודה לבדו
Va-Yite'anaf YHVH *Mea'd BeYisra'el*
Va-Yesirem Ma'al Panayv Loa' Nish'ar
Raq Shevet Yehuwdah Levado –"The Lord was incensed at Israel and He banished them from His presence; none was left but the tribe of Judah alone" (2 Kings 17:18)

4309–4722

4721 באה הצפירה אליך יושב הארץ
בא העת קרוב היום מהומה
Ba'ah Hatzefiyrah 'Aleyka Yoshev Ha'Aretz
Ba' Ha'et Qariov HaYom Mehomah

[1080] This verse was traditionally used in the expulsion of demons.

ולא־הד הרים *Velo'-Hed Hariym* –"The cycle has come around for you, O inhabitants of the land; the time has come; the day is near. There is panic on the mountains, not joy." (Meaning uncertain – Ezek. 7:7)

4722–5053

5054 חזון עובדיה כה אמר אדוני יהוה לאדום שועה שמענו מאת יהוה וציר בגויים שולח קומו ונקומה עליה למלחמה *Chazon 'ovadyah. Koh 'amer Adonai* YHVH *le-'adom, shevuw'ah shama'nuw me'et* YHVH *ve-tziyr bagoyim: shuvlach, qomo ve-naquwmah 'aleyah, lamilchamah.* -"The prophecy of Obadiah. We have received tidings from the Lord, And an envoy has been sent out among the nations: 'Up! Let us rise up against her for battle.'" (Obadiah 1:1)

5055–5162

5163 אבגיתץ־קרעשטן־נגדיכש בטרצתג־חקדטנע־יגלפזק־שקוצית *Abgitatz-qerashaten-negadikesh-batratztag-chaqdatna-yaglepzeq-shequtzit* –The name of God of 42 letters

5164–5190

5191 אשר עשה האלקים את האדם ישר והמה בקשו חשבונות רבים *Asher 'oseh Ha'Elqiym 'eth HaAdam Yosher ve-Hamah Beqso Chashvonot Raviym* –"That God has made man upright, but they have sought out many schemes" (Ecc. 7:29)

5192

5193 –The number of occurences of YHVH alone in the *Tanakh*[1081]

5194–5520

5521 –The number of occurrences of YHVH in the *Tanakh* (according to James Eshelman in The Magical Pantheons, p. 206)

5765

5766 –The number of occurences of YHVH in the *Tanakh* (according to Mitchell, Word Frequency List of Biblical Hebrew, Zondervan.).

5767–5786

5787 –The number of occurences of YHVH in the *Tanakh* (including proper names of persons and places)

5788–6717

[1081] i.e. without prepositional phrases, direct objects, etc.

6718 יברכב יהוה וישמרכ יאר יהוה
פניו אליכ ויחנכ ישא יהוה
פניו אליכ וישמ לכ שלומ

Yebarakak YHVH *ve-Yishmarak Ya'ar* YHVH
Peniyv 'aliyk ve-Yichnak Yisha' YHVH
Peniyv 'aliyk ve-Yisham Lak Shelom –"May God bless you and guard you. May God shine His Countenance upon you and give you grace. May God turn His Countenance toward you and grant you peace." (Num. 6:24 – 26)

6719

6720 –The number of asses brought out of exile (Ezra 2:67)

6721–6822

6823 –The number of occurences of YHVH in the Bible (according to The Jewish Encyclopedia, Godwin's Cabalistic Encyclopedia)

6824–7336

7337 –The number of servants and maids who returned from exile (Ezra 2:65)

7338–9146

9147 19 ויסע מלאכ האלהימ ההלכ
לפני מחנה ישראל וילכ
מאחריהמ ויסע עמוד הענ נ
מפניהמ ויעמד מאחריהמ
20 ויבא בינ מחנה מצרימ ובינ
מחנה ישראל ויהי הענ נ והחשכ

ויאר את־ הלילה ולא־קרב זה
אל־ זה כל־הלילה
21 ויט משה את־ ידו על־הימ
ויולכ יהוה את־הימ ברוח
קדימ עזה כל־ הלילה וישמ
את־הימ לחרבה ויבקעו המימ

Vayisa' Male'ak ha-Elohim ha-holek
lifeneiy machaneh Yisra'el veyelak
me'achareyhem veyisa' 'amod he'anan
mipneyhem vaya'amod me'achareyhem
Vayavo' veyn machaneh mitzrayim ve-beyn
macheneh Yisra'el va-yehiy he'anan
vehachshek
vaya'ar 'eth-Ha-laylah veloa'-qarav zeh
'el-zeh Kal-Ha-lalayelah
Ve-yet Mosheh 'eth yado 'al-hayam
vayolek YHVH *'eth-Hayam beruach*
qadiym 'azah kal-Halaylah vayasem
'eth-hayam lecharavah vayivaqe'ow hamayim –"The angel of God, who had been going ahead of the Israelite army, now moved and followed behind them; and the pillar of cloud shifted from in front of them and took up a place behind them, and it came between the army of the Egyptians and the army of Israel. Thus there was the cloud with the darkness, and it cast a spell upon the night, so that the one could not come near the other all through the night. Then Moses held out his arm over the sea and the Lord drove back the sea with a strong east wind all that night, and turned the sea into dry ground. The waters were split" (Ex. 14:19-21)

9148–14,582

14,583 –The sum of the names of *Shem HaMeforash*

14,584–20306

20,307
19 ויסע מלאך האלהים ההלך
לפני מחנה ישראל וילך
מאחריהם ויסע עמוד הענן
מפניהם ויעמד מאחריהם
20 ויבא בין מחנה מצרים ובין
מחנה ישראל ויהי הענן והחשך
ויאר את־הלילה ולא־קרב זה
אל־זה כל־הלילה
21 ויט משה את־ידו על־הים
ויולך יהוה את־הים ברוח
קדים עזה כל־הלילה וישם
את־הים לחרבה ויבקעו המים

Vayisa' Male'ak ha-Elohim ha-holek
lifeneiy machaneh Yisra'el veyelak
me'achareyhem veyisa' 'amod he'anan
mipneyhem vaya'amod me'achareyhem
Vayavo' veyn machaneh mitzrayim ve-beyn
macheneh Yisra'el va-yehiy he'anan
vehachshek
vaya'ar 'eth-Ha-laylah veloa'-qarav zeh
'el-zeh Kal-Ha-lalayelah
Ve-yet Mosheh 'eth yado 'al-hayam
vayolek YHVH *'eth-Hayam beruach*
qadiym 'azah kal-Halaylah vayasem
'eth-hayam lecharavah vayivaqe'ow hamayim –"The angel of God, who had been going ahead of the Israelite army, now moved and followed behind them; and the pillar of cloud shifted from in front of them and took up a place behind them, and it came between the army of the Egyptians and the army of Israel. Thus there was the cloud with the darkness, and it cast a spell upon the night, so that the one could not come near the other all through the night. Then Moses held out his arm over the sea and the Lord drove back the sea with a strong east wind all that night, and turned the sea into dry ground. The waters were split" (Ex. 14:19-21)

20,308–22,119

22,200 –The total number of Simeonites counted in Numbers 26:14

22,201–22,999

22,300 –The total number of Levites counted in Numbers 26:62

22,301–31,408

31,409 –The total gematria of all the letters in the 231 Gates, without finals

31,410–32,499

32,500 –The total number of Ephraimites counted in Numbers 26:37

32,501–40,499

40,500 –The total number of Gadites counted in Numbers 26:18

40,501–42,359

42,360 –The total number who returned from exile (Ezra 2:64)

42,361–43,729

43,730 –The total number of Reubenites counted in Numbers 26:7

43,731–45,399

45,400 –The total number of Naphtalites counted in Numbers 26:50

45,401–45,599

45,600 –The total number of Benjaminites counted in Numbers 26:41

45,601–52,699

52,700 –The total number of Manassites counted in Numbers 26:34

52,701–53,399

53,400 –The total number of Asherites counted in Numbers 26:47

53,401–60,499

60,500 –The total number of Zebulunites counted in Numbers 26:27

60,501–64,299

64,300 –The total number of Issacharites counted in Numbers 26:25

64,301–64,399

64,400 –The total number of Dan's descendants counted in Numbers 26:43

64,401–76,499

76,500 –The total number of Judah's descendants counted in Numbers 26:22

76,501–78,063

78,064 –The total number of Hebrew letters in the book of Genesis

78,065 – 102,605

102,606 –The sum of the first chapter of Genesis

601,730 –The total Israelites counted in Numbers 26:51

Biblical and Midrashic Bibliography

3,458 Bible People & Places. Nashville, TN: Thomas Nelson, Inc., 1993.

As the title suggests, this little book gives all the names and places in the Bible, including variations on each. Unfortunately, it does not give the original Hebrew and Greek spellings, so often the reader must refer to various Biblical passages (which are listed in the book) to find meaning and the real spelling. It is an excellent reference for the reader however, and comes highly recommended for its cross-referenced and basic information.

Anderson, Bernhard W. Understanding the Old Testament. Englewood Cliffs, NJ: Prentice-

Hall, 1957.

Despite its age, this book is an excellent analysis of the Tanakh from a Christian scholarly perspective. It has been reproduced with supplemental material various times since it was written and newer editions than the one listed here give more material that is relevant to the student of the Tanakh. It is more of an historical analysis than a Kabbalistic one, but the student will find passages and information that are relevant.

Brown, Francis. Brown-Driver-Briggs Hebrew and English Lexicon. Hendrickson, 1999.

One of the many Hebrew lexicons available, this book was originally written in 1906, so some of the interpretations have changed due to archaeological finds, linguistic discoveries, etc., but this is still an excellent book for the inquiring student of *gematria.*

Eadie, John, ed. Cruden's Compact Concordance. Grand Rapids, MI: Zondervan, n.d.

This book gives the reference to each English word in the Bible. Unfortunately, this book as well as lexicons will show, there are various interpretations of each word, even in context. Nevertheless, this book should be useful for the student of *gematria.*

Hammer, Reuven. The Classic Midrash. New York, NY: Paulist Press, 1995.

A great introduction to Midrash, this book gives only the interpretations of the Pentateuch or Torah. It contains both legendary and legal material relevant to Jewish interpretation of Torah. A few of the Midrashic references contained within my book can be found in here, but many more are found on the websites listed in this section.

Lockyer, Herbert. All the Divine Names and Titles in the Bible. Grand Rapids, MI: Zondervan

Publishing House, 1975.

As its title suggests, this book is of exceptional use to the student of *gematria.* While there are no listings in Hebrew, Greek, or Aramaic, and considering it is a purely Christian analysis of the Names, it is still exceptionally useful because it gives the passages and locations of each Name, along with full explanations of each.

Meyers, Rick. E-Sword (program). 10 March 1998. <http://e-sword.net/index.html>.

This free program gives various translations of the Bible, including the original Hebrew/Aramaic (without Masoretic points), and gives the user the possibility of downloading various dictionaries, commentaries, and graphics. A definite must-have for the student of *gematria* and Biblical scholarship. Plus, it's absolutely free and easy to use!

Soulen, Richard N. Handbook of Biblical Criticism. Atlanta, GA: John Knox Press, 1981.

While not of exceptional use to the student of *gematria*, one will eventually come across a term or phrase unfamiliar, and that's where this book comes in. This book covers nearly every term in biblical criticism from "eschatologize" to "hermeneutics" and gives full explanations of the terms used.

Strong, James. New Strong's Exhaustive Concordance of the Bible. Thomas Nelson, Inc., Nashville, TN., 1990.

This work is the basis of my book and explores each word of the Hebrew Bible and its meaning. The book itself was published in 1890 and thus is outdated in many aspects. The reader is urged to reference every term in the text with a modern lexicon to give more accurate meanings to words mistranslated here. However, due to its vast scope and staying power, this book is highly recommended.

Tanakh: JPS Hebrew-English Tanakh. Philadelphia, PA: Jewish Publication Society, 2000.

"Before one learns Kabbalah, he should learn Torah, Midrash, and Talmud." The Hebrew Bible comes in many forms and translations, the majority of which are translated from a Christian viewpoint. This translation is not only faithful to the original Hebrew and Aramaic, but gives them alongside the English translation as well. The only translation of the Tanakh to own.

Telushkin, Rabbi Joseph. Biblical Literacy. New York: William Morrow, 1997.

An excellent introduction to Jewish interpretation of the Bible. Keep in mind that no one book can give all the possible interpretations or even a definitive reading of a passage or section of the Bible. However, R. Telushkin does an excellent job of giving an overview.

Wigoder, Geoffrey, ed. Illustrated Dictionary & Concordance of the Bible. Jerusalem: Reader's Digest Assoc., 1986.

An excellent overview of people, places, things, and concepts in the Bible, this dictionary is in reality a mini encyclopedia. Useful for not only its insight into current belief and archaeological findings, but also gives the reader an excellent basis for understanding the Bible itself.

Hebrew Language Bibliography

Ben-Yehuda, Ehud. Ben-Yehuda's Pocket English-Hebrew Hebrew-English Dictionary. New York: Simon & Schuster, 1964.

Just what the title suggests, a dictionary of modern Hebrew. Interested readers will note the differences given for words that are Biblical versus modern and the use of new words such as "Internet" and "television."

Kittel, Bonnie, Vicki Hoffer. Biblical Hebrew: A Text and Workbook. London: Yale University Press, 1989.

Mansoor, Menahem. Biblical Hebrew. Vols. 1, 2. Grand Rapids, MI: Baker Book House, 1979.

Both of these books give a solid foundation in translation and reading Hebrew and Aramaic. They are highly recommended, especially the Kittel book, although it is rather complicated and academic, gives the reader a good basis in the linguistic structure of these languages.

Traditional Jewish Gematria Bibliography

Ginsburgh, R. Yitzchak. The Alef-Beit. Northvale, NJ: Gal Einai Publications, 1991.

An excellent introduction to the complexities of the Hebrew letters and their meanings, solidly grounded in Kabbalistic and Rabbinical literature. Highly recommended for the student of *gematria.*

Hoffman, Edward. The Kabbalah Deck. San Francisco, CA: Chronicle Books, 2000.

Hoffman gives a card similar to a Tarot card with each letter of the Hebrew alphabet and the names of the Sefirot. Of particular interest are the meditations and divinations given in the rear of the book. These are particularly helpful for one still learning the Hebrew letters, but also to one who wants new insight into each.

Locks, Gutman. The Spice of Torah – Gematria. New York, NY: Judaica Press, 1985.

One of the best *gematria* books available, this book takes every word in the Torah and gives its corresponding *gematria.* My book takes a few examples from this book, but the format and information given is greatly different. Nevertheless, this book should be used in conjunction with mine.

Munk, Rabbi Michael. The Wisdom in the Hebrew Alphabet. Brooklyn, NY: Mesorah

Publications, 1998.

Judaic Kabbalah Bibliography

Idel, Moshe. Kabbalah: New Perspectives. London: Yale University Press, 1988.

With the publication of this book, Idel established himself as the premier scholar of Kabbalah since the death of Gershom Scholem. This excellent book is a veritable encyclopedia of the new school of thought about Kabbalah. While it only briefly touches on the subject of *gematria*, any reader interested in scholarly Kabbalah needs to read it. Especially important is Idel's use of phenomenological theory to analyze Kabbalistic literature.

Kaplan, Aryeh. Jewish Meditation. New York, NY: Schocken Books, 1985.

Kaplan, Aryeh. Meditation and the Bible. York Beach, ME: Samuel Weiser, 1988.

Kaplan, Aryeh. Meditation and Kabbalah. York Beach, ME: Samuel Weiser, 1982.

Kaplan, Aryeh. Sefer Yetzirah. York Beach, ME: Samuel Weiser, 1997.

Kaplan, Aryeh. The Bahir. York Beach, ME: Samuel Weiser, 1979.

Any and all of Kaplan's books are extremely helpful and highly recommended. Kaplan, who was the youngest physicist employed by the United States government, turned to Kabbalah later in his life, applying scientific examination of ancient texts. His translations of the Book of Formation and the Bahir are unsurpassed in their explanations and analyses. Any serious student of Kabbalah and *gematria* should have all his books on their shelves.

Sheinkin, David. Path of the Kabbalah. St. Paul, MN: Paragon House, 1986.

As several references in my book explain, there are a great number of excellent parts of Judaic Kabbalah that Sheinkin goes through. Of especial import is his chapter "In the Beginning," an explanation of the book *Bereshit*, wherein he explains Kabbalistic thought of the creation of the Universe. This section alone makes this book one of the most valuable books on Kabbalah ever written in English.

Scholem, Gershom. Kabbalah. New York: Penguin, 1978.

Scholem, Gershom. Major Trends in Jewish Mysticism. New York, NY: Schocken, 1995.

Scholem, Gershom. On the Kabbalah and its Symbolism. New York, NY: Schocken, 1996.

Scholem, Gershom. On the Mystical Shape of the Godhead. New York, NY: Schocken, 1991.

Scholem was and remains for many people the premier Kabbalistic scholar. While many moderns take his historical aspect critically, his books are still the starting point for those interested in scholarship of the Kabbalah. Many of his writings are still not translated from German and Hebrew, but the books listed here are probably the most important texts he wrote on the subject. For the beginner, the books Kabbalah and On the Mystical Shape of the Godhead are of extreme interest, while the others are more scholarly and may need more background to appreciate fully.

Western Hermetic Gematria Bibliography

Crowley, Aleister. 777. York Beach, ME: Samuel Weiser, 1996.

Crowley's book is the first of its kind, examining words and their *gematria.* Unfortunately, there are a number of misprints in this book, some purposely by Crowley himself (פוך or "Fuk" for the fiftieth Goetic demon – this is rather indicative of Crowley's sense of humor as well as his mindset) and some misplace letters from editorial mistakes. One should never use the words in here indiscriminately as *gematria* for that reason alone. However, this book is an excellent introduction to the way in which my book and nearly every one after it is formatted and created.

Godwin, David. Godwin's Cabalistic Encyclopedia. St. Paul, MN: Llewellyn Publications,

1997.

What can one say about Godwin's book besides giving an excellent review? Of all the books relating to *gematria,* this is the first real encyclopedia of the western esoteric schools. While Crowley's book came first, Godwin's book cross-references various spellings of words and phrases. Especially important are his sections "Transliterated Hebrew" and "Hebrew." These two sections give more information than my book could possibly hold. Highly recommended.

Hulse, David Allen. The Eastern Mysteries. St. Paul, MN: Llewellyn Publications, 2000.

Second Edition

Hulse, David Allen. The Western Mysteries. St. Paul, MN: Llewellyn Publications, 2000.

Second Edition

Hulse is one of those exceptional persons who has attempted to undertake the combination of all the languages which contain the possibilities for *gematria.* In The Eastern Mysteries, he covers Hebrew, Cuneiform, Arabic, Sanskrit, Tibetan, and Chinese. In The Western Mysteries, Greek, Coptic, Runes, Latin, Enochian, the Tarot and English are covered. While these books are not formatted like mine nor Godwin's, the information given could easily keep the student of *gematria* filling his or her own book full of references across all these languages. Highly recommended.

Regardie, Israel. The Golden Dawn: A Complete Course in Practical Ceremonial

Magic. St. Paul: Llewellyn, 1995.

Regardie was the first member of the Golden Dawn to fully publish the materials that group espoused. This book is a veritable encyclopedia of the western esoteric school of thought. There are a great number of Hebrew God-names, angels, spirits, etc. used in this book that I referenced quite often. Highly recommended for anyone interested in the western esoteric school of High Magic.

Robin. Robin's Links to the Mystical Internet – Gemcalc.exe. 1 May 1997

<http://www.mysticalinternet.com/software/cag.htm>.

Robin's webpage gives a number of extremely useful programs for various western esoteric practices, including a Thelemic calendar, a concordance building tool, and most important for my book, the gemcalc program. This program will give the *gematria* of any word in Hebrew, Greek, Enochian, English, or a custom language program (which is especially useful for *aiq bekar* and other *gematria* permutations). Highly recommended because of its low cost and excellent user-friendly format.

Guide to the Comprehensive Index

This index is separated into the following subject areas:

- *Alchemy* – All references to alchemical philosophy.
- *Angels and Archangels* – Many of the names of the angels, archangels and demigods mentioned in the Hebrew Bible, Talmud and some Kabbalistic works.
- *Aramaic Language* – Important words and phrases of the Aramaic/Chaldee language.
- *Biblical Characters* – As the name suggests, this section contains every reference in the book to any person in the Hebrew Bible (except kings, judges, angels, gods and goddesses and other important names separated into other more applicable sections).
- *Biblical Locations* – Every place mentioned in the entire Tanakh.
- *Cardinal Points* – North, south, east and west and the references to them.
- *Crowley, Aleister* – This section contains words that Crowley used in *777* that are incorrectly spelled or are inaccurate, but also includes words and phrases that he created for his gematria.
- *Deities (both Biblical and extra-Biblical)* – Includes Baal, Ashtroeth, etc. I have not included the Pharaohs or Roman emperors, only abstract notions of deity, organized by nation and name.
- *Demon Kings of the Elements and Cardinal Points (Goetia)*
- *Edenic Rivers* – The four rivers leading out from Eden.
- *Edom* – The kings, dukes and places associated with this early kingdom.
- *Elements* – All five (air, water, earth, fire, and spirit).
- *God* – References to and information about, including the important subcategory "Names and Descriptors of."
- *Goetic Demons* – Names of the so-called Demons from the Goetia (see the bibliography for more information)
- *Heavenly Mansions*
- *Heavens* – Both Crowley's and the Zohar's references.
- *Hebrew Alphabet*
- *Hebrew Language* – Important terms and words used in the language.
- *High Priest* – References to the High Priest and his paraphenalia.
- *Important Biblical Terms*
- *Important Jewish Terms*
- *Important Kabbalistic Terms*
- *Important Kabbalistic Texts*
- *Israel* – This expansive subject area includes the following subcategories: Babylonian exile (every reference to the exile); Judges of; Kings of; Tribes of;
- *Israel, United Kingdom of* – This entry refers to the kingdom that existed before the split into Judah and Israel, and covers the three main kings of that era, Saul, David, and Solomon
- *Musical Instruments* – David was an avid musician himself and used music to accompany many important parts of the Biblical story. Since there are so many types of instruments listed, I have compiled them in one place.
- *Planets* – Including the subcategories Traditional and Nontraditional, this area contains much information about the spheres, including earth and Sol.
- *Qlippoth* – All references to the infernal spirits.
- *Tabernacle in the Wilderness* – While traversing from Egypt to the Promised Land, Moses and the Israelites had a sacred space built according to God's specifications. I have tried to include all references to this "traveling holy building" in this subsection.
- *Tanakh* – As the introduction explained, the Tanakh is the Hebrew Bible (or Old Testament). This category includes all quotes taken from the book, as well as references to it in my text. The books themselves are subcategorized according to their position in the Jewish text in the following order:

  Torah – Genesis, Exodus, Leviticus

  Neviim – Joshua, Judges, 1 and 2 Samuel, 1 and 2 Kings, Isaiah, Jeremiah, Ezekiel, Hosea, Joel, Amos, Obadiah, Jonah, Micah, Nahum, Habakkuk, Zephaniah, Haggai, Zechariah, Malachi

  Kethuvim – Psalms, Proverbs, Job, Song of Songs, Ruth, Lamentations, Ecclesiastes, Esther, Daniel, Ezra, 1 and 2 Chronicles

  Some important points about this category:

1. Some of the biblical quotes will not match up with Christian translations. This is because I have adhered to the Jewish translations wherever possible. The differences usually lie in the Psalms, where the titles are not versed in Christian Bibles, but are in Jewish ones. This should not prove too difficult to any reader, as most verses are either one or two verses off.
2. Because of the limitations of the index itself, I had to number chapters and verses like so: 01.24, which would mean chapter 1, verse 24. I hope this somewhat unorthodox representation does not prove a problem for readers.

- *Tarot Cards* – Includes references to both Major and Minor Arcana.
- *Temple of Solomon* – All citations to the Holy Temple, both first and second ones.
- *Weights, Measurements, and Currency* – From Adarkan to Zereth, this subsection includes the amount the unit compares to others.

COMPREHENSIVE INDEX

abandon
  (to), 271
abashed
  (to be), 233
  (to feel), 233
abate
  (to), 227, 262, 449
abated
  (and), 462
abdomen, 135, 265
abhor
  (to), 58, 124, 157, 183, 215, 242, 290, 317, 481, 491
  (you shall a it), 476
  (you shall), 462
abhorred
  (and I), 183, 491
  (you made), 419, 528
abhorrence, 221, 472
abide, 397
  (to), 105, 249, 277, 326, 414, 495
  (you shall), 401
abiding, 80
ability, 75, 399
  to stand, 342
able
  (to be), 74, 78
abode, 75, 80, 245, 421, 528
  (and you), 405
  (lofty), 64
  (of God), 293, 500
  (settled), 238, 245
  of flocks, 80
  of shepherd, 75
  of shepherds, 80
abolished
  (to be), 442
abominable
  (to be), 317
  (to make), 323, 527
  thing, 324, 528
abomination, 318, 320, 323, 324, 463, 527, 528
abominations
  (as the), 467
  (the), 322, 464
  (their), 474, 540
  (with), 463
abortion, 169
about, 94
  three, 499
above, 109, 121, 123, 159, 415
abroad
  (shall break out), 391
absent
  (we are), 402
abstain
  (to a from food), 153, 393
abundance, 30, 42, 51, 56, 64, 123, 159, 185, 213, 311, 312, 356, 359, 362, 375, 421, 501
  (to be in), 201, 226
  of God, 136
abundant
  (and will make you over), 370, 375, 508, 510
  (to be), 291, 384
abundantly
  (to bring forth), 353, 535
abuse, 318
  (subject to), 87, 408
abyss, 311, 493
acacia
  tree, 395
  wood, 250, 395
accept
  (will), 393
accept
  (to a favorably), 237
acceptance, 161
accident, 243, 264
accomplish
  (to), 74, 279
accomplished
  (to be), 74
according
  to, 121
accordingly, 132, 149
account, 275, 494
  (an a of not), 307
  (on a of), 50, 229
  (to), 246
accounted, 403
accumulation, 320
accusation, 274
accuser, 271, 492
acknowledge
  (to a offense), 262, 468
  (to), 225
acknowledged
  (and he), 207
acquaintance, 220
acquire
  (to a by paying price), 212
  (to), 107, 154, 164, 166, 233, 491
acquired
  (thing), 192, 459
acquisition, 143, 192, 306, 459
across
  (in reference to a region), 226
act, 187
  (mighty), 197
  (saving), 299
action, 282, 339, 504
  (of God in history), 137
  (to separate by distinguishing), 133
  prescribed, 189
active
  (to become), 184, 492
activity, 208
add
  (to), 162, 461
adder, 335, 337, 510, 514
addition, 62, 355
  (in a to), 50
additional, 179, 470
adjuration, 54
admirable, 167
admonish
  (and you shall), 367
  (to), 194, 225
adorn
  (to), 190, 230
adornment, 190, 195
adultery, 134, 149, 198, 426, 456, 478
  (to commit), 149, 456
advance
  (to), 98, 146, 325, 348
advanced, 348, 350
advantage, 363, 383, 529
advantageous
  (to be), 334
adversary, 163, 201, 225, 234, 271, 403, 492
  (an), 36
  (and I will be an), 399
  (to be an), 237
advice, 172, 187
advise, 109, 347
  (to), 108, 109, 173, 347, 486
affair, 127, 187, 258, 336, 503
affection
  (to have inordinate), 94
afflict
  (to), 35, 144
afflicted, 144, 148, 386
  (to be), 144
affliction, 148, 336
afford, 417
afraid, 193, 194
  (I was), 365
  (to be), 55, 64, 193, 194, 195, 348, 442
  (to make), 61
  (you shall be), 358, 425, 545
  (you were a of), 361
  (you were), 377, 519
  (you will be), 383, 529
after, 189, 198
  the following part, 189
afterbirth, 264
  (and in her), 421
after-growth, 168, 302
aftermath, 302
  (to take the), 302

afterwards, 83, 405
    (of time), 189
again, 98, 474
against, 114, 121, 132, 384
    (motion or direction of a hostile character), 50
    (of one's presence), 50
    (over), 412
    YHVH, 46
    you, 532
agate, 65, 246
age, 62, 251
    (for), 183, 455
    (from), 112, 417
    (old), 153, 171, 434
    (your old), 329
aged, 350, 358, 364
    one, 364
ages, 183, 423
agile
    (to be), 114
agitation, 192
aglow
    (to be), 128
agony, 67, 286, 518
agree
    (to a together), 105
    (to a with), 248
    (to), 292
agreeable, 173, 412
agreement, 35
ah
    now!, 71
    that!, 67
ah!, 19, 23, 27, 39
aha!, 31
aid
    (to lend), 279
aim, 225
Ain. *See* Kabbalah:The Ten *Sefirot*:0 *Ain*
Ain Sof. *See* Kabbalah:The Ten *Sefirot*:00 *Ain Sof*
Ain Sof Aur. *See* Kabbalah:The Ten *Sefirot*:000 *Ain Sof Aur*
air. *Also See* Elements: Air (*Ruach*)
    (to beat the), 210
alabaster, 355, 359
alarm, 61, 388
    (the), 390
    (to), 55
    (you shall sound an), 390
alarmed, 55
alarms, 337, 503
alas!, 23, 25, 27, 34, 39, 90
Alchemy, 136
    'Azoth (first matter), 295, 318
    'Dung of the Horse', 404
    Elements
        Mercury
            as part of the three main elements, 15
        Salt
            as part of the three main elements, 15
        Sulfur
            as part of the three main elements, 15
    VITRIOL, 410
Alef. *See* Hebrew Alphabet:01 *Alef*
alert, 300
    (to be), 33, 148, 479
alien, 225, 230
alienate
    (to), 226
alienated
    (to be), 177, 199
alike, 46
alive, 35
    (I will make), 48
    (they will keep), 53
    (to be), 41, 46
    (to remain), 41, 46
    (you keep), 47
alkali
    (used in washing), 360
    used in smelting metal, 185
all, 69, 109
    sorts of things, 140
    together, 40
    witnesses, 336
alleviation, 49
alliance, 360
    (unlawful), 354
allot
    (to), 153
allotment, 350
allow
    me, 448
allowance, 195
alloy, 65
allure
    (to), 315
almighty, 194
    living God, 273
almond
    tree, 62, 290
    wood, 62
almonds, 290
    (to bear ripe), 92
almug
    tree, 142, 147, 389, 391
    wood, 142, 389
aloe
    tree, 104, 374
aloes, 104, 374
alone, 19, 25, 59, 62
    (to let), 267, 289
along
    (to bear), 62
already, 201, 317
also, 62, 100, 355, 439
altar, 73, 76, 207, 210, 266
    (cover of), 19
    (side of), 247
    (tongs for a use), 177
    hearth, 207, 210
altars, 322, 498
alter
    (to), 268, 270
alternately, 130
although, 121, 149
altogether, 40, 240
amaze
    (to), 59
amazed
    (to be), 308
ambassadors, 287, 498
amber, 280
ambivalence, 192, 477
ambivalent, 192, 477
ambuscade, 185
ambush, 211
    (to), 185
ambushing, 130
amen, 111, 416
amerce
    (to), 298
amercing, 298
amethyst, 103
amidst
    us, 301
among, 23, 80, 241, 404
    all, 71
Amos. *See* *Tanakh: 02 Neviim:* 12 Amos
amount, 471
    (measured), 317, 509
amours, 22
amulet, 192
amulets
    (covered), 319
ancestor, 15
ancient, 160, 163, 167, 186, 350, 399, 402, 407
    things, 158, 398
and, 19, 20
angel, 111, 230, 348
angels, 104, 296, 374, 396
Angels and Archangels
    Abaddon (Angel of the bottomless pit), 81, 404
    Abdaron (2nd Decanate Aquarius), 222, 472
    Aboha (3rd Decanate Sagittarius), 31
    Adnakhiel (Archangel of Sagittarius), 136
    Akaiah (1st Quinance Virgo, day angel 8 Pentacles), 55
    Aldiah (4th Quinance Virgo, night angel 9 Pentacles), 68
    Alinkir (3rd Decanate Cancer), 253
    Amamiah (4th Quinance Aries, night angel 3 Wands), 171
    Ambriel (Archangel of Gemini), 231
    Amnitziel (Archange of Pisces), 205
    Anael (Angel of Venus, Friday), 101

Ananaurah (1st Quinance Virgo), 249
Anevel (3rd Quinance Gemini, day angel 9 Swords), 167
Aniel (1st Quinance Aquarius, night angel 5 Swords), 112
Ansuel (11th astrological house), 161
Aral (Angel of Fire), 205
Aralim (Angelic choir associated with *Binah*), 231, 454
Araziel (Angel of Taurus), 214
Ariel (4th Quinance Pisces, night angel 9 Cups), 248
Asaliah (5th Quinance Pisces, day angel 10 Cups), 296
Asmodel (Archangel of Taurus), 157
Auriel (Archangel of North, Earth), 213
Avamel (6th Quinance Sagittarius, night angel 10 Wands), 96
Avron (2nd Decanate Pisces), 222, 472
Ayel (1st astrological house), 61
Ayoel (1st Quinance Cancer, day angel 2 Cups), 133
Barkiel (Archangel of Scorpio), 222
Behahemi (2nd Decanate Aries, night angel 6 Swords), 80
Beney HaElohim (Sons of God), 405
Beni Elohim (Angelic choir associated with *Hod*), 161, 400
Beton (3rd Decanate Gemini), 316, 474
Bihelami (1st Decanate Pisces), 105
Cassiel (Angel of Saturn, Saturday), 141
Chabuyah (2nd Quinance Cancer, night angel 2 cups), 50
Chabuyah (2nd Quinance Cancer, night angel 2 Cups), 50
Chahaviah (6th Quinance Scorpio, night angel 7 Cups), 53
Chamiah (2nd Quinance Aquarius, night angel 5 Swords), 150
Chashmalim (Angelic choir associated with *Hesed*), 302, 488
Chassan (Angel of Air), 271, 492
Chayoth HaQodesh (Angelic choir associated with *Keter*), 452
Chedeqiel (Angel of Libra), 165
Damabiah (5th Quinance Gemini, day angel 10 Swords), 80
Daniel (2nd Quinance, night angel 2 Wands), 115
Elemiah (4th Quinance Leo, night angel 6 Wands), 166
Elohim (choir assoc. with *Netzach* & Venus), 104, 374
Eshim (Angelic choir of *Malkut*), 268, 472
Gabriel (Archangel of *Yesod*, Luna, the West and Water), 212
Gerodiel (3rd Decanate Aquarius), 216
Giel (3rd astrological house), 63
Haayah (2nd Quinance Sagittarius, night angel 8 wands), 40
Hahahel (5th Quinance Aquarius, day angel 7 Swords), 65
Hamaliel (Archangel of Virgo), 136
Hanael (Archangel of Capricorn), 105, 116
Haniel (Archangel associated with *Netzach*, Venus), 117
Haqmiah (4th Quinance Libra, night angel 3 Swords), 168
Hariel (3rd Quinance Libra, day angel 3 Swords), 212
Hayayel (5th Quinance Cancer, day angel 4 cups), 74
Haziel (3rd Quinance Virgo, day angel 9 Pentacles), 72
Hechashiah (3rd Decanate Aries, day angel 3 Wands), 256
Herachiel (5th Quinance Taurus, day angel 7 Pentacles), 211
Hihayah (6th Quinance Virgo, night angel 10 Pentacles), 115
In reference to Jacob's ladder, 362, 562
In reference to the angel who went ahead of Israel, 570, 571
In reference to the two who arrived in Sodom, 371, 517
Ir (watcher, angel), 230
Kael (4th astrological house), 141
Kaliel (6th Quinance Libra, night angel 4 Swords), 111
Kamael (Archangel associated with *Giburah*), 111
Kambriel (Archangel of Aquarius), 242
Kamotz (1st Decanate Scorpio), 166, 483
Kashenyayah (Angel of 10th astrological house), 315
Kedamidi (1st Decanate Taurus), 96
Kehethel (2nd Quinance Virgo, night angel 8 Pentacles), 312
Keradamidi (1st Decanate Taurus – Regardie's spelling), 229
Kerubim (Angelic choir of *Yesod*), 229, 453
Keveqiah (4th Quinance Aquarius, night angel 6 Swords), 157
Lahat (flame of sword of), 63
Laviah (5th Quinance Libra, day angel 4 Swords), 72
Laviah (5th Quinance Virgo, day angel 10 Pentacles), 72
Lehachiah (4th Quinance Capricorn, night angel 3 Pentacles), 77
Lehahel (6th Quinance Leo, night angel 7 Wands), 117
Lekabel (1st Quinance Capricorn, day angel 2 Pentacles), 102
Losanahar (1st Decanate Leo), 268
Luviah (1st Quinance Scorpio, day angel 5 Cups), 76
Mahashiah (5th Quinance Leo, day angel 7 Wands), 272
Malakh HaElohim (Angel of God), 178, 520
Malakh HaMaschith (Angel of destruction), 456
Malakh HaMashith (Angel of destruction), 530
Malakim (Angels, messengers), 157, 396
Malkidiel (Archangel of Aries), 151
Mathravash (1st Decanate Cancer), 480
Mebahel (2nd Quinance Libra, day angel 2 Swords), 96
Mebahiah (1st Quinance Taurus, day angel 5 Pentacles), 81
Melahel (5th Quinance Scorpio, day angel 7 Cups), 128
Melek (Messenger), 111, 348
Melekim (Angelic choir of *Tiferet*), 155, 394
Mendel (6th Quinance Capricorn, night angel 4 Pentacles), 143
Menqel (6th Quinance Gemini, night angel 10 Swords), 200
Metatron (Archangel of *Keter*), 249, 483
Mevamiah (6th Quinance Cancer, night angel 4 Cups), 123
Michael (6th Quinance Aquarius, night angel 7 Swords), 123
Michael (Angel of Sol, Sunday), 123
Michael (Archangel of *Hod*, Mercury, the South, and Fire), 123
Mihael (6th Quinance Pisces, night angel 10 Cups), 105
Minacharai (2nd Decanate Taurus), 250
Mishpar (3rd Decanate Virgo), 365
Mishrath (1st Decanate Sagittarius), 479
Misnin (1st Decanate Capricorn), 191, 458
Mispar (3rd Decanate Virgo), 280
Mitzrael (6th Quinance Taurus, night angel 7 Pentacles), 273
Mochayel (4th Quinance Gemini, night angel 9 Swords), 108
Muriel (Archangel of Cancer), 233
Nanael (5th Quinance Aries, day angel 4 Wands), 149

Nelakiel (3rd Quinance Scorpio, day angel 6 Cups), 149
Nemamiah (3rd Quinance Taurus, day angel 6 Pentacles), 159
Nithael (6th Quinance Aries, night angel 4 Wands), 323
Nithahiah (1st Quinance Sagittarius, day angel 8 Wands), 316
Nundohar (2nd Decanate Scorpio), 255
Oel (5th astrological house), 129
Ofan (Wheel), 153, 434
Ofanim (Angelic choir associated with *Chokmah*), 180, 419
Pahaliah (2nd Quinance Scorpio, night angel 5 Cups), 148
Pakiel (Angel of Cancer), 157
Pasiel (Angel of 12th astrological house), 299
Phorlakh (Angel of Earth), 260, 447
Poyel (2nd Quinance Taurus, night angel 5 Pentacles), 145
Qaddish (angels in the human sense), 296
Rafael (Archangel of *Tiferet*, Sol, the East, Air, angel ruling Mercury, Wednesday), 248
Rahadetz (2nd Decanate Cancer), 239, 507
Rahael (3rd Quinance Cancer, day angel 3 Cups), 208
Rayadyah (2nd Decanate Virgo), 205
Raziel (Archangel of *Chokmah*), 214
Rehael (3rd Quinance Aquarius, day angel 6 Swords), 244
Reyayel (5th Quinance Sagittarius, day angel 10 Wands), 216
Sachiel (Angel associated with Jupiter, Thursday), 130
Sagarash (1st Decanate Gemini), 346
Saharnatz (2nd Decanate Libra), 290, 519
Sahiah (4th Quinance Sagittarius, night angel 9 Wands), 253
Sahiber (3rd Decanate Leo), 228
Saitziel (Angel of Scorpio), 185
Saliah (3rd Quinance Pisces, day angel 9 Cups), 128
Samael (Angel of death), 149
Sameqiel (Angel of Capricorn), 210
Sandalfon (Archangel of *Malkut*), 230, 476
Sansenoy (Angel invoked against Lilith), 207
Saraf (Fiery serpent), 351, 527
Sarayel (Angel of Gemini), 241
Saritiel (Angel of Sagittarius), 253
Saspam (1st Decanate Aquarius), 209, 438
Satander (3rd Decanate Aries), 254
Satrip (3rd Decanate Pisces), 271, 502
Semangelof (Angel invoked against Lilith), 225, 488
Senoy (Angel invoked against Lilith), 144
Senoy, Sansenoy, Semangelof (Three angels invoked against Lilith), 369, 525, 526, 532, 567
Serafim (Angelic choir associated with *Giburah*), 368, 516
Shachdar (3rd Decanate Libra), 331
Sharatiel (Angel of Leo), 344
Sharhiel (Angel of Aries), 343
Shehadani (2nd Decanate Gemini), 276
Shelathiel (Angel of Virgo), 429
Shinanim (Angelic choir associated with *Tiferet*), 311, 493
Sitael (3rd Quinance Leo, day angel 6 Wands), 132
Sizajasel (9th astrological house – misprint), 208
Sosul (8th astrological house), 171
Soyasel (Angel of 9th astrological house), 208
Taliahad (Angel of Water), 76
Tarasni (1st Decanate Libra), 257
Tarshishim (Angelic choir associated with *Netzach*), 524, 554
'These are Michael, Gabriel, and Rafael', 395
Toel (2nd astrological house), 65
Tzadqiel (Archangel of *Hesed*, Jupiter), 206
Tzafqiel (Archangel of *Binah*, Saturn), 248
Tzakmiqiel (Angel of Aquarius), 235
Uthrodiel (3rd Decanate Scorpio), 380
Vahaviah (1st Quinance Leo, day angel 5 Wands), 51
Vakabiel (Angel of Pisces), 87
Vavaliah (1st Quinance Pisces, day angel 8 Cups), 75
Vehrin (2nd Decanate Sagittarius), 225, 475
Vehuel (1st Quinance Aries, day angel 2 Wands), 66
Vemibael (1st Quinance Gemini, day angel 8 Swords), 97
Verkiel (Archangel of Leo), 224
Veshriah (2nd Quinance Capricorn, night angel 2 Pentacles), 335
Veyel (6th astrological house), 66
Yahel (7th astrological house), 65
Yakasaganotz (3rd Decanate Taurus), 208, 499
Yasaganotz (3rd Decanate Taurus), 177, 451
Yasgedibarodiel (3rd Decanate Capricorn), 261
Yasnadibarodiel (3rd Decanate Capricorn), 283
Yasyasyah (2nd decanate Capricorn), 166
Yebamiah (4th Quinance Cancer, night angel 3 Cups), 85
Yechaviah (3rd Quinance Capricorn, day angel 3 Pentacles), 58
Yehoel (Angel of *Keter* in the world of *Briah*), 71
Yehohel (2nd Quinance Gemini, night angel 8 Swords), 70
Yelahiah (2nd Quinance Pisces, night angel 8 Cups), 78
Yelayel (2nd Quinance Leo, night angel 5 Wands), 100
Yerathel (3rd Quinance Sagittarius, day angel 9 Wands), 372
Yeyalel (4th Quinance Taurus, night angel 6 Pentacles), 100
Yeyayel (4th Quinance Scorpio, night angel 6 Cups), 80
Yeyazel (4th Quinance Aquarius, night angel 6 Swords), 77
Yezalel (1st Quinance Libra, day angel 2 Swords), 96
Zachi (2nd Decanate Leo), 115
Zamael (Angel of Mars, Tuesday), 96
Zazer (1st Decanate Aries), 195
Zuriel (Archangel of Libra), 217
anger, 68, 72, 100, 137, 162, 195, 222, 225, 386, 439, 473, 488
(burning heat of God's), 222, 473
(of Moses), 232, 491
(slow to), 200
(to be kindled with), 361
(to become emotionally agitated with), 220
(to provoke to), 162
angle, 52
angrily
(to speak), 28, 33
angry, 167, 462
(did make), 386
(to be), 133, 148, 162, 195, 225, 298, 456, 488, 501
(will you be), 385, 534
(you made), 406, 525
anguish, 67, 87, 100, 174, 180, 207, 230, 285, 286, 408, 518
(to be in), 44
animal, 35, 37, 44, 71, *Also See* Important Jewish Terms:Clean; Unclean
(sacrificial - the caudate lobe of the liver of), 492
(to break the neck of), 267, 501
(to sacrifice an), 30
hide, 401
torn by beasts, 236

animals, 41, 300
(to kneel down to rest of), 234
animosity, 286
ankle, 285
chain, 173
anklet, 163, 173
annihilate
(to), 161
annihilation, 74, 136, 417, 426
anoint
(and you shall), 422
(to), 96, 105, 266, 269, 346, 490
(you shall), 420
(you), 419
anointed, 271, 284
(one), 155, 365
one, 155, 271, 365
ones, 238
anointing
(and of the), 422
(their), 435, 531
(to pour in), 105, 346
oil, 269
portion, 269
another, 18, 28, 43, 189, 198, 219, 220, 358, 388, 448, 471
(over), 45
answer, 171, 187
(an), 405
(to), 144
ant, 143
antelope, 274, 493
antimony, 128, 352
antiquity, 156, 160, 162, 394, 399
anvil, 181, 420
anxiety, 29, 51, 198
(extreme), 198
anxious
(to be), 22, 55
care, 29, 198
anything, 64, 112, 119
apalled
(to be), 281, 479
apallment, 264, 303, 502
apart, 19
(set), 374
(you shall set), 380
from, 136
apartness, 290
ape, 180, 303, 470
aphrodisiac
(mandrake as an), 42
apostasy, 223, 269
apostate, 243
apparel, 261, 280, 320
appear
(and let), 360
(to make), 174, 449
(to), 370
appearance, 39, 188, 193, 199, 204, 212, 355
(an), 224
appears
(where there), 360
appease
(will), 393
appendage, 492
appetite, 302
apple, 323, 341, 506
(of the eye), 23
tree, 323, 341, 506
appoint, 187
(and I will), 422
(and you shall), 425
(to), 103, 116, 164, 179, 266, 471, 505
(you shall), 368, 516
appointed, 395
(to be), 105, 375
place, 140, 202
place (in army), 140
time, 105, 140, 375
to destruction, 143, 454
appointment, 135, 202
apportion
(to), 153
approach
(an), 244
(his), 401
(shall), 401
(to stop the), 121, 350
(to), 74, 241, 269
(when they), 418, 528
(you shall), 397
appropriate, 86, 407
aprons, 360
Aramaic Language
htn) – You, thou (2nd person sing.), 312
Nwtn) (you, thou - 2nd person plural), 328, 513
archer, 185, 438
architect, 117, 419
ardor, 167
are
(there), 247
argument, 187, 304
arise
(to), 160, 196, 399
arising, 235, 388
ark, 218, 468, 470
(holy), 385, 530
(the a cover), 398
(the), 295
of, 439
Ark of Noah, 292
height of in cubits, 49
length of in cubits, 240
number of days spent on, 59
number of years to build, 140
width of in cubits, 69
Ark of the Covenant, 215, 218, 385, 470, 529, 530
(as Ark of the Testimony), 413, 534
(as Holy Ark), 382
(slab on top of – the Mercy Seat), 394
(when inside Solomon's Temple – the Holy of Holies), 187, 197
covering of, 143
doorkeeper of (Hosah), 92
gatekeeper of
Jehiah, 52
head Levite when David brought it to the Temple (Chenaniah), 151, 157
Levite with David in moving of (Eliy'el), 91
musician who participated in the return of to the Temple (Azaziah), 127
musician who participated in the return of to the Temple (Aziel), 138
musician who participated in the return of to the Temple (Obed-edom), 145, 390
number of people from Beth-Shemesh struck down for looking into, 88
one who helped bring it from the house of Obed-edom (Amminadab), 176
one who helped bring it to the Temple (Amasai), 298
one who helped bring it to the Temple (Asaiah), 282
one who helped bring it to the Temple (Shebaniah), 278
one who helped bring it to the Temple (Shemaiah), 301
one who housed for three months (Obed-edom), 145, 390
one who preceded it to the Temple (Joshaphat), 290
one who was struck dead after touching (Uzza), 97
person who cared for (Eleazar), 245
place where Uzzah was struck dead for touching (Chidon), 109, 415
priest who helped bring into the Temple (Jaziel), 84
priest who helped move (Eliezer), 251
priest who helped to bring from Obed-edom (Jehoshaphat), 293
trumpet blower (Nethaneel), 338
wood of which it was made (cypress), 231
arm, 19, 227, 231
(you will a yourself), 338
armaments, 336
armed, 265
armies
(space between two), 124, 381
armlet, 173
armor, 158, 159, 198, 253, 437, 484
(coat of mail), 358

(for the body), 346, 519
(leg), 158
(not sanctionted by God), 314
(used in warfare not sanctioned by YHVH), 312
armory, 237, 310, 336
arms, 386
army, 66, 103, 114, 153, 250, 440
(appointed place in), 140
(wing of an), 103, 440
aroma, 198
arrange
(and you shall), 393
(to), 234, 428
arrangement, 223, 257, 320, 443
array
(to set in), 234, 428
arrive
(to), 291
arrogance, 30, 85, 188, 228, 407
arrogant, 27, 202, 348
(to be), 34
one, 139
arrogantly
(to talk), 144, 191, 477, 495
arrow, 118, 130, 180, 470
(flaming), 129, 141
arrows
(to shoot), 180, 489
art
(magic), 329
(originator of an), 15
article, 78
pledged as security for debt, 106
artifice, 188
artificer, 117, 329, 419
artificial
man, 97, 371
artisan, 111, 329, 416
artist, 111, 416
as, 49, 84
(according), 84
(and), 54
far as, 93
ascend
(to), 127, 181, 191
ascent, 61, 127, 159, 355
ascribe, 29
(to), 35
ashamed
(to be), 91, 109, 233, 241, 245, 376
ashes, 119, 230, 267, 272
ash-heap, 432
ash-heaps, 448
aside
(shall go), 405
(to be thrust), 162, 461
(to go), 395
(to lay), 141, 211
from, 55
ask
(and), 414
(do you), 413
(shall a of you), 421, 521
(to), 92, 95, 258
asked
(thing a for), 260
asleep
(to be), 212, 272, 440, 492
asp, 287
asphalt, 213, 321
(to cover with), 213
(to smear with), 213
pitch, 239
ass
(female), 312, 506
(male), 217, 230
(wild), 227, 230, 231
assail
(to), 440
assault
(object of), 182
assay
(to), 135
assayer, 84, 406
assemble
(to), 103, 152, 182, 395, 490
assembling, 320
assembly, 88, 152, 156, 176, 183, 187, 262, 266, 274, 424, 492
(solemn), 274
assessable, 169
assessment, 163
Assiah. *See* Kabbalah:Worlds: *Assiah*
assign
(to), 116, 153
assistance, 231
associate, 191, 196, 316, 334
(to a with), 228
association, 191, 196
astonish, 67, 358
astonished, 418
astound, 67, 358
astounded
(to be), 308
astral
body, 170, 409
astray
(to go), 20, 129, 244, 246, 383
(to wander), 103, 318
astrologer, 219, 259, 281, 447, 505
(to be an), 188
astrologers, 328, 501
asylum, 177
at, 50, 66, 95, 109, 305, 416
atonement, 239, 243, 297
(to make an), 239
(you shall make), 395
atonements
(many), 266, 471
attach
(to a to), 161
(to), 372, 517
attached, 70
attached
(to be a to), 292
attack, 208
(to), 27, 29, 191
attain
(to a to), 149
(to), 69, 314, 479
attend
(to a to), 179
attendance, 165
attendant
maidens, 232
attention, 289
attentive, 289
(to be), 289
attentiveness, 289
attire, 280
(gorgeous), 144
attractive, 275, 356, 455
Atzilut. *See* Kabbalah:Worlds: *Atzilut*
aught, 64
aunt, 36
aurochs
(great – now extinct), 210, 439
authority, 343, 351, 527
autumn, 233, 492, *Also See* Seasons:Fall (*Sethev*)
shower, 200
avail
(to), 131
avaunt!, 119, 125, 470, 473
avenge
(to a oneself), 181, 420
(to), 52, 181, 420
avenged
(to be), 181, 420
aversion, 221, 472
(held in), 273
avouched
(you have), 374
await
(to), 52
awake
(to), 183, 184, 228, 491, 492
awaken
(to), 184, 228, 492
away, 33
(and you shall put), 387
(sending), 264
(to be put), 492
(to carry), 73
(to go), 56
(to sweep), 25, 33, 104, 159, 231, 348, 490
from, 76, 94
awe, 118
(religious), 118
(to be in), 113
awe-inspiring, 276, 515
awesome, 276, 515
awful
shock, 290
awl, 288
axe, 155, 186, 217, 220, 264, 272, 458, 469, 471
(battle), 191, 495
axes

(large), 155, 458
axle, 247, 483
Ayin. See Hebrew Alphabet:16 *Ayin*
baboon, 303
babouche, 235
baby
(the), 68
back, 18, 23, 30, 102, 267, 273, 275, 439, 475, 501
(bring), 404
(to hold), 75, 169, 178, 256, 442
(to keep), 169
part, 384
side, 195
backbone, 171
backslide
(to), 87, 134
backsliding, 243, 269
backturning, 243
backwards, 384
bad, 225, 249
(and the), 388, 390
(and), 389
(to be), 242, 262
(to smell), 242
badness, 225
bag, 109, 159, 166, 203, 225, 484
(as packed), 324
(leather), 211
bait, 308
(to lay), 291
bait-layer, 297
bake
(to), 98, 105, 258
baked, 144
(thing), 144
piece, 355, 523
balance, 348, 419
(to), 116, 174
balanced
verity, 293
balances, 119, 166, 419
balancing, 310
bald, 29, 245, 249
(be), 60
(in the head), 402
(to be), 245
(to make), 214, 245
in the forehead, 295
spot, 401
baldness, 249
(back), 401
(on his), 406
of head, 401
ball, 101, 191, 202, 439
ball-shaped
carved wood, 215
balm, 240
balsam, 240, 263, 468
tree, 41, 263, 468
ban
(to), 213, 442
band, 29, 34, 58, 103, 155, 191, 224, 230, 244, 246, 319, 440
for a woman's head, 278
of soldiers, 177, 414
bandage, 230, 307
(to remove a b from a wound), 29
(to), 246
bands, 173, 177, 354
bangle, 163
bangles
(to shake), 163
banish
(to), 81
banishment, 441
banner, 55, 132
banners, 55
banquet, 418
(to give a), 202
bar, 19, 234, 504
(hammered), 108
(to), 162
(wrought iron), 108
of tribulation, 199
of yoke, 74, 79
barb, 156, 159, 255, 435
barbarous
(to be), 226
barber, 53
bare, 211, 247, 251, 462
(to be laid), 228
(to be), 227
(to lay), 284, 506
(to make), 214, 284, 316, 506
(to), 214
of children, 322
place, 228
bared
(to be), 228
barefoot, 119, 273, 447
bareness, 285
bargain
(to b over), 202
bark
(laying bare of), 302, 512
(to), 79
barley, 31, 349, 365, 515
(young b ears), 31
barn, 123, 216, 381, 469
barn-floor, 216, 469
barren, 276
barrenness, 102
base, 73, 88, 98, 135, 141, 182, 204, 398, 402, 408
basic, 244
basin, 73, 155, 171, 174, 207, 211, 265, 397, 458
basins
(and its), 427
(the), 421
basket, 30, 77, 78, 109, 179, 211
(in the), 112
(in which the baby Moses was placed), 292
saddle, 199
bastard, 233
bat, 180, 471
battering-ram, 199
(stroke of), 77
battering-rams, 150
battle, 146, 241
(arrayed for b by fives), 265
(in b array), 265
(to do), 96, 371
battle-line, 250, 259
battlement, 201
bay, 148, 355, 479
bdellium, 63
be, 33, 43
(and let them), 45
(and they shall), 55
(and will), 44
(and), 44
(far b it from me), 102
(let it not), 102
(let it), 44
(let there), 44
(shall they), 50
(to), 28, 38, 39, 43, 299
beacon, 377, 527
beads
(string of), 200
beam, 18, 90, 181, 237, 248
(to), 218
work, 264
beams, 344, 367
(hewn), 367
(to build with), 243
laid over, 320, 517
beans, 137
bear, 19, 28, 412
(shall), 396
(to), 63, 108, 113, 191, 268, 364
(you shall), 400
beard, 153, 434
(their), 183, 423
bearing, 263
(in), 397
beast, 44, 71, 297
(and), 50
(wild), 132
beasts, 231, 308, 309
(howling of), 87
(wild), 229, 325, 500
(young or offspring of wild), 327
beat, 181, 420
(and he shall b him), 61
(and you shall), 445
(to), 37, 94, 179, 251, 281, 448
it, 48
beaten
(and were), 61
out, 451
beating
(to crush by), 448
beautiful, 81, 115, 252
(of foliage), 353
(to be), 75, 169, 351, 408
(very), 182
beautifully
formed, 83, 406

beautify
(to), 80, 230
beauty, 71, 86, 120, 124, 169, 351, 390, 407, 408, 503
(and for), 508
beaver, 81
became
(and there), 50
(and they), 55
(and), 44
because, 49, 121, 147, 175, 431
(and), 54
of, 53, 147, 149, 229, 431
of that, 22
that, 49, 121, 147, 149, 431
because...not, 307
becloud
(to), 97
become
(to), 28, 38
much or abundant, 62, 355
becoming
great, 55
bed, 73, 176, 184, 273, 348
(to make a), 173
bedust
(to), 124
befall
(and shall), 400
(to), 241, 243, 244
befallen
(and have), 425
us, 423
befit
(to), 33
befitting
(to be), 33, 75
before, 22, 76, 97, 149, 158, 173, 214, 217, 317, 318, 344, 398, 443, 446, 518
(from), 76
(to be), 149
(to go), 158
that, 214, 217, 443, 446
that time, 318
befouled, 365
(thing), 365
beg
(to), 258
beget
(to), 63
begin
(to), 60, 86, 326
(will), 57
beginning, 60, 93, 307, 355, 472
(from the), 480
(in the), 473, 565
(to make a), 60
beginnings, 328
beguile
(to), 212, 268
beguiled
me, 403
behalf
(on b of), 97
behavior, 75
beheld
(and they), 56
(has), 44
behind, 94, 219, 223, 471, 473
(of place), 189
(shall be left), 468
behold, 55, 188
(and), 84
(does he), 50
(to), 33, 38, 194
behold!, 19, 55, 74, 78, 398
being, 247
(living), 302
alone, 19
strong, 139
belie
(to), 256
bell, 171
(on High Priest's robe), 209, 465
bellows, 150
belly, 80, 85, 129, 135, 265, 334, 403, 407
beloved, 22, 29, 30, 35, 36, 40, 46
(one dearly), 300
(one), 46
(the), 42
below, 73, 82, 455
belt, 158, 198
(to put on a), 193
be-mantle
(to), 216
bend, 123, 449
(to b down), 82, 177, 272, 287, 467, 488
(to b together), 287
(to), 82, 101, 162, 172, 177, 184, 194, 201, 234, 318, 397, 438, 467
bending, 320
beneath, 442, 455
beneficial
(to be), 34
benefit, 35, 319
(to be of), 148, 431
(to), 131
benevolence, 15
bent
(to be), 177, 318, 467
(to make), 287
benumbed
(to be), 108
benumbing, 113, 114
bereave
(shall), 420
bereaved, 270
(I am), 425
(to be), 267
(you have), 435, 532
bereavement, 273
berry, 291
(olive), 291
beseech
(I/we b you), 71
beside, 114, 121, 132, 141, 305, 384
besides, 19, 55, 66, 98, 136, 363
besiege
(to), 237, 323
(you shall), 393
besmear
(to), 41
besmeared
(to be), 41
besom, 79
besprinkle
(to), 152, 457
best, 80, 214, 472
(in the), 36
bestow
(they shall), 268
(to b upon), 29
(to), 29
Bet. See Hebrew Alphabet:02 *Bet*
betroth
(to), 103, 325
(you shall), 468
betrothals, 111
betrothed
(to be), 233, 491
better, 76, 363
between, 80, 124, 381, 404
(from), 80, 404
(in), 50
bevelled
work, 214
bewail, 57
(to), 45
beware
(to), 247, 461
lest, 148, 432
bewitched
(I shall be), 289, 509
beyond, 121
(in reference to a region), 226
bezel, 320, 517
Bible. *See Tanakh*
Biblical, 468
Biblical Characters
Aaron, 218, 221, 470, 472
ancestor of (Amram), 267, 472
brother-in-law of (Naashon), 296, 501
descendant of (Adaiah), 108
descendant of (Bukki), 133
descendant of (Buzi), 43
descendant of (Jakim), 168, 408
descendant of (Maasai), 298
descendant of (Malchiah), 127
descendant of (Meraioth), 379
descendant of (Meshullam), 293, 484
descendant of (Shallum), 280, 478
father-in-law of (Amminadab), 176
grandson of (Phinehas), 189

head of a family of (Jachin), 108, 415
head of a family of (Jehoiarib), 211
number of Israelites who rebelled against, 215
one who rebelled against (Korah), 245
one who rebelled against (On), 75, 399
one who tried to overthrow (Dathan), 311, 505
sister of (Miriam), 234, 456
son of (Abihu), 43
son of (Eleazar), 245
son of (Ithamar), 377
son of (Nadab), 75
son of (Putiel), 152
wife of (Elisheba), 295
Abagtha, 292
Abda, 96
Abdeel, 56, 129
Abdi, 105
Abdiel, 137
father of (Guni), 87
Abdon, 149, 432, *Also See:* Israel: Judges of: 11 Abdon
father of (Micah), 94
Abeasaph, 165, 462
Abed-nego, 151, 152
as Azariah, 235
Abel, 51, 55
brother of (Cain), 170, 444
Abi, 28
father of (Zechariah), 210
Abi Albon, 174, 449
Abi Gibon, 261, 488
Abiah
son of (Ashur), 332
Abiathar, 361
son of (Ahimelech), 130, 352
son of (Jonathan), 335, 515
Abida, 105
Abidan, 85, 407
father of (Gideoni), 153
Abiel, 63
Abiezer, 234
descendant of (Abi Haezri), 243
Abigail, 64, 74
father of (Nahash), 271
son of (Ithra), 360
Abihail, 76, 80
Abihu, 43
(and), 50
one who carried body of (Mishael), 281
Abihud, 46
Abijah, 35, *Also See:* Judah: Kings of: 02 Abijam
father of (Zechariah), 210
Abijam. *Also See:* Judah: Kings of: 02 Abijam
Abimael, 103
Abimelech, 124, 351
captain of the army of (Pichol), 156
friend of (Ahuzzath), 296
number of Gideon's sons killed by, 88
number of silver coins given to by the people of Shechem, 88
one who escaped from (Jotham), 312, 494
one who led a rebellion against (Gaal), 124
one who rebelled against (Ebed), 95
place where covenant was made with Isaac (Shebah), 246
Abinadab
son of (Ahio), 43
son of (Eleazar), 245
Abinoam, 175, 413
Abiram, 216, 445
father of (Eliab), 63
Abishag, 250
Abishai, 249, 254
Abishalom, 284, 480
Abishua, 284
son of (Bukki), 133
Abishur, 334
son of (Ahban), 80, 403
wife of (Abihail), 76
Abital, 70
son of (Shephatiah), 290
Abitub, 48
Abner, 216, 222
father of (Ner), 215
one slain by (Asahel), 291
Abraham (Abram), 177, 213, 441
(and), 216, 445
age of father when he was born, 88
as Abram, 211, 439
birthplace of (Ur), 188
brother of (Haran), 217, 219, 469, 470
brother of (Nahor), 223
brother of (Tebah), 37
burial cave of (Machpelah), 175
father of (Terah), 358
grandfather of (Nahor), 223
grandson of (Dedan), 400
grandson of (Dedan), 76
grandson of (Ephah), 171
grandson of (Epher), 267
grandson of (Hadad), 33
grandson of (Hadar), 194
grandson of (Sheba), 242
great-grandfather of (Serug), 330
hill where he was to sacrifice Isaac (Moriah), 217, 221
land given to (Canaan), 180
nephew of (Chesed), 255
nephew of (Hazo), 39
nephew of (Jidlaph), 143, 454
nephew of (Lot), 64
niece of (Iscah), 115
number of nations given to, 25
number of years lived by, 176
one from whom he bought a field (Zohar), 238
one who helped (Eshcol), 268
place where he took Isaac to be sacrificed (Adonai-Jireh), 210
servant of (Eliezer), 251
son of (Abida), 105
son of (Isaac), 298
son of (Ishbak), 295
son of (Ishmael), 311
son of (Jokshan), 313, 507
son of (Medan), 114, 418
son of (Midian), 125, 422
son of (Shuah), 249
son of (Zimran), 237, 480
three men confronting him, 395
wife of (Keturah), 253
wife of (Sarah), 328
wife of (Sarai), 331
Absalom, 280, 478
commander of army of (Amasa), 295
forest where slain (Ephraim), 258, 465
mother of (Maachah), 151
place where servants of killed Ammon (Baal Hazor), 291
place where sought refuge, 401
Achan, 156, 435
place where stoned (Achor), 237
Achar, 234
Achbor, 238
son of (Baal-Hanan), 345, 555
son of (Elnathan), 338, 516
Achish, 257
father of (Maachah), 151
father of (Maoch), 152, 363
Achsah, 166
Adah, 98
Adaiah, 108, 116
father of (Jeroham), 219, 447
Adalia, 64
Adam, 63, 356
number of years lived by, 477
rib of, 181
son of (Abel), 51, 55
son of (Cain), 170, 444
son of (Seth), 395
wife of (Eve), 37
wife of (Lilith), 319

Adam and Eve, 87, 368
Addan, 73, 80, 398, 403
Ader, 227
Adiel, 136
Adin, 150, 433
Adina, 151, 156
Adino, 90
Adlai, 135
Admatha, 308
Adna, 144
Adnah, 147
Adoni-bezek, 175
Adonijah, 87, 94
mother of (Haggith), 299
place where he sacrificed animals (Zoheleth), 308
Adonikam, 186, 426
Adoniram, 243, 460
alternate name (Adoram), 212
alternate name for (Adoram), 440
father of (Abda), 96
Adoni-zedek, 219
Adoram, 212, 440
Adriel, 250
father of (Barzillai), 214
woman given to (Merab), 211
Adullamite, 165
Agag, 20
descendent of (Agagite), 33
Agagite, 33
Agee, 18
Agur, 190
father of (Jakeh), 135
Ahab. *Also See:* Israel: Kings of: 07 Ahab
father of (Kolaiah), 164
Aharah, 197
Aharhel, 213
Ahasai, 44
Ahasbai, 100
Ahashtariy, 474
Ahasuerus, 225, 442, 449, *See Also:*Biblical Characters:Cambyses
advisor of (Dalphon), 173
chamberlain of (Bigtha), 291
chamberlain of (Bigthan), 312, 506
chamberlain of (Bigthana), 312
chamberlain of (Carcas), 239
chamberlain of (Harbona), 224
chamberlain of (Hatach), 300, 469
chamberlain of (Hegai), 35
chamberlain of (Hege), 23
chamberlain of (Mehuman), 157, 436
chamberlain of (Shaashgaz), 388
eunuch of (Biztha), 292
eunuch of (Zethar), 357
number of provinces of, 145
prime minister of (Haman), 115, 418
wife of (Vashti), 406
Ahaz, 32, *Also See:* Judah: Kings of: 11 Ahaz
son of (Jarah), 232
son of (Jehoadah), 120
Ahaziah. *Also See:* Judah: Kings of: 06 Jehoahaz, *Also See:* Israel: Kings of: 08 Ahaziah
Ahban, 80, 403
Aher, 189
Ahiam, 78, 364
Ahian, 87, 408
Ahiezer, 237
father of (Ammishaddai), 304
Ahihud, 50, 52
Ahijah, 42
Ahikam, 168, 408
Ahilud, 73
Ahimaaz, 198, 496
son of (Azariah), 235
wife of (Basmath), 417
Ahiman, 130
son of (Anak), 424
Ahimelech, 130, 352
Ahimoth, 315
Ahinadab, 93
Ahinoam, 177, 415
father of (Ahimaaz), 198, 496
son of (Ishvi), 256
Ahio, 43
Ahira, 233
Ahiram, 219, 448
son of (Aharah), 197
Ahiramites, 224
Ahisamach, 154, 364
Ahishahar, 336
Ahishar, 334
Ahithophel, 337
Ahitub, 54
son of (Zadok), 184
Ahlai, 67
son of (Attai), 319
Ahoah, 41
Ahohite, 52
Aholiab, 67
Ahumai, 83
Ahuzam, 74, 362
Ahuzzath, 296
Aiah, 33
Ajah, 33
Akan, 199, 461
Akkub, 177
Alai
son of (Zabad), 30
Alameth, 340
Alian, 169, 443
Allon, 105, 414
Almodad, 103
Alvan, 167, 441
Amal, 156
Amalekites, 215
Amariah, 218, 221
Amasa, 295
father of (Hadlai), 71
Amasai, 298
Amashai, 319
Amasiah, 179
Amassa
father of (Ithra), 360
mother of (Abigail), 360
Amaziah. *Also See:* Judah: Kings of: 08 Amaziah
Amelek, 209
Ami, 70
form of (Amon), 117, 419
Amittai, 78
Ammiel, 164
father of (Gemalli), 102
Ammihud, 152
Ammihur, 259
Amminadab, 176
father of (Ram), 209, 439
Ammishaddai, 304
Ammizabad, 150
Ammon, 172, 447
king defeated by (Nahash), 271
place where killed (Baal Hazor), 291
Ammonites, 176
Ammonitess, 349
Ammorites, 235
ancestor of (Ben-ammi), 175, 449
god of (Molech), 109, 347
king of (Sihon), 146, 150, 431, 433
Amnon, 160, 167, 437, 441
mother of (Ahinoam), 177, 415
one violated by (Tamar), 372
Amok, 197
Amon, 117, *Also See:* Judah: Kings of: 14 Amon
Amorite, 215
Amorites, 456
Amos, 176
Amoz, 153, 480
Amram, 267, 472
number of years lived by, 153
Amramite, 272
Amramites
(the), 274
Amraphel, 267
Amzi, 156
Anah, 144
Anaiah, 152
Anak, 199
ancestor of (Arba), 227
son of (Ahiman), 424
son of (Anak), 130
Anakim, 204
ancestor of (Anak), 199

Anakite, 204
Anamim, 192, 428
Anan, 174, 449
Anani, 178
Ananiah, 179
Anath, 334
Anathoth, 476
priest of (Hilkiah), 168
Aner, 253
Aniam, 174, 412
Antothijah, 477
Antothite, 477
Anub, 146
Apharsachites, 277, 428
Aphiah, 119
Appaim, 148, 392
Ara, 185
Arabian, 231
Arad, 227
Arah, 189
Aram, 209, 439
son of (Gether), 355
son of (Uz), 172, 485
Aramitess, 215
Aran, 215
Araunah, 84, 221, 222
Arba, 227
Arbathite, 389
Arbite, 194
Archevite, 207
Archite, 205
Ard, 186
Ardites, 195
Ardon, 221, 472
Areli, 210
Arelites, 210
Argob, 187
Aridai, 202
Arieh, 196
Ariel, 209, 210
Arioch, 207, 407
Arisai, 230
Arkites, 281
Arnan, 241, 481
Arod, 192
Aroerite(s), 344
Arphaxad, 356
(and), 360
Artaxerxes, 533, 547
chancellor of (Rehum), 217, 445
Arvadite, 200
Arza, 235
Asa. *Also See:* Judah: Kings of: 03 Asa
Asahel, 291
son of (Zebadiah), 46
Asahiah, 282
Asaiah, 282
Asaph, 156, 459
ancestor of (Adaiah), 108
ancestor of (Baaseiah), 283
ancestor of (Michael), 123
descendant of (Jeiel), 141
descendant of (Mattaniah), 327
father of (Berachiah), 207
father of (Berekyahu), 211
son of (Asarelah), 339
son of (Jesharelah), 342
son of (Joah), 44
son of (Joseph), 166, 462
son of (Kore), 241, 244
Asareel, 338
Asarelah, 339
Asenath, 331
son of (Ephraim), 258, 465
Aser
descendant of (Suah), 93
Ashbaal, 289
Ashbel, 259
Ashbelites, 263
Ashdodites, 255
Asher, 325
daughter of (Serah), 330
mother of (Zilpah), 142
son of (Imna), 126
son of (Ishvi), 255
wife of (Helah), 63
Asherites, 331
Ashkenaz, 280
Ashpenaz, 305
Ashriel, 341
Ashur, 332
descendant of (Achashtariy), 474
grandson of (Ethnan), 325, 513
one in the line of (Amal), 156
son of (Ahuzam), 74, 362
son of (Temeni), 331
wife of (Naarah), 255
Ashurbanipal, 285
Ashurites, 333
Ashvath, 430
Asiel, 294
Asmaveth
father of (Adiel), 136
Asnah, 136
Asnapper or Osnapper, 285
Aspatha, 341
Asriel, 341
Asrielites, 341
Assir, 225
Asterathite, 534
Atarah, 231
Ater, 190
Athaiah, 321
Athaliah, 332, 335, *Also See:* Israel: Kings of: 12 Athaliah
Athlai, 331
Attai, 319
Avites, 105
Azaliah, 152
Azaniah, 92
Azarael, 245
Azareel
father of (Jeroham), 219, 447
Azariah, 235, 238, *Also See:* Judah: Kings of: 09 Azariah, *Also See:* Judah: Kings of: 06 Jehoahaz
ancestor of (Meraioth), 379
as Abed-nego, 151, 152
father of (Hoshaiah), 287
father of (Maaseiah), 300
father of (Obed), 101
father of (Oded), 103
son of (Amariah), 218, 221
Azaz, 103
Azaziah, 127
Azbuk, 179
Azel, 141
father of (Elasah), 291
son of (Azrikam), 301, 487
son of (Bocheru), 203
Azgad, 103
Aziel, 138
Aziza, 116
Azmaveth, 336
Azriel, 252
Azrikam, 301, 487
Azubah, 109
Azzan, 145, 431
Azzur, 228, 231
Baal, 124
Baal-hanan, 190, 458
Baalis, 175
Baana
father of (Hushai), 254
Baanah, 145
Baara, 227
Baaseiah, 283
Baasha. *Also See:* Israel: Kings of: 03 Baasha
Bachrites, 205
Baharumite, 223
Bakbakkar, 290
Bakbuk, 190
Bakbukiah, 198
Balaam, 157, 396
father or (Beor), 229
king who he had curse Israel (Balak), 149
residence of (Pethor), 390, 392
Baladan, 105, 414
Balak, 149
father of (Zippor), 279
Bani, 80
number of children who returned from exile, 373
one in the line of (Eliashib), 268
son of (Uel), 56
son of (Vaniah), 90
Barachel, 216
Barak, 241
father of (Abinoam), 175, 413
Barhumite, 220

Bariah, 199
Barkos, 275
Baruch, 203, 400
father of (Col-hozeh), 87
father of (Neriah), 223, 226
father of (Zabbai), 37
grandfather of (Mahseiah), 142
one sent to capture (Azriel), 252
one sent to capture (Shelemiah), 285
Barzillai, 214
dwelling place of (Rogelim), 231, 454
son of (Adriel), 250
Basmath, 417
(and), 419
son of (Reuel), 244
Bathsheba, 429
alternate name of (Bathshua), 431
father of (Ammiel), 164
father of (Eliam), 163, 403
son of (Solomon), 279
Bathshua, 431
Bavai, 35
Bazlith, 338
Bazluth, 337
Bealiah, 137
Bebai, 30
son of (Athlai), 331
Becher, 200
son of (Alameth), 340
son of (Anathoth), 476
son of (Elioenai), 182
son of (Jeremoth), 379
son of (Zemira), 222
Bechorath, 367
Bedad, 25
Bedan, 74, 398
Bedeiah, 39
Beeliada, 179
Beera, 185
Beerah, 188
Beeri, 194
Beerites, 235
Beerothite, 361
Bela, 123
descendant of (Huram), 217, 445
son of (Ahijah), 42
son of (Ahoah), 41
son of (Ard), 186
son of (Gera), 186
son of (Jeremoth), 382
son of (Uzziel), 138
Belaites, 133
Belshazzar, 366
Belteshazzar (Daniel), 369
Ben, 71, 396
Ben-Abinadab, 141, 428
Benaiah, 85, 92
father of (Jehoiada), 126
Ben-ammi, 175, 449
Ben-dekar, 270, 491
Ben-geber, 218, 470
Ben-Hadad, 83, 405
father of (Tabrimmon), 244, 482
grandfather of (Hezion), 100, 412
murderer of (Hazael), 65, 70
Ben-Hail, 120, 420
Ben-Hesed, 143, 429
Ben-Hur, 223, 474
Beninu, 137
Benjamin, 170, 439, 444
grandfather of (Hananiah), 142
grandson of (Alameth), 340
grandson of (Huram), 217, 445
grandson of (Naaman), 191, 458
grandson of (Uzziel), 138
mother of (Rachel), 208
one of the tribe of (Ucal), 70
original name of (Ben-oni), 139, 427
overseer of the descendants of (Joel), 66
son of (Aharah), 197
son of (Ard), 186
son of (Ashbel), 259
son of (Becher), 200
son of (Bela), 123
son of (Ehi), 36
son of (Gera), 186
son of (Jediael), 143
son of (Muppim), 173, 412
son of (Naaman), 191, 458
son of (Nohah), 87
son of (Rapha), 231
son of (Shephuphan), 333, 514
son of (Shupham), 328, 501
son of (Shuppim), 303, 488
Benjamite, 175, 177, 178, 320, 449, 450, 511
Ben-oni, 139, 427
Ben-zoheth, 315, 508
Beor, 229
Bera, 226
Berachiah, 207
father of (Shimea), 295
Beraiah, 198
Bered, 187
Berekyahu, 211
Beri, 193
Beriah, 199
son of (Jeremoth), 379
Berites, 193
Berodach-Baladan, 249, 538
Berothite, 360
Besai, 91
Besodeiah, 105
Beth Rapha, 392
Bethelite, 312
Bethlehem, 322, 499
Bethlehemite, 327
Bethshemite, 501
Bethuel, 305
Bezai, 124
Bezaleel, 164
Bichri, 205
Bidkar, 243
Bigtha, 291
Bigthan, 312, 506
Bigthana, 312
Bigvai, 39
son of (Uthai), 321
Bildad, 58
Bilgah, 58
Bilgai, 64
Bilhah, 61
son of (Ahishahar), 336
Bilhan, 105, 414
son of (Chenaanah), 182
Bilshan, 282, 496
Bimhal, 95
Binea, 142
Bineah, 145
Binnui, 86
son of
Noadiah, 159
Birsha, 348
Birzavith, 362
Bishlam, 278, 477
Bithiah, 297
Biztha, 292
Boaz, 97
father of (Salma), 278
father of (Salmon), 301, 502
father of (Zalmon), 197, 460
son of (Obed), 101
wife of (Ruth), 356
Bocheru, 203
Bohan, 75
Bukki, 133
son of (Uzzi), 106
Bukkiah, 137
Bunah, 81
Buni, 86
Bunni, 81
Buz, 32
Cain, 170, 444
brother of (Abel), 51
descendant of (Mehujael), 115
land fled to after murder of Abel (Nod), 79
son of (Enoch), 103, 346
Cainan, 192, 459
father of (Enos), 270
number of years lived by, 472
son of (Mahalaleel), 152
Calcol, 120
Caleb, 71, 117
brother of (Othniel), 346

concubine of (Ephah), 171
concubine of (Maachah), 151
daughter of (Achsah), 166
descendant of (Bethlehem), 322, 499
descendant of (Geshan), 273, 493
descendant of (Gibea), 95
descendant of (Ishma), 268
descendant of (Jalon), 116, 418
descendant of (Jehudijah), 53
descendant of (Jekuthiel), 345
descendant of (Jether), 359
descendant of (Keilah), 196
descendant of (Machbenah), 134
descendant of (Mehir), 219
descendant of (Raham), 214, 442
descendant of (Regem), 211, 439
descendant of (Shammai), 267
descendant of (Shimon), 291, 500
father of Jephunneh, 159
grandfather of (Caleb), 71
grandfather of (Chelubai), 86
grandson of (Gazez), 34
grandson of (Kenaz), 167
grandson of (Ziph), 447
one defeated by (Talmai), 320
son of (Ardon), 221, 472
son of (Gazez), 34
son of (Haran), 217, 219, 469, 470
son of (Hareph), 233, 491
son of (Hur), 195
son of (Iru), 232
son of (Jesher), 330
son of (Mesha), 298
son of (Naam), 169, 408
son of (Salma), 278
son of (Shaaph), 311, 514
son of (Sheva), 248
son of (Shobab), 247
son of (Shobal), 261
wife of (Azubah), 109
wife of (Ephrath), 388, 390
wife or concubine of (Jerioth), 393
Calebite, 77, 81
Cambyses, 442, 449, *See Also:*Biblical Characters:Ahasuerus
Canaan, 180, 453
son of (Heth), 292
Canaanite, 184
Canaanites, 208, 438
Caphtorim, 420, 528
Caphtorite, 402
Carcas, 239
Carmelite, 239
Carmelites, 394
Carmi, 225
father of (Zabdi), 41
Carshena, 348
Casluhim, 172, 411
Chaldean, 114, 259
Chaldeans, 259, 280
Chaldees, 278, 477
Chedorlaomer, 346
Chelal, 98
Chelluh, 90
Chelub, 77
brother of (Shuah), 252
Chelubai, 86
Chenaanah, 182
Chenani, 147
Chenaniah, 151, 157
Cheran, 225, 475
Cherethites, 368
Chesed, 255
Chileab, 72
Chilion, 136, 426
Chimham, 127, 382
Chislon, 172, 446
Chittim, 302, 305
Col-hozeh, 87
Conaniah, 160
Coniah. *Also See:* Judah: Kings of: 18 Jehoiachin
Cozbi, 58
Cush, 256
descendant of (Dedan), 76, 400
son of (Nimrod), 236, 239
son of (Sabta), 315, 316
son of (Sabtecha), 320
son of (Seba), 82
Cushan, 279, 495
Cushan-Rishathaim, 535
Cushi, 260
Cushite, 412
(female), 414
(the), 413
Cushites, 260
Cyrus, 334, 336
Dalphon, 173, 448
Dan, 73, 397
mother of (Bilhah), 61
son of (Hushim), 271, 474
son of (Shuham), 270, 473
Daniel, 103, 115
Babylonian companion of (Mishael), 281
Babylonian name of (Belteshazzar), 369
Danites, 82
Dara, 227
Darda, 228
Darius, 334
father of (Ahasuerus), 442
Darkon, 271, 492
Dathan, 311, 505
father of (Eliab), 63
David. *Also See:* Israel, United Kingdom of: Kings of: 02 David
Debir, 187, 197
Deborah, 193, 198, *Also See:* Israel: Judges of: 04 Deborah
burial place of (Allon Bachuth), 332, 514
Dedan, 76, 400
son of (Letushim), 282, 480
son of (Leummim), 141, 388
Dehavites, 33
Dekar, 242
Delaiah, 67
father of (Mehetabel), 118
Delaiahu, 73
Delilah, 97
Deuel, 132
Diblaim, 105, 374
Dibri, 197
Diklah, 154
Dimnah, 119
Dinah, 87
one who defiled (Shechem), 273, 475
Dinaite, 93
Dishon, 269, 271, 274, 276, 490, 492, 493, 494
son of (Aran), 215
son of (Cheran), 225, 475
son of (Eshban), 268, 490
son of (Hamran), 238, 480
son of (Uz), 172, 485
Dodanim, 129, 383
Dodavah, 29
Dodo, 37
son of (Elkanan), 154, 435
Doeg, 22, 30
Donikam
leader of the clan of (Eliphalet), 162, 168
Ebed, 95
son of (Gaal), 124
Ebed-Melech, 172, 375
Eber, 191, 226
son of (Joktan), 173, 448
son of (Peleg), 134
Ebiasaph, 164, 462
son of (Assir), 225
Eden, 143, 429
Edom, 64, 356
Edomite, 73, 80
Edomites, 218
Eglah, 130
son of (Ithream), 408, 525
Eglon, 168, 443
Egyptian, 416
(the), 264, 418
Ehi, 36
Ehud. *Also See:* Israel: Judges of: 02 Ehud

Eker, 276
Ekronite, 302, 305
Eladah, 131
Elah. *Also See:* Israel: Kings of: 04 Elah
father of (Uzzi), 106
Elam, 160, 163, 402
son of (Elijah), 70
Elasah, 291
father of (Shaphan), 303, 496
Eldaah, 131
Eldad, 57
Elead, 126
Eleasah
son of (Azel), 141
Eleazar, 245
father of (Dodo), 37
father of (Phinehas), 189
father-in-law of (Putiel), 152
Eli, 132
son of (Hophni), 161
son of (Phinehas), 189
Eliab, 63
father of (Helon), 103, 106, 413, 414
Eliada, 135
Eliahbah, 70
Eliakim, 181, 420, *Also See:* Judah: Kings of: 17 Jehoiakim
Eliam, 163, 403
Eliasaph, 178, 468
father of (Deuel), 132
Eliashib, 268
son of (Jehohanan), 146, 431
Eliathah, 309
Elidad, 67
father of (Chislon), 172, 446
Eliel, 91
Elienai, 178
Eliezer, 251
descendant of (Zichri), 207
father of (Dodavah), 29
father of (Zichri), 207
son of (Rehabiah), 202, 205
Elihoreph, 256, 499
Elihu, 65, 72
father of (Barachel), 216
Elijah, 70
(to put one's knees betwen one's knees like), 189
place where birds fed (Cherith), 368
the prophet, 139
Elika, 157
Elimelech, 148, 359
Elioenai, 182
son of (Hodaiahu), 61
son of (Johanan), 143, 429
son of (Pelaiah), 144
Eliphal, 163, 170
Eliphalet, 162, 168
Eliphaz, 145
mother of (Adah), 98
son of (Amelek), 209
son of (Kenaz), 167
son of (Korah), 245
son of (Timnah), 346
son of (Zephi), 178
son of (Zepho), 176
Elisha, 265, 294
father of (Shaphat), 284
home of (Abel-Meholah), 141
servant of (Gehazi), 46, 56
Elishah, 297
Elishama, 311
father of (Ammihud), 152
Elishaphat, 302
father of (Zichri), 207
Elisheba, 295
Eliychoref, 538
Eliyzaphan, 472
Elizaphan, 221
Elizur, 260
Elkanah, 179
son of (Ahimoth), 315
son of (Amasai), 298
wife of (Peninnah), 179
Elkanan, 154, 435
father of (Dodo), 37
father of (Jaare-Oregim), 341, 505
father of (Jair), 200
Elnaam, 181, 421
Elnathan, 338, 515
father of (Achbor), 238
Elon, 111, 117, 416, 419, *Also See:* Israel: Judges of: 10 Elon
daughter of (Adah), 98
daughter of (Basmath), 417
Elonites, 111, 117
Elpaal, 192
son of (Hezeki), 143
son of (Zebadiah), 46
Eluzai, 143
Elzabad, 63
Emims, 123, 381
Enan, 178, 451
Enoch, 103, 346
descendant of (Irad), 231
number of years lived by, 275
Enos, 270
number of years lived by, 469
Enosh
son of (Cainan), 192, 459
Ephah, 171
Ephai, 172
Epher, 267
Ephlal, 156
Ephod, 103
Ephraim, 258, 465
grandson of (Eran), 253, 484
grandson of (Tahath), 442
son of (Becher), 200
son of (Ezer), 229, 235
son of (Shuthelah), 418
Ephraimite, 392
Ephrath, 388, 390
Ephrathite, 392
Ephron, 291, 500
father of (Zohar), 238
Er, 225
wife of (Tamar), 372
Eran, 253, 484
Esar-Haddon, 257, 486
Esau, 279
descendant of (Homam), 111, 377
descendant of (Hori), 198
descendant of (Husham), 269, 473
descendant of (Nahath), 313
grandson of (Amelek), 209
grandson of (Gatam), 332, 502
grandson of (Shammah), 264
grandson of (Teman), 325, 512
mother of (Rebekah), 244
son of (Adah), 98
son of (Eliphaz), 145
son of (Jeush), 283
son of (Korah), 245
son of (Reuel), 244
wife of (Adah), 98
wife of (Anah), 144
wife of (Basmath), 417
wife of (Beeri), 194
wife of (Judith), 304
wife of (Mahalath), 319
Eshban, 268, 490
Eshcol, 268
Eshek
son of (Jeush), 283
Eshkalonites, 324
Eshtaulites, 417
Eshton, 423, 536
son of (Beth Rapha), 392
Esther, 381
cousin of (Jair), 200
father of (Abihail), 80
Hebrew name of (Hadassah), 93
Etam, 251
daughter of (Hazelelponi), 241
son of (Idbash), 251
Ethan, 314, 507
father of (Kishi), 298
father of (Quwshayahu), 302
grandfather of (Abdi), 105
Ethbaal, 326
daughter of (Jezebel), 68
Ethnan, 325, 513
father of (Jair), 232
Ethni, 314
Eve, 37
son of (Abel), 51
son of (Seth), 395

Evi, 34
Evil-Merodach, 247, 436
Ezbai, 37
Ezbon, 158, 161, 436, 438
alternate name for (Ozni), 86
Ezekiel, 166
vision of
number of elders seen in, 88
wheel of (*Ofan*), 153, 434
wicked prince of Judah (Jaazaniah), 102
Ezer, 229, 235
son of (Akan), 199, 461
son of (Jaakan), 204, 463
Ezra, 229
ancestor of (Azariah), 235
ancestor of (Shallum), 280, 478
companion of (Ebed), 95
companion of (Nathan), 325, 512
man who stood by (Urijah), 200, 203
one who assisted with the Law (Hanan), 129, 423
one who helped read the Law (Hashum), 265, 471
one who helped teach the Law (Buni), 86
one who returned with (Adin), 150, 433
one who returned with (Hashabiah), 255
one who returned with (Uthai), 321
one who stood with (Anaiah), 152
one who stood with (Hilkiah), 165
one who stood with (Mishael), 281
priest who stood with (Maaseiah), 300
son of (Mered), 211
son of (Shammai), 267
wife of (Jehudijah), 53
Ezrah, 231
Ezrahite, 202
Ezri, 233
father of (Chelub), 77
Gaal, 124
father of (Ebed), 95
Gabbai, 32
Gad, 20
(to), 55
chief of (Riblah), 299, 486
mother of (Zilpah), 141
son of (Areli), 210
son of (Arod), 192
son of (Ezbon), 158, 161, 436, 438
son of (Haggi), 39
son of (Ozni), 86
son of (Shuni), 275
son of (Zephon), 203, 462
son of (Ziphion), 207, 464
Gaddi, 34
Gaddiel, 66
Gadi, 34
Gadites, 34, 40
Gaham, 70
Gahar, 193
Galal, 81
Gamul, 97
Gareb, 186
Garmite, 216
Gashmu, 266
Gatam, 332, 502
Gazathite, 321
Gazez, 34
Gazite, 321
Gazzam, 68, 358
Geber, 186
father of (Uri), 197
Gedaliah, 71
captain of the force who joined (Jaazaniah), 107
captain of the forces who joined (Jezaniah), 101, 107
captain who allied with (Johanan), 143, 429
father of one of the captains of (Tanhumeth), 466
one who joined (Jonathan), 333, 514
Gedaliahu, 76
Gedar, 172
Gederathite, 363
Gederite, 197
Gedor, 188, 194
Gehazi, 46, 56
Gemalli, 102
Gemariah, 219
father of (Hilkiah), 165
father of (Shaphan), 303, 496
Gemaryahu, 222
Genubath, 312
Gera, 186
Gers
descendant of (Joah), 44
Gershom, 341, 343, 505, 507
descendant of (Eden), 143, 429
son of (Shebuel), 261
Gershon, 345, 518
descendant of (Baaseiah), 283
descendant of (Iddo), 98
descendant of (Jeaterai), 365
descendant of (Jehiel), 78
descendant of (Jeush), 283
descendant of (Lael), 80
descendant of (Shelomoth), 430
descendant of (Zerah), 196
grandson of (Shimi), 298
member of the family of (Zimnah), 71
son of (Shimi), 298
Gershonite, 346
Geshan, 273, 493
Geshem, 263, 469
Geshurite, 401
Geshurites, 408
Gether, 355
Geuel, 60
Gezrite(s), 199
Gibbar, 186
Gibea, 95
Gibeathite, 321
Gibeon
brother of (Nadab), 75
father of (Abi Gibon), 261, 488
son of (Kish), 294
Gibeonite, 151
Giblites, 64
Giddalti, 309
Giddel, 55
Gideon. *Also See:* Israel: Judges of: 05 Gideon
Gideoni, 153
son of (Abidan), 85, 407
Gilalai, 92
Gilead, 128
grandson of (Zelophehad), 194
son of (Hepher), 233
Gileadite, 137
Gilonite, 124
Ginath, 314
Ginnetho, 313
Ginnethon, 330, 513
descendant of (Meshullam), 293, 484
Girgashite, 333
Girgashites, 345, 508
Gishpa, 282
Gittite, 295
Gizonite, 95
Gog, 28
Goliath, 307
brother of (Lahmi), 107
home of (Gath), 290
one who killed (Jair), 232
place where David slew (Elah), 54
slayer of (Jair), 200
Gomer, 211
son of (Ashkenaz), 280
son of (Riphath), 323, 392
son of (Togarmah), 376, 378
Guni, 87
Gunites, 87
Habaiah, 43
Habakkuk, 197
Habazaniah, 171
Hachaliah, 92
Hachmonite, 150

Hadad, 29, 33
as son of Bedad, 93
one who received (Tahapanes), 354, 356, 357
Hadadezer, 234
father of (Rehob), 192
Hadar, 194
wife of (Matred), 216
wife of (Mehetabel), 118
wife of (Mezahab), 83
Hadarezer, 321
captain of the army of (Shobach), 256, 442
captain of the army of (Shophach), 291, 464
Hadassah, 93
Hadlai, 71
son of (Amasa), 295
Hadoram, 214, 217, 442, 446
Hagab, 30
Hagabah, 35
Hagar, 189
son of (Ishmael), 311
well of (Beer Lahai Roi), 314
Hagarite, 198, 199
Haggai, 39
(and), 45
Haggi, 39
Haggiah, 44
Haggites, 39, 44
Haggith, 299
Hakkatan, 171, 445
Hakkoz, 185, 493
Hakupha, 182
Hallohesh, 266
Ham, 67, 357
descendant of (Sheba), 242
son of (Canaan), 180, 453
son of (Cush), 256
son of (Mizraim), 280, 478
son of (Phut), 116
Haman, 115, 418
'Cursed be', 326, 513
father of (Hammedatha), 310
son of (Adalia), 64
son of (Aridai), 202
son of (Aridatha), 362
son of (Arisai), 230
son of (Aspatha), 341
son of (Dalphon), 173, 448
son of (Parmasta), 495
son of (Parshandatha), 497
son of (Poratha), 391
son of (Shubael), 261
son of (Vajezatha), 300
wife of (Zeresh), 329
Hamath Rabah, 379
descendant of (Rechab), 201
Hamathite, 313
Hammedatha, 310
Hammoleketh, 323
Hamor, 217
son of (Shechem), 273, 475
Hamran, 238, 480
Hamuel, 104
Hamul, 103
Hamulites, 114
Hamutal, 113, 117
father of (Jeremiah), 226
Hanameel, 146
Hanan, 129, 423
(son of), 168, 539
Hanani, 138
Hananiah, 139, 142, 144
father of (Azzur), 231
father of (Shelemiah), 283
name given to (Shadrach), 336, 490
Hananiahu, 146
Hannah, 82
Hanniel, 119
father of (Ephod), 103
Hanochites, 107
Hanun, 134, 426
Happizzez, 223, 502
Haran, 217, 219, 469, 470
daughter of (Iscah), 115
daughter of (Milcah), 116
Hararite, 296, 297
Harbona, 224
Harbonah, 225
Hareph, 233, 491
town founded by (Beth-Gader), 364
Harhaiah, 204
Harhas, 228
Harhur, 299
Harim, 213, 442
as Senir, 345
descendant of (Benjamin), 170, 439, 444
son of (Eliezer), 251
son of (Elijah), 70
Hariph, 238, 494
Harnepher, 339
Harodite, 201
Haroeh, 193
Harorite, 299
Harsha, 330
Harum, 212, 440
son of (Isshiah), 255, 258
Haruphite, 242
Haruz, 242, 508
home of (Jotbah), 45
Hasbadana, 275
Hashabiah, 255, 257
Hashabiahu, 257
Hashabnah, 274
Hashabniah, 279
Hashem, 264, 469
Hashub, 250
Hashubah, 250
Hashum, 265, 470
line of (Eliphalet), 162, 168
Hashupha, 284, 286
Hasrah, 227
Hasshub, 250
Hatach, 300, 469
Hathath, 442
Hatipha, 129
Hatita, 56
Hattil, 75
Hattush, 254
Hazael, 65, 70
son of (Ben-Hadad), 83, 405
Hazaiah, 48
Hazelelponi, 241
Haziel, 75
Hazo, 39
Heber, 191
daughter of (Shua), 280
son of (Shemer), 340
wife of (Jael), 131
Heberites, 199
Hebron, 223, 474
descendant of (Jeriah), 202, 205
father of (Mareshah), 342
son of (Jaziel), 84
son of (Korah), 245
son of (Rekem), 262
son of (Shema), 294
Hebronites, 225, 228
Hegai, 35
Hege, 23
Helah, 63
son of (Zohar), 238
Helam, 97, 106, 371, 375
Heldai, 71
Heleb, 58
Helek, 153
Helem, 94, 96, 370, 371
son of (Amal), 156
Helez, 145, 478
son of (Elasah), 291
Helkai, 161
Helkite, 161
Helon, 103, 106, 413, 414
son of (Eliab), 63
Hemam, 115, 378
son of (Hothir), 362
Heman, 126, 422
son of (Bukkiah), 137
son of (Giddalti), 309
son of (Hothir), 365
son of (Jehiel), 74
son of (Joshbekashah), 407
son of (Mattaniah), 331
son of (Romamtiezer), 485
Hemdan, 124, 421
Hen, 76, 400
Henadad, 84
Hepher, 233
Hepherites, 238
Hephzibah, 182
Heresh, 329

Hermonites, 269, 473
Heth, 292
Hezeki, 143
Hezekiah, 147, 155, *Also See:* Judah: Kings of: 12 Hezekiah
 father of (Shallum), 277
Hezion, 100, 412
Hezir, 202
Hezrai, 242
Hezro, 242
Hezron, 269, 490
 descendant of (Jehu), 40
 descendant of (Tirhanah), 382
 son of (Ashur), 332
 son of (Azubah), 109
 son of (Caleb), 71
 son of (Chelubai), 86
 son of (Jerahmeel), 233
 son of (Shammai), 267
Hezronites, 274
Hiddai, 36
Hiel, 68
 son of (Abiram), 216, 445
 son of (Segub), 248
Hilkiah, 165, 168
 son of (Azariah), 235
 son of (Eliakim), 181
 son of (Seraiah), 332
Hillel, 83
Hinnom, 115, 378
Hirah, 201
Hiram, 219, 447
Hittite, 297
Hittites, 297, 313, 494
Hivite, 42
 (the), 47
Hivites, 42, 82, 366
Hizki, 143
Hobab, 28
Hod, 32
Hodaiahu, 61
Hodaviah, 54
 father of (Senuah), 137
Hodesh, 248
Hodevah, 44
Hodiah, 48
Hodijah, 48
Hoglah, 65
Hoham, 74, 362
Homam, 111, 377
Hophni, 161
Horam, 212, 440
Hori, 198, 201
Horite, 198
Horonite, 224
Hosah, 92
Hosea, 281
 daughter of (Lo-ruhamah), 231
 father of (Beeri), 194
 father-in-law of (Diblaim), 105, 374
 son of
 Lo-Ammi (symbolic name meaning 'not my people'), 163
 son of (symbolic name of – Jezreel), 251
 wife of (Gomer), 211
Hoshaiah, 287
Hoshama, 299
Hoshea. *Also See:* Israel: Kings of: 20 Hoshea
Hotham, 312, 493
Hothir, 362, 365
Hozai, 50
Hul, 44
Huldah, 66
 father-in-law of (Tikvah), 331
 father-in-law of (Tikvath), 472
 husband of (Harhas), 228
 husband of (Shallum), 277
Hupham, 150, 392
Huphamites, 158
Huppah, 113
Huppim, 153, 393
Hur, 195
 father of (Caleb), 71
 grandson of (Bezaleel), 164
 son of (Caleb), 71
 son of (Ethnan), 325, 513
 son of (Shobal), 261
 son of (Uri), 197
Hurai, 201
Huram, 217, 445
Huri, 201
Hushah, 252
Hushai, 254
Hushathite, 407
Hushim, 265, 271, 274, 471, 474, 475
Ibhar, 199
Ibneiah, 95
Ibnijah, 95
Ibri, 231
Ibzan. *Also See:* Israel: Judges of: 09 Ibzan
Ichabod, 63
Idbash, 251
 brother of (Ishma), 268
Iddo, 27, 38, 98, 100, 104, 114, 162
 father of (Zechariah), 210
 son of (Ahinadab), 93
Igal, 63
 father of (Nathan), 325, 512
Igdaliah, 86
Ikkesh, 316
Ilai, 140
Imla, 100
Imlah, 104
Immanuel, 183
Immer, 209
 son of (Pashur), 353
Imna, 126, 173
Imrah, 217
Imri, 215
Iphedeiah, 130
Ir, 230
Ira, 230
 father of (Ikkesh), 316
Irad, 231
Iri, 234
Irijah, 207
Ir-Nahash, 371
Iru, 232
Isaac, 189, 298
 mother of (Sarai), 331
 number of years lived by, 178
 place where covenant was made with Abimelech (Shebah), 246
 place where taken to be sacrificed (Adonai-Jireh), 210
 son of (Esau), 279
 well dug by (Eshek), 316
 well dug by (Rehoboth), 363
 wife of (Rebekah), 244
Isaiah, 286
 father of (Amoz), 153, 480
 name given to Egypt by (Rahab Hem Shebeth), 482, 542
 priest who he took as a witness (Urijah), 200, 203
 son of (Immanuel), 183
 son of (Maher-Shalal-Hash-Baz – a symbolic name), 475
 son of (Shear-Jashub), 448
Iscah, 115
Ishbah, 252
Ishbak, 295
Ishbi-Benob, 278
Ishbosheth, 493
 as Ashbaal (alternate name), 289
 captain in army of (Baanah), 145
 murderer of (Rechab), 201
Ishi, 284
 father of (Appaim), 148, 392
 son of (Ben-zoheth), 315, 508
Ishma, 268
Ishmael, 311
 daughter of (Basmath), 417
 daughter of (Mahalath), 319
 father of (Jehohanan), 146, 431
 father of (Nethaniah), 332, 335
 mother of (Hagar), 189
 number of years lived by, 153
 son of (Abdeel), 56
 son of (Hadad), 33
 son of (Hadar), 194
 son of (Jetur), 202
 son of (Kedar), 242

son of (Kedemah), 162
son of (Massa), 263
son of (Mibsam), 282, 479
son of (Mishma), 310
son of (Nebaioth), 314, 316
son of (Tema), 311
son of (Zebadiahu), 53
Ishmaelite, 314
Ishmaiah, 304, 306
Ishmerai, 345
Ishod, 255
Ishpan, 305, 503
Ishvah, 253
Ishvi, 255
Ismachiah, 163
Ispah, 286
Israel, 340
Israelite, 344
(female), 481
Issachar, 451
(and), 452
(of), 458
son of (Jashub), 254
son of (Job), 36
son of (Phuvah), 113
son of (Puah), 112
son of (Shimron), 354
son of (Tola), 328
Isshiah, 255, 257
Ithamar, 377
(and unto), 390
(and), 380
Ithiel, 311
Ithmah, 312
Ithra, 360
Ithran, 381, 528
(and), 382, 529
Ithream, 408, 525
mother of (Eglah), 130
Ithrite, 364
Ittai, 294, 299
father of (Ribai), 201
Izeharites, 250
Izhar, 243
descendant of (Shelomoth), 430
son of (Zichri), 207
Izrahiah, 208
Izrahite, 202
Izri, 246
Jaakan, 204, 463
Jaakobah, 180
Jaala, 132
Jaalah, 135
Jaalam, 162, 402
Jaanai, 155
Jaare-Oregim, 341, 505
Jaasau, 283
Jaazaniah, 102, 107
father of (Shaphan), 303, 496
grandfather of (Habazaniah), 171
Jaaziah, 130
Jaaziel, 146
Jabal, 62
father of (Lamech), 109, 347
mother of (Adah), 98
Jabesh, 248
Jabez, 175, 486
Jabin, 91, 409
captain of the army of (Sisera), 258
Jachan, 162, 438
Jachin, 108, 415
Jachinites, 120
Jacob, 178
as Israel (alternate name), 340
brother of (Edom), 64, 70, 359
brother of (Esau), 279
combined gematria of Abraham, Isaac, and, 371
concubine of (Zilpah), 141
daughter of (Dinah), 87
ladder of
in regards to Sinai, 148
mother of (Joseph), 208
mother of (Rebekah), 244
name given to altar by (*El elohey Yisra'el*), 364
number of days the Egyptian nation mourned after the death of, 88
number of direct descendants of who accompanied into Egypt, 88
number of words in dream of heaven, 88
number of years he worked for Laban, 38
number of years lived by, 160
place where God revealed himself to (*El Betel*), 317
place where he camped (Migdal Eder), 269
place where he camped (Migdol), 95, 102
son of (Asher), 325
son of (Benjamin), 170, 439, 444
son of (Ben-oni), 139, 427
son of (Dan), 73
son of (Gad), 20
son of (Issachar), 451
son of (Joseph), 166, 170, 462, 463
son of (Reuben), 220, 471
the God of, 203
twin brother of (Edom), 356
wife of (Leah), 55
wife of (Rachel), 208
Jada, 103
Jaddua, 108
Jadon, 87, 408
Jael, 131
husband of (Eber), 191
one murdered by (Sisera), 258
Jahath, 298
son of (Ahumai), 83
Jahaziah, 59
father of (Tikvah), 331
father of (Tikvath), 472
Jahaziel, 84
grandfather of (Benaiah), 85, 92
Jahdai
son of (Jotham), 312, 494
son of (Pelet), 139
Jahdiel, 82
Jahdo, 46
Jahleel, 97
Jahleelites, 108
Jahmai, 86
Jahzeelites, 161
Jahzerah, 44, 204
Jahziel, 161
Jair, 200, 232, *Also See:* Israel: Judges of: 07 Jair
place where he was buried (Camon), 183, 455
son of (Elkanan), 154, 435
Jairite, 200
Jakeh, 135
son of (Agur), 190
Jakim, 168, 408
Jalon, 116, 418
Jamin, 131, 424
Jaminites, 139
Jamlech, 120, 350
Janum, 384
Japheth, 322
son of (Gomer), 211
son of (Javan), 84, 406
son of (Madai), 73
son of (Magog), 72
son of (Meshech), 272, 453
son of (Tiras), 384
son of (Tubal), 304
Japhia, 173
Japhlet, 146
son of (Ashvath), 430
Japhletites, 154
Jarah, 232
Jareb, 194
Jared, 195
father of (Mahalaleel), 152
number of years lived by, 483
son of (Enoch), 103, 346
Jareshiah, 353
Jarha, 233
son of (Attai), 319
Jarib, 201
Jaroah, 201
Jashen, 272, 492
Jashobeam, 299, 486
father of (Zabdiel), 73
name given to (Adino), 90

Jashub, 252, 254
Jashubi-Lehem, 287, 482
Jashubites, 254
Jassiel, 299
Jathniel, 326
Javan, 84, 406
son of (Dodanim), 129, 383
son of (Elisha), 265
son of (Rodanim), 243, 460
son of (Tarshish), 519
Jaziel, 84
Jaziz, 53
Jeaterai, 365
Jeberechiah, 216
Jebusite, 107
Jebusites, 146, 391
Jecholiah, 100, 104
Jeconiah. *Also See:* Judah: Kings of: 18 Jehoiachin
Jedaiah, 47, 119
Jediael, 143
Jedidah, 52
father of (Adaiah), 108
son of (Allon), 105, 414
Jeduthun, 316, 318, 319, 509, 510
son of (Hashabiah), 257
son of (Mattithiah), 457, 459
son of (Uzziel), 138
Jeezer, 233
Jehaleel, 117
Jehaleleel, 128
son of (Ziph), 447
son of (Ziphah), 124
Jehdai, 47
Jehdeiah, 62
Jehezekel, 166
Jehiah, 52
Jehiel, 74, 78, 399
son of (Baal), 124
son of (Zur), 237
wife of (Maachah), 151
Jehoadah, 120
father of (Ahaz), 32
Jehoaddan, 159, 166, 437, 440
Jehoahaz. *Also See:* Judah: Kings of: 16 Jehoahaz, *Also See:* Judah: Kings of: 06 Jehoahaz, *Also See:* Israel: Kings of: 11 Jehoahaz
Jehoash. *Also See:* Judah: Kings of: 07 Joash, *Also See:* Israel: Kings of: 13 Joash
Jehohanan, 146, 431
Jehoiachin. *Also See:* Judah: Kings of: 18 Jehoiachin, *Also See:* Judah: Kings of: 18 Jehoiachin
Jehoiada, 126
captain of (Elishaphat), 302
father of (Paseah), 161
father of a captain who aided (Jehoiada), 116
son of (Zechariah), 210
Jehoiakim. *Also See:* Judah: Kings of: 17 Jehoiakim
Jehoiarib, 211
Jehonadab, 95
Jehoshabeath, 436
Jehoshaphat, 293, *Also See:* Judah: Kings of: 04 Jehoshaphat
Jehosheba, 286
Jehozabad, 53
mother of (Shimrith), 481
mother of (Shomer), 340
Jehozadek, 196
Jehu, 40, *Also See:* Israel: Kings of: 10 Jehu
Jehubbah, 44
Jehucal, 90
Jehudi, 54
father of (Nethaniah), 332
great-grandfather of (Cushi), 260
Jehudijah, 53
Jeiel, 137, 141
son of (Abdon), 149, 432
son of (Zacher), 203
Jekameam, 220, 448
Jekamiah, 171
Jekuthiel, 345
Jemimah, 126
Jemuel, 106
Jeohoram. *Also See:* Judah: Kings of: 05 Jeohoram, *Also See:* Israel: Kings of: 09 Joram
Jephthah. *Also See:* Israel: Judges of: 08 Jephthah
Jephunneh, 159
descendant of (Sheber), 326
son of (Caleb), 71
Jerah, 198
Jerahmeel, 233
descendant of (Azariah), 235
descendant of (Nadab), 75
descendant of (Nathan), 325, 512
descendant of (Sisamai), 174
descendant of (Zabad), 30
grandson of (Jada), 103
member of the family of (Ishi), 284
son of (Bunah), 81
son of (Jether), 359
son of (Onam), 111, 377
son of (Oren), 215
son of (Ozem), 149, 392
son of (Ram), 209, 438
wife of (Atarah), 231
Jerahmeelites, 239
Jeremai, 220
Jeremiah, 223, 226
birthplace of (Anathoth), 476
cousin of (Hanameel), 146
father of (Hilkiah), 168
friend and scribe of (Baruch), 203, 400
one sent to capture (Seraiah), 335
one sent to capture (Shelemiah), 285
one who arrested (Irijah), 207
one who charged with false prophecy (Azariah), 236
one who imprisoned (Gedaliah), 71
one who opposed (Hananiah), 142
one who rescued (Ebed-Melech), 172, 375
son of (Jaazaniah), 102
uncle of (Shallum), 277
Jeremoth
father of (Azriel), 252
Jeremoth, 379
Jeremoth, 382
Jeriah, 202, 205
Jeribai, 205
Jeriel, 215
Jerioth, 393
Jeroboam. *Also See:* Israel: Kings of: 14 Jeroboam, *Also See:* Israel: Kings of: 01 Jeroboam
Jeroham, 219, 447
son of (Athaliah), 332
son of (Elijah), 70
son of (Ibneiah), 95
Jerubbaal, 248, *Also See* Israel: Judges of: 05 *Gideon*
Jerubbesheth, 472
Jerusha, 333, 335
father of (Zadok), 184
Jesaiah, 286, 289
Jesharelah, 342
Jeshebeab, 250
Jesher, 330
Jeshishai, 368
Jeshoaiah, 261
Jeshua, 283
ancestor of (Joiada), 120
descendant of (Jonathan), 333, 514
father of (Azaniah), 92
father of (Jehozadek), 196
father of (Jozadak), 191
priest in the days of (Hashabiah), 255
son of (Joiakim), 176, 414
Jesimael, 285
Jesse, 252
daughter of (Zeruiah), 248
father of (Obed), 101
son of (Nethaneel), 338
son of (Shammah), 264
son of (Shimea), 295
son of (Shimeah), 296
Jesuites, 255
Jesus, 383, 521
(Greek), 465
Jether, 359

son of (Ara), 185
Jethro, 363
Jetur, 202
Jeuel, 137
Jeush, 283
Jeuz, 176, 487
Jevanite, 95
Jezaniah, 101, 107
father of (Hoshaiah), 287
Jezebel, 68
daughter of (Athaliah), 332, 335
father of (Ethbaal), 326
Jezer, 239
Jezerites, 246
Jeziah, 51
Jeziel, 73
Jezliah, 82
Jezrahiah, 208
Jezreel, 251
brother of (Ishma), 268
Jezreelite, 256
Jezreelitess, 411
Jibsam, 268, 472
Jidlaph, 143, 454
Joab, 37
(Ataroth the house of), 508
one who warred against (Hadadezer), 234
Joah, 44
father of (Asaph), 156, 459
Joash, 251, *Also See:* Judah: Kings of: 07 Joash, *Also See:* Israel: Kings of: 13 Joash
Job, 36
(and), 42
daughter of (Jemimah), 126
daughter of (Keren-Happuch), 314
daughter of (Kezia), 228
daughter of (Uzzen-Happuch), 546
man who rebuked (Elihu), 65, 72
Temanite friend of (Eliphaz), 145
Jobab, 38
father of (Zerah), 196
Jochebed, 62
Joed, 108
Joel, 66
brother of (Nathan), 325, 512
descendant of (Gog), 28
father of (Azariah), 238
father of (Pethuel), 333
father of (Zichri), 207
son of (Shemaiah), 301
Joelah, 142
Joezer, 236
Jogli, 72
Joha, 44
Johanan, 143, 429
father of (Hakkatan), 171, 445
Joiada, 120
Joiakim, 176, 414
Joiarib, 208
Jokim, 172, 411
Jokshan, 313, 507
son of (Dedan), 76, 400
Joktan, 173, 235, 448
son of (Abimael), 103
son of (Diklah), 154
son of (Hadoram), 217, 446
son of (Jerah), 198
son of (Jobab), 38
son of (Obal), 130, 133
son of (Ophir), 232, 237
son of (Shelaph), 294, 510
son of (Uzal), 63
Jonadab, 91
descendant of (Jeremiah), 226
Jonah, 90
burial place of (Halhul), 101
father of (Amittai), 78
home of (Gittah Hepher), 393
Jonathan, 333, 335, 514, 515
descendant of (Alameth), 340
descendant of (Binea), 142
descendant of (Bineah), 145
descendant of (Eliphalet), 162, 168
father of (Asahel), 291
father of (Gershom), 341, 505
father of (Uzziah), 119
site of farewell between David and, 56
son of (Peleth), 331
Jorah, 200
Jorai, 202
Joram. *Also See:* Judah: Kings of: 05 Jeohoram, *Also See:* Israel: Kings of: 09 Joram
Jorkeam/Jorkoam, 298, 486
Joseph, 166, 170, 462, 463
alternate name (Zaphenath), 365
alternate name of (Zaphenath-Paneah), 452
alternate name of (Zaphnath-Paaneah), 451
amount of silver he was sold for, 38
ephodic stone *Shoham* (malachite), 264, 469
father-in-law of (Potipherah), 312
last name given by Pharaoh (Panach), 189
master of (Potiphar), 282
number of years lived by, 132
place where he was sold into slavery (Dothan), 312
shout made to announce chariot of, 201, 397
son of (Ephraim), 258, 465
son of (Manasseh), 286
wife of (Asenath), 331
Joshah, 253
father of (Amaziah), 159, 164
Joshaphat, 290
Joshaviah, 260
Joshbekashah, 407
Josheb Basshebeth, 494
Joshua, 285, 287
burial place of (Gaash), 278
city captured by Chezib, 58
father of (Nun), 128, 423
home and burial place of (Timnath-Serah), 513
king defeated by (Debir), 187, 197
king defeated by (Horam), 212, 440
king defeated by (Jabin), 91, 409
king defeated by (Japhia), 173
king slain by (Hoham), 74, 362
one conquered by (Jobab), 38
original name of (Hosea), 281
town captured by (Geder), 188
town captured by (Gedor), 194
Josiah, 255, *Also See:* Judah: Kings of: 15 Josiah
son of (Zephaniah), 206
Josiphiah, 174
Jotham, 312, 494, *Also See:* Judah: Kings of: 10 Jotham
place where sought refuge (Beer), 185
Jozabad, 47
father of (Jeshua), 283
Jozachar, 211
Jozadak, 191
Jubal, 67
father of (Lamech), 109, 347
mother of (Adah), 98
Jucal, 84
Judah, 48
friend of (Hirah), 201
grandson of (Segub), 248
great grandson of (Caleb), 71
son of (Er), 225
son of (Hur), 195
son of (Ishvah), 253
son of (Onan), 128, 423
son of (Perez), 276, 515
son of (Shelah), 260, 261
son of (Shobal), 261
son of (Zerah), 196
wife of (Bathshua), 431
wife of (Shua), 279
Judaite, 54
Judith, 304
father of (Beeri), 194
Jushab-Hesed, 284
Kadmiel, 179

Kadmonites, 186
Kaleb
as My [God's] servant, 158
Kallai, 156
Kareah, 245
Kari, 204
Kedar, 242
Kedemah, 162
Keilah, 196
Kelaiah, 159
Kelita, 163
Kemuel, 177
father of (Shiphtan), 305, 503
son of (Hashabiah), 255
Kenezite, 172
Kenite, 174
Keren-Happuch, 314, 546
Keros, 272, 277
Keturah, 253
son of (Jokshan), 313, 507
son of (Medan), 114, 418
son of (Midian), 125, 422
son of (Shuah), 249
son of (Zimran), 237, 480
Kezia, 228
Kish, 294
father of (Abdi), 105
son of (Jerahmeel), 233
Kishi, 298
Kittim, 302, 305
Koa, 176
Kohath, 327
chief of the sons of (Uriel), 213
descendant of (Azariah), 238
descendant of (Hashabiah), 257
descendant of (Mahath), 309
descendant of (Micah), 94
descendant of (Shelomith), 432
descendant of (Tahath), 442
grandson of (Korah), 245
son of (Amminadab), 176
son of (Uzziel), 138
Kohathites, 332
Kolaiah, 164
Korah, 245
brother of (Nepheg), 150
descendant of (Elam), 163, 402
descendant of (Jediael), 143
father of
Izhar, 243
son of (Abeasaph), 165, 462
son of (Assir), 225
son of (Elkanah), 179
Korahite, 252
Kore, 241, 244
father of (Imna), 126
Koz, 183, 491
Laadah, 130
son of (Mareshah), 342
Laadan, 165, 440
son of (Zetham), 309
son or grandson of (Zetham), 491
Laban, 101, 413
daughter of (Leah), 55
pile of stones erected by (Jegar-Sahadutha), 476
Lael, 80
Lahad, 58
Lahmi, 107
Lamech, 109, 347
daughter of (Naamah), 171
father of (Methusael), 431
number of years lived by, 431
son of (Jubal), 67
son of (Noah), 77
son of (Tubal-Cain), 354, 523
wife of (Adah), 98
wife of (Zillah), 144
Lappidoth, 337
Leah, 55
(and), 61
daughter of (Dinah), 87
father of (Laban), 101, 413
handmaid of (Zilpah), 141
son of (Reuben), 220, 471
Lebanah, 102, 106
Lehabim, 106, 375
Lemuel, 129
Letushim, 282, 480
Leummim, 141, 388
Levi, 65
number of years lived by, 153
porter of (Uri), 197
sister of (Dinah), 87
son of (Gershom), 343, 507
son of (Gershon), 345, 518
son of (Kohath), 327
son of (Merari), 310
son of (Micah), 94
son of (Mushi), 266, 270
Levites, 105, 375
Libni, 112
son of (Jahath), 298
son of (Shimi), 299
Libnite, 112
Likhi, 161
Lilith the Younger
father of (Qaftzaphi), 297
Lo-Ammi, 163
Lo-Ruhamah, 231
Lot, 64
son of (Ammon), 172, 447
son of (Ben-ammi), 175, 449
son of (Moab), 68
Lotan, 115, 418
son of (Hemam), 115, 378
Lubims, 62, 67
Lud, 59
Lydians, 69, 78
Maachah, 151
father of (Imla), 100
father of (Imlah), 104
man commanded to imprison (Joash), 251
Maachathite, 337, 340
Maadai, 143
Maadiah, 146
Maai, 140
Maasai, 298
father of (Adiel), 136
Maaseiah, 300, 303
Maaz, 184, 492
Maaziah, 154
Macbannite, 142
Machbanai, 142
Machbenah, 134
Machi, 88
son of (Gehooale), 60
Machir, 225
father of (Ammiel), 164
son of (Gilead), 128
son of (Peresh), 351
wife of (Maachah), 151
Machnadebai, 144
Madai, 73
Magog, 72
Magor-Missabib, 273
Magpiash, 327
Mahalah, 102
Mahalaleel, 152
Mahalath, 319
Mahaleel
number of years lived by, 466
Maharai, 217
Mahath, 309
Mahavite, 125, 382
Mahazioth, 317
Maher-Shalal-Hash-Baz, 475
Mahlah, 102
Mahli, 107
Mahlites, 107
Mahlon, 150, 433
wife of (Ruth), 356
Mahol, 103
Mahseiah, 142
Makirite, 230
Malachi, 123
Malatiah, 114
Malcham, 147, 391
Malchiah, 127
son of (Pashur), 353
Malchiel, 149
Malchielite, 157
Malchijah, 132
Malchiram, 261, 467
Malchishua, 318
Mallothi, 321
Malluch, 117, 349
Mamre, 230
brother of (Eshcol), 268
Manahath, 324

Manasseh, 286, *Also See:* Judah: Kings of: 13 Manasseh
grandson of (Peresh), 351
grandson of (Shemida), 300
son of (Ashriel or Asriel), 341
son of (Maachah), 151
son of (Machir), 225
Manassites, 288
Manoah, 125
Maoch, 152, 363
Maon, 172, 446
Mara, 210
Mareshah, 342
Marsena, 268
Mash, 261
Massa, 263
Matred, 216
mother of (Mezahab), 83
Matri, 220
Mattan, 322, 511
Mattaniah, 327, 330, 331
ancestor of (Zabdi), 41
Mattathah, 455
Mattenai, 325
Mattithiah, 457, 459
Mebunnai, 124
Mecherathite, 384
Mecholathite, 322
Medad, 77
Medan, 114, 418
Mede, 73
Median, 73
Medianite, 134
Mehetabel, 118
grandfather of (Mezahab), 83
husband of (Qaftzaphoni), 297
mother of (Matred), 216
Mehida, 82
Mehir, 219
Mehujael, 115, 119
father of (Irad), 231
Mehuman, 157, 436
Mehunites, 176
Melchizedek, 236
city of (Salem), 277
Melek, 109, 347
Melicu, 128
Memucan, 167, 440
Menachem. *Also See:* Israel: Kings of: 17 Menachem
Meonothai, 349
Mephibosheth, 449, 452
grandson of (Melek), 109, 347
son of (Mica), 90
Merab, 211
husband of (Barzillai), 214
Meraiah, 218
Meraioth
son of (Amariah), 218
Meraioth
father of (Ahitub), 54
Meraioth, 379
Merari, 112, 310
descendant (Shoham), 264, 469
descendant of (Amaziah), 159, 164
descendant of (Asaiah), 282
descendant of (Azrikam), 302, 488
descendant of (Bani), 80
descendant of (Ibri), 231
descendant of (Jaaziah), 130
descendant of (Jehaleleel), 128
descendant of (Jesaiah), 286
descendant of (Shemaiah), 301
descendant of (Shimea), 295
descendant of (Uzzah), 101
descendant of (Zakkur), 206
descendant of (Zuriel), 261
grandson of (Ader), 227
son of (Mahli), 107
son of (Mushi), 266, 270
Merarite, 310
Mered, 211
wife of (Bithiah), 297
Meremoth, 390
father of (Urijah), 200, 203
Meres, 239
Meriaoth
son of (Amariah), 221
Merib-Baal, 269
son of (Micah), 94
Merodach, 222
Merodach-Baladan, 268, 540
father of (Baladan), 105, 414
Meronothite, 394
Mesha, 268, 298
Meshach, 276, 456
Meshech, 272, 453
Meshelemiah, 301, 303
son of (Elioenai), 182
Meshezabeel, 285
Meshillemith, 448
Meshillemoth, 446
Meshobab, 266
Meshullam, 293, 484
father of (Shephatiah), 290
father of (Zadok), 184
Meshullemeth, 443
Mesobaite, 160
Methusael, 431
(and), 433
Methuselah, 433
number of years lived by, 483
Mezahab, 83
Miamin, 155, 435
Mibhar, 214
Mibsam, 282, 479
Mica, 90
Micah, 94
son of (Ahaz), 32
son of (Melek), 109, 347
son of (Pithon), 343, 517
son of (Shamir), 343
son of (Tahrea), 387
son of (Tarea), 385
Michael, 123
Michaiah, 100, 104
father of (Uriel), 213
Michal, 120
Michri, 225
Midian, 125, 422
son of (Eldaah), 131
son of (Epher), 267
Midianite, 125
Mikloth, 349
Mikneiah, 193
Milalai, 131
Milcah, 116
sister of (Iscah), 115
son of (Chesed), 255
son of (Uz), 172, 485
Miniamin, 184, 456
Miriam, 234, 456
ancestor of (Amram), 267
Mirma, 232
Mishael, 281
as Meshach, 276, 456
brother of (Eliytsaphan), 472
brother of (Elizaphan), 221
Misham, 310, 492
Mishma, 310
Mishmannah, 304
Mishraites, 365
Mispar, 280
Mispereth, 431
Mithnite, 325
Mithredath, 498
Mitsrite, 261
Mizraim, 280, 478
descendant of (Lehabim), 106, 375
descendant of (Pathrusim), 435, 532
descendants of (Anamim), 192, 428
son of (Naphtuhim), 352, 512
Mizzah, 72
Moab, 68
Moabite, 78, 82, 313
Moadiah, 151
Molid, 109
Morashthite, 482
Mordecai, 227
(blessed be), 326, 486
father of (Jair), 200
grandfather of (Shimi), 299
great-grandfather of (Kish), 294
Moses, 264
(age of at the time of Exodus), 99
(age when he could 'no longer come and go', 140
(age when he died, 140

(anger of), 232, 491
(like), 274
ancestor of (Amram), 267
basket into which he was placed, 292
brother of (Aaron), 218, 470
burning bush of, 136
chief of Simeon appointed to assist (Shelumiel), 295
descendant of (Joram), 218, 446
father-in-law of (Hobab), 28
father-in-law of (Jethro), 363
grandson of (Jesaiah), 289
mother of (Jochebed), 62
name of altar built by (YHVH *Nissi* – YHVH is my banner), 159
number of Israelite leaders that accompanied to the base of Sinai, 88
number of Israelite leaders that accompanied to the Tabernacle, 88
one who rebelled against (Abiram), 216, 445
one who rebelled against (Korah), 245
our teacher, 361
place where he explained the Law (Suph), 160, 460
place where he gave his farewell speech (Dizahab), 46
place where he saw the burning bush (Horeb), 191
place where he smote the rock (Meribah), 219, 378
serpent made by (Nehushtan), 442, 539
sister of (Miriam), 234, 456
son of (Eliezer), 251
son of (Gershom), 341, 505
staff created by (*Nachash*), 271
successor of (Joshua), 285, 287
wife of (Zipporah), 279
Muppim, 173, 412
Mushi, 266, 270
son of (Jeremoth), 379, 383
Mushite, 270
Naam, 169, 408
brother-in-law of (Hodiah), 48
Naamah, 171
Naaman, 191, 458
Naamathite, 347
Naamites, 174
Naarah, 255
Naarai, 257
Naashon, 296
Nabal, 101
wife of (Abigail), 64, 74
Naboth, 313
Nachon, 144, 430
Nadab, 75, *Also See:* Israel: Kings of: 02 Nadab
one who carried body of (Mishael), 281
son of (Appaim), 148, 392
Naham, 119, 380
Nahamani, 168
Naharai, 224
Nahash, 271
Nahath, 313
Nahbi, 88
father of (Vophci), 166
Nahor, 223
concubine of (Reumah), 197
son of (Bethuel), 305
son of (Buz), 32
son of (Chesed), 255
son of (Gaham), 70
son of (Hazo), 39
son of (Jidlaph), 143, 454
son of (Kemuel), 177
son of (Maachah), 151
son of (Pildash), 296
son of (Tebah), 37
son of (Thahash), 401
son of (Uz), 172, 485
wife of (Milcah), 116
Nahum, 126, 382
Naomi, 174
daughter-in-law of (Orpah), 270
husband of (Elimelech), 148, 359
name assumed by (Mara), 210
son of (Chilion), 136, 426
Naphish, 306
Naphtali, 347
mother of (Bilhah), 61
son of (Guni), 87
son of (Jahzeel), 154
son of (Jahziel), 161
son of (Jezer), 239
son of (Shallum), 277
Naphtuhim, 352, 512
Nathan, 325, 512
Nathan-Melech, 352, 551
Neariah, 259
son of (Elioenai), 182
son of (Hezekiah), 147
Nebadiah, 90
Nebaioth, 314, 316
Nebat, 80
Nebo, 77
Nebuchadnezzar, 297, 299, 300, 349, 350
captain of the guard of (Arioch), 207, 407
prince of the eunuchs of (Ashpenaz), 305
Nebushazban, 297, 501
Nebuzaradan, 253, 484
Necho, 95
Nehelamite, 154
Nehemiah, 134
assistant of (Imri), 215
brother of (Hanani), 138
chief or family who sealed the covenant (Hanan), 423
chief or family who sealed the covenant with (Hanan), 129
father of (Azbuk), 179
father of (Hachaliah), 92
High Priest in time of (Eliashib), 268
man who sealed the covenant with (Baruch), 400
one who defied (Mehetabel), 118
one who sealed covenant with (Hanan), 129, 423
one who sealed the covenant with (Bigvai), 39
one who sealed the covenant with (Hashabiah), 255
one who sealed the covenant with (Hosea), 281
one who sealed the covenant with (Obadiah), 112
one who sealed the covenant with (Shobek), 292
one who sealed the covenant with (Zadok), 184
priest who assisted (Eliakim), 181
scribe of (Zadok), 184
servant who opposed (Tobiah), 51
Nehum, 126, 382
Nehushta, 424
Nekoda, 170
Nemuel, 145
Nemuelite, 153
Nepheg, 150
Nephisesim, 342, 506
Nephusim, 215, 443
Ner, 215
Nergal-Sharezer, 502
Neriah, 223, 226
Nethaneel, 338
father of (Zuar), 275
Nethaniah, 332, 335
son of (Ishmael), 311
Nethinims, 328, 330, 513
Netophathite, 343
Nimrod, 236, 239
city belonging to (Calneh), 127, 128
city built by (Akkad), 43
city built by (Calah), 77
Nimshi, 288
Noadiah, 159
Noah, 77, 143

age at the time of the Flood, 355
descendant of (Elisha), 265
father of (Lamech), 109, 347
grandfather of (Methuselah), 433
grandson of (Canaan), 180, 453
grandson of (Tarshish), 519
son of (Ham), 67, 357
son of (Japheth), 322
son of (Shem), 262, 468
Nobah, 79
Nogah, 77
Nohah, 87
Non, 128, 423
Nun, 128, 423
Obadiah, 111, 118
(of), 118
Obal, 130, 133
Obed, 101
Obed-edom, 145, 390
son of (Ammiel), 164
son of (Nethaneel), 338
son of (Peulthai), 353
son of (Rephael), 248
Ocran, 262, 488
Oded, 97, 103
Og, 98
Ohad, 25
(and), 33
Ohel, 54
Omri, 253, *Also See:* Israel: Kings of: 06 Omri
father of (Michael), 123
son of (Ammihud), 152
On, 75, 399
father of (Peleth), 331
Onam, 111, 377
grandson of (Jonathan), 333, 514
mother of (Atarah), 231
son of (Jada), 103
Onan, 128, 423
Ophir, 232, 235, 237
Ophrah, 270
Oreb, 226
Oren, 215
Ornan, 241, 481
Orpah, 270
husband (Chilion), 136
husband of (Chilion), 426
Othni, 337
Othniel. *Also See:* Israel: Judges of: 01 Othniel
Owbiyl, 67
Ozem, 149, 392
Ozni, 86
Paarai, 272
Padon, 156, 435
Pagiel, 182
Pahath-Moab, 339
son of (Bezaleel), 165
Palal, 156
father of (Uzai), 42
Palluites, 141
Palti, 147
Paltiel, 169
Paltite, 147
Parmasta, 495
Parnach, 267, 451
Parosh, 376
line of (Eleazar), 245
Parshandatha, 497
Paruah, 236
Pasach, 169, 372
Paseah, 161
Pashur, 353
alternative name of (Magor-Missabib), 273
father of (Malchiah), 127
father of (Malchijah), 132
Pathrusim, 435, 532
Pathrusite, 420
Pedahel, 140
Pedaiah, 120
son of (Joed), 108
Pekah. *Also See:* Israel: Kings of: 19 Pekah
Pekahiah. *Also See:* Israel: Kings of: 18 Pekahiah
Pekod, 181
Pelaiah, 144, 145
Pelaliah, 166
Pelatiah, 150, 156
father of (Benaiah), 85, 92
Peleg, 134
son of (Reu), 228
Pelet, 139
Peleth, 331
Pelethites, 334
Pelonite, 176
Peninnah, 179
Penuel, 172, 175
Peresh, 351
Perez, 276, 515
descenant of (Baruch), 400
descendant of (Baruch), 203
descendant of (Ephlal), 156
descendant of (Maaseiah), 300
descendant of (Omri), 253
descendant of (Peleth), 331
descendant of (Shephatiah), 290
descendant of (Zechariah), 210
grandson of (Caleb), 71
mother of (Tamar), 372
son of (Hamul), 103
son of (Hezron), 269, 490
son of (Sisamai), 174
Perizzite, 238
Perizzites, 260, 467
Persian, 267, 270
Peruda, 235, 236
Pethahiah, 327
Pethuel, 333
Peulthai, 353
Phallu, 137
Pharaoh, 270
daughter of (Bithiah), 297
wife of (Tahapanes), 354, 356, 357
Pharaoh-Hophra, 405
Pharaoh-Necho, 303
Pharaoh-Nechoh, 302
Pharzite, 281
Philistine, 449
Philistines, 459, 537
king of (Abimelech), 124, 351
Phinehas, 189
descendant of (Gershom), 341, 505
one slain by (Zimri), 219
one slain by (Zur), 237
son of (Abishua), 284
son of (Ahitub), 54
son of (Ichabod), 63
Phoenicians
god of (Molech), 109, 347
Phurah, 232
Phut, 116
Phuvah, 113
Pichol, 156
Pilcha, 139
Pildash, 296
Piltai, 147
Piram, 253, 463
Pirathonite, 447
Pispah, 202
Pithon, 343, 517
Pochereth-Zebaim, 456, 536
Poratha, 391
Potiphar, 282
Potipherah, 312
Puah, 112, 170
Puhites, 324
Pul, 137
Punites, 160
Putiel, 152
Qaftzaphoni, 297
Quwshayahu, 302
Raamiah, 255
Rabbith, 361
Rabmag, 212
Rabsaris, 338
Rabshakeh, 357
Rachel, 208
father of (Laban), 101, 413
handmaiden of (Bilhah), 61
son of (Ben-oni), 139, 427
son of (Joseph), 166, 170, 462, 463
Raddai, 195
Rahab, 192
Raham, 214, 442

son of (Jorkeam/Jorkoam), 298, 486
Ram, 209, 438, 439
descendant of (Jamin), 131, 424
son of (Eker), 276
son of (Maaz), 184, 492
Ramathite, 377
Ramiah, 218
Ramoth-Negeb, 396
Rapha, 231, 232
descendant of (Saph), 156, 458
descendant of (Sippai), 162
son of (Elasah), 291
son of (Ishbi-Benob), 278
Raphu, 233
Reaiah, 197
son of (Jahath), 298
Reba, 227
Rebekah, 244
brother of (Laban), 101, 413
Rechab, 201
descendant of (Jehonadab), 95
descendant of (Jonadab), 91
Reeliah, 250
Refaim, 231
Regem, 211, 439
Regem-Melech, 259, 533
Rehabiah, 202, 205
Rehob, 192, 197
Rehoboam. *Also See:* Judah: Kings of: 01 Rehoboam
Rehum, 217, 445
Rei, 230
Rekem, 262, 468
Remaliah, 235
Rephael, 248
Rephah, 233
Rephaiah, 237
father of (Hur), 195
Resheph, 351, 527
Reu, 228
father of (Peleg), 134
son of (Serug), 330
Reuben, 220, 471
son of (Carmi), 225
son of (Hezron), 269, 490
son of (Phallu), 137
Reubenites, 225
Reuel, 244
father of (Ibnijah), 95
Reumah, 197
Rezia, 241
Rezin, 267, 489
Rezon, 222, 473
Ribai, 201
Rinnah, 218
Riphath, 323, 392
(and), 393
Rizpah, 279
father of (Ajah), 33
son of (Mephibosheth), 450
Rodanim, 242, 460
Rohgah, 199
Romamtiezer, 485
Rosh, 326
Ruth, 356
father-in-law of (Elimelech), 359
husband of (Boaz), 97
husband of (Elimelech), 148
husband of (Mahlon), 150, 433
mother-in-law of (Naomi), 174
son of (Obed), 101
Sabean, 93, 249
Sabta, 315, 316
Sabtecha, 320
Sacar, 335
Sallai, 118
Sallu, 117, 121
Salma, 278
son of (Bethlehem), 322, 499
Salmon, 301, 502
Samaritans, 354
Samgar-Nebo, 273
Samson. *Also See:* Israel: Judges of: 12 Samson
Samuel, 280
ancestor of (Azariah), 235
ancestor of (Eliy'el), 91
ancestor of (Joel), 66
ancestor of (Toah), 296
ancestor of (Tohu), 296
ancestor of (Uzziah), 113
ancestor of (Zephaniah), 206
brother of (Zophai), 180
brother of (Zuph), 176, 467
father of (Elkanah), 179
grandfather of (Jeroham), 219, 447
great-grandfather of (Elihu), 65, 72
king of Amalek killed by (Agag), 20
mother of (Hannah), 82
place where prophets gathered around (Naioth), 315
son of (Joel), 66
son of (Vashni), 275
Sanballat, 164
servant who opposed Nehemiah (Tobiah), 51
Saph, 156, 458
Sarah, 328
maid of (Hagar), 189
son of (Isaac), 298
Sarai, 331
Saraph, 351, 527
Sardites, 227
Sargon, 252, 483
Sarsechim, 368, 516
Satan, 271, 492
(as *Theli* the dragon), 306
(the essence of), 424, 536
Satrap, 373, 526
Saul. *Also See:* Israel, United Kingdom of: Kings of: 01 Saul
Seba, 82
Segub, 248
Seir, 351
(from), 365
descendant of (Alian), 169, 443
descendant of (Alvan), 167, 441
descendant of (Bilhan), 105, 414
descendant of (Hemdan), 124, 421
descendant of (Manahath), 324
descendant of (Onam), 111
descendant of (Seir), 381, 528
descendant of (Shephi), 285
descendant of (Shepho), 283
descendant of (Zaavan), 150, 433
grandson of (Akan), 199, 461
grandson of (Dishon), 269, 272, 274, 276, 490, 492, 493, 494
grandson of (Hemam), 115, 378
grandson of (Onam), 377
son of (Anah), 144
son of (Dishon), 269, 271, 274, 276, 490, 492, 493, 494
son of (Ezer), 229, 235
son of (Shobal), 261
son of (Uz), 172, 485
son of (Zibeon), 198, 461
Seled, 114
Semachiah, 157
Senir, 345
Sennacherib, 257
Esar-Haddon, 257, 486
son of (Sharezer), 436
Senuah, 137, 142
Seorim, 365, 515
Sepharvite, 270
Serah, 330
Seraiah, 332, 335
father of (Azriel), 252
Sered, 223
Serug, 330
father of (Reu), 228
Seth, 395
(and to), 414
descendant of (Jared), 195
number of years lived by, 472
son of (Enos), 270
Sethur, 383
Shaalbonite, 314
Shaaph, 311, 514
Shaashgaz, 388
Shabbethai, 404
Shachia, 251

Shadrach, 336, 490
original name of (Hananiah), 139, 144
Shage, 243
Shaharaim, 345, 508
son of (Jeuz), 176, 487
wife of (Baara), 227
wife of (Hodesh), 248
wife of (Hushim), 271, 274, 474, 475
Shallum, 277, 280, 478, *Also See:* Judah: Kings of: 16 Jehoahaz, *Also See:* Israel: Kings of: 16 Shallum
father of (Col-hozeh), 87
father of (Zadok), 184
grandfather of (Harhas), 228
grandfather of (Hasrah), 227
Shallun, 283, 497
Shalmai, 281
Shalman, 298, 501
town destroyed by (Beth-Arbel), 374
Shalmaneser, 388
Shamariah, 346
Shamgar. *Also See:* Israel: Judges of: 03 Shamgar
Shamhuth, 421
Shamir, 343
Shamma, 263
Shammah, 264
Shammai, 267
son of (Abishur), 334
son of (Maon), 172, 446
Shammoth, 419
Shammua, 297
father of (Zakkur), 206
Shamsherai, 456
Shapham, 299, 486
Shaphan, 303, 496
father of (Azaliah), 152
grandfather of (Shaphan), 293
son of (Elasah), 291
Shaphat, 284
father of (Adlai), 135
Sharai, 331
Sharar, 395
son of (Ahiam), 364
son of (Jehiel), 78
Sharezer, 436
Sharonite, 347
Shashai, 359
Shashak, 395
son of (Antothijah), 477
son of (Ishpan), 305, 503
Shavsha, 357, 386
Sheal, 258
Shealthiel, 429
Sheariah, 352
Shear-Jashub, 448
Sheba, 242
Shebaniah, 275, 278
Sheber, 326
Shebna, 269
Shebnah, 271
Shebuel, 261
Shechaniah, 282, 285
Shechem, 273, 475
father of (Hamor), 217
Shechemites, 277
Shedeur, 335
Shehariah, 336
Shelah, 260, 261
(to), 274
descendant of (Joash), 251
father of (Arphaxad), 356
son of (Er), 225
village inhabited by descendant of (Chozeba), 49
Shelanites, 285
Shelaph, 294, 510
Shelemiah, 283, 285
father of (Abdeel), 129
Shelesh, 368
Shelomi, 281
Shelomith, 432, 434
Shelomoth, 430
son of (Jahath), 298
Shelumiel, 295
father of (Zurishaddai), 365
Shem, 262, 468
descendant of (Almodad), 103
descendant of (Gether), 355
descendant of (Obal), 130, 133
descendant of (Sheba), 242
descendant of (Shelaph), 294, 510
grandson of (Hul), 44
great-grandson of (Eber), 226
son of (Aram), 209, 439
son of (Arphaxad), 356
son of (Elam), 163, 402
son of (Lud), 59
son of (Uz), 172, 485
son or grandson of (Mash), 261
son or grandson of (Meshech), 272, 453
Shema, 294
Shemaiah, 301, 304
ancestor of (Buni), 86
father of (Delaiah), 67
father of (Delaiahu), 74
father of (Hashub), 250
father of (Joel), 66
son of (Bariah), 199
son of (Elihu), 65, 72
son of (Othni), 337
Shemariah, 345
Shemeber, 341
Shemer, 340
Shemida, 300
Shemidaites, 304
Shemiramoth, 489
Shemuel, 280
Shenazar, 373
Shephatiah, 290, 294
father of (Maachah), 151
Shephi, 285
Shepho, 283
Shephuphan, 333, 514
Sherah, 328
town founded by (Uzzen-Sherah), 346, 519
Sherebiah, 333
Sheresh, 438
Sheshan, 377, 527
daughter of (Ahlai), 67
grandson of (Attai), 319
Sheshbazzar, 466
Shethar, 468
Shethar-Boznai, 485
Sheva, 248
Shilhi, 266
Shillemites, 281
Shiloni, 285
Shilonite, 291
Shilshah, 370
Shimah, 265
Shimea, 295
son of (Jonathan), 335, 515
Shimeah, 296
brother of (Rechab), 91
son of (Jehonadab), 95
Shimeam, 282, 479
Shimeath, 444
son of (Jozachar), 211
Shimeathites, 449
Shimeites, 299
Shimhi (Adaiah), 108
Shimi, 298
father of (Gera), 186
son of (Elienai), 178
son of (Jahath), 298
son of (Zina), 86
son of (Zizah), 47
Shimon, 291, 500
son of (Ben-Hail), 120, 420
Shimrath, 479
Shimri, 344
son of (Jedaiah), 47
Shimrith, 481
Shimron, 354, 522
(of), 365, 524
Shimronites, 354
Shimshai, 377
Shinab, 269
Shiphi, 303
father of (Allon), 105, 414
Shiphmite, 303
Shiphrah, 352
Shiphtan, 305, 503
Shisha, 360
Shishak, 399, 403
Shitrai, 334
Shiza, 252

son of (Adina), 151, 156
Shobab, 247
Shobach, 256, 442
Shobai, 249
Shobal, 261
son of (Alian), 169, 443
son of (Alvan), 167, 441
Shobek, 292
Shobi, 249
Shoham, 264, 469
Shomer, 340, 343
Shophach, 291, 464
Shua, 279, 280
Shuah, 249, 252
Shual, 291
Shubael, 261
Shuham, 270, 473
Shuhamites, 274
Shuhite, 255
Shulamite, 434
Shumathites, 420
Shunamite, 441
Shuni, 275
Shunites, 275
Shupham, 328, 501
Shuphamite, 305
Shuppim, 303, 488
Shuthalhites, 419
Shuthelah, 418
(of), 429
Shuthelahites
(the), 421
Sia, 157
Siaha, 160
Sibbechai, 112
Sidonian, 171
Sihon, 146, 150, 431, 433
Simeon, 315, 508
captain of the sons of (Uzziel), 138
sister of (Dinah), 87
son of (Jachin), 108, 415
son of (Jamin), 131, 424
son of (Jemuel), 106
son of (Mibsam), 282, 479
son of (Nemuel), 145
son of (Ohad), 25
son of (Saul), 261
son of (Zohar), 238
Sinite, 148
Sippai, 162
Sisamai, 174
Sisera, 258
Sithri, 384
(and), 386
So, 86
Sodi, 98
Solomon. *Also See:* Israel, United Kingdom of: Kings of: 03 Solomon
Sophereth, 416
Sotai, 104
Suah, 93
Sukkites, 109
Susanchites, 390
Susi, 152
Syrian, 215
language of, 377
Tabbaoth, 321
Tabeal, 62
Tabrimmon, 244, 482
Tachmonite, 337
Tahan, 313, 506
Tahanites, 316
Tahapanes, 354, 356, 357
Tahath, 442
(from), 455
(in), 443
Tahrea, 387
Talmai, 320
father of (Ammihur), 259
Talmon, 151, 433
Tamar, 372
(to), 384
Tanhumeth, 466
Taphath, 322
husband of (Ben-Abinadab), 141, 428
Tappuah, 323
Tarea, 385
Tarpelites, 257
Tarshish, 519
(and), 520
Tartan, 499, 550
Tatnai, 459
Tebah, 37
Tebaliah, 81
Tehinnah, 315
Tekoite, 352
Telah, 305
Telem, 97, 371
Tema, 311
Teman, 325, 512
father of (Eliphaz), 145
Temanite, 331
Temeni, 331
Terah, 358
(from), 376
(in), 358
age of when son Abraham (Abram) was born, 88
Teresh, 468
Thahash, 401
Thamah, 309
Tibni, 314
father of (Ginath), 314
Tidal, 327
Tiglath-Pileser, 518
another name for (Pul), 137
prince taken by (Beerah), 188
Tikvah, 331
son of (Jahaziah), 59
Tikvath, 472
Tilon, 323, 512
Timnah, 346
Timnite, 325
Tiras, 384
(and), 386
Tirathite, 502
Tirhakah, 403
Tirhanah, 382
Tiria, 365
Tirshatha, 527
Tirzah, 393
(and), 396
Tishbite, 404
Tizite, 331
Toah, 296
Tob-Adonijah, 113
Tobiah, 51, 57
son of (Jehohanan), 146, 431
Tobiahu, 57
Togarmah, 376, 378
(and), 378
Tohu, 296
Tola, 328, *Also See:* Israel: Judges of: 06 Tola
descendant of (Joel), 66
Tolaites, 333
Tou, 320
son of (Hadoram), 217, 446
son of (Jehoram), 221, 449
Tubal, 304, 305
Tubal-Cain, 354, 523
Ucal, 70
Uel, 56
Ulam, 95, 370
Ulla, 123
son of (Arah), 189
Ur of the Chaldees, 351, 511
Uri, 197
son of (Bezaleel), 164
Uriel, 213
Urijah, 200, 203
father of (Shemaiah), 304
one sent to bring from Egypt (Achbor), 238
wife of (Bathsheba), 429
wife of (Bathshua), 431
Uthai, 321
Uz, 172, 485
Uzai, 42
Uzal, 63
Uzza, 97
Uzzah, 101
Uzzi, 106
Uzzia, 107
Uzziah, 113, 119, *Also See:* Judah: Kings of: 09 Azariah
Uzziel, 138
father of (Harhaiah), 204
son of (Eliytsaphan), 472
son of (Elizaphan), 221
son of (Isshiah), 255, 258
Uzzielites, 146
Vajezatha, 300

Vaniah, 90
Vashni, 275
Vashti, 406
Vophsi, 166
Yemenite, 139, 303
Zaavan, 150, 433
Zabad, 30
Zabbai, 37
Zabdi, 41
  son of (Mica), 90
Zabdiel, 73
Zabud, 37
Zaccai, 56, 57
Zachariah. *Also See:* Israel: Kings of: 15 Zachariah
Zacher, 203
Zadok, 184
  ancestor of (Azariah), 235
  father of (Ahitub), 54
  father of (Baanah), 145
  son of (Ahimaaz), 198, 496
Zaham, 71, 360
Zakkur, 206
  father of (Imri), 215
Zalaph, 184, 475
Zalmon, 197, 460
Zalmunna, 230
Zamzummim, 114, 378
Zanoah, 90
Zaphenath, 365
Zaphenath-Paneah, 452
Zaphnath-Paaneah, 451
Zarchite, 202
Zattu, 295
  one in the line of (Eliashib), 268
  son of (Aziza), 116
Zebadiah, 46
  father of (Ishmael), 311
Zebadiahu, 53
Zebah, 34
Zebina, 87
Zebudah, 46
Zebul, 57
Zebulun, 115, 418
  descendant of (Parnach), 267
  son of (Elon), 111, 117, 416, 419
  son of (Sered), 223
Zechariah, 210
  daughter of (Abi), 28
  father of (Berachiah), 207
  father of (Berekyahu), 211
  father of (Jeberechiah), 216
  father of (Shiloni), 285
  grandfather of (Iddo), 100
  staff named by (*Chebel*), 58
  staff named by (*No'am*), 169, 408
Zedekiah, 190, 196, *Also See:* Judah: Kings of: 19 Zedekiah
  father of (Chenaanah), 182
Zeeb, 25
Zelek, 199
Zelophehad, 194
  daughter of (Hoglah), 65
  daughter of (Mahlah), 102
  daughter of (Milcah), 116
  daughter of (Noah), 144
  daughter of (Tirzah), 393
Zemarite, 262
Zemira, 222
Zephaniah, 206, 210
  ancestor of (Amariah), 218, 221
  father of (Cushi), 260
  grandfather of (Gedaliah), 71
  great-grandfather of (Hezekiah), 147
  priest replaced by (Jehoiada), 126
  son of (Hen), 76, 400
  son of (Josiah), 255
Zephi, 178
Zepho, 176
Zephon, 203, 462
Zephonites, 207
Zerah, 196
  descendant of (Izrach), 202
  son of (Dara), 227
  son of (Jeaterai), 365
  son of (Zimri), 219
Zerahiah, 204
Zeresh, 329
Zereth, 392
Zeri, 240
Zeruah, 277
Zerubbabel, 209
  ancestor of one returning with (Hagab), 30
  daughter of (Shelomith), 432
  descendant of (Hodaiahu), 61
  father of (Pedaiah), 120
  father of (Shealthiel), 429
  grandson of (Jesaiah), 286
  head of family who returned with (Bigvai), 39
  one who came up with (Azariah), 236
  one who came up with (Binnui), 86
  one who came up with (Judah), 48
  one who returned with (Adna), 144
  one who returned with (Baanah), 145
  one who returned with (Bakbukiah), 198
  one who returned with (Giddel), 55
  one who returned with (Iddo), 101, 104
  one who returned with (Jedaiah), 119
  one who returned with (Melicu), 128
  one who returned with (Nehum), 126, 382
  one who returned with (Rehum), 217, 445
  one who returned with (Sallu), 117, 121
  priest who returned with (Jehohanan), 146, 431
  son of (Hananiah), 142
  son of (Hashubah), 250
  son of (Jushab-Hesed), 284
  son of (Ohel), 54
Zeruiah, 248
  father of (Nahash), 271
  son of (Abishai), 249, 254
  son of (Asahel), 291
  son of (Joab), 37
Zetham, 309, 491
Zethan, 316, 508
Zethar, 357
Zia, 105
Zibeon, 198, 461
  daughter of (Anah), 144
  son of (Anah), 144
Zibiah, 125, 129
Zichri, 207
  son of (Amasiah), 179
  son of (Mica), 90
  son of (Micah), 94
Zidkijah, 190
Zidon, 169, 444
Ziha, 120, 131
Zillah, 144
  daughter of (Naamah), 171
Zilpah, 141
Zilthai, 337
Zimnah, 71
Zimran, 237, 480
Zimri, 219, *Also See:* Israel: Kings of: 05 Zimri
Zina, 86
Ziph, 117, 447
Ziphah, 124
Ziphim, 128
Ziphion, 207, 464
Ziphite, 128
Zippor, 279
Zipporah, 279
  son of (Gershom), 341, 505
Ziza, 43
Zizah, 47
Zobebah, 120
Zohar, 238
Zoheth, 296
Zophah, 179
  son of (Hod), 32
  son of (Ithran), 381, 528
  son of (Shilshah), 370
  son of (Shual), 291
  son of (Suah), 93

Zophai, 180
Zophar, 279
Zorite, 240
Zorites, 277, 428
Zuar, 275
Zuph, 176, 467
Zur, 237
Zuriel, 260
father of (Abihail), 80
Zurishaddai, 365
Zuzims, 82, 366
Biblical Locations
Abaddon, 81, 404
Abana, 76
Abarim, 254, 464
Abel Mayim, 142, 389
Abel Mizraim, 295, 485
Abel of Beth-Maachah, 350
Abel-Keramim, 263, 469
Abel-Meholah, 141
Abel-Shittim, 287, 482
Abez, 113, 469
Accho, 117
Achmetha, 309
Achor, 237
Achzib, 58
Adadah, 165
Adamah, 68
Adami, 73
Adithaim, 338, 504
Adonai Shalom, 289, 483
Adonai-Jireh, 210
Adoraim, 221, 449
Adullam, 158, 398
Adummim, 115, 378
Aham-Naharaim, 342, 549
Ahava, 29
Ahlab, 60
Ai, 99
Aiath, 319
Aija, 104
Aijalon, 117, 419
Ain, 148, 432
Akkad, 43
(and), 50
Akshaph, 289, 509
Alammelech, 141, 355
Alamoth, 342
Allon Bachuth, 332, 514
Almon, 182, 455
Almon Diblathaim, 388, 530
Alush, 260
Amad, 179
Amalek
king of (Agag), 20
Amam, 100, 372
Amana, 116
Anab, 142
Anaharath, 380
Ananiah, 179
Anathoth, 476
Anem, 169, 409
Aner, 253
Anim, 174, 412
Aphekah, 179
Aphik, 178
Arad, 227
Aram, 209, 439
Aramzobah, 263, 469
Ararat, 293
Aridatha, 362
Arkites, 281
Armoni, 241
Arnon, 241, 244, 481, 482
Aroer, 340, 342, 343
Arpad, 232
Aruboth, 358
Arumah, 216
Arvad, 193
Ashan, 298, 501
Ashbea, 278
Ashdod, 250
Ashdothpisgah, 459
Asher, 325
Ashkelon, 321, 511
Ashnah, 270
Ashteroth
(in), 533
Ashtoreth Karnaim, 552, 562
Askalon, 321, 511
Assyria, 325, 328
king of (Shalmaneser), 388
Astaroth, 534
Atad, 36, *Also See* Biblical Locations: Goren HaAtad
Ataroth, 387, 389
Ataroth Addar, 465
Athach, 322, 484
Atroth-Shophan, 509, 552
Ava, 96
Avim, 144, 390
Avith, 321
Ayah
(and), 40
Azal, 141
Azekah, 178
Azmon, 215, 218, 467, 470, 499
Aznoth-tabor, 501
Baal Gad, 130
Baal Hamon, 185, 457
Baal Hazor, 291
Baal Hermon, 291, 500
Baal Meon, 229, 476
Baal Perazim, 335, 503
Baal Shalisha, 414
Baal Tamar, 417
Baal Zephon, 256, 486
Baalah, 128
Baalath, 326
Baalath Beer, 398
Baale Yehuwdah, 157
Babel, 52
Babylon, 52
alternate name for (Sheshack), 365, 505
symbolic name for (Merathaim), 391, 523
Babylonia, 63
Baca, 41
Bahurim, 220, 223, 448, 450
Balah, 55
Bamah, 66
Bamoth, 309
Bamoth Baal, 343
Bashan, 268, 490
king of (Og), 98
Bath Rabbim, 378, 519
Bealoth, 329
Beer, 185
Beer Elim, 231, 454
Beer Lahai Roi, 314
Beeroth, 358
(from), 373
Beeroth Bene Jaakan, 466, 544
Beersheba, 349
Beeshterah, 485
Bela, 124
Bene Berak, 274
Bene Jaakan, 235, 479
Beon, 141, 429
Berachah, 203
Berothah, 361
Berothai, 360
Besor, 329
Betah, 36
Beten, 80, 403
Beth Anath, 477
Beth Anoth, 478
Beth Arabah, 392
Beth Aram, 380, 520
Beth Astaroth, 553
Beth Aven, 316, 509
Beth Azmaveth, 477
Beth Baal Meon, 387, 530
Beth Barah, 364
Beth Car, 369
Beth Dagon, 317, 509
Beth Diblathaim, 467, 539
Beth Eden, 339, 516
Beth Eked, 352
Beth Emek, 367
Beth Gamul, 323
Beth Haccerem, 386, 522
Beth Haran, 383, 529
Beth Hogla, 312
Beth Horon, 388, 530
Beth le-Aphrah, 456
Beth Maachah, 343
Beth Marcaboth, 503
Beth Meon, 350, 521
Beth Merhak, 426
Beth Millo, 320, 322
Beth Pazzez, 385, 540
Beth Peor, 427
Beth Shemesh, 499

Beth Tappuah, 470
Beth Zur, 400
Beth-Arbel, 374
king who sacked (Shalman), 298, 501
Beth-Birei, 367
Bethel, 307
Bether, 355
Beth-Ezel, 339
Beth-Gader, 364
Beth-Gilgal, 305
Beth-Jeshimoth, 516
Bethlehem, 322, 499
alternate name for (Ephrath), 388, 390
Beth-Marcaboth, 502
Beth-Nimrah, 399
Beth-Palet, 338
Beth-Rehob, 367
Beth-Shan, 425, 536
Beth-Shean, 425, 536
Beth-Shemesh
number of people from struck down by God, 88
Beth-Shittah, 412
Bethuel, 305
Bezek, 130
Bezer, 235
Bileam, 157, 396
Bilhah, 61
Bithron, 380, 528
Biziothiah, 305
Bochim, 91, 369
Bozez, 180, 489
Bozkath, 353
Bozrah, 237
Buz, 32
Cabbon, 96, 411
Cabul, 77
Cain, 170, 444
Calah, 77
Caleb Ephrathah, 415
Calneh, 127, 128
Camon, 183, 455
Canaan, 180, 453
Canneh, 94
Caphtor, 394, 399
(from), 415
Carchemish, 352
Carmel, 234
Casiphia, 174
Chaldea
Lev Kamay (*Atbash* for), 178
Chebar, 201
Chephar Haammonai, 320
Chephirah, 250
Cherith, 368
Cherub, 204
Chesalon, 172, 446
Chesil, 139
Chesulloth, 333
Chezib, 58
(at), 60
Chidon, 108, 415
Chilmad, 114
Chinnereth, 384, 386
Chisloth Tabor, 507
Chorashan, 375, 527
Chozeba, 49
Cubit, 65
Cush, 256
Cushan, 279, 495
Cushan-Rishathaim, 564
Cuth, 301
Cuthah, 303
Dabbesheth, 398
Daberath, 356
Damascus, 307, 310, 374
Dan, 73
Dan Jaan, 179, 541
Dannah, 77
Debir, 187, 197
Dedan, 82
Diblah, 60
Dibon, 84, 91, 406, 409
Dilean, 165, 440
Dimon, 131, 424
Dimonah, 135
Dinhabah, 84
Dizahab, 46
Dophkah, 180
Dor, 186, 191
Dothan, 311, 315, 505, 507
Dura, 193
Ebal, 133
Ebenezer, 259, 487
Ebron, 254, 485
Ebronah, 256
Ecbatana, 309
Eden, 143, 429
Eder, 227
Edom, 70, 359
capital of (Bozrah), 237
capital of (Sela), 169
Edrei, 232
king defeated at (Og), 98
Eglaim, 103, 373
Egypt, 280, 478
alternate name for (Rahab Hem Shebeth), 482, 542
alternate names (Matsor), 260
name used in poetry (Ham), 64, 356
Ekron, 301, 502
El Elohe Israel, 364
Elah, 54
Elath, 306, 308
Elealah, 149, 152
Elef, 132, 451
Elim, 100, 372
Elkoshite, 306
Ellasar, 235
Elon Beth Hanan, 363, 556
El-Paran, 278, 495
Eltekeh, 338, 339
Eltekon, 351, 521
Eltolad, 317
En Eglaim, 231, 541
En Haddah, 160, 437
En Hakkore, 307, 504
En Hatannim, 370, 555
En Hazor, 304, 503
En Rimmon, 301, 551
En Rogel, 273, 493
En Shemesh, 428, 537
En Tappuah, 366, 525
En-Dor, 259, 262, 487, 488
En-Gannim, 206, 538
En-Gedi, 160, 437
alternate name for (Hazazon Tamar), 462, 464
alternate name for (Hazezon Tamar), 543
Ephes Dammim, 206, 437
Ephraim, 258, 465
Ephrath, 388, 390
alternate name for (Bethlehem), 322, 499
Eshcol, 268
Eshean, 299, 502
Eshek, 316
Eshtaol, 413, 414
Eshtemoa, 418, 444, 447
Etam, 147, 391
Eth Kazin, 409, 533
Etham, 306, 490
Ether, 384
Ethiopia
king of (Zerah), 196
Euphrates, 388
Ezel, 56, 141
Ezem, 184
Ezem, 424
Ezion Geber, 303, 503
Gaash, 278
Gaba, 93
Gaderowth, 357
Galil, 92
Galilee, 96
Gallim, 102, 373
Gath, 290
Gath Rimmon, 394, 531
Gaza, 101
Geba, 93
Gebal, 53
Gebim, 73, 362
Geder, 188
Gederah, 193
Gederoth, 361
Gederothaim, 380, 520
Gedor, 194
Gehenna, 383, 385
Geliloth, 319
Gerar, 289
Gerizim, 220, 448
Geshur, 401

king of (Talmai), 320
Gezer, 190
Giah, 39
Gibbethon, 314, 507
Gibeah, 93, 94
Gibeath, 318
Gibeon, 149, 432
Gidom, 137, 386
Gihon, 85, 95, 407, 411
Gilboa, 126
Gilead, 128
Gilgal, 84
Giloh, 56, 66
Gimzo, 74
Gittah Hepher, 393
Gittaim, 311, 493
Goath, 96
Gob, 18, 27
Gog, 28
symbolic name of (Hamonah), 128
Gog and Magog, 87
Golan, 107, 415
Golgotha, 315
Gomorrah, 250
destruction of, 162
Goshen, 268, 490
Gozan, 84, 406
Gudgod
(the), 42
Gudgodah, 36
Gur, 190
Gur Baal, 248
Habor, 197
Hachilah, 92
Hadashah, 251
Hadid, 44
Hadrach, 205, 404
Haggidgad, 36
Hahiroth, 366
Halah, 65
Halak, 153
Halhul, 101
Hali, 67
Ham, 64, 67, 356, 357
Hamath, 309
king of (Tou), 320
Hamath Zobah, 344
Hammiphkad, 204
Hammon, 125, 422
Hammoth dor, 378
Hamon Gog, 134, 425
Hamonah, 127
Hananel, 154
Hanes, 135, 138
Hannathon, 329, 513
Haphraim, 261, 467
Hara, 187
Haradah, 198
Haran, 217, 219, 469, 470
Harmown, 241, 481
Harosheth, 470
Hashmonah, 290
Hauran, 222, 473
Havilah, 77
Havoth-Jair, 372
Hazar Addar, 326
Hazar Enan, 318, 321, 510, 511
Hazar Gaddah, 246
Hazar Hatticon, 435, 538
Hazar Susah, 302
Hazar Susim, 317, 497
Hazarmaveth, 417
Hazazon Tamar, 462, 464
Hazeroth, 397
(and), 397
(from), 415, 418
(in), 394, 398
Hazezon Tamar, 543
Hazor, 242
Hazor Hadattah, 409
Hebron
early name for (Kirjath-Arba), 487
early name of (Kirjath-Haarba), 488
Helbah, 64
Helbon, 116, 418
Heleph, 138, 453
Heliopolis, 70, 395
Helkath, 339
Helkath-Hazzurim, 464, 538
Hena, 143
Hepher, 233
Heres, 224
Hereth, 357
Hermon, 242, 481
Heshbon, 275, 494
village near (Elealah), 149, 152
Heshmon, 290
Hethlon, 322, 511
Hiddikel, 157
Hilen, 118, 419
Hinnom, 115, 378
Hobab
(to), 62
Hobah, 39
Hodu, 32
Holon, 106, 114, 414, 417
Hor, 187
Hor Hagidgad, 203
Horeb, 191
Horem, 214, 442
Hormah, 216
Horonaim, 245, 460
Hukkok, 189, 198
Humtah, 81
Ibleam, 164, 404
Iim, 148, 391
Ije-Abarim, 263, 297, 469, 486
Ijon, 152, 434
Immer, 209
Ir Hammelech, 273
Ir Hatemariym, 485, 543
Ir Shemesh, 475
Ir-Nahash, 371
Iron, 224, 474
Irpeel, 253
Ish-Tob, 256
Ithnan, 330, 513
Ivah, 101
Jaazer, 232, 237
Jabbok, 133
Jabez, 175, 486
Jabneel, 113
Jabneh, 85
Jagur, 199
Jahaz, 126, 473
Jahazah, 131
Jahzeel, 154
Janoah, 93
Janohah, 97
Janum, 131
Japha, 116
Japhia, 173
Jarmuth, 379
Jattir, 364
Javan, 84, 406
Jearim, 257, 465
Jebus, 96
Jegar-Sahadutha, 476
Jehud, 37
Jehudite, 54
Jekabzeel, 206
Jericho, 202, 206
alternate name for (Ir Hatemariym), 485, 543
one who rebuilt (Hiel), 68
Jeruel, 213
Jerusalem, 352, 353, 512, 513
(the land of), 220
alternate name (Ariel), 209
cleansers of
Elam, 163, 402
early name for (Jebus), 96
governor of (Gedaliah), 71
name of (Ariel), 210
one who helped rebuild the wall of (Col-hozeh), 87
one who helped rebuild the wall of (Pedaiah), 120
one who helped repair the wall (Jadon), 87
spring outside of (Gihon), 85, 95, 407, 411
symbolic name of (YHVH *Shammah* - Adonai is there), 277
symbolic names for (Oholibah), 72
two who repaired the wall of (Zadok), 184
Jeshanah, 274
Jeshua, 283
Jethlah, 308
Jezerite, 238
Jezreel, 251

Jiphthah-el, 337
Jogbehah, 44
(and), 50
Jokdeam, 201, 433
Jokmeam, 220, 448
Jokneam, 225, 451
Joktheel, 340
Joppa, 118
Jordan, 222, 473
Jotbah, 45
Jotbathah, 301
Juttah, 43, 48
Kabzeel, 201
Kadesh, 290
Kadesh Barnea, 411
Kanah, 166
Karkaa, 317
Karkor, 354
Kartah, 398
Kartan, 420, 535
Kattath, 330
Kedemoth, 344
Kehelathah, 340
Keilah, 196
Kenath, 344
Kerioth, 407
Keziz, 234, 504
Kibroth, 401
(and in), 402
(from), 417, 419
(in), 397
Kibroth-Hattaavah, 509
Kibzaim, 211, 439
Kidron, 272, 492
Kinah, 172
Kinnereth
(from), 402
Kir, 247
Kir-Haraseth, 520
Kir-Haresh, 448
Kiriathaim, 425, 529
Kirjath Arba
founder of (Arba), 227
Kirjath Sannah, 450
Kirjath Sepher, 499
Kirjath-Arba, 487
Kirjath-Arim, 496, 545
Kirjath-Baal, 445
Kirjath-Haarba, 488
Kirjath-Huzoth, 519
Kirjath-Jearim, 498, 546
Kishion, 315, 508
Kishon, 315, 508
Kithlish, 424
Kitron, 275, 493
Laban, 101, 413
Lachish, 272
Lahmam, 138
Lahmas, 154
Laish, 260, 261
Lakum, 176, 414
Lamam, 387
Lasha, 287
Lebanon, 154, 435
Lebaoth, 305
Lebonah, 113
Lehi, 67
Lekah, 74
Leshem, 276, 476
Libnah, 106
Libya
(as Phut), 116
Lod, 53
Lo-Debar, 207, 208, 210
Luhith, 307, 312
Luz, 62
Maachah
king of (Maachah), 151
Maaleh-Acrabbim, 347, 510
Maarath, 402
Machbenah, 134
Machpelah, 175
Madmannah, 154
Madmen, 150, 433
Madmenah, 154
Madon, 120, 420
Magbish, 270
Magog, 72
Mahanaim, 161, 401
Mahaneh-Dan, 167, 441
Makaz, 204, 497
Makheloth, 349
(from), 362
Makkedah, 162
Maktesh, 424
Manahath, 324
Maon, 172, 446
Marah, 212
(to), 374
Maralah, 264
Mareshah, 342
Maroth, 375
Mashal, 276
Masrekah, 374
(from), 389
Massah, 127
Mattanah, 324
Meah, 65
Mearah, 250
Medeba, 76
Megiddo, 72, 125, 421
Me-Jarkon, 299, 502
Mekonah, 135
Memphis, 140, 148, 453, 456
Mephaath, 353
Merathaim, 391, 523
Meribah, 219, 378
Merodach, 418
Merom, 232, 455
Meroz, 216
Mesha, 263, 268
Mesopotamia
river in (Chebar), 201
Metheg-Ammah, 323
Michmas, 169
Michmash, 287
Michmethath, 467
Middin, 125, 422
Midian, 125, 422
Migdal Eder, 269
Migdalel, 130
Migdalgad, 103
Migdol, 95, 102
Migron, 239, 480
Minni, 121
Minnith, 324
Misgab, 264
Mishal, 277
Misrephoth-Maim, 508, 549
Mithkah, 342
Mizar, 288
Mizpeh, 196
Moab, 68
Moladah, 104
Moreh, 215
Moresheth-Gath, 532
Moriah, 217, 221
Mosera, 248
Moseroth, 399
(from), 418
(in), 400
Mount of Olives, 297
Mount Sinai, 259
Mozah, 151
Naamah, 171
Naaran, 276, 495
Nachon, 144, 430
Nahaliel, 146
Naioth, 315
Neah, 143
Neballat, 111
Neiel, 170
Nekeb, 74, 164
Neptoah, 342
Netaim, 177, 415
Netophah, 158
Nezib, 164
Nibshan, 289, 499
Nile, 193
Nimrah, 236
Nimrim, 262, 467
Nineveh, 141
Nob, 72
Nobah, 79
Nod, 79
Noph, 148, 456
Nophah, 154
Oboth, 289
Oholah, 60
Oholibah, 72
On, 75, 399
On-Heliopolis, 223
Ono, 75, 81
Ophel, 178
Ophir, 232, 235, 237
(gold of), 248

Ophni, 192
Ophrah, 270
Oreb, 226
Padan, 150, 433
Padan-Aram, 279, 545
Pai, 169
Palestine
as Pelesheth, 443
Palmyra, 372
Parah, 232
Paran, 258, 486
Parbar, 320
Parvaim, 260, 466
(red-orange gold from), 266, 471
Pas-Dammim, 206, 436
Pathros, 418
Pau, 167
Pelesheth, 443
Penimith
(the), 353
Penuel, 172, 175
Peor, 270
Perazim, 298, 486
Perez-Uzzah, 309, 524
Pethor, 390, 392
(from), 411
Pharpar, 345
Phoenicia
city of (Tyre), 234, 237
Pibeseth, 344
Pi-hahiroth, 397
Pirathon, 441, 539
Pisgah, 161
Pithom, 334, 502
Prath, 388
Pul, 137
Punon, 180, 452
Qeren, 267, 489
Rabbah, 188
Rachal, 215
Rahab Hem Shebeth (alternate name for Egypt), 482, 542
Rakkath, 395
Rakkon, 270, 491
Ramah, 212
Ramathaim-Zophim, 474, 559
Ramath-Lehi, 391
Rameses, 302
Ramoth, 373, 375
Ramoth-Gilead, 419, 421
Rechah, 202
Rehob, 192
Rehoboth, 359, 363
(of), 379
Rekem, 262, 468
Remeth, 372
Rephidim, 264, 469
(from), 278, 477
Resen, 247, 483
Rezeph, 277, 503
Riblah, 208
Rimmon, 237, 480
Rimmono, 242
Rimmon-Parez, 381, 560
Rissah, 223
Rithmah, 374
(from), 389
(in), 375
Rogelim, 231, 454
Rumah, 216
Sahadutha, 407
Salcah, 136
Salem, 277
Samaria, 354, 522, 523
prophet of (Oded), 97
Sansannah, 202
Saphir, 353
Sarid, 332
Sea of Galilee
early name for (Chinnereth), 384, 386
Seba, 82
Secacah, 127
Sechu, 256
Seirath, 352
Sela, 169
Sela-Hammahlekoth, 420
Senaah, 137
Seneh, 136
Sephar, 262
Sepharad, 263
Sepharvaim, 287, 482
Shaalabim, 311, 314, 493, 507
Shaaraim, 365, 515
Shahazimah, 308, 491
Shalim, 310, 493
Shalisha, 370
Shalleketh, 420
Shamir, 344
Sharon, 345, 518
Sharuhen, 346, 519
Shaveh, 248
Shaveh-Kiriathaim, 502, 547
Sheba, 242
Shebah, 246
Shebam, 263, 468
Shebarim, 344, 507
Shechem, 273, 475
(to), 275
ruler of (Zebul), 57
Shema, 294
Shen, 267, 489
Shepham, 299, 486
Shepher, 351
Sheshack, 365, 505
Shicron, 349, 521
Shihon, 275, 494
Shihor, 329, 332, 336
Shihor-Libnath, 491
Shilhim, 284, 480
Shiloah, 261
Shiloh, 260, 264, 265
Shimon-Meron, 466, 561
Shimron, 354, 522
Shinar, 365
king of (Amraphel), 267
Shittim, 271, 475
Shoa, 279
Shocho, 255, 258, 259
Shual, 291
Shunem, 287, 482
Shur, 328
Shushan, 380, 528
Sibmah, 265
Sibraim, 249, 461
Siddim, 269, 473
Silla, 111
Sin, 140, 428
Sinai, 148
Sinim, 174, 412
Siphmoth, 450
Sirah, 223
Sirion, 346, 347, 519, 520
Sitnah, 274
Sodom, 126, 382
destruction of, 162
Sorek, 356
Succoth, 319, 321
Suph, 160, 460
Sur, 224
Syene, 137, 141, 426
Syria
king of (Rezin), 267, 489
Taanach, 340, 495
Taanath-Shiloh, 516
Tabbath, 294
Taberah, 387
(and at), 389
Tabor, 357
Tadmor, 372, 374
Tahtim-Hodshi, 515
Tamar, 372
Taralah, 370
Tarshish, 519
Tekoa, 349
Telaim, 108, 376
Telassar, 477
Tel-Aviv, 308
Tel-Harsa, 478
Tel-Melah, 330
Tema, 307
Thebes, 70
Thebez, 323, 527
Tibhath, 298
Tigris, 157
Timnah, 324
(to), 466
Timnath-Heres, 513
Timnath-Serah, 513
Tipsah, 343
Tirzah, 393
Tob, 34
Tochen, 317, 509
Tolad, 306
Tophel, 331

Tophet, 464
Topheth, 463
Tyre, 234, 237
jewels imported from, 162, 368
king of (Hiram), 219, 447
king of (Huram), 217, 445
number of years forgotten by God, 88
Ulai, 65
Ummah, 136
Unni, 148
Uphaz, 114
Ur, 188
Uruk, 200, 395
Uz, 172, 485
Uzzen-Sherah, 346, 519
Vaheb, 29
Vedan, 78, 402
Zaanan, 182, 454
Zaannanim, 220, 247, 449, 461
Zabad, 29
Zair, 277
Zalmon, 197, 460
Zalmonah, 196
Zaphon, 202, 462
Zared, 193
Zarephath, 428
Zareth-Shahar, 518
Zarthan, 416, 534
Zebaim, 164, 404
Zeboiim, 158, 397
Zeboim, 158, 164, 194, 396, 404, 429
king of (Shemeber), 341
Zedad, 119
Zelah, 181
Zelzah, 198
Zemaraim, 479
Zenan, 181, 454
Zephath, 348
Zephathah, 349
Zer, 234
Zereda, 239, 395
Zererath, 324
Ziba, 125
Ziddim, 158, 398
Zidon, 165, 169, 440, 444
king of (Ethbaal), 326
Ziklag, 201, 206
Zimri, 219
Zin, 156, 435
Zion, 167, 441
Zior, 276
Ziph, 117, 447
Ziphron, 260, 487
Ziz, 181, 489
Zoan, 192, 459
Zoar, 272
(to), 275
early name of (Bela), 124
Zoba, 118, 120, 121
Zoheleth, 308
Zophim, 200, 432
Zorah, 275
Zuph, 176, 466
bid, 187
bier, 73, 273
billow, 52
Binah. See Kabbalah:The Ten *Sefirot*:03 *Binah*
bind, 103
(and you shall b them), 498, 546
(and you shall), 406, 498, 546
(to b around or upon), 143
(to b around), 216
(to b on), 246, 290
(to b together), 133, 191, 354
(to b up), 246
(to), 22, 58, 90, 143, 151, 175, 221, 230, 237, 239, 246, 290, 322, 324, 354, 368, 372, 395, 517
up, 393
binder, 217
binders, 292
binding, 29
obligation, 221
bird, 277, 279, 293
(alimentary canal of), 212
(crop or craw of), 212
(to nip off the head of), 173
of prey, 108, 187, 343, 481
cormorant, 267, 451
vulture, 262
trap, 107
birds, 167, 290, 462
(young), 233
birth, 319
(according to their), 467, 539
(as untimely), 169
(I shall give), 53
birthplace
(and to your), 339
birthright, 203, 205
(his), 367, 376
(my), 369
(your), 373, 509
bit, 320
bite
(to), 276, 456
bitter, 209, 313, 453
(to be), 306
herb, 306
thing, 306, 308, 319
bitterly, 209
bitterness, 209, 212, 230, 306, 319, 372, 455, 457
bitumen, 213
black, 73, 329, 332, 362
(to be b hot), 220
(to be), 256, 329, 442
paint (eye cosmetic), 128, 352
blackish, 508
blackness, 316, 329
of hair (indicating youth), 473
blade, 56
blaspheme
(to), 164, 233, 491
blasphemy, 160
blast, 348
blasted, 435
(and), 437
blasting, 284
blaze
(to b up), 63
(to), 63
bleached
(something b white), 355
blemish, 105, 106, 114, 375
bless, 205, 404
(and b you), 213, 411
(and he will b himself), 369, 507
(and He will), 204, 400
(and I will b her), 373
(and I will b you), 380, 511
(and I will), 371
(and you will), 384, 521
(and), 367
(may b you), 373, 509
(shall b me), 389
(to), 200, 396
(you b me), 389
(you shall), 368
(you), 366, 505
them, 387
blessed, 203, 381, 400
(and He), 208, 407
(and shall be), 371
(I have), 369
(you have), 366
be Mordecai, 326, 486
blessedness, 325
blessing, 203, 366
(according to his), 376
(according to the), 373
(my), 369
(your), 373, 509
over food, 411, 534
blessings
(the), 369
blight
(to), 282, 506
blighted, 284
thing, 284
blind, 228
(hunter's), 211
(to make), 228
(to), 228
blinded
(to be), 306
blindness, 258, 386, 487
(sudden), 251
blister, 357
blistered
(to become), 182
blisters, 162
block
(to), 121, 350
blood, 63, 356

(outpouring of), 302
bloodshed, 302
bloom, 181, 489
(to), 160, 233, 482
blossom, 155, 159, 181, 182, 454, 481
(to), 160, 180, 482, 489
blotted
(be b out), 82
blow, 83, 146, 150, 196, 200, 457
(and you shall), 494, 545
(to), 114, 154, 268, 302, 348, 512
(you did), 451
(you shall), 485
blows, 140
blue, 456
(and), 457
(in), 456
(the), 457
blunt
(to be), 132
blush
(to), 109, 376
blusterer, 188
boar, 202
board, 63, 354
(to a), 368
boards, 252, 354, 377, 519
(for the b of), 372
(its), 363
(the), 379, 519
of, 359
boast, 127
(to), 83
boastful
(to be), 83
bodies
(heap of dead), 375
body, 23, 42, 80, 102, 114, 263, 326, 403, 439, 451, 469
(dead), 42
(ear), 76, 400
(member of the), 68, 358
(members of the), 239
(stepping region of - hip), 324
(to cut off of b part), 364
(to mutilate a part of the), 213, 442
armor, 346, 519
of forced laborers, 121
of subjects, 456
bodyguard, 37, 456
boil, 357
(to b up), 34, 95
(to), 34, 213, 258, 357
(you shall), 413
boiled, 258, 413
(and he), 45
(thing), 91
boiling, 357
boils, 162, 275, 494
boisterous, 75
bold, 348
(to be), 148, 479
bolt, 182
(to), 162
bond, 71, 221, 224, 229, 243, 244
(of the covenant), 394
bondage, 320
(to bring into), 254
bondman, 225
bonds, 71, 173
bondswoman
(his), 309
bondwomen
(and for), 451
bone, 166, 184, 211, 424
bones, 184, 424
(and their), 381, 520
(as hollow - fig.), 181
(my), 359
(number of in the human body), 195, 361
(number of in the human face), 31
(to break), 211
(to gnaw), 211
bonus, 493
book, 97, 262, 263
boot
(of soldier), 137, 427
booth, 98, 104, 253, 345, 438
booty, 18, 23, 30, 93, 179, 290, 294
(the), 31
border, 53, 58, 60, 65, 96, 162, 183, 188, 283, 317, 324, 397, 461
(and the), 60
(its), 60
(the), 400
(to its), 415
(to), 53
bore
(to b through), 86
(to), 86, 164, 202, 266
boring
out, 465
boring-instrument, 288
born, 69
(to be b first), 200
borne
(what is b about), 273
borrow
(to), 60, 258
bosom, 25, 70, 138, 161, 438
of a garment, 161, 438
bottle, 74, 121, 186, 309, 350
(water skin), 23
bottles, 72
bottom, 138, 243, 317, 388
bough, 67, 184, 196, 199, 232, 296, 461, 475
boughs, 288
(network of), 254, 439
(to go over the), 230
(to lop off), 191, 477
bound, 53, 58, 60, 65, 190
(and), 491
(being b up), 465
(is b up), 360
(the utmost), 441
(to be), 90, 259, 323, 368
(to), 53, 114
boundary, 130, 183, 188, 257, 295
bounds
(set), 58
bow, 293, 438
(and b down), 412
(and with my), 447
(and you will b down), 511
(and your), 450, 528
(for hunting or war), 438
(his), 441
(my), 444
(shall b down), 412, 509
(the), 440
(to b down), 130, 177, 234, 241, 249, 467, 512
(to), 82, 234, 251
bowed, 43
(and b down), 413
(and he b down), 412
(and they b down), 411, 515, 554
(to be b down), 144, 249
(to be), 177, 467
bowels, 80, 103, 135, 374, 403
bowing
(were b down), 440, 533
bowl, 52, 56, 73, 103, 155, 174, 244, 265, 337, 339, 397, 458
(and your kneading), 483
(for kneading), 479
(sacrificial), 354
bowls
(and its), 366
(its), 363
(your kneading), 487, 540
bowman, 438
box, 192
boy, 63, 137, 152, 253
(crying), 265
(young), 137
boyhood, 253
bracelet, 158, 173, 328
bragging, 176, 450
braid, 171
braided
work, 327
bramble, 30, 40
branch, 67, 73, 127, 154, 164, 184, 196, 198, 199, 219, 232, 248, 263, 332, 459, 475, 478
(always fig.), 262
(to b off), 232
branches, 288
(full of), 184, 475
brand, 27
(to), 50
branding, 49, 60
scar, 60
brass, 424, 426
(and in), 426
(and), 426
brassy, 427
brave

(to be), 148, 216, 479, 500
bray
(to), 166, 408
brazen, 426
brazier, 23
breach, 127, 178, 276, 515
(place of), 341
(to), 276, 515
(you have made a), 428
breaches, 298, 423, 486
bread, 18, 68, 96, 371
(as disc or cake), 97
(bit or morsel of), 320
(to cook), 53
(unleavened), 151
(white), 198
of anguish, 189
wafers, 293
without leaven, 339
breadth, 192, 322
break
(and I will), 474
(and you shall b down), 487, 544
(they shall), 333
(to b away), 281
(to b down), 223, 244, 276, 330, 334, 340, 515, 532
(to b forth with), 177
(to b in), 440
(to b through), 175, 223, 276, 515
(to b up), 175, 220, 463
(to cause to b forth), 177
(to), 104, 138, 156, 176, 199, 211, 223, 232, 262, 306, 319, 334, 344, 374, 487, 496, 523
(you did), 469
(you shall b down), 467, 480, 546
(you shall b in pieces), 469
(you shall), 464, 471
forth, 27, 39
of day, 188
breaker, 281, 341
breaking, 311
(a b in), 498
(in b in), 499
camp, 173
forth
(place of), 341
in upon, 281
of sea, 341
out, 391
out (of stones), 173
breast, 22, 40, 43
(as), 59
(of animals), 38
(to shrivel of women's b's), 209
of (and the), 44
of an animal sacrifice, 38
breastpiece, 271, 492
breastplate, 271, 492
of decision, 434, 538
breath, 55, 195, 285, 286
(to take), 302
of, 435
breathe
(to b hard), 119
(to b heavily), 281, 505
(to b out), 130
(to), 28, 37, 114, 119, 154
breathing
out, 146
brethren
(and his), 50
(and my), 43
(his), 43
(my), 36
(your), 57, 334
Briah. See Kabbalah:Worlds: *Briah*
briars, 268, 490
bribe, 239, 298, 501
(receiving of), 161
(to give a), 249
brick, 106
kiln, 142, 429
mold, 142, 429
bricks
(to make), 101, 413
bride, 74
bridegroom, 313, 506
bridle, 307
brief
time, 279
brier, 40, 133, 160, 222, 225, 264, 437
briers, 268, 490
bright, 119, 197
(and to a b spot), 373
(to be), 66, 115, 161, 337
(to make), 289
spot, 357
brightening
(source of), 324
brightness, 41, 77, 82, 93, 171, 194, 357
brilliant, 118
(of light), 197
brimstone
(of judgment), 392
bring, 22, 41, 42
(and b it), 47
(and he shall b it), 47
(and he shall), 42
(and I will b back), 410
(and will b you back), 417, 520
(and you shall), 405
(and you will b down), 381, 520
(and), 48, 437, 532
(he shall b it), 42
(shall b it), 46
(shall they), 47
(then b forth), 329
(they b in), 47
(to b forth), 58, 63
(to b out), 180
(to b up), 204
(to), 62, 154, 174, 226, 449
(will I), 30
(will), 404
(you shall b near), 397
(you shall b them back), 421, 528
(you shall), 389, 404, 408, 424, 536
(you), 420, 528
back, 397
out
(and I will), 333
them (and), 48
bringing
about, 137
up, 116
brings
(he), 41
bristle
(to b up), 239
bristling, 239
broad, 281
place, 215
place or plaza, 192
broidered
work, 264
broke
(and he), 333
broken, 228, 292
(to be b into), 20
(to be), 43, 47, 222, 442
crumb, 281
off, 234
piece, 355, 523
bronze, 271, 274, 276, 280, 287, 498
brooch, 33
brood, 237, 492
(to gather together as a), 188
brook, 120
broom, 79
broth, 261, 281
brother, 23
(against his), 45
(against your), 60
(and against his), 52
(and his), 50
(her), 42
(his), 43
(my), 36
(over his), 45
(your), 57, 334
of, 36
of (and), 43
brotherhood, 37
brother-in-law, 71, 361
brothers
(her), 42
(stars of), 67
brought, 35
(and he b her), 42
(and he), 37
(and I), 25
(and they), 43, 53
(he has), 42
(he shall be), 38
(they were), 38

(they), 42
(to be b down), 155
(to be), 50, 331
(was), 31
(will be), 37
us up, 170
brow, 154
bruise, 196, 200, 209
(shall), 454
(to), 209, 283, 506
bruised, 217
bruising
(for b me), 376
(to wound by), 209
brushwood, 126
brutish
(to be), 226
person, 226
brutishness, 226
bubble
(to b up), 142
forth, 112, 468
bubbles, 112, 468
buck, 351
bucket, 43, 63, 155, 435
buckler, 113, 159, 229, 417
buckthorn, 30
bud, 126, 233
(appearing to), 401
(shall), 238
(to), 233
build
(to), 72, 75
builder, 81
of bulwarks, 242
builders, 129, 383
building, 85, 118, 133, 425
(leak in a), 127
bulb, 394
bull, 230, 328
(young), 230
bull-calf, 125
bullock, 230
bulls
(wild – now extinct), 210, 439
bulrush, 120, 420
bulwark, 57, 72, 134, 155
bundle, 159, 324
bundles, 467
of grain, 323
burden, 31, 35, 108, 113, 118, 123, 196, 198, 263, 417, 449
(to), 198
bearing, 118
burden-bearer, 113
burdened, 289, 483
(to be), 198
with guilt, 195
burdens
(with their), 338, 504
burdensome
(to be), 45
burglary, 498
burial, 249
site, 249
buried
(and she was), 400
(I), 404
(you shall be), 397
burn, 60
(and you shall), 410, 487
(and), 372
(to), 50, 63, 127, 134, 150, 218, 226, 236, 262, 292, 310, 324, 351, 361, 500, 527
(you shall b it), 497
(you shall), 408, 486, 487, 497, 549, 550
scar, 90
thoroughly, 362
burned
(and), 387
(shall be), 486, 550
(the), 370, 517
(to be b up), 331, 501
(to be), 190
burning, 49, 60, 135, 139, 162, 228, 352, 367, 392, 486
(of anger), 198
bush of Moses, 136
coal, 60, 306
heat, 182, 326
mass, 162
of anger (God's), 222, 473
burnished, 170
burnt
(and let her be), 487, 550
(shall be made to), 402
(she shall be), 486, 550
offering, 127, 243
spot, 90
burrower, 291
burst
(to b forth), 20, 27
(to b out), 468
(to b through), 233
(to cause to b forth), 177
(to), 276, 515
forth, 112, 468
bursting
forth, 276, 515
bury
(and b me), 427
(to), 119, 241, 420
(you shall b him), 424
me, 425
burying-place
(in their), 417, 528
bush, 136, 252
(juniper or cypress), 342
(the), 139
(thorn), 183, 491
(thorny), 136
bushes
(thorn), 403
busied
(to be b with), 144
business, 117
but, 39, 49, 51, 95, 104, 210, 325, 370, 413, 439
butcher
(to), 37
butter, 73, 308
buttock, 324
buttocks, 395, 398
buttress, 253
buy
(to), 77, 154, 164, 166, 202, 402
(you shall), 367, 471
buzzard, 158
buzzing, 209
by, 33, 50, 66, 95, 109, 121, 141, 416
itself, 19
reason of, 109, 416
turns, 130
YHVH, 46
byssus, 118, 470
byword, 276
cage, 77, 225
with hook, 225
cake, 62, 95, 134, 167, 198, 411
(flat), 352
(of bread), 97
(perforated), 62
(sacrificial), 95, 411
(to bake a), 98
cakes, 68
(to bake), 53
(to make), 53
calamity, 31, 38, 61, 132, 136, 225, 244, 291, 500
calculate
(to), 246, 348
calf, 125
call
(and I will), 407
(and shall), 400
(and you shall), 400
(to), 177, 221, 241
(you shall), 396
called, 248
(and he), 251
(and she), 400
(and they), 423, 536
(I c you), 413, 519
(I have), 404
one, 248
calling
together, 262
calm, 107, 240
came, 15
(and he), 37
(and I), 25
(and they c in), 43
(and they c near), 424, 536
(and when they c near), 420, 528
(I), 29
(when he), 27
(when I), 31
(when), 48
near (and), 402

camel, 92
(hump of), 398
(young female), 203
(young male), 200
camp, 130
canal, 134, 193
candlestick, 236, 344, 391
cankerworm, 155
canopy, 113, 434
cap, 216
capital, 394
crown, 495
of a pillar, 394, 495
caprice, 339
captain, 86, 185, 272, 290, 372
captains
(and c of the hosts), 386, 522
(his), 375
captive, 225, 249
(and you have taken), 407
(shall carry you away), 410, 518
(to take), 244
captives, 249, 251, 305, 401
(as though), 415
captivity, 56, 63, 102, 249, 251, 305, 401
(into), 405
(your), 411, 518
capture, 73
(to), 73
caravan, 195, 358
carbuncle, 134, 162, 368, 396
carcass, 42, 106, 231, 343
carded, 362
Cardinal Points
East (*Mizrach*), 217
Archangel
Rafael, 248
as *Qadiym*, 165, 405
as *Qadmon*, 182, 454
as *Qidmah*, 162
Demon King (Goetia)
Amaimon, 161, 437
God Name(s)
Shaddai El Chai, 273
North (*Tzaphon*), 202, 462
Archangel
Auriel, 213
Demon King
Amaimon, 161, 437
Demon King (Goetia)
Zimimay, 137
God Name(s)
Adonai HaAretz, 273, 514
South (*Darom*), 214, 443
Archangel
Michael, 123
Demon King
Paimon, 180
Demon King (Goetia)
Goap, 108, 443
God Name(s)
YHVH *Tzabaoth*, 336
West (*Ma'arab*), 249
Archangel
Gabriel, 212
Demon King
Ariton, 228, 476
Korson, 488
Demon King (Goetia)
Korson, 263
God Name(s)
Elohim Tzabaoth, 352, 512
care, 29, 51, 180, 244
(tender), 118
(to c for), 179
(to lead with), 104
(to seek with), 327
carefulness, 29
carmine, 239
carnelian, 64, 356
carpet, 351
carried
(what is c about), 273
carrion
vulture, 214, 442
carry, 42, 412
(and you shall c me), 447
(shall c you away captive), 410, 518
(to c it), 400
(to), 62, 174, 226, 268
back, 408
cart, 130
carve
(to), 134, 184, 322
carving, 323, 372, 470
(and in), 474
case
(in that), 35
casing, 320, 517
cassia, 131, 228
cast
(and she), 422, 522
(and), 400
(I have), 368
(to be vilely c away), 124
(to c away), 107, 194, 271, 442
(to c down), 47, 271, 330, 340, 532
(to c forth), 35
(to c off), 83, 271
(to c out), 107, 244, 326, 442
(to c up), 140, 326
(to), 37, 64, 184, 196, 211, 212, 267, 451
(you shall c him), 429
(you will), 441, 540
out, 78
cast
(to be c down), 169
casting, 207, 209
(for), 365
(of metal), 187
castle, 194
catch, 34
(to c up), 159
(to), 66, 118, 432, 447
caterpillar, 155
cattle, 71, 132, 182, 231, 241, 309, 451
(bellow of), 96
(in), 183
(small), 193, 459
(to bellow of), 96
dung, 212
caught
(and she c him), 517
cauldron, 30, 340
cause, 193, 297
caution, 367
cautious
(to be), 25
cave, 195, 250, 402
(in the), 404
cavern, 102
cavity, 164
cease, 407
(and he shall), 42
(and I will cause to), 410
(and I will make), 416
(I would make), 407
(to c to be), 61
(to cause to), 68
(to), 60, 61, 68, 74, 156, 160, 184, 211, 271, 460
ceased
(he), 397
ceasing, 113, 156
cedar, 188, 215, 468, 470
panels, 194
work, 194
celebrate
(to), 31
(you shall), 506
celestial
appearance, 260
cell, 270, 279, 315
cellar, 237, 245
cement, 98, 213
censer, 57, 311, 334, 420
(his), 457
censers, 457
census, 262
center, 51, 198
certain, 116, 133
(to make), 124
one, 148, 174, 186, 192
certainly, 49
certainty
(to gain), 124
cessation, 61, 73, 114, 417
cesspool, 217
chaff, 228, 288, 357
as driven by wind, 147, 478
chain, 129, 143, 356, 395, 398, 406, 440, 491
(by analogy), 304
(for necklace), 197
chains, 168, 407, 461, 517, 535
(stepping), 173
chair
(royal), 230

chalk, 185
chamber, 113, 194, 270, 279, 289
  (underground), 245
chameleon
  (and the), 517
chamois, 213
champion, 186, 193, 247
chance, 165, 243, 264
change, 150
  (of garments), 150
  (to), 126, 138, 212, 268, 270, 352, 453
changes, 333
channel, 134, 181
chant
  (to), 234
chaplet, 282
charcoal, 146, 391
charge, 282, 486
  (and the), 487
  (and their), 495, 545
  (in), 486
  (my), 488
  (to give c to), 123
  (to lay), 123
  (to), 123
chariot, 204, 222, 224, 265, 489
  (his), 384
  (in the), 382
charioteering, 119
chariotry, 201
chariots, 159, 381, 437
  (of their), 387
charm, 76, 400
  (to), 261
charmer, 191
  (to be a), 191
charmers, 25
charming, 261
charred
  (to be), 292
chase
  (and you shall), 412, 526
  (to c away), 195
  (to), 34, 37, 190, 195
chasm, 33, 275, 515
chasten
  (to), 225
chastening, 244
chastise
  (and I will), 390
check
  (to keep in), 256, 442
cheek, 67
cheer, 41
cheerfulness, 324
  (source of), 324
cheese, 58, 78, 283
chequer
  work, 436, 546
chequered
  work, 305
cherish
  (to), 28
cherished, 40
Cherub. *See* Important Kabbalistic Terms:*Kerub* (angel – sing.)
Cherubim. *See* Important Kabbalistic Terms:*Kerubim* (angels – pl.)
cherubs, 229
chest, 40, 192, 218, 470
chests, 78
Chet. *See* Hebrew Alphabet:08 *Chet*
chew
  (to), 310
Chiah. *See* Kabbalah:Souls: *Chiah*
chief, 15, 60, 132, 137, 148, 185, 186, 193, 215, 230, 272, 290, 325, 326, 424, 451, 453, 468, 472
  one, 319
  ruler, 94, 410
chiefly
  poor, 87, 408
chieftan, 233
child, 58, 63, 71, 152, 396
  (illegitimate), 233
  (sucking), 128
  (to act the), 148
  (to be with), 191
  (to play the), 148
  (to wean a), 92
  of incest, 233
childhood, 310
childless, 270, 322
  (to make), 267
childlessness, 273
children, 107, 443
  (bare of), 322
  (little), 107, 443
  of Israel, 355
    variant *gematria*, 359
chiliarch, 132, 451
chimney, 188
chin, 153, 434
chirp
  (to), 215, 484
chisel, 198
choice, 218, 350
  fruits, 216
  gold, 346, 533
  grapes, 355
  one, 199
  products, 216
  thing, 124
choicest, 214
choir, 176
Chokmah. *See* Kabbalah:The Ten *Sefirot*:02 *Chokmah*
choose
  (and), 362
  (to), 190, 289
chop
  (to), 95
chosen, 199
  one, 199
Chronicles. *See* *Tanakh: 03 Kethuvim:* 12 1 Chronicles, 13 2 Chronicles
chrysolite, 119, 519
chrysolites, 524, 554
churning, 95, 411
cincture, 377
cinnamon, 221, 472
circle, 34, 191
  (to describe a), 34
  (to make a), 34
circle-instrument, 81
circlet, 188
circuit, 34, 93, 353
  (in the), 93
  (in), 93
circumcise
  (to), 94, 95, 140
circumcised
  (every c male), 172
  (to be), 140
  (to let oneself be), 95
circumcision, 100, 104
circumstance, 148, 432
circumvent, 175
cistern, 19, 185, 188
citadel, 194, 237, 480
cities
  appointed (of refuge), 143
city, 80, 230, 248, 250, 395
  (fortified), 258
  (from the), 420
clamor, 64, 356, 399
clamorous
  (to be), 68
clamp, 217
clan, 304
clangers, 318, 507, 510
clap
  (to), 209, 348
clarified
  (what is), 330
clarity, 194
clasp
  (to), 131
class, 178, 350
  (originator of a), 15
  (reference to the lowest), 87, 408
claw, 233
clay, 46, 87, 161, 213, 408, 420, 460
  flooring, 98
  pottery, 329
clean, 45, 107, 164, 169, 185, 199, 329, 356, 364, 442
  (and you shall be), 381, 520
  (he is), 205
  (to be), 51, 66, 195, 337, 354
  (to), 66, 337
  (you shall be), 365
cleaning
  (his), 364
cleanness, 185, 356
cleanse
  (and), 364
  (to), 289
  away by rinsing, 35
cleansing, 139, 298, 356
  (for his), 366, 376

clear, 119, 185, 330
(she shall be), 362
(to be), 51, 54, 166
(to c away), 280
(to c up), 189
(to make), 185, 189
clearness, 352
clear-sighted, 180
cleavage, 138
cleave, 127
(to), 25, 120, 138, 175, 303
cleft, 178, 199, 303, 478
(in a), 421
(of a rock), 220
clefts, 34
cliff, 169, 237, 292
climb
(to), 127
cling, 127
clip
(to), 139, 227, 387
clipped
(to become), 140
cloaca, 217
cloak, 186, 339, 356
close, 107, 442
(and you shall), 418, 528
(keep), 127
(to be), 117, 470
(to c off), 188
(to c up), 272
(to keep), 325, 500
(to), 68, 222, 225, 246, 358, 502
closed, 399
closet, 113
closing, 171
cloth, 63, 279
(netted), 222
(variegated), 213, 441
(white), 195
clothe, 188
(and you shall c them), 433, 531
(and you shall), 417
(to), 258
clothed, 198
(to be), 258
clothes, 97, 279, 371
(his), 43
(in their), 444, 533
(their), 444, 533
(your), 454, 535
clothing, 261, 280, 321, 511
(innermost piece of), 195
(to put on), 258
(used indiscriminately), 23
cloud, 51, 91, 174, 176, 272, 281, 292, 449, 502
(and a), 27
(heavy or dark), 281
(theophanic), 174
cloud-mass
(of theophanic cloud), 174, 449
clouds, 313, 494
cloudy, 174, 176, 449
clout, 94
cloven, 431
clovenfooted, 303, 451
club, 191, 199, 442, 495, 496
clusters, 356, 421
(its), 426
coal, 60, 146, 306, 391
(burning), 60, 306
(live), 279
coals, 351, 527
(to snatch up), 295
coast, 27, 53, 58, 60, 65, 96, 114, 445
coat, 235, 287
(his), 462
(to), 41
of mail, 358
coating, 45
cobra, 337, 510
coerced, 452
coercion, 272
coffer, 192
coffin, 218, 470
cognomen
(to give a), 94
cohabitation, 149
coin, 141, 195
coins, 337
cold, 240, 243
(of snow), 159
colleague, 316
collect
(to), 133, 147, 395
collecting, 159
collection, 62, 156, 159, 163, 332, 355, 459
collections, 52
collective, 109
colonnade, 272, 492
color, 171
(red), 438
colored, 173
(to be), 59
fabric, 42
colorless, 49
column, 140, 207, 372, 379
combed, 362
come, 15, 23, 28
(and c upon us), 183
(and I will c down), 368
(and they shall c near), 274
(and they shall), 32
(and when he would), 27
(and when you c near), 400
(and you), 32
(as you), 46
(has), 15
(he shall), 23
(I will), 17, 25
(let), 446
(may), 209
(shall), 30, 31, 37
(things that are to), 462
(thou be), 41, 326
(to c in), 22, 148
(to c out), 123
(to c to pass), 28, 38
(to c upon), 69
(to), 22, 35, 50, 52, 58, 74, 78, 291, 331, 339, 340
(when I), 52
(will c to pass), 44
(you are), 404, 524
(you did c near), 396
(you shall), 402
forth, 27, 39
in, 23
out, 23
upon, 23
comely, 81
(to be), 75
comes
(and he that), 31
(there), 385
comfort, 125, 126, 382
(and c yourselves), 159
(to), 119, 150, 380
comforted
(to be), 119, 380
coming
(as they were), 18
(those), 29
(through c near), 398
(which is), 29
forth, 132
forth of the faithful of God, 205
in, 22, 67, 72
of, 27
round, 353
command, 117, 139, 187, 209, 230, 336, 387, 503
(royal), 290
(to), 123, 209
commander, 215, 270, 468
commandment
(of God, of man, of code of wisdom), 157
(the), 159
commandments
(his), 344
commands
(these are the), 350
commissioner, 182
common, 57, 341
commonness, 57
commune, 187
(to), 249
communicate
(to), 207
communication, 449
community, 35
compact
(to be), 191
compactness, 137
companies, 183, 492
companion, 191, 196, 225, 232, 247, 316, 358
company, 58, 62, 132, 155, 191, 196, 355, 451

(in), 327
(mixed), 226
(to keep c with), 189
(travelling), 195
compare
(to), 111, 234, 428
compass, 34, 81
(to), 194, 204, 481
compassion, 102, 126, 142, 214, 217, 238, 382, 442, 445, 458
(object of), 138
(to have c on), 79, 96
(to have), 93
(to l upon with), 93
(to look upon with), 93
compassionate, 245
woman, 245
compel
(to), 132
compensation, 396
complain, 123, 421
(to), 105, 414
complaint, 252
complete, 306, 465, 490
(to be), 74, 277, 306, 477, 490
(to make), 98
(to), 98, 104, 211
destruction, 74
completed
(to be), 160, 460
completeness, 115, 140, 312
completion, 74, 136, 312, 426, 459, 479
composition
(according to its), 474
(and according to its), 475
compound
(to), 246
compounding, 269, 419
compression, 200
compulsory
service, 118
computation, 140, 143
compute
(to), 155
comrade, 191
conceal
(to), 51, 104, 119, 156, 381, 394, 420
concealed
(to be), 156, 394
of the concealed, 351, 522
concealment, 39, 95, 411
(places of), 34
conceive
(to), 76, 191, 364
conceived, 367
(and she), 360
(having c seed), 391
(she had), 358
(to be), 191
concept, 287
conception, 221, 472
(mental), 293
(physical), 221, 472
concern, 244
concerned
(to be), 22
concerning, 50, 121
conclusion, 160, 460
concubine, 65, 113, 246, 300
condemn
(to), 157, 298, 481
(will), 372, 526
condemnation
(exposed to), 35
condense
(to), 178
condition, 148, 432
(parched), 153
of rest, 125
conduct
(to), 77
coney, 303, 496
confession, 293
confidant, 247
confidence, 42, 78, 93, 131, 135, 410
(his), 136
(object of), 70
confident
(to be), 36
confidential
friend, 247
confine
(to), 237
confinement, 70
(place of), 350
confirm, 116
(to), 111, 416
confirmation, 321
confiscation, 298
confound
(to), 80
confounded
(to be), 20, 233
confounding, 93
confront
(to), 158
confuse
(to), 46, 80, 104, 329, 355, 374
confused
(to be), 20, 46, 329
confusion, 93, 115, 117, 314
(to be put to), 109, 376
congelation, 178
congratulations, 114
congregation, 98, 152, 156
(entire), 336
conjugal
rights, 149
conjure
(to), 174, 261, 449
conjurer, 281, 505
connecting, 221
conquer
(to), 23
conscience
(stumbling because of), 181
consciousness, 267
consecrate
(to), 219, 290
consecrated, 222, 417
(and shall be), 371
one, 224
ones, 238
portion, 269
consecration, 107, 219
consent
(to), 22, 292
consequence, 175
(as a c of), 175
(as a), 175
consequently, 175
consider
(and c it), 405
(to), 76, 80, 105, 187, 241, 267, 375, 400, 404
consolation, 315
consolations, 315
console
(to c oneself), 119, 380
consort, 259, 358
conspicuous
(to be), 76
(what is), 76
conspicuousness, 299
conspiracy, 354
conspire
(to), 327, 354
constant, 177, 314, 315, 507
constellation, 96
constellations, 101, 216, 320
constrain, 183
(to), 132
constraint, 183, 207
consult
(to), 173, 486
consume
(to), 74, 104, 118, 159, 188, 226, 374
consumed
(I have), 389
(will be), 368
consumption, 74, 136, 426, 436
(with), 435
contain
(to), 75
contemplate
(to), 267
contemplation
(song of), 288
contempt, 32, 37, 93, 160, 247, 410
(held in), 126
(to hold in), 30, 31
(to treat with), 247
contemptible, 221
contend, 328, 490
(and), 361
(to), 189, 194, 316, 395
(you), 492
with, 328
contended

(they), 463
contender, 201
contention, 114, 120, 125, 151, 219, 339, 418, 420, 422
contentious
(to be), 212
continually, 312
continuance, 98
(and long), 183, 423
continue, 128, 423
(to cause to), 75
(to), 67
continuous
(to be), 195
contract
(to), 175
contraction, 224, 450
contrariness, 126, 247, 352
contrariwise, 51
contrary, 126, 352
contribution, 377, 381, 506, 549
(the), 382
contrite, 43
(to be), 43, 47
contrive
(to), 20
control, 288
controversy, 194, 361
contumely, 160
contusion, 154
convert
(and your), 204, 401
convex
surface, 18
convocation, 262
convoking, 262
cook, 37, 42
(female), 42
(to), 258
(you shall), 413
(you will), 415
cooked, 258
(and he), 45
(pieces), 355, 523
cooking
furnace, 204
places, 280
pot, 195
cool, 240
cooling, 264
coolness, 159, 264
coping, 118
copiousness, 501
copper, 271, 276, 424
coppery, 427
copulation, 410
copy, 286, 369, 526
corals, 181, 212, 454
cord, 41, 58, 128, 277, 317, 334, 376
cordage, 317
cords, 98
(and their), 403, 524
(its), 383
(their), 398, 524
coriander, 20
cormorant, 267, 326, 451
corn, 75, 185, 399
(ear of), 413
floor, 216, 469
corner, 105, 148, 152, 162, 300, 432, 461
(inner c buttress), 244
(place of c structure), 243, 244
(to be put or thrust into a), 461
(to be put or thrust into), 162
buttress, 243, 244
cornered
(to be), 162, 221, 461
corners
(for the), 412
(its), 361
(the), 398
(to be set in), 221
cornet, 67
corporeal, 284, 480
corpse, 42, 106, 114, 231
corpses, 375
corrals
(and), 361
correct, 197
corrected
(you will be), 385
correction, 239, 244, 304
corresponding
to, 76
corrupt
(it was), 426
(the), 405
(to be c morally), 57
(to be), 153, 458
(to), 227, 401
(you will become), 515, 554
corrupted
(and was), 507
(had), 410
corruption, 419
(their), 435, 531
corruptly
(and shall deal), 424, 529
(have dealt), 401
(to deal), 58
(you deal), 514, 554
costly, 451
cottage, 202
cotton, 272
couch, 73, 176, 184, 273, 348
coucheth
(that), 392
council, 88
counsel, 88, 99, 109, 172, 193, 308, 347
(to give), 173, 486
(to take crafty), 247, 461
(to), 108, 109, 172, 347, 485
counsellor, 108, 193
counselor, 296
count, 471
(and you shall), 434, 531
(to), 116, 246, 262
countenance, 123, 454
(his), 160
country, 96
(far), 266
(open), 192, 236
couple, 151
(and you shall), 362
coupled
(to be), 191
coupling
(its), 379
courage
(and be of good), 483, 545
courageous
(to be), 148, 479
course, 260, 350, 512
(of life), 262
(of stones), 95, 345
of life, 190
court, 238
(officer of the), 272
covenant, 360
(and your), 371, 508
(bond of), 394
(for a), 373
(his), 364
(in the), 361
(my), 366
(oath of), 54
(the), 363
(to cut a), 364
cover, 181, 454
(and I will), 414
(and they), 112
(of vessel), 158
(to c in), 181, 303, 454, 496
(to c over), 41, 87
(to), 59, 103, 104, 107, 108, 113, 121, 124, 167, 173, 176, 178, 181, 239, 262, 303, 350, 421, 454, 462, 465, 467, 468, 496
in, 181, 454
of an altar, 19
covered, 113
(and she c herself), 464
amulets, 319
with boards or panelling, 113, 181, 454
covering, 64, 95, 116, 119, 140, 143, 230, 321, 354, 381, 411, 428
(his), 383
(of the Ark, of the skins of the Tabernacle), 143
(outer), 116
coverlet, 212, 222, 279
(thick), 279
covers
(that which), 143
(the), 444
covert, 98, 104, 147, 185, 345, 359
covet, 27
(to), 71
covetous

(to be), 170
cow, 232
cowed
(to be), 45
cows, 388, 390
(the), 392
crab, 252, 483
craft, 121, 260
craftiness, 177, 247, 250, 461
craftsman, 329
(of metal), 329
crafty, 251, 462
(to be), 121, 247, 461
crag, 169
cramp, 286, 518
(to), 237
crane, 229
crash, 290
crashing, 53
craving, 444
crawl
(that will), 479
(to c away), 64
cream, 283
create
(to), 166, 185
created
(I have), 361
thing, 198
creation, 171, 198
creature, 302
(leaping), 209
(living), 311
(moving), 353, 535
creatures
(flying), 167, 462
(living), 300
(moving), 42
creditor
(to be a), 268, 270
creep
(to), 240
creepeth
(the creeping thing that), 503
creeping
(the c thing that creepeth), 503
thing, 340, 353, 535
things, 340
creeps, 479
crevice, 40, 270
crevices, 239
crib, 86, 193
crier, 132
crime, 70, 257
criminal, 169, 195, 348
crimson, 239, 273
crocodile, 57
crocus, 337
crooked, 182, 187, 257, 316, 379, 389, 479, 528
(and), 480
(to be), 318
(to make), 316, 318
dealing, 174, 465
place, 330
things, 330
crooked-backed, 73, 398
crookedness, 174, 307, 462, 465
crop
(after-growth of), 302
(its), 375
(of greening of), 31
crops, 443
cross, 292
crossbred, 389
crossroad, 281
crossroads, 60, 355
cross-wise
(to lay), 267
crouch
(to c down), 251
(to), 272
crowd, 98, 123, 133, 345, 421
of Gods, 181
Crowley, Aleister, 13
777, 128, 431
Ab-gi-tatz-qerashamen-kegadikesh-bamratztag-haqamamna-yaglepzeq-sheqi-ayeth
42-Letter name of God, 568
Abrahadabra, 297
Aiwass
author of the Book of the Law, 96
Ashtaroth
Archdemon of *Giburah*, 528
Ayeth
name of God associated with *Malkut*, 319
Babalon, 166
Bamratztag
name of God associated with *Tiferet*, 413
Boleskine, 297, 501
Chioa
archdemon of *Tiferet*, 44
Da'ab, 20
Dobe', 20
Fukh
Goetic Demon #50, 352
Haqamamna
name of God associated with *Netzach*, 243
Isheth Zenunim
Archdemon corresponding to *Chokmah*, 460, 537
Kedadikesh
name of God associated with *Giburah*, 271
Malka be-Tarshishim ve-Ad be-Ruach Sheharim
Intelligence of the Intelligences of Luna, 566
masculine unity according to, 35
number of magic according to, 27
number of magic force according to, 48
Qerashamen
name of God associated with *Hesed*, 425, 536
Ra'ash, 348
Sabnock
Goetic Demon #43, 459
Goetic Demon 43, 282
Samael
Archdemon of *Chokmah*, 149
Sefer Sefirot (Book of the Numbers), 504
Seven Earths
Gaye, 30
Sheqi
name of God associated with *Yesod*, 294
Stolas
Goetic Demon #36
Crowley's spelling, 381
Tzelilimiron
Qlippoth of Gemini, 507
crown, 13, 188, 219, 231, 282, 365
(to give a), 229
(to), 229
of head, 189
crucible, 156, 293, 510
cruel, 208, 290, 373, 440
(to be), 153, 480
cruelty, 129, 239, 373, 432
crumble
(to), 463
crumbled
(thing easily), 165
things, 165
crumbs, 165
crush
(to c fine), 448
(to c to pieces), 448
(to), 43, 47, 85, 104, 176, 186, 195, 199, 232, 261, 262, 281, 283, 374, 407, 505, 506, 516
crushed, 42, 125, 217, 327
(and), 338, 452, 531
(thing that is), 198
(to be), 43, 47, 222
fragments, 315
crushing, 47, 53, 259, 326
noise, 282
cry, 223, 240, 381, 481
(of joy), 215, 468
(their), 383, 447, 534
(to c aloud), 68, 126
(to c out), 126, 166, 177, 221, 240, 279, 481
(to c shrilly), 31, 144
(to make), 40, 326
(to), 31, 45, 163, 166, 177, 221, 238
(whether according to the c of it), 391
(you), 381
for help, 282
of grief or despair, 34
of joy, 218
of them, 395, 524

crying, 166
(in his), 52
boy, 265
cryptology, 377
crystal, 103, 250, 311
cubits, 309
cuckow, 284, 506
cucumber, 289
cucumbers
(field or place of), 308
cud, 189
cumin, 131, 183, 424
cunning, 121
cup, 103, 105, 174, 349
(sacrificial), 354
cup-bearer, 308
cups, 199, 432
shaped like almond blossoms, 290
curb
(to), 91, 369
curd, 73, 78
curd-like, 114
cure, 253
(to), 29
curse, 54, 172, 212, 282, 305, 355
(to utter a c against), 126
(to), 17, 54, 126, 164, 200, 289, 396
cursed, 292
cursing, 60
curtain, 125, 184, 236, 394
curtains, 391
(of the), 392
(the), 393
curve, 165
curving, 165
custody, 180
custom
duty, 74, 339
cut, 182, 245, 330, 508
(and c down), 367
(and she c off), 495
(and they will be c off), 389
(and they), 373
(and), 369
(he will c off), 372
(he), 364
(I have), 368
(let us), 386
(shall be c off), 386, 388
(shall c off), 371
(something), 34
(they c down), 367
(thing), 245, 508
(to be c off), 95, 138, 140, 166
(to c away), 107
(to c down), 27, 51, 94, 95, 107, 120, 326, 364, 376
(to c in pieces), 313
(to c in two), 95, 125, 355
(to c in), 134, 329
(to c off), 32, 34, 51, 68, 77, 95, 170, 180, 182, 191, 200, 211, 230, 326, 364, 471, 477, 503
(to c out), 120, 189, 364
(to c short), 125
(to c through), 25
(to c up), 313, 326
(to), 27, 37, 95, 134, 138, 139, 174, 190, 191, 238, 276, 313, 326, 330, 364, 387, 506
(will be c off), 368, 495
(you c off), 497
(you shall c down), 502, 551
(you shall c off), 495
(you shall c yourselves), 447
(you shall), 458
down, 372
off, 196, 367
out, 190
cutting, 34, 40, 196, 412
(and in), 474
instrument, 217
cuttings, 471
cypress, 231, 329, 342, 357, 361, 470
Daat. See Kabbalah:The Ten *Sefirot: Daat*
dainties, 168, 184, 408, 424
daintiness, 142, 337
dainty, 142, 143, 429
(of food), 171
(to be), 142
bit, 259
Dalet. See Hebrew Alphabet:04 *Dalet*
damage, 58, 167
damask, 213, 307, 441
damsel, 68, 255
dance, 102, 103, 120, 471
(to), 31, 44, 298
dancing, 102, 103
dandling, 118
danger, 107, 234
(to incur), 148, 431
dangle
(to), 57, 83
Daniel. *See Tanakh: 03 Kethuvim:* 09 Daniel
dappled, 148, 479
dark, 132
(to be), 49, 163, 167, 242, 256, 442, 462
(to become), 163, 256, 442
(to grow), 163, 226, 242, 402
brown, 73, 362
color, 73, 362
place, 275, 455
darken
(to), 163, 402
darkened, 73, 362
(and was), 413, 519
(to be), 49, 256, 442
dark-flashing, 118
darkness, 91, 132, 136, 163, 171, 172, 181, 182, 256, 259, 275, 281, 316, 402, 442, 445, 454, 455, 474
(deep), 172, 347
(gross), 281
(thick), 135, 281
dart, 108, 173, 335, 415
(to d greedily), 108
(to), 250
through the air, 25
dash
(and d in pieces), 542
(and d with pieces), 480
(and you shall), 405
(to d to pieces), 27, 330
(to make a), 284
(to), 199, 496
(you shall d into pieces), 482, 547
(you shall), 400
of horse, 190
dashing, 53, 195
date-cake, 351
daub
(to), 213
daubed
(and d it), 380
daughter, 289
(d's husband), 313, 506
(to make oneself a d's husband), 313, 506
of the voice, 124, 339
daughter-in-law, 74
daughters
(and to your), 333, 489
(our), 333
of man, 329, 501
dawn, 329, 343, 459
dawning, 196
day, 75, 363
(break of), 188
(by), 116, 379
(from the d before), 402, 524
(good), 92, 369
(in the ninth), 430
after, 376
of rest, 86, 397
daylight, 77, 220
days
(seven), 280
(these), 318
daytime, 116, 379
(in the), 116, 379
dazzling, 119
(to be), 128
dead, 306
(be), 97
(ghosts of the), 231
(like), 285, 498
(realm of the), 308
(to be), 308
body, 42
deaf, 329
(to be), 329
deal
(to d corruptly), 58
(to d falsely), 256, 354
(to d fully with), 92
(to d tyrannically with), 247
(to d with severely), 148

(to d wrongly with), 202
falsely, 490
dealing, 208
dealt
(he d well), 54
(you have d ill), 387
ill, 386
dear, 252
dearth, 385
death, 308, 321, 456
(angel of), 149
(by suffocation or strangling), 183
(gates of), 496
(personified), 308
(shadow of), 347
(sudden), 132, 425
(to stone to), 181
(valley of the shadow of), 350
shadow of, 347
death-shadow, 347
debt, 33, 272
(release from), 270
(thing given as security for), 106
(to give a pledge for a), 100
debtor, 33
debts
(heavy), 121
decade, 349
decay, 155, 242, 268, 286, 490
(to), 208, 401
decayed, 268, 490
(to be), 174
deceit, 23, 185, 188, 232, 287, 374, 498
deceitful, 31, 48, 175, 256
(to be), 121, 153
deceitfully
(to act), 23
(to get), 316
deceive, 304
(to), 212, 256, 268, 304, 321, 340
deception, 48, 256, 354
deceptions, 319
deceptive, 48, 256
thing, 48
decide
(to d for), 190
(to), 57, 238, 506
decision, 166, 242, 508
(breastplate of), 434, 538
(strict), 242
decisive
(to be), 238, 506
deck
(to), 188
declaration, 37, 352
(of prophet), 111, 377
declare, 187
(and they shall), 53
(they shall), 52
(to), 32, 37, 185, 350, 359
declaring, 37
decline
(to), 82, 195, 395
decrease
(to), 224, 262, 449
decree, 139, 163, 187, 189, 196, 221, 290, 336, 387, 402, 503
(to), 189, 238, 506
of restriction, 221
decrees
(interpreter of), 356
decrepit, 358
dedicate
(to), 96, 219, 345
dedication, 102, 107
deed, 159, 166, 173, 178, 362
(extortionate), 406
(in very), 95, 370
(wicked), 70
deeds
(noble), 90
deep, 149, 192, 199, 311, 493
(to be), 192
(to make), 192
mysteries, 199
sleep, 376
things, 199
deeply
(to love), 214, 442
deeps, 455
deer, 60, 64, 267, 306
(a kind of), 222
defamation, 27
defeat, 266
defect, 106, 254, 375, 485
defection, 223
defend
(to), 124, 421
defender, 41
defense, 187
defer
(to), 189, 198
defiant, 188
deficiency, 254, 485
deficient, 229
defile
(to), 52, 86, 154, 458
it, 133, 385
defiled
(to be), 153, 313, 458, 495
defilement, 53
defiling, 53
defraud
(to), 316
defy
(to), 233, 491
degenerate
(to), 224
degradation, 296
dehydration, 153
Deities (both Biblical and extra-Biblical)
Ammorite
Molek (god), 109, 347
Arvite
Tartaq (god of unknown), 505
Assyrian
Kiyuwn (Saturnian deity), 105, 414
Nisrok (god of unknown), 257, 443
Babylonian
Anammelech (god of Luna), 192, 391
Astarte (goddess)
groves of worship of (*'asherah*), 328
images of, 328
Bel (chief god), 51
Gad (god of fortune), 20
Meni (god of destiny), 121
Merodak (god of Mars), 222, 418
Nergal (god of Mars), 231
Sukkowth benowth (goddess of unknown), 479
Canaanite
Astarte (goddess of fortune and happiness)
groves of worship of (*'asherah*), 328
Baal (god of wind, rain and fertility), 124
(dwelling of), 251
(to), 149
dwelling place of, 350, 387, 521, 530
Resheph (lord of the underworld), 351, 527
Edomite
Lilith (goddess of the night), 207, 319
(out), 350, 351, 534, 535
angel invoked against (*Sansenoy*), 207
angel invoked against (*Semangelof*), 225, 488
angel invoked against (*Senoy*), 144
angels invoked against (*Senoy, Sansenoy, Semangelof*), 369, 532
formula used against, 525, 526, 567
Egyptian
Amon (chief god), 117, 419
Nu (goddess of the sky), 75
Nuit (goddess of the sky), 315
Ra-Hoor (god of Sol), 298
Hamath
Ashima (unknown deity), 268
Lucifer (Morning Star), 370, 526
(as brightness or morning star, 93
Moabite
Baal Peor (god of fertility), 313, 316
(to), 322
Chemosh (god of unknown), 275, 276
Nibhaz (an idol), 85

Philistinian
Dagon (god), 82, 405
Phoenician
Ashtoreth, 533
Milcom (god), 147, 391
Molek (god), 109, 347
Shechemite
Ba'al Beriyth (god of the covenant), 405
Berith (unknown), 360
Syrian
Hadad (god of storms), 29
Rimmown (god of wind rain and storm), 237, 480
delay, 362
(to), 69, 189, 198
(you shall), 358
delectable
food, 168, 408
delicacies, 184, 321, 424
delicacy, 18
(of woman), 200, 395
delicate, 142, 200, 395
(to be), 142
delicately
(to treat), 204
delight, 71, 142, 143, 171, 177, 265, 337, 416, 429, 445, 488, 489
(exquisite), 142
(to d in), 71, 177, 488
(to d oneself), 143, 429
(to take d in), 306
delightful, 173, 412
(to be), 169, 408
delightfulness, 169, 408
delighting
in, 177, 488
delineate
(to), 237, 355
deliver
(to d up), 113, 239, 417
(to), 98, 108, 113, 139, 165, 174, 246, 417
(you shall), 385
him, 441
deliverance, 139, 147, 151, 280, 285, 299, 432
from trouble, 87, 408
delivered
(and you shall be), 466, 539
(to be), 98, 280
deluge, 96
delusion, 479
demand, 260
demeaning, 296
demolish, 425
demon, 167, 243, 351
Mahalath, 319
of prostitution (*Isheth Zenunim*), 460, 537
Demon Kings of the Elements & Cardinal Points (Goetia)
Amaimon (East, Air), 161, 437
Goap (South, Fire), 108, 443
Korson (West, Water), 263, 488
Zimimay (North, Earth), 137
demoniacal
works, 427, 530
demons, 367, 368, 376, 473, 516, 519
(class of - *Lilin*), 147, 431
(class of - *Mazziqin*), 198, 460
(class of - *Ruachin*), 227, 475
(*Mezziqim*), 188
(queen of - Agrath), 541
(queen of – Naamah), 171
(world of), 431, 531
Mezziqim, 427
prince of (Samael), 149
queen of (*Agrath*), 356
Shedim, 269
den, 18, 185, 216, 239, 250
denied
(then), 413
denounce
(to), 137, 386
dense, 184, 475
with foliage, 317
density, 91
deny
(to), 169, 256
depart
(I will), 112
(to d early), 277
(to), 56, 62, 77, 178, 224, 265
departing
(those), 228
departure
(point of), 60, 355
deposit, 209, 465, 512
depository, 237
depravity, 144, 430
depressed, 160, 246
(to be), 85, 342
depression, 463
deprive
(to), 250, 270
depth, 192, 520
(ocean), 149
depths, 192, 214, 455
(and), 456
deputation, 431
deputy, 182
deride
(to), 125, 160
derision, 125, 181, 182, 304
(object of), 309
derisive
song, 168
descend
(to), 161, 195, 313
descendents, 305
descending, 313
descent, 214
desecrate
(to), 52, 86
desert, 127, 229, 297, 501
plain, 229
desert-dweller, 132
deserted, 281, 479
design, 241
designated, 414
desirable, 71, 112
(that which is), 75
thing, 112
desirableness, 71
desire, 20, 22, 27, 71, 75, 76, 93, 112, 279, 292, 295, 302, 444, 468
(and you have a), 445
(failing with), 74
(his), 519
(in a bad sense), 33
(to hungrily), 162, 438
(to), 30, 71, 92, 95, 114, 177, 289, 488
(you did), 413
(you shall), 445
(you), 362
(your), 521, 550
desired, 22
(thing), 292
desiring, 177, 488
desist
(to), 61
desolate, 51, 102, 191, 281, 479
(be), 416, 527
(the), 285, 498
(to be), 166, 191, 262, 266, 281, 468, 471, 479
(to make), 51, 159, 191
house, 144
place, 297, 501
desolation, 109, 191, 196, 252, 268, 283, 295
(and bring to), 427
(and I will bring), 425
despair, 261
(cry of), 34
(to), 248
despairing, 121
despise, 247
(to treat with), 247
(to), 30, 31, 62, 123, 157, 481
despised, 30, 126
(and he), 43
(to be), 152
despoil
(to), 246
dessert, 239
destiny, 96
(god that represented), 121
destitute, 340, 342
(to leave), 227
destitution, 385
destory, 506
destroy, 20
(and he shall), 46
(and he will d it), 408
(and I will), 426
(and so you will), 422, 529
(and), 374
(do not), 510
(I will d them), 438, 532

(I will), 408
(that I may d them), 289, 483
(thou must not), 511
(to completely), 213, 442
(to d an enemy), 34
(to d it), 417
(to d utterly), 213, 442
(to utterly), 161
(to), 58, 68, 104, 159, 189, 223, 244, 246, 247, 264, 340, 374, 381, 382, 401, 415, 435, 532
(will d you), 419, 521
(will you), 509
(will), 424, 438, 532
(you shall), 380, 394, 508, 520, 524
you, 417, 521
destroyed, 401
(and He d them), 82, 366
(and I shall be), 443
(has d them), 274
(he has), 46, 274
(one), 68
(shall be), 439, 539
(to be), 20
(when), 402
destroyer, 223, 422
(the), 425
destruction, 20, 38, 53, 58, 61, 75, 81, 114, 117, 133, 136, 143, 223, 241, 243, 292, 311, 388, 399, 401, 404, 419, 424, 426, 454
(always of Sodom & Gomorrah), 162
(angel of), 530
(fig.), 33
(one quieted by), 68
(pit of), 472
(place of), 81, 404
(to dedicate for), 213, 442
detain
(to), 272
determine, 190
(to), 74, 238, 302, 471, 506
detest
(to), 323, 527
(you shall d it), 480
(you shall), 467
detestable
(you shall make), 467
thing, 323, 324, 527, 528
Deuteronomy. *See Tanakh: 01 Torah: 05 Deuteronomy*
devastate
(to), 149, 244, 246, 247
devastated, 281, 479
devastating
storm, 249
devastation, 243, 244, 282, 283, 396
deviate
(to d from), 128
deviation, 307
device, 71, 112, 193, 270, 275, 494
(wicked), 105, 375
devices, 223
devious, 257
devise
(to), 20, 29, 105, 329, 375
devote
(and I will), 384
(to), 213, 442
devoted
one, 224
devotion, 11, 254
to study, 57
devour, 70, 131
(to), 70, 130
devouring
(fig. for ruin), 123
dew, 57
(drops of), 257
diamond, 104, 374
die, 97
(I), 309
(let), 454
(to), 308
(you shall), 455, 456
(you), 467, 544
died
(and), 455
difference, 126, 352
difficult
(and), 51
question, 45
difficulty, 301
(when she was having), 444
dig
(and you shall), 394
(to d about), 177
(to d out), 120
(to d through), 202
(to), 27, 120, 202, 233, 244, 266, 357
dignity, 287, 396, 518
diligent, 242, 507
diligently, 197, 285
(do), 44
dim, 49
(to be), 49
(to grow), 49, 256, 442
(to), 163, 402
(were), 51
diminish
(shall), 387
(to), 227
(you shall), 385
diminished
(to be), 139
dinner, 70
dip
(to d into), 60
(to), 60, 173
dipping, 478
direct
(to), 234, 428
direction, 308
(to change), 83
directly
ahead of, 86, 407
dirge, 172
(to chant a), 167, 441
dirt
(damp), 46
disable
(to), 261
disallow
(to), 75
disappear
(to), 184
disappointed
(to be), 245
disappointing, 48
(to be), 256
disappointment, 354
disaster, 33, 114, 225
disc
of bread, 97
discern
(to), 80, 225, 404
discernment, 85
discharge, 32, 431
(to), 176
discipled, 98
discipline, 239, 244
(to), 225
disclosed
(to be), 177
discomfit
(to), 70, 104, 360, 374
discomfited, 121
discomfiture, 117
disconcerted
(to be), 245
discouraged
one, 121
discourse, 155, 458
discover
(to), 228
discretion, 112
disdain
(to), 30
disdained, 126
disease, 74, 102, 142
(eruptive), 224
diseased
(to be), 57, 62
(to become), 62
diseases, 308
disfigurement
(of face), 419
disgorge
(to), 129, 136
disgrace, 115, 180, 234, 324, 453, 479
(to), 152
disguise
(to d oneself), 284
(to), 225
disgusting, 348
thing, 318
dish, 279, 337, 428, 478
disheartened

(to be), 45
dishes
(and its snuff), 461
(its snuff), 459
(its), 434
(the), 430
dishonor, 115, 180, 230, 453
(to), 152
dishonored
(to be), 152
disinherit
(to), 330
disk, 72, 397
dismay, 28, 61, 303, 318, 502
(to), 55, 317
dismayed, 292
(be), 442
(to be), 442
disobedient
(to be d towards), 212
disperse
(to), 190, 194, 199, 233, 496
dispersed
(to be), 176, 194, 487
disperser, 199, 496
dispersion, 349
displace
(to), 41
displease
(to), 171
displeased
(to be), 148, 225, 456, 488
displeasing
(to be), 242
displeasure
(my), 460
dispossess
(shall d them), 483
(to), 330
dispossession, 329
dispute, 194
disquieted
(to be), 68
disquieting
thoughts, 351, 527
disquietude, 117
dissemble
(to), 256
dissimulation, 287, 498
dissipate
(to), 97
dissolve
(to), 169, 261
dissolving, 325
distaff, 339
distance, 201, 203, 245, 266, 397
(at a d from), 76
(at a), 76
distant, 245, 252
place, 266
distill
(to), 106, 155, 188, 458
distinct
(to be), 136
(to make), 185, 350, 351
distinction, 74
(men of), 289, 483
distinguish
(to d oneself), 161
(to), 350, 351
distinguished
(to be), 136
distort
(to), 101, 174, 465
distorted, 316
distorting, 164
distortion, 101, 462
distract
(to), 70, 359
distracted
(to be), 152, 434
distress, 31, 146, 174, 183, 200, 207, 210, 234, 237, 240, 257, 305, 318, 391, 478
(expression of physical), 82
(howling of), 94
(my), 395
(to be in), 322
(to cause), 323
distressed
(to be), 239
district, 130, 148, 359
disturb, 427
(to), 55, 227, 234
disturbed
(to be), 55
ditch, 18, 27, 242, 508
divan, 348
divide
(and d into three parts), 497
(to d in three parts), 368
(to), 25, 54, 105, 120, 125, 134, 153, 175, 180, 188, 190, 232, 262, 302, 303, 313, 319, 471, 489
divided, 192, 477
(and he), 364
opinion, 192, 477
divination, 184, 208, 271, 425, 426, 438
(practicing a form of), 215, 444
(to practice), 184, 271, 425
divine
(to), 184, 271, 425
ones, 104, 374
presence, 282
revelation (the receiver of), 76, 400
diviner, 25, 158, 219, 296, 447
division, 138, 158, 192, 327, 350, 477
(of priests and Levites), 178
(of priests for service), 168
(point of), 60, 355
divorce, 496
(to), 326
do, 452
(and d them), 450, 455, 535
(and to), 444
(and), 432, 434
(that you might), 458, 537
(that you should), 438
(that), 430
(to d again), 99, 162, 270, 461
(to d away), 226, 227
(to d it), 440
(to), 95, 178, 279, 440
(will), 430
(you shall), 430, 432, 450, 540
(you will), 450, 540
you look upon one another, 491
docile, 132, 137, 451, 453
document, 262, 299
doe, 64, 129, 306
dog, 72
cage, 77
doing, 87, 159, 178
(by its), 430
(from), 443, 446
(so), 449, 534
dominate
(and), 197
(to), 190, 261, 453
domineer
(to), 261
domineering, 266, 415
dominion, 151, 276, 284, 293, 296, 339, 342, 497
(to have), 190, 276
done
(being), 450
(have you), 451, 540
(I have), 420, 435
(shall be), 430
(she has), 430
(will be), 452
(you have), 432
door, 304, 320, 348, 385, 517
(and from the), 338
(at the), 334
(lintel of), 336, 522
(supporters of), 116
(the hated one at the), 382, 534
(to the), 334
post, 60
doorkeeper, 385
doorpost, 83
doorway, 322
double, 147, 286
(to d over), 147
(to fold), 147
(to), 147
double-dealer, 383
doubling, 147
dough, 264
(of your), 435, 532
(the), 183
(to knead), 260
(unleavened), 182
(your), 438, 532
dove, 90
d's dung, 91, 259, 409, 466

down
(and let), 358
(and went), 358
(let), 42
(to beat), 161, 189, 223, 340, 438, 461, 532
(to bring), 310
(to cut), 27, 51, 94, 95, 107, 120, 326, 364, 376
(to go), 161, 195, 313, 369
(to hew), 27, 95
(when he came), 360
downfall, 401
downpour, 213, 284, 317, 441, 507, 516
downtreading, 134
downwards, 73
dowry, 30
(to give a), 212
drag
(to d away), 289
(to d oneself along), 113
(to), 88, 272, 289, 453
dragon, 306, 324, 331, 512, 514
(great), 311
drain
(to d out), 151, 199, 496
(to), 151
drank, 509
(and he), 406
(and I), 400
(and), 409, 506
(they), 407
drape, 184, 236
draught
house, 217
draw
(and I will d out), 412
(thing to d aside), 77
(to d near), 269
(to d off or away or apart), 343
(to d off), 145, 280, 294, 478, 510
(to d out), 145, 260, 284, 294, 344, 478, 506, 510
(to d together), 175, 225, 502
(to d up), 175
(to), 264, 271, 272, 453
(you d near), 397
nigh, 397
up, 27, 39
drawers, 173
drawing, 272, 453
near, 244
place of water, 263
up, 272, 453
up a trail, 272, 453
drawn, 264
(has), 274
(to be), 355
sword, 323
dread, 74, 118
(I was in d of), 366
(to be in), 113
(to), 113, 195, 306, 348, 523
dreaded, 363, 515
dreadful, 70, 275, 359, 515
(to make), 61
event, 61
dream, 96, 103, 371, 374
(interpretation of), 351
(to), 34, 96, 371
dreamer, 41
dreams
(interpreted our), 341
dregs, 340
dress
(and you shall), 417
(to), 258
drew
(and she), 402
(I d him), 425
(then d near), 426
(when they d near), 417, 528
dried, 248, 404
(to be d up), 191
drink, 63, 82, 291, 297, 308, 418
(and gave him), 447
(and I may), 510
(and she [gave to]), 440
(and they made to), 460, 542
(and to), 404
(and you may), 513, 550
(mixed), 169, 372
(shall we), 422
(shall), 406
(she made), 443
(strong or intoxicating), 335
(that I may), 404
(that may), 403
(that we may), 425
(to d heavily), 82
(to d largely), 82
(to d one's fill), 193
(to give him), 454
(to give to), 291
(to), 291, 398, 510, 511
(you shall give her to), 449
(you shall), 505, 506
offering, 143
drinking, 403
(mode or manner or amount of), 406
bout, 403
drink-offering, 169, 372
drinks, 406, 506
(and), 409
drip, 242, 495
(to), 155, 267, 452, 458, 501
dripping, 134, 242, 452, 495
drive
(and I shall d them out), 476
(and I will d out), 474
(and you shall d them out), 482, 542
(to d asunder), 150, 457
(to d away), 34, 37, 81, 145, 150, 190, 195, 326, 457
(to d from), 195
(to d on), 112, 444
(to d out), 29, 326
(to), 77, 107, 150, 201, 269, 442, 457
(you will d out), 475
away, 78
driven
(and you have d them out), 482, 542
away, 133, 385
out, 469
driver, 201
driving, 119
storm, 199, 496
dromedary, 200, 203, 308
camel, 308
droop
(to), 90
drooping, 120, 420
drop, 52, 155, 165, 209, 242, 458, 495
(of silver), 168
(to d down), 101
(to d off), 280
(to), 106, 134, 155, 267, 452, 458, 501
dropping, 134, 452
dross, 65
(usually of silver), 93
drought, 127, 191, 224, 308, 385, 474
drown
(to), 100
drowsiness, 123
drowsy
(to be), 117, 379
drug, 121, 381
drum
(to), 346, 525
drunk
(may be), 406
(to be), 335
(to become), 335
(you have), 512, 550
drunkard, 335
drunken, 335
drunkenness, 348, 520
dry, 191, 248
(to be), 191, 248, 420
(to become), 248
(to d up), 114, 178, 190, 191, 209, 349, 416
(to make), 248
earth, 267
ground, 196
ground or land, 251
land, 196
regions, 292
valley, 271, 475
dryness, 121, 127, 167, 191, 278, 441, 495
duality, 14
due, 130

dug
(I have), 372
(I), 393
dugout
holes, 239
dull, 49, 118
(to be), 132
dullard, 139
dulling, 49
dullness, 323
dumb, 90, 108, 368, 376
(to be), 103, 329, 373
(to grow), 103, 373
dumb-founded
(to be), 308
dung, 52, 114, 190, 259, 351, 417, 466
(heap of), 81
(of cattle), 212
(their), 365, 515
hill, 154
pit, 154
place, 154
dungeon, 242
dunghill, 112, 432
durable, 348, 350
duration
(long), 160, 399
of life, 62
during, 93
dust, 43, 124, 267, 272, 292
(gold), 373
(to), 267
duties
(regarding their), 495, 545
duty
(his), 487
(your), 489, 540
dwell, 252
(and go to the place that God has chosen to), 389
(and shall), 410
(and we will), 278
(and you shall), 423, 529
(and you), 407
(that I may), 434
(that they may), 413
(to d in), 413
(to d within), 28
(to), 80, 144, 191, 249, 277, 295, 417, 495
(when you), 426, 530
(you shall), 397, 401
(you to d in), 421, 522
dwellers, 266
dwelling, 64, 80, 172, 174, 185, 186, 191, 245, 266, 277, 446, 495
(one), 502
(toward the), 413
in eternity, 310, 505
place, 214, 236, 258, 266, 293, 500, 505, 512
dwelling-place, 266
dwellings
(in their), 435, 532
(out of your), 458, 536
(your), 453, 529
dwelt
(and she), 400
(and), 407
(you have), 397
(you), 421, 528
dying, 308
each, 28, 247
eagerly, 285
eagerness, 320
eagle, 343, 347
(black), 158
(the), 344
eagles
(like), 364, 515
ear, 76, 400
(piece of), 54
(tip or lobe of), 318, 482
(to pierce the), 273
(to uncover the e to reveal), 76, 400
as organ of hearing, 76, 400
of corn, 413
of grain, 259, 323
of wheat, 135, 323
eared
owl, 308, 514
early
(and you may rise up), 444, 533
(rise up), 274, 476
(to depart), 277
(to go), 277
(to rise or start), 273, 475
fig, 203, 205
life, 253, 256
earnestly, 197
earnings, 102
earring, 118, 134, 380
earth, 68, 225, 235, 241, 267, 272, 404, 505, *Also See* Elements: Earth (*Aretz*)
(as a fortress or prison), 199
(clod of), 187, 249
(clod or lump of), 246
(dry), 267
(nethermost), 514
as rising, 30
Earth. *Also See* Planets: Nontraditional: Earth
(nethermost), 557
earthen
vessel, 329
earthenware, 329
earthquake, 348
ease, 260, 263
(at), 260, 289, 304, 499, 503
(to be at), 268, 490
(you shall have), 389
east, 162, 165, 182, 405, 454
(the), 158, 398
wind, 165, 405
eastern, 186
eastward, 162
easy
(to be), 80, 403
eat
(to cause to), 139, 387
(to e up), 123
(to), 70, 96, 139, 188, 371, 387
eaten
(something), 103, 374
eating, 84
out, 465
ebony, 75, 399
Ecclesiastes. *See Tanakh: 03 Kethuvim:* 07 Ecclesiastes
echo, 124
ecstatic
(vision in the e state), 79
Edenic Rivers
Gihon (Water), 85, 93, 95, 407, 410, 411
Hiddikel (Air), 157
Phrath (Earth), 388
Pison (Fire), 308, 504
edge, 80, 105, 162, 179, 183, 210, 252, 283, 432, 461
(in the), 432
(its), 434
(of a sword), 116
edict, 290, 299, 336, 503
Edom, 70, 359
Chief of
Mizzah, 72
Chiefs of
Anah, 144
Jaalam, 162, 402
Lotan, 115, 418
Dukes of
01 Alvah (Daat), 133
as Aliah (alternate spelling), 136
01 Jetheth (Daat), 443
01 Timnah (Daat), 333, 346
02 Aholibamah (Hesed), 113
03 Elah (Giburah), 54
04 Pinon (Tiferet), 181, 454
05 Kenaz (Netzach), 167
06 Teman (Hod), 325, 512
07 Magdiel (Yesod), 107
07 Mibzar (Yesod), 258
08 Eram (Malkut), 253, 463
Kings of
01 *Bela* (*Daat*), 123
as son of *Beor*, 304, 503
city (*Dinhabah*), 84
father of (Beor), 229
02 *Yobab* (*Hesed*), 38
as son of Zerah, 232, 478
city (Bozrah), 237
father of (Zerah), 196
03 *Husham* (*Giburah*), 264, 469
alternate spelling (Chusham), 265, 471
alternate spelling (Chuwsham), 269, 473

city (*Temani*), 331
04 *Hadad* (*Tiferet*), 29
alternate spelling ('Adad), 23
as son of *Bedad*, 25, 93, 410
city (*Avith*), 321
son of (Genubath), 312
05 *Samlah* (*Netzach*), 279
city (*Masreqah*), 374
06 *Saul* (*Hod*), 261
city (*Rehoboth*), 363
07 *Baal-Hanan* (*Yesod*), 190, 458
as son of Achbor, 345, 555
father of (Achbor), 238
08 *Hadar* (*Malkut*), 190, 194
city (*Pai*), 169
city (*Pau*), 167
wife (*Matred*), 216
wife (*Mehetabel*), 118
wife (*Mezahab*), 83
efficiency, 66
egg, 128
eight, 287, 435
(and), 437
eighteen, 483, 485
eighth, 287, 294
(the), 440
eighty, 306, 489
either, 20
elder, 153, 434
elders, 188, 427
(and your), 205, 436
(to the e of), 183
elect
(to), 190
electrum, 280
elegy, 172
Elements
Air (*Ruach*), 15, 195
Angel
Chassan, 271, 492
Archangel
Rafael, 248
as 11th Path, 27, 85
as Tarot Card The Fool, 13
Demon King (Goetia)
Amaimon, 161, 437
Demon Prince
Azazel, 136
Edenic River
Hiddikel, 157
God Name
Shaddai El Chai, 273
Ruler
Ariel, 210
Earth (*Aretz*), 235, 505
Angel
Phorlakh, 260, 447
Archangel
Auriel, 213
Demon King
Amaimon, 161, 437
Demon King (Goetia)
Zimimay, 137
Demon Prince
Mahazael, 102
Edenic River
Phorlakh, 388
God Name
Adonai HaAretz, 273, 514
Ruler
Kerub, 204
Fire (*Esh*), 15, 241
Angel
Aral, 205
Archangel
Michael, 123
as 31st Path, 50, 324
as Tarot Card Judgement, 38
Demon King
Paimon, 180, 453
Demon King (Goetia)
Goap, 108, 443
Demon Prince
Samael, 149
Edenic River
Pison, 308, 504
God Name
YHVH *Tzabaoth*, 336
Ruler
Seraf, 351, 527
number of (including spirit), 18
number of (not including spirit), 17
Spirit, 289
Water (*Maim*), 15, 109, 376
Angel
Taliahad, 76
Archangel
Gabriel, 212
as 23rd Path, 42, 228
as Tarot card The Hanged Man, 28
Demon King
Ariton, 228, 476
Demon King (Goetia)
Korson, 263, 488
Demon Prince
Azael, 130
Edenic River
Gihon, 85, 93, 95, 407, 410, 411
God Name
Elohim Tzabaoth, 352, 512
Ruler
Tharsis, 484
elevation, 18, 64, 102, 152, 213, 396, 439, 441, 457
eleven, 351, 432
(to), 443
eleventh, 432
(and in the), 431
eliminate
(to), 364
else, 51
emanation, 270, 296, 485
emanations, 423
embalm
(to), 85
embalming, 85
ember, 60, 146, 306, 391
embrace
(to), 131
embroidered
with needlework, 262, 468
emerald, 396
eminence, 74, 161, 345
eminency, 74
eminent, 348, 350
emotion, 302
emplacement, 136, 426
employment, 106, 117, 208
emptied
(and she), 386
emptily, 267, 472
(to act), 55
emptiness, 29, 134, 165, 247, 252
empty, 72, 185, 247, 403
(and you shall), 363, 515
(that which is), 333
(to be), 166
(to e out), 244
(to make), 244
(to), 185, 228
talk, 19
enactment, 134
encamp
(to), 82
encamping, 315
encampment, 130, 201, 315
encampments
(and by their), 383, 521
(their), 380, 520
encasement, 225
enchanter, 25, 281, 505
enchantment, 58, 271
encircle
(to), 34, 83
encircling, 353
rope, 206
enclose
(to), 173, 188, 194, 235, 465
enclosed
garden, 264
space with steps or ladder, 84
enclosure, 72, 117, 225, 231, 237, 238, 242, 253, 297, 397, 438
encompass, 188
(to), 34, 170, 194, 463
encompassing, 130
all worlds, 345, 519
encounter, 247
(to), 74, 165, 241, 243, 244, 282
end, 77, 156, 160, 181, 182, 183, 224, 292, 324, 353, 364, 459, 460, 474, 489
(at the), 215, 467
(but his), 368
(in the), 365
(in your later), 372, 509
(in), 183

(my), 368
(their latter), 391, 523
(their), 380, 520
(to b to an), 104, 118, 123
(to be at an), 74
(to come to an), 156, 160, 211, 460
(to), 74, 211
ended
(and was), 455, 535
(to be), 74
endow
(to e with), 29
(to), 29
endowment, 30
ends
(its), 361, 473
(the), 467
endure
(to), 78, 135
enduring, 161, 163, 168, 348, 402
(to be), 161
enemies
(his), 47
(my), 41
(their), 183, 423
(your), 52, 331
enemy, 36, 225, 234
(either personal or national), 29
(to be an e to), 29
(to be an), 395
(to destroy an), 34
(your), 52, 331
energy, 171, 351, 410, 527
engage
(to), 226, 325
engender
(to), 63
engrave
(and you shall), 466
(to), 189, 322, 329, 357
(you shall), 465
engraved, 476
engraver, 329
engraving, 323
tool, 198
engulf
(to), 123, 284, 507
enigma, 176
enigmatic
saying or question, 45
enjoy
(and shall be), 393, 542
enjoyment, 416
enlarge
(and I will), 368
enlighten, 367
enmity, 35, 274, 286, 314
(and), 42
(be at), 392
(in), 37
(to watch with), 236
enough, 30, 73, 80, 403
(what is), 73
enquire
(to), 95, 241, 258, 327
enquiry, 245
enrage
(to), 192
enraged
(to be), 167, 462
enrich
(to), 348
enriched, 487
enroll
(to), 299
ensign, 131, 292
ensigns
(with), 439
ensnare
(to), 117, 310
ensnared
(you shall be), 456
enter
(to e into), 124, 241
(to), 22, 58
entered
(and is), 47
(when), 42
entering, 22, 67, 68, 72
entice
(to), 293, 315, 321
enticement, 77
entire, 109, 319, 498
entirely, 319, 498
entirety, 109
entrance, 22, 61, 67, 68, 72, 156, 316, 322, 355, 458, 508
(at the), 52
entreat, 22, 392
(and I will), 504
(and), 393
(shall I), 388
(to), 165, 384
entreated
(and he), 390
(and let be), 390
entreaty, 292
entrenchment, 72, 149, 158, 260
entry, 72
(of the temple), 22
entwine
(to), 305
enumeration, 262
enumerator, 262
envelop, 64
(to e oneself), 103, 168, 463
(to), 64
envoy, 240
(to act as an), 240
envy
(to watch with), 236
(to), 164
enwrap
(to), 64, 103, 305
ephod
(priestly garment), 108, 111
girdle or band of, 246
epithet
(to give an), 94
equal
(to), 234, 428
equalize
(to), 344, 517
equip, 188
equipment, 310
equipped
(to be e with), 310
equity, 343
eranite, 257
ere
(of time), 217, 446
that, 93
err
(to), 103, 244, 246, 318
(you shall), 402
error, 87, 252, 257, 269
(his), 404
(their), 418, 528
(to commit), 244
errors, 479
errs
(that), 403
eruption, 343, 352
escape, 139, 147, 151, 168, 324
(place of), 168
(to), 98, 137, 139, 233, 327
escaped
one, 147
espousals, 111
essence, 184, 289, 424
of glory, 208, 437
establish
(to e firmly), 81
(to), 75, 93, 125, 146, 150, 158
established
(to be), 95, 411
place, 136, 426
estate, 88, 408
esteem, 247
(to), 234, 246, 428
Esther. *See Tanakh: 03 Kethuvim:* 08 Esther
estimate, 163, 234, 428
(to), 155
estranged
(to be), 199
eternal, 168
eternity, 160, 161, 399
(dwelling in), 310, 505
ether, 197
eunuch, 257
even
as, 19
to, 93
evening, 226
(to become), 226
evenness, 343
ever, 160, 167, 399, 407
ever-flowing, 314, 507
everlasting, 160, 167, 399, 407
everlastingness, 161

evermore, 160, 167, 399, 407
every, 69
man, 315
one, 69
evil, 137, 225, 228, 249, 427
(be), 249
(gone to the grave in), 361
(shall be), 385
(to be), 242, 262
(to do), 394
inclination, 347
plan, 71, 105, 375
possessing spirit, 141
report, 27
spirit, 322
evils, 386
(the), 388
ewe, 208, 485
ewe-lamb, 256
ewe-lambs, 410
exact
(to), 269, 289
(you shall), 397
statement, 352
exactly, 197
exactness
of gold, 75
exalt
(to), 57, 116, 140, 314
(you e yourself), 346
exaltation, 78, 232, 396, 402, 455
exalted, 64, 314, 436
(and they shall be), 423
(to be e in triumph), 23
(to be), 25, 230, 454
exaltedly
(to dwell), 57
examine
(to), 78, 124, 245, 402
excavate
(to), 202
excavation, 245, 341
exceed, 25, 33
(to), 224
exceedingly, 64, 364
excel
(to), 161
excellence, 66
(and the), 362
excellency, 25, 32, 78, 383, 402, 491, 529
excellent
thing, 124
except, 49, 66, 85, 104, 132, 136, 307, 384, 413
that, 66
exception
(with the e of), 66
excess, 224, 228, 363, 501
(to be in), 165, 462
excessive
fat, 152
exchange, 377
(and its), 500
(articles of), 249
(in e for), 138, 453
(to), 212, 214, 226
exchanged
(that which is), 377
(thing), 229
excited
(to be sexually), 259
excitement, 192, 230
exclude, 78
excrement, 124, 190, 370, 526
(human), 117
excuse
me please, 28
execration, 54, 172
executed
(to have one), 308
executioner, 37, 152, 480
exempt, 169
exercise
(to e in), 94
exhaling
(of life), 146
exhausted, 72, 169, 463
(to be), 90, 231
exile, 56, 63, 305
exiled
(and he e them out), 422, 529
exiles, 305
exist
(to), 28, 38
existence, 166, 247, 406
(absolute nullification of), 485
(nullification of), 353
existing, 170, 409
exists
(that which), 166, 406
exit
(to), 123
Exodus. *See Tanakh: 01 Torah:* 02 Exodus
exorcist, 281, 505
expanse, 192
expanses, 215
expansion, 281, 284
expect
(to), 67
expectation, 70, 331
expel
(to), 107, 326, 420, 443
expense, 205
expenses, 179
expensive
robe, 338
experience
(to learn by), 271
experienced, 107, 347
experimental, 180
expiring, 146
explain
(to), 32, 189
export, 153
exposed
(to be), 228
to condemnation, 35
exposition, 341
expression, 199, 204
of satisfaction, 50, 331
expulsion, 329
(act of), 329
extend
(to), 82, 118, 252, 348
extended, 43
extension
(to make), 67
extent
(to the e of), 53
exterior, 185
exterminate
(and you shall), 387
(to), 213, 442
external, 171, 366, 445, 496
belly, 135
extinct
(to be), 117, 350
extinguish
(to), 117, 350
extinguished
(to be), 46, 114, 117, 349, 350
extolling, 232, 455
extort
(to), 316
extortion, 317, 318, 406
extortionate
deed, 406
extortioner, 318
extract
(to), 260
extraordinary, 141, 364
(to be), 133
extravagance, 326
extreme
anxiety, 198
heat, 297
old age, 153, 434
extremely, 364
extremity, 105, 162, 182, 461
extricate
(to), 174
exult
(to), 129, 181, 489
exultant, 129, 137
exultation, 356, 375, 377, 527
eye, 88, 148, 432
(to), 144, 430
cosmetic (stibium), 128, 352
eyelid, 239, 342, 495
eyes
(flash of), 213, 441
(from before the e of), 76
(his), 160
(to close the), 184, 424
(to make the e sparkle), 180, 489
(to open the), 180
(to paint), 77
(to put the e out), 228
(to shut the), 184, 424
Ezekiel. *See Tanakh: 02 Neviim:* 09 Ezekiel

Ezra. *See Tanakh: 03 Kethuvim:* 10 Ezra
fabric
(colored), 42
(dark-hued), 42
(mixed), 334
(torn pieces of), 277
fabricated
(something), 428
face, 100, 123, 148, 156, 178, 312, 416, 439, 454, 456, 515
(before your), 76
(his), 160
(to the f of), 173
faces, 328, 501
faceward, 179
facing, 76
fade
(to), 101
fail
(to), 48, 49, 74, 169, 184, 211, 227, 256, 384
failing, 136, 426
with desire, 74
failure, 256
of mental energy, 28
faint, 32, 37, 168, 169, 463
(to be), 49, 168, 169, 231, 463
(to grow), 49
(to), 59, 83
fainted, 179
faintness, 28, 82, 168, 405, 463
fair, 115, 353
(to be), 115
fairness, 352
faith, 116, 123
(former of), 183, 455
faithful, 101, 111, 157, 416, 436
(to be), 111, 416
faithfulness, 91, 111, 117, 306, 416, 419
falcon, 33, 36
(the), 39
fall, 291, 358, 500, *Also See* Seasons:Fall (*Sethev*)
(to f away), 250
(to fall out), 38
(to fall upon), 283, 317, 506
(to let), 271
(to wither and), 101
(to), 124, 169
fallow
(and let it lie), 427
(to lie), 271
false, 45, 256
(to be), 354
god, 61
phylacteries, 319
falsehood, 48, 244, 320, 354
falsely, 368
(deal), 490
(to do), 354
(you shall deal), 413
falter
(to), 49
fame, 294
families, 451, 452
(according to your), 476, 541
(after their), 473
(and of the), 473, 540
(and their), 540
(by their), 467, 469, 539, 540
(of the), 460
(of), 458
(their), 460, 537
family, 295, 304
(according to its), 462
(and against his), 454
(and the f of), 452
(his), 452
(of his), 462
(of the), 451
(to the), 458
famine, 162, 227, 254, 438, 485
famished
(and was), 387
famous, 252
fan
(to), 194
fanciful, 139
fancy, 293
fangs, 342
fantasy, 293
far, 245, 252
(so), 44
(which are), 405
(you shall go), 410
(you shall keep you), 401
country, 266
off, 252
farmer, 200
fashion, 241
(to), 171, 237, 239, 279
fast, 153, 393
(to), 153, 393
fasten
(to), 146, 151, 451
fasting, 153, 296, 393
ascetic practice of, 477
fastingly, 296
fastness, 150, 155, 397
fat, 59, 67, 193, 194, 231, 285, 498
(and the), 366
(and), 364
(excessive), 152
(super abundance of), 152
(the), 364, 366
(to be), 96, 269, 284, 285, 490, 498
(to become), 269, 285, 490, 498
(to grow), 269, 285, 490, 498
(to), 269, 490
(you are covered with), 412, 519
(you did grow), 435
ashes, 269, 490
one, 67
piece, 302, 502
fatally
(to wound), 86
wounded, 86
fate, 96
father, 15, 29
(and her), 42
(and the f of), 36
(but his), 43
(his), 36
(my), 29
(to a), 52
(to the), 52
(your f's), 51, 331
(your), 51, 331
and mother, 70
f's sister, 36
in law, 67, 357
of an individual, 15
of fathers, 104
fatherless, 312, 494
fatigue, 168, 463
fatigued, 168, 463
(to be), 168, 463
fatling, 67, 215
fatness, 269, 302, 490, 502
fat-tail
(of sheep), 65
fatten
(to), 81
fatter, 193, 194
fault, 114, 257
(through your), 214, 443
fault-finder, 228
faulty
(and obliged to offer a guilt-offering), 262, 468
favor, 40, 76, 142, 169, 265, 315, 358, 400, 408, 489
(to show), 129, 423
(you shall), 358
favorable
(to be f to), 237
(to be), 35
favorably
(to accept), 237
favority, 35
fawn, 267
fear, 22, 29, 113, 118, 197, 198, 213, 214, 217, 292, 295, 365
(and the f of you), 370, 508
(and you shall), 363
(his), 363
(to make), 61
(to shake from), 193
(to), 44, 64, 113, 115, 192, 193, 195, 306, 523
(you shall), 360, 362, 363, 380, 520
(you will), 383, 529
(you), 360, 363
of, 360
them, 377, 519
feared, 363, 515
(but they), 383, 529

fearful, 194, 199
(to be), 208
fearing, 193, 197, 199
feast, 27, 96, 202, 371, 418
(and on the), 37
(in your), 52, 331
(my), 39
(on the), 29
(that they may hold a), 52
(to give a), 202
(to hold a), 31
feather, 181, 489
feathers, 163
fecal
matter, 351
feces, 117, 370, 526
fed, 193, 194
(and they), 416
(as he), 387
feeble, 123, 358
(to be), 108, 168, 463
feed, 125, 179, 421
(to f sweetly), 340
(to), 70, 81, 82, 139, 387, 399, 405
feeding
trough, 86
feel
(to), 265, 266, 355, 372
feeling, 332
(sinking), 252
feet, 229
(place at the), 229
(trodden with the), 314
fell
(I f down), 485
(and when), 360
felling
of tree, 420
fellow, 191, 196, 334
fellowship
(to have f with), 191
felt, 343
(and he), 379
(you have), 497
female, 167, 243
(issue of - menstruation), 31
companion, 386
goat, 123
mule, 234
servant, 255
slave, 65
temple prostitute, 292
fence, 188, 297
(to f about), 87, 121, 350
(to f up or about), 253, 438
(to), 235
ferment
(to), 142, 213
ferret, 166
fertile
place, 302, 502
fertility, 208
fester
(to), 208
festival, 27
(to hold a), 31
prayer book, 221
festival-gathering, 27
festoons, 55
fetch
(to), 154
fetter, 33, 40, 71, 243
fetters, 71, 141
fever, 241, 297, 331
few, 139, 251
(to be), 139
fewness, 139
fidelity, 116, 123
field, 32, 185, 246, 266, 342
(plowed), 32
of cucumbers, 308
fields
(and of the f of), 435
(the), 401
fierce, 96, 209
(to be), 106, 290
fierceness, 109, 373
fiery, 218, 219
(the), 370, 517
serpent, 351, 527
fifteen, 475
fifth, 265, 275, 423, 427
(and a f part of it), 427
(its), 422, 426
(the), 425
(to take one), 265
part, 265
thereof, 422
fifty, 287, 482
fig
(early or ripe), 203
fig-cake
(pressed), 60
fight
(to), 96, 114, 191, 371
figs
(lump of pressed), 60
(to gather), 112
figure, 176, 355, 428, 459
figured
(their), 443, 533
figures
(sculpted), 253
filigree
work, 305
fill
(to have one's), 193
(to), 90
filled
(you shall be), 431
fillet, 292, 319
fillets, 292
fills
(that which), 90
film, 244
filth, 117, 118, 124
filthiness, 78, 87
filthy, 118, 210
fin, 288
finality, 156, 479
find
(to f out), 124
(to), 149, 256
fine, 125, 298
(of flax), 362
(to), 298
glass, 311
gold, 225
finely
decorated cultic objects of gold or silver, 308
finery, 143, 429
finger, 171
(little), 168, 443
fingernail, 233, 298, 501
fining, 298
finish
(to f off), 118
(to), 74, 98, 123, 170
finished
(to be), 74, 306, 490
fir, 329, 357
tree, 215, 468
fire, 218, 228, 241, 243, *Also See* Elements: Fire (*Esh*)
(set on), 188
(to set on), 324
offering, 243
firebolt, 351, 527
firebrand, 27, 141
fire-holder, 311
firepan, 311
firepans, 455, 457
(and its), 461
(the), 457
fire-places, 448
fire-pot, 23
firm, 73, 80, 111, 188, 193, 194, 398, 403, 416
(to be made), 188
(to be), 95, 135, 188, 411
(to grow), 135
strength, 77
firmament
(of water above), 281
firmness, 116, 123, 160, 306
first, 28, 165, 307, 344, 345, 346, 472, 518
(and), 474
(as the), 350, 521
(like unto the), 365, 516
(of the), 481
(on the), 31
(the), 35, 483
part of them, 481, 542
ripe fig, 203
year, 423
firstborn, 203, 207, 233
(of women), 207
(to be), 200
firstfruits, 203, 205

firstling, 203, 233
firstlings
(and the), 367
(of the), 384
first-ripe
fig, 205
fish, 20, 22, 28, 128, 423
(and the), 41
(great), 68
(scale of), 517
(the), 34
for, 34
of, 34
fisher, 29
fisherman, 29, 34
fishes, 75, 363
fishhook, 35, 52, 126
fishing
net, 394
fissure, 127, 178
fist, 204, 231, 490, 498
fit
(to f out), 277, 503
(to f together), 277, 503
fitting, 200, 395
fittings, 452
five, 265, 269, 419
(and), 422
(to arrange in multiples of), 265
fix
(to), 93, 103, 146
fixed, 177
(to be), 105, 375
place, 136, 320, 426
resting place, 141
flag, 62
flagpole, 377, 527
flake
(to f off), 189
flame, 56, 62, 188, 249, 277, 351, 414, 503, 527
(of angelic sword), 63
(to), 63
flames, 268, 472
flaming
arrow, 129, 141
flank, 131, 205, 206
(and his), 373
flash
(of eyes), 213, 441
flashing
up, 486
flask, 105, 121, 186, 347, 350
flat
(of the hand or foot), 156
cake, 352
roof, 19
flatcakes, 293
flattering, 153
flattery, 153, 158, 227
(words of - fig.), 114
flax, 433
(and the), 437
(strand of), 408
(the), 452, 535
flea, 376
fled
(and he), 202
(and she), 363
flee, 358
(to), 77, 79, 115, 137, 160, 190, 482
fleece, 25, 32
fleeing, 199
one, 140
fleet, 148
of ships, 80
fleeting, 61
flesh, 32, 42, 46, 326
(and my), 333
(piece of), 313
flexible
containers (for grain), 455
flies
(lord of the), 139
flight, 167, 170, 214
(to put to), 190
fling
(to), 267, 451
flint, 234, 284, 344
float
(to), 176, 466
floats, 193
flock, 157, 193, 227, 459, 485
(one of a), 243
flocks, 193, 459
(and the), 533, 534
(small or little), 284, 506
flood, 96, 145, 234, 284, 317, 507, 516
(to f away), 213, 441
(to), 176, 466
of rain, 213, 441
floods
(to pour forth in), 213, 441
floor, 317
flooring
(clay), 98
flour, 161
(fine), 322
flourishing, 277, 495
flow, 32, 216, 410
(to f forth or down), 106
(to f forth), 127
(to), 32, 76, 106, 123, 142, 176, 184, 216, 218, 291, 466, 487
flower, 181, 182, 489
flowers
(cluster of), 270
flowing, 293
down, 209
skirt, 259
stream, 259
flute, 96
(to play the), 86
flutter
(to), 77, 79, 250
flux, 32
fly, 34
(and it caused to), 44
(to f about), 167, 462
(to f away), 167, 462
(to), 157, 159, 160, 233, 482
net, 205
swiftly, 25
flying
creatures, 167, 462
foam
(to), 213
fodder, 91, 179
foe, 36, 225, 234
(to treat as), 237
fold, 117, 237
(to f double), 147
hands, 131
folding
(of leaves of doors), 92
folds
(and), 361
foliage, 164, 169, 317
follow
(to f at the heel), 175
(to), 232, 490
(you shall), 389, 535
followed
(I had), 461
following, 189, 220, 223, 471, 473
follows
(as), 88, 132, 408
folly, 106, 131, 132, 135, 281, 305, 333
food, 18, 70, 74, 84, 96, 103, 111, 125, 126, 130, 197, 202, 233, 322, 326, 357, 371, 374, 421, 492
(as boiled), 90
(burned at offering), 205
(dainty), 171, 445
(delectable), 168, 408
(for king), 321
(lack of), 254, 485
(richly prepared), 302, 502
(tasty or savory), 168, 408
(to abstain from), 153, 393
(to be gorged with), 255
(to use as), 96, 371
(type of - pastry), 150
stuff, 322
supply, 70
fool, 101, 132, 139
(to be a), 132
(to make a f of someone), 148
foolish, 65, 322, 331, 333
(to be), 60, 101, 131, 132
man, 65
foolishly
(to act), 60
foolishness, 101, 305, 333, 336
fools, 173, 412
(to become), 60
foot, 88, 181, 206, 408, 420
(at the f of), 520
(flat of), 156
(on), 211

(to f it), 206
(to go on), 206, 369
footed, 416
foothold, 165
footman, 211
footprint, 175
footstep, 175
footstool, 68, 254, 358
for, 49, 76, 95
(as), 95, 370
a judge, 169
a moment, 227
it, 55
naught, 56
nothing, 118, 380
the sake of, 81
forbear
(to), 61
forbearance, 200, 395
forbearing, 61
forbid
(to), 70, 75
forbidden, 399
force, 64, 75, 139, 174, 197, 227, 399, 486
(to), 254
forced
labor, 118
service, 121
forcing, 112
ford, 228, 249
forearm, 231
forego
(to), 61
forehead, 154
(bald in the), 295
(to be high in the), 29
foreign, 188, 225, 230
(that which is), 225
(to act as), 225
(to treat as), 225
foreignness, 225
forescore, 306, 489
foreskin, 243, 394
(having), 239
(his), 399
(their), 416, 527
(to count as), 239
(your), 425, 529
forest, 230, 232, 264, 329
forever, 93, 156, 160, 167, 394, 399, 407
(to live), 41, 46
forfeit
(to), 35
forfeited
(be), 440
forge, 202
(smelting), 278, 495
hammer, 125
forgehammer, 287
forget, 256
(and did), 413
(and you), 413
(to), 250, 256, 270
(you shall), 411
(you), 411, 413
forgetful, 256
forgetting, 256
forgive
(ready to), 119
(then I will), 427
(to), 119
forgiven
(and shall be), 393, 542
(you have), 423
forgiving, 119
forgo
(to), 271
forgotten
(I have), 415
(it shall be), 411
fork
(three-pronged - a sacrificial implement), 98
forks, 320, 510
form, 182, 239, 241, 326, 355, 459, 467
(to), 171, 185, 237, 239
(without), 295
formation, 250
formed
(things), 253
former, 165, 186, 345, 518
situation, 162
state, 162
time, 162
formerly, 318, 344, 518
forming, 239
forms, 239
fornication, 134, 314, 426, 459
(to commit), 81
fornications, 314
forsake
(to), 98, 271
forsaken, 141, 428
(of a widow), 141, 428
forsakenness, 109
fort, 150, 178
forth
(and it shall bring), 430
(sending), 282
(then bring), 329
(to bring or come), 204
(to burst), 27
(to come), 196
(to go), 114
fortification, 258
fortified, 392, 393
(and the), 401
(and), 393, 397
city, 258
place, 385
fortify
(to), 235
fortress, 67, 237, 258, 385, 480
(high), 241, 481
(of the earth - fig.), 199
fortune, 20, 264
is come, 23
fortuneteller, 25
fortunetelling
(to practice), 271
forty, 254, 464
forward, 162, 348
(to set), 177
foul
(to be), 71, 360
odor, 165, 242
thing, 139
found
(shall be), 183, 455
(to), 93
foundation, 93, 98, 104, 125, 131, 135, 136, 241, 243, 246, 359, 398, 426
(laying of), 131
(to lay), 93
laying of, 131
Foundation of Beauty, 514
foundations
(secret), 397
founded
(that being), 93
(to be), 139
founder
of a household, 15
fountain, 52, 88, 148, 265, 432
of life, the, 296, 485
four, 227, 229, 385
sides, 226
fourfold, 410, 525
fourteen, 455
fourth, 236
(and the), 391
(the f part), 389
(the), 390
(with the f part), 389
part, 226
fowl, 167, 279, 290, 462
fowler, 297
fox, 291
fragment, 257, 281, 320
fragmented
(something), 228
fragments
(pulverised), 315
fragrance, 198
frail
(to be), 268
frame, 320, 517
framework, 239, 320, 517
frankincense, 106, 113
(the), 112
frantic
(to be f at), 440
fraternity, 37
fraud, 374
free, 287
(place where animals are let), 282
(to be), 166, 284, 376
(to go), 224
(to set), 176, 233

(to), 328
from, 169
run, 293
to work, 239
freeborn
one, 189
freed
(to be), 284
freedom, 286, 436
freely, 118, 380
(to offer), 75
free-will
offering, 80
fresh, 15, 31, 57, 193, 199, 248, 277, 495
(to be grown), 352
(to become), 352
(to grow), 352
green, 15
oil, 243
fresher
new wine, 472
freshly
picked, 233, 492
plucked, 233, 492
freshness, 15, 57
fresh-plucked, 233, 492
fret, 465
(to), 167, 462
friend, 35, 132, 137, 191, 220, 225, 356, 451, 453
(to be a special), 228
confidential, 247
of the king, 228
frighten
(to), 55
frightful, 70, 359
fringe, 353
(for a), 365
frivolity, 153, 326
frogs, 308
from, 109, 415, 416
frond, 127
front, 95
(as far as in f of), 97
(as far as the f of), 76
(be in f of), 97, 102
(from the f of), 76
(in f of oneself), 76
(in f of), 76, 95, 97, 149
(in), 76, 158
(to the), 97
(towards the f of), 97
(what is in f of), 76
frontlets, 177
(as), 338
frost, 145, 244, 245
frothiness, 116
frothy
(to be), 116
fruit, 15, 67, 77, 111, 234, 237, 314
(to bear), 77, 231, 232
Egyptian (watermelon), 48
of a tree, 310, 524
of a tree yielding seed, the, 490, 554
orchard, 234
fruitage, 458
fruitful, 388
(and I will make), 396, 403
(and we shall be), 268
(to be), 231, 232
fruits, 443
(choice), 216
(of the choicest), 390
fruit-stalk
(of date trees), 199, 461
frustrate
(to), 75, 319
fuel, 323
(pile of), 217
fugitive, 147, 199, 214
fulfilled
(to be), 160, 460
full, 90
(to be), 90
end, 74
moon, 100
of marrow, 73
produce, 95
strength, 77
fuller
(to perform the work of a), 101
(to perform the work of), 101
fullness, 42, 90, 95, 159, 317
function, 165, 486
furnace, 156, 202, 278, 312, 380, 495, 506
(cooking), 204
(for smelting), 202
furnish
(to), 180, 234, 428
(you shall), 368
furrow, 34, 40, 317, 496
further, 60
furthermore, 100, 439
fury, 228
future
(as continuing), 93
(in the), 214
futurity, 160, 399
gain, 102, 143, 224
(to), 77, 131, 402
(unjust), 170
acquired by violence, 170
from merchandise, 224
galbanum, 115
gall, 308, 326
gallery, 328
galloping
(of riders), 195
gallows, 169, 484
(the), 171, 485
game, 126
gang
of forced laborers, 121
gap, 276, 515
gape
(to), 267
garden, 72, 76, 397
(enclosed), 264
bed, 231
terrace, 231
Garden of Eden, 177, 540
garden-growth, 234
garden-land, 234
garland, 64
garment, 23, 63, 68, 69, 261, 279, 287, 315, 403, 428, 511
(and the), 38
(and), 32
(bosom of a), 161, 438
(by his), 34
(his), 31, 430
(in a g of), 27
(in his), 431
(in the g of), 27
(linen wrapper), 143
(linen), 429
(outer), 279
(the), 31
(to his), 440
(to rend), 253, 463
(torn pieces of), 277
garments, 428, 462
(and g of), 44
(and his), 50
(change of), 150
(his), 434
(their), 444, 533
of, 36
garner, 73, 237
garrison, 149, 164
gasp, 75
(to), 281, 505
gate, 18, 304, 348, 385
(from the), 359
gatekeeper, 348
gatepost, 83
gates
(within your), 373, 518
of death, 496
gather, 335
(and), 404
(to g in), 156, 459
(to g together), 179
(to g up), 154
(to), 37, 147, 152, 154, 156, 182, 185, 187, 235, 276, 302, 395, 412, 459, 490
(you shall g them), 394
(you shall), 392
gathered
(and he was), 167, 462
(and you shall be), 370, 517
(to be g together), 152
(what is), 156, 459
gathering, 98, 156, 159, 183, 416, 459, 492
(in), 163, 461
place, 61, 355

gaunt, 125
gave
(and she), 457, 542
(you), 457
gaze
(to g at), 279
(to), 180, 248, 370, 489
gazelle, 124, 129, 213, 274, 493
gecko, 166
gem, 396
settings, 305
gems, 209, 438
genealogically
(to reckon), 252
genealogies, 305
genealogy, 252
general, 109
generation, 186, 191
(in his), 365
(third), 368
generations, 452, 454, 455
(according to their), 469, 471, 540
(their), 463, 538
(throughout his), 376
(throughout their), 385, 522
(throughout your), 398, 524
(unto), 369
(your), 385, 522
generator, 15
generous, 85
Genesis. *See Tanakh: 01 Torah:* 01 Genesis
genitals
(male), 263
genius, 402
gentile
people or nation, 29, 36
gentiles, 87, 368
gentleness, 25
get
(to), 154, 166, 170
out!, 214
ghost
(give up the), 97
ghosts, 365
of the dead, 231
giant, 186, 193
giants, 174, 191, 231, 428
Giburah. See Kabbalah:The Ten *Sefirot*:05 *Giburah*
gift, 30, 31, 78, 125, 247, 323, 324, 335, 421, 454, 472
(my), 369
(of a harlot's bribe), 125, 422
(parting), 264
(your), 506, 549
offering, 377
gifts, 322, 465, 498, 511
(as), 471
(my), 500
(of the sacred), 498
(your), 483, 543
Gimel. See Hebrew Alphabet:03 *Gimel*
gird, 103, 188
(and you shall), 363
(to g on), 193
(to g oneself), 193
(to g up), 294
(to), 193
girded, 198, 300
(and you), 366
girder, 173
girding, 377
girdle, 80, 83, 198, 246
girl, 68, 255, 289
(marriageable), 68
girt, 198, 300
give, 28, 29, 187, 439
(and I will), 460
(and to g you), 457, 530
(and to), 452
(and you shall), 457, 459
(he will), 454
(I g it), 460
(I will), 458
(I), 444
(that you shall), 466, 539
(then I should), 456
(to g away), 23
(to g up), 154
(to), 35, 113, 325, 417, 451, 512
(when will), 439
(you shall g it), 469
(you shall), 457
(you will), 456, 541
given
(have g it), 460
(I have g them), 467, 539
(I have), 458
(shall be), 470
(that is g by you), 482, 543
(that which is), 35
gives
(when he), 441
giving
a decision, 172
of rest, 86
glad, 266
(to be), 28, 39, 57, 62, 266
gladden
(to), 30
gladness, 41, 269, 377, 527
(and with), 43
(your), 442, 533
glance
(to), 180, 489
glaring
surface, 137
glass, 311
gleam
(to), 53, 118, 204, 428, 498
gleaming, 118
glean
(to), 148, 154, 302
gleaning, 152, 154
glide, 22
over, 22
glisten
(to), 236
glitter
(to), 127
gloom, 132, 167, 182, 402, 462, 474
gloominess, 136, 316
gloomy, 132
glorified
(will be), 45
glorify
(to), 190, 230
glorious, 51, 56, 188
(to be), 45
gloriousness, 56
glory, 30, 51, 96, 124, 186, 190, 195, 356, 390
(and for), 508
(and the), 57
(essence of), 208, 437
(from your), 94, 345
(have you this), 390
(his), 51
(in my), 56
(my), 62
(your), 65, 336, 457, 530
glow, 137, 140, 321, 388
(fiery), 134
(to), 127, 128
glowing, 119
stone, 277, 503
glue
(to), 139
gnash
(to), 245
gnat, 88, 124, 408
gnats, 88, 408
gnat-storm, 88, 408
gnaw
(to), 310
go, 15, 311, 477
(and when you g over), 407, 525
(and you), 36
(as you g toward), 46
(for I will), 391
(let him), 437
(that I may g in), 39
(to g about), 56, 83, 99, 206, 224
(to g around), 83, 204, 224, 481
(to g in), 22, 52, 148
(to g on from), 138, 453
(to g on), 98, 325
(to g one way or another), 29
(to), 22, 50, 56, 74, 78, 87, 134, 189, 246, 250, 331, 339, 340
(you g about), 493
(you shall g back), 401
(you shall g over), 385
(you shall let him), 437
(you shall make g through), 391
(you shall), 387
away!, 119, 125, 470, 473
down, 23
go!, 214
goad, 224, 320, 472, 510

goat, 96, 243, 486
(female mountain), 135
(female), 96, 123, 352
(male), 281, 319, 351
(the), 40
(wild), 128
(young), 34
goats, 45
(female), 40
goblet, 103, 155, 458
god, 54, 61, 104, 374
(false), 61
false, 54
God, 54
(abode of), 293, 500
(alarms occasioned by), 337, 503
(and G said), 263, 469
(and G saw), 242, 459
(and), 55, 112, 377
(angel of), 178, 520
(anger of), 148, 222, 456, 473
(armor not sanctioned by), 314
(as father of his people), 15
(as Lord), 210
(as), 52
(coming forth of the faithful of), 205
(commandment of), 157
(compassion of), 217, 445
(cutting of), 344
(deliverance by), 87, 408
(dwelling place of), 302, 502
(elect of), 199
(for I am YHVH, your), 201, 433
(forbid that), 102
(furnace of wrath of), 380
(great of), 249
(His love to His people), 29
(house of), 295, 307, 324
(image of), 212, 263, 533, 539
(increase the concealment of), 87
(innocence in sight of), 52
(jealousy of), 164
(king of the hand of), 151
(knowledge of), 97
(lion of), 209
(lioness of), 209
(mighty G of Israel), 364
(my), 60
(of the House of God, the) (*El Betel*), 317
(omniscience of), 67
(on G's order), 197
(one G, one soul), 309
(pearls of), 265
(praise), 105
(refuge of), 264
(son of), 153, 531
(sons of), 164, 405
(spirit of), 240, 459
(throne of – on the Ark), 394
(to blaspheme), 105, 441
(to breathe hard of G's anger), 148, 456
(to glorify), 190
(to), 80
(union with), 46
(voice of), 339
(water of), 233
(word of), 212
(work or action of in history), 137
(works or special possessions of), 104, 374
(wrath of), 225, 488
(your), 382
Names and Descriptors of
12-Letter Name of God
Resheliyiyzadigna'yav (God), 367
22-Letter Name of God, 542, 564
01 *Anaqtam* 1-5, 353, 513
02 *Patsam* 6-9, 350, 511
03 *Paspasim* 10-15, 257, 465
04 *Dionsim* 16-22, 177, 415
Anaqtam Pastam Paspasim Dionsim, 549, 568
33-Letter Name, 504, 548
42-Letter Name of God, 568, 569
13-18 *Kegadikesh*, 271
13-18 *Negadikesh*, 283
1-6 *Abgitatz*, 328, 529
19-24 *Bamratztag*, 413
19-24 *Batratztag*, 397
25-30 *Chaqbatna*, 208
25-30 *Chaqdatna*, 209
25-30 *Haqamamna*, 243
31-36 *Yaglepzeq*, 204
37-39 *Sheqi*, 294
37-39 *Shequ*, 291
37-42 *Yaglepzeq*, 470
40-42 *Tzit*, 325
40-42 *Yaglepzeq*, 319, 325
5-6 *Tatz*, 323, 527
7-12 *Qerashamen*, 425, 536
7-12 *Qerashaten*, 411, 534
Days of the Week
01 *Abgitatz* (Sunday), 328, 529
02 *Qerashaten* (Monday), 411, 534
03 *Negadikesh* (Tuesday), 283
04 *Batratztag* (Wednesday), 397
05 *Chaqbatna* (Thursday), 208
(as according to Trachtenberg), 209
06 *Yaglepzeq* (Friday), 204
07 *Shequitzit* (Saturday), 470
Sefirot
01 *Ab* (*Keter*), 15
02 *Gi* (*Chokmah*), 29
03 *Tatz* (*Binah*), 323, 527
04 *Qerashamen* (*Hesed*), 425, 536
05 *Kegadikesh* (*Giburah*), 271
06 *Bamratztag* (*Tiferet*), 413
07 *Haqamamna* (*Netzach*), 243
08 *Yaglepzeq* (*Hod*), 204
09 *Sheqi* (*Yesod*), 294
10 *Ayeth* (*Malkut*), 319
Abir (The Almighty), 194
Achad Hua Elohim ('He is One God'), 132
Achad Rosh Achdotho Rosh Ichudo Temurahzo Achad (One is His Beginning, etc.), 561, *Also See* God:Names and Descriptors of: *Ararita*
Achath Ruach Elohim Chayyim (One is the Spirit of the Living God), 430, 531
Adon Awlum (Lord of the World), 188, 531
Adonai (Lord), 83
Adonai HaAretz (Lord of the Earth), 273, 514
Agla, 53, *Also See* God:Names and Descriptors of: *Ateh Gibor le-Olam Adonai*
Aha (Initials of *Adonai HaAretz*), 20, *Also See* God:Names and Descriptors of: *Adonai HaAretz*
Ahadonhai (Combination of YHVH and *Adonai*), 111
'ahuw-ah (secret name from Creation), 33
Anoki YHVH *Eloheka* ('I am the Lord thy God'), 175, 378
Ararita, 445, *Also See* God:Names and Descriptors of: *Achad Rosh Achdotho Rosh Ichudo Temurahzo Achad*
Ateh Gibor le-Olam Adonai (Thou art mighty forever, O Lord), 457, 536, *Also See* God: Name of: *Agla*
Ba'ali (my Lord), 133
Eheieh ('I Am'), 39
Eheieh Asher Eheieh ('I Am What I Am'), 341
Eheieh Yah YHVH *Elohim*, 161, 400
Ehyahweh (Combination of *Eheieh* and YHVH), 51

El (God), 50
(and), 55
El Elyon (Most High God), 183, 455
El Melek Ne'eman (The Lord and faithful king), 221, 417
El Qanna (A Jealous God), 178
El Shaddai (God Almighty), 264
Number of Occurences of, 67
'elifuw Shel 'olam (Master of the Universe), 354, 513
Eloah (God), 54, 61
Elohi Abraham (The God of Abraham), 236, 457
Elohi Abraham Elohi Itzchaq ve-Elohi Yaaqob (The God of Abraham, the God of Isaac, and the God of Jacob), 432, 531
Elohi HaIbrim (God of the Hebrews), 278, 477
Elohi Itzchaq (The God of Isaac), 216
Elohi Yaaqob (The God of Jacob), 203
Elohikam (Your God), 127, 382
Elohim (God), 104, 374
full spelling of, 239
number of occurences of, 561
Elohim Gibor (Almighty God), 237, 457
initials of, 17
Elohim Tzabaoth (God of Hosts), 351, 512
Elokim, 178, 416
Elyon (Most High God), 172, 446
Haqabah, 133, *Also See* God:Names and Descriptors of: *HaQadosh Barukh Hu*
HaQadosh Barukh Hu ('The Holy One, Blessed Be He'), 379, 511
HaShem (The Name), 264, 469
Hu' (He), 28
'illay (Most High), 132
Kuzu Bemuksuk Kuzu (*Aiq Bekar* of *Adonai Elohainu Adonai*), 195
Matz Patz, 239, *Also See* God:Names and Descriptors of: YHVH
Na, 70
Shaddai (Almighty), 249
Shaddai El Chai (Almighty Living God), 273
Shem HaMeforash, 483, 543
01 *Vehu*, 34
02 *Yeli*, 69
03 *Sit*, 98
04 *Alem*, 156, 394
05 *Mahash*, 264
06 *Lelah*, 83
07 *Aka*, 39
08 *Kahath*, 300
09 *Hezi*, 40
10 *Elad*, 53
11 *Lav*, 56
12 *Hehau*, 98
13 *Yezel*, 66
14 *Mebah*, 66
15 *Hari*, 196
16 *Haqem*, 159, 398
17 *Lau*, 56
18 *Keliy*, 78
19 *Levo*, 62
20 *Pahel*, 136
21 *Nelakh*, 121, 350
22 *Yeyaya*, 49
23 *Melah*, 94
24 *Chaho*, 37
25 *Nethah*, 312
26 *Haa*, 20
27 *Yereth*, 358
28 *Shaah*, 244
29 *Riyi*, 200
30 *Aum*, 70, 357, 359
31 *Lekab*, 72
32 *Vesher*, 328
33 *Yecho*, 43
34 *Lehach*, 62
35 *Keveq*, 144
36 *Menadh*, 114
37 *Ani*, 80
38 *Cham*, 138, 387
39 *Reha*, 228
40 *Yeyaz*, 45
41 *Hehah*, 32
42 *Mik*, 88, 343
43 *Vaval*, 61
44 *Yelah*, 64
45 *Sael*, 111
46 *Eri*, 230
47 *Ashel*, 288
48 *Miah*, 74
49 *Vaho*, 34
50 *Dani*, 82
51 *Hachash*, 249
52 *Amem*, 163, 402
53 *Nena*, 123
54 *Nith*, 313
55 *Mabeh*, 66
56 *Poi*, 117
57 *Nemem*, 147, 391
58 *Yeyal*, 69
59 *Harach*, 195
60 *Metzer*, 257
61 *Vameb*, 66
62 *Yehah*, 38
63 *Anu*, 144
64 *Mechi*, 77
65 *Dameb*, 65
66 *Menaq*, 180
67 *Aya*, 100
68 *Chebo*, 33
69 *Raah*, 187
70 *Yebem*, 71, 361
71 *Hayeya*, 43
72 *Mum*, 105, 375
Biblical Quote of source, 570
number of names in, 92
sum of the names of, 570
Shem Yehoshuah (The name Yehoshuah), 383, 521
Tzedkosaynuw (our righteousness), 383
Tzevakot (Hosts), 354
Yah
(daughter of), 297
Yah Adonai (Lord God), 98
Yeya, 38
YHVH (The Tetragrammaton), 45
(against), 46
(and), 51
(by), 46
(in), 46
(with my life I will praise), 145
armor not sanctioned by, 312
breath of (as brimstone), 392
by 'filling', 64, 82, 91
by 'filling,' and spelled out, 71
by 'preceding numbers addition', 179
by small numbers, 41
count of gematria + the number of letters in the Name, 49
for I am Y, your God, 201, 433
holy to, 314
name by *Temurah - Kuzu*, 507
number of occurences of, 569, 570
number of occurences of with grammatical additions, 569
number of occurences of without grammatical additions, 569
permutation by *Aiq Bekar*, 170, 221, 359, 395, 403, 438, 500, 513, 514, 523, 546, 550
permutation by *Temurah - Kuzu*, 58
rebellion against, 211

reconciling of Israel and, 394
the masculine consonants spelled out, 62
the three consonants spelled out, 62
throne room of, 187, 197
total plus *tefillah*, 341
YHVH *Achad* (YHVH is One), 57
YHVH *Eloah va-Daath* (Lord God of Knowledge), 343
YHVH *Elohim* (The Lord God), 133, 385
YHVH *Ish Milchamah* ('The Lord is a man of war'), 313
YHVH *Ish Milchamah* YHVH *Shemo* (The Lord is a Man of War, YHVH is His Name), 452
YHVH *Ra'ah* ('The Lord My Shepherd'), 244
YHVH *Rafak* ('God Thy Healer'), 255
YHVH *Raphak* ('God Thy Healer'), 441
YHVH *Shammah* ('Adonai is there'), 277
YHVH *Shemo* ('YHVH is His Name'), 278
YHVH *Tzabaoth* (Lord of Hosts), 336
YHVH *Tzabaoth HaMessiach* (God of hosts, the messiah, 465
of winter, 256, 499
one slain by (Er), 225
quotes about
by signs troubles the mind the Almighty, 494
I am thankful before You, Living and Eternal King, 347, 560
references to
I will be like the One on High, 212, 466
rejection of Israel represented by Hosea's daughter, Lo-Ruhamah, 231
Shem HaMeforash
Biblical Quote of source, 571
wisdom of, 200, 395
goddess, 54, 94, 104, 374
godless, 153, 458
godlessness, 153, 158, 458
godlike
one, 104, 374
god-like
one, 50
godly, 101
gods, 104, 374
(sons of the), 161, 400
(their), 112
(worthless), 85
goes
(when he), 27
(when), 48
Goetic Demons
01 *Bael*, 52
A.S. spelling, 124
02 *Agares*, 186
03 *Vassago*, 250
04 *Gamigin*, 136, 426
A.S. spelling, 150, 433
05 *Marbas*, 211
06 *Valefor*, 251
A.S. spelling, 250
07 *Amon*, 117, 419
08 *Barbatos*, 334
09 *Paimon*, 180, 453
A.S. spelling, 180, 452
demon king attendant upon (*Abalim*), 102, 373
demon king attendant upon (*Labal*), 81
10 *Buer*, 190
11 *Gusion*, 151, 433
12 *Sitri*, 337
A.S. spelling, 351, 354
13 *Beleth*, 304
14 *Leraikha*, 221, 416
A.S. spelling, 220, 415
15 *Eligos*, 266
16 *Zepar*, 233
A.S. spelling, 232
17 *Botis*, 256
18 *Bathin*, 314, 507
19 *Sallos*, 371
A.S. spelling, 370
20 *Purson*, 373, 526
A.S. spelling, 370, 526
21 *Marax*, 258, 512
A.S. spelling, 260, 512
22 *Ipos*, 287
23 *Aim*, 70, 359
A.S. spelling, 74
24 *Naberius*, 216
25 *Glasya Labolas*, 170
26 *Bime'*, 71, 360
27 *Ronove*, 227
A.S. spelling, 224
28 *Beriyth*, 360
29 *Ashtaroth*, 528
30 *Forneus*, 371
A.S. spelling, 369
31 *Foras*, 352
A.S. spelling, 351
32 *Asmodai*, 141
A.S. spelling, 273
variant spelling, 344
33 *Gaap*, 165, 462
34 *Furfur*, 349
35 *Marchosias*, 344
36 *Stolas*, 377
A.S. spelling, 180
Crowley's spelling, 381
37 *Phenex*, 141, 496
A.S. spelling, 140, 496
38 *Halphas*, 136, 452
39 *Malphas*, 163, 461
40 *Raum*, 213, 441
A.S. spelling, 247, 461
41 *Focalor*, 263
42 *Vepar*, 232
A.S. spelling, 232
43 *Sabnock*, 280, 458
Crowley's spelling, 282, 459
44 *Shax*, 285, 517
45 *Vine'*, 85
46 *Bifrons*, 238
A.S. spelling, 263, 488
47 *Uvall*, 56
48 *Haagenti*, 337
49 *Crocell*, 228
50 *Furcas*, 244, 434
Crowley's enumeration, 109
Crowley's spelling, 128, 352
51 *Balam*, 157, 396
A.S. spelling, 157, 396
52 *Alloces*, 75, 339
53 *Camio*, 100, 412
54 *Murmus*, 232, 455
A.S. spelling, 266, 471
55 *Orobas*, 196
A.S. spelling, 258
56 *Gamori*, 214
57 *Voso*, 248
58 *Avnas*, 75, 399
59 *Oriax*, 244, 508
60 *Naphula*, 172
A.S. spelling, 169
61 *Zagan*, 80, 404
A.S. spelling, 78, 402
62 *Valu*, 55
A.S. spelling, 61
63 *Andras*, 217
A.S. spelling, 345
64 *Haures*, 194
as *Flauros* (alternate name) A.S. spelling, 281
65 *Andrealphus*, 275, 503
66 *Kimaris*, 228
A.S. spelling, 261
67 *Amdukias*, 90, 344
68 *Belial*, 92, 157
69 *Decarbia*, 206
A.S. spelling, 208
70 *Seere*, 326
71 *Dantalion*, 321
A.S. spelling, 344, 517
72 *Andromalius*, 258
number of, 92
going, 87, 115, 325, 349
(act or place of going out or forth), 153
(its g out), 473
(place of g out from), 157
forth, 296, 485

in, 155
out, 324
round, 98
gold, 27, 31, 235, 313, 495
(and in), 40
(and), 38
(arabic), 248
(armlets of), 92
(choice), 346, 533
(exactness of), 75
(fine), 225
(good), 50
(in poetic sense), 242, 508
(in), 33
(pure), 313, 495
(red-orange from Parvaim), 266, 471
(refined or pure), 106
(refined), 230, 476
(the), 36
and silver, 177, 467
dust, 373
of (the), 31
of Ophir, 248
golden, 27, 38
city, 75
image, 175, 413
ornament, 92
Golden Dawn
Hebrew name of (*Chevrah Zerach Boqer Aur*), 478
goldsmiths, 281
golem, 92, 97, 369, 371
gone
(to be), 28
good, 27, 35, 36, 40
(and the), 46
(and was), 56
(and), 41
(as), 56
(do), 44
(for), 36
(I do), 51
(is), 45
(shall do), 60
(that it was), 66
(the), 39, 45
(to be), 28, 34, 39, 91
(to do), 65
(what is), 40
(you do), 304
day, 92, 369
for nothing, 90
luck, 114
news, 328, 331
pleasure, 386
thing, 35
things, 35
will with no limit, 310, 552
goodliness, 351
goodly, 34
goodness, 35, 91, 351
(my), 45
(the), 45
(to do), 65
goods, 75, 151, 336, 399, 433
gopher, 231
wood, 231
gore
(to), 80
(will), 39
gorged
(to be g with food), 255
gorgeous
attire, 144
garment, 140
stuff, 140
gorgeously, 144
gorget, 108, 415
goring
(apt or addicted to), 80
got, 335
gourd, 225, 475
gourds, 218
gourd-shaped
carved wood, 215
govern
(to), 189, 246
government, 342
governor, 114, 134, 284, 426, 497
grace, 76, 86, 400, 407
(act of), 319
gracious, 134, 315, 426
(to be), 129, 315, 423
graduation, 423
grain, 75, 96, 185, 237, 280, 326, 371, 399
(a row of fallen), 253
(bundles of), 323
(ear of), 259, 323
(flexible containers for), 455
(of sand), 135
(parched), 156
(roasted), 156
(standing), 159
of seed, 234
granary, 73, 130, 217, 233
grandson, 71, 396
grape, 142
(unripe), 222
blossom, 242
bud, 242
grapes, 142
(choice), 355
(cluster of), 270
(sour), 222
(to press), 199
(unripe or sour), 222
grapple
(to), 124
grasp, 33
(to g with a twisting motion), 330
(to), 103, 204, 314, 330, 479, 498
grasped, 139
grass, 243, 245, 276, 278, 290
(dry), 357
(in the reed), 34
(mown), 25
(new), 243
(put forth), 398
grasshopper, 27, 30
(the), 35
grating, 222
grave, 241, 249, 258, 401
(gone to the g in evil), 361
(her), 400
(his), 401
of, 396
gravel, 180, 489
graven, 357, 362
image, 178
graver, 329
graving
tool, 198
graze
(to), 228
great, 45, 53, 55, 60, 61, 62, 81, 185, 195, 205, 290
(of God), 249
(to be), 186
(to become), 55, 186
(to do g things), 55
dragon, 311
fish, 68
man, 247
number, 378
one, 195
owl, 308, 514
toe, 75, 399
tooth, 341
tree, 105, 414
while, 201
greater, 185
(I will be), 56
light, the, 236
greater, the, 61
greatness, 55, 66, 185, 189, 378
(by the), 57
greave, 158
greedily
(to swallow), 94, 130, 370
greedy
(to be), 27, 170
green, 57, 247
(of growing), 31
(pale), 358
(to grow), 243, 277, 495
fig, 103
grass, 245
herb, 243, 389
plants, 247, 251, 278
shoots, 15
thing, 251
greenery, 15
greening, 15
greenish, 358, 492
greenish-yellow, 358
greenness, 247
greens, 251
greived
(to be), 183, 491

grevious
(to be), 45
grey
(to be), 249
hair, 251
griddle, 310
grief, 87, 160, 162, 212, 296, 408, 437
(cry of), 34
(expression of), 82
(place of), 188
(to show), 79
grieve
(to cause), 20, 35
(to), 20, 22, 35, 171
grieved
(to be), 54, 62, 134, 136, 162, 168, 285, 385
(to become), 62
grieving, 315
grievous, 50
griffon-vulture, 343
grind
(to), 85, 407
grinding
(handmills for), 195
mill, 92, 410
grits, 326
groan, 167
(in pain or grief), 75
(to), 116, 163, 166, 379
groaning, 82, 121, 166, 167
groats, 326
groove, 164
grope, 387
(to), 355, 372
gropes, 376
gross
(to be), 96, 284
ground, 68, 225, 267, 272
(dry), 196, 251
(parched), 167, 180, 326, 441, 453
(plowing), 171
(standing), 139, 165
(thirsty), 180, 453
(tillable or untilled or fallow), 220
group, 155
(member of a), 71, 396
grouse, 334
grow
(and let them), 47
(let), 55
(to g up), 23, 138, 154, 453
(to), 55, 243, 246
growing
up, 55
growl
(to), 29, 68, 116, 253, 379
growling, 29, 116, 121, 379
grown
(to be g fresh), 352
up, 55
growth, 154
from spilled kernels, 168
grudge
(shall bear), 358
grumble
(to), 105, 414
guard, 130, 153, 214, 282, 342, 350, 353, 486
(and they), 344
(to keep), 220
(to), 262, 340
post, 350
you, 347, 499
guardian, 272
guardroom, 289
guardsman, 37
guardsmen, 37
guidance, 308
guide
(to), 77, 82, 104
guile, 287, 498
guilt, 262, 265, 348, 349, 468
(burdened with), 195
(to incur), 35
of iniquity, 144, 430
guiltiness, 262, 265, 468
(to bring), 428
guilty, 195, 262, 468
(his being), 419
(to be), 33, 262, 468
(to make), 33
gull, 284, 506
gulp
(to), 94, 370
gum, 155, 458
(tragacanth), 317
resin, 63
gums, 46, 329
gush
(to g forth), 142
(to), 32
ha!, 39
Habakkuk. *See Tanakh: 02 Neviim:* 17 Habakkuk
habitation, 64, 75, 80, 172, 174, 358, 446
habitations
(according to their), 444, 533
(your), 445, 447, 533, 534
had
(and she), 60
haft, 158
Haggai. *See Tanakh: 02 Neviim:* 19 Haggai
haggle
(to), 440
haggler, 378, 527
hail, 250, 265
(to), 187
hailstone, 101, 439
hair, 57, 267, 348
(as yellow), 118
(grey), 251
(lock of), 195, 356
(locks of), 185
(long), 267
(single), 349
(well-dressed or well-set), 308
hairdo
(artistry of), 308
hairs
(grey), 404
(my grey), 410
hairy, 351, 484
crown, 189
one, 351
ones, 368, 516
half, 130, 134, 327, 343
(of their), 368, 516
of spoils, 158
half-hearted, 192, 477
hall, 270
hallelujah, 105
hallow
(and you shall), 456, 536
hallowed
(and I will be), 461
(I), 448
(to be), 290
halter, 247, 483
hamlet, 236
hammer, 125, 160, 191, 287, 320, 341, 495
(forge), 125
(to), 94, 251, 261, 370
hammered, 281
work, 308
hamstring
(to), 276
hand, 31, 38, 49, 120, 330, 448
(and his), 44
(and in his), 40
(and the), 40, 43
(and you shall), 455
(and), 38
(by or into the), 33
(by the h of), 33
(by), 33
(closed), 204, 498
(flat of), 156
(her), 37
(his), 38, 40
(hollow of), 288
(hollow or flat of), 120, 448
(in her), 39
(in your), 54, 333
(into my), 44
(into the), 33
(is the ?), 36
(my), 43
(out of), 189
(palm of), 120, 156, 448
(the), 36
(them who took in), 436
(to direct out with the), 31
(to feel with the), 355
(to take the right), 111, 416
(to use the right), 111, 416
(width of), 118

(your), 53, 57, 332
breadth, 118
mill, 92, 410
handclapping, 209
hand-drum, 320, 517
handed
(and you shall be h over), 466, 539
forward, 348
handful, 204, 288, 498
(to take a), 204, 498
handfuls, 154, 434
handicapped
(to be), 154
handle, 432
(to), 234, 310, 428
handmaid, 65
(her), 436
(his), 437
of, 435
handmaids
(his), 440
(the), 438
handmills
for grinding, 195
hands, 243
(and his), 54
(clasping of the), 131
(folding), 131
(her), 47
(his), 48, 51
(my), 43
(to clap the), 68
(to cross), 267
(to strike or clap), 68
(with her), 50
of (and the), 48
handsome, 115
(to be), 115
hang
(shall), 384
(to h down), 82
(to), 82, 305
hanging, 184
work, 214
hapless, 77
happen
(to), 38
happening, 165, 264
happiness, 325
(house of), 473
happy, 331
(to be), 35
harass, 392
them, 412, 526
hard, 290
(to be), 45, 148, 290, 479
pebble, 234
harden
(to), 135, 178, 227, 416
hardened
(and he), 61, 149
(then he), 55
(to be), 351, 527
hardly, 51
hardness, 136
hardship, 171, 198, 305, 318, 461
hare, 378
(the), 380
harem, 246
harlot, 292
(price of), 312
(to be a), 81
(to play the), 81
harlotry, 314, 424, 459
harm, 70, 137, 427
(his), 386
harmony, 307, 490
harrow, 245, 508
(to), 246
harsh, 205, 337
(to be), 177, 467
harshness, 208, 239, 432
hart, 60
(young), 267
harvest, 156, 163, 288, 459, 461
(and you), 452, 535
(and), 291
(do not), 450
(to remain in h time), 233, 491
(to spend h time), 233, 491
(to), 179, 285
time, 233, 492
harvesting, 288
haste, 72, 214
(in), 163, 439
(to make), 249, 251
(to), 117, 249, 251, 470
hasten
(and you shall), 392, 523
(to h to), 318
(to), 55, 111, 112, 115, 212, 279, 444, 468
hastened
(and she), 377
(you), 374
hastening, 212
hastily, 72
hasty
vow, 72
hate, 270
(in), 421
(shall), 421
(to), 268
hated, 273
(and he), 274, 476
(because he), 439
(the h one at the door), 382, 534
(you have), 436, 532
one, 158, 459
hateful
(to be), 268
hating, 36, 270
hatred, 35, 270
haughtily, 212
haughtiness, 32, 213, 297, 441
haughty, 25, 33, 87, 202, 408
haunt, 245
have
(I), 59
haven, 80
having
pleasure in, 177, 488
hawk, 33, 155, 187, 481
he, 27, 28
(and), 35
head, 189, 315, 325, 326, 331
(above his), 482
(around his), 482
(bald in the), 402
(baldness of), 401
(for my), 444
(place at the), 342, 468
(to put one's h between one's knees (like Elijah), 189
(under his), 482
back of, 180, 470
of a household, 15
of the house, 473
of wheat, 135
place, 342
headbands, 354
headdress, 204, 230, 481
head-gear, 140
headlong
(to push), 199
heal
(to), 231
healing, 29, 49, 205, 253, 391, 392
(of new flesh), 328
health, 29, 253
(to be restored to), 41, 46
healthful
(to make), 231
healthy, 364
(to be), 96, 371
heap, 52, 73, 140, 213, 216, 236, 247, 251, 461
(of stones), 214
(the), 57
(to h up), 191, 236, 247, 461
of dung, 81
of ruins, 99, 101
of stones, 233
heaped
(to be h up), 247, 461
hear
(and I will h it), 452
(and I will), 450
(and let), 446
(and), 446
(causing to), 449
(to), 76, 289, 294, 400
(you shall), 460, 542
(you would), 456, 536
heard, 444
(and you h it), 446
(I have h you), 454, 529
(I have), 449
(I), 449
(they), 304

(thing), 310
you have, 444
hearing, 294
hearken
(will), 444, 447
(you shall), 447
(you will), 444
(you would), 456, 536
(you), 460, 542
hearkened
(I have), 449
you have, 444
heart, 51, 53, 56
(and he hardened his), 333
(and in the), 58
(in his), 58, 61
(my), 62
(the), 52, 57
(to his), 57, 59
(to), 53
(with all your), 159, 398
that understands knowledge, 357, 524
hearth, 162, 166, 210, 266
he-ass, 217, 230
heat, 23, 67, 72, 140, 191, 222, 241, 321, 357, 388, 473
(burning or scorching), 326
(burning), 182
(extreme), 297
(of anger), 198
(raging), 182
of the sun, 72
heaven, 277, 285, 288, 481, 499
(night mist of), 57
(the), 286, 482
heavenly
man, 170, 409
Heavenly Mansions
01 *Hekel Qadesh Qadeshim* (Supernals), 476, 541
02 *Hekel Ahbah* (*Hesed*), 96
03 *Hekel Zakoth* (*Giburah*), 324
04 *Hekel Ratzon* (*Tiferet*), 294, 500
05 *Hekel Etzem Shamaim* (*Netzach*) – from Ex. 24 10, 378, 552
06 *Hekel Gonah* (*Hod*), 146
07 *Hekel Lebanath HaSafir* (*Yesod* and *Malkut*) – from Ex.24 10, 468
heavens
(masters of the), 328, 501
(vault of the), 34
Heavens (Crowley)
01 *Arabhoth* (Supernals), 387
02 *Makhon* (*Hesed*), 136, 426
03 *Maon* (*Giburah*), 172, 446
04 *Zebuwl* (*Tiferet*), 64
05 *Shechaqim* (*Netzach*), 313, 494
06 *Raqia* (*Hod*), 281
07 *Tebel Vilon Shamaim* (*Yesod* and *Malkut*), 338, 551
07 *Vilon* (*Yesod* and *Malkut*), 124, 421
Heavens (*Zohar*)
01 *Shekinah* (*Keter*), 282
02 *Metatron* (*Chokmah*), 249, 483
03 *Avir* (*Binah*), 197
04 *Arabhoth* (*Hesed*), 387
05 *Makhon* (*Giburah*), 136, 426
06 *Maon* (*Tiferet*), 172, 446
07 *Zebuwl* (*Netzach*), 64
08 *Shechaqim* (*Hod*), 313, 494
09 *Raqia* (*Yesod*), 281
10 *Vilon* (*Malkut*), 124, 421
heaviness, 29, 45, 296, 301, 316, 318, 477
heavy, 45
(and), 51
(to be), 45
debts, 121
showers, 195
Hebrew, 231
(the H women), 390, 392
Hebrew Alphabet
01 *Alef*, 13, 132, 451, 489
(as 11th Path), 27, 85
(as part of 'masculine unity'), 35
as Mother Letter, 15
as Tarot card The Fool, 13
02 *Bet*, 14, 295
(as 12th Path), 28, 97
as Tarot card The Magician, 13
03 *Gimel*, 15, 92
(as 13th Path), 30, 112
as Tarot card The High Priestess, 14
04 *Dalet*, 17, 304
(as 14th Path), 31, 127
as Tarot card The Empress, 15
05 *Heh*, 18, 25
(as 15th Path), 32, 140
as Tarot card The Emperor, 17
06 *Vav*, 19, 28
(as 16th Path), 33, 153
(as part of 'masculine unity'), 35
as Tarot card The Hierophant, 18
07 *Zayin*, 20, 85, 407
(as 17th Path), 35, 165
as Tarot card The Lovers, 19
08 *Chet*, 22, 297
(as 18th Path), 36, 175
as Tarot card The Chariot, 20
09 *Teth*, 23, 298
(as 19th Path), 37, 181
as Tarot card Strength, 22
10 *Yod*, 25, 31, 38
(as 20th Path), 38, 192
(as part of 'masculine unity'), 35
as Tarot card The Hermit, 23
11 *Kaf*, 38, 120, 324, 448
(as 21st Path), 39, 205
as Tarot card The Wheel of Fortune, 25
12 *Lamed*, 49, 93
(as 22nd Path), 40, 216
as Tarot card Justice, 27
13 *Lamed*
notarikon for, 357
13 *Mem*, 59, 109, 354, 376
(as 23rd Path), 42, 228
as final letter in middle of word (*Lemarbah*), 453
as Mother Letter, 15
as Tarot card The Hanged Man, 28
14 *Nun*, 69, 128, 394, 423
(as 24th Path), 43, 240
as Tarot card Death, 30
15 *Samekh*, 79, 140, 354
(as 25th Path), 44, 255
as Tarot card Temperance, 31
16 *Ayin*, 88, 148, 432
(as 26th Path), 45, 268
as Tarot card The Devil, 32
17 *Peh*, 99, 104, 438
(as 27th Path), 46, 280
as Tarot card The Tower, 33
18 *Tzaddi*, 109, 126, 467
(as 28th Path), 47, 292
as Tarot card The Star, 35
19 *Qof*, 121, 180, 470
(as 29th Path), 48, 305
as Tarot card The Moon, 36
20 *Resh*, 184, 331
(as 30th Path), 49, 315
as Tarot card The Sun, 37
21 *Shin*, 240, 273, 493
(as 31st Path), 50, 324
as Mother Letter, 15
as Tarot Card Judgement, 38
22 *Tau*, 288
(alternate spelling of), 292
(as 32nd Path), 51, 337
as Tarot card The Universe, 39
first and last letters of, 289
Hebrew name for (*Alef Bet*), 335, 522
sum of all, 541
Hebrew Language, 304
accusative case
(word used to mark -ty), 293
Conjunction
-w (and...), 19
Definite Article
-h (the), 18
Direct Object
(word used to indicate -t)), 289
(word used to mark -ty), 293
hnt) – you (f. pl.), 312
Lamow (poetic form of inseparable preposition), 95
Participles
yty) (denotes existence), 299

Personal Pronouns
)nxn) (we – 1st person plural), 131
)wh (he – m. sing.), 28
)yh (she – f. sing.), 33
ht) (thou, you – f. sing.), 289
ht) (you – m. sing.), 291
Mh (they – m. pl.), 64, 356
Mt) (you – m. pl.), 306, 490
Nh (they – f. pl.), 74, 398
wnxn) (we – pl.), 135
yn) (I), 80, 100
Prepositions
Inseparable
-b (in, with), 14
-k (as, like), 38
-l (to, for), 49
-m (from), 59
Separable
l((upon, over), 121
l) (to), 50
M((with (beings)), 384
-M((with (beings)), 132
-Nm (from), 109, 416
txt (under, instead of), 442
ylb (without), 61
–teen
(in combination with other numbers), 348
Hebrewess, 231
hebrews, 254
Hebrews, 464
hedge, 149, 193, 277
(to h up or about), 253, 438
(to), 121, 350
hedgehog, 181
heed
(and take h of yourselves), 497, 546
(to give), 340
(to), 289
heedless
(to be), 178
heel, 175
(take by the), 175
(to follow at the), 175
he-goat, 281, 319, 351, 403
he-goats, 368, 516
(and), 426, 530
(the), 367, 426, 516, 530
Heh. See Hebrew Alphabet:05 *Heh*
heifer, 130, 232
height, 25, 33, 64, 66, 102, 121, 151, 152, 164, 212, 213, 232, 337, 439, 441, 455, 457
(secure), 264
heighty, 375
heir, 185, 306
he-lamb, 199
hell, 134, 258, 383, 385
helmet, 119, 127, 216
help, 60, 229, 231
(cry for), 221, 282, 447
(my), 308
(needing), 87, 408
(their cry for), 534
(to call for), 177
(to come to), 279
(to cry for), 221
(to shout for), 279
(to), 227, 228, 318
(your), 238, 431
hemlock, 166
hemorrhoid, 178
hemorrhoids, 198
henna
plant, 239
heptad, 19, 20, 280
heptagon, 20
her
(and lay hold on), 436
(and to), 60
(to give), 452
(to meet), 414
(to), 54
(with), 20
herald, 206
(to), 203
herb, 278
(bitter), 306
(green), 389
herbage, 245, 247, 276, 278
herbs, 247
herd, 227, 241
herdsman, 241, 245
here, 28, 30, 44, 78, 94, 104, 292, 370
(and), 50
(from), 104
heretofore, 318
heritage, 114
hermit, 352
hero, 205
heron, 152
herself
(and she thrust), 338, 531
Hesed. See Kabbalah:The Ten *Sefirot*:04 *Hesed*
hesitate
(to), 189
hew
(to h in pieces), 306, 514
(to h into shape), 174
(to h off), 95
(to), 95, 120, 174, 202
hewed, 298
hewer
(to), 120
hewing, 155
hewn
(of stones), 155
beams, 367
stone, 298
hexagon, 19
hexagram, 129, 423
hid
(and he), 386
(shall I be), 381
(then she h him), 370
hidden, 167, 402
(and those that are), 428, 530
(to be h from view), 162, 461
(to be), 156, 256, 394, 442
light, 274
recesses, 40
stores, 162, 438
thing, 159, 204, 342, 437, 463
treasure, 159, 162, 220, 437, 438, 471
hide, 228, 382
(and h yourself), 481
(and I will), 503
(I will), 385, 386
(one who causes people to), 394
(to h oneself), 32
(to), 27, 32, 51, 104, 119, 156, 200, 303, 381, 394, 420, 461, 496
hiding, 39, 95, 394, 411
(act of), 394
place, 40, 70, 95, 185, 381, 394, 411
high, 25, 32, 172, 446
(to be inaccessibly), 243
(to be), 25, 190, 213, 243, 441
place, 66, 212, 264, 285
places, 322, 498
high places
(their), 327
High Priest, 142, 429
(bell on robe of), 209, 465
(blessing of the), 419, 528
(division of for service), 168
(Eleazar), 245
breastplate of (*Chosen*), 271, 492
Ephod, 108, 111
girdle or band of, 246
stones
(number of letters on), 92
01 *Odem* (Sardius), 64, 356
02 *Pitdah* (topaz), 119
03 *Bareqath* (carbuncle), 396
04 *Nofek* (emerald), 162, 368
05 *Sappiyr* (sapphire), 267
06 *Yahalom* (pearl), 104, 374
07 *Leshem* (amber or jacinth), 276, 476
08 *Shebuw* (agate), 246
09 *Achlamah* (amethyst), 103
10 *Tarshish* (beryl), 519
11 *Shoham* (malachite), 264, 469
12 *Yashefeh* (jasper), 286
item used for divination (Thummim), 323, 499
item used for divination (Urim), 218, 447

place where he sprinkled on the Day of Atonement - Mercy Seat, 394
skirt of robe of (*Shuwl*), 260
turban of, 381
waist band of, 80
High Priestess, 336
higher, 25, 33
part, 155
highest, 132, 172, 446
branch, 412
highway, 151, 172
hill, 98, 178, 187, 290
country, 187, 290
hilly, 175
hilt
of sword, 158
him, 22
(and he brought), 58
(and sanctify), 446
(and to), 31
(and unto), 61
(from), 309
(let h go), 278
(to meet), 414
(to minister to), 478
(to), 55
(under), 450
(upon), 20, 22
himself
(he has shown), 360
hind, 64, 306
hinder, 189, 362
(and for the h part), 386
(for the h part), 402, 524
(in the h part), 388, 522
(to), 75, 169
part, 175
hindmost chamber, 187, 197
hindrance, 291
hinge, 240
hinges, 320
hip, 238, 324, 506
joint, 238, 506
hips, 322, 511
hire, 219, 312, 335
(to), 335
hired
(I h you), 481, 537
his
offering, 327
hiss
(to), 355
hissing, 356, 360
hit
(thing), 182
(to), 94
hither, 78, 94, 104, 370
hitherto, 143, 429
ho!, 39
hoarded
(to be), 138, 427
hoarfrost, 244
hoary
(to be), 249
Hod. See Kabbalah:The Ten *Sefirot*:08 *Hod*
hoe, 245, 249, 508
(to), 227
hog, 202
hold
(and I took), 434
(take), 33
(to h back), 75, 169, 178, 256, 442
(to h in), 75, 91, 363, 369
(to h out), 123, 252
(to), 178, 314, 479
hole, 102, 164, 195, 250, 270, 322, 341, 465
(light), 216
holiday, 86
making, 86
holiness, 290, 294
(in), 291
hollow, 138, 171, 195, 356, 463, 465
(to h out), 73
hand, 288
of a rock, 120, 448
of the hand, 154, 434
way, 308
holocaust, 109, 127
holy, 294, 296
(it is holy, most), 461, 537
(the), 296
Ark, 382
ark (of the covenant), 529
living creatures, 452
one, 101, 294
place, 308
sign of the covenant, 537
spirit, 366
Holy Incense
Chelbenah (Galbanum - ingredient), 115
Levanah (Frankincense - ingredient), 106, 113
Nataf (stacte - ingredient), 155, 458
Sam (Spice -ingredient), 121, 381
Shecheleth (Onycha - ingredient), 415
(and), 417
Holy of Holies, 187, 197
Holy Place
(from the), 308
homage
(to do), 86
home, 295
homeborn, 207
honest, 87, 408
honey, 244, 337
(flowing), 337
from the comb, 337
honeycomb, 176, 232, 244, 337, 466
honor, 45, 51, 124, 190, 247, 252
(and for), 508
(and), 362
(seat of), 98, 100
(to), 57, 190
(your), 65, 336
honorable
(to be), 45
honored
(and I will be), 57
(to be), 45
hoof, 175
of horses, 264
hoofed, 416
hoofs, 418
hook, 28, 33, 40, 52, 159, 225, 272
fastened in jaw, 52
hooks, 40, 81, 366
hoop, 134
hope, 93, 131, 163, 331, 410, 453
(object of), 70
(to), 67, 133
hopeless
(it is), 248
hoping, 76
hordes, 103, 320, 440
horn, 67, 267, 351, 489
hornets, 275
horns, 420, 423
(its), 427
(lofty), 345
horrible
thing, 372
horrid, 348
thing, 372, 432
horror, 106, 264, 282, 303, 490, 502
horse, 144, 350
(dash of), 190
(dung of the), 404
horseman, 201, 350
horsemen, 368, 516
(the), 370, 517
horses, 335
(hoof of), 264
Hosea. *See Tanakh: 02 Neviim:* 10 Hosea
host, 114
hostage, 387
hostile
(to be h to), 29
hostility
(to show h to), 237
(to show h toward), 323
hosts
(and captains of the), 522
hot, 67, 357
(make), 23
(to be), 76, 107, 220, 271, 292, 364, 376, 492
(to become), 107, 220, 376
(to grow), 220
displeasure, 72
stove, 277, 503
houpee, 334
hour, 279
house, 103, 295, 314, 507
(desolate), 144

(head of the), 473
(storage), 176
(wall of), 247, 310
of bonds, 224
of God, 295
of happiness, 473
of influence, 460
of roundness, 223
household, 295
(head or founder of), 15
affairs, 295
housetop, 19
hover
(to), 233, 492
hovered, 411
how, 53, 54, 64, 332
(and), 55
long? (of time), 70, 395
how!
(interj. – in lamentation), 50, 331
how?, 27, 50, 331
howbeit, 39, 51, 95, 325, 370
howdah, 199
however, 51
howl
(to), 87
howling
animal, 23
beast, 27
of beasts, 87
of distress, 94
hub, 329
of a wheel, 329
human
being, 268
humble, 144, 148
(to be), 155, 192
(to h thyself), 262
(to), 144
humbled
(to be), 144, 155, 294
humiliate
(to), 109, 376
humiliated
(to be), 98, 109, 345, 376
humiliation, 296
humility, 149
humor
(out of), 167, 462
(to be out of), 167, 462
hump
of camel, 398
hump-backed, 73, 398
hunchback, 369
hundred, 65
(and a), 309
-fold, 365, 515
hundreds, 309
hunger, 162, 227, 254, 438, 485
(painful), 162, 438
(to), 162, 438
hungrily, 296
hungry
(to be), 162, 227, 438
hunt
(to), 121
hunter, 126
(blind of), 211
hunting, 126
implement, 155
hurl
(to h forth), 184
(to), 40, 64, 212, 267, 451
hurled, 274, 455
hurling, 102
hurried
(to be), 55
flight, 163, 439
hurriedly, 163, 439
hurry
(to h away), 190
(to), 55, 111, 112, 115, 117, 249, 251, 444, 468, 470
hurrying, 212
hurt, 58, 137, 171, 346, 427
(I have), 389
(to), 58, 171
hurtful
act, 70
husband, 124, 313, 506
h's brother, 71, 361
h's father, 67, 357
h's mother, 312
husbandman, 27, 200
(to be a), 32
hush, 87
(to), 87
hush!, 243
husks, 25
hut, 111, 149
huts, 323
hymn
of praise, 306
hypocrisy, 153, 158, 458
hypocrite, 153, 458
hypocritical, 114, 153, 458
hyrax, 303, 496
hyssop, 32
(and with the), 35
(and), 33, 40
(the), 32
I, 70, 80, 100
ice, 245
(piece of), 250
crystal, 245
idea, 287, 515
idle, 247
talk, 19
idleness, 447
idol, 81, 87, 90, 118, 148, 170, 171, 174, 178, 240, 243, 323, 324, 409, 419, 428, 527, 528
(scraping tool used in fashioning of), 243
(wickedness of), 75, 399
idolatrous
priest, 220
idolatry, 412, 414, 526, 527
idols, 85, 412, 414, 526, 527
if, 20, 55, 56, 60, 74, 78, 355, 398
(and), 54
not, 60, 65, 85
only!, 56
so be, 60, 65
ignominy, 115, 324
ignore, 30
(to), 256, 267
ill
(to be), 32
(you deal so), 406, 525
illegitimate
child, 233
ill-humored, 220
ills, 386
illuminating, 219
illumination, 188, 339
(to receive), 385
illusions, 319
image, 118, 131, 148, 170, 171, 174, 178, 240, 260, 293, 409, 419, 424, 428
(cast), 143
(molted), 155, 365
(molten), 147, 359
images, 253, 412, 414, 526, 527
imaginary, 139
imagination, 428
imagine
(to), 29, 246
imagining, 293
imbibe
(to), 82
immodesty, 322
impatience, 285
impatient, 285
(and became), 437
(to be), 54, 285
impeded, 190
impel
(to), 75, 81, 181, 420
imperious, 415
impious, 65
implacable, 220
implement, 78
(of winnowing), 151
implements, 76, 400
important
(to become), 55
Important Biblical Terms
'Ashdowdiyth (language of Ashdod), 410
Atharim
(the) - an unknown term, 379, 519
Behemowth (land-monster), 311
Bereshith (in the beginning), 473, 565
Birkat Kohaniym (the Priest's blessing), 419, 528
Gan Eden (Garden of Eden), 177, 540

Gey-Tzalmaveth (Valley of the Shadow of Death), 350
Ketuvim (Hagiographia), 319, 497
Leviathan (great sea-monster), 324, 512
Miktam (a technical term found in psalm titles), 325, 500
Nazarite, 224
(to be a), 219
Nazariteship, 219
Nefilim (Giants), 191, 428
Nefiyl (Giants), 174
Nehushtan, 442, 539
Ofan (wheel - one of the *Ofanim*), 153, 434
Qadosh Qadeshim (Holy of Holies), 460, 537
Ruach Elohim (Spirit of God), 240, 459
Sheol (the underworld), 258
Tanakh (Jewish Bible), 317, 481
Tebeth (ancient Hebrew tenth month), 294
Teraphim (idols), 412, 526
(and), 414, 527
(the), 413, 527
Thummim, 323, 499
Tohu (desolation), 295
Urim, 218, 447
Yisra'eliyth (female Israelite), 481
Important Jewish Terms
Abib (month), 31
Aggadah & *Halakhah* (two types of presentation in the *Talmud*), 92
Aggadah (legend), 29
Alef Bet (Hebrew Alphabet), 335, 522
Amidah (a prayer), 147
Ashkenazi (German Jew), 283
Ashkenazim (German Jews), 302, 488
'Ashrei (prayer consisting of Ps. 145), 331
Baal Shem (Master of the Name), 490
Baal Shem Tov (Master of the Good Name), 313, 494
Ba'al Teshuvah (one who returns to Judaism), 446
Ba'alei Teshuvah (people who return to Judaism), 450
Baraita (Tanaic and other traditions not included in the Misnah), 366
Baraitot (Tanaic and other traditions not included in the Mishnah), 496
Bava Kama (the first gate), 159
Birkat HaMazon (blessing over food), 411, 534
Chabad (a branch of *Chassidut*), 31
Challah (bread), 62
Chanukah (festival of 8 days), 107
Chassidut (lovingkindness), 322
Clean Animals
(antelope, gazelle, mountain goat), 274, 493
Derush (Torah interpretation focusing on verbal analogy), 330
Gemara (Mishnah commentary), 211
Goy (gentile), 29, 36
Goyim (gentiles), 87, 368
Haftorah (reading of the prophets), 239
Haggadah (Telling), 34
Hakafot (encircling), 353
Halakhah (practice), 78
Halchot (Talmud section dealing with matters of Law), 314
HaNeirot Halalu (liturgy recited at *Chanukkah*), 413
Hanukkah (day of rest), 86
HaRab (the Rabbi), 188
Hasid (pious), 101
HaTorah (the Torah), 362
Hoshanah Rabbah (seventh day of *Sukkot*), 371
'Ibri
Hebrew, 231
'Ibrim (Hebrews), 254, 464
Jew, 54
Keneset (Synagogue), 337
Ketuvim (Hagiographia), 319, 497
Kibbutz (assembly), 183, 492
Kippah (skullcap or yarmulka), 127
Kohen (priestly line), 94, 410
Kosher (ritually clean), 334
Ladino (language of the Sephardic Jews), 120
Lulav ve-Etrog (two of the four plants waved during *Sukkot*), 389
Machzor (festival prayer book), 221
Magen David (Star of David), 129, 423
Mazzel Tov (Good Luck), 114
Menorah (candlestick), 236
Meshiyach (Messiah), 271
Messiah, 271
(lineage of), 297, 485
(stars of), 67
Mezuzah (doorpost), 83
Midrash (study), 341
Mishnah & *Gemara* (the Talmud), 371
Mishnah (Jewish law), 286
Mishneh Torah (the Rambam's codification of the Oral Torah), 491
Mitzvah (Commandment), 157
Mitzvot (Commandment), 339
Modeh Ani (I acknowledge – prayer), 136
Musaf (Additional - a prayer added during certain times), 179, 470
Neilah (final prayer recited on *Yom Kippur*), 171
Perek Shirah (chapter of song - Midrash tractate), 466
Pesach (Passover), 161, 306, 461
(the), 165
Peshat (Literal Torah interpretation), 284
Pirkei Avot (Mishnah tractate, 438
Purim (holiday of deliverance), 257, 260, 465, 466
Qedushah (a prayer extolling God's holiness), 292
Qiddush (prayer recited on Sabbath), 294
Remez (Torah interpretation focussing on hints and allusions), 213
Rosh Chodesh (first day of the Jewish month), 445
Sabbath (day of rest), 397
(in your), 515, 551
(its), 508
(my), 507
(of every), 402
(she insulted the), 407
(the), 399
(your), 425, 530
Sefardi (Spanish Jew), 269
Sefardim (Spanish Jews), 286, 482
Sefer (book), 262
Selah (musical term), 116, 261
Shabatot (Sabbaths), 505
Shalom, 279
Shavuot (weeks), 433
Shavu'ot (weeks), 429
Shema Israel (Hear, Israel), 481, 508
Shemoneh Esreh (portion of the liturgy consisting of 19 blessings), 485
Sheol (the underworld), 258
Shichih Lavrak Yamiym Toviym Amen (may he live for long and good days, Amen), 455, 565
Shlita (notarikon for a living sage), 267
Shmini Atzeret (eight day gathering), 514
Shmitah (the sabbatical year), 274
Shofar (ram's horn), 351, 352
Shulchan Aruch (The Jewish Law - book), 389, 554
Simchat Torah (Rejoicing of the Torah), 532
Sukah (place resided in during *Sukkot*), 111
Sukkot (8-day festival of the harvest), 323
Talmud, 320
Aggadah and *Halakhah*, 92

Tanakh (Jewish Bible), 317, 481
Tannaim (teachers in the Mishnah), 326, 500
Tefillah (prayer), 333
Tefillin, 351, 521
Tefillin (Phylacteries), 348, 520
Terumah (contribution), 506, 549
Teruw'ah (one of three types of shofar blast), 388
Tiqqun (restoration), 345, 518
Tu b'Shevat (fifteen days of *Shevat*), 256
Tzaddik (righteous one), 186
Unclean Animals
cuckow, gull, sea-gull, 284, 506
ferret, shrewmouse, gecko, 166
hawk, 155, 481
heron, 152
hide made out of, 401
houpee, grouse, 334
lizard, 47, 75
lizard or tortoise, 113
osprey, black eagle, buzzard, 158
ostrich, 147, 330, 431
owl, 105
owl, ostrich, 151
pelican, cormorant, 326
swan, mole, 516
VaYakhel (and he gathered together - a Torah portion), 163
Yarmulka (skullcap), 311
Yehuwd (Jew), 47
Yehuwdiyth (Jew's language - Hebrew), 304
Yiddith (Yiddish), 300
Yisra'eliyth (female Israelite), 481
Yisre'eliy (Israelite), 344
Yod Rosh (two places where the *tefillim* are placed on the body), 332
Yom HaKipurim (the Day of Many Atonements), 294, 543
Yom Kippur (Day of Atonement), 273, 475
Yom Kippurim (Day of the Atonements), 295, 543
Zot Chanukah (This is the dedication - last day of *Chanukkah*), 324
Important Kabbalistic Terms
Abrakala (original name of Abracadabara), 336
Adam Illah (heavenly man), 170, 409
Adam Qadmon (archetypal man), 212, 539
1st face – Intellectual World, 341, 505
2nd face – Moral World, 393, 524
3rd face – Natural World, 229, 453
initials of, 123
Ain Ain Sof Ain Sof Aur (Nought without limit light without limit, 385, 568
Aiq Bekar (Kabbalistic type of cipher), 259, *See* Introduction
Arik Anpin (The Vast Countenance), 299, 544
Aur Oguwl (circular light) initials of, 90
Baal Shem (Master of the Name), 307, 490
Baal Shem Tov (Master of the Good Name), 313, 494
Boq - Daughter of the Voice, 124
Chayoth (Living Creatures), 300
Chokmah Nisetarah (Secret Wisdom), 434
Dibbuk (possessing demon), 141
Etz HaChayim (Tree of Life), 206, 546
Gematria, 222
Gilgul (reincarnation), 91
Gilgul Hanefesh (rolling or transmigration of the soul – reincarnation), 329
Golem (shapeless man), 92, 97, 369, 371
HaMaor HaQaton (the lesser light), 297, 501
Idra Rabba Qadisha (Greater Holy Assembly – section of the *Zohar*), 450
Idra Zuta Qadisha (Lesser Holy Assembly – section of the *Zohar*), 373
Kabbalah (tradition), 153
Kamea (magical square), 192
Korub (angel sing.), 204
Kol-Dabarim Be-Kol-Dabarim (All things in all things), 362, 551
Lilith (night demon), 319
Malakim (Angels), 396
Mekubbaliym (Kabbalists), 201, 432
Melek (one of the *Melekim*), 109, 111, 347, 348
Merkab (chariot), 222
Meruba (the "square" Hebrew alphabet), 252
Notarikon, 303, 503, *See* Introduction
Pardes (four levels of Torah study), 264
Paroket (curtain), 394
Qlippoth (shells), 367
Ruach Elohim (Spirit of God), 240, 459
Ruach HaQodesh (holy spirit), 366
Sefirah (number - also the singular of *Sefirot*), 264
Sefirah (sphere), 270
Sefirot (spheres), 423, *Also See* Kabbalah: The Ten *Sefirot*
Senoy, Sansenoy, Semangelof (three angels invoked against Lilith), 369, 532
Senoy, Sansenoy, Semangelof! Adam and Eve! Out, Lilith (a formula invoked against Lilith), 525, 526, 567
Seraf (angel – sing.), 351, 527
Serafim (angels – pl.), 368, 516
Shi'ur Komah (measure of height or body), 410
Sod (secret), 88
Temurah (Permutation), 377
total gematria of Sarah, Rebecca, Rachel, and Leah, 503
Tzelem (the astral body), 170, 409
Tzimtzum (contraction), 224, 450
Yehoshuah (Jesus according to Hermeticism), 255
Yehovashah (Jesus according to Hermeticism), 255
Yetzer Ra (evil inclination), 347
Zauir Anpin (The Lesser Countenance), 296, 501
Zohar (splendor), 194
impossible, 27
impression, 345, 449
imprints
(and), 450
imprison
(to), 221
imprisonment, 70, 80, 224
improvise
(to i carelessly), 234
impure, 68, 87
(to become), 68
impurity, 78, 87
in, 14, 66, 95
(and), 401
(when you come), 43
addition to, 121
the ... is, 22
in order
that, 53
inaccessible, 238
(to make), 235
inactive
(to be), 249
inactivity, 447
inarticulately
(speaking), 125
inasmuch
as, 149
inaugurate
(to), 96, 345
incense, 246, 253, 266, 384, 402, *Also See* Holy Incense
(and for the), 418
(and the), 406, 408
(for), 415
(the), 405
(to burn), 246

incense-altar, 118, 246, 419
incise
(to), 330
incision, 262, 330
incisors, 342
incite
(to), 75, 228, 315
inclination
(evil), 347
incline, 27, 159
(to), 82, 172, 355
inclined, 85
(to be), 114
in-coming, 68
incomprehensible, 141
increase, 213, 378, 485, 492
(and for), 381
(and the i of), 451
(and the), 446
(and), 494
(may), 380, 528
(of your), 451, 528
(our), 460
(to), 28, 128, 162, 188, 243, 246, 423, 461
thereof, 446
increased
(and they i abundantly), 360
(you be), 390
increases, 443
increment, 493
indeed, 39, 90, 100, 116, 148, 325, 392, 409, 439
indemnity, 298
indignant
(to be), 137, 162, 386
indignation, 72, 167, 462
(to express), 137, 386
indistinctly
(to speak), 129
indolence, 123
indulge
(to), 204
ineffective, 85
infinity, 188, 545
inflamed
spot, 275, 494
inflammation, 275, 297, 338, 494
influence
(house of), 460
influential, 54
inform
(to), 32
ingatherings
(as the), 444
ingenious
work, 246
inhabitant, 277, 495
inhabited, 424
inherit
(and you shall i them), 478, 541
(and), 474
(that you may), 480, 537
(to i it), 477
(to), 107, 330
(you shall), 466
(you will), 474
inheritance, 114, 332
(and from the), 338
(you receive), 466
iniquity, 106, 133, 144, 430
(to commit), 101
injurer, 167
injurers, 188, 427
injury, 58, 167, 317, 346
(to suffer), 167
injustice, 128, 129, 133
ink, 38
inkhorn, 345
inkwell, 345
inmost
part, 80, 403
inn, 144, 430
inner, 181
corner buttress, 243
man, 51, 53
part, 241
regions, 40
innermost
part, 194
piece of clothing, 195
innocence, 52, 185, 306, 490
(in God's sight), 52
innocency, 197, 460
innocent, 107, 169, 306, 442, 490
(to be), 166
inquire
(and you shall), 471
(to), 338
(you), 469
insane
(to be), 278
inscribe
(to), 189, 340, 505
inscription, 449
insect
(stinger of), 285, 517
insects, 167, 462
insensitive
(to be), 284
insert, 22
(to), 148
insidious, 175
insidiously
(to assail), 175
insidiousness, 177
insight, 154, 267, 441
insignia, 62
insignificant, 168, 256, 277, 296, 442, 443
(to be), 85, 168, 272, 443
(to grow), 272
(to hold as), 31
insipid, 331
insolence, 85, 407
(to show), 177, 467
insolent, 27, 95, 411
inspect
(to), 179
install
(to), 147, 359
installation, 90
instant
(in an), 344
(to act in an), 227
instead, 459
of, 442, 445
instigate
(to), 315
instruct
(to), 225
instructed, 107, 347
instruction, 215
instructions
(and your), 497, 542
instrument, 78
(leveling), 461
(of opening - key), 337
(sharp cutting), 245, 508
(to play a stringed), 125, 421
instrumental
music, 213
insufficient
(to be), 256
insult, 115
(to), 109, 376
integrity, 308
intellectual, 287
intelligence, 267
intelligences, 288, 483
intelligent
(to become), 53
intend
(to), 222
intent, 169, 193, 315, 443
intercession
(to make), 165
interdict, 221
interest, 276, 456, 493
(lending on), 263
(to give), 276, 456
(to lend for), 276, 456
(to lend on), 268
interfere, 427
intermediate, 145
internal
light, 287
organs, 135
interpose
(to), 156
interpret
(and one to), 390
(one who could), 390
(to), 32, 351, 355, 402
interpretation, 351, 534
(according to the), 422, 535
(its), 414
(of dream), 351
interpretations, 432, 531
interpreted
(and he), 393
(he had), 388

our dreams, 341
interpretion, 414
intertwine
(to), 201
intertwined
(to be), 327
intervene
(to), 156
interweave
(to), 101, 346
interwoven
foliage, 317
foliage (having), 317
intestines, 103, 135, 374
intimate, 132, 137, 451, 453
into, 50
intoxicating
drink, 335
invade
(to), 27, 29, 284
invent
(to), 246
(in a bad sense), 20
invention, 275, 494
investigate
(to), 124, 245
investigation, 245
inwards
(metaphor), 295
iron, 139, 208, 251
(tool of), 208
irredeemably, 482
irreligious, 153, 458
irrigate
(to), 291
irrigation, 308
irritate
(to), 209
is
(and he), 35
(and), 40
(it), 44
(there), 247
(which), 33
it?, 53
Isaiah. *See Tanakh: 02 Neviim:* 07 Isaiah
island, 27
isles, 39
isolated
(to be), 25
isolation, 25
Israel, 340
(all of), 353
(at beginning,), 503
(Children of - using variant *gematria*), 359
(Children of), 355
(for I began), 503
(for the people of), 361, 515
(hardness they suffered at the hands of the Egyptians), 136
(land of), 452, 548
(mighty God of), 364
Alummah (sheaf – fig. as returning from exile), 94
Babylonian exile
Ariel (a chief of the returning exiles), 209
Jeshua (priest who accompanied Zerubbabel back from), 283
number of asses brought out, 570
number of camels brought out, 305
number of children of Adin who returned, 312
number of children of Adonikam who returned, 383
number of children of Anathoth who returned, 146
number of children of Arah who returned, 430
number of children of Asaph who returned, 146
number of children of Ater who returned, 119
number of children of Azgad who returned, 520
number of children of Azmaveth who returned, 62
number of children of Bani who returned, 373
number of children of Bebai who returned, 366
number of children of Betel and Ai who returned, 201
number of children of Bethlehem who returned, 142
number of children of Bigvai who returned, 559
number of children of Elam who returned, 523
number of children of Gibbar who returned, 116
number of children of Harim who returned, 253, 494
number of children of Hashum who returned, 201
number of children of Immer who returned, 499
number of children of Jedaiah who returned, 485
number of children of Jericho who returned, 265
number of children of Jorah who returned, 134
number of children of Kirjatharim, Chephirah, and Beeroth who returned, 417
number of children of Lod, Hadid, and Ono who returned, 410
number of children of Magbish who returned, 167
number of children of Nebo who returned, 72
number of children of Netophah who returned, 75
number of children of Pahathmoab who returned, 565
number of children of Parosh who returned, 561
number of children of Pashur who returned, 523
number of children of Pelaiah, Tobiah, and Nekuda who returned, 378
number of children of Ramah and Gaba who returned, 365
number of children of Senaah who returned, 567
number of children of Shephatiah who returned, 278
number of children of the other Elam who returned, 523
number of children of the porters who returned, 155
number of children of Zaccai who returned, 425
number of children of Zattu who returned, 480
number of horses brought out, 414
number of Levites who returned, 93
number of maids and servants who returned, 570
number of men of Michmas who returned, 142
number of mules brought out of, 212
number of temple servants and sons of Solomon's servants who returned, 286
total number who returned, 571
Zaccai, 56, 57
Zerubbabel (leader of the returning exiles), 209
capital of (Tirzah), 393
Judges of
01 Othniel, 346
brother of (Seraiah), 332
father of (Kenaz), 167
husband of (Achsah), 166
son of (Hathath), 442
02 *Ehud*, 32, 36
descendant of (Uzza), 97

father of (Gera), 186
member of the family of (Ahihud), 50, 52
place where he fled to (Seirath), 352
03 *Shamgar*, 341
father of (Anath), 334
04 *Deborah*, 193, 198
general of (Barak), 241
husband of (Lappidoth), 337
king defeated by (Jabin), 91, 409
05 *Gideon*, 150, 433
altar built by (YHVH *Shalowm*), 289, 483
ancestor of (Hammoleketh), 323
father of (Joash), 251
name given to (Jerubbaal), 248
name given to by those who wanted to avoid saying his other name Jerubbaal (Jerubbesheth), 472
number of sons of, 88
one slain by (Oreb), 226
one slain by (Zalmunna), 230
one slain by (Zebah), 34
one slain by (Zeeb), 25
place where the Midianites stayed after he attacked (Tabbath), 294
servant of (Phurah), 232
son of (Jether), 359
son of (Jotham), 312, 494
06 *Tola*, 328
descendant of (Jibsam), 268, 472
father of (Phuvah), 113
grandfather of (Dodo), 37
son of (Rephaiah), 237
07 *Jair*, 200
08 *Jephthah*, 324
father of (Gilead), 128
place where he slaughtered the Ammonites (Minnith), 324
09 *Ibzan*, 158, 436
10 *Elon*, 105, 111, 117, 414, 416, 419
place where he was buried (Aijalon), 117, 419
11 *Abdon*, 149, 432
father of (Hillel), 83
number of donkeys that sons and grandsons rode upon, 88
place where he was buried (Pirathon), 441, 539
12 *Samson*, 393, 531
burial place of (Eshtaol), 413, 414
downfall of (Delilah), 97
father of (Manoah), 125
number of foxes he let loose, 240
place where he slew many Philistines (Lehi), 67
place where he slew many Philistines (Ramath-Lehi), 391
spring that God brought forth in answer to prayer of (En Hakkore), 307, 504
Kings of
01 *Jeroboam*, 254, 464
father of (Nebat), 80
mother of (Zeruah), 277
02 *Nadab*, 75
place where he was assassinated (Gibbethon), 314, 507
03 *Baasha*, 278
prophet who brought tidings of disaster to (Jehu), 40
04 *Elah*, 51, 54
captain who slew (Zimri), 219
housekeeper of (*Artsa*), 235
05 *Zimri*, 219
06 *Omri*, 253
one who rivaled (Tibni), 314
owner of the hill that he bought (Shemer), 340
07 *Ahab*, 27, 28
governor of (Obadiah), 118
man commanded by to imprison Maachah (Joash), 251
number of descendants in Samaria, 88
prophet during the time of (*Elijah*), 70
prophet who encouraged him to attack the Syrians (Zedekiah), 190, 196
wife of (*Jezebel*), 68
08 *Ahaziah*, 50, 55
king who rebelled against (Mesha), 298
misspelling of (*Azariah*), 235
town where Jehu killed relatives of (Beth Eked), 352
09 *Joram*, 214, 218, 443, 446
as *Jeohoram* (alternate name), 221, 449
son of (Jaershiah), 353
10 *Jehu*, 40
ancestor of (Nimshi), 288
captain in the service of (Bidkar), 243
father of (Hanani), 138
father of (Jehoshaphat), 293
grandfather of (Asiel), 295
11 *Jehoahaz*, 51, 56
12 *Athaliah*, 332, 335
13 *Joash*, 248, 251
as *Jehoash*, 254
14 *Jeroboam* II, 254, 464
15 *Zachariah*, 210
alternate spelling, 213
16 *Shallum*, 277, 280, 478
alternate spelling, 477
17 *Menachem*, 154, 394
(father of), 34
18 *Pekahiah*, 185
officer of (Argob), 187
19 *Pekah*, 180
father of (Remaliah), 235
man in the army of (*Tabe'el*), 62
man killed by (Arieh), 196
one slain by (Argob), 187
one who fought Judah with (Rezin), 267, 489
20 *Hoshea*, 281
number counted in Num. 26.51, 572
number of weeks before holy, 88
number of years of slavery in Egypt, 137
number of years that the nation fasted and lamented their sins, 88
number of years that the nation was desolate, 88
number of years that the nation will serve Babylon, 88
Tribes of
01 Judah, 47, 48
chief captain of (Jehohanan), 146, 431
ephodic stone *Nofek* (emerald), 162, 368
father of a chief of (Shimi), 299
head of a clan of (Eber), 191
head of a family of (Jabez), 175, 486
in association with Leo, 48
in association with the month *Av*, 15
man of (Hepher), 233
man who led half of the princes of (Hoshaiah), 287
number counted in Num. 26.22, 572

prince of (Azariah), 236
prince of (Ben-Hail), 120, 420
prince of (Judah), 48
prince of (Shephatiah), 290
prince of (Sheshbazzar), 466
prince of (Zechariah), 210
prince of the tribe of (Amminadab), 176
prince of the tribe of (Seraiah), 332
wicked prince of (Jaazaniah), 102
02 Issachar, 451
chief of (Michael), 123
chief of (Obadiah), 111
ephodic stone *Sappiyr* (sapphire), 267
head of a family of (Shemuel), 280
in association with Cancer, 451
in association with the month *Tammuz*, 311
number counted in Num. 26.25, 572
prince of (Paltiel), 169
tribal leader of (Jahmai), 86
03 Zebulun, 115, 418
chief of (Ishmaiah), 306
ephodic stone *Yahalom* (pearl), 104, 374
in association with Capricorn, 115, 418
in association with the month *Elul*, 85
leader of in the wilderness (*Eliab*), 63
man of (Obadiah), 118
number counted in Num. 26.27, 572
prince of (Helon), 106, 414
prince of the tribe of (*Helon*), 103, 413
town of (Hannathon), 329
04 Reuben, 220, 471
chief in the wilderness of (*Elizur*), 260
chief of (Jeiel), 141
chief of (Joel), 66
chief of (Zechariah), 210
ephodic stone *Odem* (sardius), 64, 356
in association with Aquarius, 220, 471
in association with the month *Shevet*, 248
number counted in Num. 26.7, 572
05 Simeon, 315, 508
captain of (Pelatiah), 150
captain of (Rephaiah), 237
chief of (Shelumiel, 295
chief of (Ziza), 43
ephodic stone *Pitdah* (topaz), 119
head of a family of (Benaiah), 85, 92
head of a family of (Shimri), 344
in association with Pisces, 315, 508
in association with the month *Adar*, 186
number counted in Num. 26.14, 571
prince of (Asaiah), 282
prince of (Jamlech), 120, 350
prince of (Shephatiah), 294
06 Gad, 20
chief of (Joha), 284
chief of (Jorai), 202
ephodic stone *Achlamah* (amethyst), 103
head of a family of (Abihail), 80
head of a family of (Eber), 191
in association with Aries, 20
in association with the month *Tevet*, 294
number counted in Num. 26.18, 571
07 Ephraim, 257, 258, 465
chief of (Azariah), 238
chief of (Hosea), 281
in association with Taurus, 257, 258, 465
in association with the month *Iyar*, 192
man of (Zabad), 30
number counted in Num. 26.37, 571
prince of (Kemuel), 177
prince of the tribe of (*Ammihud*), 152
08 Manasseh, 286
captain of (Iddo), 38, 98
chief of (Azriel), 252
chief of (Epher), 267
chief of (Hodaviah), 54
chief of the tribe of (*Eliy'el*), 91
in association with Gemini, 286
in association with the month *Iyyar*, 192
number counted in Num. 26.34, 572
prince of (Hanniel), 119
prince of (Joel), 66
prince of the tribe of (*Gamaliel*), 134
09 Benjamin, 164, 439
ancestor of (Michri), 225
chief of (Gabbai), 32
chief of (Sallai), 118
ephodic stone *Yashefeh* (jasper), 286
in association with Sagittarius, 164, 439
in association with the month *Sivan*, 144, 430
leader of (Jaasiel), 299
man of (Ithiel), 311
number counted in Num. 26.41, 572
prince of the tribe of (Abidan), 85, 407
two chiefs of the tribe of (*Eliy'el*), 91
10 Dan, 73, 397
ephodic stone *Leshem* (amber or jacinth), 276, 476
in association with Scorpio, 73, 397
in association with the month *Cheshvan*, 274, 493
number counted in Num. 26.43, 572
prince of (Azarael), 245
prince of (Jogli), 72
prince of the tribe of (Ahiezer), 237
prince of the tribe of (Ammishaddai), 304
11 Asher, 325
chief of (Pagiel), 182
chief of (Rohgah), 199
ephodic stone *Tarshish* (beryl), 519
in association with Libra, 325
in association with the month *Kislev*, 136
number counted in Num. 26.47, 572
one from the tribe of, 325
prince of (Ahihud), 50, 52
12 Naphtali, 347
chief of the tribe of (*Achira*), 233
ephodic stone *Shebuw* (agate), 246
fortress of (Horem), 214
in association with the month *Nisan*, 173, 449
in association with Virgo, 348
number counted in Num. 26.50, 572
prince of (Pedahel), 140

prince of the tribe of (*Enan*), 178, 451
ruler of (Azriel), 252
ruler of (Jeremoth), 382
spy for (*Nahbi*)
father of (Vophsi), 166
Levi (priestly tribe), 65
ephodic stone
Bareqath (carbuncle), 396
in association with the month *Tishri*, 472
Levites, 105, 375
number counted in Num. 26.62, 571
prince of (Hashabiah), 255
total gematria of, 566
Yesherown (a fig. phrase for Israel), 346, 520
Israel, United Kingdom of
Kings of
03 Solomon. *Also See:* Temple of Solomon
Israel, United Kingdom of, 340
Kings of
01 Saul, 261
ancestor of (Abdon), 149, 432
ancestor of (Abiel), 63
ancestor of (Bechorath), 367
ancestor of (Gedor), 188, 194
ancestor of (Jeiel), 137
ancestor of (Matri), 220
captain of the army under (Abner), 216, 222
commander of the warriors who left to join David (Joash), 251
commander-in-chief of (Ner), 215
concubine of (Rizpah), 279
daughter of (Merab), 211
daughter of (Michal), 120
descendant of (Ahio), 43
descendant of (Azmaveth), 336
descendant of (Bocheru), 203
descendant of (Jeush), 283
descendant of (Obadiah), 111
descendant of (Rapha), 232
descendant of (Sheariah), 352
descendant of (Tahrea), 387
descendant of (Tarea), 385
father of (Kish), 294
grandfahter of (Ner), 215
grandson of (Mephibosheth), 452
grandson of (Merib-Baal), 269
great-grandson of (Pithon), 343, 517
king of Amalek spared by (Agag), 20
one of the family of (Azrikam), 301, 487
one of the family of (Shimah), 265
one of the family of (Shimea), 295
one of the family of (Shimeam), 282, 479
place where he consulted a witch (En-Dor), 259, 262, 487, 488
place where he gathered his forces (Bezek), 130
place where he gathered his forces (Telaim), 108, 376
place where he passed (Shalisha), 370
place where he searched for his father's donkeys (Shalim), 310, 493
place where he searched for his father's donkeys (Zuph), 176, 467
servant of (Doeg), 22, 30
site of death of (Gilboa), 126
son of (Alameth), 340
son of (Armoni), 241
son of (Ashbaal), 289
son of (Bineah), 145
son of (Ishbosheth), 493
son of (Jonathan), 335, 515
son of (Malchishua), 318
son of (Mephibosheth), 449
steward of (Ziba), 125
wife of (Ahinoam), 177, 415
02 David, 30, 42
(King), 125
ancestor of (Ram), 209, 438
Benjamite warrior of (Eluzai), 143
bodyguards of (Kari), 204
brother of (Eliab), 63
brother of (Elihu), 65, 72
brother of (Ozem), 149, 392
brother of (Raddai), 195
captain of (Ammizabad), 150
captain of (Shamhuth), 421
captain of the army of (Joab), 37
captain of the Temple guard of (Ira), 230
captain who joined (Adnah), 147
captain who joined (Amasai), 298
captain who joined (Zilthai), 337
chief in army of (Eliy'el), 91
chief of (Elkanan), 154, 435
chief shepherd of (Jaziz), 53
commander of the warriors who left Saul to join (Joash), 251
companion of the sons of (Jehiel), 78
concubine of (Abishag), 250
counselor of (Jehoiada), 126
daughter of (Tamar), 372
descendant of (Anani), 178
descendant of (Arnan), 241, 481
descendant of (Eliashib), 268
descendant of (Hattush), 254
descendant of (Hodaiahu), 61
descendant of (Neariah), 259
descendant of (Obadiah), 111
descendant of (Pelatiah), 150
enemy of (Cush), 256
enemy of (Hanun), 134, 426
father of (Jesse), 252
father of a mighty warrior of
Ezbai, 37
father-in-law of (Talmai), 320
friend and counselor of (Hushai), 254
friend and supporter of (Chimham), 127, 382
friend of (Ahimelech), 130, 352
friend of (Ammiel), 164
friend of (Barzillai), 214
friend of (Jonathan), 335, 515
friend of (Rei), 230
Gadite warrior of (Eliab), 63
Gilonite warrior of (Eliam), 163, 403

guard of (Ithmah), 312
head of a family of the house of (Rephaiah), 237
hero of (Hanan), 129, 423
hero of (Hepher), 233
hero of (Igal), 63
hiding place of (Ezel), 141
High Priest in the time of (Zadok), 184
leader of army of (Benaiah), 85, 92
Levite with (Eliy'el), 91
loyal officer of (Shimi), 299
man who joined (Shephatiah), 294
manager of camels of (Owbiyl), 67
Manassite warrior of (Elihu), 65, 72
member of the royal line of (Adaiah), 108
might man of (Ilai), 140
mighty men of (Agee), 18
mighty warrior of
Abi Albon, 174, 449
Abiel, 63
Abiezer, 234
Abishai, 249
Adina, 151, 156
Ahiam, 364
Azmaveth, 336
Baanah, 145
Bani, 80
Benaiah, 85, 92
Eleazar, 245
Eliahbah, 70
Elika, 157
Eliphal, 163
Eliphalet, 162, 168
Elkanah, 179
Gareb, 186
Helez, 145, 478
Hezro or Hezrai, 242
Hiddai, 36
Hurai, 201
Ira, 230
Ittai, 294, 299
Jaasiel, 299
Jashen, 272, 492
Jediael, 143
Jehiel, 78
Jeiel, 137
Jeribai, 205
Joel, 66
Jonathan, 335, 515
Josheb Basshebeth, 494
Mibhar, 214
Naarai, 257
Paarai, 272
Shammah, 264
Shammoth, 419
Zabad, 30
musician in service of (Nethaniah, 335
musician in the court of (Eliylathah), 309
nephew of (Amasa), 295
officer of (Chelub), 77
one appointed by (Jeremoth), 379, 383
one appointed by as musician and seer (Heman), 126, 422
one appointed by to be musician (Jesharelah), 342
one defeated by (Ishbosheth), 493
one from whom he bought land (Ornan), 241, 481
one of the family of (Azrikam), 302, 488
one of the family of (Shaphat), 284
one promised to (Merab), 211
one who cursed (Shimi), 298
one who formed an alliance with (Huram), 217, 445
one who helped (Shobi), 249
one who joined (Ahiezer), 237
one who joined (Attai), 319
one who joined (Jaziel), 84
one who joined (Jehu), 40
one who joined (Jeremiah), 226
one who joined (Jeremoth), 382
one who joined (Jeziel), 73
one who joined (Jozabad), 47
one who joined (Michael), 123
one who joined (Obadiah), 111
one who joined (Pelet), 139
one who joined (Zebadiah), 46
one who joined at Ziklag (Elzabad), 63
one who joins (Jehoiada), 126
one who married the wife of (Paltiel), 169
one who married wife of (Palti), 147
one who warred against (Hadadezer), 234
one who was loyal to (Merib-Baal), 269
overseer of donkeys of (Jehdeiah), 62
place where he hid (Maon), 172, 446
priest in reign of (Eliashib), 268
priest of (Benaiah), 85, 92
priest of (Delaiah), 67
priest of (Delaiahu), 73
priest to (Ira), 230
prophet and advisor to (Nathan), 325, 512
recorder of (Jehoshaphat), 293
royal scribe for (Shavsha), 386
scribe of (Seraiah), 332
scribe of (Shavsha), 357
scribe of (Sheva), 248
sister of (Abigail), 74
site of farewell between Jonathan and, 56
soldier in army of (Urijah), 200, 203
son of (Abishalom), 284, 480
son of (Absalom), 280, 478
son of (Adonijah), 87, 94
son of (Amnon), 160, 167, 437, 441
son of (Beeliada), 179
son of (Chileab), 72
son of (Daniel), 103, 115
son of (Eliphalet), 162, 168
son of (Elishah), 297
son of (Elishama), 311
son of (Elyada), 135
son of (Ibhar), 199
son of (Ishvi), 256
son of (Ithream), 408, 525
son of (Japhia), 173
son of (Jeremoth), 382
son of (Nathan), 325, 512
son of (Nepheg), 150
son of (Nogah), 77
son of (Shammua), 297
son of (Shephatiah), 290
son of (Shimeam), 295
son of (Shobab), 247
son of (Solomon), 279
storekeeper of (Zabdi), 41
stronghold captured by (Metheg-Ammah), 323
superintendent of forced labor under (Hadoram), 214, 442
two who joined (Johanan), 143, 429
uncle of (Jonathan), 335, 515
valiant man of (Joha), 44
valiant man of (Joshaphat), 290
valiant man of (Joshaviah), 260

valiant man of (Nathan), 325, 512
valiant man of (Uzzia), 107
valiant man of (Zelek), 200
warrior of (Maharai), 217
warrior of (Obed), 101
warriors of
father of (Maachah), 151
wife of (Abigail), 64, 74
wife of (Abital), 70
wife of (Bathsheba), 429
wife of (Bathshua), 431
wife of (Eglah), 130
wife of (Haggith), 299
wife of (Maachah), 151
wife of (Michal), 121
03 Solomon, 279
birds fattened for table of, 290
city captured by (Hamath Zobah), 344
craftsman employed by (Huram), 217, 445
daughter of (Basmath), 417
daughter of (Taphath), 322
district belonging to (Aruboth), 358
father of the enemy of (Elyada), 135
friend and officer of (Zabud), 37
merchant of (Baanah), 145
name given by God to, 62
number of talents of gold he received in one year, 383
officer of (Jehoshaphat), 293
officers of
Hur, 195
one of twelve officers of (Ben-Abinadab), 141, 428
one who formed an alliance with (Huram), 217, 445
place where he built the Temple (Moriah), 217, 221
possible alternate name for (Lemuel), 129
ruler of the officers of (Azariah), 238
scribe in court of (Eliychoref), 538
scribe in the court of (Elihoreph), 257, 499
servant of (Ami), 70
servant of (Darkon), 271, 492
servant of (Jaala), 132
servant of (Jaalah), 135
servant of (Shephatiah), 290
servant of (Sophereth), 416
son of (Rehoboam), 253, 451
superintendent of forced labor under (Hadoram), 214, 442
supply officer of (Ben-Hesed), 143, 429
tribute officer of (Adoniram), 243, 460
wife of (Naamah), 171
wise man in the time of (Ethan), 314, 507
wise man with whom he was compared of (Heman), 126, 422
Israelite
(the), 482
Israelites
number of years they ate manna, 59
issue, 23, 32, 153, 178
(and the), 38
(female), 31
(her), 31, 38
(his), 39
(in his), 41
(of semen), 216
(to), 32, 180
(will), 44
isthmus, 257
it, 27, 54
(and be in), 31
(and i is), 35
(and sanctify), 446
(for), 54
(in), 20, 22
(on), 22
(to take), 446
(to), 55
(with), 20, 22
(wouldn't), 61
(you shall make), 450
is, 44
shall be, 48
itch, 186, 224
itself
(in), 22
(thing), 289
ivory, 292, 483
jacinth, 276, 476
jackal, 27, 311, 505
jackals, 325, 500
jail, 350
jambs, 60
jar, 43, 101, 290, 339, 350, 388
(large), 43
jars, 441
(and its), 450
jasmine, 43
jasmines, 45
jasper, 104, 286, 374
javelin, 108, 415
jaw, 67, 179
jealous, 167
(only of God), 164
(to be), 164
jealousy, 167
jeer
(to), 160
jeopardise
(to), 233, 491
Jeremiah. *See Tanakh: 02 Neviim:* 08 Jeremiah
jest
(to), 124
Jew, 54
(to become a J in fact or in fraud), 37
jewel
(setting of), 95
jewelry, 67, 72
jewels, 72, 181, 454
job, 178, 451
Job. *See Tanakh: 03 Kethuvim:* 03 Job
Joel. *See Tanakh: 02 Neviim:* 11 Joel
join
(to j together), 161, 226
(to), 40, 41, 60, 151, 161, 191, 271, 282
joined, 429
(thing), 358, 376
(to be j together), 259
(to be), 40, 60, 191, 259
joining, 127, 141, 148, 362
(in the), 360, 377
(of bases), 259
(place of), 376
joint, 127, 217, 246, 376
(such as elbow, etc.), 148
joke
(to), 124
Jonah. *See Tanakh: 02 Neviim:* 14 Jonah
Joshua. *See Tanakh: 02 Neviim:* 01 Joshua
journey, 115, 173, 201, 349, 397
(to), 177, 189
journeyed
(and he), 159
journies, 177
joy, 41, 57, 62, 66, 269, 307, 375, 377, 527
(cry of), 218
(shout of), 23
(to leap for), 114
(to shout for), 240, 481
joyful, 266
(to be), 34, 57, 62
jubilant, 129, 137
Judah
Kings of
01 *Rehoboam*, 253, 451
child of (Shelomith), 432
mother of (Naamah), 171
son of (Attai), 319, 345

son of (Jeush), 283
son of (Zaham), 71, 360
son of (Ziza), 43, 76
superintendent of forced labor under (Hadoram), 214, 442
wife of (Mahalath), 319
02 *Abijam*, 72, 362
as *Abijah* (alternate name), 35
03 *Asa*, 80
mother of (Maachah), 151
one cast into prison because of (Hanani), 138
one who warred with (Zerah), 196
prophet who went with (Azariah), 238
04 *Jehoshaphat*, 293
captain of (Amasiah), 179
chief captain of (Adnah), 147
chief captain of (Jehoash), 53
father of (Ahilud), 73
father of (Paruah), 236
grandfather of (Zechariah), 266
Levite sent by to teach the Law (Nethaniah), 335
Levite sent by to teach the Law (Tobiahu), 57
Levite sent by to teach the Law (*Towb Adoniyahuw*), 113
Levite sent to teach by (Zebadiahu), 53
mother of (Azubah), 109
one sent by to teach the Law (Shemiramoth), 489
one who encouraged to fight the Moabites (Jaziel), 84
prince sent by to teach the Law (Nethaneel), 338
prince sent by to teach the Law (Obadiah), 111
prince sent by to teach the Law (Zechariah), 210
prophet who spoke to (*Eliyezer*), 251
son of (Azariah), 238
son of (Jehiel), 78
son of (Michael), 123
son of (Shephatiah), 294
son of (Zechariah), 210
valley named by (Berachah), 203
05 *Jeohoram*, 221, 449
as *Joram* (alternate name), 214, 218, 443, 446
place where he defeated the Edomites (Zair), 277
daughter of (Jehoshabeath), 436
daughter of (Jehosheba), 286
06 *Jehoahaz*, 51, 56
as *Ahaziah* (alternate name), 50, 55
hill where Jehu killed (Gur), 190
as *Azariah* (alternate name), 235
07 *Joash*, 248, 251
as *Jehoash* (alternate name), 254
servant who killed (Jehozabad), 53
captain who helped make king (Maaseiah), 303
collaborator in the slaying of (Jozachar), 211
mother of (Zibiah), 129
one who helped conceal (Jehoshabeath), 436
one who helped conceal (Jehosheba), 286
one who helped make king (Obed), 101
place where he was murdered (Silla), 111
two who helped place him on the throne (Azariah), 238
wife of (Jehoaddan), 159, 166, 437, 440
08 *Amaziah*, 159, 164
father of (Zichri), 207
mother of (Jehoaddan), 159, 166, 437, 440
09 *Azariah*, 235
as *Uzziah* (alternate name), 113, 119
mother of (Jecholiah), 100, 104
officer of (Hananiahu), 146
officer of (Maaseiah), 303
one who opposed (Azariah), 238
scribe of (Jeiel), 137
son of (Athaiah), 321
wife of (Jerusha), 333, 335
wife of (Zadok), 184
grandfather of (Ananiah), 179
10 *Jotham*, 312, 494
mother of (Zadok), 184
11 *Ahaz*, 32
priest under (Urijah), 200, 203
son of (Maaseiah), 303
the governor of the house of (Azrikam), 302, 488
wife of (Abi), 28
12 *Hezekiah*, 147, 152, 155, 160
master of household of (Eliakim), 420
master of the household of (Hilkiah), 168
mother of (Abi), 29
overseer under (Ismachiah), 163
possible alternate name for (Lemuel), 129
scribe of (Shebna), 269
scribe of (Shebnah), 271
13 *Manasseh*, 286
mother of (Hephzibah), 182
prophet who recorded events of (Hozai), 50
wife of (Meshullemeth), 443
14 *Amon*, 111, 117, 416, 419
mother of (Meshullemeth), 443
15 *Josiah*, 255, 258
contemporary of (Pharaoh-Necho), 303
contemporary of (Pharaoh-Nechoh), 302
governor of Jerusalem under (Maaseiah), 303
grandfather of (Pedaiah), 120
mother of (Adaiah), 108
mother of (Jedidah), 52
officer in court of (Ahikam), 408
officer in the court of (Ahikam), 168
officer under (Pedaiah), 352, 551
official sent by (Abdon), 149, 432
prophet during the reign of (Habakkuk), 197
prophetess in the days of (Huldah), 66
son of (*Eliakim*), 181, 420
son of (Johanan), 143, 429
wife of (Hamutal), 113, 117
wife of (Zebudah), 46
16 *Jehoahaz*, 51, 56
as *Shallum* (alternate name), 277, 279, 477, 478
17 *Jehoiakim*, 174, 412
as *Eliakim* (alternate name), 181, 421

brother of (*Mattaniah*), 327, 330
descendant of (Berachiah), 207
descendant of (Berekyahu), 211
descendant of (Malchiram), 261, 467
descendant of (Meshullam), 293, 484
descendant of (Nebadiah), 90
military commander under (*Elnathan*), 338, 516
officer of (Jerahmeel), 233
prophet during the reign of (Habakkuk), 197
prophet who offended (Urijah), 200, 203
secretary of (*Elishama*), 311
wife of (Nehushta), 424
18 *Jehoiachin*, 128, 132, 422, 425
as *Coniah* (alternate name), 111
as *Jeconiah* (alternate name), 115, 123
descendant of (Pedaiah), 120
grandson of (Shimi), 299
son of (Hoshama), 299
son of (Shealthiel), 429
son or grandson of (Pedaiah), 120
son or grandson of (Shenazar), 373
grandfather of (Elnathan), 338, 515
maternal grandfather of (*Elnathan*), 338, 515
mother of (Nehushta), 424
son of (Assir), 225
19 *Zedekiah*, 190, 196
ambassador of (Gemariah), 219
ambassador of (Jucal), 222
as *Mattaniah* (alternate name), 327, 330
contemporary of (Pharaoh-hopra), 405
eunuch of (Ebed-Melech), 172, 375
messenger of (Jucal), 84, 90
priest whose son was sent by (Maaseiah), 301
servant of (Elasah), 291
Judaised
(to become), 37
judge, 78, 82, 163, 284, 356, 402, 405
(and I will), 440
(and you will), 452, 535
(diviner), 296
(office of), 166
(to), 57, 78, 82, 402, 405
(you shall), 435
judgements
(and with), 309, 491
judges, 104, 305, 374, 489
(the), 307, 490
Judges. *See Tanakh: 02 Neviim:* 02 Judges
judgment, 82, 139, 166, 284, 302, 387, 405
(calling for), 169
(pronouncement of), 172
(to make a), 246
judicial, 169
judicious
(to be), 219, 470
jug, 350
(a kind of), 290
(small oil), 105, 347
juice, 134, 259, 342
(of grapes), 161
(pressed out), 199
(slime), 294
cooked from meat, 261
juicy, 193
bit, 259
jump
(to), 114
junction, 358
juniper, 329, 342, 357, 372, 517
tree, 372, 517
Jupiter. *See* Planets: Traditional: 06 Jupiter
just, 87, 186, 408
(to be), 182, 330
justice, 82, 182, 183, 302, 405
(righteous), 366
juxtaposition, 136
Kabbalah
231 Gates
01 (*Ab*), 15
02 (*Ag*), 17
03 (*Edh*), 18
04 (*Ah*), 19
05 (*Av*), 20
06 (*Az*), 22
07 (*Ach*), 23
08 (*At*), 25
09 (*Ai*), 27
10 (*Akh*), 39, 325
100 (*Vak*), 44, 328
101 (*Val*), 54
102 (*Vam*), 65, 356
103 (*Van*), 74, 398
104 (*Vas*), 84
105 (*Va'*), 95
106 (*Vap*), 105, 440
107 (*Vatz*), 116, 470
108 (*Vaq*), 128
109 (*Var*), 187
11 (*Al*), 50
110 (*Vash*), 244
111 (*Vath*), 291
112 (*Zach*), 32
113 (*Zat*), 33
114 (*Ziy*), 34
115 (*Zak*), 45, 329
116 (*Zal*), 56
117 (*Zam*), 66, 357
118 (*Zan*), 75, 400
119 (*Zas*), 85
12 (*Em*), 60, 355
120 (*Za'*), 95
121 (*Zap*), 106, 441
122 (*Zatz*), 117, 470
123 (*Zaq*), 129
124 (*Zar*), 188
125 (*Zash*), 244
126 (*Zath*), 292
127 (*Chat*), 34
128 (*Chai*), 35
129 (*Chak*), 46, 329
13 (*An*), 70, 395
130 (*Chal*), 57
131 (*Cham*), 67, 357
132 (*Chan*), 76, 401
133 (*Chas*), 86
134 (*Cha'*), 96
135 (*Chap*), 107, 442
136 (*Chatz*), 118, 470
137 (*Chaq*), 130
138 (*Char*), 189
139 (*Chash*), 245
14 (*As*), 80
140 (*Chath*), 292
141 (*Tiy*), 37
142 (*Tak*), 47, 330
143 (*Tal*), 57
144 (*Tam*), 68, 358
145 (*Tan*), 77, 402
146 (*Tas*), 87
147 (*Ta'*), 97
148 (*Taf*), 107, 443
149 (*Tatz*), 119, 471
15 (*Ao*), 90
150 (*Taq*), 130
151 (*Tar*), 190
152 (*Tash*), 246
153 (*Tath*), 292
154 (*Yak*), 49
155 (*Yal*), 59
156 (*Yam*), 69, 358
157 (*Yan*), 78, 402
158 (*Yas*), 87
159 (*Ya'*), 98
16 (*Af*), 100, 439
160 (*Yaf*), 108, 443
161 (*Yatz*), 120, 471
162 (*Yaq*), 131
163 (*Yar*), 191
164 (*Yash*), 247
165 (*Yath*), 293
166 (*Kal*), 69
167 (*Kam*), 78, 364

168 (*Kan*), 88, 408
169 (*Kas*), 98
17 (*Atz*), 111, 468
170 (*Ka'*), 109
171 (*Kaf*), 120, 448
172 (*Katz*), 131, 475
173 (*Kaq*), 139
174 (*Kar*), 199
175 (*Kash*), 253
176 (*Kath*), 298
177 (*Lam*), 88, 368
178 (*Lan*), 98, 412
179 (*Las*), 109
18 (*Aq*), 123
180 (*La'*), 120
181 (*Lap*), 131, 451
182 (*Latz*), 140, 476
183 (*Laq*), 147
184 (*Lar*), 204
185 (*Lash*), 257
186 (*Lath*), 302
187 (*Man*), 109, 415
188 (*Mas*), 121
189 (*Ma'*), 131
19 (*Ar*), 185
190 (*Maf*), 140, 453
191 (*Matz*), 147, 478
192 (*Maq*), 155
193 (*Mar*), 209
194 (*Mash*), 262
195 (*Math*), 306
196 (*Nas*), 132
197 (*Na'*), 140
198 (*Naf*), 148, 456
199 (*Natz*), 155, 481
20 (*Ash*), 241
200 (*Naq*), 162
201 (*Ner*), 215
202 (*Nash*), 266
203 (*Nath*), 310
204 (*Sa'*), 148
205 (*Saf*), 156, 459
206 (*Satz*), 163, 483
207 (*Saq*), 169
208 (*Sar*), 220
209 (*Sash*), 272
21 (*Ath*), 289
210 (*Sath*), 313
211 (*'Ap*), 163, 461
212 (*'Atz*), 169, 484
213 (*'Aq*), 174
214 (*'Ar*), 225
215 (*'Ash*), 276
216 (*'Ath*), 317
217 (*Patz*), 174, 486
218 (*Paq*), 178
219 (*Par*), 230
22 (*Bag*), 18
220 (*Pash*), 281
221 (*Path*), 320
222 (*Tzaq*), 181
223 (*Tzar*), 234
224 (*Tzash*), 285
225 (*Tzath*), 323
226 (*Qar*), 240
227 (*Qash*), 288
228 (*Qath*), 325
229 (*Rash*), 325
23 (*Bad*), 19
230 (*Rath*), 354
231 (*Shath*), 395
24 (*Bah*), 20
25 (*Bow*), 22
26 (*Baz*), 23
27 (*Bach*), 25
28 (*Bat*), 27
29 (*Biy*), 28
30 (*Bak*), 40, 326
31 (*Bal*), 51
32 (*Bam*), 61, 355
33 (*Ban*), 71, 396
34 (*Bas*), 81
35 (*Bo'*), 91
36 (*Baf*), 101, 439
37 (*Batz*), 112, 468
38 (*Baq*), 124
39 (*Bar*), 185
40 (*Bash*), 241
41 (*Bath*), 289
42 (*Gad*), 20
43 (*Geh*), 22
44 (*Gav*), 23
45 (*Gaz*), 25
46 (*Gach*), 27
47 (*Gat*), 28
48 (*Gi*), 29
49 (*Gak*), 41, 326
50 (*Gal*), 52
51 (*Gam*), 62, 355
52 (*Gan*), 72, 397
53 (*Gas*), 81
54 (*Go*), 92
55 (*Gaph*), 102, 439
56 (*Gatz*), 113, 469
57 (*Gaq*), 125
58 (*Gar*), 185
59 (*Gash*), 242
60 (*Gath*), 290
61 (*Dah*), 23
62 (*Daw*), 25
63 (*Daz*), 27
64 (*Dach*), 28
65 (*Dat*), 29
66 (*Day*), 30
67 (*Dakh*), 42, 327
68 (*Dal*), 53
69 (*Dam*), 63, 356
70 (*Den*), 73, 397
71 (*Das*), 82
72 (*Dea'*), 93
73 (*Dap*), 103, 440
74 (*Datz*), 114, 469
75 (*Doq*), 125
76 (*Dar*), 186
77 (*Dash*), 242
78 (*Dath*), 290
79 (*Hoo*), 27
80 (*Haz*), 28
81 (*Hach*), 29
82 (*Hat*), 31
83 (*Hiy*), 32
84 (*Hak*), 43, 327
85 (*Hal*), 53
86 (*Ham*), 64, 356
87 (*Han*), 74, 398
88 (*Has*), 83
89 (*Ha'*), 94
90 (*Hap*), 104, 440
91 (*Hatz*), 115, 469
92 (*Haq*), 126
93 (*Har*), 187
94 (*Hash*), 243
95 (*Hath*), 290
96 (*Vuz*), 29
97 (*Vuch*), 31
98 (*Vat*), 32
99 (*Vaw*), 33
number of, 205
total gematria of, 571
32 Paths of Wisdom
01 *Sekhel Mopla*, 329
02 *Sekhel Mazohir*, 357
03 *Sekhel HaQodesh*, 426
04 *Sekhel Qavua*, 337
05 *Sekhel Nesharash*, 517
06 *Sekhel Shefa Nivdal*, 464
07 *Sekhel Nisetar*, 500
alternate name (*HaKachoth HaSekhelim*), 454, 535
08 *Sekhel Shalem*, 409, 525
phrase used to describe – *Tekunath HaQadmuth*, 538
09 *Sekhel Tahur*, 348
10 *Sekhel Mitnotzetz*, 495, 554
11 *Sekhel Metzochtzoch*, 353
12 *Sekhel Bahir*, 347
13 *Sekhel Manhig HaAchdoth*, 464
14 *Sekhel Meir*, 355
15 *Sekhel Maamid*, 332
16 *Sekhel Nitzchi*, 329
17 *Sekhel HaHergesh*, 459
18 *Sekhel Beth HaShefa*, 520
19 *Sekhel Sod HaPauloth HaRuachnioth*, 550
20 *Sekhel HaRatzon*, 396, 532
21 *Sekhel HaChafutz HaMevuqash*, 487, 553
22 *Sekhel Ne'eman*, 323, 511
23 *Sekhel Qayyam*, 331, 501
24 *Sekhel Qayyam* (Imaginative Intelligence), 317
25 *Sekhel Nisyoni*, 339
26 *Sekhel Mechudash*, 401
27 *Sekhel Morgash*, 467
28 *Sekhel Motba*, 318
29 *Sekhel Mughsham*, 415, 527

30 *Sekhel Kelali*, 306
31 *Sekhel Temidi*, 446
32 *Sekhel Ne'evad*, 318
number of, 51
Olympic Spirits
Arathron (Saturn), 457, 542
Bethor (Jupiter), 364
Hagith (Venus), 299
Och (Sol), 31
Ophiel (Mercury), 145
Phaleg (Mars), 134
Phul (Luna), 137
Souls
all five combined, 504
Chiah, 41
Nefesh, 302
Neshamah, 286
Ruach, 195
Yechidah, 56
Texts
Esh Metzaref (Purifying Fire), 403, 537
Sefer HaBahir (Book of Illumination), 346
Sefer HaZohar (Book of Splendor), 194, 345
(in reference to *alef*), 13
number of keys mentioned within, 541
number of mysteries mentioned in, 385
secret name of God from (*'ahuw-ah*), 33
section of (*Safra Detzniuta*), 485
Sefer Yetzirah (Book of Formation)
(first and last letters of), 40, 326
(number of elements mentioned in), 15
(number of gates mentioned in), 205
former of faith (quote from), 183, 455
Sifra Dtzenioutha (Book of Concealed Mystery), 369
The Ten *Sefirot*
0 *Ain*, 80, 403
Qlippoth
Qemetiel, 181
00 *Ain Sof*, 188, 545
initials of, 80
Qlippoth
Belial, 92, 157
000 *Ain Sof Aur*, 295, 553
Qlippoth
Athiel, 331
01 *Keter*, 365, *Also See* Kabbalah:The Ten *Sefirot*: Supernals
(as 1st Path), 13
(as part of 11th Path), 27, 85
(as part of 12th Path), 28, 97
(as part of 13th Path), 30, 112
(as part of Supernals), 424
42-Letter Name of God
Ab, 15
Alternate Titles of
Amen, 111, 416
Arik Anpin, 299, 544
Arik Apim, 273, 535
Atik Yomin, 363, 552
Atiqa, 351
Atiqa de-Atiqin, 521, 555
Atiqa Qadisha, 489
Aur Mopla, 274
Aur Pashot, 355
Aur Penimi, 287
'elyown, 172, 447
Hu', 28
Kabodh Rishon, 352, 522
Neqedah Peshutah, 345
Neqedah Rishonah, 409
Pele, 133
Risha, 331
Risha Dela, 343
Risha Havurah, 413
Rom Maalah, 285, 481
Tath Zel, 453
Temira de-Temirin, 351, 522
Angelic Choir(s)
Chayoth HaQodesh, 452
Archangel(s)
Metatron, 249, 483
Archdemon(s)
Moloch, 109, 347
Satan, 271, 492
God Name(s)
Eheieh, 39
Eheieh Asher Eheieh, 341
Kabbalistic Soul
Yechidah, 56
Material World(s)
Rashith HaGilgam, 497, 546
Number of Appearances in *Tanakh*, 365
Qlippoth
Thaumiel, 322
World of *Briah*
Angel (*Yehoel*), 71
02 *Chokmah*, 92, *Also See* Kabbalah:The Ten *Sefirot*: Supernals
(as 2nd Path), 14, 15
(as part of 11th Path), 27, 85
(as part of 14th Path), 31, 127
(as part of 15th Path), 32, 140
(as part of 16th Path), 33, 153
(as part of Supernals), 424
42-Letter Name of God
Gi, 29
Alternate Titles of
Ab, 15
HaAchdoth Zohar (as 2nd Path), 373
Kockmah, 92
Angelic Choir(s)
Ofanim, 180, 419
Archangel(s)
Raziel, 214
Archdemon(s)
Adam Belial, 137, 387
Beelzebub, 139
Isheth Zenunim, 460, 537
Samael, 149
God Name(s)
Yah, 32
Kabbalistic Soul
Chiah, 41
Material World(s)
Mazloth, 320
Number of Appearances in *Tanakh*, 92
Qlippoth
Ogiel, 140
03 *Binah*, 85, *Also See* Kabbalah:The Ten *Sefirot*: Supernals
(as 3rd Path), 15, 19
(as part of 12th Path), 28, 97
(as part of 14th Path), 31, 127
(as part of 17th Path), 35, 165
(as part of 18th Path), 36, 175
(as part of Supernals), 424
42-Letter Name of God
Tatz, 323, 527
Alternate Titles of
Aima, 70
Ama, 61
Korsia, 237
Angelic Choir(s)
Aralim, 231, 454
Archangel(s)
Tzafqiel, 248
God Name(s)
YHVH *Elohim*, 133, 385
Material World(s)
Shabbathai, 405
Number of Appearances in *Tanakh*, 85
Qlippoth
Satariel, 397
04 *Hesed*, 91

(as 4th Path), 17, 25
(as part of 16th Path), 33, 153
(as part of 19th Path), 37, 181
(as part of 20th Path), 38, 192
(as part of 21st Path), 39, 205
42-Letter Name of God
Qerashamen, 425, 536
Alternate Titles of
Gedulah, 66
Angelic Choir(s)
Chashmalim, 302, 488
Archangel(s)
Tzadqiel, 206
Archdemon(s)
Ashtaroth, 528
Dukes of Edom
Aholibamah, 113
God Name(s)
El, 50
Heaven(s)
Makhon, 136, 426
Heavenly Mansion(s)
Hekel Ahbah, 96
Hell(s)
Abaddon, 81, 404
Kings of Edom
Yobab, 38
as son of Zerah, 232, 478
father of (Zerah), 196
Number of Appearances in *Tanakh*, 91
Qlippoth
Gasheklah, 302
Seven Earths
Adamah, 68
05 *Giburah*, 197
(as 5th Path), 18, 32
(as part of 18th Path), 36, 175
(as part of 19th Path), 37, 181
(as part of 22nd Path), 40, 216
(as part of 23rd Path), 42, 228
42-Letter Name of God
Kedadikesh, 271
Alternate Titles of
Diyn, 82, 405
Pachad, 113
Angelic Choir(s)
Serafim, 368, 516
Archangel(s)
Kamael, 111
Archdemon(s)
Ashtaroth, 528
Asmodai, 141
Dukes of Edom
Elah, 54
God Name(s)
Elohim Gibor, 237, 457
Heaven(s)
Maon, 172, 446
Heavenly Mansion(s)
Hekel Zakoth, 324
Hell(s)
Bar Shachath, 472
Kings of Edom
Husham, 264, 469
Number of Appearances in *Tanakh*, 197
Qlippoth
Golachab, 67
Seven Earths
Charabhah, 196
Gaye, 30
06 *Tiferet*, 503
(as 6th Path), 19, 39
(as part of 13th Path), 30, 112
(as part of 15th Path), 32, 140
(as part of 17th Path), 35, 165
(as part of 20th Path), 38, 192
(as part of 22nd Path), 40, 216
(as part of 24th Path), 43, 240
(as part of 25th Path), 44, 255
(as part of 26th Path), 45, 268
42-Letter Name of God
Bamratztag, 413
Alternate Titles of
Adam, 63, 356
Adidyuron, 510
Adiryaron, 320
Ben, 71, 396
Ish, 247
Melek, 109, 347
Rachamim, 238, 458
Seir Anpin, 429, 537
Shakanom, 297, 486
Zahorariel, 312
Zauir Anpin, 296, 501
Angelic Choir(s)
Melekim, 155, 394
Shinanim, 311, 493
Archangel(s)
Rafael, 248
Archdemon(s)
Belphegor, 253
Chioa, 44
Dukes of Edom
Pinon, 181, 454
God Name(s)
YHVH *Eloah va-Daath*, 343
Heaven(s)
Zebuwl, 64
Heavenly Mansion(s)
Hekel Ratzon, 294, 500
Hell(s)
Tit HaYaven, 119, 420
Kings of Edom
Hadad, 29
as son of *Bedad*, 93, 410
Material World(s)
Shemesh, 372
Number of Appearances in *Tanakh*, 503
Qlippoth
Tageriron, 461, 542
Seven Earths
Neshiah, 274
Tziah, 127
07 *Netzach*, 161
(as 7th Path), 20, 47
(as part of 21st Path), 39, 205
(as part of 24th Path), 43, 240
(as part of 27th Path), 46, 280
(as part of 28th Path), 47, 292
(as part of 29th Path), 48, 305
42-Letter Name of God
Haqamamna, 243
Angelic Choir(s)
Elohim, 105, 374
Tarshishim, 524, 554
Archangel(s)
Haniel, 117
Archdemon(s)
Asmodai, 141
Baal, 124
Baal-Hanan, 190, 458
Dukes of Edom
Qenaz, 167
God Name(s)
YHVH *Tzabaoth*, 336
Heaven(s)
Shechaqim, 313, 494
Heavenly Mansion(s)
Hekel Etzem Shamaim, 378, 552
Hell(s)
Shaare-Maveth, 496
Kings of Edom
Samlah, 279
Number of Appearances in *Tanakh*, 161
Qlippoth
Oreb Zaraq, 350
Seven Earths
Tziah, 127
Yabbashah, 251
08 *Hod*, 32, 55
(as 8th Path), 22

(as part of 23rd Path), 42, 228
(as part of 26th Path), 45, 268
(as part of 27th Path), 46, 280
(as part of 30th Path), 49, 315
(as part of 31st Path), 50, 324
42-Letter Name of God
Yaglepzeq, 204
Angelic Choir(s)
Beni Elohim, 161, 400
Archangel(s)
Michael, 123
Archdemon(s)
Adramelek, 236, 430
Belial, 92, 157
Dukes of Edom
Teman, 325, 512
God Name(s)
Elohim Tzabaoth, 352, 512
Heaven(s)
Raqia, 281
Heavenly Mansion(s)
Hekel Gonah, 146
Hell(s)
Tzal-Maveth, 347
Kings of Edom
Saul, 261
Number of Appearances in *Tanakh*, 32
Qlippoth
Samael, 149
Seven Earths
Arqa, 241
09 *Yesod*, 98
(as 9th Path), 23, 64
(as part of 25th Path), 44, 255
(as part of 28th Path), 47, 292
(as part of 30th Path), 49, 315
(as part of 32nd Path), 51, 337
42-Letter Name of God
Sheqi, 294
Alternate Titles of
Tzadiq-Yesod-Olam, 302, 488
Yesod Olam, 202, 434
Angelic Choir(s)
Kerubim, 229, 453
Archangel(s)
Gabriel, 212
Archdemon(s)
Lilith, 319
Dukes of Edom
Magdiel, 107
Mibzar, 258
God Name(s)
Shaddai El Chai, 273
Heaven(s)
Tebel Vilon Shamaim, 338, 551
Vilon, 124, 421
Heavenly Mansion(s)
Hekel Lebanath HaSafir, 468
Hell(s)
Ge-Hinnom, 134, 383, 385
Kings of Edom
Baal-Hanan, 190, 458
as son of *Achbor*, 345, 555
Number of Appearances in *Tanakh*, 98
Qlippoth
Gamaliel, 134
Seven Earths
Cheled, 62
Tebhel, 304
10 *Malkut*, 324
(as 10th Path), 25, 74
(as part of 29th Path), 48, 305
(as part of 31st Path), 50, 324
(as part of 32nd Path), 51, 337
42-Letter Name of God
10 *Ayeth*, 319
Alternate Titles of
Atarah, 231
Ayyal, 60
Be'ayr, 185
Betulah, 307
Kallah, 74
Malkah, 115
Panin, 181, 454
Shar, 348
Shekinah, 282
Throa, 385
Angelic Choir(s)
Eshim, 268, 472
Archangel(s)
Sandalfon, 230, 476
Archdemon(s)
Naamah, 171
Dukes of Edom
Eram, 253, 463
God Name(s)
Adonai HaAretz, 273, 514
Heaven(s)
Tebel Vilon Shamaim, 338, 551
Vilon, 124, 421
Heavenly Mansion(s)
Hekel Lebanath HaSafir, 468
Hell(s)
Ge-Hinnom, 134, 383, 385
Kings of Edom
Hadar, 190
Mezahab, 83
Material World(s)
Cholam Yesodoth, 346, 509
Olam Yesodoth, 369, 517
Number of Appearances in *Tanakh*, 324
Qlippoth
Lilith, 319
Seven Earths
Cheled, 62
Tebhel, 304
Chokmah
(letters spelled out), 357, 556
Daat, 317
Dukes of Edom
Alvah, 133, 136
Timnah, 333
Yetheth, 443
Kings of Edom
Bela
as son of *Beor*, 503
as son of *Beor*, 304
Bela', 123
Number of Appearances in *Tanakh*, 317
second, third and pseudo-*sephiroth*, 364
Supernals (*Keter*, *Chokmah*, *Binah*)
combined into one word, 424
Heaven(s)
Arabhoth, 387
Heavenly Mansion(s)
Hekel Qadesh Qadeshim, 476, 541
Seven Earths
Aretz, 235, 505
Tunnels of Set
11 *Amprodias*, 289
12 *Baratchial*, 220
13 *Gargophias*, 286, 518
14 *Dagdagiel*, 73
15 *Hemethterith*, 499
16 *Uriens*, 286
17 *Zamradiel*, 235
18 *Characith*, 371
19 *Temphioth*, 358
20 *Yamatu*, 149
21 *Kurgasiax*, 250
22 *Lafcursiax*, 385, 540
23 *Malkunofat*, 244
24 *Niantiel*, 169
25 *Saksaksalim*, 239, 458
26 *A'ano'nin*, 208, 464
27 *Parfaxitas*, 310
28 *Tzuflifu*, 241
29 *Qulielfi*, 224
30 *Raflifu*, 291

31 *Shalicu*, 325
Tannim (Denizens of), 325, 500
32 *Thantifaxath*, 498
Worlds
Assiah, 282, 339, 504
Ben (Secret Name), 71, 396
Atzilut, 339, 389, 522
Ab (Secret Name), 91
Briah, 198, 276, 476
Seg (Secret Name), 82
Notariqon for all four (Abia), 102
Yetzirah, 250, 315, 495
Mah (Secret Name), 64
kabbalist, 175
kabbalists, 201, 432
Kaf. *See* Hebrew Alphabet:11 *Kaf*
keen
(to be), 33
keep
(and I will k you), 485, 539
(and shall k you), 489
(and shall), 405
(and you shall), 480
(to k back), 169
(to k under), 254
(to keep back), 70, 227
(to), 220, 262, 340, 438
(whether you would), 479
(you shall k you far), 401
(you shall), 479, 480, 489, 548
kept
(to be k on), 290
(to be), 492
kernels, 265, 489
Keter. *See* Kabbalah:The Ten *Sefirot*:01 *Keter*
kettle, 30, 340
key, 337
khan, 144, 430
kick
(to k at), 100
(to), 51, 100
kid, 34, 486
(the), 40
kidneys, 83
kids, 40, 45
kill
(and I will), 366
(and k it), 50
(and you shall), 361
(I would k you), 371, 508
(shall), 394
(to k ruthlessly), 37
(to), 34, 68, 94, 155, 189, 238, 251, 308, 364
(you shall), 382
killing, 189, 195, 407
kills, 54
kiln
(pottery or lime), 278, 495
kin
(near), 326
kind, 75, 101, 121, 400, 420
(of what), 64
(to be), 91
(what), 116
kindle, 188
(to), 63, 133, 134, 226, 310, 324
(you shall), 387
kindled
(to be), 133, 134, 220, 226
kindness, 40, 91, 169, 408
kindred, 57, 132, 319, 334, 384
(my), 453
(of my), 463
king, 109, 347
(against the), 112, 348
(concubine of), 259
(food for), 321
(friend of), 228
(power of), 138, 427
(the), 115, 349
(to be or become), 109, 347
(wife of), 259
kingdom, 117, 151, 324, 339
kingly
office, 108
kings, 121, 155, 394
Kings. *See* *Tanakh: 02 Neviim:* 05 1 Kings, 06 2 Kings
kingship, 108
kinship, 334
kinsman, 70, 132, 384
(his), 58
(to do the part of a), 52
kinsman-redeemer
(to act as), 52
kinswoman, 328
kiss, 315
(to), 310
kite, 25, 33, 187
(and the), 48
(the), 32
knave, 87
knavery, 121
knavish
(to be), 121
kneading
trough or bowl, 479
knee, 200, 203, 396
kneel
(to), 200, 234, 396
knees
(to knock of), 310
(to sink down to one's), 234
knew
(and he), 207
knife, 168, 191, 281, 323, 463, 496
(pruning), 235
knob, 394
(and a), 398
knobs
(its), 406
(their), 422, 529
knob-shaped
carved wood, 215
knock
(to), 179, 310
knot, 246
know
(to), 103, 225
(you), 338, 516
knowing
(power of), 171
knowledge, 93, 134, 171
known
(to make), 37, 76
labor, 100, 171, 198, 461
(and she had hard), 440
(to), 102, 156
band, 121
to bring forth, 27, 39
laborer, 156, 171
(hired), 337, 339
laborers
(body or gang of forced), 121
lack, 224
(for l of), 80, 403
(to), 224, 328
(you shall), 384
of, 224
of food, 485
lacked
(you have), 384
lacking, 61, 224, 229
(shall you suffer to be), 507
(the thing), 254, 485
(to be), 224, 227
lad, 253
ladder, 391
laden, 119, 289, 421, 483
lady, 356
laid
(and she), 418, 528
(to be), 139
lair, 98, 185, 345
lamb, 28, 59, 63, 199, 209, 243, 254, 256
lame, 306
(to be), 181
Lamed. *See* Hebrew Alphabet:12 *Lamed*
lament, 52, 79, 88
(and to), 314
(to), 40, 51, 54, 77, 79, 158, 167, 326, 441
lamentation, 32, 83, 84, 88, 166, 172
Lamentations. *See* *Tanakh: 03 Kethuvim:* 06 Lamentations
laments, 102, 373
lamp, 215, 220
stand, 241, 344
lamps, 376
(its), 382
(the), 379, 381
(these), 413
lance, 214
land, 68, 235, 246, 505
(and), 237, 506
(common or open), 341
(dry), 196, 251, 404

(parched), 167, 185, 441
(scorched), 141
(upon the dry), 405
landing
place, 293, 520
landmark, 53, 58, 60, 65
lands
(in their), 413, 526
(in), 392
(the), 393, 396
language, 283, 387, 530
(Syrian), 377
(their), 449, 534
languish
(to), 51, 59, 82, 90, 101
languishing, 37, 82, 405
lap, 161, 200, 396, 438
(to l up), 204
(to), 204
large
(to be), 192
(to grow), 192
shield, 159
vaulted tent, 129
veil, 198
last
(in the), 365
night, 262
late, 141
(of), 318
latter, 364
lattice, 188, 229, 401
latticework, 222, 254, 256, 439
laud
(to), 247
laudanum, 58
laugh
(to), 183, 292
laughing, 296
stock, 183, 292
laughter, 183, 292, 296
laver, 207
lavish
(to), 62
law, 290, 360, 491
(and the), 366
(fiery), 398
(fire of a), 398
(fire was a), 398
(in my), 494
(the), 362
lawful, 186
laws, 329
(and my), 495
(and the), 494
(and your), 497, 542
(his), 495
(the), 493
lawyer, 356
laxness, 218
lay, 505
(and she l down), 393, 542
(and), 411
(he), 411
(I), 413
(then they shall l hold), 436
(to l down), 301
(to l hold of), 154
(to l out), 176
(to l over), 121, 176, 350
(to l up), 235
(to), 140, 354
(you shall), 441, 540
layer, 95, 234, 345, 410, 428
laziness, 182, 354
lazy, 181
lead, 185, 423
(as), 430
(the), 422
(to l on), 356
(to), 62, 77, 82, 104, 194, 201, 267, 356, 397
leader, 60, 86, 130, 233, 267, 270, 272, 325
(to act as), 267
lead-weight, 90, 344
leaf, 127, 212, 233, 492
leafage, 127, 169
leafy, 317
league
(to be in), 191
lean, 194, 240
(and), 404
(the), 403
(to become), 194
(to grow), 194, 256
(to l on), 299, 502
(to l upon), 140, 354
(to move), 194
(to), 140, 354
leanness, 198, 219, 229, 256, 470
leap, 120, 471
(to), 55, 81, 114, 167, 387
learn
(to l by experience), 271
(to), 94, 132, 451
learned, 98
learning, 154
least
(not in the), 20
leather
(a kind of), 401
bag, 211
leave, 359
(and what they), 379, 520
(he shall), 367
(to give me), 453
(to), 98, 211, 271, 289, 363
leave!, 214
leaven, 153, 326, 480
(without), 151
leavened
(thing), 153, 480
(to be), 153, 480
led
(and he), 159
leech, 193
leek, 245
lees, 340
left, 280, 282
(and he was), 366
(but some), 371
(had), 365
(on the), 282
(shall be l behind), 468
(the), 434
(to go to the), 278
(to take the), 278
(you shall be), 489, 544
side, 278, 282
left over
(to be), 326
left-hand, 278
(the l side), 280
left-handed
(fig.), 190
leg, 234, 291
(lower), 288
armor, 158
legend, 29
lend
(and), 112
(to), 60, 270
(you do), 398
lending
on interest, 263
length, 200, 395
lengthening, 200
lentil, 278
leopard, 234
leper
(to be a), 272
leprosy, 425
(and for the), 437
(scall of), 344
(the), 426
(to break out of), 233
(to break out with), 233
leprous, 438
(to be), 272
(was), 438
lesion, 343
lessening, 49
lesser, 41
light, 297, 501
lest, 148, 432
let
(and l it), 50
(and she l down), 363
(and you shall l her go), 420
(to l go), 261, 266, 267
(you shall l go), 415
letter, 186, 289, 356, 441, 539
letters
(to spell), 17
on a tablet, 185
level, 461
(to be), 330
(to make), 174
Leviticus. *See Tanakh: 01 Torah:* 03 Leviticus
levy, 121

(and), 377
lewdness, 322
liar, 19
(to be a), 48
(to be found a), 48
liars
(to be found), 256
libation, 143, 147, 155, 359, 365
liberty, 293
license
(unbridled), 116
lick
(to l up), 77, 339
(to), 77, 204, 339
lie, 19, 48, 354
(and you shall l down), 427, 530
(he), 411
(she will), 410
(to l down with sexually), 254
(to l down), 226, 236, 259, 505
(to l in wait), 120, 185
(to l stretched out), 226
(to l with), 259
(to tell a), 48
(to), 48, 169, 256, 368
(you shall), 491
life, 35, 41, 86, 302, 311, 367
(and), 42
(course of), 190, 262
(duration of), 62
(early), 253, 256
(exhaling of), 146
(fountain of), 296, 485
(having the vigor of), 41
(his), 53
(in my), 48
(it is your very), 107, 375
(preservation of), 82
(price of a), 239
(to be restored to), 41, 46
(to have), 41, 46
(to live half of one's), 125
(to lose), 154
(to sustain), 41, 46
lifetime
(in her), 53
lift
(to l up), 116, 140, 178, 180, 470
(to), 108, 268, 344
(you shall), 377
up, 396
lifted
(and it was l up), 375, 518
(and she), 400
(I have l up), 379
(I l up), 382
(one l up), 272
(something l up), 131
(to be l up), 173, 178, 230, 454
(very l up), 245
up, 396
lifting, 155, 263
up, 263
light, 79, 148, 188, 213, 220, 223
(is the), 361
(returning), 302
(straight), 407
(the), 216
(to be), 85, 194
(to make l of), 116
(to send out), 194
(to), 218
in extension, 239
LVX (Latin), 83
of the sun, 185
light-bearer, 93
lightness, 153
lightning, 51, 118, 130, 241, 470
(to cast forth), 241
(to flash), 241
flash, 51, 130
lights, 218, 372, 447
(for), 386
(the), 374
ligure, 276, 476
like, 84, 131, 424
(the l of which), 84
(to be), 68, 248, 276
(to), 22
as, 19, 310
this, 64
liken
(to), 276
likeness, 310, 326, 459
(in the l of), 310
lily, 380, 528
limb, 19, 68, 358
lime, 185, 250
limit, 53, 60, 130, 134, 188, 295
limitless
light, 295, 553
limp
(to), 181, 306
limping, 181
line, 41, 128, 133, 327, 412
(measuring), 128
linen, 19, 84, 355, 406, 433, 451, 534
(and), 452, 535
(fine), 272
(of), 452, 458, 535
(the), 452, 535
(white kind made in Egypt), 118, 470
(white), 19
linger
(to), 69
lintel, 320, 336, 517, 522
lion, 62, 193, 196, 261
(as a), 207
(like a), 205, 207
(young), 247
l's whelp, 300
of God, 209
lioness, 62
of God, 209
lion-like, 209
lip, 283, 432
lips, 451, 534
(her), 437
(quivering motion of), 83
(with), 452, 535
(your), 444, 526
liquid
(to spread a), 266
liquified
(to be), 261
liquor, 82, 478
listen
(to), 76, 294, 400
listeners, 456
litter, 113, 265, 489
little, 139, 232, 251, 277, 296, 303, 522
(of quantity or of time), 232
littleness, 139
live
(and he), 42
(and it), 53
(and may), 42
(and they), 48
(and you shall), 47
(and), 42, 48
(let), 47
(shall), 52
(then she shall), 47
(to l forever), 41, 46
(to), 37, 41, 46
lived
(and), 53
(they), 42
lively, 41
liver
(as heaviest organ), 45
(the), 50
lives
(at the cost of their own), 461, 538
(of your), 476, 541
livestock, 182
lividness, 270, 474
living, 35, 41, 46, 300
(the), 41
being, 302
creature, 311
creatures, 300
substance, 166, 406
thing, 35
things, 41
lizard, 64, 75
(a kind of), 435
lo, 188
lo!, 19, 55, 74, 78, 398
load, 113, 196, 263, 273
(to bear a), 113
(to carry a), 174
(to), 146, 174, 431
loaf
(round), 167
loan, 264, 265
loath
(to), 290
loathe

(to), 58, 71, 124, 136, 168, 183, 360, 491
loathing, 124, 189
(to feel a), 136, 168, 183, 491
(to feel), 58
loathsome
(to be), 71, 129, 360, 423
thing, 189
lobe
(and the), 494
(the), 493
of the ear, 318, 482
lock, 171, 185, 353
(to), 162
of hair, 195, 356
locking, 171
locks, 267
locksmith, 242
locust, 18, 27, 30, 129, 184, 209, 424
(a kind of), 188, 209
(as whirring), 209
swarm, 188
locusts, 68, 358
lodge, 149
(to), 105, 292, 414
lodging
(place of), 144, 430
place, 358
loftiness, 25, 297
of pride, 248
lofty, 25, 297, 314
(to be), 213, 441
abode, 64
place, 151
stature, 375
loin, 204, 205, 238, 402, 506
loincloth, 198
loins, 131, 145, 322, 478, 511
long
(and you shall have been), 456, 536
(as l as), 132, 384
(may be), 232, 478
(of God's wisdom - fig.), 200, 395
(of time - fig.), 395
(of time), 200
(pinions), 200, 395
(to be), 200, 395
(to l after), 168, 463
(to l for), 30, 83, 168, 227, 290, 292, 463
ago, 201
duration, 160, 399
hair (of head), 267
longed
(you), 362
longing, 22, 74, 257, 292, 386, 444, 486
(to faint with), 83
for, 74
look, 33, 55, 199, 204
(and I will l upon it), 369
(and you shall), 380, 520
(to l after), 179
(to l at), 144, 279, 430
(to l down or out), 320, 517
(to l for), 133
(to l on), 283, 506
(to l out or about), 176
(to l out), 25
(to), 38, 80, 187, 360
looked
(and they), 57
looking, 193
lookout, 179
point, 196
post, 179
loom, 185
loop
(used in attaching curtains to hooks), 85
loose
(place of letting or turning), 282
(to be), 376
(to hang), 271
(to let), 267, 328, 376
(to), 98, 376
(you shall break), 362
loosed
(to be), 271
loosen
(to), 326
lord, 80, 124, 195, 247, 312, 403, 483, 506
(of king, of God), 210
(to l it over), 261
of the flies, 139
lost, 20
(something), 27
thing, 27
lot, 35, 153, 205, 337
cast for certain decisions, 205, 208
lots, 371
(to throw), 35
lottery, 371
lotus
(a kind of), 141
loud
(to be), 68
louder, 135
love, 22, 29, 30, 35
(and he will l you), 53, 332
(object of deep), 138
(object of), 300
(pleasures of), 22
(sensuous), 94
(to become emotionally agitated with), 220
(to l deeply), 214, 442
(to l fervently), 28
(to), 22, 214, 292, 442
loved
(and he l her), 47
(and he), 42
object, 22
lovely, 46, 173, 412
(to be), 169, 408
loves, 22
(and), 31
(he l you), 46
him, 30
lovingkindness, 322
loving-one, 35
low, 53, 246, 256, 259, 294, 442, 448
(one who is), 53
(to be), 85, 98, 144, 155, 294, 342, 345
(to become), 294
(to), 96
place, 296, 465
lower, 448, 458, 537
part, 243
lowest, 57, 448
lowland, 192, 296
lowliest
(of station), 294
lowliness, 296
lowly, 246
(to be), 192
loyal, 157, 436
luck, 96
luminaries, 372
luminary, 213
luminous, 188
luminousness, 193
lump, 101, 439
Luna. *See* Planets: Traditional: 04 Luna
lure, 308
(to lay a), 293
(to), 291, 293
lurk
(to), 185
lust, 27, 295, 424
(to have inordinate), 94
(to), 76, 364
lustful, 255
lustfulness, 98
luxuriant, 277, 495
luxuriate
(to), 143, 429
luxuriously
(to grow), 224
luxury, 143, 337, 429
lye, 185, 360
lying, 45, 256
(act of l for sexual contact), 273
(act of l with another person sexually), 256
(place of l down), 236, 258, 505, 512
(your carnal), 417, 520
down, 273
in wait, 130, 185
mace, 442
mad
(to be), 278
made, 430
(and), 430
(have I m you), 463, 532

(I have m them), 449, 534
(I have), 435
(I m him), 423
(shall be), 430, 433
(thing), 199
madness, 87, 95, 300, 317, 318, 502
magazine, 176
maggot, 212
magic
art, 329
square, 192
magician, 191, 219, 281, 329, 447, 505
magician-astrologer, 219, 447
magistrate, 465
magnificence, 66, 186
magnify
(to), 55, 243
magus, 63
maid, 286
(and m servants), 438
(your), 442, 526
maidens
(and her), 416
(attendant), 232
(song), 483
maidservant, 65, 286
maidservants
(and), 436
mail
(coat of), 358
maim
(to), 238, 506
maimed
(and), 369
maintain
(to), 220
majestic, 195
(to be), 186
one, 195
majesty, 32, 78, 190, 293, 402
make
(and I will m him), 461
(and I will m of you), 464, 533
(and I will), 422
(and to m you), 457, 530
(and you shall), 434
(to), 95, 120, 171, 178, 266, 279, 376, 471
(you shall), 430, 457
(you), 428
Malachi. *See Tanakh: 02 Neviim:* 21 Malachi
malachite, 264, 469
male, 203, 206, 306
(every circumcised), 172
(issue of - semen), 31
(of humans and animals), 203
(you shall sanctify the), 367
(young), 137
ass, 230
calf, 125
genitals, 263
organ, 290
temple prostitute, 290
malignant, 388
Malkut. See Kabbalah:The Ten *Sefirot*:10 *Malkut*
mallet, 320
mallow, 103
maltreat
(to), 83
man, 186, 193, 247, 268, 270, 306
(and a poor), 58
(artificial), 97, 371
(daughters of), 329, 501
(great), 247
(inner), 53
(of uprightness), 186
(old), 364
(poor), 173, 448
(rich), 350
(semblance of a), 248, 461
(skin of), 55
(strong), 60, 186
(to be a), 247
(wise), 86, 96, 368, 371
(young), 137, 156, 197, 394
manacles, 168, 407
mandrake
(as an aphrodisiac), 42
mandrakes, 43, 45
mane, 270
maneh, 116
manger, 86, 193
manipulate
(to), 247
mankind, 268, 270
manna, 109, 415
manner, 193, 201, 397
(in this), 44
mansion, 83
mantle, 143, 186, 216, 235
(like a), 367
(to put a m on), 216
manure, 212
many, 185, 205
(the), 361
(to be), 186, 188, 201
(to become), 186, 188
mar
(you shall), 508
marauding
band, 34
marble, 355
(red), 33
(white), 355
march
(to), 171, 194, 201, 310, 397
marching, 173
mare, 149
mariner, 97
mark, 142, 182, 214, 262, 289, 297, 449
(and shall m out), 460, 537
(to describe with a), 27
(to m off), 162, 438
(to m out), 292
(to), 27
(you shall m out), 441
marked, 187
(to be m out), 136
with points (of sheep and goats), 165
marker, 327
market, 167, 441
place, 391
marks, 177
marriage, 315
(to perform levirat), 71, 361
marriageable
girl, 68
marriages
(and make you), 462
marrow, 67
(full of), 73
marry
(shall), 524, 556
(to), 124, 154
Mars. *See* Planets: Traditional: 05 Mars
marsh, 117
plants, 31
marshal, 266
marvel, 133, 198
marvelous
(to be), 133
masculine
unity, 35
masculinity
(to show), 247
mason
(to), 120
mass, 45, 332
(collected), 163
(shapeless), 97, 371
mast, 58, 377, 527
mastaba, 153, 338
master, 80, 266, 325, 403
(to be), 261
of the name (*Baal Shem*), 307, 490
workman, 117, 419
masters
of the heavens, 328, 501
master-workman, 111, 416
mastery, 197, 284, 497
(having), 266
(to have), 261
match
(to), 306, 490
mate, 356, 386
(and his), 405
mated
(to be), 43
material, 145
materialized, 284, 480
matter, 119, 127
maw, 129
may
(what), 64
be, 60, 65
me
(against), 416

(at), 28
(by), 28
(for), 59
(in), 28
(remember), 390
(to), 59, 60
(with), 28
meadow, 51, 75, 199
meadow-saffron, 337
meal, 70, 84, 161, 195, 264
(coarse), 264
flour, 161
meant
(you), 420, 528
measure, 63, 68, 344
(the m of wisdom), 339
(to), 67, 75, 317, 509
of body, 410
of height, 410
measured
amount, 317, 509
portion, 351
measurement, 68, 103, 317, 471, 509
meat, 32, 42, 46, 84, 111
(juices cooked from), 261
(piece of), 351
(slaughtered), 32, 42, 46
offering, 125
meddle
(to), 124, 189
mediate
(to), 252
medicinal
(plant), 32
medicine, 29, 232
meditate
(to), 29, 249, 299
meditation, 11, 39, 93, 252, 254, 295, 410, 450
meekness, 149
meet
(to m her), 414
(to m him), 414
(to m them), 428, 530
(to m us), 434
(to m you), 421, 521
(to), 74, 103, 158, 165, 200, 243, 244, 282, 395, 412
meeting, 140
(unforeseen), 264
melody, 216, 236, 375
melt
(to cause to), 68
(to), 68, 169, 183, 261
melted
(to be), 316, 481
melting, 303, 325, 472
Mem. *See* Hebrew Alphabet:13 *Mem*
member, 68, 276, 358
of a group, 71, 396
of the body, 68, 358
members
(of the body), 239
memorandum, 230, 476
memorial, 203, 231, 477
offering, 205
part of it, 369
memory
of, 383
men
(to revile), 105, 441
of distinction, 289, 483
mend
(to), 127
menstrous, 32, 78
menstruation, 93
mental
conception, 293
mention
(and m me), 393
(you shall), 373
mercenary, 337, 339
merchandise, 218, 220, 229, 245, 249
merchant, 215
merciful, 217, 445
Mercury. *See* Planets: Traditional: 02 Mercury
mercy, 91, 102
(and I will show), 382
(to have), 214, 442
Mercy Seat, 394
merit, 304
merry, 266
mesh, 288
message, 326
messenger, 111, 240, 348
messengers, 396
met
(I), 436
metal
(casting of), 187
(molten), 143
(piece of), 313
(plate of), 107
(shining), 280
craftsman, 329
ornament, 215
plating, 180
metals
(inspector and valuer of), 84, 406
Micah. *See Tanakh: 02 Neviim:* 15 Micah
mid-, 327
midday, 237
middle, 23, 130, 241, 327, 343
middle, the, 23
midnight, 180, 327, 350
(about), 334
midst, 138, 198, 241
(in the m of), 80, 404
might, 47, 64, 66, 75, 96, 109, 139, 184, 186, 187, 194, 197, 276, 351, 399, 424, 515, 527
(and according to your), 380, 511
(and), 378
(my), 57
mighty, 55, 96, 109, 135, 146, 148, 156, 185, 187, 194, 205, 353, 386, 427, 431, 446, 479, 481, 527
(to be), 184, 186, 424
(used only to describe God), 194
act, 197
God of Israel, 364
man, 186, 193
one, 50, 186, 193
power, 197
things in nature, 50
mild, 306, 490
mildew, 270, 474
(and with), 278, 495
mildness, 306, 490
milk, 58
(in the m of), 61
(sour), 58
mill, 91, 92, 410
millet, 81, 404
mill-stone, 138, 201
mina, 116
mind, 51, 53, 302
(to call to), 203
(to get a), 53
(troubled), 241
mindful
(be m of), 480
mine, 59
mingle
(to), 80, 140, 354
mingled
(to be), 201, 396
minister, 478
(and his), 481
(and m unto you), 479, 537
(and will), 470
(his), 480
(they shall), 475
(they), 474
(to act as m in priest's office), 94, 410
(to m for), 138
(to m to him), 478
(to m to), 468
(to m unto them), 484, 543
(to), 372, 468, 476
ministered
(and he), 474
ministry, 193, 468
(religious), 468
(the), 469
miracle, 292, 336
miraculous
signs, 289
mire, 46, 84, 112, 351, 406, 468
mirer, 84, 406
mirror, 193, 212
mirrors
(in the), 373
mirth, 269, 296
miscarriage, 169
mischief, 137, 247, 427
(to imagine), 440

mischievous
purpose, 71
misconstrue
(to), 225
misery, 148, 225
misfortune, 225
mislead
(to), 212, 260
miss
(to m the way), 35
(to), 35
missile, 141, 173, 261
missive, 186, 262, 356
mist, 18, 272, 502
(and a), 27
as rising, 272
of heaven, 57
mistake, 266
mistress, 128
(her), 358
(my), 362
(of servants), 356
(your), 367, 506
misuse
(to), 340
mitre
(and with the), 384
(the), 382
mix
(to m by pounding), 408
(to), 80, 140, 201, 226, 246, 354, 396
mixed
(to be), 201, 396
company, 226
mixture, 69, 123, 140, 226, 354, 381
moan
(to), 29, 77
moaning, 29
moat, 242, 508
mock
(to), 125, 160, 181, 183, 292, 304
mocked
(you have), 477
mocker, 140, 304, 476
(as a), 489
mockery, 209, 304, 479
(I made a), 479
mocking, 125, 182, 209, 292
song, 168, 175
modest, 192
(to be), 192
moist, 57, 193
(to be), 193
moisten
(to), 253
moistness, 57
moisture, 192
mole, 62, 232, 516
(as digger), 233
molten
(to be), 316, 481
image, 155, 365
metal, 143
support, 207
moment, 227, 279
money, 168, 463
(the), 171, 464
month, 198, 248
monthly, 248
Months of the Jewish Calendar
01 *Tishri*, 472
02 *Cheshvan*, 274, 493
03 *Kislev*, 136
04 *Tevet*, 294
05 *Shevet*, 248
06 *Adar*, 186
07 *Nisan*, 173, 449
08 *Iyar*, 192
09 *Sivan*, 144, 430
10 *Tammuz*, 311
11 *Av*, 15
12 *Elul*, 85
Veadar (intercalary month), 193
monument, 167, 231, 441
moon, 106, 198, 345, 518, *See Also* Planets:Traditional:04 Luna
(crescent - as ornament), 345, 518
(new), 248
Moon. *See* Planets: Traditional: 04 Moon
moral, 343
more, 363
(so much the), 439
than, 109, 415, 416
moreover, 363
morning, 188, 241
(early), 459
star, 93
morrow, 376
(and on the), 392
(on the), 391
morsel, 320
mortal
man, 270
mortar, 87, 98, 213, 267, 272, 424
(to beat in), 48, 330
mortgage
(to), 226
moth, 140, 276
mother, 60, 61, 355
(thy), 80, 340
of pearl, 186
mother-in-law, 312
(his), 460
motion
(to set in), 229, 401
moufflon, 213
moulding, 188
mound, 144, 303
mount, 178, 187, 290
(in their), 309, 491
(to m and ride), 201
mountain, 187, 196, 290
(summit of), 215
clefts, 239
goat, 131, 213, 274, 493
peak, 126, 422
sheep, 213
mourn
(to), 20, 51, 68, 74, 158, 175
mourned, 45
mournfully, 426
mourning, 51, 52, 84, 88, 315
(song of), 88
(the), 56
song, 83
mournings, 102, 373
mouse, 236
moustache, 299, 486
mouth, 46, 104, 140, 179, 212, 329, 388
(your), 132, 353
mouths
(to make m at), 144, 191, 477, 495
move
(to m about), 194, 240
(to m away), 87, 134
(to m lightly), 240
(to m noisily), 104, 374
(to m on), 348
(to m slowly), 29
(to m to and fro), 79, 152, 457
(to make), 144
(to), 77, 87, 134, 144, 177, 238, 246, 348, 488, 506
gently, 22
moved
(to be), 68, 70, 360
moves
(that), 479
moving
(to keep), 329
away, 93, 249
back, 93
creature, 353, 535
things, 42, 340
mowing, 25
much, 64, 185, 205, 213, 366
(and too), 363
(to be), 201
muchness, 64
mud, 46, 112, 351, 468
mulct
(to), 298
mule, 232
female, 234
mules, 69, 221, 358, 416
multiply
(and I will), 369
(and m you), 205, 373, 405, 509
(and to), 376
(and), 364, 380, 520
(to), 28, 188, 201, 453
multitude, 98, 117, 185, 190, 312, 345, 378, 419
(connected), 159
murder
(shall), 394
(to), 189, 238
murderer, 189

murmur, 123, 421
(to), 68, 70, 105, 216, 242, 360, 414, 469, 481
murmured
(and you), 382
murmurers
(as), 360, 515
murmuring, 39, 323
murmurings, 464
(their), 476, 541
(your), 481, 542
murrain, 187
muscle, 403
muse, 124, 472
(to), 29, 249
muses, 483
(the nine), 552
music, 138, 213, 216, 375
(of instruments), 78
(resounding), 93, 410
(to make), 213
musical, 173, 412
notation, 444
Musical Instruments
Bachatzotzruwt (brass - trumpets), 437
Chaliyl (wind - pipe, flute), 96
Chatsotserah (brass – trumpet or clarion), 286
Chatzotzrot (brass - trumpets), 436
(and the), 438
(with), 435
Dachavah (stringed - unknown), 41
Gittiyth (string – harp), 445
harp
(string of), 109, 415
Kinnowr (string – lyre or harp), 228
Mena'ana' (percussion – rattle), 230
Metseleth (drums – cymbals), 345
Nebel (string – harp, lute, or guitar), 101
Pisanteriyn (string – lyre or harp), 313, 507
Qiyatharos (string – zither or lyre), 493
Qiytharos (string – zither or lyre), 428
Sabbeka (string – trigon), 102
Shaliysh (unknown), 372
Shemiyniyth (unknown), 444
Siyfoneya (wind – bagpipe, double pipe, panpipes), 193
Suwmponeyah (wind – bagpipe, double pipe, or panpipes), 216
Suwpowneyah (wind – bagpipe, double pipe, or panpipes), 219
Taqowah (wind – trumpet), 348
Tof (percussion – hand-drum, bezel, timbrel, tambourine, 320, 517
'uwgab (wind - flute, reed-pipe, or panpipe), 101
musing, 39, 93, 252, 295, 410
muster, 202
(to), 179
mustering, 180
musterings, 179
muster-officer, 262
mute, 90, 368
mutilate
(to m a part of the body), 213, 442
mutilated
(to be), 238, 506
mutter
(to), 29
muzzle, 165, 405
(to), 130, 384
myriad, 189, 190
myriads, 359
(from the), 374
myrrh, 58, 209
myrtle
tree, 87
myself
(and I hid), 35
mysteries
(deep), 199
mysterious, 192
mystery, 58, 59
mystical, 167
Nahum. *See Tanakh: 02 Neviim:* 16 Nahum
nail, 28, 233, 261, 296, 352
naïveté, 322, 466
naked, 251, 253, 342, 462, 463
place, 247
thing, 266, 471
nakedness, 230, 232, 247, 250, 251, 253, 266, 386, 463, 471
(and the), 389
(her), 388
(his), 389
(their), 411, 533
(your), 393, 515
name, 187, 262, 468
(after their), 424
(and by), 419
(the), 264
of unity, 269, 473
names, 416, 419
(according to the), 430
(by their), 432, 531
(by), 419
(from their), 448, 534
(in), 417
(their), 432, 434, 531
nard, 217
narrow, 234
(to be), 322
(to make), 322
(to), 285, 517
way, 308
narrowness, 183
nation, 29, 36, 65, 90, 132, 369, 384
(and), 43
(the), 42
(with a), 39
nations, 47, 87, 368
native, 196
(as a), 207
(like the n born), 207
natron, 376
natural, 145
nature
(mighty things in), 50
nausea, 189
nave, 83, 329
navel, 198, 325, 395
(for your), 343, 496
navel-band, 307
nay
rather, 51
Nazarite
(to live as a), 219
near, 141, 245, 289, 305
(and you came), 426, 536
(to come), 241, 417
nearness, 141
neck, 199, 220, 238, 267, 270, 416, 444, 471, 501
(back of), 238, 267, 501
(then you shall break its), 425
necklace, 143, 199, 356
(beaded), 200
(to serve as a), 199
neck-pendant, 199
necromancer, 23, 128, 158, 281, 505
need, 247, 249, 435
(in n of), 224
(to have a), 224
(to have), 250
(to), 250
needed
(thing), 249, 250
(things), 409
needlework, 264
(embroidered with), 262, 468
needy, 87, 144, 408
person, 87, 408
Nefesh. See Kabbalah:Souls: *Nefesh*
neglect, 260
(to), 260
negligent
(to be), 260
Nehemiah. *See Tanakh: 03 Kethuvim:* 11 Nehemiah
neigh
(to), 144
neighbor, 277, 334, 495
(her), 388
(of her), 446
neighing, 173
neither, 50, 56, 177, 331, 414
Neptune. *See* Planets: Nontraditional: Neptune
nerve, 270
nervous
(to be), 55
Neshamah. See Kabbalah:Souls:*Neshamah*

nest, 163, 438
  (to make a), 184, 456
net, 155, 209, 216, 239, 254, 256, 394, 439, 468, 499
  prey, 155
nethermost
  earth, 557
netted
  (something), 205
  cloth, 222
netting, 254, 256, 439
nettle, 264
nettles, 211, 308, 324, 512
network, 254, 256, 439, 468
  (the), 469
  of boughs, 254, 439
Netzach. *See* Kabbalah:The Ten *Sefirot*:07 *Netzach*
nevertheless, 210, 439
new, 57, 199, 248, 295
  (to be), 248
  thing, 198, 248
news, 294, 299, 328, 331
  (to bear), 326
next
  (the), 361, 378
night, 88, 94, 100, 226
  (to pass the), 105, 292, 414
  watch, 340
night-watch, 342
nine, 428, 430
  (and), 430
  (to), 517
nineteen, 531
ninety, 449, 534
  (and), 450, 534
ninth, 436
  (the), 437, 516
nipper, 285, 517
nipping, 285, 517
nipple, 22
nitre, 376
no, 50, 51, 55, 61, 177, 331, 414
  (with), 52
nobility, 90, 339
  (world of), 389, 522
noble, 85, 189, 252, 312, 409, 506, 525
  (to be), 186
  deeds, 90
  one, 85
nobleman, 409, 525
nobleness, 90
nobles
  fig., 148
noise, 153, 395, 399
  (to make a great), 70, 359
  (to make a), 104, 374
  (to make), 68
nonad, 428
Non-Biblical Characters
  Christian, 270
  Christian Rosenkreutz
    number of years hidden from his followers, 140
  Hiram Abiff, 227, 452
  Mormon, 270
  Mormonism, 423
  Nero Caeser, 383, 529
  Pope John Paul II, 382, 529
  Teitan, 383
noon, 237
noose, 178, 416
nor, 50, 177, 331, 414
north
  (of direction), 202, 462
northern, 207
  one, 207
northerner, 207
northward, 202, 462
nose, 100, 148, 439, 456
  ring, 33, 118, 380
nostril, 100, 224, 439
not, 27, 50, 51, 55, 56, 60, 61, 80, 148, 177, 307, 331, 355, 403, 414, 432
  (and), 55, 56
  (do), 50
  (has), 54
  (have), 50
  (is it), 61
  (is), 54
  (must I), 54
  (so as), 307
  (until), 307
  in, 52
  in the least, 20
  in), 52
  withstanding, 121
  yet, 214, 217, 443, 446
not?
  (have you), 80, 403
  (is there), 80, 403
  (is), 58
note
  (to), 340, 505
nothing, 50, 80, 403
  (as wish or preference), 50, 331
  (good for), 90
no-thing, 80
no-thing, 403
nothingness, 105
nought, 80, 403
  (of), 90, 163
nourishment, 116
now, 70, 78, 105, 155, 318, 340, 435
  (and), 340
  (until), 155, 435
nude
  (to be), 227
nudity, 230, 232
nullification
  of somethingness, 273
numb
  (to grow), 108
number, 162, 202, 264, 270, 280, 438
  (and you shall), 418
  (counted), 116
  (to), 111, 116, 179
  (you shall n them), 367, 516
  (you shall), 416, 419
numbers, 423
Numbers. *See Tanakh: 01 Torah:* 04 Numbers
numerous, 187, 427
  (to be), 184, 424
Nun. *See* Hebrew Alphabet:14 *Nun*
nurse
  (to), 128, 167, 168
nursing, 363
nuts, 33
O!, 39
oak, 54, 105, 414
oar, 270
oath, 54, 282, 429
  (from my), 450
  (the), 60
  (with), 429
  of covenant, 54
Obadiah. *See Tanakh: 02 Neviim:* 13 Obadiah
obedience, 139
obedient
  ones, 456
obey
  (to), 294
object, 171
oblation, 125, 268, 490
obligation, 221, 486
obscure, 256, 259, 442
obscurity, 256, 314, 442
observance, 350
observe, 480
  (and you shall), 487, 544
  (to diligently), 271
  (to o signs), 271
  (to), 176, 187, 340, 440
  (you shall), 479, 480, 489, 548
obstinancy, 294
obstinate
  (to be), 124
obtain
  (to o by paying purchase price), 212
occasion, 127, 312
occupation, 117, 178, 451
occupied
  (to be), 144
occupy
  (to), 226
occurence, 420
occurrence, 165, 181
ocean-deep, 149
odious
  (to become), 83
odor, 198, 384
  (foul), 165
  (sweet), 263, 468
  of sacrifice, 402
of, 95
  (and), 309
off, 109, 415
  (and you will take), 434
  (let them take), 436

(to beat), 37
(to break), 170
(to go), 56
offal, 98, 351
offend
(to), 58, 262, 468
offended
(to be), 54
offenders
(reckoned as), 35
offense, 262, 265, 468
offensive, 348
offer, 45
(to o freely), 75
(to o sacrifice), 30, 147, 359
(to), 147, 239, 359
(will), 404
(you shall), 404, 407
offered
(and he), 52
offering, 31, 41, 125, 230, 268, 377, 478, 490
(and a gift), 380
(and the), 499
(and you give your free will), 484
(burnt), 127
(drink), 143
(for a sin), 309
(for the), 502
(free-will), 80
(his), 327
(libation or drink), 147, 359
(like the meal), 334
(meat), 125
(memorial), 205
(my), 500
(peace), 277, 477
(Pesach o to YHVH), 186
(sacrificial), 31
(sin), 41, 46
(the gift), 379
(the), 379
(votive), 217
(wave), 478
(whole burnt), 109, 127
(your meal), 334, 489
made by fire, 243
offerings, 322, 498, 511
(and o of), 498
(with their meal), 341, 505
office, 88, 165, 408
of judge, 166
officer, 182, 330, 372
(principal), 94, 410
of the court, 272
official, 257, 266, 284, 330, 497
offscourings, 97
offshoot, 212, 276
offspring, 58, 63, 131, 178, 228, 234, 276, 319, 327, 424
(robbed of), 270
of wild beasts, 327
ogle
(to), 354
oh
now!, 71
that!, 56
that…!, 67
would that!, 67
oh!, 27, 28, 34, 36, 39
oil, 266, 285, 498
(for anointing), 269
(fresh or pure), 243
(shining), 243
(small o jug), 105, 347
(the), 286, 498
(to press out), 236
(to press), 236
vessel, 52
ointment, 246, 269
pot, 269, 419
ointment-maker, 246, 249
old, 54, 160, 167, 272, 350, 399, 407, 440, 492
(of humans), 153, 434
(of), 318
(three years), 501
(to be), 153, 434
(to become), 54, 153, 348, 434
age, 153, 171, 251, 434
man, 364
olive, 297
berry, 291
tree, 297
omen
(to take as an), 271
on
account of, 81, 109, 121, 147, 415, 431
account of this, 73, 397
behalf of, 94, 121
high, 121
the ground of, 121
the inside, 295
the right, 139
the side of, 109, 415
this account, 104, 413
what account?, 140
once, 28
one, 28, 29, 292, 432
(and the), 42
(and), 36
(as), 46, 52
(certain), 148, 174, 186, 192
(discouraged), 121
(hated), 158, 459
(in o of), 31
(noble), 85
(only), 51
(shining), 93
(thankless), 160, 437
(the o who falls), 171
(the), 35
(unjust, perverse, unrighteous), 128
(young), 185, 190
anointed, 155, 365
of, 29
who has a familiar spirit, 158
one hundred, 65
one third, 377
oneness, 298
ones
(little), 107, 443
oneself
(in front of), 76
(to delight), 143, 429
onion, 141
only, 39, 51, 60, 62, 210, 240, 325, 355, 439
onset, 208
onslaught, 208
onto, 121
onycha, 415, 417
onyx, 104, 374
opal, 276, 476
open
(to be), 321
(to break), 175, 192, 428
(to o wide), 267, 320
(to), 176, 233, 322, 416, 527
(you shall), 465
opened, 236
(and she), 466
(and were), 376
(is), 416
opening, 320, 322, 337, 341, 517
instrument, 337
through which one may look, 229, 401
open-minded, 322
opens
(that which first), 234
(that), 391
opinion, 93
(divided), 192, 477
opponent, 201
opportune
(to be), 74
opportunity, 312
opposite, 76, 126, 352
to, 76, 97
opposition, 247, 314
oppress, 133, 146
(to), 83, 132, 144, 153, 183, 269, 281, 306, 316, 478, 480, 516, 523
(you shall), 461
oppressed, 42, 327
oppression, 146, 176, 183, 208, 259, 272, 299, 317, 318, 468, 478
(subject to), 87, 408
oppressor, 152, 158, 234, 318, 480, 482
or, 20, 60, 355
oracle, 117, 263
orchard, 76, 234, 264
ordain
(to), 234, 428, 432
order, 223, 234, 428

(in o not), 307
(in o that), 229
(in o to), 229
(things that are set in), 234, 428
(to lay in), 234, 428
(to put in), 234, 428
(to set in), 234, 428
(to), 123, 234, 428
orders
(to give), 123
ordinance, 130, 134, 302
ore
(precious), 235
organ
(male), 290
origin, 60, 88, 157, 226, 355
originator
of a class, 15
of a profession, 15
of an art, 15
ornament, 67, 165, 190, 230
(metal), 215
(to adorn with a neck), 199
ornaments, 92, 103
orphan, 312, 494
osprey, 158
ostrich, 147, 151, 330, 431
other, 189, 198, 220, 362, 471
otherwise, 20
out
(breaking), 391
(to be put), 46
(to beat), 37, 189
(to break), 177, 196, 334, 468
(to call), 241
(to go or come), 204
(to go), 114, 123, 180, 349
(to look), 25
Lilith!, 534
of, 109, 415, 416
there, 60
out!, 119, 125, 470, 473
outcast
(to), 34, 37
outcome, 224, 474
outcry, 130, 223
(to), 177
outer, 171, 445
(at the), 215, 467
outermost
(at the), 215, 467
outflow
(to), 176
outgoing, 324
outgrowth, 56
outhouse, 112
outlay, 205
outline, 355
outpouring, 168, 228
outside, 125, 185, 473
outspreading, 73
outstretching, 282
outward, 125, 171, 445, 473
outwards, 60
oven, 380
(in), 380
ovens
(and in your), 392, 515
over, 76, 121
(and passed), 387
(bring us), 411
(to break), 276, 515
(you shall pass), 387
overcome
(to), 29, 78, 240, 351, 481, 527
overdrive
(and if they o them), 207, 437
overflow, 228
(to), 176, 466, 487
overflowing, 317, 516
overhand, 320, 492, 517
overhang
(to), 224
overhanging, 224
overlaid
(and he o it), 183
overlay
(to), 41, 113, 176
(you shall o it), 367
overlook
(to), 320, 517
overpower
(to), 351, 527
overreach
(to), 175
overreacher, 175
overrun
(to be), 224
overseer, 182, 230, 282, 353, 424
(to be), 161
overshadow
(to), 121, 350
oversight, 180, 282, 353
overspread
(to), 199, 496
overtake
(and when you o them), 422, 529
(to), 269
overthrow, 131, 162, 223, 343, 388
(to), 34, 37, 126, 211, 223, 340, 352, 532
(you), 382
overthrown, 286
(something), 286
overtunic, 186
overturn
(to), 126, 174, 352, 465
overwhelm
(to), 440
owl, 151, 180
(and the horned), 518
(eared), 308, 514
(great), 308, 514
(the horned), 517
own
(to), 124
owner, 124
(female), 128
ox, 132, 241, 328, 451
(and his), 333
goad, 93, 135
oxen, 132, 241, 451
pace
(to), 171
pacify
(to), 127
pack, 159
pact, 44
paid
(and shall be), 393, 542
pail, 43, 155, 435
pain, 58, 67, 70, 82, 100, 171, 198, 346, 395, 461
(mental and physical), 42
(place of), 188
(to be in), 42, 209
(to have), 42
(to), 171, 209
pained
(to be), 44
paint
(to adorn with), 77
pair, 151
paired
(to be), 43
palace, 83, 151, 194, 237, 314, 433, 480, 507
palanquin, 199, 265, 489
palate, 46, 329
pale
(to grow), 195
paleness, 270, 474
palisade, 149
palm, 120, 156, 448
branch, 127
frond, 127
of the hand, 156
stalk and citron, 389
tree, 107, 372
tree figure, 372
pamper
(to), 204
pan, 207, 310, 321, 478
(in the stewing), 480
(stew), 480
panel, 181, 454
(to), 303, 496
panelling, 344
pang, 58, 240, 243
panic, 198
pant
(to p after), 227
(to), 281, 285, 481, 505
papyrus, 22, 63
parable, 45, 276
parables
(to speak in), 276
parallel
to, 76
paramour, 300
(royal), 259
parapet, 196

parcel, 158, 324
parch
(to), 152
parched, 125
(to be), 420
condition, 153
grain, 156
ground, 167, 326, 441
land, 167, 441
place, 292
pardon
(to), 119
park, 264
parlor, 194
part, 116, 153, 158, 353
(after), 364
(highest), 198
(inward), 194
(of the parts of an animal cut in half for a sacrifice), 355
(to), 176, 303, 320
cut off, 138
parted, 431
(they p from each other), 244
parting
gift, 264
of ways, 281
partition, 394
partner
(in trade), 191
partridge, 241
parts
(and divide into three), 497
(extreme), 206
(hanging), 162
(inward), 40, 135
party-wall, 129, 474
pass, 249
(and you shall cause to), 410, 526
(to p away), 94, 138, 453
(to p between), 158
(to p by), 98, 138, 226, 453
(to p on), 94, 98, 138, 453
(to p over), 138, 226, 306, 453
(to p through), 138, 226, 453
(to p within), 158
(you shall p on), 387
(you shall), 385
over, 33
through, 229
passed
(I p over), 389
(you), 404, 524
passing, 249
away, 143, 454
passion, 295, 302
past
(in times), 384, 521
pastry, 150
pasturage, 250, 408
pasture, 75, 80, 135, 187, 199, 230, 250, 282
(to), 228
pasturing, 408
patch
(to), 59
path, 190, 263, 314, 316
paths, 285, 460, 481
pathway, 314
patience
(self-restraint of), 200, 395
patient, 200, 395
pattern, 459
(after their), 469, 540
(to), 277, 503
pause, 73
pavement, 106, 279, 443
pavilion, 253, 438
(royal), 434
pay
(to p out), 303
(to), 276, 456
payment, 195
peace, 279, 478
(hold), 87
(shall hold your), 483, 547
(to be at), 277, 293, 477
(to be in a covenant of), 277, 477
(will make), 432, 531
offering, 277, 477
peacefulness, 73
peacock, 303
peak, 126, 422
pearl, 104, 181, 186, 250, 374, 454
(mother of), 186
pebble, 234, 324
pedestal, 73, 88, 141, 398, 408
peel
(to), 184, 189
peep
(to), 180, 215, 484, 489
peg, 28, 296
Peh. See Hebrew Alphabet:17 *Peh*
pelican, 326
penalty, 298
pendant, 165
penetrate
(to), 27
penis, 290
Pentateuch. *See Tanakh:* Torah
people, 29, 36, 65, 90, 132, 369, 384
(a), 309
(in your), 157, 366
(mixed), 226
(the), 135, 386
peradventure, 60, 65
perceive
(to), 38, 139, 187, 387
percent, 33
(the), 39
perennial, 314, 507
perfect, 109, 277, 306, 477, 490
(thing made), 140
(to make), 98
(to), 98, 211
thing, 140
without blemish, 322
perfection, 115, 140, 144, 306, 312, 459, 490
perfectly, 144
perforate
(to), 164
perforation, 341
perforator, 341
perform
(to), 211
perfume, 246, 263, 266, 468
perfumer, 246, 249
perfumery, 246
perhaps, 60
period, 186, 191
perish, 20, 97
(to), 20, 68
(will), 20
(you shall), 495
(you), 20, 45, 328
perished, 76
(and they), 47
perishing, 27
permanent, 314, 507
permission, 345, 519
permit
(to), 271
permitted
(have I p you), 463, 532
permutation, 377
perpetual, 160, 167, 168, 314, 315, 399, 407, 507
(to be), 161
perpetuity, 93, 156, 161, 394
(in), 479, 482, 484
perplex
(to), 46, 329
perplexed
(to be), 152, 355, 434
perplexing
saying or question, 45
perplexity, 93
persecution, 255, 498
persecutor, 234
persist, 328
persistently
(to beat), 181, 420
person, 102, 270, 302, 312, 439, 451, 515
(needy), 87, 408
personification
(stars of), 67
persons, 328, 501
(of your), 467, 539
(the), 454
perspiration, 106
persuade
(to), 321
pertain
(to p to), 33
perverse, 316, 469
(to be), 316
(to declare), 316
(to prove), 316
one, 128, 137

thing, 331
perverseness, 126, 174, 352, 465
perversion, 73
perversity, 106, 126, 144, 307, 331, 352, 430
pervert
(to), 82, 101, 174, 316, 318, 465
perverted, 73, 182, 187, 316, 389
(that which is), 73
perverting, 164
pestilence, 146, 187
pestle, 132
petition, 96, 279
(to make), 92, 95
(to), 91
phylacteries, 177, 348, 520
(false), 319
pick
(to p out), 266
(to p up), 154
(to), 266
picture, 428
(mental), 293
piebald
(of color), 148, 479
piece, 54, 190, 195, 234, 313, 320, 504
(of an ear), 54
pieces
(dashes in), 425, 545
(tear in), 277
(to beat in), 199, 496
(to break in), 105, 186, 350
(to cleave in), 105
(to cut in), 313
(to cut into), 23
(to dash to), 27, 330
(to fall into), 186
(to fall to), 131
(to hew in), 306, 514
(to tear in), 284
pierce
(to p through), 242
(to), 86, 100, 146, 164, 202, 242, 350, 431
pierced, 86
piercing, 266
(something), 159
piety, 306, 490
pigeon, 90
pile, 234, 236, 247, 251, 428, 461
(to p up), 81, 236, 295
(to), 191, 247, 461
pilgrimage
(to make), 31
pilgrim-feast, 27
(to keep a), 31
pillar, 60, 116, 140, 153, 164, 175, 207, 338, 379, 395
(capital of), 394, 495
(plated capital of), 348
pillaster, 60
pillory, 215
pillow, 205
pin, 28, 296
pinch
(to), 285, 517
pine, 329, 357
(to p away), 208
(to), 20
away, 28
pining, 136, 426
pinion, 185, 188
pinions
(her), 358
(long), 200, 395
pins
(and its), 452
(and their), 458, 537
(the), 448
of, 445
pious, 101, 306, 490
pipe, 96, 209, 265, 379, 418
(to play the), 86
(to), 355
piping, 360
pistachio nuts, 80, 403
pit, 18, 185, 188, 223, 252, 254, 258, 322, 329, 401, 405, 407
of destruction, 472
of water, 234
pitch, 213, 321
(and p it), 398
(to cover over with), 239
(to), 82
pitched
(and he), 43
pitcher, 101
(her), 48
(with her), 54
pitchfork, 216
(three-pronged), 320, 510
pitied
(thing), 138
pits
(the), 361
pity, 102
(object of), 138
(to), 93, 96, 129, 315, 423
pivot
of door, 240
place, 58, 65, 88, 125, 180, 295, 355, 408, 418
(and a), 38
(appointed), 202
(bare), 228
(distant), 266
(from his), 460
(head), 468
(his secret), 383
(his), 38
(holy or sacred), 308
(in his), 450
(in its), 450
(in the p of), 445
(level), 345
(lodging), 358
(lofty), 151
(naked), 247
(of hiding), 185
(open), 192
(parched), 292
(roomy), 215
(to), 124, 125, 248, 266, 432, 471
(treading or stepping), 222, 418
laid waste, 196
of going out from, 157
possessed, 319
to ride, 222
to tread on, 222, 418
to walk, 115, 349
placed
(be p upon), 406
(something), 164
places
(after their), 376, 519
(bare), 145
of concealment, 34
round about, 93
placing
(in the), 512
plague, 142, 146, 150, 187, 457
spot, 142
plain, 105, 175, 177, 414
(open), 250
(to make), 185
plains
(from the), 404
(in the p of), 385
(in the), 387
of, 385
plait, 171, 282
plaited
work, 305, 327
plan, 71, 193, 257, 443, 459
(evil), 71, 105, 375
(to), 105, 172, 246, 375, 428, 485
planet, 96
plane-tree
(as stripped of bark), 275
as stripped of bark, 494
Planets
Nontraditional, 404
Earth, 62, 235, 505
Neptune, 182, 455
Pluto, 149
Uranus, 254
Traditional
01 Sol, 372
Angel
Michael, 123
Archangel
Rafael, 248
as 30th Path, 49, 315
as Tarot Card The Sun, 37
Chammah (alternate name), 72
Cheres (alternate name), 224
Intelligence
Nakhiel, 133
magic square

number of squares in, 55
sum of, 133
sum of numbers on, 383
metal
Zahab (gold), 31
Olympic Spirit
Och, 31
Spirit
Sorath, 383
Uwr (alternate name), 188
02 Mercury, 67
Angel
Rafael, 248
Archangel
Michael, 123
as 12th Path, 28, 97
as Tarot Card The Magician, 13
Intelligence
Tiriel, 220
magic square
number of squares in, 83
sum of numbers on, 560
metal
Kaspith (Mercury), 347
Olympic Spirit
Ophiel, 145
Spirit
Tafthartharath, 560
03 Venus, 83
Angel
Anael, 101
Archangel
Haniel, 117
as 14th Path, 31, 127
as Tarot Card The Empress, 15
God Name
Aha, 20
Elohim, 105
Intelligence
Hagiel, 68
magic square
number of squares on, 68
sum of, 176
sum of numbers on, 521
metal
Nechosheth (Copper), 424
Olympic Spirit
Hagith, 299
Spirit
Kedemel, 176
04 Luna, 106
(the Moon), 112
Angel
Gabriel, 212
Archangel
Gabriel, 212
as 13th Path, 30, 112
as Tarot Card The High Priestess, 14
full, 100
Intelligence of Intelligences
Malka be-Tarshishim ve-Ad be-Ruach Shehaqim, 566
Shed HaShedim HaLebanah, 422, 529
magic square
number of squares in, 101
sum of, 276
metal
Kesef (Silver), 168, 463
new, 248
Olympic Spirit
Phul, 137
Saharon (alternate name), 345, 518
Spirit
Chasmodai, 276
Spirit of Spirits
Ruach HaRuachoth HaLebanah, 477
Shed Barshehmath Sharthathan, 566
Shed Barshemath HaSharthathan, 566
Yerach (alternate name), 198
05 Mars, 114, 378
Angel
Zamael, 96
Archangel
Kamael, 111
as 27th Path, 46, 280
as Tarot Card The Tower, 33
Intelligence
Graphiel, 11, 255
magic square
number of squares in, 44
sum of, 83
sum of numbers on, 255
metal
Barzel (Iron), 208
Olympic Spirit
Phaleg, 134
Spirit
Bartzabel, 11, 255
06 Jupiter, 182
Angel
Sachiel, 130
Archangel
Tzadqiel, 206
as 21st Path, 39, 205
as Tarot Card The Wheel of Fortune, 25
Intelligence
Iophiel, 152
magic square
number of squares in, 33
sum of, 53
sum of numbers on, 153
metal
Bediyl (Tin), 65
Olympic Spirit
Bethor, 364
Spirit
Hismael, 152
07 Saturn, 405
Angel
Cassiel, 141
Archangel
Tzafqiel, 248
as 32nd Path, 51, 337
as Tarot Card The Universe, 39
Intelligence
Agiel, 63
magic square
number of squares in, 23
sum of, 32
sum of numbers on, 64
metal
Abar (Lead), 185
Olympic Spirit
Arathron, 457, 542
Spirit
Zazel, 64
plank, 63, 354
plant, 147, 155, 160, 169, 225, 252, 412, 460, 475, 484
(to cut off of), 107
(to), 146, 412
(young), 172, 175, 346
sarpad (unknown desert plant), 263
used for medicinal and religious purposes, 32
plantation, 139, 147, 234
planted
(to be), 100
planting, 147
(place or act of), 139
plants
(marsh), 31
(to cut off of), 107
(volunteer), 168
plaster, 45, 195
(and), 41, 402
(to p over), 139
(to), 41
plastered
(it is), 46
(was), 40
plate, 428
(flat), 310
of metal, 107
plated
capital of pillar, 348
plating

of metal, 180
platter, 279
play
(to), 183, 292
plaza
(open), 192
pleasant, 35, 71, 75, 173, 226, 412
(thing), 342
(to be), 35, 169, 226, 408
thing, 112
pleasantness, 142, 169, 191, 408, 458
please, 70
(if it), 28
(to), 28, 334
pleased
(and you were p with me), 422
(to be p with), 177, 237, 488
(to be), 114
pleasing
(to be or become), 340
(to be), 34, 39, 226, 351
(would it have been), 54
pleasure, 177, 265, 488, 489
(to take p in), 71, 177, 488
pleasures
of love, 22
pledge, 58, 106, 229, 256, 360, 387, 486, 512
(the), 112
(to give in), 226
(to lay), 58
(to take a), 58, 100
(to take on), 226
(to), 226
pledges
(to give), 226
plenteous, 193, 194
plenty, 30, 159
plot, 112, 230, 284
(to), 29, 327
plow
(to freshly), 220
(to), 329
(you shall), 471
plowing, 333
ground, 171
time, 333
plowman, 200
plowshare, 289, 344, 480
pluck
(to p down), 223
(to p off), 180, 471
(to p out), 180, 471
(to p up), 276, 344, 420
(to), 187, 214, 233, 276, 492
plumage, 163, 240, 481
plumb, 90, 344
plumbline, 90, 344
plummet, 90, 344, 461
plump, 364
plunder, 33, 281, 290, 294
(thing taken as), 65
(to), 23, 153, 174, 273, 299, 355
plunge
(to), 60
Pluto. *See* Planets: Nontraditional: Pluto
poem, 288
(mocking), 175
poetry
(to speak in sentences of), 276
point, 62, 168, 171
(to p out), 292
(to the p that), 93
of departure, 60, 355
of division, 60, 355
pointed, 40
poising, 310
poison, 72, 121, 308, 326, 381
pole, 74, 79
polish
(to), 214, 261, 289
polished, 170, 217
pollute
(to), 52, 86
polluted
(to be), 153, 458
pollution, 158
pomegranate, 234, 479
pommel, 56
pond, 112, 203, 468
(stagnant), 63, 355
pool, 19, 63, 203, 355
(troubled), 63, 355
poor, 53, 57, 77, 144, 148, 173, 448
(chiefly), 87, 408
(to be), 85, 148, 328, 342, 431
(to grow), 85, 342
man, 173, 448
poorest, 57
poplar, 106, 226
populace, 132, 384
population
(rural), 263, 488
porch, 90, 95, 100, 272, 328, 368, 370, 372, 492
porcupine, 181
porphyry, 33
portent, 336
porter, 348, 385
portico, 100, 372
portion, 30, 109, 116, 153, 158, 190, 205, 269, 322, 381, 415, 417
(as something taken up), 421
(measured), 351
(the), 382
(to p out), 32
portions
(than the), 432
portray
(to), 189
position, 292
possess
(and you shall p it), 475
(and), 474, 482, 542
(to p it), 477
(to), 107, 124, 166, 476
(you shall), 483, 547
possesses
(who), 471
possession, 39, 114, 119, 153, 192, 306, 319, 332, 342, 344, 459
(his), 474
(take), 33
(to get as a), 107
(to have of), 80, 403
(to his), 480
(to take p of), 138, 330, 427
possessions, 336
(and they got them), 57
(and you get), 52
post, 149, 164, 372
posterity, 93, 131, 424
pot, 103, 195, 207, 225, 340, 388
(for smelting), 202
(seething), 30
for ink, 345
potash, 185, 360
potentate, 219, 470
pots
(its), 390
(the), 386
potsherd, 161, 329, 385, 460
pottage, 90
potter, 233
pouch, 166, 324
pound, 116
(to p fine), 408
(to), 48, 330, 408
pounded
fine (in a mortar), 451
pounding
(to mix by), 408
of waves, 53
pour
(and p upon), 440
(to p down), 216
(to p forth), 127, 316, 481
(to p out), 62, 142, 147, 183, 184, 213, 228, 288, 316, 359, 441, 463, 481
(to), 142, 147, 184, 196, 216, 288, 359, 463
(you shall p it out), 457
(you shall p out), 439, 525
poured
(something p out), 147, 148, 359
(to be p out), 316, 481
(to be), 96, 316, 481
out, 155, 365
pouring, 143
(place of), 288, 463
poverty, 148, 224, 249, 331, 347
(you come to), 470
powder, 129, 267, 272
(to), 267
powders
(aromatic), 129
power, 20, 47, 50, 66, 75, 138, 174, 184, 187, 197, 227, 351, 399, 424, 427, 446, 486, 527
(have), 328

(in), 48
(mighty), 197
(my), 57
(royal), 138, 324, 427
(sovereign), 324
(to have), 395
(with his), 54
(with), 48
of knowing, 171
of the king, 138, 427
to stand, 342
powerful, 55, 109, 205
(to be), 186
(to make), 55
strength, 508, 559
practice, 78, 173, 314
praise, 90, 93, 127, 232, 293, 306, 454, 455
(song of), 375
(song or hymn of), 306
(songs of), 42
(to sing), 213
(to), 32, 55, 83, 200, 247, 396
(your), 457, 530
the Lord, 105
praised
(and they), 226
praises, 452
pray
(I or we), 70
(to), 28, 91, 92, 95, 141, 156, 384
excuse me, 28
now!, 71
prayer, 11, 96, 254, 333
prayers, 315
preach
(to), 155, 326, 458
preacher, 339
preaching, 251
precept, 181
precious, 75, 284
(very), 252
ore, 235
stone, 132, 536
thing, 112
preciousness, 71, 247
precipice, 292
precipitate
(to be), 199
(to), 199
pre-eminence, 375
preeminent
(to be), 161
prefect, 134, 164, 426
prefer
(to), 27
pregnancy, 221, 472
pregnant, 191
(and she became), 360
(became), 385, 530
(to become), 191
preparation, 257, 320, 443
of principles, 538
prepare
(to), 116, 234, 317, 428
for this, 28
prepared, 319, 321
(I have), 394
(she had), 430
prescribed
(something), 130, 134
presence
(from the), 177
(in the p of), 76
present, 125, 472
(and you shall bring), 421, 528
(to give a), 249
presents, 322, 511
preservation
of life, 82
preserve, 264
preserved, 266
press, 123, 449
(to p by treading), 199
(to p down and out), 195
(to p out), 251
(to p together), 287
(to p upon), 316
(to), 111, 117, 147, 183, 195, 199, 269, 276, 279, 359, 468, 470, 478
pressed
fig-cake, 60
pressing, 155, 480
(with sense of p down), 359
pressure, 123, 146, 176, 183, 200, 449, 478
(to exert demanding), 269
presume
(to), 178
presumptuous, 27
(to be), 34
presumptuously
(comes), 39
(shall), 50
(to act), 34
presumptuousness, 85, 407
prevail
(to), 78, 135, 186, 306, 351, 523, 527
prey, 23, 58, 93, 155, 179, 233, 322, 492, 518
(they took for a), 39
(to), 23
upon, 33
price, 219, 220, 247, 282
(of a harlot), 312
of redemption, 57
prick, 133, 184, 456
(to), 209
pride, 23, 25, 30, 32, 78, 85, 188, 287, 402, 407, 518
(loftiness of), 248
object of, 188
priest, 94, 220, 410, *Also See* High Priest
(idolatrous), 220
(to act as a), 94, 410
(to act as minister in p's office, 94, 410
priestess, 318, *Also See* High Priestess
priesthood, 98
primary, 344, 345, 518
primogeniture, 203, 205
primordial
(dwelling place of the), 538
prince, 86, 155, 272, 273, 325, 365, 395, 506
(to act as), 395
(to be a), 395
princes, 238, 289, 483
princess, 328
principal, 193
officer, 94, 410
prison, 214, 223, 224, 225, 350
(of the earth - fig.), 199
(your), 372, 517
prisoner, 225
prisoners
(collective), 225
private, 262
parts, 263
privates, 263
privilege, 304
prized
(to be), 246
problem, 246
proceed
(to), 348
proceedings, 305
procession, 314
proclaim
(and you shall), 419, 528
(to), 203, 241
(you shall), 389, 400
proclamation, 251
(to make), 203
produce, 56, 67, 113, 178, 229, 234, 296, 314, 326, 446, 458
(and as the), 452
(and the), 446
(its), 446
(of the soil), 67
(of your), 451, 528
(to p by mixing), 140, 354
(to), 174, 449
producing
thousands, 132, 451
product, 113, 296
profane, 57, 153, 458
(to), 86
profaned, 86
(to be), 153, 192, 458
profaneness, 57, 153, 158, 458
(and he broke the), 382
profession
(originator of a), 15
profit, 170, 224, 349, 375, 383, 521, 529
(to be of), 148, 431
(to), 131
acquired by violence, 170

progenitor, 191
progeny, 93, 160, 437, 492
(stars of), 67
progress
(to make), 325
prolong
(and you may), 385, 522
(that you may), 369
(to), 200, 395
(you may), 369, 371, 507
(you shall), 388, 530
prolongation, 200
prolonging, 200
prominence
(in belly - contemptuous), 55
promise, 209
promises
(fine), 158, 227
promote
(to), 55, 180
prompt, 217
pronounce, 187
pronouncement
of judgment, 172
pronouncing, 62
proof, 292
(to put to the), 135
prop, 140, 354
propagate
(to), 128, 423
proper, 200, 395
(to be p to), 334
(to be), 334
(what is), 40
property, 39, 114, 119, 147, 332, 336
prophecy, 83, 90, 409
prophesy
(to utter a), 111, 377
(to), 38, 73, 111, 155, 377, 458
prophesying, 83
prophet, 44, 81, 82, 187
(declaration of), 111, 377
(to speak as a), 111, 377
prophetess, 86
proportion, 471
to be paid, 140
prosper
(to), 146, 260, 267
(you may), 427
prosperity, 193, 215, 260, 263, 338
prosperous, 260
(to become), 269, 490
prosperously
(to live), 41, 46
prostitue
(price or hire of), 325, 513
prostitute
(female temple), 292
(male temple), 290
prostitution, 134, 426
prostrate
(to be), 261
(to p oneself in worship), 86
(to p oneself), 86, 189
(to), 161, 261, 461
prostrated
(and p myself), 410
(and they p themselves), 413
prostration, 266
protect
(to), 173, 465
protection, 15, 142, 381, 382
(to flee for), 245
proud, 17, 23, 25, 27, 33, 87, 95, 188, 202, 408, 411
proudly, 212
(to act), 34
(to behave), 188
prove
(he might p you), 337, 492
(to), 57, 76, 78, 135, 189, 289, 400, 402
proverb, 276
(to speak in a), 276
(to use a), 276
Proverbs. *See Tanakh: 03 Kethuvim:* 02 Proverbs
provide
(to), 35, 38
providing
for (as a parent), 116
province, 130
provision, 126, 130
provisions
(to supply oneself with), 240
provocation, 162
provoke, 386
proximity, 141
prudence, 250, 267
prudent, 80, 404
(to be), 247, 267, 461
prune
(to), 213
(you shall), 375
pruning, 218
knife, 235
psalm, 218, 236, 306
Psalms. *See Tanakh: 03 Kethuvim:* 01 Psalms
public
speaker, 339
publish
(to), 326
puddle, 112, 468
pudenda, 230, 320, 322
pudendum, 251
puff
(to), 119
puffing
out, 130
pull
(to p away), 138
(to p down), 223, 340, 532
(to p off or away or apart), 343
(to p off), 214
(to p out), 177
(to p up), 177, 420
pulling
up (of stakes), 173
pulverised
fragments, 315
pulverize
(to), 186, 292
punish
(to), 179, 298
punished
(to be), 181, 420
punishment, 118, 304, 396, 470
(disciplinary), 396
of iniquity, 144, 430
purchase, 182
(to), 164
price for wife, 212
pure, 45, 107, 164, 185, 329, 356, 442, 451
(to be), 51, 66, 166, 195, 337, 354
gold, 106, 313, 495
oil, 243
one, 45, 329
purely, 185
pureness, 356
purge
(to), 239, 289
purging, 139
purification, 354, 356
purified, 199
(and he), 53
purify
(and he shall p him), 48
(to p from uncleanness), 35
(to), 188, 289
(you shall p yourselves), 450
yourselves, 450
purifying, 354, 356
purity, 52, 185, 354, 356
purple, 220, 236, 471, 479
purpose, 112, 116, 169, 172, 225, 239, 443
(in your p with), 76
(to), 105, 375
purse, 109, 166, 203
purslane, 321
pursue
(to hotly), 150
(to), 195, 232, 490
(you shall), 389, 535
pursued
(hotly), 338
push, 153
(to p away), 36
(to), 80, 107, 181, 276, 420, 442
put, 395, 505
(and he), 406
(and I will p you), 430, 524
(and she p off), 382
(and she p on), 414
(and she), 418, 528
(and you shall p upon them), 433, 531
(and you shall), 418, 434, 457, 531

(and), 48
(I had p forth), 419
(I have), 420
(I will), 403
(shall), 408
(thing p forth), 326
(to p away), 326
(to p forth), 252
(to p out), 46
(to put together), 310
(to), 266, 325, 403, 432, 471, 512
(you shall p away), 385, 508
(you shall p out), 418
(you shall p them), 433, 531
(you shall), 423, 441, 540
(you will p out), 420
(you will), 456, 541
away, 78
on, 399
out of mind, 30
putting
away, 66
puzzle, 46
pyre, 217
Qlippoth
01 *Qemetiel* (*Ain*), 181
02 *Belial* (*Ain Sof*), 92, 157
03 *Athiel* (*Ain Sof Aur*), 331
04 *Thaumiel* (*Keter*), 322
05 *Ogiel* (*Chokmah*), 140
06 *Satariel* (*Binah*), 397
07 *Gasheklah* (*Hesed*), 302
08 *Golachab* (*Giburah*), 67
09 *Tageriron* (*Tiferet*), 461, 542
10 *Oreb Zaraq* (*Netzach*), 350
11 *Samael* (*Hod*), 149
12 *Gamaliel* (*Yesod*), 134
13 *Lilith* (*Malkut*), 319
14 *Beiriron* (Aries), 343, 517
15 *Adimiron* (Taurus), 253, 484
16 *Tzelilimiron* (Gemini), 313, 318, 507, 510
17 *Shichiriron* (Cancer), 433, 538
18 *Shalhebiron* (Leo), 355, 523
19 *Tzafiriron* (Virgo), 370, 526
20 *Abiriron* (Libra), 343, 517
21 *Necheshthiron* (Scorpio), 495, 549
22 *Nachashiron* (Sagittarius), 366, 525
23 *Dagdagiron* (Capricorn), 230, 476
24 *Bahimiron* (Aquarius), 11, 254, 485
25 *Nashimiron* (Pisces), 383, 529
Qof. *See* Hebrew Alphabet:19 *Qof*
quadrangle, 142, 429
quail, 260
quake, 192
(to), 83, 85, 102, 193, 194, 227, 278, 348
quaking, 192, 196, 198
quantity, 312
quarrel, 363
(do you), 384, 529
(to), 316
quarry, 173
(to), 120
quarrying, 173
quarter, 53, 60, 105
queen, 111, 115, 199, 259, 322, 356
(to be or become), 109, 347
quench
(to), 46
quenched
(to be), 46
quenching, 49
question
(difficult), 45
(enigmatic), 45
(perplexing), 45
quick, 217
quickened
(to be), 41, 46
quickly, 212, 251
quiet, 73, 227, 260, 262, 289, 293, 304, 499, 503
(to be), 249, 260, 268, 293, 438, 490
quiet!, 243
quieting, 101
quietness, 83, 262, 263, 293
quilt, 205
quit
(to), 271
quiver, 192, 306
(for arrows), 283
(to), 102, 144, 163, 230, 240
quivering, 192, 196, 250
motion of lips, 83
tendrils, 93
rabble, 159
race, 260, 512
radiant, 219
raft, 266
rafter, 173, 248
rafters, 252
rafts, 193
rag, 94, 97
rage, 68, 72, 167, 192, 462
(to), 68, 192, 257, 327
raging, 75, 95, 167, 192, 411, 462
heat, 182
rags, 56
raid
(to make a), 271
(to), 284
rail
(to), 233, 491
raiment, 280, 428
(and), 430
rain, 214, 215, 263, 469
(as the small), 372
(early), 200
(latter or spring), 318
(steady or persistent), 228
(the r showers), 265, 470
(to drop of), 316, 481
(to), 214, 263, 469
raindrops, 351
rained
(to be r upon), 263, 469
rainment, 261
(and), 32
(your), 435, 524
rain-shower, 213, 441
rainshowers, 351
rainstorm, 98, 213, 441
rainy
season, 315
raise
(to r up), 180, 470
(to), 180, 470
(you do r yourself up), 513
raised
way, 151
raisin-bunch, 207
raisin-cake
(sacrificial cake), 362
raisins
(bunch of), 207
ram, 60, 67, 199, 201, 319
(young), 254
r's horn, 67, 351
rampart, 57, 67, 72, 262
ran
(and), 393, 542
range, 204, 266
rank, 193, 194, 259, 364
(of soldiers), 330
ransom, 121, 156, 239, 322, 394
(to give a), 249
(to), 52, 108
rare, 70, 252
rash
utterance, 72
rashly
(to speak), 28, 33, 131
rather, 20
ration, 195
rattle
(to), 163, 218
ravage
(to), 252, 463
rave
(to), 34
raven, 226
ravine, 171, 181, 275, 515
ravines, 239
ravish
(to), 53, 259
raw, 70
(the), 41
raze
(to), 228
razor, 215, 384
reach, 405, 417
(to), 69, 123, 142, 165, 190, 200, 269, 395
read
(to), 241

(you shall), 396
reading, 262
ready, 217, 319, 321
(to be), 80, 317, 403
(to make), 317
to forgive, 119
realized, 284, 480
realm, 296
of the dead, 308
reap
(shall r it), 437
(to), 285
(you shall), 437
(you), 436
rear, 175, 195, 384
of a troop, 175
rearing, 116
reason, 193
(to r out), 348
reasoning, 172, 275, 494
rebatement, 252
rebel, 222, 246, 377
(to), 211, 310, 313
rebelled
(and you), 378
(you), 391, 523
rebellion, 211, 215, 310, 376
(against YHVH), 211
(no), 177, 414
rebellious, 211, 220, 372
(to be r against), 212
(to be), 211, 212, 313
rebelliously
(to act), 34
(to be r proud), 34
rebelliousness, 376
rebuild
(to), 75
rebuke, 57, 229, 304, 405
(and the), 407
(to), 57, 227
recall
(to), 203
receive
(to), 149, 154, 156, 459
receiver
of divine revelation, 76, 400
recently, 262, 318
receptacle, 295, 388
recess, 252
recite
(to), 241
reckless
(to be), 116
recklessness, 326
reckon
(to), 111, 116, 155, 179
reckoned
(shall be), 408
as offenders, 35
reckoning, 275, 494
reclessness, 116
recline
(to), 301
recognize, 368
(to), 225
recompense, 179, 277, 477
(to), 92
reconciliation
(to make), 239
record, 230, 341, 476
(to), 299
recount
(to), 262
recurrence, 405
red, 63, 126, 239, 356
(to be), 63, 153, 356, 480
color, 438
marble, 33
reddened
(to be), 213
reddish, 107, 355, 376
(be), 107, 376
reddish-gray, 238
redeem
(and shall), 58
(to), 52, 108
redeemed
(to be), 301
(who has), 57
redemption, 57, 156, 304, 322, 394
(price or right of), 57
redness, 323
red-purple, 220, 236, 471, 479
reed, 22, 63, 160, 166, 460
reeds, 31
reel
(to), 144, 180, 240
reeling, 240
(in terror), 28
reference
(in r to), 50, 95
refine
(to), 114, 188, 277, 501
refined
(to be), 114
gold, 106, 230, 476
reflection, 11, 254
refractory
(to be), 212, 313
refrain
(to r himself), 363
(to), 70, 169, 256, 272, 442
refresh
(to r oneself), 302
(to), 104
refreshment, 291, 297
refuge, 78, 134, 140, 142, 147, 167, 172, 174, 177, 317, 446
(cities appointed for), 143
(his), 158, 436
(of God), 264
(place of), 167
(to bring to), 103
(to seek), 103, 245
(to take), 103
refugee, 215
refuse, 129, 139, 162
(to), 111, 123, 416
heap, 112, 432
refusing, 111, 416
regard, 80, 404
(in r to), 50
(to), 80, 225, 279
regarding
him, 55
region, 27
(open), 236
beyond or across, 226
regret
(to), 119, 380
regulation, 290
reign, 117, 151, 324, 339
(to), 109, 276, 347
reincarnation, 91
reins, 83
reject, 30
(to), 83, 86, 123, 271
rejected, 61
rejoice
(and you shall), 422
(and you will), 436, 532
(to), 30, 34, 57, 62, 129, 169, 181, 266, 370, 489
(will), 364
rejoiced
(and he), 46
rejoicing, 66, 90, 215, 307, 375, 377, 468, 527
relate
(to), 209, 262
relation, 334
relative, 70
relatives, 35, 319
relax
(to), 232, 233, 492
release, 274
(from debt), 270
(shall), 420
(to), 266
reliable, 133
reliably, 133
relief, 114, 199
religious
(plant used for r purposes), 32
awe, 118
ministry, 468
uncleanness, 74
remain, 359
(shall), 363, 495
(that), 501
(they shall), 482
(to r behind), 189
(to r over), 165, 363, 462
(to), 135, 249, 326
(will), 495
(you let), 495
remainder, 326, 359, 472
(and from the), 379
(and the), 383
(the), 381, 500
remained, 379

(and she), 400
remaining
(and the), 360, 515
(the), 395, 403, 524
remains, 375
(and that which), 381
(which), 482
remedy, 232
remember, 205
(and I will), 373
(and you shall), 369
(and), 385, 522
(I will), 203
(I), 353
(to), 203
(you may), 369
(you shall), 367
remembered
(and you shall be), 410, 525
remembrance, 203, 231, 477
reminder, 231, 477
remissness, 260
remnant, 326, 332, 359, 470, 472
(and in the), 364
(and the), 501
(from the), 376
remote, 245
removal, 66
(entire), 136
(with the r of), 66
remove, 56
(and I will), 388
(to), 29, 41, 98, 145, 156, 177, 233, 265, 388, 459, 478
removed, 56, 63, 350
(to be r far away), 54
(to be r far off), 54
(to be), 348
rend, 411
(to r garment), 253, 463
(to), 233, 492
renew
(to), 248
renewed, 271
rent, 127
repair
(to), 41, 98, 248
repay
(and), 396
repeat
(to), 99, 270
repeated, 425
repel
(to), 35
repent
(to), 119, 380
repentance, 119, 246, 380
repetition, 286
repetitions, 289
repititions, 499
replacement, 150
report, 294, 299, 449
(evil), 27
repose, 83, 252
(to), 227
represent
(to), 276
representative, 111, 348
reproach, 91, 115, 236
(my), 394
(to), 233, 491
reproached
(to be), 91, 109, 376
reproof, 229, 304, 405
reprove
(to), 227
reprover, 228
reproves
(one who), 228
reptile, 47
request, 96, 258, 260, 279, 292, 468
(to), 91, 92, 95, 289
require
(did you r it), 457
(to), 289, 327
(you shall r it), 458
required
(that which is), 409
requirements, 409
requital, 280, 478
requittal, 277, 279, 477
rescue, 280
(to r you), 179, 382
(to), 108, 145, 174, 478
rescued
(to be), 145, 478
resemblance, 131, 424
resemble
(to), 68
resentful, 220
reserve
(to), 141, 211, 220
supply, 52
reservoir, 163
Resh. See Hebrew Alphabet:20 *Resh*
residence, 64, 172, 446
residue, 326, 359, 472
resin, 101, 439
resolute
(to be), 135
resolve, 189
resort
(to r to), 327
resounding
music, 93, 410
respect
(to), 225
(you shall), 370
respite, 199
resplendent, 386, 541
respond
(to), 144
response, 171
rest, 61, 73, 114, 130, 252, 326, 359, 400, 472
(and the), 362
(and will you make), 421, 529
(it shall have), 505
(place of), 252
(shall), 505
(solemn), 424, 536
(the r of), 500
(to be at), 260
(to bring to a), 104
(to cause to), 104
(to give), 104
(to kneel down to), 234
(to r safely), 81
(to), 80, 83, 86, 140, 227, 268, 354, 490
(you shall have), 389
(you shall let it), 440
(you shall), 505
rested
(and he), 407
(and they), 410
(he), 397
restful, 227
resting
place, 83, 125, 130, 135, 236, 258, 505, 512
restlessly
(to wander), 192
restlessness, 215
restoration, 205, 251, 345, 518
restore
(and you shall r it), 408
(to), 98
(you shall r it), 427
restored, 271
(to be r to life or health), 41, 46
restrain
(to keep), 169
(to), 70, 75, 91, 178, 227, 235, 246, 256, 272, 363, 369, 442
restrained
(to be), 49
restrains
(something that), 247, 483
restraint, 70, 272, 288, 291
restrict
(to), 70
results, 305
retain
(to), 272
retainer, 253
retirement, 249
retreat, 170, 264
(to), 77
retreats, 34
retribution, 279
return, 244, 405
(and you shall), 419, 528
(and you will), 400
(in r for), 138, 453
(so that I), 407
(to), 99, 246
(will), 401
(you shall), 401
returned
(and you), 405
(and), 400

his, 399
returnee, 446
returnees, 450
reveal
(to uncover the ear to), 76, 400
revealed
(I r myself), 189
revelation
(vision as a mode of), 212
revelry, 218
revenge
(to), 52, 181, 420
revenue, 296, 338, 516
revere
(to), 113, 138, 193
reverence, 213
(to kneel in), 234
(to pay r to), 138
reverent, 193
reversed, 126, 352
revile
(to r men), 105, 441
reviling
words, 105, 112, 113, 118, 441, 445
revilings, 105, 112, 113, 118, 441, 445
revolt, 472
(against YHVH), 211
(to), 211, 310
revolter, 246
revolting
(those), 228
revolve
(to), 153, 434
revolving, 91
reward, 85, 179, 279, 280, 298, 312, 454, 478, 501
for good news, 328, 331
rewarded
(have you), 444, 533
rib, 174
(of Adam), 181
ribs, 265
(of his), 375
rich, 285, 350, 498
(to be), 45, 348
(to become), 348
(to pretend to be), 348
man, 350
robe, 338
riches, 20, 56, 80, 138, 147, 348, 362, 403, 427
ridden
(you have), 366
riddle, 45, 46
(to propose or propound), 35
ride
(to mount and), 201
(to), 201
ridge, 66, 317, 496
ridicule, 181
(to), 125
riding, 203
(act of), 203
seat, 222
right, 87, 97, 102, 120, 131, 139, 304, 381, 408
(doing), 183
(the), 183
(to be), 35, 330, 334
(to choose the), 120, 420
(to choose to the), 111, 416
(to go to the), 111, 120, 416, 420
(to take the r hand), 111, 416
(to turn aside from the r path), 62
(to turn), 111, 416
(to use the r hand), 111, 416
doing, 183
hand, 120, 139, 381
of redemption, 57
of the first born, 203, 205
on, 97
side, 120, 131, 381, 424
righteous, 186
(the), 214, 345, 443, 509
(to be), 182
(you shall eat the), 383
justice, 366
ones, 217, 445
people, the (a fig. phrase for Israel), 346, 520
righteousness, 182, 183
(in your), 362, 504
(our), 383
(the), 183
right-hand, 131, 424
right-handed
(to be), 120, 420
rightness, 182
rim, 80, 188, 210, 317, 397
ring, 33, 40, 118, 134, 170, 320, 380
(for nose), 33
(to r again), 70, 359
ring-gold, 235
ringing
cry, 215, 218, 468
shout, 243
rinse, 35
(to), 284, 507
rip
(to r up), 175
(to), 253, 284, 463
ripe, 141
(to grow), 258
ripen
(to), 85, 92, 258
rise
(and you may r up early), 444, 533
(to r early), 273, 475
(to r up), 23
(to), 160, 196, 210, 213, 399, 439, 441
up early, 274, 476
rising, 396
(and for a), 414
(in the), 397
against, 334
earth, 30
mist, 272
up, 32, 166
ritual, 112
ritually
clean, 334
rival, 237
river, 57, 138, 193, 218
(the), 197
bank, 28, 40
rivers
(the), 380
(their), 393, 523
road, 201, 397
public, 151
roam
(to), 192
roar, 123, 225, 421
(to), 68, 70, 238, 243, 360
roaring, 98, 116, 246, 379
sound, 98
roast, 148
(and you shall), 414
(to), 145, 152, 229, 258, 401
roasted, 148
grain, 156
rob
(to), 58, 175
robbed
of offspring, 270
robber, 178, 281, 322, 416, 518
robbery, 23, 58, 64, 65
(in), 61
robe, 162, 216
(rich or expensive), 338
of state, 175
robust, 285, 498
rock, 40, 120, 169, 237, 284, 448
(cleft of), 220
(in), 238
(the), 171, 241
(to), 232, 491
badger, 303, 496
rod, 173, 198, 248
(the), 77
(wrought metal), 108
rode
(and they), 389
roebuck, 124
roll, 97
(to), 41, 293, 326
rolling, 167
over, 91
roof, 19, 237, 326
(flat), 19
(my), 403
(to cover with a), 87
(to), 87
roof-chamber, 136, 330
roof-room, 136, 330
room, 113, 194, 270, 279, 289
(underground), 245
(vaulted), 315
roomy

place, 215
root, 94, 139, 276, 428, 438
(to r out), 344, 420
(to r up), 276
(to take), 438
rooted
(and he r them out), 422, 529
(to be r up), 276
rope, 58, 206, 317
(by analogy), 304
(encircling), 206
rose, 337
rot
(to), 208, 242
rotten
(to be), 213, 441
rotteness, 242
rottenness, 155, 268, 490
rough, 205, 239
places, 230
roughly, 441
round, 125, 167, 208
(that which is), 124
(to draw), 34
(to), 204, 481
about, 93, 94, 124, 130
loaf, 167
thing, 124
roundhouse, 223
roundness, 223
(house of), 223
rouse
(to r oneself), 228
rove
(to r about), 250
row, 95, 196, 234, 259, 328, 345, 412, 428
(of soldiers), 330
(the), 413
(to), 250, 357
rowing, 252
rows, 414
royal
chair, 230
command, 290
paramour, 259
pavilion, 434
power, 138, 324, 427
steeds, 482, 547
royalty, 108, 117, 324
Ruach. *See* Kabbalah:Souls: *Ruach*
rub, 217
(to r away), 292
(to), 214
rubbing, 265, 419
rubbish, 267, 272
rubies, 181, 209, 454
ruby, 64, 65, 356
ruddy, 126
(of man, horse, heifer, garment, water, lentils), 63, 356
rug, 279, 351
rugged
strength, 77
ruin, 33, 53, 76, 81, 99, 101, 114, 140, 166, 196, 230, 243, 244, 251, 268, 286, 311, 343, 388, 396, 401, 404, 419, 424
(sudden), 61
(to), 174, 246, 247, 266, 465, 471
ruined, 223
(was), 506
ruins, 52
(heap of), 99, 101
(to be in), 191
(to make all in), 159
rule, 296, 342, 343
(according to), 50
(and to), 291
(and you shall), 430
(may), 428
(shall), 428
(to r over), 124
(to), 190, 276, 395, 453
(you shall), 358, 541
ruler, 15, 86, 134, 215, 219, 247, 284, 293, 325, 426, 468, 470, 483, 497
(subordinate), 134, 426
rulers, 104, 374
(the), 291, 483
ruling, 506
rumbling, 29
rumor, 294, 299, 310
run
(to r about), 325
(to r away), 190
(to), 123, 216, 235, 237, 506
running, 260, 262, 306, 512
sore, 62
runnings, 62
rural
people, 263, 488
population, 263, 488
rush, 63, 120, 160, 190, 420, 460
(to r to and fro), 325
(to r upon), 108
(to), 146, 250
rushes, 31
rushing, 98, 195, 306
sound, 98
water, 192
rust, 63
Ruth. *See Tanakh: 03 Kethuvim:* 05 Ruth
ruthless, 158, 276, 482, 515
(to be), 153, 480
ruthlessly
(to kill), 37
sack, 225, 288, 484
(his), 457
(in my), 459
(in the s of), 456
sackcloth, 288
sacking, 288
sacks, 455
(in our), 474
(in your), 475, 540
(our), 473
(your), 474, 540
sacred, 294
place, 308
sacredness, 290
sacrifice, 30, 34, 45, 125
(and they shall), 52
(and they), 47
(animal piece for), 355
(his), 41
(my), 45
(odor of), 402
(smoke of), 253
(that they may), 57
(the), 40
(to offer), 30, 147, 359
(to s an animal), 30
(to slaughter for), 34
(to), 34, 246
(will), 404
(you shall), 407, 408
(you), 41
of, 45
sacrificed
(and they), 57
(they), 52
sacrifices
(their s of well-being), 503
(to burn), 246
sacrificial
bowl or cup, 354
cake, 95, 411
cake (raisin), 362
implement (three-pronged fork), 98
offering, 31
sacrum, 171
sad, 120, 209, 420
(to be), 45, 167, 462
saddle
(basket), 199
(to), 246
saddle-bags, 448
sadness, 209
safety, 36, 300
(means or place of), 142
saffron, 230, 453
said, 215
(and she), 375
(and they), 393, 396, 531
(and you), 378
(and), 360
(has), 373
(I), 377
(you have), 374, 518
(you), 372
sail, 132
sailor, 58, 97
saint, 101, 294
saints, 296
sake, 193
(for the s of), 229
(for your), 214, 443
sale, 239, 394

saliva, 240
salt, 97
(to eat), 97
(to), 97
pit, 223
saltiness, 102
saltness, 102
salute
(to), 200, 396
salvation, 280, 285, 432, 434
(for your), 452, 529
(his), 434
salve, 240
same, 28, 74, 78, 398
(the), 64, 356
Samekh. See Hebrew Alphabet:15 *Samekh*
Samuel. *See Tanakh: 02 Neviim:* 03 1 Samuel, 04 2 Samuel
sanctification, 294
sanctified
(and), 298
(to be), 290
(you), 454, 535
sanctify
(and I will), 448
(and s it/him), 446
(and s yourselves), 523, 554
(and you shall), 443
(to), 290
(you shall), 446
themselves, 448
yourself, 446
sanctuary, 83, 308
sand, 44, 57
(grain of), 135
sandal, 137, 162, 427
thong, 335, 490
sandals
(to furnish with), 162
sandalwood, 142, 389
sapphire, 267
sardius, 64, 356
sash, 80, 377
sashes, 354
sat
(and she), 400
(when we), 424
Satan. *See:*Biblical Characters:Satan
sated
(to become), 255
satiated
(to be), 193
satire, 175
satisfaction
(expression of), 50, 331
satisfied
(you will be), 431
satisified
(and be), 431
saturated, 193
saturation, 200, 242, 495
Saturn. *See* Planets: Traditional: 07 Saturn
saucepan, 480
save
(to), 98, 139, 174, 211, 235, 280
saved
(and you shall be), 461, 538
(to be), 280
saving
act, 299
saw, 342
(and God), 459
(and I), 189
(and s me), 383
(and she s him), 364
(for stone cutting), 214
(when she), 369
(you), 360
say, 187
(and I shall), 380
(and you shall), 390, 523
(shall), 215
(then shall you), 375
(to), 111, 209, 334, 377
(will), 215
(you shall), 375, 393, 531
(you should), 373
saying, 209
(enigmatic), 45
(perplexing), 45
scab, 186, 334, 343, 344, 352, 392
(to cause a), 161
(to smite with), 161
scalded, 381
scale, 119, 419
(of fish or water animals), 517
scales, 119, 161, 334, 401, 419
(accurate), 218
(and)...(as on a fish), 518
(just), 218
scall
(of leprosy), 344
scalp, 189
scantness, 219, 470
scapegoat, 136
scar, 357
of a sore, 392
scarcity, 347
scarlet, 470
(and), 470
(the), 274, 472
(to be clad in), 325
scatter
(to s abundantly), 244
(to s seed), 228
(to), 176, 187, 190, 194, 199, 233, 244, 350, 487, 496
scattered
(something), 234
(to be), 176, 194, 199, 283, 487, 496
scatterer, 199, 216, 496
scattering, 199, 253, 496
scent, 198
sceptre, 335
scholar, 321
scoff
(to), 181
scorch
(to), 50, 63, 236, 282, 506
scorched, 141
(to be), 190, 292, 331, 501
region, 185
scorching, 392
heat, 326
scorn, 209, 236
(to), 144, 191, 477, 495
scorned, 30
scorning, 176, 450
scorpion, 278
scoundrel, 87
scour
(to), 261
scoured, 217
scourge, 246, 252
(to), 91
scrape
(to s off), 221
(to s out), 190
(to), 93, 188, 221, 283
scraping, 265, 419
tool, 243
scratch
(to), 188, 330
scream
(to), 108, 166
screen
(of the Tabernacle), 140, 354
(to), 121, 350
scribe, 262, 266
scroll, 97
sculpted
figures, 253
scum, 63
scurf, 334
sea, 69, 358
(breaking of), 341
sea-gull, 284, 506
seal, 309, 312, 492, 493
(signet), 455
(to affix a), 309, 492
(to s up), 213, 309, 492
(to), 309, 492
seals, 424, 529
(the), 426, 457, 530
sealskin
(the), 405
seal-skin, 401
seam, 376
seaman, 58, 97
sea-monster, 331, 514
search, 245
(and make), 405
(to s for), 233, 245, 284
(to s out), 245, 284
(to), 124, 245, 284, 363
searched
(thing to be s out), 245
searching, 245
seashore, 114, 445

season, 106, 140, 375
(to), 97
seasoned, 161, 482
seasoning, 269, 419
seasons, 173, 412
Seasons
Fall (*Sethav*), 315
Spring (*Aviv*), 31
Summer (*Qayitz*), 184, 493
Winter (*Choref*), 233, 492
seat, 98, 100, 266
(toward the), 413
of honor, 98, 100
second, 273, 286, 331, 514
(the s time), 474
(the), 274, 426
secrecy, 58, 59, 275, 381, 455
(in), 381
secret, 25, 88, 188, 198, 402
(his s place), 383
(in), 381
(the s things), 508
(to be), 156, 394
foundations, 397
parts, 320
place, 394
thing, 159, 342, 437
wisdom, 434
secretary, 262
secretly, 329
(and), 409
(to do), 107
section, 138
secure, 163, 289, 304, 402, 499, 503
height, 264
securely, 36
security, 36, 256, 300, 486, 512
(thing given as), 106
sedan, 265, 489
sedition, 472
seduction, 77
seductiveness, 153
see, 78
(and when I), 367
(and you shall), 363, 380, 383, 520, 529
(I have caused you to s it), 374, 510
(to s it), 370
(to s them), 385, 521
(to), 33, 38, 187, 369, 370
(when they), 373, 518
(you may s them), 380
(you), 365, 505
seed, 228, 234
(bearing), 344
(grain of), 234
(having conceived), 391
(white), 271, 492
(your), 237, 430
seed-land, 251
seeds, 265, 489
seeing, 48, 180, 187, 193
(from), 373
(place of), 79
seek
(and you will), 455, 536
(do you), 439
(to s out), 95, 370
(to), 91, 92, 95, 241, 245, 289, 327, 329
(you s him), 483
(you shall s out), 442
(you shall), 469, 472
seeking, 244
seemly, 81
seen
(and shall be), 381
(and when you have), 366
(and you have), 361
(have I), 365
(have), 360
(I have), 363, 379, 519
(you have), 377, 519
him, 367
seer, 38, 44, 187
seers, 50
sees
(when he), 369
seethe
(to), 34, 154
seize, 33
(to), 58, 73, 75, 118, 154, 162, 295, 322, 330, 447, 518
select
(to), 289
self, 102, 211, 302, 439
(lifting up of), 388
selflessness, 66
self-nullification, 66
self-possessed, 240
self-restraint
(of patience), 200, 395
sell
(to), 220
(you shall s her), 406
(you shall s to me), 483
(you shall), 383
semblance, 326
of a man, 248, 461
semen
(issue of), 216
(to scatter), 228
send, 415
(and I will), 422, 424
(let him), 437
(to s away), 261
(to), 261
(will), 415
(you did), 415
(you s forth), 415
(you shall let him), 437
(you shall), 418
(you will), 415
sending, 282, 431
away, 264, 431
forth, 282
sensation, 332
sensed, 343
senseless, 101
(to be), 101
senselessness, 106
sensible, 251, 462
sent
(and he s him forth), 274
(and I will s you), 274, 455
(and she), 417
(and you have s me away), 443
(have s you), 427, 523
(I), 419
(that I might have s you away), 274, 455
(you), 431, 531
me away, 438
separate, 296
(and you shall), 309
(thus you shall), 380, 520
(to be), 25
(to s by distinguishing action), 133
(to), 29, 54, 176, 219, 232, 233, 350
place, 100
separated
(to be), 136
separateness, 436
separates
(that which), 233
separation, 19, 25, 196, 219
sepulchre, 241
serenity, 82
serfdom, 121
serpent, 271, 298, 331, 351, 514, 527
(poisonous), 209
(the), 310
(venemous), 337, 510
servant, 95, 253
(but my), 112
(female), 255
(trained), 107, 347
servants
(and maid), 438
(household), 100
serve
(that they may), 472
(to), 95, 114, 138, 372, 468
(you shall), 335, 503
service, 100, 112, 165, 173, 447, 486
(to be of), 148, 431
in the Tabernacle, 468
servitude, 320
set, 15
(and he s forward), 159
(and I will), 406
(and s him), 414
(and you shall s apart), 392, 523
(as that which is s aside), 501
(I have), 420
(in the), 360, 377
(the), 362
(to be s apart), 290

(to be s over), 158
(to be), 134
(to s apart), 239
(to s oneself), 124
(to s out), 177
(to), 103, 124, 125, 147, 189, 248, 266, 325, 359, 403, 432, 471, 505, 512
(you shall s apart), 389
(you shall), 420, 528
apart, 78, 294
bounds, 58
on fire, 188
over, 164
time, 105, 375
setting, 90, 317
(my), 403
(of jewel), 95
out, 173
place, 249
settings, 164, 452, 453
(the), 453, 454
settle
(to s down), 100, 277, 495
settled
(to be), 100
(what is), 330
abode, 238, 245
settlement, 238
settler, 401
(and for the), 417
(and to your), 426, 522
(as a), 411
settlers
(and), 426, 530
seven, 280, 305, 429
(and), 431
(in), 278
(to), 439
days or years, 280
times, 450, 534
Seven Earths
Crowley Attributions
01 *Aretz* (Supernals), 235, 505
02 *Adamah* (*Hesed*), 68
03 *Gaye* (*Giburah*), 30
04 *Neshiah* (*Tiferet*), 274
05 *Tziah* (*Netzach*), 127
06 *Arqa* (*Hod*), 241
07 *Cheled* (*Yesod* and *Malkut*), 62
Midrash Konen Attributions
01 *Aretz* (Supernals), 235, 505
02 *Adamah* (*Hesed*), 68
03 *Charabhah* (*Giburah*), 196
04 *Tziah* (*Tiferet*), 127
05 *Yabbashah* (*Netzach*), 251
06 *Arqa* (*Hod*), 241
07 *Cheled* (*Yesod* and *Malkut*), 62
07 *Tebhel* (*Yesod* and *Malkut*), 304
sevenfold, 450, 534
seventeen, 480
seventh, 285
(and in the), 436
(the), 399, 434
seventy, 300, 487
severe, 50, 290
(to be), 290
wound, 154
severed
piece, 54
severely
(to act), 148
(to deal with), 148
(to treat), 292
(to wound), 154
severity, 197, 239, 432
sew
(to s together), 388
sewed
(and they), 396
sewer, 217
sexual
(act of lying down for s contact), 273
uncleanness, 74
union, 22
sexuality
(the act of lying with another person), 256
sexually
(to be s excited), 259
(to lie down with), 254
shackling, 221
shade, 140, 163
(to have), 87
(to seek), 87
shadow, 140, 163
(deep), 347
of death, 347
shaft, 84
shake
(to s out or off), 253
(to), 69, 74, 79, 83, 85, 135, 144, 232, 240, 253, 278, 348, 376, 491
shaking, 74, 121, 253
shall
(it s be), 48
shame, 91, 115, 180, 230, 234, 249, 270, 324, 396, 453, 479
(to be put to), 109, 376
(to put to), 245
(to), 109, 376
shamed
(you have), 477
shamefully
(to act), 241
shamelessness, 322
shape, 182, 355
(to hew into), 174
(to stretch into), 171
(to), 171, 185
shard, 329
share, 130, 153, 350
(to), 153
shared, 191
sharp, 28, 40, 192, 242, 459, 507
(to be), 29, 33
sharpen
(to), 238, 261, 288, 499, 506
sharpened, 40
sharp-pointed, 242, 507
shatter
(to), 105, 154, 199, 261, 262, 273, 438, 496, 514
shattered, 292
(to be), 131, 186, 442
shattering, 239
(of type of weapon), 191, 495
shave, 34, 60
(to s off), 95
off, 60
shawl, 215, 484
she, 27, 33
(and), 35, 40
sheaf, 247
(as something bound), 94
shear, 25
(to), 34, 59, 139, 182, 387
shearers, 45
she-ass, 312, 506
she-asses, 456
(and), 457
sheath, 125, 130, 384, 422
sheaves
(to bind), 247
shed
(you), 441
she-donkey, 312, 506
sheep, 28, 157, 193, 243, 254, 256, 459
(among), 278, 477
(young), 243
sheep-dealer, 165
sheepfold, 193, 237
sheepfolds, 448
(the), 462, 538
sheep-raiser, 165
sheep-tender, 165
she-goat, 96, 352
shekel, 303, 337
shells, 367
shelter, 134, 140, 317, 381
(place of), 399
(to), 173, 465
Shem HaMeforash. See God:Names and Descriptors of: *Shem HaMeforash*
shepherd, 230
(abode of), 75
shepherding, 408
shepherds
(abode of), 80
shield, 113, 159, 229, 261, 417
(to), 173, 465
carrier, 372
Shin. See Hebrew Alphabet:21 *Shin*
shine, 188
(to s forth or out), 168

(to), 27, 54, 77, 83, 118, 133, 168, 180, 194, 196, 201, 204, 218, 243, 262, 267, 351, 397, 425, 489, 498
shining, 171, 194, 196, 197
(to be), 194
(to make), 144
oil, 243
one, 93
surface, 137
shiny, 430
(to be), 428
ship, 84, 121, 187, 260
shirt, 162, 222, 461
shiver
(to), 239, 348
shock
(awful), 290
shoe, 162, 180
(to), 162
shoot, 93, 94, 139, 212, 219, 232, 263, 428
(always fig.), 262
(to), 37, 40, 186, 188, 190, 212, 233, 243
(young), 175, 346
shore, 27, 40, 114, 283, 445
short, 285
(to be), 285
(too), 436
sword, 108, 415
shortness, 285
shoulder, 231, 273, 275, 324, 475, 520
(her), 275
blade, 275
shoulder-blade, 324, 520
shoulder-pieces, 467, 470
shout, 23, 41, 130, 215, 240, 388, 468, 481
(for joy), 243
(to s at), 440
(to), 126, 144
made to announce Joseph's chariot, 201, 397
of joy, 23
shouted
(they), 226
shouting, 41, 225
shovel, 98, 256, 357
show, 403
(to s forth), 326
(to s you), 392, 523
(to), 32, 37, 372, 373
me, 223
you, 367, 506
shower, 263, 469
(autumn), 200
showers
(copious), 195
(heavy), 195
shown
(you have been), 362
show-piece, 428
shrewd, 251, 462
(to be), 247, 461
device, 284
shrewdness, 247, 250, 461
shrewmouse, 166
shriek
(to), 108
shrink
(to s back), 64
shrivel
(to s of women's breasts), 209
(to), 278
shrub, 252
shudder
(to), 184, 492
shuddering, 180, 356, 490
shut, 107, 190, 442
(and was s up), 384
(let her be s up), 382
(to s in), 121, 246, 350
(to s off), 121, 350
(to s oneself in or off or up), 142, 429
(to s up), 68, 70, 148, 225, 325, 358, 431, 500, 502
(to), 68, 171, 222, 225, 272, 358, 502
(you shall), 385, 540
up, 190
shutter
(to), 23
shutting
up, 242
shuttle, 185
sick
(and of her that is), 44
(to be), 57, 62, 173, 257, 268, 270, 511
(to become), 62
(to make), 257, 511
sickle, 93, 343
sickness, 67, 74, 102, 107
side, 105, 114, 148, 181, 204, 205, 206, 226, 324, 402, 520
(from every), 93
(of altar), 247
sides
(it), 411
sidewall, 134
siege, 260
(to lay s against), 82
enclosure, 260
towers, 87, 408
wall, 134
work, 149
works, 155, 260, 262
sieve, 151, 203
sieze
(to), 272, 432, 453
sift
(to), 144
sifter, 203
sigh, 27, 75
sighing, 82
sight, 193, 212, 299
(in s of), 76
(in the s of), 76, 97
(to catch s of), 283, 506
(to remove from), 381
sign, 132, 289, 292, 336
(the), 291
(to), 27, 340, 505
signal, 131, 388
pole, 131
signet, 312, 320, 493
seal, 455
signet-ring, 177, 312, 320, 455, 493
signets
(the), 457
signpost, 167, 441
signs, 439, 441
(and the), 444
(and with), 446
(by), 439
(for), 451
(his), 447
(I have observed the), 427
(my), 444
(the), 440, 444
(to observe), 271
silence, 73, 83, 107, 108, 376, 446
(in), 90, 368
(keep), 87, 243
silence!, 83
silenced
(one), 68
silent, 90, 337, 368, 441
(be), 87
(to be), 103, 249, 319, 329, 373, 438
silently, 329
silk, 266, 307
sill, 155, 458
silliness, 305
silly, 65, 333
silver, 168, 463
(drop of), 168
(dross of), 93
(gold and), 177, 467
similitude, 310
(and the), 466
simple, 306, 322, 490
(to be), 321
light, 355
simpleton, 139
simplicity, 306, 322, 466, 490
sin, 35, 38, 41, 45, 87, 248, 262, 265, 297, 468
(and), 47
(his), 42
(in his own), 44
(inadvertent), 248
(shall), 47
(to commit), 244
(to), 35
offering, 41, 46
since, 49, 109, 415
sincere, 185, 306, 490
sincerity, 306, 490

sinew, 34, 403
(in the), 36
sinful, 35, 41
sing
(to), 144, 213, 331
singe
(to), 229, 401
singer, 213
singing, 173, 338, 412
single, 28
sink
(to s down), 100, 101, 232, 249, 317
(to s into), 100
(to), 100, 163, 232, 294, 317
sinking, 262, 447, 488
feeling, 252
sinned
(has), 47
(they), 42
(you have), 313, 494
sinners, 35
sins
(my), 46
(to break off), 281
(when he), 43
sister, 296
(father's), 36
sit, 397
(to s up), 259
(to), 249, 295
(when you), 410, 518
sits, 404
(when he), 411
six, 355, 356, 490
(about), 364
(and), 360, 491
(for), 368, 496
(the), 358
sixteen, 515
sixth, 359
(the), 362, 493
(to give the s part of), 356
sixty, 377, 425, 519, 536
(and), 379, 520
size, 68, 120, 420
skill, 349, 521
skilled, 217
workman, 117, 419
skin, 74, 228, 401
(bright spot on), 357
(harmless eruption of), 128
(of man), 55
(to be diseased of), 272
(white patch of), 357
eruption, 344
spot, 128
skin-bag, 101
skin-bottle, 74
skins, 25, 384, 386
(and), 386
(their), 402, 524
skip
(to s about), 243
(to), 173, 465
skull, 315
skullcap, 127, 311
sky, 277, 285, 288, 481, 499
slab, 63, 428
slack, 232
slackening, 218
slackness, 218
slain, 86
(have I), 364
(was), 48
(will be), 44
slander, 221
(to), 280, 496
slanderer, 221
slap
(to), 209
slaughter, 32, 37, 42, 46, 78, 83, 146, 155, 189, 195
(and you shall), 410
(and), 43
(to s for sacrifice), 34
(to), 34, 37, 251
(you shall), 410
slaughtered, 407
(thing), 42
meat, 32, 42
slaughtering, 37, 407
place, 78
slave, 95
(and treats as a), 409
(female), 65
(you shall treat as a), 507
slavegirl, 286
slay
(to), 37, 94, 155, 189, 191, 238
(you shall), 362, 456
slayer, 189
slaying
(act of), 407
sleep, 117, 268, 270, 326, 420
(and a deep), 379
(and when I), 414
(deep), 376
(my), 425
(out of his), 437
(she will), 410
(to), 34, 272, 379, 492
sleeping, 272, 492
sleeplessness
(tossing of), 77
sleet, 145
slice
(to), 138
slide
(to), 135
sliding, 334
slight
(to be), 170
slime, 213
sling, 184, 233
(to), 184
slinger, 184
slingstones, 184
slip, 412
(to s away), 98, 139
(to s off), 280
(to), 74, 135
slipperiness, 227
slippery
(to be), 153, 169, 484
slit
(to), 213, 442
slope, 214, 243, 246, 324, 520
(steep), 275, 515
slopes, 398
slow
(and), 51
to anger, 395
sluggish, 181
(to be), 20, 181
sluggishness, 182, 354
sluice, 188
slumber, 117, 326
(to), 379
sly, 175, 251, 462
small, 125, 168, 232, 443
(to be), 139, 168, 443
(to become), 139
(to grow), 272
thing, 288, 296
Small
thing, 131
smear
(to), 139, 266
smeared
(to be s over), 306
smell
(sweet), 263, 468
(to have a bad), 242
(to s bad), 242
smelt
(to), 277, 501
smelting
pot or furnace, 202
smile
(to), 53
smiling, 324
smite, 48, 54, 146
(and I will), 45, 329
(and), 48, 50, 54, 61, 331
(to s down), 191
(to s through), 154
(to s with scab), 161
(to), 68, 91, 94, 150, 370, 457
him, 61
smiters, 302
smith, 242
smitten, 94
(and he be), 54
smoke, 250, 252, 298, 402, 501
(and you shall make), 408
(place of sacrificial), 266
(shall be made to), 402
(thick), 250, 252
(to), 298, 501
of sacrifice, 253
smoking, 298, 501

smooth, 114, 153, 217, 430
(to be), 153, 169, 428, 484
(to make), 214
part, 158
smoothness, 153, 158, 227
smote
(and they), 61
(and), 48
(they), 50
snail, 275
snake, 166, 180, 271, 337, 510
(horned), 335, 514
snap
(to), 138
snapping, 228
snare, 107, 178, 209, 239, 308, 323, 416, 499
(to lay a), 293
(to lay), 291
(to), 293
snared
(you be), 441
snares, 230
snatch
(to s away), 159, 174, 322, 518
(to), 154
sneeze
(to), 292
sneezing, 286
sniff
(to s at), 154
snorting, 219
snow, 259, 304
(to), 259
snuff
(its s dishes), 459, 461
dish, 311
snuffers, 235
(for lamps in Temple or Tabernacle), 177
so, 87, 88, 105, 132, 408
(and), 50
be it, 111, 416
much the more, 100
that even, 93
that not, 109, 415
soaking, 242, 478, 495
soap, 360
society, 191
of the shining light of dawn. *See* Golden Dawn: Hebrew name of
socket, 73, 164, 398
sockets, 320
soda, 376
(carbonate of), 376
sodden
(thing), 90
soft, 200, 395
(to be), 142, 209, 409
(to grow), 233, 492
softness, 25, 200, 395
soil
(one rising from the), 196
(to), 154, 458
sojourn, 251
sojourned
(and of her that), 376
(I have), 361
sojourner, 185, 401
(and a), 405
sojourning, 214
place, 214
Sol. *See* Planets: Traditional: 01 Sol
sold
(and he), 333
(and you shall be), 507
(be), 394
(shall be), 381
(thing), 239
(you), 394, 524
solder, 127
soldier
(boot of), 137, 427
soldiers
(band of), 177, 414
sole, 120, 156, 448
solid
(to be), 148, 479
solitary, 51, 102
solution, 351
solved
(and he), 393
some, 366
someone, 148
something, 64
somethingness
(nullification of), 273
somnolence, 123
son, 63, 71, 185, 396
of possession, 306
song, 138, 216, 218, 331, 375
(and), 378
(mocking or derisive), 168
(mocking), 175
(mourning), 83
(taunting), 138
maidens, 483
of contemplation, 288
of mourning, 88
of praise, 306, 375
Song of Songs. *See Tanakh: 03 Kethuvim:* 04 Song of Songs
song-maiden, 472
songs
of praise, 42
son-in-law, 313, 506
(to become a), 313, 506
sons
of the gods, 161, 400
soon
(so), 393, 531
soot, 119
sooth
(to), 127
soothe
(to), 247
soothing, 101
soothsayer, 25, 158, 190
soothsaying
(to practice), 174, 449
sorcerer, 287, 308, 509
sorceress, 128, 345
sorceries, 310, 492
sorcery, 287, 509
(to practice), 287, 509
sore, 334
(and), 51
(to be), 42, 135
sorrel, 355
sorrow, 22, 28, 29, 37, 42, 58, 67, 70, 75, 82, 87, 119, 171, 198, 296, 346, 380, 395, 399, 405, 408, 461
sorrowful
(to be), 20, 42
sorry
(to be), 62, 119, 380
(to become), 62
sort, 75, 400
soujourner, 397
soul, 53, 302, *Also See* Kabbalistic Souls
(the), 304
souls, 451, 452, *See Also* Kabbalah:Souls
(of your), 467, 539
(our), 466
(the), 454
sound, 78, 123, 148, 153, 170, 294, 348, 421
(and you shall), 409, 525
(to be), 277, 477
(to make a clear), 238
(to make a shrill), 238
(to), 68
soundness, 319, 498
soup, 90
sour
(to be), 153, 480
milk, 58
source, 60, 88, 153, 355
(thy), 80, 340
of brightening or cheerfulness, 324
south, 74, 214, 220, 325, 471, 512
south-country, 74
southward, 325, 512
sovereign
power, 324
sovereignty, 151, 284, 339, 497
sow
(and you shall), 410, 526
(to), 228
(you shall), 387, 389
sowing, 228, 231
(place of), 251
sown
(that is), 387
(that which is), 231
(thing), 231
(you have), 387
space, 53, 60, 195, 266

(bare), 250
spacious
(to be), 321
spade, 289
span, 118
(and a), 361
spare
(to), 93, 96
spark, 63, 141, 212, 500
sparkle, 134
(to make the eyes), 180, 489
(to), 180, 204, 489, 498
spatter
(to), 81
speak, 187
(and I will), 366
(and you shall), 360
(and you), 378, 519
(I will), 362
(shall you), 381, 528
(to be unable to), 90, 368
(to s indistinctly or unintelligibly), 129
(to), 29, 144, 207, 209, 249, 252, 334
speaker, 81
speaking
inarticulately, 125
spear, 170, 192, 209, 214, 255, 316, 335, 444, 459
(head of), 62
(tip of), 56
species, 75, 121, 400, 420
of hardwood tree, 358
of tree – perhaps cypress or cedar, 470
specify
(to), 351
speckled, 165, 173
speech, 94, 209, 212, 283, 432
(my), 377
speechless
(to be), 329
speed, 214
speedily, 212
speedy, 212
spell, 191
spelt, 334
spent
(to be), 74
sperm, 271, 492
sphere, 270
spheres, 423
spice, 121, 246, 263, 266, 381, 468
(cassia), 131, 228
(to), 85
(tragacanth gum), 317
mixture, 246
spicery, 246
spices
(aromatic), 266
spice-seasoning, 269, 419
spicy
(to make), 85
spider, 129, 435
spied
(you have s out), 498, 546
spies, 377, 519
(the), 379, 519
spikenard, 217
spill
(to), 288, 463
(you), 441
spilled
(and s it), 405
spin
(did), 39
(to), 38
spindle-wheel, 339
spine, 171
spirit, 195, 285, 286, *Also See* Elements: Spirit
(evil), 322
(one that has a familiar), 23
spirits, 231, 365
(the), 364
spiritual, 227
unreceptivity, 132
spit, 463, 464
(to), 247, 288
spite
(in s of), 132, 384
spitting
(act of), 463, 464
spittle, 240, 294
splendid, 350
splendor, 30, 32, 41, 74, 171, 190, 194, 390
(with), 47
Splendor of Unity, the, 373
splintering, 228
split, 22
(to), 134, 175, 192, 213, 303, 319, 428, 442
spoil, 18, 23, 30, 33, 290, 294
(and you shall), 363, 515
(its), 275
(the), 274
(to take), 273, 355
(to), 58, 247, 273, 299, 355
spoiled
(and they), 50
spoiling, 23
spoils, 158
(half of), 158
spoke, 292
(and she), 360
(and), 201
(you), 388, 522
of a wheel, 292
to, 226
spoken
(I have), 362
(you have), 374, 518
spokesman, 81
sport
(to), 306
spot, 106, 375
(in the bright), 358
(peeled), 187
(the bright), 360
(to), 59
spots, 297
spotted, 187
(to be), 59
spout, 265
spread, 212, 359
(and you shall s abroad), 430
(be), 433
(shall s abroad), 434
(something), 198
(thing s out), 365
(to be), 188, 283
(to s abroad), 251, 271
(to s out), 82, 173, 271, 281, 284, 309, 350
(to s over), 41
(to s something over), 262, 468
(to), 118, 188, 194, 232, 251, 282, 350
out, 455
spreading, 73, 352
out, 73, 155, 365, 458
place, 273
spring, 52, 56, 88, 91, 120, 148, 153, 173, 185, 265, 344, 432, 448, 471, *Also See* Seasons:Spring (*Aviv*)
(to s about), 283
(to s over), 306
(to s up), 154, 376
(to), 81, 114, 142, 167
of water, 138
rain, 318
spring-crop, 302
springs, 91, 344
sprinkle, 34
(and he shall), 41
(he shall), 40
(to), 81, 244
sprinkled, 40
(and he), 41
sprout, 154, 233, 261
(always fig.), 262
(to), 154, 233, 243
spue
(to s out), 129
spun
(that which is), 79
spurn
(to), 83, 157, 215, 481
spurt
(to), 81
spy
(that they may s out), 366
(to s out), 206, 369, 370
(to), 176
spying
(from), 375
squander
(to), 23
square, 252

(magic), 192
(to), 226
squared
(to be), 226
squeeze
(to), 146, 147, 195, 251, 279, 285, 359, 478, 517
squeezer, 152, 480
squeezing, 155, 480
sshamed, 494
stab, 266
stable, 170, 388, 409
(to be), 95, 411
stack, 251
stacte, 155, 458
staff, 73, 173, 248, 313, 315, 507
(and your), 207, 437
(his), 460
stag, 60, 267
stagger, 181
(to), 31, 144, 266
staggering, 181, 398
stained
(to be deeply), 313, 495
(to be), 313, 495
stair, 159
staircase, 84
stairway, 127
stake, 296
stalk, 166, 169, 484
stall, 388
(for animals), 193, 263
stalwart
ones, 269, 490
stammer
(to), 234
stammering, 125
stamp
(to), 281, 351
stamping
(of hoofs), 282
(to foul by), 351
stand, 88, 408
(ability or power to), 342
(to be at a), 135
(to make), 124
(to s still), 124
(to s up), 160, 239, 399
(to s upright), 158
(to take one's), 135, 158
(to), 135, 158, 160, 399
standard, 55, 132, 292
(according to), 50
standards, 55
standing, 342
grain, 159
ground, 139
place, 135, 180, 418
standing-place, 149
stank
(and), 402
Star of David, 423
stare
(to), 248
stars
(of Messiah, brothers, youth, numerous progeny, personification, God's own omniscience), 67
start
(to s early), 273, 475
(to s up), 376
(to), 229, 401
startle
(to), 59, 317
startled
(to be), 194
state
of rest, 125
statement
(exact), 352
station, 149
(to bring to a), 104
statue, 148
stature, 68, 120, 163, 402, 420
(lofty), 375
statute, 117, 130, 134, 181, 189
statutes, 329
(my), 333
staves
(its), 39
(with their), 468, 539
of, 33
stay, 397
(to), 150, 272
stayed
(and was), 426
stead
(in his), 450
(in their), 455, 536
steadfastness, 116, 123
steadiness, 116, 123
steady-handed
one, 111, 416
steal
(to s away), 73
(to), 73
stealthily
(to watch), 236
steed, 350
steeds, 221, 335, 416
(royal), 482, 547
steel, 139
steep, 175, 216, 292
place, 214, 216
slope, 275, 515
steer, 230
stela, 231
stem, 98
stench, 165, 242
(to emit), 83
step, 83, 159, 181, 186, 310, 325, 341, 420
(to s forward), 310
(to), 81, 171, 310
steppe, 229
stepping
chains, 173
place, 222, 418
steps, 127
(to take quick little), 118, 173, 465
sterile, 102, 276
stibium, 128, 352
stick, 148, 169, 359, 484
(to), 139
closer, 127
stiffen
(you should), 441
still, 98, 143, 429
(to be), 103, 249, 373
waiting, 83
sting
(to), 350
stinger
(of insect), 285, 517
stink
(to), 83, 242
stinkberries, 268, 473
stinking
things, 245, 268, 472
stinkweed, 245
stir
(to s up), 61, 189, 227, 234
(to), 201, 329, 396
stirred
(to be s up), 20, 189
stock, 94, 98, 139, 169, 276, 428, 484
stocks, 215
(as instrument of torture), 341
(for feet), 83
stolen
(thing), 78
stomach, 129
stone, 72, 101, 234, 253, 397, 439
(and you shall s them), 370, 517
(costly), 33
(glowing), 277, 503
(hewn), 298
(large or small), 72, 397
(precious - agate), 246
(precious - amethyst), 103
(precious - beryl), 519
(precious - carbuncle), 396
(precious - corals, rubies, jewels), 181, 454
(precious - emerald), 162, 368
(precious - emerald, carbuncle), 396
(precious - jacinth), 276, 476
(precious - jasper), 286
(precious - jasper, onyx, diamond), 104, 374
(precious - malachite), 264, 469
(precious - pearl), 104, 374
(precious - ruby, agate), 65
(precious - sapphire), 267
(precious - sardius), 64, 356
(precious - topaz), 119
(precious), 132, 536
(to s to death), 181
(to), 211, 439

(used in paving [w/marble]), 384
stones
(course of), 345
(heap of), 214, 233
(hewing of), 155
stoning
(to kill by), 211, 439
(to put to death by), 181
(to slay by), 211, 439
stood
(and he), 333
(and she), 464
(that), 183, 423
stool, 68, 98, 100, 358
stoop
(to s down), 272
(to), 172
stop
(to s over), 105, 414
(to s the approach), 121, 350
(to s up), 130, 148, 225, 325, 384, 431, 500, 502
(to), 61
stopped
(to be s up), 73
stopping, 113
storage, 176, 272, 492
house, 176
store, 156, 180, 209, 237, 272, 459, 465, 492
(to s up), 139, 200, 235
(to), 461
stored
(to be), 138, 427
storehouse, 123, 130, 156, 217, 233, 237, 381, 459
stores, 52
storing, 156, 459
stork, 106
(the), 112
storm, 51, 257, 349
(devastating), 249
(driving), 199, 496
(to rush of s winds), 151
(to s away), 348
(to), 257, 348
stormily
(to act), 188
storming, 167, 462
story, 341
stout, 135
(among the), 285, 498
(the), 285, 498
(to be), 148, 479
stove, 204
(hot), 277, 503
straight, 97, 102, 330
(to go), 325, 330
(to make), 344, 517
forward, 76
in front, 102
straightforward, 76
straightness, 97, 102, 330, 343
strain
(to), 188
strait, 183
straiten
(to), 183
straitened
(to be), 323
straitness, 174, 207, 210
straits, 174, 207, 210, 234, 237, 257
(to be in), 239
(to bring into), 183
strange, 188, 195
(but he made himself), 390
(to act as), 225
(to be), 195
(to treat as), 225
stranger, 397
(to be a), 195, 208
strangers, 390
(the), 426, 530
strangle
(to s oneself), 168
(to), 168
strangling, 183
straw, 288
heap, 323, 512
stray
(to), 77, 103, 246
strayed
(and), 462
straying, 215
streaked, 175
streaks
(penetrating), 525
stream, 57, 62, 67, 120, 138, 193, 218
(to), 76, 218
street, 125, 291, 473
strength, 20, 47, 50, 55, 60, 66, 75, 96, 103, 109, 135, 138, 139, 148, 152, 161, 171, 174, 187, 197, 208, 211, 231, 308, 340, 351, 393, 399, 410, 427, 479, 486, 527
(firm or rugged), 77
(full), 77
(her), 52
(like the), 485
(powerful), 508, 559
(to have), 186
strengthen
(to), 135, 150, 306
stress, 174, 207, 210
stretch
(to s into shape), 171
(to s oneself out), 236, 505
(to s out), 82, 251, 348
(to), 67, 350
stretched
(to lie s out), 226
out, 43
strew
(to), 244
stricken, 91, 94
strict
decision, 242, 507
strictness, 468
stride
(to), 171
strife, 114, 120, 125, 151, 219, 339, 418, 420, 422
(in the s of), 378
(to cause), 189
strike, 146
(to s down), 94, 370
(to s off), 204, 481
(to), 68, 73, 91, 94, 142, 150, 204, 310, 348, 370, 457, 481
striking, 150, 457
off, 204, 481
string, 41, 376
of harp, 109, 415
strings
(to play), 125, 421
(to strike), 125, 421
strip
(to s off), 159, 200, 284, 376, 506
(to s oneself), 316
(to), 174, 284, 316, 506
stripe, 187, 196, 200, 297
striped, 175
stripped, 322, 340, 342
(what is s off a person in war), 158
stripping, 302, 512
strive, 39, 194
(to), 189, 194, 316, 327
striven
(you have), 472
striving, 257, 386, 486
stroke, 142, 181, 420
(to), 306, 355
of a battering-ram, 77
strokes, 140
strong, 73, 80, 96, 135, 138, 139, 146, 148, 156, 187, 188, 192, 227, 398, 403, 427, 431, 459, 479, 481
(to be), 96, 103, 106, 135, 148, 178, 186, 216, 306, 371, 479, 500
(to grow), 351, 527
(used only to describe God), 194
drink, 335
man, 60, 186
one, 186, 193
stronger, 135
(and the), 381, 520
(the), 499
stronghold, 142, 150, 155, 178, 258, 262, 265, 489
structure, 85, 118, 133, 344, 425
(covered), 147, 359
struggle
(to), 159, 327
struggled
(and they), 439
stubble, 288
stubborn, 220
(to be), 313
stubborness, 294
stubbornness

(in the), 506
study, 57, 341
(devotion to), 57
studying, 57
stuff
(woven), 143
stumble, 181
(to), 180, 266
stumbling, 40, 181, 287, 291, 500
(means of), 76
(means or occasion of), 287
(occasion of), 76
(of qualm of conscience), 181
stumbling-block, 284, 286, 287
stump, 77, 153, 338
stunted
(to be), 154
stupid
(to be), 131, 226
fellow, 139
stupidity, 131, 135, 226, 281, 336
stylus, 98, 198, 327
point, 298, 501
subdue
(to), 127, 254, 261
subdued
(be), 358
(to be), 155
subject
(to), 254
to oppression and abuse, 87, 408
subjection
(to be brought into), 155
subjects, 456
subjugation, 134
submerged
(to be), 163
submit
(to s thyself), 262
subsequent, 220, 223, 471, 473
subside
(to), 189, 262, 317, 449
substance, 75, 80, 184, 247, 399, 403, 424
(living), 166, 406
(shining), 280
yet being unperfect, 92, 369
substitute, 377
subtle, 251, 462
(to be), 247, 461
subtlety, 177, 247, 461
suburb, 341
subversion, 320
succeed
(and you do s them), 482, 542
(to), 146, 334
success, 349, 521
succor, 229, 231
(to), 228, 318
such, 22, 28, 30, 292
suck
(to give), 128
(to s up), 174
(to), 168, 199, 496
sucked
out, 72
sucker, 172
sucking
child, 128
suckle
(to), 128, 167, 168
suckling, 128, 172
sudden
terror or ruin, 61
suddenly, 337, 503
suddenness, 337, 344, 503
suet, 231
suffer
(to), 35, 57, 271
me, 448
sufferer, 156
suffering, 107, 121
suffice, 405, 417
sufficiency, 30, 73, 80, 261, 403
(and), 38
sufficient, 261
sufficiently, 73
suffocation, 183
suitable, 86, 407
(to be), 334
sulfur, 392
sullen, 220
sultry, 337
sum, 326
summer, 139, *Also See* Seasons:Summer (*Qayitz*)
(to spend the), 183, 491
summer-fruit, 184, 493
summit, 126, 326, 345, 422
(of tree or mountain), 215
summoned, 248
sun, 72, 188, 372, *See* Planets: Traditional: 01 Sol
(and to the), 386
(heat of), 72
(light of), 185
(the), 374
sun-pillar, 118, 419
sunrise
(place of), 217
sunset, 67, 226, 378
super
abundance of fat, 152
superiority, 363, 375
Supernals. *See* Kabbalah:The Ten *Sefirot*: Supernals
supplant, 175
supplanter, 175
supple
(to be), 114
supplicant, 384
supplicate
(to), 384
supplication, 315
supply, 176, 209, 465
support, 116, 140, 151, 175, 239, 253, 313, 354, 398, 507
(molten), 207
(of every kind), 315
(of tree), 94, 139, 428
(to), 111, 140, 150, 228, 281, 299, 314, 354, 416, 479, 502
supported, 315
supporters
of the door, 116
supporting, 144, 356
suppose, 65
suppress
(to), 83
sure, 116, 133
surely, 39, 49, 51, 90, 95, 133, 148, 240, 325, 370, 392, 409
(and), 45, 329
surety, 229, 387
(to be), 226
(to become), 226
surface
(shining or glaring), 137, 145
surname
(to), 94
surnamed
(to be), 94
surpassing, 348, 350
(to be), 133
surprisingly, 337, 503
surround
(to), 83, 124, 170, 173, 194, 229, 364, 421, 463, 465
surrounded
(to be), 134
surrounding, 124, 130
surrounds
(that which), 124
survive
(to), 327
survivor, 332
sustain
(to), 150
sustenance, 82, 125, 421
swaddled
(to be), 305
swaddling-band, 307
swallow, 63, 131, 144, 229, 293
(to s down), 123, 128
(to s greedily), 94, 130, 370
(to s up), 123
(to), 128
swallowed
(thing), 123
swallowing, 123
swamp, 112, 117, 468
swan, 516
swarm, 226
swarms
(that), 488
swath, 253
swaying, 310
swear
(made me), 309
(to), 17, 54
(you did), 450
(you shall), 429, 431
swears, 429

sweat, 101, 106
sweep
  (to s away), 25
  (to s bare), 283
  (to s together), 104
  (to), 33, 104, 231, 490
sweet, 173, 226, 263, 342, 412, 468
  (to be or become), 340
  (to be), 169, 226, 408
  odor, 263, 468
  smell, 263, 468
  thing, 350
  wine, 199
sweetly
  sounding, 173, 412
sweetness, 340, 342, 350
swell, 183
  (to cause s to), 95
  (to s up), 118
  (to), 27, 95, 118, 178, 182
swelling, 118, 396
swerve
  (to), 250
swerver, 246
swift, 144, 148, 212
  (to be), 170
swim
  (to), 249
swimming, 250
swine, 202
swinging, 341
swollen, 118
swoop
  (to s upon), 108
  (will s down), 38
swooper, 108
sword, 85, 191, 323, 407
  (drawn), 323
  (edge of), 116
  (hilt of), 158
  (short), 108, 415
  (their), 406, 525
  (they killed with the), 301
swords, 223, 363
sworn
  (have I), 452
sycamore
  tree, 306, 490
synagogue, 337
tabernacle, 293, 321, 500
Tabernacle in the Wilderness, 293, 321, 500
  (screen of), 140
  (service in), 468
  architect of - Bezaleel, 165
  curtain pieces of, 358
  gatekeeper of (Hilkiah), 168
  gatekeeper of (Nethaneel), 338
  height in cubits of the curtains in, 47
  number of Israelite leaders that accompanied Moses to, 88
  number of shekels of gold used in the construction of, 412
  number of shekels of silver used in the construction of, 553
  number of talents of gold used in the construction of, 48
  one who helped build (Ahisamach), 154, 364
  rings clasping a pillar of, 292
  screen of, 354
  snuffers for lamps used in, 177
  the covering (the skins), 143
table, 119, 199, 284, 420, 497
tablet, 63, 119, 420
  (letters on), 185
tablets, 92
taboo
  (to make someone), 234
tail, 77
  (of sheep), 65
tainted
  (to be), 57
take, 330
  (and they shall t down), 207
  (to t away), 154, 226, 295, 322, 518
  (to t everything), 302
  (to t from), 227
  (to t hold of), 295
  (to t hold upon), 269
  (to t off), 145, 294, 478, 510
  (to t up), 66
  (to), 73, 149, 154, 226, 268, 322
  (you shall), 397
  (you will), 341
  hold, 33
  it (and), 40
  out, 27, 39
taken
  away, 350
taking, 73, 161
tale, 29, 280, 471
tale-bearer, 221
talk, 187
  (empty), 19
  (idle), 19
  (to t arrogantly), 144, 191, 477, 495
tamarisk
  tree, 257
tambourine, 320, 517
tame, 132, 137, 451, 453
Tanakh, 317, 481
  (number of negative commandments in), 275
  01 Torah, 360
    (and), 363
    (as word of God), 212
    (book of the), 482
    (number of books in), 18
    (the), 362
    01 Genesis
      Baba'ahaweh (initials of first seven words), 39
      Hebrew name of (*Bereshit*), 473, 565
      number of days the earth was created, 19
      number of letters in, 547
      number of letters in the account of the days of creation, 552
      Quotes
        01.10, 12, 18, 21, 25
          And God saw that it was good, 266, 471
        01.12
          And the earth brought forth grass, 505, 556
        01.16
          Two great lights, 504, 548
        01.21
          The great sea monsters, 375, 552
        01.22
          Be fruitful and multiply, 325
        01.22, 28
          And God blessed them, 426, 562
        01.26
          And God said, 561
          And God said let us make man in his own image, 496
          Let us make man in our image, 523
          Let us make the earth creature in our image, 391
        01.27
          In the image of God created he them, 458, 557
          Male and female created He them, 497, 546
          So God created man in his own image, 475, 559
        01.29
          Every herb bearing seed, 485
        01.3
          Let there be light, 205
        01.4
          ...was good, and God separated the light from the darkness, 458, 566
          divided the light and divided the darkness, 563

the light and divided the darkness, 361, 386, 551
01.7, 9, 11, 15, 24, 30
And it was so, 123, 421
02.12
Good gold, 50
02.2
His work which He had made, 533
02.20
But for the man there was not, 133, 385
02.9
And from the ground the Lord God caused to grow, 294, 547
07.12
Forty days and forty nights, 428, 563
08.20
And he, Noah, built an altar to YHVH, 208, 465
12.3
I will bless those who bless you, 336, 491
12.8
Noah built an altar to YHVH, 335, 504
13.2
was rich in silver, 180, 471
18.2
And behold, three, 395
19.1
The two angels arrived in Sodom, 371, 517
14.10, 11; 18.20
Sodom and Gomorrah, 301, 487
22.1
And God tested, 361, 515
And God tested Abraham, 386, 557
22.7, 8
God will see to the sheep, 375, 518
22.9
And Abraham built an altar there, 509, 561
25.8
Old, wise and satisfied, 339, 516
28.10
From Beer-Sheba, 362
28.11
And lay down in that place, 341, 505
28.12
Angels of God were going up and down on it, 362, 562
28.13
I am the Lord, the God of your father Abraham, 295, 539
28.16
And I did not know it, 360
Surely the Lord exists in this place, 360, 554
31.24
The fear of Isaac, 244
33.20
He erected there an altar, 327, 501
The mighty God of Israel, 364
39.2, 21
YHVH was with, 313
YHVH was with Joseph, 362, 530
39.23
YHVH made it prosper, 186
45.27
the spirit of their father Jacob revived, 462, 538
47.23
Take for yourselves seed, 278, 477
49.18
For Your salvation do I hope, God, 534, 555
49.24
Mighty One of Jacob, 286
49.33
And, breathing his last, he was gathered to his people, 292, 510
He was gathered to his people, 249, 497
01.28
Be fruitful and multiply and replenish the earth, 525, 560
sum of the first chapter of, 572
total number of Hebrew letters in, 572
02 Exodus
Hebrew name of (*Shemoth*), 419
number of judgment from, 42
Quotes
02.10
And he became to her as a son, 161, 438
From the waters, 179, 535
02.16
Seven daughters, 451
02.3
With tar and pitch, 418
03.3, 4
Moses turned aside, 360
03.5
This shall be My name forever, This My appellation for all eternity, 521, 553
03.6
The God of Abraham, the God of Isaac, and the God of Jacob, 432, 531
12.48
Passover to YHVH, all his males must be circumcised, 361
13.14
I will be what I will be, 341
13.17
The people might change their minds, 269, 560
14.10
Greatly frightened, 229
14.19-21
The angel of God...waters were split, 570, 571
09.12, 10.20, 27; 11.10
And the Lord stiffened the

heart of Pharaoh, 480
15.10
They sank like lead in mighty waters, 526, 563
15.3
The Lord is a man of war, 452
20.12
Honor thy father and thy mother, 476, 556
20.13
Thou shalt not bear false witness against thy neighbor, 543, 558
Thou shalt not murder, 411
20.15
All the people witnessed the thunder (or voices), 533, 563
20.3
Thou shalt have no other gods before me, 393, 562
20.4
Thou shalt not make unto thee any graven image, 495, 542
21.1
And these are the laws, 336, 503
22.19
I will make all My goodness pass before you, 388, 514
25.8
And let them make Me a sanctuary that I may dwell among them, 560, 564
28.15
breastplate of decision, 434, 538
30.10
It is Holy, most Holy, 461, 537
30.29
Whatever touches them shall be consecrated, 371, 517
31.6
And all skillful, 166, 406
33.13
Pray let me know Your ways, 454, 530
33.18
He said, 'Oh, let me behold Your presence!', 495, 541
Oh, let me behold Your presence!, 426, 522
33.19
And I will proclaim before you the name YHVH, 525, 562
25.3
Gold and silver, 177, 467
38.16
Capitals were silver, 407, 558
40.2
Set up the Tabernacle of the Tent of Meeting, 532, 563
40.6
Open the door to the Tabernacle of the Tent of Meetings, 499, 550
03 Leviticus
Hebrew name of (*Vayiqra*), 251
Quotes
09.1
On the eighth day, 327, 501
11.44, 45
Holy am I, 326
18.30
And you shall not defile yourselves through them, 340, 504
19.26
You shall not practice divination, 437
21.8
I am YHVH who makes you holy, 353, 513
24.5
The pure table, 360
06.10, 18, 22; 7.1, 6; 10.12, 17; 14.13
It is Holy, most Holy, 461, 537
25.42
For they are My servants, 170, 409
11.44; 20.7; 24.22; 25.17
for I am YHVH, your God, 201, 433
26.4
And the earth shall give of its produce, 458
26.42
And I will remember the land, 337, 531
04 Numbers
Hebrew name of (*Bamidbar*), 213
Quotes
06.24 – 26)
May God bless you and guard you. May God shine His Countenance upon you and give you grace. May God turn His Countenance toward you and grant you peace., 564, 570
06.26
May YHVH bestow His favor upon you, 307, 475
09.23
On a sign from the Lord they made camp and on a sign from the Lord they broke camp, 380
10.2
Two trumpets of silver, 548, 563
13.2
All were leaders, 313, 494
14.22
and have disobeyed me, 355
14.9, 112, 348
19.2
In which there is no defect, 378, 555
21.14
The Book of the Wars of the Lord, 466
21.28
Lords of the High Places, 345
22.2
Balak, son of Zippor, 345, 518

24.5
How fair are your tents, O Jacob, Your dwellings, O Israel!, 549, 564
31.22, 23
And the lead, everything that goes through the fire, 561
33.1
The leadership of Moses and Aaron, 366, 525
05 Deuteronomy
Hebrew name of (*Devarim*), 218, 446
Hebrew name of (*Eleh Hadevarim*), 237, 457
Quotes
04.12
You heard the sound of words but perceived no shape, 553, 568
04.45
(Moses) spoke to the children of Israel, 453
07.13
He will favor you and bless you and multiply you, 332, 557
07.9
Know, therefore, that only the Lord your God is God, 360, 504
10.17
For the Lord your God is the God of gods and the Lord of lords, the Almighty, the great..., 347, 562
16.20
So that you might thrive, 361, 524
16.3
Bread of anguish, 189, 427
21.20, 157
Glutton and drunkard, 161
26.2
And go to the place, 389, 522
26.3
That I have entered the land, 427, 545
29.22
Sodom and Gomorrah, 301, 487
29.28
...with overt acts, it is for us and our children ever, 481, 542
30.12
Who will go up for us to heaven?, 373
30.2
and heed His command with all your heart and soul, 482
31.29
You will become corrupt, 554
31.6
Your God [YHVH] Himself marches with you He will not fail you or forsake you, 382, 564
33.2
YHVH came from Sinai, 183
33.30
How does one pursue a thousand?, 311, 556
34.9
Yeheshua son of Nun was filled with the spirit of wisdom, 473, 561
first and last letters of, 51
first two letters of, 185
02 Neviim
01 Joshua
Hebrew name of (*Yehoshua*), 285
Quotes
06.27
YHVH was with, 313
10.13
The Book of Jashar, 482
10.27
Going down of the sun, 378
02 Judges
Hebrew name of (*Shofetim*), 308, 491
Quotes
01.19
YHVH was with, 313
03 1 Samuel
Hebrew name of (*Shemuel*), 280
04 2 Samuel
Hebrew name of (*Shemuel*), 280
Quotes
01.18
The Book of Jashar, 482
05.11
Hiram, King of Tyre, 374, 549
05 1 Kings
Hebrew name of (*Melekim*), 157, 396
Quotes
07.14
Widow's son, 320, 511
10.18
Refined gold, 230, 476
10.22
Gold and silver, 177, 467
11.41
The Book of the Annals of Solomon, 544
05.15
Hiram, King of Tyre, 374, 549
06 2 Kings
Hebrew name of (*Melekim*), 157, 396
Quotes
01.10
fire from heaven, 434, 558
17.18
and [He] banished them from His presence, 355, 514
The Lord was incensed at Israel and He banished them from His presence, 565, 568
18.4
Brazen serpent, 509
07 Isaiah
Hebrew name of (*Yeshayah*), 286
Quotes
06.3
Holy, holy, holy is God..., 562, 565
09.5
Prince of Peace, 462, 538
14.12

Son of the Dawn, 370, 526
24.16
From the end of the earth we have heard songs, the desire of the *tzaddik*, 557, 567
25.9
Behold, this is our God that we have been waiting for, 318
29.19
The humble shall increase joy in God, 408, 525
30.26
Light of the sun, 223
32.2
Refuge from gales, 223
34.16
Book of YHVH, 275
52.8
Eye to eye, 222, 544
08 Jeremiah
Hebrew name of (*Yirmeyah*), 223
Quotes
01.14
Evil begins from the north, 538, 560
06.29
The lead comes whole from the fire, 543, 560
23.6
The Lord is our Vindicator, 228
49.18
Sodom and Gomorrah, 301, 487
09 Ezekiel
Hebrew name of (*Yechzqiel*), 166
Quotes
01.14
Dashing to and fro [among] the creatures was something that looked like flares, 537
01.26
Semblance of a man, 248, 461
There was the semblance of a human form, 504, 548
07.7
The cycle has come around for you..., 562, 569
22.18
And lead in the middle of the furnace, they are the dross of silver, 550, 567
22.20
And the lead into the middle of the furnace to blow the fire on it to melt it, 565, 568
27.12
Lead they gave for your wares, 537, 556
16.13
Gold and silver, 177, 467
10 Hosea
Hebrew name of (*Hoshea*), 281
11 Joel
Hebrew name of (*Yoel*), 66
Quotes
02.20
The eastern sea, 223, 450
12 Amos
Hebrew name of (*Amos*), 176
Quotes
07.7
and in his hand a lead plumbline, 119, 350
13 Obadiah
Hebrew name of (*Obadyah*), 111
Quotes
01.1
The prophecy of Obadiah. We have received tidings from the Lord, and an envoy has been sent out among the nations 'Up! Let us rise up against her for battle.', 566, 569
14 Jonah
Hebrew name of (*Yonah*), 90
15 Micah
Hebrew name of (*Miykah*), 94
16 Nahum
Hebrew name of (*Nachum*), 126, 382
17 Habakkuk
Hebrew name of (*Chabaqquwq*), 197
Quotes
02.19
Gold and silver, 177, 467
20 Zechariah
Hebrew name of (*Zekaryah*), 210
Quotes
05.7
A lead cover was lifted up, 551
05.8
Lead stone on its mouth, 478, 545
14.14
Gold and silver, 177, 467
21 Malachi
Hebrew name of (*Meleaki*), 123
Quotes
03.16
Book of Remembrance, 366, 525
03.6
I am God, I have not changed, 465
03 Kethuvim
01 Psalms
145
name of a prayer consisting of, 331
Hebrew name of (*Tehillim*), 321, 498
musical terms
Al-taschith (do not destroy – unknown meaning), 511
Selah, 261
Quotes
103.1, 2, 22
My soul, bless God, 504
111.3
His beneficence is everlasting, 521
115.10-13
He (God) is their help and shield, 316, 545
118.22
The stone that the builders rejected, 227, 541
The stone that the builders rejected has become the chief cornerstone, 532, 563
12.7

Silver refined in an earthen furnace, 489, 566
133.1
Together in unity, 83, 367
135.1
The Name of the Lord, 427, 530
137.4
The song of YHVH, 339
147.5
Great is our Lord and abundant in strength, 551, 563
19.3
Speaks out, 326
19.7
The Law of the Lord, 497
22.17
Dogs surround me, a pack of evil ones closes in on me, like lions [they maul] my hands and feet, 556, 565
Like a lion, they are at my hands and my feet, 336
22.2
My God, my God, why hast thou forsaken me?, 496, 497
24.1
World and all its inhabitants, 427
29.3
The voice of YHVH is over the waters, 271, 474
29.4
The voice of the Lord is majesty, 278
The voice of the Lord is power, 182
29.5
The voice of the Lord breaks cedars, 475, 541
29.7
The voice of YHVH kindles flames of fire, 491
29.8
The voice of YHVH convulses the wilderness, 315
29.9
The voice of YHVH causes hinds to calve, 392
30.2
I will exalt You, God, for You have lifted me up, 460, 531
32.2
And in whose spirit there is no deceit, 341, 517
33.18
The eye of the Lord is on those who fear Him, 296, 501
56
Yownath (title of), 315
56.1
Yownath 'elem rechoqiym (Title – meaning uncertain), 466, 558
60
Lily of the testimony (title), 511, 553
69.29
Book of Life, 309, 492
80
Lilies of the testimony (title), 516, 552
80.17
Your right hand, 341, 495
84.12
A sun and shield are YHVH Elohim, 456, 559
85.11
Justice and well-being kiss, 497, 546
85.2
O Lord, You will favor Your Land, restore Jacob's fortune, 567, 568
53.1
Mahalath (catchword used in), 317
90.17
May the favor of the Lord, our God, be upon us, 336, 503
90.4
A thousand years in Your eyes are as a day of yesterday, 521, 567
96.9
Bown down to God in a sacred splendor, 553
02 Proverbs
Hebrew name for (*Mishle*), 280
Quotes
02.4
If you seek her as silver, 399, 537
04.5
Acquire wisdom, acquire discernment, 310
08.10
Choice gold, 533
10.20
Choice silver, 298, 511
16.16
Understanding to be chosen above silver, 337, 523
17.3
Fining pot is for silver, 354, 559
03 Job
Quotes
19.24
With an iron and lead pen, 502
22.24
Gold dust, 373
26.7
He suspends the earth on nothingness, 473, 551
28.1
A mine for silver, 256, 498
28.3
He has set an end to darkness, 465, 564
28.6
Its rocks are a source of sapphires, 339, 504
32.2, 6
Elihu, son of Barakel, 271, 491
33.33
Be still and I will teach you wisdom, 410, 518
04 Song of Songs

Hebrew name for (*Shir HaShirim*), 502, 547
Quotes
05.11
Pure gold of the head, 343, 506
05.3
I had bathed my feet, 532
I had taken off my robe, 560
06.3
I am my beloved's..., 179
05 Ruth
Hebrew name of (*Ruth*), 356
06 Lamentations
Hebrew title of (*'ekah*), 54
07 Ecclesiastes
Hebrew name for (*Qoheleth*), 339
Quotes
01.1
Vanity of vanities, says Ecclesiasted, vanity of vanities, all is vanity, 508, 561
07.29
That God has made man upright, but they have sought out many schemes', 567, 569
08 Esther
Hebrew name of (*Esther*), 381
Quotes
01.6
Gold and silver, 177, 467
03.1
Haman son of Hammedatha the Agagite, 364, 556
09 Daniel
Hebrew name of (*Daniel*), 115
Quotes
02.32
Its breasts and its arms were of silver, 329, 521
02.49
Shadrach, Meshach, and Abed-nego, 497, 558
03.5, 7, 10, 12, 14, 18
Golden image, 175, 413
03.6, 11, 15, 17, 21, 23, 26
Fiery furnace, 405, 533
05.25
Numbered, numbered, weighed, and divisions, 508, 510, 552, 553
08.27
And I, Daniel, was broken and became sick for many days, 523, 554
10 Ezra
Hebrew name of (*Ezra*), 229
11 Nehemiah
Hebrew name of (*Nechemiyah*), 134
12 1 Chronicles
Hebrew name of (*Debere HaYamim*), 254, 463
Quotes
02.52
Half of the Menuhoth, 363
02.54
Half of the Manahethites, 365
14.1
Hiram, King of Tyre, 374, 549
17.21
One nation in the land, 255, 511
18.10
Gold and silver, 177, 467
29.4
Arabic gold, 248
13 2 Chronicles
Hebrew name of (*Debere HaYamim*), 254, 464
Quotes
03.6
Red-orange gold from Parvaim, 266, 471
09.15
Beaten gold, 260
09.14, 21
Gold and silver, 177, 467
Aramaic (*Targum*), 376, 518
Flood, 96
year of creation at, 548
number of books in, 43, 58
number of scrolls in the original, 40
Quotes
And God made, 317, 496
The Ten Commandments, 521, 553
01 Thou shalt have no other gods before me, 393, 562
02 Thou shalt not make unto thee any graven image, 495, 542
03 Thou shalt not take the name of the Lord thy God in vain, 556, 565
04 Remember the sabbath day, to keep it holy, 554, 563
05 Honor thy father and thy mother, 476, 556
06 Thou shalt not murder, 411
07 Thou shalt not commit adultery, 346, 525
08 Thou shalt not steal, 321
09 Thou shalt not bear false witness against thy neighbor, 543, 558
Number of Letters in, 365
Number of Words in, 175
Tablets they were written upon, 307
Thou shalt not covet, 320
The Ten Plagues of Egypt (taking the first letter of each), 326, 486
01 *Dam* (Blood), 63, 356
02 *Tzefardea* (Frogs), 308
03 *Kinnim* (Vermin), 139, 387
04 *Arov* (Wild beasts), 229
05 *Dever* (Murrain), 187
06 *Shechin* (Boils), 275, 494
07 *Baradh* (Hail), 187
08 *Arbeh* (Locusts), 188
09 *Choshek* (Darkness), 256, 442
10 *Makath be-Khoroth* (Slaying of the Firstborn), 504
tar, 321
target, 182, 214
Tarot Cards, 40
Major Arcana
0 The Fool, 13
as 11th path, 27
01 The Magician, 13
as 12th Path, 28
02 The High Priestess, 14
as 13th Path, 30
03 The Empress, 15
as 14th Path, 31
04 The Emperor, 17
as 15th Path, 32
05 The Hierophant, 18
as 16th Path, 33
06 The Lovers, 19
as 17th Path, 35
07 The Chariot, 20
as 18th Path, 36
08 Strength, 22
as 19th Path, 37

09 The Hermit, 23
as 20th Path, 38
10 The Wheel of Fortune, 25
as 21st Path, 39
11 Justice, 27
as 22nd Path, 40
12 The Hanged Man, 28
as 23rd Path, 42
13 Death, 30
as 24th Path, 43
14 Temperance, 31
as 25th Path, 44
15 The Devil, 32
as 26th Path, 45
16 The Tower, 33
as 27th Path, 46
17 The Star, 35
as 28th Path, 47
18 The Moon, 36
as 29th Path, 48
19 The Sun, 37
as 30th Path, 49
20 Judgement, 38
as 31st Path, 51
21 The Universe, 39
as 32nd Path, 51
Minor Arcana
Cups
02
day angel (*Vaho*), 133
night angel (*Chabuyah*), 50
03
day angel (*Rahael*), 208
night angel (*Yebamiah*), 85
04
day angel (*Hayayel*), 74
night angel (*Mevamiah*), 123
05
day angel (*Luviah*), 76
night angel (*Pahaliah*), 148
06
day angel (*Nelakiel*), 149
night angel (*Yeyayel*), 80
07
day angel (*Melahel*), 128
night angel (*Chahaviah*), 53
08
day angel (*Vavaliah*), 75
night angel (*Yelahiah*), 78
09
day angel (*Saliah*), 128
night angel (*Ariel*), 248
10
day angel (*Asaliah*), 296
night angel (*Mihael*), 105
Pentacles
02
day angel (*Lekabel*), 102
night angel (*Veshriah*), 335
03
day angel (*Yechaviah*), 58
night angel (*Lehachiah*), 77
04
day angel (*Keveqiah*), 157
night angel (*Mendel*), 143
05
day angel (*Mebahiah*), 81
night angel (*Poyel*), 145
06
day angel (*Nemamiah*), 159
night angel (*Yeyalel*), 100
07
day angel (*Herachiel*), 211
night angel (*Mitzrael*), 273
08
day angel (*Akaiah*), 55
night angel (*Kehethel*), 312
09
day angel (*Haziel*), 72
night angel (*Aldiah*), 68
10
day angel (*Laviah*), 72
night angel (*Hihayah*), 115
Swords
02
day angel (*Mebahel*), 96
day angel (*Yezalel*), 96
03
day angel (*Hariel*), 212
night angel (*Haqmiah*), 168
04
day angel (*Laviah*), 72
night angel (*Kaliel*), 111
05
day angel (*Aniel*), 112
night angel (*Chamiah*), 150
06
day angel (*Rehael*), 244
night angel (*Yeyazel*), 77
07
day angel (*Hahahel*,), 65
night angel (*Michael*), 123
08
day angel (*Vemibael*), 97
night angel (*Yehohel*), 70
09
day angel (*Anevel*), 167
night angel (*Mochayel*), 108
10
day angel (*Damabiah*), 80
night angel (*Menqel*), 200
Wands
02
day angel (*Vehuel*), 66
night angel (*Daniel*), 115
03
day angel (*Hechashiah*), 256
night angel (*Amamiah*), 171
04
day angel (*Nanael*), 149
night angel (*Nithael*), 323
05
day angel (*Vahaviah*), 51
night angel (*Yelayel*), 100
06
day angel (*Sitael*), 132
night angel (*Elemiah*), 166
07
day angel (*Mahashiah*), 272
night angel (*Lehahel*), 117
08
day angel (*Nithahiah*), 316
night angel (*Haayah*), 40
09
day angel (*Yerathel*), 372
night angel (*Sahiah*), 253
10
day angel (*Reyayel*), 216
night angel (*Avamel*), 96
total number of, 97
tarry, 397
(and you), 407
(to), 69, 189, 198
task, 130, 178, 451
(place for), 171
taskmasters, 121
taskwork, 121
taskworkers, 121
tassel, 353
tassels, 55
taste, 46, 139, 329, 387
(to), 139, 387
tastlessness, 331
tattoo, 262
(to), 330
Tau. *See* Hebrew Alphabet:22 *Tau*
taught, 98
(ones who), 119, 419
taunt, 118, 138, 296
(to), 233, 491
(would t her), 252
taunting, 176
song, 138
tawny, 238, 355

tax, 140
(to), 234, 428
teach, 187
(and I will t you), 380, 511
(and I will), 370
(and that he may), 375
(and you shall), 455, 535
(that you may t them), 388, 522
(to), 94, 194, 372
teacher, 119, 194, 215, 311, 419
(Moses our), 361
teaching, 154, 320
team, 151, 201
tear
(to t apart), 252, 281, 463
(to t away), 97, 138, 281
(to t down), 223, 330
(to t in pieces), 284
(to t off or away or apart), 343
(to t off), 252, 281, 463
(to), 175, 233, 253, 277, 284, 463, 492
away, 58
in pieces, 277
tears, 139
(dripping of), 134
(to drip of), 134
(to shed), 45
teat, 22, 243
teeling, 398
teeth, 342
(number of human), 51
(to break out), 340, 532
(to grind the), 245
tekel, 337
tell, 45, 46, 51, 187
(and), 46, 47
(that I may), 47
(to), 32, 37, 76, 116, 209
(you may), 416
telling, 34
tempest, 257
temple, 83, 194, 243, 295
of the head, the, 243
Temple of Solomon, 307
architect of (Hiram), 219, 447
area containing officials' chambers and cattle stalls (Parbar), 320
attendant of (Hashabiah), 255
builder of (Bannah), 145
captain of guard of (Ira), 230
captain of the service of (Heldai), 71
chief priest of (Jehoiada), 126
cleansers of
Azariah, 238
Joel, 66
Kish, 294
Mattaniah, 331
Shemaiah, 301
Shimi, 299
Shimri, 344
Uzziel, 138
Zechariah, 210
Zimnah, 71
doorkeeper of (Elioenai), 182
entry of, 22
gatekeeper for the sanctuary of (Obadiah), 112
gatekeepers of
Ahiman, 130, 424
Hatita, 56
guard of (Bakbukiah), 198
head of family that helped rebuild (Henadad), 84
heighth of the entrance to, 59
Holy Sanctuary, 308
innermost sanctuary (Holy of Holies or Sanctuary), 28, 187, 197
Levite in charge of the dedicated things (Jehiel), 78
musicians of
Azarael, 245
Benaiah, 85, 92
Bukkiah, 137
Eliashib, 268
Ethni, 314
Hanani, 138
Heman, 126
Jaaziel, 146
Jeremoth, 383
Mahazioth, 317
Mallothi, 321
number of years from the Exodus to the building of, 320
officers of
Hanan, 129, 423
Maaseiah, 303
one entrusted with sacred vessels of (Noadiah), 159
one in charge of courses of (Giddalti), 309
one who brought gifts to (Jedaiah), 119
one who cared for vessels of (Sheshbazzar), 466
one who helped rebuild (Kadmiel), 179
overseer in work done on (Obadiah), 118
overseer of building of (Meshullam), 293, 484
overseer of servants of (Gishpa), 282
overseer of the dedicated things of (Jozabad), 47
overseer of the offerings at (Nahath), 313
owner of land upon which was built (Ornan), 241, 481
person who had a 'chamber' in (Igdaliah), 86
place built (Moriah), 217, 221
place where gold was obtained for (Parvaim), 260, 466
porters of
Akkub, 177
Talmon, 151, 433
priest who weighed the gold and silver vessels of (Meremoth), 390
priests of
Harim, 213, 442
Hashabiah, 255
Jeremoth, 382
Jeshua, 283
Shammua, 297
Shimi, 299
rebuilders of
Adiel, 136
Zerubbabel, 209
repairer of (Jahath), 298
servants of (Nethinims), 328, 330, 513
Barkos, 275
Shalmai, 281
snuffers used for lamps used in, 177, 235
the pillars of
Boaz, 97
Jachin, 108, 415
three Levites who participated in the worship at (Bani), 81
treasurer or official of (Obed-edom), 145, 390
west gate of (Shalleketh), 420
tempt
(to), 135
temptation, 176, 450
ten, 348, 349, 484
thousand, 186, 189, 190
thousands, 359
tenant, 400, 401
tend
(to), 228
tender, 200, 395
(to be), 209, 409
(to grow), 220
care, 118
tenderness, 200, 395
tendon, 34, 270
tendril, 278, 332
tendrils, 93
(quivering), 93
of a vine (as spread out), 278
tens, 484
tent, 54, 129
(his), 60, 61
(in the), 56
(its), 61
(the), 60
(to move a), 54
(to pitch a), 54
of meetings, 166
village, 37
tent, the, 65
tentative, 180
tenth, 349, 353, 486
(and a t part), 367, 369, 506, 525

(and the), 489
(I will give a), 367
(to take the t part of), 348
part, 359, 367, 525
parts, 384, 521
teraphim. *Also See:* Important Biblical Terms: *Teraphim*
terebinth, 54, 60, 105, 414
tree, 54
termination, 74
terrible, 70, 325, 359
(the), 381
(to make), 61
terrified, 292
(be), 447, 540
(to be), 115, 194, 306, 523
(you be), 427
terrify
(to), 55, 317
terrifying, 276, 515
territory, 58, 96, 153
terror, 28, 61, 74, 100, 188, 197, 213, 214, 217, 290, 292, 295, 311, 318, 442, 446, 447
(object of), 106
(sudden), 61
(to be in), 102, 113
(to be overtaken by sudden), 317
of, 442
terrors, 337, 503
terror-striking, 276, 515
test, 261
(to put to the), 135
(to), 76, 135, 277, 289, 400, 501
tested, 78, 402
testicle, 253, 439
testify
(to), 144
testimony, 98, 319, 321
(my), 121, 350
testing, 78, 402
Teth. See Hebrew Alphabet:09 *Teth*
tether, 206
than, 109, 415
thank, 32
(I will), 32
thankless
one, 160, 437
thanks, 47
(to give), 32
thanksgiving, 293, 444
that, 27, 34, 49, 93, 109, 175, 325, 410, 415
(and), 50, 54
(would), 61
in it, 22
the, 18
the one...the other, 28, 292
thee
(by), 40, 326
theft, 78
them, 61, 70, 308, 355, 491
(and do), 534
(and put), 434, 531
(in), 61, 355
(then make), 434, 531
(to do), 453, 535
(to meet), 428, 530
(unto), 370
(upon), 61, 355
themselves, 308, 491
(to), 55
then, 20, 22, 35, 49, 83, 105, 149, 262, 405, 468
(and), 31
theophanic
cloud, 174, 449
there, 78, 262, 468
are, 241, 299
is, 241, 299
therefore, 73, 87, 104, 147, 362, 397, 408, 413, 431
thereupon, 83, 405
these, 50, 54, 60, 64, 70, 74, 78, 100, 111, 128, 337, 356, 398, 412, 423
(and), 61
(by), 56
are, 54
they, 64, 68, 70, 74, 78, 128, 356, 398, 423
thick
(to be), 96
thicken
(to), 178
thicket, 40, 91, 98, 101, 104, 230, 232, 345, 346
thickness, 101, 137
thief, 73
thigh, 113, 204, 205, 291, 402
(tendon in the), 270
thin, 53, 125, 240
cake, 294
wall, 129, 474
thing, 94, 119, 187
think, 187
(to), 222, 246, 428
third, 377
(and the), 498
(and), 390, 522
(pertaining to), 368
(the), 374, 379, 498
(to do a t time), 368
(to the), 500
part, 377, 498
time, 377
thirst, 149, 153
thirsty
(to be), 149
thirteen, 518
thirtieth, 388, 522
thirty, 388, 522
(and), 390, 522
this, 18, 22, 28, 30, 34, 42, 61, 66, 73, 93, 292, 327, 397, 410
(as), 51
(for), 30
(with), 30
is, 28
one, 18, 28, 35, 61, 66, 292
this...that, 28, 292
thistles, 292, 308, 324, 512
thither, 262, 468
thorn, 30, 40, 133, 156, 160, 183, 184, 225, 253, 435, 437, 438, 456, 491
bush, 40, 183, 244, 491, 508
bushes, 403
thorns, 292, 344
thorny
bush, 136
thoroughly, 285
those, 50, 70, 100, 111, 128, 337, 412, 423
(and), 309, 491
thou, 289, 312, 328, 513
though, 100, 439
(as), 49
(contrary to fact), 55
thought, 134, 225, 246, 257, 270, 450, 486, 515
(I), 344
(to have a), 105, 375
thoughtlessly
(to speak), 28, 33
thoughts, 159, 351, 420, 527
(disquieting), 351, 527
thousand, 132, 451
(to make t fold), 132, 451
thousands
(producing), 132, 451
(to bring forth), 132, 451
of thousands, 289, 499
thread, 41, 84, 244, 334, 406
threads, 57
(twisted), 55
three, 368, 370, 496
(about), 391
(and), 370, 372, 497
(for), 381
(of), 382
(the), 370, 371
(to divide in t parts), 368
(to do t times), 368
(you), 504, 548
days ago, 384, 521
years old, 384, 501
threescore, 377, 425, 519, 536
thresh, 246, 249
(to), 37, 186, 243
threshed
(that which is), 266
(thing), 266
thresher, 214
threshing
(the process), 249
floor, 186, 216, 469
threshing-sledge, 214
threshold, 156, 347, 458, 520
(to stand at or guard the), 199, 478
throat, 120, 220, 471
throne, 98, 100, 230
throng, 98, 117, 327, 345, 419

through, 94
(and t her), 29
(to go), 138, 190, 453
throw
(to t down), 60, 223, 340, 532
(to), 37, 196, 211, 212, 244, 267, 451
(you will), 441, 540
thrown, 274, 455
thrum, 57
thrust, 133, 153, 229, 266
(and she t herself), 338, 531
(thing t forth), 326
(to be t aside), 162, 461
(to t away), 60, 107, 326, 443
(to t down), 60
(to t in), 148
(to t out), 60
(to t through), 242
(to t upon), 148
(to), 34, 37, 80, 81, 107, 148, 181, 420, 442
aside, 78
thumb, 75, 399
thunder, 247, 461
(to), 247, 461
thunderbolt, 51
thunderstorm, 213, 441
thus, 44, 64, 87, 88, 132, 408
(and), 50
tidings, 328, 331
(to bear), 326
tie
(to t up), 143
(to), 175, 221, 246, 354
tied, 467
Tiferet. See Kabbalah:The Ten *Sefirot*:06 *Tiferet*
tight, 234
tile, 106
till
(to freshly), 220
(to), 32
timber, 90, 169, 484
timbrel, 320, 517
(to play the), 346, 525
time, 75, 105, 116, 143, 317, 363, 375, 429
(at that), 22
(at this), 155, 435
(before that), 318
(before the), 318
(brief), 279
(from that), 83, 405
(in t to come), 214
(little), 131
(loss of his), 401
(past), 318
(second), 425
(set or appointed), 375
(the second), 474
(to appoint a), 105, 375
timely, 148, 319, 432
tin, 65
tingle
(to), 163
tinkle
(to), 163
tip
of the ear, 318, 482
tired, 113
tiring, 107
tithe, 359, 367, 525
(of his), 379
(the), 362
(to give a), 348
(to take a), 348
(to), 348
(you shall), 484
tithes
(your), 502, 548
title
(to give a flattering), 94
(to), 94
to, 50, 95, 121, 305
toe, 171
(big or great), 75, 399
together, 40, 46, 62, 355
(and to be), 53
(to agree), 105, 375
(to be gathered), 152
with, 121, 289
toil, 113, 171, 198, 305, 318, 461
(to), 102, 156, 198
toiler, 171
toiling, 156
token, 229, 292
tokens, 439
told, 40
(and he), 41
(and they), 47
(and was), 41
(when it is), 35
toll, 74, 339
tomb, 241, 251
tomorrow, 214
tone, 170
tongs
(for altar use), 177
tongue, 283, 387, 497, 530
(hold), 87
(to use the), 280, 496
tongues
(according to their), 456, 536
took
(and they t off), 439
tool, 78
(engraving), 198
(graving), 198
(leveling), 461
of iron, 208
tools, 76, 400
tooth, 179, 267, 273, 341, 489, 493
top, 18, 19, 102, 215, 326, 328, 412, 439
of head, 189
topaz, 119
topmost, 328
Torah. *See Tanakh:* Torah
torch, 143
torn
(that which is), 236
torrent, 107
tortuous, 479
toss
(to t aside), 116
(to), 211, 244
tossing
(of sleeplessness), 77
total, 326
totter
(to cause to), 176
(to), 34, 37, 74, 135, 144, 176, 180, 266
tottering, 181
touch
(to), 142, 266
tow
(as shaken from flax when beaten), 408
toward, 50, 132, 384
(of direction, not necessarily physical motion), 50
the inside, 179
towards, 121
the front of, 97
tower, 95
town, 37, 230, 238, 250, 395
track, 158, 355
trade, 218
(place of), 391
(to get by), 202
(to go about in), 224
(to), 202
(you shall), 386
tradition, 248
traffic, 218, 224
tragacanth
gum, 317
train, 259
(to), 96, 345
trained, 107, 347
servant, 107, 347
training, 116
tramp
(to), 133, 425
trample
(to t down), 86, 262
(to t on), 243
(to), 81, 240, 246, 273, 281, 505
trampling, 261
place, 261
trance, 376
tranquil
(to be), 293
tranquility, 293
tranquilizing, 101
transform
(to), 126, 352
transgress
(to), 155, 226, 310
transgressed

(I), 389
transgression, 87, 246, 257, 310
transient, 61
translate
(to), 355
translation, 376, 518
transmigration, 91
transplant
(to), 412
trap, 107, 178, 216, 323, 416
(to), 117
trapper, 297
trash, 129
travail, 58
(to), 44, 58
travel
(to t about in), 224
(to), 192, 459
traveller, 74, 314, 339
travelling
company, 87, 195
traverse, 335, 490
tray, 311
treacherous, 31, 48, 296
act, 155
treacherously
(to act), 23, 155
(to deal), 23
treacherousness
of treacherous behavior, 296
treachery, 23, 185, 232, 374
tread, 246, 249
(to t down), 47, 86, 199, 246, 273, 330
(to t on), 243
(to t out), 199
(to t upon), 23
(you shall), 367, 368, 506
treading
(to foul by), 351
(to press by), 199
(to wash by), 101
down, 401
place, 222, 418
treason, 354
treasure, 78, 138, 159, 204, 220, 237, 316, 427, 437, 463, 471
(hidden), 162, 220, 438, 471
(to t up), 200
(to), 200, 461
house, 237
of the primordial, 538
treasured
(to be t up), 138, 427
treasurer, 190, 194
treasures, 147
(in my), 401
treasuries, 338, 516
treasury, 78, 98, 338, 345, 516
treat
(to t delicately), 204
(to t hardly), 292
(to t lightly), 23
(to t severely), 292
(to t violently), 83, 129
tree, 105, 111, 169, 414, 416, 484
(acacia), 395
(almond), 290
(almug), 142, 147, 389, 391
(aloe), 104, 374
(apple), 323, 341, 506
(balsam), 41, 263, 468
(cedar), 215, 468
(cypress), 361
(felling of), 420
(fir), 215, 468
(fruit of), 310, 490, 524, 554
(great - oak), 105, 414
(great), 105, 414
(juniper or cypress), 342
(juniper), 372, 517
(mighty), 60
(myrtle), 87
(olive), 297
(palm), 107, 372
(species of hardwood), 358
(summit of), 215
(support of - root), 94, 139, 428
(sycamore), 306, 490
(tamarisk), 257
(terebinth), 54, 60
(vine), 150, 433
(willow), 264
from Lebanon - almug tree, 142, 147, 389, 391
Tree of Knowledge, 371, 539
Tree of Life, 206, 546
(from the), 227, 548
Tree of the Knowledge of Good and Evil, 477, 551
trees, 172
(palm), 392, 523
(the palm), 393, 523
(to tend sycamore), 112
treetop, 412
tremble, 192
(to cause to), 306, 523
(to), 44, 85, 102, 113, 144, 184, 193, 194, 227, 230, 306, 376, 492, 523
trembling, 100, 106, 192, 194, 196, 198, 356, 489
(object of), 106
tremendous
(the), 381
trench, 27, 242, 508
trepidation, 163, 439
trespass, 155
(to commit a), 155
(to), 262, 468
triad, 368
trial, 176, 450
tribe, 65, 73
tribulation
(bar of), 199
tributary, 121
tribute, 56, 68, 74, 121, 125, 140, 247, 263, 339
trick, 188, 284
(to), 354
trickle
(to), 106, 127, 267, 501
tried, 78, 107, 347, 402
trifle, 251
trim
(to), 139, 213, 387
trimming, 218
trip
(to), 118, 173, 465
triumph
(to be exalted in), 23
(to), 129
trodden
with the feet, 314
troop, 34
(rear of), 175
(shall), 35
trouble, 75, 117, 192, 237, 399
(deliverance from), 87, 408
(to), 54, 104, 234, 326, 374
troubled
(to be), 68
(you have), 412
(your), 526
mind, 241
troubles
(and), 396
trough, 195, 356
(feeding), 86
(kneading), 264
(the), 440
(watering), 438
troughs
(in the), 518
trousers, 173
true, 87, 116, 133, 408
truly, 51, 90, 95, 111, 116, 133, 148, 306, 370, 392, 409, 416
(and), 309
trumpet, 67, 348, 352
(to sound a), 238
(to sound), 238
blast, 348, 503
trust, 42, 78, 93, 410
(to t in), 299, 502
(to), 36, 238, 506
trusting, 42, 117, 419
truth, 133, 293, 296, 306
(and), 309
(in), 306
(to know the), 124
try
(to), 78, 135, 402
(you did t him), 366
tubies, 438
tumor, 178
tumors, 198
tumult, 117, 123, 421
(to be in a), 327
(to be in), 327
(to), 68
tunic, 287

(and a), 462
tunics, 461
(in their), 472, 540
(the), 462
turban, 66, 140, 204, 216, 230, 481
(of the High Priest), 381
turbid
(to make), 61
turbulent, 95, 411
turn
(and you t aside), 398, 524
(at the t of), 487
(I will t aside), 223
(to t about, around, aside, back, towards), 83
(to t around), 161
(to t aside from the right path), 62
(to t aside), 168, 224, 395, 463
(to t away), 161, 246
(to t back), 87, 134, 246
(to), 41, 82, 83, 126, 152, 326, 330, 352, 395
(you shall t aside), 383
(you shall turn aside), 383
(you will t away), 424, 536
of affairs, 86, 137
of events, 86
turned
(to be), 134
(you are t away), 417, 527
(you are t back), 417, 527
(you had t aside), 394, 524
away, 43
in, 43
work, 308
turner
t's work, 308
turning, 92, 353
aside, 223
away, 269
back, 269
over, 91
turtle-doves, 377, 519
(the), 379, 519
twelve, 484, 543
twentieth, 365, 515
twenty, 365, 368, 515, 525
(and), 367, 516
(for), 366, 516
(the), 367, 516
twenty-one, 371, 517
twenty-two, 495, 560
twig, 93, 175, 198, 219, 278, 332, 346
twilight, 302, 512
twins, 324, 500
twist
(to), 44, 101, 162, 174, 184, 316, 329, 330, 331, 335, 438, 465, 490
twisted, 98, 316, 330, 479
(to be), 329
twisting, 304
two, 288, 381, 403, 420, 483, 528
(and), 406, 422, 529
(for), 404, 415
(to break in), 262
(to cut in), 95, 125, 355
kinds, 123, 381
years, 438, 532
tyrant, 247, 483
Tzaddi. See Hebrew Alphabet:18 *Tzaddi*
ulcer, 62
umbilical
cord, 325, 395
umpire
(office of), 166
unbridled
license, 116
uncircumcised, 239, 243
(to count), 239
(to remain), 239
uncle, 22, 30
(his), 30
u's wife, 36
unclean, 68
(he is), 81
(to be), 68, 73
(to become), 68
thing, 323, 527
uncleanness
(sexually and religiously), 74
(through their), 112, 377
(to purify from), 35
unconscious
(to be), 212, 440
uncover, 56
(to), 227
unctuous, 114
under, 442
(and), 445
(from), 455
(to be), 155
(was u them), 459, 537
part, 442
undergarments, 461
underground
chamber, 245
room, 245
underneath
(and), 457
understand
(to), 80, 404
understanding, 51, 53, 85, 267
(ones who gave), 119, 419
(words of), 251
undertake
(to u for), 226
undertaking, 282
underwear, 173
underworld, 258
undo
(to), 376
undone
(to leave), 61
undressed, 287
unfaithful
act, 155
unfaithfully
(to act), 155
unfathomable, 192
unfolding, 322
unforeseen
meeting or event, 264
unformed
mass, 92, 369
unfortunate
person, 77
unfruitful
valley, 271, 475
unguent, 246
unhewn, 430
unholy, 57
unimportant, 168, 443
union, 40, 58
(sexual), 22
with God, 46
unite
(to), 40, 191
united, 191
(to be), 40
unitedness, 40
unity, 13, 29, 36, 298
(name of), 269, 473
universal, 109
unjust
gain, 170
one, 128, 137
unjustly
(to act), 128
unlawful
alliance, 354
unleavened
bread or cake, 151
unless, 60, 65, 85
unmindful
(you are), 403
unoccupied, 239
unreceptivity
(spiritual), 132
unrestrained
(to be), 224
unrighteous
one, 128
unrighteousness, 128, 133
unripe
fig, 103
unseasoned, 331
until, 93
when?, 70, 395
unto, 54
(and), 55
(idea of motion to), 50
(of motion), 50
them, 94
untrue
(to be), 256
untruth, 48
unwell, 32
(to be), 32
unwilling
to obey, 111, 416

up
(he lifts himself), 425
(I have lifted), 425
(something lifted), 131
(to be laid), 138, 427
(to bear), 108, 268
(to burn), 70
(to come), 181, 191
(to go), 127, 135
(to rise), 23, 135, 160, 196, 213, 399, 441
(what comes), 159
(you do raise yourself), 513
to, 93
to the time that, 93
upbraid
(to), 233, 491
uphold, 116
(to), 140, 354
uplifted, 265
uplifting, 235, 265, 388, 417
upon, 121
upper, 132, 172, 446
part, 155
uppermost
parts, 183
upright, 330
(to be), 330
uprightness, 330, 332, 343, 345, 355
(and in), 333
uprising, 417
(no), 177, 414
uproar
(to be in an), 68
uproot
(to), 438
uprooting, 441
upwards, 121
Uranus. *See* Planets: Nontraditional: Uranus
urethra, 290
urge, 123, 449
(to), 111, 141, 161, 468, 477, 482
urgency, 123, 449
urgent
(to be), 177, 467
urinate
(to), 420, 535
urine, 273, 493
us
(between), 338
(to meet), 434
(you sent), 436
usage, 290
use
(to be of), 148, 431
usury, 263, 276, 456, 493
(to lend for), 276, 456
(to lend on), 268
utensil, 78, 111, 416
utter, 45, 187
(to u tunefully), 144
(to), 29, 209, 334
utterance, 94, 111, 209, 212, 263, 295, 337, 377, 417
(rash), 72
uttering, 62
utterly, 223
vain, 247
(to be in), 48
(to be), 55
(to become), 55
vainly, 267, 472
vale, 192
valiant, 194
man, 186, 193
one, 205
valley, 29, 30, 107, 177, 192, 296
(dry and unfruitful), 475
(dry or unfruitful), 271
(in the), 31, 33
(level), 177
(of the), 36
(the), 36
of the shadow of death, 350
valuable, 348
(to be), 246
value, 220, 247
(to), 234, 428
vanish, 20
(to), 184
vanishing, 143, 454
vanity, 55, 75, 247, 399
vapor, 18, 55, 272
variegated, 173
vast, 187, 427
(to be), 184, 424
vault
of the heavens, 34
vaulted
room, 315
Vav. See Hebrew Alphabet:06 *Vav*
vegetables, 247
(as sown), 228
vegetation, 243
vehicle, 201
veil, 124, 125, 133, 143, 152, 215, 243, 394, 421, 484
(as spread out), 182
(large), 198
(long), 182
(the), 398
(to the), 412
vein, 270
(in the), 36
vengeance, 181, 182, 420
(to take), 181, 420
venom, 326
Venus. *See* Planets: Traditional: 03 Venus
verily, 51, 111, 116, 148, 392, 416
veritable, 88, 408
vermilion, 438
vermin, 139, 387
vessel, 43, 78, 111, 171, 187, 211, 416
(cover of), 158
vestibule, 90, 95, 100, 368, 370, 372
vestment, 320
vestments, 280
vesture, 315
vex
(to), 104, 171, 323, 374
vexation, 117, 162
vexed, 117, 167, 462
(to be), 162, 167, 285, 462
vexer, 237
vial, 121, 350
vibration, 250
victim, 230
victory, 161
view, 299
(in your), 76
vigil, 340
vigor, 32, 57, 77, 160, 399
vigorous, 41, 269, 490
vile, 126, 348
(to be), 85
vileness, 307
vilification, 172
village, 37, 238, 239, 247
(unwalled), 236
villages, 265, 470
vine, 150, 433
(and unto the choice), 372
(insignificant product of), 25
(product that is insignificant), 265, 489
row, 328
tree, 150, 433
vinegar, 153, 480
vines
(to dress), 220, 448
(to tend), 220, 448
vine-tendrils, 356
vineyard, 220, 448
vineyards
(to dress), 220, 448
(to tend), 220, 448
vintage, 238, 241
violate
(to), 259, 316
violence, 58, 96, 129, 139, 243, 329
(profit acquired by), 170
(thing taken away by), 58, 64
(to do v to), 129
(to do), 316
(to gain by unrighteous), 170
violent, 209
heat, 297
one, 281
perverting, 58
violently
(to treat), 83, 129
violets, 43, 45
viper, 166, 287, 337, 510
virgin, 307
(a v of), 453
virginity, 322, 498
virgins
(the), 454
virtues, 310

visibility, 299
vision, 39, 90, 100, 187, 212, 299, 409, 412
(as mode of revelation), 212
(in the ecstatic state), 79
visionary, 41
visions, 299
(in the), 373
visit
(to), 179
visitation, 180
voice, 148, 153
(my), 160
void, 20, 29, 165
(and), 36
place, 216, 469
voluntariness, 80
volunteer
(to), 75
plants, 168
voluptuous, 150, 433
vomit, 123, 133
(to v up), 129, 136
vomited
(what is v up), 123
voracious
(to be), 227
votive
offering, 217
vow, 217
(hasty), 72
(to make a), 217
(to), 217
(you), 359, 378
vulture, 25, 36, 214, 262, 343, 442
wadi, 107
wafer, 294, 352
wages, 335, 482
(my), 484
(your), 486, 539
wagging, 121
wagon, 113, 130
wail
(to), 54, 79, 87, 158, 314
wailing, 32, 79, 83, 88, 94, 179
wainscotted, 113, 181, 454
wainscotting, 181, 454
waist
band, 80, 195
cloth, 195
wait
(to lie in), 120, 185
(to w for), 52
(to), 52, 67, 69, 103, 133, 167, 364, 373, 441
longingly, 27
waiting, 76
wake
(to w up), 183, 491
wakeful
one, 230
waking, 230
walk, 115, 349
(and I will), 462
(to), 50, 74, 78, 325, 331, 339, 340
walked
(I had), 461
wall, 57, 67, 73, 77, 129, 188, 193, 310, 328, 344, 474
(to build a), 188
(to w off), 188
(to w up), 188
of house, 247, 310
wallet, 166
walls
(in the), 404
wander
(to w abroad), 77
(to w astray), 103, 318
(to w restlessly), 192
(to), 79, 103, 144, 189, 192, 459
wanderer, 215
wandering
(of aimless fugitive), 79
wands, 173, 349
want, 27, 224
(in w of), 224
(in), 87, 408
(to be in), 328
of, 224
wanted, 229
wanton
(to be), 116, 354
wantonness, 116, 159, 339
war, 96, 142, 146, 241, 371
(to arm for), 145, 478
(to equip for), 145, 478
(to make), 96, 371
(to wage), 114
(what is stripped off a person in), 158
club, 191, 495
ward, 214
wardrobe, 320
ware, 165, 239
wares, 151, 433
warhorse, 350
warm, 67, 357
(to grow), 220
warmed
(to be), 190
warmth, 67, 357
warn
(to), 194
warp, 403
(in the), 404
(the), 406
warped
(that which is), 73
warping, 164
warrior, 186, 233
wars
of, 334
was
(and there), 50
(there), 44, 300
wash
(and you shall), 397
(to w away), 238, 506
(to w by treading), 101
(to w off), 238, 506
(to), 238, 284, 506, 507
washed
(to be), 101
washing, 35, 238, 242, 506
waste, 29, 191, 196, 264, 283, 297, 501
(place laid), 196
(to be), 191
(to lay), 120, 149, 191, 244
(to w away), 278, 384
(to), 149
wasted
(to be), 191
wasting, 219, 229, 470
watch, 153, 342, 350, 486
(a period of time), 342
(in the), 479
(to keep), 176
(to w over), 262
(to w stealthily), 236
(to w with enmity or envy), 236
(to), 176, 262
watcher, 230
watchful, 230
watching, 340
watchtower, 78, 87, 179, 196, 351, 402, 408
(and the), 202
water, 160, 376, 460, *Also See* Elements: Water (*Maim*)
(an accumulation of), 332
(drawing place of), 263
(in), 112
(pit of), 234
(place to draw), 263
(rushing), 192
(spring of), 138
(the), 115, 378
(to draw of), 57
(to draw), 242
(to), 291, 454
conduit, 265
hole, 18
of God, 233
watercourse, 62
watered, 193
watering
(to guide to a w place or station), 104
place, 135
trough, 438
watermelon, 48
waters, 376
(in the), 112
(in), 377
waterskin, 309
waterskins, 289
watery
pit, 234
wave, 52

(to), 144, 152, 457
waver
(to), 79, 144
wavering, 74
waves
(pounding of), 53
waving, 341
wavy, 459
wax, 82
way, 87, 190, 201, 263, 397
(the), 204, 401
(to miss the), 35
(which turned every), 480
side, 49, 330
ways
(parting of), 281
we, 75, 135
weak, 53, 123, 144, 200, 261, 367, 395
(to be), 49, 62, 90, 209, 261, 268, 409
(to become), 62
(to grow), 49, 168, 463
from fear, 200, 396
weaken
(to), 94, 261
weakness, 220, 266, 281, 416
wealth, 50, 56, 66, 75, 80, 138, 143, 348, 362, 399, 403, 427
wealthy, 350
(to be), 348
(to become), 348
wean
(to w a child), 92
weaned, 350
(to be), 92
weaning, 107
weapon, 261, 346, 442, 519
(shattering of), 191, 495
(tip of), 56, 62
weapons, 76, 159, 223, 310, 336, 400, 437
wear
(to w away), 52
(to w out), 52, 54
(to), 258
(you shall), 413
weariness, 168, 318, 463
(what a), 318
wearing
out, 61
wearisome, 102
weary, 102, 113, 168, 169, 463
(to be), 54, 102, 168, 169, 463
(to grow), 102, 168, 463
(was), 20
weasel, 62
weave
(and you shall), 437
(to w together), 121, 317, 350
(to), 147, 185, 286, 317, 359, 518
web, 143, 244, 334
wedding, 315
money, 212
weed
(a kind of), 211
weeds, 211
(stinking or noxious), 245
week, 280
weeks, 429, 431, 433, 434, 506
(in your), 454, 535
(the), 433
weep
(to cause to), 40, 326
(to), 45, 134, 314
weeping, 45, 51, 304
(they be), 57
weigh
(to w out), 303
(to), 76, 111, 116, 174, 303, 337, 400
weighed
(something w out), 116
weight, 45, 108, 316, 318
of pledges, 121
Weights, Measurements, and Currency
Adarkan (Drachma (or Daric) - 4.32 grams), 227, 252, 476, 484
Ammah (Cubit – 18 in.), 65
Bad, 19
Bath (40 litres), 289
Beqa' (1/2 shekel), 175
Chomer (65 imperial gallons), 213
Ephah, 116
gerah, 189
Gomed (Cubit), 66
Hin (5 quarts), 83, 406
Kikker (talent), 208
Kor, 199
Lethek (1/2 homer), 310, 476
Log (basin – 1/2 liter), 52
Maneh (60 shekels), 116
Maneh or *Mina* (50 or 60 shekels), 111
Omer (1/10 ephah), 247
Peh (1/3 of a shekel), 104
Peras (1/2 shekel), 262
Qab, 124
Qesiytah (unknown value), 300
Seah (1/3 *ephah*), 85
Sha'ar, 348
Zereth (1/2 cubit), 357
weighty, 54
(to be), 45, 219, 470
welfare, 35, 40
benefit, 35
well, 52, 88, 185, 188
(and dealt), 56
(do), 44
(may be), 50
(they have said), 61
(to be), 39
well-fed, 215
went, 15
(and they w in), 43
wept, 45
(and he), 57, 333
were, 39
(as it), 84
west, 249
western, 220, 223, 471, 473
westward, 249
wet
(to w something), 173
whale, 325, 331, 500, 514
what, 60, 64
what?, 109, 415
whatever, 60, 64
wheat, 40, 86
(and the), 52
(ear of), 323
(ear or head of), 135
wheel, 72, 84, 153, 397, 434
(hub of), 329
wheels, 180, 419
whelp, 185, 189, 190
when, 49, 60, 84, 355
(and), 54
when?, 70, 310, 395
whence?, 27, 80, 403
where, 32
(and), 40
[is] he? (and), 41
where?, 27, 70, 80, 116, 395, 403
(of persons, things), 33
(rhetorical), 33
wherefore, 95, 370
wherefore?, 140
wherein, 325
whet
(I), 427
(to), 261, 288, 499
whether, 20, 74, 398
which, 28, 30, 64, 257, 292, 325
(of), 30
which?, 27, 69
while, 93, 98
whip, 246
whirl
(to w away), 348
(to), 44, 298
of spindle, 148, 359
whirlwind, 257
whirring, 209
whisper, 25, 39, 107, 303, 304, 522
(to), 216, 242, 261, 469, 481
whispering, 27, 261, 304
whistle
(to), 355
whistling, 356, 360
white, 101, 195, 238, 413
(something bleached), 355
(to be), 101, 195, 413
(to grow), 195
bread, 198
cloth, 195
linen, 19
marble, 355
patch of skin, 357
poplar, 106

stuff, 195
whitewash
(to), 250
whither?
(of place), 70, 395
who, 64, 74, 78, 257, 356, 398
who?, 69, 109, 415
whoever, 69, 109, 415
whole, 69, 109, 277, 306, 430, 477, 490
burnt offering, 109, 127
wholeness, 306, 490
wholesome, 334
whom
(of), 30
whom?, 69
whoredom
(woman of), 460, 537
whose, 325
whosoever, 69, 109, 247, 415
why, 64
why?, 140
wicked, 348
(be), 386
(the), 367, 516
(to be), 348
deed, 70
device, 105, 375
ones, 365, 515
wickedly, 34
(to act), 348
wickedness, 71, 136, 348, 349, 384, 492
(and for the), 486
(his), 485
(in regards to an idol), 75, 399
(in), 484
wide, 215
(to be), 186, 192, 321
(to grow), 192
widow, 144
widowed, 141, 428
widowhood, 141, 336, 428
width, 322, 359
of the hand, 118
wield, 112
wife, 237, 243, 246, 358
(against the), 401
(and for his), 417
(and his), 405
(and the), 400
(and your), 411, 518
(his), 399
(my), 403
(of his), 414
(or his), 406
(purchase price for), 212
(to his), 401
(to take a), 154
(uncle's), 36
(your), 409, 517
of, 395
wild, 209
ass, 227, 230, 231
beast, 132
beasts, 229, 325, 500
wilderness, 212, 297, 501
(wasteland in the), 112
wildgrapes, 268, 473
wildness, 229
wiliness, 121
will, 51, 53, 386
(and I w be), 45
(good w with no limit), 310, 552
(not necessarily evil), 27
willing, 85
(to be), 22, 114
(to make), 75
(will be), 35
willingness
(to show), 60
willow, 226
(a kind of), 264
tree, 264
wilted, 179
wind, 195
(to w around), 200, 479
(to w up together), 200, 479
(to), 317
winding, 202, 257
stair, 84
window, 25, 45, 79, 114, 188, 417
casing, 320, 517
lattice, 268
windows
(and the), 358
winds
(to rush of storm), 151
wine, 82, 87, 199, 213, 408, 472
(and your), 477, 536
(and), 474, 475
(as blood - fig.), 63, 356
(fresh or new), 472
(mixed), 69, 169, 372
(of the), 474
(your), 477, 536
press, 133, 290
vat, 133, 290
winepress, 235
wing, 162, 181, 185, 188, 461, 489
(of bird), 102, 439
winged, 162, 461
wings
(to flap the), 210
(to fly by moving), 185
(with his), 359
wink
(to), 213, 441
winnow
(to), 194
winnowing
implement, 151
winter, 233, 492, *Also See* Seasons:Winter (*Choref*)
(to), 233, 491
wipe
(to w out), 73
(to), 73
wiped
(be w out), 82
wisdom, 75, 92, 93, 267, 317, 399
(secret), 434
(the measure of), 339
wise, 86, 96, 368, 371
(and), 93, 369
(to be), 86, 368
man, 86, 96, 368, 371
ones, 188, 427
wish, 27
witch, 287, 509
witchcraft, 184, 287, 425, 509
(to practice), 287, 509
(to use), 287, 509
witchcrafts, 310, 492
with, 14, 132, 135, 289, 305, 384
withdraw
(to), 25, 27, 32, 117, 141, 145, 161, 227, 470, 478
withdrawal, 25, 223, 249
wither
(to w and fall), 101
(to), 178, 248, 256, 416
withered
(to be), 174
withheld, 411
withhold
(to), 70, 141, 169, 256, 272, 442
within, 22, 179, 194, 295
(in), 50
(to), 50
without, 52, 61, 80, 136, 403
(to be), 224
cause, 118, 380
leaven, 151
witness, 93, 98, 246
(to bear), 99
witnesses
(all), 336
wives, 288, 293, 482, 500
wizard, 158
woe!, 23, 27, 28, 34, 36, 39, 90
wolf, 25
woman, 243
(compassionate), 245
(young), 159
of, 395
w's veil, 152
womb, 60, 80, 85, 214, 216, 355, 403, 407, 442
(and of the), 217, 445
(opening of), 341
women, 288, 289, 482
(the Hebrew), 390, 392
(the), 400
(young), 289
wonder, 133, 289, 336
wonderful, 141, 167
(to be), 133
wondrous
work, 167
wood, 90, 169, 172, 230, 232, 329, 484
(pile of), 217

wooded
area, 329
height, 230, 232, 329
woof
(as knitted material), 226
wool, 247, 257
word, 94, 187, 193, 209, 212, 230
(sharp), 296
(to pick up a), 66
(your), 132, 353, 381, 511
cutting, 296
words, 218, 446
(reviling), 105, 112, 113, 118, 441, 445
(your), 386, 513
work, 95, 112, 113, 117, 178, 179, 199, 336, 362, 503
(braided), 327
(broidered), 264
(chequered), 305
(filigree), 305
(of God in history), 137
(plaited), 305, 327
(to), 95, 438
(wondrous), 167
working
(skillful), 470
workmanship, 420
works, 420
(demoniacal), 427, 530
world, 62, 160, 167, 225, 399, 407
(Lord of the), 188, 531
(this), 171, 410
worlds, 183, 423
(encompassing all), 345, 519
worm, 212
(the), 469
wormwood, 166
wormy
(to be), 213, 441
worn
out, 54
out things, 56
worship, 112, 173, 447
(and we will), 430
(and you will), 511
(to prostrate oneself in), 86
(to), 86, 138, 171
worshipped
(and he), 412
(and you w them), 515, 551
(and), 412
worshipper, 384
worshippers, 191
worthless, 85, 90, 163, 221
(something), 85
(to be), 85
gods, 85
things, 268, 472
worthlessness, 307
(fig.), 230
would
that, 69
wound, 83, 118, 196, 200, 209, 216, 346, 470
(severe), 154
(to remove a bandage from a), 29
(to w by bruising), 209
(to w fatally), 86
(to w severely), 154
(to), 209
woven
material, 403
stuff, 143
wrap, 143
(to w closely), 64
(to w oneself), 103
(to w tightly), 64
(to w up together), 200, 479
(to), 147, 200, 479
together, 92, 369
wrapped, 139
(and w herself), 487, 550
(thing), 202
wrapper, 215, 484
(linen), 143, 429
wrapping, 377
wrath, 72, 228
(and their), 407, 525
(he was filled with), 391
(of God), 225, 488
(to provoke to), 162
wreath, 64, 70, 188, 282
diadem, 231
wreathen, 462
wrest
(to), 171
wrestle
(to), 124
wrestled
(have I), 484
wrestlings, 346
wretched, 148
one, 156
wretchedness
(in my), 389
wringing, 155, 480
write
(and I will), 453
(and you shall), 450, 460, 537
(to), 299
(you shall), 450
writhe
(to), 44
writhing, 67, 100
writing, 97, 262, 299, 314
(a), 299
written
(I have), 452
(may you be), 451
(thing), 314
(you have), 449
wrong, 70, 128, 129, 348
(to do), 101
(to go), 35
(to), 129, 316
wrongdoing, 265
wrongfully
(to act), 128
wrongly
(to do), 129
wroth
(to be), 162, 167, 298, 462, 501
wrought, 298
iron bar, 108
yard, 84, 406
yarmulka, 127
yarn, 79
(and in), 473
(and), 472
(in), 470
yea, 100, 439
year, 75, 270, 363, 423
(first), 422
(from the), 435
(in the y of), 421
old, 423
yearn
(to y for), 168, 463
(to), 220
years, 288, 483
(and), 291, 483
(seven), 280
(two), 438, 532
of, 423
Yechidah. *See* Kabbalah:Souls: *Yechidah*
yellow, 118
(of hair), 118
yelper, 132
Yesod. *See* Kabbalah:The Ten *Sefirot*:09 *Yesod*
yesterday, 262, 317, 318
(before), 386, 522
(day before), 384, 521
yet, 39, 98, 143, 325, 429
Yetzirah. *See* Kabbalah:Worlds: *Yetzirah*
yield, 229, 326, 439
(to), 279
yielding, 279
Yod. *See* Hebrew Alphabet:10 *Yod*
yoke, 121, 151
(bar of), 74, 79
yonder, 61, 66
you, 306, 312, 328, 490, 513
(against), 436, 532
(among), 40, 326
(and against), 46, 329
(and upon), 52
(and), 46, 309, 329, 491
(in), 40, 326
(over), 40, 326
(shall bring), 52, 332
(to meet), 421, 521
(under), 453, 529
(when y come in), 327
(where are), 54
young, 15, 58, 168, 233, 243, 277, 443, 485
your
old age, 45

yourselves
(to), 476, 541
youth, 160, 197, 220, 253, 256, 279, 310, 362, 366, 399, 448
(according to his), 434
(blackness of hair indicating), 473
(stars of), 67
youthful, 160, 399
Zayin. *See* Hebrew Alphabet:07 *Zayin*
zeal, 167
Zechariah. *See Tanakh: 02 Neviim:* 20 Zechariah
Zephaniah. *See Tanakh: 02 Neviim:* 18 Zephaniah
Zodiac, 216, 320
Constellations
Ayish (Arcturus), 276, 281
Ben Ayish (Ursa Minor), 304, 503
Kesilim (Orion), 173, 412
Kesiyl (Orion), 139
Kiymah (Pleiades), 94
Mazzel (constellations or planet), 96
Houses
01
angel (*Ayel*), 61
02
angel (*Toel*), 65
03
angel (*Giel*), 63
04
angel (*Kael*), 141
05
angel (*Oel*), 129
06
angel (*Veyel*), 66
07
angel (*Yahel*), 65
08
angel (*Sosul*), 171
09
angel (*Sizajasel* – misprint), 208
angel (*Soyasel*), 208
10
angel (*Kashenyayah*), 315
11
angel (*Ansuel*), 161
12
angel (*Pasiel*), 299
number of decanates in, 55
number of quinances in, 92
Signs
01 Aries, 63
Angel
Sharhiel, 343
Angels of Decanates
01 *Zazer*, 195
02 *Behahemi*, 80
03 *Satander*, 11, 254
Angels of Quinances
01 *Vehuel*, 66
02 *Daniel*, 115
03 *Hechashiah*, 256
04 *Amamiah*, 171
05 *Nanael*, 149
06 *Nithael*, 323
Archangel
Malkidiel, 151
as 15th Path, 32, 140
as 28th Path, 47, 292
as Tarot Card The Emperor, 17
in association with the month *Nisan*, 173, 449
in association with the tribe Gad, 20
Lord of Triplicity by Day (*Sateraton*), 287, 498
Lord of Triplicity by Night (*Sapatavi*), 207
Qlippoth
Beiriron, 343, 517
Shem HaMeforash
1st Quinance (*Vaho*), 34
2nd Quinance (*Dani*), 82
3rd Quinance (*Hachash*), 249
4th Quinance (*Amem*), 163, 402
5th Quinance (*Nena*), 123
6th Quinance (*Nith*), 313
02 Taurus, 328
Angel
Araziel, 214
Angels of Decanates
01 *Kedamidi*, 96
Keradamidi (Regardie's spelling), 229
02 *Minacharai*, 250
03 *Yakasaganotz*, 208, 499
Yasaganotz (Regardie's spelling), 177, 451
Angels of Quinances
01 *Mebahiah*, 81
02 *Poyel*, 145
03 *Nemamiah*, 159
04 *Yeyalel*, 100
05 *Herachiel*, 211
06 *Mitzrael*, 273
Archangel
Asmodel, 157
as 16th Path, 33, 153
as Tarot Card The Hierophant, 18
in association with the month *Iyar*, 192
in association with the tribe *Ephraim*, 257, 258, 465
Lord of Triplicity by Day (*Raydel*), 212
Lord of Triplicity by Night (*Totath*), 300
Qlippoth
Adimiron, 253, 484
Shem HaMeforash
1st Quinance (*Mabeh*), 66
2nd Quinance (*Poi*), 117
3rd Quinance (*Nemem*), 147, 391
4th Quinance (*Yeyal*), 69
5th Quinance (*Harach*), 195
6th Quinance (*Metzer*), 257
03 Gemini, 324, 500
Angel
Sarayel, 241
Angels of Decanates
01 *Sagarash*, 346
02 *Shehadani*, 276
03 *Beton*, 316, 474
Angels of Quinances
01 *Vemibael*, 97
02 *Yehohel*, 70
03 *Anevel*, 167
04 *Mochayel*, 108
05 *Damabiah*, 80
06 *Menqel*, 200
Archangel
Ambriel, 231
as 17th Path, 35, 165
as Tarot Card The Lovers, 19
in association with the month *Sivan*, 144, 430
in association with the tribe Manasseh, 286
Lord of Triplicity by Day (*Sarash*), 368
Lord of Triplicity by Night (*Ogarman*), 305, 503
Qlippoth
Tzelilimiron, 314, 318, 507, 510
Shem HaMeforash
1st Quinance (*Vameb*), 66
2nd Quinance (*Yehah*), 38
3rd Quinance (*Anu*), 144
4th Quinance (*Mechi*), 77
5th Quinance (*Dameb*), 65
6th Quinance (*Menaq*), 180
04 Cancer, 252, 483
Angel
Pakiel, 157
Angels of Decanates

01 *Mathravash*, 480
02 *Rahadetz*, 239, 507
03 *Alinkir*, 253
Angels of Quinances
01 *Vaho*, 133
02 *Chabuyah*, 50
03 *Rahael*, 208
04 *Yebamiah*, 85
05 *Hayayel*, 74
06 *Mevamiah*, 123
Archangel
Muriel, 233
as 18th Path, 36, 175
as Tarot Card The Chariot, 20
in association with the month *Tammuz*, 311
in association with the tribe Issachar, 451
Lord of Triplicity by Day (*Raadar*), 317
Lord of Triplicity by Night (*Akel*), 141
Qlippoth
Shichiriron, 433, 538
Shem HaMeforash
1st Quinance (*Aya*), 100
2nd Quinance (*Chebo*), 33
3rd Quinance (*Raah*), 187
4th Quinance (*Yebem*), 71, 361
5th Quinance (*Hayeya*), 43
6th Quinance (*Mum*), 105, 375
05 Leo
Angel
Sharatiel, 344
Angels of Decanates
01 *Losanahar*, 268
02 *Zachi*, 115
03 *Sahiber*, 228
Angels of Quinances
01 *Vahaviah*, 51
02 *Yelayel*, 100
03 *Sitael*, 132
04 *Elemiah*, 166
05 *Mahashiah*, 272
06 *Lehahel*, 117
Archangel
Verkiel, 224
as 19th Path, 37, 181
as Tarot Card Strength, 22
in association with the month *Av*, 15
in association with the tribe Judah, 48
Lord of Triplicity by Day (*Sanahem*), 166, 406
Lord of Triplicity by Night (*Zalbarhith*), 378
Qlippoth
Shalhebiron, 355, 523
Shem HaMeforash
1st Quinance (*Vehu*), 34
2nd Quinance (*Yeli*), 69
3rd Quinance (*Sit*), 98
4th Quinance (*Alem*), 156, 394
5th Quinance (*Mahash*), 264
6th Quinance (*Lelah*), 83
06 Virgo, 307
Angel
Shelathiel, 429
Angels of Decanates
01 *Ananaurah*, 249
02 *Rayadyah*, 205
03 *Mishpar*, 365
Micpar (Regardie's spelling), 280
Angels of Quinances
01 *Akaiah*, 55
02 *Kehethel*, 312
03 *Haziel*, 72
04 *Aldiah*, 68
05 *Laviah*, 72
06 *Hihayah*, 115
Archangel
Hamaliel, 136
as 20th Path, 38, 192
as Tarot Card The Hermit, 23
in association with the month *Elul*, 85
in association with the tribe Naphtali, 348
Lord of Triplicity by Day (*Laslara*), 253
Lord of Triplicity by Night (*Sasia*), 149
Qlippoth
Tzafiriron, 370, 526
Shem HaMeforash
1st Quinance (*Aka*), 39
2nd Quinance (*Kahath*), 300
3rd Quinance (*Hezi*), 40
4th Quinance (*Elad*), 53
5th Quinance (*Lav*), 56
6th Quinance (*Hehau*), 98
07 Libra, 161, 401
Angel
Chedeqiel, 165
Angels of Decanates
01 *Tarasni*, 257
02 *Saharnatz*, 290, 519
03 *Shachdar*, 331
Angels of Quinances
01 *Yezalel*, 96
02 *Mebahel*, 96
03 *Hariel*, 212
04 *Haqmiah*, 168
05 *Laviah*, 72
06 *Kaliel*, 111
Archangel
Zuriel, 217
as 22nd Path, 40, 216
as Tarot Card Justice, 27
in association with the month *Tishri*, 472
in association with the tribe Asher, 325
Lord of Triplicity by Day (*Thergebon*), 381, 528
Lord of Triplicity by Night (*Achodraon*), 228, 476
Qlippoth
Abiriron, 343, 517
Shem HaMeforash
1st Quinance (*Yezel*), 66
2nd Quinance (*Mebah*), 66
3rd Quinance (*Hari*), 196
4th Quinance (*Haqem*), 159, 398
5th Quinance (*Lau*), 56
6th Quinance (*Keliy*), 78
08 Scorpio, 278
Angel
Saitziel, 185
Angels of Decanates
01 *Kamotz*, 166, 483
02 *Nundohar*, 255
03 *Uthrodiel*, 380
Angels of Quinances
01 *Luviah*, 76
02 *Pahaliah*, 148
03 *Nelakiel*, 149
04 *Yeyayel*, 80
05 *Melahel*, 128
06 *Chahaviah*, 53
Archangel
Barkiel, 222
as 24th Path, 43, 240
as Tarot Card Death, 30
in association with the month *Cheshvan*, 274, 493
in association with the tribe Dan, 73, 397
Lord of Triplicity by Day (*Betchon*), 318, 510
Lord of Triplicity by Night (*Sahaqnab*), 198
Qlippoth
Necheshthiron, 495, 549
Shem HaMeforash
1st Quinance (*Levo*), 62
2nd Quinance (*Pahel*), 136
3rd Quinance (*Nelakh*), 121, 350

4th Quinance (*Yeyaya*), 49
5th Quinance (*Melah*), 94
6th Quinance (*Chaho*), 37
09 Sagittarius, 438
Angel
Saritiel, 253
Angels of Decanates
01 *Mishrath*, 479
02 *Vehrin*, 225, 475
03 *Aboha*, 31
Angels of Quinances
01 *Nithahiah*, 316
02 *Haayah*, 40
03 *Yerathel*, 372
04 *Sahiah*, 253
05 *Reyayel*, 216
06 *Avamel*, 96
Archangel
Adnakhiel, 136
as 25th Path, 44, 255
as Tarot Card Temperance, 31
in association with the month *Kislev*, 136
in association with the tribe Benjamin, 164, 439
Lord of Triplicity by Day (*Ahoz*), 36
Lord of Triplicity by Night (*Lebarmim*), 254, 464
Qlippoth
Nachashiron, 366, 525
Shem HaMeforash
1st Quinance (*Nethah*), 312
2nd Quinance (*Haa*), 20
3rd Quinance (*Yereth*), 358
4th Quinance (*Shaah*), 244
5th Quinance (*Riyi*), 200
6th Quinance (*Aum*), 70, 357, 359
10 Capricorn, 34
Angel
Sameqiel, 210
Angels of Decanates
01 *Misnin*, 191, 458
02 *Yasyasyah*, 166
03 *Yasgedibarodiel*, 261, 283
Angels of Quinances
01 *Lekabel*, 102
02 *Veshriah*, 335
03 *Yechaviah*, 58
04 *Lehachiah*, 77
05 *Keveqiah*, 157
06 *Mendel*, 143
Archangel
Hanael, 105
as 26th Path, 45, 268
as Tarot Card The Devil, 32
in association with the month *Tevet*, 294
in association with the tribe Zebulun, 115, 418
Lord of Triplicity by Day (*Sandali*), 202
Lord of Triplicity by Night (*Aloyar*), 213
Qlippoth
Dagdagiron, 230, 476
Shem HaMeforash
1st Quinance (*Lekab*), 72
2nd Quinance (*Vesher*), 328
3rd Quinance (*Yecho*), 43
4th Quinance (*Lehach*), 62
5th Quinance (*Keveq*), 144
6th Quinance (*Menadh*), 114
11 Aquarius, 63
Angel
Tzakmiqiel, 235
Angels of Decanates
01 *Saspam*, 209, 438
02 *Abdaron*, 222, 472
03 *Gerodiol*, 216
Angels of Quinances
01 *Aniel*, 112
02 *Chamiah*, 150
03 *Rehael*, 244
04 *Yeyazel*, 77
05 *Hahahel*, 65
06 *Michael*, 123
Archangel
Kambriel, 242
as 15th Path, 32
as 28th Path, 47, 292
as Tarot Card The Star, 35
in association with the month *Shevet*, 248
in association with the tribe Reuben, 220, 471
Lord of Triplicity by Day (*Athor*), 386
Lord of Triplicity by Night (*Polayan*), 174, 449
Qlippoth
Bahimiron, 11, 254, 485
Shem HaMeforash
1st Quinance (*Ani*), 80
2nd Quinance (*Cham*), 138, 387
3rd Quinance (*Reha*), 228
4th Quinance (*Yeyaz*), 45
5th Quinance (*Hehah*), 32
6th Quinance (*Mik*), 88, 343
12 Pisces, 75, 363
Angel
Vakabiel, 87
Angels of Decanates
01 *Bihelami*, 105
02 *Avron*, 222, 472
03 *Satrip*, 271, 502
Angels of Quinances
01 *Vavaliah*, 75
02 *Yelahiah*, 78
03 *Saliah*, 128
04 *Ariel*, 248
05 *Asaliah*, 296
06 *Mihael*, 105
Archangel
Amnitziel, 205
as 29th Path, 48, 305
as Tarot Card The Moon, 36
in association with the month *Adar*, 186
in association with the tribe Simeon, 315, 508
Lord of Triplicity by Day (*Ramara*), 306
Lord of Triplicity by Night (*Nathdorinel*), 421
Qlippoth
Nashimiron, 383, 529
Shem HaMeforash
1st Quinance (*Vaval*), 61
2nd Quinance (*Yelah*), 64
3rd Quinance (*Sael*), 111
4th Quinance (*Eri*), 230
5th Quinance (*Ashel*), 288
6th Quinance (*Miah*), 74

Printed by BoD™in Norderstedt, Germany